INSIDE

American Democracy Now offers privileged access to the tough questions, the daily conversations, and the real participation of the most influential players in our government. Every chapter features an article from *National Journal* that highlights an important, current topic so students can get an insider's perspective on that issue and consider it in context.

DID YOU KNOW. . .

■ **That the youth vote is considered a hot commodity? See page 36**

■ **That you may soon need a national ID card, which is pitting state rights advocates against the national government? See page 126**

■ **That the battle between warrantless surveillance of your e-mail and your civil liberties is far from over? See page 166**

■ **That you could work for a powerful lobby—the video game industry? See page 276**

■ **That public opinion changes a lot faster than foreign policy? See page 642**

AMERICAN DEMOCRACY NOW

AMERICAN DEMOCRACY NOW

BRIGID CALLAHAN HARRISON

Montclair State University

JEAN WAHL HARRIS

University of Scranton

SUSAN J. TOLCHIN

George Mason University

WITH

SUZANNE U. SAMUELS
Ramapo University

ELIZABETH BENNION
Indiana University at South Bend

 Higher Education

Boston   Burr Ridge, IL   Dubuque, IA   New York   San Francisco   St. Louis
Bangkok   Bogotá   Caracas   Kuala Lumpur   Lisbon   London   Madrid   Mexico City
Milan   Montreal   New Delhi   Santiago   Seoul   Singapore   Sydney   Taipei   Toronto

Mc Graw Hill **Higher Education**

Published by McGraw-Hill, a business unit of The McGraw-Hill Companies, Inc., 1221 Avenue of the Americas, New York, NY 10020. Copyright © 2009 by The McGraw-Hill Companies, Inc. All rights reserved. No part of this publication may be reproduced or distributed in any form or by any means, or stored in a database or retrieval system, without the prior written consent of The McGraw-Hill Companies, Inc., including, but not limited to, any network or other electronic storage or transmission, or broadcast for distance learning.

Some ancillaries, including electronic and print components, may not be available to customers outside the United States.

This book is printed on acid-free paper.

1 2 3 4 5 6 7 8 9 0 DOW/DOW 0 9 8

ISBN: 978-0-07-352627-0
MHID: 0-07-352627-4

Editor in Chief: *Michael Ryan*
Director, Editorial: *Beth Mejia*
Sponsoring editor: *Mark Georgiev*
Marketing manager: *Bill Minick*
Director of development: *Rhona Robbin*
Developmental editors: *Sylvia Mallory and Carla Kay Samodulski*
Editorial coordinator: *Briana Porco*
Media project manager: *Ron Nelms*
Production editor: *Leslie LaDow*
Manuscript editor: *Judith Brown*
Designers: *Cassandra Chu and Linda Beaupré*
Cover designers: *designworksgroup and Cassandra Chu*
Art manager: *Robin Mouat*
Photo research coordinator: *Alexandra Ambrose*
Photo researcher: *David Tietz*
Production supervisor: *Tandra Jorgensen*
Composition: *10/12 ITC Legacy Serif Book by Thompson Type*
Printing: *45# Influence Gloss by R.R. Donnelley & Sons*
Back cover image: *Copyright © Shutterstock*

The credits for this book begin on page C-1, a continuation of the copyright page.

Library of Congress Cataloging-in-Publication Data

American democracy now / Brigid Callahan Harrison . . . [et al.].
    p.   cm.
  Includes bibliographical references and index.
  ISBN-13: 978-0-07-352627-0 (alk. paper)
  ISBN-10: 0-07-352627-4 (alk. paper)
  1. United States—Politics and government—Textbooks.   2. Political participation—
United States—Textbooks.   I. Harrison, Brigid C.
  JK276.A43   2008
  320.473—dc22
                                                                                    2008047487

The Internet addresses listed in the text were accurate at the time of publication. The inclusion of a Web site does not indicate an endorsement by the authors or McGraw-Hill, and McGraw-Hill does not guarantee the accuracy of the information presented at these sites.

JOIN THE CONVERSATION

As seasoned instructors of American government, we have learned a great deal about what works best with our students. In creating *American Democracy Now,* we aim to share with our fellow instructors a text built on an approach that teaches students to **think critically** by encouraging them to **inquire, converse** with one another, and, finally, **participate** in American government. Especially given the excitement surrounding the 2008 presidential election, students are more eager than ever to participate in civic life; *American Democracy Now* gives them the skills and tools.

As we began writing this text, we thought about the main goal we always set for ourselves as instructors: by the end of the semester we want our students to be skilled and confident enough to **join the conversation of American political life,** a conversation that starts with the discussion and debate that we promote in the classroom. It is the freedom to engage in a good conversation that allows us as instructors to reproduce in lectures—both large and small—the intimate teaching and learning experience we have enjoyed for years. And it is a good conversation that leads students to think about, discuss, and eventually participate in political processes that go on around us every day.

To join this conversation, students need to learn to ask thoughtful, **critical questions.** *American Democracy Now* teaches students the essential elements, institutions, and dynamics of American government. As they gain an understanding of the fundamental character of our political process, however, they also learn to ask the questions that make their understanding of American government meaningful to them. They learn how the fundamental principles of American democracy inform their understanding of the politics and policies of today so they can think about the policies they would like to see take shape tomorrow. In short, they learn to **inquire:** how does **then** and **now** shape what's going to happen **next**?

This critical thinking approach—then, now, next—serves as the basis for student participation. We take a broader view of participation than the textbooks we have used in the past. To us, participation encompasses a variety of activities from the modest, creative, local, or even personal actions students can take to the larger career choices they can make. By inquiring and conversing, students define what participation means to them and make active choices about where, when, and how to participate.

Joining the conversation makes American government matter. As the students in our American Government classroom become ever more diverse, the challenge is not to appeal directly to their personal backgrounds; the challenge is to hone their critical thinking skills and foster and harness the energy behind a smart question and a sudden insight so they learn to make the scholarly material we present to them their own. We know we have succeeded when students apply their learning and sharpened skills to consider the outcomes they—as students, citizens, and participants—would like to see.

Joining the conversation also means joining students where they are. Facebook, YouTube, and many other technologies are not only powerful social networking tools, they are powerful political and educational tools. New technologies help politicians to communicate with citizens, citizens to communicate with each other, and you to communicate with your students. And we invite you to do so as well.

Brigid Callahan Harrison
Jean Wahl Harris
Susan J. Tolchin

BRIEF CONTENTS

CONTENTS

Part I: Foundations of American Democracy

Part II: Fundamental Principles

Part III: Linkages Between People and the Government

6 POLITICAL SOCIALIZATION AND PUBLIC OPINION   208

7 INTEREST GROUPS   242

Part IV: Institutions of Government

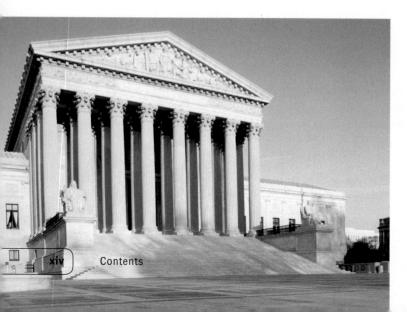

Contents

Part V: Public Policy

15 ECONOMIC POLICY 532

16 DOMESTIC POLICY 568

17 FOREIGN POLICY AND NATIONAL SECURITY 604

Part VI: State and Local Government

"Democracy begins in conversation."

— JOHN DEWEY

Critical Thinking in American Government

American Democracy Now is designed to enable students to think critically about American government so they can better inquire, converse, and participate in American government. Learning about American government means more than developing an academic understanding of our democratic system; it means learning how to participate in the conversation of American political life that takes place around us every day. This conversation is both ongoing and constantly changing, shifting its direction according to the way we understand the issues of yesterday, the problems of today, and the policies of tomorrow. Whatever the topic, however, good conversations always begin with good questions. This is how we approach the teaching of American government: with questions that lead to conversations, and with conversations that in turn lead students to an enduring understanding of our democracy and of the politics and policies that shape it, as well as instill confidence about the informed and creative ways in which they can participate in our democratic system.

Critical thinking enables students to better participate in the great conversation of American political life, and we developed *American Democracy Now* to cultivate the knowledge and thinking skills required to do so in an informed and effective way. Specifically, to prepare them for this lifelong conversation, we ensure that they leave the course with three core proficiencies: a firm grasp of the fundamental principles of American democracy and the historical context in which they arose; the ability to evaluate contemporary issues and events by referring to those founding principles and the historical arena of their development; and the power to think critically about the future outcomes of policies and politics so that they can make sound decisions about these matters now and well beyond their college years.

> With a critical thinking approach, we aim to introduce students to the great conversation of American political life.

> Students learn to participate in our national political conversation by using a framework of political inquiry: *Then, Now, Next.*

A Commitment to Stimulating Inquiry

We designed the text to hone students' skills in political inquiry—to help them shape those critical questions that will bring them to a closer understanding of how American government works and how they can participate in it. Our method is systematic, clear, and consistent. It rests on a framework of political inquiry that organizes students' reading and guides their navigation through the narrative. This framework at the same time allows instructors to harness the content of the course for their students' better understanding of American government.

Chapter-opening pages introduce the then-now-next framework.

A set of chapter-opening statements and questions frames students' reading and stimulates their critical evaluation of the material, prompting them to consider:

- What was the situation **then**?
- How does **then** connect us to **now,** and what is the current situation?
- How does considering what happened **then** and what exists **now** help us to determine what should or willcome **next**?

> **Students learn the tools of inquiry in order to participate in our national political conversation and explore the avenues for further political and community engagement.**

This political-inquiry approach asks students to consider what foundational principles are at stake, how these foundations inform our understanding of policies and events taking place now, and how the foundations from then and the issues and events taking place now can guide us in choosing the political outcomes we want to happen next. Together the intersection of these questions provides the scaffolding for a deliberative, critical approach to American government—one that places students in the ongoing political conversation, which is both the aim of the course and the key to cultivating a better-informed citizenry. ***American Democracy Now*** shows how the past provides guidance, how the ever-changing present demands decision, and how both shape consequences in the future. When students have learned to guide themselves by using political inquiry, not only will they have excelled in American government, they will have joined the conversation as active and informed citizens.

Then, Now, . . . Next? tables suggest ways to compare facts and data.

These provocative tables compare political or policy data or information from some time in the past (then) with present-day reality (now) and ask students to think about what the future (next) will bring. Making these comparisons and considering these questions help students to build their political-inquiry skills.

Political Inquiry questions teach students to critically evaluate visual information.

Selected graphs, charts, photographs, cartoons, and maps throughout the text are accompanied by questions that prompt students to consider them closely and evaluate their meaning on various levels. Students learn to inquire as to the nature of the visual information and data and to form questions that will lead to better conversations.

A Commitment to Enabling the Conversation of Democracy

American Democracy Now emphasizes the importance of civic discourse, or what we call the *conversation of democracy*. Our goal is to encourage students to exploit the best aspects of the information revolution—during this course and in their lives afterward—and to deliberate, discuss, and actively listen to others, especially to those who do not share their views. An ongoing conversation of democracy is a crucial channel of civic participation: Students learn how they and others form opinions. They come to understand where compromise is possible—and where it is not.

Exploring the Sources activities help students learn to evaluate data, primary documents, and other types of information.

These exercises focus on analyzing and interpreting a wide variety of sources—everything from graphs, tables, and primary documents to photographs, political cartoons, and political artifacts. Students are led through the steps needed to ensure they consider their evidence critically and present solid arguments. They learn to appreciate past contexts, to observe current trends, and to assess future directions.

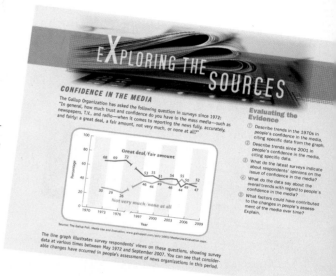

Articles from the *National Journal* provide an insider's perspective on policy and issues.

Appearing at the end of each chapter, an article from the *National Journal,* a premier source of information for government officials, journalists, and other Washington insiders, offers students rare insight and perspective on the chapter's topic. Students learn that the conversation works best when it is informed and nonpartisan.

> Political participation also means learning how to form political positions and understanding how others form theirs.

In *The Conversation of Democracy* sidebars, students consider important policy questions or other issues related to the chapter themes.

The sidebars present various points of view on the issue, showing students that political conversation is seldom neatly two-sided and always developing and changing, shifting direction as we reevaluate issues in light of what we know of the past (then), what we understand of the present (now), and what we expect of the future (next).

A Commitment to Encouraging Civic Participation

American Democracy Now recognizes that a full, sophisticated understanding of the dynamics of the American political system requires students to appreciate the importance and value of everyday civic participation. But it also recognizes that students must learn to use critical thinking to define what form of participation is meaningful to them. This book discusses participation in the broadest sense of the term, emphasizing that participation in civic life has varied faces and that political life is deeply entwined with nonpolitical civic life.

> **Inquiry and conversation help students decide what forms of civic participation are meaningful to them.**

Civic participation comprises activities ranging from the relatively passive—say, paying one's taxes—to the very active—for example, running for office. But civic engagement also includes day-to-day activities such as signing a "Web petition" to stop genocide in Darfur, attending a student government meeting, learning about a policy issue such as crime prevention, and organizing a church clothing drive.

On the Job interviews profile individuals whose careers embody civic participation.

Rather than profiling high-level government officials, *American Democracy Now* highlights former students of American government who are employed in interesting occupations relevant to each chapter. These profiles tap directly into students' desire to answer the questions "How is this information relevant to the real world?" and "What am I going to do when I graduate from college?" Legislative aides, a White House intern, and interest group employees reveal how they got their jobs, describe their day-to-day responsibilities, and comment candidly on what they like and dislike about their work. Typical salaries for that type of work are also included.

American Democracy Now vignettes showcase a dramatic episode of civic action by one or more persons or a group.

Appearing at the beginning of each chapter, these vignettes spotlight a wide range of opportunities and motivations for participating in our democratic system and civil society.

Suggestions for *Doing Democracy* offer students practical tips for getting involved in their communities.

These helpful sidebars give students concrete ideas and guidelines for hands-on civic participation related to the theme of each chapter.

Keep the conversation going, in and out of class.

American Democracy Now provides both traditional and innovative tools for success in a complete teaching and learning support system.

The Tools for Success accompanying *American Democracy Now* is an integrated program.

This innovative program offers invaluable support to instructors teaching and students studying American government. The instructors who make up the author team offer a depth and breadth of experience in all types of American government classrooms. Keeping to the nature and theme of the text, the tools for instructors and students all facilitate ways for students to learn, study, and apply information. The tool kit includes a full test item bank tied to Bloom's taxonomy and an Instructor's Manual that goes beyond lecture topics and outlines by tying all text features to individual and group projects in and out of class. BlackBoard, WebCT, and other course management cartridges are available along with simulations and other online activities. Video resources feature the authors discussing key concepts in the course to help students better understand the central principles and core terms of American government.

Facebook for Instructors and for Students harnesses the power of social networking for the American government classroom.

Terri Towner, professor of political science at the Oakland University (Michigan), has assistant researched the value of using Facebook in the American government classroom. Why Facebook? Your students already use networking sites to converse and share information. Now you can use Facebook as an educational tool. We guide you in creating an innovative learning opportunity for your students, who will experience the conversation of American government in a media-rich social and learning network—a place they enjoy visiting every day.

Dynamic, highly visual PowerPoints fully explain complicated concepts and ideas that enhance and support your lecture.

Combining subject matter expertise from political scientists and instructional design, the PowerPoints build on themselves much like overhead transparencies but provide a richer learning experience for your students. In addition, a separate set of lecture outline PowerPoints is available.

ACKNOWLEDGMENTS

We owe a debt of thanks to all of the people who have contributed their thoughts and suggestions during the stages of this book's development and whose many ideas have improved it immeasurably.

Manuscript Reviewers

Janet Adamski, *University of Mary Hardin-Baylor*
M. Ahad Hayaud-Din, *Brookhaven College*
Ahrar Ahmad, *Black Hills State University*
Susan Allen, *Texas Tech University*
Jeffrey Ashley, *Eastern Illinois University*
Lawrence Becker, *California State University–Northridge*
Nancy Bednar, *Del Mar College*
Steven S. Berizzi, *Norwalk Community College*
Jeffrey C. Berry, *South Texas College*
John Bolen, *San Jacinto College–South*
Shannon Bow, *University of Texas–Austin*
Robert C. Bradley, *Illinois State University*
Lynn Brink, *North Lake College*
Teresa Bush-Chavy, *American River College*
Richard D. Caldwell, *Eastern Illinois University*
Jamie Carson, *University of Georgia*
Anita Chadha, *University of Houston, Downtown*
June Cheatham, *Dallas County Community College*
Grace Cheng, *Hawaii Pacific University*
Ann V. Clemmer, *University of Arkansas at Little Rock*
Robert Collins, *College of the Canyons*
Paul W. Cooke, *Cy Fair College*
James W. Corey, *High Point University*
Beatriz Cuartas, *El Paso Community College*
Denise DeGarmo, *Southern Illinois University–Edwardsville*
Louis DeSipio, *University of California–Irvine*
Robert E. Dewhirst, *Northwest Missouri State University*
Kevin Dockerty, *Kalamazoo Valley Community College*
Thomas Doleys, *Kennesaw State University*
Nelson Dometrius, *Texas Tech University*
Cecil Dorsey, *San Jacinto College–South*
Duane Emmons, *San Jacinto College–North*
John Forshee, *San Jacinto College–Central*
Jeffrey Fox, *Fort Lewis College*
Kevin Fridy, *University of Florida–Gainesville*
David Garrison, *Collin County Community College*
Donald V. Gawronski, *Mesa Community College*
Dana K. Glencross, *Oklahoma City Community College*

Amy Glenn, *Tyler Junior College*

Craig Goodman, *Texas Tech University*

Charles Greenawalt, *Millersville University*

Anke L. Grussendorf, *Georgia State University*

Willie Hamilton, *Mount San Jacinto College*

Michelle Kukoleca Hammes, *St. Cloud State University*

Margaret Hankenson, *University of Wisconsin–Waukesha*

Randy Hopkins, *Oklahoma City Community College*

William T. Horner, *University of Missouri*

Terri Johnson, *University of Wisconsin–Green Bay*

Aaron Karp, *Old Dominion University*

Matthew Kenney, *Austin Peay State University*

Manoucher Khosrowshahi, *Tyler Junior College*

Richard Kiefer, *Waubonsee Community College*

Jason Kirksey, *Oklahoma State University–Stillwater*

Patricia Knol, *Triton College*

Judith Kullberg, *Eastern Michigan University*

Lisa Langenbach, *Middle Tennessee State University*

Aie-Rie Lee, *Texas Tech University*

John Linantud, *University of Houston, Downtown*

Shari L. MacLachlan, *Palm Beach Community College–Lake Worth*

Daniel McIntosh, *Slippery Rock University*

Nathan Melton, *Utah Valley State College*

Todd Meyers, *Grossmont College*

Eric Miller, *Blinn College–Bryan*

Layna Mosley, *University of North Carolina–Chapel Hill*

Leah Murray, *Weber State University*

Christopher Newman, *Elgin Community College*

Sunday P. Obazuaye, *Cerritos College*

William D. Pederson, *Louisiana State University–Shreveport*

Shannon Peterson, *Utah State University–Logan*

Clarissa Peterson, *DePauw University*

Jason Pigg, *Louisiana Tech University*

Leonard Riley II, *Pikes Peak Community College*

Chris Saladino, *Virginia Commonwealth University*

Frauke Schnell, *West Chester University*

Ronnee Schreiber, *San Diego State University*

James Scott, *Oklahoma State University–Stillwater*

Margaret E. Scranton, *University of Arkansas at Little Rock*

Patrick L. Shade, *Edison Community College*

Henry Sirgo, *McNeese State University*

Markus Smith, *Oklahoma City Community College*

Michael W. Sonnleitner, *Portland Community College*

John Speer, *Houston Community College–Southwest*

Joseph L. Staats, *Valdosta State University*

Henry Steck, *SUNY Cortland*

Judy Tobler, *NorthWest Arkansas Community College*

Dennis Tombs, *San Jacinto College–North*

John Vanzo, *Bainbridge College*

Ronald W. Vardy, *University of Houston*

Rick Vollmer, *Oklahoma City Community College*

David G. Wigg, *St. Louis Community College*

Van Allen Wigginton, *San Jacinto College–Pasadena*

Linda Williams, *University of Maryland*

Francisco Wong, *City College of San Francisco*

Zhiqun Zhu, *University of Bridgeport*

Design Reviewers

Marilyn Gaar, *Johnson County Community College*
Kenneth Hicks, *Rogers State University*
John Linantud, *University of Houston, Downtown*
Shari L. MacLachlan, *Palm Beach Community College–Lake Worth*
Michael McConachie, *Collin County Community College*
Maurice Mangum, *Southern Illinois University–Edwardsville*
Henry Sirgo, *McNeese State University*
John Speer, *Houston Community College–Southwest*
Judy Tobler, *Northwest Arkansas Community College*
Elizabeth Williams, *Santa Fe Community College*

American Government Symposium

In October 2006 and October 2008 McGraw-Hill conducted two American Government Symposiums for instructors from across the country. These events offered forums for instructors to exchange ideas and experiences with colleagues they might not have met otherwise. They also provided an opportunity for editors from McGraw-Hill to gather information about the needs and challenges of instructors of American Government. The feedback we received has been invaluable and has contributed—directly and indirectly—to the development of *American Democracy Now* and its supplements. We would like to thank the participants for their insights.

Robert Ballinger, *South Texas College*
Kathleen Collihan, *American River College*
Vida Davoudi, *Kingwood College*
Karry Evans, *Austin Community College*
William Gillespie, *Kennesaw State University*
Dana K. Glencross, *Oklahoma City Community College*
Larry Gonzalez, *Houston Community College–Southwest*
Michelle Kukoleca Hammes, *St. Cloud State University*
Wanda Hill, *Tarrant County Community College*
John Hitt, *North Lake College*
Brenda Jones, *Houston Community College-Central*
Franklin Jones, *Texas Southern University*
Lynn Jones, *Collin County Community College*
Chien-Pin Li, *Kennesaw State University*
Eric Miller, *Blinn College*
Kay Murnan, *Ozarks Technical Community College*
Blaine Nelson, *El Paso Community College*
Ray Sandoval, *Richland College*
Louis Schubert, *City College of San Francisco*
Thomas Simpson, *Missouri Southern University*
Henry Sirgo, *McNeese State University*
John Speer, *Houston Community College-Southwest*
Beatrice Talpos, *Wayne Community College*
Judy Tobler, *Northwest Arkansas Community College*
Matthew Turgeon, *University of North Texas*
Van Allen Wigginton, *San Jacinto College–Central Campus*
John Wood, *Rose State College*
Ann Wyman, *Missouri Southern State University*
Kathryn Yates, *Richland College*

Supplements Team

American Democracy Now is supported by a highly collaborative and integrated program of supplements for instructors teaching and students studying American Government. The conversation within the text is continued within the supplements, resulting in a set of tools that will help instructors communicate with students and students both learn the material and join the national conversation.

The **Tools for Success** accompanying *American Democracy Now* is an integrated program offering support to instructors teaching and students learning American Government. The tool kit includes an Instructor's Manual that goes beyond lecture topics and outlines by tying all text features to individual and group projects in and out of class and a full test item bank tied to Bloom's taxonomy.

- The **Instructor's Manual** by **Dana K. Glencross,** *Oklahoma City Community College,* **Beatriz Chasius-Cuartes,** *El Paso Community College,* **Michelle Kukoleca Hammes,** *St. Cloud State,* and **Ronald W. Vardy,** *University of Houston,* includes chapter summaries, chapter outlines, lecture outlines with integrated PowerPoints, and abundant class activities.

- The **Test Bank** by **Paul W. Cooke,** *Cy Fair College,* **Elizabeth McLane,** *Wharton County Junior College,* **Michelle Kukoleca Hammes,** *St. Cloud State,* and **Ronald W. Vardy,** *University of Houston,* includes over 1000 multiple-choice and short-answer questions to accompany the chapters in *American Democracy Now,* along with questions to be used in class (with PowerPoints) and student self check questions.

- **Facebook for Instructors and Students** by **Terri Towner,** *Oakland University (Michigan),* harnesses the power of Facebook as a classroom tool and guides you in creating an innovative learning opportunity for your students.

Expert Reviewers

Brian J. Brox, *Tulane University*
Brett Curry, *Georgia Southern University*
Brian Fogarty, *University of Missour–St. Louis*
Mark R. Joslyn, *University of Kansas*
Hans Noel, *Georgetown University*
Jason MacDonald, *Kent State University*
Franco Mattei, *University of Buffalo*
Lawrence Rothenberg, *University of Rochester*
Saundra K. Schneider, *Michigan State University*
Robert Whaples, *Wake Forest University*
Jeff Worsham, *West Virginia University*

Personal Acknowledgments

We must thank our team at McGraw-Hill: Steve Debow, president of the Humanities, Social Science, and Languages group; Judy Ice, national sales manager; Mike Ryan, vice president and editor-in-chief; and Lisa Pinto, executive director of development have supported this project with amazing talent and resources. Beth Mejia, Director, Editorial, went the distance for this project and became a dear friend in the process. With kind and thoughtful leadership and sharp intellect, Mark Georgiev, sponsoring editor, took us by the hand and gently led us to where we needed to be. We benefited from steady guidance and wisdom from Rhona Robbin, director of development, and Lisa Moore, publisher for special projects. Senior development editor Carla Samodulski's enormous patience, sweet disposition, and impeccable insight made our book and our lives better. Editor Sylvia Mallory contributed her considerable skill and vast body of knowledge to improve every chapter in *American Democracy Now*. Marketing manager Bill Minick's enthusiasm, encouragement, and support have meant a great deal to us. Leslie LaDow, our production editor, and her team showed innovation and flexibility. We would particularly like to thank Cassandra Chu and Linda Beaupré, our designers; Robin Mouat, our art manager; Judith Brown, our copy editor; and Alex Ambrose and David Tietz, our photo researchers. Briana Porco, Rachel Bara, and Elena Mackawgy provided invaluable support with good humor. We are extraordinarily grateful to all of you.

We would also like to thank our contributors: Suzanne U. Samuels at Ramapo College, Elizabeth Bennion at Indiana University, and Carol Whitney.

For their patience, understanding, and support, the authors also wish to thank: Ken, Caroline, Alexandra, and John Harrison, Rosemary Fitzgerald, Patricia Jillard, Kathleen Cain, John Callahan, Teresa Biebel, Thomas Callahan, Paula Straub, Sarah Griffith, Deborah Davies, Michael Harris, Jim and Audrey Wahl and the Wahl "girls"—Eileen Choynowski, Laura McAlpine, Audrey Messina, and Jaimee Conner; Bryan D. Smith; Aaron M. Arnold; and Martin Tolchin.

John and Rosemary Callahan and Jim and Audrey Wahl first began the conversation of democracy with us and we thank them and all of the students and colleagues, friends and family members, who continue that conversation now.

Brigid Callahan Harrison
Jean Wahl Harris
Susan J. Tolchin

ABOUT THE AUTHORS

Brigid Callahan Harrison

Brigid Harrison specializes in the civic engagement and political participation of Americans, especially the Millennial Generation, the U.S. Congress, and the Presidency. Brigid has taught American government for over fourteen years. She takes particular pride in creating in the classroom a learning experience that shapes students' lifelong understanding of American politics, sharpens their critical thinking about American government, and encourages their participation in civic life. She enjoys supervising student internships in political campaigns and government and is a frequent commentator in print and electronic media on national and New Jersey politics. She received her B.A. from The Richard Stockton College, her M.A. from Rutgers, The State University of New Jersey, and her Ph.D. from Temple University. Harrison lives in Galloway, NJ and has three children: Caroline (14), Alexandra (8), and John (5). Born and raised in New Jersey, Harrison is a fan of Bruce Springsteen and professor of political science and law at Montclair State University.

Jean Wahl Harris

Jean Harris's research interests include political socialization and engagement, federalism, and the evolution and institutionalization of the first ladyship and the vice presidency. She regularly teaches introductory courses in local, state, and national government and upper level courses in public administration and public policy. In the classroom, Jean seeks to cultivate students' participation in the political conversation so vital to American civic life and to convey the profound opportunities that the American political system affords an active, critical, and informed citizenry. She earned her B.A., M.A., and Ph.D. from the State University of New York at Binghamton. In 1994 the University of Scranton named her its CASE (Council for Advancement and Support of Education) professor of the year. She was an American Council on Education (ACE) Fellow during the 2007–08 academic year. Jean lives in Nicholson, Pennsylvania with her husband Michael. She enjoys reading on her deck overlooking the Endless Mountains of Northeast Pennsylvania.

Susan J. Tolchin

Susan Tolchin's research interests focus on public policy theory, federal government, federal regulation, and ethics. She enjoys teaching public policy and the processes that create good governance. She is the co-author, with Martin Tolchin, of seven books, including *Dismantling America: The Rush to Deregulate* (1983); *Buying Into America: How Foreign Money is Changing the Nation* (1988); *Selling Our Security: The Erosion of America's Assets* (1992); and *Glass Houses: Congressional Ethics and the Politics of Venom* (2001). She was elected a fellow and board member of the National Academy of Public Administration. In 1997, she received the Marshall Dimock Award from the American Society for Public Administration for the best lead article in the Public Administration Review for 1996, and in 1998, the Trachtenberg Award for Research from George Washington University.

CHAPTER

1

People, Politics, and Participation

THEN

Cynicism, distrust, and apathy have characterized Americans' relationship with their government for the past generation.

NOW

New information technologies, new political leadership, and a diversifying population give cause for optimism as the nation responds to the challenges of a new millennium.

NEXT

Will the present generation break the cycle of cynicism that has pervaded the politics of the recent past?

Will new information technologies facilitate and energize political participation?

Will the face of American politics change as the nation's population grows and shifts?

3

Defining the Millennial Generation

Social scientists do not know what to call the generation born between 1980 and 1995. Some call it Generation Y, because its members were born after the group known as Generation X (those who came into the world between 1965 and 1980). Others call it the Internet Generation; still others, the 9/11 Generation. One social scientist even dubbed it "Generation We."* But perhaps the term *Millennial Generation* best describes individuals who came of age in the new century, for a couple of reasons. First, names that define this generation in relation to other generations are inadequate. Second, characterizing an entire generation based on its relationship to technology or to a single event does a disservice to its complexity, opinions, and priorities. Besides, the Millennial Generation sounds cooler than those other labels. ❙ You may or may not be a millennial. Whether you are or aren't, *American Democracy Now* is about *you*. Like the Baby Boom Generation (Americans born between 1945 and 1964) that has defined U.S. politics since the late 1960s, the Millennial Generation will influence politics and political participation disproportionately for the next fifty years. If you are not part of this generation, you might have relatives who are. Whatever your relationship to the millennials, you will need to understand them as they make their mark on the country's political life. ❙ "But wait," you might be saying, "a lot of my friends aren't interested in politics. They don't vote. They're too busy to talk about political issues; they couldn't care less." Though this might be true for many in this generation, and the media might reinforce these ideas, the following statistics demonstrate otherwise:

> Members of the millennial generation often participate in the civic life of their communities by volunteering, as this Syracuse, New York, college student does.

■ In 2005, 76 percent of all high school seniors had volunteered in their community, compared with 65 percent in 1976.**

■ In 2005, over 13 percent of high school seniors *regularly* volunteered in their community, nearly double the rate a generation ago (7.8 percent in 1975).***

■ College students volunteer in a wide variety of activities, including tutoring and mentoring children, helping religious organizations, and assisting social or community organizations to provide services.[†]

■ The most common reason young people give for volunteering is "to help other people."[†]
❙ Forty-one percent of 18- to 20-year-olds who were eligible to vote in 2004 voted. Although this turnout was not as high as the turnout in the 1972 presidential election (48 percent), which occurred immediately after people in this age group were granted the legal right to vote, it was higher than turnout among young people in the 1976 presidential election (38 percent).[§] ❙ Many members of the Millennial Generation also differ from their older peers in *how* they are engaged in their communities. For example, college-age volunteers are more likely than older adults to volunteer with religious, social, community, and environmental organizations and less likely to volunteer with traditional political institutions, such as campaigns and party organizations. They rely on nontraditional sources such as the Internet and YouTube for their news (and entertainment). They also rely on social-networking sites such Facebook to communicate with others.

*Carl M. Cannon, "Generation 'We': The Awakened Giant," *National Journal,* March 9, 2007: 20–27; **Mark Hugo Lopez and Karlo Barrios Marcelo, "Volunteering Among Young People," Circle: the Center for Information & Research on Civic Learning & Engagement, www.civicyouth.org/PopUps/FactSheets/FS07_Volunteering.pdf; ***Ibid; †Mark Hugo Lopez, Peter Levine, Deborah Both, Abby Kiesa, Emily Kirby, and Karlo Marcelo, "The 2006 Civic and Political Health of the Nation: A Detailed Look at How Youth Participate in Politics and Communities," www.civicyouth.org/PopUps/2006_CPHS_Report_update.pdf; †Lopez and Marcelo, "Volunteering Among Young People"; §*Statistical Abstract of the United States,* Table 405, "Voting-Age Population, Percent Reporting Registered, and Voted: 1972 to 2004," www.census.gov/compendia/statab/tables/07s0405.xls.

The United States was founded

by individuals who believed in the power of democracy to respond to the will of citizens. Historically, citizen activists have come from all walks of life, but they have shared one common attribute: the belief that, in the ongoing conversation of democracy, their government listens to *people like them*. This idea is vital if individuals are to have an impact on their government; people who don't believe they can have any influence rarely try. From the Pilgrims' flight from religious persecution, to the War for Independence, to the Civil War, to the Great Depression, to World War II, and to the great movements for social justice—civil rights, women's liberation, and more—the story of the United States is the story of people who are involved with their government, who know what they want their government to do, and who have confidence in their ability to influence its policies.[1] *American Democracy Now* tells the story of how today's citizen activists are participating in the "conversation of democracy"—in the politics, governance, and civic life of their communities and their nation during a time of technological revolution and unprecedented global change. This story is the next chapter in America's larger story.

The history of democracy in the United States is rife with examples of ordinary people who have made and are making a difference.[2] Throughout this book, we describe the impact that individuals and groups have had, and continue to have, in creating and changing the country's institutions of government. We also explore how individuals have influenced the ways in which our governments—national, state, and local—create policy.[3] These stories are important not only in and of themselves but also as motivators for all of us who want to live in a democracy that responds to all of its citizens.

A fundamental principle underlying this book is that your beliefs and your voice—and ultimately how you use those beliefs and that voice—matter. Whatever your beliefs, it is important that you come to them thoughtfully, by employing introspection and critical thinking. Similarly, however you choose to participate, it is crucial that you take part in the civic life of your community. This book seeks both to inform and to inspire your participation. A sentiment voiced by American anthropologist Margaret Mead expresses a powerful truth: "Never doubt that a small group of thoughtful, committed citizens can change the world. Indeed, it's the only thing that ever has." This sentiment demonstrates our respect for the importance of your activism in the civic and political life of the United States and our desire to nurture that activism.

This chapter provides a framework for your study of American government in this textbook.

FIRST, we delve into the basic question, *why should you study American democracy now?*

SECOND, we explore *what government does.*

THIRD, we explain how political scientists categorize the various *types of government.*

FOURTH, we consider the *origins of American democracy,* including the ideas of natural law, a social contract, and representative democracy.

FIFTH, we examine *political culture and American values,* which centrally include liberty; equality; consent of the governed; capitalism; and the importance of the individual, the family, and the community.

SIXTH, we focus on *the changing face of American democracy* as the population grows and diversifies.

SEVENTH, we look at *ideology as a prism* through which American politics can be viewed.

y shd u stdy am dem now? Or, Why Should You Study American Democracy Now?

Politics as practiced today is not your parents' brand of politics. **Politics**—the process of deciding who gets benefits in society and who is excluded from benefiting—is a much different process today than it was even a decade ago. Advances in technology have altered the political landscape in many ways, including how voters and candidates communicate with each other, how governments provide information to individuals, how people get their news about events, and how governments administer laws. The political landscape has also

politics
the process of deciding who gets benefits in society and who is excluded from benefiting

changed because of world events. In particular, the terrorist attacks of September 11, 2001, and the wars in Iraq and Afghanistan have markedly changed many aspects of American life. Color-coded terror alerts are now routine; Americans have become immune to the latest reports of suicide bombings in Iraq, Afghanistan, and elsewhere; and they have become all too familiar with reports of local soldiers killed in war. These shifts in how Americans interact with government and in what issues concern them represent distinct changes that make the study of politics today interesting, exciting, and important.

How Technology Has Changed Politics

It would be difficult to overstate the impact of the technological revolution on politics as it is practiced today. In electoral politics, faster computers and the Internet have revolutionized a process that, until the advent of the personal computer and the World Wide Web, was not that different in 1990 from the way it was carried out in 1890. Today, many voters get a good portion of their information from Internet-based news sites and Weblogs. Campaigns rely on e-mail; instant and text messaging; Web sites; and social-networking pages on MySpace, Facebook, BlackPlanet, Cyloop, and similar sites to communicate with and organize supporters. State governments rely on computers to conduct elections.

>Today's political candidates need to meet voters where they live: on the Internet. Candidates for federal office typically maintain Web sites, and many have a presence in other virtual communities such as MySpace, Facebook, Flickr, YouTube, Eons, and Twitter. If a candidate wins an election in SecondLife, is it binding IRL?

But the impact of technology is not limited to elections. Would you like to help your grandfather apply for his Social Security benefits? You no longer need to go to the local Social Security office or even mail an application; instead, you can help him apply online, and his check can be deposited into his bank account electronically. Do you want to communicate your views to your representatives in Congress? You do not need to call or send a letter by snail mail—their e-mail addresses are available online. Do you want to find out which government agencies are hiring recent college graduates? Go to usajobs.gov. Do you need to ship a package using the U.S. Postal Service? The postal service Web site provides guidelines.

Because of these unprecedented shifts in the ways politics happens and government is administered, Americans today face both new opportunities and new challenges. How might we use technology to ensure that elections are conducted fairly? How might the abundance and reach of media technology be directed toward informing and enriching us rather than overwhelming us or perpetuating the citizen cynicism of recent years? What privacy rights can we be sure of in the present digital age? Whatever your age, as a student, you are a member of one of the most tech-savvy groups in the country, and your input, expertise, and participation are vital to sorting out the opportunities and obstacles of this next stage of American democracy.

The Political Context Now

September 11, 2001, and the subsequent wars in Iraq and Afghanistan have had a marked effect on the U.S. political environment. These events have been a catalyst for changes in the attitudes of many Americans, including young Americans, about their government and their role in it.

Since the early 1970s—a decade blemished by the intense unpopularity of the Vietnam War and by scandals that ushered in the resignation of President Richard Nixon in 1974—Americans' attitudes about government have been dismal.[4] Numerous surveys, including an ongoing Gallup poll that has tracked Americans' opinions, have demonstrated low levels of trust in government and of confidence in government's ability to solve problems.[5] Young people's views have mirrored those of the nation as a whole. In 2000, one study of undergraduate college students, for example, showed that nearly two-thirds (64 percent) did not trust the federal government to do the right thing most of the time, an attitude that reflected the views of the larger population.[6] Distrust; lack of **efficacy,** which is a person's belief that he or she has the ability to achieve something desirable and that the government genuinely listens to individuals; and apathy among young people were reflected in the voter turnout for the 2000 presidential election, when only 36 percent of eligible college-age voters went to the polls.

The events of 9/11 jolted American politics and the nation, and the altered political context provoked changes in popular views—notably, young people's opinions. "The attacks of 9/11 . . . changed the way the Millennial Generation thinks about politics. Overnight, their attitudes were more like [those of] the Greatest Generation [the generation of Americans who lived through the Great Depression and World War II]," observed John Della Volpe, a pollster who helped Harvard University students construct a national poll of young people's views.[7]

As patriotic spirits soared, suddenly 60 percent of college students trusted government to do the right thing. Ninety-two percent considered themselves patriotic. Some 77 percent thought that politics was relevant to their lives.[8] In the immediate aftermath of the 9/11 attacks, President George W. Bush and Congress enjoyed record-high approval ratings. Roughly 80 percent of young people and nearly that same percentage of all Americans supported U.S. military actions in Afghanistan. Beyond opinions, actions changed as well:

- More than 70 percent of college students gave blood, donated money, or volunteered in relief efforts.
- Nearly 70 percent volunteered in their communities (up from 60 percent in 2000).
- Eighty-six percent believed their generation was ready to lead the U. S. into the future.[9]

Technology and Political Participation

THEN (1970s)	NOW (2009)
47 percent of 18- to 20-year-olds voted in the 1976 presidential election.	About 53 percent of 18- to 20-year-olds voted in the 2008 presidential election.
People got their national news from one half-hour-long nightly news broadcast.	People get their news from an array of sources, including twenty-four-hour news networks and Internet news services available on demand on computers and cell phones.
Many people participated in civic life primarily through demonstrations, protests, and voting.	People still participate through demonstrations and protests but now also through volunteerism, Internet communities, and targeted purchasing; and a competitive Democratic primary in 2008 generated record-breaking voter participation and interest.

WHAT'S NEXT?

> How might advancing media technologies further transform the ways that people "consume" their news?

> Will the upswing of voter participation by 18- to 20-year-olds continue?

> What new forms of civic participation will emerge?

> Will the highly competitive 2008 presidential race motivate a new wave of voters to remain active participants in the electoral process?

Then the political context changed again, over months and then years, as wars in Afghanistan and Iraq wore on, as casualties mounted, and as military spending skyrocketed. Trust in government, particularly of the president, plummeted. The changes after 9/11 continued to affect how Americans, particularly young Americans, participate in politics.

An important trend is visible in one of the most easily measured contexts: voter turnout. Figure 1.1 shows the jump in participation by young voters in the 2004 presidential election. (In contrast, for voters aged 66–74, participation actually *de*creased in 2004.) Among voters aged 18–21, the largest increases in turnout occurred among 19-year-olds, whose turnout rivaled that of voters in their 30s. Americans are debating the importance of this upswing in turnout over the long haul (see "The Conversation of Democracy"). In 2008, that trend continued, with estimates indicating that voters aged 18–20 increased by 2.2 million, surpassing the young voter turnout since 18-year-olds voted for the first time in 1972.

As these statistics demonstrate, lingering media characterizations of a cynical young electorate are off the mark. The evidence indicates that many young people are enthusiastic

efficacy
citizens' belief that they have the ability to achieve something desirable and that the government listens to people like them

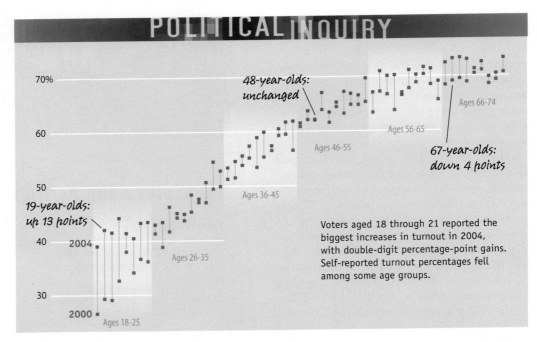

70%

48-year-olds: *unchanged*

Ages 66-74

60

Ages 56-65

Ages 46-55

67-year-olds: *down 4 points*

19-year-olds: *up 13 points*

50

Ages 36-45

Voters aged 18 through 21 reported the biggest increases in turnout in 2004, with double-digit percentage-point gains. Self-reported turnout percentages fell among some age groups.

40 2004

Ages 26-35

30

2000 Ages 18-25

FIGURE 1.1 ■ **VOTER TURNOUT 2000–2004 BY VOTER AGE** In 2008, turnout for the 18–29 age group was about 53 percent, while overall turnout rate increased to 64 percent, the highest rate in at least 48 years. What trends led to this increased turnout?

Source: Carl M. Cannon, "Generation 'We': The Awakened Giant," *National Journal*, March 9, 2007. © 2007 by National Journal Group, Inc. All rights reserved.

participants in civic and political life.[10] Witness the strong political support that the presidential campaign of Senator Barack Obama (D-Illinois) garnered from young people, some of whom packed their bags and traveled with the Obama team during the primary season that led to the Democratic convention in August 2008. Others are taking part in ways that have not traditionally been thought of, and measured as, participation. These include, for example, Internet activism and using one's power as a consumer to send political messages. For many students, that foundation of political participation, volunteerism, or community action has already provided them with a rationale for increasing their knowledge of, and participation in, their communities.

Individuals who engage in politics and civic life experience many benefits. Engaged citizens are knowledgeable about public issues; actively communicate with policy makers and others; press government officials to carry out the people's will; advocate for their own self-interest and the interests of others; and hold public officials accountable for their decisions and actions. You will find that advocating for your own interests or working with others in similar situations will sometimes (perhaps to your surprise) lead to desired outcomes. This is efficacy in action. And you will discover that with experience you will become more effective at advocacy—the more you do, the better you get. Furthermore, you will derive social and psychological benefits from being civically engaged.

In addition, and importantly, local communities, states, and the nation benefit from an engaged populace. Governments are more effective when people voice their views. As we explore throughout this book, American democracy provides citizens and others more opportunities to influence governmental action than at any other time in history. If you have the knowledge and tools, you should be able to make the most of these opportunities.

What Government Does

In this brief section, we look at the nature of government and the functions a government performs. Let's start with some important definitions. **Government** is an institution that creates and implements the policy and laws that guide the conduct of a nation and its citizens. **Citizens** are those members of a political community—town, city, state, or country—who,

government
the institution that creates and implements policies and laws that guide the conduct of the nation and its citizens

citizens
members of the polity who, through birth or naturalization, enjoy the rights, privileges, and responsibilities attached to membership in a given nation

THE CONVERSATION OF DEMOCRACY

DOES THE YOUTH VOTE MATTER?

The Issue: Organizations targeting the "youth vote" abound. David D. Burstein, a 19-year-old Haverford College student, traveled the country interviewing members of Congress, reporters, student activists, and apathetic college students for his film *18in08*. The documentary turned into an organization, 18in08, which is (according to 18in08's Web site) "a truly unprecedented national peer-to-peer effort to register, engage, and mobilize young voters for the 2008 election and beyond."[11] This youth mobilization has primarily occurred through screenings of the film paired with follow-up talk-back sessions in which political leaders engage with students and voter registration opportunities are extended.

Claims about the impact of the youth vote and about the effectiveness of organizations such as 18in08 are questioned by some in the media, who point to the failure of young voters to live up to their potential. For example, in 2004, young voters preferred Democratic nominee John Kerry by a ten-point margin, and they were widely expected to deliver the White House to the Democrats—who were ultimately defeated. During that 2004 presidential race, through an organization called Citizen Change, rapper P. Diddy started a mobilization campaign called Vote or Die—an allusion to the high stakes of the 2004 election, which emphasized the issue of the war in Iraq. Like 18in08, Vote or Die was designed to "make voting hot, sexy and relevant to a generation that hasn't reached full participation in the political process" according to the campaign's Web site.[12]

With all this intensive effort as a backdrop, the question arises: Has the youth vote genuinely made a difference in recent elections?

Yes: The youth vote has mattered. The 2008 election serves as evidence of the importance of the youth vote. Barack Obama's candidacy would have faltered early on were it not for the support of young voters, particularly those in early primary and caucus states such as Iowa and New Hampshire, where Obama enjoyed overwhelming support from young voters. As for the 2004 youth vote, the media have portrayed it inaccurately. That year, there was an 11 percent increase in the turnout rate among voters under the age of 25.

Young voters have made a difference in the outcomes of a number of hotly contested political races, including the 2006 U.S. Senate race in Virginia. During the campaign, incumbent Republican senator George Allen called S. R. Sidarth, a volunteer working for Democrat Jim Webb's campaign, a "macaca," a term thought to be derived from the name of a kind of monkey. Sidarth, an Indian American college student conducting opposition research for Webb, shot video of the speech in which Allen uttered the slur, and the video was subsequently posted on YouTube. Webb's Senate victory is frequently attributed to minority voters' opposition to Allen's candidacy. But Webb also won sizeable victories in cities with college campuses, including a large plurality of the vote in Charlottesville, where Sidarth was a senior at the University of Virginia.

No: The youth vote has failed to live up to its potential. Young voters were important to Barack Obama's candidacy, but in other elections, they have failed to vote in sufficient numbers to influence results. The media were correct in blaming John Kerry's 2004 loss on insufficient turnout by young voters. Election exit-poll data showed that a large percentage of young people had not voted.

CBS News appropriately asked the question "Are young voters has-beens?" Matt Drudge, who maintains the influential conservative Weblog *The Drudge Report,* justifiably ridiculed Diddy's campaign as "Vote or Die or Whatever."*

Other approaches: The youth vote is ill informed and should not be encouraged. The social scientists who advocate repealing the Twenty-Sixth Amendment, which extended the franchise to citizens 18 years of age or older in 1971, have a point: that young people lack the knowledge and experience to be informed voters. Timothy Furnish, a history professor at Georgia Perimeter College, advocates this point of view:

> Democracy works when KNOWLEDGEABLE citizens vote, as was recognized as long ago as Plato's and Aristotle's time. Can any rational member of the human species watch Jay Leno's *Jaywalking*—in which he roams the streets of Southern California, interviewing folks who don't know the vice president's name, which hemisphere they live in—and possibly think it's a good idea for these people to be left alone with a voting machine of any kind?
>
> As a college history professor, I can cite examples of 18- and 19-year-olds' ignorance that make the Jaywalkers look like the Founding Fathers . . . The point is that we allow such uninformed people to vote! Indeed, we encourage it: MTV's "Rock the Vote," P. Diddy's "Vote or Die." There's even an organization, Youthrights.org, that demands we lower the voting age to 16! (Just what we need: presidential candidates taking stands on their preferred anti-acne medication.)**

What do you think?

① What was the impact of the youth vote on the 2008 election? How can campaigns more effectively mobilize young voters?

② What issues motivate young voters to vote? Do campaigns like 18in08 and Rock the Vote make any difference? Explain.

③ What is the effect of allowing uninformed voters to vote?

④ Do you agree with Professor Furnish's assessment of young potential voters? Why or why not?

*The Drudge Report, www.sfgate.com/cgi-bin/article.cgi?file=/news/archive/2004/11/02/politics2059EST0779.DTL&type=printable, November 3, 2004.
**Timothy Furnish, "Should We Take Away the Right to Vote of 18 Year Olds?" George Mason University's History News Network, http://hnn.us/articles/8491.html.

DOING DEMOCRACY

MAKE A DIFFERENCE ANY DAY OF THE YEAR

FACT:

Each year in late October, students and other volunteers give up part of their Saturday to help make their communities a better place. Make a Difference Day, a national day of service, was created in 1997 by Gannett's *USA Weekend Magazine*. In 2007, millions of people participated, volunteering for hundreds of organizations throughout the country. Make a Difference Day promotes volunteerism and community-building for groups and individuals alike.

College students volunteered for a number of projects. Students from the College of Lake County in Illinois salvaged food that humans couldn't eat from a local food bank to feed the big cats at the Valley of the Kings Sanctuary and Retreat in southeastern Wisconsin. Fraternity and sorority members from Eastern Kentucky University helped build a Habitat for Humanity home. Students from Black Hills State University in South Dakota volunteered at a local nursing home. Volunteers from Herkimer County Community College in New York cleaned up the Herkimer Mini Park, and students from West Virginia University, Parkersburg, contributed their time and muscle to building a town playground.

> Two engineering students from Case Western University volunteer to repair and adapt toys for disabled children.

Act!

You need not wait until Make a Difference Day to start making a difference. Participating in the life of your community has many benefits. Being an active participant will make you feel empowered in terms of the impact your actions can have on your own life and the lives of others. Individuals involved in local activities can improve a school, a community, a state, and the nation. It goes even further: the cumulative efforts of those who take part make for a better world. If you are not motivated by altruism, then become engaged for selfish reasons: research conducted by Circle: The Center for Information and Research on Civic Learning and Engagement finds that students who volunteer in their communities are more likely to graduate from college and that they get better grades than their non-volunteering peers.*

Where to begin

- Many colleges and universities provide clearinghouse services that offer nonprofits and other organizations seeking volunteers the opportunity to recruit students. Start by asking your dean of students or the career planning office if such a service is available at your school.
- The national United Way maintains a volunteer database that matches volunteers with member agencies. Go to http://national.unitedway.org/volunteer/ and enter your zip code.
- Volunteermatch.org (www.volunteermatch.org) posts a wide variety of volunteer positions. Enter your zip code and select an area of interest in which you would like to volunteer. The site offers opportunities ranging from animal protection, to gay rights, to disaster relief. There are even assignments for virtual volunteers who can use the Internet to help various organizations.
- The "Doing Democracy" feature throughout this book provides specific steps you can take to become active in your community, particularly through political participation.

*Alberto Davila and Marie T. Mora, "Civic Engagement and High School Academic Progress: An Analysis Using NELS Data," Circle: the Center for Information & Research on Civic Learning & Engagement, www.civicyouth.org/PopUps/WorkingPapers/WP52Mora.pdf.

through birth or naturalization, enjoy the rights, privileges, and responsibilities attached to membership in a given nation. **Naturalization** means becoming a citizen by means other than birth, as in the case of immigrants. Although governments vary widely in how well they perform, most national governments share some common functions.

To get a clear sense of the business of government, consider the following key functions performed by government in the United States and many other national governments:

- **To protect their sovereign territory and their citizenry and to provide national defense.** Governments protect their *sovereign territory* (that is, the territory over which they have the ultimate governing authority) and their citizens at home and abroad. Usually they carry out this responsibility by maintaining one or more types of armed services, but governments also provide for the national defense through counterterrorism efforts.

    In the United States, the armed services include the Army, Navy, Marines, Air Force, and Coast Guard. In 2008, the U.S. Department of Defense budget was approximately $480 billion. This excludes about $235 billion in emergency appropriations for military operations in Iraq and Afghanistan, plus about $38 billion in funding for the Department of Homeland Security.

    Governments also preserve order domestically. In the United States, domestic order is preserved through the National Guard and federal, state, and local law enforcement agencies.

- **To preserve order and stability.** Governments also preserve order by providing emergency services and security in the wake of disasters. For example, after Hurricane Katrina struck the Gulf Coast and the city of New Orleans in August 2005, the National Guard was sent in to provide security in the midst of an increasingly dangerous situation (though in the eyes of many critics, including local and state elected officials, the action came too late to "preserve order"). Governments also maintain stability by providing a political structure that has **legitimacy:** a quality conferred on government by citizens who believe that its exercise of power is right and proper.[13]

- **To establish and maintain a legal system.** Governments create legal structures by enacting and enforcing laws that restrict or ban certain behaviors. In the United States, the foundation of this legal structure is the federal Constitution.[14] Governments also provide the means to implement laws through the actions of local police and other state and national law enforcement agencies. By means of the court system, governments administer justice and impose penalties.

- **To provide services.** Governments distribute a wide variety of services to their citizens. In the United States, government agencies provide services ranging from inspecting the meat we consume to ensuring the safety of the places where we work. Federal, state, and local governments provide roads, bridges, transportation, education, and health services. They facilitate communication, commerce, air travel, and entertainment.

    Many of the services governments provide are called **public goods** because their benefits, by their nature, cannot be limited to specific groups or individuals. For example, everyone enjoys national defense, equal access to clean air and clean water, airport security, highways, and other similar services. Because the value and benefits of these goods are extended to everyone, government makes them available through revenue collected by taxes. Not all goods that government provides are public goods, however; some goods, like access to government-provided health care, are available only to the poor or to older Americans.

- **To raise and spend money.** All of the services that governments provide, from national protection and defense to health care, cost money.[15] Governments at all levels spend money collected through taxes. Depending on personal income, between

> Children are socialized to the dominant political culture from a very early age. When children emulate firefighters, for example, they begin the process of learning about the functions governments perform.

25 and 35 cents of every dollar earned by those working in the United States and earning above a certain level goes toward federal, state, and local income taxes. Governments also tax *commodities* (commercially exchanged goods and services) in various ways—through sales taxes, property taxes, sin taxes, and luxury taxes.

■ **To socialize new generations.** Governments play a role in *socialization,* the process by which individuals develop their political values and opinions. Governments perform this function, for example, by providing funding for schools, by introducing young people to the various "faces" of government (perhaps through a police officer's visiting a school or a mayor's bestowing an honor on a student), and by facilitating participation in civic life through institutions such as libraries, museums, and public parks. In these ways, governments transmit cultural norms and values such as patriotism and build commitment to fundamental values such as those we explore later in this chapter. For a detailed discussion of political socialization, see Chapter 6.

Types of Government

When social scientists categorize the different systems of government operating in the world today, two factors influence their classifications. The first factor is *who participates in governing or in selecting those who govern.* These participants vary as follows, depending on whether the government is a monarchy, an oligarchy, or a democracy:

■ In a **monarchy,** a member of a royal family, usually a king or queen, has absolute authority over a territory and its government. Monarchies typically are inherited—they pass down from generation to generation. Most modern monarchies, such as those in Great Britain and Spain, are *constitutional monarchies* in which the monarch plays a ceremonial role but has little actual say in governance, which is carried out by elected leaders. In contrast, in traditional monarchies, such as the Kingdom of Saudi Arabia, the monarch is both the ceremonial and the governmental head of state.

- In an **oligarchy,** an elite few hold power. Some oligarchies are *dictatorships,* in which a small group, such as a political party or military junta, supports a dictator. North Korea and Myanmar (formerly Burma) are present-day examples of oligarchies.
- In a **democracy,** the supreme power of governance lies in the hands of citizens. The United States and most other modern democracies are *republics,* sometimes called *representative democracies,* in which citizens elect leaders to represent their views. We discuss the idea of a republican form of government in detail in Chapter 2.

Social scientists also consider *how governments function* and *how they are structured* when classifying governments:

- Governments that rule according to the principles of **totalitarianism** essentially control every aspect of their citizens' lives. In these tyrannical governments, citizens enjoy neither rights nor freedoms, and the state is the tool of the dictator. Totalitarian regimes tend to center on a particular ideology, religion, or personality. North Korea is a contemporary example of a totalitarian regime, as was Afghanistan under the Islamic fundamentalist regime of the Taliban.
- When a government rules by the principles of **authoritarianism,** it holds strong powers, but they are checked by other forces within the society. China and Cuba are examples of authoritarian states because their leaders are restrained in their exercise of power by political parties, constitutions, and the military. Individuals living under an authoritarian regime may enjoy some rights, but often these rights are not protected by the government.
- **Constitutionalism,** a form of government structured by law, provides for **limited government**—a government that is restricted in what it can do so that the rights of the people are protected. Constitutional governments can be democracies or monarchies. In the United States, the federal Constitution created the governmental structure, and this system of government reflects both the historical experiences and the norms and values of the founders.

The Constitution's framers (authors) structured American government as a *constitutional democracy.* In this type of government, a constitution creates a representative democracy in which the rights of the people are protected. We can trace the roots of this modern constitutional democracy back to ancient times.

monarchy
government in which a member of a royal family, usually a king or queen, has absolute authority over a territory and its government

oligarchy
government in which an elite few hold power

democracy
government in which supreme power of governance lies in the hands of its citizens

totalitarianism
system of government in which the government essentially controls every aspect of people's lives

authoritarianism
system of government in which the government holds strong powers but is checked by some forces

constitutionalism
government that is structured by law, and in which the power of government is limited

limited government
government that is restricted in what it can do so that the rights of the people are protected

The Origins of American Democracy

The ancient Greeks first developed the concept of a democracy. The Greeks used the term *demokratia* (literally, "people power") to describe some of the 1,500 *poleis* ("city-states"; also the root of *politics*) on the Black and Mediterranean seas. These city-states were not democracies in the modern sense of the term, but the way they were governed provided the philosophical origins of American democracy. For example, citizens decided public issues using majority rule in many of the city-states. However, in contrast to modern democracies, the Greek city-states did not count women and slaves as citizens. American democracy also traces some of its roots to the Judeo-Christian religion and the English common law, particularly the ideas that thrived during the Protestant Reformation.[16]

Democracy's Origins in Popular Protest: The Influence of the Reformation and the Enlightenment

We can trace the seeds of the idea of *modern* democracy almost as far back as the concept of monarchy—back to several centuries ago, when the kings and emperors who ruled in Europe claimed that they reigned by divine sanction, or God's will. The monarchs' claims

divine right of kings
the assertion that monarchies, as a manifestation of God's will, could rule absolutely without regard to the will or well-being of their subjects

social contract
an agreement between people and their leaders in which the people agree to give up some liberties so that their other liberties are protected

natural law
the assertion that standards that govern human behavior are derived from the nature of humans themselves and can be universally applied

> In his scientific work, Sir Isaac Newton demonstrated the power of science to explain phenomena in the natural world and discredited prevalent ideas based on magic and superstition. Newton's ideas laid the foundation for the political philosophers of the Enlightenment.

reflected the political theory of the **divine right of kings,** articulated by Jacques-Benigne Bossuet (1627–1704), who argued that monarchies, as a manifestation of God's will, could rule absolutely without regard to the will or well-being of their subjects. Challenging the right of a monarch to govern or questioning one of his or her decisions thus represented a challenge to the will of God.

At odds with the theory of the divine right of kings was the idea that people could challenge the crown and the church—institutions that seemed all-powerful. This idea took hold during the Protestant Reformation, a movement to reform the Catholic Church. In October 1517, Martin Luther, a German monk who would later found the Lutheran Church, posted his *95 Theses,* criticizing the harmful practices of the Catholic Church, to the door of the church at Wittenberg Castle. The Reformation continued throughout the sixteenth century, during which time reform-minded Protestants (whose name is derived from *protest*) challenged basic tenets of Catholicism and sought to *purify* the church.

In England, some extreme Protestants, known as Puritans, thought that the Reformation had not gone far enough in reforming the church. Puritans asserted their right to communicate directly with God through prayer rather than through an intermediary such as a priest. This idea that an individual could speak directly with God lent support to the notion that the people could govern themselves. Faced with persecution in England, congregations of Puritans, known to us today as the Pilgrims, fled to America, where they established self-governing colonies, a radical notion at the time. Before the Pilgrims reached shore in 1620, they drew up the Mayflower Compact, an example of a **social contract**—an agreement between people and their leaders, whereby the people give up some liberties so that their other liberties will be protected. In the Mayflower Compact, the Pilgrims agreed to be governed by the structure of government they formed, thereby establishing consent of the governed.

In the late seventeenth century came the early beginnings of the Enlightenment, a philosophical movement that stressed the importance of individuality, reason, and scientific endeavor. Enlightenment scientists such as Sir Isaac Newton (1642–1727) drastically changed how people thought about the universe and the world around them, including government. Newton's work in physics, astronomy, math, and mechanics demonstrated the power of science and repudiated prevalent ideas based on magic and superstition. Newton's ideas about **natural law,** the assertion that the laws that govern human behavior are derived from the nature of humans themselves and can be universally applied, laid the foundation for the ideas of the political philosophers of the Enlightenment.

The Modern Political Philosophy of Hobbes and Locke

The difficulty of individual survival under the rule of an absolute monarch is portrayed by British philosopher Thomas Hobbes (1588–1679) in *Leviathan* (1651). Hobbes, who believed in the righteousness of absolute monarchies, argued that the strong naturally prey upon the weak and that through a social contract, individuals who relinquish their rights can enjoy the protection offered by a sovereign. Without such a social contract and without an absolute monarch, Hobbes asserted, anarchy prevails, describing this state as one lived in "continuall feare, and danger of violent death; And the life of man, solitary, poore, nasty, brutish, and short."[17]

John Locke (1632–1704) took Hobbes's reasoning concerning a social contract one step further. In the first of his *Two Treatises on Civil Government* (1689), Locke systematically rejected the notion that the rationale for the divine right of kings is based on scripture. By providing a theoretical basis for discarding the idea of a monarch's divine right to rule, Locke paved the way for more radical notions about the rights of individuals and the role of government. In the second *Treatise,* Locke argued that individuals possess certain unalienable (or natural) rights, which he identified as the rights to life, liberty, and property. He stressed that these rights are inherent in people as individuals; that is, government can neither bestow them nor take them away. When people enter into a social contract, Locke said, they do so with the understanding that the government will protect their natural rights. At the same time, according to Locke, they agree to accept the government's authority; but if the government fails to protect the inherent rights of individuals, the people have the right to rebel.

The French philosopher Jean-Jacques Rousseau (1712–1778) took Locke's notion further, stating that governments formed by social contract rely on **popular sovereignty,** the theory that government is created by the people and depends on the people for the authority to rule. **Social contract theory,** which assumes that individuals possess free will and that every individual possesses the God-given right of self-determination and the ability to consent to be governed, would eventually form the theoretical framework of the Declaration of Independence.

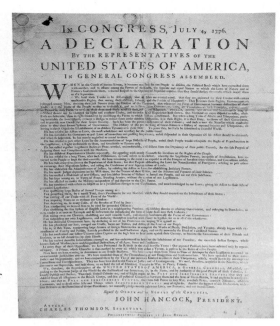

The Creation of the United States as an Experiment in Representative Democracy

The people who settled the American colonies that eventually rebelled against Great Britain and became the first thirteen states were shaped by their experiences of living under European monarchies. Many rejected the ideas of absolute rule and the divine right of kings, which had been central to rationalizing the monarchs' authority. The logic behind the rejection of the divine right of kings—the idea that monarchs were not chosen by God—was the idea that people could govern themselves.

In New England, where many colonists settled after fleeing England to escape religious persecution, a form of **direct democracy,** a structure of government in which citizens discuss and decide policy through majority rule, emerged in *town meetings* (which still take place today). In every colony, the colonists themselves decided who was eligible to participate in government, and so in some localities, women and people of color who owned property participated in government well before they were granted formal voting rights under amendments to the federal Constitution.

Beyond the forms of direct democracy prevalent in the New England colonies, nearly all of the American colonies had councils structured according to the principle of representative democracy, sometimes called **indirect democracy,** in which citizens elect representatives who decide policies on their behalf. These representative democracies foreshadow important political values that founders like Thomas Jefferson and James Madison would incorporate into key founding documents, including the Declaration of Independence and the Constitution.

Political Culture and American Values

On September 11, 2002, the first anniversary of the terrorist attacks on the United States, the *New York Times* ran an editorial, "America Enduring." The author described how the United States and its residents had weathered the difficult year after 9/11. "America isn't bound together by emotion. It's bound together by things that transcend emotion, by principles and laws, by ideals of freedom and justice that need constant articulation."[18] These ideals are part of American **political culture**—the people's collective beliefs and attitudes about government and the political process. These ideals include liberty, equality, capitalism, consent of the governed, and the importance of the individual (as well as family and community).

popular sovereignty
the theory that government is created by the people and depends on the people for the authority to rule

social contract theory
the idea that individuals possess free will, and every individual is equally endowed with the God-given right of self-determination and the ability to consent to be governed

direct democracy
a structure of government in which citizens discuss and decide policy through majority rule

indirect democracy
sometimes called a *representative democracy,* a system in which citizens elect representatives who decide policies on behalf of their constituents

political culture
the people's collective beliefs and attitudes about government and political processes

> Thomas Jefferson's ideas about the role of government shaped the United States for generations to come. In 1999, descendants of Thomas Jefferson, including those he fathered with his slave, Sally Hemings, posed for a group photo at his plantation, Monticello, in Charlottesville, Virginia.

Liberty

The most essential quality of American democracy, **liberty** is both freedom from government interference in our lives and freedom to pursue happiness. Many of the colonies that eventually became the United States were founded by people who were interested in one notion of liberty: religious freedom. Those who fought in the War for Independence were intent on obtaining economic and political freedom. The framers of the Constitution added to the structure of the U.S. government many other liberties,[19] including freedom of speech, freedom of the press, and freedom of association.[20]

There is evidence all around us of ongoing tensions between people attempting to assert their individual liberty on the one hand and the government's efforts to exert control on the other. For example, issues of religious freedom are in play in school districts where some parents object to the teaching of the theory of evolution because the theory contradicts their religious beliefs. Issues of freedom of the press have arisen as the government has attempted to prevent the news media from photographing the flag-draped coffins of soldiers killed in Iraq. The struggle for privacy rights—and how these rights are defined—continues unabated as the government's counterterrorism efforts result in officials' seeking greater access to our communications.

Throughout history and to the present day, liberties have often conflicted with efforts by the government to ensure a secure and stable society by exerting restraints on liberties. When government officials infringe on personal liberties, they often do so in the name of security, arguing that such measures are necessary in order to protect the rights of other individuals, institutions (including the government itself), or society as a whole. As we consider in Chapter 4, these efforts include, for example, infringing on the right to free speech by regulating or outlawing hate speech or speech that compels others to violence. Governments may also impinge on privacy rights; think of the various security measures that you are subject to before boarding an airplane.

The meaning of liberty—how we define our freedoms—is constantly evolving. In light of 9/11 and the digital revolution, difficult questions have arisen about how much liberty

liberty
the most essential quality of American democracy; it is both the freedom from governmental interference in citizens' lives and the freedom to pursue happiness

Americans should have and how far the government should go in curtailing liberties to provide security. Should law enforcement officers be allowed to listen in on an individual's phone conversations if that person is suspected of a crime? Or should they be required to get a warrant first? What if that person is suspected of plotting a terrorist attack—should the officer be required to obtain a warrant first in that situation? What if one of the suspected plotters is not a U.S. citizen?

> In 2003, New Yorkers and others from across the nation were moved by the Tribute in Light memorial at the site of the World Trade Center on the second anniversary of the September 11 terrorist attacks. Many Americans began to change their views about their country on September 11, 2001. These views are still evolving today.

Equality

The Declaration of Independence states that "all men are created equal . . ." But the founders' notions of equality were vastly different from those that prevail today. Their ideas of equality evolved from the emphasis the ancient Greeks placed on equality of opportunity. The Greeks envisioned a merit-based system in which educated freemen could participate in democratic government rather than inheriting their positions as a birthright. The Judeo-Christian religions also emphasize the idea of equality. All three major world religions—Christianity, Judaism, and Islam—stress that all people are equal in the eyes of God. These notions of equality informed both Jefferson's assertion about equality in the Declaration of Independence and, later, the framers' structuring of the U.S. government in the Constitution.[21]

The idea of equality evolved during the nineteenth and twentieth centuries. In the early American republic, all women, as well as all men of color, were denied fundamental rights, including the right to vote. Through long, painful struggles—including the abolition movement to free the slaves; the suffrage movement to gain women the right to vote; various immigrants' rights movements; and later the civil rights, Native American rights, and women's rights movements of the 1960s and 1970s (see Chapter 5)—members of these disenfranchised groups won the rights previously denied to them.

Several groups are still engaged in the struggle for legal equality today, notably gay and lesbian rights organizations and groups that advocate for fathers', children's, and immigrants' rights (see "On the Job"). And historic questions about the nature of equality have very modern implications: Are certain forms of inequality, such as preventing gay couples from enjoying the rights of married heterosexual couples, acceptable in American society? Are the advantages of U.S. democracy reserved only for citizens, or should immigrants living legally in the United States also enjoy these advantages?

Beyond these questions of legal equality, today many arguments over equality focus on issues of economic equality, a concept about which there is substantial disagreement. Some in the United States believe that the government should do more to eliminate disparities in wealth—by taxing wealthy people more heavily than others, for example, or by providing more subsidies and services to the poor. Others disagree, however, and argue that although people should have equal opportunities for economic achievement, their attainment of that success should depend on factors such as education and hard work, and that success should be determined in the marketplace rather than through government intervention.

Capitalism

Although the founders valued the notion of equality, capitalism was equally important to them. **Capitalism** is an economic system in which the means of producing wealth are privately owned and operated to produce profits. In a pure capitalist economy, the marketplace

capitalism
an economic system in which the means of producing wealth are privately owned and operated to produce profits

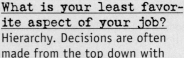

ON THE JOB

TINA HUANG, CHILD ADVOCATE

<u>Name:</u> Tina Huang

<u>Age:</u> 24

<u>Hometown:</u> New York City

<u>College:</u> Wesleyan University, Middletown, Connecticut

<u>Major:</u> Government and East Asian Studies (BA)

<u>Job title:</u> Staff Associate for Communications, Citizens' Committee for Children of New York, Inc. (CCC)

<u>Typical salary for jobs like this:</u> $45,000

<u>Day-to-day responsibilities:</u> I coordinate our annual Community Leadership Course (CLC), and I also work with designers and public relations consultants to design brochures, newsletters, and annual reports. In addition, I supervise college interns in the summer as they develop curricula and help plan the CLC course. Throughout the year, I communicate with 3,000 New Yorkers weekly via our CCC E-Action Network, a communications and action portal for New Yorkers to take action for children through e-alerts and e-newsletters, among my many other responsibilities for recruiting volunteers and for outreach.

<u>How did you get your job?</u> I replied to the job opening posted by another Wesleyan graduate and current CCC employee at Wesleyan's Career Resources Center.

<u>What do you like best about your job?</u> My favorite part is working with the interns and volunteers who are such a vital part of CCC. I love the opportunity to teach and mentor interns as they learn about children's advocacy work. Addition-ally, I love learning from CCC's cadre of volunteers, many of them retired professionals who have incredible insight into New York City's social and economic environment and the needs of children and families.

<u>What is your least favor-ite aspect of your job?</u> Hierarchy. Decisions are often made from the top down with little input from staff members who are working on the imple-mentation side. The creative and unique perspectives of new, young employees are often dismissed in favor of the status quo.

<u>What advice would you give to students who would like to do what you are doing?</u> When in-terviewing for communications/public relations positions in a nonprofit organization, take time to investigate how much priority the organization places on professional development for both young and longer-term employees. Although many nonprofits are strained for resources, they should *never* cut cor-ners when it comes to professional development for *all* of their employees over the entire course of their time at the organiza-tion. Also, as exciting as the job description may sound, you need to find out who your future supervisor will be (his or her type of personality and working style). Your future supervisor should be someone who can mentor you and with whom you see yourself developing a good relationship.

determines the regulation of production, the distribution of goods and services, wages, and prices. In this type of economy, for example, businesses pay employees the wage that they are willing to work for, without the government's setting a minimum wage by law. Although capitalism is an important value in American democracy, the U.S. government imposes cer-tain regulations on the economy: it mandates a minimum wage, regulates and inspects goods and services, and imposes tariffs on imports and taxes on domestically produced goods that have an impact on pricing.

property
anything that can be owned

One key component of capitalism is **property**—anything that can be owned. There are various kinds of property: businesses, homes, farms, the material items we use every day, and even ideas are considered property. Property holds such a prominent position in Ameri-can culture that it is considered a natural right, and some aspects of property ownership are constitutionally protected.

Consent of the Governed

The idea that, in a democracy, the government's power derives from the consent of the people is called the **consent of the governed.** As we have seen, this concept, a focal point of the rebellious American colonists and eloquently expressed in Jefferson's Declaration of Independence, is based on John Locke's idea of a social contract. Implicit in Locke's social contract is the principle that the people agree to the government's authority, and if the government no longer has the consent of the governed, the people have the right to revolt.

The concept of consent of the governed also implies **majority rule**—the principle that, in a democracy, only policies with 50 percent plus one vote are enacted, and only candidates who attain 50 percent plus one vote are elected. Governments based on majority rule include the idea that the majority has the right of self-governance and typically also protect the rights of people who are in the minority. A particular question about this ideal of governing by the consent of the governed has important implications for the United States in the early twenty-first century: Can a democracy remain stable and legitimate if less than a majority of its citizens participate in elections?

consent of the governed
the idea that, in a democracy, the government's power derives from the consent of the people

majority rule
the idea that in a democracy, only policies with 50 percent plus one vote are enacted, and only candidates that win 50 percent plus one vote are elected

Individual, Family, and Community

Emphasis on the individual is a preeminent feature of American democratic thought. In the Constitution, rights are bestowed on, and exercised by, the individual. The importance of the individual—an independent, hearty entity exercising self-determination—has powerfully shaped the development of the United States, both geographically and politically.

Family and community have also played central roles in the U.S. political culture, both historically and in the present day. A child first learns political behavior from his or her family, and in this way the family serves to perpetuate the political culture. And from the earliest colonial settlements to today's blogosphere, communities have channeled individuals' political participation. Indeed, the intimate relationship between individualism and community life is reflected in the First Amendment of the Constitution, which ensures individuals' freedom of assembly—one component of which is their right to form or join any type of organization, political party, or club without penalty.

The Changing Face of American Democracy

In the spring of 2006, thousands of demonstrators took to the streets in cities across the United States, demanding reform of the nation's immigration laws. Immigration reform has become a hot-button issue in recent years. Advocates for the rights of undocumented immigrant workers have called on legislators to pass an amnesty law that would provide a structure for the legalization of these illegal immigrants. The immigrant-rights supporters have noted that the withdrawal of "undocumented workers" from the workforce would cripple the U.S. economy, in particular the agricultural and restaurant industries. On the other side of the controversy are countless concerned citizens who worry that low-income "illegal aliens" are draining the resources of already hard-pressed communities that suddenly must provide services to these individuals. Further, many of these citizens say that the undocumented immigrants are breaking the law and thus should not be rewarded with amnesty.

Though the debate has been passionate, it is not new, nor is the intense reaction to it by recent immigrants, both legal and undocumented. The questions and anxieties about demographic (population) change owing to immigration are as old as the nation itself. Figure 1.2 shows how the U.S. population has grown since the first census in 1790. At that point there were fewer than 4 million Americans. By

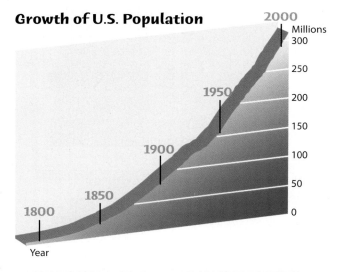

Growth of U.S. Population

POLITICAL INQUIRY

FIGURE 1.2 ■ **From 1790 to 1900, the population of the United States increased gradually, and it did not reach 100 million until the second decade of the twentieth century. What factors caused the steep rise during the twentieth century? How will these forces continue to affect the size of the U.S. population during this century?**

Source: U.S. Census, www.census.gov/population/www/documentation/twps0056 .html.

2000, the U.S. population had reached 281 million, and it will soar well over 300 million by the next census, in 2010.

Immigrants have always been part of the country's population growth, and over the centuries they have made innumerable contributions to American life and culture.[22] Immigrants from lands all around the world have faced the kind of struggles that today's undocumented immigrants encounter. Chinese Americans, for example, were instrumental in pioneering the West and completing the construction of the transcontinental railroad in the mid-nineteenth century, but they were excluded by law from becoming U.S. citizens by the Chinese Exclusion Act of 1881. Faced with the kinds of persecution that today would be considered hate crimes, Chinese Americans used civil disobedience to fight against the so-called Dog Tag Laws that required them to carry registration cards. In one incident, in 1885, they fought back against unruly mobs that drove them out of the town of Eureka, California, by suing the city for reparations and compensation.[23]

A Population That Is Growing— and on the Move

Between 1960 and 2000, the population of the United States increased by more than 50 percent. As the population rises, measures of who the American people are and what percentage of each demographic group makes up the population have significant implications for the policies, priorities, values, and preferred forms of civic and political participation of the people. All of the factors contributing to U.S. population growth—including immigration, the birth rate, falling infant mortality rates, and longer life spans—have broad implications for both politics and policy as the ongoing debate about immigration reform shows. Generational differences in preferred methods of participation are yet another, as is the national conversation about the future of Social Security.

Although it is difficult to measure the impact of illegal immigration on the total U.S. population, the census attempts to count all residents, whatever their status. As Table 1.1 shows, the total foreign-born population counted by the U.S. census in 2000 increased slightly over 1990, with foreign-born residents accounting for 11 percent of the population (versus 8 percent in 1990).

Accompanying the increase in population over the years has been a shift in the places where people live. For example, between 1990 and 2000, 684 of the nation's 3,142 counties, most of them in the Midwest and Plains states, reported a loss in population. But 80 counties, primarily in the West and the South, had population growth of more than 50 percent. In five counties, two in Georgia and three in Colorado, the population jumped by more than 100 percent.

An Aging Population

As the U.S. population increases and favors new places of residence, it is also aging. Figure 1.3 shows the distribution of the population by age and by sex as a series of three pyramids for three different years. The 2000 pyramid shows the "muffin top" of the baby boomers, who were 36 to 55 years old in that year. A quarter-century later, the echo boom of the millennials, who will be between the ages of 30 and 55 in 2025, is clearly visible. The pyramid evens out and thickens by 2050, showing the effects of increased population growth and the impact of extended longevity, with a large number of people (women in particular) expected to live to the age of 85 and older.

Some areas of the United States are well-known meccas for older Americans. For example, the reputation of Florida and the Southwest as the premier retirement destinations in the United States

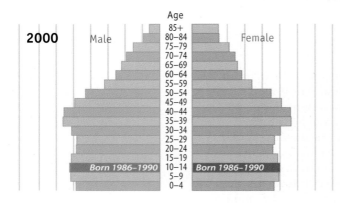

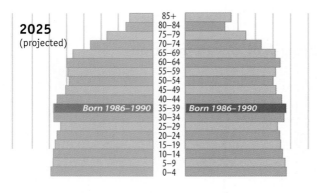

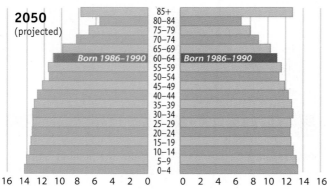

16 14 12 10 8 6 4 2 0   0 2 4 6 8 10 12 14 16

Population (in millions)

FIGURE 1.3

The Aging U.S. Population, 2000–2050

Source: U.S. Census Bureau, National Population Projections, www.census.gov/population/www/projections/natchart.html.

Nativity and Citizenship Status, 1990–2000

TABLE 1.1

	1990 Number (millions)	1990 Percentage	2000 Number (millions)	2000 Percentage
Total population	**249**	**100%**	**281**	**100%**
Total native population	**229**	**92**	**250**	**89**
Total foreign-born population	**20**	**8**	**31**	**11**
Naturalized	8	3	13	4
Non-naturalized	12	5	19	7

Source: www.CensusScope.org, Social Science Data Analysis Network, University of Michigan, www.ssdan.net.

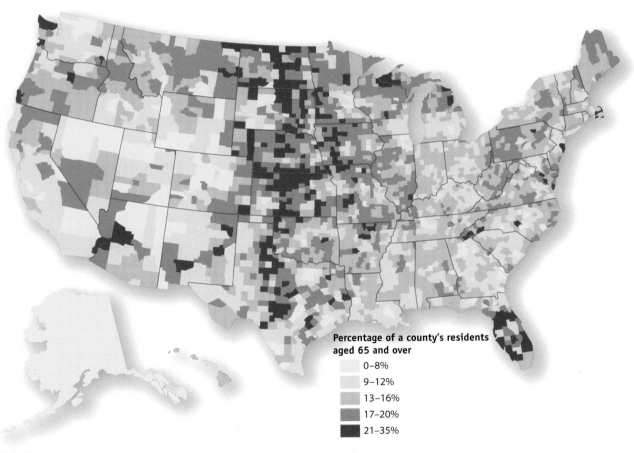

Percentage of a county's residents aged 65 and over

- 0–8%
- 9–12%
- 13–16%
- 17–20%
- 21–35%

FIGURE 1.4

Where the Older Americans Are

Source: www.CensusScope.org, Social Science Data Analysis Network, University of Michigan, www.ssdan.net.

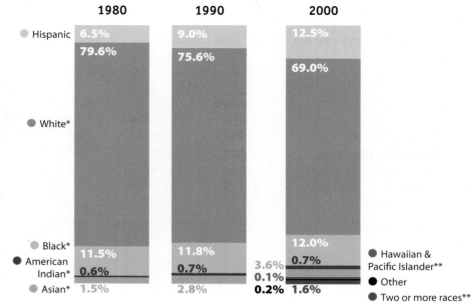

FIGURE 1.5

Population by Race Since 1980

Source: www.CensusScope.org, Social Science Data Analysis Network, University of Michigan, www.ssdan.net.

is highlighted in Figure 1.4, which shows that older Americans are concentrated in these areas, as well as in a broad north–south band that runs down the United States' midsection. Older people are concentrated in the Midwest and Plains states because of the high levels of emigration from these areas by younger Americans, who are leaving their parents behind to look for opportunity elsewhere.

A Changing Complexion: Race and Ethnicity in the United States Today

The population of the United States is becoming not only older but also more racially and ethnically diverse. Figure 1.5 shows the racial and ethnic composition of the U.S. population in 2000. Notice that Hispanics* now make up a greater proportion of the U.S. population than do blacks. As Figure 1.5 also shows, this trend has been continuous over the past several decades. Figure 1.5 also indicates that the percentage of Asian Americans and Pacific Islanders has nearly doubled in recent decades, from just over 2 percent of the U.S. population in 1980 to nearly 4 percent today. The Native American population has increased marginally but still constitutes less than 1 percent of the whole population. Figure 1.5 also shows the proportion of people reporting that they belonged to two or more racial groups, a category that was not an option on the census questionnaire until 2000.

As Figures 1.6 and 1.7 show, minority populations tend to be concentrated in different areas of the United States. Figure 1.6 shows the concentration of non-Hispanic African Americans. At 12 percent of the population, African Americans are the largest racial minority in the United States (Hispanics are an ethnic minority). As the map illustrates, the African American population tends to be centered in urban areas and in the South, where, in some counties, African Americans constitute a majority of the population.

---

* A note about terminology: When discussing data for various races and ethnicities for the purpose of making comparisons, we use the terms *black* and *Hispanic,* because these labels are typically used in measuring demographics by the Bureau of the Census and other organizations that collect this type of data. In more descriptive writing that is not comparative, we use the terms *African American* and *Latino* and *Latina,* which are the preferred terms at this time. Although the terms *Latino* and *Latina* exclude Americans who came from Spain (or whose ancestors did), these people compose a very small proportion of this population in the United States.

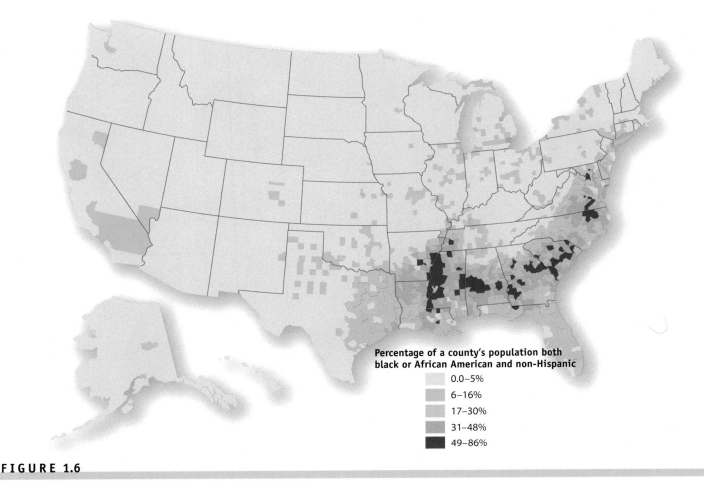

Percentage of a county's population both black or African American and non-Hispanic

- 0.0–5%
- 6–16%
- 17–30%
- 31–48%
- 49–86%

FIGURE 1.6

Where African Americans Live

Source: www.CensusScope.org, Social Science Data Analysis Network, University of Michigan, www.ssdan.net.

Hispanics, on the other hand, tend to cluster in Texas and California along the border between the United States and Mexico and in the urban centers of New Mexico, as shown in Figure 1.7 (on page 24). Concentrations of Hispanic populations are also found in Florida and the Northeast. Hispanics are the fastest-growing ethnic group in the United States, with nearly 13 percent of respondents to the 2000 census identifying themselves as Hispanic, an increase of nearly 4 percent since 1990. Among people of Hispanic ethnicity, Mexicans make up the largest number (7 percent of the total U.S. population in 2000), followed by Puerto Ricans (1 percent in 2000) and Cubans (0.4 percent).

Changing Households: American Families Today

The types of families that are counted by the U.S. census are also becoming more diverse. The *nuclear family*, consisting of a stay-at-home mother, a breadwinning father, and their children, was at one time the stereotypical "ideal family" in the United States. Many—though hardly all—American families were able to achieve this cultural ideal during the prosperous 1950s and early 1960s. But since the women's liberation movement of the 1970s, in which women sought equal rights with men, the American family has changed drastically. As Figure 1.8 on page 25 shows, these changes continued between 1990 and 2000, with the percentage of married couples declining from 55 percent to 52 percent. Explanations for this decline include the trend for people to marry at an older age and the fact that as the population ages, rising numbers of individuals are left widowed. The percentage of female householders without spouses (both with and without children) remained constant between 1990 and 2000 after experiencing a significant increase from 1970 through 1990. The proportion of male householders without spouses increased slightly, and men without

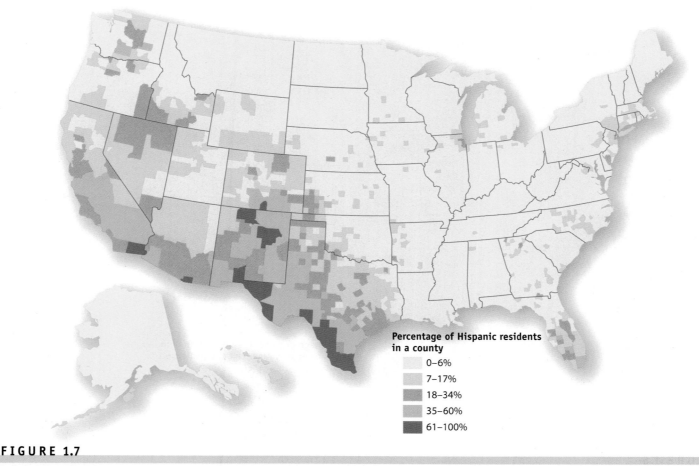

**Percentage of Hispanic residents
in a county**

- 0–6%
- 7–17%
- 18–34%
- 35–60%
- 61–100%

FIGURE 1.7

Where Hispanics Live

Source: www.CensusScope.org, Social Science Data Analysis Network, University of Michigan, www.ssdan.net.

a spouse are more likely to be raising children than they were in 1980. Finally, the proportion of the population living in nonfamily households, both those living alone and with others, rose slightly.

Why the Changing Population Matters for Politics and Government

Each of the changes to the U.S. population described here has implications for American democracy. As the nature of the electorate shifts, different priorities may become important to a majority of the nation's people, and various policies may become more and less important (see "Exploring the Sources" on page 26). For example, swift U.S. population growth means that the demand for the kinds of services government provides—from schools, to highways, to health care—will continue to increase. The aging of the population will inevitably increase the burden on the nation's Social Security and Medicare health care systems, which will be forced to support the needs of that rising population.

Changes in the population's racial and ethnic composition also matter, as does the concentration of racial minorities in specific geographic areas. The racial and ethnic makeup of the population (along with other influences) can significantly affect the nation's political culture and people's political attitudes (see "Global Comparisons" on page 27). It has implications, too, for who will govern, as more and more representatives of the country's various racial and ethnic groups become candidates for political office and as *all* political candidates must reach out to increasingly diverse groups of voters—or possibly pay the price at the ballot box for failing to do so.

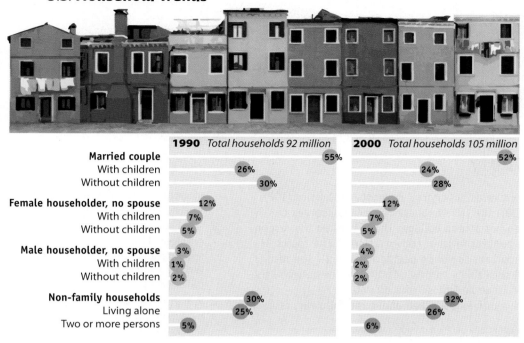

U.S. Household Trends

	1990 Total households 92 million	2000 Total households 105 million
Married couple	55%	52%
With children	26%	24%
Without children	30%	28%
Female householder, no spouse	12%	12%
With children	7%	7%
Without children	5%	5%
Male householder, no spouse	3%	4%
With children	1%	2%
Without children	2%	2%
Non-family households	30%	32%
Living alone	25%	26%
Two or more persons	5%	6%

POLITICAL INQUIRY

FIGURE 1.8 ■ **What factors might explain the increase in male householders without spouses between 1990 and 2000? What factors might explain the increase in nonfamily households? What impact, if any, might these trends have on policy in the future?**

Source: www.CensusScope.org/us/chart_house.html, Social Science Data Analysis Network, University of Michigan, www.ssdan.net.

Ideology: A Prism for Viewing American Democracy

Besides focusing on the demographic characteristics of the U.S. population, another way of analyzing political events and trends is by looking at them through the prism of ideology. **Political ideology** is an integrated system of ideas or beliefs about political values in general and the role of government in particular. Political ideology provides a framework for thinking about politics, about policy issues, and about the role of government in people's everyday lives. In the United States, one key component of various ideologies is the extent to which adherents believe that the government should have a role in people's everyday lives, in particular, the extent to which the government should promote economic equality in society.

For all of the twentieth century, the ideologies of liberalism and conservatism dominated U.S. politics. Although liberalism and conservatism have remained powerful ideologies in the early years of the twenty-first century, neoconservatism has also become increasingly important. Table 1.2 on page 28 summarizes the key ideologies we consider in this section.

Liberalism

Modern **liberalism** in the United States is associated with the ideas of liberty and political equality; its advocates favor change in the social, political, and economic realms to better protect the well-being of individuals and to produce equality within society. They emphasize the importance of civil liberties, including freedom of speech, assembly, and the press, as outlined in the Bill of Rights. Modern liberals also advocate the separation of church and state, often opposing measures that bring religion into the public realm, such as prayer in the public schools. In addition, they support political equality, advocating contemporary

political ideology
integrated system of ideas or beliefs about political values in general and the role of government in particular

liberalism
an ideology that advocates change in the social, political, and economic realms to better protect the well-being of individuals and to produce equality within society

WHAT CURRENT EVENTS DO YOUNG PEOPLE TALK ABOUT?

The following data show responses to Harvard University's Institute of Politics (IOP) poll of young people aged 18–24. In 2007, the IOP conducted a national survey of college students and individuals who do not attend college. The IOP asked the respondents a variety of questions about the content of their conversations.* The topics of their conversations indicate what is important to young people in general. The results of the poll also suggest some real (and sometimes surprising) differences between the concerns of young people who attend college and those who do not.

In the last few weeks, have you and your friends talked about the following issues?

*Institute of Politics at Harvard University, "Attitudes Towards Politics and Public Service: A National Survey of College Undergraduates," April 11–20, 2000, www.iop.harvard.edu/pdfs/survey/2000.pdf.

THE SITUATION IN IRAQ

	NON-COLLEGE	COLLEGE
Yes	54%	64%
No	46	36

GENOCIDE IN DARFUR

	NON-COLLEGE	COLLEGE
Yes	15	25
No	85	75

U.S. POLITICS

	NON-COLLEGE	COLLEGE
Yes	51	66
No	49	34

CELEBRITY GOSSIP

	NON-COLLEGE	COLLEGE
Yes	52	56
No	48	44

GLOBAL WARMING AND THE ENVIRONMENT

	NON-COLLEGE	COLLEGE
Yes	49	59
No	51	41

THE JOB MARKET AND THE ECONOMY

	NON-COLLEGE	COLLEGE
Yes	48%	51%
No	52	50

THE 2008 PRESIDENTIAL CAMPAIGN

	NON-COLLEGE	COLLEGE
Yes	53	63
No	47	37

RELATIONS BETWEEN THE UNITED STATES AND IRAN

	NON-COLLEGE	COLLEGE
Yes	24	30
No	76	70

LATEST SPORTS NEWS

	NON-COLLEGE	COLLEGE
Yes	41	53
No	59	47

Source: "The 12th Biannual Youth Survey on Politics and Public Service," www.iop.harvard.edu/pdfs/survey_s2007_topline.pdf, accessed August 20, 2007.

Evaluating the Evidence

① Which topic was the most talked about among the young college students? Among young people who do not attend college?

② On which topics were there the greatest differences between college students and nonstudents? What do you think explains the differences?

③ Which topics were talked about by similar proportions of college students and nonstudents? Can you think of any reasons why the results for these two groups would be similar?

④ Ask yourself the questions in the survey. For each issue, which groups does your response match? Why do you think this is the case? Are your responses similar to those of the college students who were polled? Why or why not?

GLOBAL COMPARISONS

WHAT CITIZENS IN HIGH-POLLUTING COUNTRIES DO TO HELP PRESERVE THE ENVIRONMENT

The United States, China, India, Russia, and Japan are the world's top five polluting countries in terms of carbon dioxide emissions. Studies indicate that these five nations alone generate 54 percent of the world's emissions of carbon dioxide, the pollutant responsible for global warming.

The Gallup polling organization asked survey respondents in these countries what activities they had undertaken in the past year to help the environment. The finding: self-reported "green" activities varied a great deal among respondents in the five nations. Americans and the Japanese were most likely to report having recycled (nearly 90 percent in each nation) or having refrained from using environmentally harmful products (roughly 70 percent in each country). Indians and Russians were among the least likely to report activities designed to decrease their carbon footprint. Respondents from all five countries indicated that, of the various activities measured, they are least likely to have been active in organizations that work to protect the environment. As you can see, these lows range from about 18 percent in the United States to 6 percent in Russia.

Source: Magali Rheault, The Gallup Organization, "In Top Polluting Nations, Efforts to Live 'Green' Vary," April 22, 2008, www.gallup.com/poll/106648/Top-Polluting-Nations-Efforts-Live-Green-Vary.aspx.

* Will the continuation of the earth as we know it demand stronger efforts by world citizens to preserve and protect the environment?

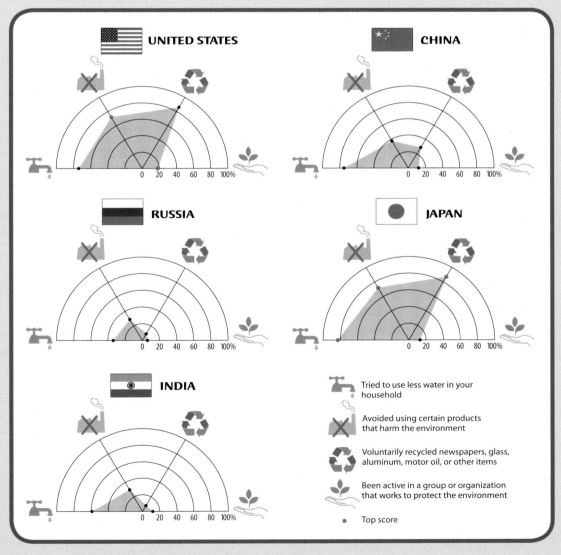

The Traditional Ideological Spectrum

TABLE 1.2

	Socialism	Liberalism	Middle of Road (Moderate)	Conservatism	Libertarianism
Goal of government	Equality	Equality of opportunity, protection of fundamental liberties	Nondiscrimination in opportunity, protection of some economic freedoms, security, stability	Traditional values, order, stability, economic freedom	Absolute economic and social freedom
Role of government	Strong government control of economy	Government action to promote opportunity	Government action to balance the wants of workers and businesses; government fosters stability	Government action to protect and bolster capitalist system, few limitations on fundamental rights	No governmental regulation of economy, no limitations on fundamental rights

A Social Safety Net

Should the government care for those who can't care for themselves?

☐ Yes, it should.

☐ No, it shouldn't.

Source: "Trends in Political Values and Core Attitudes: 1987–2007," http://people-press .org/reports/pdf/312.pdf.

conservatism

an ideology that emphasizes preserving tradition and relying on community and family as mechanisms of continuity in society

movements that promote the political rights of gay and lesbian couples and voting rights for the disenfranchised.

The historical roots of modern liberalism reach back to the ideas of classical liberalism, which emerged from the Enlightenment. The classical liberal ideals that emerged from the Enlightenment—freedom of thought and the free exchange of ideas, limited governmental authority, the consent of the governed, the rule of law in society, the importance of an unfettered market economy, individual initiative as a determinant of success, and access to free public education—were founding ideals that shaped American democracy as articulated in the Declaration of Independence and the Constitution.

Modern liberalism, which emerged in the early twentieth century, diverged from its classical roots in a number of ways. Most important, modern liberals expect the government to play a more active role in ensuring political equality and economic opportunity. Whereas classical liberals emphasized the virtues of a free market economy, modern liberals, particularly after the Great Depression that began in 1929, advocated government involvement in economic affairs. Today we see this expectation in action when liberals call for affirmative action; increases in social welfare programs such as Social Security, Medicare, and Medicaid; and government regulation of business and workplace conditions.

Conservatism

Advocates of **conservatism** recognize the importance of preserving tradition—of maintaining the status quo, or keeping things the way they are. Conservatives emphasize community and family as mechanisms of continuity in society. Ironically, some conservative ideals are consistent with the views of classical liberalism. In particular, the emphasis on individual initiative, the rule of law, limited governmental authority, and an unfettered market economy are key components of both classical liberalism and contemporary conservatism.

Traditionally one of the key differences between modern liberals and conservatives has been their view of the role of government. In fact, one of the best ways of determining your own ideology is to ask yourself the question, To what extent should the government be involved in people's everyday lives? Modern liberals believe that the government should play a role in ensuring the public's well-being, whether through the regulation of industry or the economy, through antidiscrimination laws, or by providing an economic "safety net" for the neediest members of society. By contrast, conservatives believe that government should play a more limited role in people's everyday lives. They think that government should have a smaller role in regulating business and industry and that market forces, rather than the government, should largely determine economic policy. Conservatives believe that families, faith-based groups, and private charities should be more responsible for protecting the neediest and the government less so. When governments must act, conservatives prefer decentralized action by state governments rather than a nationwide federal policy. Conservatives also believe in the importance of individual initiative as a key determinant of success. Conservative ideas are the fundamental basis of policies like the Welfare Reform Act of 1996, which placed the development and administration of welfare (Temporary Aid to Needy Families, or TANF) in the hands of the states rather than the federal government.

Other Ideologies on a Traditional Spectrum: Socialism and Libertarianism

Although liberals and conservatives dominate the U.S. political landscape, other ideologies reflect the views of some Americans. In general, those ideologies tend to be more extreme than liberalism or conservatism. Advocates of certain of these ideologies call for *more* governmental intervention than modern liberalism does, and supporters of other views favor even *less* governmental interference than conservatism does.

For example, **socialism**—an ideology that stresses economic equality, theoretically achieved by having the government or workers own the means of production (businesses and industry)—lies to the left of liberalism on the political spectrum.[24] Although socialists play a very limited role in modern American politics, this was not always the case.[25] In the early part of the twentieth century, socialists had a good deal of electoral success. Two members of Congress (Representative Meyer London of New York and Representative Victor Berger of Wisconsin), more than 70 mayors of cities of various sizes, and numerous state legislators (including five in the New York General Assembly and many municipal council members throughout the country) were socialists. In 1912, Socialist Party presidential candidate Eugene Debs garnered 6 percent of the presidential vote—six times what Green Party candidate Ralph Nader netted in 2004.

According to **libertarianism,** on the other hand, government should take a "hands-off" approach in most matters. This ideology can be found to the right of conservatism on a traditional ideological spectrum. Libertarians believe that the less government intervention, the better. They chafe at attempts by the government to foster economic equality or to promote a social agenda, whether that agenda is the equality espoused by liberals or the traditional values espoused by conservatives. Libertarians strongly support the rights of property owners and a *laissez-faire* (French for "let it be") capitalist economy.

socialism
an ideology that advocates economic equality, theoretically achieved by having the government or workers own the means of production (businesses and industry)

libertarianism
an ideology whose advocates believe that government should take a "hands-off" approach in most matters

neoconservatism
an ideology that advocates military over diplomatic solutions in foreign policy and is less concerned with restraining government activity in domestic politics than traditional conservatives

Neoconservatism

The term *neoconservatism,* which emerged in the early 1970s, describes the "new conservatives," or "neo-cons"; the prefix *neo* indicates that many of the prominent thinkers who developed this ideology were new to conservatism. Many people who espouse neoconservative ideology were previously socialists or liberal Democrats who then turned to a more traditional perspective.

Neoconservatives differ from traditional conservatives in several ways. Whereas traditional conservatives tend to advocate an isolationist foreign policy and reliance on traditional foreign policy tactics such as diplomacy, neoconservatives are often characterized as "hawks" because they tend to advocate military over diplomatic solutions. Often, too, neoconservatives press for unilateral (one-sided) military action rather than the collective effort of a multinational military coalition. And unlike traditional conservatives, who emphasize a limited role for government, particularly in social policy, neoconservatives are less concerned with restraining government activity than they are with taking an aggressive foreign policy stand. During the Cold War, neoconservatives were

"I'm using my website to spread Marxist propaganda. I'm a dot commie."
www.cartoonstock.com

defined by their militaristic opposition to communism. Today they are defined by their fierce advocacy of U.S. superiority and their stance against predominantly Arab states that are alleged to support or harbor terrorists or pose a threat to the state of Israel.

The ideology of neoconservatism has been an increasingly powerful force in the Republican Party since George W. Bush's election in 2000. Indeed, the U.S. war in Iraq is often cited as an example of the power of neoconservatives in the administration of George W. Bush.

A Three-Dimensional Political Compass

The rise of neoconservatism demonstrates the limitations of a one-dimensional ideological continuum. For example, although an individual may believe that government should play a strong role in regulating the economy, he or she may also believe that the government should allow citizens a high degree of personal freedom of speech or religion. Even the traditional ideologies do not always fit easily into a single continuum that measures the extent to which the government should play a role in citizens' lives. Liberals supposedly advocate a larger role for the government. But although this may be the case in matters related to economic equality, liberals generally take a more laissez-faire approach when it comes to personal liberties, advocating strongly for privacy and free speech. And while conservatives support less governmental intervention in the economy, they sometimes advocate government action to promote traditional values, such as constitutional amendments to ban flag burning and abortion and laws that mandate prayer in public schools.

Scholars have developed various *multidimensional scales* that attempt to represent peoples' ideologies more accurately.[26] Many of these scales measure people's opinions on the proper role of government in the economy on one axis and their beliefs about personal freedom on a second axis. As shown in Figure 1.9, these scales demonstrate that traditional liberals (upper left quadrant) and traditional conservatives (lower right quadrant) believe in social liberty and economic equality, and economic liberty and social order respectively. But the scale also acknowledges that some people prioritize economic equality and social order, while others embrace economic liberty and social order. One Web site, *The Political Compass* (www.politicalcompass.org), allows visitors to plot their ideology on the site's multidimensional scale.

Multi-Dimensional Ideological Scale

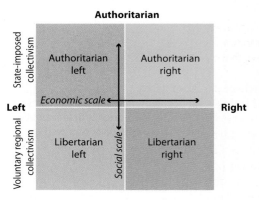

POLITICAL INQUIRY

FIGURE 1.9 ■ Where would you place yourself on this scale? How has your socialization formed your ideology? Can you imagine future circumstances that might cause your views to change?

Source: http://politicalcompass.org/analysis2, accessed August 20, 2007.

Civic Engagement: Acting on Your Views

One vitally important goal of this book is to encourage you to engage in a respectful, continuing conversation about your views and to make the connection between having ideas and opinions and acting on them. Political scientist Michael Delli Carpini has defined **civic engagement** as

> individual and collective actions designed to identify and address issues of public concern. Civic engagement can take many forms, from individual voluntarism to organizational involvement to electoral participation. It can include efforts to directly address an issue, work with others in a community to solve a problem or interact with the institutions of representative democracy.[27]

civic engagement
individual and collective actions designed to identify and address issues of public concern

The possibilities for citizen involvement are so broad and numerous that the idea of civic engagement encompasses a whole range of activities. Everything from tutoring an underprivileged child to volunteering at a conservative think tank exemplifies civic engagement. In this book, we focus in particular on civic engagement that takes the form of **political engagement**—that is, citizen actions that are intended to solve public problems through political means. As you will find as you read the book, a wide variety of political actions are possible, from boycotting and *buycotting* (buying goods produced by companies whose policies you agree with) to running for office.

political engagement
citizen actions that are intended to solve public problems through political means

In conclusion, we hope that this book not only empowers you by teaching you about the institutions, policies, and processes of the government but also inspires you to become civi-

cally and politically engaged. You can take part in your democracy by organizing a fund-raising event, joining a volunteer group, volunteering for a campaign, calling or writing to an elected official, or even participating in a protest march, to name just a few of the many options available to you. Consider which potential volunteer activities pique your interest. Think about what might best suit your schedule, lifestyle, and personal and professional goals. By taking part, you will ensure that your voice is heard, and you will derive the satisfaction of knowing that your community and the nation benefit from your actions as well.

CONCLUSION
CONTINUING THE CONVERSATION

Now is an exciting time to study American democracy. And the fast-paced changes in American society today make participation in government and civic life more vitally important than ever. The effects of participating in the continuing conversation of American democracy through both words and actions are unequivocally positive—for you, for others, and for the government—and can have large ripple effects.

Generational changes, particularly the distinctive political opinions of the millennial generation, underscore why it is essential for members of that generation to voice their views. Millennials are participating in the civic life of their communities and the nation through unprecedented—and efficacious—new forms of political participation and community activism. Technology will continue to play a significant role in how they and the population at large communicate and participate in politics and how government creates and administers policy. Exciting changes have come to pass in the political realm, and there is no end to them in sight.

Demographic changes in American society—particularly the aging and growing diversity of the U.S. population—are giving rise to new public policy demands and creating new challenges. Challenges mean opportunities for those who are ready for them, and citizens who respond to those challenges will have an impact on the future of the nation.

STUDY NOW

Summary

1. y shd u stdy am dem now? Or, Why Should You Study American Democracy Now?
American democracy is at a crossroads with respect to the impact of technology, war, and the continuing terrorist threat on politics. The young Americans of today differ from earlier generations in notable ways, and their fresh opinions and means of organizing and communicating with one another make them a significant political force.

2. What Government Does
Governments perform a variety of essential functions. They provide for the national defense, preserve order and stability, establish and maintain a legal system, distribute services, raise and spend money, and socialize new generations of citizens.

3. Types of Government
In categorizing governmental systems, political scientists evaluate two factors. One factor is who participates in governing or in selecting those who govern. In a monarchy, a king or queen has absolute authority over a territory and its government (though most of today's monarchies are constitutional), whereas in an oligarchy, an elite few hold power. In a democracy, the people hold and exercise supreme power. Scholars also categorize governmental systems according to how governments function and are structured. Totalitarian governments effectively control every aspect of their citizens' lives. Authoritarian governments have strong powers but are checked by other forces within the society. In democracies, the people have a say in their governance either by voting directly or, as in the United States, by electing representatives to carry out their will.

4. The Origins of American Democracy
American democracy was shaped by individuals who believed in the right of citizens to have a voice in their government. Through principles developed by Enlightenment philosophers such as Thomas Hobbes, John Locke, and Jean-Jacques Rousseau, the key tenets of American democracy emerged, including the idea of a social contract creating a representative democracy.

5. Political Culture and American Values
Political culture refers to the people's collective beliefs and attitudes about the government and the political process. Though aspects of political culture change over time, certain fundamental values have remained constant in American democracy. These include liberty, which is both freedom *from* government interference in daily life and also freedom *to* pursue happiness; and equality, the meaning of which has fluctuated significantly over the course of U.S. history. Capitalism—an economic system in which the means of producing wealth are privately owned and operated to produce profits—is also a core value of American political culture, as is consent of the governed, with its key components of popular sovereignty and majority rule. Finally, the American political system values the importance of the individual, the family, and the community.

6. The Changing Face of American Democracy
The population of the United States is growing, aging, and becoming increasingly diverse. Hispanics now make up the country's largest ethnic minority. U.S. families have undergone fundamental structural alterations, as the number of nonfamily households and of households headed by single people has increased in recent times. These changes have already had an impact on communities, and their effect on government policies will intensify. The demographic shifts may create demand for changes in current policies, or they may indicate that the nature of the electorate has shifted and that different priorities are favored by a majority of the people.

7. Ideology: A Prism for Viewing American Democracy
Liberals emphasize civil liberties, separation of church and state, and political equality. Conservatives prefer small government, individual initiative, and an unfettered market economy. Socialists advocate government intervention in the economy to promote economic equality, whereas libertarians argue that government should take a "hands-off" approach to most matters. Neoconservatism, with its emphasis on military rather than diplomatic solutions in foreign policy, and with its comparatively small concern for restraining government

activity, has become a growing force in politics and government. Some social scientists prefer to use a three-dimensional framework rather than a two-dimensional continuum for understanding and analyzing political ideology. Regardless of their ideology, citizens can and should act upon their views through civic and political engagement.

Key Terms

authoritarianism 13	indirect democracy 15	political culture 15
capitalism 17	legitimacy 11	political engagement 30
citizens 8	liberalism 25	political ideology 25
civic engagement 30	libertarianism 29	politics 5
consent of the governed 19	liberty 16	popular sovereignty 15
conservatism 28	limited government 13	property 18
constitutionalism 13	majority rule 19	public goods 11
democracy 13	monarchy 13	social contract 14
direct democracy 15	natural law 14	social contract theory 15
divine right of kings 14	naturalization 11	socialism 29
efficacy 7	neoconservatism 29	totalitarianism 13
government 8	oligarchy 13	

For Review

1. In what ways has technology changed how politics happens and how government works? What impact did September 11 and the subsequent war on terror have on how Americans thought—and think—about their government?

2. Explain the functions that governments perform.

3. Describe how social scientists categorize governments.

4. How did the ideas of the Enlightenment shape people's views on the proper role of government?

5. Explain the fundamental values of American democracy.

6. Describe the general trends with regard to population change in the United States.

7. Contrast liberals' and conservatives' views on government. How do the views of neo-conservatives differ from these other perspectives?

For Critical Thinking and Discussion

1. In what ways do you use technology in your daily life? Do you use technology to get information about politics or to access government services? How? If not, what information and services may be obtained using technological tools?

2. Have the events of September 11, 2001, changed how you think about government? Explain. Have the wars in Iraq and Afghanistan changed how you view government? Describe.

3. Why do governments perform the functions they do? Can you think of any private entities that provide public goods?

4. Think of the advantages and disadvantages of direct versus indirect democracies. Do you participate in any form of direct decision making? If so, how well, or poorly, does it work?

5. Examine the demographic maps of the United States in this chapter, and describe what they reveal about the population in your home state.

MULTIPLE CHOICE: Choose the lettered item that answers the question correctly.

1. Governments that have strong powers but are checked by certain internal forces are called
   a. democracies.
   b. totalitarian states.
   c. authoritarian states.
   d. monarchies.

2. The economic system in which the means of producing wealth are privately owned and operated to produce profits is
   a. capitalism.
   b. monetarism.
   c. socialism.
   d. communism.

3. Emphasizing the importance of preserving tradition and of relying on community and family as mechanisms of social continuity is known as
   a. communism.
   b. conservatism.
   c. liberalism.
   d. libertarianism.

4. Citizens' belief that they have the ability to achieve something desirable and that the government listens to them is called
   a. popular sovereignty.
   b. democracy.
   c. civic engagement.
   d. efficacy.

5. A system in which citizens elect representatives who decide policies on behalf of their constituents is referred to as
   a. an indirect democracy.
   b. a representative democracy.
   c. consent of the governed.
   d. both (a) and (b).

6. A belief by the people that a government's exercise of power is right and proper is
   a. authoritarianism.
   b. democracy.
   c. popular sovereignty.
   d. legitimacy.

7. The principle that the standards that govern human behavior are derived from the nature of humans themselves and can be universally applied is called
   a. the social contract.
   b. neoconservatism.
   c. natural law.
   d. representative democracy.

8. The ideology that advocates military over diplomatic solutions in foreign policy and is unconcerned with restraining government activity in domestic politics is called
   a. liberalism.
   b. socialism.
   c. neoconservatism.
   d. conservatism.

9. An agreement between the people and their leaders in which the people agree to give up some liberties so that other liberties are protected is called
   a. popular sovereignty.
   b. a social contract.
   c. republicanism.
   d. natural law.

10. A form of government that essentially controls every aspect of people's lives is
    a. socialism.
    b. neoconservatism.
    c. liberalism.
    d. totalitarianism.

FILL IN THE BLANKS.

11. _____ is individual and collective actions designed to identify and address issues of public concern.

12. _____ is the institution that creates and implements policy and laws that guide the conduct of the nation and its citizens.

13. _____ is the idea that in a democracy, only policies with 50 percent plus one vote are enacted, and only candidates elected with 50 percent plus one vote are elected.

14. _____ are services governments provide that are available to everyone, such as clean air, clean water, airport security, and highways.

15. A form of government that is structured by law, and in which the power of government is limited, is called _____.

Answers: 1. c; 2. a; 3. b; 4. d; 5. d; 6. d; 7. c; 8. c; 9. b; 10. d; 11. Civic engagement; 12. Government; 13. Majority rule; 14. Public goods; 15. constitutionalism.

RESOURCES FOR RESEARCH AND ACTION

Internet Resources

American Democracy Now Web site
http://www.mhhe.com/harrison1e   Consult the book's Web site for study guides, interactive activities, simulations, and current hotlinks for additional information on American politics and political and civic engagement in the United States.

Circle: the Center for Information & Research on Civic Learning & Engagement
www.civicyouth.org   Circle is the premier clearinghouse for research and analysis on civic engagement.

Institute of Politics, Harvard University
www.iop.harvard.edu   Harvard's IOP provides a host of information about civic participation, but particularly useful are its surveys of American youth (look under Research and Publications).

American Association of Colleges and Universities
www.aacu.org/resources/civicengagement/index.cfm   The AACU's Web site offers a clearinghouse of Internet resources on civic engagement.

American Political Science Association
www.apsanet.org/section_245.cfm   The professional association for political scientists offers many resources on research about civic engagement, education, and participation.

The Statistical Abstract of the United States
www.census.gov/compendia/statab   This is "the authoritative and comprehensive summary of statistics on the social, political, and economic organization of the United States." It provides a plethora of data about the population of the United States.

Recommended Readings

Levine, Peter. *The Future of Democracy: Developing the Next Generation of American Citizens.* Medford, MA: Tufts University Press (UPNE), 2007. An examination of how today's youth are participating in politics differently from previous generations and of how they lack the skills necessary to facilitate some forms of civic participation. The author proposes educational, political, and institutional changes to correct this problem.

Norris, Pippa. *Digital Divide: Civic Engagement, Information Poverty, and the Internet Worldwide.* Cambridge: Cambridge University Press, 2001. A comparative analysis probing how access to information and technology have an impact on civic and political engagement.

Putnam, Robert D. *Bowling Alone: The Collapse and Revival of American Community.* New York: Touchstone, 2000. A classic volume demonstrating the decline in traditional forms of civic participation.

Verba, Sidney, Kay Lehman Schlozman, and Henry E. Brady. *Voice and Equality: Civic Voluntarism in American Politics.* Cambridge, MA: Harvard University Press, 1995. An analysis of how people come to be activists in their communities, what issues they raise when they participate, and how activists from various demographic groups differ.

Zukin, Cliff, Scott Keeter, Molly Andolina, Krista Jenkins, and Michael X. Delli Carpini. *A New Engagement? Political Participation, Civic Life and the Changing American Citizen.* Oxford: Oxford University Press, 2006. A study of participation and political viewpoints across generations.

Movies of Interest

V for Vendetta (2005)
Actor Natalie Portman becomes a revolutionary in this thriller, which depicts an uprising against an authoritarian government.

If I Had a Minute with the President (2004)
In this downloadable documentary (www.archive.org/details/lu_if_i_had_a_minute_with_the_president), middle school students respond to a series of questions concerning their political viewpoints about life in the United States. The political voice of the youngest members of the Millennial Generation is given fascinating expression by the filmmaker.

Blue Collar (1978)
This classic film tracing the experience of three autoworkers in the late 1970s explores racial and economic strife in the United States.

Man of Marble (1977)
This film by Andrzej Wajda documents Poland's Solidarity movement and shows how a small group of committed citizens can genuinely change the world.

GENERATION 'WE': THE AWAKENED GIANT

During the first presidential campaign of the new millennium, Harvard students Erin Ashwell and Trevor Dryer, like their counterparts at colleges across the country, eagerly awaited the thrill of voting in a national election for the first time. Their anticipation was tempered, however, by dismissive talk about the apparent political disaffection of young people and the youth vote's irrelevance in the 2000 elections.

This didn't strike Ashwell and Dryer as the whole story. "In 2000, there was a lot of press about how young people don't vote, don't get involved, don't care about politics," Ashwell recalls. "Trevor and I wanted to know if it was true. It didn't seem right: All of our friends were into community service." Although they were only college sophomores—or perhaps because they were college sophomores—the pair decided to test conventional wisdom. They also sought to shed light on the paradox of a generation of young activists who devoted hours each week to tutoring underprivileged children, volunteering at food banks, and promoting environmental activism—but who couldn't be bothered to register or vote.

Ashwell and Dryer began delving into the attitudes of their fellow collegians via a nationwide survey, a project Harvard continued after they graduated. Over the ensuing years, the poll by the Institute of Politics at the John F. Kennedy School of Government has penetrated more deeply than other surveys, using the Internet and other innovative techniques, such as having undergraduates help formulate the questions.

The survey has drawn a picture of a unique generation. Today's youth are an underrated force in American civic life—difficult to stereotype, with attitudes markedly different from those of their predecessors. College students overwhelmingly favor the partial privatization of Social Security, a conservative Republican position and one at odds with the preferences of older Americans. Yet they are far more supportive of gay marriage, gay adoption, and gays' being allowed to serve openly in the military

than any other age group, views that place them in the vanguard of Democratic liberalism. In many respects, they are available to both major parties and, judging by their weak party affiliation, would be receptive to an independent presidential candidate. The 2006 IOP poll went even further, concluding that the traditional labels of "liberal" and "conservative" don't adequately capture the complexity of college students' attitudes. One in four college students identify themselves as "religious centrists," a stance that indicates deep concern over the moral direction of the country—and that encompasses issues such as environmental protection, universal health care, and free trade.

Today's college students are not isolationist, but they are the furthest thing from unilateralists. The Institute of Politics poll shows that college students are twice as likely as older Americans to favor a United Nations solution to a foreign crisis than a plan conceived in Washington.

These young people are so little understood that many of the 2006 congressional campaigns ignored them utterly, although candidates who did paid a price for their inattention. Social scientists can't even agree on what to call this generation. Some label those ages 18 to 29 "Generation Y," to distinguish them from the Generation X-ers who preceded them. Others call them "Millennials." The Pew Research Center calls them simply "Generation Next." They are certainly not the "Me Generation." Harvard professor David C. King, research director at the Institute of Politics, calls them "Generation We." Is that an exaggeration?

Released in April 2000, "Attitudes Toward Public Service: A National Survey of College Undergraduates" found that although 59.5 percent of the students surveyed had participated in active community service in the previous 12 months, only 16 percent had signed on to a government, political, or issue-oriented organization and only 6.5 percent had volunteered for any kind of political campaign. The students' attitudes toward government ranged from cynicism to antipathy:

Almost two-thirds of them said they didn't trust the federal government to "do the right thing" all or most of the time. Asked about the motivations of politicians, three-fourths of the respondents said that elected officials "seem to be motivated by selfish reasons." More than 70 percent said that America's political institutions were unconcerned with the desires of college students.

A study by the National Association of Secretaries of State, moreover, showed that turnout among young voters in the 1996 presidential election was the lowest on record, and hinted at an even worse performance in 2000. Eight years of Bill Clinton's White House, a contentiously partisan Congress, and a scandal-mongering media had produced nearly the opposite effect that Clinton's boyhood hero JFK had had on the nation's young people. "They were just turned off to politics," pollster John Della Volpe says. "Community service was something they could get their hands on. You could feed a hungry person or teach a struggling high school kid his math problem, and it was tangible. Political success was more ephemeral. We'd get these responses in the focus groups: 'What difference does it make who the president is? It's just some old white guy.' To them, politics wasn't ever cool, and it wasn't very fun."

The dismal forecast for November 2000 came true. According to the Census Bureau's supplemental information (available several months after each election), the turnout among voters ages 18 to 24 stayed at the all-time-low 1996 figure of 36 percent—and turnout among 18-to-21-year-olds fell below 30 percent for the first time.

Then the planes hit.

On September 11, 2001, former Sen. David Pryor of Arkansas was director of the Institute of Politics. Acting on gut instinct, he ginned up the poll again. The results this time couldn't have been more different. "The attacks of 9/11 totally changed the way the Millennial Generation thinks about politics," Della Volpe says today. "Overnight, their attitudes were more like the Greatest Generation."

A stunning 60 percent of college students in the institute's new survey said they had faith in the government to do the right thing all or most of the time, compared with 36 percent in 2000. Fully three-fourths of them expressed "trust" in the military, 69 percent said they trusted the president, and 62 percent said they trusted Congress. Four out of five supported U.S. military action in Afghanistan, and the same number rated terrorism as the top issue facing the United States.

Yet two intriguing elements in the 2001 poll were little noticed at the time. First, the college students' newfound hawkishness did not replace their altruism; it supplemented it. The number participating in community service increased, to 69 percent. The second facet that, in hindsight, seems significant is that in the days just after 9/11, college students' support for a military solution, while quite high, was noticeably lower than that of older voters.

By the spring of 2003, 65 percent of college students supported the war (compared with 78 percent of the entire country), but a trend toward multinationalism—particularly support for the United Nations—was building among the students.

The Millennials were, in Della Volpe's words, "creating a unique political voice of their own." By then, the institute was polling twice a year, and the October survey underscored the point about the students' singular identity. In that poll, college students revealed themselves to be more pro-Bush than their older counterparts but simultaneously more skeptical of the Iraq war. The youth vote in the impending presidential race, it seemed, was up for grabs, and by the time of the April 2004 institute poll, John Kerry had emerged on college campuses as a 10-point favorite.

Inside the Kerry campaign and in groups such as Rock the Vote, the high expecta-

Today's youth are an underrated for in American civic life—difficult to stereotype, with attitudes markedly different from those of their predecessors.

tions were palpable: The 18-to-24-year-olds were going to lead Democrats back into the White House. But Election Day brought heartburn to liberals, starting with erroneous early exit polls that seemed to presage a big Kerry win and then compounded by a widely distributed news service article (also based on exit polls) asserting that the youth-vote surge had not materialized.

But this interpretation was mistaken. David King, the Harvard professor, whose specialty is analyzing voting patterns, says that exit polls weren't taken near college campuses. Furthermore, Election Night stories confused turnout with vote share. Months later, after the Census Bureau released its supplemental information, it became apparent that the number of voters younger than 25 had jumped 11 points—compared with an increase of 4 points among those 25 and older. "One of the missed angles of the 2004 election is that college-age people drove the increase in voter turnout nationally," Jeanne Shaheen, the institute's current director, said at the time.

In 2002, David W. Nickerson made a name for himself as a graduate student at Yale by writing a thesis showing that young voters were just as susceptible to the blandishments of politicians as anyone else, but that it was three times as costly for a political campaign to reach them. If one also

considers that young voters are more fickle than older ones—studies have shown that they are more likely to change their preferences in midcampaign—only a very stubborn campaign manager would spend money wooing the young. But five years can be a long time in politics, especially when a nation is at war, and most especially when technology is developing rapidly. "That calculus is wrong now," King said. "This is the stock you want to invest in—the young."

What has happened in the meantime? Well, Iraq, and the online YouTube and Facebook, to name three things.

It's common political wisdom that George Allen of Virginia narrowly lost his Senate seat—and the Republican majority along with it—after he was videotaped calling one of Democrat Webb's volunteers a "macaca." What's often forgotten is that Webb's campaign, not knowing quite what to do with the footage, simply posted it on YouTube. The effect was devastating.

King has just finished work on a study in which 56 campaign managers involved in 2006 congressional races were interviewed about their outreach efforts aimed at young voters. The questions ranged from what technology they employed to how many of their staffers were younger than 30. Did they upload to YouTube, make appeals on MySpace, or set up a Facebook page, and raise money online?

King's and Della Volpe's assessment is not that e-mails and podcasts have replaced political volunteers at the grassroots. It's that the new technology has altered Nickerson's cost-benefit analysis. It is now far less expensive to reach young volunteers and voters. But a candidate still must have charisma and a message, and be able to translate high-technology methods into good, old-fashioned ground organizing.

■**THEN:** Generation We is bigger than Generation X, and a surge in the birthrate that began in 1989 (sometimes called the "echo boom") means that a large group of potential voters is coming of age just in time for the 2008 election.

■**NOW:** If young people not attending college have political attitudes that are the same as their classroom-bound colleagues, 2008 might be a watershed year in American politics.

■**NEXT:** Will Generation We be more involved in politics than previous generations?
Will campaigns increasingly use internet technology to successfully mobilize the youth vote, thereby increasing the participation of future generations of young voters?
What effect will the presidential election of 2008 have on the participation of tomorrow's college students in the political process?

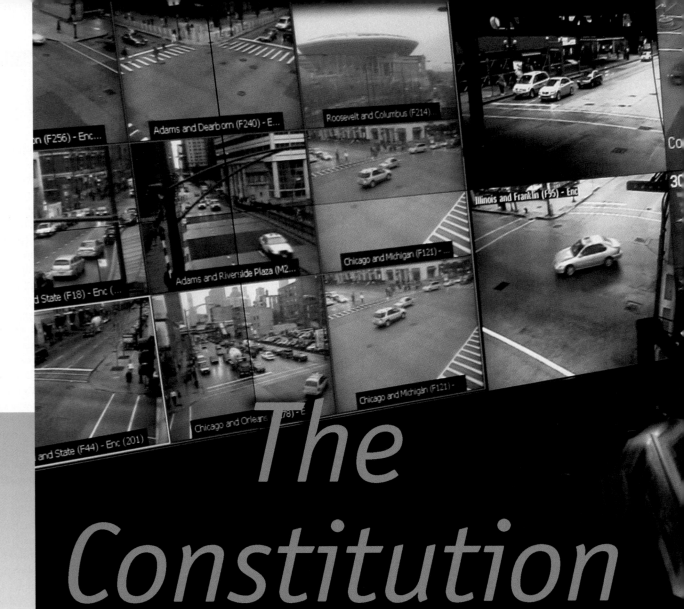

CHAPTER

2

The Constitution

THEN

The Constitution's framers distributed government power and created checks and balances to ensure a representative democracy.

NOW

The courts continue to probe and interpret the Constitution's meaning, and members of Congress introduce proposed constitutional amendments annually.

NEXT

Will an amendment be ratified guaranteeing equal rights under the law for women?

Will an amendment be ratified requiring presidential election by direct popular vote rather than by the Electoral College?

Will the Constitution's third century witness a greater volume of ratified constitutional amendments as the people's efforts to create "a more perfect union" continue?

Relaunching the Drive for the Equal Rights Amendment

On March 26, 2007, the National Council of Women's Organizations (NCWO) sponsored the Women's Equality Summit in Washington, D.C. The convention attracted more than 400 participants—including the leaders of over 200 women's organizations from throughout the country, senior activists in the women's rights movement, young feminists, and members of Congress. They joined a dialogue on the need for an amendment to the U.S. Constitution guaranteeing equality of rights under the law for women. The next day, after fiery speeches by Democratic and Republican members of the Congressional Women's Caucuses of the House and the Senate, Representative Carolyn Maloney (D-New York) announced the reintroduction of the Equal Rights Amendment (ERA), first proposed in Congress in 1923, under a new name, the Women's Equity Amendment (WEA). ▌ Media outlets from the Associated Press to the *Washington Post,* and from Comedy Central's *Colbert Report* to popular Web sites such as WomensENews, reported on the events. If 290 members of the House and 67 senators vote in support of the WEA, it will go to the states' legislatures for deliberation and a vote on ratification. If thirty-eight state legislatures ratify the amendment, it will become the twenty-eighth constitutional amendment. ▌ Meanwhile, other groups are pursuing a different path toward ratification of an equal rights amendment. 4ERA and the ERA Campaign Network are focusing on a "three-state strategy" on the reasoning that a previously introduced ERA that Congress sent to the states in 1972 needs only three more states' approval to become the Twenty-Eighth Amendment. These groups point out that even though the ERA ratification period established by Congress expired in 1982, the *Twenty-Seventh* Amendment, which limits Congress's authority to give itself a pay raise, was ratified in 1992—203 years after its initial submission to Congress. This set a precedent that, when applied to the Equal Rights Amendment, makes the ERA still legally viable. ▌ The legal reasoning behind the three-state strategy is rooted in the research of third-year law school students Allison Held, Sheryl Herndon, and Danielle Stager in 1995.* The fact that Congress accepted, and national archivist Don Wilson certified, the validity of the 203-year ratification period for the Twenty-Seventh Amendment led the three students to question the time limit that Congress had imposed on the ratification of the ERA. The students discovered that the Supreme Court had ruled in a 1939 decision (*Coleman v. Miller*)** that Congress may determine that the states' ratification of an amendment has occurred in a reasonable time as long as the members of Congress judge the amendment to be relevant to societal conditions at the time of ratification. Three-state strategy supporters argue that the ERA is still relevant and needed and that Congress has the authority to accept the ERA's addition to the Constitution as valid whenever three more states ratify it.

> Proponents of the Equal Rights Amendment gather under the dome of the Arkansas State Capitol to rally for the ERA.

*www.4era.org/threestate.html.
**Coleman v. Miller, 307 U.S. 433 (1939)

The Constitution of the United

States has been formally amended, meaning that its wording has been modified by congressional and state approval, only twenty-seven times over its 220-year history. More than eighty years after the first introduction in Congress of a proposed amendment guaranteeing equality of rights under the law for women, the campaign to ratify the ERA is again heating up. Citizens are debating whether the amendment is a necessary legal foundation for women to gain equality of rights. Opponents say that the Constitution already guarantees women equal rights. But on the other side, proponents argue that as yet, the U.S. courts have not interpreted the Constitution as guaranteeing women equal rights, and so it needs to be formally amended.

Whether an equal rights amendment is necessary really depends on how the majority of justices on the U.S. Supreme Court—the ultimate interpreters of the Constitution—construe current constitutional language. To date, when interpreting the equal protection clause of the Constitution's Fourteenth Amendment (ratified in 1868), the majority of justices have used one test to determine instances of illegal discrimination against citizens due to the color of their skin, their ethnicity, or their religion, and a different, weaker test to determine cases of discrimination against women. Supporters of the ERA and WEA argue that an additional amendment, specifying equality of rights for women, is essential if women are to be guaranteed equal protection. If three more states ratify the 1972 ERA, the U.S. Supreme Court will undoubtedly have the opportunity to review a lawsuit, brought by ERA opponents, challenging the constitutionality of the ERA ratification process.

The U.S. Constitution is the supreme law of the land, meaning that all laws and the procedures used to approve all laws must be in compliance with it. Yet because the authors of the Constitution had to negotiate and compromise to win approval of the document, much of the language in the Constitution is vague and ambiguous. As a result, conflicts have erupted over its meaning—and hence over what the supreme law of the land is—since even before the Constitution was ratified, and they continue unabated today. The courts resolve many such conflicts when they are presented to them in lawsuits. Constitutional amendments are another means of resolving conflict over what the supreme law of the land is. Amendments clarify or even change that law.

What Is a Constitution?

A **constitution** is a document that describes three basic components of an organization: the organization's mission, its foundational structures, and its essential processes. Typically, constitutions begin with a description of the *mission,* the long-term goals of the organization as envisioned by its founders. Second, constitutions detail *foundational structures,* which are the bodies that will do what is necessary to accomplish the mission; and constitutions also articulate the relationships among these bodies. For example, the U.S. Constitution describes three bodies, or branches, of government—legislative, executive, and judicial—and gives each responsibility for a different governmental function. The Constitution also describes how these bodies will monitor and check one another. Third, constitutions establish *essential processes,* which include the procedures for selecting the members of the organization, as well as the processes that the members will follow to fulfill their assigned functions. For example, the U.S. Constitution describes the basic procedures for electing

We trace various constitutional conflicts throughout this textbook. So that you can understand these conflicts, this chapter concentrates on the roots of the U.S. Constitution and the basic governing principles, structures, and procedures it establishes.

FIRST, we probe the question *what is a constitution?* by considering the three main components of constitutional documents: descriptions of mission, foundational structures, and essential procedures.

SECOND, we discuss the underlying governing principles upon which the Constitution is based and examine the mission, foundational structures, and essential processes established in *the Constitution of the United States of America.*

THIRD, we explore the political, economic, and social factors that were the catalysts for *the creation of the United States of America.*

FOURTH, we survey the *crafting of the Constitution* and the processes of *compromise, ratification, and quick amendment.*

FIFTH, we focus on *the Constitution as a living, evolving document*—a vitality that derives from the alteration (formal amendment) of its written words and from the Supreme Court's (re)interpretation of its existing language to create new meaning.

constitution
a document that describes three basic components of an organization: its mission, foundational structures, and essential processes

and appointing officials to the three branches, making laws, resolving conflicts over the implementation and meaning of laws, and ratifying and amending the Constitution.

Approval (ratification) of any constitution gives birth to the organization described in the constitution, just as ratification of the U.S. Constitution gave birth to a new government. The legitimacy of a constitution and of the organization it creates depends on the means by which the organization came into existence, including what process was used to approve the constitution. Legitimacy of the organization also rests on its continued compliance with its constitution.

If you review your school's student government constitution or the constitution of any of your college's student clubs, you will find these same three components: a mission statement, foundational structures, and essential processes. Typically, colleges establish ratification processes for clubs and governance bodies. If the people attempting to create a new organization follow the established procedures, the college and its community members will view the newly created organization as legitimate, as long as it adheres to the mission, foundational structures, and essential processes described in the approved constitution.

Today, the legitimacy of the national government created by the U.S. Constitution is clear. An overwhelming majority of U.S. citizens have complied with the laws made by the national government for more than 200 years (with the exception of the Civil War period) without governmental coercion or force, because they perceive the government to be legitimate. This compliance does not mean that the national government has served all citizens well, nor does it mean that all citizens have agreed with the government's interpretation or implementation of the Constitution all the time. In fact, citizens (as individuals and as members of a group) regularly question the constitutionality of government actions.

Mike Luckovich Editorial Cartoon © 2006 Mike Luckovich. Used with the permission of Mike Luckovich and Creators Syndicate.

Moreover, government officials frequently lock horns over the proper interpretation of the Constitution. They are "trying to undermine the age-old checks and balances that the founding fathers placed at the center of the Constitution and the Republic," Senator Charles E. "Chuck" Schumer (D-New York) argued in 2005 when Republicans questioned the constitutionality of Democratic senators' use of the *filibuster* (a nonstop speech to prevent a vote in the Senate) to block Senate confirmation of the president's nominees.[1] Another battle over the proper interpretation of the Constitution broke out in 2006 over President George W. Bush's use of "signing statements," a political device whose constitutionality some citizens and some members of Congress questioned. The signing statements that President Bush attached to legislation as he signed it into law asserted that the president would not implement specific pieces of the law he was signing. Also during the George W. Bush years, some citizens challenged the constitutionality of federal government practices such as wiretapping phones without warrants, and others spoke out against state and local government laws aimed at reducing unauthorized immigration to the United States.

Complicating the matter of constitutional interpretation is the fact that some of the language in the Constitution is vague and ambiguous and hence subject to varying interpretations. The reason for this vagueness and ambiguity is that the Constitution is the product of vigorous deliberation, negotiation, and compromise, as we consider later in this chapter. Before we tune in to the conversations and compromises that produced this language, though, we first examine the governing principles that inspired the authors of the Constitution and the mission, structures, and essential governmental processes they established.

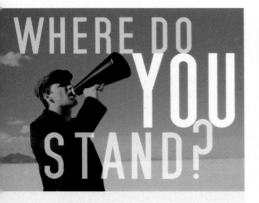

The State of American Democracy

How satisfied are you with the way democracy works in the United States?

☐ Very satisfied

☐ Somewhat satisfied

☐ Neither satisfied nor unsatisfied

☐ Somewhat dissatisfied

☐ Very dissatisfied

Source: "Americans Assess Democracy in the U.S.," www.gallup.com/poll/9574/Americans-Assess-Democracy-US.aspx.

The Constitution of the United States of America

In March 1789, the United States began to function under the Constitution of the United States of America. This bold new blueprint for the federal government replaced the nation's first constitution, the Articles of Confederation, which had been in effect since 1781. The mission of the government that was created by the Constitution shared many characteristics with the national government's mission as described in the Articles of Confederation. But the organizational structure and essential processes that the authors of the Constitution—the *framers*—articulated were new, innovative, and unprecedented. Moreover, these structures and processes successfully established a system that has evolved into a government by and for the people, one that many Americans claim is the best government in the world.

Mission of the Constitution

If a foreign visitor asked you to tell her why the United States is a good country in which to live, what would you say? When U.S. citizens are asked what is good about their country, there are several common responses. They say that government in the United States

> The preamble to the Constitution is set in stone to welcome visitors to the National Constitution Center in Philadelphia. Visitors to this interactive history museum can explore the Constitution then and now.

- is by and for the people;
- is democratic;
- protects individual liberties such as freedom of speech, freedom of religion, and freedom of the press;
- protects people from unreasonable governmental searches and seizures of property;
- guarantees the right of citizens to participate in government;
- allows citizens to elect a large number of government officials, through regular, free elections, to represent and serve them;
- ensures through its court systems that all people uphold the Constitution because no one is above the law.

These typical responses dovetail with the principles of government developed by philosophers John Locke (1632–1704) and Jean-Jacques Rousseau (1712–1778) and articulated in the Declaration of Independence and the Constitution of the United States. Recall from Chapter 1 that a key tenet of Locke and Rousseau is that people agree to create a government as a way to protect their **natural rights** (also called *unalienable rights*), which are rights possessed by all humans as a gift from nature, or God, including the rights to life, liberty, and the pursuit of happiness. Viewed in this light, a government created by the people is a government *for* the people. In addition to expecting that their government will be *for the people*, U.S. citizens are guaranteed by their Constitution a government that will be *carried out by the people*. This kind of government, in which sovereign power is in the hands of the people, not a monarch or some other leader, is called a **republic.** In a republic, voters elect government officials to represent them in the processes by which laws are made. As we saw in Chapter 1, another common name for the U.S. system is *representative democracy.*

Built on the foundational principles of government for and by the people, the U.S. Constitution, in its *preamble* (introductory statement), lays out the mission of the newly created national government of the United States:

> We the People of the United States, in Order to form a more perfect Union, establish Justice, insure domestic tranquility, provide for the common defence, promote the general Welfare and secure the Blessings of Liberty to ourselves and our Posterity, do ordain and establish this Constitution for the United States of America.

As we shall see, the vision of a government by and for the people—a government that would provide justice, tranquility, defense, and liberty—would be at the heart of colonial Americans' dissatisfaction with the British crown. This vision would not only spark the War for Independence but also deeply motivate how the framers would shape the new national government.

natural rights
(also called *unalienable rights*), the rights possessed by all humans as a gift from nature, or God, including the rights to life, liberty, and the pursuit of happiness

republic
a government that derives its authority from the people and in which citizens elect government officials to represent them in the processes by which laws are made; a representative democracy

A Key Foundational Structure: Separation of Powers with Integrated Checks and Balances

separation of powers
the Constitution's delegation of authority for the primary governing functions among three branches of government so that no one group of government officials controls all the governing functions

The Constitution's framers created a republic with governmental structures aimed at ensuring that a majority of the population could not pass laws that would take away the life, liberties, and pursuit of happiness of a minority of the population. Borrowing from French political thinker Baron de Montesquieu's (1689–1755) *The Spirit of the Laws* (1748), the framers separated the primary governing functions among three branches of government—referred to as the **separation of powers**—so that no one group of government officials controlled all the governing functions. Under the terms of the separation of powers, each branch of the

Separation of Powers with Checks and Balances

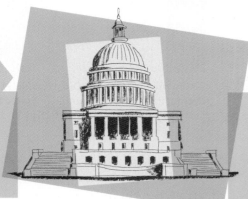
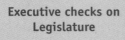

Executive checks on Legislature

Veto power

Vice president as president of Senate

Calling of emergency sessions of both houses

Authority to force adjournment when both houses cannot agree on adjournment

Legislative checks on Executive

Impeachment (House); trials for impeachment (Senate)

Overriding of vetoes

Approval of appointments, treaties, and ambassadors (Senate)

Judicial checks on Legislature

Judicial review of statutes

Legislative checks on Judiciary

Approval of federal judges (Senate)

Impeachment of federal judges (House) and impeachment trials (Senate)

Initiation of constitutional amendments

Creation of inferior courts

Determination of jurisdiction of federal courts

Legislative Functions

Passage of federal legislation

Establishment of federal courts lower than the Supreme Court

Judicial checks on Executive

Judicial review of executive orders, administrative regulations, and the implementation of laws

Executive checks on Judiciary

Appointment of judges

Power to pardon

Executive Functions

Making foreign treaties

Enforcement of federal laws and court orders

Service as commander in chief

Judicial Functions

Interpretation of U.S. Constitution and federal laws

Trying of federal lawsuits

POLITICAL INQUIRY

FIGURE 2.1 ■ Why did the Constitution's framers separate powers among the three branches of the national government? What specific powers does each branch have? What is the purpose of the Constitution's checks and balances? For each branch of the government—legislative, executive, judicial—name a specific check that it can exert on each of the other two.

government has specific powers and responsibilities that allow it to operate independently of the other branches: the legislative branch has authority to formulate policy; the executive branch has authority to implement policy; the judicial branch has authority to resolve conflicts over the law.

As suggested by Montesquieu's work, once the framers separated the primary functions, they established various mechanisms by which each branch can monitor and limit the functions of the other branches in order to ensure that no branch acts to the detriment of citizens' natural rights. These mechanisms collectively form a system of **checks and balances.** If one branch tries to move beyond its own sphere or to behave tyrannically, this arrangement ensures that the other branches can take action to stop it.

The following brief review of the first three of the seven articles that compose the Constitution should help to clarify the system of separation of powers, with its integrated checks and balances. For a complete compilation of the separation of powers and specific checks and balances, see Figure 2.1.

ARTICLE I: THE LEGISLATIVE BRANCH   Article I of the Constitution delegates lawmaking authority to Congress, describes the structure of the legislative branch, and outlines the legislative process. Article I specifies that the legislature is **bicameral,** that is, composed of two chambers, which are the House of Representatives and the Senate. Each state is represented in the House based on its population. Seven states have the required minimum of one representative (Alaska, Delaware, Montana, North Dakota, South Dakota, Vermont, and Wyoming). California has the largest representation with 53 House members. In contrast, state representation in the Senate is equal, with each state having two senators. Today, all citizens eligible to vote can participate in the election of one of their state's representatives in the U.S. House and both of their state's U.S. senators.

According to Article I, a proposed piece of legislation—a *bill*—requires simple majority votes (50 percent plus one vote) in both the House and the Senate in order to become a law. This requirement means that the House and the Senate can check each other in the legislative process, because even if one chamber garners a majority vote, the other chamber can kill the bill if its majority does not support it. Because all pieces of legislation supported by the majority of the House and the majority of the Senate go to the president for approval or rejection, the president has a check on the legislative authority of Congress.

ARTICLE II: THE EXECUTIVE BRANCH   Article II of the Constitution describes the authority of the president. This article gives the president authority to ensure that the laws are faithfully executed, to appoint people to assist in administering the laws, to negotiate treaties, and to command the military. In addition to these executive functions, Article II allows the president several checks on the power of the other two branches of government.

As already noted, the president checks the legislative authority of Congress. All pieces of legislation approved by the House and the Senate are forwarded to the president's desk. The president has ten days to act on a bill, or it will automatically become law. Within those ten days, the president can either sign the bill into law or send it back to Congress—**veto** it—with his objections noted. Because Congress has primary responsibility for legislative functions, it can set aside the president's veto, that is, override the veto, by achieving positive supermajority votes of two-thirds of House members and two-thirds of the senators.

With respect to the legislature's checks on the executive, the Constitution gives the Senate a check on presidential authority to negotiate treaties by specifying that the Senate can approve or reject any negotiated treaties. The Senate also checks the executive power through its constitutional authority of **advice and consent,** which is the power to approve or reject the president's appointments. The Senate's advice and consent authority extends to the president's judicial nominees as well. Although the president nominates the individuals who will serve as judges in the federal judicial branch—ultimately, the people who will interpret the Constitution—the Senate must formally approve these candidates.

ARTICLE III: THE JUDICIAL BRANCH   Article III describes the judicial branch. More specifically, Article III establishes the U.S. Supreme Court, and it delegates to

checks and balances
mechanisms by which each branch of government can monitor and limit the functions of the other branches

bicameral
composed of two chambers

Whom Do You Trust?

Which branch of government do you trust the most?

☐ The executive branch

☐ The legislative branch

☐ The judicial branch

Source: "Low Trust in Government Rivals Watergate Era," www.gallup.com/poll/28795/Low-Trust-Federal-Government-Rivals-Watergate-Era-Levels.aspx.

veto
the president's rejection of a bill, which is sent back to Congress with the president's objections noted

advice and consent
the Senate's authority to approve or reject the president's appointments

Congress the authority to establish other, inferior (lower) courts. The Supreme Court and the other federal courts established by Congress have the authority to resolve lawsuits arising under the Constitution, federal laws, and international treaties. In 1803, in the case of ***Marbury v. Madison,*** the Supreme Court interpreted Article III to mean that the Court has the authority to determine whether an action taken by any government official or governing body violates the Constitution; this is the power of **judicial review.**

In the *Marbury* case, the justices considered a portion of one of the first laws passed by Congress, the Judiciary Act of 1789. In its *Marbury* decision, the Court struck down the portion of the Judiciary Act that gave the Supreme Court new authority that was not specified in the Constitution. In so doing, the justices determined that it is in the Court's power to make rulings on what the Constitution means—that is, to interpret its often vague provisions. With its power of judicial review firmly established in *Marbury,* the Supreme Court has the authority to strike down laws, or portions of laws, approved by the other two branches (as well as by state and local governments) that it views as in violation of the Constitution. Some analysts consider the power of judicial review the ultimate check on the other two branches of government.

The framers intended that the national government created by the Constitution, with its separation of primary functions among the three branches, complemented by an integration of checks and balances, would work alongside the existing state governments. The Constitution did not describe the mission, foundational structures, or essential processes of the state governments because the states' own constitutions already did so. But the Constitution did spell out the distribution of authority between the national and state governments in this innovative governing system, as we now consider.

Another Key Structure: The Federal System

The framers created a federal system—a two-tiered government, comprising the national and state levels, each with ultimate authority over different matters. Article I of the Constitution lists the matters over which the national legislature (Congress) has ultimate lawmaking authority, such as regulating interstate and foreign commerce, coining money, raising and funding an army, and declaring war. Article I also prohibits state governments from engaging in certain specific activities, such as negotiating treaties. (Chapter 3 focuses on the constitutional distribution of power between the national and state governments.)

Yet the primary constitutional clause that acknowledges the establishment of a federal system of government is the Tenth Amendment, which in its entirety reads, "The powers not delegated to the United States by the Constitution, nor prohibited by it to the States, are reserved to the States respectively, or to the people." In this amendment, *United States* refers to the national government. Because there is no list of state responsibilities in the Constitution, the vagueness of the Tenth Amendment's "reserved to the states" clause has led to a perpetual battle between the national government and state governments over who is responsible for what.

Essential Processes of the National Government

In addition to the legislative process, the Constitution lays out the procedures governing the selection of national government officials. It also describes two procedures that have been vital for achieving representative democracy—the processes for formal amendment of the Constitution and for constitutional ratification. Consider that until the Constitution was amended, the national government had *no* authority to determine voting rights; *state law* determined who could vote in local, state, and national elections. Today, through the ratification of various key amendments over time, the Constitution specifies that all citizens—no matter what their race or color (Fifteenth Amendment, ratified in 1870) and regardless of their sex (Nineteenth Amendment, ratified in 1920)—who are at least 18 years of age (Twenty-Sixth

> Charnisha Thomas signs in to vote in New Orleans during Louisiana's 2008 presidential primary. Before the Constitution was formally amended, it did not guarantee any citizen the right to vote. Rather, state governments determined voting rights. Today the Constitution guarantees the right to vote to citizens who are at least 18 years old (Twenty-Sixth Amendment), regardless of their race (Fifteenth Amendment) or gender (Nineteenth Amendment).

Amendment, ratified in 1971) have the right to vote and cannot be charged a fee to vote (Twenty-Fourth Amendment, ratified in 1964). The ratification of each of these amendments, which are so crucial for citizens' free participation in the act of voting, followed strong public criticism of the legal barriers to representative democracy.

SELECTION OF NATIONAL GOVERNMENT OFFICIALS Members of the House and the Senate are elected by winning the majority of the people's direct vote (the popular vote) in their district and state, respectively. But when you cast your vote for a presidential candidate (which is an automatic vote for that candidate's vice-presidential running mate), you are not directly electing the president. Instead, in nearly every state your presidential vote, combined with the votes of other citizens from your state, determines which political party's slate of representatives (*electors*) will participate on behalf of your state in the **Electoral College,** the body that actually selects the president and the vice president.

"I believe strongly that in a democracy, we should respect the will of the people, and to me, that means it's time to do away with the Electoral College and move to the popular election of our president," declared Senator Hillary Clinton (D-New York) in response to the outcome of the 2000 presidential election.[2] In that election, Democratic presidential candidate Al Gore won the popular vote, but Republican candidate George W. Bush ultimately won the electoral vote. In order to reform or eliminate the Electoral College, the Constitution would have to be formally amended by one of the methods we next consider.

Electoral College
a group of people elected by voters in each state to elect the president and the vice president

ARTICLE V: THE AMENDMENT PROCESS The Constitution's framers wanted to ensure that widespread deliberation among the American people would precede any and all changes in the written Constitution. Thus, they made it no easy matter to amend the U.S. Constitution formally—that is, to change its written language.

Amendment is a two-step process, entailing, first, the proposal of the amendment and, second, the ratification of the proposed amendment. Article V describes two different procedures for *proposing* an amendment (see Figure 2.2). The first method requires a two-thirds majority vote in both the House and the Senate, after which the congressionally approved proposal is sent to the states for ratification. The second method (which has never been used) requires a special constitutional convention. If two-thirds of the state legislatures petition Congress to consider an amendment, such a convention, where state delegates vote on the possible amendment, takes place; an approved proposal then goes to the states for ratification.

Article V also outlines two avenues by which the second step, ratifying a proposed amendment, may occur. An amendment is ratified by a vote of approval in either three-quarters of the state legislatures or three-quarters of the special state conventions. Citizens have no vote in the process by which the U.S. Constitution is amended, nor did they have a vote in the original Constitution's ratification. In contrast, many countries and forty-nine of the fifty states in the United States do mandate citizen approval of constitutional amendments, as well as new constitutions. See "Global Comparisons" for recent examples of constitutional change in other countries.

After the required number of states have ratified a constitutional amendment, the archivist of the National Archives is authorized to certify the amendment and add it to the Constitution. The National

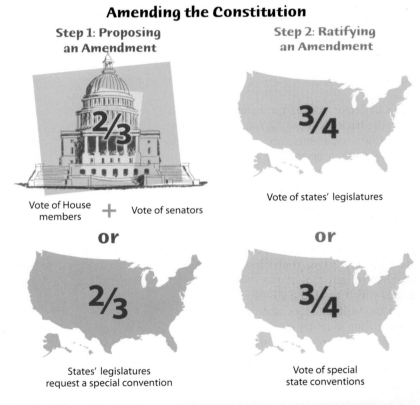

Amending the Constitution

Step 1: Proposing an Amendment

2/3

Vote of House members ＋ Vote of senators

or

2/3

States' legislatures request a special convention

Step 2: Ratifying an Amendment

3/4

Vote of states' legislatures

or

3/4

Vote of special state conventions

POLITICAL INQUIRY

FIGURE 2.2 ■ **What steps are involved in proposing a constitutional amendment? In what two ways can an amendment be ratified? Who has the authority to ratify amendments to the Constitution? Why is the designation of this authority important to the balance of power between the national and state governments? Explain.**

CONSTITUTIONAL CHANGE TODAY

In late October 2007, thousands of protesters converged on the National Assembly in downtown Caracas, Venezuela, and began throwing rocks and bottles at police. Led by students, the protesters were vehemently opposing sixty-nine constitutional amendments that President Hugo Chavez had proposed. These amendments, among other things, would eliminate the presidential term limit, thereby allowing Chavez to run for reelection indefinitely. They would also give the president authority to suspend *due process rights*—rights that protect citizens against the government's taking away their life, liberty, and property without following legal procedures—during states of emergency. Thousands of demonstrators turned out again in early November 2007, after the National Assembly's approval of Chavez's proposals.

Will constitutional upheaval continue to be the norm in many nations throughout the world?

To these opponents, the constitutional changes would severely weaken democracy and violate individuals' civil liberties—two foundational governing principles of the current Venezuelan constitution. In addition, the anti-Chavez forces charged that the collection of sixty-nine amendments amounted to nothing less than the creation of a new constitution that would replace the current law of the land, which was written in 1999, barely a decade ago. Shortly after the student-led protests, Chavez supporters, including government workers, marched to rally around the sixty-nine proposed amendments, one of which created a six-day workweek.

In the United States, such amendments to the federal Constitution must be ratified by *representatives of the people,* either in the state legislatures or in special state conventions. In contrast, in Venezuela, *citizens themselves* (not their representatives) must approve proposed constitutional changes by popular vote before they can take effect. In a December 2, 2007, Venezuelan constitutional referendum, the voters narrowly handed Chavez his first major electoral defeat in the nine years of his presidency. The 56 percent of registered voters who cast their ballot rejected the sixty-nine proposed amendments by 51–49.

Meanwhile, also in fall 2007, the citizens of the central Asian country of Kyrgyzstan, like their Venezuelan counterparts, participated in a constitutional referendum. Governing officials in Kyrgyzstan reported that almost 80 percent of the country's registered voters voted on the referendum and that 85 percent cast their ballot in support of the new constitution. This vote occurred only one month after President Kurmanbek Bakiyev had presented the people with the proposed new constitution. The president's plan of government replaced the national constitution that voters had ratified in 1993. Bakiyev and supporters claimed that the new constitution strengthened the country's parliament (national legislature) and balanced power between the legislative and executive branches. Opponents of the new constitution, however, argued that it shifted additional power to the president by allowing him to appoint judges and local bureaucrats and to dismiss the government when he deems it necessary. Non-Kyrgyzstani election observers cited many polling place irregularities, with ballot stuffing rampant (in addition to the ballots that individual voters put in the ballot box, extra ballots were "stuffed" in the box to ensure a desired outcome). It is not surprising that opponents of the new constitution are challenging not only the validity of the vote but also the legitimacy of the new constitution.

In Pakistan, a period of constitutional crisis began when President Pervez Musharraf suspended the constitution and established martial law in November 2007. Under martial law, the military takes control of the administration of justice; at the time, Musharraf was not only president but also the top-ranking military officer. He claimed his action was necessary to eradicate the extremists and terrorists threatening the nation's domestic tranquility. Musharraf directed security forces to detain hundreds of opposition political figures, lawyers protesting the suspension of the constitution, and human rights advocates. He postponed elections and disbanded the supreme court. Musharraf took all these actions after the court's unanimous decision that he was ineligible to continue serving as president

These three recent cases of constitutional upheaval highlight two remarkable characteristics of the Constitution of the United States—its longevity and its force. The long life and continuing vitality of the U.S. Constitution, and its status as the supreme law of the land that no one is above—not even the president—stand in contrast to the status of constitutions in many other nations.

> A young woman in Caracas takes part in a rally against the constitutional amendments promoted by Venezuelan president Hugo Chavez.

Archives is the home of the Constitution, the Declaration of Independence, and other historic documents.

ARTICLE VII: THE CONSTITUTIONAL RATIFICATION PROCESS According to Article VII of the Constitution, ratification of the Constitution required the affirmative vote of special conventions in nine of the thirteen original states. Notably, the ratification process did not authorize the state legislatures—whose elected officials might understandably have felt threatened by the new national government that the Constitution would create to work alongside them—to vote on the adoption of the Constitution. Instead, ratification would require special state conventions whose delegates would be selected by each state in a manner of its own determination.

The national-state competition underlying the ratification process exemplifies the many tensions and conflicts sparked by the plan to replace the Articles of Confederation (the nation's first constitution) with the Constitution of the United States. To appreciate the strength of this uneasiness requires a review of the history of the United States' founding.

The Creation of the United States of America

Understanding the American colonists' experiences in the period before the War for Independence (1775–1783) is central to comprehending the governments created by their first and second constitutions. Unlike their brothers and sisters in England, the colonists, most of whom viewed themselves as British subjects, were largely shut out of participating in the political processes taking place in England. As the eighteenth century unfolded, this exclusion increasingly rankled the American colonists, especially as an increasing number of the British government's policies put more and more restrictions on their freedoms and pursuit of economic well-being. Eventually the colonists' public debates—in homes, taverns, town squares, and newspapers—coalesced around the principles of government by and for the people.

Colonization and Governance of America

In the 1600s, waves of Europeans undertook the dangerous sea voyage to America to start new lives. Some people with connections to the king of England were rewarded with large grants of land and the authority to govern. Many more voyagers came as *indentured servants,* who would work for a number of years for a master who paid for their passage. Others came to create communities with people of the same religion so that they could practice their faith without government interference. Countless others—Africans who were brought to the colonies as slaves—came against their will. In short, a diversity of people and a mix of economic classes migrated to the colonies, joining the Native American peoples who had lived there since ancient times.

By the early eighteenth century, a two-tier system of governing the American colonies had evolved, with governance split between the colonies and Britain. The colonists elected local officials to assemblies that had the authority to rule on day-to-day matters (including criminal law and civil law) and to set and collect taxes. Back in England, Parliament, with no representatives from the colonies, enacted laws with which the colonists had to comply. Governors appointed by the king oversaw the enforcement of British law in the colonies. Initially, these laws focused on international trade—the regulation of colonial imports and exports. But that focus would soon shift.

British Policy Incites a Rebellion

The towering costs of waging the Seven Years' War in Europe and its colonial extension, the French and Indian War (1756–1763), combined with costs of maintaining peace in America as westward-moving colonists encroached on Indian lands, convinced the British Parliament to turn to the colonies for increased revenues. The first new tariff imposed after the end of the war came by way of the Sugar Act (1764). In addition to increasing the taxes on such imported goods as molasses, coffee, and textiles, the Sugar Act directed that all the taxes thus collected be sent directly to Britain instead of to the colonial assemblies, as had been the practice until then.[3] Almost immediately, the colonists condemned the law, saying that because they had no representatives in Parliament, they had no obligation to pay taxes imposed by that body. Their anger intensified in 1765 when Parliament passed the Stamp Act, which taxed the paper used for all legal documents, bills of sale, deeds, advertisements, newspapers, and even playing cards.[4] The Stamp Act introduced a new level of British involvement (some thought interference) in the day-to-day matters of the colonies.

The colonists responded to the Sugar and Stamp acts by boycotting imported goods. Women, including groups of upper-class women known as Daughters of Liberty, substituted homegrown or homespun goods for the banned items. Although the boycotts were largely peaceful, other acts of resistance were not. The Sons of Liberty, founded by Boston brewer Samuel Adams in 1765, opposed the Stamp Act through intimidation of British stamp commissioners and sometimes violence. Most of the rebellious actions occurred on the local level, but in October 1765, delegates of nine of the colonies assembled in New York at the Stamp Act Congress and adopted the slogan "No taxation without representation!"[5] People in every colony would proclaim this pledge in the coming years as Britain took even more extreme measures to increase revenues from the colonies.

Parliament followed the Sugar and Stamp acts with passage of the Quartering Act in 1765. The Quartering Act directed each colonial assembly to provide supplies to meet the basic needs of the British soldiers stationed within its colony. Parliament expanded this law in 1766 to require the assemblies to ensure housing for the soldiers.[6] Throughout the colonies, violent reactions to the quartering law erupted.[7] Since 1791, the Third Amendment to the Constitution has protected U.S. citizens from being required to quarter soldiers during times of peace.

Although Parliament repealed the hated Stamp Act in 1766, it paired this repeal with passage of the Declaratory Act. This new law gave Parliament the blanket power to assert control over colonies "in any way whatsoever."[8] This development was a clear indication that the two-tier system of colonial government, in which the colonies exerted some local governing authority, was dissolving. The next year, the colonists understood how momentous this law was, as Parliament used the Declaratory Act as the basis for a new series of laws that would culminate in war. Significant among these laws was the Townshend Duties Act of 1767, which not only expanded the list of imported goods that would be taxed but also stated that Parliament had unilateral power to impose taxes as a way of raising revenue and that the colonists had no right to object.[9] With this new law, the colonists dramatically stepped up their civic resistance.

A "MASSACRE" AND A TEA PARTY

By 1770, more than 4,000 British soldiers were quartered in the homes of the 16,000 civilians living in Boston. To make matters worse, the British soldiers quartered in the city sought additional work as rope makers and in other crafts, competing with the colonists for these jobs.[10] On March 5, 1770, an angry mob of nearly 1,800 struggling colonists clashed with the British soldiers, who shot into the crowd, leaving five dead and six wounded.

Almost immediately Samuel Adams—an expert at "spinning" a news story—condemned the event as "the Boston Massacre." Partnering with Adams to shape public opinion were silversmith Paul Revere and wealthy shipping merchant John Hancock. The communications of the two men stressed that the colonists respected the rule of law but emphasized that the British king, George III, cared more about preserving his own power than about his subjects' well-being. Therefore, Revere and Hancock asserted, there could be no assurance that he would respect the colonists' rights and

DOING DEMOCRACY

STAGE A PEACEFUL PROTEST TO RAISE AWARENESS

FACT:

On April 16, 2007, Virginia Tech student Seung-Hui Cho killed thirty-two people with guns that he had purchased in just three minutes. The massacre sparked numerous investigations and public discussions—of the privacy rights of students with a history of mental problems, of college and university emergency notification plans, and of issues related to the Second Amendment of the Constitution, specifically gun control laws. Abigail Spangler, a cellist with a doctorate from Columbia University, organized a simple, hard-hitting demonstration to shed light on the ease with which Americans can purchase guns. Her demonstration took the form of a "lie-in." Spangler's lie-in involved thirty-two people (representing the thirty-two individuals whom Cho had killed) dressing in black and lying on the ground for three minutes (highlighting the time it takes

> During his deadly rampage at Virginia Tech University in April 2007, Seung-Hui Cho paused between shootings to send this photo. This horrific episode refueled the ongoing debate on gun control laws and sparked discussion of students' privacy rights.

to purchase a gun in the United States). Protesters have staged lie-ins to ignite awareness of what they see as lax gun control laws in numerous cities and on several college campuses, and Spangler yearns for more college student activism on this issue: "We hope that college students will be inspired by our social movement . . . because we need their help" to lobby the government for changes in gun laws.* Spangler is using Facebook.com and the Internet generally to engage and mobilize young people. At the same time, other citizens are challenging the constitutionality of gun control laws through lawsuits (see "Exploring the Sources," p. 64).

Act!

Whatever issue gets your blood boiling and inspires you to take action, you need first to do your research on current, relevant laws in order to be effective. Research is made easier by the Internet and its variety of search engines. Of course, you want to be sure that the Web sites you visit are reputable. Once you have a sure understanding of the issue and of the relevant laws and policies, you can use your knowledge to mobilize like-minded individuals and to organize a public demonstration to bring attention to your concern. You can also benefit from Abigail Spangler's "protest in a box" resource—a straightforward guide to organizing a protest in general and a lie-in specifically. Her protest in a box provides motivated individuals with

a step-by-step process for organizing a public protest, from sample letters for mobilizing people, to sample press releases, to avenues for contacting elected officials. Whatever issue has moved you, Spangler's protest in a box is a great primer for an inexpensive, manageable, legal public demonstration.

Where to begin

To learn more about organizing a protest, begin with Spangler's protest in a box, which you can find at www.protesteasyguns .org/inabox.html.

*"Bringing the Gun Debate Back to Campus," *Inside Higher Education*, November 1, 2007, www.insidehighered.com/layout/set/rpint/news/2007/11/01/guns.

liberties. This problem, they argued, could be rectified only by the American colonists' ending their relationship with Britain.

In 1772 Adams created the Massachusetts Committee of Correspondence, a group dedicated to encouraging and maintaining the free flow of information and the spread of calls for rebellion among the Massachusetts colonists. Radicals in other colonies followed his lead.[11] Revere published pamphlets aimed at keeping the colonists together in their battle with the Crown, talking boldly about "our rights," "our liberties," and "our union."[12] These communication networks served as a kind of colonial-era Internet, facilitating the sharing of news among the colonists. But in this case, the swift transmission of information occurred by way of riders on horseback and printers at their presses rather than by the keystrokes of citizens typing on computers—today's vital communication network for rallying people behind a cause and mobilizing political activism.

Adding fuel to the fire, in 1773 Parliament passed the Tea Act, which gave the East India Tea Company a monopoly on tea imported into the colonies. The questioning of the act's legitimacy by the Sons of Liberty successfully swayed public opinion and became the catalyst for an event that would become known as the Boston Tea Party. In November 1773, the first post–Tea Act shipment of tea arrived in Boston Harbor on three East India tea ships. Under cover of darkness on the night of December 16, 1773, fifty colonists, dressed as Mohawk Indians, boarded the three ships, broke open hundreds of crates, and dumped thousands of pounds of tea into the harbor.[13] The Boston Tea Party had a cataclysmic effect, not only on the relationship between Britain and the colonies but on the relationship among the colonists themselves.

Parliament responded with the Coercive Acts (Intolerable Acts), which closed the port of Boston and kept it closed until the colonists paid for the lost tea. In addition, the new laws imposed martial law, shut down the colonial assembly, and banned virtually all town meetings, thus curtailing legal opportunities for political engagement.[14] At the same time, the Crown stepped up enforcement of the Quartering Act.

THE CONTINENTAL CONGRESSES AND COLONIAL DEMANDS FOR POLITICAL RIGHTS Sympathy for Massachusetts's plight, along with rising concerns about how the Crown was generally abusing its powers, reinforced the colonists' growing sense of community and their shared consciousness of the need for collective action. The Massachusetts and Virginia colonial assemblies requested a meeting of delegates from all the colonies to develop a joint statement of concern that would be sent to the king. In September 1774, every colony but Georgia sent delegates to what became known as the First Continental Congress. The Congress (the assembled delegates) called for a boycott of all British goods and created Committees of Enforcement to impose the ban. Moreover, the Congress drafted and sent to the king a document demanding that the American colonists should have political rights to petition the government and to assemble, the right to select representatives to formulate tax policy, a guarantee of trial by peers, and freedom from a standing army.[15] The Congress also scheduled a second meeting—the Second Continental Congress—to discuss the king's response to these demands.

When the king refused to address the Congress's demands, civic discourse on the prospect of pursuing independence from Great Britain increased. On April 19, 1775, before the Second Continental Congress met, shots rang out at Lexington and Concord, Massachusetts, as British troops moved inland to seize the colonists' store of guns and ammunition. On May 10, 1775, the Second Continental Congress convened. The assembled delegates empowered the Congress to function as an independent government and to prepare for war with Britain, appointing George Washington to command the to-be-created Continental Army.

The Common Sense of Declaring Independence

In July 1775, the Second Continental Congress made one last effort to avert a full-blown war. The Congress petitioned King George III to end hostile actions against the colonists. The king refused and sent even more troops to the colonies to put down the rebellion. Yet even as the Congress made preparations for a likely war, many colonists remained unsure about whether the colonies should cut their ties with Britain. A brief pamphlet written by

Thomas Paine, a recently arrived radical from Britain, and published in January 1776 transformed many such wavering colonists into patriots. Paine's *Common Sense* argued that war with Great Britain was not only necessary but unavoidable. Without war, the colonies and their people would continue to suffer "injuries" and disadvantages. Only through independence would Americans attain civil and religious liberty.[16]

In May 1776, Virginia delegate to the congress Richard Henry Lee asserted "that these united Colonies are, and of right ought to be free and independent States, [and] that they are absolved from all allegiance from the British crown."[17] This "declaration of independence," which congressional delegates from other colonies subsequently echoed, led the congress to approve a resolution empowering a committee of five to write down, in formal language, a collective declaration of independence. The committee selected Virginia delegate Thomas Jefferson, a wealthy plantation owner, to draft the declaration.

Unanimously endorsed by the Second Continental Congress on July 4, 1776, Jefferson's Declaration of Independence drew upon the work of John Locke and Jean-Jacques Rousseau, as Table 2.1 highlights. The declaration was a radical statement. Its two central principles—that all men are equal and have rights that are unalienable (that is, fundamental) and that all government must be based on consent of the governed—may seem obvious from the vantage point of the twenty-first century. But in 1776, the idea that the people had a right not only to choose their government but to abolish it made the Declaration of Independence unlike anything before it.

After establishing these two central principles, the Declaration spelled out a list of grievances against King George in an attempt to convince the colonists and the European powers that the break with England was necessary and justified. The Declaration fulfilled this

> Jefferson's Declaration of Independence, drawing on the work of philosophers John Locke and Jean-Jacques Rousseau, delivered the radical message that people have a right not only to choose their government but also to abolish it when it no longer serves them.

POLITICAL INQUIRY

TABLE 2.1

The Theories of Locke and Rousseau as Applied by Jefferson

What ideas did Jefferson take from Locke and Rousseau with respect to human rights and liberties? How would you summarize the views of the three men on the purposes of government and the source of government power?

John Locke's Theories: *Two Treatises of Government* (1690)

All people are born free and equal.

All people are born into a "state of nature" and choose to enter into government for protection against being harmed.

Every person has the right to "life, liberty and property," and government may not interfere with this right.

Jean-Jacques Rousseau's Theories: *The Social Contract* (1762)

All power ultimately resides in the people.

People enter into a "social contract" with the government to ensure protection of their lives, liberties, and property.

If government abuses its powers and interferes with the people's exercise of their civil liberties, then the people have both the right and the duty to create a new government.

Thomas Jefferson's Application of Locke and Rousseau: Declaration of Independence (1776)

All men are created equal.

All men are endowed with certain unalienable rights, among which are life, liberty, and the pursuit of happiness.

To secure these rights, men create governments, which derive their powers from the consent of the governed.

King George III failed to respect the unalienable rights of the American colonists and instead created an "absolute tyranny" over them.

If government is destructive of people's rights, the people can alter or abolish it and create a new government.

purpose of winning the hearts and minds of people both in the colonies and abroad. Until this point, the patriots had united in their hatred toward Britain but had little else around which to rally. The Declaration provided that rallying point by promising a new government that would be based on consent of the people, with liberty and equality as its central goals.

In 1777, as a brutal war over colonial independence raged between England and the colonies, the Second Continental Congress turned to the pressing task of establishing a new, *national* government by drafting a constitution, the Articles of Confederation. By that year, too, eleven colonies had written and ratified constitutions establishing new *state* governments, although two colonies continued to function under the structures and procedures established by their *royal charters* (constitutional documents initially approved by the British king).[18] In these ways, the colonies had become thirteen states with independent, functioning governments. It is to these governments that the Second Continental Congress sent the Articles of Confederation for ratification in 1777.

The State Constitutions

The states stood at the center of American politics when the nation was born. Every state constitution established a *mission* for the state government; *foundational structures* (including three branches of government, each with distinct primary governing functions and checks on the other branches), to organize the government and distribute power within it; and *essential processes* by which the government would operate. The state constitutions provided the governments they created with only limited powers, however. Most of these powers rested in the legislatures because of the prevailing view of people of the times that this was where the best prospects for representative government could be found.

Ensuring liberty was a crucial aspect of the mission of all the state governments. To this end, each state constitution included a *bill of rights*—a section enumerating the individual liberties with which the new state government could not interfere, including freedom of speech, press, and assembly; protection against unreasonable searches and seizures and taxation without representation; and the right to a jury trial. As you can see, the authors of the state constitutions wrote into them limits on the state governments to prevent these governments from infringing on individuals' life, liberties, and pursuit of happiness as the British Crown had done. Hence the inclusion of a written list of citizens' liberties established a limited government by ensuring that both the people and the government knew what freedoms the government could not violate. In addition, most state constitutions explicitly asserted that power was held by the people, who created government and whom government served.

The states of the new American republic used their new constitutions to guide them in handling their day-to-day domestic matters. Meanwhile, members of the Second Continental Congress turned their attention to creating a national government that would allow the states to collectively address international affairs.

> This flag represents the original five nations of the Iroquois Confederacy: Seneca, Cayuga, Onondaga, Mohawk, and Oneida. The needles of the white pine, in the middle, grow in clusters of five. The influence of the Iroquois Confederacy is evident in the first four articles of the first constitution of the United States, the Articles of Confederation.

The Articles of Confederation (1781–1789)

Because of the colonists' bitter experience under the British Crown, the people and their delegates to the Second Continental Congress were leery of a strong, distant central government; they had a preference for government that was close to their homes. The delegates nevertheless recognized the need for a unified authority in the realms of international trade, foreign affairs, and defense. For a model of government, they needed to look no further than a league formed by several Indian tribes of the northeastern United States and eastern Canada.

The Iroquois League was an alliance of five tribes. Under the league, the tribes pursued their own self-interest independently of one another, and the only condition was that they maintain peace with each other. Presiding over the league was a Grand Council of fifty representatives who were chosen by the tribes and who had very limited authority. This council served as a unified front and was charged simply with keeping intertribal peace—and later, with negotiating with the Europeans.[19]

The influence of the Iroquois League is evident in the first four articles in the Articles of Confederation, which was submitted to the states for ratification in 1777 and ratified by the required thirteen states by 1781. The Articles of Confederation established a **confederation:** a national government composed of a league of independent states and in which the central government has less power than the member states. Through the Articles of Confederation, the states created an alliance for mutual well-being in the international realm yet continued to pursue their own self-interest independently. Article II asserts that "each state retains its sovereignty, freedom, and independence" and that every power not specifically given to the central government is retained by the states. In addition, the national Congress that the Articles of Confederation established, like the Iroquois League's Grand Council, had the authority to negotiate treaties with other nations.

STRUCTURE AND AUTHORITY OF THE CONFEDERATION Structurally, the new national government had only one body, a Congress. Under the articles, the Congress was **unicameral,** meaning that it had only one chamber, and every state had from two to seven delegates but only one vote in this body. Each state determined how its delegates would be selected. Approving policies and ratifying treaties required nine affirmative votes. The articles did not create a judicial branch, an executive branch, or a chief executive officer. Conflicts of law were to be addressed by the state court systems, and national policies would be implemented and paid for by state governments. There was to be a president—one of the congressional members selected by his peers to preside over the meetings of Congress. Finally, and important to remember, amending the Articles of Confederation required unanimous agreement among all thirteen states.

What authority did the new national government have by way of this unicameral body? The answer is a very limited authority. Congress could approve policies relevant to foreign affairs, defense, and the coining of money. It was not authorized, however, to raise revenue through taxation; only state governments could levy and collect taxes. Therefore, in order to pay the national government's bills, Congress had to request money from each state. Moreover, the value of the money coined by the national government was not insured, because the national government did not control a source of money to back the value.

WEAKNESSES OF THE CONFEDERATION Under the Articles of Confederation, the states retained ultimate authority in matters of commerce. As a result, other nations were not willing to negotiate trade policies with national officials. In addition, each state taxed all goods coming into the state from foreign nations and from other states. Moreover, the states issued their own money and required the use of this currency for all business within the state. The cumulative effect of these state policies hampered interstate and international commerce severely, putting the nation's economic health in jeopardy.*

In Massachusetts, economic pressures reached a head in 1786 when small farmers, many of whom had fought in the War for Independence, could not pay their legal debts and faced bankruptcy and the loss of their land. Farmer and war veteran Daniel Shays led an uprising of these debt-burdened farmers, today known as Shays's Rebellion. The rebels broke into county courthouses and burned all records of their debts. They then proceeded to the federal arsenal. Massachusetts asked Congress for assistance in putting down the rebellion. Congress appealed to each state for money to fulfill this request, but only Virginia complied. While eventually, through private donations, Massachusetts raised enough money to hire a militia to end the rebellion, the weaknesses of the national confederacy and a rationale for a stronger central government were becoming apparent.

In an attempt to deal with the weakness of the Articles, delegates from five states met in Annapolis, Maryland, in 1786. The delegates signed a resolution that called for a

confederation
a national government composed of a league of independent states and in which the central government has less power than the member states

unicameral
a legislative body with a single chamber

---

*For an excellent discussion of how the Articles benefited the states, see Keith L. Dougherty, *Collective Action under the Articles of Confederation* (Cambridge University Press, 2000), p. 76–82.

constitutional convention to be held in Philadelphia in 1787 and attended by all thirteen states. This resolution had a sweeping objective: delegates to the constitutional convention were to consider changes not only in commercial regulation but also in the overall structure of the new government that the Articles of Confederation had established.

Crafting the Constitution: Compromise, Ratification, and Quick Amendment

The delegates to the Constitutional Convention in 1787 were among the most elite Americans. Some 80 percent had served as members of the Continental Congress, and the vast majority were lawyers, businessmen, or plantation owners. Many were engaged in highly lucrative international trade, and all were wealthy. These elites contrasted sharply with the masses, who included the country's hard-pressed farmers and struggling local merchants and tradespeople. As a matter of fact, historian Charles Beard contended in 1913 that the Constitution's framers succeeded in forging a government that protected their elite status.[20]

Indeed, the delegates did write into the new constitution a much greater role for Congress in creating and maintaining a healthy economy, something that would be good for the delegates as well as the nation. For example, the new constitution gave Congress the authority to lay and collect taxes, regulate interstate and foreign commerce, coin money, and develop a system of weights and measures.

But although the delegates widely agreed about the need to create a stronger economic role for the national government, they differed significantly over other issues that loomed large in the new nation. There was considerable disagreement in particular about what powers to give the central government, how to ensure a representative democracy, and what to do about the entrenched institution of slavery. Delegates from southern states worried that the northern states would create barriers to their states' economic interests by either insisting on the abolition of slavery or diluting the voting strength of the South. In the North, a region on the cusp of the Industrial Revolution, people were concerned about how the new government's trade and tax policies would affect them. These regional concerns reflected continuing unease about the relative power of the national government and state governments and about the powers of the states relative to one another. These power concerns played out in the compromises written into the Constitution and in the ratification battle as well.

Many convention delegates, including James Madison of Virginia, believed that a closed environment would be necessary for hammering out the compromises that would be essential for creating an improved system of government. Therefore, the delegates met in secret. The framers ultimately succeeded in producing a new constitution by bargaining and by forging compromises on several thorny issues. Thereafter, proponents of the Constitution would win its ratification only after acknowledging the need to amend the ratified Constitution quickly by adding a bill of rights to limit the power of the national government.

Conflict and Compromise over Representative Democracy

Among the delegates' top points of contention was disagreement over representation in the national government.

THE VIRGINIA AND NEW JERSEY PLANS AND THE CONNECTICUT COMPROMISE Virginian James Madison arrived at the convention with a plan in hand for restructuring the national government. His proposal called for a radically revamped government, consisting of a bicameral legislature (Congress), a chief executive officer, and a separate national judiciary. Madison's proposal, which became known as the **Virginia Plan,** favored states with larger populations, because it called for the determination of state representation in the national legislature on the basis of population. The lower house would be chosen through popular election, but the members of the upper house would be elected by the lower house. Madison argued forcefully for a separation of powers, believing this arrangement to be the key to limiting the authority of the much expanded national govern-

Virginia Plan
James Madison's proposal at the Constitutional Convention for a new governmental structure, which favored states with larger populations

ment and to protecting individual rights and liberties.

The states with smaller populations quickly and aggressively responded to Madison's Virginia Plan with their own proposal, which became known as the **New Jersey Plan.** The small states' concerns about the Virginia Plan were obvious. Because Madison's plan based representation in Congress on state population, the small states stood to lose significant power (remember that under the Articles of Confederation, each state, no matter what its population and no matter how many representatives it had in the legislature, had one vote). Unlike the Virginia Plan, the New Jersey Plan was not a radical proposal—it essentially reworked the Articles of Confederation. Under the New Jersey proposal, a unicameral national legislature would remain the centerpiece of the government, and all states would have an equal voice (equal representation) in this government.

The conflict and negotiation over the Virginia and New Jersey plans resulted in several compromises, most notably the **Connecticut Compromise** (also known as the *Great Compromise*). This compromise created today's bicameral Congress, with state representation in the House of Representatives based on state population and equal state representation in the Senate (two senators per state).

THE CONSTITUTION'S CHECKS ON REPRESENTATIVE DEMOCRACY

At the heart of representative democracy is the participation of citizens in electing their government officials. Yet the framers built a number of checks into the Constitution that significantly *limited* representative democracy, and in doing so they effectively took most of the institutions of governing out of the hands of the people. Although the Constitution allowed citizens to elect members of the House directly, it specified the election of senators by the state legislatures. This protocol remained in effect until 1913, when the ratification of the Seventeenth Amendment to the Constitution gave voters the power to elect the members of the Senate, too. And as we have seen, the Electoral College system that the framers devised for the election of the president and vice president prevented citizens from directly selecting the nation's chief executive and the second-in-command.

In addition to limiting the number of officials elected by citizens, the framers also effectively limited voting rights to a minority of citizens. Existing state constitutions had established that only property-owning white men could vote. The one exception was New Jersey, where property-owning white women could also vote until 1807, when the state constitution was amended to deny women the right to the franchise. The framers left to the states the authority to determine eligibility to vote. Hence, women and many men, including Native Americans as well as slaves, were denied the right to vote under the new Constitution.

The delegates spent most of the first two months of debate arguing about the national legislature and primarily focused on the question of state representation in Congress. They devoted less than a month to the rest of the issues before them, including the structure of

The Changing Face of Popular Representation

	CONSTITUTIONAL CONVENTION (1787)	110TH CONGRESS (2007–2008)	CURRENT U.S. POPULATION*
Women	0%	16%**	51%
African Americans	0%	8%†	12%
Asian Americans	0%	2%	4%
Hispanics	0%	5%	15%
Native Americans	0%	0.2%	0.8%

*U.S. Census Bureau, 2006 American Community Survey.
**www.cawp.rutgers.edu/Facts2.html.
†www.ethnicmajority.com/congress.htm.

WHAT'S NEXT?

> What is different about the composition of the delegates to the Constitutional Convention and the composition of the 110th Congress? What explains the differences?

> Why do you think the demographic representation among lawmakers in the 110th Congress does not mirror the composition of the U.S. population at large more closely?

> Do you think future Congresses will be more "representative"? Explain.

New Jersey Plan
the proposal presented by states with smaller populations at the Constitutional Convention in response to James Madison's Virginia Plan

Connecticut Compromise
(also known as the *Great Compromise*), the compromise between the Virginia Plan and the New Jersey Plan that created a bicameral legislature with one chamber's representation based on population and the other having two members for each state

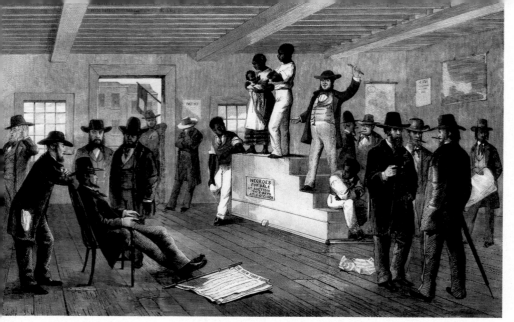

> Because the northern and southern delegates to the Constitutional Convention did not resolve their conflict over slavery, the institution remained constitutional. The Constitution also prohibited Congress from banning slave importation until 1808. With the legal importation of slaves banned in 1808 through congressional legislation, the demand for native-born slaves and their children grew.

the executive and judicial branches; the relationship between the federal and state governments; the process for amending the new plan of government, should the need arise to do so; the procedures for the Constitution's ratification; and a series of compromises over the slave trade.[21]

Conflict and Compromise over Slavery

Another major disagreement among the Constitutional Convention delegates centered on the "peculiar institution" (as Thomas Jefferson called it) of slavery. In 1790, slaves made up almost 20 percent of the U.S. population, and the overwhelming majority of slaves resided in the southern states.[22] The southern states' delegates worried that a strong central government would threaten the institution of slavery. During the constitutional debates, they therefore refused to budge on the slavery issue. Meanwhile, northern delegates, who were widely concerned that a weak national government would affect the United States' ability to engage in commerce and international trade, believed that the nation needed a more powerful central government than had existed under the Articles of Confederation. Ultimately, to get the southern states to agree to a stronger central government, the northern states compromised on the slavery issue.

A provision in Article I, Section 9, of the Constitution postponed debate on the legality of slavery—and consequently kept it legal—by prohibiting Congress from addressing the importation of new slaves into the United States until January 1, 1808. Moreover, Article IV, which deals with interstate relations, established the states' obligation to deliver all fugitive slaves back to their owners. This measure aimed to ensure that people in non-slaveholding states would continue to respect the property rights of slaveholders—including the right to own slaves, who were legally property, not people with natural rights.

Three-Fifths Compromise
the negotiated agreement by the delegates to the Constitutional Convention to count each slave as three-fifths of a free man for the purpose of representation and taxes

Although the slaves were legally property, Article I, Section 2, established a formula for "counting" slaves for purposes of representation in the House of Representatives, apportionment of electors for the Electoral College, and the allocation of tax burdens among the states. This **Three-Fifths Compromise** counted each slave as three-fifths of a free man. The southern states benefited by this compromise: they gained greater representation in the House and the Electoral College than they would have if only nonslaves were counted. The benefit to the northern states was that the South would pay more taxes than they would if only nonslaves were counted in taxation formulas.

James Madison, while deploring slavery, argued that the delegates' "compromise" over slavery was "in the spirit of accommodation which governed the Convention." He insisted that without the compromise, the Constitution would never have been signed.

So in the delegates' debates and deliberations, they resolved some disagreements, such as the large state–small state conflict over congressional representation. They put on hold other differences, such as their divisions over slavery. In the end, the document that the framers sent to the states for ratification described a government structure that aimed to fulfill the principles of the Declaration of Independence, for a select group of people. Foremost among these principles was the idea that it is up to the people to found a government that protects their natural rights to life, liberty, and the pursuit of happiness. To ensure these rights, which were initially meant only for white, property-owning men, the framers devised two key arrangements: the separation of powers with an integrated system of checks and balances, and a federal system in which the national and state governments had distinct, ultimate authorities.

> James Madison, Alexander Hamilton, and John Jay authored *The Federalist Papers,* a series of newspaper articles that justified and argued for the governing structures and procedures established in the U.S. Constitution. Because Madison and Hamilton had attended the Constitutional Convention, they had an insider's view of the arguments for and against the Constitution.

The Federalist–Anti-Federalist Debate

Signed by thirty-nine delegates on September 17, 1787,* the Constitution was published two days later in a special issue of a newspaper called the *Pennsylvania Packet.* Almost immediately, opponents of the proposed Constitution began to write letters, issue pamphlets, and make stirring speeches urging the state legislatures to reject the document. The debate developed as one between the Federalists and the Anti-Federalists. The **Federalists** supported the Constitution as presented by the convention delegates. The **Anti-Federalists** opposed the Constitution on the grounds that it gave the national government too much power—power that would erode states' authority and endanger individual freedoms.

It was in the Pennsylvania debate between the Federalists and the Anti-Federalists that the call first clearly emerged for the inclusion of a bill of rights that would limit the powers of the federal government. Geared toward addressing the main Anti-Federalist complaints about the Constitution, the proposal for a bill of rights became the dominant point of contention in the ratification campaign. In the end, the success or failure of the ratification process would hinge on it.

***THE FEDERALIST PAPERS:* IN SUPPORT OF A STRONG NATIONAL GOVERNMENT**   The Federalists made their most famous arguments in a series of essays known as *The Federalist Papers,* which appeared in newspapers across the new nation. The authors, James Madison, Alexander Hamilton, and John Jay, knew that achieving ratification depended on convincing the public and state legislators that the Constitution would empower the new nation to succeed. They also understood that many of the Anti-Federalists' concerns centered on how much power the national government would have under the Constitution and how that authority would affect the states and individual freedoms. Consequently, they approached the ratification debate strategically, penning eloquently reasoned essays (in the form of letters) to speak to these specific issues.[23]

Addressing fears of lost state power, Hamilton argues in *Federalist* No. 9 that "a FIRM Union will be of the utmost moment to the peace and liberty of the States, as a barrier against domestic faction and insurrection." Similarly, in *Federalist* No. 51, Madison explains

Federalists
individuals who supported the new Constitution as presented by the Constitutional Convention in 1787

Anti-Federalists
individuals who opposed ratification of the Constitution because they were deeply suspicious of the powers it gave to the national government and of the impact these powers would have on states' authority and individual freedoms

The Federalist Papers
a series of essays, written by James Madison, Alexander Hamilton, and John Jay, that argued for the ratification of the Constitution

---

* In 2004, the national government approved a law establishing September 17th as Constitution Day. The law mandates that all educational institutions receiving federal funds, which includes almost every college in the country, must provide educational programs about the Constitution on that day.

> Mercy Otis Warren was one of the rare, respected, politically engaged women of the eighteenth century. Her significant influence extended to the citizenry and to the authors of the Constitution and the Bill of Rights, with many of whom she discussed and debated governance and politics. Her political writings include the *Anti-Federalist Papers* and her extraordinary *History of the Rise, Progress, and Termination of the American Revolution* (1805).

how the Constitution's provision of both a separation of powers and a system of checks and balances would prevent the national government from usurping the powers of the states and also ensure that no one branch of the federal government would dominate the other two.[24]

With regard to protecting individual rights, in *Federalist* No. 10, Madison reassuringly details how the republican government created by the Constitution would ensure that many views would be heard and that a majority of the population would not be permitted to trample the rights of the numerical minority.[25] And writing in *Federalist* No. 84, Hamilton argues that because "the people surrender nothing, and as they retain every thing" by way of the Constitution, there was no danger that the new government would usurp individual rights and liberties.[26]

THE ANTI-FEDERALIST RESPONSE: IN OPPOSITION TO A STRONG CENTRAL GOVERNMENT On the other side of the debate, Anti-Federalists penned countless letters, speeches, and essays warning of the dangers of the new government and urging Americans to reject it. Anti-Federalists agonized that the Constitution ceded much too much power to the national government, at the expense of both the states and the people. Without a bill of rights, they reasoned, there was no way of truly limiting the actions the new government might take to achieve its goals. Some Anti-Federalists reminded Americans that the framers had exceeded their mandate when they decided to scrap the Articles of Confederation and start again. The Constitutional Convention, they stressed, had authorized *amendment* of the articles, not wholesale rejection of them.

Articulating Anti-Federalist views, Thomas Jefferson insisted that the inclusion of a bill of rights in the Constitution was essential. Federalist Alexander Hamilton countered that listing these rights might in fact endanger the very kind of individual freedoms and rights they sought to safeguard. It was possible, Hamilton reasoned, that the list would be incomplete and that at some future time people might legitimately argue that because a given right was not specifically enumerated, it did not exist. (Was Hamilton correct? Consider the debate today about abortion.) Jefferson's response was that "half a loaf is better than no bread" and that "if we cannot secure all our rights, let us secure what we can."[27]

Along with Jefferson, Mercy Otis Warren was among the most influential Anti-Federalists. In addition to influencing public debate over declaring independence from Great Britain and ratifying the Articles of Confederation and the Constitution, Warren was a catalyst for the development of the Bill of Rights. She published her *Anti-Federalist Papers* under the pen name "A Columbian Patriot." The circulation of her pamphlet was larger than that of Hamilton, Madison, and Jay's *Federalist Papers*.

In the end, Jefferson's and Warren's views and the larger civic discourse about states' rights and individuals' liberties placed significant pressure on the Federalists to reconsider their opposition to a bill of rights. With the proviso that a bill of rights would be the first order of

Concept Summary

WHY THE ANTI-FEDERALISTS FOUGHT FOR, AND SECURED, A BILL OF RIGHTS

Bill of Rights: The first ten amendments to the Constitution, all ratified within two years of the Constitution's ratification.

— Anti-Federalists argued that without an enumeration (a list) of individual freedoms with which the new central government could not interfere, the government would not respect individual freedoms, just as the British king had not.

— Anti-Federalists preferred strong state governments that were close to the people and feared a powerful central government. They worried that without a list of individual freedoms, the proposed central government would have more power than would the state governments, which were limited by their constitutions' own bills of rights.

— In order to achieve ratification of the Constitution by the states of Massachusetts, Maryland, South Carolina, and New Hampshire, Federalists had to compromise with Anti-Federalists and support the enumeration of specific freedoms with which the government could not interfere.

business for the new Congress, four holdout states, Massachusetts, Maryland, South Carolina, and New Hampshire—the last four states of the nine needed to ratify the Constitution—ratified it in 1788. Ultimately, all original thirteen states ratified the Constitution.

The Bill of Rights (1791): Establishing Civil Liberties

In the opening days of the first session of the newly constituted Congress in March 1789, Virginia congressman James Madison introduced a bill of rights. Comprising twelve amendments, this proposed addition to the Constitution powerfully reflected the public concerns voiced during the ratification debates by (1) enumerating limits on the government's right to infringe on the natural rights of life, liberty, and the pursuit of happiness, and (2) preserving the states' authority. Congress passed all twelve amendments and sent them to the states for approval. By 1791, the required number of states had quickly ratified ten of the twelve amendments, which we refer to today as the **Bill of Rights.**

The Bill of Rights establishes the government's legal obligation to protect several specific liberties to which the Declaration of Independence referred when it stated that men were "endowed by their creator with certain unalienable rights." These natural rights became government-protected liberties, *civil liberties,* through the ratification process. Chapter 4 focuses in depth on the civil liberties established in the Bill of Rights.

Bill of Rights
the first ten amendments to the Constitution, which were ratified in 1791, constituting an enumeration of the individual liberties with which the government is forbidden to interfere.

The Constitution as a Living, Evolving Document

The authors of the Constitution were pragmatic men who were willing to compromise to resolve the problems confronting the new nation.[28] To garner the votes needed to move the document from first draft through ratification, the framers had to negotiate and compromise over constitutional language. As a result of this give-and-take, the Constitution is replete with vague and ambiguous phrases, which the framers expected judges to interpret later. Alexander Hamilton wrote, "A constitution is in fact, and must be, regarded by judges as a fundamental law. It therefore belongs to them to ascertain its meaning as well as the meaning of any particular act proceeding from the legislative body. . . . The courts must declare the sense of the law. . . ."[29] As Supreme Court justice Charles Evans Hughes (1862–1948) more recently observed, "The Constitution is what the Judges say it is."[30]

Judges—and principally the justices sitting on the U.S. Supreme Court, which has the ultimate authority to rule on what the Constitution means—have reinterpreted the Constitution many times. The Constitution has been formally amended only twenty-seven times, however. The reason for the relatively low number of constitutional amendments is that the framers established a difficult amendment process, requiring supermajority votes in Congress and among the states. They did so to ensure that nationwide public discourse would take place before the Constitution, the supreme law of the land, could be formally changed.

The alteration of this document—through both the formal passage of amendments and the less formal, but no less important, judicial reinterpretation of key clauses—derives from a continuing conversation among citizens about the core beliefs and principles of the framers and the generations that have followed them, including Americans today. In 2007, political scientist Larry Sabato, in his book *A More Perfect Constitution: 23 Proposals to Revitalize Our Constitution and Make America a Fairer Country,* tried to energize public discourse on the need to amend the Constitution so as to make the country "a more perfect union."[31] In this concluding section, we consider the amendments that have been approved to date as the American people have undertaken efforts to perfect the union established by the Constitution, and we look at the process by which these amendments became a reality.

Formal Amendment of the Constitution

Every term, members of Congress introduce between 100 and 200 proposals for new constitutional amendments. Collectively, since 1789, this amounts to more than 10,000 proposals! Members of Congress who oppose a ruling by the U.S. Supreme Court or a law that engenders a great deal of public debate may propose an amendment to supersede the

DO WOMEN AND MEN HAVE EQUAL PROTECTION UNDER THE LAW?

The Issue: The Declaration of Independence states that "all men are created equal" and that they are endowed with natural rights to life, liberty, and the pursuit of happiness. The Constitution created a government in which the Declaration's "all men" truly meant white males, not all human beings, when it established the rights and liberties that would be guaranteed for citizens of the United States. Women, as well as minority men, have been fighting throughout U.S. history to gain equal protection of the laws. The Fourteenth Amendment to the Constitution (1868) guarantees equal protection of the law to all people. But do women genuinely receive the same legal protections as men?

Yes: Although initially the courts did not interpret the Fourteenth Amendment to guarantee women the same legal protections as men, today equal protection does exist. Thanks to Title VII of the Civil Rights Act of 1964, women are provided the same protection against discrimination in employment decisions—or, put positively, are guaranteed the same consideration for employment decisions—as are men. Moreover, Title IX, added to the Civil Rights Act in 1972, ensures that women's opportunity for public education is equal to that of men. Today, women earn the majority of bachelor's and master's degrees. Clearly, educational opportunity is equally protected. Because education is the building block for economic opportunities, equal protection in education leads to equal economic opportunity because discrimination is prohibited in employment decisions.

No: Women with the same educational background earn less on average than men. Moreover, domestic violence, a crime for which women disproportionately are victims, does not get the same treatment under the law as assaults against strangers. Rape, another crime that is disproportionately perpetrated against women, has one of the lowest "go to trial" rates of all felony crimes. Beyond the fact that such women victims do not receive equal protection of the law, some research suggests that women found guilty of violence against intimate partners receive harsher punishments than men found guilty of comparable crimes.*

Other approaches: The written law in most cases does not differentiate between male and female, black and white, or any other demographic characteristic. The question of equal protection of the law is really a question of how the people in government *implement* the law, how citizens *comply with* it, and how the judges sitting in courtrooms *interpret* it. The reality is that all people have biases—we all experience life differently and so develop different understandings, stereotypes, preferences, and prejudices. Our biases influence how we behave, consciously or not. Therefore, because many laws, at least since the ratification of the Fourteenth Amendment, have mandated equal protection, a major barrier to equal protection is the fact that people with various inevitable biases must interpret and implement the law.

What do you think?

① Will an amendment to the Constitution specifically granting women equal protection of the laws ensure that women and men have equal economic, political, and legal status? Explain.

② Would women's protection under the law look more like men's protection if more women were formulating the law (as elected officials), implementing the law (as government workers), and interpreting the law (as judges)? Why or why not?

③ What does this Conversation of Democracy reveal about the legal status of other groups that are underrepresented among elected officials, bureaucrats, and judges, such as African Americans, Latinos, persons with disabilities, and low-income Americans? Do these other underrepresented groups enjoy equal protection of the laws? Explain.

*"Women Prisoners: Facts and Figures at a Glance," *Legal Services for Prisoners with Children*, www.prisonerswithchildren.org/pubs/womgen.pdf.

Court ruling or the law. Often members of Congress introduce these amendments knowing that they will never be ratified but wanting to appease their core constituencies by at least instigating public discourse about how our government should function and what rights and freedoms individuals possess. One amendment that has been introduced repeatedly since 1923 calls for equality of rights for women, which the "American Democracy Now" vignette at the beginning of the chapter explores. The "Conversation of Democracy" selection looks at the arguments from the public debate over the need for such an amendment.

Only a tiny fraction of the 10,000-plus proposed amendments have cleared Congress—in fact, only thirty-three have achieved the two-thirds vote necessary in Congress—and, as noted, only twenty-seven have been ratified by the states. The amendments that the states have ratified fit into one of three categories: they have (1) extended civil liberties and civil rights (equal protection of laws for citizens), (2) altered the selection or operation of the branches of the national government, or (3) dealt with important policy issues. Table 2.2 summarizes

What Would the Nation's Founders Think?

Do you think the signers of the Declaration of Independence would generally agree or disagree with the way the Constitution of the United States is interpreted today?

☐ Agree

☐ Disagree

Source: "Americans Are Widely Patriotic, but Many Think Founding Fathers Would Frown on Modern America," www.gallup.com/poll/3745/Americans-Widely-Patriotic-Many-Think-Founding-Fathers-Would.aspx.

TABLE 2.2

The Eleventh Through Twenty-Seventh Amendments to the Federal Constitution

AMENDMENTS THAT PROTECT CIVIL LIBERTIES AND CIVIL RIGHTS

Thirteenth	1865	Banned slavery
Fourteenth	1868	Established that all people have the right to equal protection and due process before the law, and that all citizens are guaranteed the same privileges and immunities
Fifteenth	1870	Guaranteed that the right to vote could not be abridged on the basis of race or color
Nineteenth	1920	Guaranteed that the right to vote could not be abridged on the basis of sex
Twenty-third	1961	Defined how the District of Columbia would be represented in the Electoral College
Twenty-fourth	1964	Outlawed the use of a poll tax, which prevented poor people from exercising their right to vote
Twenty-sixth	1971	Lowered the voting age to 18 years

AMENDMENTS THAT RELATE TO THE SELECTION OF GOVERNMENT OFFICIALS OR THE OPERATION OF THE BRANCHES OF GOVERNMENT

Eleventh	1795	Limited federal court jurisdiction by barring citizens of one state from suing another state in federal court
Twelfth	1804	Required the electors in the Electoral College to vote twice: once for president and once for vice president
Seventeenth	1913	Mandated the direct election of senators by citizens
Twentieth	1933	Set a date for the convening of Congress and the inauguration of the president
Twenty-second	1951	Limited to two the number of terms the president can serve
Twenty-fifth	1967	Established the procedures for presidential succession in the event of the disability or death of the president; established the procedure for vice-presidential replacement when the position becomes vacant before the end of the term
Twenty-seventh	1992	Required that there be an intervening election between the time when Congress votes itself a raise and when that raise can be implemented

AMENDMENTS THAT ADDRESS SPECIFIC PUBLIC POLICIES

Sixteenth	1913	Empowered Congress to establish an income tax
Eighteenth	1919	Banned the manufacture, sale, and transportation of liquor
Twenty-first	1933	Repealed the ban on the manufacture, sale, and transportation of liquor

CONSTITUTIONAL PRINCIPLES IN A RECENT SECOND AMENDMENT CASE

Consider the following chronology related to the Second Amendment and its legal protections. Has the court made the meaning of the Second Amendment clear and unambiguous?

1791 **Second Amendment** passes, stating that "a well regulated Militia, being necessary to the security of a free State, the right of the people to keep and bear Arms, shall not be infringed."

1976 **Washington, D.C., law** is passed, banning all handguns in homes unless they were registered before 1976. The law's intent is to decrease gun violence.

2007 **Majority opinion of the U.S. Court of Appeals for D.C. Circuit,** *Parker v. District of Columbia,* finds the 1976 Washington, D.C., ban unconstitutional and explains, "We . . . take it as an expression of the drafters' view that the people possessed a natural right to keep and bear arms, and that the preservation of the militia was the right's most salient political benefit—and thus the most appropriate to express in a political document."*

2008 **Majority opinion of the U.S. Supreme Court in** *Distrinct of Columbia and Adrian M. Felty v. Dick Anthony Heller* declares "There seems to us no doubt, on the basis of both text and history, that the Second Amendment conferred an individual right to keep and bear arms." The decision goes on to say, "Like most rights, the Second Amendment right is not unlimited. It is not a right to keep and carry any weapon whatsoever in any manner whatsoever and for whatever purpose."**

**Parker v. District of Columbia 478 F. 3d 370 (D.C. Circuit 2007).*
***District of Columbia and Adrian M. Fenty v. Dick Anthony Heller 544 U.S.*

Evaluating the Evidence

① What do you think was the intent of the authors of the Second Amendment? Did they intend to protect a natural, individual right to bear arms? Did they mean to ensure that resources (that is, people with the right to bear arms) for protecting domestic tranquility and national defense would be readily available? Did they seek to ensure both?

② What do you imagine the majority of Americans think the Second Amendment means? Why? Where might you get data to support your prediction?

③ Do you agree with the majority opinion in the *Parker* case or the majority opinion in the *D.C. v. Heller* case? Explain.

④ What impact on public safety will the divergent interpretations of the Second Amendment have?

---

the eleventh through the twenty-seventh constitutional amendments and organizes them by category.

Interpretation by the U.S. Supreme Court

Beyond the addition of formal amendments, the Constitution has changed over time through reinterpretation by the courts. This reinterpretation began with the U.S. Supreme Court's landmark *Marbury v. Madison* decision in 1803, in which the Court established the important power of judicial review—the authority of the courts to rule on whether acts of government officials and governing bodies violate the Constitution. Although the U.S. Supreme Court's interpretation is final, if the Supreme Court does not review constitutional interpretations made by lower federal courts, then the interpretations of these lower courts are the final word.

How do judges decide what the Constitution means? To interpret its words, they might look at how courts have ruled in past cases on the phrasing in question or what the custom or usage of the words has generally been. They might try to ascertain what the authors of the Constitution meant. Alternatively, the judges might consider the policy implications of differing interpretations, gauging them against the mission presented in the Constitution's

ON THE JOB

CHELSEA J. ANDREWS, GOVERNMENT ATTORNEY

Name: Chelsea J. Andrews, Esq.

Age: 30

Hometown: Fort Lauderdale, Florida

College: Florida A&M University; George Washington University

Majors: Business Administration (BS and MBA); Law (JD)

Job Title: Assistant State's Attorney, Prince George's County State's Attorney's Office, Upper Marlboro, Maryland

Salary range for jobs like this: $45,000–$70,000

Day-to-day responsibilities: I prosecute adult and juvenile offenders of felony and misdemeanor criminal, traffic, and municipal infractions.

How did you get your job? While in my last year of law school, I applied for a clerkship. It was one of the best decisions of my life. I was hired to clerk for the Honorable Zinora Mitchell-Rankin in the Superior Court for the District of Columbia. I had an opportunity to watch and evaluate hundreds of trials and litigators. Most importantly, I gained a life mentor, who connected me with the State's Attorney's Office.

What do you like best about your job? I enjoy making a positive impact on the community every day. I help ensure that Prince George's County residents live in a safer community. The cases are always interesting, and no two days are the same.

What is your least favorite aspect of your job? It's difficult to work with victims of crimes on a daily basis.

It makes you emotionally connected to each case. However, it's this connection that keeps you grounded and fuels you to be passionate about ensuring that justice prevails in each case.

What advice would you give to students who would like to do what you are doing? I would encourage anyone interested in the legal profession to be proactive about obtaining professional mentors. Follow up with people you meet, and cultivate relationships so that you will have many mentors to guide you through your career path.

Personally, every professional experience I have had can be attributed to a professional mentor. For example, as an undergrad, I worked part time for a local PR consulting company. The company's president became my mentor and years later connected me with my first internship in law school. Through her, I was able to work at the NAACP in the Education Department during one of the most exciting and historical times for the organization—the fiftieth anniversary of *Brown v. Board of Education*. I assisted with planning the commemorative activities, but most significantly, I drafted legal memoranda on cases leading up to the *Brown* decision and the impact the decision has had on America. Overall, each opportunity, each job, and each mentor has helped pave the path that I am on and has had a significant impact on my life journey.

---

preamble. In any given case, the deciding court must determine which of these points of reference it will use and how it will apply them to interpret the constitutional principles under consideration. For a taste of how the courts determine the meaning of the Constitution, see "Exploring the Sources."

The power of judicial review has allowed the courts to continue to breathe life into the Constitution to keep up with societal norms and technological change. For example, in 1896 the Supreme Court decreed that the Fourteenth Amendment allowed laws requiring the segregation of white and black citizens.[32] Then in 1954, in the case of *Brown v. The Board of Education of Topeka, Kansas,*[33] the Supreme Court declared such segregation to be an unconstitutional violation of the Fourteenth Amendment. (Chelsea J. Andrews highlights the celebration of the fiftieth anniversary of this landmark reinterpretation of the Constitution in her "On the Job" interview.)

> Congress or state legislatures sometimes defy U.S. Supreme Court rulings by passing legislation that counteracts the Court's decision. The foreigners detained by the national government at the U.S. naval base in Guantánamo Bay, Cuba, are in the middle of such a battle. In 2008 the Supreme Court ruled that the Guantánamo detainees had the constitutional right to challenge their imprisonment in U.S. federal courts.

Technology also drives constitutional reinterpretation. The framers naturally never conceived of the existence of computers and artificial intelligence. Yet by reviewing and freshly interpreting the Fourth Amendment, which prohibits unreasonable searches and seizures by government officials, the courts have uncovered the principles behind this amendment that apply to our technologically advanced society. Consequently, this provision, whose original intent was to limit governments' physical searches of one's property and person, can be used today to determine, for example, whether governmental surveillance of computer databases is permissible.

Sometimes the Supreme Court's opinions ignite a debate or intensify a debate already under way. Court decisions that are viewed as a "win" for one side and a "loss" for the other often generate fierce responses in the other branches or levels of the government. For example, the executive branch might decide not to implement a Court decision. Or perhaps the legislative branch might write a new law that challenges a Court decision. Unless a lawsuit allows the Court to find the new law unconstitutional, the new law takes effect.

Consider the ongoing issue of the foreign citizens being held at the U.S. Naval base at Guantánamo Bay in Cuba. In January 2002, the United States began to detain at Guantánamo foreigners who had been captured in Afghanistan and other countries and who were labeled by the government as "enemy combatants." Lawyers for these prisoners challenged their detention through federal lawsuits, but the federal courts countered they did not have the jurisdiction (legal authority) to decide these cases. In 2004, however, the Supreme Court found that the federal courts did have jurisdiction in these cases. In response to this decision, Congress and President Bush approved a law in 2005 that removed from federal court jurisdiction lawsuits brought by foreign detainees. In response, in 2006 the Supreme Court ruled that Congress improperly established this new law and that it therefore was unconstitutional. Then, later in 2006, Congress passed another law removing the detainee lawsuits from federal court jurisdiction. In its 2007–2008 term, the Court ruled that the federal courts, not U.S. military courts, had jurisdiction over the detainees.[34] Therefore, the Guantánamo detainees had the constitutional right to challenge the legality of their imprisonment in the federal courts.[35]

Although controversial Court decisions often capture significant media attention, in the vast majority of cases, the Court's rulings are in step with public opinion. Analysts note that the Court does not often lead public opinion—in fact, it more often follows it.[36] And even if the justices wanted to take some very controversial and unpopular action, the system of checks and balances forces them to consider how the other branches would react. Recall that the Court has the power to interpret the law; it does not have the power to implement or to enforce the law and must be concerned about how the other branches might retaliate against it for highly unpopular decisions. Therefore, for the most part, changes to the Constitution, both formal and informal, are incremental and further the will of the people because they are the product of widespread public discourse—an ongoing conversation of democracy.

CONCLUSION *CONTINUING THE CONVERSATION*

Ratified in 1788 and in effect since 1789, the Constitution is remarkable for its long life—a longevity that owes much to the genius of its framers. They established a government that, in its mission, foundational structures, and essential processes, successfully addressed the problems of governance experienced under the British Crown and the Articles of Confederation. The structures and governing procedures the framers established, including the process by which the courts are able to interpret constitutional language in the context of contemporary societal values and technological advances, have allowed the Constitution to survive (with only twenty-seven amendments) for more than two centuries.

Over the centuries, through judicial interpretation of the Constitution and formal constitutional amendment, the underlying principles of government by and for the people have become a reality for an ever-growing diversity of people in the United States. Each year thousands of lawsuits make their way to the Supreme Court. From this number the justices select between eighty and one hundred cases to hear. The cases they choose are those they deem most important to upholding the foundational principles of the Constitution. Congress receives on average about fifty proposals to amend the Constitution each year. This volume of lawsuits and proposed amendments ensures that the Constitution is a living, evolving document, not one that sits on a shelf accumulating dust.

As technology advances, as globalization's international interdependence spreads, and as the population of the United States grows and diversifies, will ongoing interpretation of the Constitution's mission, foundational structures, and essential processes continue to protect the people's natural rights and to perfect government by and for the people?

Summary

1. What Is a Constitution?
A constitution is a document that describes the mission, foundational structures, and essential processes of an organization—including, as in the case of the U.S. Constitution, a government.

2. The Constitution of the United States of America
In 1788, the required nine states ratified the Constitution of the United States of America, which replaced the Articles of Confederation (the nation's first constitution). Social contract theory is the foundation for the governing principles of the Constitution. The Constitution gives these principles explicit form by specifying the U.S. government's foundational structures: (1) the separation of powers, (2) an integrated system of checks and balances, and (3) the federal system of government.

3. The Creation of the United States of America

By the mid-eighteenth century the American colonists were protesting the impact of British rule on their lives and livelihoods. The colonists were persuaded by pamphlets, newspaper articles, public discourse, and eloquent revolutionaries that it was common sense, as well as their obligation, to declare their independence from Britain and to create a new government. Yet the weak national government established by the country's first constitution, the Articles of Confederation, did not serve the people well, as the government under the Articles had no authority to levy taxes, establish a common currency, or regulate intrastate trade, and generally lacked the authority to ensure domestic tranquility and to govern effectively.

4. Crafting the Constitution: Compromise, Ratification, and Quick Amendment

In response to severe economic problems and tensions among the states, and to growing desires for a more perfect union of the states, representatives from the states met in Philadelphia in 1787 to amend the Articles of Confederation. Debate and deliberation led to compromise and a new constitution, supported by the Federalists and opposed by the Anti-Federalists. The addition of the Bill of Rights two years after the Constitution was ratified addressed the primary concerns about individual liberties and states' authority that the Anti-Federalists had raised during the debates over ratification of the Constitution of the United States (the country's second constitution).

5. The Constitution as a Living, Evolving Document

The Constitution of the United States has been formally amended a mere twenty-seven times over its 220-plus years of life. This rare occurrence of formal change to the Constitution's written words belies the reality of its perpetual revision through the process of judicial review and interpretation. The U.S. Supreme Court ultimately decides what the written words in the Constitution mean, and through this authority, the Court clarifies and modifies (hence, revises) the Constitution yearly.

Key Terms

advice and consent 45	Electoral College 47	separation of powers 44
Anti-Federalists 59	*The Federalist Papers* 59	Three-Fifths Compromise 58
bicameral 45	Federalists 59	unicameral 55
Bill of Rights 61	judicial review 46	veto 45
checks and balances 45	*Marbury v. Madison* 46	Virginia Plan 56
confederation 55	natural rights	
Connecticut Compromise	(unalienable rights) 43	
(Great Compromise) 57	New Jersey Plan 57	
constitution 41	republic 43	

For Review

1. Describe the three main components of a constitution.

2. Describe the mission, governing principles, foundational structures, and essential processes outlined in the Constitution of the United States of America.

3. How did the events leading up to the War for Independence shape the core principles of the U.S. Constitution?

4. Why do we say that conflict and compromise characterize the drafting and ratification of the Constitution? What specific issues caused conflict and required compromise for their resolution?

5. What are the formal and informal mechanisms for changing the Constitution?

For Critical Thinking and Discussion

1. What was the relationship between the state constitutions, many of which were created right after the signing of the Declaration of Independence, and the U.S. Constitution, which was written more than a decade later?

2. Think about important debates in the American polity today. Describe one that you think is linked in some way to the compromises upon which the Constitution is based.

3. Pretend that you are a young adult living during the revolutionary era who is writing an article for a newspaper in England, and you are trying to explain why the colonists have destroyed thousands of pounds of British tea at the Boston Tea Party. How might you, as an English citizen living in England, characterize the colonists' motives? How might you, as an English citizen living in the colonies, characterize the colonists' motives?

4. The contest between the Federalists and Anti-Federalists over ratification of the Constitution was a very close one. What do you think would have happened had the Anti-Federalists prevailed? What kind of government would they have shaped? How would this government have dealt with the difficult issues facing the new republic—slavery, concerns about mob rule, and continuing hostility in the international community?

MULTIPLE CHOICE: Choose the lettered item that answers the question correctly.

1. According to the Declaration of Independence, the natural, unalienable rights include all of the following except
   a. liberty.
   b. life.
   c. property.
   d. the pursuit of happiness.

2. The existence of three branches of government, each responsible for a different primary governing function, is the implementation of the foundational organizational structure called
   a. judicial review.
   b. the federal system.
   c. representative democracy.
   d. separation of powers.

3. *Marbury v. Madison* (1803) is a landmark case because it
   a. clarified the Electoral College system.
   b. clarified congressional legislative authority.
   c. clarified the courts' judicial review authority.
   d. clarified presidential appointment authority.

4. Ratification of an amendment to the U.S. Constitution requires
   a. approval of the majority of citizens voting in a referendum.
   b. approval of three-quarters of the members of Congress.
   c. approval of three-quarters of either the House or the Senate.
   d. approval of three-quarters of the state legislatures or special conventions.

5. All of the following were authors of *The Federalist Papers* **except**
   a. John Jay.
   b. Thomas Jefferson.
   c. Alexander Hamilton.
   d. James Madison.

6. The document (or set of documents), grounded in social contract theory and stating that citizens have an obligation to replace their government if it is not serving them and protecting their unalienable rights, is
   a. the Articles of Confederation.
   b. the Constitution of the United States of America.
   c. the Declaration of Independence.
   d. *The Federalist Papers*.

7. At the Constitutional Convention, the delegates devoted the bulk of their time to resolving the issue of
   a. procedures for electing the president and vice president.
   b. representation in the national legislature.
   c. the necessity for a bill of rights.
   d. slavery.

8. The ultimate authority to interpret the meaning of constitutional language, and hence to decide what is the supreme law of the land, comes from
   a. the majority of members of Congress.
   b. the majority of members of state legislatures.
   c. the majority of justices on the U.S. Supreme Court.
   d. the president of the United States.

9. The required nine states ratified the Constitution of the United States in
   a. 1776.   c. 1788
   b. 1781.   d. 1791.

10. One check that the Senate has on both the executive branch and the judicial branch is its power of
   a. advice and consent.
   b. impeachment.
   c. ratification of treaties.
   d. veto override.

FILL IN THE BLANKS.

11. Currently there are _____ amendments to the U.S. Constitution, and the last amendment was added in the year _____.

12. The United States' first constitution was the _____.

13. _____ is the authority of courts to declare actions of government officials and governing bodies unconstitutional.

14. The Virginia delegate to the Second Continental Congress who wrote the Declaration of Independence was _____.

15. Many of the Anti-Federalist criticisms of the Constitution were addressed in 1791 with the ratification of the _____.

Answers: 1. c; 2. d; 3. c; 4. d; 5. b; 6. c; 7. b; 8. c; 9. c; 10. a; 11. 27 and 1992; 12. Articles of Confederation; 13. Judicial review; 14. Thomas Jefferson; 15. Bill of Rights.

RESOURCES FOR RESEARCH AND ACTION

Internet Resources

American Democracy Now Web site
http://www.mhhe.com/harrison1e   Consult the book's Web site for study guides, interactive activities, simulations, and current hot-links for additional information on contemporary issues involving the Constitution.

FindLaw
www.findlaw.com   This site offers links to news regarding current cases before the U.S. Supreme Court as well as access to decisions of all federal and state appellate courts.

Library of Congress Memory Project
www.loc.gov/rr/program/bib/ourdocs/PrimDocsHome.htm
This comprehensive Web site, created by the Library of Congress and part of its Memory Project, includes a wealth of information about the early American republic, including primary documents such as *The Federalist Papers.*

The U.S. Constitution Online
www.USConstitution.net   This interesting site helps to place the U.S. Constitution in a contemporary context. Its current events section discusses how the pending issues are affected by constitutional principles.

ConstitutionFacts.com
www.constitutionfacts.com   This site includes all kinds of information about the U.S. Constitution and the constitutions of the states and other nations.

Recommended Readings

Breyer, Stephen. *Active Liberty: Interpreting Our Democratic Constitution.* New York: Random House, 2005. A short, readable book in which Supreme Court justice Stephen Breyer argues that constitutional interpretation must be guided by the foundational principle of government by the people and that the courts must ensure that they protect and facilitate citizens' participation in government.

Hamilton, Alexander, James Madison, and John Jay. *The Federalist Papers.* Cutchogue, NY: Buccaneer Books, 1992. A compilation of the eighty-five newspaper articles written by the authors to convince the voters of New York to ratify the proposed Constitution of the United States, featuring a comprehensive introduction that puts the articles in context and outlines their principal themes—and hence, the underlying principles of the Constitution.

Morgan, Edmund S. *The Birth of the Republic: 1763–89,* 3rd ed. Chicago: University of Chicago Press, 1992. An excellent chronicle of the pre-revolutionary period, as well as the Revolution, the Articles of Confederation, and the Constitution, explaining how discourse among Americans about governance changed over time and how the confederation of independent states finally gave way to an independent nation.

Pasley, Jeffrey L., Andrew W. Robertson, and David Waldstreicher. *Beyond the Founders: New Approaches to the Political History of the Early American Republic.* Chapel Hill, NC: University of North Carolina Press, 2004. Essays exploring the ways in which ordinary Americans engaged in politics, including an account of the making of a mammoth piece of cheese that was presented to Thomas Jefferson at his inauguration in 1801 and a look at how clothing and appearance conveyed one's political ideals.

Roberts, Cokie. *Founding Mothers: The Women Who Raised Our Nation.* New York: Perennial Press, 2004. An examination of the Revolution and its aftermath, focusing on how women contributed to the war effort and to wider discussions about how the new government should be structured and what goals it should advance.

Sabato, Larry. *A More Perfect Constitution: 23 Proposals to Revitalize Our Constitution and Make America a Fairer Country.* New York: Walker Publishing, 2007. An exploration by political scientist Larry Sabato into why a constitutional convention is needed. The book includes proposals for 23 amendments—many of which citizens support, according to a poll commissioned by the author—that Sabato argues will perfect the Constitution. His real goal in writing the book was to kindle a national conversation on what he perceives as the deficiencies in U.S. representative democracy.

Movies of Interest

National Treasure (2004)
Starring Nicholas Cage, this adventure-packed film traces a hunt for treasure that a family's oral history says the nation's founding fathers buried. Clues are found hidden in the country's early currency and even on the back of the Declaration of Independence. The hunt exposes the viewer to the workings of the National Archives and its Preservation Room and features images of the founding fathers not typically reproduced in textbooks.

Return to the Land of Wonder (2004)
This documentary follows Adnan Pachachi's return to Iraq in 2003, after thirty-seven years in exile, to head a committee charged with drafting a new constitution and bill of rights. The movie focuses on the tortuous process of trying to resolve conflicts created by the demands of the United States and the expectations of Iraqis, as well as the realities of everyday life in Iraq in 2003.

An Empire of Reason (1998)
A thought-provoking answer to an intriguing "what if?" question: What if the ratification debates were held using the media tools of the twenty-first century, specifically television?

Amistad (1997)
This film depicts the mutiny and subsequent trial of Africans aboard the ship *Amistad* in 1839–1840. Viewers get a glimpse of the intense civic discourse over slavery in the period leading up to the Civil War.

National Journal

Is Judicial Review Obsolete?

The big Supreme Court decision that the Second Amendment protects an individual right to keep a loaded handgun for self-defense at home is the high-water mark of the "original meaning" approach to constitutional interpretation championed by Justice Antonin Scalia and many other conservatives. At the same time, the decision may show "originalism" to be a false promise.

Scalia's 64-page opinion for the five-justice majority was a tour de force of originalist analysis. Without pausing to ask whether gun rights is good policy, Scalia parsed the Second Amendment's 27 words one by one while consulting 18th-century dictionaries, early American history, the 1689 English Bill of Rights, 19th-century treatises, and other historical material.

And even the lead dissent for the Court's four liberals—who are accustomed to deep-sixing original meaning on issues ranging from the death penalty to abortion, gay rights, and many others—all but conceded that this case should turn mainly on the original meaning of the 217-year-old Second Amendment. They had little choice, given the unusual absence of binding precedent.

But in another sense, the case, *District of Columbia v. Heller* belies the two great advantages that originalism has been touted as having over the liberals' "living Constitution" approach. Originalism is supposed to supply first principles that will prevent justices from merely voting their policy preferences and to foster what Judge Robert Bork once called "deference to democratic choice." But the gun case suggests that originalism does neither.

First, even though all nine justices claimed to be following original meaning, they split angrily along liberal-conservative lines perfectly matching their apparent policy preferences, with the four conservatives (plus swing-voting Anthony Kennedy) voting for gun rights and the four liberals against.

These eight justices cleaved in *exactly* the same way—with Kennedy tipping the balance from case to case—in the decision the same day striking down a campaign finance provision designed to handicap rich, self-funded political candidates; decisions earlier in 2008 barring the death penalty for raping a child and striking down the elected branches' restrictions on judicial review of Guantánamo detainees' petitions for release; and past decisions on abortion, affirmative action, gay rights, religion, and more.

This pattern does not mean that the justices are *insincerely* using legal doctrines as a cover for politically driven votes. Rather, it shows that ascertaining the original meaning of provisions drafted more than 200

not definitively resolve the ambiguity inherent in the amendment's curious wording: "A well-regulated militia, being necessary to the security of a free state, the right of the people to keep and bear arms, shall not be infringed."

And even if there is a clear right answer, the voting pattern suggests that conservative and liberal justices will never agree on what it is. More broadly, even when there is no dispute as to original meaning, it is often intolerable to liberals and conservatives alike. For example, no constitutional provision or amendment was ever designed to prohibit the federal government from discriminating based on race (or sex). This has not stopped conservatives from voting to strike down

If originalism **does not deliver on its promises** to channel judicial discretion and constrain judicial usurpations of elected officials' power, what good is it?

years ago, in a very different society, is often a subjective process on which reasonable people disagree—and often reach conclusions driven consciously or subconsciously by their policy preferences. And some of us have trouble coming to confident conclusions either way.

Scalia's argument for striking down the District of Columbia's gun laws—the strictest in the country—was persuasive. But so were the dissents by liberal Justices John Paul Stevens and Stephen Breyer. Scalia and the two dissenters all made cogent arguments while papering over weaknesses in their positions. Scalia may have won on points. But more study might tip an observer the other way.

The reason is that the justices' exhaustive analyses of the text and relevant history do

federal racial preferences for minorities (by seeking to extend liberal precedents) any more than it stopped liberals from striking down the federal laws that once discriminated against women.

Second, the notion that originalists would defer more to democratic choices than would the loosey-goosey liberals has come to ring a bit hollow. The originalists began with a compelling critique of the liberals' invention of new constitutional rights to strike down all state abortion and death-penalty laws, among others. But the current conservative justices have hardly been models of judicial restraint.

They have used highly debatable interpretations of original meaning to sweep aside a raft of democratically adopted laws. These include federal laws regulating campaign money and imposing monetary liability on states. And in 2007's 5–4 decision striking down two local school-integration laws, the conservative majority came close to imposing a "colorblind Constitution" vision of equal protection that may be good policy but which is hard to find in the 14th Amendment's original meaning.

In the gun case, as Justice Breyer argued, "the majority's decision threatens severely to limit the ability of more knowledgeable, democratically elected officials to deal with gun-related problems." (Of course, Breyer's solicitude for elected officials disappears when the issue is whether they should be able to execute rapists of children or ban an especially grisly abortion method.)

If originalism does not deliver on its promises to channel judicial discretion and constrain judicial usurpations of elected officials' power, what good is it?

Indeed, it seems almost perverse to be assessing what gun controls to allow based not on examining how best to save lives but on seeking to read the minds of the men who ratified the Bill of Rights well over 200 years ago.

The originalist approach seems especially odd when it comes down to arguing over such matters as whether 18th-century lawyers agreed (as Scalia contends) that "a prefatory clause does not limit or expand the scope of the operative clause" and whether (as Stevens contends) the phrase "'bear arms' most naturally conveys a military meaning" and "the Second Amendment does not protect a 'right to keep *and* to bear arms,' but rather 'a right to keep and bear arms'" (emphasis in original). The justices may as well have tried reading the entrails of dead hamsters.

> Indeed, not one of the nine justices seems to have a modest understanding of his or her powers to set national policy **in the name of enforcing the Constitution.**

Is the answer to embrace liberals' "living Constitution" jurisprudence, which roughly translates to reading into the 18th-century document whichever meaning and values the justices consider most fundamental?

By no means. Rather, in the many cases in which nothing close to consensus about the meaning of the Constitution is attainable, the justices should leave the lawmaking to elected officials.

Now it seems that the originalist view of the Constitution is indeed incapable of telling today's judges what to do—not, at least, with any consistency from one judge to the next. So is judicial review itself obsolete?

Not quite. Judicial review remains valuable, perhaps indispensable, because it helps provide the stability and protection for liberty inherent in our tripartite separation of powers, with the legislative, executive, and judicial branches serving as the three legs of a stool and with each potent enough to check abuses and excesses by the others.

The June 12 decision rebuffing President Bush's (and Congress's) denial of fair hear-

ings to Guantánamo detainees proclaiming their innocence is a case in point. But the broad wording of Kennedy's majority opinion, joined by the four liberals, went too far by flirting with a hubristic vision of unprecedented judicial power to intrude deeply into the conduct of foreign wars.

Indeed, not one of the nine justices seems to have a modest understanding of his or her powers to set national policy in the name of enforcing the Constitution. But the other branches, and most voters, seem content with raw judicial policy-making—except when they don't like the policies. For better or worse, what Scalia has called "the imperial judiciary"—sometimes liberal, sometimes conservative—seems here to stay.

Given this, the best way to restrain judicial imperialism may be for the president and the Senate to worry less about whether prospective justices are liberal or conservative and more about whether they have a healthy sense of their own fallibility.

■ **THEN:** Judicial review is a cornerstone of our democractic process and essential to the separation of powers in modern government.

■ **NOW:** The claim to knowing the original meaning of the constitution is fraught with difficulties and often appears colored by political agendas.

■ **NEXT:** Do the intentions of the Constitution's framers still matter in considering issues like gun control? When they're ambiguous, how would you attempt to deduce what those intentions were?

Do you think the constitution is a "living document" or are you an "originalist"?

Should the 2nd Amendment be read to mean that every individual has a right to a firearm? Where should that protection begin and end?

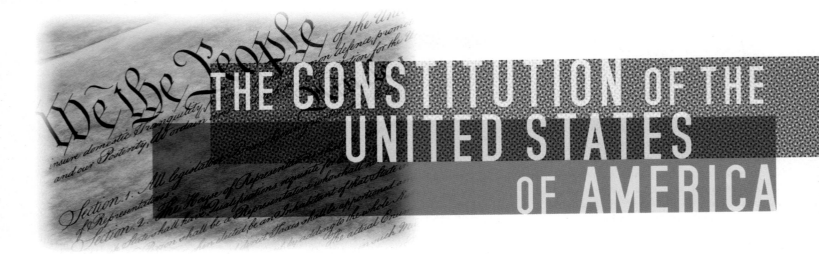

THE CONSTITUTION OF THE UNITED STATES OF AMERICA

> The Preamble states that "the People" are creating a new government, which is described in the Constitution. The Preamble also decrees that it is the mission of this new government to serve the people better than did the government established by the Articles of Confederation, which had been in effect since before the end of the War for Independence.

> The Constitution divides the responsibility for the three inherent functions of government—making laws, administering laws, and resolving conflicts in the interpretation of laws as well as judging violations of them—among three branches. Article I presents the organization, procedures, and authority of the lawmaking branch, the Congress, a bicameral (two-chamber) legislature comprising the House of Representatives and the Senate.

> House members are elected to serve a two-year term. Initially, only those citizens eligible to vote for members of their state's legislature were eligible to vote for members of the House of Representatives. Today, all citizens 18 years of age and older are guaranteed the right to vote in all national elections.

> The Constitution specifies only three qualifications to be elected to the House: you must be at least 25 years old; you must be a U.S. citizen for at least seven years (so a foreign-born, naturalized citizen can be a House member) and you must be a resident of the state you will represent. By tradition, House members live in the district that they represent.

> The number of seats in the House increased as the population of each state grew until 1911, when Congress set the number of House seats at 435. Congress distributes these seats among the fifty states according to each state's share of the total population, as determined by a census (official count of the country's inhabitants) conducted every ten years. Every state must have at least one seat in the House. The "three-fifths" clause decreed that when conducting the census the government would not count Native Americans and would count each slave as three-fifths of a person while counting every other inhabitant as one person. The Thirteenth Amendment (1865) abolished slavery, and the Fourteenth Amendment (1868) repealed the three-fifths clause. Today every inhabitant of the United States is counted as one person in the census, and House seats are redistributed every ten years based on the census to ensure that each House member is elected by (and therefore represents) approximately the same number of people.

Preamble

We the People of the United States, in Order to form a more perfect Union, establish Justice, insure domestic Tranquility, provide for the common defence, promote the general Welfare, and secure the Blessings of Liberty to ourselves and our Posterity, do ordain and establish this Constitution for the United States of America.

ARTICLE I. (Legislative Branch)

Section 1. (Bicameral Legislative Branch)
All legislative Powers herein granted shall be vested in a Congress of the United States, which shall consist of a Senate and House of Representatives.

Section 2. (The House of Representatives)

Clause 1: The House of Representatives shall be composed of Members chosen every second Year by the People of the several States, and the Electors in each State shall have the Qualifications requisite for Electors of the most numerous Branch of the State Legislature.

Clause 2: No Person shall be a Representative who shall not have attained to the age of twenty five Years, and been seven Years a Citizen of the United States, and who shall not, when elected, be an Inhabitant of that State in which he shall be chosen.

Clause 3: Representatives and direct Taxes shall be apportioned among the several States which may be included within this Union, according to their respective Numbers, which shall be determined by adding to the whole Number of free Persons, including those bound to Service for a Term of Years, and excluding Indians not taxed, three fifths of all other Persons. The actual Enumeration shall be made within three Years after the first Meeting of the Congress of the United States, and within every subsequent Term of ten Years, in such Manner as they shall by Law direct. The Number of Representatives shall not exceed one for every thirty Thousand, but each State shall have at Least one Representative; and until such enumeration shall be made, the State of New Hampshire shall be entitled to chuse three, Massachusetts eight, Rhode-Island and Providence Plantations one, Connecticut five, New-York six, New Jersey four, Pennsylvania eight, Delaware one, Maryland six, Virginia ten, North Carolina five, South Carolina five, and Georgia three.

Clause 4: When vacancies happen in the Representation from any State, the Executive Authority thereof shall issue Writs of Election to fill such Vacancies.

Clause 5: The House of Representatives shall chuse their Speaker and other Officers; and shall have the sole Power of Impeachment.

> Governors have the authority to call for a special election to fill any of their state's House seats that become vacant.

> House members select their presiding officer, the Speaker of the House. The Speaker is in line to succeed the president if both the president and the vice president are unable to serve. The Constitution gives the House a check on officials of the executive and judicial branches through its power of impeachment: the power to accuse such officials formally of offenses such as treason, bribery, and abuse of power. If the officials are subsequently found guilty in a trial held by the Senate, they are removed from office.

POLITICAL INQUIRY: *Because members of the House of Representatives run for reelection every two years, they are perpetually raising money for, and worrying about, their next election campaign. Recently an amendment was introduced that would increase their term from two to four years. What would be the consequences of such a change? How would this change make members of the House more, or less, responsive to their constituents' concerns?*

Section 3. (The Senate)

Clause 1: The Senate of the United States shall be composed of two Senators from each State, chosen by the Legislature thereof, for six Years; and each Senator shall have one Vote.

Clause 2: Immediately after they shall be assembled in Consequence of the first Election, they shall be divided as equally as may be into three Classes. The Seats of the Senators of the first Class shall be vacated at the Expiration of the second Year, of the second Class at the Expiration of the fourth Year, and of the third Class at the Expiration of the sixth Year, so that one third may be chosen every second Year; and if Vacancies happen by Resignation, or otherwise, during the Recess of the Legislature of any State, the Executive thereof may make temporary Appointments until the next Meeting of the Legislature, which shall then fill such Vacancies.

Clause 3: No Person shall be a Senator who shall not have attained to the Age of thirty Years, and been nine Years a Citizen of the United States, and who shall not, when elected, be an Inhabitant of that State for which he shall be chosen.

Clause 4: The Vice President of the United States shall be President of the Senate but shall have no Vote, unless they be equally divided.

Clause 5: The Senate shall chuse their other Officers, and also a President pro tempore, in the Absence of the Vice President, or when he shall exercise the Office of President of the United States.

Clause 6: The Senate shall have the sole Power to try all Impeachments. When sitting for that Purpose, they shall be on Oath or Affirmation. When the President of the United States is tried the Chief Justice shall preside: And no Person shall be convicted without the Concurrence of two thirds of the Members present.

Clause 7: Judgment in Cases of Impeachment shall not extend further than to removal from Office, and disqualification to hold and enjoy any Office of honor, Trust or Profit under the United States: but the Party convicted shall nevertheless be liable and subject to Indictment, Trial, Judgment and Punishment, according to Law.

> Initially, senators were selected by the members of their state's legislature, not by their state's voters. The Seventeenth Amendment (1913) changed this election process; today, senators are elected by the voters in their state. This amendment also authorized each state's governor to call for elections to fill vacancies as well as authorizing the state's legislature to determine how its state's vacant Senate seats would be temporarily filled until the election of a new senator.

> Every even-numbered year, congressional elections are held in which one-third of the Senate's 100 seats and all 435 House seats are up for election. Every state elects two senators, who serve six-year terms.

> Senators must be at least 30 years old, either natural-born citizens or immigrants who have been citizens for at least nine years, and—like members of the House—residents of the state they are elected to represent.

> The vice president serves as the president of the Senate, with the authority to preside over meetings of the Senate and to vote when there is a tie.

> Although the first few vice presidents did preside over daily meetings of the Senate, the vice president rarely does so today, leaving that task instead to the president pro tempore, a senator elected by the other senators to preside in the vice president's absence.

> The Senate exercises a check on officials of the executive and judicial branches of the federal government by trying them once they have been impeached by the House of Representatives.

> If the Senate convicts an impeached official, he or she is removed from office and may be subject to prosecution in the criminal courts.

POLITICAL INQUIRY: *The framers of the Constitution, who did not expect members of Congress to serve more than one or two terms, would be shocked to learn that Strom Thurmond served in the Senate for forty-seven years and was 100 years old when he retired in 2003. Senator Robert C. Byrd (D-West Virginia), who was first elected to the Senate in 1959, is now the longest-serving* senator. Concerned about such longevity in office, some have proposed a constitutional amendment that would limit the number of times a House member or a senator could win reelection to the same seat. How would term limits benefit citizens? What problems might term limits cause?

> Though states have the authority to organize and conduct elections, today they rely heavily on local governments to assist them. Congress has passed numerous laws to ensure constitutionally guaranteed voting rights. The first such law was passed shortly after ratification of the Fifteenth Amendment to criminalize attempts to deny black men their newly won right to vote. Congress has also enacted laws to make voter registration easier. For example, a 1996 federal law requires states to allow citizens to register to vote through the mail.

Section 4. (Congressional Elections)

Clause 1: The Times, Places and Manner of holding Elections for Senators and Representatives, shall be prescribed in each State by the Legislature thereof; but the Congress may at any time by Law make or alter such Regulations, except as to the Places of chusing Senators.

POLITICAL INQUIRY: *Voter turnout (the percentage of eligible voters that vote on election day) has increased in Oregon since that state changed its laws to allow voters to vote by mail. Proponents of allowing citizens to vote by mail argue that democracy is enhanced when more citizens participate in elections. What are some additional arguments that could be made in support of a national law allowing citizens to vote by mail? What are some arguments that could be made against such a national law?*

> Congress must meet at least once each year. Since ratification of the Twentieth Amendment (1933), the regular annual session of Congress begins on January 3 of each year; however, the Twentieth Amendment gives Congress the authority to change the date on which its session begins.

Clause 2: The Congress shall assemble at least once in every Year, and such Meeting shall be on the first Monday in December, unless they shall by Law appoint a different Day.

Section 5. (Powers and Responsibilities of the House)

Clause 1: Each House shall be the Judge of the Elections, Returns and Qualifications of its own Members, and a Majority of each shall constitute a Quorum to do Business; but a smaller Number may adjourn from day to day, and may be authorized to compel the Attendance of absent Members, in such Manner, and under such Penalties as each House may provide.

> Each chamber decides whether the election of each of its members is legitimate. A majority of the members of each chamber must be present to conduct business: at least 218 members for the House and 51 senators for the Senate.

Clause 2: Each House may determine the Rules of its Proceedings, punish its Members for disorderly Behaviour, and, with the Concurrence of two thirds, expel a Member.

> After each congressional election, both the House and the Senate determine how they will conduct their business, and each chamber selects from among its members a presiding officer. Moreover, the members of each chamber establish codes of behavior, which they use to judge and—if necessary—punish members' misconduct.

Clause 3: Each House shall keep a Journal of its Proceedings, and from time to time publish the same, excepting such Parts as may in their Judgment require Secrecy; and the Yeas and Nays of the Members of either House on any question shall, at the Desire of one fifth of those Present, be entered on the Journal.

> The House and the Senate must keep and publish records of their proceedings, including a record of all votes for and against proposals, except those that they decide require secrecy. However, if one-fifth of the members of a chamber demand that a vote be recorded, it must be recorded. Congress publishes a record of its debates called the *Congressional Record*.

Clause 4: Neither House, during the Session of Congress, shall, without the Consent of the other, adjourn for more than three days, nor to any other Place than that in which the two Houses shall be sitting.

> To close down business for more than three days during a session, or to conduct business at another location, each chamber needs to get approval from the other one. This ensures that one chamber cannot stop the legislative process by refusing to meet.

Section 6. (Rights of Congressional Members)

Clause 1: The Senators and Representatives shall receive a Compensation for their Services, to be ascertained by Law, and paid out of the Treasury of the United States. They shall in all Cases, except Treason, Felony and Breach of the Peace, be privileged from Arrest during their Attendance at the Session of their respective Houses, and in going to and returning from the same; and for any Speech or Debate in either House, they shall not be questioned in any other Place.

> Today, each member of Congress earns $150,000 per year, paid by taxes collected by the national government. Members of Congress are protected from civil lawsuits and criminal prosecution for the work they do as legislators. They are also protected from arrest while Congress is in session except for a charge of treason, of committing a felony, or of committing a breach of the peace.

Clause 2: No Senator or Representative shall, during the Time for which he was elected, be appointed to any civil Office under the Authority of the United States, which shall have been created, or the Emoluments whereof shall have been encreased during such time; and no Person

> To ensure the separation of basic governing functions, no member of Congress can hold another federal position while serving in the House or Senate. Moreover, members of Congress cannot be appointed to a position in the executive or judicial branch that was created during their term of office.

holding any Office under the United States, shall be a Member of either House during his Continuance in Office.

Section 7. (The Legislative Process)

Clause 1: All Bills for raising Revenue shall originate in the House of Representatives; but the Senate may propose or concur with amendments as on other Bills.

Clause 2: Every Bill which shall have passed the House of Representatives and the Senate, shall, before it become a law, be presented to the President of the United States: If he approve he shall sign it, but if not he shall return it, with his Objections to that House in which it shall have originated, who shall enter the Objections at large on their Journal, and proceed to reconsider it. If after such Reconsideration two thirds of that House shall agree to pass the Bill, it shall be sent, together with the Objections, to the other House, by which it shall likewise be reconsidered, and if approved by two thirds of that House, it shall become a Law. But in all such Cases the Votes of both Houses shall be determined by Yeas and Nays, and the Names of the Persons voting for and against the Bill shall be entered on the Journal of each House respectively. If any Bill shall not be returned by the President within ten Days (Sundays excepted) after it shall have been presented to him, the Same shall be a Law, in like Manner as if he had signed it, unless the Congress by their Adjournment prevent its Return, in which Case it shall not be a Law.

Clause 3: Every Order, Resolution, or Vote to which the Concurrence of the Senate and House of Representatives may be necessary (except on a question of Adjournment) shall be presented to the President of the United States; and before the Same shall take Effect, shall be approved by him, or being disapproved by him, shall be repassed by two thirds of the Senate and House of Representatives, according to the Rules and Limitations prescribed in the Case of a Bill.

> This section details the legislative process.

> While all revenue-raising bills, such as tax bills, must originate in the House, the Senate reviews them, has the authority to make modifications, and ultimately the House and the Senate must approve the identical bill for it to become law.

> After both the House and the Senate approve, by a simple majority vote in each chamber, the identical bill, it is sent to the president for approval or rejection. The president has ten days in which to act, or the bill will automatically become law (unless Congress has adjourned, in which case the bill dies—a pocket veto). If the president signs the bill within ten days, it becomes law. If the president rejects—vetoes—the bill, he or she sends it back to the chamber of its origin with objections. Congress can then rewrite the vetoed bill and send the revised bill through the legislative process. Or Congress can attempt to override the veto by garnering a supermajority vote of approval (two-thirds majority) in each chamber.

> The president must approve or veto everything that Congress approves except its vote to adjourn or any resolutions that do not have the force of law.

POLITICAL INQUIRY: *The presidential veto power is limited to an all-or-nothing decision. Presidents must either approve or veto entire bills; they cannot approve part of a bill and veto other parts of it. Many who worry about the national debt have called for a new type of presidential veto: a line-item veto. This type of veto would authorize the president to overrule parts of a bill that provide spending authority while approving other parts of the same bill. Would giving the president authority to exercise a line-item veto make it easier for the national government to enact a balanced annual budget (a budget in which the money spent in the budget year is equal to or less than the money raised in that year)? Why or why not? What arguments might members of Congress make against giving the president a line-item veto, hence giving up their final say on spending bills?*

Section 8. (The Lawmaking Authority of Congress)

Clause 1: The Congress shall have Power To lay and collect Taxes, Duties, Imposts and Excises, to pay the Debts and provide for the common Defence and general Welfare of the United States; but all Duties, Imposts and Excises shall be uniform throughout the United States;

Clause 2: To borrow Money on the credit of the United States;

> This section specifies the constitutionally established congressional powers. These powers are limited to those listed and any other powers that Congress believes are "necessary and proper" in order for Congress to fulfill its listed powers. Congress has used the "necessary and proper" clause (Clause 18) to justify laws that expand its listed powers. Laws that appear to go beyond the listed powers can be challenged in the courts, with the Supreme Court ultimately deciding their constitutionality.

> The power to raise money and to authorize spending it for common defense and the general welfare is one of the most essential powers of Congress. The Sixteenth Amendment (1913) authorizes a national income tax, which was not previously possible given the "uniformity" requirement in Clause 1.

> Today, after years of borrowing money to pay current bills, the national government has a debt of over $9 trillion.

POLITICAL INQUIRY: *Some economists, politicians, and citizens fear that the national debt harms the United States by limiting the amount of money available to invest in growing the economy. Moreover, citizens worry that their children and grandchildren, saddled with the obligation of paying back this debt,*

> With the Supreme Court's support, Congress has interpreted Clause 3 in a way that has allowed it to expand its involvement in the economy and the daily lives of U.S. citizens, using this clause to regulate business as well as to outlaw racial segregation. However, state governments have frequently challenged Congress's expansion of power by way of the commerce clause when they believe that Congress is infringing on their constitutional authority.

> Congress has the authority to establish the process by which foreigners become citizens (Clause 4). Recently, national legislation has made it more difficult for individuals to file for bankruptcy.

> The authority to make and regulate money as well as to standardize weights and measures is essential to the regulation of commerce (Clause 5).

Clause 3: To regulate Commerce with foreign Nations, and among the several States, and with the Indian Tribes;

Clause 4: To establish an uniform Rule of Naturalization, and uniform Laws on the subject of Bankruptcies throughout the United States;

Clause 5: To coin Money, regulate the Value thereof, and of foreign Coin, and fix the Standard of Weights and Measures;

Clause 6: To provide for the Punishment of counterfeiting the Securities and current Coin of the United States;

Clause 7: To establish Post Offices and post Roads;

Clause 8: To promote the Progress of Science and useful Arts, by securing for limited Times to Authors and Inventors the exclusive Right to their respective Writings and Discoveries;

Clause 9: To constitute Tribunals inferior to the supreme Court;

Clause 10: To define and punish Piracies and Felonies committed on the high Seas, and Offences against the Law of Nations;

Clause 11: To declare War, grant Letters of Marque and Reprisal, and make Rules concerning Captures on Land and Water;

Clause 12: To raise and support Armies, but no Appropriation of Money to that Use shall be for a longer Term than two Years;

Clause 13: To provide and maintain a Navy;

Clause 14: To make Rules for the Government and Regulation of the land and naval Forces;

Clause 15: To provide for calling forth the Militia to execute the Laws of the Union, suppress Insurrections and repel Invasions;

Clause 16: To provide for organizing, arming, and disciplining, the Militia, and for governing such Part of them as may be employed in the Service of the United States, reserving to the States respectively, the Appointment of the Officers, and the Authority of training the Militia according to the discipline prescribed by Congress;

> Congress exercised its authority under Clause 9 to create the federal court system other than the Supreme Court, which was established under Article III of the Constitution.

> Every nation in the world possesses the authority to establish its own laws regarding crimes outside its borders and violations of international law (Clause 10).

> Clauses 11 through 15 collectively delegate to Congress the authority to raise and support military troops, to enact rules to regulate the troops, to call the troops to action, and to declare war. However, the president as commander in chief (Article II) has the authority to wage war. Presidents have committed armed troops without a declaration of war, leading to disputes over congressional and presidential war powers. Clause 11 also provides Congress with the authority to hire an individual for the purpose of retaliating against another nation for some harm it has caused the United States—that is, to provide a *letter of Marque,* an outdated practice.

> Clauses 15 and 16 guarantee the states the right to maintain and train a militia (today's National Guard), but state control of the militia is subordinate to national control when the national government needs the support of these militias to ensure that laws are executed, to suppress domestic uprisings, and to repel invasion.

POLITICAL INQUIRY: *Several state governments, specifically states that have needed their National Guard troops to help with crises such as massive forest fires, have raised questions about the right of the national government to send National Guard troops to Iraq. Imagine you are arguing in front of the Supreme Court on behalf of the states. What argument would you make to support the states' claim that the national government does not have the right to send National Guard troops to Iraq? Now imagine that you are arguing in front of the Court on behalf of the national government. What argument would you make to support the right of the national government to send National Guard troops anywhere in the world?*

> Congress has the authority to govern Washington D.C., which is the seat of the national government. Today citizens living in Washington D.C. elect local government officials to govern the city with congressional oversight. The national government also governs federal lands throughout the states that are used for federal purposes, such as military installations.

Clause 17: To exercise exclusive Legislation in all Cases whatsoever, over such District (not exceeding ten Miles square) as may, by Cession of Particular States, and the Acceptance of Congress, become the Seat of the Government of the United States, and to exercise like Authority over all Places purchased by the Consent of the Legislature of the State in which the Same shall be, for the Erection of Forts, Magazines, Arsenals, dock-Yards and other needful Buildings;—And

POLITICAL INQUIRY: *Article IV of the Constitution delegates to Congress the authority to admit new states to the union. The citizens of Washington D.C. have petitioned Congress to become a state. What would be the benefits of making Washington D.C. a state? What problems might arise if Washington D.C. were to become a state?*

Clause 18: To make all Laws which shall be necessary and proper for carrying into Execution the foregoing Powers and all other Powers vested by this Constitution in the Government of the United States, or in any Department or Officer thereof.

> Clause 18 grants Congress authority to make all laws it deems necessary and proper to fulfill its responsibilities under the Constitution, including those listed in Section 8. This clause also authorizes Congress to pass laws it deems necessary to ensure that the other two branches are able to fulfill their responsibilities. Congress has also used this clause to expand its powers.

Section 9. (Prohibitions on Congress)

> Article I, Section 9 limits Congress's lawmaking authority and mandates that Congress be accountable to the people in how it spends the public's money.

Clause 1: The Migration or Importation of such Persons as any of the States now existing shall think proper to admit, shall not be prohibited by the Congress prior to the Year one thousand eight hundred and eight, but a Tax or duty may be imposed on such Importation, not exceeding ten dollars for each Person.

> Clause 1 barred Congress from passing laws to prohibit the slave trade until 1808 at the earliest. The Thirteenth Amendment (1865) made slavery illegal.

Clause 2: The Privilege of the Writ of Habeas Corpus shall not be suspended, unless when in Cases of Rebellion or Invasion the public Safety may require it.

> Clauses 2 and 3 guarantee protections to those accused of crimes. Clause 2 establishes the right of imprisoned persons to challenge their imprisonment in court (through a *writ of habeas corpus*). It notes that Congress can deny the right to a writ of habeas corpus during times of a rebellion or invasion if public safety is at risk.

Clause 3: No Bill of Attainder or ex post facto Law shall be passed.

Clause 4: No Capitation, or other direct, Tax shall be laid, unless in Proportion to the Census of Enumeration herein before directed to be taken.

> Congress cannot pass laws that declare a person or a group of people guilty of an offense (Bills of Attainder). Only courts have the authority to determine guilt. Congress is also prohibited from passing a law that punishes a person tomorrow for an action he or she took that was legal today (ex post facto law).

Clause 5: No Tax or Duty shall be laid on Articles exported from any State.

> Clause 4 prohibits Congress from directly taxing individual people, such as imposing an income tax. The Sixteenth Amendment (1913) authorized congressional enactment of a direct income tax on individual people.

Clause 6: No Preference shall be given by any Regulation of Commerce or Revenue to the Ports of one State over those of another: nor shall Vessels bound to, or from, one State, be obliged to enter, clear or pay Duties in another.

> Congress is prohibited from taxing goods that are exported from any state, either those sent to foreign lands or to other states (Clause 5).

> Congress cannot favor any state over another in its regulation of trade (Clause 6).

Clause 7: No Money shall be drawn from the Treasury, but in Consequence of Appropriations made by Law; and a regular Statement and Account of the Receipts and Expenditures of all public Money shall be published from time to time.

> The national government can spend money only as authorized by Congress through enacted laws (no more than authorized and only for the purpose authorized) and must present a public accounting of revenues and expenditures.

Clause 8: No Title of Nobility shall be granted by the United States: And no Person holding any Office of Profit or Trust under them, shall, without the Consent of the Congress, accept of any present, Emolument, Office, or Title, of any kind whatever, from any King, Prince or foreign State.

> Congress cannot grant individuals special rights, privileges, or a position in government based on their heredity (birth into a family designated as nobility), which is how kings, queens, and other officials were granted their positions in the British monarchy. In addition, federal officials cannot accept gifts from foreign nations except those Congress allows (which today are gifts of minimal value).

Section 10. (Prohibitions on the States)

Clause 1: No State shall enter into any Treaty, Alliance, or Confederation; grant Letters of Marque and Reprisal; coin Money; emit Bills of Credit; make any Thing but gold and silver Coin a Tender in Payment of Debts; pass any Bill of Attainder, ex post facto Law, or Law impairing the Obligation of Contracts, or grant any Title of Nobility.

> Clause 1 specifically prohibits states from engaging in several activities that the Constitution delegates to the national government, including engaging in foreign affairs and creating currency. In addition, it extends several of the prohibitions on Congress to the states.

Clause 2: No State shall, without the Consent of the Congress, lay any Imposts or Duties on Imports or Exports, except what may be absolutely necessary for executing its inspection Laws: and the net Produce of all Duties and Imposts, laid by any State on Imports or Exports, shall

> Clause 2 prevents states from interfering in foreign trade without congressional approval.

> States cannot, without congressional approval, levy import taxes, sign agreements or treaties with foreign nations, or enter into compacts (agreements) with other states.

> Article II outlines the authority of the president and the vice president and the process of their selection.

> The Constitution delegates to the president the authority to administer the executive branch of the national government. The term of office for the president and his vice president is four years. No term limit was specified; until President Franklin D. Roosevelt there was a tradition of a two-term limit. President Roosevelt served four terms.

> The Electoral College system was established as a compromise between those who wanted citizens to elect the president directly and others who wanted Congress to elect the president. Each state government has the authority to determine how their state's electors will be selected.

> Electors, who are selected through processes established by the legislatures of each state, have the authority to select the president and the vice president. Citizens' votes determine who their state's electors will be. Electors are individuals selected by officials of the state's political parties to participate in the Electoral College if the party wins the presidential vote in the state. Before passage of the Twelfth Amendment (1804), each elector had two votes. The candidate receiving the majority of votes won the presidency, and the candidate with the second highest number of votes won the vice presidency. Today, when the electors meet as the Electoral College, each elector casts one vote for the presidency and one vote for the vice presidency. If no presidential candidate wins a majority of the electoral votes, the House selects the president. If no vice-presidential candidate wins a majority of the electoral votes, the Senate selects the vice president.

be for the Use of the Treasury of the United States; and all such Laws shall be subject to the Revision and Controul of the Congress.

Clause 3: No State shall, without the Consent of Congress, lay any Duty of Tonnage, keep Troops, or Ships of War in time of Peace, enter into any Agreement or Compact with another State, or with a foreign Power, or engage in War, unless actually invaded, or in such imminent Danger as will not admit of delay.

ARTICLE II. (Executive Branch)

Section 1. (Executive Powers of the President)

Clause 1: The executive Power shall be vested in a President of the United States of America. He shall hold his Office during the Term of four Years, and, together with the Vice President, chosen for the same Term, be elected, as follows:

Clause 2: Each State shall appoint, in such Manner as the Legislature thereof may direct, a Number of Electors, equal to the whole Number of Senators and Representatives to which the State may be entitled in the Congress: but no Senator or Representative, or Person holding an Office of Trust or Profit under the United States, shall be appointed an Elector.

Clause 3: The Electors shall meet in their respective States, and vote by Ballot for two Persons, of whom one at least shall not be an Inhabitant of the same State with themselves. And they shall make a List of all the Persons voted for, and of the Number of Votes for each; which List they shall sign and certify, and transmit sealed to the Seat of the Government of the United States, directed to the President of the Senate. The President of the Senate shall, in the Presence of the Senate and House of Representatives, open all the Certificates, and the Votes shall then be counted. The Person having the greatest Number of Votes shall be the President, if such Number be a Majority of the whole Number of Electors appointed; and if there be more than one who have such Majority, and have an equal Number of Votes, then the House of Representatives shall immediately chuse by Ballot one of them for President; and if no Person have a Majority, then from the five highest on the List the said House shall in like Manner chuse the President. But in chusing the President, the Votes shall be taken by States, the Representatives from each State having one Vote; a quorum for this Purpose shall consist of a Member or Members from two thirds of the States, and a Majority of all the States shall be necessary to a Choice. In every Case, after the Choice of the President, the Person having the greatest Number of Votes of the Electors shall be the Vice President. But if there should remain two or more who have equal Votes, the Senate shall chuse from them by Ballot the Vice President.

POLITICAL INQUIRY: *The Electoral College system is criticized for many reasons. Some argue that deciding the presidential election by any vote other than that of the citizens is undemocratic. Others complain that in 2000 the system allowed George W. Bush to become president, even though he had not won the popular vote. Many argue that the Electoral College system should be eliminated and replaced by direct popular election of the president and the vice president. What is(are) the benefit(s) of eliminating the Electoral College? What might be the potential harm to the nation of eliminating the Electoral College?*

Clause 4: The Congress may determine the Time of chusing the Electors, and the Day on which they shall give their Votes; which Day shall be the same throughout the United States.

Clause 5: No Person except a natural born Citizen, or a Citizen of the United States, at the time of the Adoption of this Constitution, shall be eligible to the Office of President; neither shall any person be eligible to that Office who shall not have attained to the Age of thirty five Years, and been fourteen Years a Resident within the United States.

> Today, by law, national elections are held on the Tuesday following the first Monday in November, in even-numbered years. During presidential election years, the electors gather in their state capitals on the Monday after the second Wednesday in December to vote for the president and the vice president. When Congress convenes in January after the presidential election, its members count the electoral ballots and formally announce the newly elected president and vice president.

> The president (and the vice president) must be at least 35 years old and must have lived within the United States for at least fourteen years. Unlike the citizenship qualification for members of the House and Senate, the president and vice president must be natural-born citizens; they cannot be immigrants who have become citizens after arriving in the United States. Therefore, prominent public figures such as California governor Arnold Schwarzenegger, who was born in Austria, Madeleine Albright, secretary of state under President Clinton, who was born in what is now the Czech Republic, and Senator Mel Martinez (R-Florida), who was born in Cuba, could never be elected president.

POLITICAL INQUIRY: *With the success of foreign-born politicians like Governor Arnold Schwarzenegger, Secretary of State Madeleine Albright, and Senator Mel Martinez, some have argued for a constitutional amendment to allow foreign-born citizens to be eligible for the presidency. Congress has proposed an amendment that would allow a non–native-born citizen who has been a citizen for at least twenty years to be eligible for the presidency. Should the Constitution be amended so that foreign-born citizens would be eligible to become president of the United States? Why or why not? How would such an amendment change the nature of the presidential office?*

Clause 6: In Case of the Removal of the President from Office, or of his Death, Resignation, or Inability to discharge the Powers and Duties of the said Office, the Same shall devolve on the Vice President, and the Congress may by Law provide for the Case of Removal, Death, Resignation or Inability, both of the President and Vice President, declaring what Officer shall then act as President, and such Officer shall act accordingly, until the Disability be removed, or a President shall be elected.

> Clause 6 states that the powers and duties of the presidency are transferred to the vice president when the president is no longer able to fulfill them. It also states that Congress can pass legislation to indicate who shall act as president if both the president and the vice president are unable to fulfill the president's powers and duties. The "acting" president would serve until the disability is removed or a new president is elected. The Twenty-Fifth Amendment (1967) clarifies when the vice president acts as president temporarily—such as when the president undergoes surgery—and when the vice president actually becomes president.

Clause 7: The President shall, at stated Times, receive for his Services, a Compensation, which shall neither be encreased nor diminished during the Period for which he shall have been elected, and he shall not receive within that Period any other Emolument from the United States, or any of them.

> Currently the president's salary is $400,000 per year plus numerous benefits including a nontaxable expense account.

Clause 8: Before he enter on the Execution of his Office, he shall take the following Oath or Affirmation:—"I do solemnly swear (or affirm) that I will faithfully execute the Office of President of the United States, and will to the best of my Ability, preserve, protect and defend the Constitution of the United States."

Section 2. (Powers of the President)

Clause 1: The President shall be Commander in Chief of the Army and Navy of the United States, and of the Militia of the several States, when called into the actual Service of the United States; he may require the Opinion, in writing, of the principal Officer in each of the executive Departments, upon any Subject relating to the Duties of their respective Offices, and he shall have Power to Grant Reprieves and Pardons for Offences against the United States, except in Cases of Impeachment.

> Under the Constitution, the authority to ensure that laws are carried out is delegated to the president. The president and the vice president are elected to serve concurrent four-year terms. The call for a term limit followed President Franklin Roosevelt's election to a fourth term. The Twenty-Second Amendment (1951) established a two-term limit for presidents.

> The president is the commander of the military and of the National Guard (militia of the several states) when it is called to service by the president. When they are not called to service by the president, the state divisions of the National Guard are commanded by their governors. The president is authorized to establish the cabinet, the presidential advisory body comprising the top officials (secretaries) of each department of the executive branch. As the chief executive officer, the president can exercise a check on the judicial branch by decreasing or eliminating sentences and even pardoning (eliminating guilty verdicts of) federal prisoners.

POLITICAL INQUIRY: *It has become a tradition for presidents to pardon numerous individuals just before leaving office. A constitutional amendment to require the approval of a two-thirds majority of the Supreme Court for any pardon granted by the president has been proposed in Congress. Should the president's authority to pardon federal prisoners be checked by the Supreme Court? Why or why not?*

> The Constitution provides a check on the president's authority to negotiate treaties and appoint foreign ambassadors, top officials in the executive branch, and Supreme Court justices by requiring that treaties be ratified or appointments confirmed by the Senate. Congress can create additional executive branch positions and federal courts and can decree how these legislatively created positions will be filled.

> If vacancies occur when the Senate is not in session and is therefore not available to confirm presidential appointees, the president can fill the vacancies. The appointees serve through the end of the congressional session.

Clause 2: He shall have Power, by and with the Advice and Consent of the Senate, to make Treaties, provided two thirds of the Senators present concur; and he shall nominate, and by and with the Advice and Consent of the Senate, shall appoint Ambassadors, other public Ministers and Consuls, Judges of the supreme Court, and all other Officers of the United States, whose Appointments are not herein otherwise provided for, and which shall be established by Law: but the Congress may by Law vest the Appointment of such inferior Officers, as they think proper, in the President alone, in the Courts of Law, or in the Heads of Departments.

Clause 3: The President shall have Power to fill up all Vacancies that may happen during the Recess of the Senate, by granting Commissions which shall expire at the End of their next Session.

POLITICAL INQUIRY: *In recent years, Presidents Clinton and Bush have both taken advantage of the constitutional loophole that allows presidents to appoint people without Senate confirmation to make controversial appointments. Should the Constitution be amended to limit further the time an appointee who has not been confirmed can serve by requiring the Senate to consider the appointment when it next reconvenes? Why or why not?*

> As chief executive officer of the nation, the president is required to ensure that laws are properly implemented by overseeing the executive-branch agencies to be sure they are doing the work of government as established in law. The president is also required from time to time to give an assessment of the status of the nation to Congress and to make recommendations for the good of the country. This has evolved into the annual televised State of the Union Address, which is followed within days by the presentation of the president's budget proposal to Congress. The president can also call special sessions of Congress.

Section 3. (Responsibilities of the President)
He shall from time to time give to the Congress Information on the State of the Union, and recommend to their Consideration such Measures as he shall judge necessary and expedient; he may, on extraordinary Occasions, convene both Houses, or either of them, and in Case of Disagreement between them, with Respect to the Time of Adjournment, he may adjourn them to such Time as he shall think proper; he shall receive Ambassadors and other public Ministers; he shall take Care that the Laws be faithfully executed, and shall Commission all the Officers of the United States.

> Presidents, vice presidents, and other federal officials can be removed from office if the members of the House of Representatives formally accuse them of treason (giving assistance to the nation's enemies), bribery, or other vaguely defined abuses of power ("high Crimes and Misdemeanors") and two-thirds of the Senate find them guilty of these charges.

Section 4. (Impeachment)
The President, Vice President and all Civil Officers of the United States, shall be removed from Office on Impeachment for and Conviction of, Treason, Bribery, or other high Crimes and Misdemeanors.

> Article III presents the organization and authority of the U.S. Supreme Court and delegates to Congress the authority to create other courts as its members deem necessary.

ARTICLE III. (Judicial Branch)

> To ensure that judges make neutral and objective decisions, and are protected from political influences, federal judges serve until they retire, die, or are impeached by the House and convicted by the Senate. In addition, Congress cannot decrease a judge's pay.

Section 1. (Federal Courts and Rights of Judges)
The judicial Power of the United States, shall be vested in one supreme Court, and in such inferior Courts as the Congress may from time to time ordain and establish. The Judges, both of the supreme and inferior Courts, shall hold their Offices during good Behaviour, and shall, at stated Times, receive for their Services, a Compensation, which shall not be diminished during their Continuance in Office.

POLITICAL INQUIRY: *Although age discrimination is illegal, the government has allowed a retirement age to be established for some positions. For example, there is a retirement age for airline pilots, and most states have established retirement ages for state judges. What would be the arguments for or against amending the Constitution to establish a retirement age for federal judges?*

Section 2. (Jurisdiction of Federal Courts)

Clause 1: The judicial Power shall extend to all Cases, in Law and Equity, arising under this Constitution, the Laws of the United States, and Treaties made, or which shall be made, under their Authority;—to all Cases affecting Ambassadors, other public ministers and Consuls;—to all Cases of admiralty and maritime Jurisdiction;—to Controversies to which the United States shall be a Party;—to Controversies between two or more States;—between a State and Citizens of another State;—between Citizens of different States;—between Citizens of the same State claiming Lands under Grants of different States, and between a State, or the Citizens thereof, and foreign States, Citizens or Subjects.

> Federal courts have the authority to hear all lawsuits pertaining to national laws, the Constitution of the United States, and treaties. They also have jurisdiction over cases involving citizens of different states and citizens of foreign nations. Note that the power of judicial review, that is, the power to declare acts of government officials or bodies unconstitutional, is not enumerated in the Constitution.

POLITICAL INQUIRY: *Today there are nine Supreme Court justices, yet the Constitution does not set a specific number for Supreme Court justices. With the increasing number of cases appealed to the Supreme Court, what would be the arguments for or against increasing the number of Supreme Court justices?*

Clause 2: In all Cases affecting Ambassadors, other public Ministers and Consuls, and those in which a State shall be Party, the supreme Court shall have original Jurisdiction. In all the other Cases before mentioned, the supreme Court shall have appellate Jurisdiction, both as to Law and Fact, with such Exceptions, and under such Regulations as the Congress shall make.

> The Supreme Court hears cases involving foreign diplomats and cases in which states are a party. Today, such cases are rare. For the most part, the Supreme Court hears cases on appeal from lower federal courts.

Clause 3: The Trial of all Crimes, except in Cases of Impeachment, shall be by Jury; and such Trial shall be held in the State where the said Crimes shall have been committed; but when not committed within any State, the Trial shall be at such Place or Places as the Congress may by Law have directed.

> Defendants accused of federal crimes have the right to a jury trial in a federal court located in the state in which the crime was committed.

Section 3. (Treason)

Clause 1: Treason against the United States, shall consist only in levying War against them, or in adhering to their Enemies, giving them Aid and Comfort. No Person shall be convicted of Treason unless on the Testimony of two Witnesses to the same overt Act, or on Confession in open Court.

> This clause defines treason as making war against the United States or helping its enemies. At least two witnesses to the crime are required for a conviction.

Clause 2: The Congress shall have Power to declare the Punishment of Treason, but no Attainder of Treason shall work Corruption of Blood, or Forfeiture except during the Life of the Person attainted.

> This clause prevents Congress from redefining treason. Those found guilty of treason can be punished, but their family members cannot be (no "Corruption of Blood").

ARTICLE IV. (State-to-State Relations)

Section 1. (Full Faith and Credit of legal proceedings and decisions)
Full Faith and Credit shall be given in each State to the public Acts, Records, and judicial Proceedings of every other State. And the Congress may by general Laws prescribe the Manner in which such Acts, Records and Proceedings shall be proved, and the Effect thereof.

> Article IV establishes the obligations states have to each other and to the citizens of other states.

> States must respect one another's legal judgments and records, and a contract agreed to in one state is binding in the other states.

POLITICAL INQUIRY: *States have had the authority to legally define marriage since before the Constitution was ratified. Today, one of the many issues being debated is whether states with laws defining marriage as a contract between one man and one woman need to give full faith and credit to a same-sex marriage contract from a state where such marriages are legal, such as Massachusetts. The 1996 federal Defense of Marriage Act (DOMA) decrees that state governments*

Section 2. (Privileges and Immunities of Citizens)

Clause 1: The Citizens of each State shall be entitled to all Privileges and Immunities of Citizens in the several States.

> No matter what state they find themselves in, all U.S. citizens are entitled to the same privileges and rights as the citizens of that state.

Clause 2: A Person charged in any State with Treason, Felony, or other Crime, who shall flee from Justice, and be found in another State, shall on Demand of the executive Authority of the State from which he fled, be delivered up, to be removed to the State having Jurisdiction of the Crime.

> If requested by a governor of another state, a state is obligated to return an accused felon to the state from which he or she fled.

Clause 3: No Person held to Service or Labour in one State, under the Laws thereof, escaping into another, shall, in Consequence of any Law or Regulation therein, be discharged from such Service or Labour, but shall be delivered up on Claim of the Party to whom such Service or Labour may be due.

> The Thirteenth Amendment (1865) eliminated a state's obligation to return slaves fleeing from their enslavement in another state.

Section 3. (Admission of New States)

Clause 1: New States may be admitted by the Congress into this Union; but no new State shall be formed or erected within the Jurisdiction of any other State; nor any State be formed by the Junction of two or more States, or Parts of States, without the Consent of the Legislatures of the States concerned as well as of the Congress.

> Congress can admit new states to the union, but it cannot alter established state borders without the approval of the states that would be affected by the change.

Clause 2: The Congress shall have Power to dispose of and make all needful Rules and Regulations respecting the Territory or other Property belonging to the United States; and nothing in this Constitution shall be so construed as to Prejudice any Claims of the United States, or of any particular State.

> The federal government has authority to administer all federal lands, wherever they are located, including national parks and historic sites as well as military installations.

Section 4. (National Government Obligations to the States)
The United States shall guarantee to every State in this Union a Republican Form of Government, and shall protect each of them against Invasion; and on Application of the Legislature, or of the Executive (when the Legislature cannot be convened) against domestic Violence.

> The national government must ensure that every state has a representative democracy, protect each state from foreign invasion, and assist states in addressing mass breaches of domestic tranquility. Under this section, Congress has authorized the president to send in federal troops to protect public safety. During the civil rights movement, for example, federal troops ensured the safety of black students attending newly desegregated high schools and colleges.

ARTICLE V. (Formal Constitutional Amendment Process)

> Article V details the process by which the Constitution can be amended.

The Congress, whenever two thirds of both Houses shall deem it necessary, shall propose Amendments to this Constitution, or, on the Application of the Legislatures of two thirds of the several States, shall call a Convention for proposing Amendments, which, in either Case, shall be valid to all Intents and Purposes, as Part of this Constitution, when ratified by the Legislatures of three fourths of the several States, or by Conventions in three fourths thereof, as the one or the other Mode of Ratification may be proposed by the Congress; Provided that no Amendment which may be made prior to the Year One thousand eight hundred and eight shall in any Manner affect the first and fourth Clauses in the Ninth Section of the first Article; and that no State, without its Consent, shall be deprived of its equal Suffrage in the Senate.

> Amendments can be proposed either by Congress or by a special convention called at the request of the states. States have the authority to ratify amendments to the Constitution; three-fourths of the state legislatures must ratify an amendment for it to become part of the Constitution. Every year dozens of constitutional amendments are proposed in Congress, yet only twenty-seven have been ratified since 1789.

ARTICLE VI. (Supremacy of the Constitution)

Clause 1: All Debts contracted and Engagements entered into, before the Adoption of this Constitution, shall be as valid against the United States under this Constitution, as under the Confederation.

Clause 2: This Constitution, and the Laws of the United States which shall be made in Pursuance thereof; and all Treaties made, or which shall be made, under the Authority of the United States, shall be the supreme Law of the Land; and the Judges in every State shall be bound thereby, any Thing in the Constitution or Laws of any state to the Contrary notwithstanding.

Clause 3: The Senators and Representatives before mentioned, and the Members of the several State Legislatures, and all executive and judicial Officers, both of the United States and of the several States, shall be bound by Oath or Affirmation, to support this Constitution; but no religious Test shall ever be required as a Qualification to any Office or public Trust under the United States.

ARTICLE VII. (Constitutional Ratification Process)

Clause 1: The Ratification of the Conventions of nine States, shall be sufficient for the Establishment of this Constitution between the States so ratifying the same.

Clause 2: Done in Convention by the Unanimous Consent of the States present the Seventeenth Day of September in the Year of our Lord one thousand seven hundred and Eighty seven and of the Independence of the United States of America the Twelfth. In witness whereof We have hereunto subscribed our Names,

> Article VI decrees that the Constitution is the supreme law of the land.

> This provision states that the new federal government created by the Constitution was responsible for the financial obligations of the national government created by the Articles of Confederation.

> The Constitution, and all laws made to fulfill its mission that are in compliance with it, is the supreme law of the land; no one is above the supreme law of the land.

> All national and state officials must take an oath promising to uphold the Constitution. This article also prohibits the government from requiring officeholders to submit to a religious test or swear a religious oath, hence supporting a separation of government and religion.

> Article VII outlines the process by which the Constitution will be ratified.

> When the Constitutional Convention presented the proposed second constitution, the Constitution of the United States, to the states for ratification, the Articles of Confederation (the first constitution) were still in effect. The Articles required agreement from all thirteen states to amend it, which some argued meant that all thirteen states had to agree to replace the Articles of Confederation with the Constitution. Yet the proposed second constitution decreed that it would replace the Articles when nine states had ratified it. The first Congress met under the Constitution of the United States in 1789.

G. Washington—Presid't.
and deputy from Virginia

Delaware	George Read
	Gunning Bedford, Jr.
	John Dickinson
	Richard Bassett
	Jacob Broom
Maryland	James McHenry
	Daniel of St. Thomas Jenifer
	Daniel Carroll
Virginia	John Blair
	James Madison, Jr.
North Carolina	William Blount
	Richard Dobbs Spaight
	Hugh Williamson
South Carolina	John Rutledge
	Charles Cotesworth Pinckney
	Charles Pinckney
	Pierce Butler
Georgia	William Few
	Abraham Baldwin

New Hampshire	John Langdon
	Nicholas Gilman
Massachusetts	Nathaniel Gorham
	Rufus King
Connecticut	William Samuel Johnson
	Roger Sherman
New York	Alexander Hamilton
New Jersey	William Livingston
	David Brearley
	William Patterson
	Jonathan Dayton
Pennsylvania	Benjamin Franklin
	Thomas Mifflin
	Robert Morris
	George Clymer
	Thomas FitzSimons
	Jared Ingersoll
	James Wilson
	Gouverneur Morris

Amendments to the Constitution of the United States of America

THE BILL OF RIGHTS: AMENDMENTS I–X (RATIFIED IN 1791)

> Government cannot make laws that limit freedom of expression, which includes freedom of religion, speech, and the press, as well as the freedom to assemble and to petition the government to address grievances. None of these individual freedoms is absolute, however; courts balance the protection of individual freedoms (as provided for in this Constitution) with the protection of public safety, including national security.

Amendment I (1791)

Congress shall make no law respecting an establishment of religion, or prohibiting the free exercise thereof; or abridging the freedom of speech, or of the press; or the right of the people peaceably to assemble, and to petition the Government for a redress of grievances.

POLITICAL INQUIRY: *Currently, freedom of speech protects symbolic speech such as the burning of the U.S. flag to make a statement of protest. What reasons are there to amend the Constitution to make burning the flag unconstitutional and hence a form of speech that is not protected by the Constitution? What reasons are there not to do so?*

> Today, states and the federal government balance the right of the people to own guns with the need to protect the public.

Amendment II (1791)

A well regulated Militia, being necessary to the security of a free State, the right of the people to keep and bear Arms, shall not be infringed.

POLITICAL INQUIRY: *Does the phrase "a well regulated Militia" limit the right to bear arms to those engaged in protecting public peace and safety? Why or why not?*

> Military troops cannot take control of private homes during peacetime.

Amendment III (1791)

No Soldier shall, in time of peace be quartered in any house, without the consent of the Owner, nor in time of war, but in a manner to be prescribed by law.

Amendment IV (1791)

The right of the people to be secure in their persons, houses, papers, and effects, against unreasonable searches and seizures, shall not be violated, and no Warrants shall issue, but upon probable cause, supported by Oath or affirmation, and particularly describing the place to be searched, and the persons or things to be seized.

> Government officials must obtain approval before they search or seize a person's property. The approval must come either from the person whose private property they are searching or seizing or from a judge who determines that the government is justified in taking this action in order to protect public safety and therefore signs a search warrant.

POLITICAL INQUIRY: *Since the terrorist attacks on September 11, 2001, the national government has tried to balance the right of people to be secure in their person and property with public safety and national security. What reasons have the president and members of Congress offered in defense of allowing intelligence agencies to bypass the requirement to get judicial permission to conduct searches or seizures of phone records of suspected terrorists? How valid are those reasons? In your opinion, can they be reconciled with constitutional protections?*

Amendment V (1791)

No person shall be held to answer for a capital, or otherwise infamous crime, unless on a presentment or indictment of a Grand Jury, except in cases arising in the land or naval forces, or in the Militia, when in actual service in time of War or public danger; nor shall any person be subject for the same offence to be twice put in jeopardy of life or limb; nor shall be compelled in any criminal case to be a witness against himself, nor be deprived of life, liberty, or property, without due process of law; nor shall private property be taken for public use, without just compensation.

Amendment VI (1791)

In all criminal prosecutions, the accused shall enjoy the right to a speedy and public trial, by an impartial jury of the State and district wherein the crime shall have been committed, which district shall have been previously ascertained by law, and to be informed of the nature and cause of the accusation; to be confronted with the witnesses against him; to have compulsory process for obtaining witnesses in his favor, and to have the Assistance of Counsel for his defence.

> The Fifth Amendment provides much more than the familiar protection against self-incrimination that we hear people who are testifying before Congress and the courts claim by "taking the Fifth." For example, before the government can punish a person for a crime (take away a person's life, liberty, or pursuit of happiness), it must follow certain procedures specified in law; it must follow *due process of the law.* The federal government guarantees those accused of federal crimes a grand jury hearing in which the government presents its evidence to a selected group of citizens who determine whether there is sufficient evidence to go to trial. If a defendant is found not guilty of a specific criminal offense, he or she cannot be brought to trial again by the same government for the same offense. If the government determines it needs private property for a public use, the owner is compelled to sell the land, and the government must pay a fair price based on the market value of the property.

> The Sixth Amendment outlines additional procedures that the government must follow before taking away a person's life, liberty, or pursuit of happiness. People accused of crimes have the right to know what they are accused of doing, to hear from witnesses against them, and to defend themselves in a trial that is open to the public within a reasonable amount of time after the accusations are made. An indigent (very poor) person is guaranteed a government-provided lawyer in serious criminal cases. It is assumed all others can afford to hire a lawyer.

POLITICAL INQUIRY: *The resources needed to provide an adequate defense in a criminal case can be quite steep. For example, to ensure a fair trial, a lawyer may use government money to pay for expert witnesses. Argue for or against the need to limit such expenditures for indigent defendants accused of serious crimes.*

Amendment VII (1791)

In Suits at common law, where the value in controversy shall exceed twenty dollars, the right of trial by jury shall be preserved, and no fact tried by a jury, shall be otherwise re-examined in any Court of the United States, than according to the rules of the common law.

> Either party (the complainant or the person accused of causing harm or violating a contract) in a federal civil lawsuit involving more than $20 can demand a jury trial.

Amendment VIII (1791)

Excessive bail shall not be required, nor excessive fines imposed, nor cruel and unusual punishments inflicted.

> The Eighth Amendment protects those accused of crimes as well as those found guilty from overly punitive decisions. Bail, a payment to the government that can be required to avoid incarceration before and during trial, cannot be set at an excessively high amount, unless the judge determines that freedom for the accused would jeopardize public safety or that he or she might flee. The punishment imposed on those convicted of crimes is expected to "fit" the crime: it is to be reasonable given the severity of the crime. Punishment cannot be excessive or cruel.

POLITICAL INQUIRY: *When the Constitution was written, imprisonment was viewed as cruel and unusual punishment of the convicted. Today there is debate over whether the death penalty (capital punishment) is cruel and unusual. Whatever your opinion is of the death penalty itself, consider some of the techniques used by the government to put people to death. Are they cruel and unusual? Make a case for or against the use of lethal injection, for example.*

Amendment IX (1791)

The enumeration in the Constitution, of certain rights, shall not be construed to deny or disparage others retained by the people.

Amendment X (1791)

The powers not delegated to the United States by the Constitution, nor prohibited by it to the States, are reserved to the States respectively, or to the people.

> The Ninth Amendment acknowledges that there are additional rights, not listed in the preceding eight amendments, that the government cannot deny to citizens. The Supreme Court has interpreted the First Amendment, Fifth Amendment, and the Ninth Amendment to collectively provide individuals with a right to privacy.

> The Tenth Amendment acknowledges that state governments retain all authority they had before ratification of the Constitution that has not been delegated to the national government by the Constitution. This amendment was demanded by the Anti-Federalists, who opposed ratification of this Constitution. The Anti-Federalists feared that the national government would infringe on people's freedoms and on the authority of the state governments. The vagueness of the rights retained by the states continues to cause tensions and disputes between the state governments and the national government.

> The courts have interpreted this amendment to mean that federal courts do not have the authority to hear lawsuits brought by citizens against their own state or against another state, or brought by foreigners against a state.

> The presidential election in 1800 ended with a tie in Electoral College votes between Thomas Jefferson and Aaron Burr. Because the candidate with the most votes was to become president and the candidate with the second highest number of votes was to become vice president, the tie meant that the job of selecting the president was turned over to the House of Representatives. The House selected Jefferson. Calls to change the procedure were answered by the enactment of this amendment. Today, each elector has two votes; one for a presidential candidate and one for a vice-presidential candidate. The presidential candidate who wins the majority of electoral votes wins the presidency, and the same is true for the vice-presidential candidate. If no presidential candidate wins a majority of the votes, the House selects the president. If no vice-presidential candidate wins a majority of the votes, the Senate selects the vice president.

> This amendment abolished slavery.

> This amendment extends the rights of citizenship to all those born in the United States and those who have become citizens through naturalization. States are prohibited from denying U.S. citizens their rights and privileges and must provide all people with due process before taking away their life, liberty, or pursuit of happiness. States must also treat all people equally and fairly. The courts have also used this section of the Fourteenth Amendment to require that states ensure citizens their protections under the Bill of Rights.

Amendment XI (1795)

The Judicial power of the United States shall not be construed to extend to any suit in law or equity, commenced or prosecuted against one of the United States by Citizens of another State, or by Citizens or Subjects of any Foreign State.

Amendment XII (1804)

The Electors shall meet in their respective states and vote by ballot for President and Vice-President, one of whom, at least, shall not be an inhabitant of the same state with themselves; they shall name in their ballots the person voted for as President, and in distinct ballots the person voted for as Vice- President, and they shall make distinct lists of all persons voted for as President, and of all persons voted for as Vice-President, and of the number of votes for each, which lists they shall sign and certify, and transmit sealed to the seat of the government of the United States, directed to the President of the Senate;—The President of the Senate shall, in the presence of the Senate and House of Representatives, open all the certificates and the votes shall then be counted;—The person having the greatest Number of votes for President, shall be the President, if such number be a majority of the whole number of Electors appointed; and if no person have such majority, then from the persons having the highest numbers not exceeding three on the list of those voted for as President, the House of Representatives shall choose immediately, by ballot, the President. But in choosing the President, the votes shall be taken by states, the representation from each state having one vote; a quorum for this purpose shall consist of a member or members from two-thirds of the states, and a majority of all the states shall be necessary to a choice. And if the House of Representatives shall not choose a President whenever the right of choice shall devolve upon them, before the fourth day of March next following, then the Vice-President shall act as President, as in the case of the death or other constitutional disability of the President—The person having the greatest number of votes as Vice-President, shall be the Vice-President, if such number be a majority of the whole number of Electors appointed, and if no person have a majority, then from the two highest numbers on the list, the Senate shall choose the Vice-President; a quorum for the purpose shall consist of two-thirds of the whole number of Senators, and a majority of the whole number shall be necessary to a choice. But no person constitutionally ineligible to the office of President shall be eligible to that of Vice-President of the United States.

Amendment XIII (1865)

Section 1. Neither slavery nor involuntary servitude, except as a punishment for crime whereof the party shall have been duly convicted, shall exist within the United States, or any place subject to their jurisdiction.

Section 2. Congress shall have power to enforce this article by appropriate legislation.

Amendment XIV (1868)

Section 1. All persons born or naturalized in the United States and subject to the jurisdiction thereof, are citizens of the United States and of the State wherein they reside. No State shall make or enforce any law which shall abridge the privileges or immunities of citizens of the United States; nor shall any State deprive any person of life, liberty, or property, without due process of law; nor deny to any person within its jurisdiction the equal protection of the laws.

Section 2. Representatives shall be apportioned among the several States according to their respective numbers, counting the whole number of persons in each State, excluding Indians not taxed. But when the right to vote at any election for the choice of electors for President and Vice President of the United States, Representatives in Congress, the Executive and Judicial officers of a State, or the members of the Legislature thereof, is denied to any of the male inhabitants of such State, being twenty-one years of age, and citizens of the United States, or in any way abridged, except for participation in rebellion, or other crime, the basis of representation therein shall be reduced in the proportion which the number of such male citizens shall bear to the whole number of male citizens twenty-one years of age in such State.

> This section of the Fourteenth Amendment is the first use of the term "male" in the Constitution. This section requires that if a state denies men over the age of 21 the right to vote, its representation in the House will be diminished accordingly. The Fifteenth Amendment makes this section unnecessary.

Section 3. No person shall be a Senator or Representative in Congress, or elector of President and Vice President, or hold any office, civil or military, under the United States, or under any State, who, having previously taken an oath, as a member of Congress, or as an officer of the United States, or as a member of any State legislature, or as an executive or judicial officer of any State, to support the Constitution of the United States, shall have engaged in insurrection or rebellion against the same, or given aid or comfort to the enemies thereof. But Congress may by a vote of two-thirds of each House, remove such disability.

> The intent of this section was to prevent government officials who supported the Confederacy during the Civil War from serving in government. In 1898 Congress voted to eliminate this prohibition.

Section 4. The validity of the public debt of the United States, authorized by law, including debts incurred for payment of pensions and bounties for services in suppressing insurrection or rebellion, shall not be questioned. But neither the United States nor any State shall assume or pay any debt or obligation incurred in aid of insurrection or rebellion against the United States, or any claim for the loss or emancipation of any slave; but all such debts, obligations and claims shall be held illegal and void.

Section 5. The Congress shall have power to enforce, by appropriate legislation, the provisions of this article.

> All male citizens meeting their state's minimum age requirement are guaranteed the right to vote.

> This amendment authorizes the national government to establish taxes on personal and corporate income.

> Since the ratification of the Seventeenth Amendment in 1913, senators are elected by the citizens in each state rather than by state legislatures. The amendment also allows each state legislature to establish the process by which vacancies in the Senate will be filled, either through special election or by gubernatorial appointment.

> The "Prohibition" amendment—making it illegal to manufacture, sell, or transport alcoholic beverages in the United States—was widely disobeyed during the years it was in effect. The Twenty-First amendment repealed this amendment.

> All female citizens meeting their state's minimum age requirement are guaranteed the right to vote.

> The first two sections of the Twentieth Amendment establish new starting dates for the president's and vice president's terms of office (January 20) as well as for members of Congress (January 3). Section 2 also decrees that the annual meeting of Congress will begin on January 3 unless Congress specifies a different date.

Amendment XV (1870)

Section 1. The right of citizens of the United States to vote shall not be denied or abridged by the United States or by any State on account of race, color, or previous condition of servitude.

Section 2. The Congress shall have power to enforce this article by appropriate legislation.

Amendment XVI (1913)

The Congress shall have power to lay and collect taxes on incomes, from whatever source derived, without apportionment among the several States, and without regard to any census or enumeration.

Amendment XVII (1913)

The Senate of the United States shall be composed of two Senators from each State, elected by the people thereof, for six years; and each Senator shall have one vote. The electors in each State shall have the qualifications requisite for electors of the most numerous branch of the State legislatures.

When vacancies happen in the representation of any State in the Senate, the executive authority of such State shall issue writs of election to fill such vacancies: Provided, That the legislature of any State may empower the executive thereof to make temporary appointments until the people fill the vacancies by election as the legislature may direct.

This amendment shall not be so construed as to affect the election or term of any Senator chosen before it becomes valid as part of the Constitution.

Amendment XVIII (1919)

Section 1. After one year from the ratification of this article the manufacture, sale, or transportation of intoxicating liquors within, the importation thereof into, or the exportation thereof from the United States and all territory subject to the jurisdiction thereof for beverage purposes is hereby prohibited.

Section 2. The Congress and the several States shall have concurrent power to enforce this article by appropriate legislation.

Section 3. This article shall be inoperative unless it shall have been ratified as an amendment to the Constitution by the legislatures of the several States, as provided in the Constitution, within seven years from the date of the submission hereof to the States by the Congress.

Amendment XIX (1920)

The right of citizens of the United States to vote shall not be denied or abridged by the United States or by any State on account of sex. Congress shall have power to enforce this article by appropriate legislation.

Amendment XX (1933)

Section 1. The terms of the President and Vice President shall end at noon on the 20th day of January, and the terms of Senators and Representatives at noon on the 3d day of January, of the years in which such terms would have ended if this article had not been ratified; and the terms of their successors shall then begin.

Section 2. The Congress shall assemble at least once in every year, and such meeting shall begin at noon on the 3d day of January, unless they shall by law appoint a different day.

Section 3. If, at the time fixed for the beginning of the term of the President, the President elect shall have died, the Vice President elect shall become President. If a President shall not have been chosen before the time fixed for the beginning of his term, or if the President elect shall have failed to qualify, then the Vice President elect shall act as President until a President shall have qualified; and the Congress may by law provide for the case wherein neither a President elect nor a Vice President elect shall have qualified, declaring who shall then act as President, or the manner in which one who is to act shall be selected, and such person shall act accordingly until a President or Vice President shall have qualified.

> Sections 3 and 4 of this amendment establish that if the president elect dies before his or her term of office begins, the vice president elect becomes president. If the president elect has not been selected or is unable to begin the term, the vice president elect serves as acting president until the president is selected or is able to serve.

Section 4. The Congress may by law provide for the case of the death of any of the persons from whom the House of Representatives may choose a President whenever the right of choice shall have devolved upon them, and for the case of the death of any of the persons from whom the Senate may choose a Vice President whenever the right of choice shall have devolved upon them.

Section 5. Sections 1 and 2 shall take effect on the 15th day of October following the ratification of this article.

Section 6. This article shall be inoperative unless it shall have been ratified as an amendment to the Constitution by the legislatures of three-fourths of the several States within seven years from the date of its submission.

Amendment XXI (1933)

Section 1. The eighteenth article of amendment to the Constitution of the United States is hereby repealed.

> With this amendment, the Eighteenth Amendment's prohibition of the manufacture, sale, and transportation of alcoholic beverages was repealed.

Section 2. The transportation or importation into any State, Territory, or possession of the United States for delivery or use therein of intoxicating liquors, in violation of the laws thereof, is hereby prohibited.

Section 3. This article shall be inoperative unless it shall have been ratified as an amendment to the Constitution by conventions in the several States, as provided in the Constitution, within seven years from the date of the submission hereof to the States by the Congress.

Amendment XXII (1951)

Section 1. No person shall be elected to the office of the President more than twice, and no person who has held the office of President, or acted as President, for more than two years of a term to which some other person was elected President shall be elected to the office of the President more than once. But this Article shall not apply to any person holding the office of President, when this Article was proposed by the Congress, and shall not prevent any person who may be holding the office of President, or acting as President, during the term within which this Article becomes operative from holding the office of President or acting as President during the remainder of such term.

> This amendment established a two-term limit for the presidency, or in the case of a vice president succeeding to the presidency and then running for reelection, a maximum limit of ten years in office.

Section 2. This article shall be inoperative unless it shall have been ratified as an amendment to the Constitution by the legislatures of three-fourths of the several States within seven years from the date of its submission to the States by the Congress.

POLITICAL INQUIRY: *Critics of term limits in general argue that they are undemocratic because they may force out of office an official whom the voters want to keep in office as their representative. Other critics of term limits for the president argue that forcing out a popular, successful president during a time of war may be harmful to the nation. Argue for or against eliminating the two-term limit for the presidency.*

Amendment XXIII (1961)

Section 1. The District constituting the seat of Government of the United States shall appoint in such manner as the Congress may direct: A number of electors of President and Vice President equal to the whole number of Senators and Representatives in Congress to which the District would be entitled if it were a State, but in no event more than the least populous State; they shall be in addition to those appointed by the States, but they shall be considered, for the purposes of the election of President and Vice President, to be electors appointed by a State; and they shall meet in the District and perform such duties as provided by the twelfth article of amendment.

Section 2. The Congress shall have power to enforce this article by appropriate legislation.

Amendment XXIV (1964)

Section 1. The right of citizens of the United States to vote in any primary or other election for President or Vice President, for electors for President or Vice President, or for Senator or Representative in Congress, shall not be denied or abridged by the United States or any State by reason of failure to pay any poll tax or other tax.

Section 2. The Congress shall have power to enforce this article by appropriate legislation.

POLITICAL INQUIRY: *Several states have enacted laws requiring voters to show a photo ID in order to vote. Indiana, for one, requires voters to produce a government-issued photo ID such as a driver's license or passport. Does requiring a government-issued photo ID create an unreasonable barrier to a person's constitutionally guaranteed right to vote? For example, does this pose a barrier to those who do not tend to have such IDs or an easy way to obtain them, including the elderly, the poor, and urban residents? Is requiring voters to pay for a government ID that they must show in order to vote similar to a poll tax? Why or why not? What argument is used to justify requiring a voter to show a photo ID in order to vote?*

Amendment XXV (1967)

Section 1. In case of the removal of the President from office or of his death or resignation, the Vice President shall become President.

Section 2. Whenever there is a vacancy in the office of the Vice President, the President shall nominate a Vice President who shall take office upon confirmation by a majority vote of both Houses of Congress.

> Citizens living in Washington D.C. are given the right to elect three voting members to the Electoral College. Before this amendment, these citizens were not represented in the Electoral College.

> Governments are prohibited from requiring a person to pay a tax in order to vote.

> The vice president becomes president if the president resigns or dies.

> The president can nominate a person to fill a vice-presidential vacancy. Congress must approve the nominee. President Richard Nixon appointed and Congress confirmed Gerald Ford to the vice presidency when Vice President Spiro Agnew resigned. When President Nixon resigned, Vice President Ford, who had not been elected, became president. He subsequently appointed and Congress confirmed Nelson Rockefeller to be vice president.

Section 3. Whenever the President transmits to the President pro tempore of the Senate and the Speaker of the House of Representatives his written declaration that he is unable to discharge the powers and duties of his office, and until he transmits to them a written declaration to the contrary, such powers and duties shall be discharged by the Vice President as Acting President.

Section 4. Whenever the Vice President and a majority of either the principal officers of the executive departments or of such other body as Congress may by law provide, transmit to the President pro tempore of the Senate and the Speaker of the House of Representatives their written declaration that the President is unable to discharge the powers and duties of his office, the Vice President shall immediately assume the powers and duties of the office as Acting President.

Thereafter, when the President transmits to the President pro tempore of the Senate and the Speaker of the House of Representatives his written declaration that no inability exists, he shall resume the powers and duties of his office unless the Vice President and a majority of either the principal officers of the executive department or of such other body as Congress may by law provide, transmit within four days to the President pro tempore of the Senate and the Speaker of the House of Representatives their written declaration that the President is unable to discharge the powers and duties of his office. Thereupon Congress shall decide the issue, assembling within forty-eight hours for that purpose if not in session. If the Congress, within twenty-one days after receipt of the latter written declaration, or, if Congress is not in session, within twenty-one days after Congress is required to assemble, determines by two-thirds vote of both Houses that the President is unable to discharge the powers and duties of his office, the Vice President shall continue to discharge the same as Acting President; otherwise, the President shall resume the powers and duties of his office.

Amendment XXVI (1971)

Section 1. The right of citizens of the United States, who are eighteen years of age or older, to vote shall not be denied or abridged by the United States or by any State on account of age.

Section 2. The Congress shall have power to enforce this article by appropriate legislation.

Amendment XXVII (1992)

No law varying the compensation for the services of the Senators and Representatives shall take effect, until an election of Representatives shall have intervened.

> If the president indicates in writing to Congress that he or she cannot carry out the duties of office, the vice president becomes acting president until the president informs Congress that he or she is again fit to resume the responsibilities of the presidency.

> If the vice president in concert with a majority of cabinet officials (or some other body designated by Congress) declares to Congress in writing that the president is unable to fulfill the duties of office, the vice president becomes acting president until the president claims he or she is again fit for duty. However, if the vice president and a majority of cabinet officials challenge the president's claim, then Congress must decide within three weeks if the president can resume office.

> The Twenty-Sixth Amendment guarantees citizens 18 years of age and older the right to vote.

> Proposed in 1789, this amendment prevents members of Congress from raising their own salaries. Approved salary increases cannot take effect until after the next congressional election.

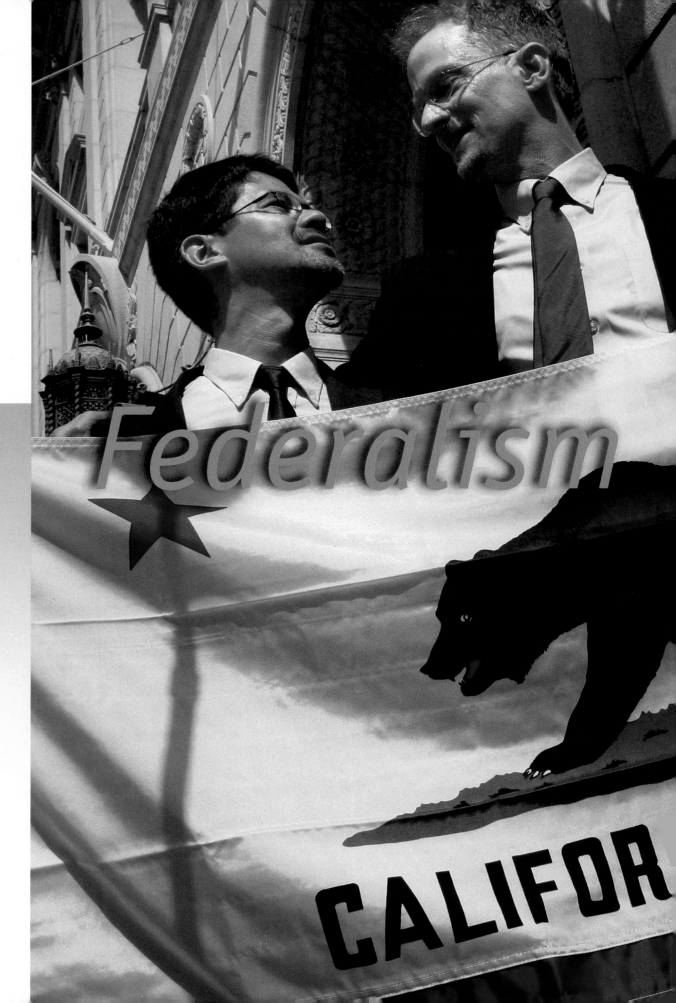

CHAPTER

3

Federalism

THEN

The newly created national government and the preexisting state governments acted independently as they implemented the innovative federal system of government established in 1789.

NOW

National, state, and local governments challenge one another regularly over the proper interpretation of the Constitution's distribution of power in the federal system.

NEXT

Will Supreme Court justices continue to issue conflicting interpretations of federalism?

Will increasing national inaction on domestic policy issues force state and local governments to boost their efforts to be laboratories for the creation of effective policies?

Will intergovernmental relations evolve so that government can provide more efficient, effective public service?

Fighting for Her Home: Susette Kelo Challenges Eminent Domain

In 2005, the U.S. Supreme Court resolved a lawsuit that questioned the definition of the phrase *public use* in the case of *Kelo v. New London*.* The events that led to the case were highly controversial. The city government of New London, Connecticut, had condemned homes in a stable working-class neighborhood to make way for the private development of high-priced houses and commercial properties. Attorneys for the city of New London argued that this use of *eminent domain*—the government's takeover of private property even when the owner does not want to sell it—would create jobs and bring much-needed tax revenue. Such economic development, the city's lawyers insisted, was for a public use. But some New London residents strongly disagreed. Seven homeowners, led by Susette Kelo, opted to sue the city, claiming that the city's condemnation of the property was not a proper use of the Fifth Amendment's eminent domain clause. Kelo stressed that she would sell her property to the government without a fight for a firehouse or improved roads, which she saw clearly as a public use. But she steadfastly argued that she should not be forced to sell her property to the government "so someone else can enjoy [her] view."** | The Supreme Court's ruling in the case favored the defendant, the city of New London. In their opinion, the justices held that *state* governments have the authority to determine what "public use" means with regard to state and local application of eminent domain. In this way the Court affirmed the Connecticut State Supreme Court's earlier finding that the New London economic development project was a public use. But all was not lost for Kelo and her co-plaintiffs. For although the Court had cleared the way for New London authorities to take the properties of Kelo and her neighbors, with just compensation provided, Connecticut governor M. Jodi Rell imposed a moratorium on the property seizure, allowing Kelo to hold on to her salmon-pink cottage with its scenic water view. | Despite her loss in court, Susette Kelo chalked up an important gain for American democracy.

> Susette Kelo took her case all the way to the U.S. Supreme Court to prevent the city of New London, Connecticut, from taking her salmon-pink cottage.

Indeed, her actions have opened up a passionate civic conversation concerning property rights—a dialogue directed at *all* levels of government—that is ongoing. Local governments, pleased with the *Kelo* decision's support of economic development, find themselves at odds with state legislators, who are formulating and debating bills and state constitutional amendments to limit the definition of public use in state and local eminent domain cases. These state lawmakers are responding to interest groups fighting to protect private property rights, such as the Institute for Justice and the Property Rights Foundation of America, as well as to individual voters who fear that local governments will seize their property and turn it over to private developers. The U.S. Senate Judiciary Committee invited Kelo to testify at its September 2005 hearings on several bills that would limit the availability of federal funds for private development projects approved by local and state governments, which presents a real threat to the economic development efforts of these governments. Therefore, the Supreme Court's *Kelo* decision and Congress's reaction to it have forced state and local governments to reassess their use of eminent domain.

*Kelo v. New London, 545 U.S. 469 (2005).
**Susette Kelo, "Eminent Domain Up Close," *The Washington Times*, September 20, 2005, A14.

The conflict over the term *public*

use in the *Kelo* case is just one example of many battles that have arisen between U.S. citizens and their governments over the proper interpretation of constitutional language. The case focuses attention on the three levels of government in the U.S. federal system—national, state, and local—and on questions about the constitutional distribution of authority among these governments.

With more than 89,000 distinct governments in the United States today—one national, 50 state, and over 89,476 local governments—and given vague constitutional language regarding the proper authority of national and state governments, the courts frequently must interpret the framers' intent with respect to the distribution of authority. Among the conflicts over jurisdiction that have reached the courts are disagreements over which level of government has the authority to set the legal drinking age, to establish gun-free school zones, to legalize the medical use of marijuana, and to determine which votes count in a presidential election.

Wherever you live in the United States, at least four or five governments collect taxes from you, provide services to you, and establish your rights and responsibilities. With so many governments in action, citizens who are interested in influencing public policies have many access points. Yet which government has the authority to address your concerns may not be clear to you. It may not even be clear to government officials. Ultimately, the Constitution, as interpreted by the U.S. Supreme Court justices, determines which government is responsible for which matters.

Even as the wrangling continues over the proper interpretation of the constitutional distribution of authority between governments, the U.S. national, state, and local governments engage every day in *collaborative* efforts to fulfill the complex, costly needs of the people whom they serve. Such intergovernmental efforts are essential in today's world. But they complicate attempts to clarify which level of government is ultimately responsible for which services and policies.

This chapter examines the nature and evolution of the constitutional distribution of authority between the national and state governments in the U.S. federal system of government.

FIRST, we take an *overview of the U.S. federal system* and its distinct dual sovereignty.

SECOND, we explore the details of dual sovereignty by considering the *constitutional distribution of authority* between the national and state governments.

THIRD, we focus on the *evolution of the federal system* and see how national and state governments' power relationships have changed over time.

FOURTH, we survey the complex intergovernmental relations that dominate *today's federalism: the good, the bad, and the inevitable.*

An Overview of the U.S. Federal System

The U.S. Constitution established an unprecedented government structure characterized by a federal system of governance. A **federal system** has two constitutionally recognized levels of government, each with **sovereignty**—that is, ultimate governing authority, with no legal superior—over different policy matters and geographic areas. According to the Constitution, the national government has ultimate authority over some matters, and the state governments hold ultimate authority over different matters. The existence of two governments, each with ultimate authority over different matters—an arrangement called **dual sovereignty**—is what distinguishes the federal system of government from the two other most common systems of government, known as unitary and confederal. The American colonists' experience with a unitary system, and subsequently the early U.S. citizens' life under a confederal system (1781–1788), led to the creation of the innovative federal system.

Unitary System

Colonial Americans lived under Great Britain's unitary system of government. In fact, the majority of the world's nations today also have unitary governments. In a **unitary system,** the central government is sovereign—it is the ultimate governing authority, with no legal

federal system
a governmental structure with two levels of government and in which each level has sovereignty over different policy matters and geographic areas

sovereignty
having ultimate authority to govern, with no legal superior

dual sovereignty
the existence of two governments, each with authority over different matters at the same time; neither level is sovereign over the other

unitary system
a governmental structure in which one central government has sovereignty, although it may create regional governments to which it delegates responsibilities

superior. It can create other governments (regional governments) and delegate powers and responsibilities to them. The central government in a unitary system can also unilaterally take away any responsibilities it has delegated to any regional governments it creates and can even *eliminate* the regional governments.

Indeed, under Britain's unitary system of government during the American colonial period, the British Crown (the sovereign government) created colonial governments and gave them authority to handle day-to-day matters such as regulating marriages, resolving business conflicts, providing for public safety, and maintaining roads. As the central government in Britain approved tax and trade policies that harmed the colonists' quality of life, growing public discourse and dissension spurred the colonists to protest. It was their failed attempts to influence the central government's policies—by lobbying the king's selected colonial governors, sending petitions to the king, and boycotting certain goods—that eventually sparked more radical acts such as the Boston Tea Party and the colonists' declaration of independence from Great Britain.

Confederal System

When the colonies declared their independence from Great Britain in 1776, each became an independent sovereign state and adopted its own constitution. As a result, no state had a legal superior. In 1777, delegates from every state except Rhode Island met in a convention and agreed to a proposed alliance of the thirteen sovereign state governments. In 1781, the thirteen independent state governments ratified the Articles of Confederation, the first U.S. constitution, which created a confederal system of government.

confederal system
a structure of government in which several independent sovereign governments agree to cooperate on specified governmental matters while retaining sovereignty over all other governmental matters within their jurisdictions

In a **confederal system,** several independent sovereign governments (such as the thirteen state governments in the American case) agree to cooperate on specified matters while each retains ultimate authority over all other governmental matters within its borders. The cooperating sovereign governments delegate some responsibilities to a central governing body. Each sovereign government selects its own representatives to the central governing body. The sovereign governments retain ultimate authority in a confederal system for the simple reason that they can recall their delegates from the central government at any time and can either carry out or ignore the central government's policies.

As detailed in Chapter 2, the effectiveness of the confederation created by the Articles of Confederation increasingly came into question. In February 1787 the national Congress passed a resolution calling for a constitutional convention "for the sole and express purpose of revising the Articles of Confederation" in order to preserve the Union. Clear-eyed about the failures of the unitary and confederal systems, the colonists decided to experiment with a unique government system—a federal system. The federal system created by the Constitution of the United States has succeeded in preserving the union for over 220 years.

Federal System

The state delegates who met in Philadelphia in 1787 drafted a new constitution that created an innovative federal system of government with dual sovereignty. The Constitution's framers established dual sovereignty by detailing a new, sovereign national government for the United States and modifying the sovereignty of the existing state governments. The national government thus created has no legal superior on matters over which the Constitution gives it authority, and the state governments have no legal superior on the matters over which they are granted authority by the Constitution.

Such dual sovereignty does not exist in unitary and confederal systems, where sovereignty is held by one level of government (the central government in a unitary system and the regional governments in a confederal system). The federal system gives both the central (national) government and the regional (state) governments ultimate authority over different matters (see Figure 3.1).

The European Union (EU), or United States of Europe, represents the most recent innovation in governmental systems. See "Global Comparisons" for a look at this new governing system.

Unitary System	Confederal System	Federal System

The central government is sovereign, with no legal superior. It may create state governments and delegate legal authority to them. It can also eliminate such governments.

An alliance exists among independent sovereign governments, which delegate limited authority to a central government of their making. The independent sovereign governments retain sovereignty, with no legal superior, over all matters they do not delegate to the central government.

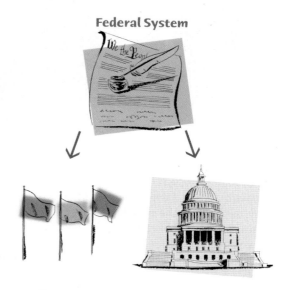

State governments are sovereign in specified matters, and a central (national) government is sovereign in other specified matters. The matters over which each government is sovereign are set forth in a constitution, which is the supreme law of the land. Dual sovereignty is the distinguishing characteristic of a federal system.

POLITICAL INQUIRY

FIGURE 3.1 ■ **Who is sovereign in a unitary system of government? In a confederal system of government? In a federal system of government? Which of the systems of government does the United States have, and why?**

The federal system, as it works in the United States today, can be confusing—not only to citizens but also to elected officials and even Supreme Court justices. The confusion begins with the fact that in addition to the one national and fifty distinct state governments that are operating in the country today, more than 89,000 local governments are functioning, even though the Constitution does not mention local governments.

It is *state constitutions* that authorize states to create local governments. State governments delegate some of their responsibilities to these local governments through legislation and/or the approval of a *charter,* which is a local government's version of a constitution. At the same time, state governments have the authority to take back delegated responsibilities and even to eliminate local governments. Because the state government retains ultimate authority over all the matters it delegates to its local governments and can eliminate its local governments, the relationship between a state government and its local governments is *unitary* (following a unitary system of governmental structure).

INTERGOVERNMENTAL RELATIONS (IGR) In order to govern, a government must have the authority to formulate and approve a plan of action, to raise and spend money to finance the plan, and to hire workers to put the plan into action. In the U.S. federal system today, the responsibility for these three elements of any given public policy—the policy *statement,* the policy *financing,* and the policy *implementation*—may rest entirely with one level of government (national, state, or local), or it may be shared in a collaborative effort by two or more of these levels. Political scientists label the collaborative efforts of two or more levels of government working to serve the public **intergovernmental relations (IGR).**

The provision of elementary and secondary public education serves as an example of IGR. Although education is a policy matter that the U.S. Constitution distributes to the states, in all but four states the state governments have created school districts—which are local-level governments—to implement elementary and secondary school policies. Funding

intergovernmental relations (IGR)
collaborative efforts of two or more levels of government working to serve the public

GLOBAL COMPARISONS

THE UNITED STATES OF EUROPE

Clearly not a unitary system, the European Union (EU) claims to be "more than just a confederation of countries, but . . . not a federal State."* The principles, institutions, and power relationships of the EU have developed over the last fifty years through a series of treaties among European nations. The current twenty-seven EU member states have delegated some of their national sovereignty to several shared institutions (each with legislative, executive, and/or judicial functions) through a series of treaties, not in one single document such as the Constitution of the United States.

*What are some potential future impacts of EU membership-- good and bad-- for EU member nations?

Each European country that joins the EU has its own constitution and maintains its national sovereignty—with all inherent powers of sovereignty—in order to further its national interests. (Each state in the United States has its own constitution; however, the Constitution of the United States is the supreme law of the land and distributes sovereignty between the national government and the state governments.) Yet when a country joins the EU, it agrees to follow the decisions of the EU institutions, which focus on the *collective* interests of European nations.

The roots of the EU reach back to 1951. That year, six countries—Belgium, the Federal Republic of Germany, France, Italy, Luxembourg, and the Netherlands—signed a treaty establishing among themselves a common market for their coal and steel. By the 1960s, these six countries had signed additional treaties in which they expanded their common market to a wide range of goods and services, eliminated import taxes on each other's goods, and established common trade and agricultural policies. The success of these policies soon led to agreement on common social and environmental policies as well. Moreover, additional European countries joined what the world knew as the European Economic Community (EEC).

By 1990, twelve European countries belonged to the EEC, and they turned their attention to negotiating a new treaty to clarify the principles and institutions of their government system. In 1992, the presidents and prime ministers of the EEC countries signed the Treaty on European Union, better known as the Treaty of Maastricht, for the Dutch city in which it was signed. The Treaty of Maastricht, which took effect in 1993, defines the foundations for the current EU institutions and the relationships among these bodies, which are as follows:

- The *European Council of Ministers* represents the member states and officially initiates major EU international policies. The council's focus is the discussion of current world problems, and its objective is to speak with one European voice on international issues. In addition to its authority to conclude international agreements, the council shares legislative power (to approve regulations and directives) and responsibility to formulate the EU budget with the European Parliament.

- The *European Parliament* is a body elected by and representing the citizens of the EU member countries. The parliament shares lawmaking authority and the "power of the purse" with the European Council of Ministers.

- The *European Commission* is the EU's executive arm. It must ensure the proper implementation of legislation adopted by the European Council of Ministers and the European Parliament.

- The *Court of Justice* resolves conflicts over the meaning and implementation of EU law. This body ensures that the EU collects and spends its revenues legally.

Originally, the collaborative efforts of European countries focused on a common European market for the sale of goods and services, as noted above. Today, however, EU policies range well beyond economic considerations. Indeed, the EU targets a wide range of policy areas, including environmental protection, public health, consumer rights, transportation, education, economic development, and fundamental human rights.

> Traditionally, the number twelve is a symbol of perfection, completeness, and unity. The circle of twelve gold stars on the European Union flag represents solidarity, harmony, and unity among the peoples and nations of Europe.

Source: "Europe in 12 Lessons," *Europa*, http://europa.eu/abc/12lessons/index_en.htm.

for the majority of school districts comes predominantly from local taxes, but these are supplemented by grants of money collected by the federal and state governments through their taxes. In the majority of public school districts, only teachers certified by the state government can teach. These state-certified teachers, hired by local school districts, implement national policy mandating equal educational opportunity for all students (required by Titles VI and IX of the Civil Rights Act and the Individuals with Disabilities Education Act) and proficiency tests (mandated by the No Child Left Behind Act). They also implement state policy with respect to curricula and the school calendar, as well as school district policy regarding school uniforms and discipline. The United States thus delivers the public service of elementary and secondary education through intricate intergovernmental relations, where three levels of government share policy making and policy financing and where school district employees implement the policies.

We can measure the scope of IGR today by looking at the distribution of the workers whom national, state, and local governments hire to deliver specific public services. The graphs in Figure 3.2 show some policies that are purely national, one that is purely local, and several that are truly intergovernmental. Another gauge of the extent of IGR is the percentage of national grant money that state and local governments spend on the delivery of specific services.

Who Employs the Public Servants?

National defense — 100%

Postal service — 100%

Space research & technology — 100%

Elementary & secondary education 1% — 99%

Hospitals 14% 37% 50%

Higher education 81% 19%

Police protection 14% 9% 77%

Fire protection — 100%

Streets & highways 1% 42% 57%

▮ % = National ▮ **%** = State ▮ **%** = Local

FIGURE 3.2 ▦ What proportion of employees working on space research and technology is national? What proportion of employees working in elementary and secondary education is national? What explains the difference in these two cases?

Source: U.S. Census Bureau, "Federal, State and Local Governments, Public Employment Data for 2005," www.census.gov/compendia/stat.ab/tables/08s0448.xls.

Education Today

How satisfied are you with the state of education in the United States today?

☐ Satisfied

☐ Not satisfied

Source: "Slim Majority Dissatisfied with Education in the U.S.," www.gallup.com/poll/18421/Slim-Majority-Dissatisfied-Education-US.aspx.

> National legislation mandates equal educational opportunities for all children regardless of their race, color, ethnicity, religion, sex, or disability. State and local governments share with the national government the cost of providing equal educational opportunities. School districts hire the teachers who implement equal educational opportunity policies.

For example, in the policy area of public elementary and secondary education, the national government supplies approximately 9 percent of the funds needed; state governments provide 48 percent on average; and local governments contribute 42 percent on average.[1]

WHAT A FEDERAL SYSTEM MEANS FOR CITIZENS   For citizens, living in a federal system of government means that their legal rights and liberties and their civic responsibilities vary depending on where they live. The majority of U.S. citizens live under the jurisdiction of at least five governments: national, state, county (called *borough* in Alaska and *parish* in Louisiana), municipal or township, and school district. Each of these governments can impose responsibilities on the people living in its jurisdiction. The most obvious responsibility is to pay taxes to several governments. These taxes can include the national personal income tax; state sales and personal income taxes; and county, municipal, township, and school district property taxes. Each government can also guarantee personal liberties and rights. The Constitution lists individual liberties in the Bill of Rights. In addition, every state constitution has its own bill of rights, and some local governments offer further protections to their citizens. For example, some cities and counties prohibit discrimination based on an individual's sexual orientation, yet most states do not, nor does the national government.

In some cases a citizen must fulfill a responsibility to one government before he or she can enjoy certain rights and privileges guaranteed by another government. A case in point is selective service registration. National law requires all male citizens and all male noncitizens residing in the United States to register for *selective service*—the draft—within thirty days of their 18th birthday (with a few exceptions, such as for males with disabilities). Males who do not register are ineligible for any form of college assistance as provided under the federal Higher Education Act. In addition to forfeiting eligibility for national financial assistance, males violating the national mandate to register for the draft can also lose their driver's licenses and state identification cards in twenty-seven states; twenty-four states deny such males state financial aid for higher education; and eighteen state governments will not hire males who flout the national draft registration mandate.[2] No matter what state they live in, males must register with selective service according to national law. The punishment for not registering, however, varies depending on one's state of residence.

Thus, the federal system can be confusing for citizens. It can also be confusing for the many governments created to serve the people. Which government is responsible for what services and policies? Because the Constitution of the United States is the supreme law of the land, it is to the Constitution that we must turn to answer this question. Yet constitutional language is not always clear. As we saw in Chapter 2, the framers hammered out the Constitution through intensive bargaining and compromise that produced a text that is often vague and ambiguous.

Also as discussed in Chapter 2, the U.S. Supreme Court has the authority to determine what the constitution means and hence what is constitutional. This authority came from the Court's decision in the *Marbury v. Madison* case (1803), in which the justices found that the Constitution gives them, sitting as the Supreme Court, the ultimate authority to determine the Constitution's meaning and intent.[3] Significantly, and specifically, the *Marbury* case established the principle of judicial review: the Court's authority to determine whether an action of any government operating within the United States violates the Constitution.

Although the Supreme Court is the final interpreter of the Constitution, the Court's *constructions* (interpretations) have changed over time. For example, it is true that dual sovereignty—and therefore a federal system—still exists in the United States today, but the courts have interpreted the Constitution in such a way that the authority of the national government has expanded significantly over the last 220-plus years. In addition, the determination of which government has ultimate authority over specific matters has become even less clear due to the evolution of a complex arrangement of various levels of government working together to meet the various responsibilities that the Constitution delegates, implies, or reserves to them.

Later in this chapter, we consider this evolution of the U.S. federal system. Before we do, it is useful for us to examine the constitutional distribution of authority to the national and state governments.

The Return of the Draft

Do you support or oppose a return to the military draft in the United States today?

☐ Support the draft
☐ Oppose the draft

Source: "Vast Majority of Americans Opposed to Reinstating Draft," www.gallup.com/poll/28642/Vast-Majority-Americans-Opposed-Reinstituting-Military-Draft.aspx.

Constitutional Distribution of Authority

By distributing some authority to the national government and different authority to the state governments, the Constitution creates the dual sovereignty that defines the U.S. federal system. The Constitution specifically lists the several matters over which the national government has ultimate authority, and it implies additional national authority. The Constitution spells out just a few matters over which the state governments have authority. The lack of constitutional detail on state authority is partially explained by the fact that at the time of the Constitution's drafting, the states expected to retain their authority, except for matters that, by way of the Constitution, they agreed to turn over to the newly created national government.

To fulfill their responsibilities to their citizens, both the national and the state governments have the authority to engage in the functions inherent to all sovereign governments. This authority extends to the concurrent powers, our first topic in this section.

Concurrent Sovereign Authority

In order to function, sovereign governments need the authority to make policy, raise money, establish courts to interpret policy when a conflict arises about its meaning, and implement policy. These authorities are recognized as *inherent* to all governments—they are defining characteristics of governments. In the U.S. federal system, we designate these inherent governing functions as the **concurrent powers** because the national and the state governments hold these powers jointly and each can use them at the same time. For example, national and state governments make their own public policies, raise their own revenues, and spend those revenues to implement their policies. (State governments delegate these authorities, in limited ways, to the local governments they create so that they can function as governments.)

A particular concurrent authority established by the Constitution is **eminent domain**—the power of a government to purchase private property for public use, even when the property owner refuses to sell. Citizens have turned to the courts to resolve conflicts over whether the constitutionally required "just compensation" paid for a given property is fair, as well as to settle disagreements over the definition of "public use," as we saw in the "American Democracy Now" vignette on Susette Kelo.

Just as the Court has had to step in to resolve conflicts over areas of concurrent authority, it must also resolve conflicts between the national and state governments over the constitutional powers that establish national and state sovereignty, as we now consider.

National Sovereignty

The Constitution distributes powers that are (1) enumerated, or specifically listed, and (2) implied for the national government's three branches—legislative, executive, and judicial. For example, Article I of the Constitution enumerates (lists) the matters over which Congress holds the authority to make laws, including interstate and foreign commerce, the system of money, general welfare, and national defense. These matters are **enumerated powers** of the national government. The Constitution also gives Congress **implied powers**—that is, powers that are not explicitly described but may be interpreted to be necessary to fulfill the enumerated powers. Congress specifically receives implied powers through the Constitution's **necessary and proper clause**, sometimes called the **elastic clause** because the national government uses this passage to stretch its enumerated authority. The necessary and proper clause states that Congress has the power to "make all laws which shall be necessary and proper" for carrying out its enumerated powers.

Articles II and III of the Constitution also enumerate certain powers of the national government. Article II delegates to the president the authority to ensure the proper implementation of national laws and, with the advice and consent of the U.S. Senate, the authority to make treaties with foreign nations and to appoint foreign ambassadors. With respect to the U.S. Supreme Court and the lower federal courts, Article III enumerates jurisdiction over

concurrent powers
basic governing functions of all sovereign governments, in the United States they are held by the national, state, and local governments and include the authority to tax, to make policy, to implement policy, and to exercise the power of eminent domain

eminent domain
the authority of government to compel a property owner to sell private property to a government to further the public good

enumerated powers
the powers of the national government that are listed in the Constitution

implied powers
powers of the national government that are not enumerated in the Constitution but that Congress claims are necessary and proper for the national government to fulfill its enumerated powers in accordance with the necessary and proper clause of the Constitution

necessary and proper clause (elastic clause)
a clause in Article I, Section 8, of the Constitution that gives Congress the power to do whatever it deems necessary and constitutional to meet its enumerated obligations; the basis for the implied powers

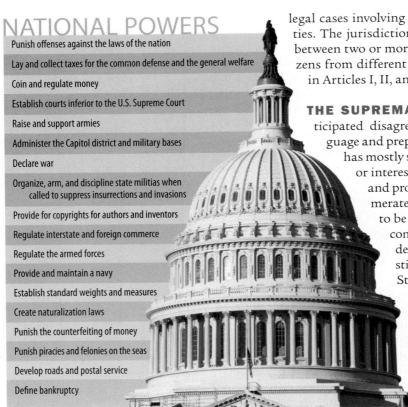

NATIONAL POWERS

Punish offenses against the laws of the nation

Lay and collect taxes for the common defense and the general welfare

Coin and regulate money

Establish courts inferior to the U.S. Supreme Court

Raise and support armies

Administer the Capitol district and military bases

Declare war

Organize, arm, and discipline state militias when called to suppress insurrections and invasions

Provide for copyrights for authors and inventors

Regulate interstate and foreign commerce

Regulate the armed forces

Provide and maintain a navy

Establish standard weights and measures

Create naturalization laws

Punish the counterfeiting of money

Punish piracies and felonies on the seas

Develop roads and postal service

Define bankruptcy

FIGURE 3.3

Enumerated Powers of National Government

> This engraving portrays a meeting of Sioux, Arapaho, and Cheyenne chiefs with U.S. army generals at North Platte, Nebraska. Recognizing Native American tribes as sovereign nations, the federal government has negotiated hundreds of treaties with numerous Indian nations, and state and local governments must comply with these agreements.

legal cases involving constitutional issues, national legislation, and/or treaties. The jurisdiction of the Supreme Court also extends to disagreements between two or more state governments, as well as to conflicts between citizens from different states. Figure 3.3 lists the national powers enumerated in Articles I, II, and III of the Constitution.

THE SUPREMACY CLAUSE The country's founders obviously anticipated disagreements over the interpretation of constitutional language and prepared for them by creating the Supreme Court. The Court has mostly supported the national government when states, citizens, or interest groups have challenged Congress's use of the necessary and proper clause to take on new responsibilities beyond its enumerated powers. Unless the Supreme Court finds a national law to be outside of the enumerated or implied powers, that law is constitutional and hence the **supreme law of the land,** as defined by the **supremacy clause** in Article VI of the Constitution: "This Constitution, and the laws of the United States which shall be made in pursuance thereof; and all treaties made, or which shall be made, under the authority of the United States, shall be the supreme law of the land." State and local governments are thereby obligated to comply with national laws that implement national enumerated and implied powers, as well as with treaties—including treaties with Native American nations.

NATIONAL TREATIES WITH INDIAN NATIONS Throughout U.S. history, the national government has signed treaties with Native American nations, which are legally viewed as sovereign foreign nations. As with all treaties, treaties with Native American nations are supreme law with which the national government and state and local governments must comply. The core issue in the majority of these treaties is the provision of land (reservations) on which the native peoples could resettle after non-Indians took their lands during the eighteenth and nineteenth centuries. Today, the federal government recognizes more than 550 Indian tribes. Although the majority of Native Americans no longer live on reservations—most native peoples have moved to cities—approximately 300 reservations remain, in thirty-four states.[4]

Even though Indian reservations lie within state borders, national treaties and national laws, not state or local laws, apply to the reservation populations and lands. State and local laws, including laws having to do with taxes, crime, and the environment, are unenforceable on reservations. Moreover, Native American treaty rights to hunt, fish, and gather on reservations and on public lands supersede national, state, and local environmental regulations.[5]

Treaties entered into by the national government (including those negotiated with Indian nations residing within the states) and constitutional national laws are the supreme law of the land. Tensions frequently flare between the national government and state governments over the constitutionality of national laws. We now look at constitutional powers delegated and reserved to the states.

State Sovereignty

The Constitution specifies only a few state powers. It provides the states with a role in national politics and gives them the final say on formally amending the Constitution. The fact that the state governments were already functioning when the states ratified the Constitution partly explains the lack of constitutional specificity regarding state authority. Other than those responsibilities that the states agreed to delegate (and to imply) to the newly created federal government through their ratification of the Constitution, the states expected to retain their sovereignty over all the day-to-day matters internal to their borders that they were already handling. Yet the original Constitution did not speak of this sovereignty explicitly.

POWERS DELEGATED TO THE STATES   The state powers enumerated in the Constitution give the states a distinct voice in the composition and priorities of the national government. Members of Congress are elected by winning a plurality of votes in their home state (in the case of senators) or their home district (in the case of representatives in the House). Voters also participate in the election of their state's Electoral College electors, who vote for the president and vice president on behalf of their state, as we saw in Chapter 2. Because electors are selected in state elections, presidential campaigns focus tirelessly on the concerns of citizens on a state-by-state level. Overall, state voters expect that the officials whom they elect to the national government will carefully consider their concerns when creating national policy. This is representative government in action.

In addition to establishing the various electoral procedures that give voice to state interests in the national policy-making process, the Constitution creates a formal means by which the states can ensure that their constitutional authority is not changed or eliminated without their approval. Specifically, the Constitution stipulates that three-fourths of the states (through votes in either their legislatures or special conventions, as discussed in Chapter 2) must ratify amendments to the Constitution. By having the final say in whether the supreme law of the land will be changed through the passage of amendments, the states can protect their constitutional powers. Indeed, they did just that when they ratified the Tenth Amendment (1791).

POWERS RESERVED TO THE STATES   The Constitution's extremely limited attention to state authority caused concern among citizens of the early American republic. Many people feared that the new national government would meddle in matters for which states had been responsible, in this way compromising state sovereignty. Citizens were also deeply concerned about their freedoms, corresponding to the protections listed in each state constitution's bill of rights. Anti-Federalists argued that without a bill of rights in the Constitution, the national government would trample the people's natural rights to life, liberties, and the pursuit of happiness. As described in Chapter 2, the states ratified the Bill of Rights, the first ten amendments to the Constitution, in response to Anti-Federalist concerns.

The Tenth Amendment asserts that the "powers not delegated to the United States by the Constitution, nor prohibited by it to the states, are *reserved to the states* [emphasis added] respectively, or to the people." This **reserved powers** clause of the Tenth Amendment acknowledged the domestic matters over which the states had exercised authority since the ratification of their own constitutions. These matters included the ordinary, daily affairs of the people—birth, death, marriage, intrastate business, commerce, crime, health, morals, and safety. The states' reserved powers to protect the health, safety, lives, and property of their citizens are referred to as their **police powers.** It was over these domestic matters, internal to each state, that the states retained sovereignty according to the Tenth Amendment. In addition, state courts retained sovereignty over legal cases that involve their state's constitution and legislation (and that do not also raise issues involving the U.S. Constitution). Figure 3.4 summarizes the constitutionally reserved and enumerated powers of the states at the time of the Tenth Amendment's ratification.

supreme law of the land
the Constitution's description of its own authority, meaning that all laws made by governments within the United States must be in compliance with the Constitution

supremacy clause
the paragraph in Article VI that makes the Constitution, and the treaties and laws created in compliance with it, the supreme law of the land

reserved powers
the matters referred to in the Tenth Amendment over which states retain sovereignty

police powers
the states' reserved powers to protect the health, safety, lives, and properties of residents in a state

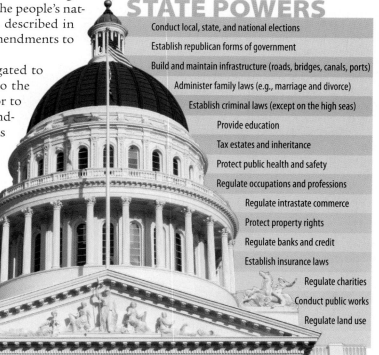

STATE POWERS

Conduct local, state, and national elections
Establish republican forms of government
Build and maintain infrastructure (roads, bridges, canals, ports)
Administer family laws (e.g., marriage and divorce)
Establish criminal laws (except on the high seas)
Provide education
Tax estates and inheritance
Protect public health and safety
Regulate occupations and professions
Regulate intrastate commerce
Protect property rights
Regulate banks and credit
Establish insurance laws
Regulate charities
Conduct public works
Regulate land use

FIGURE 3.4

Constitutionally Delegated and Reserved State Powers

The Tenth Amendment's affirmation of state sovereignty is brief and vague, and the Supreme Court continues to this day to resolve conflicts over its interpretation. New cases, leading to fresh interpretations, come before the Court when state governments challenge national laws that the states deem to infringe on their reserved powers but that the national government claims to fulfill its enumerated or implied powers. New interpretations by the Court also arise when the national government or citizens challenge the constitutionality of a state or local government action (just as citizens challenged their city and state in the *Kelo* case). Citizens, local governments, state governments, and the national government persistently ask the courts to resolve constitutional conflicts in order to protect their liberties, their rights, and, in the case of governments, their sovereignty.

The Supreme Court's Interpretation of Enumerated, Implied, and Reserved Powers

McCulloch v. Maryland
established that the necessary and proper clause justifies broad understandings of enumerated powers

The landmark case of ***McCulloch v. Maryland*** (1819) exemplifies a Supreme Court ruling that established the use of the implied powers to expand the national government's delegated authority.[6] The case stemmed from Congress's establishment of a national bank, and in particular a branch of that bank located in the state of Maryland, which the Maryland state authorities tried to tax. Attorneys for the state of Maryland argued that if the federal government had the authority to establish a national bank and to locate a branch in Maryland, then Maryland had the power to tax the bank. On a more basic level, Maryland's legal counsel asserted that Congress did not have the constitutional authority to establish a national bank, noting that doing so was not an enumerated power. Lawyers for the national government in turn argued that federal authority to establish a national bank was implied and that Maryland's levying a tax on the bank was unconstitutional, for it impinged on the national government's ability to fulfill its constitutional responsibilities by taking some of its financial resources.

>In 1995, the U.S. Supreme Court ruled the national Gun-Free School Zones legislation unconstitutional and affirmed that the Constitution reserves to the *states* the power to establish gun-free school zones. Notice the bilingual gun-free and drug-free school zone signs at this Phoenix, Arizona, school.

The Supreme Court decided in favor of the national government. The justices based their ruling on their interpretation of the Constitution's necessary and proper clause and the enumerated powers of Congress to "lay and collect taxes, to borrow money . . . and to regulate commerce among the several states." The Court said that combined, these powers implied that the national government had the authority to charter a bank and to locate a branch in Maryland. In addition, the Court found that Maryland did not have the right to tax that bank, because taxation by the state would interfere with the exercise of federal authority. In addition to establishing that the necessary and proper clause justifies broad understandings of the enumerated powers, the Court affirmed once and for all that in the event of a conflict between national legislation (the law chartering the national bank) and state legislation (Maryland's tax law), the national law is supreme *as long as* it is in compliance with the Constitution's enumerated and implied powers.

THE POWER TO REGULATE COMMERCE A few years later, in the case of *Gibbons v. Ogden* (1824), the Supreme Court again justified a particular national action on the basis of the implications of an enumerated power.[7] The *Gibbons* case was the first suit brought to the Supreme Court seeking clarification on the constitutional meaning of *commerce* in the Constitution's clause on the regulation of interstate commerce. The Court established a broad definition of commerce: "all commercial intercourse—meaning all business dealings." The conflict in this case concerned which government, New York State or the national government, had authority to regulate the operation of boats on the waterways between New York and New Jersey. The Court ruled that regulation of commerce implied regulation of navigation and that therefore the national government had authority to regulate it, not New York State.

Following the *Gibbons* decision, the national government frequently justified many of its actions by arguing that they were necessary to fulfill its enumerated powers to regulate interstate commerce, and the Court typically agreed. The case of *United States v. Lopez* (1995) is an example, however, of the Court's recent trend of being more critical of Congress's attempts to use the commerce clause to justify a national law.[8] The context for the case is the national Gun-Free School Zones Act of 1990, which mandated gun-free zones within a specified area surrounding schools. The lawyers for Alfonso Lopez, a twelfth-grader charged with violating this national law by bringing a .38-caliber handgun to school, successfully argued that the law was unconstitutional. The Court rejected the national government attorney's argument that the 1990 law was a necessary and proper means to regulate interstate commerce. Instead, the Court found that the law was a criminal statute, for which the state governments, not the national government, have authority.[9]

THE POWER TO PROVIDE FOR THE GENERAL WELFARE Another enumerated power that has expanded through Court interpretation of what the Constitution implies is the power of the national government to provide for the general welfare. The national government's landmark Social Security Act of 1935 was a response to the Great Depression's devastating impact on the financial security of countless Americans. The congressional vote to establish Social Security was overwhelmingly favorable. Yet the constitutionality of this very expansive program, which has become the most expensive national program, was tested in the courts shortly after its passage. In 1937, the Supreme Court had to decide: Was Social Security indeed a matter of general welfare for which Congress is delegated the authority to raise and spend money? Or was Social Security a matter for the state governments to address?[10] The Court found the national policy to be constitutional—a reasonable congressional interpretation, the justices wrote, of the enumerated and implied powers of the national government.

The Supreme Court's decisions in the *McCulloch, Gibbons,* and Social Security cases set precedents for the expansion of national power in domestic policy matters by combining the necessary and proper clause with such enumerated powers as the regulation of commerce and providing for the general welfare. The Court continues today to support Congress's use of the elasticity provided by the implied powers clause to expand its delegated powers. The Court also continues to protect national enumerated powers. Yet Congress does not always get its way, as the justices' decision in the *Lopez* case indicates.

In addition to establishing dual sovereignty and creating two independently operating levels of government, the Constitution enumerates some obligations that the national government has to the states—the topic to which we now turn.

National Obligations to the States

On August 27, 2005, the day before Katrina (a powerful category 3 hurricane) hit the Gulf Coast states, National Hurricane Center director Max Mayfield personally called the governors of Mississippi and Louisiana and the mayor of New Orleans. Mayfield wanted to be sure that these state and local officials understood the severity of the approaching storm.[11] That same day, President George W. Bush declared a national state of emergency

Concept Summary

DUAL SOVEREIGNTY AND NATIONAL SUPREMACY

— The Constitution distributes sovereignty (ultimate governing authority) between the national government and the state governments.

— National sovereignty is defined in the powers enumerated and implied in the Constitution and applies to matters of defense, diplomacy, interstate commerce, foreign commerce, general welfare, and the U.S. monetary system.

— State sovereignty is defined in the Tenth Amendment's reserved powers clause and includes the day-to-day domestic matters internal to each state.

— The result of the constitutional distribution of power is two levels of government, each with distinct, constitutionally established sovereignty.

— National law is supreme when it fulfills enumerated or implied powers. State law is supreme when it fulfills reserved powers.

— In this federal system of dual sovereignty, the national government cannot eliminate the state governments, and the state governments cannot eliminate the national government, without a constitutional amendment.

> This sign raised by desperate apartment dwellers in Biloxi, Mississippi, five days after Hurricane Katrina battered the Gulf coastline sought to publicize the fact that FEMA's limited initial efforts were focusing on New Orleans, Louisiana, and leaving Mississippians to fend for themselves. **What does this photo show? What is FEMA, and why have people posted a sign asking "Where are you, 'FEMA'?"**

for the area, and Mississippi governor Haley Barbour did the same for his state. Louisiana governor Kathleen Blanco had declared a state of emergency for her state the day before. New Orleans mayor Ray Nagin ordered a mandatory evacuation of the city's 485,000 residents.[12] Federal Emergency Management Administration (FEMA) director Michael Brown told state and local officials in the Gulf states that FEMA was ready with all available assistance and was "going to move quick . . . and going to do whatever it takes to help disaster victims."[13]

Even with this apparent readiness at all levels of government, the impact of Katrina's subsequent flooding in New Orleans due to a levee break (which government reports predicted would result from a hurricane with even less force than Katrina) was devastating: over 1,200 people dead, more than 1 million evacuees, and an estimated $200 billion-plus of damage.[14]

In light of Katrina's destruction of property and devastating human toll, the media and citizens throughout the country directed a hurricane of criticism at the failure of local, state, and national governments to work together effectively during and after the crisis. State and local officials complained about unacceptable—and deadly—federal delays in responding to their urgent requests for help. The devastation also prompted questions about the national government's obligations to local and state governments (and citizens) in times of disaster. The Constitution describes several obligations that the national government has to the states, including assistance during times of domestic upheaval (see Table 3.1).

TABLE 3.1

National Obligations to the States

The federal government:

- must treat states equally in matters of the regulation of commerce and the imposition of taxes
- cannot approve the creation of a new state from the property of an existing state without the consent of the legislatures of the states concerned
- cannot change state boundaries without the consent of the states concerned
- must guarantee a republican form of government
- must protect states from foreign invasion
- at their request, must protect states against domestic violence

Department of Homeland Security (DHS) secretary Michael Chertoff explained four days after Katrina hit that the national government steps in "to assist local and state authorities. Under the Constitution, state and local authorities have the principal first line of response obligation. DHS has the coordinating role, or the managing role. The president has, of course, the ultimate responsibility for all the federal effort here. I want to emphasize the federal government does not supersede the state and local government."[15]

There is no denying the national government's constitutional obligation to assist state and local governments in times of domestic upheaval. Yet does the national government have to wait for state or local officials to ask for help before it takes action? The Constitution is not clear about this question, and to date the courts have not rendered an interpretation on the matter.

Just as the Constitution establishes national obligations to the states, it also defines state-to-state obligations, our next subject.

State-to-State Obligations: Horizontal Federalism

In Article IV, the Constitution sets forth obligations that the states have to each other. Collectively, these state-to-state obligations and the relationships they mandate are forms of what scholars call **horizontal federalism.** For example, state governments have the right to forge agreements with other states, known as **interstate compacts.** Congress must review and approve interstate compacts to ensure that they do not harm the states that are not party to them and the nation as a whole. States enter into cooperative agreements to provide services and benefits for each other, such as monitoring paroled inmates from other states; sharing and conserving natural resources that spill over state borders, such as water; and decreasing pollution that crosses state borders. For example, in 2005, to improve air quality, the states of Connecticut, Delaware, Massachusetts, New Jersey, New York, Rhode Island, and Vermont agreed to an interstate compact establishing emissions caps on power plants in their states—caps that were higher than national standards.

States also cooperate through a procedure called **extradition,** the legal process of sending individuals back to a state that accuses them of having committed a crime, and from which they have fled. The Constitution establishes a state governor's right to request the extradition of an accused criminal. Yet the courts have also supported governors' refusals to extradite individuals.

The Constitution asserts, too, that each state must guarantee the same **privileges and immunities** to all U.S. citizens—that is, citizens from other states who visit or move into the state—that it provides its own citizens. This guarantee does not prohibit states from imposing reasonable requirements before extending rights to visiting or new state residents. For example, states can and do charge higher tuition costs to out-of-state college students. In addition, in many states, new state residents must wait thirty days before they can register to vote. Yet no state can deny new state residents who are U.S. citizens the right to register to vote once they meet a reasonable state residency requirement.

Today, one very controversial state-to-state obligation stems from the full faith and credit clause of Article IV, Section 1, of the Constitution. The **full faith and credit clause** asserts that each state must recognize as legally binding (that is, valid and enforceable) the public acts, records, and judicial proceedings of every other state. For example, states must recognize the validity of out-of-state driver's licenses. Currently, public debate is ongoing about the impact of the full faith and credit clause on same-sex marriage contracts, and hence the constitutionality of the national Defense of Marriage Act (DOMA) of 1996, which allows states to determine whether they will recognize same-sex marriage contracts or same-sex civil union contracts legalized in other states (see "The Conversation of Democracy").

horizontal federalism
the state-to-state relationships created by the U.S. Constitution

interstate compacts
agreements between states that Congress has the authority to review and reject

extradition
the return of individuals accused of a crime to the state in which the crime was committed upon the request of that state's governor

privileges and immunities clause
the Constitution's requirement that a state extend to other states' citizens the privileges and immunities it provides for its own citizens

full faith and credit clause
the constitutional clause that requires states to comply with and uphold the public acts, records, and judicial decisions of other states

> Protesters from both sides of the same-sex marriage debate lobbied the Massachusetts legislature to enact their opinions into law. Vagueness and ambiguity of language in the U.S. Constitution fuels debate and tensions among citizens, between state governments, and between state governments and the national government as to who has authority to define marriage and what that definition should be.

THE CONVERSATION OF DEMOCRACY

SHOULD SAME-SEX COUPLES HAVE THE RIGHT TO A MARRIAGE CONTRACT AND TO THE BENEFITS THAT OPPOSITE-SEX COUPLES ENJOY?

The Issue: Marriage is a contract—a legal agreement—between two individuals. Each state determines the content of its marriage contract, and courts have traditionally interpreted the Constitution's full faith and credit clause as requiring other states and the national government to recognize each state's marriage contracts. Traditionally, and now legally in all states except Connecticut, Massachusetts, and California, state law (through legislation or the state constitution) makes the marriage contract available only to opposite-sex couples.* State and national laws define the benefits—the legal rights and protections—that are provided to the two individuals who agree to a marriage contract. Such benefits include Social Security, Medicare, family leave, medical decision making for an incapacitated spouse, hospital visitation rights, property distribution rights in divorce, the right to obtain joint insurance policies and joint credit, and the spousal privilege not to be required to testify against a spouse in a court of law.

Should same-sex couples have the same right to a marriage contract, and to the benefits that come with it, that opposite-sex couples have?

Yes: The Fourteenth Amendment guarantees "equal protection of the laws" to all people and the same "privileges and immunities" to all citizens. In the Supreme Court case *Loving v. Virginia* (1967), the justices ruled as unconstitutional a state law that limited the right of a black citizen to marry a white citizen.** According to Chief Justice Earl Warren, who voted with the majority in the *Loving* case, the freedom to marry is a legal right that the Fourteenth Amendment guarantees to all people and that is essential to an individual's pursuit of happiness. The Constitution guarantees all people the same civil rights. But only a marriage contract guarantees the *benefits* of marriage. So for a culture that distributes many legal and societal benefits based on a person's marital status, only a marriage contract can guarantee true equality. The supreme law of the land must not be compromised.

No: Marriage is a social institution regulated by government as well as by religious institutions. Its purpose is to encourage the perpetuation of the human race. To provide legal status to same-sex unions ignores the purpose of marriage and devalues the contribution to the well-being of society made by husbands and wives, who can procreate. There are other means to obtaining some of the benefits that same-sex couples seek. These partners can agree to own property jointly, and they can choose who will make health care decisions when they are incapacitated and who will receive their property after death. The government could even rewrite the laws so that Social Security, Medicare, and insurance benefits are available to same-sex partners. Recognition of same-sex unions through a marriage contract (or civil union contract) threatens the sanctity of marriage and the stability of family life, as well as the stability of society and the human race. Society cannot afford to validate same-sex partnerships.

Other approaches: Although same-sex couples should not be able to marry, if for no other reason than tradition, these couples should have access to the same benefits as married couples. A civil union contract provides the same-sex couple with the legal benefits of marriage and divorce without labeling the relationship a marriage. Further, religious institutions have no obligation to recognize a civil union contract. Only governments need recognize this contract. Yes, this is a compromise, but is not all public policy the product of compromise?

What do you think?

① Is marriage a right equally guaranteed to all people by the Fourteenth Amendment? Is marriage a liberty, protected by the Bill of Rights as a privacy right? Explain.

② If the Constitution does protect same-sex marriage, should the Constitution be amended to deny it? Why or why not?

③ Does the constitutional distribution of sovereignty reserve to the state governments the authority to define marriage, so that states where the majority of citizens support same-sex marriage could legalize it and states without such a majority could ban it?

④ No freedom or right is absolute—the government can limit liberties and rights when it is necessary to achieve a compelling public good. Does banning same-sex marriage achieve a compelling public good? Would such a ban be the only way to achieve this compelling public good? Explain.

*www.lambdalegal.org/nationwide-status-sex-relationships.html.
**Loving v. Virginia, 388 U.S. 1 (1967).

The debates over same-sex marriage and civil unions raise several challenging constitutional questions. Because the Constitution is supreme, answers to these questions will eventually come from the Supreme Court's interpretation of the Constitution. Recently, the Supreme Court ruled that while the Constitution *is* the supreme law, state and local governments can guarantee their citizens more liberties and rights than are found in the Constitution, which guarantees only the required minimum.

The New Judicial Federalism

Political scientists use the phrase **new judicial federalism** to describe the practice whereby state judges base decisions regarding citizens' legal rights and liberties on their state constitutions when these laws guarantee more than the minimum rights or liberties enumerated in the U.S. Constitution. In fact, many state and local governments grant more liberties and rights than the Constitution guarantees, and can do so, according to the Supreme Court.

In *Pruneyard Shopping Center and Fred Sahadi v. Michael Robins et al.* (1980), the Court considered the case of a group of politically active high school students who had set up tables in a mall to hand out informational pamphlets and obtain signatures on a petition.[16] The pamphlets and petition dealt with opposition to the United Nations' stand on Zionism—that is, the existence of the Jewish state of Israel. After the owner of the shopping center asked the students to leave his private property, the students sued him on the basis of their belief that the California state constitution specifically protected their freedom of speech and expression, even in a privately owned shopping center. The Supreme Court agreed with the students that California's constitution gave its citizens more freedom of expression than the U.S. Constitution guaranteed, and judged that greater freedom to be constitutional.

New judicial federalism expands the authority of state governments in an era when the Supreme Court is ever more frequently being asked to clarify the constitutional distribution of authority. As we have seen, the delineation among national powers (enumerated and implied) and the states' reserved powers has never been clear. To complicate matters, over the course of U.S. history, national, state, and local governments' interactions have evolved into collaborative efforts whereby the creation, financing, and implementation of a given public policy are shared by two or more levels of government. We now explore the evolution of intergovernmental relations in the U.S. federal system.

new judicial federalism
the practice whereby state judges base decisions regarding civil rights and liberties on their state's constitution, rather than the U.S. Constitution, when their state's constitution guarantees more than minimum rights

Evolution of the Federal System

Evolution means to change slowly and continuously, often from the simple to the complex. The federal system established by the Constitution has evolved from a simple system of *dual federalism* to a complex system of *conflicted federalism*. The figure in "Exploring the Sources" on page 112 models both the original, simple federal system established in the Constitution and the current system, with its complex arrangement of intergovernmental relations. Specifically, evolution has occurred in the power relationship between the national government and the states. Yes, the United States is still a federal system of government with dual sovereignty. However, the power relationship between the federal and state governments has changed over the years, as we now consider. We first survey four types of federalism, characterized by four different power relationships that have evolved in the U.S. federal system, all of which continue to this day. We then explore various means by which the national government has altered the power relationship between it and the state governments.

Dual Federalism

Initially, the dual sovereignty of the U.S. federal system was implemented in such a way that the national and state governments acted independently of one another, as in Deil Wright's coordinate model (see "Exploring the Sources"). Political scientists give the name **dual federalism** to this pattern of implementation of the federal system, whereby the national government takes care of its enumerated powers and the states independently take care of

dual federalism
the relationship between the national and state governments, dominant between 1789 and 1932, whereby the two levels of government functioned independently of each other to address their distinct constitutional responsibilities

THREE MODELS OF INTERGOVERNMENTAL RELATIONS IN A FEDERAL SYSTEM

The diagram below presents Deil Wright's models of intergovernmental relations in the United States.* The "coordinate" model, indicates that the relationship between the national government and state governments is one of independence. Each government has autonomy over its functions. The "overlapping" model, shows the interdependent relationships among all three levels of government in the United States. Wright argues that the authority pattern in the overlapping model is based on bargaining between the national and state governments. Finally, the "inclusive" model shows dependent relationships with a hierarchical pattern of authority.

*Deil Wright, *Understanding Intergovernmental Relations*, 3rd ed. © 1988 Wadsworth, a part of Cengage Learning, Inc.

Evaluating the Evidence

① Which of Wright's models do you think the Constitution's framers— the creators of the U.S. federal system— had in mind? Justify your selection.

② Which of Wright's models do you think best presents the relationships among the national, state, and local governments today? Explain.

③ Which model displays the relationships and pattern of authority that you believe will best serve you and your family? Justify your selection.

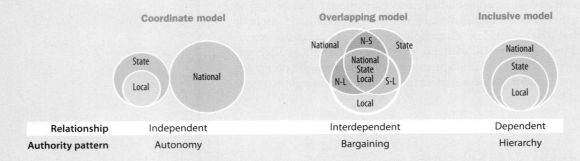

	Coordinate model	Overlapping model	Inclusive model
Relationship	Independent	Interdependent	Dependent
Authority pattern	Autonomy	Bargaining	Hierarchy

their reserved powers. From 1789 through 1932, dual federalism was the dominant pattern of national-state relations. Congresses and presidents did enact some laws that states argued infringed on their powers, and the Courts typically found in favor of the states in these cases. Yet as the 1819 *McCulloch* case shows, sometimes the Court ruled in favor of the national government.

Cooperative Federalism

A crippling economic depression that reached global proportions, known as the Great Depression, began in 1929. To help state governments deal with the domestic problems spawned by the economic collapse, Congress and President Franklin D. Roosevelt (1933–1945) approved numerous policies, collectively called the New Deal, that infringed on states' traditional reserved powers. Through these policies, the independent actions of national and state governments to fulfill their respective responsibilities evolved into cooperative efforts. **Grants-in-aid**—transfers of money from one level of government to another (also known as **intergovernmental transfers**)—became a main mechanism of President Roosevelt's New Deal programs.

grant-in-aid (intergovernmental transfer) transfer of money from one government to another government that does not need to be paid back

The national grants of money offered to the state governments, and eventually also to local governments, during the Great Depression had few specific terms and conditions and did not need to be paid back. State and local governments welcomed the national grants, which assisted them in addressing the domestic matters that fell within their sovereignty while allowing them to make most of the specific program decisions to implement the policy. The era of federalism that began during the Depression, with its growing number of collaborative, intergovernmental efforts to address domestic matters reserved to the states, is the period of **cooperative federalism** (1932–1963), described by Wright's overlapping model.

Centralized Federalism

By the time of Lyndon Johnson's presidency (1963–1969), a new kind of federalism was replacing cooperative federalism. In this new form of federalism, the national government imposed its own policy preferences on state and local governments. Specifically, in **centralized federalism,** directives in national legislation, including grant-in-aid programs with ever-increasing conditions or strings attached to the money, force state and local governments to implement a particular national policy. Wright's inclusive model comes closest to diagramming centralized federalism.

Presidents since Richard Nixon (1969–1974) have fought against this centralizing tendency by proposing to return policy responsibilities (policy making, policy financing, and policy implementation) to state and local governments. Presidents Nixon and Ronald Reagan (1981–1989) gave the name *new federalism* to their efforts to revert such obligations to state and local governments, and today we use the term **devolution** to refer to the return of policy responsibilities to state and local governments.

Republicans and Democrats (including presidents, members of Congress, and state and local lawmakers) broadly support devolution, but they debate *which elements of the policy-making process* should be devolved: policy creation, financing, and/or implementation. They also butt heads over *which policies* to devolve. The legislation and court decisions that result from these debates make for a complicated coexistence of dual federalism, cooperative federalism, and centralized federalism. In the evolution of federalism, we are now experiencing what David B. Walker, a preeminent scholar of federalism and intergovernmental relations, calls **conflicted federalism.**[17]

Conflicted Federalism

Because present-day national-state relations frequently feature conflicting tendencies, the label **conflicted federalism** has been used to describe intergovernmental relations today. Efforts to centralize policy making at the national level are evident, as are efforts to decentralize the implementation of national policies to the state and local levels. For some policy matters, the national and state governments operate independently of each other, and hence dual federalism is at work. For the majority of policies, however, intergovernmental efforts are the norm. These efforts may be voluntary and a means to advance state policy priorities (cooperative federalism), or they may be compelled by national legislation (centralized federalism).

The era of conflicted federalism has seen a jump in the number of legal challenges to national legislation that mandates state and local action. In the various cases that the Supreme Court has heard, the justices have ruled inconsistently, sometimes upholding or even expanding state sovereignty and at other times protecting or expanding national sovereignty. For example, in 1976 the Supreme Court ruled in *National League of Cities v. Usery* that state and local governments were not legally required to comply with the national minimum wage law—hence protecting state authority.[18] Then nine years later, in the *Garcia v. San Antonio Transportation Authority* (1985) case, the Court ruled that national minimum wage laws did apply to state and local government employees—thus expanding national authority.[19]

> With the unemployment rate climbing as high as 25 percent, thousands of Americans relied on soup kitchens and other charities to survive the Great Depression. Through new grant-in-aid programs, the federal government worked with state and local governments to provide urgently needed services.

cooperative federalism
the relationship between the national and state governments whereby the two levels of government work together to address domestic matters reserved to the states, driven by the policy priorities of the states

centralized federalism
the relationship between the national and state governments whereby the national government imposes its policy preferences on state governments

devolution
the process whereby the national government returns policy responsibilities to state and/or local governments

conflicted federalism
the current status of national-state relations that has elements of dual and cooperative federalism, with an overall centralizing tendency at the same time that elements of policy are devolved

Another policy matter that has been subject to conflicting Court decisions is the medical use of marijuana. California has fought an up-and-down battle with the national government over medical uses of marijuana. In 1996, California voters approved the Compassionate Use Act, allowing people to grow, obtain, or smoke marijuana for medical needs, with a doctor's recommendation. Then in 2001, the U.S. Supreme Court ruled that the national government could charge people who distributed marijuana for medical use with a crime, even in California, where the state law allowed such activity.[20] The Court found that national narcotics laws took precedence over California's law, which California had argued was grounded in the reserved police powers of the states. But in 2003, the Court refused to review a case challenging a California law allowing doctors to recommend marijuana use to their patients.[21] As a consequence of the Court's refusal to take on the case, the decision from the lower court prevailed. The lower court's ruling had been that doctors could *not* be charged with a crime for recommending marijuana to patients. To add to the confused legal status of medicinal marijuana in California, the U.S. Supreme Court in 2005 upheld the right of the national government to prosecute people who smoke the drug at the recommendation of their doctors, as well as those who grow it for medical purposes.[22]

In the case of medicinal marijuana, national and state actions and intents have been in clear conflict. Further, U.S. Supreme Court decisions have not yet clarified the confusion over constitutional authority to regulate medicinal marijuana. How did the federal system evolve from dual federalism to the conflicted federalism that is sharply in evidence today?

Landmarks in the Evolution of Federalism: Key Constitutional Amendments

Understanding the U.S. federal system's evolution from dual federalism to conflicted federalism requires a brief review of the tools the national government uses to expand its authority to direct state and local governments' domestic policies. Although the formal language of the Constitution with regard to the distribution of national and state sovereignty remains essentially as it was in 1791 (when the Tenth Amendment was ratified), three amendments—the Fourteenth, Sixteenth, and Seventeenth—have had a tremendous impact on the power relationship between national and state government. The Civil War, which was a catalyst for the ratification of the Fourteenth Amendment, also influenced the national-state power relationship.

THE CIVIL WAR AND THE POSTWAR AMENDMENTS   The military success of the northern states in the Civil War (1861–1865) meant the preservation of the union—the United States of America. The ratification of the Thirteenth Amendment (1865) brought the legal end of slavery in every state. In addition, the Fourteenth Amendment (1868), which extended the rights of citizenship to individuals who were previously enslaved, also placed certain limits and obligations on state governments.

The Fourteenth Amendment authorizes the national government to ensure that the state governments follow fair procedures (due process) before taking away a person's life, liberty, or pursuit of happiness and that the states guarantee all people the same rights (equal protection of the laws) to life, liberties, and the pursuit of happiness, without discrimination. In addition, the amendment guarantees the privileges and immunities of U.S. citizenship to all citizens in all states. Accordingly, since the Fourteenth Amendment's ratification, Congresses and presidents have approved national laws that direct the states to ensure due process and equal protection. This legislation includes, for example, laws mandating that all government buildings, including state and local edifices, provide access to all persons, including individuals with physical disabilities. In addition, the Supreme Court has used the Fourteenth Amendment to justify extending the Bill of Rights' limits on national government to state

Medical Marijuana

Are you for or against the legalization of marijuana for medicinal purposes?

☐ For legalization
☐ Against legalization

Source: "Americans Support Legalization of Marijuana for Medicinal Use," www.gallup.com/poll/2902/Americans-Support-Legalization-Marijuana-Medicinal-Use.aspx.

and local governments (under incorporation theory, which Chapter 4 considers). And in *Bush v. Gore* (2000), the Supreme Court used the amendment's equal protection clause to end a controversial Florida ballot recount in the 2000 presidential election.[23]

In that electoral controversy, Democratic presidential candidate Al Gore first won a lawsuit in Florida State Supreme Court that challenged the official Florida vote count. As a result, ballots not initially counted were to be counted. In turn, Republican presidential candidate George W. Bush challenged the Florida Supreme Court's finding and asked the U.S. Supreme Court to determine the constitutionality of Florida's election law as interpreted by the state's supreme court. In its decision, the U.S. Supreme Court ruled that the Florida recount violated the Constitution's equal protection clause by not ensuring that each vote would be treated equally. The Court's ruling put an end to the recount, and candidate Bush became President Bush. (For more on the 2000 election, see Chapter 9.)

THE SIXTEENTH AMENDMENT   Passage of the Sixteenth Amendment (1913) powerfully enhanced the ability of the national government to raise money. It granted Congress the authority to collect income taxes from workers and corporations without apportioning these taxes among the states on the basis of population (which had been mandated by the Constitution before this amendment).

The national income tax provides the national government with access to tremendous financial resources. The national government uses these resources as leverage over state and local governments, encouraging or coercing them to pursue and implement policies that the national government thinks best. Specifically, by offering state and local governments grants-in-aid, national officials have gained the power to determine many of the policies these governments approve, finance, and implement. For example, by offering grants to the states for highways, the federal government encouraged each state to establish a legal drinking age of 21 years.

> A Broward County, Florida, election official attempts to determine whether there is a countable vote on this ballot during the 2000 presidential election. The Florida Supreme Court called for a recount of ballots in several counties, but the U.S. Supreme Court stopped the Florida recount, finding that the subjectivity of election officials determining which votes were countable violated the Constitution's equal protection clause.

THE SEVENTEENTH AMENDMENT   Before ratification of the Seventeenth Amendment in 1913, the Constitution called for *state legislators* to select U.S. senators. By this arrangement, the framers strove to ensure that Congress and the president would take the concerns of state governments into account in national policy making. Essentially, the original arrangement provided the state legislatures with lobbyists in the national policy-making process who would be accountable to the states. Once ratified, the Seventeenth Amendment shifted the election of U.S. senators to a system of popular vote by the citizens in a state.

With this change, senators were no longer directly accountable to the state legislatures because the latter no longer selected the senators. Consequently, state governments lost their direct access to national policy makers. Some scholars of federalism and intergovernmental relations argue that this loss has decreased the influence of state governments in national policy making.[24]

Further Evolutionary Landmarks: Grants-in-Aid

In 1837 the national government shared its revenue surplus with the states in the form of a monetary grant. But the government did not make a habit of such financial grants-in-aid until the Great Depression of the 1930s. Today, there is growing controversy over the strings attached to the various kinds of grants issued by the federal government.

CATEGORICAL GRANTS   Historically, the most common type of grant-in-aid has been the **categorical formula grant**—a grant of money for a narrow purpose, as defined by the national government. The legislation that creates such a grant includes a formula determining how much money is available to each grant recipient. The formula is typically based on factors related to the purpose of the grant, as well as political considerations (which assist in gaining the majority vote required to approve the legislation). Categorical grants come with strings—that is, rules and regulations with which the recipient government must comply.

categorical formula grant
money granted by the national government to state and local governments for a specified program area and in an amount based on a legislated formula

Federal Homeland Security Grants to State and Local Governments

	THEN		NOW
	2001 (MILLIONS)	2004 (MILLIONS)	2007 (MILLIONS)
Total outlays for home- land security grants to state and local governments	$3,010*	$5,490**	$9,514**

*U.S. Census Bureau, *Statistical Abstract of the United States 2004–2005*, Table 424.
**U.S. Census Bureau, *Statistical Abstract of the United States 2008*, Table 419.

WHAT'S NEXT?

> Why is 2001 an important year with regard to homeland security grants? Why have these grants increased since that year?

> Do you think that with the election of a new president to succeed George W. Bush, there will be a noticeable change in the level of home- land security grant money provided to state and local governments? Why or why not?

categorical project grant
money granted by the national govern- ment to state and local governments for a specified program area for which recipients compete by proposing spe- cific projects they want to implement

block grant
money granted by the national gov- ernment to states or localities for broadly defined policy areas, with fewer strings than categorical grants, and in amounts based on complicated formulas

One typical condition is a matching funds requirement, which obligates the grant recipi- ent to spend some of its own money to match a specified percentage of the grant money pro- vided. Matching funds requirements allow the national government to influence the bud- get decisions of state and local governments by forcing them to spend some of their own money on a national priority, which may also be a state priority, in order to receive national funding.

Medicaid, the health insurance program for qualified low-income U.S. citizens, is an example of a categorical formula grant with a matching funds requirement. Created in 1965, this national grant-in-aid program gives participating states national funds to help pay the health insurance costs of citizens entitled to Medicaid. Although states voluntarily par- ticipate in this grant program, some states, in light of the increased cost of medical care, are finding it difficult to meet the matching funds requirement. In fact, many states are now spending almost as much on Medicaid as they spend on education, which had been the most expensive state budget item for decades.

Since the 1960s, the national government has also offered categorical project grants. Like the categorical formula grant, a **categor- ical project grant** covers a narrow purpose (program area), but unlike the formula grant, a project grant does not include a formula specifying how much money a recipient will receive. Instead, those interested in receiving such a grant must compete for it by writing a proposal detailing what program they wish to implement and what level of funding they need. A categorical project grant has strings attached to it and typically offers much less funding than a categorical formula grant.

BLOCK GRANTS Another type of formula-based intergovernmental transfer of money, the **block grant,** differs from categorical formula and categorical project grants in that the use of the grant money is less narrowly defined by the national government. While a cat- egorical grant might specify that the money is to be used for a child care program, a block grant gives the recipient government more discretion to determine what program it will be used for within a broad policy area such as assistance to economically needy families with children. When first introduced by the Nixon administration in the 1970s, the block grant also had fewer strings attached to it than the categorical grants. Today, however, the num- ber and specificity of conditions included in block grants are increasing.

State and local governments have grown dependent on national financial assistance, and so grants are an essential tool of national power to direct state and local government activ- ity. Although the states welcome federal grant money, they do not welcome the strings at- tached to the funds.

STATE ATTEMPTS TO INFLUENCE GRANT-IN-AID CONDITIONS State government opposition to the strings attached to national grants came to a head in 1923 in the case of *Massachusetts v. Mellon*.[25] In this case the Supreme Court found the conditions of national grants-in-aid to be constitutional, arguing that grants-in-aid are voluntary cooperative arrangements. By voluntarily accepting the national grant, the justices ruled, the state government agrees to the grant conditions. This 1923 Court decision was essential to the proliferation of national grants in subsequent years and to the evolution of federalism and intergovernmental relations as well. But the Court's decision did not end states' challenges to grant conditions.

In 1987, South Dakota challenged a 1984 national transportation law that penalized states whose legal drinking age was lower than 21 years. The intent of the national law was to decrease "drinking while intoxicated" (DWI) car accidents. States with legal drinking ages lower than 21 years would lose 5 percent of their national grant money for transportation. South Dakota argued that Congress was using grant conditions to put a law into effect that Congress could not achieve through national legislation because the law dealt with a power reserved to the states—determining the legal age for drinking alcoholic beverages.

In its decision in *South Dakota v. Dole,* the Court found that the national government could not impose a national drinking age because setting a drinking age is indeed a reserved power of the states.[26] Yet, the Court ruled, the national government could *encourage* states to set a drinking age of 21 years by threatening to decrease their grants-in-aid for highway construction. In other words, conditions attached to voluntarily accepted grants-in-aid are constitutional. Ultimately, the national policy goal of a 21-year-old drinking age was indeed accomplished by 1988—not through a national law but through a condition attached to national highway funds offered to state governments, funds on which the states are dependent.

Over time, the number and specificity of the grant conditions have grown. State and local governments have increasingly lobbied national lawmakers during the policy-making processes that create and reauthorize grants. One goal of this **intergovernmental lobbying** is to limit the grant conditions—or at least to influence them to the states' advantage. In other words, lobbyists for an individual state work to ensure that the conditions, including the grants' formulas, benefit that state. Beyond the efforts of lobbyists hired by individual states, coordinated lobbying on behalf of *multiple* states, municipal governments, and county governments is common. The National Governors Association is just one group involved in intergovernmental lobbying. See "On the Job" for insight into the work of the National Governors Association.

If a state does not want to comply with a grant condition, then it need not accept the grant. The problem for state and local governments is that they have come to rely on national grant funds. Today, approximately 31 percent of state and local general revenue comes from national grants.[27] Yet the national government has no constitutional obligation to offer grants-in-aid to state or local governments. Therefore, intergovernmental lobbies persistently lobby Congress to ensure not only favorable grant formulas but also the survival of grants-in-aid on which state and local governments depend. They also lobby to prevent the passage of national laws mandating specific state and local actions.

> The Constitution reserves to the states the authority to establish the legal drinking age. However, the national government's grant-in-aid for highways requires states to set 21 years as the age when people can legally purchase alcohol, or the states risk losing a percentage of their highway grant dollars. Today, all states have established 21 years as the legal drinking age.

intergovernmental lobbying
efforts by groups representing state and local governments to influence national public policy

Federalism's Continuing Evolution: Mandates

In our earlier analysis of the constitutional distribution of sovereignty, we considered specific examples of the Court's expansion of national authority through its decisions in cases involving conflicts over constitutional interpretation. The constitutional clauses most often questioned are

- the necessary and proper clause (Article I, Section 9);
- the national supremacy clause (Article VI);
- the general welfare clause (Article I, Section 8);
- the regulation of interstate commerce clause (Article I, Section 8).

With these Court decisions in hand, the national government is able to *mandate* certain state and local government actions. In addition, through a process known as *preemption,* the federal government can take away states' and localities' policy authority and impose its policy choices on state and local governments.

ON THE JOB

JODI OMEAR, SENIOR PRESS SECRETARY

Name: Jodi Omear

Age: 31

Hometown: Moundsville, West Virginia

Colleges: West Liberty State College; George Washington University

Majors: Journalism and English (BS); Political Management (MA)

Job title: Senior Press Secretary for the National Governors Association (NGA)

Salary range for jobs like this: $60,000–$90,000

Day-to-day responsibilities: My job priorities include working on NGA's lobbying efforts; responding to press inquiries regarding NGA's policy positions; creating communications plans and strategies for the Office of Federal Relations and the association's annual meetings; and serving as liaison to governors' press secretaries across the country.

How did you get your job? I was the press secretary for former West Virginia governor Bob Wise, and we worked closely with the National Governors Association. I worked directly with the Office of Communications there and was offered the job when an opening became available.

What do you like best about your job? I enjoy working on a variety of lobbying efforts, which will affect the daily lives of citizens all over the country. I also enjoy working with governors' press secretaries across the country.

What is your least favorite aspect of your job? It's not so much something I like least about my job, but I would say recognizing that things won't always turn out the way I want or expect is the least favorite part of any job. It is difficult to accept that sometimes the idea is good but the practicality is not. Sometimes it's how you handle Plan B that's important.

What advice would you give to students who would like to do what you are doing? I would advise students to find something they really enjoy and devote themselves to it. If you don't like what you are doing, you inevitably won't do it well and you won't be happy. I would say study a lot and learn as much about your craft as possible. Perhaps, most importantly, take the time to learn from others. Recognize at the beginning of your career that there are others with more experience and more knowledge than you. Take a moment to learn from them and earn your stripes; your time will come.

---

mandates
clauses in legislation that direct state and local governments to comply with national legislation and national standards

National **mandates** are clauses in national laws that direct state and local governments to do something specified by the national government. Most mandates relate to ensuring citizens' civil rights and civil liberties, as in the case of the mandate in the Rehabilitation Act of 1973 requiring that all government buildings, including those of state and local authorities, must be accessible to persons with disabilities. When the national government assumes the entire cost of a mandate, it is a *funded mandate*. When the state or local government must cover all or some of the cost, it is an *unfunded mandate*.

Also common is the federal government's use of preemption and partial preemption.
Preemption means that a national policy supersedes a state or local policy because it deals with an enumerated or implied national power. Therefore, people must obey, and states must enforce, the national law even if the state or local government has its own law on the matter. **Partial preemption** gives the states the authority to set and implement their own standards, but if a state's standards are less protective than the national standards, the state must implement the national standards. For example, as noted earlier, several states in the Northeast signed an interstate compact establishing power plant emission standards that were higher

preemption
constitutionally based principle that allows a national law to supersede state or local laws

than national standards. But if states have no standards, the law directs them to apply the national standards. If the states do not implement standards that meet or exceed the national standards, the national government can step in and enforce its standards in the state.

The Supreme Court typically has supported the federal government's arguments that the national supremacy clause and the necessary and proper clause—coupled with the powers delegated to the national government to provide for the general welfare and to regulate interstate commerce—give the federal government the authority to force state and local governments to implement its mandates. The Court has also supported the national government's argument that it can attach conditions to the grants-in-aid it offers state and local governments, hence forcing those that voluntarily accept national grants to implement policies established by national lawmakers.

partial preemption
the authority of the national government to establish minimum regulatory standards that provide state and local governments the flexibility either to enforce the national standards or to establish their own more stringent standards, which they must enforce

Today's Federalism: The Good, the Bad, and the Inevitable

With more than 89,000 individual governments operating in the United States today, citizens have numerous opportunities to engage with government to ensure that it serves them. There are millions of government jobs for citizens who want to be in the front line of making or implementing public policy. There are multiple channels for citizens' requests for assistance, lobbying efforts, and complaints. Moreover, as the ongoing public conversation on immigration policy shows (see "Doing Democracy"), if one level of government does not respond, there are numerous other governments to approach. Ultimately, the courts may be called in to determine which government has the authority and responsibility to respond to citizens' specific requests.

The federal system also encourages public policy experimentation. A state or local government can act as a policy laboratory, and then other governments—state, local, and/or national—can choose to adopt a successful policy, without the expense of conducting their own experiments. For example, the 1990s witnessed numerous states' experimentation with public assistance programs for low-income families with children. A national welfare reform law passed in 1996, the Personal Responsibility and Work Opportunity Reconciliation Act, adopted some of the most successful of these state-level experiments. Today state, county, and city governments across the nation continue to experiment with innovative policies targeting such objectives as protecting the environment, preventing illegal immigration, and making health insurance affordable and available to all.

The United States' multiple governments increasingly offer redundant and overlapping protection of civil rights and civil liberties. (Chapters 4 and 5 explore these rights and liberties, including past and current initiatives to expand civil rights to groups historically denied equal protections.) Moreover, the involvement of multiple levels of government can also yield a widely varying quality and quantity of services for the people. Because state constitutions require balanced state budgets, in any policy area for which state governments are sovereign, there is the potential for a "race to the bottom," in which the winner is the state that regulates and taxes businesses the least (thus achieving a low unemployment rate) and provides fewer and less responsive services to the poor (thus discouraging poor outsiders from entering the state). Differing financial capacities and political ideologies from state to state lead to policy variation across the states. A given state or local policy might fulfill citizens' needs and expectations, but it might also support unacceptable inequalities.

The *Kelo* decision, which devolved to the states the authority to define public use in eminent domain cases, may lead to state-to-state variations over whose private property is and is not protected from government condemnation. Rep. Maxine Waters (D-California), one of the leading House critics of *Kelo*, called the decision "one of the most un-American things that one can imagine." This is so, Waters explains, because the "blighted" properties developed through eminent domain are statistically more likely to include minority-owned private properties than properties owned by others. The National Association for the Advancement of Colored People (NAACP) predicted that the taking of private property for economic

ENGAGE WITH GOVERNMENT OFFICIALS ON IMMIGRATION POLICY

FACT:

"There's going to be a barrage of local laws dealing with immigration policy," warned U.S. senator Lindsey Graham (R-South Carolina) after the 2007 Senate immigration reform bill stalled in the Senate. Indeed, frustrated with congressional inaction on immigration policy reform, citizens across the country have turned to their state and local governments for action. Whatever the objective (whether the goal is attempting to decrease illegal immigration by fining property owners who rent to illegal immigrants or trying to assist illegal immigrants in assimilating by creating safe havens for them), citizens successfully lobbied state legislators in all fifty states to propose immigrant-related legislation in 2007 and 2008. In addition to the thousands of state proposals, hundreds of county, city, township, and borough governments throughout the country have also proposed various immigration-related laws—again, some aimed at decreasing illegal immigration and others aimed at supporting illegal immigrants.

But some citizens and government officials are questioning the constitutionality of these state and local actions. Outspoken county commissioner Tony Peraica (R-Cook County, Illinois), for example, stresses that "the Constitution clearly states under Article IV that immigration laws are solely reserved for [the] U.S. Congress to determine."* Even in the face of such challenges, citizens are forcing state and local governments to act.

> After the national government failed to enact new immigration laws in 2007, state and local governments proposed and debated thousands of pieces of legislation that would affect unauthorized immigrants.

ACT!

There are multiple arenas for civic activism on immigration issues. Citizens are attending local government meetings and calling for action. They are lobbying their state legislatures by e-mail and phone and in face-to-face visits. Letters to the editor variously support and oppose action on the part of government officials. In addition, individual citizens and interest groups are suing state and local governments over the constitutionality of their immigration laws. You can engage any of your multiple governments in these—as well as many other—ways.

Where to begin

Before you can make your voice heard in the civic conversation about immigration policy, you need to identify your multiple

governments and the appropriate officials in each government and find out how best to contact them.

■ Numerous Web sites can assist you in identifying your local, state, and national officials. A point of entry for a comprehensive Web search is **www.firstgov.gov,** the national government's one-stop Web site for government information.

■ Your local phone book is a great starting point for the development of a directory of your government officials. Phone books typically include a section on government officials—local, state, and national.

*Esther J. Cepeda, "County Joining City as Immigrant Haven?" *The Chicago Sun-Times,* June 19, 2007.

development, as allowed by *Kelo,* would "disproportionately affect and harm the economically disadvantaged and, in particular, racial and ethnic minorities and the elderly."[28]

Citizens may like overlap and redundancy when these characteristics protect their liberties and rights. But like quickly turns to dislike if the result is higher taxes and an inefficient use of tax dollars as more than one level of government spends money to address the same problems. Overlap and redundancy in the provision of homeland security may be a good thing if it means that numerous levels of public officials are ensuring domestic tranquility. Yet an overlap of responsibilities requires careful coordination and communication to ensure a sharing of information and resources so that the public is served effectively and efficiently. As the experience of Hurricane Katrina has shown, coordination and communication problems are endemic to dual sovereignty implemented through intergovernmental efforts during crises.

Today's vexing societal problems demand the expertise and resources of multiple governments. From addressing environmental problems, to providing medical care, to preparing for and dealing with disasters of natural and human origin, intergovernmental relations are essential to the provision of government service in the United States today. Yet conflicts over which government is ultimately in charge—has sovereignty—pervade public policy making and fill the docket of the Supreme Court.

CONCLUSION *CONTINUING THE CONVERSATION*

The *dual sovereignty* established by the creators of the U.S. federal system remains in effect today. Yet *dual federalism* no longer dominates relations between the national government and the states. *Conflicted federalism* best describes the variety of intergovernmental relations (IGR) that prevails in the U.S. federal system today.

Throughout the nation's history, state and local governments have challenged national encroachments on matters they deemed reserved to the states. On an annual basis, these governments, as well as individual citizens, continue to bring lawsuits to the courts, questioning the constitutionality of national laws. Although the general pattern of Supreme Court decisions over the Constitution's 220-plus-year history has been in favor of expanding national power in domestic policy areas, the Court's decisions since the 1970s have been mixed, with national legislation being upheld in some cases and states' sovereignty being upheld in others.

The federal system of government has evolved into a system of conflicted federalism featuring complex intergovernmental relations. The recognition of the interconnectedness across the states of so many societal problems is the reason for this complicated arrangement. Even with technological advances, coordination and communication problems pose huge barriers for effective and efficient intergovernmental relations. Yet the continuation of IGR seems inevitable as the 89,000-plus governments in the United States attempt to fulfill the mission of the Constitution in the context of the present-day realities of worldwide interdependence.

Will globalization lead to a new phase in the evolution of the U.S. federal system of government? Will problems associated with global interdependence require the shift of more federal dollars toward international issues and away from domestic problems? If so, will the states increase their experimentation in shaping innovative policies that successfully address the needs of a growing, changing population?

Summary

1. An Overview of the U.S. Federal System
Dual sovereignty is the defining characteristic of the United States' federal system of government. Under a federal system, the national government is sovereign over specific matters, and state governments are sovereign over different matters. Today it is often difficult to differentiate between national sovereignty and state sovereignty.

2. Constitutional Distribution of Authority
The vagueness of the U.S. Constitution's language providing for enumerated and implied national powers, reserved state powers, concurrent powers, and national supremacy has provoked ongoing conflict between the federal government and the states over the proper distribution of sovereignty. The U.S. Supreme Court has the final word on the interpretation of the Constitution—and hence the final say on national and state sovereignty.

3. Evolution of the Federal System
The Supreme Court's interpretations of the Constitution's distribution of authority have reinforced the ability of national officials to compel state and local governments to implement national policy preferences. Mandates and preemption, as well as conditions placed on voluntarily accepted national grants-in-aid, require states to assist in financing and implementing national policies. As a result, relations between the national government and the states have evolved from a simple arrangement of dual federalism to a complex system of intergovernmental relations (IGR).

4. Today's Federalism: The Good, the Bad, and the Inevitable
For citizens, federalism provides many benefits but creates some burdens and confusion. Yet given the complexity of today's societal problems, problems that cut across state lines and nations' borders, the IGR that is a characteristic of today's federal system is essential to efficient and effective government.

Key Terms

block grant 115
categorical formula grant 115
categorical project grant 116
centralized federalism 113
concurrent powers 103
confederal system 98
conflicted federalism 113
cooperative federalism 113
devolution 113
dual federalism 111
dual sovereignty 97
eminent domain 103
enumerated powers 103
extradition 109

federal system 97
full faith and credit
  clause 109
grants-in-aid
  (intergovernmental
  transfers) 112
horizontal federalism 109
implied powers 103
intergovernmental
  lobbying 117
intergovernmental relations
  (IGR) 99
interstate compacts 109
mandates 118

McCulloch v. Maryland 106
necessary and proper clause
  (elastic clause) 103
new judicial federalism 111
partial preemption 119
preemption 118
police powers 105
privileges and immunities
  clause 109
reserved powers 105
sovereignty 97
supremacy clause 105
supreme law of the land 105
unitary system 97

For Review

1. In terms of which government is sovereign, differentiate among a unitary system, a confederal system, and a federal system of government.

2. To which level of government does the Constitution distribute the enumerated powers? Implied powers? Concurrent authorities? Reserved powers? Provide several examples of each power and authority.

3. What matters fall within the scope of state sovereignty?

4. Differentiate among dual federalism, cooperative federalism, centralized federalism, and conflicted federalism.

5. How does the national government use grants-in-aid, mandates, and preemption to direct the policy of state and local governments?

6. What do we mean by intergovernmental relations (IGR)? Why is the term a good description of U.S. federalism?

For Critical Thinking and Discussion

1. Is the federal system of government that provides citizens with the opportunity to elect a large number of officials each year a benefit or a burden for citizens? Explain your answer.

2. Would the amount of money citizens pay for their governments through taxes and fees decrease if there were fewer levels of governments serving them? Defend your answer.

3. Would the quality or quantity of government services decrease if there were fewer levels of government in the United States? Why or why not?

4. Note at least three societal problems you believe the national government can address best (more effectively and efficiently than state or local governments). Discuss why you believe the national government is best suited to address these problems. Do these problems fit in the category of delegated national powers? Explain your answer.

5. Note at least three societal problems you believe state or local governments can address best (more effectively and efficiently than the national government). Discuss why you believe state or local governments are best suited to address these problems. Do these problems fit in the category of powers reserved to the states? Explain your answer.

MULTIPLE CHOICE: Choose the lettered item that answers the question correctly.

1. The characteristic that distinguishes a federal system of government from both a unitary and a confederal system is
   a. dual sovereignty.
   b. the existence of three levels of government.
   c. sovereignty held by only the central government.
   d. sovereignty held by only the regional governments.

2. The authorities to make policy, raise money, establish courts, and implement policy that are inherent to all governments are examples of
   a. concurrent powers.
   b. enumerated powers.
   c. implied powers.
   d. reserved powers.

3. The necessary and proper clause of the Constitution establishes the
   a. enumerated powers of the national government.
   b. implied powers of the national government.
   c. implied powers of the state governments.
   d. reserved powers of the state governments.

4. The authority to coin and regulate money, to regulate interstate and foreign commerce, and to make treaties with foreign nations (including Native American nations) are examples of
   a. concurrent powers.
   b. enumerated powers.
   c. implied powers.
   d. reserved powers.

5. The Supreme Court used implied powers to confirm the national government's authority to establish a national bank, and applied the national supremacy clause to deny state authority to tax branches of the national bank, in the case of
   a. *Gibbons v. Ogden.*
   b. *Kelo v. New London.*
   c. *Marbury v. Madison.*
   d. *McCulloch v. Maryland.*

6. The state-to-state obligations detailed in the Constitution create state-to-state relationships known as
   a. centralized federalism.
   b. cooperative federalism.
   c. dual federalism.
   d. horizontal federalism.

7. The current debate over states' recognizing same-sex marriage contracts from other states may eventually force the Supreme Court to interpret the Article IV clause that concerns
   a. extradition.
   b. full faith and credit.
   c. interstate compacts.
   d. privileges and immunities.

8. The powers that the Tenth Amendment to the Constitution establishes are the
   a. enumerated powers.
   b. concurrent powers.
   c. implied powers.
   d. reserved powers.

9. Political scientists label today's federalism as
   a. centralized federalism.
   b. conflicted federalism.
   c. dual federalism.
   d. horizontal federalism.

10. _____ provide(s) state governments with the most discretion over their policy actions (including policy formulation, policy financing, and policy implementation).
    a. National block grants
    b. National categorical grants
    c. National mandates
    d. National preemption

FILL IN THE BLANKS.

11. _____ is the name political scientists give to the collaborative efforts of two or more levels of government working to serve the public.

12. All national, state, and local laws must comply with the Constitution of the United States, for the Constitution is the _____ .

13. In the case of *Kelo v. New London,* the U.S. Supreme Court was asked to clarify constitutional language regarding the power of _____—specifically, to clarify for what purposes local governments can take private property when the property owner does not want to sell it.

14. The national government has used the _____ clause of the Constitution, also known as the elastic clause, to stretch its enumerated powers.

15. Beginning in the 1970s, state governments and presidents began to respond to centralized federalism by calling for _____, which is the return of policy creation, financing, and/or implementation to the state governments.

Answers: 1. a; 2. a; 3. b; 4. b; 5. d; 6. d; 7. b; 8. d; 9. b; 10. a; 11. Intergovernmental relations; 12. supreme law of the land; 13. eminent domain; 14. necessary and proper; 15. devolution.

RESOURCES FOR RESEARCH AND ACTION

Internet Resources

American Democracy Now Web site
www.mhhe.com/harrison1e   Consult the text's Web site for study guides, interactive activities, simulations, and current hotlinks for additional information on federalism in the United States.

Bureau of the Census
www.census.gov   Access the *Statistical Abstract of the United States* as well as other sources of data about national and state governments at this site.

Council of State Governments
www.csg.org   This site is a place where state officials can share information on common problems and possible solutions.

National Conference of State Legislatures
www.ncsl.org/statefed/statefed.htm   This site is dedicated to state-federal issues and relationships.

National Governors Association (NGA)
www.nga.org   The NGA lobbies the national government on behalf of governors and also provides the governors with opportunities to share information on policies.

Recommended Readings

O'Toole, Laurence J. *American Intergovernmental Relations: Foundations, Perspectives, and Issues,* 3rd ed. Washington, DC: CQ Press, 2000. A collection of readings giving a comprehensive overview of U.S. federalism and intergovernmental relations, covering historical, theoretical, and political perspectives as well as fiscal and administrative views.

Rehnquist, William H. *The Supreme Court: Revised and Updated.* New York: Vintage Books, 2001. A history of the Supreme Court by the deceased chief justice, probing the inner workings of the Court, key Court decisions in the evolution of federalism, and insights into the debates among the justices.

Walker, David B. *The Rebirth of Federalism: Slouching Toward Washington,* 2nd ed. Washington, DC: CQ Press, 2000. Both a history of U.S. federalism and an assessment of the status of U.S. federalism today.

Zimmerman, Joseph F. "The Nature and Political Significance of Preemption." *PS: Political Science and Politics,* 37, no. 3 (2005): 359–62. An overview of federalism that includes a concise explanation of preemption.

Movies of Interest

When the Levees Broke: A Requiem in Four Acts (2006)
This Spike Lee documentary critically examines the responses of federal, state, and local governments to Hurricane Katrina. Through images of the disaster, interviews with Katrina's victims, and clips of government officials' media interviews, Lee focuses on racial issues and intergovernmental ineptitude—from the poor construction of the levees to the delayed and inadequate federal, state, and local response.

Hoxie: The First Stand (2003)
This documentary presents one of the first integration battles in the South post–*Brown v. Board of Education of Topeka, Kansas.* The opponents are the Hoxie Board of Education, which in the summer of 1955 decided to integrate its schools, and grassroots citizens' organizations that resisted integration through petitions, harassment, and threats of violence against the school board members, their families, and the school superintendent.

Dances with Wolves (1990)
Sent to command the U.S. Army's westernmost outpost in the 1860s, Lieutenant John Dunbar witnesses, as an observer and a participant, the conflicts created in the Dakota Territory as white settlers encroach on territory of the Sioux Indians. Movie critics and historians praised Kevin Costner (the movie's director and lead actor) for correcting the erroneous image of Native Americans presented in classic Hollywood Westerns.

National Journal

IDENTITY PROBLEMS

Sen. Lamar Alexander argues that in the post-9/11 world the United States needs a national identification card to help prevent terrorist attacks. But the Tennessee Republican vehemently opposes Real ID, the leading federal program to create fraud-resistant identification cards for tens of millions of Americans.

Alexander is co-sponsoring legislation to repeal key sections of the Real ID Act of 2005, which requires states to follow federal standards in verifying someone's identity before issuing a driver's license. The senator complained to National Journal that the law turns motor vehicle department workers "into little CIA agents" and burdens states with expensive new unfunded mandates. "If the federal government thinks this is such a good idea, the federal government ought to pay for it," he said.

In theory, at least, beefing up identification requirements for travel, work, and voting is quite popular. In the most recent national poll on the subject, Gallup found in 2005 that two-thirds of Americans support the creation of a national ID card. Many countries already require them. Advocates in the U.S. tout such cards as a way to fight terrorism and more-conventional crime, reduce illegal immigration, prevent election fraud, and curb identity theft.

In practice, however, efforts to outfit virtually all Americans with more-reliable identification have been fraught with headaches and controversy. And Alexander is far from alone in crying foul.

For example, the Real ID Act has spawned a mini-rebellion at the state level. Ten states have enacted statutes declaring that they will not comply with the federal law.

Invariably, the struggle over IDs bumps up against big, even philosophical, questions: How can identity be proved? Can the government ever really be sure that individuals are who they say they are? If so, at what cost—in terms of lost freedom and privacy, not just dollars and cents?

As Sen. George Voinovich, R-Ohio, noted dryly at a congressional hearing earlier this year, improving American ID security is "easier said than done." It's not a new undertaking. Attempts to expand the federal use of Social Security numbers, a system created in 1935 to make it easier to track and distribute federal retirement benefits, have sometimes failed. President Carter opposed the idea of turning Social Security cards into national identification cards; President Reagan opposed the creation of any form of national ID. But in 2001, the September 11 terrorist attacks heightened the intensity of the national ID debate. All but one of the hijackers had carried some form of ID issued by a government agency in this country, such as a Virginia driver's license. Some of the IDs were fraudulently obtained. The 9/11 commission recommended in 2004 that Congress tighten the security of driver's licenses.

Yet even as ID requirements proliferate, the backlash against them has grown. Some experts argue that there are better, more-direct ways to improve security. Others contend that the only way to create truly fraud-proof IDs is to collect DNA or biometrics from all Americans at birth—a Big Brother scenario that smacks of a surveillance society.

Whatever the ideal model in the long run, America's ID policy is at a crossroads. Americans may eventually embrace a national ID card, as Britons have done recently. Or, U.S. citizens may find themselves carrying multiple smart cards with different uses, as privacy experts prefer. In the meantime, ID wars are breaking out on many fronts.

When officials at the Indiana Bureau of Motor Vehicles set out to check the records of the state's 6.4 million licensed drivers last July, the effort began smoothly. The bureau had just upgraded its computer system and could now verify the Social Security numbers of drivers online, as the Real ID Act would soon require.

The records matched for 97 percent of drivers. In most of the other cases, a simple error—such as a typo or the person's failure to alert the Social Security Administration about a name change—caused a mismatch that was easily corrected. But that still left 34,000 Indiana drivers with records that didn't match. The bureau warned them that their licenses would be revoked if they didn't fix the problem within 30 days. When South Bend lawyer Lyn Leone received a notice, she promptly contacted the American Civil Liberties Union. Leone's Social Security card reads "Mary Lyn Leone." But Leone has been known as Lyn all her life, she says, and she maintains that she has a legal right to go by that name on her driver's license.

"They are basically trying to erase my identity," said Leone, 60, now a plaintiff in an ACLU lawsuit challenging the Indiana Bureau of Motor Vehicles. The licenses of thousands of Indiana drivers could be revoked for similar reasons, said Kenneth Falk, legal director of the Indiana ACLU. "If you are named 'William' but you've always used 'Bill,' and your license is in 'Bill,' you will be terminated."

Although few observers disagree with the basic premise of Real ID—before issuing a driver's license, states should obtain the applicant's identifying documents, such as a birth certificate and proof of legal residency, and verify their authenticity—Indiana's experience spotlights the things that can go wrong when a requirement becomes law with no public debate or hearings. Congress initially set out to bring state officials, privacy experts, and other stakeholders together in what's known as a negotiated rule-making. But in 2005, Real ID Act proponents in the House abruptly attached it to a must-pass appropriations bill funding the Iraq war and tsunami relief.

The Homeland Security Department fielded about 21,000 public comments on Real ID before issuing final regulations in January. By then, state governments were in such an uproar that DHS pushed back its deadline for taking the first steps toward full compliance—from May 11, 2008, to December 31, 2009. The final deadlines for states that pass certain benchmarks will be 2014 for drivers under 50 and 2017 for older ones. The extension averted what would have been a public-relations disaster, because anyone from a state not issuing Real IDs would have been barred from boarding a plane or entering a federal building.

Both the National Governors Association and the National Conference of State Legislatures have decried Real ID as a massive, unfunded mandate. The law is expected to cost at least $4 billion to implement, according to DHS, but less than $200 million in federal money has been set aside for the changeover. States may use their federal homeland-security money for Real ID, but many governors object.

"It makes our state less homeland-secure," said South Carolina Gov. Mark Sanford, "because while we don't know if we're going to get struck by a terrorist, what we do unquestionably know is that we are going to get struck by another hurricane." In an April 3 letter to members of Congress, the Republican governor called Real ID "the worst piece of legislation I have seen during the 15 years I have been engaged in the political process."

Sen. Daniel Akaka, D-Hawaii, has introduced legislation to repeal Real ID and return to the drawing board by having the negotiations on the issue that were skipped three years ago. Akaka and other critics of Real ID warn that it would create an extraordinary target for hackers and ID thieves: a huge new database loaded with personal information. That's because the states would be forced to link their databases in order to enforce the law's ban on drivers holding licenses from more than one state.

"We believe that this, if ever implemented, is the coming national ID card system," said Tim Sparapani, senior legislative counsel at the ACLU. Bush administration officials strongly disagree. "The notion that

Ten states have enacted statutes declaring that they will not comply with the federal law.

there's going to be a national database is just wrong," said Stewart Baker, assistant secretary for policy at DHS. Only "a very narrow" number of state employees will be able to check the databases, and those databases have proven fairly resistant to tampering, he said. Because of the threats posed by terrorism and identity theft, Baker continued, "there's an enthusiasm for good ID that, I think, is going to continue to grow."

Of course, his department's current deadline for final implementation isn't until December 1, 2017, more than 16 years after the 9/11 attacks.

Some experts are convinced that a national, biometric ID card is the answer to the simmering "identity" crisis. "Right now, we are proceeding in hundreds of different ways, for dozens of different IDs, at tremendous expense," said Robert Pastor, co-director of the Center for Democracy and Election Management at American University. It makes more sense to "do it right, once," he maintains.

Pastor's AU colleague Curtis Gans, who heads the university's Center for the Study of the American Electorate, wants to establish a high-level, bipartisan commission to examine the issue of a mandatory biometric government ID. At least theoretically, Americans are receptive, polling shows. Gans is a vigorous advocate: "If we set up this national

biometric ID, we could get rid of identity theft; we could deal with immigration better than the feds; we could provide for success in criminal prosecution and exoneration; we might constructively use it for medical records; we could eliminate the need for physical enumeration in the census. The uses are many and manifold, including the voting process."

But a growing number of scientists and privacy experts insist that requiring a single ID for multiple purposes would actually make Americans less safe. Skeptics liken a national ID to using a skeleton key for one's office, home, and safe deposit box: Lose it—or have it stolen—and you're vulnerable everywhere. The better model, they argue, is using multiple IDs for discrete uses, just as most people carry several keys.

"Uniformity in IDs across the country would create economies of scale" for prying eyes, warns Jim Harper, director of information policy studies at the Cato Institute and author of Identity Crisis: How Identification Is Overused and Misunderstood. "We want to prevent that uniformity. We want to prevent the tools for that surveillance society from being built."

Harper contends, "There's no practical way in a free country to defeat identity fraud." Illegal immigrants, terrorists, and garden-variety criminals forge birth certificates, Social Security cards, and other IDs all too easily, he notes. Reports abound, moreover, of motor vehicle department officials accepting bribes to assist fraud rings.

"Try to prevent it by locking down everybody's ID, and you have to build this cradle-to-grave biometric tracking system," Harper said.

■THEN: Opponents of strict ID rules are quick to invoke the danger of an Orwellian, show-me-your-papers scenario reminiscent of Nazi Germany or South Africa under apartheid. "We're investing these federal agencies with an unprecedented level of authority to decide: Can we work, can we fly?" said Peter Zamora, the Washington, D.C., regional counsel for the Mexican American Legal Defense and Educational Fund. "And these are agencies that have not been proven to be flawless."

■NOW: But even in the absence of a national ID, Americans will likely find that in more and more places they will be asked, "May I see your ID?"

■NEXT: Would you support a mandatory biometric ID? Or would you see one as an invasion of your privacy?
Would you rather your state or the Federal Government supply your ID? Why?
Would a Federal ID be a violation of State sovereignty? What arguments might the Federal Government advance in favor of its right to issue one?

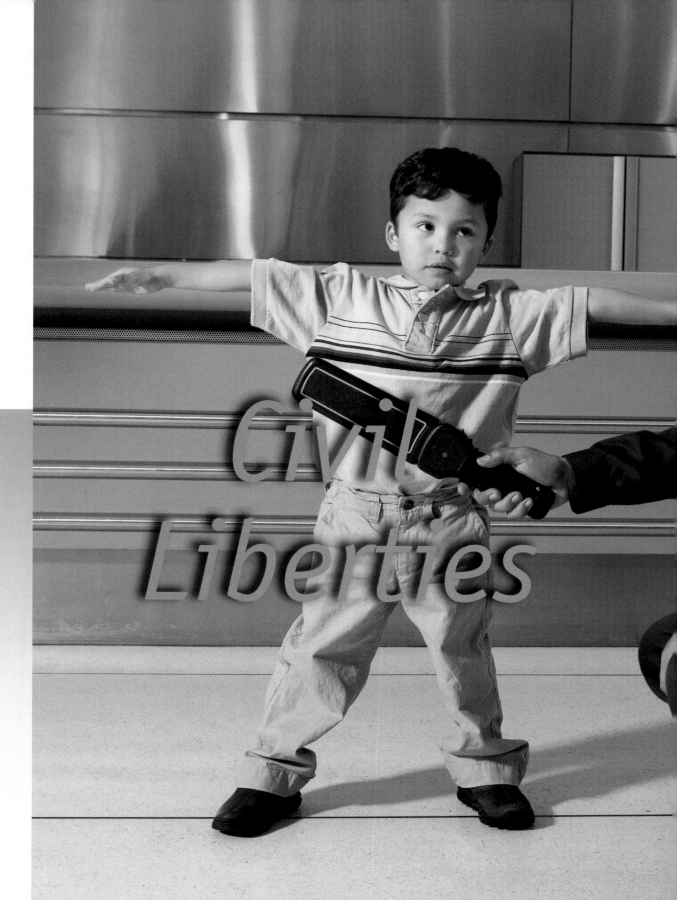

Civil
Liberties

THEN

The Bill of Rights protected citizens' rights to speak and act without undue monitoring or interference from the national government.

NOW

As part of a global war on terrorism, the national government increasingly monitors the words and actions of citizens and others.

NEXT

Will the Supreme Court uphold new laws allowing the president to place terrorist suspects under surveillance without a court order?

Will airports and national security agencies further develop and deploy security systems based on methods such as thumb print and eye scan technology?

Will the Court uphold new laws that require Internet providers to secretly share personal information about their clients with the FBI?

Exercising Their Right to Dissent:
Jeffery and Nicole Rank and the First Amendment

On August 16, 2007, the American Civil Liberties Union (ACLU) announced the resolution of the case of Jeffery and Nicole Rank, a Texas couple arrested on the West Virginia Capitol grounds on July 4, 2004, for peacefully expressing their opposition to President George W. Bush. According to the settlement agreement, the U.S. government will pay the Ranks $80,000. | The Ranks, who wanted to attend the president's Fourth of July address without being mistaken for supporters of his policies, had worn homemade T-shirts bearing the international "no" symbol (a circle with a diagonal line across it) superimposed over the name "Bush." One T-shirt said "Love America, Hate Bush" on the back, and the other read "Regime Change Starts at Home." | Event staff and law enforcement officers ordered them either to leave the event or to remove or cover their shirts. The couple responded by insisting that they had a First Amendment right to remain and to express their views. The two were arrested for trespassing, handcuffed, and hauled away in a police van. | "This is a simple case," said ACLU Senior Staff attorney Chris Hansen, the lead counsel in the case. "Two Americans went to see their president and to express their disagreement with his policies respectfully and peacefully. They were arrested at the direction of federal officials. That is precisely what the First Amendment was adopted to prevent."* | "We couldn't believe what was happening to us," said Nicole Rank. "We tried to tell them we had a right to express our opinion in a peaceful way, but they wouldn't listen to us." | The ACLU filed a lawsuit in federal court on behalf of the Ranks, alleging that the government's actions violated their rights under the First Amendment to the Constitution. The ACLU took this legal action after obtaining a copy of the *Presidential Advance Manual* from the Department of Justice. The manual outlined the government's policy of excluding dissenters from public presidential appearances. Among other things, the manual asserts that proper ticket distribution is vital to "deterring potential protesters from attending events" and outlines procedures for minimizing demonstrators and shielding them from the press. "As a last resort," the policy says, "security should remove the demonstrators from the event." | "This settlement is a real victory not only for our clients but for the First Amendment. The outcome of the case speaks for itself," said Andrew Schneider, Executive Director of the ACLU of West Virginia. "As a result of the Ranks' courageous stand, public officials will think twice before they eject peaceful protestors from public events for exercising their right to dissent."

> Nicole and Jeffery Rank wear the T-shirts that caused their arrest and removal from the West Virginia Capitol grounds.

*This and following quotations from www.aclu.org/freespeech/protest/11462prs20040914.html.

As the Ranks' story demon-

strates, a strong belief in civil liberties is deeply embedded in our understanding of what it means to be an American. Civil liberties protect people from government intrusion and allow them to follow their own belief systems. Civil liberties also empower people to speak out against the government, as long as they do not harm others.

Since the nation's founding, political discourse among the people has often focused on the ideals of liberty and freedom. The colonists took up arms against Britain because the king and Parliament refused to recognize their liberties as English citizens—freedoms their counterparts in Great Britain took for granted: freedom of speech and assembly and the right to be free from unrestrained governmental power, especially in the investigation and prosecution of crimes. As scholar Stephen L. Carter noted, by declaring their independence, the colonists engaged in the ultimate act of dissent.[1] Withdrawing their consent to be governed by the king, they created a new government that would tolerate political discourse and disagreement and that could not legally disregard the collective or individual will of citizens.

Ideologies of liberty and freedom inspired the War of Independence and the founding of the new nation.[2] As the nation matured, Americans found that these freedoms were not absolute and would need to be tempered by other goals and values, perhaps most importantly by the goal of order and the need to protect people and their property. Following the terrorist attacks of September 11, 2001, the national government enacted laws aimed to protect American citizens and property from further attack. But these laws have had a dramatic impact on individual freedoms and rights, in some cases overturning decades of legal precedent in the area of civil liberties.

The subject of this chapter is civil liberties, the personal freedoms that protect citizens from government interference and allow them to participate fully in social and political life.

FIRST, we discuss the protection of *civil liberties in the American legal system*—including the freedoms protected by the Bill of Rights and the application of these protections to state governments.

SECOND, we explore *the freedoms of speech, assembly, and the press: First Amendment freedoms in support of civic engagement.*

THIRD, we examine how the *freedoms of religion, privacy, and criminal due process* strengthen civil society by encouraging inclusiveness and community engagement.

FOURTH, we consider *freedoms in practice* by looking at *the controversy over the Second Amendment and the right to bear arms.*

FIFTH, we consider the changing nature of *civil liberties in post-9/11 America.*

Civil Liberties in the American Legal System

Civil liberties are individual liberties established in the Constitution and safeguarded by state and federal courts. We also refer to civil liberties as *personal freedoms* and often use the concepts of "liberty" and "freedom" interchangeably.

Civil liberties are different from civil rights. **Civil liberties** are constitutionally established guarantees that protect citizens, opinions, and property *against* arbitrary government interference. In contrast, civil rights (the focus of Chapter 5) reflect positive acts of government (in the form of constitutional provisions or statutes) *for* the purpose of protecting individuals against arbitrary or discriminatory actions. For example, the freedom of speech, a liberty established in the First Amendment to the U.S. Constitution, protects citizens against the government's censorship of their words, in particular when these words are politically charged. In contrast, the right to vote, which the Constitution protects in a number of places, requires the government to step in to ensure that all citizens be allowed to vote, without restriction by individuals, groups, or governmental officials.

civil liberties
constitutionally established guarantees that protect citizens, opinions, and property against arbitrary government interference

The Freedoms Protected in the American System

The U.S. Constitution, through the Bill of Rights, and state constitutions explicitly recognize and protect civil liberties. As Table 4.1 summarizes, the first ten amendments to the Constitution strictly limited the power of the legislative, executive, and judicial branches of the national government.

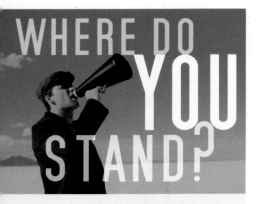

TABLE 4.1

The Bill of Rights: Limiting Government Power

Amendment I: Limits on Congress	Congress cannot make any law establishing a religion or abridging the freedom of religious exercise, speech, assembly, or petition.
Amendments II, III, IV: Limits on the Executive	The executive branch cannot infringe on the right of the people to bear arms (II), cannot house soldiers in citizens' houses (III), and cannot search for or seize evidence without a legal warrant from a court of law (IV).
Amendments V, VI, VII, VIII: Limits on the Judiciary	The courts cannot hold trials for serious offenses without providing for a grand jury (V), a trial jury (VII), a fair trial (VI), and legal counsel (VI). The accused also have the right to hear the charges against them (VI), to confront hostile witnesses (VI), and to refrain from giving testimony against themselves (V); and they cannot be tried more than once for the same crime (V). In addition, neither bail nor punishment can be excessive (VIII), and no property can be taken from private citizens without "just compensation" (V).
Amendments IX, X: Limits on the National Government	Any rights not listed specifically in the Constitution are reserved to the states or to the people (X), and the enumeration of certain rights in the Constitution should not be interpreted to mean that those are the only rights the people have (IX).

POLITICAL INQUIRY

Broadly speaking, what do the Bill of Rights amendments aim to recognize and protect? What do they aim to limit? Which amendments limit the powers of the legislative branch; of the executive branch; of the judicial branch?

The freedoms established by the Bill of Rights are essential to individuals' and groups' free and effective participation in the larger community. Consider how the absence of freedom to speak one's mind or the absence of protection against the arbitrary exercise of police powers might affect the nature and extent of people's engagement in political and civic discourse. Without these protections, citizens could not freely express their opinions through rallies, protests, letters, pamphlets, public meetings, blogs, e-mail, and other forms of civic engagement. The Constitution's framers, who had been denied these liberties under British rule, saw them as indispensable to forming a new democratic republic.

These precious freedoms have had shifting meanings over the course of U.S. history, as presidents, legislators, judges, and ordinary citizens have changed their minds about how much freedom the people should have. When Americans have not perceived themselves as being under some external threat, they generally have adopted an expansive interpretation of civil liberties. At these times, citizens tend to believe that the government should interfere as little as necessary in individuals' lives. Accordingly, they strongly support people's right to gather with others and to speak their minds, even when the content of this speech is controversial. When the nation has been under some perceived threat, citizens have sometimes allowed the government to limit freedom of speech and assembly.[3] Limits have also extended to many criminal **due process** protections—legal safeguards that prevent the government from arbitrarily depriving people of life, liberty, or property without adhering to strict legal procedures. In this chapter, we consider not only the historical context for our

due process
legal safeguards that prevent the government from arbitrarily depriving citizens of life, liberty, or property; guaranteed by the Fifth and Fourteenth amendments

civil liberties but also recent changes in how Congress, the president, and the courts are interpreting these liberties.

The Historical Basis for American Civil Liberties: The Bill of Rights

The framers vividly remembered the censorship and suppression of speech that they had suffered under British rule. Criticism of the British government, through both speech and the publication of pamphlets, had been harshly punished, often by imprisonment and the confiscation of property but sometimes even by death. The framers understandably viewed liberty as a central principle guiding the creation of a new democratic republic. Federalists such as Alexander Hamilton saw the Constitution itself as a bill of rights because it delegated specific powers to the national government and contained specific provisions designed to protect citizens against an abusive government (see Table 4.2).

The protections listed in Table 4.2 were designed to protect people from being punished, imprisoned, or executed for expressing political beliefs or opposition. However, the Anti-Federalists still stressed the need for a written bill of rights. As we saw in Chapter 2, the ratification of the Constitution stalled because citizens were worried about how the government might use its expanded powers to interfere with individual freedoms, particularly those associated with political speech and engagement. The First Amendment, which ensures freedom of religion, the press, assembly, and speech, was essential to political speech and to discourse in the larger society.

The freedoms embodied in the Bill of Rights are broad principles rather than specific prohibitions. From the nation's beginnings, the vagueness of the Bill of Rights led to serious disagreement about how to interpret its amendments. For example, the First Amendment's establishment clause states simply that "Congress shall make no law respecting an establishment of religion." Some commentators, most notably Thomas Jefferson, argued that the clause mandated a "wall of separation between church and state" and barred any federal support of religion. Others more narrowly interpreted the clause as barring only the establishment of a national religion or the requirement that all public officials swear an oath to some particular religion. This disagreement about the breadth of the establishment clause is ongoing today, as courts and lawyers continue to try to determine what the proper relationship should be between church and state.

Other freedoms, too, have been subject to differing interpretations, including the First Amendment guarantees of freedom of speech, assembly, and the press. These conflicting interpretations often arise in response to public crises or security concerns. Security concerns also affect the protections offered to those accused of threatening the safety of the nation. For example, the USA PATRIOT Act, passed by Congress almost immediately after the 9/11 attacks and amended in 2002, allows law enforcement a good deal of legal leeway. It permits agents to sidestep well-established rules that govern how searches and seizures may be conducted and to restrict criminal due process protections severely, particularly for persons suspected of involvement in organizations thought to have ties to suspected terrorists. Civil liberties advocates such as Gavin Rose worry

TABLE 4.2

Citizens' Protections in the Original Constitution

Clause	Protection
Article I, Sec. 9	Guarantee of *habeas corpus*—a court order requiring that an individual in custody be brought into court and told the cause for detention
Article I, Sec. 9	Prohibition of *bills of attainder*—laws that declare a person guilty of a crime without a trial
Article I, Sec. 9	Prohibition of *ex post facto laws*—retroactive laws that punish people for committing an act that was legal when the act was committed
Article III	Guarantee of a trial by jury in the state where the crime was committed

> According to the Supreme Court, public schools cannot sponsor religious activities, including teacher-led school prayer, without violating the First Amendment's establishment clause. Here, children at a Christian school in California bow their heads in prayer. Does the ban on prayer in public schools violate the free exercise clause, in your view?

Incorporation of the Bill of Rights to Apply to the States

The framers intended the Bill of Rights to restrict the powers of only the *national* government. They did not see the Bill of Rights as applicable to the state governments. In general, there was little public worry that the states would curtail civil liberties, because most state constitutions included a bill of rights that protected the individual against abuses of state power. Further, it was common thinking that because the state governments were geographically closer to the people than the national government, they would be less likely to encroach upon individual rights and liberties.

The Bill of Rights was assumed to apply to the national government, not the states, through most of early U.S. history. This assumption is illustrated by the case of *Barron v. Baltimore* (1833), in which a wharf owner named Barron sued the city of Baltimore. Barron claimed that the city had violated the "takings clause" of the Fifth Amendment, which bars the taking of private property for public use without just compensation. *Barron* argued that by paving its streets, the city of Baltimore had changed the natural course of certain streams; the resulting buildup of silt and gravel in the harbor made his wharf unusable. The case centered on the idea that the Fifth Amendment protects individuals from actions taken by both the national and state or local governments. The Supreme Court disagreed, ruling that the Fifth Amendment was restricted to suits brought against the federal government.[4]

In 1868, three years after the Civil War ended, the Fourteenth Amendment was added to the U.S. Constitution. The Fourteenth Amendment reads as if it were meant to extend the protections of the Bill of Rights to citizens' interactions with *state* governments:

> No State shall make or enforce any law which shall abridge the privileges or immunities of citizens of the United States; nor shall any State deprive any person of life, liberty, or property, without due process of law; nor deny to any person within its jurisdiction the equal protection of the laws.

> Since September 11, 2001, Americans have struggled to balance national security with civil liberties. Here, a demonstrator protests the PATRIOT Act, warrantless wiretapping, and other government initiatives they believe violate the freedoms guaranteed by the Bill of Rights.

Although this language sounds like an effort to protect citizens' rights and liberties from arbitrary interference by state governments, the Supreme Court rejected the doctrine of **total incorporation:** that is, the application of *all* of the protections contained in the Bill of Rights to the states. Instead, beginning with a series of cases decided by the Court in the 1880s, the justices formulated a narrower approach, known as **selective incorporation.**[5] This approach considered each protection individually, one case at a time, for possible incorporation into the Fourteenth Amendment and application to the states. In each case, the justices rejected the plaintiff's specific claims of protection against the state. But they held that due process mandates the incorporation of those rights that serve the fundamental principles of liberty and justice, those that were at the core of the "very idea of free government" and that were unalienable rights of citizenship.

Despite these early cases, the Supreme Court continued to embrace the idea that although citizenship meant being a citizen of a state and of the nation as a whole, the Bill of Rights protected citizens only against the national government. As Table 4.3 shows, not until 1925 did the Court gradually begin the process of incorporation, starting with the First Amendment protections most central to democratic government and civic engagement. That year, in the case of *Gitlow v. New York,* the Court held that freedom of speech is "among the fundamental personal rights and 'liberties' protected by the due process clause of the Fourteenth

total incorporation
the theory that the Fourteenth Amendment's due process clause requires the states to uphold all freedoms in the Bill of Rights; rejected by the Supreme Court in favor of selective incorporation

selective incorporation
the process by which, over time, the Supreme Court applied those freedoms that served some fundamental principle of liberty or justice to the states, thus rejecting total incorporation

GAVIN M. ROSE, ACLU STAFF ATTORNEY

<u>Name:</u> Gavin M. Rose

<u>Age:</u> 27

<u>Hometown:</u> Indianapolis, Indiana

<u>Colleges:</u> University of California, Davis; Indiana University School of Law—Bloomington

<u>Major:</u> Political Science (BA, minors in Philosophy and Comparative Literature); Law (JD)

<u>Job title:</u> Staff Attorney and Director of Legislation, ACLU of Indiana

<u>Salary range for jobs like this:</u> $35,000–$85,000

<u>Day-to-day responsibilities:</u> As an attorney, I am responsible both for litigating cases in state and federal court and for rendering advice to needy citizens on countless concerns. The cases themselves concern a wide assortment of issues: free speech, voting rights, equal protection, and disability rights are several that crop up routinely. As a lobbyist, I am responsible for monitoring developments at the state legislature and aggressively advocating legislation aimed at expanding civil liberties and opposing legislation that will curtail these liberties.

<u>How did you get your job?</u> Shortly after graduating law school, I applied for a one-year position as a disability rights attorney with the ACLU of Indiana. I interviewed on a Friday morning about ten days before the bar exam and was offered the position that afternoon. I must have done something right during that year because they asked me to stay on.

<u>What do you like best about your job?</u> I get to wake up every morning glad to be going to work and knowing that before I go home that night I will have done something to make the world a better place.

<u>What is your least favorite aspect of your job?</u> Few jobs so often require being put in touch with the more gruesome aspects of human nature—from homelessness and poverty to racism and sexism to greed and corruption. Faced with such tragedies of human existence, and armed with the knowledge that you can't help everyone, far too much of the time is spent running to stand still.

<u>What advice would you give to students who would like to do what you are doing?</u> Have the courage of your convictions, stand strong in the face of adversity, and never underestimate the importance of being in the right place at the right time.

Amendment from impairment by the states."[6] In 1931, in its decision in *Near v. Minnesota,* the Court added freedom of the press, and in 1937 it added freedom of assembly to the list of incorporated protections.[7]

Incorporation progressed further with the landmark case of *Palko v. Connecticut* (1937), in which the Court laid out a formula for defining fundamental rights that later courts have used time and time again in incorporation cases, as well as in due process cases more generally. The justices found that fundamental rights were rooted in the traditions and conscience of the American people. Moreover, if these rights were eliminated, the justices argued, neither liberty nor justice could exist.[8] Judges in subsequent cases have used this formula to determine which Bill of Rights protections should be applied to the states. In case after case, the justices have considered whether such a right is fundamental—that is, rooted in the American tradition and conscience and essential for liberty and justice. The objectives of civic engagement and political participation are central to this judicial calculation, as the justices have tried to determine whether the right at issue is necessary for participation in the larger civil society.

What do we mean by *selective incorporation*? According to the table, the Supreme Court incorporated most Bill of Rights protections over time. What are some exceptions?

Selective Incorporation of the Bill of Rights

TABLE 4.3

Amendment	Liberty	Date	Key Case
I	Freedom of speech	1925	*Gitlow v. New York*
	Freedom of the press	1931	*Near v. Minnesota*
	Freedom of assembly and petition	1937	*DeJonge v. Oregon*
	Freedom to practice religion	1940	*Cantwell v. Connecticut*
	Freedom from government-established religion	1947	*Everson v. Board of Education*
II	Right to bear arms		Not incorporated
III	No quartering of soldiers		Not incorporated
IV	No unreasonable searches and seizures	1949	*Wolf v. Colorado*
	Exclusionary rule	1961	*Mapp v. Ohio*
V	Right to just compensation (for property taken by government)	1897	*Chicago, B&Q RR Co. v. Chicago*
	No compulsory self-incrimination	1964	*Malloy v. Hogan*
	No double jeopardy	1969	*Benton v. Maryland*
	Right to grand jury indictment		Not incorporated
VI	Right to a public trial	1948	*In re Oliver*
	Right to counsel in criminal cases	1963	*Gideon v. Wainwright*
	Right to confront witnesses	1965	*Pointer v. Texas*
	Right to an impartial jury	1966	*Parker v. Gladden*
	Right to a speedy trial	1967	*Klopfer v. North Carolina*
	Right to a jury in criminal trials	1968	*Duncan v. Louisiana*
VII	Right to a jury in civil trials		Not incorporated
VIII	No cruel and unusual punishments	1962	*Robinson v. California*
	No excessive fines or bail		Not incorporated

Concept Summary

SELECTIVE INCORPORATION OF THE BILL OF RIGHTS

Selective incorporation: The process by which, over time, the Supreme Court applied those freedoms that served some fundamental principle of liberty or justice to the states.

— The Bill of Rights was written to restrain the power of the national government.

— Ratification of the 14th Amendment in 1868 paved the way for incorporation of the Bill of Rights to the states.

— Over time, the Supreme Court ruled that specific freedoms were also protected from infringement by state governments.

— Most of the freedoms protected in the Bill of Rights now apply to state governments.

Over time, the Supreme Court has incorporated most Bill of Rights protections, as Table 4.3 summarizes. Even rights that once were not incorporated—such as the right to compensation for the government's taking of private property—have now been incorporated. Yet a few notable exceptions to the trend of incorporation remain. For example, the Third Amendment's prohibition against the quartering of soldiers in citizens' homes has not been an issue since colonial times. The Fifth Amendment's provision for a grand jury indictment runs counter to a trend in state criminal cases away from grand juries, and is not required to guarantee that states adhere to Fifth and Sixth Amendment protections during the arrest, interrogation, and trial of criminal defendants. Similarly, the Seventh Amendment's provision of a jury in a civil trial is widely viewed as less important than the Sixth Amendment's guarantee of a jury trial in criminal cases in which life and liberty may be at stake.

Freedoms of Speech, Assembly, and the Press: First Amendment Freedoms Supporting Civic Discourse

Civic discourse and free participation in the political process have certain requirements. As we consider in this section, an individual must be able to express his or her political views through speech, assembly, and petition. The person must also live in a society with a press that is independent of government censorship. Freedom of speech, assembly, petition, and the press is essential to an open society and to democratic rule. These freedoms ensure that individuals can discuss the important issues facing the nation and try to reach agreement about how to address these matters. Scholars have referred to this sharing of contrasting opinions as the **marketplace of ideas.** It is through the competition of ideas—some of them radical, some even loathsome—that solutions emerge. Freedom of the press allows for the dissemination and discussion of these varying ideas and encourages consensus building.

> **marketplace of ideas**
> a concept at the core of the freedoms of expression and press, based on the belief that true and free political discourse depends on a free and unrestrained discussion of ideas

The marketplace of ideas serves as a means by which people can voice concerns and views freely and where individuals can reconsider their ideas on important national and local issues. The centrality of the freedom of political expression to the First Amendment reflects the founders' belief that democracy would flourish only through robust discussion and candid debate.

The First Amendment and Political Instability

Over time, the Supreme Court has distinguished between political expression that the First Amendment protects and expression that the government may limit or even prohibit. The government has tried to limit speech, assembly, and the press during times of national emergency, when it has viewed this expression as more threatening than it would be in normal times.

THE TENSION BETWEEN FREEDOM AND ORDER A fundamental tension exists between the Bill of Rights, with its goal of protecting individual freedoms, and the government's central goal of ensuring order. Not even a decade had gone by after the Constitution's ratification when Congress passed the Alien and Sedition Acts (1798). These laws placed the competing goals of freedom and order directly in conflict. The Sedition Act, for example, criminalized all speech and writings judged to be critical of the government, Congress, or the president. This was just the first of many times in U.S. history that lawmakers sacrificed free speech and freedom of the press in an effort to ensure national security and order. For example, President Abraham Lincoln attempted to silence political dissidents during the Civil War by mandating that they be tried in military courts, without the due process protections afforded in a civilian court. Lincoln also suspended the writ of **habeas corpus** (Latin, meaning "you have the body"), an ancient right that protects an individual in custody from being held without the right to be heard in a court of law.[9] Again, it was political dissidents who were targeted for indefinite detention without trial.

> **habeas corpus**
> an ancient right that protects an individual in custody from being held without the right to be heard in a court of law

The struggle for a balance between freedom and order continues today as the United States fights a global war on terrorism. Part of the 1789 Alien and Sedition Acts, known as the Alien Enemies Act, empowered the president to deport aliens suspected of threatening the nation's security or to imprison them indefinitely.[10] After the 9/11 terrorist attacks on U.S. soil, President George W. Bush invoked these same powers for combatants, insurgents, and suspected terrorists captured in the United States or abroad. Like President Lincoln, President Bush also argued that military combatants and suspected terrorists should be tried in military tribunals and denied the protections of civilian courts, including the right to a speedy and public trial.[11]

THE HISTORICAL CONTEXT FOR FREE SPEECH LAWS The Supreme Court's willingness to suppress or punish political speech has changed over time in response to perceived internal and external threats to the nation. During World War I, the Court upheld the conviction of socialist and war protester Charles Schenck for distributing a pamphlet to recently drafted men urging them to resist the draft.[12] For the first time, the Court created

clear and present danger test
a standard established in the 1919 Supreme Court case *Schenck v. U.S.* whereby the government may silence speech or expression when there is a clear and present danger that this speech will bring about some harm that the government has the power to prevent

bad tendency test
a standard established in the 1925 case *Gitlow v. New York* whereby any speech that has the tendency to incite crime or disturb the public peace can be silenced

through its ruling a test to evaluate such government actions, called the **clear and present danger test.** Under this standard, the government may silence speech or expression only when there is a clear and present danger that this speech will bring about some harm that the government has the power to prevent. In the *Schenck* case, the Court noted that the circumstances of war permit greater restrictions on the freedom of speech than would be allowable during peacetime. The justices ruled that Schenck's actions could endanger the nation's ability to carry out the draft and prosecute the war.

Soon after the *Schenck* case, a majority of the justices moved toward a far more restrictive test that made it easier to punish citizens for the content of their speech. This test, known as the **bad tendency test,** was established in the case of Benjamin Gitlow, who was convicted of violating a New York State criminal anarchy law by publishing pamphlets calling for a revolutionary mass action to create a socialist government.[13] The political context of Gitlow's conviction is revealing: a so-called red scare—fears that the socialist revolution in the Soviet Union would spread to other nations with large populations of workers—was sweeping the nation. Gitlow's lawyer contended that there was no proof that Gitlow's pamphlet created a clear and present danger of a violent uprising. The Court disagreed, however, ruling that any speech that had the tendency to incite crime or disturb the public peace could be silenced.

This highly restrictive test required only that the government demonstrate that some speech may at some time help to bring about harm. The threat did not need to be immediate or even direct. The test sacrificed the freedoms of speech and the press to concerns about public safety and protection of the existing order. The bad tendency test lasted only a short while; by the late 1930s, the Court had reverted to the clear and present danger test, which the justices interpreted more broadly to protect speech and participation. The relative peace and stability of the period between the two world wars is apparent in the Court's handling of speech and press cases, as the justices required government officials to demonstrate that the speech clearly posed a danger to public safety.

Even after the Court reverted to the clear and present danger test, however, it still allowed concerns about national security to dominate its handling of First Amendment cases. In the wake of World War II, a war of conflicting ideologies emerged between the United States and the Soviet Union. Termed the *Cold War* because it did not culminate in a direct military confrontation between the countries, this development nevertheless created a climate of fear and insecurity in both nations. Concerns about the spread of communism in the United States led to prosecutions of individuals deemed to be sympathetic to communism and socialism under the Smith Act of 1940. This federal law barred individuals from advocating or teaching about "the duty, necessity, desirability, or propriety of overthrowing or destroying any government in the United States by force or violence."

In the most important case of this period, the Supreme Court upheld the conviction of several individuals who were using the writings of German philosophers Karl Marx and Friedrich Engels, along with those of Soviet leaders Vladimir Lenin and Josef Stalin, to teach about socialism and communism.[14] In upholding the convictions, the justices found that although the use of these writings did not pose a risk of imminent danger to the government, it created the *probability* that such harm might result. Because there was a probability that these readings might lead to the destruction of the government, the Court reasoned, the speech could be barred. The seriousness of the evil was key to the test that came out of this ruling, known as the **clear and probable danger test.** Because the government was suppressing speech to avoid the gravest danger, an armed takeover of the United States, the Supreme Court majority ruled that it was justified in its actions—even if the risk or probability of this result was relatively remote.

clear and probable danger test
a standard established in the 1951 case *Dennis v. U.S.* whereby the government could suppress speech to avoid grave danger, even if the probability of the dangerous result was relatively remote; replaced by the imminent lawless action (incitement) test in 1969

As the Cold War subsided and concerns diminished about a potential communist takeover of the United States, the Court shifted to a broader interpretation of the First Amendment speech and press protections. Beginning with *Brandenburg v. Ohio* (1969), the Court signaled that it would give more weight to First Amendment claims and less to government concerns about security and order. In this case, the Court considered the convictions of the leaders of an Ohio Ku Klux Klan group who were arrested after they made a speech at a televised rally, during which they uttered racist and anti-Semitic comments and showed guns and rifles. Local officials charged them with violating a state law that banned speech that disturbed the public peace and threatened armed overthrow. In overturning the convictions, the Court reverted to a strict reading of the clear and present danger test. The justices held that government officials had to demonstrate that the speech they sought to silence went beyond mere advocacy, or words, and that it created the risk of imminent disorder or lawlessness.[15]

THE STANDARD TODAY: THE IMMINENT LAWLESS ACTION TEST

The Brandenburg test, known as both the **imminent lawless action test** and the **incitement test,** altered the clear and present danger test by making it even more stringent. Specifically, after the *Brandenburg* decision, any government in the United States—national, state, or local—trying to silence speech would need to show that the risk of harm from the speech was highly likely and that the harm was imminent or immediate. The imminent lawless action test is the standard the courts use today to determine whether speech is protected from government interference.

Even though the Brandenburg test is well established, the issue of whether speech is protected continues to be important. For example, since the 9/11 attacks, public attention has increasingly focused on Web sites operated by terrorists and terrorist sympathizers, especially members of militant Islamic groups. Some of these sites carry radical messages; for example, one site urges viewers to eliminate all "enemies of Allah" by any necessary means and gives instructions on loading weapons. Do First Amendment guarantees protect such sites? Courts examining this question must determine not only whether the speech intends to bring about a bad result—we would probably all agree that intent is there—but also whether the speech incites lawless action that is imminent.

Freedom of Speech

The freedom to speak publicly, even critically, about government and politics is central to the democratic process. Citizens cannot participate fully in a political system if they are unable to share information, opinions, advice, and calls to action. Citizens cannot hold government accountable if they cannot criticize government actions or demand change.

PURE SPEECH VERSUS SYMBOLIC SPEECH

The Supreme Court has made a distinction between pure speech that is "just words" and advocacy that couples words with actions. With respect to civic discourse, both are important. When speech moves beyond words into the realm of action, it is considered to be **symbolic speech:** nonverbal "speech" in the form of an action such as picketing or wearing an armband to signify a protest.

Unless words threaten imminent lawless action, the First Amendment will likely protect them. But in civic discourse, words are often combined with action. For example, in the 1960s, antiwar protesters were arrested for burning their draft cards to demonstrate their refusal to serve in Vietnam, and public high school students were suspended from school for wearing black armbands to protest the war. When the two groups brought their cases to the Supreme Court, the justices had to determine whether their conduct rose to the level of political expression and merited First Amendment protection. Together, these cases help to define the parameters for symbolic speech.

In the first of these cases, *U.S. v. O'Brien,* the justices considered whether the government could punish several Vietnam War protesters for burning their draft cards in violation of the Selective Service Act, which made it a crime to "destroy or mutilate" these cards. The Court balanced the free expression guarantee against the government's need to prevent the destruction of the cards. Because the cards were critical to the nation's ability to raise an army, the Court ruled that the government had a compelling interest in preventing their destruction. Moreover, because the government had passed the Selective Service Act to facilitate the draft and not to suppress speech, the impact of the law on speech was incidental. When the justices balanced the government's interest in making it easy to raise an army against the incidental impact that this law had on speech, they found that the government's interest overrode that of the political protesters.[16]

> Cleveland police officers stand guard as Ku Klux Klan demonstrators exercise their rights to free speech and assembly. Even unpopular and racially intolerant groups like the Klan are protected by the First Amendment.

imminent lawless action test (incitement test)
a standard established in the 1969 *Brandenburg v. Ohio* case whereby speech is restricted only if it goes beyond mere advocacy, or words, to create a high likelihood of imminent disorder or lawlessness

symbolic speech
nonverbal "speech" in the form of an action such as picketing, flag burning, or wearing an armband to signify a protest

Despite several congressional attempts to outlaw the burning and desecration of the American flag, the Supreme Court has ruled that flag burning is a protected form of symbolic political speech. Here, antiwar protesters in Washington, D.C., burn a U.S. flag in protest of the war in Iraq.

In contrast, when the Court considered the other symbolic speech case of this era, *Tinker v. Des Moines,* they found that the First Amendment did protect the speech in question. In this case, the justices ruled that the political expression in the form of the students' wearing black armbands to school to protest the Vietnam War was protected.[17] On what basis did the justices distinguish the armbands in the *Tinker* case from the draft cards in the *O'Brien* case? They focused on the fact that there were legitimate reasons for the government to ban the burning of draft cards: in a time of war, these cards were especially important to aid in the military draft. But there were no comparable reasons to ban the wearing of armbands, apart from the school district's desire to curb or suppress political expression. School officials could not show that the armbands had disrupted normal school activities.[18] For this reason, the Court argued, the symbolic speech in *Tinker* warranted more protection than that in *O'Brien*.

The highly controversial case of *Texas v. Johnson* (1989) tested the Court's commitment to protecting symbolic speech of a highly unpopular nature. At issue was a man's conviction under state law for burning the American flag at the Republican National Convention in 1984 to emphasize his disagreement with the policies of the administration of President Ronald Reagan (1981–1989). The Supreme Court overturned the man's conviction, finding that the flag burning was political speech worthy of protection under the First Amendment.[19] After the *Johnson* decision, Congress quickly passed the Flag Protection Act in an attempt to reverse the Court's ruling. Subsequently, however, in the case of *U.S. v. Eichman* (1990), the Court struck down the new law by the same 5–4 majority as in the *Johnson* ruling.[20]

The decisions in these flag-burning cases were very controversial and have prompted Congress to pursue the only remaining legal avenue to enact flag protection statutes—a constitutional amendment. Indeed, each Congress since the *Johnson* decision has considered creating a flag desecration amendment. Since 1995, the proposed amendment has been approved biennially by the two-thirds majority necessary in the U.S. House of Representatives, but it has consistently failed to achieve the same constitutionally required supermajority vote in the U.S. Senate. Senate opponents of the ban argue that ratification of the amendment would undermine the principles for which the flag stands.

NOT ALL SPEECH IS CREATED EQUAL: UNPROTECTED SPEECH The Supreme Court long ago rejected the extreme view that all speech should be free in the United States. Whereas political speech tends to be protected against government suppression, other forms of speech can be limited or prohibited.

The courts afford **commercial speech,** that is, advertising statements, limited protection under the First Amendment. According to the Supreme Court, commercial speech may be restricted as long as the restriction "seeks to implement a substantial government interest, directly advances that interest, and goes no further than necessary to accomplish its objective." Restrictions on tobacco advertising, for example, limit free speech in the interest of protecting the health of society.

Other forms of speech, including libel and slander, receive no protection under the First Amendment. **Libel** (written statements) and **slander** (verbal statements) are false statements that harm the reputation of another person. In order to qualify as libel or slander, the defamatory statement must be made publicly and with fault, meaning that reporters, for example, must undertake reasonable efforts to verify allegations. The statement must extend beyond mere name calling or insults that cannot be proven true or false. Those who take a legal action on the grounds that they are victims of libel or slander, such as government officials, celebrities, and people involved with specific public controversies, are required to prove that the defendant acted with malice—with knowledge that the statement was false or recklessly disregarded the truth or falsity of the statement.

Obscenity, indecent or offensive speech or expression, is another form of speech that is not protected under the First Amendment. After many unsuccessful attempts to define

commercial speech
advertising statements that describe products

libel
false written statements about others that harm their reputation

slander
false verbal statements about others that harm their reputation

obscenity
indecent or offensive speech or expression

obscenity, in 1973 the Supreme Court developed a three-part test in *Miller v. California*.[21] The Court ruled that a book, a film, or another form of expression is legally obscene if

- the average person applying contemporary standards finds that the work taken as a whole appeals to the prurient interest—that is, tends to excite unwholesome sexual desire;
- the work depicts or describes, in a patently offensive way, a form of sexual conduct specifically prohibited by an anti-obscenity law;
- the work taken as a whole lacks serious literary, artistic, political, or scientific value.

Of course, these standards do not guarantee that people will agree upon what materials are obscene. What is obscene to some may be acceptable to others. For this reason, the Court has been reluctant to limit free speech, even in the most controversial cases.

The Court may also ban speech known as **fighting words**—speech that inflicts injury or results in public disorder. The Court first articulated the fighting-words doctrine in *Chaplinsky v. New Hampshire* (1942). Walter Chaplinsky was convicted of violating a New Hampshire statute that prohibited the use of offensive, insulting language toward persons in public places after he made several inflammatory comments to a city official. The Court, in upholding the statute as constitutional, explained the limits of free speech: "These include the lewd and obscene, the profane, the libelous, and the insulting or fighting words—those which by their very utterance inflict injury or tend to incite an immediate breach of the peace."[22] Thus the Court ruled that like slander, libel, and obscenity, "fighting words" do not advance the democratic goals of free speech.

Even the types of "unprotected" speech we have considered enjoy broad protection under the law. Although cigarette ads are banned from television, a wide variety of products are sold through every media outlet imaginable. Though a tabloid such as the *National Inquirer* sometimes faces lawsuits for the false stories it prints, most celebrities do not pursue legal action because of the high burden of proving that the paper knew the story was false, intended to damage the subject's reputation, and in fact caused real harm. Even though network television is censored for broadcasting objectionable material, the Supreme Court has ruled that the government cannot ban (adult) pornography on the Internet or on paid cable television channels.[23] The Court even struck down a ban on the transmission of "virtual" child pornography, arguing that no real children were harmed in the creation of these photographic or computer-generated images.[24] And, despite continued reaffirmation of the fighting-words doctrine, the Supreme Court has declined to uphold any convictions for fighting words since *Chaplinsky*. In short, the Court is reluctant to do anything that might limit the content of adults' free speech and expression, even when that speech is unpopular or offensive.

fighting words
speech that is likely to bring about public disorder or chaos; the Supreme Court has held that this speech may be banned in public places to ensure the preservation of public order

Freedom of Assembly and Redress of Grievances

The First Amendment says that people have the freedom to assemble peaceably and to seek redress of (compensation for) grievances against the government, yet there are limits placed on assembly. As the Supreme Court has considered the parameters of free assembly cases, it has been most concerned about ensuring that individuals and groups can get together to discuss their concerns and that they can take action in the public arena that advances their political goals.

The Court's stance in free speech cases provides insight into its leanings in cases concerning freedom of assembly. The Court is keenly aware of the need for order in public forums and will clamp down on speech that is intended and likely to incite public unrest and anger. This is one reason the Court has reaffirmed the fighting-words doctrine. Although officials cannot censor speech before it occurs, they can take action to limit speech once it becomes apparent that public disorder is going to erupt. In its rulings, the Court has also allowed content-neutral **time, place, and manner restrictions**—regulations regarding when, where, or how expression may occur. Such restrictions do not target speech based on content, and in order to stand up in court, they must be applied in a content-neutral manner. For example, people have the right to march in protest, but not while chanting into bullhorns at four o'clock in the morning in a residential neighborhood.

time, place, and manner restrictions
regulations regarding when, where, or how expression may occur; must be content neutral

DOING DEMOCRACY

WRITE A LETTER TO THE EDITOR

FACT:

Newspapers are the leading news source for the United States' political elite. Local and national newspapers shape the agenda for television news broadcasts and political leaders. Newspapers regularly publish short editorial pieces from citizens in the form of letters to the editor. Publishing your opinion or story can lead to connections with other interested citizens, media outlets, and political activists, giving you increased influence over the policies that matter to you most.

Act!

Hala Saadeh was ordered off a commuter train to Boston, where she was a summer school student at Tufts University, after someone on the train reported a "suspicious person." Hala was wearing a traditional Muslim *hijab* with her jacket and blue jeans and was studying for a midterm exam. Although the experience frightened and humiliated her, Hala refused to remain silent and brought the incident to the public's attention by writing letters to the editors of her local newspaper and the *Boston Globe.*

After the episode, Hala was a featured speaker at a rally in downtown Boston and at a screening of Robert Greenwald's documentary *Unconstitutional,* a film arguing that the USA PATRIOT Act endangers civil liberties by taking away checks on law enforcement. She was also featured in a special episode of *Chronicle,* an ABC TV/Boston Channel 5 weekly program, which the station broadcast on the third anniversary of the signing of the USA PATRIOT Act. "Being an activist for civil liberties is not just a label," said Hala. "I truly feel as if it is inherently a part of me, and I am honored to assume that position."

Where to begin

First, pick an issue that interests you. Next, go online to find the "Letter to the Editor" guidelines for your local or campus newspaper(s). Finally, write your letter, keeping in mind the following advice:

Keep it short and on one subject. Many newspapers strictly limit the length of letters because they have limited space to publish them. Keeping your letter brief will help ensure that the newspaper does not cut out your important points.

Make it legible. Word process or e-mail your letter if your handwriting is difficult to read.

Include your contact information. Many newspapers will print a letter to the editor only after calling the author to verify his or her identity and address. Newspapers will not give out that information, however, and will usually only print your name and city should your letter be published.

Make references to the newspaper. Although some papers print general commentary, many will print only letters that refer to a specific article. For example: "I was disappointed to see that *The Post*'s May 18 editorial 'School Vouchers Are Right On' omitted some of the key facts in the debate."

The Court's rulings in these various cases illustrate how the government is balancing the freedom of public assembly against other concerns, notably public safety and the privacy rights of certain individuals. The Court is carefully weighing the freedoms of one group of individuals against another and attempting to ensure the protection of free public expression.

Freedom of the Press

Throughout American history, the press has played a crucial role in the larger debate about political expression. Before the War for Independence, when the British monarchy sought to clamp down on political dissent in the colonies, the king and Parliament quickly recognized the urgency of silencing the press. A free press is essential to democratic ideals, and democracy cannot survive when a government controls the press. The First Amendment's guarantees of a free press ensure not only that American government remains accountable to its constituents but also that the people hear competing ideas about how to deal with matters of public concern. Indeed, local and state newspapers include editorial pages where ordinary citizens can share their views on important political issues (see "Doing Democracy").

Ensuring a free press can complicate the work of government. Consider the challenge presented to the George W. Bush administration when the *New York Times* broke a story in late 2005 that the National Security Agency (NSA) had been using futuristic spy technology against individuals inside the United States.[25] The NSA is responsible for monitoring the communications of foreigners outside U.S. borders and does not have authority to engage in surveillance of Americans in the United States. Moreover, the Fourth Amendment protects American citizens against searches without either a warrant or a court order.

Certain well-established principles govern freedom of the press in the United States. First and foremost, the courts almost never allow the government to engage in prior restraint. **Prior restraint** means censorship—the attempt to block the publication of material that is considered to be harmful. The Supreme Court established this rule against censorship in 1931 in the landmark case of *Near v. Minnesota*.[7] After editor Jay Near wrote a story in the *Saturday Press* alleging that Jews were responsible for corruption, bribery, and prostitution in Minneapolis, a state judge barred all future sales of the newspaper. The Court overturned the state judge's ruling, finding that the sole purpose of the order was to suppress speech. Because freedom of the press has strong historical foundations, the Court concluded, censorship is clearly prohibited.

In the *Near* ruling, the Court recognized, however, that there might be times when governmental officials could limit the publication of certain stories. Specifically, such censorship might be justified under extraordinary circumstances related to ensuring public safety or national security or in cases involving obscenity. In reality, though, the Court has disallowed prior restraint in the vast majority of cases. For example, in the most important case examining the national security exception, *New York Times v. U.S.* (1971), the Court rejected the government's attempt to prevent publication of documents that detailed the history of the United States' involvement in Vietnam. In this case, also known as the Pentagon Papers case, the government argued that censorship was necessary to prevent "irreparable injury" to national security. But the Court dismissed this argument, asserting that full disclosure was in the interest of all Americans and that publication of the documents could contribute to the ongoing debate about the U.S. role in the Vietnam War.[26] In their ruling, the justices recognized that some materials are clearly necessary for full and fair discussion of issues facing the nation, while others are far less important to political discourse. (The Court, for example, has allowed the government to censor publications that are far less central to public debate, such as obscene materials.)

The Court is far more willing to allow the government to impose constraints on broadcast media than print media. Why should a distinction be made between print and broadcast media? Probably the most important justification is that only a limited number of channels can be broadcast, and the government is responsible for parceling out these channels. Because the public owns the airwaves, the people may also impose reasonable regulations on those who are awarded licenses to operate these channels.

The Court views the Internet to be more like print media than broadcast media. Thus far, the Court has signaled its interpretation that the Internet is an enormous resource for democratic forums, one that allows users access to virtually unlimited sites at very low cost (*Reno v. ACLU*, 1997). The Court's fine distinctions are between media that allow more versus less access to individuals and groups to engage in political discourse. The Court's assumption is that print media and the Internet provide relatively cheap and virtually unlimited access and enable people to tap easily into discussions about issues facing the nation. In contrast, broadcast media, with much scarcer channels, represent a much more limited arena for dialogue and thus can reasonably be regulated.

prior restraint
a form of censorship by the government whereby it blocks the publication of news stories viewed as libelous or harmful

Freedoms of Religion, Privacy, and Criminal Due Process: Encouraging Community and Civic Engagement

The Constitution's framers understood that the government they were creating could use its powers to single out certain groups for either favorable or unfavorable treatment and in this way could interfere with the creation of community—and with citizens' engagement within that community. The founders' commitment to community building and citizens' engagement lies at the heart of several constitutional amendments in the Bill of Rights. Specifically these are the amendments establishing the freedom of religion, the right to privacy, and the right to due process for individuals in the criminal justice system.

The First Amendment and the Freedom of Religion

The religion clauses of the First Amendment—the establishment clause and the free exercise clause—essentially do two things. First, they bar the government from establishing or supporting any one religious sect over another, and second, they ensure that individuals are not hindered in the exercise of their religion. While the establishment clause requires that the government be neutral toward religious institutions, favoring neither one specific religion over others nor all religious groups over nonreligious groups, the free exercise clause prohibits the government from taking action that is hostile toward individuals' practice of their religion. As we now consider, there is a tension between these two clauses.

establishment clause
First Amendment clause that bars the government from passing any law "respecting an establishment of religion"; often interpreted as a separation of church and state but increasingly questioned

THE ESTABLISHMENT CLAUSE   Stating only that "Congress shall make no law respecting an establishment of religion," the **establishment clause** does little to clarify what the relationship between church and state should be. The Constitution's authors wanted to ensure that Congress could not create a national religion, as a number of European powers (notably France and Spain) had done; the framers sought to avoid this level of government entanglement in religious matters. Further, many colonists had immigrated to America to escape religious persecution in Europe, and although many were deeply religious, uncertainty prevailed about the role that government should play in the practice of religion. This uncertainty, too, is reflected in the brevity of the establishment clause. The question arises, does the clause prohibit the government from simply preferring one sect over another, or is it broader, encompassing any kind of support of religion?

This is a crucial question because religious institutions have always been important forums for community building and engagement in the United States. Americans continue to be a very religious people. In 2007, over 82 percent of Americans surveyed said religion was fairly or very important in their lives.[27] But even given their strong religious affiliations, most Americans believe in some degree of separation between religious organizations and the government. The real question has centered on what amount of separation the establishment clause requires.

Over time, scholars and lawyers have considered three possible interpretations of the establishment clause. One interpretation, called separationism, is that the establishment clause requires a *strict separation of church and state* and bars most or all government support for religious sects. Supporters of the strict separationist view invoke the writings of Thomas Jefferson, James Madison, and others that call for a "wall of separation" between church and state.[28] They also point to societies outside the United States in which religious leaders dictate how citizens may dress, act, and pray (see "Global Comparisons") as examples of what can happen without strict separation.

A second, and more flexible, interpretation allows the government to offer support to religious sects as long as this support is neutral and not biased toward one sect. This interpretation, known as *neutrality* or the *preferential treatment standard,* would permit government support provided that this support extended to all religious groups. The third interpretation is the most flexible and reads the establishment clause as barring only establishment

MODESTY CODES IN IRAN

Iranian reporter Azadeh Moaveni moved to Tehran in 2005 after being raised in the United States. During the summer of 2007, she was stopped by a policewoman in a black *chador,* who pronounced her plain cotton head scarf too thin and decided to arrest her for this violation of Islamic modesty laws (*hijab*).

Can the Iranian people realistically hope to restore their shattered civil liberties?

After her husband pleaded with the officer not to separate Moaveni from her baby, a male officer noted that her sleeves, which fell a few inches from her wrists, were also too short. Before the authorities would release her, they forced Moaveni to sign a commitment that she would not repeat her mistake.

In 2005, men with long hair and women with brightly colored head scarves had moved about freely in Iranian society. However, in the summer of 2007, convinced that the United States was seeking to destabilize their Islamic system, ruling clerics began retaking control of the public sphere by clamping down on dress codes, confiscating satellite dishes linking Iranians to the outside world, searching houses without a warrant or warning, and detaining Iranian American academics for plotting to overthrow the government through support for a civil society. Since the crackdown, even couples celebrating a wedding with upbeat music, fancy evening wear, and energetic dancing must fear police raids for undignified dress and behavior.

The booking or detention of women whom authorities judge to be insufficiently clad is part of security officials' campaign against "bad *hijab,*" which extends to youths sporting "Western-style" haircuts, rock-music fans, shopkeepers selling indecent garments, and unmarried couples caught holding hands in public. The seriousness of the modesty code is illustrated by signs outside public hospitals declaring that only women wearing the head-to-floor *chador,* and not merely the head scarf, will be helped.

Without a bill of rights protecting individuals' basic civil liberties, ordinary Iranian citizens are subject to the whims of the ruling religious authorities. As a theocracy that rejects the notion of a separation between church and state, Iran subjects all citizens to the dictates of its religious leaders and to their rulings on basic personal decisions about clothing, hairstyle, music, and television.

Whereas the First Amendment's prohibition on state-established religion bars the U.S. government from enforcing religious laws, the government in Iran is committed to upholding Islamic values. And while the First Amendment's guarantee of a free press allows Americans to access network, cable, and satellite television as they wish, the state-controlled communications networks in Iran empower the government to restrict Internet and television access.

Iranian president Mahmoud Ahmadinejad has intensified a campaign to reimpose the moral fervor of the 1979 Islamic revolution's early years. Iran officially became an Islamic republic on April 1, 1979, when Iranians, upset with what they perceived as anti-Islamic, Western dominance over their affairs, overwhelmingly approved a national referendum to make it so. The year 2007 saw the largest crackdown on civil liberties since the 1980s. The government uses fear of the West and of a U.S. attack as a justification for limiting free speech. Under President Ahmadinejad, authorities curbed Internet access, shut down almost all liberal newspapers, jailed Iranian American scholars, and kept activists under close surveillance and frequently summoned them for questioning.

Although some offenders, like Moaveni, are released after signing pledges of good behavior, complaints of brutality have surrounded much police action. In many cases documentary evidence, such as graphic footage of beatings posted on dissidents' Web sites, has confirmed the abuses. Without due process protections for the criminally accused, the number of executions, including mass public hangings, has skyrocketed, making Iran the world's heaviest user of capital punishment per capita.

of a state religion. This interpretation, known as *accommodationism,* allows the government to offer support to any or all religious groups provided that this support does not rise to the level of recognizing an official religion.[29]

Which of these three vastly different interpretations of the establishment clause is correct? Over time, the Supreme Court has shifted back and forth in its opinions, usually depending on the kind of government support in question. Overall, the courts have rejected the strictest interpretation of the establishment clause, which would ban virtually any form of aid to religion. Instead, they have allowed government support for religious schools, programs, and institutions if the support advances a secular (nonreligious) goal and does not specifically endorse a particular religious belief.

For example, in 1974, the Court upheld a New Jersey program that provided funds to the parents of parochial school students to pay for bus transportation to and from school.[30] The Court reasoned that the program was necessary to help students to get to school safely and concluded that if the state withdrew funding for any of these programs for parochial school students, it would be impossible to operate these schools. The impact would be the hindrance of the free exercise of religion for students and their parents.

In another landmark case, *Lemon v. Kurtzman* (1971), however, the Court struck down a state program that used cigarette taxes to reimburse parochial schools for the costs of teachers' salaries and textbooks. The Court found that subsidizing parochial schools furthered a process of religious teaching and that the "continuing state surveillance" that would be necessary to enforce the specific provisions of the laws would inevitably entangle the state in religious affairs.[31]

In the *Lemon* case ruling, the Court refined the establishment clause standard to include three considerations. First, does the state program have a secular, as opposed to a religious, purpose? Second, does it have as its principal effect the advancement of religion? And third, does the program create an excessive entanglement between church and state? This three-part test is known as the **Lemon test.** The programs most likely to withstand scrutiny under the establishment clause are those that have a secular purpose, have only an incidental effect on the advancement of religion, and do not excessively entangle church and state.

More recently, the Court upheld an Ohio program that gave vouchers to parents to offset the cost of parochial schooling.[32] The justices ruled that the purpose of the program was secular, not religious, because it was intended to allow parents an alternative to the Cleveland public schools. Any aid to religious institutions—in this case, mostly Catholic schools—was in-direct, because the primary beneficiaries were the students themselves. Finally, there was little entanglement between the church and state, because the parents received the vouchers based on financial need and then were free to use these vouchers as they pleased. There was no direct relationship between the religious schools and the state.

So where the government program offers financial support, the Court has tended to evaluate this program by using either the preferential treatment standard or the accommodationist standard. Where the program or policy involves prayer in the school or issues related to the curriculum, however, the Court has adopted a standard that looks more like strict separationism. Table 4.4 summarizes the Court's decisions in a variety of school-related free exercise and establishment clause cases.

As Table 4.4 illustrates, a series of cases beginning with *Engel v. Vitale* (1962) has barred formalized prayer in the school, finding that such prayer has a purely religious purpose and that prayer is intended to advance religious, as opposed to secular, ideals.[33] For this reason, the Court has barred organized prayer in public elementary and secondary schools on the grounds that it constitutes a state endorsement of religion.

Recently, courts have begun to grapple with the decision of some school boards to mandate the inclusion of intelligent design in the curriculum.[34] **Intelligent design** is the theory that the apparent design in the universe and in living things is the product of an intelligent cause rather than of an undirected process such as natural selection. Though not stated by some of its primary proponents, many supporters believe that the designer is God, and they seek to redefine science to accept supernatural explanations.

Lemon test
a three-part test established by the Supreme Court in the 1971 case *Lemon v. Kurtzman* to determine whether government aid to parochial schools is constitutional; the test is also applied to other cases involving the establishment clause

intelligent design
theory that the apparent design in the universe and in living things is the product of an intelligent cause rather than of an undirected process such as natural selection; its primary proponents believe that the designer is God and seek to redefine science to accept supernatural explanations

Advocates of intelligent design claim that unlike **creationism,** which defends a literal interpretation of the biblical story of Genesis, intelligent design is a scientific theory. For this reason, they say, school boards should be permitted to include it in the curriculum, alongside evolution. Opponents claim that intelligent design is just another form of creationism, as it is based upon a belief in a divine being, does not generate any predictions, and cannot be tested by experiment. Mandating that schools teach intelligent design, critics argue, constitutes an endorsement of religion by the state.

THE FREE EXERCISE CLAUSE A real tension exists between the establishment and free exercise clauses. Whereas the establishment clause bars the state from helping religious institutions, the **free exercise clause** makes it illegal for the government to enact laws prohibiting the free practice of religion by individuals. Establishment clause cases often raise free exercise claims, and so courts must frequently consider whether by banning state aid, they are interfering with the free exercise of religion.

Although free exercise and establishment cases raise many of the same concerns, they are very different kinds of cases whose resolution depends on distinct legal tests. Establishment clause cases typically involve well-established and well-known religious institutions. Because establishment clause cases often center on state aid to religious schools, many involve the Roman Catholic Church, which administers the largest number of private elementary and secondary schools in the country. In contrast, free exercise clause cases tend to involve less mainstream religious groups, among them Mormons, Jehovah's Witnesses, Christian Scientists, and Amish. These groups' practices tend to be less well known—or more controversial. For example, free exercise clause cases have involved the right to practice polygamy, to use hallucinogens, to refuse conventional medical care for a child, and to refuse to salute the flag.

The Supreme Court has refused to accept that the government is barred from *ever* interfering with religious exercise. Free exercise claims are difficult to settle because they require that courts balance the individual's right to free practice of religion against the government's need to adopt some policy or program. First and foremost, the Court has always distinguished between religious beliefs, which government may not interfere with, and religious actions, which government is permitted to regulate. For example, although adults may refuse lifesaving medical care on the basis of their own religious beliefs, they may not refuse medical procedures required to save the lives of their children.[35]

In assessing those laws that interfere with religiously motivated action,

creationism
theory of the creation of the earth and humankind based on a literal interpretation of the biblical story of Genesis

free exercise clause
First Amendment clause prohibiting the government from enacting laws prohibiting an individual's practice of his or her religion; often in contention with the establishment clause

TABLE 4.4

Religion and Schools: Permissible and Impermissible Activities

Public Funding Not Permitted	Supreme Court Case	Year
Parochial school salaries	Lemon v. Kurtzman	1971
Parochial school textbooks	Lemon v. Kurtzman	1971
Public Funding Permitted	**Supreme Court Case**	**Year**
Parochial school busing	Everson v. Board of Education	1947
Parochial/private school computers	Mitchell v. Helms	2000
Public/private school vouchers	Zelman v. Simmons-Harris	2002
Public School Activities Not Permitted	**Supreme Court Case**	**Year**
Teacher-led nondenominational prayer	Engel v. Vitale	1962
Banning the teaching of evolution	Epperson v. Arkansas	1968
Requiring teaching of creationism	Edward v. Aguillard	1987
Requiring Ten Commandments posting	Stone v. Graham	1980
Official graduation ceremony prayers	Lee v. Weisman	1992
Moment of silence for voluntary prayer	Wallace v. Jaffree	1985
Student-led prayers using PA system	Santa Fe School District v. Doe	2000
Requiring all students to say the Pledge	W. Virginia Board of Ed. v. Barnette	1943
Public School Activities Permitted	**Supreme Court Case**	**Year**
Off-campus release-time religion classes	Zorach v. Clauson	1952
After-school student-led religion club	Board of Education of Westside Community Schools v. Mergens	1990
Use of public school building by religious groups (after hours)	Lamb's Chapel v. Center Moriches School District	1993
Public school teachers teaching in parochial schools	Agostini v. Felton	1997
Voluntary after-school Bible study	Good News Club v. Milford Central School	2001

> In April 2008, after allegations of child abuse and underage marriage arose, law enforcement agents descended on the Eldorado, Texas, ranch inhabited by 1,951 members of the Fundamentalist Church of Jesus Christ of Latter Day Saints, a polygamist Mormon sect. Authorities temporarily removed 416 children from the compound. The episode provoked debate about the limits of civil liberties such as freedom of religion and freedom from unreasonable search and seizure.

the Court has distinguished between laws that are neutral and generally applicable to all religious sects and laws that single out one sect for unfavorable treatment. In *Employment Division, Department of Human Resources v. Smith* (1990), the Court allowed the state of Oregon to deny unemployment benefits to two substance abuse counselors who were fired from their jobs after using peyote as part of their religious practice. Oregon refused to provide benefits because the two men had been fired for engaging in an illegal activity. The Court concluded that there was no free exercise challenge, because Oregon had good reason for denying benefits to lawbreakers who had been fired from their jobs. The justices concluded that the state was simply applying a neutral and generally applicable law to the men as opposed to singling them out for bad treatment.[36]

In summary, people are free to hold and profess their own beliefs, to build and actively participate in religious communities, and to allow their religious beliefs to inform their participation in politics and civil society. However, individual *actions* based on religious beliefs may be limited if these actions conflict with existing laws that are neutrally applied in a nondiscriminatory fashion.

The Right to Privacy

right to privacy

the right of an individual to be left alone and to make decisions freely, without the interference of others

So far in this section, we have explored the relationship between civil liberties and some key themes of this book: civic participation, inclusiveness, community building, and community engagement. We now shift our focus somewhat to consider the **right to privacy,** the right of an individual to be left alone and to make decisions freely, without the interference of others. Privacy is a core principle for most Americans, and the right to make decisions, especially about intimate or personal matters, is at the heart of this right. Yet the right to privacy is also necessary for genuine inclusiveness and community engagement, because it ensures that each individual is able to act autonomously and to make decisions about how he or she will interact with others.

The right to privacy is highly controversial and the subject of much public debate. In large part, the reason is that this right is tied to some of the most divisive issues of our day, including abortion, aid in dying, and sexual orientation. The right to privacy is also controversial because, unlike the freedoms of speech, the press, assembly, and religion, it is not explicitly mentioned anywhere in the Constitution. A further reason for the debate surrounding the right to privacy is that the Supreme Court has only recently recognized it.

THE EMERGENT RIGHT TO PRIVACY   For more than one hundred years, Supreme Court justices and lower court judges have concluded that the right to privacy is implied in all of the other liberties spelled out in the Bill of Rights. Not until the landmark Supreme Court case *Griswold v. Connecticut* (1965) did the courts firmly establish the right to privacy. The issue in this case may seem strange to us today: whether the state of Connecticut had the power to prohibit married couples from using birth control. In their decision, the justices concluded that the state law violated the privacy right of married couples seeking to access birth control, and they struck down the law. The Court argued that the right to privacy was inherent in many of the other constitutional guarantees, most importantly the First Amendment freedom of association, the Third Amendment right to be free from the quartering of soldiers, the Fourth Amendment right to be free from unreasonable searches and seizures, the Fifth Amendment protection against self-incrimination, and the Ninth Amendment assurance of rights not explicitly listed in the Bill of Rights. Justice William O. Douglas and his colleagues effectively argued that a zone of privacy surrounded every person in the United States and that government could not pass laws that encroached upon this zone.[37]

In its ruling, the Court asserted that the right to privacy existed quite apart from the law. It was *implicit* in the Bill of Rights and fundamental to the American system of law and justice. The right to privacy hinged in large part on the right of individuals to associate with one another, and specifically the right of marital partners to engage in intimate association.

In a 1984 case, the Supreme Court ruled that the Constitution protects two kinds of freedom of association: (1) intimate associations and (2) expressive associations.[38] The protection of intimate associations allows Americans to maintain intimate human relationships as part of their personal liberty. The protection of expressive associations allows people to form associations with others and to practice their First Amendment freedoms of speech, assembly, petition, and religion.

THE RIGHT TO PRIVACY APPLIED TO OTHER ACTIVITIES   The challenge for the Court since *Griswold* has been to determine which activities fall within the scope of the privacy right, and this question has placed the justices at the center of some of the most controversial issues of the day. For example, the first attempt to extend the privacy right, which raised the question whether the right protected the right to abortion, remains at least as controversial today as it was in 1973 when the Court decided the first abortion rights case, *Roe v. Wade*.[39] In *Roe* and the many abortion cases the Court has heard since, the justices have tried to establish whether a woman's right to abortion takes precedence over any interests the state may have in either the woman's health or the fetus's life. Over time, the Court has adopted a compromise position by rejecting the view that the right to abortion is absolute and by attempting to determine when states can regulate, or even prohibit, access to abortion. In 1992, the Court established the "undue burden" test, which asks whether a state abortion law places a "substantial obstacle in the path of a woman seeking an abortion before the fetus attains

> Public debate over abortion was not settled by the Supreme Court's 1973 decision in *Roe v. Wade*. In this photo taken more than three decades later, pro-life and pro-choice activists in Washington, D.C., hold signs supporting their differing viewpoints. Abortion rights advocates frame the issue in terms of a woman's right to privacy and to control her own body. Abortion rights opponents view abortion as murder and frame the issue in terms of the rights of an unborn child.

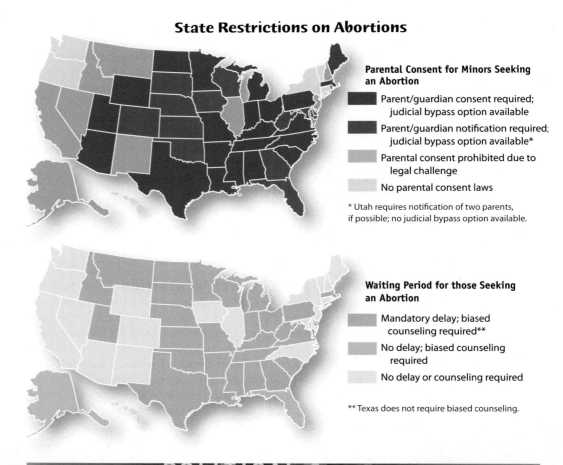

State Restrictions on Abortions

Parental Consent for Minors Seeking an Abortion

- Parent/guardian consent required; judicial bypass option available
- Parent/guardian notification required; judicial bypass option available*
- Parental consent prohibited due to legal challenge
- No parental consent laws

* Utah requires notification of two parents, if possible; no judicial bypass option available.

Waiting Period for those Seeking an Abortion

- Mandatory delay; biased counseling required**
- No delay; biased counseling required
- No delay or counseling required

** Texas does not require biased counseling.

POLITICAL INQUIRY

FIGURE 4.1 ■ **What are three states that require both a mandatory delay and parental consent for abortion? What are three that require one or the other only? What restrictions does your home state put on abortions?**

viability."[40] Although spousal notification requirements were struck down using this standard, Figure 4.1 shows that other requirements, including waiting periods, mandatory counseling, and parental consent, have been upheld by the Court.

The Court has also stepped gingerly around other privacy rights, such as the right to choose one's sexual partners and the right to terminate medical treatment or engage in physician-assisted suicide. Both of these rights have been presented to the Court as hinging on the much broader right to privacy. With respect to the right to terminate medical treatment, the Court has been fairly clear. Various Court decisions have confirmed that as long as an individual is competent to terminate treatment, the state may not stop him or her from taking this action, even if stopping treatment will lead to the person's death.[41] The Court has been less clear in its rulings when an incompetent person's right is advanced by another individual, such as a spouse, parent, or child. In these circumstances, the Court has accepted the state's argument that before treatment may be terminated, the state may require that the person seeking to end life show that his or her loved one would have wanted this course of action.[42] When a person's wishes are not clear, loved ones may wage legal battles over whether to discontinue life support (see Chapter 14).

In cases involving the right to engage in consensual sexual activities with a partner of one's choosing, the Supreme Court has also employed a less than absolute approach. For many years the Court allowed states to criminalize homosexual activity, finding that the right to engage in consensual sexual activity did not extend to same-sex partners.[43] In a 2002 case, *Lawrence v. Texas,* the Court changed course by ruling that the right to engage in intimate sexual activity was protected as a liberty right, especially when the activity occurred inside one's home, and that states could not criminalize this activity.[44] Yet beyond the *Lawrence* decision, states are still free to prohibit a range of sexual activities, including prostitution, child sexual abuse, and sex in public places.[45] In the Court's view, these activities can be prohibited primarily because they are not consensual or not taking place in the home, a place that accords special protection by the privacy right.

The right to privacy remains very controversial. Cases brought under the right to privacy tend to link this right with some other civil liberties issue, such as the protection against unreasonable search and seizure, the right to free speech, or the protection against self-incrimination. In other words, the privacy right, which the justices themselves created, seems to need buttressing by other rights that the Bill of Rights *explicitly* establishes. The explanation for this development may be the contentiousness of Americans' civic discourse about abortion, aid in dying, and other privacy issues. In short, continuing civic disagreement may have forced the Court to fall back on rights that are well established and more widely accepted.

Public discourse about privacy is constantly evolving as people voluntarily share more and more information about themselves through online networking sites such as Facebook, MySpace, and YouTube (see "Then, Now, Next").

Sharing Personal Information on the Internet

WEB SITE	THEN (2003)	NOW (2009)
MySpace	0 accounts	> 200 million accounts
Facebook	0 active users	> 75 million active users
YouTube	0 videos shared	> Hundreds of millions of videos shared daily

WHAT'S NEXT?

> Will social-networking Web sites be required to share personal information about their clients, and their clients' Internet behavior, with federal investigators?

> How will our conceptions of privacy (and privacy rights) change as people post increasing amounts of information about themselves on the Web?

> Will the courts continue to protect virtually unlimited speech on the Web?

Users share stories, photos, and videos of themselves—as well as of others, who may be unaware that they are the subject of a Weblog or video. Civil libertarians worry about the misuse and theft of personal information in a high-tech society where people's financial, employment, consumer, legal, and personal histories are so easily accessible. Government and law enforcement agencies are still deciding how they may use such materials in criminal investigations. Legal implications remain unclear.

The Fourth, Fifth, Sixth, and Eighth Amendments: Ensuring Criminal Due Process

The last category of civil liberties that bear directly on civic engagement consists of the criminal due process protections established in the Fourth, Fifth, Sixth, and Eighth amendments. Does it surprise you that so many of the Bill of Rights amendments focus on the rights of individuals accused of crimes? The context for this emphasis is the founders' concern with how the British monarchy had abused its power and used criminal law to impose its will on the American colonists. The British government had used repeated trials, charges of treason, and imprisonment without bail to stifle political dissent. The founders therefore wanted to ensure that there were effective checks on the power of the federal government, especially in the creation and enforcement of criminal law. As we have seen, the Bill of Rights amendments were incorporated to apply to the states and to their criminal codes through the process of selective incorporation. Thus, criminal due process protections are the constitutional limits imposed on law enforcement personnel.

These four amendments together are known as the **criminal due process rights** because they establish the guidelines that the government must follow in investigating, bringing

criminal due process rights safeguards for those accused of crime; these rights constrain government conduct in investigating crimes, trying cases, and punishing offenders

to trial, and punishing individuals who violate criminal law. Each amendment guides the government in administering some facet of law enforcement, and all are intended to ensure justice and fairness in the administration of the law. Criminal due process is essential to guarantee that individuals can participate in the larger society and that no one person is singled out for better or worse treatment under the law. Like the First Amendment, due process protects political speech and freedom. Without these liberties, government officials could selectively target those who disagree with the laws and policies they advocate.

Moreover, without these rights, there would be little to stop the government from using criminal law to punish those who want to take action that is protected by the other amendments we have examined in this chapter. For example, what good would it do to talk about the freedom of speech if the government could isolate or punish someone who spoke out critically against it without having to prove in a public venue that the speech threatened public safety or national security? The criminal due process protections are essential to ensuring meaningful participation and engagement in the larger community and to safeguarding justice and fairness.

THE FOURTH AMENDMENT AND THE PROTECTION AGAINST UNREASONABLE SEARCHES AND SEIZURES

The Fourth Amendment requires police to get a warrant before engaging in a search and guides law enforcement personnel in conducting criminal investigations and in searching an individual's body or property. It has its roots in colonial history—specifically, in the British government's abuse of its law enforcement powers to prosecute and punish American colonists suspected of being disloyal.

The Fourth Amendment imposes significant limits on law enforcement. In barring police from conducting any unreasonable searches and seizures, it requires that they show probable cause that a crime has been committed before they can obtain a search warrant. The warrant ensures that police officers can gather evidence only when they have probable cause. Further, a judicially created ruling known as the **exclusionary rule** compels law enforcers to carry out searches properly. Established for federal prosecutions in 1914, the exclusionary rule forbids the courts to admit illegally seized evidence during trial.[46] This rule was extended to state court proceedings in the Supreme Court decision *Mapp v. Ohio* (1961).[47] In this case, the Court overturned an Ohio court's conviction of Dollree Mapp for the possession of obscene materials. Police had found pornographic books in Mapp's apartment after searching it without a search warrant and despite the defendant's refusal to let them in. Critics of the exclusionary rule note that securing a warrant is not always necessary or feasible and that guilty people sometimes go free due to procedural technicalities. They argue that reasonable searches should not be defined solely by the presence of a court-ordered search warrant.[48]

What are "reasonable" and "unreasonable" searches under the Fourth Amendment? Over time, the U.S. Supreme Court has established criteria to guide both police officers and judges hearing cases. The strictest definition of reasonableness requires that there is a warrant: where there is no warrant, the search is considered to be unreasonable. However, the Supreme Court has ruled that even without a warrant, some searches would still be reasonable. In 1984, for example, the Court held that illegally obtained evidence could be admitted at trial if law enforcers could prove that they would have obtained the evidence legally anyway.[49] In another case the same year, the Court created a "good faith" exception to the exclusionary rule by upholding the use of evidence obtained with a technically incorrect warrant, because the police officer had acted in good faith.[50]

More broadly, a warrantless search is valid if the person subjected to it has no reasonable expectation of privacy in the place or thing being searched. From colonial times to the present, the assumption has been that individuals have a reasonable expectation of privacy in their homes. Where there is no reasonable expectation of privacy, however, there can be no unreasonable search, and so the police are not required to get a warrant before conducting the search or surveillance. Since the 1990s, the Court has expanded the situations in which there is no reasonable expectation of privacy and hence no need for a warrant. For example, there is no reasonable expectation of privacy in one's car, at least in those areas that are in plain view such as the front and back seats. There is also no expectation of privacy in public places such as parks and stores, because it is reasonable to assume that a person knowingly exposes his

exclusionary rule
criminal procedural rule stating that evidence obtained illegally cannot be used in a trial

or her activities to public view in these places. The same is true of one's trash: because there is no reasonable expectation of privacy in the things that one discards, police may search this material without a warrant.[51]

In instances where there is a reasonable expectation of privacy, individuals or their property may be searched if law enforcement personnel acquire a warrant from a judge. To obtain a warrant, the police must provide the judge with evidence that establishes probable cause that a crime has been committed. Further, the warrant must be specific about the place to be searched and the materials that the agents are seeking. These requirements limit the ability of police simply to go on a "fishing expedition" to find some bit of incriminating evidence.

As society changes, expectations of privacy change as well. For example, technological innovation has given us e-mail and the World Wide Web, and Fourth Amendment law has had to adapt to these inventions. Is there a reasonable expectation of privacy in our communications on the Web? This is an important question, especially in light of citizens' heightened concerns about terrorism and white-collar crime.

THE FIFTH AND SIXTH AMENDMENTS: THE RIGHT TO A FAIR TRIAL AND THE RIGHT TO COUNSEL
The Fifth and Sixth amendments establish the rules for conducting a trial. These two amendments ensure that criminal defendants are protected at the formal stages of legal proceedings. Although less than 10 percent of all charges result in trials, these protections have significant symbolic and practical importance, because they hold the state to a high standard whenever it attempts to use its significant power to prosecute a case against an individual.

The Fifth Amendment bars **double jeopardy** and compelled self-incrimination. These safeguards mean, respectively, that a person may not be tried twice for the same crime nor forced to testify against himself or herself when accused of a crime. These safeguards are meant to protect people from persecution, harassment, and forced confessions. A single criminal action, however, can lead to multiple trials if each trial is based on a separate offense.

The Sixth Amendment establishes the rights to a speedy and public trial, to a trial by a jury of one's peers, to information about the charges against oneself, to the confrontation of witnesses testifying against oneself, and to legal counsel. The protection of these liberties is promoted by the **Miranda rights,** based on the Supreme Court decision in *Miranda v. Arizona* (1966).[52] In the *Miranda* case, the Court outlined the requirement that "prior to questioning, the person must be warned that he has a right to remain silent, that any statement he does make may be used against him, and that he has a right to the presence of an attorney, either retained or appointed." Later cases have created some exceptions to *Miranda* (see Table 4.5).

Together, the Fourth, Fifth, and Sixth amendments ensure the protection of individuals against abuses of power by the state, and in so doing they promote a view of justice that the community widely embraces. Because these rights extend to individuals charged with violating the community's standards of right and wrong, they promote a broad sense of inclusiveness—a respect even for persons who allegedly have committed serious offenses, and a desire to ensure that the justice system treats all people fairly.

The Court has considered the community's views in reaching its decisions in cases brought before it. For example, through a series of Supreme Court cases culminating with *Gideon v. Wainwright* (1963), the justices interpreted the right to counsel to mean that the government must provide lawyers to individuals who are too poor to hire their own.[53] The justices adopted this standard because they came to believe that the community's views of fundamental fairness dictated this result.

double jeopardy
to be tried again for the same crime that one has been cleared of in court; barred by the Fifth Amendment

Miranda **rights**
criminal procedural rule, established in the 1966 case *Miranda v. Arizona,* requiring police to inform criminal suspects, on their arrest, of their legal rights, such as the right to remain silent and the right to counsel; these warnings must be read to suspects before interrogation

TABLE 4.5

Cases Weakening Protection Against Self-Incrimination

Year	Case	Ruling
1986	*Moran v. Burbine*	Confession is not inadmissible because police failed to inform suspect of attorney's attempted contacts.
1991	*Arizona v. Fulminante*	Conviction is not automatically overturned in cases of coerced confession if other evidence is strong enough to justify conviction.
1994	*Davis v. U.S.*	Suspect must unequivocally and assertively state his right to counsel to stop police questioning.

The Death Penalty

Do you favor or oppose the death penalty for persons convicted of murder?

☐ Favor the death penalty

☐ Oppose the death penalty

☐ Unsure/Don't know

Source: "Capital Punishment's Constant Constituency: An American Majority," http://pewresearch.org/pubs/523/capital-punishments-constant-constituency-an-american-majority.

THE EIGHTH AMENDMENT: PROTECTION AGAINST CRUEL AND UNUSUAL PUNISHMENT The meaning of *cruel* and *unusual* has changed radically since the Eighth Amendment was ratified, especially with regard to the imposition of capital punishment—the death penalty. Moreover, Americans have always disagreed among themselves about the death penalty itself. Throughout the country's history, citizens and lawmakers have debated the morality of capital punishment as well as the circumstances under which the death penalty should be used. Central to the public debate have been the questions of which crimes should be punished by death and how capital punishment should be carried out.

Generally, the Court has supported the constitutionality of the death penalty. An exception was the landmark case *Furman v. Georgia* (1972), in which, in a 5–4 decision, the Court suspended the use of the death penalty.[54] Justices Brennan and Marshall believed the death penalty to be "incompatible with evolving standards of decency in contemporary society." The dissenting justices argued in turn that capital punishment had always been regarded as appropriate under the Anglo-American legal tradition for serious crimes and that the Constitution implicitly authorized death penalty laws because of the Fourteenth Amendment's reference to the taking of "life." The majority decision came about due to concurring opinions by justices Stewart, White, and Douglas, who focused on the arbitrary nature with which death sentences had been imposed. The Court's decision forced the states and the national legislature to rethink their statutes for capital offenses to ensure that the death penalty would not be administered in a capricious or discriminatory manner.[55] Over time, the courts have also interpreted the Eighth Amendment as requiring that executions be carried out in the most humane and least painful manner. Public discourse and debate have strongly influenced thinking about which methods of execution are appropriate.

Recent studies, however, suggest that states' administration of the sedative sodium pentothal has left individuals conscious and in agony but paralyzed and thus unable to cry out while they are dying. But in 2008, the Supreme Court ruled in a 7–2 decision that lethal injection does not constitute cruel and unusual punishment,[56] paving the way for ten states, which had halted lethal injections pending the case's outcome, to resume executions. The 2008 decision marked the first time the Supreme Court reviewed the constitutionality of a method of execution since 1878, when the Court upheld Utah's use of a firing squad.[57] In that ruling, the Court said the Constitution prohibits executions that involve torture, such as burning alive or drawing and quartering an individual, as well as other infliction of "unnecessary cruelty" that the justices did not define. In the recent case, lawyers for the Kentucky inmates argued that the state is violating that standard by using drugs that pose a risk of extreme pain if something goes wrong and by failing to provide adequate safeguards. But in its decision in April 2008, the Court ruled that there is no Eighth Amendment requirement that a government-sanctioned execution be pain free, only that it does not involve a "substantial" or "objectively intolerable" risk of serious harm—a risk greater than possible alternatives.

Freedoms in Practice: Controversy over the Second Amendment and the Right to Bear Arms

The fierce debate today over gun control illustrates much about the nature of political discourse and citizen action in the United States. Americans disagree about how to interpret the Second Amendment of the Constitution, but they do agree to have their disputes settled through laws and court rulings rather than armed conflict. Private citizens and political interest groups voice their opinions about the place of guns in society by using their First Amendment freedoms of speech and assembly. They also work behind the scenes to influence elected officials through campaign contributions and lobbying (see Chapter 7). At the heart of this debate is the question of the role guns play in creating a safe and free society.

FIGURE 4.2

State Conceal and Carry Gun Legislation
There are forty right-to-carry (RTC) states. Of these, thirty-six have "shall issue" laws, which require that carry permits be issued to applicants who meet uniform standards established by the state legislature. Alabama, Connecticut, and Iowa have "discretionary-issue" carry permit systems. Vermont allows citizens to carry without a permit. (Alaska, which has a shall-issue provision for purposes of permit reciprocity with other states, adopted a no-permit-required law in 2003.) Of the ten non-RTC states, eight have discretionary-issue systems; two prohibit carrying altogether.
Source: www.nraila.org.

Right-to-Carry States

Shall issue (36 including AK)

Discretionary issue (3)

No permit required (AK does not require a permit but has a shall-issue permit system)

Non-Right-to-Carry States

Right restricted–very limited issue (8)

Right infringed/non-issue (2)

Competing Interpretations of the Second Amendment

Americans disagree about the purpose and contemporary significance of the Second Amendment, which reads

> A well regulated Militia, being necessary to the security of a free State, the right of the people to keep and bear Arms, shall not be infringed.

Some people argue that the amendment gives individual citizens the right to bear arms, free from government control.[58] On the opposing side, others stress that the Second Amendment's original purpose was to ensure that state militias could back the government in maintaining public order.[59] These people suggest that the right to bear arms is thus a group right subject to regulation by Congress and the states.[60] The unorganized militia has not been activated since before the Civil War, and the government now has adequate weapons to defend the nation, these critics say.

As Figure 4.2 illustrates, states differ widely in the degree to which citizens have access to guns. Some states allow residents to carry concealed weapons for personal protection, but others do not. In 1976, Washington, D.C., passed the nation's toughest gun control laws, including a ban on handguns, rifles, and automatic weapons, except for individuals with a special permit—mostly police and security guards. In March 2007 a federal appeals court struck down the district's handgun ban, rejecting the city's argument that the Second Amendment right to bear arms applies only to militias (see Chapter 2, "Exploring the Sources"). The city appealed the decision to the U.S. Supreme Court, which, in a 2008 ruling, affirmed the appeals court's ruling. In a 5–4 decision, the Supreme Court ruled that "the right of the people to keep and bear arms" is not limited to state militias but rather is a part of "the inherent right of self-defense."[61]

Citizens Engaged: Fighting for a Safer Nation

This disagreement over the Second Amendment's meaning is reflected in the actions of ordinary citizens and organized interest groups. For example, the Million Moms and the Second Amendment Sisters are two interest groups with clashing views on the issue of gun control. The Million Moms see stronger gun control laws as a way to prevent the alarmingly high number of U.S. deaths of young people from gun violence, an estimated ten deaths per day.[62] The Second Amendment Sisters believe that guns are a woman's best tool for self-defense and give her the ability to protect herself and her family.[63] Both groups have joined vocally in the public debate, exercising their freedom of speech and assembly to influence opinions about guns in the United States. They disagree over how best to protect themselves and their families in a dangerous world. Each group struggles to interpret the Second Amendment to fit its members' own understandings of social needs and problems today.

Owning a Gun in America

Does the Second Amendment guarantee to *all* U.S. citizens the right to own a gun? Or does it protect that right only in the case of state militias such as the National Guard?

☐ Guarantees the right to all Americans

☐ Guarantees the right exclusively to state militias

☐ Do not know/no opinion

Source: "Public Believes Americans Have Right to Own Guns," www.gallup.com/poll/105721/Public-Believes-Americans-Right-Own-Guns.aspx.

> The Second Amendment Sisters and the Million Mom March represent women on different sides of the gun control debate. What are your views on gun control?

Civil Liberties in Post-9/11 America

Public discussion about the proper balance between individual freedom and public safety is not limited to gun control policies. Debate has intensified as the nation struggles with the aftermath of the 9/11 terrorist attacks and the continuing global war on terror. Citizens and government leaders are rethinking their beliefs about the proper scope of government power.

In the course of U.S. history, liberty and security have perennially coexisted in a state of tension. In the wake of 9/11, this tension has become more acute, as the federal, state, and local governments have taken certain actions that directly intrude upon individual freedoms. The government argues these actions are necessary to protect life and property. But civil libertarians shudder at what they see as unprecedented violations of individual freedoms and rights.

Perceived Intrusions on Free Speech and Assembly

Following 9/11, a number of government agencies engaged in the surveillance of political groups in the United States. In late 2005, the media exposed a program by the Bush administration and the National Security Administration (NSA) to target U.S. civilians for electronic surveillance without judicial oversight. Members of the Bush administration claimed that they had monitored only communications where one party was suspected of links to terrorism and was currently overseas. Beginning in 2005, however, the American Civil Liberties Union (ACLU) issued a series of reports detailing how the Federal Bureau of Investigation (FBI) spied not only on people suspected of taking part in terrorist plots but also on individuals involved in peaceful political activities.[64] In one instance, the FBI monitored the organizers of an antiwar protest who had gathered at a Denver bookstore, and agents compiled a list with the descriptions and license plates of cars in the store's vicinity. The ACLU has released similar reports describing the Pentagon's database of peaceful war protesters.[65]

The ACLU and other critics of the domestic surveillance program have argued that the federal government is targeting political protest, not domestic terrorism plots. Opponents of the policy warn that the FBI and other agencies are infringing upon free speech, assembly, and expression. But former attorney general John Ashcroft and others in the Bush administration defended the government's expanded investigation and enforcement activities. They claimed that the threats to national security are grave and that the government must be given the power it needs to protect against these dangers.[66]

Perceived Intrusions on Criminal Due Process

Even though several years have passed since 9/11, concern lingers about another terrorist attack on U.S. soil, and many Americans are willing to accept some infringement on their freedoms if it makes them safer. These citizens assume that real criminal activity may be afoot and that the surveillance is not being used to target groups that are politically unpopular or critical of the administration. Much of the debate about the surveillance activities of the FBI and other groups centers on this distinction.

To what extent must administration officials provide evidence of real criminal intent before placing a suspect under surveillance? Since 9/11, the laws that govern domestic spying have been modified in such a way that the government has much more leeway in conducting searches and investigations, even where there is no real proof of criminal activity.

The 9/11 terrorism led to important shifts in U.S. policy. One example is the USA PATRIOT Act, which Congress passed six weeks after the 9/11 attacks with little debate in either the House or the Senate.[67] This law, reauthorized in 2005, allows the FBI and other intelligence agencies to access personal information and records without getting permission from, or even informing, targeted individuals. Much of the data come from private sources, which are often ordered to hand over their records. For example, the USA PATRIOT Act authorized the FBI to order Internet service providers to give information about their clients to the FBI. The USA PATRIOT Act also empowered intelligence agencies to order public libraries to hand over records of materials that the targeted individuals borrowed or viewed.

In addition, the Foreign Intelligence Surveillance Act (FISA) of 1978, which empowers the government to conduct secret searches where necessary to protect national security, has significantly broadened the powers of law enforcement agencies. Agencies must go before a specialized court, the Foreign Intelligence Surveillance Act Court, to justify the secret search. Civil libertarians are concerned about the FISA court's secret location and sealed records, as well as its proceedings, in which the suspect is never told about the investigation and probable cause is not required to approve surveillance or searches of any person suspected of having some link to terrorism.

On July 28, 2007, President Bush called on Congress to pass legislation to reform the FISA in order to ease restrictions on the surveillance of terrorist suspects in cases where one

POLITICAL INQUIRY

What is the cartoonist's view of how civil liberties have changed since 9/11? Do you agree with this view? How might policies affecting civil liberties change in the new presidential administration? Why?

© Ed Stein, Rocky Mountain News, http://blatanttruth.org.

Privacy Versus Security

Which is more important in the United States today—national security or personal privacy?

☐ Security is more important

☐ Privacy is more important

☐ Not sure

Source: "51% Say Security More Important than Privacy," www.rasmussenreports.com/public_content/politics/current_events/general_current_events/51_say_security_more_important_than_privacy.

party or both parties to the communication are located overseas. The Protect America Act of 2007, signed into law on August 5, 2007, essentially legalized ongoing NSA practices.[68] Under the act, communications that begin or end in a foreign country may be wiretapped by the U.S. government without supervision by the FISA court. The act removes from the definition of "electronic surveillance" in FISA any surveillance directed at a person reasonably believed to be located outside the United States. As such, surveillance of these communications no longer requires an order from the FISA court. This means that the government may listen to conversations without a court order as long as the U.S. attorney general approves the surveillance. Supporters stress that flexibility is needed to monitor the communications of suspected terrorists and their networks. Critics, however, worry that the law is too vague and provides the government with the ability to monitor any group or individual it opposes, regardless of whether it has links to terrorism.

Although many Americans are concerned about domestic surveillance, especially in situations where it targets political speech and expression, these laws remain on the books, and this surveillance likely will continue. For the time being, the line between suspected criminal activity and purely political expression remains blurred. Civic discourse about how to balance liberty and national security continues to play out as Americans consider how much freedom they should sacrifice to protect public safety (see "Exploring the Sources").

In addition to conversations about search and surveillance procedures, the nation is struggling with larger questions about the rights of detainees accused of conducting or supporting terrorist activities. Some political commentators argue that the torture of these individuals is appropriate in specific situations.[69] They point to a "ticking time bomb" scenario, in which the torture of a single suspect known to have information about the location of a nuclear bomb would be justified in order to save thousands or millions of innocent lives. Critics of this logic note that information obtained through torture is unreliable and not worth the price of violating our moral codes. Further, they argue that if the United States legalizes torture, Americans will lose their standing as a moral society and alienate potential allies in the war against terror.[70]

The debate over torture resulted in passage, by Congress and the president, of the Detainee Treatment Act of 2005, which bans cruel, inhuman, or degrading treatment of detainees in U.S. custody.[71] Despite this legislation, questions remain. For example, the Hollywood film *Rendition* (2007) dramatized a controversial practice involving the transfer of custody of suspected terrorists to other nations for imprisonment and interrogation. Critics charge that the goal of such "extraordinary rendition" (which is based on an actual program the media uncovered in 2006) is to circumvent U.S. law, which requires due process and prevents torture. Former secretary of state Condoleezza Rice denied that U.S. officials transfer suspects to places where they know these individuals will be tortured.[72] But according to a February 2007 European Parliament report, the CIA conducted 1,245 flights over European territory between 2001 and April 2006, many of them to destinations where suspects could face torture.[73] The 2007 confirmation hearings of Attorney General Michael Mukasey focused on the related issue of what constitutes torture. Critics of the nominee were upset by his refusal to define waterboarding—a controversial practice that simulates drowning—as illegal. Unquestionably, the global war on terror has caused U.S. citizens and public officials to rethink the boundaries of acceptable behavior as they balance the need to protect the civil liberties of the accused with the desire to prevent terrorist attacks.

Perceived Discrimination Against Muslim Americans

Members of the Bush administration repeatedly said that the war on terror was not a war on immigrants or a war on Islam. Despite assurances, civil libertarians and leaders in the Muslim American community criticized administration policies targeting Muslims. Among these were policies allowing racial profiling of Arab and Muslim men; the use of secret evidence in national security cases; widespread FBI interviews of Muslims; raids of Muslim homes, schools, and mosques; the special registration and fingerprinting of Muslims from specific Arab nations; and the detention and deportation of many Arab and Muslim nationals without the right to legal representation.[74] Members of the Bush administration

SHOULD U.S. AUTHORITIES USE ETHNIC PROFILING IN THE INTEREST OF NATIONAL SECURITY?

The Issue: In light of the ongoing terrorist threat, should airport security and law enforcement officials practice ethnic and religious profiling to prevent a hijacking or terrorist attack?

Yes: The most serious threat we face as a nation is the threat posed by militant Islamic fundamentalists. Militant Islam, or fundamentalism, is a radical ideology that teaches its adherents to apply the laws of Islam, the Shari'a, to all people by creating Islamic states.

Given the nature of the threat, it makes sense for police seeking suspects after a terrorist attack to search mosques rather than churches or synagogues and to question pedestrians who appear to be Middle Eastern or wear head scarves. To avoid an attack, it also makes sense to focus on the people most likely to threaten our safety. Heightened scrutiny for young Middle Eastern men fitting the profile of al-Qaeda recruits is reasonable. Should we require an 85-year-old grandmother from Wisconsin to remove her shoes at the airline gate simply because we just asked a 25-year-old single man from Saudi Arabia to do the same? Common sense tells us that we can more efficiently use resources by concentrating our attention on those who are most likely to pose a risk.

Although profiling may inconvenience law-abiding Muslims, they must be willing to endure mild inconvenience for the larger goal of saving lives. Indeed, integrationist Muslims who seek to live successfully within the U.S. constitutional framework react with fear and loathing when Islamist extremists commit acts of terror in the name of Islam.*

No: Racial, ethnic, and religious profiling is inefficient, counterproductive, and morally wrong. Race and ethnic appearance are poor predictors of behavior. First, it is difficult to determine a person's religion by appearance alone. People from the Middle East have a wide range of skin tones and facial features. They include Christians and Jews as well as Muslims. Cases of mistaken identity are widespread. Many of those who found themselves the victims of anti-Muslim hate crimes after 9/11 included numerous non-Muslims such as Chaldeans, Hindus, and Sikhs. More important, focusing on race and ethnicity keeps security officials' attention on a set of surface details that tell us little about a person, and draw officers' attention away from what is much more important and concrete: behavior.

Focusing on ethnic appearance can cause us to miss genuine threats. John Walker Lindh, a 20-year-old white Californian, fought with the Taliban in Afghanistan. Does an 85-year-old Middle Eastern grandmother deserve closer scrutiny than a 25-year-old white American man who has just bought a one-way ticket and looks nervous and sweaty?

Subjecting all Muslims or Middle Easterners to intrusive questioning, stops, or searches will harm our enforcement and detection efforts. First, profiling will drain enforcement efforts away from the close observation of suspicious behavior. Second, profiling will alienate law-abiding Muslims whose cooperation is critical for effective information gathering and counterterrorist intelligence. Alienating law-abiding Muslims by treating them like terrorist suspects will ultimately harm our ability to gather information about real terrorist threats.

We must find effective ways to secure the nation without giving up what is best about our country. Enacting discriminatory policies that take away individual liberty destroys the values for which we are fighting.**

Other approaches: The issue of ethnic profiling is more complicated than a yes or no answer would allow. In some cases, law enforcement use ethnic profiling based on specific threats. But law enforcement needs to recognize that ethnic profiling limits their ability to detect terror suspects who may not fit the mold of the stereotypical terrorist—including women.

What do you think?

1. Should airport security officers pay greater attention to passengers who appear to be Middle Eastern or Muslim? Why or why not?

2. Should the FBI use ethnic or religious profiling to select people to interview as part of its counterterrorism efforts?

3. Will profiling strengthen or weaken our intelligence-gathering efforts? Explain.

4. Is racial, ethnic, or religious profiling ever justified? If so, in what cases? If not, why not?

*For a fuller exposition of this argument, see Daniel Pipes, "Fighting Militant Islam, Without Bias," *City Journal*, November 2001.

**For a fuller exposition of this argument, see David A. Harris, "Flying While Arab, Immigration Issues, and Lessons from the Racial Profiling Controversy." Testimony before the U.S. Commission on Civil Rights (October 12, 2001).

EXPLORING THE SOURCES

A CHOICE BETWEEN FREEDOM AND SECURITY?

©2002 Ann Telnaes. All rights reserved. ATelnaes@aol.com

Evaluating the Evidence

1. What message is the cartoonist trying to convey?

2. Do you think citizens must choose between freedom and security? Explain.

3. Do you support the central provisions of the USA PATRIOT Act and the NSA wiretapping program? Why or why not? Do such programs increase security or threaten liberty? Explain.

explained this aggressive policing in Muslim communities as a way to catch would-be terrorists and to cause them to delay or abandon their plans. Critics argued that the policies violate the civil liberties of Muslims by denying them due process.

In addition, the administration used the USA PATRIOT Act's provision barring "material support" for terrorist organizations to crack down on Muslim charitable organizations. Several Muslim charities were shut down for allegedly providing financial or other material assistance to groups the government designates as "terrorist." Critics of this policy stressed that officials used it to lock down three of the largest Muslim American charities without investigation and without proving that these organizations had links to terrorist organizations.[75] Muslims who had been donating to these nonprofit organizations as part of their *Zakat,* an Islamic charitable obligation, later found themselves questioned by the FBI.

Critics contend that administration policies have violated Muslims' freedoms of speech, religion, and association as law enforcers monitor their words, religious ceremonies, and organizational ties and as Muslims have become targets of government interrogation and even detention. In a government profiling program designed to catch would-be terrorists, race, age, and national origin, too, can lead to interrogation. Those in the Bush administration argued that it was required to do whatever it could to protect U.S. citizens from another terrorist strike. Critics worried that racial and religious profiling would alienate the 7 million Muslim citizens and would in fact jeopardize officials' ability to gather valuable intelligence (see "The Conversation of Democracy"). The nation's struggles to balance the demands of freedom and order are clearly illustrated in the ongoing conversation about how to protect personal liberty while ensuring national security.

CONCLUSION

CONTINUING THE CONVERSATION

At the core of the U.S. political and legal system lies a strong belief in individual liberties and rights. This belief is reflected in the Bill of Rights, the first ten amendments to the Constitution. These freedoms are at the heart of civic engagement and ensure that individuals can freely participate in the political and social life of their communities. But these freedoms are also malleable, and at times the government has starkly limited them, as when officials perceive a threat to national security.

The inevitable tension between freedom and order is heightened in a post-9/11 world. Americans and their government struggle to protect essential liberties while guarding the nation against future terrorist attacks. This tension between national security and personal freedom is reflected in contemporary debates over free speech, political protest, and due process.

Do antiwar protests threaten the nation's success in Iraq? Should the government be able to track citizens' phone calls and e-mail messages? Should security officials profile Muslims and Arabs? Is torture ever justifiable? These are the questions we confront in a post-9/11 world as we struggle to maintain the commitment to liberty that defines our nation while preserving the nation itself.

Summary

1. Civil Liberties in the American Legal System
The U.S. Constitution—and more specifically, the Bill of Rights, the first ten amendments—protects individuals against the unrestrained exercise of power by the federal government. The framers intended the Bill of Rights to ensure that individuals could engage freely in political speech and civic discourse in the larger society. Although the Bill of Rights was initially interpreted as imposing limits only on the national government, over time the Supreme Court has interpreted most of its protections as applying to the state governments as well.

2. Freedoms of Speech, Assembly, and the Press: First Amendment Freedoms Supporting Civic Discourse
Civic engagement is possible only in a society that fully protects civil liberties. Some of the civil liberties guaranteed in the Bill of Rights relate specifically to political participation and discourse. Most importantly, the freedoms of speech, assembly, petition, and the press empower individuals to engage actively and freely in politics and public life. These freedoms have always existed in a state of tension with the goal of national security, however, and in times of crisis or instability, the judicial system has interpreted them narrowly.

3. Freedoms of Religion, Privacy, and Criminal Due Process: Encouraging Community and Civic Engagement
Other Bill of Rights freedoms encourage inclusiveness and community building, ensuring that individuals can be fully engaged in the social life of the nation. The freedom of religion, right to privacy, and criminal due process protections ensure that no one individual or group may be singled out for either favorable or unfavorable treatment.

4. Freedoms in Practice: Controversy over the Second Amendment and the Right to Bear Arms

Historical context is crucial to our understanding of the freedoms protected by the Bill of Rights. Americans actively disagree about the proper interpretation of the Second Amendment and about the role of guns in maintaining a free and safe society.

5. Civil Liberties in Post-9/11 America

The tension between liberty and security, always present in U.S. political culture, has become more acute since the terrorist attacks of September 11, 2001. In the wake of these attacks, federal and state law enforcement officials have limited the speech, assembly, and petition rights of some American citizens and nationals and have curtailed the due process protections of those suspected of engaging in or supporting domestic and international terrorism.

Key Terms

bad tendency test 138

civil liberties 131

clear and present danger test 138

clear and probable danger test 138

commercial speech 140

creationism 147

criminal due process rights 151

double jeopardy 153

due process 132

establishment clause 144

exclusionary rule 152

fighting words 141

free exercise clause 147

habeas corpus 137

imminent lawless action test (incitement test) 139

intelligent design 146

Lemon test 146

libel 140

marketplace of ideas 137

Miranda rights 153

obscenity 140

prior restraint 143

right to privacy 148

selective incorporation 134

slander 140

symbolic speech 139

time, place, and manner restrictions 141

total incorporation 134

For Review

1. What are civil liberties? How do civil liberties differ from civil rights?

2. How does the First Amendment support civic discourse?

3. What protections does the Bill of Rights provide to those accused of committing a crime?

4. What are the two sides of the issue of Second Amendment rights? How has the Supreme court interpreted this right?

5. How have the terrorist attacks of September 11, 2001, affected civil liberties in the United States?

For Critical Thinking and Discussion

1. Under what circumstances should the government be allowed to regulate or punish speech?

2. Should Congress pass a constitutional amendment banning flag burning? Why or why not?

3. Under what circumstances should government be able to punish people for practicing their religious beliefs?

4. Should the government be allowed to search people and property without a warrant based on probable cause that a crime was committed? Explain.

5. Do you believe that the USA PATRIOT Act and the NSA domestic surveillance program make the nation safer? Why or why not?

6. Will giving up liberty to enhance security protect the nation against terrorists, or will it destroy the fundamental values upon which the nation was founded? Defend your position.

PRACTICE QUIZ

MULTIPLE CHOICE: Choose the lettered item that answers the question correctly.

1. Civil liberties
   a. are protected only in Article III of the U.S. Constitution.
   b. entitle all citizens to equal protection of the laws.
   c. protect individuals against an abuse of government power.
   d. did not exist until the twenty-first century.

2. Which of the following is protected by the U.S. Constitution and the courts?
   a. slander
   b. libel
   c. fighting words
   d. symbolic speech

3. Teacher-led prayer in public schools is prohibited by the
   a. establishment clause.
   b. free exercise clause.
   c. due process clause.
   d. equal protection clause.

4. The right to privacy was first established in the case
   a. *Griswold v. Connecticut.*
   b. *Roe v. Wade.*
   c. *Lemon v. Kurtzman.*
   d. *Miller v. California.*

5. Criminal defendants' rights to legal counsel and a jury trial are protected by the
   a. First Amendment.
   b. Second Amendment.
   c. Fourth Amendment.
   d. Sixth Amendment.

6. Critics of the USA PATRIOT Act charge that the law violates the
   a. Second Amendment.
   b. Fourth Amendment.
   c. Eighth Amendment.
   d. Tenth Amendment.

7. Police would most likely be required to use a warrant if they wanted to collect evidence from
   a. a house.
   b. the back seat of a car.
   c. a school locker.
   d. a prison cell.

8. According to the Supreme Court, burning the U.S. flag is a form of
   a. hate speech.
   b. libel.
   c. symbolic speech.
   d. treason.

9. Citizens' disagreement about how to interpret the Eighth Amendment is reflected in the current debate over
   a. school vouchers.
   b. intelligent design.
   c. "virtual" child pornography.
   d. lethal injection.

10. The Second Amendment protects U.S. citizens'
    a. free speech.
    b. freedom from self-incrimination.
    c. freedom of religion.
    d. freedom to bear arms.

FILL IN THE BLANKS.

11. _____ refers to the process by which the Supreme Court has applied to the states those provisions in the Bill of Rights that serve some fundamental principle of liberty or justice.

12. _____ set guidelines that the government must follow in investigating, bringing to trial, and punishing those accused of committing a crime.

13. Under the _____, evidence obtained illegally cannot be used in a trial.

14. The Fifth Amendment protection against _____ ensures that criminal defendants cannot be tried again for the same crime when a court has already found them not guilty of committing that crime.

15. Speech that is likely to bring about public disorder or chaos and which may be banned in public places to ensure the preservation of public order is called _____.

RESOURCES FOR RESEARCH AND ACTION

Internet Resources

American Democracy Now Web site
www.mhhe.com/harrison1e   Consult the text's Web site for study guides, interactive activities, simulations, and current hotlinks for additional information on the civil liberties in the United States.

National Archives
www.archives.gov/national_archives_experience/charters/bill _of_rights.html   This organization is based in Washington D.C.; go to this site to read an original copy of the Bill of Rights and information about its adoption.

American Civil Liberties Union
www.aclu.org   Browse this site for information about a wide range of issues, court cases, and legislative actions affecting civil liberties in the United States, from the leading liberal civil liberties organization.

American Conservative Union
www.conservative.org   This site provides information about contemporary civil liberties issues from a conservative viewpoint.

Center for Democracy and Technology
www.cdt.org   The effect of new computer and communications technologies on American civil liberties is the subject of this site.

Electronic Privacy Information Center
www.epic.org/privacy   Find out more about privacy issues related to the Internet here.

Public Broadcasting Station
www.npr.org/news/specials/patriotact/patriotactprovisions .html   PBS provides a summary of controversial provisions of the USA PATRIOT Act, including major arguments for and against each provision.

Recommended Readings

Ackerman, Bruce. *Before the Next Attack: Preserving Civil Liberties in an Age of Terrorism.* New Haven, CT: Yale University Press, 2006. A recent work advocating the creation of an "emergency constitution" with specific time limits that would give the government enhanced national security powers in times of crisis while protecting civil liberties during normal circumstances.

Bollinger, Lee C., and Geoffrey R. Stone, eds. *Eternally Vigilant: Free Speech in the Modern Era.* Chicago: University of Chicago Press, 2002. Drawing on the work of legal scholars, an examination of the philosophical underpinnings of free speech, with a highlighting of the history of contentious free speech disputes.

Carroll, Jamuna, ed. *Privacy.* Detroit, MI: Greenhaven Press, 2006. An edited volume of point-counterpoint articles exploring a wide variety of issues, including counterterrorism measures, Internet privacy, video surveillance, and employee monitoring.

Cassel, Elaine. *The War on Civil Liberties: How Bush and Ashcroft Have Dismantled the Bill of Rights.* Chicago: Lawrence Hill Books, 2004. Argues that the USA PATRIOT Act, the Homeland Security Act, and dozens of lesser-known laws and executive orders passed as part of the "war on terrorism" have all but dismantled the Bill of Rights.

Pinaire, Brian K. *The Constitution of Electoral Speech Law.* Palo Alto, CA: Stanford University Press. Analyzes Supreme Court rulings in freedom of speech cases concerning campaigns and elections.

Spitzer, Robert J. *The Politics of Gun Control,* 4th ed. Washington, DC: CQ Press, 2007. Analysis of the gun control debate in the United States, including its history, the constitutional right to bear arms, the criminological consequences of guns, citizen political action, and the role and impact of American governing institutions.

Movies of Interest

Rendition (2007)
When an Egyptian terrorism suspect "disappears" on a flight from Africa to Washington, D.C., his American wife and a CIA analyst struggle to secure his release from a secret detention (and torture) facility somewhere outside the United States.

Enemy of the State (1998)
This film depicts the adventures of an attorney entangled in a web of national politics when a reporter friend accidentally records the murder of a senator. Unaware that he is in possession of the reporter's video, the attorney becomes the target of a National Security Agency investigation that nearly succeeds in destroying his personal and professional life.

The Siege (1998)
After the U.S. military abducts an Islamic religious leader, New York City becomes the target of escalating terrorist attacks. As the bombings continue, the U.S. government responds by declaring martial law, detaining Muslim men, and sending U.S. troops into the streets of New York City.

The People Versus Larry Flynt (1996)
This film documents the economic success, courtroom battles, and personal challenges of *Hustler* magazine publisher Larry Flynt. Flynt is obnoxious and hedonistic in ways that offend and anger "decent people," even as he fights to protect freedom of speech for all.

Guilty by Suspicion (1991)
This film tells the story of a fictional 1950s Hollywood film director caught up in the communist witch hunt sweeping Hollywood. After rebuffing the House Committee on Un-American Activities, the director cannot get work, having been blacklisted for failing to cooperate.

SURVEILLANCE STANDOFF

From 1985 to 86 the number of registered mobile-phone subscribers in the United States doubled to 500,000. Within two years after that, the number climbed to 1.6 million. By the end of the decade, the cellphone universe had skyrocketed past 4 million.

Organized crime was an early adopter of the mobile phone. In a communications technique presaging that of Islamic terrorists today, members of the Colombian Cali drug cartel operating in New York would briefly use a phone, toss it, and get a new one. To wiretap a mobile device, technicians had to install listening equipment on an "electronic port." But in most switching stations in New York, there were only half a dozen or so ports available at any one time. Federal prosecutors and agents had to stand in line at phone company offices and fight with each other over whose investigation should take priority. Some prosecutors threatened to haul company employees into court on contempt charges so they could explain to a judge why the phone company was unwilling to execute a wiretap order.

Electronic surveillance, once such a dependable, relatively easy craft, was becoming inordinately difficult. FBI Field Agent Jim Kallstrom may have been the first to alert the FBI and the Justice Department to this new reality. The digital revolution generated a constant tension that exists to this day, a push and pull between the federal government in one camp and technology corporations and civil-liberties activists in the other to control the development of the global communications system, and so the balance of power in the Information Age.

This struggle's latest manifestation is the intensely politicized effort to rewrite the Foreign Intelligence Surveillance Act. At issue is nothing less than the government's authority to broadly monitor communications networks to spot terrorists and other national security threats.

Activists and their allies in the business world have been motivated by different but mutually supportive goals: to extend constitutional safeguards to the digital realm, and to keep the government from suffocating technological development with burdensome surveillance laws. Some in those ranks would have liked, and indeed tried, to make the digital network a wiretap-free zone.

But despite the occasionally extreme positions and deeply held convictions of all of these players, the most important laws governing wiretapping, electronic surveillance, and privacy have been the product of negotiation, of people gathering in a room, sitting at a table, and talking—sometimes screaming—until they reached a settlement. The current debate, however, is missing that crucial spirit. It's not entirely clear where or why minds turned so stubborn. But to understand today's political calcification, it helps to recall a simpler time.

In the summer of 1994, the FBI and the Justice Department made a bold play to force the telecom carriers to help them conduct legal wiretaps. They put forth a proposal that would require the companies to build their networks so that law enforcement agents serving a warrant could access them in real time. The legality of wiretapping was not in question. The government wanted legal assurance that it could tap, at any time, and that the industry had an obligation under law to comply with the government's proper authority.

After months of haggling, the Communications Assistance for Law Enforcement Act passed in November 1994. CALEA would let the industry set its own standards to meet the Justice Department's needs. The department could list its surveillance requirements, but the act let companies decide how to build their equipment. Justice won the right to petition the Federal Communications Commission if its officials felt that the companies weren't fulfilling their obligations. But civil-liberties groups also secured the right to challenge the government's requirements in court.

Had the FBI and the Justice Department stopped there, had the government settled for secure access to phone networks, the history of Internet privacy and civil liberties might have turned out differently.

FBI officials knew in 1994 that they were making a mistake by leaving cyberspace out of CALEA. They understood the Internet's potential as a communications device and an intelligence tool—that is, after all, why CALEA's authors exempted "information services."

In early 1995, the Justice Department issued its list of requirements for wiretapping, known as the punch list. Not surprisingly, many telecom executives and their attorneys viewed the demands as unreasonable. Al Gidari, a lawyer representing the wireless industry, was among the first to see the FBI's requirements, during the initial meeting to develop standards for CALEA, which was held that spring in Vancouver, British Columbia. The Justice Department's wish list, he said, amounted to "the Cadillac of wiretaps."

Over the next few years, the Justice Department continued to seek increasingly sophisticated surveillance capabilities, including real-time geographical tracking of mobile phones; the ability to monitor all parties in a conference call regardless of whether they are on hold or participating; and "dialed digit extraction," a record of any numbers that a subject under surveillance punched in during a call, such as a credit card or bank account number. The government got a lot of what it wanted, but not all.

To be sure, criminals' use of new technologies helped drive the law enforcement demands. But telecom carriers worried that the cost of compliance was too high and that the FBI's technical requirements were illegally broad. CALEA, they argued, had forbidden the government from requiring specific system designs or technologies.

Justice, frustrated by its inability to get all the demands on the punch list, finally asked the Federal Communications Commission to step in. In 1997, the Cellular Telecommunications Industry Association, which then represented mobile carriers, and the Center for Democracy and Technology complained to the commission that the negotiations had deadlocked because of "unreasonable demands by law enforcement for more surveillance features than either CALEA or the wiretap laws allow." The FCC, however, sided with the Justice Department on a host of requirements that privacy groups found overly broad. The tussle dragged on for two more years and ended up in the U.S. Court of Appeals for the District of Columbia Circuit, which overruled the FCC. After the commission took up matters again, it granted some of the FBI's requests, and the CALEA standards were amended.

The level of government surveillance was so low at that time that some questioned why the FBI wanted such multifaceted access at all. In 1994, federal and state authorities were running 1,154 wiretaps nationwide, mostly for drug investigations, at an average cost of $50,000. The government was asking carriers to "design a nuclear rocket ship" for a rarely used tool, Gidari thought. "In [the FBI's] view, there was no limit to the expense the carrier should spare in order to save a life."

CALEA continued to evolve, shaped by the ongoing arguments over the terms of its birth. Activists and carriers thought that the FBI was reneging on its bargain, asking for more than the law allowed. The FBI believed that carriers were stalling when they failed to meet compliance deadlines. As all sides dug in, the meetings on implementation turned bitter.

The government asked those same questions after September 11, 2001. And this time, telecommunications carriers responded. Outside the normal FISA warrant process, which covers intelligence-gathering, carriers opened access to their networks, their

> **FBI and Justice officials slammed their hands on tables and screamed at carrier representatives,** Gidari recalls. "You're unpatriotic! What do you want to do, help the criminals?"

customer call data, and their valuable transactional information—the kind that CALEA had intended to exclude. President Bush and his administration believed that the extraordinary nature of the terrorist attacks demanded emergency actions that FISA couldn't accommodate, and the carriers answered the call from law enforcement and intelligence agencies. But government officials also seized on the post-9/11 mentality to change other surveillance laws and procedures, which they believed—just as their predecessors did in 1994—were out of step with technology and reality. About three years after 9/11, officials set their sights on rewriting CALEA.

In August 2004, in response to a petition by the Justice Department, the FBI, and the Drug Enforcement Administration, the FCC expanded CALEA to cover Internet communications, including voice calls and instant messages. The Electronic Frontier Foundation sued, along with industry, civil-liberties, and academic groups. In 2005, the Court of Appeals ruled 2–1 to defer to the FCC's reading of the law.

Many of those who had helped craft CALEA believed that the commission had

misread the law and acted on a post-9/11 impulse to give the government more, not less, access to information. But to the FCC, new Internet technologies that operate a lot like telephones blurred the distinction between "information services" and the kinds of technology that CALEA was meant to cover.

After 9/11, law enforcement and intelligence agencies took a variety of measures, apart from wiretaps, to collect and mine potentially valuable information from the Internet. With the cooperation of telecom companies, government accumulated lots of transactional data—including e-mail header information and lists of websites visited by targeted individuals—to support counter-terrorism operations. Viewed solely as a reaction to the terrorist attacks of 2001, this kind of collection might seem extraordinary. But through the longer lens of history, the government's steady march into cyberspace is not surprising.

The FISA debate hung on whether companies that assisted warrantless surveillance after 9/11 should have retroactive legal immunity for any laws they may have broken. CALEA has something to say about that, too. The law requires that carriers be able to deliver call identification information to the government remotely. According to Beryl Howell, Sen. Leahy's lead CALEA staffer, that provision was meant to keep government agents from sitting in the phone companies' offices to execute their wiretaps.

It is a basic tenet of wiretapping law, whether for intelligence or law enforcement, that the communications companies act as a buffer between their customers and the government, she says, and that telecom carriers must make their own determination whether official requests are, in fact, legal.

■ **THEN:** Electronic surveillance was once an easy craft conducted with a warrant on a limited number of possible targets.

■ **NOW:** The digital revolution has created a constant tension, a push and pull between the federal government in one camp and technology corporations and civil-liberties activists in the other to control the development of the global communications system.

■ **NEXT:** Will you support wiretaps on these new technologies? Why or why not?
In the future the courts will continue to decide the legality of wiretaps on new technologies like cell phones and Internet use.
Should telecom companies be responsible for protecting their clients' civil liberties?
Will we need to rethink the protection of our civil liberties in the information age?

CHAPTER

5

Civil Rights

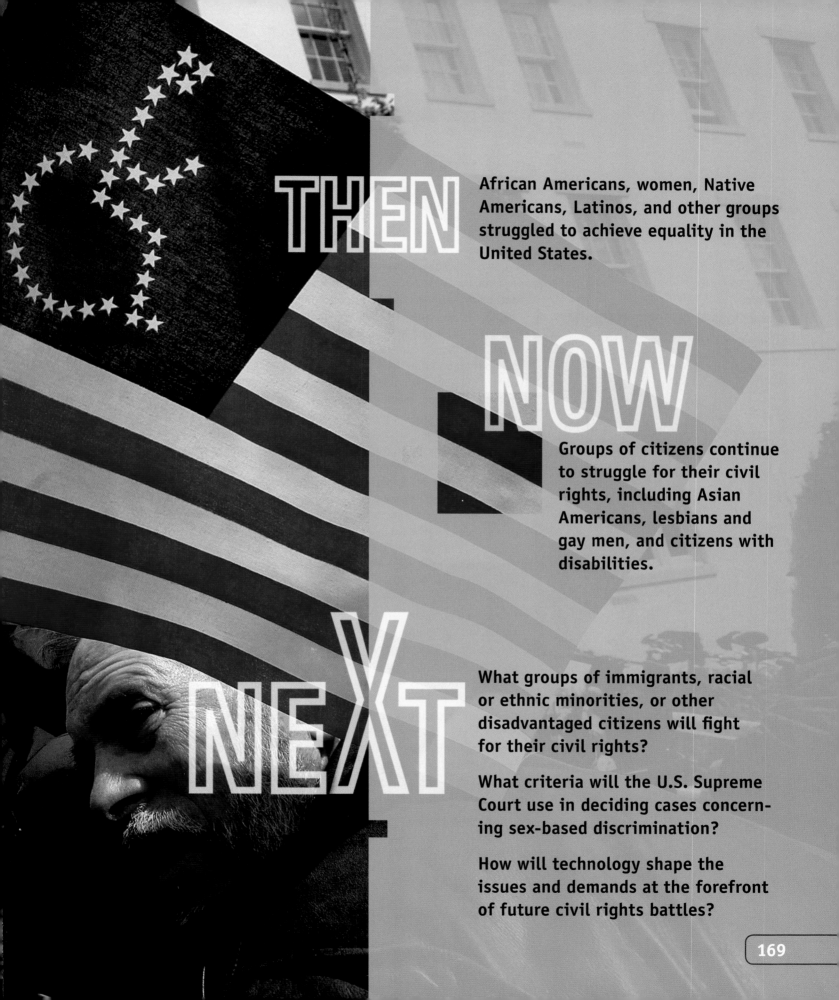

THEN

African Americans, women, Native Americans, Latinos, and other groups struggled to achieve equality in the United States.

NOW

Groups of citizens continue to struggle for their civil rights, including Asian Americans, lesbians and gay men, and citizens with disabilities.

NEXT

What groups of immigrants, racial or ethnic minorities, or other disadvantaged citizens will fight for their civil rights?

What criteria will the U.S. Supreme Court use in deciding cases concerning sex-based discrimination?

How will technology shape the issues and demands at the forefront of future civil rights battles?

Rallying for the Jena 6: An Echo of Past Protests?

On September 20, 2007, on college campuses and in cities throughout the country, people rallied for equal treatment of African Americans under the law. Was this day the anniversary of an event in the civil rights movement, which took place nearly a half century before? No, students and others who protested on that September day were rallying to support the "Jena 6," a group of African American students from Jena, Louisiana, who had become involved in a struggle that for many echoed the battle for civil rights that had occurred throughout the country during the 1950s and 1960s. I The troubles began in September 2006, when several nooses were found hanging from a tree at Jena High School. The nooses—a threat and a long-standing symbol of racial hatred—were discovered after an African American student had asked if African American students were permitted to sit under the "white tree" at the school. Three white students had hung the nooses in the tree, and the principal of the high school recommended that the three students be expelled from school. But the school board and superintendent disagreed, and the students were given a lighter punishment. Racial tensions in the community and the school grew when it was widely reported that the punishment for the offense was a three-day, in-school suspension (the actual punishment meted out was closer to six weeks, including a stint at an alternative high school and other measures). I In the days that followed these incidents, tensions at the school escalated, with frequent fights between black and white students. The situation boiled over when six African American students badly beat a white student, Juston Barker. The six students, who became known as the "Jena 6," were expelled from the school, and five were charged with attempted second-degree murder. Because of his criminal record, one student, 16-year-old Mychal Bell, was charged as an adult. A jury convicted Bell of aggravated second-degree battery and conspiracy to commit aggravated second-degree battery. He faced a possible sentence of twenty-two years in prison. Bell's sentencing was scheduled for September 20, 2007. I Before the scheduled sentencing date, Bell's convictions were overturned on the grounds that Bell should have been tried as a juvenile. But on that date in Jena and other cities and at colleges throughout the United States, tens of thousands of people rallied to protest what they perceived as race-based inequality in the justice system. Hundreds of thousands of others signed online petitions calling for justice; others contributed to legal defense funds. Six days after the protests, Louisiana governor Kathleen Blanco announced that the state would not appeal the overturned convictions. Bell eventually pled guilty to a lesser battery charge and was sentenced to eighteen months in a juvenile justice facility. Four of the remaining five students, who were 17 at the time of the crime, were charged as adults, while a 14-year-old was charged as a juvenile. As of this writing, the five are awaiting trial.

> During a rally outside the courthouse in Jena, Louisiana, a protester holds a picture of a noose while standing under a live oak tree.

Although the Declaration of

Independence promises equality, throughout U.S. history this promise has seemed just be-yond the grasp of many individuals and groups. As the story of the Jena 6 illustrates, the fact that people disagree strongly about what "equal treatment" requires is at the heart of many struggles for equality. Some define the concept of equality broadly and would bar differential treatment of any group or individual when it is based on innate characteristics. Others define equality more narrowly, allowing differential treatment of individuals or groups as long as this discrimination is not based on certain protected characteristics, specifically race, national origin, sex, or religion.

In this chapter, we examine the concept of equality under the law, focusing on how, through various types of civic activism, groups that were originally deprived of equal pro-tection in American society have been able to obtain their civil rights. For nearly the first century of our nation's history, much of the debate about equality focused on the plight of Africans and African Americans under slavery. After passage of the Thirteenth Amendment in 1865, which outlawed slavery, African Americans, Native Americans, and other disenfran-chised groups shifted their attention to the challenge of obtaining the right to vote (suf-frage). This right was granted first for male African Americans in 1870, for women in 1920, Native Americans in 1924, and for 18- to 20-year-olds in 1971. This chapter examines the struggle for the expansion of suffrage in the United States.

Over time, civil rights advocates have also pressed for equal access not only to voting, but to all realms of public and private life, including the educational system, employment, housing, and public accommodations. Modern civil rights activists contend that the right to equal protection under the law guarantees this access, though community resistance and continuing discrimination may thwart equal protection and render even the most ambitious court decisions ineffective.

The Quest for Equality Under the Law

When asked what principles or ideals they hold most dear, many Americans will mention freedom and equality, often in the same breath. As we discussed in Chapter 4, the ideal of freedom is very much at the heart of our commitment to civil liberties. Freedom of expres-sion, the press, religion, and assembly are at the core of American political culture, as is the commitment to due process for criminal defendants. As we noted in Chapter 2, the Constitution was ratified only after the framers agreed to introduce the Bill of Rights in the first session of Congress. This Bill of Rights, made up of the first ten amendments to the Constitution, essentially bars the federal government from interfering with certain basic freedoms.

While the issue of protecting civil liberties was in the forefront at the nation's founding, the issue of guaranteeing civil rights reached the national agenda much later.[1] When we talk about **civil rights** in the United States, we mean the rights and privileges guaranteed to all citizens under the equal protection and due process clauses of the Fifth and Fourteenth amendments.[2] Included in these rights is the idea that individuals are protected from dis-crimination based on inherent characteristics such as race, national origin, religion, and sex. When a person or an organization interferes with a person's civil rights, the government has an obligation to intervene to remove these obstacles.

civil rights
the rights and privileges guar-anteed to all citizens under the equal protection and due process clauses of the Fifth and Four-teenth amendments; the idea that individuals are protected from discrimination based on character-istics such as race, national origin, religion, and sex

Fighting for Their Rights: How Groups and Issues Change

THEN (1960s AND 1970s)	NOW (2009)
African Americans, women, Native Americans, and Latinos fight for equal treatment under the law.	Asian citizens, citizens with disabilities, and lesbian, gay, bisexual, and transgendered citizens fight for equal treatment under the law.
Key strategies include nonviolent civil disobedience, protests, and seeking remedy through the justice system.	Protest and lawsuits remain important strategies, but today's activists also focus on petitioning Congress and state legislatures in attempts to pass legislation.
Important issues include equal access to schools, public accommodations, voting rights, and equal pay.	Important issues include spousal rights for gays and lesbians, voting rights, and immigration policy.

WHAT'S NEXT?

> What groups will begin to seek ways of achieving their civil rights?

> How will new technologies change the strategies and tactics that civil rights activists use?

> What important issues will be at the forefront of the civil rights agenda in the future?

inherent characteristics
individual attributes such as race, national origin, religion, and gender

suspect classifications
distinctions based on race, religion, national origin, and gender, which are assumed to be illegitimate

Inherent characteristics such as race, national origin, religion, and sex merit a greater level of protection than other qualities. When people are treated differently solely because of their membership in a particular racial or religious group, or because of their ancestry or sex, this discrimination is based on assumptions about the characteristics of the group, rather than on the unique qualities of the individual member of that group. Because no real consideration is given to the individual's unique characteristics, this kind of discrimination is arbitrary and unfair.

What is the government's role in ensuring equality? Most of us agree that no government should treat people differently because of race, ethnicity, national origin, or gender. But people disagree about whether this list should also include characteristics such as disability and sexual orientation. Americans also disagree about what should happen when a private person or an organization, and not a governmental agency or official, engages in discriminatory behavior. Some believe that the government should vigorously pursue equality, even when its actions intrude upon individual freedoms or group privileges. Others accept a much more limited role for the government in these matters.

Let's use a familiar example of classifications: it may make sense for the government to require that people be at least 18 years old before they can vote because 18-year-olds have reached the level of maturity needed to make an informed decision. It makes no sense, however, to impose a blanket ban on voting by racial, ethnic, or religious groups or by women. Race, religion, national origin, and gender are **suspect classifications** because the government considers distinctions based on these characteristics to be illegitimate. To establish whether a classification is "suspect," courts consider whether it is immutable (incapable of being changed), whether the group in question has experienced a history of discrimination, and whether the group is unable to effect change through the political process. Many argue that the list of suspect classifications should be expanded to include sexual orientation, ability or disability, and native language. While some states have barred discrimination against people who fit within these categories, there is less than full agreement among the states as to whether they merit the highest level of protection under the law.

For most of our nation's history, the law not only allowed unequal treatment for different racial, ethnic, and religious groups as well as for men and women, but it also *required* this unequal treatment for a majority of the population. Women were not granted the right to vote until 1920, and they faced a wide variety of discriminatory practices. Ethnic and religious groups also faced widespread discrimination, some as a matter of law. For example, more than 120,000 people of Japanese ancestry were forcibly interned in camps during World War II. More recently, following the terrorist attacks of September 11, 2001, the federal government has detained thousands of Arabs and Arab Americans in prisons without providing any criminal due process protections. But probably the most blatant example

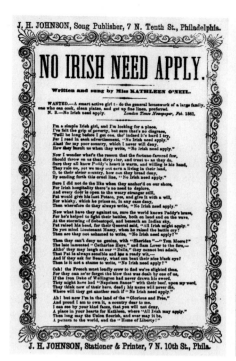

> In some places segregation extended well beyond schools and housing, affecting every aspect of daily life. Historically, people have encountered discrimination because of their ethnicity, race, or gender. In some places, Irish citizens were barred from applying for jobs, African Americans attending theaters were forced to use separate entrances (here with the ironic promise of "good shows in comfort"), and help-wanted ads were segregated based on gender.

of discrimination in U.S. history is slavery. This practice was protected under the law, and slaves were considered to be the property of their owners. They had no protection under the law and could be treated in any way their owners saw fit.

Slavery and Its Aftermath

When it was first written, the Constitution implicitly endorsed the unequal and discriminatory treatment of African Americans.[3] Some of the most important provisions of the new constitution treated people of African descent as property, allowing states to continue to permit them to be enslaved. Although the movement to abolish slavery was in its early stages in 1787, the year the Constitution was completed, by the early to mid-1800s, it had gained significant momentum in the North, largely because of the activism of various religious and humanitarian groups.[4]

Slavery in the United States

Most African Americans today are the descendants of Africans who were forcibly brought to the New World beginning in 1619, when twenty Africans arrived in Jamestown as *indentured servants,* workers with a fixed term of service. But, by the mid-1600s, slavery began to replace indentured servitude.

OPPOSITION TO SLAVERY   Many chafed at the hypocrisy of those who sought freedom and equality but kept slaves. Among the first to challenge slavery were former slaves, who staged both peaceful protests and armed insurrections throughout the late 1700s and early 1800s. These activists successfully rallied support in the North for the gradual abolition of slavery by 1804. They argued forcefully against the injustice of the slave system, moving the opponents of slavery to action by their horrifying firsthand accounts of the treatment of slaves.

Despite these arguments, the U.S. Congress, wary of the divisiveness caused by the slavery issue, sought to balance the antislavery position of the abolitionist states with the pro-slavery sentiments of the slaveholding states. One such attempt was the Missouri

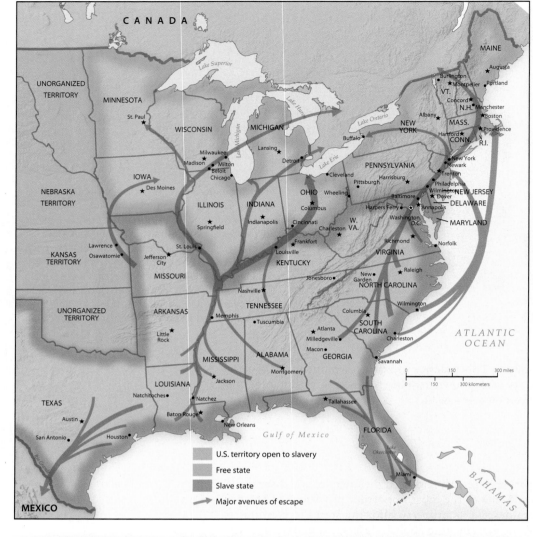

Compromise, passed by Congress in 1820. The compromise regulated slavery in the newly acquired western territories: slavery was prohibited north of the 36°30′ north parallel, except within the state of Missouri.

The abolitionists, including organizations like the American Anti-Slavery Society, objected to the efforts of Congress to accommodate the slaveholding states and called for the emancipation of all slaves. Members of the American Anti-Slavery Society were actively engaged in civil disobedience by supporting the Underground Railroad, a series of safe houses that allowed slaves to escape to the northern states and Canada. Between 1810 and 1850, an estimated 100,000 people escaped slavery through the Underground Railroad (see Figure 5.1). But in 1850, the U.S. Congress—in an attempt to stall or prevent the secession, or separation, of southern states from the Union—passed the Fugitive Slave Act. The law required federal marshals to return runaway slaves or risk a $1,000 fine (over $20,000 in today's dollars), while private citizens who harbored or abetted runaway slaves could be imprisoned for six months and fined $1,000. Passage of this law meant that "conductors" on the Underground Railroad operated in clear violation of the statute, risking their own livelihoods and property.

POLITICAL INQUIRY

FIGURE 5.1 ■ ROUTES TO FREEDOM ON THE UNDERGROUND RAILROAD Why did many escaping slaves use routes that followed the Mississippi River or the Atlantic coast? Which northern cities were important "stations" on the Underground Railroad? Why was legislation such as the Fugitive Slave Act ultimately powerless to stop this movement?

THE CIVIL WAR ERA Abolitionists were bolstered in their efforts when Harriet Beecher Stowe's popular book *Uncle Tom's Cabin* was published in 1852. Vividly depicting the harsh reality of slavery in the United States, this work inspired many to actively challenge slavery. By the late 1850s, the widespread distribution of *Uncle Tom's Cabin,* as well as the trial and execution of John Brown, a white abolitionist who tried to ignite a slave insurrection in Harpers Ferry, in what was then Virginia and is now West Virginia, had convinced many northerners that slavery was immoral.

Yet the U.S. Supreme Court ruled otherwise. In 1857, Dred Scott, an African American slave held by a surgeon in the U.S. Army, sued for his freedom, arguing that because he had lived in both a free state (Illinois) and a free territory (the Wisconsin Territory, now Minnesota), he had become a free man and as such he could not be re-enslaved when he moved to Missouri. (Figure 5.1 shows states that did and did not allow slavery at this time.) The Supreme Court rejected Scott's claim and in *Dred Scott v. Sandford,* ruled that the Missouri Compromise of 1820 was unconstitutional because the U.S. Congress lacked the authority to ban slavery in the territories.[5] It also ruled that Scott was not a U.S. citizen, asserting that slaves were property rather than citizens with **standing to sue,** or the legal right to bring lawsuits in court. While the *Dred Scott* decision appeared to be a victory for slaveholding states, it was also pivotal in mobilizing the abolitionist movement and swaying public opinion in favor of a war to prevent secession and to bring about emancipation.

standing to sue
the legal right to bring lawsuits in court

Certain that their way of life was under siege and alarmed by the election of Abraham Lincoln as president in 1860, the southern states decided that they should secede from the union. By May 1861, eleven southern states had declared their independence and created the Confederate States of America. A long and bloody civil war followed as the North fought to bring the southern states back into the union.

One of the most important turning points of the Civil War was the Emancipation Proclamation, issued by Abraham Lincoln in April 1862. This order abolished slavery in the states that had seceded from the Union. The Union army and navy were charged with implementing the order. The proclamation had several purposes: it decreed that the abolition of slavery was a goal of the war, and by doing so it effectively prevented Britain and France from intervening in the war on the southern side because these countries had both renounced the institution of slavery. When the South finally surrendered in April 1865, it did so knowing that its economic way of life, which depended on slave-based plantation farming, was over. At the end of the war, nearly 4 million slaves in the United States had been freed, and three Constitutional amendments were ratified to codify the victories won on the battlefield:

- The Thirteenth Amendment (1865), which ended slavery throughout the United States and prohibited it in the future (see "Global Comparisons").
- The Fourteenth Amendment (1868), which defines *citizens* as "all persons born or naturalized in the United States" and mandates the same privileges and immunities for all citizens and due process and equal protection for all people.
- The Fifteenth Amendment (1870), which decrees that every man has the right to vote, regardless of color.

Reconstruction and the First Civil Rights Acts

After the North won the war and Lincoln was assassinated in April 1865, members of Congress and others in government disagreed about the best way to proceed in the South. Many Republicans thought that the South should be stabilized and quickly brought back into the political fold. Like Lincoln, these moderates endorsed a plan that would enable the southern states to be quickly represented in Congress. Others, however, took a more radical view and argued that all people who had ever supported the confederacy should be kept out of national and state politics. As the 1860s drew to a close, many of these more radical Republicans had come to power and had strictly limited the people in southern states who could participate in politics. As a result of their activities, during the **Reconstruction era** between 1866 and 1877—when the institutions and the infrastructure of the South were rebuilt—freed slaves, who could easily say they had never supported the confederacy, made up a sizeable portion of both the electorate and the candidate pool in the southern states. Federal troops provided protection that facilitated their participation. During this decade, African American voters made the most of their position in the South and elected a substantial number of other African Americans to legislative offices in the local, state, and federal governments. In some places, such as in South Carolina, African American legislators outnumbered whites, giving them a majority during the Reconstruction years.

Reconstruction era
the time after the Civil War between 1866 and 1877 when the institutions and infrastructure of the South were rebuilt

Between 1865 and 1875, Congress passed a series of laws designed to solidify the rights and protections outlined in the Thirteenth, Fourteenth, and Fifteenth amendments. Congress needed to spell out the rights of African Americans because of the pervasiveness of **Black Codes,** laws passed immediately after the Civil War by the confederate states that limited the rights of "freemen," or former slaves. These codes prevented freemen from voting, owning property, or bringing suit. To remedy this situation, Congress passed laws that sought to negate the Black Codes. One law, the Civil Rights Act of 1866, extended the definition of *citizen* to anyone born in the United States (including freemen) and granted all citizens the

Black Codes
laws passed immediately after the Civil War by the confederate states that limited the rights of "freemen" (former slaves)

GLOBAL COMPARISONS

MODERN FORMS OF SLAVERY

The Universal Declaration of Human Rights makes the following statement: "No one shall be held in slavery or servitude: slavery and the slave trade shall be prohibited in all their forms." When Americans think of slavery, they think of our nation's own historical experience with the institution of slavery: slave ships, plantation life, and the Civil War. It surprises many that in the twenty-first century, slavery still exists. As former United Nations Secretary General Kofi Annan has observed:

> Nearly every day, there are shocking reports of men, women and children who are exploited, denied their basic rights and their dignity and deprived of a better future, through both ancient and modern forms of slavery.
>
> Slavery and trafficking, and related practices such as debt bondage, forced prostitution and forced labour, are violations of the most fundamental human rights: the right to life; the right to dignity and security; the right to just and favourable conditions of work; the right to health; and the right to equality. These are rights that we all possess—irrespective of our sex, our nationality, our social status, our occupation or any other characteristic.*

*Secretary-General Kofi Annan, message on the occasion of the International Day for the Abolition of Slavery, December 2, 2003.

*❋ **What can governments do to prevent modern-day slavery?**

Women and children, particularly in Asia but also in countries of the former Soviet Union, are sometimes forced to be part of prostitution rings that operate in those countries as well as in Western democracies. In some countries, young women who respond to help-wanted ads for international work as nannies or domestic servants are essentially kidnapped and forced to work as prostitutes. Often, traffickers advertise in the help-wanted sections of local newspapers, offering high-paying jobs as models, domestic servants, hotel maids, nannies, or shop clerks in Western nations and promising to help secure the required visa applications and work permits.

Traffickers rely on people's desire for a better life as a lure. Once victims are out of their homeland, they may be raped and forced into prostitution. Frequently, traffickers will confiscate the victim's identification and travel permits (often forgeries), withhold food or shelter unless the victim complies, and use the threat of imprisonment by authorities or the threat of harm to the victim's family at home as a means of ensuring compliance. The U.S. Department of State estimates that 800,000–900,000 people annually are trafficked across international borders worldwide, including an estimated 20,000 people who are brought into the United States.

---

right to sue, own property, bear witness in a court of law, and enter into legal contracts. The Enforcement Act of 1870 bolstered the Fifteenth Amendment by establishing penalties for interfering with the right to vote. The Civil Rights Act of 1872, also known as the Anti-Ku Klux Klan Act, made it a federal crime to deprive individuals of their rights, privileges, or immunities. Although the Reconstruction-era Congress sought to remedy the new forms of inequality that emerged after the Civil War, its efforts would be short-lived.

Backlash: Jim Crow Laws

Jim Crow laws
laws requiring strict separation of racial groups, with whites and "nonwhites" required to attend separate schools, work in different jobs, and use segregated public accommodations, such as transportation and restaurants

In 1877, the inauguration of President Rutherford Hayes (1877–1881) brought the Reconstruction era to a decisive end, almost immediately rolling back the gains African Americans had achieved in education and political participation. Under Hayes, the federal troops that had protected African Americans from physical reprisals were withdrawn. State and local governments throughout the South mandated racial segregation by enacting what came to be known as **Jim Crow laws.** These laws required the strict separation of racial groups, with whites and "nonwhites" going to separate schools, being employed in different jobs, and using segregated public accommodations, such as transportation and restaurants.

The idea behind the Jim Crow laws was that whites and nonwhites should occupy separate societies and have little to do with each other. Many whites feared that racial mixing would result in interracial dating and marriage, which would inevitably lead to the decline of their superior position in society; thus in many southern states miscegenation laws, which banned interracial marriage, cohabitation, or sex, were passed and severe penalties imposed for those who violated them. Interracial couples who married risked losing their property and even their liberty, since heavy fines and jail sentences were among the penalties for breaking these laws.

State and local governments in the South also found creative ways to prevent African Americans from exercising their right to vote. They relied on several tactics:

■ The **white primary** was a primary election in which only white people were allowed to vote. Because Democrats dominated politics so heavily in the post–Civil War South, the only races that really mattered were the primary races that determined the Democratic nominees. But Southern states restricted voting in these primaries to whites only.

■ The **literacy test** determined eligibility to vote. Literacy tests were designed so that few voters would stand a chance of passing the exam administered to African American voters, while the test for white voters was easy to pass. Typically, white voters were exempt from literacy tests because of a grandfather clause (see below).

■ A **poll tax,** a fee levied for voting, often presented an insurmountable obstacle to poor African Americans. White voters were often exempt from poll taxes because of a grandfather clause.

■ The **grandfather clause** exempted individuals from conditions on voting (such as poll taxes or literacy tests) if they themselves or their ancestor had been eligible to vote before 1870. Because African Americans did not have the right to vote in southern states before the Civil War, the grandfather clause was a mechanism to protect the voting rights of whites.

These laws were enforced not only by government agents, particularly police, but by nongovernmental groups as well. Among the most powerful of these groups was the Ku Klux Klan (KKK). Throughout the late 1800s and into the 1900s, the Klan was dreaded and hated throughout the southern states, and it used its powers to threaten and intimidate those African Americans and whites who dared to question its core principle: that whites are in every way superior to African Americans. The Klan's particular brand of intimidation, the burning cross and the lynching noose, was reviled throughout the southern and border states, but few could dispute the power the Klan wielded in these areas.

Governmental Acceptance of Discrimination

The federal government too had seemingly abandoned African Americans and the quest for equality under the law. In the *Civil Rights Cases* of 1883, the Supreme Court ruled that Congress lacked the authority to prevent discrimination by private individuals and organizations. Rather, Congress's jurisdiction, the Court claimed, was limited to banning discrimination in official acts of state or local governments. The Court also declared that the Civil Rights Act of 1875, which had sought to mandate "full and equal enjoyment" of a wide variety of facilities and accommodations, was unconstitutional.

In 1896, the Court struck what seemed to be the final blow against racial equality. In 1890, Louisiana passed a law that required separate accommodations for blacks and whites on railroad trains. Several citizens of New Orleans sought to test the constitutionality of the law and enlisted Homer Plessy, who was one-eighth African American (but still considered

> **This cartoon, which originally ran in *Harper's Weekly* in January 1875, comments (in an exaggerated way) on the protection federal troops provided to African Americans living in the South during Reconstruction. It suggests the danger they faced when those troops were removed following the election of Rutherford B. Hayes in 1877.**

white primary
a primary election in which a party's nominees for general election were chosen but in which only white people were allowed to vote

literacy test
a test to determine eligibility to vote; designed so that few African Americans would pass

poll tax
a fee for voting; levied to prevent poor African Americans in the South from voting

grandfather clause
a clause exempting individuals from voting conditions such as poll taxes or literacy tests if they or their ancestor had voted before 1870, thus sparing most white voters

Plessy v. Ferguson
1896 Supreme Court ruling creating the separate but equal doctrine

equal protection clause
the Fourteenth Amendment clause stating that no state shall "deny to any person within its jurisdiction the equal protection of the laws"

separate but equal doctrine
established by the Supreme Court in *Plessy v. Ferguson,* it said that separate but equal facilities for whites and nonwhites do not violate the Fourteenth Amendment's equal protection clause

"black" by Louisiana state law) to serve as plaintiff. (The choice of Plessy, who could "pass" for white, was intended to show the arbitrary nature of the statute.) On June 7, 1892, Plessy boarded a railroad car designated for whites only. Plessy was asked to leave the whites-only car, and he refused. He was then arrested and jailed, charged with violating the state law. In 1896, the U.S. Supreme Court heard *Plessy v. Ferguson,* in which Plessy's attorneys argued that the Louisiana state law violated the **equal protection clause** of the Fourteenth Amendment, which states that no state shall "deny to any person within its jurisdiction the equal protection of the laws."

In a 7–1 decision, the Court rejected Plessy's arguments, claiming that segregation based on race was not a violation of the equal protection clause. Rather, the court made this argument:

> We consider the underlying fallacy of the plaintiff's argument to consist in the assumption that the enforced separation of the two races stamps the colored race with a badge of inferiority. If this be so, it is not by reason of anything found in the act, but solely because the colored race chooses to put that construction upon it.[6]

In its decision, the Court created the **separate but equal doctrine,** declaring that separate but equal facilities do not violate the Fourteenth Amendment's equal protection clause. Under this doctrine, the Court upheld state laws mandating that the races be separated in schools and all public accommodations such as businesses, public transportation, restaurants, hotels, swimming pools, and recreational facilities. The only condition the Court placed on these segregated facilities was that the state had to provide public facilities for both whites and nonwhites. The Court paid little attention to whether the school systems or public accommodations were comparable in quality. As long as the state had some kind of facilities in place for both whites and nonwhites, the segregation was permitted. This doctrine would become the legal backbone of segregationist policies for more than five decades to come.

The Civil Rights Movement

In the early decades of the twentieth century, African Americans continued their struggle for equality. Though the movement for civil rights enjoyed some early successes, the century was nearly half over before momentous victories by civil rights activists finally began to change the status of African Americans in revolutionary ways. These victories were the result of strong leadership at the helm of the movement, the effective strategies used by activists, and a national government that was finally ready to fulfill the promise of equality embodied in the Declaration of Independence.

Fighting Back: Early Civil Rights Organizations

In the early years of the twentieth century, the political climate was open to reform, with activists in the Progressive movement calling for an end to government corruption, reforms to labor laws, the protection of children from abusive labor practices, and an expansion of rights, including the right of women to vote and the civil rights of African Americans (see Chapter 8 for more on the Progressive movement). In the dawn of that century, several influential African Americans, including W. E. B. Du Bois and William Monroe Trotter, met on the Canadian side of Niagara Falls to form the agenda for a new organization, the Niagara Movement, which would advocate for voting rights for African Americans, increased educational and economic opportunities, and the end to various forms of racism and discrimination.[7] But a schism developed within the group over one question: should whites be allowed to participate in the organization?

Du Bois believed that the group would be more effective with white participation. In 1909, he joined with Oswald Garrison Villard (publisher of the *New York Evening Post,* an influential newspaper, and grandson of the abolitionist leader William Lloyd Garrison) to form the National Association for the Advancement of Colored People (NAACP). One of the targets the NAACP would focus on over the next several decades was the separate but equal doctrine,

Race Relations

Do you think there will always be problems between African Americans and white Americans in the United States, or will there eventually be a solution?

☐ There will always be problems.

☐ There will be a solution.

which remained in place through the first half of the twentieth century. Citing the lack of graduate schools, law schools, and medical schools for African Americans, the NAACP argued that the states had violated the equal protection clause by failing to make such schools available to African Americans. During the 1930s, lawsuits brought by the NAACP in several states ended discriminatory admissions practices in professional schools.[8] Momentum in the movement for equality continued to grow, fueled in part by the growing political activism of African American soldiers returning home after fighting against fascism abroad during World War II. Many of these soldiers began to question why they were denied freedom and equality in their own country, and they mobilized for civil rights in their communities. Though the Court had not yet overturned the separate but equal doctrine, by 1950, the U.S. Supreme Court had ruled that segregating classrooms, dining rooms, or library facilities in colleges, universities, and professional schools was unconstitutional.

Taking cues from these court decisions, by the 1950s the NAACP and other groups had changed their tactics. Instead of arguing that states had to provide equivalent schools and programs for African Americans and whites, these groups began to argue that segregation itself was a violation of the equal protection clause. But it was not until 1954 that the U.S. Supreme Court struck down the separate but equal doctrine, finding it inherently unequal and therefore unconstitutional.

The End of Separate but Equal

In the fall of 1951, Oliver Brown, a welder at the Santa Fe Railroad yard in Topeka, Kansas, sought to have his daughter Linda enrolled in the third grade in an all-white public school seven blocks from their home. The act was not accidental; it was the calculated first step in a legal strategy that would result in sweeping changes to the nation's public school system, effectively shattering the segregated school system dominant in the South.[9] The Browns lived in an integrated neighborhood in Topeka, and Topeka schools were segregated, as allowed (but not required) under Kansas state law. Linda was denied admission, and instead was required to walk six blocks to a bus stop, and then travel a mile by bus to attend her segregated school. Oliver Brown had spoken with a Topeka attorney and with the Topeka NAACP, which convinced him to join a lawsuit against the Topeka Board of Education. Brown agreed and was directed to attempt to register his daughter at the all-white public school. Here Linda Brown (now Thompson) describes the beginning of the journey that would lead to the U.S. Supreme Court:

> . . . we lived in an integrated neighborhood and I had all of these playmates of different nationalities. And so when I found out that day that I might be able to go to their school, I was just thrilled. . . .
>
> And I remember walking over to Sumner School with my dad that day and going up the steps of the school and the school looked so big to a smaller child. And I remember going inside and my dad spoke with someone and then he went into the inner office with the principal and they left me out . . . to sit outside with the secretary. And while he was in the inner office, I could hear voices and hear his voice raised, you know, as the conversation went on. And then he immediately came out of the office, took me by the hand and we walked home from the school. I just couldn't understand what was happening because I was so sure that I was going to go to school with Mona and Guinevere, Wanda, and all of my playmates.[10]

But Cheryl Brown Henderson, Linda Brown Thompson's sister, cautions against a romanticized version of the events surrounding the Brown case:

> People would come to this community looking for this wonderful little story, because it's what

> *Brown v. Board of Education,* the Supreme Court case that resulted in orders to desegregate all public schools, was brought by the father of Linda Brown, here shown in her segregated classroom (front, center). The strategy and plans for this monumental case were developed by the best legal and political minds of the civil rights movement.

they believed Brown was . . . something that took 105 years to really materialize and all these attorneys. . . . And this little story in their minds was that a little girl wanted to go to school down the block, and she couldn't because she was African-American. And her father was angry about that and he sued the school board; and Thurgood Marshall rode in and decided to represent them; and the Supreme Court did the right thing. Now, the sad thing about that is—when you think about all the sacrifices that were made to bring something about like a *Brown v. Board of Education*, it trivializes something so important to this country and it negates the role played and the legal brilliance on the part of the team that came up with how best to attack Jim Crow. It also keeps people in the dark about the nearly 200 plaintiffs out there—many of whom lost jobs; their homes were burned; they were run out of their home communities because they signed a petition to be part of a court case.[11]

Brown v. Board of Education of Topeka

This 1954 Supreme Court decision ruled that segregated schools violated the equal protection clause of the Fourteenth Amendment.

But the stand taken by Oliver Brown and the other plaintiffs was not in vain. Thurgood Marshall, who would go on to become the first African American to sit on the U.S. Supreme Court, argued the case, and in a unanimous decision in 1954 the Supreme Court ruled in **Brown v. Board of Education of Topeka** that segregated schools violate the equal protection clause of the Fourteenth Amendment. In one stroke, the Court concluded that "separate but equal" schools were inherently unequal since they stamped African American children with a "badge of racial inferiority" that stayed with them throughout their lives.

In a second case the following year (sometimes called the second Brown decision or Brown II), the court grappled with the issue of how the first *Brown* decision should be implemented—recognizing that many southern states would be reluctant to enforce the decision unless they were made to do so. In its decision, the justices called on the states to dismantle the segregated school system "with all deliberate speed" but left it to local officials to determine how to achieve a desegregated system. Many have criticized the Court's unwillingness or inability to provide more concrete guidelines to local and state officials, contending that the Court's failure to act ultimately undermined the impact of the *Brown* opinion. Nevertheless, the Court's decision in this case signaled both a new era in civil rights law and a governmental climate favorable to changing centuries-long inequalities in American society.[12]

Incident on a Montgomery Bus

In December 1955, a now-legendary woman named Rosa Parks was on a bus returning home from work as a seamstress at a Montgomery, Alabama, department store. In Montgomery and throughout the South, buses were segregated, with white riders boarding in the front and sitting front to back and African American riders sitting back to front.[13] The bus driver asked the 43-year-old African American woman to give up her seat for a white man; Parks refused and was arrested for violating a local segregation law. (See "Exploring the Sources.")

The Montgomery chapter of the NAACP, of which Parks and her husband were active members, had sought a test case to challenge the constitutionality of the state's Jim Crow laws. Parks agreed to participate in the case, and her arrest came at a pivotal time in the civil rights movement. Activists were buoyed by the *Brown* decision. Momentum favored the civil rights activists in the South, and their cause was bolstered when civil rights and religious leaders in Montgomery chose a 27-year-old preacher relatively new to the city to lead a bus boycott to protest the segregated public facilities. His name was Martin Luther King Jr.[14]

Dr. Martin Luther King Jr. and the Strategy of Civil Disobedience

Over the course of the year-long bus boycott, King became a national symbol for the civil rights movement, as the boycott garnered national media attention. King's leadership skills were put to the test during the year-long battle: He was arrested. His home was bombed. Death threats were made against him. But for 381 days, the buses of Montgomery remained virtually empty, representing a serious loss in revenue to the city and causing the NAACP to be banned in the state of Alabama. African Americans walked to and from work, day in and day out, for over a year. White employers drove some domestic servants to and from work. Finally, in December 1956, the U.S. Supreme Court ruled that segregated buses were unconstitutional.[15] The bus boycott was a success on many fronts: its righteousness was con-

A FAMOUS IMAGE FROM THE CIVIL RIGHTS ERA

Chances are you have seen this famous photograph before. It is a powerful image. Rosa Parks is the African American woman who refused to obey the law requiring her to give up her seat and moving to the back of the bus for a white man. Her refusal and subsequent arrest were the catalyst for a 381-day bus boycott in Montgomery, Alabama, a boycott that ended when the Supreme Court ruled that Montgomery's segregated bus law was unconstitutional. This photo of Parks sitting on a bus in front of a white man was taken a month later.

Evaluating the Evidence

① The man sitting behind Rosa Parks is Nicholas Chriss, a reporter who was working for United Press International at the time the photograph was taken. Who do you think most people looking at this photograph assume that he is? Who did you think he was when you first saw the image?

② Journalists and civil rights advocates, who wanted to create a dramatic, lasting image of the landmark Court decision, had to talk Rosa Parks into having the picture taken. Do you think the photo's impact would be diminished if more people knew about its origin?

③ What is your opinion of the ethics of using a staged photograph such as this one? Can a staged photograph accurately depict a historic event? Why or why not?

---

firmed by the Supreme Court, the protests garnered national media attention and evoked public sympathy, and the civil rights movement had gained an articulate leader who was capable of unifying and motivating masses and who had an effective strategy for challenging the racism of American society.

NONVIOLENT CIVIL DISOBEDIENCE King believed in protesting government-sanctioned discrimination through **civil disobedience,** a philosophy that advocates actively, but in a nonviolent way refusing to comply with laws or governmental policies that are morally objectionable. In 1849, Henry David Thoreau espoused the philosophy in his essay *Civil Disobedience,* which argues that one should not support a government if one morally opposes that government's principles. Abolitionists used civil disobedience when they refused to comply with the Fugitive Slave Act of 1850. King's tactics of civil disobedience and nonviolent resistance were strongly influenced by Mahatma Gandhi, who used the strategy effectively to protest the British colonial presence in India, eventually resulting in India's independence.[16]

African American students, as well as white students and other civil rights activists from throughout the country, used the tactics of civil disobedience, including boycotts, sit-ins, and marches, to challenge the policies of segregation. One such demonstration was held in August 1963, in which hundreds of thousands of black and white Americans heard King deliver his famous "I Have a Dream" speech in the shadow of the Lincoln Memorial. (You can view

civil disobedience
active, but nonviolent, refusal to comply with laws or governmental policies that are morally objectionable

> Martin Luther King Jr. holds his son and contemplates a burned cross outside his home in Atlanta, Georgia. King and other civil rights leaders faced threats and intimidation throughout the civil rights era. King was assassinated in Memphis, Tennessee, in April 1968.

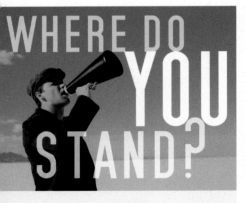

King's Dream

With regard to Martin Luther King Jr. and the 1960s civil rights movement, how many goals of that movement have been achieved so far?

☐ All
☐ Most
☐ Only some
☐ Almost none

Source: "On King Holidays, a Split Response to Civil Rights Progress," www.gallup.com/poll/103828/Civil-Rights-Progress-Seen-More.aspx.

the speech on YouTube at www.youtube.com/watch?v=PbUtL_0vAJk.)

THE REACTION TO CIVIL DISOBEDIENCE One famous series of marches occurred in early March 1965 from Selma to Montgomery, Alabama. On Sunday, March 7, about six hundred civil rights activists began a march out of Selma, protesting the policies of intimidation and violence that prevented African Americans from registering to vote. The demonstrators, led by John Lewis (now a Democratic member of Congress from Georgia), walked only six blocks to the Edmund Pettus bridge, where law enforcement officials, including Alabama State Troopers and members of the sheriff's office of Dallas County, Alabama, were waiting.[17] When the peaceful protesters attempted to cross the bridge, law enforcement officers brutally attacked them, using tear gas, bull whips, and night sticks. Dubbed Bloody Sunday, the march and the beatings were televised nationally and were instrumental in swaying public opinion in favor of civil rights. The marches sparked a renewed focus on the lack of voting rights for African Americans and ultimately helped to pressure Congress to pass the Voting Rights Act in 1965.[18]

King, who was not present at the Bloody Sunday march, returned to Selma to lead another march on the following Tuesday. When law enforcement officers again confronted the marchers at the bridge, King asked his followers to kneel in prayer and then turn around and return to their starting point. Critics charged that King was giving in to law enforcement and questioned his nonviolent tactics.[19] Differences over the use of nonviolent civil disobedience generated divisions within the civil rights movement,[20] with the more militant leaders such as Stokely Carmichael and Malcolm X advocating more aggressive tactics.[21]

While the violence used against protesters was successful in generating positive opinions of the civil rights movement, another form of violence, urban riots, eroded feelings of goodwill toward the movement. For five days in 1965, rioting in the Watts neighborhood of Los Angeles resulted in thirty-four deaths, more than 1,000 injuries, and over 4,000 arrests. Though the immediate cause of the violence was an altercation between white police officers and an African American man who had been arrested for drunk driving, the frustration and anger that spilled over had long been brewing in this poor, predominantly African American neighborhood.

On April 4, 1968, Martin Luther King was in Memphis, Tennessee, in support of African American sanitation workers who were striking for equal treatment and pay with white workers. Standing on a balcony at the Lorraine Motel, King was killed by an assassin's bullet. Heartbreak, hopelessness, and despair followed King's assassination—a feeling manifested in part by further rioting in over one hundred cities. Many Americans, both black and white, objected to the looting depicted in nightly news broadcasts. But those who sympathized with the rioters noted that because of the accumulated injustices against African Americans, the government and the rule of law had lost legitimacy in the eyes of those who were rioting.

The Government's Response to the Civil Rights Movement

The civil rights movement is credited not only with ending segregation in public schools, but also with the desegregation of public accommodations such as buses, restaurants, and hotels and with promoting universal suffrage. As a result of the movement, Congress passed the Voting Rights Act, which aggressively sought to counter nearly one hundred years of disenfranchisement, as well as the 1964 Civil Rights Act, which bars racial discrimination in accommodations and private employment, and the 1968 Civil Rights Act, which prohibits racial discrimination in housing.

The Civil Rights Act of 1964

Simultaneously expanding the rights of many Americans and providing them with important protections from discrimination, the Civil Rights Act of 1964 includes provisions that mandate equality on numerous fronts:

- It outlaws arbitrary discrimination in voter registration practices within the states.
- It bans discrimination in public accommodations, including in hotels, restaurants, and theaters.
- It prohibits state and local governments from banning access to public facilities on the basis of race, religion, or ethnicity.
- It empowers the U.S. Attorney General to sue to desegregate public schools.
- It bars government agencies from discrimination, and imposes the threat of the loss of federal funding if an agency violates the ban.
- It establishes a standard of equality in employment opportunity.

>On Sunday, March 7, 1965, Alabama state troopers move in on civil rights marchers with swinging clubs and tear gas. The ferocity of their attack, televised nationally, helped sway public opinion in favor of the marchers' cause.

The last part of the act, Title VII, which establishes the equality standard in employment opportunity, provides the legal foundation for a body of law that regulates fair employment practices. Specifically, Title VII bans discrimination in employment based on inherent characteristics—race, national origin, religion, and sex. Title VII also established the Equal Employment Opportunity Commission (EEOC), a government body that still administers Title VII today. The EEOC provides employers with guidelines on interpreting and enforcing current fair employment regulations. It is also a resource for employees who believe they have been discriminated against: Congress granted the EEOC broad investigatory powers. Thus, the EEOC can collect evidence and conduct hearings to investigate claims of discrimination in the workplace.

Other Civil Rights Legislation in the 1960s

While the Civil Rights Act of 1964 sought to address discrimination in access to public accommodations, employment, and education, many civil rights leaders believed that further legislation was necessary to protect the voting rights of African Americans in the South because they had been so systematically intimidated and prevented from participating.[22] In some southern counties, less than a third of all eligible African Americans were registered to vote, while nearly two-thirds of eligible white voters were registered in the same counties.

The Voting Rights Act of 1965 (VRA) sought to rectify this disparity in two ways. First, the VRA banned voter registration practices, like literacy tests, that discriminated based on race. Second, the VRA mandated federal intervention in any county in which less than 50 percent of eligible voters were registered. Under this tough enforcement mechanism, dozens of federal voter registration agents were sent to many southern counties. During the summer of 1965, thousands of civil rights activists, including many college students, worked to register voters. Within months, a quarter of a million new voters had been added to the voting rolls.

steering

the practice by which realtors steered African American families to certain neighborhoods and white families to others

One component of the VRA provided for periodic review of some of its tenets. After a specified period of time, Congress must pass and the president must sign an extension of the law to have these requirements remain in effect. Although the VRA permanently eliminated discriminatory practices such as literacy tests, the Department of Justice is responsible for monitoring other practices. The law includes a requirement that in some states (where less than 50 percent of eligible voters were registered)* "any voting qualification or prerequisite to voting, or standard, practice, or procedure with respect to voting..." must first be cleared with the Department of Justice.

In 1968, in the aftermath of Martin Luther King's murder on April 4, Congress passed and President Lyndon Johnson signed an additional piece of civil rights legislation. The Civil Rights Act of 1968 sought to end discriminatory practices in housing, including mortgage lending. The act banned the practice of **steering,** in which realtors would steer African American families to certain neighborhoods and white families to others. One part of the act also made it a federal crime for individuals to tamper with the civil rights of others, thus offering protection for civil rights workers.

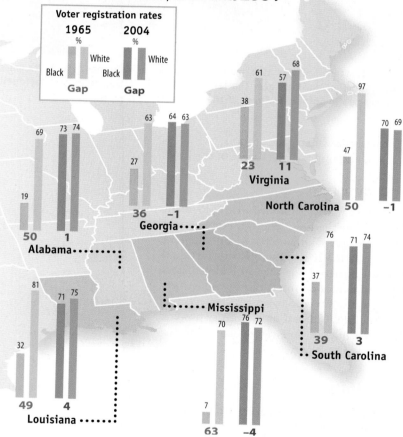

The Voting Rights Act and Voter Registration Rates, 1965 and 2004

POLITICAL INQUIRY

FIGURE 5.2 ■ In view of the profound impact of the Voting Rights Act, as indicated by the data presented here, has the act outlived its usefulness? What might be some reasons for continuing the act? For discontinuing it?

Source: www.usdoj.gov/crt/voting/intro/intro_c.htm and author's calculations based on www.census.gov/population/socdemo/voting/cps2004/tab04a.xls.

Impact of the Civil Rights Movement

The culmination of many acts of resistance by individuals and groups, the civil rights movement has had a momentous impact on society by working for the laws and rulings that bar discrimination in employment, public accommodations, education, and housing. The movement has also had a profound impact on voting rights by establishing the principle that the laws governing voter registration and participation should ensure that individuals are permitted to vote regardless of their race. As shown in Figure 5.2, as a result of the Voting Rights Act, in Mississippi, for example, the percentage of African Americans registered to vote jumped from 7 percent in 1965 to 76 percent in 2004. In some states, including Georgia, Mississippi, and North Carolina, a greater percentage of African Americans are registered than whites. In addition, all states, especially those in the south, have seen an enormous increase in the number of African Americans elected to serve in offices at the state, county, and municipal levels and in school districts. Indeed, more African Americans serve in elected office in Mississippi than in any other state, and all southern states boast among the highest numbers of African American elected officials.[23]

In addition to having a profound impact on race relations and civil rights law, the civil rights movement soon came to be regarded by other groups as a model of political engagement. Ethnic minorities, women, the disabled, and gays and lesbians have adopted many tactics of the movement in their own quest to secure their civil rights.

*These states include Alaska, Alabama, Arizona, Georgia, Louisiana, Mississippi, South Carolina, Texas, plus some counties in California, Florida, New York, North Carolina, South Dakota, and Virginia.

The Movement for Women's Civil Rights

As already noted, the pronouncement in the Declaration of Independence that "all men are created equal" initially applied only to white men, and usually only to those who owned property. Not only did the concept of equal protection of the laws not apply to nonwhite male citizens, until the Civil War amendments to the Constitution and subsequent pieces of national legislation such as the Voting Rights and Civil Rights acts, it did not apply to female citizens—white or nonwhite. Like African Americans, women had to wait until the Constitution was amended and civil rights legislation was adopted in response to the women's rights movement.

Advocates for women's civil rights began their efforts in the mid-1800s, initially focusing on gaining the right to vote for women citizens. This endeavor, the first wave of the women's rights movement, won suffrage for women in 1920. The cause of women's civil rights was rejuvenated in the 1960s, when the second wave of the movement began. This second wave continues today.

The First Wave of the Women's Rights Movement

The segregation of the women delegates at the 1840 World Anti-Slavery Conference in London was a defining moment for the first wave of the U.S. women's rights movement. Forced to sit in the balcony behind a drawn curtain, Lucretia Mott and Elizabeth Cady Stanton recognized that without improving their own legal and political status, women were not going to be successful in fighting for the legal rights of other groups of people.

In 1848, Mott and Stanton organized a meeting at Seneca Falls, New York, to talk about the lack of legal rights of U.S. citizens who happened to be born female. At the end of the convention, the participants signed the Declaration of Sentiments. This Declaration, modeled after the Declaration of Independence, listed many rights and opportunities that the law did not guarantee women, including the right to vote, educational and employment opportunities equal to those of white men, and married women's rights to own property as well as legal standing to sue. At the end of the convention, the participants signed the Declaration of Sentiments (see Appendix D).

Clearly, John Adams and the other architects of the Constitution had ignored Abigail Adams's request to her husband and his colleagues to "remember the ladies" when they created the new system of government. Adams warned her husband that not only would women not feel bound to obey laws in which they had no say but that the ladies would "foment a rebellion" if they were not provided a voice in government.

The signatories of the Declaration of Sentiments began Adams's forecasted rebellion. The document they signed insisted "that [women] have immediate admission to all rights and privileges which belong to them as citizens of these United States." For those women and men who joined this new movement for women's rights, the right to vote became the focal point. They recognized that this right was the foundational right that would enable women to win the other rights and privileges of citizenship.

Because the Constitution initially reserved for the states the authority to determine who had the right to vote as well as to be employed and obtain the best possible education, many of the initial battles for women's rights took place at the state level of government. Eventually, as the national government's responsibilities expanded through court interpretations of the Constitution, especially the Fourteenth Amendment, the federal government's role in guaranteeing civil rights expanded.

STATE-LEVEL RIGHTS Even after ratification of the Fourteenth Amendment (1868) guaranteeing equal protection of the laws for all people and the same privileges and immunities to all citizens, women's educational and work opportunities were limited by social norms as well as state laws. Education for girls prepared them to be good wives and mothers, not to be economically independent. By the late 1800s, a few colleges began to admit women, and several women's colleges were established. Yet most colleges did not offer women the same educational opportunities as men, and women who graduated and aspired to a career were limited in two ways. First, by choosing a career, these educated women gave up the possibility of marriage. They were not legally banned from marriage, but societal norms prevented them from having both a career and a husband. Second, their career choices were limited: teaching, the developing professions of nursing and social work, or missionary work.

In 1873 Myra Bradwell challenged women's limited career choices when she sued the state of Illinois over its refusal to let her practice law.[24] She argued that the Fourteenth Amendment's privileges and immunities clause protected her right to earn a living in a career of her choice. In this case, the Supreme Court found that women's God-given destiny was to "fulfill the noble and benign offices of wife and mother" and that allowing women to practice law would impinge on this destiny. The *Bradwell* case established the precedent for the Court to allow women to be treated differently from men (sex-based discrimination) if the different treatment was deemed a *rational* means by which the government could fulfill a *legitimate* public interest. This guideline for determining in a specific case whether sex-based discrimination is legal became known as the **ordinary scrutiny test** (also labeled the **rational basis test**). In the *Bradwell* case the Court deemed it legitimate for the government to protect the role of women as wives and mothers, and in order to accomplish this protection, it was rational to deny them equal employment opportunities.

In 1875 another women's rights case came before the Supreme Court. In this case, Virginia Minor of Missouri (actually her husband, because she, like all married women, did not have standing to sue) challenged the constitutionality of Missouri's law that guaranteed the right to vote only to male U.S. citizens. In this case, *Minor v. Happersett,* the Court acknowledged that women were citizens, yet it also decreed that state governments established voting rights, not the U.S. Constitution.[25] Therefore, the justices argued that the Fourteenth Amendment's privileges and immunities clause did not give women rights not established in the Constitution, hence it did not extend to women the right to vote. While by 1875 some local governments (school districts specifically) had extended voting rights to women, no state other than New Jersey had ever given women the right to vote. Women who owned property in New Jersey had the right to vote for a brief period between the end of the War for Independence and 1807, when it was taken away in response to the lobbying of politicians and professional men.

In 1890, when the Wyoming Territory became a state, Wyoming women, who had been voting in the territory since 1869, retained their voting rights. In this same year in which women were first granted the right to vote by any state, two women's suffrage organizations, both of which had been established in 1869, merged to begin a new phase in their battle for women's suffrage.

THE NINETEENTH AMENDMENT TO THE CONSTITUTION The American Women's Suffrage Association (AWSA), directed by Lucy Stone, had been leading the battle to extend the right to vote to women in the states. At the same time, the National Women's Suffrage Association (NWSA), directed by Susan B. Anthony and Elizabeth Cady Stanton, was fighting to extend to women all rights of citizenship, including but not limited to the right to vote. Unlike the AWSA, the NWSA focused its suffrage battle on the federal level, specifically on amending the U.S. Constitution. In 1890, frustrated by their lack of success in the battle to extend suffrage to women, the AWSA and the NWSA joined forces, creating the National American Women's Suffrage Association (NAWSA). The NAWSA focused its efforts on amending the U.S. Constitution.

In 1916 Alice Paul founded the National Women's Party, which adopted more radical tactics than the NAWSA had been willing to use in its fight for suffrage. Noting the lack of support on the part of national officials for suffrage, Paul's organization called on voters in the 1916 election not to vote for candidates who did not support women's suffrage, including President Wilson, who was running for reelection. In 1917, after President Wilson was reelected, Paul and other suffragists chained themselves to the White House fence and called on Wilson to support the suffrage amendment. Arrested, jailed, and force fed when they engaged in a hunger strike, the women gained media attention, which in turn brought national attention to their struggle for suffrage and the president's opposition. After several months and persistent media pressure, President Wilson called on the House and the Senate to approve the women's suffrage amendment.

ordinary scrutiny test (rational basis test)
the guidelines the courts used starting in 1873 to determine the legality of sex-based discrimination; on the basis of this test, sex-based discrimination is legal if it is a reasonable means by which the government can achieve a legitimate public interest

By June 1919, the House and the Senate approved what was to become the Nineteenth Amendment. In 1920, Tennessee became the thirty-sixth state to ratify the amendment, and it was added to the Constitution.

The Second Wave of the Women's Rights Movement

After the Nineteenth Amendment was added to the Constitution, the push for women's rights ceased to be a mass movement. Women were still organized in groups and lobbied the government for women's civil rights, but the many women's organizations were no longer working collectively toward one agreed-upon goal, such as the right to vote. Another mass women's movement did not arise until the 1960s. Several factors account for the mobilization of the second wave of the women's movement in the 1960s, which focused this time on the plethora of rights related to the social, economic, and political status of women, many of the same rights originally demanded in the Declaration of Sentiments.

By the 1960s, large numbers of women were working outside the home in the paid labor force. Working women talked with each other about their work and family lives and came to recognize common concerns and problems, including discrimination in educational opportunities, employment opportunities, and pay; lack of child care; domestic violence; the problem of rape, for which *they* were often blamed; and their inability to obtain credit (borrow money) without having a male cosign on the loan. Women recognized that as a class of citizens they did not have equal protection of the laws.

In 1961, at the prodding of Esther Peterson, the director of the Women's Bureau in the Department of Labor, President John F. Kennedy (1961–1963) established a Commission on the Status of Women, chaired by Eleanor Roosevelt. In 1963, the commission reported that women in the United States were discriminated against

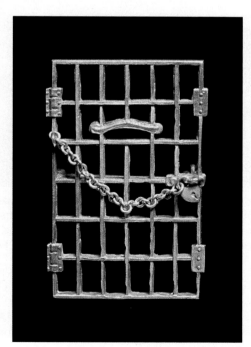

>Alice Paul designed this pin and presented it to the many suffragists arrested and imprisoned for picketing in front of the White House for women's suffrage between 1917 and 1919. The pin, a replication of a prison gate, calls attention to the injustice of being "jailed for freedom."

in many areas of life, including education and employment. In its report, the commission argued that women needed to pursue lawsuits that would allow the Supreme Court to interpret properly the Fourteenth Amendment's equal protection clause, hence prohibiting discrimination against women.

By the mid-1960s, the women's rights movement was rejuvenated with a second wave of mass activity. The goal of this second wave was equal legal rights for women. The means to achieve this goal were legislation, litigation, and an as yet unsuccessful attempt to enact the Equal Rights Amendment (ERA), which had been written by Alice Paul and first introduced in Congress in 1923.

FEDERAL LEGISLATION AND WOMEN'S RIGHTS In 1955, Edith Green (D-Oregon) introduced into Congress the first piece of national legislation written specifically to protect women, the Equal Pay Act. Enacted into law in 1963, the Equal Pay Act prohibited employers from paying women less than men were paid for the same job, which was the standard employment practice at the time. Indeed, beginning with school boards in the mid-1800s and the federal Mint during the Civil War, governments had hired women specifically because they could pay them less than men.

The 1964 Civil Rights Act as initially drafted prohibited discrimination in education, employment, and public accommodations based on race, ethnicity, and religion. Yet because of congressional women's efforts, Title VII of the proposed act was rewritten to prohibit discrimination in all personnel decisions based on *sex* as well as the other categories. Initially, the EEOC, the federal agency responsible for monitoring Title VII implementation, did not take sex-based discrimination complaints seriously. Women serving on state committees on the status of women responded by establishing the National Organization for Women (NOW) in 1966. NOW's initial statement of purpose is modeled on the requests of the 1848 Seneca Falls Declaration of Sentiments, demonstrating the continued lack of progress toward the goal of women's equality under the law.[26]

In order to take advantage of Title VII's promise of equal employment opportunities, women needed to pursue educational opportunities on an equal basis with men. Yet Title VI of the 1964 Civil Rights Act does not prohibit sex-based discrimination in institutions that receive federal funds, including educational institutions. By 1972 women's rights advocates won an amendment to the 1964 Civil Rights Act, Title IX, which prohibits such sex-based discrimination.

The Equal Pay Act, Title VII, and Title IX are landmark pieces of national legislation that provide equal protection of the law for women. At the same time that Congress was enacting laws prohibiting sex-based discrimination, the courts were reinterpreting the clause of the Fourteenth Amendment on equal protection of the law.

> During the 1960s and 1970s, the movement for women's civil rights was rejuvenated. A focal point for protests and demonstrations during the second wave has been the Equal Rights Amendment, which Congress sent to the states in 1972 for ratification. Although the attempt to win ratification failed in the 1980s, proponents of the ERA continue to lobby for it today.

WOMEN'S RIGHTS AND THE EQUAL PROTECTION CLAUSE In 1971, in the case of *Reed v. Reed,* the Supreme Court for the first time in history used the equal protection clause of the Fourteenth Amendment to find a law that discriminated against women unconstitutional.[27] In the *Reed* case, the Supreme Court found that an Idaho state law giving automatic preference to men to administer the estate of a deceased person who had not named an administrator was not a reasonable means to fulfill a legitimate government interest. Hence using the ordinary scrutiny test established in the 1873 *Bradwell* case, the court ruled this discriminatory treatment of women was unconstitutional.

In 1976, the Supreme Court developed a new test for the legality of sex-based discrimination. Oklahoma law allowed women 18 years of age to buy beer with 3.2% alcohol content. Yet men in Oklahoma had to be 21 years of age to purchase 3.2% beer. Men challenged the law, asking the Court to decide if this sex-based discrimination was constitutional. In this case, *Craig v. Boren,* the Court established a **heightened scrutiny test** (also labeled the **intermediate scrutiny test**) for sex-based discrimination cases: different treatment is legal if it is *substantially* related to an *important* government interest.[28] The Court used this intermediate scrutiny test in the *Craig* case to find the Oklahoma law unconstitutional. The Court also used the heightened scrutiny test in the 1996 *U.S. v. Virginia* case.[29] In this case the Court found the male-only admission policy of the Virginia Military Institute unconstitutional. Justice Ruth Bader Ginsburg noted in her opinion that the state of Virginia had *not* shown that this discriminatory admissions policy was *substantially related* to the *important* government objective of training soldiers.

Today, courts sometimes use the ordinary scrutiny test and other times the intermediate scrutiny test when deciding sex-based discrimination cases as well as other non–race-based discrimination cases. In comparison, the courts use the strict scrutiny test in race-based discrimination cases as well as cases regarding certain liberties: freedom of religion, press, and assembly, and privacy rights. The **strict scrutiny test** allows discrimination only if the different treatment is *necessary* to fulfill a *compelling* government interest. This test is much harder to pass than the ordinary scrutiny test.

Proponents of an ERA argue that the strict scrutiny test should be used in sex-based discrimination cases and that this will not happen until the Constitution is amended to explicitly guarantee equality of rights under the law whether a person is a man or a woman.

heightened scrutiny test (intermediate scrutiny test)
the guidelines used most frequently by the courts to determine the legality of sex-based discrimination; on the basis of this test, sex-based discrimination is legal if the government can prove that it is substantially related to the achievement of an important public interest

strict scrutiny test
the guidelines the courts use to determine the legality of all but sex-based discrimination; on the basis of this test, discrimination is legal if it is a necessary means by which the government can achieve a compelling public interest

THE PROPOSED EQUAL RIGHTS AMENDMENT

During the 1970s, as the Supreme Court was reinterpreting the implications of the Fourteenth Amendment for sex-based discrimination, lobbying for the Equal Rights Amendment increased. In 1972 Congress approved the ERA, which states that "Equality of rights under the law shall not be denied or abridged by the United States or by any State on account of sex." Finally, forty-nine years after it was first introduced in Congress, the ERA was sent to the states for ratification.

Opponents of the ERA argued it was a duplication of the Fourteenth Amendment and therefore was not needed. Opponents also claimed that passage of the amendment would make women subject to the military draft; would lead to the integration of all single-sex institutions, including schools and public bathrooms; and would result in the legalization of and public funding for all abortions. Moreover, they argued that the ERA was not needed because Congress was passing laws that guaranteed women equal protection in employment and education. Whether or not the claims of its opponents were accurate, they were successful in defeating the ERA, which had not been ratified by enough states by the deadline of 1982. The effort to ratify an ERA continues, with a recent revival of the effort, which we explored in Chapter 2.

The first wave of the women's rights movement won the vote through constitutional amendment. The second

TESTS FOR LEGAL DISCRIMINATION

— **Ordinary scrutiny** is the weakest test used by the courts to determine the constitutionality of sex-based discrimination. To pass this test, the government must show the court that treating women differently than men is a *rational way* for the government to accomplish a *legitimate public interest.*

— **Heightened scrutiny** is the intermediate test used by the courts to determine the constitutionality of sex-based discrimination. To pass this test, the government must show the court that treating women differently than men is *substantially related* to the government's ability to accomplish an *important public interest.*

— **Strict scrutiny** is the hardest test to pass, and the courts have not yet applied this test to sex-based discrimination cases. The courts use this test to determine the constitutionality of discrimination based on race, color, ethnicity, and religion. To pass this test, the government must show the court that such discriminatory treatment is *necessary* for the government to achieve a *compelling public interest.*

Concept Summary

wave successfully expanded women's civil rights through litigation and legislation. Yet many women's rights advocates argue that women still battle inequities, including unequal pay, sexual harassment, and the glass ceiling (aspiring to higher-level jobs but being unable to win them). Although the situation for women has greatly improved, some argue, not all women have benefited equally from gains in women's rights. Nonwhite women have two characteristics that can lead to discriminatory treatment: gender and color, necessitating a struggle for equal protection on two fronts: the women's rights movement and the civil rights movements of their racial group. We now explore the struggles of several other groups of citizens for equal civil rights.

Other Civil Rights Movements

Today, discriminatory treatment is still a reality for many groups of citizens. The Civil Rights Act notwithstanding, discrimination in employment, education, housing, and due process still occurs. Some employers still make personnel decisions, from hiring to setting salaries, based on sex, race, ethnicity, English fluency, as well as disability. Because of the Supreme Court's ruling in the *Brown* case, no government in the United States can write laws that segregate people based on their race or the color of their skin (unless such segregation passes the strict scrutiny test). **De jure segregation,** or segregation by law, is unconstitutional. Yet because people tend to live in neighborhoods with others of their race, religion, or ethnic group, schools are still segregated by race and color, producing **de facto segregation.** Poorer quality schools are more common in communities dominated by African American and Latino residents. Housing discrimination can come in many forms: Landlords illegally refuse to rent to, and realtors selectively show homes for sale to people based on the color of their skin or their lack of fluency in English. Law enforcement officers may also select people for stopping, questioning, and even searching based on the color of their skin (racial profiling) instead of for reasonable cause based on their actions.

Unfortunately, we cannot discuss all of the civil rights movements that have occurred in the United States. Therefore, we will explore the civil rights battles of just a few groups of citizens: Native Americans; Hispanic Americans; Asian Americans; citizens with disabilities; and lesbian, gay, bisexual, and transgendered people. The hard-fought victories and aspirations of these groups offer an overview of both the history and the breadth of contemporary civil rights movements.

Native Americans' Rights

At first, the fledgling nation recognized the native residents of the land that became the United States as members of sovereign and independent nations with inherent rights. The federal government entered into more than 370 treaties with Native American tribes between 1778 and 1870.[30] Most of these treaties promised land to tribes that agreed to move, and almost all of these promises were empty, with the government reneging on most of these agreements. In addition, in 1830, Congress passed the Indian Removal Act, which called for the forced relocation of all native peoples to lands west of the Mississippi. In the end, most Native Americans were dispossessed of their lands and wound up living on reservations. The federal government treated Indians as subhumans, relegating them to second-class status, as they had African Americans.

Until Congress passed the Indian Citizenship Act in 1924, Native Americans had no rights to U.S. citizenship, and even the laws that allowed immigrants to become citizens did not apply to Native Americans. The Indian Rights Association, founded in 1882 and active in lobbying Congress and the state legislatures until the 1930s, was one of the most important of the early groups that actively campaigned for full suffrage for native peoples, in the belief that enfranchisement would help to "civilize" them. The early 1900s also saw the founding of the Society of American Indians and the American Indian Defense Association, both of which fought for citizenship for Native Americans and then for their civil rights. However, for more than forty years after passage of the Indian Citizenship Act, the basic rights enu-

de jure segregation
segregation mandated by law

de facto segregation
segregation caused by the fact that people tend to live in neighborhoods with others of their own race, religion, or ethnic group

ON THE JOB

MICHAEL WOESTEHOFF, ADVOCATE FOR NATIVE AMERICAN EDUCATION

Name: Michael Woestehoff

Age: 24

Hometown: Ganado, Arizona

College: Northern Arizona University

Major: Political Science (BA)

Job title: Membership and Communications Coordinator, National Indian Education Association (NIEA)

Salary range for jobs like this: $30,000–$40,000

Day-to-day responsibilities: My job is to increase membership, keep the members interested by providing them with incentives, unify the membership, communicate to members, and assess the members' needs. I also work on developing and maintaining a brand for the national organization, editing a quarterly newsletter, writing articles, distributing press releases, and contacting the media as well as outreach; Web site maintenance; designing ads, posters, and mailings, and more!

How did you get your job? I wrote a cover letter to many organizations expressing my interest in their goals and missions. The National Indian Education Association was a particular focus of my efforts. I had a résumé full of internships and provided concise details of what I had done in those positions. Because of my persistence, they offered me the position.

What do you like best about your job? It is absolutely rewarding. I am an advocate for education issues that have an immediate impact on the lives of the people in my community. I provide a positive image that shows results. This organization not only unifies teachers, students, and tribal leaders through our national goals for education, but it also works for the preservation of the cultural traditions and languages of the American Indian, Alaskan Native, and Native Hawaiian peoples.

What is your least favorite aspect of your job? The most difficult part is that there is not enough time in the day to get things done. Although I leave the office every day with the belief that I have accomplished much, I still have the feeling that I should be doing more.

What advice would you give to students who would like to do what you're doing? Stay interested and motivated. Write your ideas down in a daily journal. Be your own monitor by assessing your accomplishments. If you can get in the habit of writing ideas down, you will be able to show progress.

merated in the Bill of Rights were not granted to Native Americans. In the 1960s, Indian activists became more radical, occupying government buildings, picketing, and conducting protests. In 1968, the American Indian Movement (AIM) was founded. In the same year, Congress passed the Indian Civil Rights Act, which ensured that Native Americans would have the full protection of the Bill of Rights. While this law had significant symbolic impact, it lacked an enforcement mechanism, and so native peoples continued to be deprived of basic due process protections and equal education and employment opportunites. The National Indian Education Association (NIEA), founded in 1969, confronts the lack of quality educational opportunities for Native Americans and the loss of native culture and values. Michael Woestehoff discusses his work for the NIEA in "On the Job."

During the 1970s, Native American organizations began a new effort to force the federal government to honor treaties granting Indians fishing and hunting rights as well as rights to the natural resources buried in their lands. Indians in New York, Maine, and elsewhere sued for land taken from them decades or even a century ago in violation of treaties. Starting with the 1975 Indian Self-Determination and Education Assistance Act, Congress, President

Richard Nixon (1969–1974), and subsequent presidents enacted laws that supported greater autonomy for Indian tribes and gave them more control of their assets.

The 1988 Indian Gaming Regulatory Act is the best known of the federal laws enacted to support Indian self-determination. This law authorizes Indian tribes to establish gaming operations on their property and requires them to negotiate compacts with the states in which their lands are located. The compacts typically include a profit-sharing understanding. The act mandates that the money made through gaming operations must be used for education, economic development, infrastructure (for example, roads and utilities), law enforcement, and courts. By 2003, there were 310 Indian gaming operations, operating under 198 tribe and state gaming compacts in twenty-eight states and accounting for about 10 percent of the U.S. gaming industry.[31] Clearly, one goal of the Gaming Act was to generate resources that would increase the educational and employment opportunities on Indian reservations.

Even with gaming profits, however, the prospects for many Native Americans today remain bleak. According to race and ethnic relations scholars Joe R. Feagin and Clairece Booher Feagin, "Native Americans have endured the longest Depression-like economic situation of any U.S. racial or ethnic group."[32] They are among the poorest, least educated U.S citizens. Like many other groups of U.S. citizens with characteristics that identify them as non–white European descendants, Native Americans continue to fight in the halls of government, in the courtrooms, and in the public arena for their constitutionally guaranteed rights and privileges.

Citizens of Latin American Descent

U.S. citizens of Latin American descent (Latinos) include those whose families hail from Central America, South America, or the Caribbean. Latinos are the largest minority group in the United States, making up 15 percent of the total U.S. population in 2006 (44.3 million people). Sixty percent of this Latino population is composed of natural-born U.S. citizens.[33] Latinos make up a large percentage of the population of several states, including New Mexico, California, Texas, Arizona, and Florida.

Thirty-nine percent of Latinos are eligible voters—U.S. citizens at least 18 years of age. In 2004, 47 percent of these eligible voters voted.[34] So far the elections that have occurred in the twenty-first century have been followed by numerous lawsuits claiming that individual citizens, organized groups, and local governments have prevented eligible Latino voters from voting. For example, in 2006 the national government sued Philadelphia's city government for failing to assist voters effectively—specifically Spanish-speaking voters—who had limited-English proficiency. Limited-English proficiency continues to cause problems with access to voting and equal educational and employment opportunities for many U.S. citizens, including Latino citizens. We focus here on U.S. citizens of Mexican origin—the largest Latino population in the United States today.

EARLY STRUGGLES OF MEXICAN AMERICANS   In 1846, because of land disputes sparked by white immigrants from the United States encroaching on Mexican territory, the United States declared war on Mexico. By the terms of the 1848 Treaty of Guadalupe Hidalgo, which ended the war, Mexico ceded territory to the United States for $15 million. The Mexican landowners living within this ceded territory had the choice of staying on their land and remaining in what was now the United States or relocating to Mexico. According to the treaty, those Mexicans who stayed on their land would become U.S. citizens, and their civil rights would be protected. While nearly 77,000 Mexicans chose to do so, and became U.S. citizens, their civil rights were *not* protected.[35] Thus began a long and continuing history of discrimination against U.S. citizens of Mexican descent.

At the turn of the twentieth century, Mexican Americans organized to protest the various forms of discrimination they were experiencing, which included segregated schools, inequities in employment opportunities and wages, discrimination by law enforcement officers, and barriers to their voting rights such as poll taxes and English-only literacy tests. In 1929, several Mexican American organizations combined to create the League of United Latin American Citizens (LULAC).[36]

In 1945, LULAC successfully challenged the segregated school systems in California, which provided separate schools for Mexican children that were of poorer quality than the schools for white children. In this case, *Mendez v. Westminister,* the federal court set an important precedent by using the Fourteenth Amendment to guarantee equal educational opportunities.[37] In 1954, the U.S. Supreme Court followed this lower court's precedent when it ended legal race-based segregation in public schools throughout the nation in the *Brown v. Board of Education of Topeka* case.

THE CHICANO MOVEMENT In addition to the women's rights movement and the civil rights movement for African American rights, the 1960s witnessed the birth of the Chicano Movement, the mass movement for Mexican American civil rights. The Chicano Movement was composed of numerous Latino organizations focusing on a variety of issues, including rights to equal employment and educational opportunities. One of the most widely recognized leaders in the Chicano Movement was Cesar Chavez.

Cesar Chavez began his civil rights work as a community organizer in 1952, encouraging Mexican Americans to vote and educating them about their civil rights. In the early 1960s, Chavez, along with Jessie Lopez and Dolores Huerta, founded the Agricultural Workers Organizing Committee (AWOC) and the National Farm Worker Association (NFWA). Under Chavez's leadership the AWOC and the NFWA merged to form the United Farm Workers (UFW) in 1966. The UFW organized successful protests and boycotts to improve working conditions and pay for farmworkers.[38]

>Cesar Chavez, a Mexican American born in Arizona, began his civil rights work as a community organizer in 1952 by encouraging Mexican Americans to vote and educating them about their civil rights. From the early 1960s until his death in 1993, Chavez was the leading voice for and organizer of migrant farmworkers in the United States.

The activism of Mexican American workers inspired others to call for additional civil rights protections, including access to equal educational opportunity. In 1968, Mexican American high school students in East Los Angeles staged a walkout to protest high drop-out rates of Latino students and the lack of bilingual education, Mexican American history classes, and Mexican American teachers. Though the student walkout did not lead to many immediate changes in the school system, it drew national attention, empowered the students, and inspired other protests.

Until 1971, Latinos were not legally considered a racial minority group, and therefore antidiscrimination laws, such as the 1964 Civil Rights Act, did not apply to them. In the landmark case *Corpus Christi Independent School District v. Cisneros*[39] (1971), the Supreme Court upheld a lower court's ruling that Latinos are a racial minority group; therefore, they are covered by laws protecting the rights of minority groups.[40]

EMPLOYMENT DISCRIMINATION AND OTHER CIVIL RIGHTS ISSUES Since the 1986 Immigration Reform and Control Act went into effect, organizations that work to protect the rights of Latinos and other minority citizens have been receiving increasing numbers of complaints about employment discrimination. Under this act employers who hire undocumented immigrant workers are subject to sanctions. In order to comply with this law, some employers refuse to hire—and thus discriminate against—any applicants for whom English is a second language and any who look Latino under the assumption that all such people could be undocumented immigrants. This means that employers are violating the equal employment rights of Latino citizens in many cases, for they are mistakenly assuming they are undocumented immigrants.

Today, U.S. citizens of Mexican descent continue to experience violations of their civil rights. LULAC, along with the Mexican American Legal Defense and Education Fund (MALDEF; founded in 1968), and other organizations continue to fight for laws that will provide due process and equal protection, equal access to education, and other civil rights for Latino citizens and immigrants. They also work to educate Latinos about their rights and empower them to engage in the political process. Through the efforts of these and other groups, Hispanic voter registration and turnout has significantly increased in recent elections. According to the Bureau of the Census, the only demographic group with lower voter

DOING DEMOCRACY

JOIN A CIVIL RIGHTS ORGANIZATION

FACT:

In March 2007, thousands of Latino high school students in California walked out of school and took to the streets to demand national and state holidays honoring Cesar Chavez, the migrant labor activist, who died in 1993. Currently eight states and many counties and cities honor Chavez with a holiday. In California, state government offices and colleges were closed on March 30, 2007, to honor Chavez, but the public schools remained open. The group By Any Means Necessary (BAMN) used its Web site to urge public school students to participate in the walkout. "Whether they want to close down the schools to honor the Chavez holiday or not, we are closing them and forcing everyone to recognize our Movement and honor the Chavez holiday!" declared the BAMN Web site.

Act!

According to its Web site, BAMN is a "national organization dedicated to building a new mass civil rights movement to defend affirmative action, integration, and the other gains of the civil rights movement of the 1960s and to advance the struggle for equality in American society by any means necessary." For those interested in learning more about current civil rights issues and perhaps participating in a civil rights group, the possibilities are endless.

Where to begin

- **www.bamn.com**   This is the home page of BAMN, an organization working to mobilize America's youth to make equality of rights and opportunities for women and minorities a reality.
- **www.civilrights.org/research_center/national_directory** This Web site provides a directory of civil rights organizations across the country.

---

turnout than Hispanics is Asian Americans.[41] We now turn to the history and ongoing efforts to obtain and protect the civil rights of Asian citizens.

Citizens of Asian Descent

Asian American citizens come from, or have ancestors from, a number of different countries with diverse cultures, religions, histories, and languages. Today, the largest percentage of Asian Americans have Chinese origins, followed by those of Filipino, Asian Indian, Vietnamese, Korean, and Japanese ancestry. Large numbers of immigrants from Japan came to the United States around the turn of the twentieth century, but it was not until the 1940s that the flow of immigrants from other Asian countries began to increase, beginning with the Philippines. In the 1960s the number of immigrants from Korea and India began to increase significantly, and in the 1970s—as the Vietnam War ended—immigrants from Vietnam began to arrive in large numbers. Today, 4 percent of the U.S. population is of Asian descent.

Like other U.S. citizens with non–white European ancestry, Asian Americans have had to fight continually for their civil rights, specifically for equal protection under the law and particularly for equal access to educational and employment opportunities as well as citizenship. Asian immigrants and Asian Americans created organizations to fight for citizenship and equal protection of the law, such as the Japanese American Citizens League (JACL; founded in the 1930s). One successful result of these efforts was the 1952 Immigration and Nationality Act, which allowed Asian immigrants to become citizens for the first time. Before passage of this law, only U.S.-born children of Asian immigrants could be citizens.

INTERNMENT OF JAPANESE AMERICANS DURING WORLD WAR II   As noted previously, one of the most egregious violations of the civil rights of tens of thousands of Asian American citizens occurred during World War II when Americans of Jap-

Interracial Dating

Have you ever dated someone from a different racial or ethnic background than your own?

☐ Yes

☐ No

Source: "Most Americans Approve of Interracial Dating," www.gallup.com/poll/19033/Most-Americans-Approve-Interracial-Dating.aspx.

anese ancestry were forced to move to government-established camps. Under President Franklin Roosevelt's Executive Order 9066, over 120,000 Japanese Americans, two-thirds of whom were native-born U.S. citizens, were relocated from the West Coast of the United States after Japan's attack on Pearl Harbor. During this same period the federal government also restricted the travel of Americans of German and Italian ancestry who were living on the West Coast (the United States was also fighting against Germany and Italy), but these citizens were not relocated. Many relocated Japanese Americans lost their homes and businesses.

The JACL fought for decades to obtain reparations for the citizens who were interned and for the repeal of a section of the 1950 Internal Security Act that allowed the government to imprison citizens deemed enemy collaborators during a crisis. Congress repealed the section of the 1950 law targeted by the JACL, and in 1987 President Ronald Reagan (1981–1989) signed a bill providing $1.2 billion in reparations.

CONTEMPORARY ISSUES FOR ASIAN AMERICANS   During the 1960s and 1980s, the number of organizations and coalitions pressing for the civil rights of Asian Americans grew as large numbers of new immigrants from Asian countries arrived in the United States in response to changes in U.S. immigration laws. During the 1960s, Asian Americans on college campuses organized and fostered a group consciousness about the need to protect their civil rights. During the 1980s, Asian American organizations began to pay more attention to voting rights as well as to hate crimes and employment discrimination. Then in 1996, numerous organizations, each representing Asian Americans with ancestry from one country, joined to form the National Council of Asian Pacific Americans (NCAPA), which presses for equal protection of the law for all Asians.

> Before 1952, foreign-born Asian immigrants could not become U.S. citizens; however, children born in the United States to Asian immigrants were citizens by birth. Today, both the biological and adopted children of U.S. citizens who are born abroad acquire automatic citizenship. For example, for children adopted from Asian countries, such as the young girl in this photo, U.S. citizenship is acquired automatically once the adoption process is completed.

With the exception of Korean Americans and Vietnamese Americans, Asian Americans have the highest median income compared to the population as a whole.[42] Asian Americans are also twice as likely as the population as a whole to earn a bachelor's degree or higher.[43] Moreover, Asian Americans are better represented in professional and managerial positions than any other racial or ethnic group, including white Americans. Yet like women, Asian American citizens appear to hit a glass ceiling, for they are not as well represented in the very top positions as their high levels of educational achievement would seem to predict. Therefore, those advocating for Asian American civil rights are increasingly concentrating their efforts on discrimination in employment.

Citizens with Disabilities

The civil rights movements of the 1960s and 1970s made society more aware of the lack of equal protection of the laws for diverse groups of citizens, including people with disabilities. The first law to mandate equal protection for people with physical and mental disabilities was the 1973 Rehabilitation Act, which prohibited discrimination against people with disabilities in federally funded programs. In 1990, people with disabilities achieved a significant enhancement of this earlier victory in their fight to obtain protection of their civil rights. The Americans with Disabilities Act (ADA), enacted in that year, extends the ban on discrimination against people with disabilities in education, employment, health care, housing, and transportation to all programs and organizations, not just those receiving federal funds. The ADA defines a disability as any "physical or mental impairment that substantially limits one or more of the major life activities of the individual." The ADA

Claiming that recent Supreme Court decisions have narrowed the scope of the 1990 Americans with Disabilities Act, advocates for the rights of people with disabilities toured the United States in this Road to Freedom bus. Their purpose was to educate Americans about the need to amend the act and restore it to its original intent.

does not enumerate every disability that it covers, resulting in much confusion over which conditions it covers and which it excludes.

Disability advocates disagree with recent Court decisions that specify a definition of "disability" that they believe is too narrow. The Court has determined that if an individual can take an action to mitigate an impairment (such as wearing eyeglasses for severe near-sightedness or taking medication for high blood pressure), then the impairment is not a disability requiring reasonable accommodation.[44] In response to these Court rulings, disability advocates support the ADA Restoration Act that was proposed in 2007. Among other things, this act would broaden the category of impairments that are covered by the ADA by eliminating the need for an impairment to "substantially limit one or more major life activities." To heighten awareness of the need for this law, the National Coalition of Disability Rights and ADA Watch—two organizations fighting for the civil rights of people with disabilities—undertook "the Road to Freedom" tour in 2007. The tour made more than eighty stops throughout the United States, mostly at "mainstream" locations like shopping malls, schools, sports events, and fairs. At each stop, tour participants provided audiences with opportunities to experience the obstacles faced by people with disabilities and educated them on what needs to be done to ensure equal access in transportation, education, and employment.

Despite disagreement about the breadth of the law's coverage, there is no question that the ADA has enhanced the civil rights of citizens with disabilities. Before the ADA was enacted, people with disabilities who were fired from their jobs or denied access to schools, office buildings, or other public places had no recourse. Cities were under no obligation to provide even the most reasonable accommodations to people with disabilities who sought employment or the use of public transportation systems. And employers were under no obligation to make even the most minor modifications to their workplaces for employees with disabilities. For example, if a qualified job applicant was wheelchair bound, an employer did not have to consider installing ramps or raising desks to accommodate the wheelchair but could simply refuse to hire the individual. The ADA changed this situation by requiring employers and governmental organizations to make it possible for people with disabilities to participate meaningfully in their communities through reasonable accommodations.

Lesbian, Gay, Bisexual, and Transgendered Citizens

Lesbian, gay, bisexual, and transgendered people (people whose gender identity cannot be categorized as male or female)—a group often referred to with the abbreviation LGBT or GBLT—also actively seek equal civil rights. Some of the specific rights that LGBT persons have organized to fight for include employment rights, housing rights, and marriage rights. Though the 1970s and 1980s saw some successes in these civil rights battles, there was some backlash in the 1990s and early in the twenty-first century. In this section we focus mainly on the rights of lesbians and gay men.

THE GAY PRIDE MOVEMENT Several LGBT civil rights organizations were founded after the Stonewall Rebellion. In June 1969, groups of gay men and lesbians clashed violently with police in New York City, in a protest over the routine harassment by law enforcement of members of the lesbian and gay community. This influential conflict, which started at the Stonewall bar, marked the first time that members of this community acted collectively and in large numbers to assert their rights. Shortly after this event, in 1970, Lambda Legal, a national organization fighting for full recognition of the civil rights of LGBT citizens, was founded. Within a few years, gays and lesbians began to hold gay pride marches throughout the country, and many new groups such as the Human Rights Campaign and the National Gay and Lesbian Task Force, began advocating for LGBT rights (see Chapter 7, "On the Job").

As a result of organized educational and lobbying efforts by the gay community, during the 1980s a number of state and local governments adopted laws prohibiting discrimination in employment, housing, public accommodations, and employee benefits—that is, guaranteeing equal protection of some laws—for LGBT persons. In 1982, Wisconsin was the first state to prohibit such discrimination. Yet during the same decade, numerous states had laws on the books prohibiting sex between mutually consenting adults of the same sex, typically in the form of antisodomy laws. In the 1986 case of *Bowers v. Hardwick,* the U.S. Supreme Court upheld Georgia's antisodomy law.[45] In 2003, another lawsuit challenging the constitutionality of a state antisodomy law came before the Supreme Court in the case of *Lawrence v. Texas.*[46] This time the Court overturned the 1986 *Bowers* decision, finding that the Fourteenth Amendment provides due process and equal protection for sexual privacy and therefore the Texas law was unconstitutional.

Advocates for the rights of LGBT persons hoped this 2003 ruling would lead to federal protections of LGBT citizens' civil rights. But there is still no federal law prohibiting LGBT-based discrimination in employment, housing, or public accommodations. In contrast to the lack of federal legislation, today twenty states and the District of Columbia have anti-discrimination laws guaranteeing equal access to employment, housing, and public accommodations regardless of sexual orientation.[47]

BACKLASH AGAINST THE MOVEMENT FOR LGBT CIVIL RIGHTS On the other side of the issue, in 1992, opponents of civil rights for LGBT persons succeeded in placing on the ballot in Colorado a proposed law that would prohibit all branches of the state government from adopting any law or policy making it illegal to discriminate against gay men, lesbians, bisexuals, or transgendered people. Immediately after Colorado voters approved the law, the state court placed an injunction on its implementation, preventing its enforcement, in order to allow a lawsuit challenging the law's constitutionality to work its way through the courts. In 1996, the U.S. Supreme Court, in *Romer v. Evans,* found the state law to be unconstitutional.[48] The parties who filed the suit challenging the law included the Boulder school district; the cities of Denver, Boulder, and Aspen; and the County of Denver.

Another civil rights battle for lesbians and gays is over the issue of marriage rights. The Hawaii state Supreme Court ruled in 1993 that it was a violation of the Hawaii state constitution to deny same-sex couples the right to marry. Opponents of same-sex marriage succeeded in their subsequent efforts to get a state constitutional amendment banning same-sex marriage on the ballot, and in 1996 the majority of Hawaiian voters approved it. The conflict over same-sex marriage that began in Hawaii quickly spread to other states.

Since 1998, almost three-quarters of the states have banned same-sex marriage through constitutional amendment or legislation. What this means for gay and lesbian couples is that they are not able to obtain the same rights and benefits that are available to opposite-sex couples through marriage, including tax benefits, the right to receive joint mortgages, the right to make medical decisions for a partner who is unable to make such decisions, spousal Social Security benefits, and rights of inheritance when a deceased partner has no will.

In contrast, by 2008 the states of California, Connecticut, and Massachusetts allow same-sex marriages, and Vermont and New Jersey allow civil unions. Civil unions provide same-sex couples with many of the protections that married couples enjoy. However, the 1996 national Defense of Marriage Act states that the federal government does not recognize same-sex marriages, or civil unions, legalized by any state and that states do not need to recognize same-sex marriages that were legalized in other states.

hate crime

a crime committed against a person, property, or society, where the offender is motivated, in part or in whole, by his or her bias against the victim because of the victim's race, religion, disability, sexual orientation, or ethnicity

affirmative action

in the employment arena, intentional efforts to recruit, hire, train, and promote underutilized categories of workers (women and minority men); in higher education, intentional efforts to diversify the student body

Though the LGBT community is winning some of its civil rights battles in a growing number of states, in many areas the battle has just begun. For example, in the area of family law, issues involving adoption rights and child custody as well as divorce and property rights are now battlegrounds. In addition, hate crimes continue to be a problem for members of the LGBT community as well as for citizens (and noncitizens) with non–white European ancestry (see "The Conversation of Democracy"). A **hate crime** is a crime committed against a person, property, or society as a whole, where the offender is motivated, in part or entirely, by his or her bias against the victim because of the victim's race, religion, disability, sexual orientation, or ethnicity.

Affirmative Action: Is It Constitutional?

Laws reinforcing constitutional guarantees by prohibiting discriminatory treatment are the most common objectives of civil rights battles. Nevertheless, in the 1960s the federal government also began implementing policies aimed at reinforcing equal access to employment by mandating recruitment procedures that actively sought to identify qualified minority men for government positions. This policy of **affirmative action** was extended to women in employment and then to educational opportunities. However, affirmative action policies have been and continue to be very controversial.

How Affirmative Action Works

In 1961, President John F. Kennedy (1961–1963) used the term *affirmative action* in an executive order regarding the recruitment of personnel by federal agencies and private businesses with contracts to do work for the federal government. The executive order required that these agencies and businesses do more than merely refrain from discriminating against minority men; it required that they engage in affirmative actions—intentional efforts to recruit qualified minority men for employment. The use of this term indicated the government was attempting to take *proactive* measures to ensure equal employment opportunity.

In 1965, President Lyndon B. Johnson (1963–1968) extended the affirmative action requirement to include the recruitment of qualified women. Today, affirmative action policies cover personnel processes including hiring, training, and promoting. Private companies, nonprofit organizations, and government agencies that receive federal government contracts worth at least $50,000 are required by law to have an affirmative action plan for their personnel processes.

Affirmative action does not require organizations to hire unqualified candidates, nor does it require the hiring of a qualified minority candidate over a qualified nonminority candidate. Affirmative action does require that an organization make intentional efforts to diversify its workforce by providing equal opportunity to classes of people that have been historically, and in many cases are still today, subject to discrimination. It focuses attention on an employer's history of personnel decisions. If over the years an employer with an affirmative action plan does not hire qualified underutilized workers (women and minority men), it will appear to many that the employer is discriminating and is violating Title VII of the Civil Rights Act. However, critics of affirmative action argue that it discriminates against Caucasians, and they have questioned whether the way it is applied to personnel policies as well as to college admissions policies is constitutional.

In the 1970s, institutions of higher education began to adopt intentional efforts to expand educational opportunities for both men and women from various minority groups. In addition, colleges and universities use affirmative action to ensure a student body that is

>The federal government began collecting data on hate crimes in the 1990s, highlighting the increasing incidence of such crimes. Today, hate crimes motivated by racial prejudice are the most commonly reported. The federal government does not define crimes motivated by prejudice against a person because of his or her gender or sexual orientation as hate crimes.

SHOULD HATE CRIMES BE PUNISHED MORE SEVERELY THAN OTHER CRIMES?

The Issue: In the fall of 2007, the U.S. House of Representatives and the Senate deliberated legislation that would expand coverage of the federal hate crime laws by adding sexual orientation, gender, gender identity, and disability to the list of characteristics already covered in the laws: race, color, religion, national origin, and ethnicity. If these characteristics had been added to the list, those found guilty of committing a crime and having been motivated by bias against their victims because of one of these characteristics would have had their punishment increased. Is this type of law just? Is it constitutional?

Yes: Hate crime laws further a compelling government interest. Crimes motivated by hate for a person because of an immutable characteristic are crimes against a whole group of people, not just that individual. When a Muslim is assaulted because he or she is a Muslim, fear spreads throughout the Muslim community, for any member of the community could be next. Hate crimes are intended to intimidate the victim and incite fear in all people like the victim. The government must do all it can to ensure public safety and deter threats to domestic tranquility. Hate crimes threaten domestic tranquility in a way that other crimes do not because hate crimes breed retaliatory hate crimes. The harm to public order and tranquility caused by hate crimes requires an additional punishment that indicates society will not tolerate people acting on their biases. Increased punishment may also deter others from committing hate crimes.

No: Hate crime laws violate the principle that all people are created equal. Enhancing punishment for hate crimes sends the message that some people are worth more than other people. If you commit a crime against any person, you might find the government arguing that you were motivated by your prejudice, and therefore the crime was a hate crime and you should be punished more severely. Valuing some victims more by punishing the perpetrators of crimes against them more harshly creates—rather than heals—divisions in society. Assault is assault. Does it really matter what motivated the criminal?

Other approaches: Many states have laws that make it a punishable crime to commit a *breach of the peace:* an act or behavior that seriously endangers or disturbs public peace and order or that results in community unrest or a disturbance. A legal act can disrupt the public peace and lead to a charge of breaching the peace. For example, although burning the American flag is legal, if you burn it during a Memorial Day Parade in clear view of war veterans and a scuffle ensues, you can be charged with the crime of breach of the peace in many jurisdictions. Any *illegal* act that creates community unrest, no matter what motivated the offender, should therefore result in the additional charge of breach of the peace.

What do you think?

① Do you think that increased punishment for those found guilty of a crime motivated by hate will deter future hate crimes? Explain.

② Some opponents of hate crime laws argue that they will lead to limits on free speech. Do you think this concern is valid? Explain.

---

diverse in race, color, economic status, and other characteristics. These institutions believe that having students on campus from a wide variety of backgrounds enhances all students' educational experience and best prepares them to function successfully in a nation that is increasingly diverse. Yet like affirmative action in personnel policies, affirmative action in college admission policies has been controversial.

Opposition to Affirmative Action

In the important *Bakke* decision in 1978, the U.S. Supreme Court found unconstitutional the University of California at Davis's affirmative action plan for admission to its medical school.[49] The UC Davis plan set aside sixteen of the one hundred seats in its first-year medical school class for minorities (specifically, African Americans, Latinos, Asian Americans, and Native Americans). Justice Powell noted in his opinion that schools can take race into consideration as one of several factors for admission but cannot use it as the sole consideration, as Alan Bakke argued UC Davis had done.

Ward Connerly, chairman of the American Civil Rights Institute (ACRI) argues, "There can be no middle ground about the use of race. This is not an area where one can fudge or cheat just a little bit. Either we permit the use of 'race' in American life or we don't. I say, 'We don't!'"[50] Connerly is leading the battle against affirmative action in admissions and employment procedures. Connerly founded the ACRI in 1997, one year after his successful effort to have California voters repeal their state's affirmative action policies in college admissions and employment. After anti-affirmative action victories in Washington (1998) and Michigan (2006), the ACRI has also targeted Arizona, Colorado, Missouri, Nebraska, and Oklahoma for similar efforts.[51]

Opponents have challenged affirmative action in the courts as well as through legislative processes and statewide referenda. In two cases involving the University of Michigan in 2003, the U.S. Supreme Court upheld the *Bakke* decision that universities can use race as a factor in admissions decisions, but not as the overriding factor. Using the strict scrutiny test, the Court said in the *Grutter v. Bollinger* case that the school's goal of creating a diverse student body serves a *compelling public interest:* a diverse student body enhances "cross-racial understanding . . . breaks down racial stereotypes . . . and helps students better understand persons of different races."[52]

In 2007, however, the Supreme Court found unconstitutional two school districts' policies of assigning students to elementary schools based on race to ensure a diverse student body.[53] The majority of justices argued that these policies violated the equal protection clause of the Fourteenth Amendment. Chief Justice Roberts, writing for the majority, argued that governments should not use laws to remedy racial imbalances caused by economic inequalities, individual choices, and historical biases (de facto imbalances). He stated that such laws put in place discrimination that the Court found unconstitutional in the *Brown*

POLITICAL INQUIRY

This cartoon suggests a number of the factors that colleges consider when making admissions decisions. Why is membership in a minority group controversial, whereas other factors—such as the ability to play a certain sport or being the son or daughter of a graduate—are not? In the future, how can colleges achieve the goals of a diverse campus and a fair admissions process?

case back in 1954. The justices who dissented from the majority opinion noted that today's policies are trying to ensure inclusion of minorities, not create segregation of, and hence cause harm to, minorities. The dissenters view policies that take race into account to ensure inclusion and balance as necessary means to achieving the compelling public good gained by a diverse student body.

Are affirmative action policies aimed at ensuring equal educational and employment opportunities for women and minority men constitutional, or do they violate the equal protection clause of the Fourteenth Amendment? The answer to this question depends on how the majority of the members of the Supreme Court interpret the Fourteenth Amendment. Today, in order for an affirmative action policy for minority men to be constitutional, the government must pass the strict scrutiny test by showing that affirmative action is necessary to achieve a compelling public interest. In the case of affirmative action for women, the government must pass the heightened scrutiny test by showing that the policy is substantially related to the government's achievement of an important public interest. Much depends on how the courts define these interests.

CONCLUSION
CONTINUING THE CONVERSATION

For most of U.S. history, the law allowed, and in some cases even required, discrimination against people based on inherent characteristics such as race, ethnicity, and sex. This discriminatory treatment meant that the U.S. government did not guarantee all citizens equal protection of their civil rights. In 1875, for example, while acknowledging that women were citizens, the Court ruled that denying women citizens the right to vote that male citizens enjoyed was legal. African Americans and Native Americans had first to fight for laws that identified them as citizens (enacted in 1868 and 1924, respectively) and then to fight for the rights that are assumed to come with that citizenship.

The long and continuing battles for civil rights of African Americans, Native Americans, and women are only part of the story. Latinos, Asian Americans, citizens with disabilities, and LGBT citizens are all currently engaged in political, legal, and civic activities aimed at guaranteeing equal protection of their civil rights. Numerous other groups are working to gain their civil rights as well. These include older Americans, poor Americans, and children born in the United States to parents who are in the country illegally (the Fourteenth Amendment extends citizenship, and hence civil rights, to these children). Will lack of access to, or understanding of, rapidly changing communications technology continue to be a barrier to these groups' efforts to organize and lobby? Will the courts extend the use of strict scrutiny to protect the civil rights of women—whose rights are protected by heightened scrutiny but so far not by the highest level—as well as to protect these other groups?

History tells us that an unhealthy economy, with high levels of unemployment and inflation and without real improvements in wages, as well as perceived threats to national security that are attributed to one ethnic, religious, or racial group, often trigger increased violations of civil rights and therefore new civil rights battles. When will the next civil rights movement begin? What citizens will experience violations of their civil rights as a result of future economic conditions or perceived threats to national security?

Summary

1. The Quest for Equality Under the Law

Discrimination based on inherent characteristics like race, national origin, religion, and sex merit a greater level of protection under the law than other qualities (for example, job performance). Race, religion, national origin, and sex are considered suspect classifications because distinctions based on these characteristics are assumed to be illegitimate.

2. Slavery and Its Aftermath

One legacy of slavery in the United States was a system of racial segregation. Under this system, both the states and the federal government condoned and accepted a structure of inherent inequality for African Americans in nearly all aspects of life, and they were forced to use separate facilities, from water fountains to educational institutions.

3. The Civil Rights Movement

Through the efforts of the early and modern civil rights organizations such as the NAACP, chinks appeared in the armor of the segregationists. The strategy of using the justice system to right previous wrongs proved instrumental in radically changing the nation's educational system, especially with the key *Brown v. Board of Education* decision in 1954, in which the Supreme Court ruled against segregation. In other arenas, such as public accommodations, and housing, Dr. Martin Luther King's leadership and strategy of nonviolent civil disobedience proved instrumental in winning victories in both legislatures and the court of public opinion.

4. The Government's Response to the Civil Rights Movement

The government responded to the demands for equal rights for African Americans with an important series of laws that attempted to secure fundamental rights, including voting rights and rights to employment, public accommodations, housing, and equal pay.

5. The Movement for Women's Civil Rights

The 1848 Seneca Falls Convention, which produced the Declaration of Sentiments, was the beginning of the first wave of the women's rights movement in the United States. This first wave focused on winning for women the right to vote, which was accomplished by the ratification of the Nineteenth Amendment in 1920. The second wave of the women's rights movement began in the 1960s with women organizing and lobbying for laws guaranteeing them equality of rights. The efforts of the second wave continue today.

6. Other Civil Rights Movements

In addition to African Americans and women, numerous other groups of U.S. citizens have battled for, and continue to fight for, equal treatment under the law. These groups include Native Americans, Latino and Asian American citizens, citizens with disabilities, and lesbian, gay, bisexual, and transgendered citizens. They seek equal employment opportunities, educational opportunities, housing, voting rights, and marriage rights, among others.

7. Affirmative Action: Is It Constitutional?

Since 1866, the national government has enacted civil rights laws that have prohibited discrimination. In a 1961 executive order, President John F. Kennedy introduced the nation to a proactive policy of intentional actions to recruit minority male workers, which he labeled *affirmative action*. President Lyndon B. Johnson extended affirmative action to women. Institutions of higher education also adopted the concept of affirmative action in their admissions policies. Affirmative action has been controversial, however, and a review of recent Supreme Court cases indicates that the constitutionality of affirmative action is in question.

affirmative action 198
Black Codes 175
Brown v. Board of Education of Topeka 180
civil disobedience 181
civil rights 171
de facto segregation 190
de jure segregation 190
equal protection clause 178
grandfather clause 177

hate crime 198
heightened scrutiny test (intermediate scrutiny test) 189
inherent characteristics 172
Jim Crow laws 176
literacy test 177
ordinary scrutiny test (rational basis test) 186
Plessy v. Ferguson 178

poll tax 177
Reconstruction era 175
separate but equal doctrine 178
standing to sue 175
steering 184
strict scrutiny test 189
suspect classifications 172
white primary 177

For Review

1. What is meant by *suspect classification*?

2. What tactics did whites in the South use to prevent African Americans from achieving equality before the civil rights era?

3. What strategy did the early civil rights movements employ to end discrimination?

4. What civil rights did the 1964 Civil Rights Act protect for minority, male citizens but not for female citizens?

5. Why did those fighting for women's civil rights begin their work by concentrating their efforts on state governments rather than on the national government?

6. Other than color and sex, what inherent (immutable) characteristics have been used as a basis for discriminatory treatment of citizens?

7. Explain how an approach to improving access to employment and educational opportunity based on affirmative action differs from an approach based on civil rights legislation.

For Critical Thinking and Discussion

1. Given the history of the attainment of civil rights for women and African Americans, what is your opinion of the result of the battle for the Democratic Party's presidential nominee in 2008?

2. Is it constitutional to deny any citizen the equal protection of marriage laws; is denying gay men and lesbians the right to marry a necessary means to a compelling public interest? Explain.

3. Today more women than men are in college pursuing their bachelor's degrees. Is it legal for schools to give preference to male applicants by accepting men with lower SAT scores and high school grade-point averages than women, in order to maintain sex balance in the student body? Explain.

4. Many organizations fighting for civil rights protections include in their name the phrase "legal defense and education fund." What do you think explains the common two-pronged focus of these organizations?

5. What would be the effect of using the strict scrutiny test to determine the legality of sex-based discrimination? Would sex-based affirmative action pass the test? Explain.

PRACTICE QUIZ

MULTIPLE CHOICE: Choose the lettered item that answers the question correctly.

1. The idea that individuals are protected from discrimination on the basis of race, national origin, religion, and sex is called
   a. civil liberties.
   b. civil rights.
   c. natural rights.
   d. unalienable rights.

2. Individual attributes like race, national origin, religion, and sex are called
   a. unalienable rights.
   b. inherent characteristics.
   c. indiscriminatory qualities.
   d. civil rights categories.

3. Laws that required the strict separation of racial groups, with whites and "nonwhites" attending separate schools, working in different jobs, and using segregated public accommodations such as transportation and restaurants are called
   a. Fred Samuels laws.
   b. Sally Hemmings laws.
   c. Jim Crow laws.
   d. Abraham Lincoln laws.

4. An election in which a party's nominees were chosen but in which only white people were allowed to vote is called
   a. a general election.
   b. a run-off primary.
   c. an uncontested primary.
   d. a white primary.

5. A mechanism that exempted individuals from conditions on voting (such as poll taxes or literacy tests) if they or their ancestor had been eligible to vote prior to 1870 is called
   a. a poll tax.
   b. a white primary.
   c. the grandfather clause.
   d. a literacy test.

6. Unlike sex-based discrimination, race-based discrimination must pass the
   a. heightened scrutiny test.
   b. ordinary scrutiny test.
   c. strict scrutiny test.
   d. ultimate scrutiny test.

7. Initially the courts interpreted which amendment in such a way that women were told they were citizens but that they had no constitutional right to vote?
   a. Thirteenth Amendment
   b. Fourteenth Amendment
   c. Fifteenth Amendment
   d. Nineteenth Amendment

8. What right does Title IX protect for women?
   a. equal access to credit
   b. equal access to educational opportunities
   c. equal access to employment opportunities
   d. suffrage

9. In what decade was the ERA ratified and added to the U.S. Constitution?
   a. 1920s
   b. 1970s
   c. 1980s
   d. It has not been ratified and added to the U.S. Constitution.

10. Today, citizens of what descent experience the highest educational and income level compared to the nation as a whole?
   a. African
   b. Asian
   c. Mexican
   d. Native American

FILL IN THE BLANKS.

11. _____ was the period between 1866 and 1877 when the institutions and infrastructure of the South were rebuilt after the Civil War.

12. The legal right to bring lawsuits in court is called _____.

13. To pass the strict scrutiny test, differential treatment must be _____ for the government to achieve a _____ public interest.

14. During World War II the federal government relocated citizens of _____ descent to internment camps.

15. The ADA is the _____.

Answers: 1. b, 2. b, 3. c, 4. d, 5. c, 6. c, 7. b, 8. b, 9. d, 10. b, 11. Reconstruction, 12. standing to sue, 13. necessary, compelling, 14. Japanese, 15. Americans with Disabilities Act.

RESOURCES FOR RESEARCH AND ACTION

Internet Resources

American Democracy Now Web site
www.mhhe.com/harrison1e   Consult the book's Web site for study guides, interactive activities, simulations, and current hotlinks for additional information on civil rights.

Center for American Women and Politics
www.cawp.rutgers.edu   Go to this premier Web site for historical as well as up-to-date information on women in elected and appointed positions in national, state, and local governments.

Equal Employment Opportunity Commission
www.eeoc.gov/facts/qanda.html   This federal government site offers a list of federal laws relevant to equal employment opportunities and includes answers to the most frequently asked questions regarding equal employment laws.

ERA Campaign Network
www.eracampaign.net   The Web site for the contemporary ERA movement.

Leadership Conference on Civil Rights/Leadership Conference on Civil Rights Education Fund
www.civilrights.org   Founded by the LCCR and the LCCREF, this site seeks to serve as the "online nerve center" for the fight against discrimination in all its forms.

Recommended Readings

Branch, Taylor. *Parting the Waters: America in the King Years.* New York: Simon and Schuster, 1989. A Pulitzer Prize–winning book focusing on the civil rights movement from 1954 to 1963. It includes detailed descriptions of the leadership of Martin Luther King Jr. and describes the inner workings of the movement as it organized boycotts, sit-ins, and freedom rides.

Feagin, Joe R., and Clairece Booher Feagin. *Racial and Ethnic Relations.* Upper Saddle River, NJ: Prentice Hall, 2003. A comprehensive look at the immigration of Africans, Asians, Europeans, Latin Americans, and Middle Easterners to the United States and the history of relations between Native Americans and the U. S. government. The initial chapters provide frameworks for analyzing the discrimination experienced by these groups of eventual citizens.

Harrison, Brigid. *Women in American Politics: An Introduction.* Belmont, CA: Wadsworth, 2003. *American Democracy Now* coauthor Brigid Harrison introduces the study of women's participation in American politics, including their historic and contemporary participation in political groups, as voters, and in government.

Herr, Stanley S., Lawrence O. Gostin, and Harold Hongju Koh. *The Human Rights of Persons with Disabilities: Different but Equal.* Oxford: Oxford University Press, 2003. A collection of essays explaining how Article I of the Universal Declaration of Human Rights, which states that all humans have equal and unalienable claims to dignity and freedom, defines the standard for rights for people with disabilities, including those with intellectual disabilities.

Rosenberg, Gerald. *The Hollow Hope: Can Courts Bring About Social Change?* Second ed. Chicago: The University of Chicago Press, 2008. Rosenberg supports his argument that Congress, the White House, and civil rights activists—not the courts—bring about social change by reviewing the evolution of federal policy in the areas of desegregation, abortion, and the struggle for LGBT rights.

Movies of Interest

Bury My Heart at Wounded Knee (2007)
Based on Dee Brown's book of the same name, this HBO made-for-television movie chronicles ordeals of Sioux and Lakota tribes as the U.S. government displaces them from their lands. Well-intentioned yet misguided policies and efforts culminate in the massacre of women, men, and children by the U.S. Cavalry at Wounded Knee Creek in 1890.

Iron Jawed Angels (2004)
The little-known story of the tensions between the young, militant women's suffrage advocates, led by Alice Paul, and the older, more conservative advocates of the NAWSA, such as Carrie Chapman Catt. The details of the suffrage battle during wartime, with a popular president opposed to women's suffrage, are well presented in this made-for-television movie.

Crazy in Alabama (1999)
The story takes place in 1965 Alabama. The movie follows two individuals. One is Lucille, a crazy woman (played by Melanie Griffith) who kills her abusive husband and runs away to Hollywood. The second main character is Lucille's nephew, Peejoe, who witnesses race-based crimes, including a police officer killing a young black boy. Peejoe participates in acts of civil disobedience with his black neighbors and violates the code of silence to tell the truth about who killed the young black boy. The story sheds light on issues of domestic violence, child abuse, and civil rights battles.

Malcolm X (1992)
Based on the book *The Autobiography of Malcolm X* (as told to Alex Haley), this Spike Lee film stars Denzel Washington as black power movement leader Malcolm X. The film depicts the struggle in the 1960s between the black nationalists like Malcolm X and the activists who advocated more peaceful means like Martin Luther King Jr.

Mississippi Burning (1989)
Gene Hackman and Willem Dafoe portray FBI agents sent into Mississippi in 1964 to investigate the disappearance of two civil rights workers.

A Tough Sell Gets Tougher

Black Republicans are already considered a contradiction in terms in the African-American community. And the arrival of Barack Obama as the Democratic presidential nominee made selling black voters on the GOP exponentially more difficult.

That hasn't kept a small group of vociferous conservative blacks from trying. They argue that, historically, the GOP is the true home of African-Americans. They posit an unbroken line of civil-rights victories from Abraham Lincoln's Emancipation Proclamation to George W. Bush's Leave No Child Behind initiative, and they object to the Democratic Party's claim to the mantle.

"The Democrat Party has hijacked the civil-rights record of the Republican Party," said Frances Rice, chairwoman of the National Black Republican Association, which boasts 1,000 members in 48 states. "The Democratic Party is the party of slavery, secession, segregation, and now—socialism."

The nimble historical hopscotch behind that claim irks Democratic activists and historians alike, but there's enough truth in it to keep a parlor argument going late into the night. So far, the African-American community has not bought into the story line. President Bush captured only 11 percent of the black vote in the 2004 election, and no Republican African-American lawmakers are serving in Congress.

"My job is difficult whether Barack Obama is standing there or not," said Michael Steele, chairman of GOPAC, the political action committee charged with electing Republicans to state and local offices. Steele was the first African-American lieutenant governor of Maryland and lost a 2006 U.S. Senate bid to Democrat Ben Cardin. He knows well the challenges facing black Republicans, both as candidates and citizens.

"The reality becomes very difficult when the biases toward all things black-Republican are so stark, so personal," Steele said. "People just don't even give you credit for anything."

Shamed Dogan knows these biases firsthand. He is a black Republican campaigning for state representative in Missouri's 88th district. "I tell people I'm running as a Republican and they give me 'The Look'— like they are seeing a unicorn," Dogan said. "If they talked to me for five minutes, they would realize I'm for the betterment of all people, including African-Americans."

African-American Republicans fondly recall the origins of the Grand Old Party, whose creators were fierce abolitionists.

After the Civil War, Southern Democrats returned to Congress and voted against efforts by the then-majority Republicans to pass the 14th and 15th amendments to the Constitution to grant freed slaves U.S. citizenship and full voting rights, respectively. Historians agree: This was largely a group of sullen Southern sympathizers disdainful of Lincoln's Emancipation Proclamation and the 13th Amendment, which abolished slavery. They did all they could to subjugate blacks during Reconstruction and supported local Jim Crow laws that disenfranchised blacks in the former Confederate states for the next century.

"The Democrats [who were] revived in the wake of the Civil War [belonged to] a largely Southern, white-supremacist party," said Yale history professor David Blight.

Not all of the bigotry came from below the Mason-Dixon line. "The Almighty has made the black man inferior, sir," said Rep. Fernando Wood, D-N.Y., in 1865. "By no legislation, by no military power, can you wipe out this distinction."

The so-called radical Republicans battled Democratic President Andrew Johnson and handed him 15 veto overrides, including the Civil Rights Act of 1866 and the Reconstruction Act of 1867.

Republicans remained staunchly pro-civil rights into the 1870s with the help of GOP President Ulysses S. Grant. Together they saw the adoption of the Force Act of 1871 to provide federal oversight of congressional elections, the Ku Klux Klan Act of 1871 to protect blacks from the racial vigilantes, and the Civil Rights Act of 1875. The latter, never fully enforced and ultimately declared unconstitutional in 1883, called for open access to inns, public transportation, and theaters for all races.

Here the litany of pro-black GOP policies stops until passage of the Civil Rights Act of 1964 with the instrumental support of Sen. Everett Dirksen, R-Ill. Not to be overlooked in the effort was the lobbying of Democratic President Lyndon Johnson and Senate Democrats, who wooed Dirksen relentlessly.

"Dirksen did help make the 1964 act possible," said Senate Associate Historian Donald Ritchie. "LBJ made sure Dirksen was on board, front and center," and he was willing to let the senior Republican senator take a large share of the credit in order to close the deal. It worked. The bill passed, and Dirksen appeared on the cover of Time magazine in June 1964.

Last on the checklist for black Republicans is the creation of affirmative action by Assistant Labor Secretary Art Fletcher in 1970 during the Nixon administration. The program, derived from an earlier Johnson administration plan, helped guarantee equal access for women and minorities to public- and private-sector jobs. "We created it," Steele said, "Democrats bastardized it" by letting it become a quota system.

Critics of the rosy recitation of GOP civil-rights accomplishments say the historical take is selective at best and misleading at worst. "Any use of the 'party of Lincoln' rhetoric by the current Republican Party is, frankly, an egregious twisting of history," Blight said. He explains that the original GOP underwent drastic changes from the 1870s into the early 20th century. "They became the party of Big Business interests, imperial expansionism, and ultimately turned their backs decisively on their more egalitarian origins in the Civil War era," Blight said.

The first turning point came during the Great Depression. Until the economic collapse in 1929, most African-Americans voted Republican—if they could vote at all. But blacks began to shift allegiance as President Roosevelt's progressive New Deal created jobs. FDR won 23 percent of the black vote in 1932, a figure that grew to 71 percent in

1936 and stayed high during World War II. President Truman, who ordered the desegregation of the military and aggressively investigated several high-profile lynchings, won 65 percent of the black vote in 1948.

Presidential candidate John F. Kennedy re-established a strong Democratic relationship with the black community through a phone call to Coretta Scott King in 1960, expressing his concern about the incarcera-

understatement. Sen. Strom Thurmond of South Carolina began the exodus in 1964 by joining the GOP in protest. In 1968, Republican presidential candidate Richard Nixon seized the opportunity to peel off many more disaffected white Democrats with the "Southern strategy" that equated the GOP with "law and order" and "states' rights"—widely regarded as code words for a conservative backlash against civil-rights protections.

capped block grants to states. It also required welfare recipients to enter job-training programs, mandated that states boost child-support enforcement, and limited individual benefits to five years, total. Within three years of enactment, 4.7 million Americans moved off the welfare rolls, and by 2006, caseloads declined 59 percent, according to the Health and Human Services Department.

"We're not against government programs," Steele said. "They need to be suited to the task, not wasteful; and when they've served their purpose, get rid of them."

While shrinking the government is a staple of conservative thought, the starve-the-beast rallying cry of the GOP may also quietly alienate the black community, Blight says. The federal government ended slavery, gave African-Americans the vote, and promoted civil rights in the 1860s and 1960s. "If you don't believe in government, you're not going to get many black people to vote for you," he said.

> "Some Republicans gave up on winning the African-American vote, **looking the other way or trying to benefit from racial polarization**," Mehlman said. "I am here today as the Republican chairman to tell you we were wrong."

tion of her husband in the Birmingham, Ala., jail, and subsequent calls for his release. The overture was enough to prompt Martin Luther King Sr., "Daddy King," to publicly renounce the Republican Party and support Kennedy. JFK won the election with the help of 71 percent of black voters.

"What you saw in 1958 to 1964 was more Democratic engagement in the civil-rights movement," said Julianne Malveaux, president of Bennett College for Women in Greensboro, N.C. Although key Republicans ultimately supported the landmark legislation, it was a Democratic Congress and president that made the 1964 Civil Rights Act and the 1965 Voting Rights Act law, Blight said.

President Johnson garnered an estimated 100 percent of the black vote in 1964 but famously remarked at the time that he feared that Democratic support for civil-rights legislation would cause the party to "lose the South for a generation." It was a historic

The tactic helped both Nixon and Ronald Reagan win the White House, and it became a staple of modern GOP presidential politics. "Republicans have been more likely to use race as a proxy to signal to [white] people—we've got your backs," Malveaux said.

Steele bitterly regrets the move by his party. "It was a dumb strategy," he said. "It alienated a partner. African-Americans and the GOP had been historically linked since day one."

Black Republicans say that a lot in the conservative Goldwater/Reagan doctrine strikes chords within the larger African-American community—particularly the admonition to self-sufficiency and frustrations with the welfare system that evolved from the Johnson administration's War on Poverty.

Black Republicans laud welfare reform, which congressional conservatives pushed in 1994 and President Clinton ultimately signed into law in 1996. The new system dispensed with open-ended entitlements in favor of

In 2005, the Republican National Committee made a concerted effort to woo back at least a small percentage of the black vote. Then-RNC Chairman Ken Mehlman appeared before the NAACP convention in Milwaukee and offered a striking apology for the Southern strategy. "Some Republicans gave up on winning the African-American vote, looking the other way or trying to benefit from racial polarization," Mehlman said. "I am here today as the Republican chairman to tell you we were wrong."

The contrition strategy failed. Blacks voted 89 percent Democratic in the 2006 elections that cost the GOP control of Congress. Distrust of the modern GOP still dominates in the African-American community, and few in it appear willing to countenance black- (or white-) Republican efforts to paint the party in a softer racial light.

■ THEN: Before the Great Depression, most African American voters supported the Republican party.

■ NOW: Civil rights and the civil rights movement are now Democratic platform issues.

■ NEXT: What strategies will both political parties use to win the growing Hispanic vote?

Based on your experiences with the two political parties today, which one will do more to promote the Civil Rights agenda in the next decade?

Ken Mehlman says he regrets the GOP's callousness to black voters. Are parties or politicians making similar mistakes that will hurt them in the future by alienating certain constituencies today?

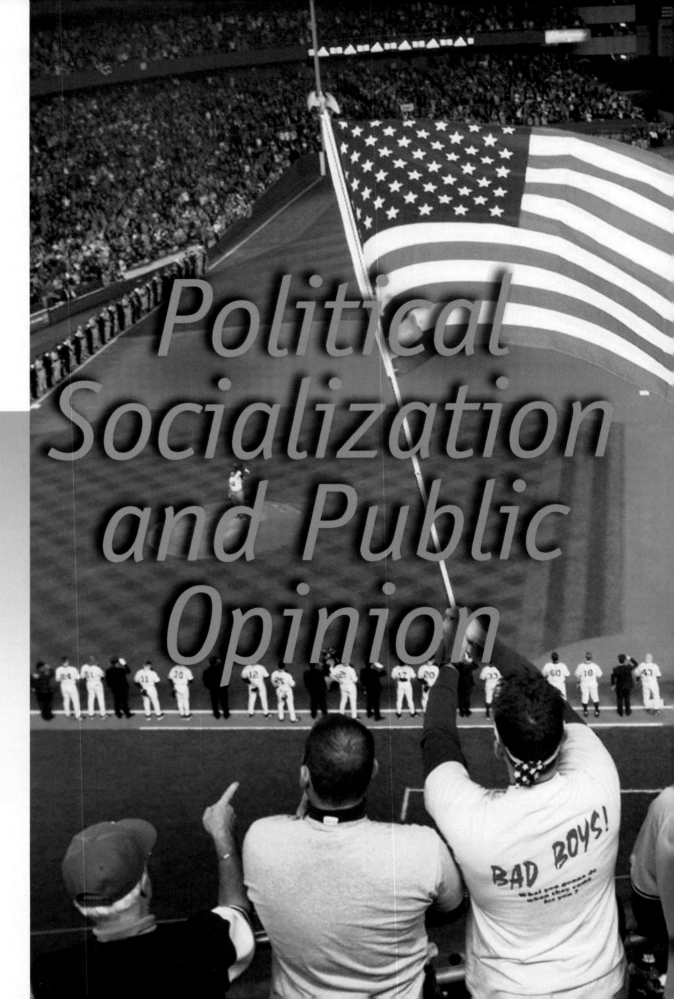

Political Socialization and Public Opinion

THEN Families and schools were the most important influences on children as they developed their political views.

NOW Families and schools remain influential, but the media have been enormously important in developing the political views of the Millennial Generation.

NEXT How will technology affect the socialization of new generations of Americans?

How will polling organizations harness the power of the Internet to predict political behavior accurately?

How can pollsters find ways to measure the opinions of "celly-onlys"—potential respondents who own only cell phones?

Using New Technology to Socialize Young Voters

Celebrities are eager to get in on the action: Justin Timberlake got an invitation to the party, as did America Ferrera of ABC's *Ugly Betty* and Hayden Panettiere of NBC's *Heroes* (who, at barely 18, almost didn't make it in). Friends include actors Jessica Alba, Scarlett Johansson, Hilary Duff, Adrian Grenier, Mandy Moore, and Kate Walsh. And Sean Kingston wrote a song just for the event. Are these stars competing for invitations to the pre-release party of next summer's blockbuster? | No, these celebrities are part of Declare Yourself (DY) (www.declareyourself.com), a national nonpartisan, nonprofit youth voter initiative founded by producer Norman Lear. Formerly, groups like the Young Republicans, College Democrats, or the League of Women Voters might come to a college or high school campus to register 18-year-olds to vote. Today, young people are increasingly being socialized to political action through electronic media such as the Internet, which facilitates the use of high-profile celebrities to educate and motivate young people to register and to vote. DY's MySpace page features celebrities explaining what motivates them to vote (www.myspace.com/declareyourself). For example, actor and singer Corbin Bleu explains why he votes for arts in education, saying, "Art in schools inspires students to learn, think, and grow . . . and I'm voting to put art back in schools." Declare Yourself's Web page summarizes key election-related news through Yahoo News! and provides a hotlink to that service's election news Web site. Its UWIRE links feature the best in student-created campaign coverage, some of which is available through YouTube. It also relies on Google and the popular Evite invitation service to harness the power of the Internet to socialize young potential voters where many of the 4 million 18-year-olds eligible to vote in 2008 live: online. | Declare Yourself and similar organizations help socialize a new generation of Americans in a variety of ways. For example, they provide information on who is eligible to vote and the various voter registration

> Actress Hayden Panettiere registering to vote in August 2007 at the Beverly Hills offices of Declare Yourself.

deadlines in each state as well as the actual voter registration forms. Through events and its celebrity spokespeople, DY also helps educate young Americans about the importance of voting, particularly the impact of the youth vote in past elections. Declare Yourself also helps mobilize young voters to "spread the word" with text alerts, e-newsletters, and downloadable widgets that can be added to individual Web pages. | Lear is known for his liberal-style politics, but he is keeping DY strictly nonpartisan. He was motivated to found Declare Yourself after having the opportunity to view (and then purchase) one of the twenty-five remaining original prints of the Declaration of Independence (DOI). He now has begun a series of DOI Roadtrips, bringing the Declaration along with live bands to more than eighteen college campuses. His twin goals are to enable students to see the Declaration of Independence for themselves and challenge them to find their *own* reasons to register and vote.

The process of developing in-

formed opinions about issues begins with the process of political socialization. Through socialization, we acquire our basic political beliefs and values. Declare Yourself is one example of an organization that seeks to socialize individuals to value the importance of democratic values like informed citizenship and voting. Through political socialization, we come to value the attributes of our own political culture. We also develop our ideological outlook and perhaps even begin to identify with a particular political party. While the process of political socialization begins in early childhood, throughout our lives, institutions, peers, and the media continue to influence our views.

Political socialization is a key component in the process of creating an engaged citizenry. Psychologist Steven Pinker once noted that ". . . no matter how important learning and culture and socialization are, they don't happen by magic."[1] Joe Zavaletta, director of the Center for Civic Engagement at the University of Texas at Brownsville, would agree with Pinker's assertion: "Democracy is not magic. Why we expect our kids to magically become engaged citizens when they turn 18 when they haven't practiced . . . doesn't make any sense."[2]

Through the process of socialization, individuals acquire the ideology and perspective that shape their political opinions. Though seemingly simple, public opinion is a fundamental building block on which American democracy rests. When we discuss public opinion, we often do so in the context of various public opinion polls that ask respondents everything from whether they approve of the president's job performance to how many sugars they take in their skim milk lattes. Political scientist V. O. Key Jr. wrote, "To speak with precision of public opinion is a task not unlike coming to grips with the Holy Ghost."[3] Key was referring to the nebulous nature of public opinion, which changes from day to day, is sometimes difficult to pinpoint, and is open to subjective interpretation. The glut in the number of "latest polls" has perhaps made us forget that the act of voting is itself simply the act of expressing one's opinion. Indeed, the word *poll* means to gauge public opinion as well as the location where one casts a ballot.

Public opinion is one of the ways citizens interact with their government. Through public opinion surveys, people express their policy priorities ("What do you think is the country's most important problem?") and their approval or disapproval of both government officials ("Do you approve or disapprove of the way the president is handling his job?") and the policies they create ("Do you agree or disagree with President Bush's 'surge strategy' in the war in Iraq?") Much of the literature bemoaning the decline of civic involvement is based on public opinion research. But studies of civic involvement reveal that public opinion is the starting point for many forms of informed participation—participation that begins when individuals learn about an issue and choose to express their views on it using a variety of media.

Political Socialization and Civic Participation

How do we acquire our political views? Though an infant would be hard pressed to evaluate the president's job performance, of course, children begin to acquire political opinions at an early age, and this process continues throughout adulthood. As noted above, the process

In this chapter, we consider the ways in which political socialization happens, including the various agents of socialization. We consider how public opinion is measured and take a look at how Americans currently view their governmental institutions.

FIRST, we examine the process of *political socialization* and how it can lead to *civic participation.*

SECOND, we consider the different *agents of socialization,* including family, the media, schools, churches, peers, community and political leaders, and demographic characteristics.

THIRD, we look at ways of *measuring public opinion.*

FOURTH, we focus on *what Americans think about politics.*

political socialization

the process by which we develop our political values and opinions throughout our lives

by which we develop our political values and opinions is called **political socialization.** As we develop our political values, we form the bedrock of what will become our political ideology. As this ideology emerges, it then shapes how we view most political subjects: what side we take on public issues, how we evaluate candidates for office, and what our opinions on policies will be.

While many tend to think that political socialization occurs as people approach voting age, in reality this process begins at home in very early childhood. Core tenets of our belief system—including our political ideology, our beliefs about people of different races and sexes, even our party identification—are often firmly embedded before we have completed elementary school.

A key aspect of political socialization is whether children are socialized to participate in politics. Simply put, civically engaged parents often have civically engaged children. Parents who engage in active forms of participation like volunteering on a campaign and passive forms like watching the nightly news or reading a newspaper demonstrate to children what matters to them. Parents who change the channel to a *Law and Order* rerun during an important presidential news conference are also socializing their children to their values. Children absorb the political views of their parents as well: a parent's subtle (or sometimes not so subtle!) comments about the president, a political news story, or a policy debate contribute to a child's political socialization by shaping that child's views.

The Process of Political Socialization

The beliefs and values we learn early in life also help shape how we view new information. While events may change our views, we often choose to perceive events in a way that is consistent with our earlier beliefs. For example, people's evaluation of which candidate "won" a debate often strongly coincides with their party identification. Thus, the process of political socialization tends to be cumulative.

> Children are socialized to the views of their parents at a very early age. Here a young boy attending an environmental rally holds a placard expressing "his" views. What opinions were you socialized to as a young child?

Historically, most social scientists have agreed that family and school have the strongest influence on political socialization. Our families teach us that it is—or is not—valuable to be an informed citizen and coach us in the ways in which we should participate in the civic life of our communities. For example, if your mother is active in Republican Party politics in your town, you are more likely to be active in the party than someone whose parents are not involved in a local party. Is your father active in charitable organizations such as the local food bank? Perhaps he might ask you to run in a 5K race to raise money to buy food for the upcoming holiday season. Schools also influence our political socialization by teaching us shared cultural values. And in recent times, the omnipresent role that the media play in everyday life warrants their inclusion as one of the prime agents of political socialization.

Participating in Civic Life

Does the process of socialization matter in determining whether individuals are active in civic life? Studies indicate that socialization does matter in a number of ways. First, children whose parents are active in politics or in their community are more likely to be active themselves. Schools also play an important role in socializing young people to become active in civic life—high school and college students are more likely to participate than young people of the same age who are not attending school. Research also indicates that socialization actually *generates* participation. People who have been socialized to participate in civic life are more likely to volunteer for a charitable or a political organization in their communities when they are invited to do so.

From our families and schools we also learn the value of becoming informed. Parents and schools, along with the media and the other agents of socialization that are discussed in the next section, provide us with important information that we can use to make decisions about our political actions. People who lack political knowledge, by contrast, tend not to be actively involved in their communities.[4] In fact, research indicates that when young people use any source of information regularly, including newspapers, radio, television, magazines, or the Internet, they are more likely to engage in all forms of civic participation. There is also a strong link between being informed and voting behavior. According to the results of one survey that measured civic engagement among young people, "youth who are registered to vote are more informed than their nonregistered peers. Eighty-six percent of young registered voters answered at least one of the knowledge questions (measuring political knowledge) correctly as opposed to 78 percent of youth who are not registered to vote."[5]

Agents of Socialization

Learning, culture, and socialization occur through **agents of socialization,** the individuals, organizations, and institutions that facilitate the acquisition of political views. Among the most important agents of socialization are the family, the media, schools, churches, peers, and political and community leaders. Our political views are also shaped by who we are: our race, ethnicity, gender, and age all influence how we become socialized to political and community life.

agents of socialization
the individuals, organizations, and institutions that facilitate the acquisition of political views

Family Influences on Activism and Attitudes

Family takes one of the most active roles in socializing us to politics and influencing our political views and behaviors. First of all, we learn whether our family members value civic activism by observing their actions and listening to their views. By example, parents show children whether community matters. The children of political activists are taught to be engaged citizens. They may see their parents attend city council meetings, host Democratic or Republican club meetings in their home, or help local candidates for office by volunteering to campaign door-to-door on a weekend afternoon. Other parents may teach different forms of political engagement—some young children might attend protests or demonstrations with their parents. Others might learn to boycott a particular product for political reasons. When political activists discuss their own involvement, they often observe that "politics is in my blood." In reality, political activism is passed from one generation to the next *through example*.

In other homes, however, parents are not involved in politics or their communities. They may lack the time to participate in political activities, or they may fail to see the value of doing so. They may have a negative opinion of people who participate in politics, constantly making comments like "all politicians are corrupt," "they're just in it for themselves," or "it's all about ego." Such opinions convey to children that politics is not valued and may in fact be frowned upon. A parent's political apathy need not necessarily sour a son or daughter on politics or civic engagement permanently, however. Instead, first-generation activists often point to external influences such as school, the media, friends, and public policies, any of which can cause someone to become involved in civic life, regardless of family attitudes.

Our families influence not only whether or not we are civically active participants in the political process but also what we believe. While parents or older siblings may discuss specific issues or policies, their attitudes and outlook also shape children's general political attitudes and ideology. Children absorb their parents' beliefs—whether their parents think the government should have a larger or smaller role in people's lives, whether they value equality between the sexes and races, whether they consider people in government to be trustworthy, and even specific opinions they have about political leaders. In fact, we can see evidence of how strongly parents' views are transmitted to their children in one of the best predictors of the results of presidential elections: each election year, the *Weekly Reader*, a current events magazine that many school districts subscribe to, conducts a nonrandomized poll of its readers. Since 1956, the first- through twelfth-grade student poll has correctly predicted the outcome of every presidential election. Children know for whom their parents will vote and mimic that behavior in their responses to the poll.

The Media's Ever-Increasing Role in Socialization

An almost ever-present fixture in the lives of young Americans today, the media contribute to the political socialization of Americans in a wide variety of ways. Television, radio, the Internet, and various forms of electronic entertainment and print media help shape Americans' political perspectives. First of all, the media, especially television, help shape societal norms. The media impart norms and values on children's shows such as *Sesame Street, Barney, Maya and Miguel,* and *Dora the Explorer,* which teach about racial diversity and tolerance. For example, Barney's friends include children with and without disabilities. These shows and others reflect changing societal standards and values. The media also reinforce core democratic values. Television programs such as *American Idol* or *The Biggest Loser,* or XM Radio's *20on20,* incorporate the principle of voting: viewers decide which contestant stays or goes, or listeners pick which songs are played. And as we saw in this chapter's *American Democracy Now* vignette, organizations are using Internet tools like Web sites and Facebook and MySpace pages to socialize individuals to the value of political participation.

Second, the media also help determine the national agenda. Whether they are covering the war in Iraq, sex-abuse scandals, global climate change, or congressional policy debates, the media focus the attention of the American public. This attention may then have spillover effects as people demand action on a policy issue. We will see in Chapter 7, for example, how media coverage of the introduction of a bill concerning immigration spawned a nationwide protest movement in favor of immigration rights.

Third, the media educate the public about policy issues. Local and national news programs, newsmagazine shows, and even comedies like *The Daily Show with Jon Stewart* (yes, it really is a comedy, *not* a news, program) inform viewers about current events, the actions of policy makers, and public policy challenges in communities, states, and the nation.

Finally, the media, particularly television, can skew people's perception of public policy priorities and challenges. The oft-quoted saying "if it bleeds, it leads" demonstrates the attention that most local news stations focus on violence. While crime rates have dropped since the 1970s, the reporting of crime, particularly violent crime, on nightly news broadcasts has increased. Even national news broadcasts and talk shows fall prey to the tendency to emphasize "visual" news—fires, floods, auto accidents, and plane crashes. Although these stories are important to those involved, they have very little long-term impact on society as a whole. But because they pique viewer interest more effectively than, say, a debate in Washington or in a state capital, news programs devote more time to them. Internet news sources also cover these dramatic events, but the sheer number of Internet news sites and blogs makes it more likely that at least some of them will also cover more important news, and people interested in political events and debates can find Internet news sources that cover such events and issues.

Schools, Patriotism, and Civic Participation

As early as kindergarten, children in the United States are socialized to believe in democracy and express patriotism. Schools socialize children to the concept of democracy by making the idea tangible for them. On Election Day, children might vote for their favorite snack and wait for the results at the end of the day. Or they might compare different kinds of apples or grapes, or different books, and then vote for a favorite. Lessons such as these introduce children to processes associated with democracy at its most basic level: they learn about comparing attributes, choosing a favorite, voting, and winning and losing.

Children also are taught patriotism as they recite the Pledge of Allegiance every day, sing patriotic songs, and learn to venerate the "founding fathers," especially George Washington and other American heroes, including Abraham Lincoln, Dr. Martin Luther King Jr., and John F. Kennedy. Traditionally, elementary and high schools in the United States have emphasized the "great men in great moments" form of history, a history that traditionally concentrated solely on the contributions of elites—usually white men in formal governmental or military settings. Increasingly, however, the curriculum includes contributions by women, African Americans, and other minorities.

Education also plays a pivotal role in determining *who* will participate in the political affairs of the community. Research indicates that higher levels of education are associated with higher levels of political activism. In a book on civic voluntarism, authors Sidney Verba, Kay Schlozman, and Henry Brady write, "Well-educated parents are more likely to also be politically active and to discuss politics at home and to produce children who are active in high school. Growing up in a politicized household and being active in high school are associated with political engagement."[6]

Churches: The Role of Religion

The impact of church and religion in general on one's political socialization varies a great deal from individual to individual. For some people, religion plays a key, defining role in the development of their political beliefs. For others, it is irrelevant.

> Reciting the Pledge of Allegiance is one way schools socialize children to express patriotism.

For many years, political scientists have examined the impact religious affiliation—whether one is Catholic or Jewish, Protestant or Muslim—has on political preferences. For example, religion is related to how people view various issues, especially the issue of abortion (see "The Conversation of Democracy"). But more recent analysis shows that a better predictor of the impact of religion on voting is not so much the religion an individual practices, but rather how regularly he or she practices it. In the 2008 presidential primaries, the regularity of church attendance was linked with candidate preference in both the Democratic and Republican nomination contests. A Gallup poll estimated that in the 2008 presidential election, white voters who attended church weekly favored John McCain over Barack Obama 65 to 28 percent, while Obama outpolled McCain among those whites who never or seldom attend church 56 to 49 percent. McCain enjoyed an edge (53 to 41 percent) among those whites who attend services nearly weekly to monthly. Similar parallels cannot be seen among highly religious black voters, who overwhelmingly favored Obama (89 percent to McCain's 5 percent).[7] But the 2008 data are reflective of a historic trend in the United States, in which the Republican party can count on the support of highly religious white voters in presidential elections.

In general, however, it seems that those who are faithful in their church attendance are more likely to share conservative values—and support Republican candidates in general elections. Gallup reports that in the 2004 presidential election, of those voters who attended church weekly or almost every week, 63 percent voted for President Bush, a Republican, while 37 percent voted for the Democratic candidate, Senator John Kerry.[8] On the other hand, among those voters who seldom or never attended church, Kerry won 60 percent of the vote to Bush's 40 percent.[9] The gap was not as wide, but was still significant, in the 2000 presidential election between Bush and Democratic candidate Al Gore, when 54 percent of those who attended church weekly or almost weekly voted for Bush, with 37 percent voting for Gore. These findings are consistent with trends throughout the 1990s that indicated that Bill Clinton's opponents also fared better among frequent churchgoers.

Research also shows that this relationship between frequency of church attendance and identification with the Republican Party is particularly strong among white Protestants, but less so among Catholics, who are generally more Democratic. African American voters are even more likely than Catholics to vote for a Democratic candidate. But African Americans are also likely to have high levels of religiosity, as measured by frequency of church

The Role of Religion

How much importance does religion have in your life?

☐ It's very important.

☐ It's somewhat important.

☐ It's not that important.

Source: "Religion Most Important to Blacks, Women, and Older Americans," www.gallup.com/poll/25585/Religion-Most-Important-Blacks-Women-Older-Americans.aspx.

SHOULD ABORTION BE LEGAL?

The Issue: In the 1973 decision *Roe v. Wade,* the Supreme Court legalized abortion, essentially ruling that abortion would be legal in the first trimester of pregnancy, that states could regulate it in the second trimester (for example, by requiring that abortions be performed in a hospital), and that states had the power to ban abortion in the third trimester. Since that time, several other cases have influenced public policy on this issue, with the Court granting states more powers to regulate the circumstances surrounding abortion. Many states now require a mandatory waiting period before obtaining an abortion and/or parental consent for minors who wish to have an abortion. The Court has also struck down some proposed regulations, including a requirement that women notify their spouses before having an abortion.

Abortion is one of the most divisive issues in the United States, and public opinion on this issue has changed very little since the decision in *Roe v. Wade* was announced in 1973. About a quarter of Americans believe that abortion should be legal under any circumstances; another 56 percent believe that it should be legal under certain circumstances, while 16 percent think it should be illegal in all circumstances.* A slim majority of Americans (53 percent) call themselves pro-choice, and 41 percent call themselves pro-life. While individuals tend to hold very strong views on the abortion issue, very few people base their vote for a candidate solely on that candidate's position on the abortion issue. The divisiveness on this issue is heightened because those who hold different positions on the abortion issue also differ on other issues as well. Consider the stances articulated below, which typify views people express on this issue:

Yes: Women are the ones affected by a pregnancy, and they should be able to make decisions about their own bodies, without interference from the government—the "pro-choice" stance. Therefore, abortion should be legal under all circumstances until the point of viability. Women should be able to choose abortion, in consultation with their doctors, up to the time when the fetus can survive outside the womb, and there should be no restrictions on a woman's options.

No: Life begins at the moment of conception, and a fetus is another human life, as worthy of protection from the law as any other human being—the "pro-life" stance. We need to value life at every stage. Abortion should be illegal except to save the life of the mother; no other exceptions should be allowed. Doctors and others who perform abortions should be subject to criminal prosecution.

Other approaches: Abortion should be legal, but states should be allowed to place various restrictions on abortion. Parents should be notified when their underage daughters are seeking the procedure, for example, and states can require providers to inform women about alternatives such as adoption or make them wait twenty-four hours before performing the procedure. In other words, the goal should be to make abortion "legal but rare."

What do you think?

① Do you consider your view to be pro-choice or pro-life, or do you favor another approach? Do you think that abortion should be legal or illegal under all circumstances, or legal but with restrictions?

② Have you or would you ever base your vote solely on a candidate's position on abortion? Why or why not?

③ Think about your own socialization process—how did family, church, peers, and events shape your views on this issue?

*"Abortion: Gallup's Pulse of Democracy: Guidance for Lawmakers," www.galluppoll.com/content/?ci=1576&pg=1.

attendance. Table 6.1 shows the breakdown in party identification by frequency of church attendance. As the table shows, while African American churchgoers are slightly more likely to identify themselves as Republican than their non-churchgoing counterparts, nearly two-thirds still identify themselves as Democrats. This presence of two conditions or traits that pull a voter toward different parties is called **cross pressuring.**

cross pressuring
the presence of two conditions or traits that pull a voter toward different political parties

Interestingly, Table 6.1 also shows that those who never attend church, particularly whites, are most likely to identify themselves as independents, with no party preference. Similarly, blacks who never attend church are more likely to identify themselves as independents than are those who attend at least occasionally.

Peers and Group Norms

Friends, neighbors, coworkers, and other peers influence political socialization. Through peers, we learn about community and the political climate and values of the area in which we live. For example, your neighbors might inform you that a particular member of the city council is a strong advocate for your neighborhood on the council,

TABLE 6.1

Party Identification by Frequency of Church Attendance and Race

Race	Church Attendance	Republican (%)	Independent (%)	Democrat (%)
White	Once a week	51	25	24
	Almost every week	46	28	26
	Once a month	37	31	31
	Seldom	32	34	33
	Never	24	43	33
Black	Once a week	9	25	65
	Almost every week	6	22	71
	Once a month	5	23	72
	Seldom	4	26	70
	Never	4	38	58

Source: www.galluppoll.com/content/default.aspx?ci=16381&pg=2.

securing funds for recreational facilities or increased police protection in your area. Or a co-worker might let you know what your member of Congress is doing to help save jobs in the industry in which you work. Much research indicates that the primary impact of peers is to reinforce our already-held beliefs and values, however. Typically, the people with whom you are acquainted are quite similar to you. While diversity exists in many settings, the norms and values of the people you know tend to be remarkably similar to your own.

Political and Community Leaders: Opinion Shapers

Political and community leaders also help socialize people and influence public opinion. Positions advocated by highly regarded government leaders hold particular sway, and the president plays an especially important role in shaping Americans' views. For example, many commentators believe that President George W. Bush's characterization of Iraq, Iran, and North Korea as an "axis of evil" in his 2002 State of the Union speech helped convince the American people to support the war in Iraq and succeeded in inflaming their opinions of Iran and North Korea. And in 2007, former vice president Al Gore was awarded the Nobel Peace Prize for educating the public and political leaders concerning the issue of global climate change. But the role of political leaders in influencing public opinion is not limited to the national stage. In your city, chances are that the views of community leaders—elected and not—influence the way the public perceives local policies. Perhaps the fire or police chief endorses a candidate for city council, or the popular football coach for the Police Athletic League makes the funding of a new football field a policy priority in your town. Often we rely on the recommendations and priorities of well-respected leaders who have earned our trust.

Demographic Characteristics: Our Politics Are a Reflection of Ourselves

Who we are often influences our life experiences, which shape our political socialization and therefore what we think. The racial and ethnic groups we belong to, our gender, our age and the events that have shaped our lives, and where we live all play a role in how we are socialized

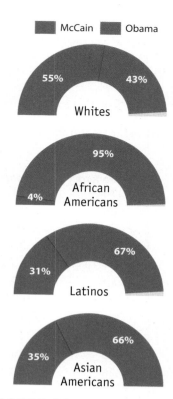

FIGURE 6.1

Support of the 2008 Presidential Candidates by Racial Group

Source: The Gallup Poll, Candidate Support by Race, http://www.gallup.com/poll/108040/Candidate-Support-Race.aspx, and Jane Junn, Taeku Lee, S. Karthick Ramakrishnan, and Janelle Wong, the National Asian American Survey, *Asian Americans and the 2008 Election*, http://www.naasurvey.com/assets/NAAS-National-report.pdf; www.cnn.com/ELECTION/2008/results/polls/USP00p1.

to political and community life, our values and priorities, and even whom we vote for. Demographic characteristics also shape our levels of civic involvement and may even help determine the ways in which we contribute to the civic life of our communities and our nation.

RACE AND ETHNICITY Whites, African Americans, Latinos, and Asian Americans prefer different candidates, hold different political views, and have different levels of civic involvement. Among the most salient of these differences are the candidate preferences of African Americans, who strongly support Democratic candidates over Republicans. But Figure 6.1 shows that in 2008, President Obama won majorities from Latinos, Asian Americans, other groups, and particularly African Americans, 95 percent of whom voted for President Obama. This proportion exceeds the share of the African American vote that Democratic presidential candidates have garnered in recent years, which has averaged 84 to 90 percent. The 43 percent of the white vote that President Obama won exceeds the 41 percent that John Kerry received in 2004, and the average of 39 percent of white votes that Democratic candidates have received since 1964.

This breakdown of 2008 voter preferences is not unique, but rather reflects well-established differences in party affiliation and ideology between racial and ethnic minorities and whites. But there are also significant differences even within racial and ethnic groups.[10] Table 6.2 shows how the various categories of Latinos differ in terms of party identification. As the table shows, Latinos who identify themselves as Puerto Rican, Dominican American, or Mexican American are very likely to be Democrats, while nearly a majority of Cuban Americans are more likely to be Republicans.

Party affiliation among ethnic groups within the Asian American community also varies somewhat, as Figure 6.2 shows. In general, about 60 percent of all Asian Americans are registered Democrats. South Asians are most likely to be Democrats, and majorities of Chinese and Koreans are Democrats as well. A quarter to a third of all Korean, Southeast Asian, Filipino, and Chinese Americans are unaffiliated with either party.

Beyond party affiliation and candidate preferences, racial and ethnic minorities and white voters also differ on other issues as well. One example is their level of satisfaction with the state of the nation. Gallup frequently

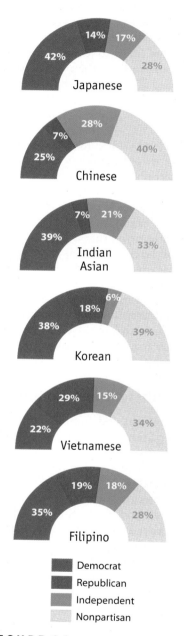

FIGURE 6.2

Asian Americans' Party Affiliation by Ethnic Group

Source: Jane Junn, Taeku Lee, S. Karthick Ramakrishnan, and Janelle Wong, the National Asian American Survey, *Asian Americans and the 2008 Election*, http://www.naasurvey.com/assets/NAAS-National-report.pdf

Latino Party Identification by National Origin, 2006

	Republican	Democratic	Independent	Other
Puerto Rican	15	48	20	6
Mexican	19	43	20	7
Cuban	49	24	17	2
Dominican	10	50	12	12

TABLE 6.2

Source: "The 2006 National Survey of Latinos: The Immigration Debate," Pew Hispanic Center, http://pewhispanic.org/files/reports/75.8.pdf.

asks the question "Are you generally satisfied or dissatisfied with the way things are going in the United States at this time?" In June 2007, about 30 percent of whites and Hispanics reported being satisfied with the state of the nation, while 68 percent of whites and Hispanics were dissatisfied. But only 11 percent of blacks were satisfied, while 87 percent reported being dissatisfied.[11]

White, African American, Latino, and Asian American youth also differ significantly in their levels of civic engagement as well as in how young people in these groups connect with their communities. Trends reported in *The 2006 Civic and Political Health of the Nation: A Detailed Look at How Youth Participate in Politics and Communities* include the following:

> Studies suggest that Asian American millennials are more likely to volunteer in their communities. Here, University of Texas at Austin students spruce up the St. John's neighborhood of northeast Austin as part of a volunteer project.

- African American youth are the most politically engaged racial or ethnic group. They are the most likely to vote, belong to political groups, make political contributions, display buttons or signs, canvass voters, and contact the media about political issues.
- Asian Americans are more likely to have been active in their communities. They are more apt to work to solve community problems, volunteer, engage in boycotts, sign petitions, and raise charitable contributions.
- Young Latinos are the least likely to be active in politics or their communities, but they are most likely to have engaged in political protests. One-quarter of Latinos (more than twice the proportion of any other group) have protested, primarily in

immigration rights demonstrations. The lack of civic involvement may be a function of barriers to participation—including the fact that many Latino youths in the United States are not citizens, which would bar them from voting. The slogan of many immigration reform marches, "Hoy marchamos! Mañana votamos!" (Today we march! Tomorrow we vote!) may be a promise of increased political participation among young Latinos in the future.

- Young white people are moderately likely to engage in many community and political activities. They are more likely than other groups to run, walk, or bike for charity, and they are also more likely to be members of a community or political group. Of the groups of young people considered here, they are the least likely to protest, the least likely to contribute money to a political cause, and the least likely to persuade others to vote.[12]

GENDER   Public opinion polls and voting behavior indicate that men and women have very different views on issues, different priorities when it comes to public issues, and often favor different candidates, particularly in national elections. This difference in men's and women's views and voting preferences is called the **gender gap,** the measurable difference in the way women and men vote for candidates and in the way they view political issues. The gender gap was first noticed by Eleanor Smeal, who at the time was president of the National Organization for Women. In the 1980 presidential election, Democratic incumbent Jimmy Carter lost to Republican challenger Ronald Reagan, but Smeal noticed that in poll after poll, women favored Carter.

Since that watershed 1980 election, the gender gap has been a factor in every subsequent presidential election: women voters are more likely than men to favor Democratic candidates. President Bill Clinton, first elected in 1992, had the smallest gender gap that year, with women voters favoring him by only 4 percent. Four years later, when he ran for reelection, he had the largest gender gap to that point, with women voters favoring him by 11 percent. In the 2008 presidential election, the gender gap continued to favor the Democratic nominee,

gender gap
the measurable difference in the way women and men vote for candidates and in the way they view political issues

with women voters favoring Barack Obama, over John McCain by 7 percent. The presence of Alaska Governor Sarah Palin as the Republican vice presidential nominee appeared not to have swayed vast numbers of women voters.

Voting turnout patterns increase the effect of the gender gap. Women in most age groups—except those under age 25—are more likely to vote than their male counterparts. In addition, on average women also live longer than men, so older women constitute an important voting bloc. The difference in women's candidate preferences and their higher likelihood of voting means that the gender gap is a political reality that any candidate seeking election cannot ignore.

Young men and women also differ in their level of civic engagement, in the ways in which they are involved with their communities, and in their perspectives on the government. While majorities of young men and women believe it is their *responsibility* (rather than their choice) to get involved to make things better for society, how they choose to get involved varies by gender. As Figure 6.3 shows, women in particular are more likely to participate in certain forms of community activism such as volunteering and running, walking, biking, or engaging in other fund-raising activities for charity. Men and women are about equally likely to work on solving a community problem, such as volunteering for a nonprofit mediation service that helps negotiate disputes between neighbors. Men are more likely than women to choose formal political forms of activism, such as voting, persuading others to vote, and contributing money to political campaigns.

Women's and men's opinions also differ on public policy issues, though often in unexpected ways. On the one hand, there is very little difference of opinion between men and women on the issue of abortion. On the other hand, men's and women's view on the optimal role of government vary greatly, with 66 percent of young women believe that government should do more to solve problems (versus 60 percent of young men), while only 27 percent of women believe that government does too many things better left to businesses and individuals, as opposed to 35 percent of men.[13] Women are also more likely to believe that the United States is at risk of another terrorist attack since September 11, and they are less likely to feel safe from terrorism. Women, too, are more likely to believe that going to war in Iraq was a mistake, and they were more likely to have reached this conclusion earlier than men were. When it comes to domestic priorities, men and women are equally likely to cite jobs and the economy as high priorities, but women are more likely to consider health care a priority. Men are about 10 percent more likely to favor the death penalty than are women.[14] Do the different life experiences of women and men help to explain some of their policy preferences, and hence their candidate preferences?

> Eleanor Smeal, president of the Feminist Majority and a former president of the National Organization for Women, coined the term "gender gap" after the 1980 presidential election. Smeal noticed that in poll after poll women favored Democratic incumbent Jimmy Carter over Republican challenger Ronald Reagan. Was there a gender gap in the 2008 presidential election?

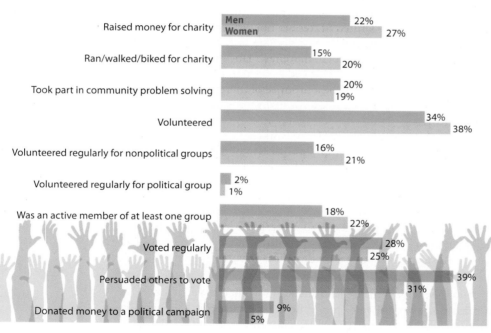

FIGURE 6.3

Participation in Civic Activities Among Young Men and Women

Source: Karlo Barrios Marcelo, Mark Hugo Lopez, and Emily Hoban Kirby, *Civic Engagement Among Young Men and Women* (College Park, MD: Circle: The Center for Information and Research on Civic Learning and Engagement, 2007).

generational effect
the impact of an important external event in shaping the views of a generation

AGE AND EVENTS Differences in the candidates voters prefer—party, gender, the age of the candidates themselves—are one reflection of age and political opinions. People's opinions are also influenced by the events they have lived through and by their political socialization; an epic event may lead to a widespread change in political views. Called the **generational**

effect (sometimes called the *age-cohort effect*), this is the impact of a significant external event in shaping the views of a generation. Typically, generational effects are felt most strongly by young people. As a result of the attacks that occurred on September 11, 2001, people who were under age 30 on that day might place a heightened priority on keeping the United States safe in the face of a new kind of threat, for instance. Other key events that have shaped the socialization of a generation include the Great Depression and World War II for the oldest Americans and the war in Vietnam and the changes in society that occurred during the 1960s for the Baby Boom Generation born between 1946 and 1964. The major events that occur while we grow up affect our socialization by shaping our viewpoints and our policy priorities.

One of the strongest examples of the generational effect is the Great Depression. The oldest Americans, who came of age during the era of Democratic president Franklin Roosevelt's New Deal social programs, remain most likely to vote Democratic. But often the impact of events is not immediately apparent. Political scientists continue to measure the effects of the September 11, 2001, terrorist attacks and the subsequent war on terror on the views of the generation socialized to politics during the first decade of the twenty-first century. In the 2008 presidential election, young voters strongly preferred Senator Barack Obama over Republican candidate Senator John McCain. But was this difference in candidate preference a result of the generational effect? Will the Americans who grew up in the wake of those attacks be more patriotic than their parents? Will they resist a militaristic foreign policy throughout their lifetimes? These types of questions will interest public opinion researchers in the decades to come.

GEOGRAPHIC REGION Since the nation's founding, Americans have varied in their political attitudes and beliefs and how they are socialized to politics, depending on the region of the United States from which they come. These differences stem in part from historical patterns of immigration: Irish and Italian immigrants generally settled in the northeastern seaboard, influencing the political culture of Boston, New York, Philadelphia, and Baltimore. Chinese immigrants, instrumental in building the transcontinental railroad in the nineteenth century, settled in California and areas of the Pacific Northwest and have had a major impact on the political life of those areas.

Among the most important regional differences in the United States is the difference in political outlook between those who live in the Northeast and those in the South. The differences between these two regions predate even our nation's founding. During the Constitutional Convention in 1787, northern and southern states disagreed as to the method that should be used to count slaves for the purposes of taxation and representation. The differences between these two regions were intensified in

AGENTS OF SOCIALIZATION

Family

— Children learn whether family members value civic activism by observing their actions and listening to their views.

— Families also influence our political beliefs.

The Media

— The media help shape societal norms.

— The media help determine the national agenda.

— The media educate people about policy issues.

— The media can skew people's perception of public policy priorities and challenges.

Schools

— Schools socialize children to democratic norms and patriotism.

— Education level helps determine who will participate in the political affairs of the community.

Churches

— The impact of church and religion in general on a person's political socialization varies a great deal from individual to individual.

— Religious denomination and frequency of church attendance are critical in determining whether religion is an important agent of socialization for any individual.

Peers

— Peers' primary impact is to reinforce already-held beliefs and values.

Political and Community Leaders

— Political and community leaders help socialize people and influence public opinion.

Demographic Characteristics

— Race and ethnicity, gender, age and life events, and the geographic region from which they come all have an impact on the way people are socialized to political opinions and behavior.

> Geographic region contributes to differences in political climate. What is the political climate of your state? Your region? How does the political climate influence the candidates who tend to win party primaries or caucuses? How does it influence those who tend to win in your state in general elections?

the aftermath of the Civil War—the quintessential manifestation of regional differences in the United States. Since the Republican Party was the party of Lincoln and the North, the South became essentially a one-party region, with all political competition occurring *within* the Democratic Party. The Democratic Party dominated the South until the later part of the twentieth century, when many Democrats embraced the civil rights movement (as described in Chapter 5). Differences in regional culture and political viewpoints between North and South remain. Today, in national elections, Republicans tend to carry the South, the West, and most of the Midwest, except for large cities in these regions. Democrats are favored in the Northeast, the West Coast, and in most major cities.

Table 6.3 illustrates one factor that contributes to these differences in regional political climate: religious affiliation. Although differences in religious affiliation are often a function of people's heritage, church membership can alter the political culture of a region through the perpetuation of values and priorities. As Table 6.3 shows, the South is much more Protestant than other regions of the United States. Not surprisingly, Republicans dominate in this area, particularly among religious Protestants, born again Christians, and Evangelicals (see the discussion of the influence of churches on political socialization on pages 215–217). Catholics and Jews tend to dominate in the Northeast along the East Coast; both groups are more frequently supporters of the Democratic Party. People without a religious affiliation, who tend to value independence and have negative views of governmental activism, tend to live in the West and vote Republican.

TABLE 6.3

Religious Affiliation in Geographic Regions of the United States

MOST PROTESTANT STATES		MOST CATHOLIC STATES		MOST JEWISH STATES		MOST NONRELIGIOUS STATES	
State	Percentage of Population	State	Percentage of Population	State	Percentage of Population	State	Percentage of Population
Alabama	76	Rhode Island	52	New York	7	Oregon	18
West Virginia	75	Massachusetts	48	New Jersey	6	Idaho	17
Mississippi	75	New Jersey	46	Massachusetts	4	Washington	16
Tennessee	72	Connecticut	46	Florida	4	Colorado	15
South Carolina	71	New York	40	Maryland	4	Maine	14
Arkansas	70	New Hampshire	38	Connecticut	3	California	14
North Carolina	70	Wisconsin	34	Vermont	3	New Hampshire	13
Georgia	68	Louisiana	33	California	3	Nevada	13
Oklahoma	67	New Mexico	32	Nevada	3	Arizona	12
Kentucky	65	Vermont	32				

Measuring Public Opinion

Public opinion consists of the public's expressed views about an issue at a specific point in time. Public opinion and ideology are inextricably linked because ideology is the prism through which people view all political issues; hence their ideology informs their opinions on the full range of political issues. Indeed, the growing importance of public opinion has even led some political scientists, such as Elizabeth Noelle-Neumann to argue that public opinion itself is a socializing agent in that it provides an independent context that affects political behavior.[15] Though we are inundated every day with the latest public opinion polls on television, on the Internet, in magazines, and even on podcasts, the importance of public opinion is not a new phenomenon in American politics.

As early as the War for Independence, leaders of the Continental Congress were concerned with what the people thought. Popular opinion mattered because support was critical to the success of the volunteer revolutionary army. As discussed in Chapter 2, after the thirteen colonies won their independence, public opinion was an important concern of political and economic leaders during the early years of the new nation. The dissatisfaction of ordinary people troubled by debt caused Shays's Rebellion in Massachusetts in 1786–87, which led to a shift in the thinking of the elites who came together in Philadelphia the following May to draft the new Constitution. And once the Constitution was drafted, *The Federalist Papers* were used as a tool to influence public opinion and generate support for the new form of government.

Public opinion is manifested in a variety of ways: demonstrators protesting on the steps of the state capitol; readers of the local newspaper writing letters to the editor on behalf of (or against) a proposal before the city council; citizens communicating directly with government officials, perhaps by telling their local city council member what they think of the town's plan to develop a recreational center or by calling their member of Congress to indicate their opinion of a current piece of legislation. One of the most important ways public opinion is measured is through the act of voting, which we discuss in Chapter 9. But another important tool that policy makers, researchers, and the public rely on as an indicator of public opinion is the **public opinion poll,** a survey of a given population's opinion on an issue at a particular point in time. Policy makers, particularly elected officials, care about public opinion because they want to develop and implement policies that reflect the public's views.[16] Such policies are more likely to attract support from other government leaders, who are also relying on public opinion as a gauge, but they also help ensure that elected leaders will be reelected because they are representing their constituents' views.[17]

The Origins of Public Opinion Polls

In his book *Public Opinion,* published in 1922, political writer Walter Lippmann stressed both the importance of public opinion for policy makers and the value of measuring it accurately. Lippman's thought informed a generation of public opinion researchers, who in turn shaped two divergent areas of opinion research: marketing research, used by businesses to increase sales, and public opinion research, used to measure people's opinions on political issues.

Among the first efforts to gauge public opinion were attempts to predict the outcomes of presidential elections. In 1916, the *Literary Digest,* a popular magazine similar in format to today's *Reader's Digest,* conducted its first successful **straw poll,** a poll conducted in an unscientific manner to predict the outcome of an election. (The term comes from the use of natural straw to determine which way the wind is blowing; so too does a straw poll indicate how the winds of public opinion are blowing.) Between 1920 and 1932, *Literary Digest* correctly predicted the winner of every presidential race by relying on its subscribers to mail in postcards indicating their vote choice. The 1936 presidential election between Democrat Franklin Roosevelt and Republican governor Alfred M. "Alf" Landon of Kansas centered on one issue, however: the government's role in responding to the Great Depression. In effect, the election was a mandate on Roosevelt's New Deal policies. The *Literary Digest* poll predicted that Landon would defeat Roosevelt by 57 to 43 percent, but Roosevelt won that election by a landslide, receiving nearly 63 percent of the popular vote.

public opinion
the public's expressed views about an issue at a specific point in time

public opinion poll
a survey of a given population's opinion on an issue or a candidate at a particular point in time

straw poll
a poll conducted in an unscientific manner, used to predict election outcomes

GLOBAL COMPARISONS

WORLD OPINION ON THE BEST AND WORST NATIONS IN THE WORLD

Americans traveling abroad are often warned not to advertise the fact that they are from the United States. In many parts of the world, opposition to what is often referred to as "the American War" in Iraq has fueled what many sense is a widely prevalent anti-American sentiment. In fact, however, while people in other countries continue to have a negative view of the influence of the United States on world affairs, their view actually improved in 2008. During that year, a poll of the residents of thirty-four nations was conducted for the British Broadcasting Company (BBC) in which the respondents were asked to evaluate whether each one of fourteen nations, including the United States, has a positive or negative influence in the world.*

> **What impact do you think the outcome of the 2008 U.S. presidential election will have on international opinion of the United States?**

In general, views of U.S. influence in the world remain negative, but among residents of eleven of the twenty-three countries in which the survey was conducted the previous year, the United States' standing improved, while it declined in only three countries. An average of 35 percent of respondents said that the United States is having a positive influence, up from 31 percent in 2007.

As shown in the accompanying figure, which gives the average poll results over several years, in 2008, 49 percent said they believed that the United States is having a negative influence, a decline from 55 percent in 2007. The second figure indicates that countries showing the sharpest increase in their positive views of the United States include South Korea (35% in 2007 to 49% in 2008), France (24% to 32%), Portugal (29% to 42%), Brazil (29% to 39%), Chile (32% to 41%), and the

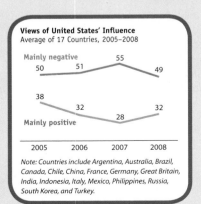

Views of United States' Influence
Average of 17 Countries, 2005–2008

Mainly negative
50   51   55   49

38   32   28   32
Mainly positive

2005   2006   2007   2008

Note: Countries include Argentina, Australia, Brazil, Canada, Chile, China, France, Germany, Great Britain, India, Indonesia, Italy, Mexico, Philippines, Russia, South Korea, and Turkey.

United Arab Emirates (25% to 37%). Steven Kull, director of the Program on International Policy Attitudes (PIPA) at the University of Maryland, one of the organizations that conducted the poll, indicated that the evaluation of the United States may actually be based on hope for the future rather than an assessment of the present. "It may be that as the U.S. approaches a new presidential election, views of the U.S. are being mitigated by hope that a new administration will move away from the foreign policies that have been so unpopular in the world."**

Which countries received the most positive evaluations? With a positive rating of 56 percent each, Germany and Japan were tied, as shown in the second accompanying figure, though Germany has a lower negative evaluation (18 percent) than does Japan (21).

The two countries with the highest negative evaluations are Iran and Israel. Twenty percent of those surveyed believe that Iran is having a positive influence in the world, and 19 percent think Israel is. Doug Miller, president of GlobeScan, PIPA's partner in conducting the poll, offered the explanation that the "poll suggests that Iran continues to pay a price for its nuclear stand-off with the United Nations. World opinion continues to see it as the country having the most negative influence."**

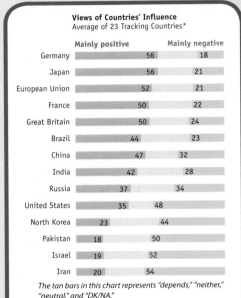

Views of Countries' Influence
Average of 23 Tracking Countries*

	Mainly positive	Mainly negative
Germany	56	18
Japan	56	21
European Union	52	21
France	50	22
Great Britain	50	24
Brazil	44	23
China	47	32
India	42	28
Russia	37	34
United States	35	48
North Korea	23	44
Pakistan	18	50
Israel	19	52
Iran	20	54

The tan bars in this chart represents "depends," "neither," "neutral," and "DK/NA."

* Averages not including views of subject country/countries (in the case of the EU)

*A total of 17,457 citizens in Argentina, Australia, Brazil, Canada, Chile, China, Costa Rica, Egypt, El Salvador, France, Germany, Ghana, Great Britain, Guatemala, Honduras, India, Indonesia, Israel, Italy, Japan, Kenya, Lebanon, Mexico, Nicaragua, Nigeria, Panama, the Philippines, Portugal, Russia, South Korea, Spain, Turkey, the UAE, and the United States were interviewed face-to-face or by telephone between October 31, 2007, and January 25, 2008. The international polling firm GlobeScan and its research partners in each country conducted polling for the BBC World Service. In sixteen of the thirty-four countries, the sample was limited to major urban areas. Given that country ratings were given by samples of about 500 per country, the margin of error per country ranges from +/−3.4 to 4.6 percent.
**www.worldpublicopinion.org/pipa/articles/views_on_countriesregions_bt/463.php?lb =btvoc&pnt=463&nid=&id=.

Source: Graphs courtesy of BBC World Service.

Where did the *Literary Digest* go wrong? The most fatal error the magazine committed was to use an unrepresentative sample to draw conclusions about the wider voting public. The straw poll respondents were derived from a list of subscribers to the magazine, automobile owners, and people listed in telephone directories. At the height of the Depression, this sample excluded most members of the working and middle classes. And class mattered in the 1936 election, with Roosevelt deriving his support primarily from poor, working-class, and middle-class voters. *Literary Digest* had committed what Lippmann termed an error of the casual mind: "to pick out or stumble upon a sample which supports or defies its prejudices, and then to make it the representative of a whole class."[18] Notice the similarity between *Literary Digest*'s faulty straw poll and many of today's voluntary Internet polls—self-selected respondents often differ dramatically in their views from those of the broader public.

Although the 1936 election destroyed the credibility of the *Literary Digest* poll, it was also the watershed year for a young Princeton-based public opinion researcher named George Gallup. Gallup's entry in political public opinion research was driven in part by a desire to help his mother-in-law, Ola Babcock Miller, win election as Iowa's secretary of state, the first woman elected to that position. In 1935, Gallup founded the American Institute of Public Opinion, which would later become the Gallup Organization. Gallup gained national recognition when he correctly predicted the outcome of the 1936 election, and scientific opinion polls, which rely on the random selection of participants rather than their own self-selection, gained enormous credibility during this era.

Gallup's credibility suffered a substantial setback, however, after the presidential election of 1948 between Democrat Harry S Truman and Republican Thomas E. Dewey. That year, the "big three" polling organizations, Gallup, Roper, and Crossley, all concluded their polls in October, and all predicted a Dewey victory. By ending their efforts early, the polls missed the swing of third-party voters back to Harry S Truman's camp in the final days of the campaign. The organizations didn't anticipate that many voters would switch back to the Democratic nominee, who wound up winning the presidency. During his administration, Truman would sometimes offer a good-natured barb at the pollsters who had prematurely predicted his demise, and George Gallup responded in kind: "I have the greatest admiration for President Truman, because he fights for what he believes. I propose to do the same thing. As long as public opinion is important in this country, and until someone finds a better way of appraising it, I intend to go right ahead with the task of reporting the opinions of the people on issues vital to their welfare."[19]

How Public Opinion Polls Are Conducted

In politics, public opinion polls are used for a variety of reasons.[20] Political scientist Herbert Asher noted "Polling plays an integral role in political events at the national, state, and local levels. In any major event or decision, poll results are sure to be a part of the news media's coverage and the decision makers' deliberations."[21] In addition, public opinion polls help determine who those decision makers will be: candidates for public office use polls to determine their initial name recognition, the effectiveness of their campaign strategy, their opponents' weaknesses, and how potential voters are responding to their message. Once elected to office, policy makers often rely on public opinion polls to gauge their constituents' opinions and as a means of measuring how well they are performing on the job.

The process of conducting a public opinion poll consists of several steps. Those conducting the poll first need to determine the **population** they are targeting for the survey—the group of people whose opinions are of interest and about whom information is desired. For example, if your neighbor were considering running for the U.S. House of Representatives, she would want to know how many people recognize her name. But she would be interested only in those people who live in your congressional district. Furthermore, she would probably narrow this population by looking only at those people in the district who are

population
in a poll, the group of people whose opinions are of interest and/or about whom information is desired

EXPLORING THE SOURCES

EXAMINING AMERICANS' IDEOLOGY

This graph shows a distribution of how Americans identify themselves by ideology, ranging from very liberal to very conservative (note that "neoconservative" was not offered as a possible response).

Source: Joseph Carroll, "Many Americans Use Multiple Labels to Describe Their Ideology," Gallup News Service, December 6, 2006.

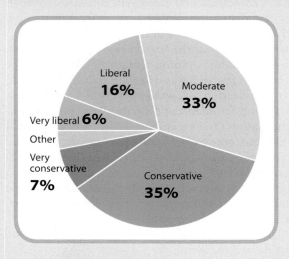

Liberal **16%**
Very liberal **6%**
Other
Very conservative **7%**
Moderate **33%**
Conservative **35%**

Evaluating the Evidence

① What does the graph indicate about how most people identify themselves? Why do you think this is true?

② If you were a candidate for the presidency, how might these data affect the policy stances you would take on specific issues?

③ The data are from a national sample of U.S. citizens. How do you think the data would vary in your state? In your community? If the sample included all U.S. residents, rather than just U.S. citizens?

---

registered to vote. She might even want to narrow her target population further by limiting her survey to likely voters, perhaps those who have voted in past congressional elections.

The sponsor of any poll, whether a candidate, a political party, an interest group, or a news organization, needs to determine what information is desired from survey respondents. Sometimes this information is relatively clear—news media organizations track presidential approval ratings each month, for example. But other times this process might be more complex (see "On the Job"). Polling organizations construct polls carefully to ensure that the questions actually measure what the client wants to know. Pollsters also recognize that many factors, including question design and question order, have an impact on the responses. For example, this chapter's "Exploring the Sources" provides data on how Americans identify themselves ideologically: 6 percent of Americans identify themselves as very liberal, 16 percent as liberal, 33 percent as moderate, 35 percent as conservative, and 7 percent as very conservative. But when the Gallup organization changed the term "liberal" to "progressive" in half of the surveys sent to respondents, those who received the questionnaire with the "progressive" alternative responded quite differently. While a consistent 8 percent identified themselves as very conservative, those who identified themselves as conservative dropped to 28 percent. Fully 10 percent more (43 percent) identified themselves as moderates, with 14 percent identifying themselves as progressives, and 5 percent identifying themselves as very progressive.[22] This simple change in terminology indicates that Americans may be more likely to identify themselves as "conservative" when the opposing term "liberal" is used rather than when the opposing term "progressive" is used.

SAMPLING   Once the target population is determined and the survey measurement instrument, or poll, is designed, pollsters then must select a sample that will represent the views of this population. Because it is nearly impossible to measure all of the opinions of any given population, pollsters frequently rely on **random sampling,** a scientific method of selection in which each member of the population has an equal chance at being included in the sample. Relying on random sampling helps to ensure that the sample is not skewed so that one component of the population is overrepresented. To demonstrate this point, sup-

random sampling
a scientific method of selection for a poll in which each member of the population has an equal chance at being included in the sample

pose the dean of students asks you as a class to conduct a public opinion survey that will measure whether students believe that parking facilities are adequate at your school. In this case, the population you need to measure is the entire student body. But clearly how you conduct the sampling will have a bearing on the responses. If you ask only students in your 8:00 a.m. American Government class, you might find that they have little trouble parking because the campus is not crowded at that hour. If you ask students who attend classes only during peak hours, you might get different, yet not necessarily representative, views as well, as these students may have more difficulty parking than average. How then would you obtain a random sample? The best way would be to ask the registrar for a list of all students, determine your sample size, randomly select every nth student from the list, contact each nth student, and ask for his or her views.

Researchers have noted, however, that one problem with polls is that even those conducted using random samples may not provide the accurate data needed to illuminate political opinions and behaviors. Part of the problem is that randomization can go only so far. One standard method for conducting telephone surveys is by using random-digit dialing of landline telephones.[23] Nearly every polling organization omits cellular lines from its population,[24] however, for a variety of reasons including the potential cost to the cell phone subscriber, the high rate of nonresponse because of the nearly universal use of caller ID, and the transportable nature of cell phones that makes their owners' willingness to participate in surveys unlikely.[25] Consider as well the population of individuals who rely exclusively on cell phones and do not use landlines. How might these people be different from those who use only landlines? People who rely exclusively on landlines are likely to be older than "celly-onlys." Indeed, one study found that 25 percent of young adults aged 18–29 years lived in celly-only households.[26] And some individuals who eliminate landlines from their homes do so in order to save money. In fact, in 2006, 17 percent of adults with household incomes below 200 percent of the federal poverty thresholds and 32 percent of low-income young adults lived in homes with only a cell phone.[27] So, by eliminating cell phone users from a potential sample, pollsters eliminate individuals who may be poorer or more concerned with the economy than those who pay to keep a landline.

One way pollsters attempt to address these types of concerns is through the use of a **quota sample,** a more scientifically sophisticated method of sampling than random sampling. A pollster using this method structures the sample so that it is representative of the characteristics of the target population. Let's say that your mother is running for mayor of your town, and you would like to conduct a poll that measures opinions of her among various constituencies. From census data, you learn that your town is 40 percent white, 35 percent African American, 20 percent Latino, and 5 percent Asian. Therefore, at a citywide event, you structure your sample so that it reflects the proportions of the population. With a sample of 200 voters, you would seek to include 80 white respondents, 70 African Americans, 40 Latinos, and 10 Asians. Pollsters routinely rely on quota sampling, though often they may not ask participants about their demographic characteristics until the end of the poll.

Another method used to address problems in sampling is **stratified sampling,** in which the national population is divided into fourths and certain areas within these regions are selected as representative of the national population. While some organizations still rely on quota sampling, larger organizations and media polls now use stratified sampling, the most reliable form of random sample. Today, nearly every major polling organization relies on U.S. census data as the basis of their four sampling regions. Stratified sampling is the basis for much of the public opinion data used by political scientists and other social scientists, in particular the General Social Survey (GSS) and the National Election Study.

SAMPLING ERROR As we have seen, to accurately gauge public opinion, pollsters must obtain an accurate sample from the population they are polling. A sample need not be large to reflect the population's views. In fact, most national polling organizations rarely sample more than 1,500 respondents; most national samples range from 1,000 to 1,500. To poll smaller populations (states or congressional districts, for example), polling organizations routinely use samples of between 300 and 500 respondents.

The key is having a sample that accurately reflects the population. Let's say that your political science instructor offers extra credit if you attend a weekly study group. The group

quota sample
a method by which pollsters structure a sample so that it is representative of the characteristics of the target population

stratified sampling
a process of random sampling in which the national population is divided into fourths and certain areas within these regions are selected as representative of the national population

Public Opinion Polling

THEN (1970s)	NOW (2009)
Telephone polls replace mail-in and door-to-door polling because most American households have landlines.	Internet polls are at the cutting edge of public opinion research, but anonymity and multiple responses from the same person can damage a poll's accuracy.
Early telephone polls overrepresent the views of homemakers and retirees, who are more likely to answer the phone during the day.	The accuracy of telephone polls is affected by the difficulty of reaching people who use only cell phones or who screen calls using caller ID.
Pollsters remedy nonrepresentative sampling through quota sampling.	Pollsters rely on stratified sampling to ensure the most representative sample of the population they are targeting.

WHAT'S NEXT?

> How will new media technologies such as YouTube and social networking sites such as Facebook shape polling in the future?

> How might pollsters overcome the obstacles associated with Internet polls, in particular, anonymous respondents giving false answers or responding to the same poll multiple times?

> How will cell phones and text messaging change the process of measuring public opinion in the future?

initially convenes immediately after your regular class session. At the conclusion of the study group, the leader asks if this is a convenient time for everyone to meet. Since everyone present has attended the study group, chances are that the time is more convenient for them than it is for those students who did not attend—perhaps because they have another class immediately after your political science class, or they work during that time period, or they have child care responsibilities. In other words, the composition of the sample—in this case, the students in the study group—will skew the responses to this question. Similarly, if a poll is administered to a nonrepresentative sample of a population, the responses will not accurately reflect the population's views.

In selecting a representative sample, pollsters need to pay particular attention to the time of day a poll is administered: afternoons yield a disproportionate number of mothers with small children and retirees, evenings may yield more affluent individuals who do not do shift work. And today's telephone technology presents pollsters with even more obstacles. As we have seen many potential respondents, particularly young people, have opted out of telephone landlines in favor of cell phones, making them a subset of the population that is more difficult for pollsters to reach. People with caller ID or both cell and landlines frequently screen out unknown numbers or those of survey research companies.

Internet polls present their own set of obstacles, including the ability of some individuals to complete surveys (or vote for their favorite reality show contestant) repeatedly.[28] Nonetheless, market research firms, public opinion polling organizations, and even political candidates are increasingly relying on the Internet as a survey research tool.[29] Some organizations, such as the Harris Poll Online, offer "memberships": poll respondents can earn rewards for completing surveys that help the organization create a representative sample of their target population (see "Doing Democracy").

To adjust for problems with sampling, every poll that relies on a sample has a **sampling error** (sometimes called a **margin of error**), which is a statistical calculation of the difference in results between a poll of a randomly drawn sample and a poll of the entire population. Most polls have a sampling error of ±3 percentage points ("plus or minus three percentage points"). This means 3 percentage points should be added and subtracted from the poll results to find the range for the population. Consider the following story reported by Reuters News Service in 1996:

> WASHINGTON (Reuters) - President Clinton, hit by bad publicity recently over FBI files and a derogatory book, has slipped against Bob Dole in a new poll released Monday but still maintains a 15 percentage point lead. The CNN/USA Today/Gallup poll taken June 27–30 of 818 registered voters showed Clinton would beat his Republican challenger if the election were held now, 54 to 39 percent, with seven percent undecided. The poll had a margin of error of plus or minus four percentage points.
> A similar poll June 18–19 had Clinton 57 to 38 percent over Dole.[30]

sampling error

also called *margin of error;* a statistical calculation of the difference in results between a poll of a randomly drawn sample and a poll of the entire population

DOING DEMOCRACY

PARTICIPATE IN ONLINE POLLING

FACT:

Because college students keep unpredictable hours and frequently lack access to landline telephones, learning about the opinions and priorities of this important demographic group is a significant challenge for pollsters. Though skepticism about online polling abounds, John Zogby, founder of the Zogby Poll, notes that using online polling to supplement telephone interviews has helped his organization more accurately predict the winners of national and local elections. He notes, "Zogby International's groundbreaking new Zogby Interactive poll is the wave of the future. . . . As a pioneer in the field, Zogby expects a certain degree of skepticism of this groundbreaking method. While caller ID, cell phones, and rapidly falling response rates foreshadow a day where telephone polling is less preferable than other methods, interactive polling is well on its way to becoming as accurate as telephone polling."*

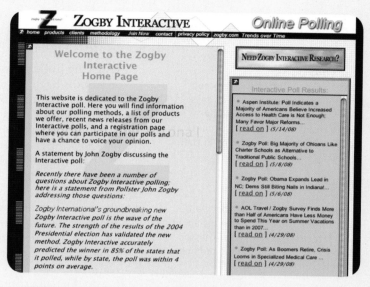

Act!

Zogby and the Harris Poll Online offer individuals the opportunity to join as members and participate in public opinion surveys.** Joining one of these online polls enables you to voice your opinion to policy makers. In addition, candidates often rely on these polling organizations as barometers of public opinion, using them to shape campaign priorities or to help them articulate their positions on issues. Participating in online polls has other benefits as well, according to the Harris Poll Online: "By participating, you'll not only have your say in matters that affect you, you'll also be able to see the results from the surveys you complete. You can then compare your opinions and experiences to many others'—people who are like, and unlike, you. Occasionally, you may participate in surveys whose results will be published in national or international media. If time permits, we'll even email the results to you before they are published."

Where to begin

- Register for the Zogby Interactive Survey (ZIS) at the organization's Web site (**http://interactive.zogby.com/index .cfm**). By doing so, you will join hundreds of thousands of other volunteer participants who may be randomly selected to participate in particular Zogby polls.

- The Harris Online Poll (**www.harrispollonline.com/ AdultReg.asp?lang=1**) has a similar registration process, and members can expect to receive two to three invitations to participate in surveys each month. Members receive reward points for participating, which can be redeemed for merchandise.

*Zogby Interactive Homepage, http://interactive.zogby.com/index.cfm . . .
**Screen captures courtesy of the Harris Polls and © 2008 Zogby International. Used with permission.

The reporter who wrote this story did not understand the sampling error. In fact, with a margin of error of 4 percentage points, Clinton's standing remained virtually the same, because 54 percent (really 50–58 percent, as 54 − 4 = 50 and 54 + 4 = 58) encompassed the 57 percent he had garnered the previous week.

Types of Political Polls

Today, the process of measuring political opinions has evolved drastically from the days of the *Literary Digest*'s straw poll or even George Gallup's first successful predictions of the results of presidential elections.[31] Political candidates, parties, and news organizations rely on several different types of polls, depending on their goals and objectives. These include tracking polls, push polls, and exit polls.

tracking polls
polls that measure changes in public opinion over the course of days, weeks, or months by repeatedly asking respondents the same questions and measuring changes in their responses

push polls
a special type of poll that both provides information to campaigns about candidate strengths and weaknesses and attempts to skew public opinion about a candidate

exit polls
polls conducted at polling places on Election Day to determine the winner of an election before the polls close

■ **Tracking polls** measure changes in public opinion over the course of days, weeks, or months by repeatedly asking respondents the same questions and measuring changes in opinion. Since the 1992 presidential election, tracking polls have been an important tool, particularly for presidential candidates seeking to glean information about how campaign strategy has affected public opinion. Tracking polls are useful in indicating the effectiveness of the media strategy, the success of a day's worth of campaigning, or whether the campaign has gotten its message across in the most recent news cycle.

■ **Push polls** are a special type of poll that both provides information to campaigns about candidate strengths and weaknesses and attempts to skew public opinion about a candidate. At their best, push polls help gauge voter priorities so that a campaign can better target its message. For example, a push poll might ask a respondent, "If you were aware that Senator John McCain was held prisoner while serving his country during the Vietnam War, would that make you more or less likely to vote for him?" Such questions enable the campaign to measure the importance to voters of a quality or stance of the candidate, in this case service in Vietnam and McCain's POW status. The campaign can then determine whether to accentuate that message. But push polls have an unsavory reputation because some campaigns have used them to smear an opponent. Doing so in the hypothetical structure of push polls enables one campaign to make often baseless accusations against an opponent without having to substantiate the charges. For example, a pollster might ask, "If you knew that Jane Jones had been arrested for driving while intoxicated, would that make you more or less likely to vote for her?" Of course, the pollster is not saying that Jones had been arrested, but the hypothetical would lead some respondents to conclude that she had.

■ **Exit polls** are conducted at polling places on Election Day to determine the winner of an election before the polls close. News organizations frequently sponsor exit polls, which help them predict the outcome of gubernatorial, congressional, and presidential elections. Because of exit polls, news organizations can frequently predict the outcome of a given election shortly after the polls have closed. Exit polls also provide the media, candidates, and political parties with information about why voters voted the way they did.

What Americans Think About Politics

Public opinion research is the means by which individuals can convey their opinions and priorities to policy makers. Consequently, polls connect Americans to their government.[32] Through public opinion polls, whether conducted by campaigns or media organizations, government officials come to know and understand the opinions of the masses.[33] Through polls, leaders learn what issues are important to people, which policy solutions they prefer, and whether they approve of the way government officials are doing their jobs.[34] The role of opinion polls in shaping citizens' involvement with their government is also circular: polls play a pivotal role in shaping public opinion, and the results of polls, frequently reported by the media, provide an important source of information for the American public.

The Most Important Problem

Several polling organizations routinely ask respondents to identify (either from a list or in their own words) what they view as "the most important problem" facing the country. Since April 2008, "the economy" was most frequently cited as the most important problem (by 43 percent of those surveyed), having risen steadily in the rankings over the previous six-month period.[35] Not surprisingly, until November 2007, the war in Iraq was the top issue, with about a third of Americans—34 percent—citing it as the most important problem. By April 2008, only 23 percent named the war in Iraq as the most important problem. Until that time, Iraq had consistently been named the top problem for the four previous years. Interestingly, however, the percentage of Americans who were concerned about the situation in Iraq was not as high as it was for other wars, as reflected in the results of previous surveys conducted during earlier armed conflicts. For example, 56 percent of respondents identified the Korean War as the most important problem in September 1951, and 62 percent named the Vietnam War as the top problem in January 1967.[36] In general, other problems Americans identify as important include the state of the economy, gas prices, health care, immigration, and terrorism.

The Mood of the Nation

In April 2008, Americans' satisfaction with the state of the nation was quite low, with 15 percent of Americans saying they were satisfied and 83 percent indicating that they were dissatisfied. Gallup reports that since it began asking the "mood of the nation" question in 1979, typically 43 percent of the American people report being satisfied.[37] When George W. Bush took office in 2001, 56 percent of Americans reported being satisfied; that percentage jumped to an unsustainable 70 percent in the aftermath of the 9/11 attacks and has since declined steadily, most precipitously in 2008. As noted, during that year the economy emerged as one cause of high levels of dissatisfaction, replacing dissatisfaction with the war in Iraq.

> Bumper stickers are a means of voicing individual opinion and provide a (very unscientific) way of observing public opinion. Why might people demur from putting bumper stickers on their cars? Does a sticker-less bumper indicate a lack of strongly held beliefs?

Public Opinion About Government

Analysts of public opinion, government officials, and scholars of civic engagement are all concerned with public opinion about the government at all levels, in particular about the institutions of the federal government. For decades, public opinion researchers have measured the public's trust in government by asking survey respondents to rate their level of trust in the federal government's ability to handle domestic and international policy matters and to gauge their amount of trust and confidence in the executive, legislative, and judicial branches of government.

The responses to these questions are important for several reasons. First, although these measures indicate public opinion about institutions rather than individuals, individual office holders nonetheless can use the data as a measure of how well they are performing their jobs. Lower levels of confidence in the institution of the presidency, for example, tend to parallel lower approval ratings of specific presidents.[38] Second, trust in government is one measure of the public's sense of efficacy, their belief that the government works for people like them, as discussed in Chapter 1. If people trust their government, they are more likely to believe that it is responsive to the needs of citizens—that it is working for people like themselves.

As indicated by the results of a survey conducted in 2007, the public's trust in the ability of the federal government to handle both international affairs and domestic problems has declined over the years. Many analysts attribute this decline to widespread dissatisfaction with both foreign policy as it relates to the war in Iraq and the economic downturn. As

ON THE JOB

LEANN ATKINSON, OPINION RESEARCHER

Name: Leann Atkinson

Age: 26

Hometown: Cassville, New York

College: Hamilton College, Clinton, New York

Major: Sociology (BA)

Job title: Project Manager, Zogby International

Salary range for jobs like this: $50,000–$60,000

Day-to-day responsibilities: Most inquiries come into our office via the Internet or by phone. Lots of times, people will call and not have a concrete idea of what they need, so I will help them determine what information they want to obtain and help figure out how to go about getting that information, whether from an Internet poll, a telephone poll, or any of our other measurement tools. I work on the project from start to finish. We price the poll, hammer out the questionnaire; and when the project begins, I remain in contact with the clients to be sure they are getting the information that will be the most useful to them. I also oversee some of our testing sessions, like the dial-testing sessions, where people use this little handheld wireless device so we get real-time responses to stimuli. I also coordinate focus groups and go to most focus groups throughout the country. If a project has any needs that fall outside a particular department—presenting clients, securing translation services—that's part of my job.

How did you get your job? Hamilton sociology students are required to write a senior thesis and also to come to Zogby and make fifteen complete survey calls. We had constructed a survey measure of Arab American youth, and it was really difficult to get people to talk about these hot-button issues right after September 11. After graduating, I knew I wanted to do research, and I moved to Los Angeles to do market research. After a while, I started thinking, "Who cares if Tigger is going to sell more than Pooh?" I knew if I were doing opinion research, I could really get into much more stuff. So I moved back home and kept calling Zogby until I was brought in for an interview.

What do you like best about your job? It's just so exciting, knowing what's going on, getting an inside look into what people think. We recently hired a former newspaper reporter who commented she would miss knowing everything that was going on. But then she realized that we are creating the news, and that's a very exciting thing.

What is your least favorite aspect of your job? There is nothing that is that bad. Though I guess there are so many clients that I don't get a chance to bring a candidate's campaign to the next level, to be involved in developing a client's marketing strategy when I feel really strongly about an issue or a candidate.

What advice would you give to students who would like to do what you're doing? If students are interested in this type of work, they should take a couple of statistics courses. We use SPSS (a statistical computer program), and it is important to learn to use it and to take a survey research course, so they have a better understanding of how polls are written. It also helps to be involved; the résumés that stand out are the ones where someone's been involved in a local political campaign. Being a creative thinker also helps—someone who can think about new ways of doing the kinds of things our clients need. For example, we're working on ways of developing text message polling and online focus groups. Of course, being well versed in technology and computers helps in this kind of career.

shown in Figure 6.4, the 2007 data, in which 51 percent of Americans expressed trust in the government's handling of international problems, continued to display a steady decline since a record-high 83 percent of the survey respondents indicated a great deal or fair amount of trust immediately following the September 11 terrorist attacks.

The public's trust in the government's ability to handle domestic matters has also declined, as shown in Figure 6.5, which indicates a decrease in the number of people who trust the government to handle domestic problems a great deal or a fair amount since the record highs after September 11, 2001. Notably, a significant dip in the assessment of the government's ability to handle domestic matters occurred in 2005, immediately after Hurricane Katrina devastated parts of Louisiana, Mississippi, and other southern states. The widely perceived inability of the government to manage this crisis is reflected in this drop in confidence, and confidence has continued to decline as the nation's worries about the economy have persisted into 2008. The low levels of confidence seen in 2007 rival the record low confidence levels of 51 to 49 percent seen in the period between 1974 and 1976, following the Watergate scandal.

The public's trust in governmental institutions has also been affected by the impact both of the

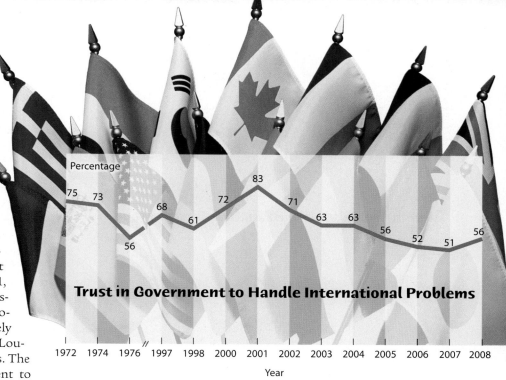

Trust in Government to Handle International Problems

Percentage

75 73 56 68 61 72 83 71 63 63 56 52 51 56

1972 1974 1976 // 1997 1998 2000 2001 2002 2003 2004 2005 2006 2007 2008

Year

FIGURE 6.4 ■ As you can see, as of 2008, public trust in the government's ability to deal with international problems matches what it was during 1976, after the end of the Vietnam War. Is the Iraq War the only contributing factor, or can you think of other events or situations that may have affected the public's judgment?

Source: Jeffrey M. Jones, "Trust in Government," The Gallup Poll, www.gallup.com/poll/5392/Trust-Government.aspx.

Trust in Government to Handle Domestic Problems

Year

1972 1974 1976 // 1997 1998 2000 2001 2002 2003 2004 2005 2006 2007 2008

70 51 49 51 65 58 77 63 58 61 53 52 47 48

Percentage

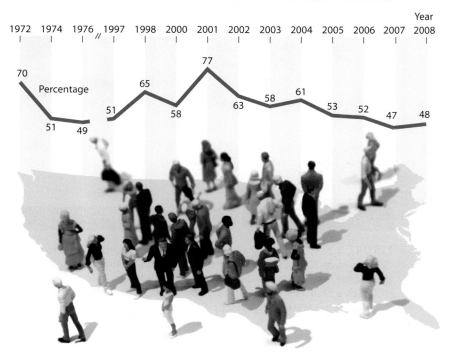

FIGURE 6.5 ■ What impact does the state of the economy have on the public's trust in the government's ability to handle domestic problems? What can you infer about the state of the economy in May 1972? In September 2004? In September 2008?

Source: Jeffrey M. Jones, "Trust in Government," The Gallup Poll, www.gallup.com/poll/5392/Trust-Government.aspx.

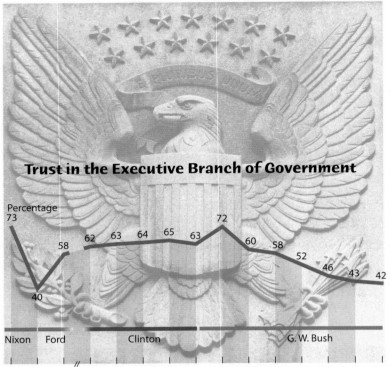

Trust in the Executive Branch of Government

Percentage
73
58
40
62 63 64 65 63
72
60 58
52
46 43 42

Nixon   Ford   Clinton   G. W. Bush

1972 1974 1976 1997 1998 1999 2000 2001 2002 2003 2004 2005 2006 2007 2008

Year

POLITICAL INQUIRY

FIGURE 6.6 ■ As the graph shows, the public's trust in the executive branch declined steeply (from 73 percent to 40 percent in two years) during the Nixon presidency as a result of the Watergate scandal. The decline during George W. Bush's presidency has been more gradual, from 72 percent to 42 percent in six years. Is this decline partly to be expected for any second-term president?

Source: Jeffrey M. Jones, "Trust in Government," The Gallup Poll, www.gallup.com/poll/5392/Trust-Government.aspx.

terrorist attacks of September 11 and weariness with the Iraq War. Indeed, in 2007 the level of public trust in the executive and legislative branches was at a near-record low. As Figure 6.6 shows, for example, in 2007 public trust in the executive branch dropped to 43 percent, marking a 9-percentage-point decline from 2005. The only time the level of public trust in the executive branch was lower (at 40 percent) since Gallup began measuring trust in institutions was in 1974, at the height of the Watergate scandal and just months before Richard Nixon resigned the presidency.[39] As previously noted, the decline in trust in the institution of the presidency is closely related to public approval of individual presidents: in the 2007 survey, only 36 percent of those surveyed approved of the way President Bush was handling his job.

Often there is an inverse relation in levels of trust between the executive and the legislative branches (when one enjoys high levels of trust, the other suffers low). This was not the case in 2007, however. As Figure 6.7 shows, trust in

Percentage
71
68
61
54
61
57
68
65 67
63
60
62
56
50
47

Trust in the Legislative Branch of Government

1972 1974 1976 1997 1998 1999 2000 2001 2002 2003 2004 2005 2006 2007 2008

Year

POLITICAL INQUIRY

FIGURE 6.7 ■ Trust in the legislative branch has plummeted from 62 percent in 2005 to 47 percent in 2008. What factors can explain this trend? Why do you believe that trust in both the executive and the legislative branches was low from 2006 to 2008, despite the fact that those branches were controlled by different political parties?

Source: Jeffrey M. Jones, "Trust in Government," The Gallup Poll, www.gallup.com/poll/5392/Trust-Government.aspx.

FIGURE 6.8 ■ Trust in the judicial branch is consistently high, but it has been lower than usual since 2003, with ratings consistently below 70 percent—especially in 2004, when the percentage almost reached the Watergate level. What could have caused these ratings to dip?

Source: Jeffrey M. Jones, "Trust in Government," The Gallup Poll, www.gallup.com/poll/5392/Trust-Government.aspx.

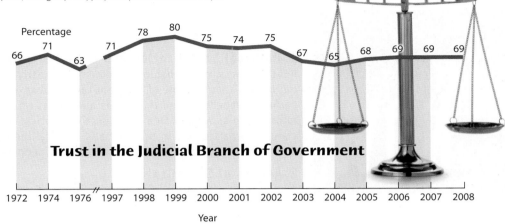

Trust in the Judicial Branch of Government

Percentage

66 71 63 71 78 80 75 74 75 67 65 68 69 69 69

1972 1974 1976 1997 1998 1999 2000 2001 2002 2003 2004 2005 2006 2007 2008

Year

the legislative branch also declined to 50 percent from 62 percent in 2005. Before 2006, part of this decline of trust could be attributed to the public's dissatisfaction with the Republican Congress's consent to Bush administration policies concerning Iraq. But since 2006, the continuing decline indicates widespread dissatisfaction with the Democratic majority in Congress. Public dissatisfaction could be attributed to the Democrats' inability to make good on their campaign promise to end the war in Iraq, as well as dissatisfaction with the U.S. economy.

The judicial branch of government consistently scores higher in levels of public trust than the other two branches. Figure 6.8 shows that confidence in the judiciary typically hovers between 65 and 75 percent, sometimes climbing into the high 70s (or even 80 percent in 1999). The judiciary's lowest rating came in 1976, when there was widespread dissatisfaction with government as a whole in the aftermath of the Watergate scandal.

CONCLUSION

CONTINUING THE CONVERSATION

The process of political socialization is quite different from even a generation ago. While some agents of socialization such as families, peers, and churches remain important, other agents, particularly the media, are more pervasive and influential than ever before. Although television and radio have played a part in socializing the average 40-year-old in 2009, today's young people are almost constantly bombarded by various forms of media, which may influence their viewpoints, priorities, behaviors, and opinions.

Technology has also drastically changed the way public opinion is measured. The advent of the computer alone—from powerful mainframes to personal computers—has revolutionized the data collection process; today computers facilitate near-instant access to polling data. They also provide the means to generate and survey increasingly representative samples in order to gauge the public's views with a high degree of accuracy.

The catch-22, however, has been the pervasiveness of public opinion polls. People's opinions are solicited by every kind of survey from cheesy Internet polls to reputable polling organizations. As a result, the public has become poll weary, dubious of the value of the pollster's next set of questions.

But technology has provided—and will continue to provide—ways to solve the problems that technology itself has generated in accurately measuring public opinion. Stratified samples and other increasingly sophisticated microsampling techniques have improved the ability of reputable pollsters to gauge public opinion. And pollsters are incorporating new technologies, including text messaging and cell phone surveys, as they work to develop new ways to accurately measure and convey the public's views to candidates, to policy makers, and, through the media, to the public itself.

Summary

1. Political Socialization and Civic Participation

Political socialization begins at home in very early childhood, when our political ideology, our beliefs about people of different races and sexes, and even our party identification can be firmly embedded, and the beliefs and values we learn early help shape how we view new information as we age. One key aspect of political socialization is whether children are socialized to participate in the civic and political life of their communities. Families, schools, and media all contribute to whether and how people participate.

2. Agents of Socialization

Among the agents of socialization—including family, the media, schools, churches, peers, community and political leaders, and demographic characteristics—the most important are the family and the media. Family shapes our political values and ideology from childhood and has a strong impact on our political perspective. The media now rival the family in the influence that they have in shaping our views and informing our opinions. A person's level of religiosity is actually a more important influence than his or her actual belief structure so that, in general, very religious people of all faiths have more in common with each other than with less religious people of the same faith. Demographic characteristics—including race and ethnicity, gender, age, and geographic region—not only contribute to how we are socialized to political and community life and our values and priorities but also influence the candidates we vote for.

3. Measuring Public Opinion

The measurement of public opinion has evolved and become increasingly complex and reliable when done scientifically, though the proliferation of questionable straw polls on the Internet, similar to the initial attempts to predict presidential elections in the early twentieth century, still offers dubious results to the gullible. In measuring public opinion, reputable pollsters identify the target population, design an accurate measure, select a sample, and administer the poll. Through various methods of sampling, pollsters attempt to select a subset of the population that is representative of the population's views. Different types of polls, including tracking polls, push polls, and exit polls, are used for different purposes in political campaigns.

4. What Americans Think About Politics

Americans identify the state of the economy as the "most important problem," replacing the war in Iraq as their top concern. Polls also indicate that their overall satisfaction with the direction the country is headed in is low. Among the three branches of government, people's trust in both the presidency and Congress is at near-record lows, while trust in the judiciary remains relatively stable.

For Review

1. How are political socialization and civic participation linked?

2. Explain in detail the agents of socialization. How does each agent have an impact on an individual's political views over a lifetime?

3. What demographic characteristics contribute to how individuals view politics?

4. How did public opinion polls evolve historically?

5. Explain how public opinion polls are conducted.

6. What factors have an impact on what Americans perceive as the "most important problem"?

7. Describe the most recent trend regarding Americans' trust in government.

For Critical Thinking and Discussion

1. Were you brought up in a family in which joining groups was important? Do your parents belong to any interest groups? Do you? If not, why do you think that is the case?

2. How have your demographic characteristics—your age, the area of the country in which you were raised—contributed to the formation of your political views? How relevant are the generalities described in the chapter to your own experience and beliefs?

3. What do you think is the "most important problem" facing the United States? Is it a problem discussed in this book? Is it one shared by your classmates?

4. What factors influence how satisfied you feel about the direction of the country?

5. Which branch of government do you trust the most? Why?

MULTIPLE CHOICE: Choose the lettered item that answers the question correctly.

1. The public's expressed views about an issue at a specific point in time are called
   a. aggregate viewpoint.
   b. net view.
   c. public opinion.
   d. cumulative opinion.

2. Individuals, organizations, and institutions that facilitate the acquisition of political views are called
   a. agents of socialization.
   b. viewfinders.
   c. transmitters.
   d. behavior shapers.

3. A statistical calculation of the difference in results between a poll of a sample and a poll of an entire population is called
   a. randomization process.
   b. quota sampling.
   c. margin of error.
   d. all of the above.

4. Polls conducted at polling places on Election Day in order to determine the winner of an election before the polls close are called
   a. exit polls.   c. push polls.
   b. tracking polls.   d. Internet polls.

5. The group of people whose opinions are of interest and/or about whom information is desired is called
   a. a random sample.
   b. the population.
   c. the measurement group.
   d. the control group.

6. A special type of poll that both provides information to campaigns about candidate strengths and weaknesses and attempts to skew public opinion about a candidate is called a(n)
   a. exit poll.   c. push poll.
   b. tracking poll.   d. straw poll.

7. A process of random sampling in which the national population is divided into fourths and certain areas are selected as representative of the national population is called
   a. random sampling.
   b. quota sampling.
   c. stratified sampling.
   d. skewed sampling.

8. A method by which pollsters structure a sample so that it is representative of the characteristics of the target population is called
   a. random sampling.
   b. quota sampling.
   c. stratified sampling.
   d. skewed sampling.

9. A poll used to predict election outcomes but conducted in an unscientific manner is called a(n)
   a. exit poll.   c. push poll.
   b. tracking poll.   d. straw poll.

10. Polls that measure changes in public opinion over the course of days, weeks, or months by repeatedly asking respondents the same questions and measuring changes in their responses are called a(n)
    a. exit polls.   c. push polls.
    b. tracking polls.   d. straw polls.

FILL IN THE BLANKS.

11. The presence of two conditions or traits that pull a voter toward different parties is called _____.

12. A _____ is a survey of a given population's opinion on an issue or a candidate at a particular point in time.

13. The impact of an important external event in shaping the views of a generation is called a _____.

14. The process by which we develop our political values and opinions is called _____.

15. A scientific method of selection in which each member of the population has an equal chance at being included in the sample is called _____.

Answers: 1. c; 2. a; 3. c; 4. a; 5. b; 6. c; 7. c; 8. b; 9. d; 10. b; 11. cross pressuring; 12. public opinion poll; 13. generational effect; 14. political socialization; 15. random sampling

RESOURCES FOR RESEARCH AND ACTION

Internet Resources

American Democracy Now Web Site
www.mhhe.com/harrison1e   Consult the book's Web site for study guides, interactive activities, simulations, and current hot-links and for additional information on socialization and public opinion in the United States.

Annenberg National Election Studies
www.electionstudies.org   The ANES Web site contains a plethora of information on American public opinion as well as a valuable user guide that can help acquaint you with using the data. It also provides a link to other election studies, including some cross-national studies at www.electionstudies.org/other_election_studies.

The Gallup Organization
www.galluppoll.com   You will find both national and international polls and analysis on this site.

The Roper Center
www.ropercenter.uconn.edu   This Web site features the University of Connecticut's Roper Center polls, the General Social Survey, presidential approval ratings, and poll analysis.

Zogby International
www.zogby.com   For a wide variety of political, commercial, and sociological data, go to this site.

Recommended Readings

Fiorina, Morris P. *Culture War: The Myth of a Polarized America.* New York: Pearson Longman, 2006. A critical view of the notion that the United States is divided along ideological lines. Fiorina asserts that Americans are generally moderate and tolerant of a wide variety of viewpoints.

Jacobson, Gary. *A Divider, Not a Uniter: George W. Bush and the American People, The 2006 Election and Beyond.* New York: Longman, 2007. A data-driven analysis that asserts that the Bush presidency has polarized politics in the United States.

Jamieson, Kathleen Hall. *Electing the President, 2004.* Philadelphia: University of Pennsylvania, 2006. A fascinating "insider's view" of how public opinion shaped the 2004 presidential campaigns by the director of the Annenberg National Election Studies.

Page, Benjamin I., and Robert Y. Shapiro. *The Rational Public: Fifty Years of Trends in Americans' Policy Preferences.* Chicago: University of Chicago, 1992. An analysis of the policy preferences of the American public from the 1930s until 1990. The authors describe opinion on both domestic and foreign policy.

Traugott, Michael W., and Paul J. Lavrakas. *The Voter's Guide to Election Polls.* New York: Chatham House, 2000. A user-friendly approach, written in question-and-answer format, that helps beginners understand the polling process and how to interpret public opinion data.

Welch, Susan, Lee Sigelman, Timothy Bledsoe, and Michael Combs. *Race and Place: Race Relations in an American City* (Cambridge Studies in Public Opinion and Political Psychology). Cambridge: Cambridge University Press, 2001. An analysis of the impact of residential changes on the attitudes and behavior of African Americans and whites.

Movies of Interest

18in08 (2008)
Haverford college student David Burstein produced this film in which students, activists, policy makers, and members of Congress discuss the importance and impact of voting (www.18in08.com).

Lions for Lambs (2007)
Directed by Robert Redford and starring Redford, Meryl Streep, and Tom Cruise, this film about a platoon of U.S. soldiers in Afghanistan demonstrates the influence educational socialization can have on individuals.

Wag the Dog (1997)
A classic Barry Levinson film featuring a spin-doctor (Robert De Niro) and a Hollywood producer (Dustin Hoffman) who team up eleven days before an election to "fabricate" a war in order to cover up a presidential sex scandal.

National Journal

THE PEOPLE V. WASHINGTON

Alexander Hamilton famously labeled public opinion "a great beast." The notion is that vital matters of state are best left to well-informed professional elites, not to the masses. And if the people don't like an adopted course of action, this reasoning goes, they can always vote out its representatives.

To give the argument its due, it is certainly true that the American public wins no medals for mastery of world geography and the intricacies of foreign politics and culture.

And yet there is a difference between knowledge and judgment. Even in a republic like the United States the unknowledgeable are presumed to possess a capacity, or at least a potential, for good judgment. Otherwise, why permit the average citizen to vote at all?

In early 2007, President Bush informed the nation of his decision to increase the number of U.S. troops in Iraq by about 20,000 as the key element in his new strategy for "a way forward" in the conflict. Bush's plan was based on extensive consultations with foreign-policy and military experts of various stripes, inside and outside the administration. No doubt he received a variety of opinions. But let's consider what "The People" think.

More than five years have passed since the 9/11 attacks, which inaugurated the administration's global war on terrorism and put into play the question of whether to invade Iraq. Over this period, all major polling outfits have been taking the public's pulse at regular intervals on just about every imaginable national security question.

These data indeed tell an interesting story, at odds with certain myths that have taken root about the public's mind-set on Iraq. Perhaps vox populi is a beast. But it is a beast with some fascinating things to say—about its initial attitudes on the Iraq war, about its sentiments as the war has ground on, about what it thinks is "a way forward" on Iraq, and, beyond Iraq, about America's role in the post-9/11 world.

On the eve of the Iraq invasion in March 2003, virtually every major opinion poll showed a solid majority of Americans—64 percent of respondents in the Gallup/CNN/USA Today poll, 59 percent in the Princeton Survey Research Associates/Pew Research Center poll—in favor of taking military action to remove Saddam Hussein from power. From these high numbers, a certain conventional wisdom developed about the public's support for the war.

The saga goes like this: The public backed a war whose rationale was sold, like a product, by the Bush administration and affiliated hucksters and never really challenged by a cowed and gullible news media.

A stream of public opinion surveys suggests . . . that **the federal government is following a misplaced set** of national security priorities.

Team Bush's own pronouncements buttress this story line. In explaining the White House's slow start in the summer of 2002 in putting together a plan to rally the public around the need to confront Saddam, Andy Card, at that point Bush's chief of staff, famously told The New York Times early in September 2002: "From a marketing point of view, you don't introduce new products in August."

According to this plot sequence, public opinion went over to the war camp as a result of the administration's fear-mongering statements about Saddam's weapons of mass destruction capabilities. Just days before the first anniversary of 9/11, on September 8, 2002, then-National Security Adviser Condoleezza Rice said on CNN, "We don't want the smoking gun to be a mushroom cloud."

The problem with this marketing-based account is that it is a myth. In the PSRA/Pew Research Center poll, public support for "military action in Iraq to end Saddam Hussein's rule" was 64 percent in an August 14-25, 2002, survey, before the administration's PR blitz, and at 64 percent in a September 12-14 survey, in the three days following Bush's Ground Zero visit. In the

September 26–27 poll, support was 63 percent. Where's the bounce?

In fact, nearly all polls recorded their highest backing for war in the months immediately after the 9/11 attacks, when Washington was not talking much about invading Iraq. In November 2001, public support for military action against Iraq was at 78 percent in the ABC News/Washington Post poll, 77 percent in Fox News/Opinion Dynamics, and 74 percent in Gallup/CNN/USA Today. During the buildup to war that culminated in the invasion 17 months later, those numbers never went higher. This suggests a fierce, if misguided, reaction to the attacks. As everyone now acknowledges, Saddam was not behind 9/11.

Just days after the invasion began on March 20, 2003, 23 percent of respondents said United States had "made a mistake"—that's the key phrase—"in view of the developments since we first sent our troops to Iraq." Because at that starting juncture, virtually no "developments" to speak of had taken place, the 23 percent can be seen as the slice of the people who had already made up their minds about the war. 75 percent said, no, the war was not a mistake. Only 2 percent registered no opinion.

The Gallup consortium kept asking that question. But despite early waves of good news—light casualties, the fall of Baghdad on April 9, Bush's declaration on May 1 of the end of "major combat"—the "mistake" number kept rising. By early October, little more than six months after the invasion, it was already up to 40 percent; and it was 42 percent in the first poll taken after the ballyhooed capture of Saddam in his spider hole in mid-December of that first year of the war. The sensational revelations of the Abu Ghraib prison torture scandal, in mid-April 2004, did not move the number much.

The "mistake" cohort reached a majority, 54 percent, for the first time in a poll taken on June 21-23, 2004—15 months after the invasion began, and a week after the 9/11 commission found "no credible evidence" of a link between Iraq and Al Qaeda, as the White House had asserted.

In his second inaugural address, Bush declared, "The survival of liberty in our land increasingly depends on the success of liberty in other lands. The best hope for peace in our world is the expansion of freedom in all the world."

In that speech and others, Bush has, in effect, offered both a diagnosis and a prescription for what ails the post-9/11 world. His premise that a freer world is a more placid one may not seem particularly controversial, or even original. Elites generally applauded. The beast, though, was unconvinced.

Eight months later, the Chicago Council on Foreign Relations released a comprehensive poll, "Americans on Promoting Democracy." In that survey, only 26 percent agreed that "when there are more democracies, the world is a safer place." This was not a reaction against democracy per se. Consider this second, more nuanced finding: 68 percent said that "democracy may make life better within a country, but it does not make the world a safer place."

So, broadly speaking, a stream of public opinion surveys suggests, and has been suggesting for several years, that the federal government is following a misplaced set of national security priorities. And while the people are not speaking with a single voice, majorities favor clear positions—and those majorities seem to be not fickle or mercurial but fairly solid.

With respect to Iraq, the balance of opinion, following the logic of accepting the war as a mistake, is clearly in favor of reducing America's involvement in Iraq. In the December 2006 CBS News poll, 57 percent of respondents favored setting a timetable for withdrawing U.S. troops. In the exit poll of midterm election voters, 55 percent said the United States should withdraw some or all troops, and only 17 percent supported "send more." And these beliefs carry some urgency: In Gallup's first poll after the midterms, Republicans, independents, and Democrats, all by very large margins, listed the situation in Iraq as the "top priority" for Washington to address.

These poll numbers are the stuff of front-page news. But they don't tell the whole story. Iraq is the most urgent public priority because it is an active, bleeding mess. But the public does not view Iraq as the key to dealing with America's principal, long-term problems in the world. The people are not saying to Washington, "Disengage from Iraq and then focus on the problems at home."

Americans have said that their No. 1 priority in the war on terrorism is "increasing CIA and FBI efforts to find and capture suspected terrorists," and the second goal was "capturing or killing Osama bin Laden." Even though Washington no longer talks much about getting the devastator of the twin towers, the public has clung to its wrath—and its demand for blood justice.

The Program on International Policy Attitudes posed the broader question, "What kind of foreign policy does the American public want?" In that survey, respondents listed the issues that they believed deserved greater attention from national policy makers. First was "working to reduce U.S. dependence on oil," followed by "port security," and "coordinating with the intelligence and law en-forcement agencies of other countries to track and capture members of terrorist groups."

The top priority, reducing U.S. reliance on oil, is a sophisticated choice. Stories about oil dependency are not what lead the evening news, and congressional committee chairmen do not make big splashes with hearings on the subject. "Reducing oil dependency"—a goal that lends itself to quantitative measurement—may sound prosaic compared with "the expansion of freedom in all of the world." No spines tingle at the phrase. But the beast, it seems, is in a mood for prose, not poetry.

The People, to boil things down, think three big things: Washington should disengage from the military conflict in Iraq, take out bin Laden and all other known terrorists who mean America lethal harm, and reduce the nation's dependence on oil.

Two days before the 2006 midterm elections, ABC's George Stephanopoulos noted in an interview with Vice President Dick Cheney, "It seems like the public has turned against" the administration's policy on Iraq. Cheney responded, "It may not be popular with the public. It doesn't matter, in the sense that we have to continue the mission and do what we think is right, and that's exactly what we're doing."

The Iraq debacle is unavoidably calling into question the horse sense of the political establishment. "I would rather be governed by the first 2,000 names in the Boston phone book than by the 2,000 members of the faculty of Harvard University," William F. Buckley Jr. once quipped. Buckley was getting at the idea that ordinary citizens in a democracy can possess a certain collective wisdom. He also once said, less notably, "The best defense against usurpatory government is an assertive citizenry."

THEN: Public opinion supported the war, and policy seemed to reflect the popular will of the people.

NOW: Public opinion has turned against the war, and one question remains, whether policy should reflect the will of the people or guide the will of the people.

NEXT: Will public opinion persuade the new administration to alter U.S. priorities in the global war on terrorism? What foreign policy initiative will the new administration work to rally the public around? Will public opinion lead policy makers and industry to find ways to reduce U.S. dependence on foreign oil?

CHAPTER

7

Interest
Groups

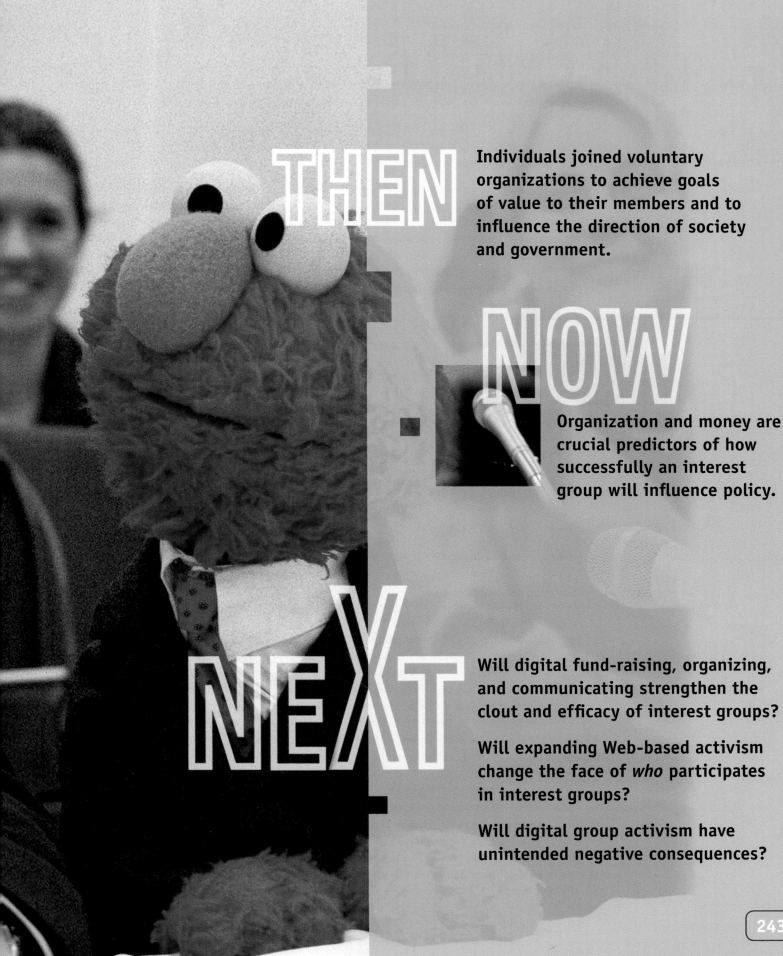

THEN

Individuals joined voluntary organizations to achieve goals of value to their members and to influence the direction of society and government.

NOW

Organization and money are crucial predictors of how successfully an interest group will influence policy.

NEXT

Will digital fund-raising, organizing, and communicating strengthen the clout and efficacy of interest groups?

Will expanding Web-based activism change the face of *who* participates in interest groups?

Will digital group activism have unintended negative consequences?

Advocating for Immigration Reform

In December 2005 Representative James Sensenbrenner (R-Wisconsin) introduced a bill in the House of Representatives that sought to "amend the Immigration and Nationality Act to strengthen enforcement of the immigration laws, to enhance border security, and for other purposes."* House Resolution 4437 passed in the House and was introduced in the Senate. If it had become law, it would have classified all undocumented workers and U.S. citizens who harbor and employ them as "aggravated felons." I Sensenbrenner's bill came about as the result of a crisis playing out in communities throughout the nation. The need for cheap labor—in the cities, as restaurant workers, landscapers, and laborers; and in the countryside, as farm workers who plant and harvest the majority of the nation's produce—has created a subeconomy in which immigration law is largely ignored by the businesses that need the labor. Consumers share culpability because without the labor of illegal aliens, the prices of many products and services would increase. And so businesses and consumers have benefited from a vast pool of cheap immigrant labor. But communities have been forced to pay the price, with low-wage immigrant workers increasing the demand for social services and taxing the resources of public schools. I Many interest groups aggressively lobbied House members to support their position and were a force in the passage of H.R. 4437 in the House. In contrast, the opposing interest groups pressing for immigrant rights were largely scattered and ineffective insofar as their impact on national policy was concerned. Nevertheless, H.R. 4437 galvanized a wide array of these groups, including immigration advocates within the Roman Catholic church, many labor unions, and Latino organizations such as the civil rights advocacy group La Raza. These diverse organizations, which seemed to have little else in common, began to unite around the cause of immigration reform. I In the spring of 2006, immigrant rights groups mobilized

> A sign warning motorists to watch for migrant workers crossing the highway near the border between California and Mexico.

hundreds of thousands of immigrants and their supporters in cities throughout the United States to rally for the defeat of H.R. 4437 in the Senate. A demonstration in Los Angeles attracted more than 500,000 people—the largest such turnout in the city's history. Rallies in Washington, D.C., New York, Chicago, Detroit, Oklahoma City, Knoxville, and several other cities drew unexpectedly large crowds supporting immigrant rights. In Sensenbrenner's home state of Wisconsin, the advocacy group Voces de la Frontera organized "A Day Without Latinos" in Milwaukee, urging Latino immigrant workers to strike so as to demonstrate the impact of their work on the city's economy. This idea spread to cities throughout the nation, and Latinos and other immigrants were urged to boycott non–immigrant-owned businesses on designated days. I As a result of the protests, H.R. 4437 died in the Senate Judiciary Committee. Further, although Congress has passed some incremental measures affecting immigration law, none of the more sweeping proposals for immigration reform have succeeded in garnering enough support. Despite the failure of comprehensive immigration reform, interest groups concerned about immigrant rights have succeeded in a number of ways—in particular, by calling attention to immigration as a pressing public policy issue. They have also given diverse groups new opportunities to work together to push for a solution. Indeed, Congress's failure to act on immigration reform demonstrates how effective groups on both sides of this issue have been at lobbying for their side: members of Congress have listened and now must struggle to create a compromise policy.

*You can read all about the bill at the Library of Congress Thomas site: http://thomas.loc.gov/cgi-bin/bdquery/z?d109:HR04437:@@@P.

Organizations that seek to

achieve their goals by influencing government decision making are called **interest groups.** Also called *special interests,* interest groups differ from political parties in that interest groups do not seek to control the government, as parties do. Interest groups simply want to influence policy making on issues. Interest groups are more important in the political process of the United States than anywhere else in the world.[1] Their strong role is partly due to the number of interest groups that attempt to influence U.S. policy.

Take just one issue—the environment, say—and chances are that you or someone in your class is a member of one of the almost 200 organizations concerned with the environment, conservation, or ecology in the United States.[2] The multitude of interest groups focused on any given issue is an important component of how government policy is formulated. Interest groups shape the policy process by helping determine which issues policy makers will act on and which options they will consider in addressing a problem.

When we think of interest groups, the typical images that come to mind are of wealthy lobbyists "schmoozing" with easily corrupted politicians. While this may sometimes be the case, this chapter's "American Democracy Now" vignette illustrates that interest groups do not require the leadership of the rich and well connected to be effective. In this case, the organized effort of the least powerful members of society demonstrated that through collective action, people from all walks of life can influence policy making. Although moneyed interests may dominate politics, interest groups play a crucial role in leveling the political playing field by providing access for organized "average" people.

In this chapter, we survey the composition, power, and strategies of interest groups in the United States. We explore the development of interest groups over time and analyze what makes an interest group successful.

FIRST, we examine *the value of interest groups* as tools of citizen participation.

SECOND, we consider the questions of *who joins interest groups, and why.*

THIRD, we examine *how interest groups succeed.*

FOURTH, we look at various *types of interest groups.*

FIFTH, we focus on *interest group strategies.*

SIXTH, we probe the intersection of *interest groups, politics, and money:* specifically, *the influence of political action committees.*

The Value of Interest Groups

The nineteenth-century French historian and writer Alexis de Tocqueville, author of the influential work *Democracy in America,* dubbed Americans "a nation of joiners" in 1835, and his analysis still rings true today.[3] Indeed, estimates indicate that about 80 percent of all Americans belong to some kind of voluntary group or association, although not every group is an interest group.[4] The key role interest groups would play in politics was foreseen by the founders—James Madison acknowledged the idea that people with similar interests would form and join groups to prompt government action. He believed that the only way to cure "the mischiefs of faction" was by enabling groups to proliferate and compete with one another.[5]

Yet despite this heritage, some contemporary scholars argue that Americans today are increasingly staying at home. Political scientist Robert Putnam, author of *Bowling Alone: The Collapse and Revival of American Community,* found a marked decrease in the number of people who belong to interest groups and other types of clubs and organizations. These organizations, Putnam argues, are essential sources of **social capital,** the relationships that improve our lives by giving us social connections with which to solve common problems. Putnam demonstrates that social capital improves individual lives in very concrete ways: those with a greater number of social ties live longer, happier, and healthier lives. But social capital also improves communities, and even larger polities, because it stimulates individuals to communicate and interact with their government. Efficacy increases, because when people are engaged and communicate with government officials, government responds by meeting their needs more effectively. This response in turn creates the feeling among individuals that government listens to people like them. And when government responds, it becomes more likely that those affected will try to influence government decisions again.[6]

interest groups
organizations that seek to achieve some of their goals by influencing government decision making

social capital
the ways in which our lives are improved in many ways by social connections

> Can a conversation over a skim latte create social capital? People may not be joining gardening clubs, but are they really less connected than in the past? Or are their connections just different?

Critics of Putnam's work have noted that although the number of people belonging to the kinds of groups Putnam analyzed may be declining, people are engaged in other types of groups and clubs and enjoy various forms of group recreation.[7] For example, it is unlikely that you are a member of a gardening club such as those that Putnam researched (but if you are, good for you!). Yet it is likely that you belong to an online community such as MySpace or Facebook. Such communities facilitate social relationships and may even provide the opportunity for participants to solve community problems. And although people may be less likely to entertain friends and relatives in their homes today (another activity Putnam measured), they are *more likely* to socialize with friends and relatives over meals in restaurants. So even if Putnam may be correct in his analysis that we are no longer socially engaged the way Americans used to be, we may still be engaged—but through different channels and in different settings. Research supports this interpretation: in 2005, more than one-quarter of college freshmen surveyed said they believed that it was important to participate in community action programs, and over two-thirds said they believed it was important to help others in need, *the highest proportion to say so in twenty-five years.*[8]

Political scientist E. E. Schattschneider has written, "Democracy is a competitive political system in which competing leaders and organizations define the alternatives of public policy in such a way that the public can participate in the decision-making process."[9] One of the key types of competitive organizations Schattschneider was describing is interest groups. Schattschneider and other political scientists study and assess the value that interest groups provide in American democracy. This value centrally includes interest groups' usefulness in channeling civic participation—serving as a point of access and a mechanism by which people can connect with their government. Political scientists also explore interest groups, on the one hand, as valuable avenues by which people can influence the policy process and, on the other hand, as resources for policy makers. In this section we consider various perspectives on the role of interest groups in a democracy, the diverse value that interest groups confer, and the drawbacks of interest groups.

Interest Groups and Civic Participation

Scholars who study civic engagement acknowledge the significant ways in which interest groups channel civic participation. Interest groups afford a way for people to band together to influence government as a *collective force*. Interest groups also seek to involve *individuals* more actively in the political process by encouraging them to vote and to communicate their views one-on-one to their elected officials. In addition, interest groups assist in the engagement of *communities* by providing a forum through which people can come together and form an association. Importantly, too, interest groups offer an alternative means of participation to individuals who are disenchanted with the two-party system.

The power of interest groups is evident in the recent initiatives of immigration rights groups, discussed in this chapter's "American Democracy Now." It is also evident in the efforts of the women's rights interest groups who successfully influenced government policy in the 1960s (see Chapter 5). By taking part in interest groups, individuals, acting together, perform important roles in the polity not only by communicating their viewpoints to policy makers but also by providing a medium that other people can use to express their opinions.

Pluralist Theory vs. Elite Theory

An interest group can represent a wide variety of interests, as in the case of a community Chamber of Commerce that serves as an umbrella organization for local businesses. Alternatively, an interest group can restrict itself to a narrower focus, as does the Society for the Preservation and Encouragement of Barbershop Quartet Singing. Scholars who support **pluralist theory** emphasize how important it is for a democracy to have large numbers of diverse interest groups representing a wide variety of views.[10] Indeed, pluralists view the policy-making process as a crucial competition among diverse groups whose members attempt to influence policy in numerous settings, including agencies in the executive branch of government, Congress, and the courts.[11] Pluralists believe that interest groups are essential players in democracy because they ensure that individual interests are represented in the political arena *even if some individuals opt not to participate*. Like some of the founders, pluralists argue that individuals' liberties can be protected only through a proliferation of groups representing diverse competing interests, so that no one group dominates.

Pluralists believe, moreover, that interest groups provide a structure for political participation and help ensure that individuals follow the rules in participating in civic society. Following the rules means using positive channels for government action rather than extreme tactics such as assassinations, coups, and other forms of violence. Pluralists also stress that groups' varying assets tend to counterbalance one another, as demonstrated in this chapter's "American Democracy Now." Pluralists contend that this is frequently the case with many policy debates. And so although an industry association such as the American Petroleum Institute, an interest group for the oil and natural gas industry, might have a lot of money at its disposal, an environmental group opposing the industry, such as Greenpeace, might have a large membership base from which to launch grassroots activism.

Proponents of elite theory dispute some claims of pluralist theory. In particular, elite theorists point to the overwhelming presence of elites as political decision makers. According to **elite theory,** a ruling class composed of wealthy, educated individuals wields most of the power in government and also within the top universities, corporations, the military, and media outlets. Elite theorists claim that despite appearances that the political system is accessible to all, elites hold disproportionate power in the United States. They also emphasize that elites commonly use that power to protect their own economic interests, frequently by ensuring the continuation of the status quo. And so while non-elites represented by interest groups may occasionally win political victories, elites control the direction of major policies directions. But elite theorists posit that there is mobility into the elite structure. They emphasize that (in contrast to the situation in aristocracies) talented and industrious individuals

How Group Participation Has Changed in the United States

THEN (1960s)	NOW (2009)
Individuals joined bowling leagues, civic associations, and community service organizations.	People join Internet-based organizations and use social-networking sites to keep in touch with others who share their personal and public interests.
Many people entertained and socialized a great deal at home.	People are more likely to visit with friends and relatives in restaurants, cafés, and other public settings, as well as online through "virtual visits."
Groups used traditional activities to communicate their interests to policy makers, including letter writing and lobbying.	Groups rely on traditional activities but also increasingly use new technologies to communicate with members, to fund-raise, and to lobby policy makers.

WHAT'S NEXT?

> What new media technologies and strategies might shape how interest groups organize and mobilize members in the future?

> Are there *negative* consequences to relying on the Internet as an organizing tool? What obstacles will some Internet-based organizations face in mobilizing their supporters around a given issue?

> In what ways will technology change how policy makers are influenced in the future?

pluralist theory
a theory that holds policy making is a competition among diverse interest groups that ensure the representation of individual interests

elite theory
a theory that holds that a group of wealthy, educated individuals wields most political power

> After their son, Ensign John Elliott, was killed by a drunk driver in 2001, Bill and Muriel Elliott campaigned to have "John's Law" passed in New Jersey. John's Law requires a twelve-hour impoundment of the vehicles driven by those arrested on DUI charges. Because of the Elliotts' Hero Campaign, many states and the federal government have passed versions of John's Law.

from nonelite backgrounds can attain elite status in a democracy, often through education. This mobility, they say, gives the political system an even greater façade of accessibility.

Although these theories offer competing explanations for the role and motivation of interest groups in the United States, many political scientists agree that aspects of both theories are true: elites do have disproportionate influence in policy making, but that power is checked by interest groups. Undisputed is that interest groups are an essential feature of American democracy and provide an important medium through which individuals can exercise some control over their government.

Key Functions of Interest Groups

Many Americans join interest groups, and yet interest groups have a generally negative reputation. For example, it has been said of many a politician that he or she is "in the pockets of the special interests." This statement suggests that the politician is not making decisions based on conscience or the public interest but rather that the individual can be "bought." This notion is closely linked to the ideas held by elite theorists, who argue that elites' disproportionate share of influence negatively impacts the ability of the "average Jill or Joe" to get the government to do what she or he wants it to. Yet despite the criticisms frequently leveled by politicians, pundits, and the populace about interest groups' efforts to influence government, they serve several vital functions in the policy-making process in the United States:

- *Interest groups educate the public about policy issues.* Messages from interest groups abound. For example, thanks to organizations such as Mothers Against Drunk Drivers (MADD), most people are aware of the dangers of drinking and driving. In educating the public, interest groups often provide a vehicle for civic discourse, so that genuine dialogue about policy problems and potential solutions is part of the national agenda.
- *Interest groups provide average citizens with an avenue of access to activism.* Anyone can join or form an interest group. Although wealthy and well-educated people are most likely to do so, interest groups can speak for all kinds of people on all kinds of issues. Historically in the United States, groups have been significant forces for advocates of civil rights for African Americans[12] as well as for supporters of equal rights for women,[13] gays and lesbians, and ethnic minorities. And like the immigration-reform activists described in this chapter's opening vignette, even you and your fellow students can form an interest group—for example, to influence the college administration to take some desired action. This is what happened at Emerson College in Boston, where students in the Emerson Alliance threatened to boycott classes to pressure the college administration to negotiate with the college faculty on pay issues.
- *Interest groups mobilize citizens and stimulate them to participate in civic and political affairs.* Some people are "turned off" by politics because they feel that neither the Democratic nor the Republican party represents their views. In these cases, interest groups, with their typically narrower area of focus, can sometimes fill the void. Moreover, interest groups nurture community involvement by encouraging the formation of local chapters of larger interest groups. They support public education activities by private citizens. And interest groups not only can facilitate the ongoing conversation of democracy between people and their government officials but also encourage voting.
- *Interest groups perform electoral functions.* By endorsing and rating candidates and advertising their positions, interest groups provide voters with cues as to which candidates best represent their views. Interest groups also mobilize campaign volunteers and voters. These activities facilitate informed civic participation.
- *Interest groups provide information and expertise to policy makers.* The private sector often has greater resources than the public sector and can be a source of meaningful data and information for policy makers on pressing social issues.

- *Interest groups can protect the common good.* The federal government is structured so that only one individual (the president) is elected from a national constituency. Interest groups can work to protect the nation's interest as a whole rather than just the needs of a specific constituency.
- *Interest groups are an integral part of the government's system of checks and balances.* Interest groups often "check" each other's influence with competing interests, and they can similarly check the actions of policy makers.

The Downside of Interest Groups

Despite the valuable functions of interest groups, certain criticisms of these organizations are valid. Interest groups do contribute to the appearance of (and sometimes the reality of) corruption in the political system. Indeed, there are various criticisms of the "interest group state." Former president Jimmy Carter bemoaned the influence of special interests, saying that they are "the single greatest threat to the proper functioning of our democratic system," while former president Ronald Reagan charged that interest groups are "placing out of focus our constitutional balance."[14]

Another criticism is that interest groups and their political action committee (PAC) fund-raising arms (which we consider briefly later in this chapter and in more detail in Chapter 9) make money a vital force in American politics. By contributing large sums of money to political campaigns, interest groups' PACs make campaigns expensive and often lopsided; candidates without well-stuffed campaign war chests have a difficult, if not impossible, task in challenging those who receive large PAC contributions. Money also changes the nature of campaigns, making them less engaging for citizens on a grassroots level and more reliant on the mass media.

Interest groups moreover are faulted with strengthening the advantages enjoyed by incumbents. Most interest groups want access to policy makers, regardless of these elected officials' party identification. Realizing that the people already in office are likely to be reelected, interest groups use their resources disproportionately to support incumbent candidates. Doing so increases incumbency advantage even further by improving the odds against a challenger.

Finally, although the option to form an interest group is open to any and all activists and would-be activists, elites are more likely to establish and to dominate interest groups than are nonelites. This fact skews the policy process in favor of elites. Interest group activism is much more prominent among the wealthy, the white, the upper-middle class, and the educated than among the poor, the nonwhite, the working class, and the less educated. Although Internet-based interest groups have been particularly effective in attracting young people and others not traditionally drawn to such organizations, many of the most effective national interest groups remain dominated by traditional interest-group populations.

Who Joins Interest Groups, and Why?

People are not all equally likely to join or form interest groups, and this reality has serious consequences for the ability of interest groups to represent everyone's views. Political scientists agree that income and education tend to be the best predictors of interest-group membership. This said, enormous diversity exists in the types of people who choose to join or form interest groups.

Patterns of Membership

Interest group participation is related to three demographic characteristics: income, social class, and education. People with higher incomes are more likely to participate in interest groups than those with lower incomes. Also, many surveys show that those who identify themselves as upper-middle or middle class are more likely to join interest groups than

WHERE DO YOU STAND?

The Influence of Special-Interest Groups

Do you think the issue of powerful special-interest groups having too much influence on politics is a crisis, a major problem, a minor problem, or not a problem?

☐ Crisis
☐ Major problem
☐ Minor problem
☐ Not a problem

Source: "Gallup's Pulse of Democracy," www .gallup.com/poll/27286/Government.aspx.

> Nancy H. Nielsen, president-elect of the American Medical Association (AMA), announcing the AMA's campaign, "Voice for the Uninsured," at the National Press Club in August 2007. Next to Nielsen is a poster the AMA is using to advertise the problem. Organizations like the AMA offer various incentives for membership, such as accreditation for qualified professionals and political advocacy for members.

those who self-identify as lower-middle or working class. Similarly, higher education levels are a strong predictor of interest group participation. But interest group participation also frequently reflects one's occupation: people tend to belong to associations related to their work.

INTEREST GROUP PARTICIPATION BASED ON OCCUPATION

There are several reasons for interest group membership patterns, some of which, as we shall see, are interconnected. For example, people with higher incomes have more disposable income to spend on membership dues for organizations. They are also likely to have occupations in which interest group activity is useful (or even required, as in some professional fields such as the law).

Doctors and lawyers, for example, are likely to be members of professional associations such as the American Medical Association (AMA) and the American Bar Association. These organizations give incentives for membership, such as accreditation of qualified professionals. They also confer benefits by providing various services to members and by attempting to influence government policy on members' behalf. The AMA accredits qualified physicians, promotes opportunities for continuing education to members, and lobbies the government on policy issues related to health care. During the 2008 presidential campaign, the AMA began a three-year media campaign designed to get the presidential candidates and the new president to tackle the issue of insurance coverage for the estimated 47 million Americans who do not have health insurance. Ads placed in the *New York Times* and *USA Today* feature a person holding a stethoscope as if it were a microphone, and part of the message says that the uninsured have "a voice and a vote."

Workers such as teachers and tradespeople are likely to belong to labor unions.[15] Many labor unions are influential in local politics, generating grassroots support for candidates through their membership base. A few of the national labor unions, especially the National Education Association (NEA), the largest teachers' union in the country, and the American Federation of Labor-Congress of Industrial Organizations (AFL-CIO), an organization of many different labor unions, are strongly influential in national politics.

Executives in business and industry are likely to be members of industry-specific and general business organizations that advocate on behalf of their members. All of these professional associations, labor unions, and business organizations are types of interest groups.

INTEREST GROUP PARTICIPATION AND SOCIAL CLASS Differentiating the influence of income from that of class can be difficult when examining the impact of social class on the likelihood of joining an interest group. But in general, people who identify themselves as working class are less likely to have been socialized to participate in interest groups, with the important exception of labor unions, which historically have been most likely to organize working-class occupations. As we considered in Chapter 6, an important predictor of political participation (and interest group participation, specifically) is whether a person learns to take part and join from a young age. If your mother participated in your town's historical preservation society, and your father attended meetings of the local Amnesty International chapter, you are likely to view those behaviors as "what people do" and do them yourself. If you come from a working-class family, you are generally less likely to see your parents engage in these participatory behaviors, rendering you similarly less likely to participate. Although scholars trace much of the lack of participation of working-class people to how they are socialized, the overlapping occurrence of working-class status and lower income is also a factor.[16] That is, working-class people are likely to have lower incomes and less job security than their middle-class counterparts. Thus they might not be able to afford membership dues and contributions to interest groups or might not have access to child care that would allow them to attend meetings. Their lower likelihood of owning a computer limits their chances of taking an active role in Internet-based groups. Or they might simply lack the leisure time to participate.

INTEREST GROUP PARTICIPATION AND EDUCATION   Educational attainment also has a strong impact on whether a person will join an interest group. One recent study surveyed 19- to 23-year-olds and found that those who were college students were more than twice as likely to join a politically motivated interest group as their age-group peers who did not attend college.[17] Individuals with higher education levels are more likely to be informed about issues and more willing to invest the time and energy in joining an interest group that represents their views. They might also be more likely to understand how important interest groups are in shaping public policy.

College students are among the most avid participants in Internet-based activist groups. But "belonging" to these groups varies a great deal (not unlike the situation in "real-world" interest groups). A member of an Internet-based interest group may play a highly active role—communicating with other members regularly, attending rallies and other campus events, and taking concrete actions such as signing an Internet petition and participating in a protest. Or members may be more passive: they may limit their activity to reading the regular e-mails from the group that inform them of issues and events, and may only occasionally participate. Or they may be members of a group in name only. But this phenomenon is not unique to Internet-based groups. Many interest groups are dominated by a cadre of committed activists supported by "sometimes-activists." And nearly every group has a contingent of "members" who signed up mainly for the free T-shirt, tote bag, or umbrella.

Motivations for Joining Interest Groups

Some people may join an interest group for the benefits they can gain. Others might gravitate to a group sponsoring a particular cause. Still others might become members of a group for the simple reason that they want to meet new people. Recognizing that individuals have various motivations for joining, interest groups typically provide a menu of incentives for membership. As Figure 7.1 shows, for example, the National Association for the Advancement of Colored People (NAACP) offers a wide range of motivations for people to join the group. In doing so, the NAACP, like many other interest groups, attempts to attract as many members as possible.

Source: www.naacp.org/get=involved/membership/fivereasons/index.htm

POLITICAL INQUIRY

FIGURE 7.1 ■ **SOLIDARY, PURPOSIVE, AND ECONOMIC INCENTIVES TO JOIN AN INTEREST GROUP**   What is the NAACP, and what does this interest group advocate? What solidary incentives does the membership appeal described in this figure mention? What purposive and economic incentives does it describe?

SOLIDARY INCENTIVES   Some people join interest groups because they offer **solidary incentives**—the feeling of belonging, companionship, friendship, and the satisfaction derived from socializing with others. Solidary incentives are closely linked to Robert Putnam's idea of social capital: both solidary incentives and social capital are related to the psychological satisfaction derived from civic participation. For example, a person might join the Sierra Club because she wants to participate in activities with other people who enjoy hiking or care deeply about wilderness protection. Your uncle might join the National Rifle Association because he likes to compete in shooting contests and wants to get to know others who do the same.

solidary incentives
motivation to join an interest group based on the companionship and the satisfaction derived from socializing with others that it offers

> Actress Pippa Black poses in an ad for vegetarianism sponsored by People for the Ethical Treatment of Animals (PETA). Many PETA members are motivated by purposive incentives.

Let vegetarianism grow on you

GOVEG.COM

PIPPA BLACK FOR *PETA AsiaPacific*

PURPOSIVE INCENTIVES People also join interest groups because of **purposive incentives,** that is, because they believe in the group's cause from an ideological or a moral standpoint. Interest groups pave the way for people to take action with like-minded people. And so you might join People for the Ethical Treatment of Animals (PETA) because you strongly object to animal abuse and want to work with others to prevent cruelty to animals. A friend who is passionately pro-life might join the National Right to Life Committee (NRLC), whereas your pro-choice cousin might join NARAL Pro-Choice America (formerly the National Abortion Reproductive Rights Action League).

The Internet is a particularly effective forum for attracting membership through purposive incentives. Accessible anyplace and anytime, the Internet provides resources for you to join an interest group even during a bout of insomnia at 3:00 a.m. Suppose a conversation earlier in the day got you thinking anew about the brutal genocidal conflict in Darfur. In those dark predawn hours, you can google "save Darfur" and within seconds have a variety of access points for becoming civically engaged by participating in an interest group. Some interest groups might ask you to contribute money; others might urge you to sign an online petition or to call the White House to make your opinions known. You can also learn about demonstrations sponsored by other groups right on your college campus and in your community. You might even find out about state and national demonstrations. The media contacts provided by online interest groups make it easy for you to write a letter to an editor, attempting to convince others of your views. Just learning about the wide variety of activities available can make you feel that you are "doing something" about a cause you believe in.

ECONOMIC INCENTIVES Many people join interest groups because of material or **economic incentives;** that is, they want to support groups that work for policies that will provide them with economic benefits. For example, the National Association of Police Organizations lobbies Congress concerning many appropriations measures that could affect its membership, including bills that would provide or increase funding for Community Oriented Policing Services (COPS) programs, bulletproof vests, and overtime pay for first responders to disasters.

Nearly all corporate and labor interest groups offer economic incentives to their members. They sometimes do so by advocating for policies that support business or labor in general, such as policies focused on the minimum wage, regulations concerning workplace conditions, and laws governing family leave or health coverage.

Other interest groups offer smaller-scale economic benefits to members. Many Americans over age 50 join the American Association of Retired Persons (AARP) because of the discounts members receive on hotels, airfares, and car rentals. Other organizations provide discounts on health insurance, special deals from merchants, or low-interest credit cards.

Most people join and remain in interest groups for a combination of reasons. A person might initially join an interest group for purposive incentives and then realize some solidary benefits and remain in the group because of the friendships formed. Or someone might join a professional association for the economic benefits but then develop rewarding social networks. Many individuals who join and stay in interest groups do so because of overlapping incentives.

purposive incentives
motivation to join an interest group based on the belief in the group's cause from an ideological or a moral standpoint

economic incentives
motivation to join an interest group because the group works for policies that will provide members with material benefits

How Interest Groups Succeed

In a single week in early 2006, the defense corporation Lockheed Martin won more than $2.5 billion worth of defense contracts from the federal government. First the Defense Department contracted with the company for a $2.1 billion project that would create a network system to connect the department's earth-based global information grid to Defense Department users around the world. Then the company won a $491 million contract to build a third spacecraft for the Advanced Extremely High Frequency satellite system.

As it happens, Lockheed Martin, with annual revenues of over $37 billion, wins more federal contracts than any other company that contracts with the federal government. Similarly to many other big businesses, Lockheed Martin acts like an interest group. That is, it attempts to influence government policy by using the kinds of strategies on which interest groups rely to sway policy makers. In Lockheed Martin's case, such strategies include joining with competitors to form the National Defense Industrial Organization for the purpose of achieving policies benefiting all member corporations.

Contrast this powerful corporate interest with the "nuclear freeze" groups that coalesced in opposition to President Ronald Reagan's proposal in the 1980s to build a space-based shield to protect the United States from nuclear attack. Dubbed "Star Wars," the proposal attracted vocal and widespread opposition from nuclear freeze activists in the nation's capital and in cities throughout the United States. Although the groups continued their "no nukes" campaign more modestly during the George H. W. Bush administration, their efforts largely fizzled during the Clinton presidency. Despite the fact that Lockheed Martin is researching what has been called the "Son of Star Wars" weapon system advocated by President George W. Bush, the effectiveness of the no nukes activists has dissipated.

Given that interest groups attempt to influence all kinds of policies, why are some interest groups better at getting what they want than others? Political scientists agree on various factors that influence whether an interest group will succeed. These factors include the interest group's *organizational resources*, the tools it has at its disposal to help achieve its goals; and its *organizational environment*, the setting in which it attempts to achieve those goals (see "Global Comparisons").

Organizational Resources

The effectiveness of interest groups in influencing government policy often depends on the resources they use to sway policy makers.[18] Interest groups rely on two key types of resources: membership, the people who belong to a given group; and financial resources, the money the group can spend to exert influence.

HOW MEMBERSHIP AFFECTS SUCCESS A large membership enhances an interest group's influence because policy makers are more likely to take note of the group's position. The age-old concept of "strength in numbers" applies when it comes to interest

GLOBAL COMPARISONS

THE ZAMBEZI SOCIETY

When we think of interest groups, we tend to think of groups dedicated to a specific national policy issue—gun control or abortion, for example. When we think of environmental interest groups, we similarly call to mind organizations whose activities focus on the United States, such as protecting endangered U.S. species or protesting oil drilling in Alaska's Arctic National Wildlife Refuge. In fact, however, environmental interest groups are among the most likely to cross international borders. The benefits of conservation and sound governmental environmental policy are public goods—they cannot be limited to people active in a particular interest group, nor even to citizens of a particular nation. And so it is logical that environmental interest groups are among the most internationally focused groups.

> ❋ **Will the future see the rise of more internationally focused interest groups like the Zambezi Society?**

One such group is the Zambezi Society, an organization headquartered in Harare, Mozambique, a country in southeastern Africa. The Zambezi Society's primary concern is the protection of the various ecosystems surrounding the Zambezi River. Among these are wetlands, woodlands, forests, savannah (grasslands), and aquatic ecosystems. During its twenty-five-year history, the Zambezi Society has strived to protect a wide variety of animal species found in the Zambezi area, including the black rhinoceros, the African elephant, cheetahs, lions, leopards, crocodiles, lechwe (a kind of antelope), and over 600 bird species. The society also has worked to protect trees and plant life surrounding the Zambezi. The group's efforts to protect animals and plants include such activities as conducting black rhino counts at watering holes and surveying human–carnivore conflict.

The issues of concern to the Zambezi Society vary, but all center on the fragile Zambezi River environment. For example, the group opposes the use of DDT for controlling the tsetse fly, citing the chemical's negative environmental impact. The society also has lobbied for a moratorium on development in the town of Victoria Falls, the Zambezi's premier tourist destination. The tourism industry has had a negative environmental impact on the area because of poor planning and a lack of basic infrastructure, including inadequate sewer and water systems.

Like many other interest groups, the Zambezi Society relies on two types of resources—membership and financial resources—to ensure that its efforts are as effective at influencing policy as they can be. The society attracts members of various nationalities by offering membership rates (currently at $40 U.S.) in dollars, euros, and British pounds. The society also works with other international and local organizations to carry out its agenda and influence environmental policy. And like many other organizations, the Zambezi Society raises money through its various funds, by which a contributor can support rhinos and elephants, or carnivores, or water and wetlands protection. The Zambezi Society's fund-raising events are similar to many used in the United States and include a bicycling fund-raiser to attract donations for the society's general fund.

groups. As we saw with this chapter's "American Democracy Now" episode, the sheer number of a group's membership is often an important factor in forcing policy makers, the media, and the public to pay attention to an issue. Among the largest U.S. interest groups is the American Association of Retired Persons (AARP), which boasts a membership of more than 35 million people. This vast size gives the organization incredible clout and historically has made policy makers unwilling to take on any issue that would unleash the wrath of AARP's formidable membership. For example, for years many economic analysts have suggested increasing the age at which people become eligible to receive Social Security. They reason that the average life span has risen significantly since the eligibility age was set, and that people are working longer because they remain healthier longer. But this potential policy solution has long simmered on the back burner. The reason? Politicians in Congress and the White House have not wanted to incur the disapproval of the AARP's members, who would widely oppose increasing the eligibility age and might respond by voting unsympathetic officials out of office. While he was Speaker of the House of Representatives, Dennis Hastert (R-Illinois) remarked that he took "the AARP very seriously"—as had Newt Gingrich when he was Speaker before—and that "Republicans had been courting AARP for some time, listening to them, engaging in a give-and-take dialogue that none of the capital's pundits even suspected was going on."[19]

But size is not the only important aspect of an interest group's membership. The *cohesion* of a group, or how strongly unified it is, also matters to participants and to policy makers.[20] For example, the Human Rights Campaign (HRC) lobbies for federal legislation to end discrimination on the basis of sexual orientation and provides research to elected officials and policy makers on issues of importance to people who are gay, lesbian, bisexual, or transgender. The HRC has a membership of about 600,000, but because the organization limits its advocacy to issues impacting gay, lesbian, bisexual, and transgender people, it is an extremely cohesive association (see "On the Job").

Another significant aspect of an interest group's membership is its *intensity*. Intensity is a measure of how strongly members feel about the issues they are targeting. Certain kinds of organizations, including pro-life interest groups such as the National Right to Life Committee, environmental groups such as the Sierra Club and Greenpeace, and animal rights groups such as People for the Ethical Treatment of Animals (PETA), are known for sustaining high levels of intensity. These organizations are more adept at attracting new members and younger members than are older, more entrenched kinds of groups. These newer, youthful members are a significant force behind the persistence and intensity of these groups.

The *demographics* of a group's membership also may increase its success. Members who know policy makers personally and have access to them mean greater influence for the group.[21] In the case of Lockheed Martin, the defense contractor discussed above, the company enjoys the benefit of having had connections with some well-placed members of the George W. Bush administration. These include Vice President Dick Cheney, whose wife, Lynne, served on Lockheed's board of directors until 2001; former transportation secretary Norman Mineta, who served as a vice president with the company; and Deputy Secretary of Homeland Security Michael Jackson, a former chief operating officer (COO) at Lockheed.

In addition to an interest group's members' connections, other demographic attributes also matter. Members who are well educated, geographically dispersed (because they can influence a broader network of policy makers than a geographically consolidated membership), or affluent tend to have more influence. Policy makers perceive these attributes as important because the groups' membership is more likely to lobby and to contribute financial resources on behalf of the organization's cause.

HOW FINANCIAL RESOURCES AFFECT SUCCESS For an interest group, money can buy power.[22] Money fuels the hiring of experienced and effective staff and lobbyists, who communicate directly with policy makers, as well as the undertaking of initiatives that will increase the group's membership. Money also funds the raising of more money.[23] For example, the Business Roundtable represents the interests of 150 chief executive officers of the largest U.S. companies, including American Express, General Electric, IBM, and Verizon. In 2007, it spent over $10 million lobbying the president, Congress, and several cabinet departments for policies that would benefit its member corporations, their shareholders,

MICHAEL COLE, COMMUNICATIONS COORDINATOR, HUMAN RIGHTS CAMPAIGN

Name: Michael Cole

Age: 25

Hometown: Stratford, Connecticut

College: American University, Washington, D.C.

Major: Political Science

Job title: Communications Coordinator, the Human Rights Campaign, an interest group that works for gay, lesbian, bisexual, and transgender equal rights.

Salary for jobs like this: Starting at $30,000

Day-to-day responsibilities: As the Communications Coordinator, I do mostly media-relations work. As there are a few of us, I work on all of the regional and local press inquiries. I provide information [and] statistics and comment on different stories. I also am the primary radio spokesperson, so I do a lot of radio interviews, primarily on conservative talk radio shows. I do both interviews and debate. I also have done a bit of video production—I produce short compilations that are used for fund-raising events.

How did you get your job? I started here as an intern in the Political Department. I interned with the federal legislation team and with the PAC [political action committee]. When I graduated, I was looking for a job, and the Communications Coordinator position became available. I have grown to love it.

What do you like best about your job? I like working in the advocacy field, and I like dealing with issues that are personally important to me. It is more than just a way to pay the bills. It is personally fulfilling.

What is your least favorite aspect of your job? I guess the biggest complaint is that I have the same conversation so many times every day. I am constantly going over the same issues. And while I've reached a certain level of expertise, I am just going over the basics at any given time every day. I guess that gets a bit tiring.

What advice would you give to students who would like to do what you're doing? The most important thing is to find the one thing that matters the most to you. What is going to make you want to go to work? And then do whatever you can, whether it's interning or volunteering, so that you eventually can get a job in that area.

---

and their member corporations' 10 million employees. Issues of concern to the Business Roundtable include policies such as Securities and Exchange Commission rules, laws concerning corporate ethics, and reform to the nation's class action lawsuit regulations.

political action committee (PAC)
a group that raises and spends money in order to influence the outcome of an election

Sometimes interest groups form a separate entity, called a **political action committee (PAC),** whose specific goal is to raise and spend money to influence the outcome of elections (see Chapter 9 for a detailed discussion of PACs). Interest groups use PACs to shape the composition of government; that is, they contribute money to the campaigns of favored candidates, particularly incumbents who are likely to be reelected.[24] While this is but one specific example of the influence that interest groups' money has on politics, interest groups representing the economic concerns of members—business, industry, and union groups—generally tend to have the greatest financial resources for all of these activities.[25]

Organizational Environment

The setting in which an interest group attempts to achieve its goals is the *organizational environment.* Key factors in the organizational environment include its leadership and the presence or absence of opposition from other groups[26] (see "The Conversation of Democracy").

SHOULD AMNESTY BE EXTENDED TO ILLEGAL WORKERS IN THE UNITED STATES?

The Issue: There are about 7.5 million unauthorized immigrant workers in the United States today, according to the Pew Hispanic Center. Unauthorized immigrant workers are citizens of other nations who have either entered the United States illegally or violated the terms of legal entry into the United States (as in the case of people who enter the United States on a tourist visa but stay after the visa has expired). Illegal aliens are in violation of the Immigration and Naturalization Act—a misdemeanor—and are subject to deportation back to their country of origin. Repeat offenders can be charged with a felony.

Recent proposals in Congress have raised the possibility of establishing an amnesty program for workers who are in the country illegally. Such a program would create a structure by which illegal immigrant workers eventually could become legal U.S. residents after paying fines. Various interest groups—some pro-amnesty and others that are opposed—have mobilized around the issue of amnesty for immigrant workers, and often in surprising ways. An intense debate thus centers on the question, should amnesty be extended to illegal workers in the United States?

Yes: Some form of amnesty for workers who are in the United States illegally makes economic sense. The U.S. economy depends upon the cheap labor provided by undocumented workers. Losing these workers would drive up costs for employers, who would then be forced to pass the costs along to consumers in the form of higher prices—with a detrimental impact on the overall economy.

A wide variety of interest groups have raised dire warnings about the economic impact of not extending amnesty. Immigration rights groups—particularly groups that advocate for the rights of Latino immigrants—support amnesty proposals. But it is not just immigrant rights groups that support amnesty proposals. The National Restaurant Association, for example, supports such a plan because so many restaurant employees are undocumented workers. The prevalence of undocumented workers as part of the workforce has meant that some labor unions support amnesty plans, including UNITE HERE, a union representing many textile, hotel, restaurant, and casino workers.

No: The United States should not give illegal workers amnesty. Proposals that grant amnesty to undocumented immigrants reward these unauthorized workers' illegal activity by granting them legal status in the United States. In addition, American citizens are losing jobs to foreign nationals, as many individual commentators and groups persuasively argue. The Coalition for the Future American Worker, for example, has convincingly asserted that "big business and immigration lawyers are conspiring to fill American jobs here at home with foreign workers."* The coalition is an umbrella organization composed of professional trade groups, population and environmental organizations, and immigration reform groups. The coalition is circulating e-petitions and urging members to write letters to the editors of local newspapers pressing legislators not to support amnesty for undocumented workers.

Other approaches: Immigrants add to the productivity of the American economy, and the United States can address this issue by changing immigration policies to permit more laborers in certain occupations to enter through a guest worker program like the limited agricultural program currently in place. Such a program would enable policy makers to identify specific occupations that need laborers and then allow those workers to come to the U.S. temporarily to work. By requiring guest workers to apply to enter, the United States would not be rewarding those who break the law.

What do you think?

① Should illegal immigrants be granted amnesty and be permitted to stay in the United States? Why or why not?

② What are the advantages of a large immigrant workforce? What are the disadvantages?

③ Why are organizations that are typically competitive—such as the National Restaurant Association and UNITE HERE, the restaurant workers' union—on the same side of this issue?

④ Why are illegal immigrants themselves at a disadvantage in participating in this debate?

*www.americanworker.org/index.html.

LEADERSHIP Strong, charismatic leaders contribute to the influence of an interest group by raising public awareness of the group and its activities, by enhancing its reputation, and by making the organization attractive to new members and contributors. An example of a dynamic leader who has increased his interest group's effectiveness is James P. Hoffa, the son of powerful Teamsters Union president Jimmy Hoffa, who disappeared without a trace in 1975. Since 1999, he has served as the president of the Teamsters Union, which primarily represents unionized truck drivers.

OPPOSITION The presence of opposing interest groups can also have an impact on an interest group's success. When an interest group is "the only game in town" on a particular issue, policy makers are more likely to rely on that group's views. But if groups with opposing views are also attempting to influence policy, getting policy makers to act strongly in any one group's favor is more difficult. Consider this example: Hotel Employees and the Restaurant Employees International Union supported increasing the minimum wage, but the National Restaurant Association, which advocates for restaurant owners, opposed a minimum wage hike, arguing that the higher wage would cut into restaurant owners' profits or limit its members' ability to hire as many employees as before. In the face of such opposing interests, policy makers are often more likely to compromise than to give any one group exactly what it wants.

Although each of these factors—organizational resources and the organizational environment—influences how powerful an interest group will be, no single formula determines an interest group's clout. Sometimes an interest group has powerful advocates in Congress who support its cause. Other times, a single factor can prove essential to an interest group's success.

Types of Interest Groups

A wide variety of political interest groups exercise their muscle in the case of virtually every type of policy question, from those concerning birth (such as what is the minimum hospital stay an insurance company must cover after a woman gives birth?) to matters related to death (such as what are the practices by funeral directors that should be banned by the government?). Despite the broad range of issues around which interest groups coalesce, political scientists generally categorize interest groups by what kinds of issues concern them and who benefits from the groups' activities. For example, some interest groups focus primarily on economic decisions that affect their members. Other interest groups pursue ideological, issue-based, or religion-based goals. Yet others lobby for benefits for society at large, while still others advocate on behalf of foreign interests.

Economic Interest Groups

When economic interest groups lobby government, the benefits for their members can be direct or indirect. In some cases the economic benefits flow directly from the government to the interest group members, as when an agricultural interest group successfully presses for *subsidies,* monies given by the government to the producers of a particular crop or product, often to influence the volume of production of that commodity. For example, as a result of the lobbying efforts of several large dairy cooperatives, including the Dairy Farmers of America, the 2007 Farm Bill Extension Act earmarked over $800 million in subsidies to large and small dairy farmers.[27]

In other instances, economic interest groups lobby for or against policies that, while not directly benefiting their members, have an indirect impact on the interest group's membership. This was the case when many unions, including the AFL-CIO, lobbied against the creation of private Social Security accounts, fearing that this privatization would result in a decrease in Social Security retirement benefits for their members.

CORPORATE AND BUSINESS INTERESTS Large corporate and smaller business interest groups are among the most successful U.S. pressure groups with respect to their influence on government. These groups typically seek policies that benefit a particular company or industry. For example, the Motion Picture Association of America (MPAA) represents the seven major U.S. manufacturers and distributors of movies and television programs. The MPAA lobbies policy makers (often by hosting prerelease screenings of films and lavish dinner receptions) with the goal of securing the passage of antipiracy laws, which aim to prevent the illegal copying of movies and to penalize individuals who sell them. This advocacy benefits the group's members and their employees, because antipiracy laws help to ensure that any copies of movies sold are legal and thus profitable for MPAA members.

Certain industries' associations are stand-alone organizations, such as the National Association of Realtors and the National Beer Wholesalers Association. But industry and business groups also commonly advocate for policies using **umbrella organizations,** which are interest groups representing groups of industries or corporations. Examples of umbrella business organizations include the Business Roundtable, which represents the chief executive officers (CEOs) of 150 large corporations, and the U.S. Chamber of Commerce, a federation of local chambers of commerce that represents about 3 million large and small businesses.

Often corporate and business groups compete against labor groups. This rivalry is a natural result of having different constituencies. Typically, corporate interests advocate on behalf of the company owners, stockholders, and officers, whereas labor unions champion employees' interests.

umbrella organizations
interest groups that represent collective groups of industries or corporations

LABOR INTERESTS   Like corporate interest groups, labor interest groups include both national labor unions and umbrella organizations of unions. The AFL-CIO, an umbrella organization made up of more than 50 labor unions, is among the nation's most powerful interest groups, although its influence has waned over the past several decades as union membership has declined generally. During the 1950s and 1960s, nearly 35 percent of all U.S. workers were union members. By 1983, membership had decreased to about 20 percent, and today about 13 percent of all U.S. workers belong to unions. In part, this decline stems from changes in the U.S. economy, with many highly unionized manufacturing jobs being replaced by less unionized service sector jobs. Given the drop in union membership, labor interest groups' influence has also waned, although the unions' reduced clout is in part due to a lack of cohesion among labor union members.

Like corporate and business interest groups, labor unions pursue policies that benefit their members, although these are frequently at odds with corporate and business interest groups' positions. And like corporate and business interest groups, labor unions sometimes press for policies that primarily benefit their own members, while at other times they promote policies that benefit all union workers and sometimes even non-union workers. For example, in 2007 the AFL-CIO successfully lobbied Congress for an increase in the federal minimum wage, which benefited the members of many unions whose contracts are based on federally mandated minimum wages but also many non-union workers who are paid the minimum wage.

AGRICULTURAL INTERESTS   Of all types of U.S. interest groups, agricultural interest groups probably have the most disproportionate amount of influence given the relatively small number of farmers and farmworkers in the country relative to the general population. And because agricultural producers in the United States are also very diverse, ranging from small farmers to huge multinational agribusinesses, it is not surprising to see divergent opinions among people employed in the agricultural sector.

The largest agricultural interest group today is the American Farm Bureau Federation (AFBF), which grew out of the network of county farm bureaus formed in the 1920s. With more than 5 million farming members, the AFBF is one of the most influential interest groups in the United States, primarily because of its close relations with key agricultural policy makers. It takes stands on a wide variety of issues that have an impact on farmers, including subsidies, budget and tax policies, immigration policies that affect farmworkers, energy policies, trade policies, and environmental policies.

In addition to large-scale, general agricultural interest groups such at the AFBF, there is an industry-specific interest group representing producers for nearly every crop or commodity produced in the agricultural sector. Table 7.1 shows that corn producers are among the most effective groups in securing subsidies for their growers. Between 1995 and 2006, more than 1.5 million corn farmers across the United States received in excess of $56 billion in government subsidies. Table 7.1 reveals as well that the producers of several other crops—wheat, cotton, soybeans, and rice—have managed to secure subsidies of more than $10 billion each from 1995 to 2006.

Top Agricultural Subsidies in the United States, 1995–2006

TABLE 7.1

Rank	Program	Number of Recipients 1995–2006	Subsidy Total 1995–2006
1	Corn subsidies	1,568,095	$56,170,875,257
2	Wheat subsidies	1,308,268	$22,051,566,200
3	Cotton subsidies	247,879	$21,329,862,262
4	Conservation Reserve Program	768,180	$20,337,282,263
5	Disaster payments	1,246,432	$15,114,518,393
6	Soybean subsidies	985,712	$14,239,702,740
7	Rice subsidies	65,533	$11,043,795,298
8	Sorghum subsidies	586,766	$ 4,569,912,363
9	Dairy program subsidies	151,737	$ 3,560,356,847
10	Livestock subsidies	754,842	$ 2,908,502,988

Source: The Environmental Working Group, http://farm.ewg.org/farm/region.php?fips=00000.

> The Sierra Club and other public interest groups that lobby Congress about environmental issues work to protect public lands such as the Denali National Wildlife Refuge, home to herds of caribou and other species.

collective goods

outcomes shared by the general public; also called *public goods*

free rider problem

the phenomenon of someone deriving benefit from others' actions

TRADE AND PROFESSIONAL INTERESTS Nearly every professional occupation—doctor, lawyer, engineer, chiropractor, dentist, accountant, and even video game developer—has a trade or professional group that focuses on its interests. These interest groups take stands on a variety of policy matters, many of which indirectly affect their membership. For example, in the aftermath of the September 11, 2001 terrorist attacks, members of the American Hotel and Lodging Association (AH&LA), a trade group representing state and city partner lodging associations, lobbied for passage of a law that would aid insurance companies in the event of a future terrorist strike. Congress subsequently passed the Terrorism Risk Protection Act, which provides up to $100 billion in subsidies to insurers in the event of a catastrophic terrorist attack. The AH&LA argued for the bill because its members would benefit from greatly reduced costs of terrorism insurance under the bill. When President George W. Bush signed the bill into law in 2002, representatives of the AH&LA attended the signing ceremony.

Public and Ideological Interest Groups

Public interest groups typically are concerned with a broad range of issues that affect the populace at large. These include social and economic issues such as Social Security reform and revision of the federal tax structure, as well as environmental causes such as clean air and clean water. Examples of public interest groups include the National Taxpayers Union, Common Cause, and the Sierra Club. Usually, the results of the efforts of a particular public interest group's advocacy cannot be limited to the group's members; rather, these results are **collective goods** (sometimes called *public goods*)—outcomes that are shared by the general public. Collective goods are "collective" and "public" because they cannot be denied to people who are not group members. For example, if the Sierra Club succeeds in winning passage of an environmental bill that improves water and air quality, *everyone* shares in the benefits. Specifically, it is impossible to make pure drinking water and clean air a privilege restricted to Sierra Club members.

The nature of collective goods—the fact that they cannot be limited to those who worked to achieve them—creates a **free rider problem,** the situation whereby someone derives a benefit from the actions of others. You are probably familiar with the free rider problem.

Suppose, for example, that you form a study group to prepare for an exam, and four of the five members of the group come to a study session having prepared responses to essay questions. The fifth member shows up but is unprepared. The unprepared group member then copies the others' responses, memorizes them, and does just as well on the exam. The same thing happens to interest groups that advocate for a collective good. The group may work hard to improve the quality of life, but the benefits of its work are enjoyed by many who do not contribute to the effort.

Economist Mancur Olson asserted in his **rational choice theory** that from an economic perspective it is not rational for people to participate in a collective action designed to achieve a collective good when they can secure that good without participating. So, in the study group example, from Olson's perspective, it is not economically rational to spend your time preparing for an exam when you can get the benefits of preparation without the work. Of course, taking this idea to the extreme, one might conclude that if no one advocated for collective goods, they would not exist, and thus free riders could not derive their benefit.

Current scholarship on civic engagement has focused on the free rider problem. Researchers have investigated the increased benefits of widespread citizen participation in interest groups, citing evidence that groups with higher levels of public participation may be more effective, and may provide greater collective benefits, than groups with lower rates of participation. Studies also indicate that through the act of participating in civic life, individuals derive some benefit themselves in addition to the benefits created by their work. So, if the fifth person in the study group prepares for the exam, too, *all* members of the group may perform better on the exam. And if more people are civically involved in groups, then their potential to have an impact on their government increases. In addition, civic engagement scholars cite the psychic benefit to an individual of knowing that a collective good was achieved in part because of *her* participation, and these researchers also mention the other benefits derived from collective action, including solidary and purposive benefits.

CONSUMER INTERESTS   Well before attorney and activist Ralph Nader gained nationwide attention as a Green Party candidate for the presidency in 2000, he founded numerous organizations to promote the rights of consumers. In the 1970s and 1980s, these organizations lobbied primarily—and successfully—for changes in automotive design that would make cars safer. One result was the mandatory installation of harness safety belts in rear seats, which then typically had only lap belts. In 1971 Nader founded the interest group Public Citizen, which lobbies Congress, the executive branch, and the courts for openness in government and consumer issues, including auto safety, the safety of prescription drugs, and energy policy. Each year in December, the group issues a list of unsafe toys to guide gift-buyers' holiday purchases.

ENVIRONMENTAL INTERESTS   Many groups that advocate for the protection of the environment and wildlife and for the conservation of natural resources came about as a result of a broader environmental movement in the 1970s, although the Sierra Club was founded more than a century ago, in 1892. Some environmental groups, particularly Greenpeace, have been criticized in the media and by their opponents for their use of confrontational tactics. But many environmental activists say that the power of corporate interests (with which they are frequently at odds) is so pervasive that they can succeed only by taking strong, direct action to protect the natural environment, thus rationalizing their sometimes extreme tactics. And so while some environmentalists follow the conventional route of lobbying legislators or advertising to raise public awareness of their causes, others camp out in trees to attempt to prevent their removal or sit on oil-drilling platforms to halt drilling into a coral reef. In addition to stalling the undesired action, the confrontational protest tactic also has the advantage of attracting media attention, which serves to increase public awareness.[28] Such environmental groups hope that they can prevent environmental destruction by embarrassing the corporation or government involved.

rational choice theory
the idea that from an economic perspective it is not rational for people to participate in collective action when they can secure the collective good without participating

RELIGIOUS INTERESTS For a long time, organized religions in the United States were essentially uninvolved in politics, partly because they were afraid of losing their tax-exempt status by becoming political entities. But formal religions increasingly have sought to make their voices heard, usually by forming political organizations separate from the actual religious organizations. Today, religious interests are among the most influential interest groups in U.S. politics.

In the early stages of their activism, Christian organizations typically were most politically effective in the Republican presidential nomination process, when the mobilization of their members could alter the outcome in low-turnout primaries. During the 1970s several conservative Christian organizations, most notably the Moral Majority, founded by the late Reverend Jerry Falwell, were a force in national politics. The Moral Majority helped to elect Ronald Reagan, a Republican, to the presidency in 1980 and was instrumental in shaping the national agenda of the Reagan years, particularly regarding domestic policy. In 1989, another conservative Christian organization, the Christian Coalition, took shape, marking a new era in the politicization of religious groups. The Christian Coalition advocates that "people of faith have a right and a responsibility to be involved in the world around them" and emphasizes "pro-family" values.[29] During its first decade, the Christian Coalition's influence grew gradually. During the 2000 election, the organization was an important supporter of George W. Bush's candidacy for the presidency, and with his election, the group's influence has grown considerably. In the 2004 presidential election, conservative Christian organizations proved enormously important in activities such as voter registration and get-out-the-vote campaigns, thus aiding President Bush's reelection efforts.

The Christian Coalition and other religious groups—including Pax Christi USA (the national Catholic peace movement), B'nai Brith (an interest group dedicated to Jewish interests), and the Council on American-Islamic Relations (CAIR, a Muslim interest group)—also advocate for the faith-based priorities of their members. Many of these organizations have become increasingly active in state and local politics in recent years. For example, since 2000, members of the Christian Coalition, recognizing the influence that local school boards have in determining how religion is integrated into the classroom, have made national headlines by running organized slates of candidates for election to local school boards, many of whom have won. By 2008, lawmakers in more than twenty states had considered various pieces of legislation that would include instruction in creationism in school curricula. Many such proposals came at the behest of Christian school board members.

Foreign Interest Groups

In the United States, advocacy by interest groups is not limited to U.S.-based groups. Foreign governments, as well as international corporations based abroad, vigorously press for U.S. policies beneficial to them. Foreign governments might lobby for U.S. aid packages; corporations might work for beneficial changes to tax regulations. Often a foreign government will rely on an interest group made up of U.S. citizens of the foreign nation's heritage to promote its advocacy efforts. Indeed, one of the more influential interest groups lobbying for foreign concerns is the U.S.-based American Israel Public Affairs Committee (AIPAC), which has 65,000 members. AIPAC lobbies the U.S. government for pro-Israel foreign policies such as the grant of nearly $2.5 billion in economic and military aid for Israel in 2007. Despite its relatively small membership, AIPAC is considered highly influential because of its financial resources and well-connected membership base, which enjoys access to many policy makers.

Sometimes it is readily apparent when foreign interests are lobbying for their own causes—as, for example, when a trading partner wants better terms. But in other cases, particularly when international corporations are lobbying, it is difficult to discern where their "American" interest ends and their "foreign" interest begins. So while only U.S. citizens and legal immigrants can contribute to federal PACs, American employees of foreign companies do form and contribute to PACs. Many people would be surprised at the large amounts of money that international corporations' PACs contribute to both of the major U.S. political parties. But because many subsidiaries of these corporations are important American businesses, their lobbying activities are not necessarily a foreign encroachment on U.S. politics.

Interest Group Strategies

Interest groups use two kinds of strategies to advance their causes. *Direct strategies* involve actual contact between representatives of the interest group and policy makers. *Indirect strategies* use intermediaries to advocate for a cause or generally to attempt to persuade the public, including policy makers, to embrace the group's position.

In the spring of 2006, many Americans who opposed Congress's plan for an amnesty provision in the immigration reform bill advocated the construction of a wall along the U.S.-Mexican border. A group called send-a-brick.com, led by University of North Texas political science major Chris Brown, engaged in a "mail a brick" campaign to members of Congress as a way to demonstrate their support. According to the Web site, by September 2007, nearly 13,000 bricks had been sent to members of Congress. U.S. senator Wayne Allard (R-Colorado) received one brick with a letter stating that while the letter writer could not take time from work to protest, "I did have time to send you this brick so that you could get started building a wall between the U.S. and Mexico." Most interest groups opt for a combination of direct strategies, such as the "mail a brick" campaign, and indirect strategies to accomplish their goals.

Direct Strategies to Advance Interests

Groups often opt for direct strategies when they seek to secure passage or defeat of a specific piece of legislation. These strategies include lobbying, entering into litigation to change a law, and providing information or expert testimony to decision makers.

LOBBYING, ISSUE NETWORKS, AND IRON TRIANGLES Interest groups hire professionals to **lobby,** or communicate directly with, policy makers on the interest groups' behalf. President Ulysses S. Grant coined the term *lobbyist* when he walked through the lobby of the Willard Hotel in Washington, D.C., and commented on the presence of "lobbyists" waiting to speak to members of Congress.

lobby
to communicate directly with policy makers on the interest group's behalf

Today lobbying is among the most common strategies that interest groups use, and the practice may include scheduled face-to-face meetings, "buttonholing" members of Congress as they walk through the Capitol, telephone calls, and receptions and special events hosted by the interest groups. The professional lobbyists whom interest groups hire are almost always lawyers, and their job is to cultivate ongoing relationships with members of Congress (and their staff) who have influence in a specific policy area. In many situations, lobbyists help navigate access to these policy makers for industry and interest group members.

Interest groups have learned that one of the most effective ways of influencing government is to hire former government officials, including cabinet officials, members of Congress, and congressional staffers, as lobbyists. Because these ex-officials often enjoy good relationships with their former colleagues and have an intimate knowledge of the policy-making process, they are particularly effective in influencing government. Frequently, this practice creates an **issue network,** the fluid web of connections among those concerned about a policy and those who create and administer the policy.

issue network
the fluid web of connections among those concerned about a policy and those who create and administer the policy

To understand how an issue network operates, let's take as an example the actual case of a technology company, Artel, that wanted to secure large federal government contracts. In this issue network, the interest group did not hire a former government official. Rather, the advocacy effort was headed up by a good friend of a powerful House member, Representative Thomas M. Davis III (R-Virginia), who chaired the Government Reform Committee, an important House committee.[30] Before winning election to the House, Davis was a corporate executive at a Virginia firm that contracted with the federal government to provide computers. During this time, he developed a close friendship with a colleague at the technology firm, Donald Upson. Shortly before Davis became chair of the House committee, Upson formed ICG Government, a consulting firm that advises technology companies seeking to win federal government contracts. ICG Government hired Davis's wife and publicly touted the firm's relationship with the congressman, going so far as to feature a photograph of Davis in front of the ICG banner on the company's Web site.

THE INFLUENCE OF ISSUE NETWORKS

To prevent the Department of Defense from canceling its $2.2 billion contract, executives at Artel, Inc., hired ICG Government, headed by Donald Upson, the good friend of Representative Thomas M. Davis III. Upson, executives at Artel, and their hired lobbying firm drafted a letter (below, left). Davis sent a letter (below, right) that contains remarkably similar language. After further lobbying efforts by Artel, their contract was renewed.

Compare the draft and the letter actually sent by Representative Davis.

Evaluating the Evidence

① What does Representative Davis's choice of language in his letter to the government official indicate about ICG's effectiveness in representing its clients to the federal government? About Davis's independence as a legislator?

② Compare ICG Government's ability to bring about a desired government action with the ability of a firm *without* such close access to a government official to influence policy.

③ Can a *private citizen* wield such influence as ICG Government achieved? Why or why not?

The Letter That Davis Sent to Lt. Gen. Croom

Congress of the United States
House of Representatives

COMMITTEE ON GOVERNMENT REFORM

2157 Rayburn House Office Building

Washington, DC 20515-6143

August 24, 2005

Lt. General Charles Croom
Director, Defense Information Systems Agency
P.O. Box 4502
Arlington, VA 22204-4502

Dear General Croom:

I received a copy of the report, "Defense Communications Satellite Services Procurement Process," released on July 29, 2005 in response to the mandate in section 803 of Ronald Regan National Defense Authorization Act for Fiscal Year 2005 (Authorization Act).

The report concludes that the existing Satellite Transmissions Services-Global (DSTS-G) contract be modified as needed, and that a separate successor procurement strategy be explored. The first part makes sense, and I hope those modifications are made in earnest and for established needs. It would make sense that these contract modifications be made prior to any "exploration" of an alternative procurement strategy.

Apparently, though, that is not the course the Defense Information Systems Agency (DISA) has elected to take.

Unfortunately, DISA moved within days of the above report with the issuance of a "Source Sought Notice" (Notice) to small businesses on a separate procurement strategy.

I have a number of questions to which I would appreciate written answers as soon as possible:

> 1) Contrary to, at least the intent if not the letter of, the Authorization Act, has DISA, under contract to any company, already prepared a draft RFP? If so, when was the draft prepared, under whose authority and for what purpose?

> 2) Do those involved with the decision to prepare the Notice see any conflict between that action and language contained in section 803 of the Authorization Act?

It is my intention to explore these and related issues in my committee. I have requested support from the Government Accountability Office. I urge that further action be withheld until Congress can fully explore the report and the determination of some in DISA to pursue an alternative and untested procurement strategy against evidence that the existing strategy, with minor modifications, can satisfy military requirements in these challenging times.

Should you have any questions, please contact John Brosman at 202-225-5074.

Sincerely,

Tom Davis
Chairman

The Draft by Lobbying Firm ICG Government

Ccontrary to at least the intent, if not the letter of last year's DoD authorization, has DISA, under contract to any company, already prepared a draft RFP? If so, when was the draft prepared, under whose authority and for what justification?

Do those involved with the decision to prepare the RFP see any conflict between that action and language contained in the DoD authorization?

It is my intention to fully explore these and related issues in my Committee. I also may request support from both the Government Accountability Office and the DoD Office of Inspector General. I would ask that further action be withheld and that the RFI be withdrawn until Congress can explore the report and unwavering determination of some in DISA to pursue an alternative and untested procurement strategy against evidence that the existing strategy, with minor modification, can satisfy military requirements in these challenging times.

Although Representative Davis enjoys a solid reputation as an advocate for clean elections and reform of the nation's lobbying laws (the interest group Public Citizen recognized him as a "true blue reformer"), his cozy relationship with ICG Government and his advocacy on behalf of the firm's clients have been called into question. For example, the *Washington Post* noted the close-knit issue network that exists among Davis, his friend and ICG Government head Upson, and Artel, Inc., a company with a $2.2 billion federal government contract to provide satellite services. When Artel believed that its federal contract was not going to be renewed, it hired ICG Government. Artel was convinced that larger satellite service companies were lobbying to get the contracts away from Artel. Artel executives and Upson worked on a draft of a letter to a lieutenant general, the director in charge of the satellite services contract renewals, stating that Representative Davis was concerned about the Department of Defense plan not to renew Artel's contract. A remarkably similar letter was sent by Davis to the lieutenant general (see "Exploring the Sources"). After further lobbying and a meeting between Davis and the lieutenant general, Artel's contract was renewed. Some analysts would argue that such an issue network creates an unfair playing field, but Davis contends that his actions are justified, as he perceives his role as an advocate for the many technology companies that operate in his northern Virginia district and employ many of his constituents.

Similarly, an interest group's efficacy often depends on its having close relationships with the policy makers involved in decisions related to the group's causes. During the rough-and-tumble policy-making process, the interaction of mutual interests among a "trio" comprising (1) members of Congress, (2) executive departments and agencies (such as the Department of Agriculture or the Federal Emergency Management Agency), and (3) organized interest groups is sometimes referred to as an **iron triangle,** with each of the three players being one side of the triangle (see Figure 7.2). Although each side in an iron triangle is expected to fight on behalf of its own interests, constituents, or governmental department, the triangle often seeks a policy outcome that benefits all parts of the triangle. Often this outcome occurs because of close personal and professional relationships that develop as a result of the interactions among the sides in an issue-based triangle. And sometimes the individual players in a triangle that is focused on a particular issue—say, military policy or subsidies for tobacco growers—share a personal history, have attended the same schools, come from the same region of the country, and have even worked together at one time. Such long-term relationships can make it difficult for opposing interests to penetrate the triangle. (See Chapter 13 for further discussion of the role of iron triangles in policy making.)

iron triangle
the interaction of mutual interests among members of Congress, executive agencies, and organized interests during policy making

LITIGATION BY INTEREST GROUPS Sometimes, interest groups challenge a policy in the courts. For example, in 2004, the Recording Industry Association of America (RIAA), a trade association representing manufacturers of music compact discs, filed five separate lawsuits against 531 defendants in Philadelphia, Orlando, Florida, and Trenton, New Jersey, claiming that the defendants had illegally swapped copyrighted songs by sharing computer files with other Internet users. The RIAA, which has continued to target college students in its lawsuits, said that the litigation was designed to protect the interests of its members, who had seen a slump in CD sales since song swapping had become more popular. By prosecuting offenders, the RIAA aimed to deter others from sharing files and hoped that law enforcement would view the issue more seriously than it had. Although few prosecutions and convictions have resulted from the RIAA lawsuits, media coverage of these legal actions is thought to have deterred some individuals from sharing copyrighted songs via the Internet.

POLITICAL INQUIRY

FIGURE 7.2 ■ **AN IRON TRIANGLE** Who are the players in an iron triangle? How do interest groups benefit from their iron triangle relationships? Why do you think the triangular relationship has been described as "iron"?

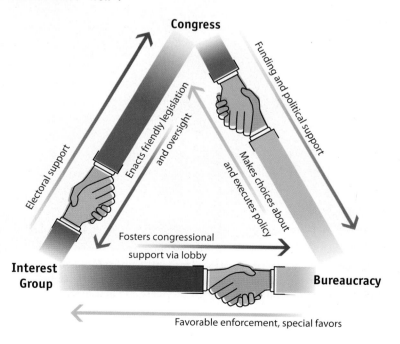

Congress

Funding and political support

Enacts friendly legislation and oversight

Electoral support

Makes choices about and executes policy

Fosters congressional support via lobby

Interest Group

Bureaucracy

Favorable enforcement, special favors

In other instances, interest groups sue to prevent a particular public policy from being enacted or to prompt a court ruling on the constitutionality of an issue. The latter was the case when in 1992, Planned Parenthood of Pennsylvania, an abortion-rights advocacy group, sued the state's governor, claiming that the state's Abortion Control Act violated the constitutional protections on abortion outlined in the Supreme Court's decision in *Roe v. Wade* (1973). In particular, Planned Parenthood argued that the clauses in the state legislation that required a pregnant woman to notify her husband, a pregnant teen to get parental consent, and any abortion seeker to satisfy a twenty-four-hour waiting period after receiving counseling presented an undue burden and violated the spirit of *Roe*. In *Roe v. Wade,* the Supreme Court had ruled that a woman's right to abortion was essentially guaranteed in the first trimester, could be regulated by the states in the second, and could be banned by the states in the third. The Supreme Court agreed to hear the Planned Parenthood case and struck down some components of the Pennsylvania legislation, including the requirement for spousal notification, while allowing other components not specified in *Roe,* including the parental consent requirement and the twenty-four-hour waiting period, to stand.

By litigating, interest groups can ensure that laws passed by legislatures and signed by executives are in keeping with current constitutional interpretation. By bringing their causes before the courts, they also can shape policy and encourage enforcement by executive agencies.

PROVIDING INFORMATION AND EXPERT TESTIMONY   Interest groups are one of the chief sources of information for policy makers. Interest groups have the resources to investigate the impact of policies. They have access to data, technological know-how, and a bevy of experts with extensive knowledge of the issues. Most interest groups provide information to policy makers, and policy makers understand that the information received is slanted toward the group's interest. But if competing interest groups supply information to policy makers, then policy makers can counterbalance the various sets of information.

Sometimes interest groups use celebrities as "experts" to testify, knowing that they will attract greater attention than most policy experts. Elmo, the furry red *Sesame Street* Muppet, testified in 2002 on behalf of a bill that would provide $2 million in federal funding to public schools for music education. The House Appropriations Subcommittee on Labor, Health and Human Services, and Education heard testimony from Elmo, who apparently is an authority on music education. Elmo told the subcommittee: "Elmo loves to sing and to dance and to make music with all his friends on *Sesame Street.* It helps Elmo learn ABCs and makes it easier for Elmo to remember things. Sometimes it makes Elmo excited, and sometimes it calms Elmo down. Elmo's teacher really likes that! My friend [American Music Conference Executive Director] Joe Lamond says some kids don't have music in school. That makes Elmo sad."[31] Other celebrities who have testified on behalf of causes important to them include Bono, the lead singer of the group U2, who testified concerning debt relief for African nations; actor Michael J. Fox, who testified about Parkinson's disease, from which he suffers; actor Goldie Hawn, who testified against granting permanent, normal trade status to China; and actor Julia Roberts, who spoke on behalf of those who suffer from Rett Syndrome, a nervous system disorder disproportionately suffered by women.

>Celebrity "experts" frequently offer testimony before Congress on many issues. School music education was the subject of Elmo's appearance before a hearing of the House Labor, Health and Human Services, and Education Appropriations Committee in 2002.

Indirect Strategies to Advance Interests

Reaching out to persuade the public that the interest group's position is right, deploying citizens as grassroots lobbyists, and electioneering are some of the indirect strategies interest groups use to pursue their public policy agendas. Indirect tactics are likely to be ongoing rather than targeted at a specific piece of legislation, although that is not always the case.

PUBLIC OUTREACH   Interest groups work hard—and use a variety of strategies—to make the public, government officials, their own members, and potential members aware of issues of concern and to educate people about their positions on the issues. Some interest groups focus solely on educating the public and hope that through their efforts people will be concerned enough to take steps to have a particular policy established or changed. In doing so, the groups promote civic engagement by informing individuals about important policy concerns, even if the information they provide is skewed toward the group's views. The groups also encourage civic discourse by bringing issues into the public arena. Often they do so by mounting advertising campaigns to alert the public about an issue. NARAL Pro-Choice America used such a strategy during the 2008 elections when the league took out ads in many traditionally Democratic states urging the election of pro-choice senators and alerting the public to the important role the U.S. Senate plays in confirming U.S. Supreme Court nominees. The ads stressed that the balance of the Court could shift in favor of an overruling of abortion protections if a sitting justice were to retire and be replaced by a pro-life justice.

Sometimes interest groups and corporations engage in **climate control,** the practice of using public outreach to build favorable public opinion of the organization or company. The logic behind climate control is simple: if a corporation or an organization has the goodwill of the public on its side, enacting its legislative agenda or getting its policy priorities passed will be easier because government will know of, and may even share, the public's positive opinion of the organization. For example, when Wal-Mart started to see opposition to the construction of its superstores in communities across the country, it relied on public relations techniques, particularly advertising, to convince people that Wal-Mart is a good corporate citizen. As critics complained about Wal-Mart's harmful effects on smaller, local merchants, the firm's ads touted Wal-Mart's positive contributions to its host communities. When opponents publicized the company's low-wage jobs, Wal-Mart countered with ads featuring employees who had started in entry-level positions and risen through the ranks to managerial posts. These ads would be viewed both by policy makers (municipal planning board members, for example) and by citizens, whose opinions matter to those policy makers. This type of climate control is designed to soften opposition and increase community goodwill.

Other groups, especially those without a great deal of access to policy makers, may engage in protests and civil disobedience to be heard, as we saw in this chapter's opening vignette. Sometimes leaders calculate that media attention to their actions will increase public awareness and spark widespread support for their cause, as was the case with the immigration reform protesters.

ELECTIONEERING   Interest groups often engage in the indirect strategy of **electioneering**—working to influence the election of candidates who support their issues. All of the tactics of electioneering are active methods of civic participation. These techniques include endorsing particular candidates or positions and conducting voter-registration and get-out-the-vote drives. Grassroots campaign efforts often put interest groups with large memberships, including labor unions, at an advantage.

Campaign contributions are considered a key element of electioneering. The importance of contributions puts wealthier interest groups, including corporate and business groups, at an advantage. Table 7.2 shows the breakdown of contributions by business, labor, and ideologically driven PACs. Business PACs and individuals with business interests compose the largest sources of revenue for political candidates and tend to favor Republicans over Democrats. Labor groups and individuals associated with them give overwhelmingly to

climate control
the practice of using public outreach to build favorable public opinion of the organization

electioneering
working to influence the elections of candidates who support the organization's issues

DOING DEMOCRACY

INVESTIGATE CANDIDATES' CAMPAIGN FUNDING

FACT:
Although "being in the pockets of the special interests" has become a cliché, the Federal Election Commission has made it easier than ever for citizens and the media to find out who is funding federal political campaigns. You can use this information to help make up your mind about whether you should support a particular candidate. You can also use it to influence others' opinions by sharing this information with campus groups, the media, and even a candidate's opposition.

Act!
First, go to the Federal Election Commission Web site, www.fec.gov, and then click on the "Campaign Finance Reports and Data" button. You can search the disclosure database by selecting a specific candidate, office, or state. You can also search the database to see which candidates received certain political action committees' contributions.

Where to begin
Information is important, but doing democracy means *using* that information. If you support a particular candidate but do not necessarily support some of his or her contributors, ask the candidate or the individual's campaign staff to explain why the contribution might have been made and why it was accepted. If a candidate whom you oppose has accepted contributions from organizations that do not seem to have constituents' views in mind, you might express your reactions by blogging about the matter or by writing a letter to the editor of a newspaper—or you can blog to ask the candidate to explain why he or she accepted that contribution.

TABLE 7.2

Contributions by Business, Labor, and Ideological Political Action Committees

	Total	Democrats	Republicans	Dem %	Repub %
Business	$1,503,597,831	$669,580,014	$828,512,346	45%	55%
Labor	$61,613,085	$53,773,797	$7,702,938	87%	13%
Ideological	$72,785,656	$35,374,037	$37,219,029	49%	51%

Source: Federal Election Commission, www.fec.gov/press/press2007/20071009pac/contrib2006.pdf.

Democratic candidates but contribute a great deal less money than do business PACs. Ideologically driven PACs and individuals are nearly evenly divided between Democrats and Republicans.

Interest groups also commonly use the tactics of endorsements and ratings to attract support for the candidates whom they favor and to reduce the electoral chances of those whom they do not. Through endorsements, an interest group formally supports specific candidates and typically notifies its members and the media of that support. An endorsement may also involve financial support from the interest group's PAC. And by the technique of rating candidates, the interest group examines candidates' responses to a questionnaire issued by the group. Sometimes a group rates members of Congress on the basis of how they voted on measures important to the group. The ratings of a liberal interest group such as the Americans for Democratic Action (ADA) or a conservative interest group such as the American Conservative Union (ACU) can serve as an ideological benchmark. So, for example, as senators in 2007, both Hillary Clinton and Barack Obama had ADA ratings of 75, while Republican John McCain had an ADA rating of 10. McCain had an ACU rating of 82, and Clinton and Obama each had about an 8. Interest group ratings are used by voters and the media to evaluate candidates and also by candidates themselves, who may advertise their rating to targeted group constituencies.

Interest Groups, Politics, and Money: The Influence of Political Action Committees

The influence of money on politics is not a recent phenomenon. Louise Overacker, one of the first political scientists to do research on campaign finance, wrote in 1932, "Any effective program of control must make it possible to bring into the light the sources and amounts of all funds used in political campaigns, and the way in which those funds are expended. . . . Negatively, it must not attempt to place legal limitations upon the size of contributions or expenditures."[32] Years later, Congress would see the wisdom of Overacker's analysis: federal regulations now stipulate that a group that contributes to any candidate's campaign must register as a political action committee (PAC). For this reason, most interest groups form PACs as one arm of their organization.

Whereas the interest group pursues the group's broad goals by engaging in a variety of activities, its PAC raises and spends money in order to influence the outcome of an election. Typically it will do so by contributing to candidates' campaigns. Funding campaigns helps

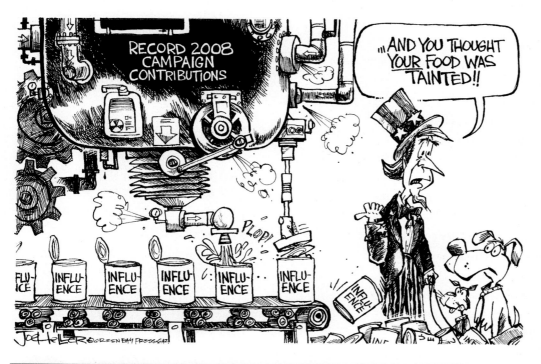

POLITICAL INQUIRY

What point does this cartoon make about the nature of 2008 political campaign contributions? Exactly what are these contributions buying, according to the cartoonist?

© Joe Heller, 2008. www.cagle.com

an interest group in various ways. For one thing, it establishes the interest group as a formal supporter of one or more candidates. And importantly, campaign contributions are a door opener for an interest group's lobbyists. For a lobbyist, access to policy makers is crucial, and campaign contributions provide a means of contact and help ensure that a phone call will be returned or an invitation responded to, even if the policy maker does not support the group's position on every issue.

Table 7.3 lists the PACs that contribute the most money to U.S. campaigns and highlights the party their contributions favor. As the table (along with Table 7.2) illustrates,

TABLE 7.3

Top Twenty-Five PAC Contributors and Their Contribution Tilt, 1989–2008

Rank	Organization Name	Total	Contribution Tilt 1989–2008
1	American Fed. of State, County & Municipal Employees	$39,165,934	🐴🐴🐴
2	AT&T Inc	$38,929,795	🏛
3	National Assn of Realtors	$31,928,656	🏛
4	American Assn for Justice	$28,539,389	🐴🐴🐴
5	Goldman Sachs	$28,367,132	🐴
6	Intl Brotherhood of Electrical Workers	$27,580,809	🐴🐴🐴
7	National Education Assn	$27,355,449	🐴🐴🐴
8	Laborers Union	$26,269,589	🐴🐴🐴
9	Service Employees International Union	$25,408,993	🐴🐴🐴
10	Carpenters & Joiners Union	$25,389,482	🐴🐴
11	Communications Workers of America	$24,817,879	🐴🐴🐴
12	Teamsters Union	$24,773,864	🐴🐴🐴
13	Citigroup Inc	$24,643,677	🏛
14	American Medical Assn	$24,511,421	🐘
15	United Auto Workers	$23,720,205	🐴🐴🐴
16	American Federation of Teachers	$23,214,443	🐴🐴🐴
17	Altria Group	$23,081,795	🐘🐘
18	Machinists & Aerospace Workers Union	$22,791,645	🐴🐴🐴
19	United Food & Commercial Workers Union	$22,082,112	🐴🐴🐴
20	United Parcel Service	$21,829,443	🐘
21	National Auto Dealers Assn	$21,790,892	🐘
22	FedEx Corp	$21,534,907	🏛
23	National Assn of Home Builders	$19,872,310	🐘
24	American Bankers Assn	$19,350,493	🐘
25	EMILY's List	$18,583,058	🐴🐴🐴

LEGEND: 🐘 Republican   🐴 Democrat   🏛 On the fence
🏛 = Between 40% and 59% to both parties
🐘 = Leans Dem/Repub (60%–69%)
🐴🐴 = Strongly Dem/Repub (70%–89%)
🐴🐴🐘 = Solidly Dem/Repub (over 90%)

Source: Center for Responsive Politics, www.opensecrets.org/orgs/list.asp?order=A.

many business and corporate PACs favor Republicans, whereas labor groups tend to support Democrats. More consistently, PACs, particularly those formed by economic interest groups, overwhelmingly favor incumbents (see "Doing Democracy"). PACs' powers-that-be know that incumbent candidates are most likely to be reelected, and thus the PACs support their reelection bids. As we will examine further in Chapter 9, interest groups rely on political action committees to channel their support to candidates that espouse their views.

CONCLUSION
CONTINUING THE CONVERSATION

Interest groups are a powerful vehicle by which individuals can join forces and collectively convince policy makers to take legislative action on their goals. As such, interest groups play a strong role in the policy-making process. Throughout U.S. history and continuing today, the prevalence of interest groups is testimony to people's desire to influence the pathways of their society and government.

Interest groups are one of the great leveling devices in U.S. politics. They are organizations that enable "regular Jills and Joes" to influence policy through collective action and organization. And although not all Americans are equally likely to join and form interest groups, interest groups represent an avenue of participation open to all, and with enough variety in tactics and strategies to offer appealing means of civic participation to a broad spectrum of the population. Particularly today, with the Internet providing a highly accessible medium for participation, interest groups give individuals the opportunity to increase their own social capital—to improve their own lives and the life of their community by making government more responsive to their needs and concerns and by increasing the effectiveness of the public policy-making process.

Although there are competing opinions about the role and value of interest groups in U.S. politics, their influence in policy-making is unquestioned. Thus interest groups offer enormous potential for people who wish to become civically engaged. The abundance of groups for virtually every cause (and the ability of anyone to form his or her own group) means that like-minded individuals can work together to ensure that government policy represents their views.

Today, through the Internet and other digital technology, interest groups can provide individuals with instantly accessed information and organizational tools. Advances in computing, telephone communications, and television have opened the doors to participation in politics and government in ways that were undreamed of a few decades ago. Thanks to technology, the potential exists for interest groups to reach new and ever-widening audiences. As we have seen, however, the potential audience, at least in the present day, excludes many members of the working class, who may not have been socialized to take part in groups and who may lack the time and means to access computer technology. This lack of access poses a challenge to interest groups as they rely ever more heavily on digital recruiting, communicating, organizing, and fund-raising.

In becoming increasingly dependent on relatively low-cost technological tools, interest groups also have to deal with the challenges of paying for the expertise needed to design, build, and maintain their Web sites and Weblogs. Once such issues are resolved, and once access is opened to those not currently wired, digital strategies will further strengthen the clout and efficacy of interest groups and these groups will speak for a broader swath of Americans.

STUDY NOW

Summary

1. The Value of Interest Groups

Interest groups offer individuals a vehicle for engaging in civic actions and improving their communities and the nation as a whole. The positive impacts of improved social capital are reciprocal: as participation benefits individuals, it also benefits communities and larger governments, which in turn provide benefits to individuals, and so on. Interest groups also have some downsides: they can allow well-organized minority views to dominate over less-well-organized majority viewpoints; they emphasize the role of money in politics; they strengthen the incumbency advantage of elected officeholders; and they tend to draw participants disproportionately from among society's elites.

2. Who Joins Interest Groups, and Why?

While interest groups serve as an accessible channel for citizen participation, not everyone is equally likely to join or form an interest group. In general, people with high incomes, individuals who are upper-middle and middle class, and those with high levels of education are more likely to join interest groups than are people with low incomes, those who are lower-middle and working class, and those who have less education. In addition, some people join interest groups related to their occupation.

People typically join interest groups for a variety of reasons that can be categorized as solidary incentives, purposive incentives, and economic incentives.

3. How Interest Groups Succeed

Interest groups succeed by using their organizational resources and maximizing the effectiveness of their organizational environment. Organizational resources consist of groups' membership and financial resources. The organizational environment comprises the group's leadership and the presence of opposing or competitive interest groups in the policy-making environment.

4. Types of Interest Groups

Interest groups typically fall into one of three categories. Economic interest groups, such as business, agricultural, or labor union groups advocate for financial benefits for their members in the form of subsidies or wage policies, for example. Public and ideological interest groups lobby for policies that affect public, or collective, goods and include abortion-rights groups and environmental groups. Foreign governments and corporations also use interest groups to influence a wide variety of policies, especially trade and military policy.

5. Interest Group Strategies

Interest groups usually combine direct and indirect strategies in their attempts to influence the policy process. Direct strategies typically involve lobbying a policy maker, while indirect strategies might include using public outreach to build favorable public opinion of the organization (climate control), using campaign contributions and electioneering to influence who will be making policy, and educating the public so that they share a group's position and can convey that view to policy makers.

6. Interest Groups, Politics, and Money: The Influence of Political Action Committees

PACs are the tool by which interest groups contribute to electoral campaigns. Some PACs are partisan, but in general PACs tend to support incumbent candidates, making it difficult for nonincumbents effectively to challenge those already in office.

Key Terms

For Review

1. Explain in detail the differences between how the pluralist and elite theories view interest groups in U.S. democracy.

2. Why do people join interest groups? Who is most likely to join an interest group? Why?

3. What kinds of interest groups exist in the United States? Which types are the most influential? Why are they most influential?

4. What resources help determine how powerful an interest group is?

5. How do political action committees attempt to influence government action?

For Critical Thinking and Discussion

1. Were you brought up in a family in which joining groups was important? Do your parents belong to any interest groups? Do you? If not, why do you think that is the case?

2. What kinds of interest groups are you and your friends most likely to be involved in (even if you are not)? Why are the issues these groups advocate important to you?

3. How has the Internet changed how interest groups operate? What kinds of groups has it made more effective? Has it made any groups less effective?

4. Select a controversial issue such as abortion or gun control, and use the Internet to search for and learn about the interest groups that represent opposing views. What tactics does each group use? Is one strategy more effective than the other?

5. The Supreme Court has ruled that political expenditures constitute a form of free speech. Do you agree? Can you think of any other ways in which "money talks"?

MULTIPLE CHOICE: Choose the lettered item that answers the question correctly.

1. To social scientists, the ways in which our lives are improved by social connections are called
   a. return of social investment.
   b. social interest.
   c. social capital.
   d. material gains.

2. The theory asserting that policy making is a competition among diverse interest groups that are important because they ensure the representation of individual interests is called
   a. Marxist theory.
   b. elite theory.
   c. pluralist theory.
   d. rational choice theory.

3. Motivations to join an interest group based on the companionship and the satisfaction derived from socializing with others are called
   a. solidary incentives.
   b. purposive incentives.
   c. networking incentives.
   d. economic incentives.

4. Motivations to join an interest group based on the belief in the group's cause from an ideological or a moral standpoint are called
   a. solidary incentives.
   b. purposive incentives.
   c. networking incentives.
   d. economic incentives.

5. Motivations to join an interest group because of the monetary benefits its members receive are called
   a. solidary incentives.
   b. purposive incentives.
   c. networking incentives.
   d. economic incentives.

6. Groups that represent collective groups of industries or corporations are called
   a. interest groups.
   b. political parties.
   c. umbrella organizations.
   d. political action committees.

7. The idea that it is not economically rational for people to participate in collective action when the resultant collective good could be realized without participating is the essence of
   a. Marxist theory.
   b. elite theory.
   c. pluralist theory.
   d. rational choice theory.

8. Outcomes that are shared by the general public are called
   a. inalienable rights.
   b. public goods.
   c. unlimited benefits.
   d. policy perks.

9. The interaction of mutual interests among members of Congress, executive agencies, and organized interests during policy making is called
   a. social networking.
   b. an iron triangle.
   c. the steel cube.
   d. a political action committee.

10. The practice of using public outreach to build a favorable public opinion of the organization is called
    a. electioneering.
    b. social networking.
    c. alliance building.
    d. climate control.

FILL IN THE BLANKS.

11. _____ are organizations that seek to achieve some of their goals by influencing government decision making.

12. The phenomenon of someone's deriving benefit from others' actions is called the _____.

13. Working to influence the election of candidates who support an organization's issues is called _____.

14. _____ is the practice of using public outreach to build favorable public opinion of the organization or company.

15. To communicate directly to policy makers on the interest group's behalf is to _____.

RESOURCES FOR RESEARCH AND ACTION

Internet Resources

American Democracy Now Web site
www.mhhe.com/harrison1e   Consult the book's Web site for study guides, interactive activities, simulations, and current hotlinks for additional information on interest groups in the United States.

Center for Responsive Politics
www.opensecrets.org   This nonpartisan Web site provides information on the campaign financing of candidates for federal office.

Common Cause
www.commoncause.org   This Web site features a special section on money and politics and provides links to sites related to its endorsed reform measures.

Federal Election Commission
www.fec.org   You'll find a plethora of information about campaign financing, including regulations, contributions and expenditures, specific candidates, individual donors, political action committees, and political parties.

Recommended Readings

Alexander, Robert M. *Rolling the Dice with State Initiatives: Interest Group Involvement in Ballot Campaigns.* Westport, CT: Praeger, 2001. A probing analysis of the impact of interest groups on gambling initiatives in California and Missouri that, unlike most treatments of interest group activity, focuses on interest group initiatives within states and on lobbying in a nonlegislative arena.

Berry, Jeffrey M., and Clyde Wilcox. *The Interest Group Society,* 4th ed. New York: Longman, 2006. Analyzes the proliferation of various types of interest groups in the United States, as well as the strategies interest groups use to sway policy makers.

Cigler, Alan J., and Burnett A. Loomis. *Interest Group Politics,* 7th ed. Washington, DC: CQ Press, 2007. A classic analysis, first published in 1983, detailing the impact of interest groups in modern American politics.

Hays, Richard A. *Who Speaks for the Poor: National Interest Groups and Social Policy.* New York: Routledge, 2001. An examination of how the poor gain political representation in the policy process through the efforts of interest groups.

Herrnson, Paul S., Ronald G. Shaiko, and Clyde J. Wilcox. *The Interest Group Connection: Electioneering, Lobbying, and Policymaking in Washington,* 2nd ed. Washington, DC: CQ Press, 2004. A collection of essays describing the role of interest groups on the federal level. The essays focus on elections, Congress, the president, and the judiciary.

Rothenberg, Lawrence S. *Linking Citizens to Government: Interest Group Politics at Common Cause.* New York: Cambridge University Press, 1992. An examination of interest group operations using the case study of the interest group Common Cause and looking into the reasons why members join and stay in a group, relations among the group members and the group leaders, and the impact of those relationships on the lobbying policies of the group.

Wright, John. *Interest Groups and Congress (Longman Classics Edition).* New York: Longman, 2002. A study of the influence of both historical and modern interest groups, asserting that interest groups' practice of providing specialized information to members of Congress increases their influence there, has an impact on the resultant policy, and shapes opinion.

Movies of Interest

Thank You for Smoking (2005)
Aaron Eckhart stars as a lobbyist in this satirical comedy about the big tobacco lobby.

Erin Brockovich (2000)
Starring Julia Roberts, this film is based on the true story of Erin Brockovich, an activist fighting for the rights of a community whose water supply has been contaminated.

The Pelican Brief (1993)
Based on the John Grisham novel of the same name, this film, starring Julia Roberts and Denzel Washington, spotlights competition between big business and the environmental movement and illuminates how interested parties can use the courts to make policy.

WHY THEY LOBBY

Thank You for Smoking, the 2005 film based on a novel by Christopher Buckley, follows the life of Nick Naylor, a chief spokesman for Big Tobacco with questionable morals, who makes his living defending the rights of smokers and cigarette-makers and then must deal with how his young son, Joey, views him. Naylor may have been a fictitious character, but Washington has its share of lobbyists arguing for the interests of industries with a perceived darker side.

The cynical response is that career decisions and political give-and-take revolve around money: Greenbacks triumph over ethics. But those who represent socially sensitive industries such as tobacco and alcohol have a lot more to say about why, out of all the potential job opportunities, they chose and often "love" what they do.

They all make it a point to note that the First Amendment sanctions lobbying: "the right of the people . . . to petition the government for a redress of grievances."

■ Tobacco

In the film, Naylor works for the Academy of Tobacco Studies, which Buckley based on the Tobacco Institute, the industry's former trade association. Andrew Zausner, who has lobbied for tobacco for 30 years, feeds off the challenge. "The more unpopular the client, the better you have to be as a lobbyist," he declares. "Believing in your client's position makes you a more forceful advocate." Although Zausner doesn't want his children to use tobacco, he notes that the "product has been continuously used in the United States before the United States existed" and says that the industry has a legitimate point of view and a constitutional right to express it.

Beau Schuyler lobbies for UST Public Affairs, a subsidiary of the holding company that owns U.S. Smokeless Tobacco and Ste. Michelle Wine Estates. A former congressional aide to two Democratic House members from his native state of North Carolina—in the heart of tobacco country—Schuyler says

that the "opportunity to work internally at one of the oldest continually listed companies on the New York Stock Exchange was just too good to pass up."

■ Gambling

James Reeder, a lobbyist at Patton Boggs, has spent about half his time over the past decade representing the gambling industry. He insists he didn't seek out this niche, adding, "I tell my grandchildren that gambling is a bad habit . . . and to go fishing."

Shortly after Reeder joined Patton Boggs, a client named Showboat called the firm looking for someone who knew about Louisiana because the company was interested in building a casino there. Reeder happened to be from the Pelican State and was put on the case. He reasoned that Louisiana has always been a home to illegal gambling, and "if the culture of the state supports the industry, [the state] might as well make it legal and reap the benefits and get more tax money."

"Whenever you take on one of these vices like booze or gambling and you just pass a law to say it is illegal," Reeder says, "you end up like in Prohibition, when the mob took over the liquor business."

Reeder excelled at lobbying for the gambling industry even though he avoids games of chance. "I don't gamble, because I am not a good card player," he says. "My friends would die laughing because I would go to offices to talk to clients on gambling and I would never go into a casino." If a lawmaker was morally opposed to gambling, Reeder wouldn't argue with him, he says.

John Pappas began working for the industry as a consultant for the Poker Players Alliance while at Dittus Communications.

Pappas calls poker a game of skill that has a rich history in America. He grew up playing cards with family members and friends, and noted during an interview that he would be playing poker with 20 lawmakers that evening at a charity tournament. "Responsibility in all aspects of life is paramount," he says.

■ Firearms

Richard Feldman's book, *Ricochet: Confessions of a Gun Lobbyist,* has been gaining the former National Rifle Association employee some attention recently. Feldman says that the gun control issue, like most, is not black and white. Working for the NRA, he says, "was the best job I ever had." The "huge power" he was able to wield "in the middle of major political battles" was more attractive to him at the time than the money he earned.

Feldman says he would sometimes play hardball but "didn't hit below the belt" in his pursuit of the gun industry's objectives. "Lobbying an issue that you have some special passion on (guns) is like waking up every day already having consumed a triple espresso," he said in an e-mail to *National Journal.* "On the other hand, if you can empathize with your client's position regardless of the issue, one can be a more convincing advocate, which I've always viewed as the more critical aspect of truly effective lobbying.

■ Video Games

Because many video games contain a fair share of gunplay and other violence, Entertainment Software Association President Michael Gallagher has had to address complaints that playing violent games causes psychological harm such as increased aggression.

His group lobbies against "efforts to regulate the content of entertainment media in any form, including proposals to criminalize the sale of certain video games to minors; create uniform, government-sanctioned entertainment rating systems; or regulate the marketing practices of industry."

Gallagher, a former assistant Commerce secretary for communications and information in the Bush administration, calls video games a great form of family entertainment. The titles are responsibly rated, he says, and the gaming consoles have easy-to-use parental controls.

"I have been playing video games all my life," Gallagher says, including with his children. He contends that his industry "leads all forms of media when it comes to disclosure on what's in the game" and says that it works with retailers to "make sure minors can't buy games that are inappropriate for them."

Alcohol

Lobbyists who work for the beer, wine, and spirits industries have to deal with a host of negative images, among them drunk-driving accidents, underage drinking, and the effects of alcohol on health.

Mike Johnson, a lobbyist for the National Beer Wholesalers Association, acknowledges that alcohol is a "socially sensitive product" and says that is why the industry operates under strict government guidelines.

"I am blessed. I get to represent some great family-owned and -operated businesses that are very active in their communities and provide some really great jobs," Johnson says. "I am completely comfortable one day having a conversation with my son about who I work for, because I can tell him what a great job that beer distributors do in ensuring a safe marketplace and in protecting consumers from a lot of the problems we see with alcohol in other places in the world."

Craig Wolf, president of the Wine & Spirits Wholesalers, calls alcohol a "great social lubricant" that "creates great environments." Wolf got involved in wine-industry issues when he was counsel for the Senate Judiciary Committee. As his job there was ending, Wolf was offered the post of general counsel at the association; he took over as president in 2006.

"The key to advocating for a socially sensitive product is doing business responsibly," Wolf says. "We spend more time and resources [on the issue of] responsible consumption of alcohol than all other issues combined."

Distilled Spirits Council President Peter Cressy says, "I was interviewed for this position precisely because the Distilled Council wanted to continue and increase its very serious approach to fighting underage drinking." As chancellor of the University of Massachusetts (Dartmouth), Cressy says, he was active in "fighting binge drinking on campuses." The opportunity to join the council, which has lobbyists in 40 states, gave him the chance to have a national audience, he says. After nine years with the council, Cressy notes, he "has not been disappointed."

Snack Foods

Nicholas Pyle stands at the policy divide where junk food meets America's bulging waistlines. "I love my job," says Pyle, a lobbyist for McKee Foods, the makers of Little Debbie, America's leading snack-cake brand.

Many of the brand's affordable treats contain a dose of sugar, along with corn syrup, partially hydrogenated oil, bleached flour, and artificial flavor. Little Debbie "has been the target of a number of folks out there who want to paint people as a victim of the foods they eat," says Pyle, who is also president of the Independent Bakers Association. Little Debbie is a "wonderful food, great product, wholesome, with a wonderful image," he says. Pyle explains that he and his children enjoy the snacks.

"The big question of obesity is all about personal responsibility and people balancing [snacking] with a healthy and active lifestyle," Pyle insists. He contends that McKee, a family-owned business, doesn't target children in its marketing. "We market to the decision makers in the household," he says, adding that the company doesn't advertise on Saturday morning cartoon shows.

Snack Food Association President and CEO Jim McCarthy says that lobbying is one of his many duties as head of the organization. "Our belief is that all foods fit into the diet," McCarthy says, and "we don't like the term 'junk food.'"

The industry has developed healthier products over the years, McCarthy says, but at "certain times consumers haven't bought these products." He attributes the obesity problem to a lack of exercise and shortcomings in educating people about the need for a balanced diet.

Challenging Stereotypes

No matter what industry they represent, lobbyists interviewed for this article said that a good practitioner of their profession knows all sides of an issue, enabling lawmakers and their staffs to make the best-informed decision.

Although many of the lobbyists acknowledge some familiar situations in *Thank You for Smoking*, they insist that the stereotypes are not altogether fair. "I think people don't understand the importance of lobbying to the system. If I don't explain what we do and I am not here to explain it to people, Congress will make uninformed decisions without understanding the consequences to the industry," a former liquor lobbyist says.

For consumers, the message that lobbyists appear to be sending is that the individual is responsible for making the right choices in life. Yet the profusion of advertising, marketing ploys, political rhetoric, and seemingly conflicting studies can be bewildering. And although the financial incentive is ever-present, lobbyists believe they fill a fundamental role in society and deserve some relief from the negative stereotypes.

THEN: Every group, like every individual, had the right to advocate or attempt to prevent legislation when it is within their interests to do so.

NOW: Not every interest group is perceived to be ethically equivalent, and some, it is claimed, place their narrow, often economic, interests above the good of the people.

NEXT: How will intensive lobbying for "sin industries" such as gambling affect legislation—and public policy—in the twenty-first century? Should certain lobbies be regulated but not others?

How will the positions put forward by the interest groups in the article affect how the public thinks about these industries?

CHAPTER

8

Political Parties

THEN

Political parties relied on patronage and voter loyalty to become powerful entities in American politics.

NOW

Voter loyalty has declined, but parties remain an important force for mobilizing citizens.

NEXT

Will the dominance of the Democratic and Republican parties continue?

Will political parties decline in their ability to perform key functions?

How will digital technologies further shape parties' strategies and expand their reach—and change the membership of parties?

Joining the Party in 2008

In the winter and spring of 2008, an extraordinary thing happened: people became riveted by the political primary process. Throughout the country, viewers watched the results of the early presidential primaries and caucuses roll in. The "day after," they gathered and gabbed around office water coolers and campus student centers as if the topic were the NFL playoffs. Later primaries—those on February 5 in particular—rose to the level of Super Bowls, with full media coverage and all the excitement of a tie game with a minute to go in the fourth quarter. I The Republicans decided on a nominee comparatively early. But even so, voter turnout was up. In all, over 20 million Republicans voted in the 2008 primaries, with John McCain winning nearly half of all Republican votes cast. Even in later primaries, turnout remained strong, although John McCain already had enough delegates to secure the nomination. I For the Democrats, the contest went down to the wire. The race, one of historic proportions in terms of race and gender, captivated the electorate and the media alike. The media neatly delineated the two camps: if you were African American or young, Barack Obama was your candidate; if you were a woman or an older voter, Hillary Clinton was your clear choice. But the reality was far more complex. As voters registered, reflected, listened to pundits, were subjected to a barrage of candidate commercials, talked to their neighbors and families, and reflected some more, they changed their minds. They changed them back again. And then they voted. More than 55 million of them. They shattered primary turnout records in well over half of the states. They waited for hours to get a seat in a caucus. Or they stood in line in the rain at a polling place. Millions of independent and unaffiliated voters declared their preference and voted in a party primary—long the bastion mainly of loyal party members—for the first time. Because the race for the Democratic nomination was so tight, Democratic turnout in most states was nearly double that of the Republican primaries. I "Historic numbers," the headlines trumpeted. "Record turnout," the blogs reported. In the end over 36 million citizens voted in the Democratic primaries, shattering the previous record of 23 million, set in the 1988 presidential primaries. I Beyond the impressive turnout, the high levels of voter interest and voter knowledge also stood out. Most polls indicated that more people than usual said they were interested in the campaign. And they were paying attention to campaign issues. People in subways talked about how the spread of the delegate count was deciphered. Googling "superdelegates" would get you 2.8 million hits. I When the confetti settled, some voters were happy with their party's nominee, but others were not. Some of the disgruntled voters took those sentiments to the polls with them in November and voted for the opposing party's candidate. But in the spring of 2008, nearly 20 million new Democratic and Republican primary voters had had a say in determining their party's presidential nominee.

> After a hard-fought primary season, Barack Obama officially became the Democratic nominee for president at the party's convention in late August 2008.

Political parties are essential

channels for the realization of American democracy. The "American Democracy Now" vignette illustrates how citizens determine their choice of presidential nominee through party processes. Political parties serve the American system in many crucial capacities, from recruiting candidates, to conducting elections, to distributing information to voters, to participating in governance. One of their essential functions is to provide an open arena for participation by civic-minded individuals, while reaching out to involve those who do not participate.

Because Americans place high value on independent thought and action, some citizens view political parties with suspicion. For such observers, the collective activity of parties brings worries about corruption and control by elite decision makers. But even though party insiders sometimes do exert considerable power, parties remain one of the most accessible forums for citizens' participation in democracy. Indeed, political scientist E. E. Schattschneider, who believed that parties represented the foremost means for citizens to communicate with political decision makers—and in this way to retain control over their government—wrote that "modern democracy is unthinkable save in terms of political parties."[1]

Parties Today and Their Functions

In the United States today, two major political parties—the Democratic and the Republican parties—dominate the political landscape. Generally speaking, a **political party** is an organization of ideologically similar people that nominates and elects its members to office in order to run the government and shape public policy. Parties identify potential candidates, nominate them to run for office, campaign for them, organize elections, and govern. But given some overlapping roles, political scientists agree that parties can be distinguished from other political organizations, such as interest groups and political action committees, through four defining characteristics.

Defining a Political Party

First, political parties run candidates under their own label, or affiliation. Most candidates who run for office are identified by their party affiliation. Running

In this chapter, we view the nature and function of contemporary U.S. political parties through several lenses. We trace party development historically and explore how parties are continuing to evolve and change in the digital age.

FIRST, we examine the *parties today and their functions.*

SECOND, we consider the *three faces of parties*—the party in the electorate, the party organization, and the party in government.

THIRD, we focus on *political parties in U.S. history*—the five party systems identified by political scientists.

FOURTH, we examine the reasons for and persistence of *two-party domination in U.S. politics.*

FIFTH, we look at various interpretations of the health of the *two-party system today.*

SIXTH, we survey *third parties in the United States*—their nature, electoral record, and influence.

SEVENTH, we probe the impact of *new ideologies and new technologies* on parties in the contemporary era.

political party
an organization that recruits, nominates, and elects party members to office in order to control the government

> Texas governor Rick Perry campaigning for office. Parties today appeal to diverse groups of supporters, including women, racial and ethnic minorities, and young people. As the leading Republican officeholder in his state, Perry runs as the head of the Republican ticket.

a candidate under the party label involves a host of party functions, including recruiting candidates, organizing elections, and campaigning.[2] And political parties typically are the only organizations that regularly run candidates under their party label.

Second, unlike interest groups, which hope to have individuals sympathetic to their cause elected but which typically do not want to govern, *political parties seek to govern.* Political parties run candidates hoping that they will win a majority of the seats in a legislature or control the executive branch. Such victories enable the party to enact a broad partisan agenda. For example, the Democratic victories in the 2006 congressional races swept the Democrats into control of both the U.S. House and Senate, paving the way for the Democratic leadership in both houses to act on the party's stated agenda, particularly in establishing a timeline for the withdrawal of U.S. troops from Iraq.

A third defining characteristic is that *political parties have broad concerns, focused on many issues.* The major parties in the United States are made up of coalitions of different groups and constituencies who rely on political parties to enact their agendas. That is to say, if we were to look at a party's **platform**—the formal statement of its principles and policy objectives—we would find its stance on all sorts of issues: war, abortion rights, environmental protection, the minimum wage, and so on. These positions are one articulation of the interests of that party's coalition constituencies. Typically, interest groups have narrower issue concerns than parties do, and some focus on only a single issue. For example, we know that the National Rifle Association opposes governmental controls on gun ownership, but what is this interest group's position on the minimum wage? On the environment? Chances are high that the NRA does not have positions on these matters because its concern is with the single issue of gun ownership.

Finally, *political parties are quasi-public organizations that have a special relationship with the government.* Some functions of political parties overlap with governmental functions, and some party functions facilitate the creation and perpetuation of government (running elections, for example). The resulting special status subjects political parties to greater scrutiny than private clubs and organizations.

platform
the formal statement of a party's principles and policy objectives

How Parties Engage Individuals

Political scientists who study the nature of Americans' civic engagement recognize that political parties represent one of the main channels through which citizens can make their voices heard. A fixture in the politics of American communities large and small, parties today are accessible to virtually everyone.

Historically, political parties excluded various groups from participating. For example, in many states, women were shut out of party meetings until the mid-twentieth century.[3] African Americans were formally excluded from voting in Democratic primaries in the South until the U.S. Supreme Court banned the practice in 1944, though it took decades before the party complied with that decision.[4] But in recent times political parties have increasingly embraced and championed diversity. They have encouraged various groups beyond the traditional white European American male party establishment to get involved formally in the party organization, to participate in campaign activities, and to vote. As a result, parties today are much more inclusive of women, ethnic and racial minorities, and students, providing an important avenue for those traditionally excluded from political life to gain valuable experience as party activists, campaign volunteers, and informed voters. This increasingly diverse participation has also contributed to the parties' health, because it has caused them to recognize that to be successful candidates must reflect the diverse identities and interests of voters.

Concept Summary

DEFINING FEATURES OF POLITICAL PARTIES

Political party: an organization that recruits, nominates, and elects party members to office in order to control the government.

— Political parties run candidates under their own label, or affiliation.

— Political parties seek to govern.

— Political parties have broad concerns.

— Political parties are quasi-public organizations that have a special relationship with the government.

What Political Parties Do

As we have seen, by promoting political activity, political parties encourage civic engagement and citizen participation and in this way foster democracy. Parties provide a structure for people at the grassroots level to volunteer on party-run campaigns, make campaign contributions, work in the day-to-day operations of the party, and run for office. During the 2008 presidential campaign, for example, the Drexel (University) Democrats and the university's College Republicans registered nearly 2,000 new voters for the Pennsylvania primary alone. Following that effort, a bipartisan coalition called Drexel Votes 2008, comprising students, faculty, and staff, joined forces to get these newly registered voters out to vote on election day in November. The coalition knew that voter turnout would likely make *the* difference in the presidential contest that year.

On the local level, a political party's ability to promote citizen participation varies with its relative influence within the community. Viable political parties—those that effectively contest and win some elections—are more effective at promoting citizen participation than weak political parties. A party that typically is in the minority in a local government—on town council, in the county legislature—will find it more difficult to attract volunteers, to bring people out to fund-raisers, and to recruit candidates. And it naturally follows that parties that are better at attracting public participation are more likely to win elections.

Political parties also foster cooperation between divided interests and factions, building coalitions even in the most divisive of times. In 2004, Democrats helped to bring together a coalition of groups—including medical researchers, physicians, support and research groups that provide services to people with diseases such as Alzheimer's and Parkinson's, and individuals with those diseases—to oppose the Bush administration's limitations on embryonic stem cell research. This coalition succeeded in lobbying Congress to pass a bill, the Stem Cell Research Enhancement Act of 2006. Although President Bush vetoed the legislation, the coalition continues to attempt to influence stem cell research policy, now concentrating on the states. Civic engagement researchers point out that political parties' work in building coalitions and promoting cooperation among diverse groups often occurs away from the bright lights of the media-saturated public arena, where the parties' differences, rather than their common causes, often are in the spotlight.

Political parties also grease the wheels of government and ensure its smooth running. Nearly all legislatures, from town councils to Congress, consist of a *majority party,* the party to which more than 50 percent of the elected legislators belong, and the *minority party,* to which less than 50 percent of the elected legislators belong. Thus, if five of the nine members of your town council are Republicans and four are Democrats, the Republicans are the majority party and the Democrats are the minority party. The majority party elects the legislature's leaders, makes committee assignments, and holds a majority on those committees.

By serving as a training ground for members, political parties also foster effective government. This role of parties is particularly important for groups that traditionally have not been among the power brokers in the government. Historically, African Americans, Latinos, and women have gained valuable knowledge and leadership experience in party organizations—by volunteering on party-run campaigns, assisting with candidate recruitment, or helping with fundraising endeavors—before running for office.[5] Party credentials established by serving the party in these ways can act as a leveling device that can help make a newcomer's candidacy more viable.

Perhaps most important, political parties promote civic responsibility among elected officials and give voters an important "check" on those elected officials. In the 2006 congressional election, voters checked President Bush's power by voting a majority of Democrats into Congress. And because many viewed that election a mandate against the administration's policy in Iraq, the president's ability to accomplish his goals was stymied by the Democrats, who rebuked his policy by calling for a timeline for withdrawal and by questioning budget allocations for the war. When an elected leader, particularly a chief executive, is the crucial

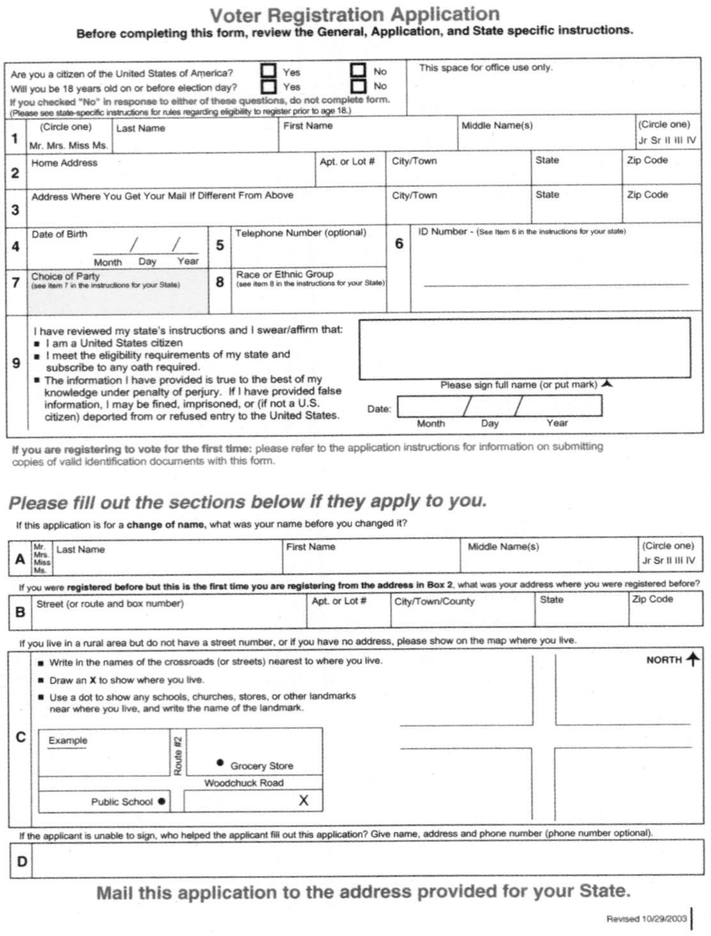

Voter Registration Application
Before completing this form, review the General, Application, and State specific instructions.

[Voter registration form with fields including citizenship questions, name, address, date of birth, telephone number, ID number, choice of party, race or ethnic group, oath/affirmation section, and additional sections A–D for change of name, prior registration address, rural area map, and applicant assistance.]

Mail this application to the address provided for your State.

Revised 10/29/2003

> Most states offer voters the opportunity to declare their party affiliation when registering to vote. Affiliated voters are the party in the electorate.

responsible party model
political scientists' view that a function of a party is to offer a clear choice to voters by establishing priorities or policy stances different from those of rival parties

party in the electorate
individuals who identify with or tend to support a party

party identifiers
individuals who identify themselves as a member of one party or the other

independent
often used as a synonym for an unaffiliated voter

player in enacting an important policy, the existence of political parties enables voters to hold party members responsible *even if that particular elected official is not running for reelection.* The system thus provides a check on the power of elected officials, because it makes them aware that the policy or position they are taking may be unpopular.

Historically, according to one theory, political parties have also made government more effective and have provided important cues for voters. The **responsible party model,** developed by E. E. Schattschneider, posits that a party tries to give voters a clear choice by establishing priorities or policy stances different from those of the other rival party or parties. Because a party's elected officials tend to be loyal to their party's stances, voters can readily anticipate how a candidate will vote on a given set of issues if elected, and can thus cast their vote according to their preferences on those issues.

The Three Faces of Parties

American political parties perform their various functions through three "faces," or spheres of operation.[6] The three components of the party include the party in the electorate, the party organization, and the party in government (see Figure 8.1).

The Party in the Electorate

All of the individuals who identify with or tend to support a particular party make up the **party in the electorate.** Several factors influence which party an individual will identify with, including personal circumstances, race, and religion, as well as the party's history, ideology, position on issues of importance to the voter, and candidates.[7]

MEASURING THE PARTY IN THE ELECTORATE The term **party identifier** refers to an individual who identifies himself or herself as a member of one party or the other; party identifiers typically are measured by party registration. In most states, party registration is a legal process in which a voter formally selects affiliation with one political party. This declaration of affiliation often occurs when a person registers to vote; the prospective voter selects his or her party identification by filling out a voter registration form or party declaration form. Depending on the state, a voter may select the Democratic or Republican Party, a variety of third parties, or no party. When a voter does not select a party, he or she is technically an unaffiliated voter, but often analysts refer to such a voter as an **independent.**

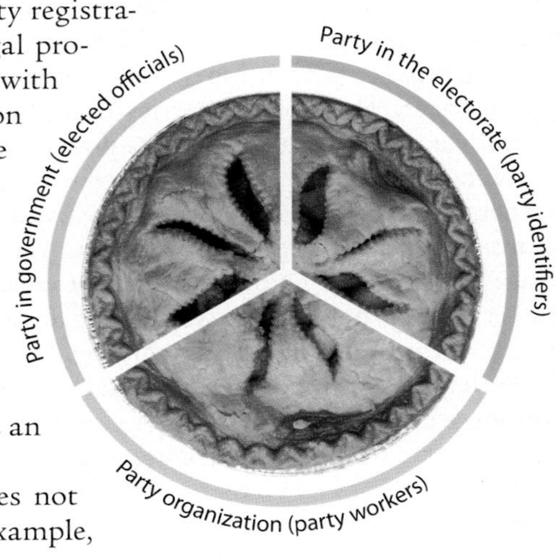

People's party identification sometimes does not match their actual voting preferences. For example, perhaps a voter never declared his or her party identification yet votes consistently for one party over the other. When we refer to the party

FIGURE 8.1

The Three Faces of Parties

[Diagram labels: party in government (elected officials); Party in the electorate (party identifiers); Party organization (party workers)]

in the electorate, we also consider those individuals who express a tendency to vote for one party or a preference for that party.

DETERMINING WHO BELONGS TO EACH POLITICAL PARTY

Although we commonly speak in terms of which groups affiliate with and "belong to" each of the political parties, these are just generalizations, with many exceptions. In general, each political party counts specific demographic groups as part of its base of support. A party will often draw party activists and leaders from the ranks of this bloc of individuals whose support can be counted on.

Figure 8.2 shows the breakdown of party membership among various groups in the United States. Although whites, men, and people with some college education are naturally found in both parties, they are more likely to be Republicans. For the Democrats, key voting blocs include African Americans, ethnic minorities, women, and people with no college education. Individuals with a college degree or more are evenly divided between the two parties. Social class also plays a role in party preference. The working class is largely Democratic; the upper-middle class, largely Republican; and the middle class, by far the largest class in the United States, is divided between the two parties. But the best predictor of a person's party identification is his or her ideology. People who identify themselves as conservative are much more likely to be Republicans; people who identify themselves as liberal are much more likely to be Democrats (see the discussion of ideology in Chapter 1).

DIFFERENCES BETWEEN DEMOCRATS AND REPUBLICANS

We can trace some of the differences—in both ideologies and core constituencies—between today's Democrats and Republicans to the 1930s. This was the era of the **Great Depression,** a time of devastating economic collapse and personal misery for people around the world. President Franklin D. Roosevelt's drive to expand the role of government by providing a safety net for the most vulnerable in society has remained part of the Democratic agenda to this day. In the past several decades, this agenda has centered on pressing for civil rights for African Americans and for the expansion of social welfare programs. Today, key components of the Democratic agenda include gay rights, environmental protection, and freedom of choice with respect to abortion.

Traditionally, Republicans have countered this position by advocating a smaller government that performs fewer social welfare functions. But a major priority for the Republican Party today is advocacy of a stronger governmental role in regulating traditional moral values. Because of this stance, a solid voting bloc within the Republican Party comprises conservative Christians, sometimes called the Christian Right or Religious Right, who agree with the Republicans' pro-life position on abortion (which includes support for an increased regulation of abortion) and appeals for a constitutional amendment banning gay marriage. Republicans also emphasize the protection of business and business owners and in general support a decreased role for the federal government, particularly with respect to the economy and social welfare issues, and a corresponding larger role for state governments.

More recent analysis of the differences between Democrats and Republicans reveals how much the world has changed in the past several years. Research on party identifiers between 2005 and 2008 shows how the perception of a party's level of assertiveness in foreign affairs is a defining characteristic of Democrats and Republicans.[8] Previous analyses, conducted before

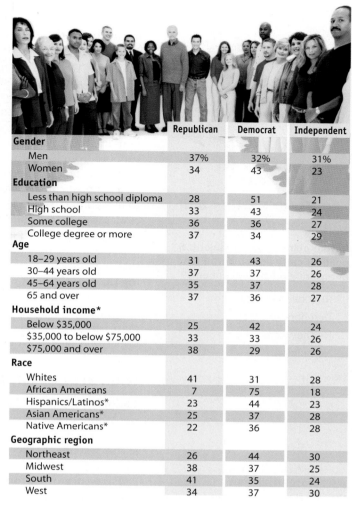

	Republican	Democrat	Independent
Gender			
Men	37%	32%	31%
Women	34	43	23
Education			
Less than high school diploma	28	51	21
High school	33	43	24
Some college	36	36	27
College degree or more	37	34	29
Age			
18–29 years old	31	43	26
30–44 years old	37	37	26
45–64 years old	35	37	28
65 and over	37	36	27
Household income*			
Below $35,000	25	42	24
$35,000 to below $75,000	33	33	26
$75,000 and over	38	29	26
Race			
Whites	41	31	28
African Americans	7	75	18
Hispanics/Latinos*	23	44	23
Asian Americans*	25	37	28
Native Americans*	22	36	28
Geographic region			
Northeast	26	44	30
Midwest	38	37	25
South	41	35	24
West	34	37	30

POLITICAL INQUIRY

FIGURE 8.2 ■ DEMOGRAPHIC CHARACTERISTICS OF PARTY IDENTIFIERS (2006) Which two racial groups are likeliest to identify with the Democratic Party? Which party do people with incomes below $35,000 per year favor? What might explain these data?

Source: The National Election Poll conducted by Edison/Mitofsky, www.washingtonpost.com/wp-srv/politics/interactives/independents/data-year-by-year.html.
*Income based on 2004 data. The National Annenberg Election Study polls conducted between October 7 and November 16, 2004, www.annenbergpublicpolicycenter.org/NewsFilter.aspx?mySubType=ALL&. Used by permission of Annenberg Public Policy Center.

Great Depression
between 1929 and 1939, a time of devastating economic collapse and personal misery for people around the world

party organization
the formal party apparatus, including committees, party leaders, conventions, and workers

the wars in Afghanistan and Iraq, showed that this factor had very little bearing on party identity. The more recent research also indicates that positions on social issues, once a defining feature of the parties, have declined tremendously as a key determinant of partisanship.

In concrete terms, these differences mean that Republicans are more likely to believe that a foreign policy emphasizing military action is the right course, and that Democrats are more likely to oppose war (such as the war in Iraq) and to believe that foreign policy should stress diplomacy over military action. In general, Democrats remain committed to a larger government role in providing an economic safety net and until 2008 were quite united in their opposition to many domestic policies advanced by the Bush administration, particularly the privatization of Social Security. Interestingly, the Republican Party is gaining support from lower-income voters who are less opposed than traditional Republican supporters to a larger governmental role in providing economic security.

It is not surprising that the base constituencies of the parties are drawn from the groups that each party's platform emphasizes. The base of the Democratic Party prominently includes women, the majority of whom, since 1980, have voted for the Democratic presidential nominee. Since Franklin Roosevelt's New Deal social welfare policy during the 1930s, African Americans have been an important voting bloc within the Democratic Party, although they have faced struggles and strife in asserting and securing their rights, particularly during the civil rights movement of the 1960s. Other ethnic minorities, including Latinos and Asian Americans, also tend to support the Democratic Party (as described in Chapter 6), as do many working-class voters. The base of the Republican Party prominently includes many small-business owners, citizens who identify themselves as being very religious, and upper-middle-class voters.[9]

The Party Organization

Thomas P. "Tip" O'Neill (D-Massachusetts), Speaker of the House of Representatives from 1977 until 1987, is often quoted as saying, "All politics is local." In no case is this statement truer than it is for American political parties.

Party organization refers to the formal party apparatus, including committees, headquarters, conventions, party leaders, staff, and volunteer workers. In the United States, the party organization is most visible at the local level. Yet county and local parties tend to be *loosely* organized—centered predominantly around elections—and may be dormant when election season passes.[10] Except during presidential elections, state and local political parties typically function quite separately from the national party. Although the number of individuals who actually participate in the party organization is quite small when compared with the party in the electorate, on the local level, political parties offer one of the most accessible means for individuals to participate in politics.

But with respect to political *power*, county and local parties are the most important components of a party organization. Theoretically, political parties' organization resembles a pyramid (see Figure 8.3), with a broad base of support at the bottom and power flowing up to a smaller group at the state level and then to an even smaller, more exclusive group at the national level.[11] In reality, the national committees of both major U.S. political parties exist separately from the committees of the state and local parties (see Figure 8.4), and real political power can usually be found at the local or county party level, as we will see in the following discussion.

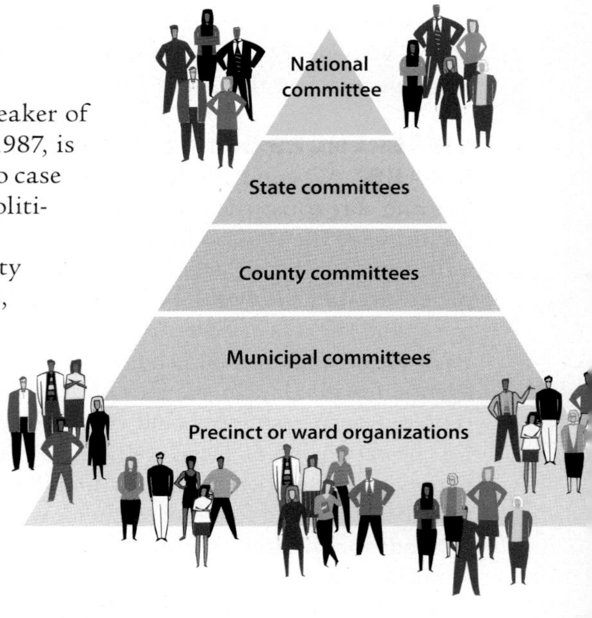

FIGURE 8.3

Theoretical Structure of Political Parties: A Hierarchical Model of Party Organizations

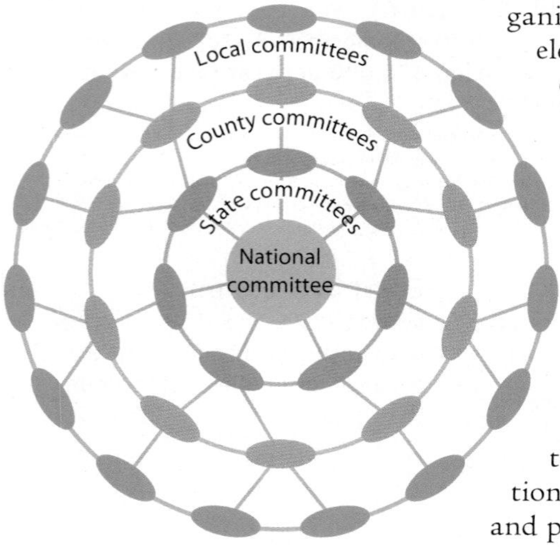

National committee
State committees
County committees
Municipal committees
Precinct or ward organizations

FIGURE 8.4

Modern Structure of Political Parties: Power Diffused Through Many Party Organizations

Local committees
County committees
State committees
National committee

EXPLORING THE SOURCES

THE PEOPLE'S OPINION OF THE PARTIES

The figure below shows the percentage of survey respondents who have a favorable view of the Republican and Democratic parties at selected dates between September 2001 and April 2008.

Evaluating the Evidence

① What is the general trend with regard to party favorability ratings? Is one political party consistently viewed more favorably than the other? What is the trend over time regarding the favorability of Democrats versus Republicans?

② Look at particular high and low points for each political party. What events may have caused people's opinions of the parties to increase or decline?

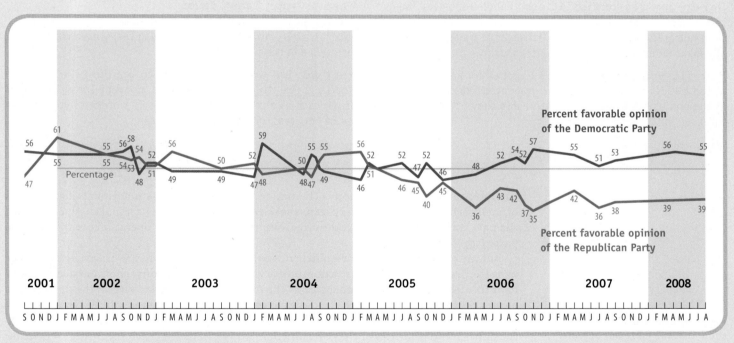

Source: "Party Images," www.gallup.com/poll/24655/Party-Images.aspx.

THE NATIONAL PARTIES Every four years, political party activists meet at a national convention to determine their party's nominee for the presidency. Here the delegates also adopt rules and develop a party platform that describes the party's policy priorities and positions on issues.

The national party committees (the Democratic National Committee, or DNC, and the Republican National Committee, or RNC) are the national party organizations charged with conducting the conventions and overseeing the operation of the national party during

JON THOMPSON, PARTY COMMUNICATIONS COORDINATOR

Name: Jon Thompson

Age: 23

Hometown: Charlotte, North Carolina

College: University of North Carolina at Wilmington

Major: Political Science (BA)

Job title: Executive Assistant to the Communications Director

Salary range for jobs like this: $40,000–$75,000

Day-to-day responsibilities: I handle reporters' inquiries, compile media clips, schedule interviews, manage interns, send out press releases, arrange for advance travel, and generally make sure the Press Office runs smoothly.

How did you get your job? I applied for an internship at the RNC for the summer after I graduated from college, and at the end of the three-month internship they offered me a full-time job.

What do you like best about your job? Being in the center of all the action. The RNC is on Capitol Hill, and I regularly see members of Congress and senators. I also speak with high-profile journalists and politicians on a daily basis. Many other employees in the building are also young staffers, and that makes for a great work environment.

What is your least favorite aspect of your job? The hours are long, but in the end, it's a very rewarding job where you feel you've made a difference in the political arena.

What advice would you give to students who would like to do what you're doing? Intern early and often, such as at the D.C. office or district office of your member of Congress, or on a local campaign.

---

the interim between conventions. The national committee elects a national chair, who is often informally selected by the party's presidential nominee. The national chair, along with the paid staff of the national committee, oversees the day-to-day operations of the political party (see "On the Job").

But the role of the national chair depends to a large extent on whether the party's nominee wins the presidency. If the party's nominee is victorious, the national chair has a less prominent role because the president serves as the most public representative of the party. If the party's nominee loses, however, the national chair may take on a more public persona, serving as the spokesperson for the **loyal opposition**—the out-of-power party's objections to the policies and priorities of the government in power. In recent years, regardless of whether the party's nominee has won or lost, one of the most important roles of the national chair has been to fund-raise. Money donated to the national parties is often redirected to the state and local parties, which use it to help contest elections and mobilize voters.

loyal opposition
a role that the party out of power plays, highlighting its objections to policies and priorities of the government in power

STATE PARTIES Both national parties have committees in each state (the Illinois State Democratic Committee, for example) that effectively *are* the party in that state. State committees act as intermediaries between the national committees and county committees. Typically, state committees are made up of a few members from each county or other geographical subdivision of a given state.

Historically, state parties were important because of their role in the election of U.S. senators, who until 1913 were elected by their states' legislatures. Since the ratification of

DOING DEMOCRACY

ATTEND A COUNTY COMMITTEE MEETING

FACT:

County party committees represent party politics at an influential and a most accessible level. County parties provide the enthusiastic grassroots volunteers and the local know-how that get national candidates elected to office—and that help citizens to network effectively with these officials, once elected. They also help aspiring politicians to gain valuable experience and identify and recruit potential candidates for office.

Act!

First, determine whether you are a Democrat or a Republican. You can start by taking the quiz "Are You Red, Blue, or Purple?" on p. 305. If you are a Democrat, go to www.democrats.org, click on "Get Involved," then "Get Local." Click on your state and then scroll through "Local Democrat Sites." If you are a Republican, go to www.gop.com/States/, click on your state and see if your county committee is listed. If you cannot find information about county committee meetings through the state party Web sites, call or e-mail your state committee, explain that you are interested in attending a county committee meeting, and inquire about the time and location.

Where to begin

A good time to attend a county committee meeting is a few months before a general election, when the committee typically has an urgent need for volunteers, or a few months before a primary election, when you can watch the candidate selection process firsthand. Introduce yourself to the county chair and explain that you are taking a course in American government and want to see what the local party is like. If you are interested in volunteering, don't hesitate to let the chair know.

---

the Seventeenth Amendment in that year, the voters of each state have directly elected their senators by popular election.

Later in the twentieth century, state political parties began a rebound of power, partly due to the U.S. Supreme Court's decision in *Buckley v. Valeo* (1976). In this case, the Court ruled that political parties are entities with special status because their functions of educating and mobilizing voters and contesting elections help to ensure democracy.[12] This ruling created the so-called **soft money loophole,** through which the political parties could raise unlimited funds for party-building activities such as voter registration drives and get-out-the-vote (GOTV) efforts, although contributions to specific candidates were limited. The Court's decision strengthened the influence of the state parties, which the national parties often relied upon to coordinate these efforts. The Bipartisan Campaign Reform Act of 2002 eliminated the soft money loophole, but until that time state parties were strengthened by their ability to channel those contributions to political parties. (See Chapter 9 for further discussion of soft money.)

soft money loophole
Supreme Court interpretation of campaign finance law that enabled political parties to raise unlimited funds for party-building activities such as voter registration drives and get-out-the-vote (GOTV) efforts

COUNTY AND LOCAL PARTIES   County committees consist of members of municipal, ward, and precinct party committees. The foot soldiers of the political parties, county committees help recruit candidates for office, raise campaign funds, and mobilize voters. The importance of a given county committee's role largely depends on whether its candidates are elected and whether its party controls the government. Party success tends to promote competition for candidates' slots and for seats on the county committee.

In most major cities, ward committees and precinct committees dominate party politics. Because city council members are often elected to represent a ward, ward committees are a powerful force in city politics, providing the grassroots organization that turns voters out in city elections. Precinct committees (a precinct is usually a subdivision of a ward) also help elect city council members.

Besides fund-raising, county and local political parties still play key roles in shaping both community engagement and individual participation in the political process, as they have done historically. During election season (in most places, from the end of August through the first week in November), county and local parties recruit and rely on volunteers to perform a host of functions, including answering phones in party headquarters, registering voters, coordinating mailings, doing advance work for candidates, compiling lists for get-out-the-vote efforts, supervising door-knocking campaigns, and phone-banking to remind voters to vote on election day.

The Party in Government

party in government
the partisan identifications of elected leaders in local, county, state, and federal government

When candidates run for local, state, or national office, their party affiliation usually appears next to their name on the ballot. After an elected official takes the oath of office, many people do not think about the official's party affiliation. But in fact, the **party in government**—the partisan identification of elected leaders in local, county, state, and national government—significantly influences the organization and running of the government at these various levels.

In most towns, the party identification of the majority of the members of the legislative branch (often called *city council* or *town council*) determines who will serve as the head of the legislature (sometimes called the *president of city council*). And in most towns, the president of city council hails from the majority party. In addition, paid professional positions such as city solicitor (the town's lawyer), town planner, and city engineer are often awarded on the basis of the support of the majority of council. Even though the entire council votes on appointments, the minority party members often defer to the majority, as appointments typically are viewed as a privilege of winning a majority. Other appointments might include positions on voluntary boards such as a town planning or zoning board.

On the state level, the party in government plays a similarly prominent role in organizing government work. Typically, state legislatures are organized around political party. Seating assignments and committee assignments are made by the majority party leadership and are based on a legislator's party affiliation. Figure 8.5 illustrates the partisan breakdown of state legislatures. In each state, the party with a majority (shown in the figure) in the legislature also has a majority on the legislature's committees, which decide the outcome of proposed legislation. Parties moreover are important in the executive branch of state government, as state governors typically appoint party loyalists to key positions in their administrations. Depending on the appointment powers of the governor, which vary from state to state, a governor may also appoint party members to plum assignments on state regulatory boards. In states where the governor appoints the judiciary, the governor also frequently selects judicial nominees from his or her own political party.

Parties perform a similar role in the federal government. Presidents draw from party loyalists to fill cabinet and subcabinet appointments and typically appoint federal judges from their own political party. Congress is organized based on the party affiliation of its members. When representatives or senators refer to a colleague "on the other side of the aisle," they are referring to a member of the other political party, as congressional Democrats and Republicans sit across the aisle from one another. As in state legislatures, the party with the majority in Congress essentially runs the legislative branch. From its ranks comes the congressional leadership, including the Senate Majority Leader, the Speaker of the House of Representatives, and the House Majority Leader (see Chapter 11).

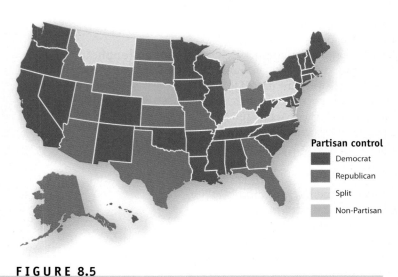

Partisan control
- Democrat
- Republican
- Split
- Non-Partisan

FIGURE 8.5

Partisan Control of State Legislatures Before the Election of 2008

Source: The National Conference of State Legislatures, www.ncsl.org/statevote/partycomptable2008.htm.

DIVIDED GOVERNMENT   There are limits to a party's power. Probably the most important check comes from the opposition party, which can openly criticize the party in power and aggressively investigate alleged misconduct on the part of its officials. During parts of the Bill Clinton and George W. Bush administrations, for example, the president and the members of Congress functioned with a **divided government,** the situation in which one party controls Congress and the other party, the presidency.[13]

Divided government prevailed after 1994 when Democrat Bill Clinton was president and Republicans won control of the House of Representatives. The Republicans not only opposed Clinton's policy priorities but also condemned his sexual improprieties with White House intern Monica Lewinsky, as well as his and Hillary Clinton's ties to a controversial land deal dubbed Whitewater. In 2000, when Republican president George W. Bush was elected, the Senate was evenly divided between Democrats and Republicans. Divided government emerged again after the 2006 midterm elections, when the Democrats won control of both houses of Congress. Democrats in Congress alleged administration misconduct when it appeared that Bush's attorney general, Alberto Gonzales, dismissed federal prosecutors for political reasons of politics rather than competence. In these instances of a divided government, both administrations' attention was diverted from pursuing policy initiatives to dealing with the scandals, and both presidents suffered a loss of prestige that negatively affected their ability to achieve their legislative priorities.

divided government
the situation that exists when Congress is controlled by one party and the presidency by the other

Political Parties in U.S. History

Modern Americans' divided opinions of political parties would not be surprising to the founders, who viewed political parties with suspicion.[14] Thomas Jefferson said, "If I could not go to heaven but with a party, I would not go there at all." This sentiment was shared by George Washington, who warned of "the baneful effects of the spirit of party."[15] Despite these reservations, political parties began to emerge in the United States during the debate over ratification of the Constitution (with both Washington and Jefferson instrumental in their creation). Those who advocated ratification and a strong central government were called Federalists, and those who opposed ratification and favored states' rights were called Anti-Federalists. Thus began the first party system in the United States. **Party system** refers to the number

party system
the categorization of the number and competitiveness of political parties in a polity

and competitiveness of political parties in a polity[16]—for example, a government may have a two-party system in which one party is ascending in power. As we will see, the demarcation of party systems typically occurs in hindsight, when social scientists recognize points where there has been a **realignment,** a shift in party allegiances or electoral support.[17]

realignment
a shift in party allegiances or electoral support

While these shifting allegiances have played a pivotal role in shaping the context of politics since the country's early days, the founders generally believed that parties threatened the stability of the fledgling democracy.[18] Most thought that political parties enabled individuals and groups to pursue self-serving interests that were often contrary to the common good. Some of the founders argued that parties discouraged independence in thought and action. Some thought that parties exacerbated conflicts and disagreements among the people rather than building consensus. Yet their formation and continued evolution testifies to their important role in achieving political and policy goals for their members.[19]

The First Party System: The Development of Parties, 1789–1828

In 1788, George Washington was elected president, but the consensus surrounding his election proved short-lived. Washington deeply opposed the idea of political parties and ruled during an era without formal parties. But he recognized that despite his popularity, he needed legislators who would push his initiatives through Congress. Washington's secretary of the treasury and close ally, Alexander Hamilton, gathered legislators into a loosely knit party, the Federalists, that favored a strong national government.

Thomas Jefferson, secretary of state during Washington's first term (1789–1793), feared a strong central government, and he and his backers opposed Hamilton's Federalists. But Jefferson's primary concern was that the new government should succeed, and so despite his opposition, he remained in Washington's cabinet during the president's first term. When Jefferson later resigned his secretarial post, in 1793, many of those who shared his apprehensions about a strong central government remained in Congress.

Although Jefferson lost to Federalist John Adams in the 1796 presidential election, he paved the way for his future electoral success by building a base of support—including partisan groups in the states and newly established political newspapers—that allowed him to get his message out.[20] This direct communication with voters marked a significant step in the civic development of the U.S. electorate. The strategy was effective: Jefferson won election to the presidency in 1800 over Adams, and Adams's defeat marked the end of the Federalist Party. Jefferson was reelected in 1804, and both of his elections demonstrated the important function that political parties would play in elections.[21] His supporters became known as Jeffersonian Republicans; later, Democratic-Republicans. The modern descendants of the Democratic-Republicans today are called Democrats.

The Jeffersonian Republicans' effective campaign tactics of communicating with voters, along with the absence of well-organized opposition, resulted in their continued dominance from 1815 to 1828. Historians call these years the Era of Good Feelings, largely because of the widespread popular support for Democratic-Republican presidents James Madison (1809–1817), James Monroe (1817–1825), and John Quincy Adams (1825–1829).

The Second Party System: The Democrats' Rise to Power, 1828–1860

populism
a philosophy supporting the rights and empowerment of the masses as opposed to elites

spoils system
the practice of rewarding political supporters with jobs

By 1828, some dissension among the Jeffersonian Republicans was becoming apparent. Members of the party, including the charismatic military general and politician Andrew Jackson of Tennessee, chafed at the elitism of the party and the era. The Jacksonian Democrats—the name for the new coalition that Jackson formed—emphasized leadership through merit rather than birth.[22] They espoused **populism,** a philosophy supporting the rights and empowerment of the masses, particularly in the area of political participation, and the **spoils system,** in which political supporters were rewarded with jobs (from the phrase "to the victor go the spoils"). The Jacksonian Democrats succeeded in mobilizing the masses, sweeping

Jackson to victory in the presidential election of 1828.[23] Political parties had become the medium through which many Americans were politicized, and in 1828, for the first time, more than one million Americans cast their ballots in the presidential contest.

Jackson's populism marked a critical step in opening up the civic life of the polity to a much wider swath of citizens.[24] It redefined not only who was eligible to succeed as political leaders but also who should be eligible to participate in the selection of those leaders. Historian Richard P. McCormick noted that the Jacksonian Democrats extended voting rights to all white adult males, changed the mechanism for selecting presidential electors to popular elections by voters instead of by the state legislatures, and increased the importance of the party convention, in effect giving party members more say in candidates' selection. And although women would not gain the right to vote until 1920, the Jacksonian era saw the formal beginnings of the women's suffrage movement with the formation of the two major women's suffrage organizations and the advent of the Seneca Falls Convention (1848) in support of expanded rights for women.[25]

During the 1830s, southern plantation owners and northern industrialists became concerned about the impact the Democrats' populism would have on economic elites.[26] Their mutual interests crystallized in the formation of the Whig Party in 1836, which succeeded in electing two presidents, William Henry Harrison (succeeded by John Tyler upon his death) and Zachary Taylor.[27] But the era of the Second Party System ultimately was defined by the long-standing effects that Jacksonian principles would have on U.S. politics, namely through the politicization of a previously excluded mass of citizens—many of whom had been initiated into the rites of full citizenship and others of whom had begun the struggle to win their own status as full citizens.[28]

The Third Party System: The Republicans' Rise to Power, 1860–1896

In the 1850s slavery became the primary concern for both the Whigs and the Democrats.[29] This highly charged issue divided the Whig Party into proslavery and abolitionist factions, and the party consequently faded away.[30] In its place, a new antislavery party, the Republicans (also called the Grand Old Party, or GOP), took shape in 1854 and gained the support of abolitionist Whigs and northern Democrats.[31] The victory of the Republican presidential nominee, Abraham Lincoln, in the election of 1860 marked the beginning of a period of dominance of the antislavery Republicans, which continued even after the Civil War.[32] During this time, the Republican Party enjoyed strong support from newly franchised African American voters. Although many African Americans in the South were prevented from exercising their right to vote through threats, intimidation, and tactics such as the white primary (see Chapter 5), African Americans in the North widely voted Republican. They would remain strong supporters of the "party of Lincoln" for decades.

During this time, political parties grew very strong, and political machines came to dominate the political landscape. A **political machine** was both a corrupt and a useful organization that dominated politics around the turn of the twentieth century, particularly in cities. Each political machine was headed by a "boss," whose power rested on a system of patronage. A party leader used **patronage** as a device to reward political supporters—rather than individuals who might demonstrate greater merit or particular competence—with jobs or government contracts. In exchange, those receiving patronage would vote for the party and might be expected to volunteer on a campaign or kick back some of their wages to the party.

political machine
big-city organization that exerted control over many aspects of life and lavishly rewarded supporters

patronage
system in which a party leader rewarded political supporters with jobs or government contracts in exchange for their support of the party

THE CURIOUS EFFECT OF CLEAN LINEN UPON THE DEMOCRATIC PARTY

POLITICAL INQUIRY

In this cartoon by the famous nineteenth-century caricaturist and cartoonist Thomas Nast, what does the tiger represent? What point is the cartoonist making about the "clean linen" the tiger is wearing?

Party Politics in Flux

THEN (1889)	NOW (2009)
Powerful political parties are in their heyday, and party bosses rule the cities with an iron fist.	The era of party politics in the United States is over, according to some scholars.
The patronage system is in high gear, and political parties derive enormous power and loyalty from the recipients of jobs and lucrative contracts.	A merit-based civil service system has largely replaced patronage, and parties are weakened because of a decline in the number of loyal members.
Elected officials toe the party line, because they depend on the party for their office.	Elected officials pride themselves on their "independence" and sometimes owe very little to their political party.

WHAT'S NEXT?

> How are advancing technologies likely to change political parties and their operations in the future? Will these weaken or strengthen the parties? Explain.

> Do you think that the voters who went to the polls in the 2008 primaries and general election will remain loyal to their parties? Why or why not?

> How do parties today help voters evaluate candidates? Will they still perform this function in the future? Will the nature of this process change? Explain.

Although political machines were known for corruption, they did accomplish some good. Richard Croker was political boss of Tammany Hall, New York City's Democratic Party political machine from 1886 until 1902. He explained: "Think of what New York is and what the people of New York are. One half are of foreign birth. . . . They do not speak our language, they do not know our laws. . . . There is no denying the service which Tammany has rendered to the Republic, there is no such organization for taking hold of the untrained, friendless man and converting him into a citizen. Who else would do it if we did not?"[33]

On that score, Croker was right. At the time, political machines provided the vital service of socializing a generation of immigrants to democracy and to the American way of political life. Some machines, including Tammany Hall, generated widespread political participation, and some allowed the participation of women.[34] Political machines helped integrate immigrants into the social, economic, and political fabric of the United States, usually by awarding jobs for loyalty to the party. And in an era when the federal government had not yet become a large-scale provider of social services, urban political machines also provided a safety net for the injured, the elderly, and widows.

The Fourth Party System: Republican Dominance, 1896–1932

The 1896 presidential election between populist Democrat William Jennings Bryan and Republican William McKinley marked the beginning of a new era in party politics. Bryan appealed widely to Protestants, southerners, midwesterners, and rural dwellers who were suspicious of Catholic, ethnic, working-class immigrants in the urban Northeast. McKinley emphasized economic growth and development and garnered support from industrialists, bankers, and even working-class factory workers, who saw his backing of business as being good for the economy. McKinley won the election handily, his victory ushering in an era of Republican dominance in presidential politics that would last until the election of 1912.

That year, Theodore Roosevelt (who had succeeded McKinley as president in 1901 after the latter's assassination, and who had been elected president as a Republican in 1904) ran in the presidential election as a Progressive. The Progressive Party advocated widespread governmental reform and sought to limit the power of political bosses. The Republicans' split between William Howard Taft's regular Republicans and Roosevelt's Progressives powered Democrat Woodrow Wilson to the presidency with only 42 percent of the popular vote.

As Wilson's Democratic administration ended up enacting many of the Progressive Party's proposals, the power of the urban political machines declined. For example, recorded voter registration and secret ballot laws were passed, the direct party primary was established, and civil service reform was expanded. The national leaders who spearheaded these measures designed them to take political power out of the bosses' hands and give it to the electorate.

After Wilson's two terms, the Republicans continued to enjoy the support of business elites and the industrial working class. They also benefited from the backing of the many African Americans in the northern cities who continued to support the party of Lincoln, and of women voters, many of whom had been activists in the Progressive movement. With this widespread and diverse support, the Republicans retained control of the presidency throughout the 1920s.

The Fifth Party System: Democratic Dominance, 1932–1968

When the stock market crashed in 1929, the economy entered the deep downturn that history remembers as the Great Depression. In the election of 1932, a broad constituency responded to the calls of the Democratic candidate, Franklin D. Roosevelt, for an increased governmental role in promoting the public welfare. Roosevelt pressed tirelessly for a **New Deal** for all Americans, a broad program in which the government would bear the responsibility of providing a "safety net" to protect the weakest members of society.

A new alignment among American voters swept "FDR" into presidential office. In fact, the **New Deal coalition**—the name for the voting bloc comprising traditional southern Democrats, northern city dwellers (especially immigrants and the poor), Catholics, unionized and blue-collar workers, African Americans, and women—would give Roosevelt the presidency an unprecedented four times.[35]

The era of the Fifth Party System significantly opened up party politics and civic activity to a widening spectrum of Americans. Notably for African Americans and women, Franklin Roosevelt's elections marked the first time that they had been actively courted by political parties, and their new political activism—particularly in the form of voting and political party activities—left them feeling they had a voice in their government.

Vice President Harry Truman assumed the presidency on Roosevelt's death in 1945 and was elected in his own right in 1948, but subsequent Democrats were unable to keep Roosevelt's coalition together. Republican Dwight Eisenhower won the White House in 1952 and again in 1956. And although Democrats John F. Kennedy and Lyndon Johnson held the presidency through most of the 1960s, the events of that decade wreaked havoc on the Democratic Party, with deep divisions opening up over the Vietnam War and civil rights for African Americans.[36]

New Deal
Franklin Roosevelt's broad social welfare program in which the government would bear the responsibility of providing a "safety net" to protect the weakest members of society

New Deal coalition
the group composed of southern Democrats, northern city dwellers, immigrants, the poor, Catholics, labor union members, blue-collar workers, African Americans, and women that elected FDR to the presidency four times

> African American voters were a key constituency in Franklin Roosevelt's New Deal coalition. Here, voters in Harlem wait to cast their ballots for President Roosevelt in 1936.

A New Party System?

Between 1968 and 2008, Republicans held the presidency for all but the Jimmy Carter (1977–1981) and Bill Clinton (1993–2001) administrations. With the passage of time and the gaining of perspective on the significance of these relatively recent events, some political scientists contend that the years since 1968 can be characterized as a period separate from the Fifth Party System—an era that has given rise to a new party system.

Other political scientists have noted certain changes within the electorate that help to explain the prevalence of Republican victories at the national level. One such change is the tendency of southern whites to vote Republican, a trend that began with Ronald Reagan's election to the presidency in 1980. The migration of southern whites—historically a core constituency of the Democratic Party—to the Republicans has provided a crucial boost for Republican nominees. In his book *Whistling Past Dixie,* political scientist Thomas F. Schaller argues that the deep conservatism of southern whites has rendered the region no longer a competitive ground for Democrats. Schaller argues that the Democrats would be better off focusing on strengthening their constituencies in the Southwest and Midwest, where their ideological positions would have greater voter appeal.[37]

Additional characteristics of this new party system, according to scholars, include *intense party competition,* in which the two major U.S. political parties have been nearly evenly matched and neither one has dominated; and *divided government,* where a president of one party has to deal with a Congress of the other. This fierce partisan competitiveness is clearly apparent in the outcomes of recent national elections. In particular, the 2000 presidential campaign demonstrated the ferocious rivalry of the two parties, with a presidential election so close that the outcome was in question for weeks after the voting had ended. That year, voters also evenly divided the Senate, electing fifty Democrats and fifty Republicans.

Moreover, some scholars see **dealignment,** the phenomenon in which fewer voters support the two major political parties and instead self-identify as independent, as a notable characteristic of this new party system.[38] Others view the increasing trend toward supporting candidates from both parties (**ticket splitting**) or from third parties as evidence of a new party system's emergence.

The period since 1968 has also been characterized by the growing importance of candidate-centered politics. The rise of **candidate committees,** organizations that candidates form to support their individual election as opposed to the party's slate of candidates, is one reflection of how politics has increasingly become candidate-centered. Candidate committees compete with political parties in many arenas. They raise and spend money, organize campaigns, and attempt to mobilize voters. One impact of their enhanced influence has been that elected officials, particularly members of Congress, are less indebted to their parties than in previous eras and thus sometimes demonstrate less loyalty when voting on bills in the legislature.

Some political scientists argue that these characteristics of the new party system demonstrate that the responsible party model (discussed earlier) is not as strong as it once was. The rise of candidate committees and the increase in ticket splitting mean that parties are less helpful to voters as they assess candidates, because the differences between Republican and Democratic candidates may dissipate in the face of constituent opinion. Yet most Americans disagree: a recent Gallup poll indicated that nearly two-thirds of those surveyed believe that there are important differences between the Democratic and Republican parties.[39] And the research of some scholars, including David Karol, Hans Noel, John Zaller, and Marty Cohen, indicates that party elites, including elected officials and former elected officials, have increased their control in selecting party presidential nominees, suggesting a potential revival of the importance of parties as players in politics today.[40]

dealignment
the situation in which fewer voters support the two major political parties, instead identifying themselves as independent, or splitting their ticket between candidates from more than one party

ticket splitting
the situation in which voters vote for candidates from more than one party

candidate committees
organizations that candidates form to support their individual election

Two-Party Domination in U.S. Politics

third party
a party organized as opposition or alternative to the existing parties in a two-party system

Since the ratification of the Constitution in 1787, the United States has had a two-party system for all but about thirty years in total. This historical record stands in marked contrast to the experience of the many nations that have third parties.[41] A **third party** is a political

GLOBAL COMPARISONS

POLITICAL PARTIES IN NORTHERN IRELAND

Although the functions and focus of political parties in the United States today are broad and important, it may be hard to envision modern parties as institutions that can change people's everyday lives and alter the course of a nation's history. But that is exactly what happened in the mid-1990s in the six counties that make up Northern Ireland. This region, which was under the rule of the British government, had been wracked by violence for decades as Catholic and Protestant paramilitary forces engaged in guerrilla warfare over a deep division among the citizenry: Catholics wanted the counties to be reunited with the Republic of Ireland, but Protestants wanted them to remain part of Great Britain.

Will Northern Ireland's bold experiment in governance by party power-sharing succeed?

Reflecting the varying preferences of the country's voters, Northern Ireland features more than a dozen political parties. Only a subset of these parties enjoys a competitive edge, however, because of their wider support among the people. In the mid-1990s, Gerry Adams and John Hume, the leaders of two of Northern Ireland's most influential political parties, began talks to explore how to end political violence in the provinces once and for all. Gerry Adams's Sinn Fein Party (pronounced "shin fane," meaning "ourselves alone" in Irish) was affiliated with the Provisional Irish Republican Army, the Catholic paramilitary group engaged in violence that sought to end British rule in Northern Ireland. John Hume's Social Democratic and Labour Party, Northern Ireland's largest political party, has a liberal ideology and has always rejected violence as a means of achieving political goals. Over the course of many months that turned into years, Adams and Hume, later joined by Ulster Unionist Party (UUP) leader David Trimble (who negotiated with Adams despite the UUP's fierce commitment to retaining British control in the region), agreed to a six-plank set of principles. Called the Mitchell Principles in honor of then-U.S. senator George Mitchell (D-Maine), who helped to broker the deal, the agreement called for the people of Northern Ireland to decide their political fate democratically and provided for the verifiable disarmament of the paramilitary groups.

The so-called Good Friday agreement was signed by the Irish and British governments and was endorsed by nearly all major political parties in 1998. In May of that year, 71 percent of the voters of Northern Ireland approved the Good Friday agreements, a major step in the Northern Ireland peace process. The way was paved for the election of a devolved Northern Irish Assembly, a legislature that would essentially govern the territory through a power-sharing agreement among the leading political parties. Until March 2007, it appeared that all of the negotiations would be undone when Democratic Unionist Party (DUP) leader Ian Paisley refused even to discuss the agreement with Adams or other Sinn Feiners. (The DUP is vehemently anti-Catholic and opposed the Good Friday agreement.) But on March 27, one day before a deadline that would have put Northern Ireland back under British control, Paisley relented and accepted the power-sharing scenario. A new era of devolved democracy thus began in Northern Ireland.

> Ian Paisley (far left) and Gerry Adams (far right), leaders of Northern Ireland's Protestant and Catholic political parties, respectively.

party organized as opposition or an alternative to the existing parties in a two-party system. Many countries even have *multi*party systems (see "Global Comparisons").

The United States' two-party system has had two contradictory influences on people's civic engagement. On the one hand, the dominance of only two strong political parties through most of American history has made it easy for individuals to find avenues for becoming civically engaged. Further, at various historical points, political parties have worked for the outright extension of political rights to groups that were excluded, although often with the foremost aim of bolstering their core supporters. On the other hand, the dominance of just two political parties that tend to be ideologically moderate discourages the political participation of some people, particularly those who are strongly ideological.

Although the grip of the United States' two-party system is frustrating to people who support a greater diversity of parties, the reasons for the two-party system are numerous and difficult to change.

The Dualist Nature of Most Conflicts

Historically, many issues in the United States have been dualist, or "two-sided," in nature. For example, the debate over ratification of the U.S. Constitution found people with two basic opinions. On one side, the Federalists supported ratification of the Constitution, which created a federal government that separated powers among three branches and shared power with state governments. They were opposed by the Anti-Federalists, who campaigned against ratification of the Constitution, supported stronger states' rights, and wanted to see states and individuals enjoy greater protections. This split provided the initial structure for the two-party system, and a multitude of issues followed that format.

Political scientists Seymour Martin Lipset and Stein Rokkan asserted that the dualist nature of voter alignments or cleavages shapes how political parties form. In particular, these alignments or cleavages concern the character of the national fabric (for example, should religious ideals or secular notions prevail?), and they are determined by function (business versus agrarian interests, for example).[42] These cleavages shaped party formation during the nineteenth century, when the dualist nature of conflict continued to be in evidence in public affairs. Some states wanted slavery; other states opposed "the peculiar institution" of human bondage. In some states, commercial and industrial interests dominated; in other states, agricultural interests held the reins of power. Immigrants, often Catholics, controlled the politics of some states, whereas native-born Protestants held sway in others.

By the twentieth century, the dualist conflict had become more ideological. Some Americans agreed with President Franklin D. Roosevelt's plan to help lift the country out of the Great Depression by significantly increasing the role of government in people's everyday lives. Others opposed this unprecedented expansion of the federal government's power. In later decades, debates over civil rights and women's rights demonstrated the continued dualist nature of conflict in American society and culture.

The Winner-Take-All Electoral System

In almost all U.S. elections, the person with the most votes wins. If a competitor gets just one vote less than the victor, he or she wins nothing. If a third party garners a significant proportion of the vote in congressional elections nationwide but does not win the most votes in any given district, the party will not win any seats in Congress.

Compare the winner-take-all system to the proportional representation system found in many nations. In a **proportional representation system,** political parties win the number of parliamentary seats equal to the percentage of the vote each party receives. So, for example, if

proportional representation system
an electoral structure in which political parties win the number of parliamentary seats equal to the percentage of the vote the party receives

Concept Summary

WHY TWO PARTIES DOMINATE IN U.S. POLITICS

— Historically, many public issues in the United States have been dualist (two-sided).

— The electoral system encourages a two-party structure.

— Individuals are socialized to belong to one of the two main U.S. parties and thus perpetuate the two-party system through the generations.

— Election laws favor the two political parties.

the Green Party were to capture 9 percent of the vote in a country's election, it would get nine seats in a one-hundred-member parliament. In a proportional representation system, the 19 percent of the vote that Reform Party candidate Ross Perot won in the 1992 U.S. presidential election would have given the Reform Party about 85 seats in the House of Representatives!

In nations with proportional representation, third parties (which we consider in more detail later in the chapter) are encouraged because such parties can win a few seats in the legislature and use them to further their cause and broaden their support.[43] In addition, in proportional representation systems, third parties sometimes form a *coalition,* or working union, with a larger party so that the two together can control a majority of a legislature. And so, for example, the Green Party that won nine seats in Parliament in the example mentioned above might form a coalition with another party that had received 42 percent of the vote, together forming a majority government. In this way, a third party can get members appointed to key positions as a reward for forming the coalition. Consequently, societies with proportional representation systems can sometimes be more inclusive of differing points of view because even those winning a small proportion of the vote achieve representation, and that representation can be pivotal in the formation of coalitions.

Continued Socialization to the Two-Party System

Another reason that the two-party system dominates in the United States is that party identification—like ideology, values, and religious beliefs—is an attribute that often passes down from one generation to the next. Hence many an individual is likely to be a Democrat or Republican because his or her parents were one or the other. Many people first learn about government and politics at home. Around the dinner table, a child may have heard her parents rail against Bill Clinton's indiscretions or criticize George W. Bush's Iraq policy. Having become socialized to their household's political culture, children are likely to mimic their parents' views.

Even children who do not share their parents' political outlook or who grow apart from it over time (as commonly occurs during the college years) have been socialized to the legitimacy of the two-party system—unless, of course, their parents routinely criticized both Democrats and Republicans or voiced dissatisfaction with the two-party system.

Election Laws That Favor the Two-Party System

At both the federal and the state level in the United States, election laws benefit the two major parties because they are usually written by members of one of those parties. Although some local governments mandate nonpartisan elections, in most cities and towns, getting on the ballot typically means simply winning the party's nomination and collecting a state-specified number of signatures of registered party members on a nominating petition. Usually, the party organization will circulate this petition for a candidate. Third parties have a much steeper climb to get their candidates in office. In the 2008 presidential election, candidate Ralph Nader, who ran as an independent, had difficulty just getting his name on the ballot in some states.

Scholars of civic engagement point to the structural impediments to the formation of third parties as key to the low level of civic engagement on the part of individuals who are dissatisfied with the two-party system. Facing seemingly insurmountable structural obstacles to the formation of successful third parties, some Americans shy away from political engagement.

The Two-Party System Today: In Decline or in Resurgence?

Given the various historical changes to the U.S. political party system that we examined above, many political scientists have inquired into what the impact of these changes will be. Do the changes signify an end to party control in American politics? Or can political parties adapt to the altered environment and find new sources of power?

The Party's Over

Some scholars argue that changes in the political environment have rendered today's political parties essentially impotent to fulfill the functions that parties performed during stronger party systems. In 1982, political scientist Gary Orren wrote, "In a world in which political scientists disagree on almost everything, there is remarkable agreement among the political science profession that the strength of American political parties has declined significantly over the past several decades."[44] Although some political scientists would subsequently challenge Orren's perspective, many agreed with him at the time.

These theorists note several key factors that have contributed to party decline. Some argue that the elimination of political patronage through the requirement of civil service qualifications for government employees has significantly hurt parties' ability to reward loyal followers with government jobs. Patronage jobs still exist, but most government positions are now awarded upon an applicant's successful performance on a civil service exam that is designed to measure qualifications based on objective criteria. Whereas the recipients of patronage jobs were among the most loyal party members in previous decades, party loyalty has decreased as political parties have lost a significant amount of control in the awarding of jobs.

Other political scientists emphasize the government's increased role over time in providing social welfare benefits as a contributor to the decline of political parties. Before President Franklin D. Roosevelt's New Deal, the government bore little if any responsibility for providing a safety net for those on the bottom economic rungs of society, a role often filled by political parties. With the coming of the New Deal and the subsequent passage of social welfare legislation, the government has come to be the largest provider of social services, and the parties typically no longer perform that function. Thus changing times have brought the elimination of another source of party loyalty.

primary election
an election in which voters choose the party's candidates who will run in the later general election

Primary elections—elections in which voters choose the party's candidates who will run in the later general election—also have decreased parties' power by taking the control of nominations from party leaders and handing it to voters. In the past, when a party machine anointed nominees at nominating conventions, those nominees became indebted to the party and typically responded with loyalty if they got elected. But today's candidates are less likely to owe their nomination to the party: instead, in many cases they have fought for and won the nomination by taking their campaign directly to primary voters.

Changes in the mass media have also meant a drastically decreased role for political parties. In their heyday, political parties were one of the most important providers of news. Parties published so-called penny papers that reported information to the public. Today, political parties may still provide some information to voters at election time, but most voters rely on other, independent media outlets—newspapers, television, radio, and Internet news sources—rather than exclusively partisan sources.

candidate-centered campaign
a campaign in which an individual seeking election, rather than an entire party slate, is the focus

The rise in candidate-centered campaigns has also weakened political parties. **Candidate-centered campaigns,** in which an individual seeking election, rather than an entire party slate, is the focus, have come about because of changes in the parties' functions, the advent of direct primaries, and trends in the mass media that have shifted the focus to individual office-seekers. Candidate-centered campaigns also must rely more heavily on paid professional campaign workers (instead of party volunteers), a reality necessitating campaign contributions to individual candidates rather than to the party.

These changes in the nature of political parties and in their ability to perform their traditional functions have led some political scientists to conclude that the era of party rule is ending. Other players, they say—including interest groups, candidate-based organizations, and the media—will come to assume the roles traditionally performed by political parties.

The Party's Just Begun

Pointing to the record-breaking turnout in the 2008 presidential primaries, other political scientists strongly disagree that U.S. parties' prime has passed.[45] While conceding that political parties' functions have changed, these theorists observe that parties have proved themselves remarkably adaptable. When the political environment has changed in the past, political parties have responded by assuming different functions or finding new avenues by which to seed party loyalty. According to this view, the parties' ability to rebound is alive and well.

These scholars also argue that the continued dominance in the United States of two political parties—through decades of threats to their survival—has demonstrated a strength and resilience that are likely to prevail. Today's Republicans, the party of Lincoln, have endured the assassinations of party leaders, the Great Depression, the four-term presidency of popular Democrat Franklin D. Roosevelt, and the Watergate scandal during the Nixon presidency. Today's Democrats are the same party that opposed suffrage for African Americans in the aftermath of the Civil War, and that survived internal divisions over civil rights through the 1960s, to become strong supporters of African American rights in recent decades. The Democrats too have endured assassinations, and scandals and have weathered Republican control of the White House for all but twelve years since 1968. Both political parties have remained remarkably competitive despite the challenges to their success.

Scholars who argue that the two main U.S. political parties are once again rebounding cite the lack of viable alternatives to the two-party system. Yes, third parties have made a mark in recent presidential elections. But the present-day party system has not seen the emergence of a strong, viable third party with a cohesive ideology that has attracted a significant portion of the vote in more than one election. And civic education scholars agree that third parties have served an important function by encouraging the political participation of people who are disenchanted with the current two-party system. They also acknowledge, however, the continued dominance of the two main parties in creating opportunities for civic engagement within communities.

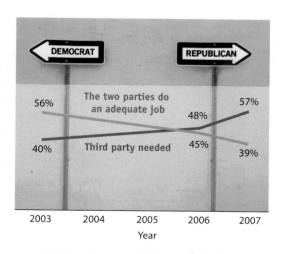

Third Parties in the United States

As we have seen, the absence of viable U.S. political parties beyond the Democrats and Republicans is a source of frustration for some Americans. This frustration is borne out by the data in Figure 8.6, which illustrates that a majority of Americans favor a third party. Notably, the data show a significant increase in popular dissatisfaction with both political parties. Why should this be the case? Most pollsters would argue that the failure of both the Republicans and the Democrats to end the war in Iraq has contributed to the electorate's growing dissatisfaction with both political parties.

Despite the fact that a majority of Americans think a third party is needed, third parties have had little success in contesting elections. In recent times, Ralph Nader was an influential candidate in 2000, not because he netted a sizeable proportion of votes but because the 3 percent that he did win was enough to change the outcome of that razor-close election. Other third-party candidacies have proved influential because of their role in focusing attention—particularly the attention of the victorious candidate—on an issue that might not otherwise have been addressed.[46] Such was the case in 1912 when Progressive Party candidate Theodore Roosevelt ran against Woodrow Wilson. Although he lost the presidency, Roosevelt succeeded in shaping public opinion so that Wilson felt compelled to enact part of the Progressives' national agenda, including sweeping changes to the nation's child labor laws.

One of the most significant obstacles to the formation of a viable third party is that people who are dissatisfied with the two dominant parties fall across the ideological spectrum: some are very liberal; others, quite conservative; still others,

DEMOCRAT **REPUBLICAN**

| 56% | The two parties do an adequate job | 48% | 57% |

| 40% | Third party needed | 45% | 39% |

2003   2004   2005   2006   2007
Year

POLITICAL INQUIRY

FIGURE 8.6 ■ **IS A THIRD PARTY NEEDED?** What trend do the polling data in this figure show? What factors in the political and social environments might explain this trend?

Source: The Gallup Poll, "Party Images," www.galluppoll.com/content/default.aspx?ci=24655, accessed October 4, 2007.

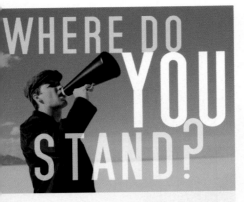
moderate. Thus, although many Americans are dissatisfied with the current parties, a third party would have difficulty attracting enough support from among these diversely dissatisfied party members.

Nonetheless, third parties have played, and continue to play, an influential role in American electoral politics. Third parties are particularly effective at encouraging the civic engagement of people who feel that the two dominant parties do not represent their views or do not listen to them. Third parties give such citizens a voice. And even though third parties often do not succeed electorally, their mere presence in the political arena enlivens civic discourse and frequently encourages debate about urgent policy issues that the two major parties ignore or slight.

Types of Third Parties

Third parties have existed in the United States since the early nineteenth century. Over the nation's history, third parties typically have fallen into one of three general categories: issue advocacy parties, ideologically oriented parties, and splinter parties.

ISSUE ADVOCACY PARTIES   Formed to promote a stance on a particular issue, many issue advocacy parties are short-lived. Once the issue is dealt with or fades from popular concern, the mobilizing force behind the party disintegrates. An example is today's Green Party, which promotes environmental protection as a primary issue and also emphasizes human rights, childhood poverty, globalization, health care, and corporate corruption and greed in its party platform. In the 2000 presidential election, the Green Party sought to win 5 percent of the vote for its presidential candidate, Ralph Nader. If the Greens had succeeded, they would have automatically qualified their party for federal matching funds in the 2004 campaign. The Green Party fell short, however, as it captured only 3 percent of the vote. Its share of the vote then dropped drastically in the 2004 presidential election.

IDEOLOGICALLY ORIENTED PARTIES   The agenda of an ideologically oriented party is typically broader than that of an issue-oriented party. Ideologically oriented parties are structured around an *ideology*—a highly organized and coherent framework concerning the nature and role of government in society (see Chapter 6). Such parties have broad views about many different aspects of government. For example, the Libertarian Party, which holds the ideological position that government should not interfere with individuals' social, political, and economic rights, advocates a very limited role for government: no guarantees of minimum wages or other forms of governmental regulation of the economy, including environmental regulation; no governmental interference in individuals' privacy; the legalization of prostitution and drugs; and the elimination of major governmental bureaucracies, including the Central Intelligence Agency, the Internal Revenue Service, and the Federal Bureau of Investigation.

Another ideologically oriented party is the Socialist Party, which lies at the other end of the ideological spectrum from the Libertarian Party. The Socialist Party, formed in 1901, is one of the longest-standing ideologically oriented parties in the United States. Socialists believe that government should play a large role in ensuring economic equality for all people. Historically, the Socialist Party has advocated various policies that ultimately were addressed in legislation by the two major parties, including Social Security, workers' compensation, disability insurance, and unemployment insurance. Currently the Socialist Party is calling for a 50 percent cut in the military budget and proposes to replace that expenditure with spending on education, child care, health care, and low-cost housing.

SPLINTER PARTIES   A splinter party is a political party that breaks off, or "splinters," from one of the two dominant parties. Often a group splinters off because of intraparty (internal, or within the party) disagreement on a particular issue. For example, in 1948, a group of southern Democrats who opposed the Democratic Party's support of civil rights for African Americans splintered from the Democratic Party to form the States' Rights Party, which quickly became known as the Dixiecrat Party. The party called itself the States'

THE CONVERSATION OF DEMOCRACY

ARE THIRD PARTIES BAD FOR THE UNITED STATES?

The Issue: The United States' political culture and electoral structure predispose the country to a two-party system. Historically, two parties have dominated, and when third parties have emerged, they have either been subsumed by the dominant parties or have simply disappeared when their primary issue of concern was no longer relevant.

The question of whether third parties are bad or good for American democracy dates back almost as far as the democracy itself. But the question has modern implications. Third-party candidates are often seen as spoilers who siphon off votes from the majority's top candidate and thereby enable the less-favored candidate to win. Many pundits allege that this very thing occurred in 2000 with the presidential candidacy of Ralph Nader. When Nader announced his run for the presidency of the United States again in 2008, he was asked by NBC's *Meet the Press* host Tim Russert whether his candidacy could lead to another Democratic defeat. Nader, a third-party fixture on the presidential ballot since 1996, replied, "Not a chance. If the Democrats can't landslide the Republicans this year, they ought to just wrap up, close down, and emerge in a different form."* Nader is not the only third-party candidate said to have delivered an election for one presidential candidate by drawing away votes from a major party candidate whose positions are close to the third-party candidate's. Similar arguments were made in 1992, when pundits charged Reform Party candidate H. Ross Perot with taking votes away from Republican George H. W. Bush and thus ushering Democrat Bill Clinton into the White House.

Do third-party candidacies hurt American democracy by skewing elections away from the third party's major party rival? Or are they good for democracy because they bring out voters who would otherwise have stayed at home and because they help ensure that issues of crucial concern to the electorate get on the national agenda?

Yes: The presence of third-party candidates on a ballot means that the major political party—Democratic or Republican—that is closest to the third party in ideology and in base of support will be hurt. This effect occurs because if the third-party candidate were not on the ballot, many of his or her supporters would vote for the candidate (Democratic or Republican) who is ideologically closest to the third-party candidate. Thus, that major party candidate is at a disadvantage, because the third-party candidate essentially siphons off or splits the vote for the major party candidate. Democracy is subverted, because often a candidate wins who is *least* appealing to the majority of voters (that is, those who voted for the losing major party candidate and those who voted for the third-party candidate). As a result, people are highly dissatisfied with both the political process and elected officials.

No: Only through third parties and third-party candidacies can voters get the national agenda they desire. In 2008, many citizens wanted issues such as universal health care, labor law reform, and corporate crime to be priorities on the federal policy agenda. Other citizens wanted serious national attention given to tort reform, the elimination of most social welfare benefits, and flat taxes. These issues were not part of the national policy debate between the two major political parties. Without third parties to spearhead such conversations of democracy, many more people will be turned off by and disaffected from the political process.

Other approaches: Third parties are a mixed blessing for the United States. Proponents of third parties are correct in asserting that they provide a safety valve for participation by those dissatisfied with the status quo. Third parties have been effective at getting specific policy concerns on the national agenda, even though frequently that has occurred because one of the major parties co-opts a third party's key issue. But supporters of third parties should realize that the electoral politics in the United States is structured to ensure the perpetuation of the two-party system, and that by supporting a third party candidate, they run the risk of spoiling the chances of their preferred major party candidate.

What do you think?

① Do you think third parties help or hurt American democracy? Why?

② What was the impact of third-party candidates in the 2008 election?

③ What kind of third party do you think would be successful in winning elections?

---

*Sarah Wheaton, "Nader to Run Again," on *The Caucus: The New York Times Political Blog,* February 24, 2008, http://thecaucus.blogs.nytimes.com/2008/02/24/nader-to-run-again/.

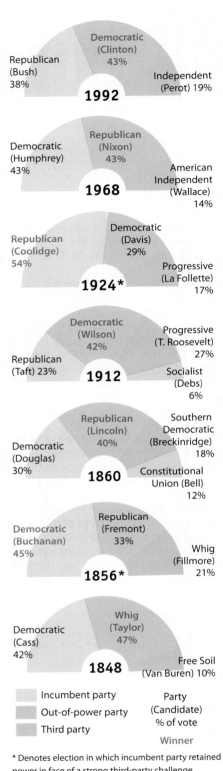

Republican (Bush) 38%
Democratic (Clinton) 43%
Independent (Perot) 19%
1992

Democratic (Humphrey) 43%
Republican (Nixon) 43%
American Independent (Wallace) 14%
1968

Republican (Coolidge) 54%
Democratic (Davis) 29%
Progressive (La Follette) 17%
1924*

Republican (Taft) 23%
Democratic (Wilson) 42%
Progressive (T. Roosevelt) 27%
Socialist (Debs) 6%
1912

Democratic (Douglas) 30%
Republican (Lincoln) 40%
Southern Democratic (Breckinridge) 18%
Constitutional Union (Bell) 12%
1860

Democratic (Buchanan) 45%
Republican (Fremont) 33%
Whig (Fillmore) 21%
1856*

Democratic (Cass) 42%
Whig (Taylor) 47%
Free Soil (Van Buren) 10%
1848

Incumbent party
Out-of-power party
Third party

Party (Candidate) % of vote

Winner

* Denotes election in which incumbent party retained power in face of a strong third-party challenge

FIGURE 8.7

Third Parties Help the Out-of-Power Party

Note: Candidate appears in parentheses; percentage is percentage of vote won by candidate.

Rights Party because it claimed that Congress had no power to interfere with the administration of laws made by the states. It used this claim to retain the policies that created a system of racial segregation in the South. Although the States' Rights Party was a separate, formal organization, many southern Democratic elected officials and party leaders who agreed with the States' Rights Party's platform supported its views from within the Democratic Party.

The Impact of Third Parties

Despite the difficulties associated with sustaining support in American electoral politics, third parties have important effects in the political arena. First, although U.S. third parties usually do not win elections, they can influence electoral outcomes. For example, given the closeness of the 2000 presidential race, many Democrats believe that Green Party candidate Ralph Nader caused Democrat Al Gore to lose the election. They reason that Nader voters would have been more likely to vote for the liberal Gore than for the conservative George W. Bush if Nader had not been a candidate. In a state such as Florida where the electorate was evenly divided, Nader's candidacy in fact could have changed the outcome of that state's balloting and thus the results of the national election as well. Of course, many third-party advocates claim that supporters of a third-party candidate may not have voted at all if their party had not been on the ballot (see "The Conversation of Democracy").

Second, third parties provide a release valve for dissatisfied voters. People who are disgruntled with the two major parties can join or form another political party. And although a third party's chances of electoral success are not great, such parties provide a mechanism for like-minded people to come together to try to effect change. Sometimes, these efforts result in a victory, especially on the local level. A well-known third-party victor is Jesse Ventura, a former professional wrestler who was elected governor of Minnesota in 1998 as a candidate of the Reform Party. With respect to the national level, the impact of third parties as a release valve for discontented voters may be seen in several elections, as shown in Figure 8.7. In U.S. history, third-party presidential candidates have won more than 10 percent of the vote seven times, the latest being in 1992, when Independent Party candidate H. Ross Perot captured 19 percent of the vote. As the figure illustrates, in five of those seven cases, the incumbent party's presidential nominee lost the presidency. Thus, third parties tend to help the major out-of-power party win election.

Finally, third parties put a variety of issues on the national political agenda. When a third party, especially an issue-oriented third party, draws attention to an issue of concern, sometimes government officials respond to that concern even if the third party fails in its election bid. In some such cases, the issue has not previously been given priority, and the attention the third party draws to it serves to create a groundswell of political pressure that forces action. In other cases, the policy makers might act to address the issue in order to woo the supporters of the third party who have expressed that particular issue concern.

Historically, the two major parties' co-option of issues that were first promoted by third parties has sometimes contributed to the demise of third parties. For example, as we have seen, the Progressives' presidential candidate, Theodore Roosevelt, lost to Democrat Woodrow Wilson in 1912, but Wilson enacted many elements of the Progressive Party's platform, including antitrust regulations, corporate law reforms, and banking regulations. Lacking a unique platform, and with comparatively little electoral success, the Progressives faded away. More recently, Reform Party candidate H. Ross Perot's activism concerning campaign finance reform eventually led the two major parties to pass the Bipartisan Campaign Finance Reform Act of 2002. The Reform Party's inability to sustain voter support over the long haul is also apparent: after the party's 2000 presidential nominee Pat Buchanan failed to net even 1 percent of the national vote, the party did not nominate a candidate in 2004, instead backing Green Party nominee Ralph Nader.

TAKE PART IN YOUR DEMOCRACY

ARE YOU RED, BLUE, OR PURPLE?

News commentators use *red* and *blue* to refer to Republicans and Democrats, respectively. Although the basis for an individual's political ideology is complex (see Chapter 1), party identification in the United States often reflects differences in viewpoint on several key issues. Do you know what each party stands for? Do you know which party best represents your views? Take this brief quiz to find out which party you lean toward. Of course, before voting for candidates of that party or even counting yourself as a party identifier, you should further investigate the positions of the parties. The Web sites listed at the end of the chapter are a good place to start.

IN GENERAL, DO YOU BELIEVE

■ that government should play a more active role in ensuring individuals' well-being	Yes	No
■ that government should actively promote equality in the workplace through affirmative action programs	Yes	No
■ that tax cuts are among the best ways to spur economic growth	Yes	No
■ that the government should regulate gun ownership	Yes	No
■ that U.S.-targeted international terrorism is linked to the Arab-Israeli conflict and that fighting terrorism should include furthering the peace process there	Yes	No

■ that the government should promote economic growth and job creation through tax and wage policies that promote domestic job growth and increase workers' salaries	Yes	No
■ that marriage should be defined as a heterosexual union	Yes	No
■ that women should have the right to an abortion	Yes	No
■ that the government should promote economic growth and job creation with tax, legal, and labor policies that businesses advocate	Yes	No
■ that the government should aggressively protect the environment, even if it means more government regulations for industries	Yes	No

New Ideologies, New Technologies: The Parties in the Twenty-First Century

American political parties have changed dramatically in recent years. Global realities such as the end of the Cold War, international and domestic terrorism, and the impact of the Internet have partly driven the changes. Within the Republican and Democratic parties, the changes have reflected an ideological shift from an era when a party's defining position was its position on social welfare policy to a time when foreign policy issues are central. Today, much emphasis is placed on the differences between the Democrats and the Republicans, but for many citizens there are shades of "purple" between the reds and the blues (see the box "Are You Red, Blue, or Purple?").

The Neoconservative Republicans

As we saw in Chapter 1, commentators often use the term *neoconservatism* to describe the ideology of the "new conservatives" or "neocons," an increasingly powerful force in the Republican Party since George W. Bush's election in 2000. *Neo-* ("new") signifies a prior identification with a liberal or even socialist political viewpoint and a newness to conservatism, although neoconservative thought has been part of American political philosophy since the 1970s.

Neoconservatives agree with traditional conservatives that government should have a limited role, particularly in social and fiscal policy. Neoconservatives are frequently defined (and distinguished from other conservatives) by their aggressive foreign policy stance, particularly in defense of Israel.[47] Neoconservatives also advocate the proactive spread of democracy.

Neoconservatives' positions sometimes put them at odds with traditional conservatives who disagree with neocons' hard-line foreign policy stance. For example, traditional conservatives complained that the Bush administration's social welfare spending was excessive and its foreign policy too aggressive or "hawkish."

During the Cold War, neoconservatives were defined by their militaristic opposition to communism. Since the terrorist attacks of September 11, 2001, neoconservatives' foreign policy position has been largely shaped by their opposition to the predominantly Arab states that are alleged to support or harbor terrorists or that pose a threat to the state of Israel. Traditional conservatives, who tend to advocate an isolationist foreign policy and traditional tactics of foreign policy such as diplomacy, also bemoan the **unilateralism,** or one-sided action, characteristic of neoconservative foreign policy. During the George W. Bush administration, many prominent neoconservatives played increasingly important roles within the Republican National Committee, and the party itself reflected the changes in its composition.

unilateralism
one-sided action, usually in foreign policy

The New Democrats

In response to the overwhelming electoral success of the Republicans in capturing the White House in recent decades, Democratic Party leaders began in the early 1990s to consider how they could successfully challenge the Republicans' grip on presidential politics. One key Democrat was then-governor Bill Clinton of Arkansas. Clinton and the so-called New Democrats (who were sometimes referred to as the Third Way, to distinguish them from both the Republicans and the traditional wing of the Democratic Party) proposed a new view of how government can best serve the needs of society in a dynamic time. Acknowledging the limitations of traditional Democratic approaches shaped during the Great Depression—government as the chief solution to social problems; advocacy of labor unions and the environment at the expense of business and economic development—New Democrats have sought to bring liberal values to bear in a changed world.

In particular, New Democrats focus on *globalization*—the continuing integration of world markets for goods, services, and financial capital—as the most significant factor today in the framing of public policy problems and the shaping of their solutions. For New Democrats, the rise of globalization has brought the need for new approaches to the policy issues that have traditionally been important to Democrats. For example, Democrats historically have sided with labor in business-labor policy struggles. But with the globalization of the economy, corporations now have the ability to pick up and move their operations abroad, where labor costs are lower. And so with respect to policies affecting both business and labor, New Democrats advocate working to ensure that *each side* gains advantages.

Further, unlike traditional Democrats, New Democrats do not see the solutions to many policy problems resting primarily in the hands of government. New Democrats are more likely to advocate cooperative solutions between business and government, as well as international cooperation. Unlike their traditional counterparts, New Democrats are also more likely to emphasize individual responsibility and to advocate solutions designed to empower individuals rather than encouraging dependence on the government.

Changing Both Parties: The Internet

The ways in which party members and voters give and get information, as well as the methods by which parties campaign, have changed drastically in recent years. More and more people in the electorate are finding information about issues on the Internet. For their part, the parties are increasingly using the Net as a tool for reaching loyalists and communicating with potential supporters. Take, for example, the "warm" stages preceding the 2008 presidential primaries. In years past, the first significant indicator that a politician was considering tossing his or her hat in the presidential ring was the formation of an exploratory committee that would test the waters with respect to public opinion and fund-raising. But in 2007, as he contemplated a presidential bid, one of the first things U.S. senator Fred Dalton Thompson (R-Tennessee) did was to establish a Weblog on his Web site fred08.com. This strategy provided a cost-effective method of communicating with voters for the media-savvy Thompson, an actor by trade. It also allowed Thompson to signal his interest in running for president while sparing him from spending the political capital of actually declaring his candidacy.

During the 2008 campaign, both the McCain and Obama campaigns used their Web sites to plug their supporters into assorted outlets for their interest and activism. Both offered downloadable widgets that allowed supporters to link their social-networking pages and to fund-raise by linking the campaign site to their own Web sites. Both also hosted a wide variety of ways for individuals to stay connected to the campaigns, including listing candidates' favorites on del.icio.us, links to campaign videos on YouTube and to Facebook and MySpace pages, a Twitter micro-blog through which the campaign sent short, updated communications to instant messaging and e-mail accounts and to the Twitter Web site, and campaign photos available at the flickr Web site.

The Internet has also democratized the party process. Partisan activism is no longer limited to individuals who can attend meetings. Whole new forms of Internet activism have emerged. People with access to the Internet can chat, organize, plan, lobby, fund-raise, contribute, and mobilize without leaving their desks.

Today, each party relies heavily on the Internet for communicating with supporters, as, for example, the Democratic Party's blog "Kicking Ass" and the Republican Party's "podcasts to go" reveal. Each party's Web site gives visitors information and plenty of opportunities to volunteer. Moreover, adopting a strategy first employed by individual candidates, parties are also using the Internet as a fund-raising tool: they solicit contributions via special e-mail accounts and on party Web sites and accept donations through online credit card payments. At the end of this chapter you will find URLs for the Web sites of the Democratic National Committee, the Republican National Committee, and a nonpartisan organization, where you can explore your own opportunities for Internet activism.

> Twitter offers candidates another means of communicating with their supporters and potential voters. While private individuals use Twitter to send micro-messages about their everyday lives ("standing in line @ bookstore behind a guy named Buster"), candidates can twit about the everyday lives of their campaigns ("just got Rev. Buster's endorsement").

CONCLUSION *CONTINUING THE CONVERSATION*

Despite the cynicism with which people often view them, political parties are a vital institution for the civic engagement of Americans and are essential to democracy. For many citizens, political parties are the gateway to political participation. For others, they provide cues that guide decisions at the ballot box. The role of parties in teaching individuals essential skills that may lead to elective office, in recruiting candidates, in contesting elections, and in governing—all these valuable functions often do not get the recognition they deserve.

The two major U.S. political parties have demonstrated enormous adaptability over time. The ability to change in response to constituent demands is a consistent trait of these two dominant parties. The cultural and structural forces that perpetuate the two-party system show little sign of relenting. And although third parties such as the Green Party provide rich fodder for political pundits who speculate about their importance, in electoral terms third parties have demonstrated very little ability to win elections. Instead, third parties commonly advocate issues that eventually are co-opted by one or both of the major parties, and they sometimes play the role of spoiler in elections.

The ability of the Democrats and Republicans to adapt to the concerns of their constituents is perhaps nowhere in better evidence than in the ideological viewpoints of the past two presidents. Democrat Bill Clinton espoused a New Democratic viewpoint that moved the party away from the Rooseveltian ideal of government as the solution to most public policy crises, in favor of the view that the workings of the global economy should be the primary factor shaping policy choices. George W. Bush, also less concerned with his party's traditional position on social welfare policy, instead advocated a neoconservative foreign policy shaped primarily by opposition to foreign states supporting terrorism. In the future, the parties will be challenged to adapt in other ways, too. In particular, they will need to adjust continually to new circumstances, as technology changes how the party organizations identify, organize, mobilize, and communicate with the party in the electorate, as well as how the party in government governs. The contemporary faces of the two major parties demonstrate their continuing evolution and responsiveness to their identifiers and constituents.

Summary

1. Parties Today and Their Functions
Political parties run candidates in elections in an effort to control government. They advance the cause of civic engagement by facilitating citizens' participation, providing unity and cohesiveness, encouraging civic discourse, and communicating important cues to voters.

2. The Three Faces of Parties
Three aspects of parties are the party in the electorate (the individuals who tend to support a particular party), the party organization (the formal party apparatus), and the party in government (the partisan identification of elected leaders).

3. Political Parties in U.S. History
Political scientists have identified five U.S. party systems. Stretching back to the eighteenth century, these systems describe the evolution of party competition and dominance. Through these party systems, we see the ideological roots and political foundations of the two dominant political parties today.

4. Two-Party Domination in U.S. Politics
Explanations of why two political parties dominate include the ideas that parties reflect the dualist nature of conflict in the United States; that the winner-take-all election system creates a two-party structure; that people are socialized to the two-party system; and that election laws strengthen and perpetuate that structure.

5. The Two-Party System Today: In Decline or in Resurgence?
Some political scientists argue that recent times show a decline in the influence of the two major U.S. parties. As factors, they cite waning constituent loyalty to parties, caused by decreases in patronage, and the advent of direct primaries and candidate-centered campaigns. Other scholars assert that parties are rebounding, and they note parties' adaptability, as well as the lack of viable alternatives to the two major parties.

6. Third Parties in the United States
Third parties, which include issue advocacy parties, ideologically oriented parties, and splinter parties, sometimes act as a spoiler for one of the two major parties. Although third-party candidates typically lose elections, they do succeed in getting various issues on the national agenda.

7. New Ideologies, New Technologies: The Parties in the Twenty-First Century
Neoconservatives are an important faction within the Republican Party. They are less concerned than traditional Republicans with constraining governmental involvement in domes-

tic policy and instead are defined by their strong militaristic stance in support of Israel and against Arab states alleged to harbor or support terrorists. New Democrats shy away from the traditional liberal advocacy of government as the chief solution to social problems and focus on globalization as a determining factor shaping public policy dilemmas and their solutions.

candidate-centered campaign 300

candidate committees 296

dealignment 296

divided government 291

Great Depression 285

independent 282

loyal opposition 288

New Deal 295

New Deal coalition 295

party identifiers 282

party in the electorate 282

party in government 290

party organization 286

party system 291

patronage 293

platform 282

political machine 293

political party 281

populism 292

primary election 300

proportional representation system 298

realignment 292

responsible party model 284

soft money loophole 289

spoils system 292

third party 296

ticket splitting 296

unilateralism 306

For Review

1. What functions do political parties perform? How do these functions encourage the civic engagement of Americans?

2. What are the three faces of political parties?

3. Explain the development of the five party systems in U.S. history. Why, historically, does the majority change from one party to another?

4. Why do two parties dominate in politics and government in the United States?

5. What are the arguments that political parties are in decline? What do opponents of these arguments contend?

6. What has been the impact of third parties in recent elections?

7. Describe the political philosophy of the neoconservatives and the New Democrats. How do these factions represent new ways of thinking about politics?

For Critical Thinking and Discussion

1. How were you socialized to the two-party system? Do your views reflect your parents' views? Were third parties even mentioned in your house when you were growing up?

2. What factors explain the demographic bases of the two major parties? How could each party expand its base of support?

3. What impact do you think the neoconservatives and New Democrats will have on third parties over time? Why?

4. What evidence is there that a new party system is emerging? Do the 2008 election results support the claim that a new party system is taking shape?

5. In what ways beyond those discussed in the chapter might the Internet be used as a communication tool between voters and parties? In your view, what are the most important uses for the Internet in partisan politics?

MULTIPLE CHOICE: Choose the lettered item that answers the question correctly.

1. Characteristics of political parties include:
   a. they are private organizations that can set limits on membership.
   b. they have narrow issue concerns.
   c. they run candidates on their own label.
   d. they support candidates only after the candidates have been elected to office.

2. The primary goal of the major political parties is to:
   a. raise large amounts of money.
   b. win the advertising wars.
   c. control government.
   d. enact a single specific policy.

3. The three faces of parties *do not* include
   a. the party in government.
   b. party-building activities.
   c. the party organization.
   d. the party in the electorate.

4. The formal party apparatus, including committees, head-quarters, conventions, party leaders, staff, and volunteer workers, is called the
   a. party in government.
   b. party-building coalition.
   c. party organization.
   d. party in the electorate.

5. The party in government is
   a. the partisan identification of elected leaders in local, county, state, and federal governments.
   b. the ability of parties to raise unlimited funds for party-building activities such as voter registration drives and get-out-the-vote.
   c. a party's objections to the policies and priorities of the government in power.
   d. a political party that breaks off from one of the two dominant parties.

6. The categorization of the number and competitiveness of political parties in a polity is called
   a. dealignment.
   b. unilateralism.
   c. a party system.
   d. the responsive party model.

7. Elections in which voters choose the party's candidates who will later run for office are called
   a. primary elections.
   b. general elections.
   c. run-off elections.
   d. special elections.

8. A corrupt yet useful organization that dominated politics, particularly in cities, around the turn of the twentieth century was known as the
   a. party system.
   b. proportional representation system.
   c. political machine.
   d. party organization.

9. The phenomenon in which fewer voters support the two major political parties and instead self-identify as inde-pendent is called
   a. proportional representation.
   b. realignment.
   c. neoconservatism.
   d. dealignment.

10. The group composed of southern Democrats, northern city dwellers, immigrants, the poor, Catholics, labor union mem-bers, blue-collar workers, and women that elected Franklin D. Roosevelt to the presidency four times was called
    a. the New Left.
    b. the Third Way.
    c. the Dixiecrat alliance.
    d. the New Deal coalition.

FILL IN THE BLANKS.

11. A _____ is a campaign in which an individual seeking election, rather than an entire party slate, is the focus.

12. In a _____, political parties win the number of parliamentary seats equal to the percentage of the vote each party received.

13. Party leaders used _____ as a device to reward political supporters with jobs or government contracts.

14. The group that emphasizes an aggressive foreign policy, particularly in support of Israel, and deemphasizes the traditional conservative focus on limited government is called _____.

15. The role that the party out of power plays, highlighting its objections to the policies and priorities of the government in power, is called _____.

Answers: 1. c; 2. b; 3. b; 4. c; 5. a; 6. c; 7. a; 8. c; 9. d; 10. d; 11. candidate-centered campaign; 12. proportional representation system; 13. patronage; 14. neoconservatives; 15. loyal opposition.

310 | CHAPTER 8 | Political Parties

RESOURCES FOR RESEARCH AND ACTION

Internet Resources

American Democracy Now Web site
www.mhhe.com/harrison1e   Consult the book's Web site for study guides, interactive activities, simulations, and current hotlinks for additional information on political parties in the United States.

Democratic National Committee
www.democrats.org   The Democrats' Web site contains hotlinks for state and local party Web sites and opportunities for volunteering, internships, and employment, as well as party position papers and platforms and candidate information.

Pew Research Center for the People and the Press
http://people-press.org/reports/display.php3?ReportID=242
This the Web site for the report "Beyond Red vs. Blue: Republicans Divided About Role of Government - Democrats by Social and Personal Values," which provides a quiz so you can determine where your political beliefs fall on Pew's typology of voters.

Project Vote Smart
www.vote-smart.org   This nonpartisan site provides independent, factual information on candidates and elected officials of all political parties.

Republican National Committee
www.gop.org   The Republicans' site also has links for state and local party sites and opportunities for volunteering, internships, and employment, as well as party position papers and platforms and candidate information.

Recommended Readings

Dionne, E. J., Jr. *They Only Look Dead: Why Progressives Will Dominate the Next Political Era.* New York: Simon & Schuster, 1995. A noted *Washington Post* columnist's theory as to how a third party will become viable in the United States, elaborating the idea that support of a third party will come from middle-class voters dissatisfied with the two-party system.

Flammang, Janet. *Women's Political Voice.* Philadelphia: Temple University Press, 1997. A well-researched account of women's political participation in general and women's participation in political parties in particular.

Hershey, Marjorie Random, and Paul Allen Beck. *Party Politics in America,* 10th ed. New York: Longman, 2003. A classic work on American political parties, analyzing the changing roles of parties in the twentieth century and the impact of the campaign finance system on political parties.

Lijphart, Arend. *Electoral Systems and Party Systems: A Study of Twenty-Seven Democracies 1945–1990.* New York: Oxford University Press, 1994. An exploration of the nature of party systems in many industrialized democracies both historically and in modern times.

Rohde, David W. *Parties and Leaders in the Postreform House.* Chicago: University of Chicago Press, 1991. Analyzes the reasons behind the realignment and resurgence of partisanship in Congress during the 1980s.

Schattschneider, E. E. *Party Government.* New York: Rinehart, 1942. A classic work that explains the nature of political parties and their impact on party government.

Shea, Daniel M., and John C. Green, eds. *The State of the Parties: The Changing Role of Contemporary Party Organizations.* Lanham, MD: Rowman and Littlefield, 1995. Analysis of changes in modern political parties in light of changes to campaign finance laws, the rise of candidate-centered campaigns, and the increased role of campaign professionals.

White, John Kenneth, and Daniel M. Shea. *New Party Politics: From Jefferson and Hamilton to the Information Age.* New York: Bedford/St. Martin's, 2000. A solid historical overview of parties, with a particular focus on the impact of the Internet on modern party politics.

Movies of Interest

Primary Colors (1998)
Starring John Travolta, and based on the anonymously written book of the same name, this popular movie—a fictionalized account of Bill Clinton's 1992 campaign—provides insight into the primary election season of a presidential nominee.

City Hall (1996)
This film starring Al Pacino and John Cusack shows the workings of a corrupt political machine—and the consequences of that corruption.

National Journal

PENNSYLVANIA: VOTER PARTICIPATION IN A SCHIZOPHRENIC STATE

Few states resisted Barack Obama more than Pennsylvania during the Democratic primary season. Partly as a result, few states are more critical to his hopes of winning the White House this fall.

Most of Pennsylvania's recent political developments, from the trend in voter registration to the latest statewide results, tilt toward the Democrats, often sharply. But the one exception to that pattern encourages Republicans: Although Democrats have carried the state in the past four presidential elections, their winning margins have dropped from about 9 percentage points under Bill Clinton in 1992 and 1996 to 4 points under Al Gore in 2000 and to just 2.5 points under John Kerry in 2004. And in John McCain, who polls well nationally among independents, Republicans may have a nominee capable of reversing the Democrats' two-decade advance in the affluent, growing, and once reliably Republican suburbs of Philadelphia—the trend most responsible for the Democratic rise in Pennsylvania.

Add to these factors Obama's weak performance in the April primary, and the state's top Democrats are cautioning the party to expect a tough fight in Pennsylvania. "I still think it's a swing state, and all you have to do is look at the trend lines . . . in presidential politics, it has been getting closer and closer," Democratic Gov. Ed Rendell told National Journal. "And McCain is the best Republican candidate they have fielded presidentially since Ronald Reagan, in the sense that his reputation as a maverick and a moderate . . . holds him in very good stead with the independents and [suburban] Republicans who have been tending to vote Democratic in the last four elections."

Yet the very ferocity of the Keystone State's Democratic presidential primary may have strengthened Obama's chances by spurring a registration surge that has swelled the Democratic lead over the GOP on the voter rolls to nearly 1.1 million, almost double the party's 2004 edge. According to Rendell, that's a record voter-registration advantage for the Democrats, and it dramatizes the extent to which Pennsylvania remains a difficult challenge for McCain, especially amid the intense disillusionment with Bush there. The state is "still in play . . . but the idea that it is evenly divided between McCain and Obama, that it is a 50-50 toss-up, I think that is just wrong," says Ruy Teixeira, an electoral analyst at the liberal Brookings Institution who co-authored a recent comprehensive study of the state's demographic and political trends. "It is a purple state leaning blue, and it may be even bluer than it was in 2004. So it is a real uphill climb for McCain in my view."

In its recent political evolution, Pennsylvania has been a tale of two states. It has simultaneously moved sharply toward the Democrats in the southeast, particularly in the comfortable Philadelphia suburbs, and sharply toward the GOP in the southwest, especially in the largely blue-collar suburbs of Pittsburgh. McCain's challenge is to reverse the first trend and reinforce the second, as well as the GOP's more modest gains in presidential races in hardscrabble northeastern counties around Scranton.

"You can play the chess game almost any way, but the Philly 'burbs, southwestern Pennsylvania, and those counties up there [around Scranton] are basically it," says G. Terry Madonna, a longtime Pennsylvania pollster who is now the director of the Center for Politics and Public Affairs at Franklin and Marshall College. "McCain has to win the [blue-collar] Reagan Democrats in the west and the northeast, and he has to win some independents, independent-minded Republicans, and Democrats in the Philly suburbs."

For generations, the Philadelphia suburbs were the home of prosperous "Main Line" moderate Republicans. But like other socially moderate, white-collar suburbs outside the South, these communities began moving toward the Democrats during Clinton's 1992 race. They have shifted even further in that direction under Bush, who has given the GOP a more Southern and more evangelical face.

In the four suburban counties immediately outside Philadelphia, the change has been profound. From 1920 through 1988, no Democratic presidential nominee won Delaware or Montgomery counties, with the exception of Lyndon Johnson in his 1964 landslide. During that period in Bucks County, the only Democratic winners were Johnson and Franklin D. Roosevelt in 1936. As late as 1988, George H.W. Bush won 60 percent of the vote in all three counties.

But starting with Clinton in 1992, Democrats have now carried that trio of counties in four consecutive elections. And their margins in Delaware and Montgomery have increased each time. "The suburbs are a place that really liked Bush 41 but couldn't relate to Bush 43," said Christopher Nicholas, a Harrisburg-based Republican consultant who ran the successful 2004 re-election campaign of Republican Sen. Arlen Specter. "They liked the Connecticut Yankee and had trouble relating to the Texan."

Over the same period, though, the state's southwest corner—the counties surrounding Pittsburgh, such as Beaver, Washington, and Westmoreland—have moved in the opposite direction. Although Pittsburgh itself has remained solidly Democratic, these counties, much less affluent and less white-collar than the Philadelphia suburbs, have responded favorably to George W. Bush's conservative cultural and national security policies.

On balance, this geographic swap has benefited Pennsylvania Democrats, because their new strongholds are bigger and are gaining population, while some of the increasingly Republican areas are shrinking. "Where population is growing, the Democrats are doing better. Where it is declining, Republicans are doing better," says Teixeira, the co-author of the Brookings analysis with demographer William Frey.

The conversion of the Philadelphia suburbs and exurbs, in addition to the Democrats' continuing dominance of Pittsburgh and heavily African-American Philadelphia, has provided the party a fragile but perceptible advantage in the state. After the 2000 election, Republicans controlled the governorship, both U.S. Senate seats, a majority of U.S. House seats, and both chambers of the state Legislature.

In 2002, Rendell captured the governorship. In 2006, Democrats re-elected Rendell, won a majority of the state House, ousted four GOP lawmakers to gain a majority of the state's U.S. House delegation, and took a U.S. Senate seat as Democrat Bob Casey routed staunchly conservative GOP Sen. Rick Santorum. The 2006 recoil from the GOP was especially powerful in the four Philadelphia suburban counties, where Democrats defeated two Republican House members and Casey annihilated Santorum by more than175,000 votes. Six years earlier, Santorum had swept those counties by nearly 152,000 votes.

In this period of Democratic advance, the one big exception was Specter's successful 2004 campaign. On the day that Bush lost the state to Kerry, Specter won re-election with nearly 53 percent of the vote. Specter, a moderate who supports abortion rights, built a much different coalition from Bush's, actually running behind him in 29 of Pennsylvania's 67 counties. Nearly all of these were culturally conservative counties either near Pittsburgh or in the heavily rural "T" that extends through the state's center. But Specter, a former Philadelphia district attorney, ran far better than Bush through all of the eastern counties, from Philadelphia

the very ferocity of the Keystone State's Democratic presidential primary may have strengthened Obama's chances by spurring a registration surge

north to Scranton and beyond to the New York border. Most important, Specter held down his losses in Philadelphia itself and amassed a nearly 150,000-vote lead in the four suburban Philadelphia counties that decisively rejected Bush.

Running against the first African-American presidential nominee of a major party, McCain has little chance of minimizing the Democratic advantage in Philadelphia as much as Specter did. But, apart from that, the Specter map may be "as good a model as McCain can find," Madonna says.

In fact, Republicans hope that McCain can do better than Specter among culturally conservative voters. "Obama's challenge is, how does he win over the working-class white folks that he didn't win [in the primary]?" says consultant Nicholas. "He is just radically different from their lives, and McCain is not. Military, father in the military, grandfather in the military: That's an arc they can understand. The Obama life story, while very unique and interesting, is not something folks in these little railroad towns can relate to."

Rendell, who openly declared during the primary that some Pennsylvania voters might not be willing to vote for a black presidential candidate, says he thinks that economic anxiety may help Obama perform better than Republicans anticipate in the Scranton and

Pittsburgh areas. But to hold the state, Rendell is mostly counting on Obama's energizing new voters and maintaining the Democratic advantage in the Philadelphia suburbs and Lehigh Valley.

Can Obama defend the Democratic beachheads outside Philadelphia? Since 2004, Democrats have posted substantial voter-registration gains in all four suburban counties, as well as across the Lehigh Valley. But in the Democratic primary, Obama did not run as well in these places as he did in white-collar communities elsewhere: Clinton split the four Philadelphia suburbs with him and swept the Lehigh Valley.

Those results worry Rendell, who was Clinton's highest-profile Pennsylvania supporter. "There is a very strong reservoir of support for Clinton among women [in these counties]," he says. "So . . . we have real work to do in the suburbs." Plus, he adds, McCain's reputation for independence will make him a "tough" competitor for moderate suburban voters.

Rendell says that Obama might win the Philadelphia suburbs "by a smaller margin than Kerry did," but he expects the senator from Illinois to run well enough there to hold Pennsylvania. Republicans hope that Rendell is wrong. Both sides agree that no matter how much ground McCain gains elsewhere, he is unlikely to capture the state unless he can run even with or better than Obama immediately outside of Philadelphia. "All roads end up pointing back to those Philly suburbs," one senior McCain campaign aide said.

Madonna agrees. "You can't just give up about 90,000 votes in the Philadelphia suburbs [as Bush did]," he says. "There are so many votes there that making up that kind of deficit elsewhere is really difficult." Such inescapable math ensures the Philadelphia suburbs a spot high on the list of the places picking the next president.

■**THEN:** Candidate preference was often linked to geography.

■**NOW:** Geography has played an important but not determining role in the 2008 presidential election.

■**NEXT:** How will increased voter mobility affect the importance of geography as a political variable?
What impact will increased mass communication and technology have on the importance of geography in future presidential elections?
What strategies will candidates need to rely on in states like Pennsylvania in the future?

CHAPTER 9

Elections, Campaigns, and Voting

RESERVED FOR VOTER PARKING

THEN

Political party–dominated campaigns and grassroots activism were deciding factors in how people voted.

NOW

Candidate-centered campaigns rely on paid professionals to shape and spin candidates' messages—and on costly media buys to disseminate it.

NEXT

How will continuously advancing technologies drive and change campaigns?

How will changes in the campaign finance structure affect how campaigns are conducted?

What new faces and voices will determine the campaign environment?

The Students of SNAP PAC

Many students would love to work on a political campaign full-time, but tuition, rent, and food expenses often get in the way. Enter SNAP PAC—Students for a New American Politics—an innovative political action committee (PAC) formed by six undergraduate students. Unlike typical political action committees, which raise money and contribute the funds to the campaigns of political candidates, SNAP PAC raises funds and grants this income to students so they can work on political campaigns. In 2008, through its Summer Internship Program, SNAP PAC funded students working on more than a half-dozen campaigns throughout the country (applications are available at www.snappac.org). These lucky individuals received stipends of up to $2,500 each for working full-time as organizers in designated congressional races. (SNAP PAC identifies "progressive" candidates that it will support and then dispatches students to work for their campaigns.) With their focus on grassroots organizing, the students make direct contact with voters and potential voters. They lead voter registration drives, canvass door-to-door for candidates, and work at phone banks and in Election Day efforts to mobilize registered voters to come out to vote. And in the summer program, students contribute their minds and muscle for ten to twelve weeks on a campaign. The SNAP PAC Web site notes:

By providing candidates with fully trained, enthusiastic, and cost-free organizers, we are helping provide the margin of victory in tight races. And by placing talented students in positions of responsibility within key campaigns, we are training and inspiring the next generation of political activists. All of the students that SNAP PAC supports are students who would not be able to participate fully in progressive campaigns were it not for receiving a summer scholarship.

Moreover, through this unique PAC's Fall Campus Mobilization program, students at ten colleges and universities (including Columbia University/Barnard College, Dartmouth College, Earlham College, Florida A&M, George Washington University, Miami University, and Pace University) worked on voter registration and grassroots mobilization drives. I SNAP PAC functions like most other political action committees in its fund-raising tactics, which include special events with well-known speakers. For example, New York City councilwoman Gale Brewer hosted a 2008 fund-raiser for SNAP PAC that featured women's rights activist Gloria Steinem. I Of the fifteen candidates that SNAP PAC student activists supported through their campaign work in 2006, ten won their races. But all of the student activists had won. They had worked for something they believed in. They had made their voices heard in the political process, helped others to participate, and learned firsthand about issues facing the people today. In the process, they gained invaluable political and life experience.

> Students participating in internship programs funded by **SNAP PAC** help to mobilize voters.

When Americans think about

politics, their first thought is often about elections, campaigns, and voting. In the eyes of many of us, these activities are the essence of political participation, because it is through the electoral process that we feel we participate most directly and meaningfully in our democracy. Often viewed as the pinnacle of the democratic experience, the act of voting is the culmination of a wide range of forms of political engagement. In this chapter's "American Democracy Now" vignette and in the discussion that follows, we see the interconnectedness of many aspects of political campaigns and elections, including fund-raising, grassroots organizing, candidate selection, and voter mobilization. These opportunities for civic participation in the democratic process are present in such a broad variety of forms that they are accessible to everyone who wants to be engaged.

Civic Engagement and Political Participation

Elections, campaigns, and voting are fundamental aspects of the civic engagement of Americans and people in other democracies. These activities represent concentrated forms of civic engagement and are important both for the polity as a whole and for the individuals who participate.[1] But intensive political engagement—working on a campaign or running for office, say—rarely represents an individual's first foray into a civically engaged life. Rather, people who are so engaged in the political process usually are initiated through smaller, less intensive steps. Perhaps a group of classmates who especially enjoy the political discussions in your American government class might continue their conversations of democracy over a cup of Starbucks after class. Those same classmates might begin regularly reading political blogs and daily newspapers to become better informed about candidates and issues. Some members of the informal group might decide to hear a candidate who is giving a speech on campus—and wind up volunteering on his or her campaign. Political engagement often begins with small steps such as these, but the cumulative results are large: they help to ensure that the government is representative of the people and responsive to their needs. Representative governments, which are the product of individuals' political engagement, tend to be more stable and to make decisions that best reflect the needs and will of the people who elect them.

Direct forms of political participation such as voting, volunteering on a campaign, and running for office are of keen interest to scholars of civic engagement. Many scholarly analysts have noticed an overall decrease in levels of political participation. As discussed in Chapter 7, political scientist Robert Putnam argues that the United States is seeing a decline in its social capital, the social networks and reciprocal relationships characteristic of a community or society. These networks are varied and include formal organizations such as clubs, fraternities, sororities, interest groups, and sports teams. But there are also informal networks such as babysitting co-ops, car pools, and study groups. Putnam details how solitary pursuits such as watching television and using a computer have pervasively replaced group activities related to civic participation.

Some scholars have challenged Putnam's assertion that social capital has declined. They point out that new forms of social capital have arisen in the form of Internet social networks, instant messaging, and Internet activism to replace the traditional social networks that Putnam studied. Despite these differing views, there is consensus that civic participation is essential and that among its most important forms is electoral political participation.

Indeed, elections offer a wealth of opportunities for citizen involvement:

- Members of political parties recruit candidates to run for election.
- Cadres of volunteers organize campaign events, including fund-raisers, rallies, and neighborhood leafleting.

In this chapter, we explore opportunities for—and the value of—citizens' participation in electoral politics; the processes of voting and running for office; and the elements of modern campaigns and elections. We also analyze the factors that determine whether an individual will vote, how voters decide among candidates, and why some people do not vote.

FIRST, we examine *civic engagement and political participation* in the electoral process.

SECOND, we consider the various kinds of *elections in the United States.*

THIRD, we focus on *the act of voting* and the impact that the type of ballot used can have on election outcomes.

FOURTH, we examine the requirements of *running for office* and making the *choice to run.*

FIFTH, we look at the *nature of political campaigns today,* paying particular attention to campaigns' extensive use of professional consultants and deep reliance on electronic media and the Internet.

SIXTH, we survey legislators' efforts at *regulating federal campaign contributions.*

SEVENTH, we probe the long duration and various stages of *presidential campaigns.*

EIGHTH, we look at *who votes*—the factors influencing voter participation.

NINTH, we delve into the question of *how voters decide* on the candidates whom they will endorse at the ballot box.

TENTH, we investigate the many reasons *why some people do not vote,* including factors such as lack of efficacy, voter fatigue, and negative campaigns.

> Are more people really *"Bowling Alone"*? Political scientist Robert Putnam has argued that the United States is experiencing a decline in social capital because its citizens are participating less in civic life. But perhaps Americans are engaged in civic life in very different ways from those of previous generations. Here, a group of Wii bowling enthusiasts compete in a friendly match in an Illinois restaurant.

GOTV
get out the vote

general election
an election that determines which candidates win the offices being sought

- Phone bank volunteers try to persuade other people to participate in the electoral process—for instance, by giving a campaign contribution, putting a candidate's sign on their lawn, or simply voting for the candidate.
- Other volunteers focus exclusively on **GOTV**—that is, they work to get out the vote. They register voters for both primary and general elections, and they provide absentee ballots to people who are ill or who will be out of town on election day. On Election Day itself, they remind people to vote by phoning them or knocking on their door and asking if they need a ride to the polls.[2]
- Others (who may be paid) volunteer to work at the polls on election day.

While each volunteer effort plays a part in ensuring the success of a democracy, a key form of political participation is running for office. Electoral contests in which more than one candidate seeks to win office are a fundamental component of a democracy.

Elections in the United States

Every state holds at least two types of elections. A *primary election* comes first and determines the party's nominees—those who will run for office. For most political offices, there is little or no competition in the primary election. But in presidential and gubernatorial primary elections, vigorous contention is often the rule, particularly within the out-of-power party. House and Senate primary elections that lack an incumbent candidate (that is, one who has been elected to that office before) are also often highly competitive as many candidates attempt to win their party's nomination.

In a **general election,** the parties' respective nominees run against each other, and voters decide who should hold office, as the person with the most votes wins. (Presidential elections, discussed later in this chapter, are a notable exception.) The degree of competition in general elections depends on a number of factors, including the presence of and strength of incumbency, the degree of party competition, and the level of the office. In recent times, presidential elections have been brutally competitive, as have been certain gubernatorial races and many congressional contests where no incumbent is seeking reelection. Some communities, particularly big cities, may also experience intense competition for office in general elections.

Nominations and Primary Elections

In a primary election, voters decide which nominees the political parties should run in the general election. But *which* voters decide varies greatly from state to state. In some states, only registered party members are eligible to vote in primary elections, whereas in other states, any registered voter can vote in any party's primary, and in North Dakota, voters are not even required to register.

In U.S. presidential primaries, voters do not vote directly for the candidate whom they would like their party to nominate. Instead, the popular vote determines which candidate's delegates will attend the party's nominating convention and vote for that party's nominee. This system of selecting delegates through primary voting is different from the earlier system, when party leaders selected the presidential nominee with little or no input from the rank-and-file party members.

The two major U.S. parties made reforms to the earlier delegate selection process after the 1968 Democratic National Convention in Chicago. Anti–Vietnam War activists outside the convention protested the presumed nomination of Vice President Hubert Humphrey as the Democratic Party's presidential candidate. Humphrey had not won any primaries but was favored among the convention's delegates who had been hand-picked by party leaders. The activists instead supported the candidacy of Senator Eugene McCarthy (D-Minnesota), an outspoken war opponent. The demonstrations turned into riots when Chicago police beat the protesters. The Democratic National Committee, in an attempt to address the concerns of those complaining that they had been excluded from the nomination process, appointed the McGovern-Fraser Commission (named after its cochairs), which recommended a series of reforms to the delegate-selection process.

The reforms, many of which both the Democratic Party and the Republican Party adopted, significantly increased the influence of party voters. Voters could now select delegates to the national conventions, a power previously restricted to the party elite. Party voters today select the delegates at statewide conventions or through primary elections or **caucuses**—meetings of party members held to select delegates to the national convention. The reforms also included provisions that would ensure the selection of a more representative body of delegates, with certain delegate slots set aside for women, minorities, union members, and young party voters. These slots roughly correspond with the proportion of support the party receives from those groups.

When an individual is elected to be a delegate at the national convention, often that delegate has pledged to vote for a specific candidate. This pledge is nonbinding, however, as delegates of a losing candidate often switch their support to the apparent victor.

TYPES OF PRIMARY ELECTIONS

In an **open primary** election, any registered voter can vote in any party's primary, as can independent voters not registered with a party. In an open primary, parties' ballots are available in the voting booth, and the voter simply selects privately or publicly one on which to register his or her preferences.

In a **closed primary** election, voting in a party's primary is limited to members of that party. In some states, voters must declare their party affiliation well in advance of the primary election—sometimes as many as sixty days before. In other states, voters can declare their party preference at the polling place on the day of the election. Such restrictions on who can vote in a party's primary originated in the parties' maneuvering to have the strongest candidate nominated. For example, if a popular incumbent president were running unopposed in a primary election, members of the president's party might choose to vote in the other party's primary as a way of scheming to get a weak candidate nominated. A closed primary aims to thwart this strategy.

PRESIDENTIAL PRIMARIES

The states determine the timing of primary elections. Figure 9.1 shows the schedule of the presidential primaries in 2008. Historically, states that held their presidential primary earlier in the year had a greater say in determining the nominee than did states with later primaries. The reason is that candidates tended to drop out if they did not win primaries, did not meet media expectations, or ran out of funds (see "The Conversation of Democracy"). In general, past presidential primaries gave great sway to the agricultural states, as many of the more urban states' primaries fell later in the season.

All of this changed in 2007 when, in an attempt to increase their political clout, a number of diverse states banded together to hold their primaries on the same day so that presidential candidates would be forced to address issues of the keenest interest to those states. These states modeled their objective on **Super Tuesday,** the day in early March on which the most presidential primary elections took place, many of them in southern states. Super Tuesday had been the fruit of a successful effort in 1988 by several southern and rural states to hold their primaries on the same day so as to increase their political importance and allow expression of southern voters' political will.[3] But in 2007, the Super Tuesday strategy was challenged by state legislators in some of the most populous states, including California, New York, Illinois, and New Jersey, who sought to have their presidential primaries on the earliest day that national political party rules allowed. In 2008, that day, dubbed "Super-Duper Tuesday" by the

> Chicago police restrained protesters during the 1968 Democratic National Convention by using tear gas, among other methods. As a result of the riots during this convention, sparked by dissatisfaction over the selection of Hubert Humphrey as the nominee by party insiders, the two major U.S. parties made major reforms to the delegate-selection process.

caucus
meeting of party members held to select delegates to the national convention

open primary
a type of primary in which both parties' ballots are available in the voting booth, and voters select one on which to register their preferences

closed primary
a type of primary in which voting in a party's primary is limited to members of that party

Super Tuesday
the Tuesday in early March on which the most primary elections were held, many of them in southern states; provided the basis for Super-Duper Tuesday in 2008

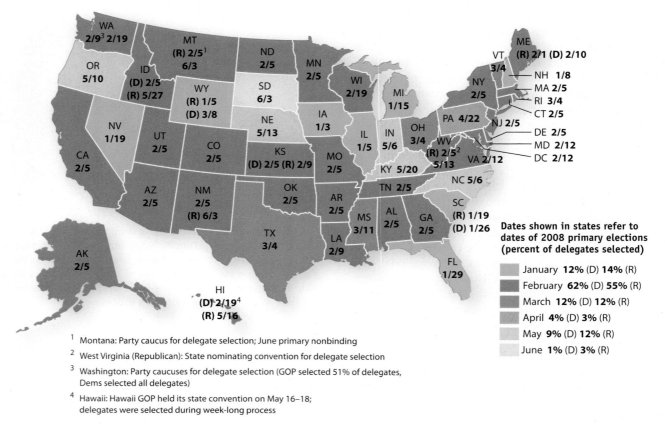

WA 2/9[3] 2/19
OR 5/10
ID (D) 2/5 (R) 5/27
NV 1/19
CA 2/5
UT 2/5
AZ 2/5
MT (R) 2/5[1] 6/3
WY (R) 1/5 (D) 3/8
CO 2/5
NM 2/5 (R) 6/3
ND 2/5
SD 6/3
NE 5/13
KS (D) 2/5 (R) 2/9
OK 2/5
TX 3/4
MN 2/5
IA 1/3
MO 2/5
AR 2/5
LA 2/9
WI 2/19
IL 1/5
MI 1/15
IN 5/6
KY 5/20
TN 2/5
MS 3/11
AL 2/5
GA 2/5
OH 3/4
WV (R) 2/5[2] 5/13
VA 2/12
NC 5/6
SC (R) 1/19 (D) 1/26
FL 1/29
PA 4/22
NY 2/5
VT 3/4
ME (R) 2/1 (D) 2/10
NH 1/8
MA 2/5
RI 3/4
CT 2/5
NJ 2/5
DE 2/5
MD 2/12
DC 2/12
AK 2/5
HI (D) 2/19[4] (R) 5/16

Dates shown in states refer to dates of 2008 primary elections (percent of delegates selected)

January 12% (D) 14% (R)
February 62% (D) 55% (R)
March 12% (D) 12% (R)
April 4% (D) 3% (R)
May 9% (D) 12% (R)
June 1% (D) 3% (R)

[1] Montana: Party caucus for delegate selection; June primary nonbinding

[2] West Virginia (Republican): State nominating convention for delegate selection

[3] Washington: Party caucuses for delegate selection (GOP selected 51% of delegates, Dems selected all delegates)

[4] Hawaii: Hawaii GOP held its state convention on May 16–18; delegates were selected during week-long process

FIGURE 9.1

Dates of Presidential Primaries, 2008

Source: National Association of Secretaries of State, http://www.nass.org/releases/2008%Presidential/%20Primaries%Calendar.pdf

media, was February 5. In all, twenty other states jumped on the early primary bandwagon, with the result that twenty-four states held their primaries and caucuses on February 5, 2008. Although under normal circumstances, such a change would have muted the impact of other primaries because the most populous states control an enormous number of delegates to the national conventions, in 2008 this was not the case. That year, the highly competitive Democratic primary between Senator Hillary Clinton (D-New York) and Senator Barack Obama (D-Illinois) meant that states such as New Mexico and Oregon (which had late primaries, in early June) were competitive and received national media coverage.

General Elections

In a general election, voters decide who should hold office from among the candidates determined in the primary election. Most general elections, including presidential elections, are held on the first Tuesday after the first Monday in November. But because the states schedule and oversee elections, you might find that your gubernatorial election, state legislative election, or town council election occurs at different times of the year.

General elections for Congress and most state legislatures feature a winner-take-all system. That is, the candidate who receives the most votes wins that office (even if that total is not a majority, or even if an opponent receives only one vote less than the victor). Thus, a member of the U.S. House of Representatives or Senate can be elected with less than a majority of the votes in his or her district, particularly when three or more candidates are seeking that seat.

Because electoral law varies from state to state, and counties and municipalities within those states have their own structures of governance, less common kinds of elections are possible and are used in some locales. For example, some states require a runoff election when no candidate receives the majority of the votes cast. In a **runoff election,** if no can-

runoff election
a follow-up election held when no candidate receives the majority of votes cast in the original election

THE CONVERSATION OF DEMOCRACY

SHOULD THE UNITED STATES HAVE A NATIONAL PRIMARY?

The Issue: The party primary process that selects each party's nominee for president was a hot-button issue in the 2008 presidential race. Historically, the primary system focused enormous attention on the states of Iowa, where the first caucus is held, and New Hampshire, where the first party primary takes place. In these states, voters have had the opportunity to gain a deep familiarity with all of the candidates seeking the parties' nominations. But critics of the system have charged that these two states' political culture does not reflect the vast majority of Americans. As a result, many of the most populous states moved their primaries to the earliest day allowed by the political parties—in 2008 that day was February 5. Other states, including Pennsylvania, Texas, West Virginia, and Kentucky, held off having their primaries, in the hopes that one state could find itself in the position of kingmaker by bringing one of the party candidates over the top in the needed delegate count. Given this structure, many citizens have asked, "Is this any way to begin electing a president?"

Should states matter when it comes to selecting the parties' nominees? One potential solution to the skewed emphasis on various states is to hold a national primary, a day like election day, when party members throughout the country can choose their nominees on the same day. People have voiced arguments for and against the idea of a national primary.

Yes: Having a national primary will help the parties, because it will ensure that the nominee chosen in each case is the best candidate for the party. With the shift to a national primary, states that currently have late primaries will no longer be forced to accept a nominee chosen by party members who might be very different from themselves. Furthermore, if more people have a say in choosing their party's nominee, voter turnout might rise in both the primary and the general election. Holding a national primary also will shorten the election season, so that voters will be less fatigued by the length of the campaign.

No: The primary system ensures that small, agricultural states have a voice in national politics. In the general election, smaller states are overshadowed because the Electoral College, which is based on state population, determines the winner. The current primary and caucus system enables voters in those states to analyze the candidates thoroughly, without the noise and distraction that would come with a large-scale, media-saturated national primary. And because the voters in states such as Iowa and New Hampshire are, after all, party members, they naturally understand that a large part of their responsibility is to select the nominee best equipped to win the general election.

Other approaches: Some have suggested the idea of holding regional primaries instead of one national primary, with a different region holding its primary election first in each presidential election year so that no region would have the influence that Iowa and New Hampshire now enjoy. Each region would include a mix of large and small states and urban and rural areas. Candidates would need to campaign throughout each region in turn rather than the entire country, thus allowing them to focus their efforts more than they would be able to with one national primary, and with three or four regional primaries, the campaign season would still be shortened significantly, thus eliminating voter fatigue.

What do you think?

① Do you believe that we should have a national primary? Explain.

② What impact would a national primary have on your home state's say in the nomination process? How will small states fare versus large states? Rural versus urban?

③ What impact do you think a national primary or regional primaries would have on voter turnout? What effect might either type of primary have on how presidential campaigns are waged? Would money be more or less important? Why?

---

didate receives more than 50 percent of the vote, several of the top vote-getters (usually the top two) run in another, subsequent election. Typically, the field of candidates is winnowed down until one candidate receives the requisite 50 percent plus one vote. Runoff elections often occur in *nonpartisan* municipal elections where candidates do not run on a party label.

Owing to advances in technology, runoff elections can occur immediately in some states when needed. In an **instant runoff election,** a computerized voting machine simulates the elimination of last-place vote-getters. How does this system work? In an instant runoff, voters rank candidates in order of preference (first choice, second choice, and so on). If any

instant runoff election
a special runoff election in which the computerized voting machine simulates the elimination of last-place vote-getters

referendum

an election in which voters in a state can vote for or against a measure proposed by the state legislature

initiative

a citizen-sponsored proposal that can result in new or amended legislation or a state constitutional amendment

proposition

a proposed measure placed on the ballot in an initiative election

recall

a special election in which voters can remove officeholders before their term is over

Australian ballot

a secret ballot prepared by the government, distributed to all eligible voters, and, when balloting is completed, counted by government officials in an unbiased fashion, without corruption or regard to individual preferences

candidate garners more than 50 percent of all of the first-choice votes, that candidate wins. But if no candidate gets a majority of first-choice votes, the candidate in last place is electronically eliminated. The voting machine computer then recalculates the ballots, using the second-choice vote for those voters who voted for the eliminated last-place finisher; in effect, every voter gets to choose among the candidates remaining on the ballot. This process is repeated until a candidate who receives more than 50 percent of the votes emerges. Today's voting machines allow this process to take place instantly.

Referendum, Initiative, and Recall

Whereas primary elections and general elections select an individual to run for and serve in office, various other kinds of elections are held for the purpose of deciding public policy questions. Although no national mechanism allows all Americans to vote for or against a given policy proposal, citizens can directly decide policy questions in their states by referendum or initiative.[4]

A **referendum** is an election in which voters in a state can vote for or against a measure proposed by the state legislature. Frequently, referenda concern matters such as state bond issues, state constitutional amendments, and controversial pieces of legislation. An **initiative,** sometimes called an initiative petition, is a citizen-sponsored proposal that can result in new or amended legislation or a state constitutional amendment. Initiatives differ from referenda in that they are typically propelled to public vote through the efforts of citizens and interest groups.[5] The initiative process usually requires that 10 percent of the number of the voters in the previous election in that state sign a petition agreeing that the **proposition,** or proposed measure, should be placed on the ballot.

A third type of special election, the recall, differs from referenda and initiatives in that it is not concerned with policy-related issues. Rather, the **recall** election allows voters to cut an officeholder's term of office short. Recall elections are typically citizen-sponsored efforts that demonstrate serious dissatisfaction with a particular officeholder. Concerned citizens circulate a petition, and after they gather the required number of signatures, an election is held to determine whether the official should be thrown out of office.

The Act of Voting

> In some states, voters can decide directly whether a policy should be enacted through the use of an initiative, added to the ballot in the form of a proposition. In Phoenix, Arizona, an elderly member of the Navajo Nation urges voters to vote against Proposition 203, which voters approved in November 2000. The proposition eliminated bilingual education in Arizona's public schools.

The process of voting begins when a voter registers to vote. Voting registration requirements vary greatly from state to state. Some states require registration months in advance of an election; others allow voters to register on the day of voting. In the United States, the voters use an **Australian ballot,** a secret ballot prepared by the government, distributed to all eligible voters, and, when balloting is completed, counted by government officials in an unbiased fashion, without corruption or regard to individual preferences. Because the U.S. Constitution guarantees the states the right to conduct elections, the mechanics and methods of voting vary widely from state to state. Some states use touch-screen technology; others employ computerized ballots or punch cards that are counted by computers. Still other states use traditional lever ballots, in which voters pull a lever to register their vote for a particular candidate. Despite these differences, all ballots are secret ballots.

Although secret ballots are the norm today, that was not always the case. From the days of the early republic through the nineteenth century, many citizens exercised their right to vote using oral votes cast in public or written votes witnessed by others; some made their electoral choices on color-coded ballots prepared by the political parties, which indicated which party the voter was supporting.

The 2000 Election and Its Impact

In the 2000 presidential election between Democrat Al Gore and Republican George W. Bush, an enormous controversy erupted over the voting in Florida. Because of the closeness of the electoral vote, the outcome of the Florida election turned out to be pivotal. But the tallies in that state's election were in question, not only because of the narrow difference between the number of votes won by each candidate but also because of the voting process itself. Florida citizens cast their vote on a punch card by poking through a **chad,** a ready-made perforation, near the name of their candidate of choice. Officials then counted the punch card ballots using a computer program that calculated votes by counting the absence of chads. But in the case of the 2000 election, thousands of ballots could not be read by the computer and needed to be counted by hand. This unexpected development put election officials in the difficult, and ultimately deeply controversial, position of gauging "voter intent." If a chad was hanging by one perforation only, did the voter intend to vote for that candidate? What if the chad was "pregnant" (that is, sticking out but not removed; see the photo)? What if the chad was dimpled, and the voter had cast his or her entire ballot by only dimpling the chads?

> The problems with chads: A hanging chad . . . and a pregnant chad.

chad
a ready-made perforation on a punch card ballot

In the end, the U.S. Supreme Court had the final say. On December 12, 2000, the Court halted the hand counting of ballots in Florida, with the Court's majority ruling that the differing standards of hand counting ballots from one county to the next and the absence of a single judicial officer charged with overseeing the hand counts violated the equal protection clause of the U.S. Constitution. The ruling meant that George W. Bush, who was leading in the count, was certified the winner of the Florida race, thus securing that state's twenty-five Electoral College votes and the presidency of the United States.

Indignation surrounding the 2000 election resulted in federal policy changes to the conduct of elections by the states. The key policy revision came through the passage of the Help America Vote Act of 2002 (HAVA). HAVA allocated $650 million to assist states in changing from punch card ballots to electronic voting systems and set a deadline of 2005 for states to comply, although some states have not yet done so.

Types of Ballots

There are two types of ballots most commonly used in general elections in the states today. The first, the **party-column ballot,** organizes the candidates by party, so that all of a given party's candidates for every office are arranged in one column. The opposing party's candidates appear in a different column.

party-column ballot
a ballot that organizes the candidates by political party

The impact of a party-column ballot is twofold. First, party-column ballots increase voters' tendency to vote the "party line," that is, to vote for every candidate of a given party for every office. In fact, some states provide a party lever, which allows a voter to vote for all of a given party's candidates simply by one pull of a lever or one press of a "vote party" button. Second, because they increase the tendency to vote the party line, party-column ballots also increase the **coattail effect,** the phenomenon where *down-ballot candidates* (candidates who are running for lower-level offices, such as city council) benefit from the popularity of a top-of-ticket nominee. Often, the composition of city councils, county legislatures, and even state legislatures changes because of a coattail effect from a popular presidential or gubernatorial candidate. Because party-column ballots strengthen political parties, parties tend to favor this type of ballot, which is the most commonly used ballot in the United States.

coattail effect
the phenomenon by which candidates running for a lower-level office such as city council benefit in an election from the popularity of a top-of-ticket nominee

Another type of general election ballot is the **office-block ballot,** which arranges all candidates for a particular office under the name of that office. Office-block ballots are more likely to encourage ticket splitting, where voters "split their ticket"—that is, divide their votes—between candidates from different parties.[6] Because office-block ballots deemphasize political parties by breaking up the party line, the parties do not tend to favor them.

office-block ballot
a type of ballot that arranges all of the candidates for a particular office under the name of that office

absentee voting
casting a ballot in advance by mail in situations where illness, travel, or other circumstances prevent voters from voting in their precinct

Why Ballot Design Matters

The 2000 presidential election voting in Florida provides evidence that not only the voting process but also the design of ballots can make a difference in outcomes. Specifically, with respect to the vote in Florida's Palm Beach County, where voters push a button on their voting machine ballot to register their vote, critics charge that the ballot in use, the *butterfly ballot* (so called because candidates are listed on two "wings" with a common "spine"), was particularly confusing to voters.

The photograph of the county's butterfly ballot in "Exploring the Sources" shows that the Democratic ticket of Al Gore and Joe Lieberman was listed second in the left column, or wing. But in order to vote for them, a voter had to select the *third* button down. Hitting the second button would have registered a vote for the Reform Party candidates. Because of the lack of ballot clarity and voters' widespread assumption that the two major party candidates would lead the ballot, many Democrats complained that this ballot layout put the Gore/Lieberman ticket at a disadvantage. Although supporters of Reform Party candidate Pat Buchanan in Palm Beach County projected that he should have received at best 1,000 votes there, Buchanan received over 3,400 votes. Many people, including Buchanan himself, believed that these votes were mistakenly cast for him and intended for Al Gore. [7]

In fact, an additional 19,000 votes were nullified in the Palm Beach County election because voters cast *two* votes for president, presumably with balloters realizing too late that they had pushed the wrong button. Buchanan himself addressed this issue, saying, "If the two candidates they pushed were Buchanan and Gore, almost certainly those are Al Gore's votes and not mine. I cannot believe someone would vote for Gore and say, 'I made a mistake, I should have voted for Buchanan.' Maybe a small minority of them would have done that. But I—I've got to think that the vast majority of those [votes] would naturally belong to Al Gore and not to me." [8]

Voting by Mail

One form of voting, **absentee voting,** is a long-standing tradition by which voters cast their ballots in advance by mail when disability, illness, school, work, service in the armed forces, or travel prevents them from casting a ballot in their voting precinct. To cast an absentee ballot, an individual must typically apply (before a specific state-designated deadline) to vote by absentee in the county where he or she usually votes. The superintendent of elections then mails a ballot to the voter, who votes and then mails the ballot back. The absentee ballots are counted and added to the votes cast in the voting precincts. Requirements for absentee ballots vary from state to state. Some states require a legitimate excuse, but increasingly many states accept ballot applications simply because absentee voting is more convenient for the voter.

A relatively recent development is the advent of statewide voting by mail, a practice that states have adopted in an attempt to increase voter participation by making voting more convenient. The first experiment with statewide vote by mail occurred in Oregon in 1996. In a special election there, where officials had predicted a turnout of less than 50 percent, more than 66 percent of voters cast their ballots. This experiment brought another benefit: it saved taxpayers more than $1 million. Oregon decided to continue the practice in the 2000 presidential election, in which voter turnout hit 80 percent, and in the 2004 presidential race, where the turnout approached 85 percent. Oregon has now taken the drastic step of abandoning voting in polling places on election day.

There are obvious advantages to voting by mail. As Oregon's experience demonstrates, more people participate when voting becomes easier. Further, increased participation may bring to office candidates who are more representative of the will of the people because more people had a say in their election.

Some scholars, however, have criticized the vote-by-mail trend. One important criticism is that voting by mail means that people vote before the final days of the campaign, thus casting their ballot before some additional last-minute information might be revealed about a candidate. Indeed, some voters may cast their ballots before the political rivals' debates occur or before candidates fully articulate their message. Consider one case in Bainbridge

THE BUTTERFLY BALLOT

The photograph shows Florida's butterfly ballot as used in the 2000 presidential election. Before reading the following material, select the button on the vertical yellow strip that would register a vote for Al Gore and Joseph Lieberman, the two candidates on the Democratic presidential ticket in 2000. In order to vote for Gore and Lieberman, you would have to select the button marked with the "5" arrow. Could you foresee circumstances in which a voter might think that the second button (marked 4) would register a vote for Gore? Reform Party candidate Pat Buchanan (candidate number 4) could. Two days after the election, Buchanan told NBC's *Today Show* host Matt Lauer that "when I took one look at that ballot on election night . . . [it was] very . . . easy for me to see how someone could have voted for me in the belief they voted for Al Gore. It's—it's quite simple. You simply hit the second dot. It's by the Gore line, it's the second line on the thing. The first is Bush. Folks would say, the second is Gore. They might not look over to the right and see that the second is actually Pat Buchanan."*

Evaluating the Evidence

① Members of both political parties in Palm Beach County approved this ballot. Why is it important that both parties signed off on the ballot's design? Does the layout of the ballot really matter?

② How can controversies such as the one over the butterfly ballot be avoided? What are the obstacles to these solutions?

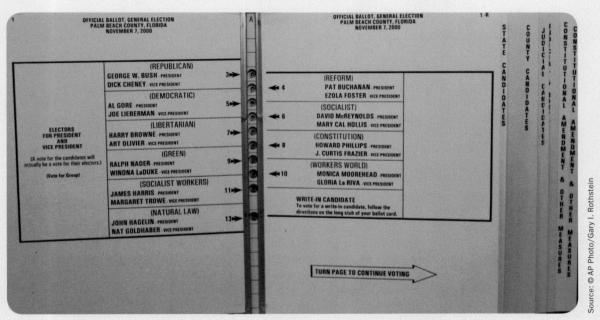

Source: © AP Photo/Gary I. Rothstein

Island, Washington, where it was revealed just days before the election that a candidate for mayor had padded his résumé. By the time the exaggerations came to light, some voters had already cast their ballots by mail.[9]

Voting by mail also increases the chances of vote fraud. Even though states take measures to ensure the principle of "one person, one vote," voting by mail presents opportunities for corruption. Voting at the polls requires a face-to-face encounter, but voting by mail does not, so ballots could be stolen from individuals' mailboxes or intercepted after having been mailed by a voter.

Voting by mail also may eliminate the privacy associated with voting in recent times. With mail balloting, the vote occurs in a less controlled setting, and the voter might feel pressured by others to select a particular candidate. In contrast, booth voting affords privacy and secrecy that go far toward ensuring that the votes cast behind the curtain reflect the individual voter's will.

Finally, voting by mail may undermine feelings of civic engagement by eliminating a source of psychological rewards for voters. Going to a polling place, signing the voting registry, entering the voting booth, and casting your vote can elicit feelings of patriotism, civic pride, and fulfillment of civic responsibility: the sense that you are doing your duty to help ensure the election of the best-qualified candidates. Although the results may be the same with voting by mail, some evidence suggests that voting by mail does not bring with it the same sense of civic satisfaction that voting at a polling place confers.

Running for Office: The Choice to Run

The reasons that individuals become political candidates vary almost as much as the individuals do. Yet four types of motivation are generally in play when a person decides to declare a candidacy:

- a sense of civic responsibility—the feeling on the candidate's part that he or she bears an obligation to govern
- a sense of party loyalty—of filling the need for parties to run viable candidates
- personal goals, and in particular, interest in electoral politics and officeholding as a career
- interest in increasing the candidate's name recognition and stature in the community, often for business reasons

Some people believe they have an obligation to put their experience, knowledge, and skills to work for the greater good of the community or country. Often these civically motivated people become politically involved out of concerns about specific issues. They might object to a specific policy or want to see the government take action on a given issue. For example, Representative Carolyn McCarthy (D-New York) ran for and won a seat in the House of Representatives after her husband was killed and her son was injured in a mass shooting on the Long Island Railroad. While nursing her adult son's injuries after the senseless tragedy, McCarthy decided to run when her congressman voted to repeal a ban on assault weapons.

Sometimes an individual may choose to run for office out of a sense of party duty. The candidate may run as a "sacrificial lamb" for a seat he or she has little chance of winning, mainly with the intent to ensure that the party offers an alternative to the favored candidate. Or an elected official may decide to run for another office because he or she has the best chance at winning an election and allowing the party to attain control of that office.

Other people are motivated to run for a particular office because of personal goals. Many of these individuals seek elected office as their career. Whereas presidents and governors typically serve no more than eight years, members of Congress, state legislators, county commissioners, and council members often serve for decades. Holding office is what they do— and because of the advantages of incumbency, once elected, many remain in office for years. Other candidates run for office because of political ambitions: a town council member who aspires to serve in the state legislature might run for county commissioner even if she thinks she will not win because she realizes that leading a viable campaign might help her in a later bid for the statehouse.

Finally, some people run for office because of the heightened stature that a candidacy brings to their "regular" careers. Lawyers may run for the state legislature, realtors for the city council, or insurance brokers for county commissioner because a candidacy makes them more successful in their daily occupations. Running for office enhances a person's name recognition so that, for example, the realtor sitting on the city council might get more business because people in the community know his name. Running for office also opens doors to networks of potential business contacts, as many candidates address civic groups and get to know people in the community. These networks can be useful in business as well as politics.

Many candidates, of course, run for office for a combination of reasons. They might believe, for example, that they have a responsibility to serve their country *and* that they have something valuable to contribute.

Formal Eligibility Requirements

Article I of the U.S. Constitution specifies some minimum criteria for those seeking election to federal office:

- President: A candidate for the presidency must be a natural-born citizen. Naturalized citizens, who are born citizens of another country and then choose to become American citizens such as Ileana Ros-Lehtinen (R-Florida), a member of the House of Representatives and a native of Cuba, cannot run for president. Presidential candidates also must be at least 35 years old and must have been a resident of the United States for fourteen years by the time of inauguration.
- Vice president: A vice-presidential candidate, like a contender for the presidency, must be a natural-born citizen and must be at least 35 years old; he or she must not be a resident of the same state as the candidate for president with whom he or she will serve.
- U.S. senator: A candidate for the Senate must have citizen status of at least nine years, must be at least 30 years old when taking office, and must be a resident of the state from which he or she is elected.
- U.S. representative: A candidate for the House of Representatives must be a citizen for at least seven years, must be at least 25 years old when taking office, and must be a resident of the state from which he or she is elected.

Typically a state's constitution determines the minimal qualifications for the governorship and state legislature, and these vary from state to state. In general, state requirements address the same issues as federal guidelines—citizenship, age, and residency.

Informal Eligibility Requirements

In addition to the legal eligibility requirements prescribed by the federal and state constitutions, informal eligibility criteria—that is, the characteristics that voters expect officeholders to have—help to determine who is qualified to run for a particular office. By and large, the eligibility pool for elected office depends on the office—and so although your car mechanic might be considered a good candidate for your town council, he would not likely meet the informal eligibility criteria to be elected president of the United States.

Generally speaking, the higher and more prestigious the political office, the greater the informal eligibility requirements are. On the local level, particularly in smaller communities, an individual would be considered eligible to run for town council if he or she were liked and respected in the community, had lived in the community long enough to know the voters, and were either gainfully employed, a homemaker, or retired.

Farther up the political office ladder, state legislative candidates in most states are expected to have some kind of professional career. Still, there is a great deal of variation from state to state, and certainly nonprofessionals occupy many state legislative seats. State legislatures tend to be dominated by lawyers and business professionals, occupations that offer the prestige to be considered part of the informal eligibility pool and that allow enough flexibility to facilitate campaigning and legislative work.

The informal eligibility requirements for federal office are even more stringent. Voters expect candidates for the House of Representatives, the U.S. Senate, and the presidency to have higher qualifications than candidates for state and local offices. Among most congressional constituencies, candidates for federal office would be viewed as "qualified" to hold office if they had a college degree, considerable professional and leadership experience, and strong communication skills. But informal qualifications vary according to the political culture in a district, with some districts favoring a particular religious affiliation, ethnicity, or other characteristic. In races for the U.S. Senate and the presidency, the popular press examines the minutest details of candidates' professional and educational background. For example, sometimes it is not enough that candidates are college graduates; where they went to college, whose

> Informal qualifications for Congress vary according to the political culture in the district. Openly gay members of Congress are a rarity. Representative Tammy Baldwin (D-Wisconsin), the only openly lesbian member of Congress, talks here with a constituent.

campaign consultant

paid professional who specializes in the overall management of political campaigns or an aspect of campaigns

campaign manager

a professional whose duties comprise a variety of strategic and managerial tasks, from fund-raising to staffing a campaign

campaign strategy

blueprint for the campaign, including a budget and fund-raising plan, advertising strategy, and staffing plan

fund-raising consultant

a professional who works with candidates to identify likely contributors to the campaign and arrange events and meetings with donors

media consultant

a professional who brings the campaign message to voters by creating handouts and all forms of media ads

university is more prestigious, and who had the higher grade point average are all fodder for the media and political pundits.

The Nature of Political Campaigns Today

Campaigns today are a different animal from the campaigns of the 1980s or even the early 1990s. The main reasons for the changes are the professionalization of campaign staffs, the dramatically expanded role of the media and the Internet, and candidates' ever-rising need for funding to keep pace with the unprecedented demands of contemporary campaigning.[10]

The Professionalization of Political Campaigns

One of the most significant changes in the conduct of campaigns is the rise in prominence of **campaign consultants,** paid professionals who specialize in the overall management of political campaigns or an aspect of campaigns, such as fund-raising or advertising. Previously, volunteers who believed in the party's ideals and in the candidate ran most campaigns. Although some volunteers may have been motivated by the expectation that they would personally benefit from the election of their candidate, their efforts focused largely on the election itself—of a single candidate or slate of candidates.

In contrast, professional consultants dominate modern campaigns for federal offices, many state offices, and some municipal offices. Typically these advisers receive generous compensation for their services. Although professional consultants may not be as dedicated to a single candidate as earlier grassroots volunteers were, these strategists are typically committed to seeing their candidate elected and often are quite partisan, usually working only for candidates of one party throughout their careers. For example, well-known Democratic political strategists James Carville and Paul Begala (both of CNN's *The Situation Room*) work only for Democratic presidential and senatorial candidates. Similarly, Ken Mehlman, who managed the 2004 Bush-Cheney reelection bid, works exclusively for Republican candidates.

One of the top jobs in a political campaign is that of **campaign manager,** a professional whose duties comprise a variety of strategic and managerial tasks. Among these responsibilities might be the development of the overall **campaign strategy,** the blueprint for the campaign, which includes a budget and fund-raising plan, an advertising strategy, and staffing objectives. Once the campaign strategy is set, the campaign manager often hires and manages the office staff; selects the campaign's theme, colors, and slogan; and shapes the candidate's image. Another crucial campaign professional is the pollster, who conducts focus groups and polls that help develop the campaign strategy by identifying the candidate's strengths and weaknesses and by revealing what voters care about.

Other professionals round out the candidate's team. A **fund-raising consultant** works with the candidate to identify likely contributors and arranges fund-raising events and meetings with donors. Policy directors and public relations consultants help to develop the candidate's stance on crucial issues and to get the candidate's positions out to the voters, and a **media consultant** brings the campaign message to voters by creating handouts and brochures, as well as newspaper, radio, and television promotions. Media consultants rely increasingly on the Internet to bring the campaign to voters through e-mail campaigns, Web-based advertising, blogs, and message boards.[11]

Media and New Technologies: Transforming Political Campaigns

Today, with the presence everywhere of the media in all its forms—television, Internet news sites, blogs, radio, podcasts, newspapers, magazines—citizens' access to information is unprecedented. Whereas our ancestors had far fewer sources of news—word of mouth and the printed newspaper dominated for most of American history—people today can choose from a wide range of information sources and a bounty of information. Today twenty-four-hour news channels such as CNN and MSNBC compete with the Internet news outlets, satellite radio programming, and news text messages to grab audience attention. But not all of this bombardment of information is accurate.

Given the abundance of information disseminated today, and in light of its diverse and sometimes questionable sources, engaged citizens have a greater responsibility to be discerning consumers of the news, including coverage of campaigns, voting, and elections. They cannot be passive listeners and spoon-fed watchers of news as it is dished out by daily newspapers, nightly newscasts, and the occasional weekly or monthly periodical. Vivé Griffith at the University of Texas at Austin's Think Democracy Project writes, "The challenge for the contemporary citizen is to be more than an audience member. Voters have unprecedented opportunities to access information and, at the same time, myriad ways to see issues obscured. An informed polity is essential to a democracy, and it can be difficult to sort through whether our media-saturated world ultimately serves to make us more or less informed."[12] We consider media coverage of elections, campaigns, and voting in detail in Chapter 10.

PERSONALITY VERSUS POLICY In sorting through the abundance of "news," citizens must also contend with changes in how information is presented by the media. When news was less available, that is, when TV networks aired a single fifteen-minute nightly news broadcast, the content tended to be policy-oriented and hard-hitting. Today, networks have much more time to fill: in addition to their nightly thirty-minute news broadcasts, most metropolitan areas have an hour and a half of local news in the evening, with two additional half-hour broadcasts in the morning and at noon. This all-day banquet of news programming does not include national morning talk shows such as *Good Morning America* and the *Today Show*, nor does it include evening news magazines such as *60 Minutes, 20/20*, and *48 Hours*. Because of the many (and sometimes endless) hours that networks and twenty-four-hour cable news shows must fill, the focus has shifted more and more from the policy stances of candidates and government officials to the personalities of these individuals. Many Americans are well equipped to describe the personality traits and lifestyle preferences of elected leaders: President George W. Bush's penchant for exercise, former president Bill Clinton's reputation as a fast-food junkie, Barack Obama's pack-a-day smoking habit. The reason for this shift is twofold: many viewers enjoy lighter content when watching so much television,

WHERE DO YOU STAND?

Source of Campaign Information

What would you say is the source of the majority of the information you learn about a presidential campaign?

☐ Television
☐ Newspapers
☐ Internet
☐ Magazines
☐ Radio
☐ Other

Source: "Internet's Broader Role in Campaign 2008," http://people-press.org/reports/display.php3?ReportID=384.

> Recognizing the enormous importance of the national media in helping to deliver his 2008 presidential campaign's message to voters, Republican candidate Senator John McCain (R-Arizona) talks to reporters while riding in his campaign bus, the Straight Talk Express, in New Hampshire.

THEN NOW NEXT

How Political Campaigns Have Changed in the Past 30 Years

THEN (1980s)	NOW (2009)
Many campaigns were managed and staffed by volunteers.	Campaigns are increasingly professionally managed by "guns for hire" and often have an extensive staff dedicated to strategy setting, fund-raising, and media relations.
Grassroots activism was the norm in all but the largest campaigns.	*Netroots* activism—political activism driven by interest groups' Web sites, blogs, and social-networking sites—uses the Internet as a complement to traditional grassroots campaign efforts.
Money was a crucial consideration in campaigns, but grassroots activism demanded fewer financial resources.	Money rules the day in most campaigns.

WHAT'S NEXT?

> How can the Internet change the need for money in political campaigns?

> Given the extent of Web activism during the 2008 campaigns, is there still a role for grassroots activism in post-2008 campaigns? Explain.

> Will campaigns continue to be dominated by professional staffers? Why or why not?

and personality-oriented coverage is less likely to offend viewers and advertisers.

REVOLUTIONIZING THE CAMPAIGN: THE INTERNET The Internet has dramatically changed the conduct of political campaigns. As its use has steadily grown, the ways in which the Internet is impacting political campaigns is continuously evolving. Among the new tools used by candidates for the presidency, the Internet is among the most valuable and powerful. The Internet serves as an efficient means by which office seekers can communicate with supporters and potential supporters, as well as a mechanism to mobilize citizens. Candidates' Web sites provide a unique and easily accessed forum where the electorate can find out about candidates' experience, views, and policy priorities—and potentially make more informed choices in the voting booth.

Internet communities provide a powerful mechanism for political engagement. Some Internet communities may be dedicated to advancing the electoral chances of a particular candidate. Other communities host forums for political discourse. People who post on the anonymous message board UrbanBaby.com, popular among mothers aged 25–45, engage in political chats (between their postings on matters such as what to do about a high fever and whether one should invest in a nanny camera), for example, about the merits of potential candidates for office and which candidates present the toughest obstacles to their favored candidates.

Candidates for government office also increasingly use the Internet for fund-raising. In 2003 Howard Dean (then Vermont governor) used the Internet to raise nearly $15 million for his thwarted presidential bid. In discussing the growth of campaign fund-raising on the Internet, Eli Pariser, founder of MoveOn. org's Peace Campaign, noted that "candidates are wasting their time with rubber-chicken donors,"[13] an allusion to the donors who contribute to candidates by paying to attend campaign dinners.

Regulating Federal Campaign Contributions

Money—lots of it—is essential in electoral races today. Money and the modern campaign are inextricably linked because of the importance of costly media advertising in modern campaigns.[14] Federal regulations require any group that contributes to candidates' campaigns to register as a political action committee (PAC), and many interest groups form PACs as one arm of their organization. Though they are a fixture in U.S. politics, PACs are a relatively recent phenomenon. But the influence of money in electoral politics goes back a long time, as do the efforts to regulate it.[15] Reformers have attempted to limit the impact of money on political campaigns for almost as long as campaigns have existed. One of the foremost obstacles to reforming the campaign finance system is that the people charged with fixing the problem—the members of Congress—have successfully used the system to get elected. The media have sometimes likened the situation to putting the vampire in charge of the blood bank. Still, despite the significant obstacles, legislators have made efforts historically and in recent times to overhaul the country's campaign finance system.

An early attempt at regulating campaign finance took root after a scandal that erupted during the administration of President Warren Harding (1921-1923). In 1921, the president transferred oil reserves at Teapot Dome, Wyoming, from the Department of the Navy to the Department of the Interior. The following year, Harding's secretary of the interior leased the oil fields without competitive bidding. A Senate investigation into the deal revealed that the lessee of the fields had "loaned" the interior secretary more than $100,000 in order to win political influence. The interior secretary was convicted and sentenced to a year in prison and a $100,000 fine. Dubbed the Teapot Dome scandal, this sordid affair led Congress to try to limit influence of money on politics through legislation.

The Federal Corrupt Practices Act of 1925 sought to prevent future wrongdoing. This act aimed to regulate campaign finance by limiting campaign contributions and requiring public disclosure of campaign expenditures, and it was one of the first attempts at campaign finance regulation. But because the act did not include an enforcement mechanism, it was a weak attempt to fight corruption, and candidates found numerous loopholes in the law.

The Political Activities Act of 1939, also known as the Hatch Act, marked another congressional attempt to eliminate political corruption. With the growth of the federal bureaucracy as a result of the New Deal programs of President Franklin D. Roosevelt, several scandals had emerged, demonstrating the

© N. Y. "Tribune."

> A *New York Tribune* cartoon titled "The First Good Laugh They've Had in Years" depicts the Democrats' jubilation over the Teapot Dome Scandal of 1921, which saddled Republicans with a reputation for corruption. The scandal led Congress to try to limit the influence of money on politics.

problems that could arise when government employees took an active role in politics. The Hatch Act banned partisan political activities by all federal government employees except the president, vice president, and Senate-confirmed political appointees. The act also sought to regulate the campaign finance system by limiting the amount of money a group could spend on an election and placing a $5,000 cap on contributions from an individual to a campaign committee. Although the Hatch Act was more effective than the Federal Corrupt Practices Act of 1925, it also contained a significant loophole: groups that wanted to spend more than the legislated limit of $3 million simply formed additional groups.

Congress again attempted to curtail the influence of special interests in 1946 with the passage of the Federal Regulation of Lobbying Act. Title III of this law stated that any person who received money in order to influence congressional legislation was a lobbyist and must register his or her activities. The law's goal was to provide for public disclosure of lobbyists' activities, but it fell short because it too lacked an enforcement mechanism.

In 1971, Congress passed the Federal Election Campaign Act (FECA), the most significant attempt at overhauling the nation's campaign finance system. The law was sponsored by Democrats in Congress who were concerned about the enormous fund-raising advantage the Republicans had had during the 1968 presidential election. This law placed considerable limitations on both campaign expenditures and campaign contributions, and it provided for a voluntary tax-return check-off for qualified presidential candidates. This provision enables you, when filling out your federal income tax return, to contribute three dollars, which will go toward the matching funds that qualified presidential candidates receive.

In 1974, FECA was amended to place more stringent limitations on individual contributions and to limit expenditures by PACs, and it revamped the presidential election process by restricting spending and providing public financing for qualified candidates who abided by the limits. The act also required public disclosure of contributions and expenditures by all candidates for federal office. Most important, the act created an enforcement mechanism in the Federal Election Commission, the agency charged with enforcing federal campaign finance laws.

In the subsequent, highly significant Supreme Court case *Buckley v. Valeo* (1976), however, the plaintiffs contended that placing limitations on the amount an individual candidate could spend on his or her own campaign violated First Amendment protections of free speech. The Court agreed, ruling that "the candidate . . . has a First Amendment right to engage in the discussion of public issues and vigorously and tirelessly to advocate his own election."[16] This ruling paved the way for the subsequent explosion in the formation of PACs that we next consider, as the Court recognized political expenditures as a protected form of speech and removed limits on overall campaign spending, on personal expenditures by an individual candidate, and on expenditures not coordinated with a candidate's campaign that are made by independent interest groups. In its *Buckley* ruling, the Court boldly overturned the limitations on expenditures that to that point had been written into law.

Regulatory Loopholes: Independent Expenditures

independent expenditures
outlays by PACs and others, typically for advertising for or against a candidate, but uncoordinated with a candidate's campaign

The determination that campaign expenditures constitute free speech uncovered an important loophole in the Federal Election Campaign Act of 1974. Because expenditures are protected from limitations, many PACs now use the independent expenditure loophole to spend unlimited sums for or against political candidates.[17] **Independent expenditures** are outlays, typically for advertising for or against a candidate, that are uncoordinated with a candidate's campaign. Although PAC contributions to a candidate are limited, a PAC can spend as much as it wants on mailings, television promotions, or other advertisements supporting (or working against) candidates for federal office. This tactic is legal if these expenditures are not coordinated with the candidates' campaigns and if they do not "expressly advocate" a candidate by saying "Vote for . . . ," "Elect . . . ," or using similar language.[18]

Regulatory Loopholes: Soft Money

Another loophole in the amended Federal Election Campaign Act of 1974 proved important in the 1990s. Soft money constitutes contributions to the political parties that are not subject to contribution limits and are designated for use on so-called party-building activities. The soft money loophole allowed donors who had contributed the maximum to federal candidates to give even more money by contributing to the national party committees. The party committees then gave the money to state parties, which subsequently spent the funds on party-building activities under more lenient state regulations. Frequently, such soft money contributions benefited federal candidates by paying for voter registration drives, polls, and general, party-based advertisements. Then, during the 1990s, the political parties began to use soft money for television advertisements that featured the presidential candidates but did not expressly advocate their election. The Bipartisan Campaign Finance Reform Act of 2002 (see pages 333–335) banned soft money contributions to political parties.

The Impact of Regulation: The Growth of PACs

Throughout the 1970s, Congress continuously sought to redress problems that arose out of the changes to the law and the *Buckley* decision through a series of amendments to the Federal Election Campaign Act. One of the most significant amendments lifted the ban on the formation of PACs by businesses and organizations that do business with the federal government. Because of this amendment and the assertion of free speech protections in the *Buckley* case, the number of political action committees shot up dramatically, as Figure 9.2 demonstrates. The figure shows that the number of corporate PACs alone nearly doubled between 1977 and 1980. Many of these PACs were formed by corporations that do business with the federal government and by associations whose members' livelihoods are significantly affected by federal regulations, including defense contractors, agricultural producers, and government employee unions.

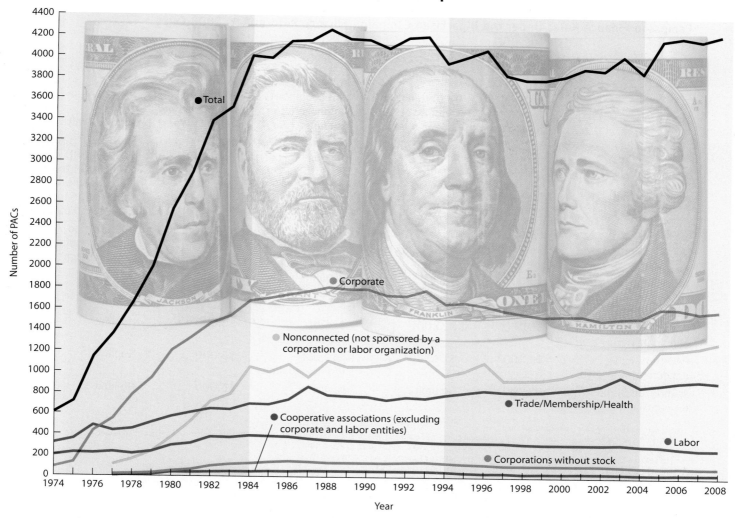

PAC Count, 1974 to present

Number of PACs (y-axis, 0 to 4400); Year (x-axis, 1974 to 2008)

Series labeled: Total, Corporate, Nonconnected (not sponsored by a corporation or labor organization), Trade/Membership/Health, Cooperative associations (excluding corporate and labor entities), Labor, Corporations without stock

POLITICAL INQUIRY

FIGURE 9.2 ■ What trends does the figure show with respect to the number of political action committees since 1977? For which groups has the growth in PACs risen most steeply?

Source: Federal Election Commission, www.fec.gov/press/press2008/20080117paccount.shtml.

The ballooning of the number of PACs over time is indicative of the increased power that PACs have wielded in campaigns for federal office since 1980. And although the growth in the number of political action committees has leveled off since 1995, there is little evidence that their influence is waning.

The Bipartisan Campaign Finance Reform Act of 2002

Throughout the 1980s and 1990s, campaign finance reform was a perennial topic in presidential campaigns, and candidates roundly criticized the role of "special interests" in politics. But members of Congress had little to gain from reforming the system that had brought them to office. Although various campaign finance proposals were considered, only one passed both the Senate and the House, in 1992, and President George H. W. Bush vetoed it.

Then in 2002, the world's largest energy-trading company and one of the nation's biggest corporations, Enron, collapsed after an internal accounting scandal, leaving in its wake

Campaign Finance Rules Under the Bipartisan Campaign Finance Reform Act, 2008 Cycle

TABLE 9.1

	To Each Candidate or Candidate Committee per Election	To National Party Committee per Calendar Year	To State, District, and Local Party Committee per Calendar Year	To Any Other Political Committee per Calendar Year[1]	Special Limits
Individual may give	$2,300*	$28,500*	$10,000 (combined limit)	$5,000	$108,200* overall biennial limit: • $42,700* to all candidates • $65,500* to all PACs and parties[2]
National Party Committee may give	$5,000	No limit	No limit	$5,000	$39,900* to Senate candidate per campaign[3]
State, District, and Local Party Committee may give	$5,000 (combined limit)	No limit	No limit	$5,000 (combined limit)	No limit
PAC (multi-candidate)[4] may give	$5,000	$15,000	$5,000 (combined limit)	$5,000	No limit
PAC (not multi-candidate) may give	$2,300*	$28,500*	$10,000 (combined limit)	$5,000	No limit
Authorized Campaign Committee may give	$2,000[5]	No limit	No limit	$5,000	No limit

*These contribution limits are indexed for inflation.
[1]A contribution earmarked for a candidate through a political committee counts against the original contributor's limit for that candidate. In certain circumstances, the contribution may also count against the contributor's limit to the PAC. 11 CFR 110.6. See also 11 CFR 110.1(h).
[2]No more than $42,700 of this amount may be contributed to state and local party committees and PACs.
[3]This limit is shared by the national committee and the national Senate campaign committee.
[4]A multicandidate committee is a political committee with more than fifty contributors which has been registered for at least six months and, with the exception of state party committees, has made contributions to five or more candidates for federal office. 11 CFR 100.5(c)(3).
[5]A federal candidate's authorized committee(s) may contribute no more than $2,000 per election to another federal candidate's authorized committee(s). 11 CFR 102.12(c)(2).

Source: Federal Election Commission, www.fec.gov/ans/answers_general.shtml#How_much_can_I_contribute.

furious stockholders, employees, and retirees whose financial health depended upon the company. Investigations revealed massive corporate fraud, including accounting improprieties that had enabled corporate leaders to lie about profits and debt. Investigations also revealed that Enron had contributed nearly $4 million to state and federal political parties for "party-building activities" through the soft money loophole. Public indignation at the scandal flared, leading to the passage of the McCain-Feingold Act. This bipartisan campaign reform proposal, named after its two sponsors, Senator John McCain (R-Arizona) and Senator Russell Feingold (D-Wisconsin), had been making its way at a snail's pace through committees before the Enron scandal broke.

The McCain-Feingold Act, formally known as the Bipartisan Campaign Finance Reform Act (BCRA) of 2002, banned nearly all soft money contributions (see Table 9.2), although PACs can contribute up to $5,000 to state, county, or local parties for voter registration and get-out-the-vote drives. Table 9.1 shows that the law also increased individual contribution limitations and regulated some independent expenditure advertising. Although BCRA sought to fix many of the system's problems, some of the remedies remain in dispute.

One aspect of the McCain-Feingold Act became the subject of a series of legal challenges. In 2003, Senator Mitch McConnell (R-Kentucky), an opponent of the act, and a variety of groups affected by the new law (including the National Rifle Association and the California State Democratic Party) filed *McConnell v. the Federal Election Commission*.[19] The suit alleged that McCain-Feingold was a violation of the plaintiffs' First Amendment rights. One aspect of the law to which the groups objected was a ban on independent issue ads (thirty days before a primary election and sixty days before a general election), in which a group purchases advertising targeting a particular candidate for federal office. But the Supreme Court upheld the constitutionality of McCain-Feingold in a 5–4 decision.

Then in 2007, the Court (in another 5–4 decision) did an about-face and created an exception to the ban on issue-based ads. In *Federal Election Commission v. Wisconsin Right to Life, Inc.*,[20] the justices held that advertising within the thirty- and sixty-day window could not be prohibited, thus paving the way for its extensive use in the 2008 presidential race.

Regulatory Loophole: 527s

Another loophole in the campaign finance law became apparent with the emergence of a new form of political group, the so-called 527. Named after the section of the Internal Revenue Service tax code that regulates such organizations, a **527** is a tax-exempt group that raises money for political activities, much like those allowed under the soft money loophole. If a 527 engages only in activities such as voter registration, voter mobilization, and issue advocacy, it does not have to report its activities to the Federal Election Commission, only to the government of the state in which it is located or to the IRS. Disclosure to the FEC is required only if a 527 engages in activities expressly advocating the election or defeat of a federal candidate, or in electioneering communications.

In 2004, two 527s—Swift Boat Veterans and POWs for Truth, which opposed the presidential bid of Senator John Kerry (D-Massachusetts), and MoveOn.org, which opposed President George W. Bush's candidacy—grabbed national attention as each ran television "issue advocacy" advertisements across the country targeting the opposing candidate. Many observers viewed the emergence of these and other 527s as attempts to get around the ban on unlimited soft money contributions to political parties. Campaign finance reform advocates note that several 527s have been partially funded by large contributions from a few wealthy individuals, a claim bolstering the charge that 527s are a way to evade the soft money ban. In 2008, 527s spent about $200 million to influence the outcome of federal elections through voter registration and mobilization efforts and through ads that, while purportedly issue based, typically criticized a candidate's record.

527
a tax-exempt group that raises money for political activities, much like those allowed under the soft money loophole

Presidential Campaigns

To many Americans, presidential campaigns epitomize the democratic process. In presidential election years, nonstop campaigning affords ample opportunities for the public to learn about the candidates and their positions. Campaigns also provide avenues for participation by the people—for example, by volunteering in or contributing to candidates' campaigns or even just by debating candidates' views around the water cooler. Although these opportunities for citizen engagement are especially abundant during a presidential election, they arise well before, because potential candidates typically position themselves years in advance of a presidential election to secure their party's nomination and to win the general election.

Party Conventions and the General Election Campaign

As Figure 9.3 illustrates, political parties hold conventions to select their party's nominee for president of the United States. As discussed in Chapter 8 and as reviewed earlier in this chapter, the delegates to the national conventions are chosen by citizens in each state who vote in their party's primary election. After the conventions are over and the nominees have been decided (typically by late August or early September of the election year), the nominees and their vice-presidential running mates begin their general election campaign. Usually the parties' choice of nominee is a foregone conclusion by the time of the convention. Eligible incumbent presidents (who have served only one term) are nearly always renominated, and the nominee of the opposing party is often determined by the primary results.

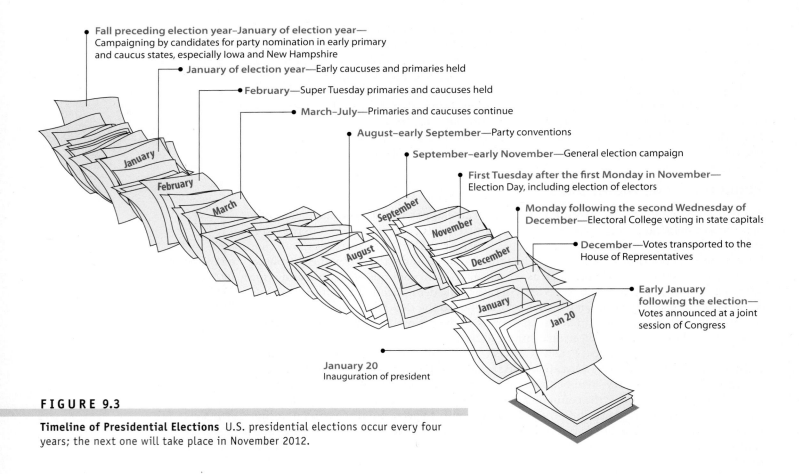

- Fall preceding election year–January of election year—Campaigning by candidates for party nomination in early primary and caucus states, especially Iowa and New Hampshire
- January of election year—Early caucuses and primaries held
- February—Super Tuesday primaries and caucuses held
- March–July—Primaries and caucuses continue
- August–early September—Party conventions
- September–early November—General election campaign
- First Tuesday after the first Monday in November—Election Day, including election of electors
- Monday following the second Wednesday of December—Electoral College voting in state capitals
- December—Votes transported to the House of Representatives
- Early January following the election—Votes announced at a joint session of Congress

January 20
Inauguration of president

FIGURE 9.3

Timeline of Presidential Elections U.S. presidential elections occur every four years; the next one will take place in November 2012.

The Electoral College

The votes tallied on Election Day determine which presidential candidate's slate of electors will cast their ballots, in accordance with state law. There are 538 electors in the Electoral College because the number of electors is based on the number of members of Congress—435 in the House of Representatives, 100 in the Senate—plus 3 electors who represent the District of Columbia. A presidential candidate needs a simple majority of votes (270) to win.

On the Monday following the second Wednesday of December, the slate of electors chosen in each state meets in the state capital and casts their electoral votes. The results are then announced in a joint session of Congress in early January. In most presidential elections, however, the winner is known on election night, because analysts tabulate the outcome in each state and predict the electoral vote. The winner takes the oath of office as president in inaugural ceremonies on January 20.

>Every four years, electors determined by popular presidential elections in the states convene at state capitals in December and cast their votes for president. In Austin, Texas, Marjorie Chandler, a member of the Electoral College, casts her vote for President George W. Bush in 2004.

Who Votes? Factors in Voter Participation

Not all people are equally likely to participate in the process of voting for the president or other government officials. Yet of all the forms of political participation, the act of voting has been analyzed perhaps more than any other.[21] Scholars such as Angus Campbell, Philip E. Converse, Warren Miller, and Donald Stokes have examined what factors influence who votes and

DOING DEMOCRACY

BECOME A DELEGATE TO THE NEXT NATIONAL PARTY CONVENTION

FACT:

Both major U.S. political parties encourage political participation by young people (particularly college students), who have networks of friends and who also make energetic campaign volunteers.

Delegates to the national party conventions are usually chosen in one of two ways. Often, they are "pledged" to a particular presidential primary candidate and go to the convention if that candidate wins the state primary election (although state laws vary between winner-take-all and proportional election systems for delegates). But in other cases, state party officials select delegates, and these officials sometimes must abide by national party guidelines about the demographic diversity of the delegate slate. Sometimes, state parties *actively seek* young people to attend as convention delegates.

Act!

When Smith College student Maura Spiegelman was 18, she was selected as one of the youngest delegates attending the 2004 Democratic National Convention in Boston. A native of New Hampshire, Spiegelman was one of sixty candidates to file a petition to become one of New Hampshire's thirty-three convention delegates. The New Hampshire delegates were chosen on the basis of a thirty-second "speech." In her remarks, Spiegelman noted that "people always talk about wanting younger voters involved in the process and by electing me, this is your chance."*

You can become a delegate to your party's next national convention. If you are not successful or prefer a different form of activism, both political parties rely heavily on volunteers to work the convention, and these opportunities are readily available. Serving as a delegate or a volunteer provides avenues for various specific forms of civic engagement: getting to know state and national party leaders and how the system works; learning about pressing national issues and the party's position on them; and networking and volunteering.

Where to begin

The Democratic National Committee (www.democrats.org/) and the Republican National Committee (www.gop.com) both have links to state committees. These sites provide contact information where you can inquire about becoming a delegate from your state to your party's national convention.

Presidential candidates' Web sites (use an Internet search engine to help you find them) may also provide information on becoming a pledged delegate to the national party convention.

*Molly Wienberg, "NH Delegate Is Young, Interested, and Involved," *Scholastics News*, http://teacher.scholastic.com/scholasticnews/indepth/election_kidscover/delegates/index.asp?article=spiegelman.

---

how voters decide.[22] They and others have analyzed how characteristics such as education level, income, age, race, and the degree of party competitiveness in a given election influence whether a person will vote.[23] Of course, in considering demographic characteristics such as voter age and income level, we must remember that these are merely generalizations.

Education Level— the Number One Predictor of Voting

An individual's level of education is the best predictor of whether that person will vote. Table 9.2 shows that in 2006, half of U.S. citizens with an eighth-grade education or less were registered to vote, and only 29 percent actually voted. As education increases,

TABLE 9.2

U.S. Voters' Rate of Registering and Voting by Educational Attainment, 2006

	Total Number (millions)	Percent Registered	Percent Voted
Eight years or less	7	50	29
Less than high school graduate	17	47	27
High school graduate or GED	65	40	40
Some college or associate degree	58	71	49
Bachelor's or advanced degree	43	79	64

Source: "Voting-Age Population, Percent Reporting Registered, and Voted, 2006," *Statistical Abstract of the United States*, www.census.gov/compendia/statab/tables/08s0404.xls.

ON THE JOB

SARAH SAHEB, REGIONAL DIRECTOR, ROCK THE VOTE

Name: Sarah Saheb

Age: 21

Hometown: Kirksville, Missouri

College: Truman State University, Kirksville, Missouri

Major: Political Science and Communication Studies (BA)

Job: Midwest Regional Director, Rock the Vote

Typical salary for jobs like this: $55,000

Day-to-day responsibilities: My day-to-day responsibilities depend on whether we are in an election. During an election, I handle all of the Rock the Vote operations throughout the Midwest. Every state and every major city has a street team leader, plus a high school team and college team. I oversee all of these teams and make sure they are implementing our national field plan. I do different things every day, talking to the leaders in different communities, managing events, networking with elected officials. In some ways it's like strategic warfare—we're trying to get people to reach out to young people, to make young people's issues their priority.

How did you get your job? When I was 17, I read an article about Rock the Vote and decided that this was something I wanted to do. I started out on a street team in Chicago and then was appointed the Chicago Street Team leader; then I just started seeing opportunities—why don't we have a street team here? And we would start one. After a while, they asked,

"How about you as the Midwest director?" So I worked my way up the ladder.

What do you like best about your job? I like the creativity. I like being able to show youth they are capable of doing a lot. It's not like sitting in a cubicle from nine to five—I couldn't do that. This is fun. And you know you are doing something good. You're exhausted at the end of the day, but you know that you're making a difference.

What is your least favorite aspect of your job? I don't like dealing with the internal bureaucracy of organizations. I don't like dealing with paperwork—making sure people are paid, or the six hours of conference calls!

What advice would you give to students who would like to do what you're doing? If you are passionate about something, get out and do it! Take the initiative. Be a leader about things; find ways to get things done. Ask yourself, "How can *I* do things?" Do it. Don't sit around and wait for someone to ask you to help. Academia can only take you so far—then you need to go out and apply that information, make it work for you.

---

so too does the likelihood of voting, with measurable differences even between those who have only attended college and those who have graduated, particularly in the proportion registered to vote. Among those with a college or an advanced degree, nearly three-quarters are registered, and about one-half vote.

The Age Factor

During any presidential campaign, you will hear much about age as a factor in the likelihood of voting. Despite efforts by organizations such as MTV's Rock the Vote (see "On the Job"), and despite campus-focused initiatives by presidential campaigns, young adults are less likely to vote than Americans who are middle-aged and older though that figure has increased in recent years.[24] But in the 2008 election, we saw that the turnout rate among young Americans—those aged 18 to 29—continued to climb, reaching about 53 percent, the highest turnout rate for voters of that age group since 18-year-olds were first granted the right to vote in 1972. While the turnout rate may not have broken records, the youth vote was key in

FIGURE 9.4 ■ AGE AND VOTING IN THE 2008 PRESIDENTIAL ELECTION For which age group was the percentage of people voting highest? For which age group was the voting percentage lowest? What overall pattern does the graph show? How do you explain it? In 2008, about 53 percent of individuals aged 18 to 29 voted, compared with a national average of 62 percent. Is this in keeping with the 2004 trend? Why did the youth vote matter in 2008?

Source: U.S. Census Bureau, www.census.gov/compendia/statab/tables/08s0404.xls.

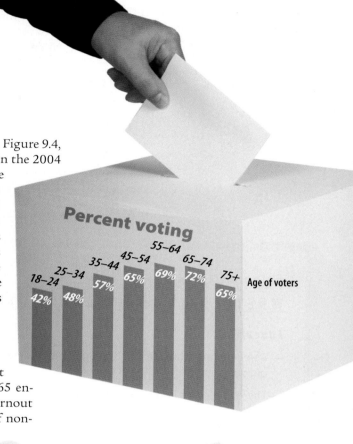

President Obama's election: 66 percent of young voters favored Obama. Figure 9.4, which plots the percentage of people in various age groups who voted in the 2004 presidential election, shows a historic trend: as Americans age, they are more likely to vote. While 42 percent of individuals aged 18 to 24 years reported that they had voted, more than 70 percent of people aged 65 to 74 said that they had. There are numerous reasons why young people do not vote. Among 18- to 24-year-olds, the reason most often cited is that they were too busy or had a schedule conflict, but members of this age group are also more likely to report that they forgot to vote or were out of town. Age also is related to mobility—young people might move when they leave for college or to start a new job, and mobility depresses voter turnout.

Race and Voter Participation

As the 2008 presidential contest demonstrated, race plays a significant role in voter turnout. For decades after the Voting Rights Act of 1965 ensured that African Americans could freely exercise the right to vote, turnout rates among African Americans lagged substantially behind those of non-Hispanic white Americans. Today, however, voter participation among African Americans nearly equals that of whites, as Figure 9.5 indicates. The figure also shows that voting participation among Hispanics and Asian Americans lags behind that of whites and African Americans.

Figure 9.5 shows that the percentage of non-Hispanic whites who reported they voted in the 2004 presidential election was 68 percent, and for African Americans the voting rate was 60 percent. But the 2008 election saw increases in the turnout rate among all racial and ethnic groups. Importantly, in addition to increased turnout by African Americans, Barack Obama's candidacy netted him 95 percent of all votes cast by African Americans.

Income—a Reliable Predictor of Voting

Besides education, income is one of the best predictors of whether an American will vote.[25] Typically in recent years, U.S. citizens with the lowest income level have had voter turnout levels of 50–60 percent; whereas, those with the highest income level have had turnout levels above 85 percent.[26] As income increases, so too does the likelihood of voting.

The reasons for the close correlation between income and likelihood of voting are complex.[27] One possibility is that people with lower incomes may have less belief than higher-income earners that the government listens to people like them. Another factor may be that individuals with lower

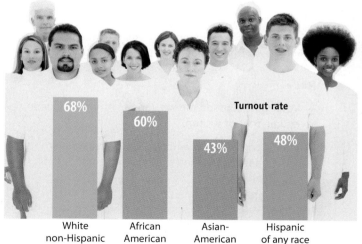

FIGURE 9.5 ■ VOTER TURNOUT IN THE 2004 PRESIDENTIAL ELECTION, BY RACE Which demographic group had the highest turnout of the four groups shown? Which had the lowest? Which groups do you believe increased the most in the 2008 election? Why? Looking ahead to the next presidential election in 2012, what do you predict about the voting turnout rates for each of the groups shown?

turnout rate
the proportion of eligible voters who actually voted

prospective voting
a method of evaluating candidates in which voters focus on candidates' positions on issues important to them and vote for the candidates who best represent their views

incomes have less leisure time in which to learn about candidates and issues and even to vote. Further, in contrast to the situation in many European democracies, U.S. political parties and political organizations tend not to be highly class based. Whereas European voters are often mobilized—by class-based trade unions and by the parties themselves—to vote on the basis of their economic interests, in the United States, the lowest-income workers are less likely to be members of organized labor unions and thus are less likely to be mobilized to vote on the basis of their own economic interests.

Party Competitiveness and Voter Turnout

Finally, researchers have found that party competitiveness in elections also influences voter turnout.[28] In tight contests, in which either party has a viable chance of winning, voter turnout typically is high because the race generates more voter interest than an election in which the winner is a foregone conclusion. Sometimes turnout is high in competitive elections because voter efficacy is higher—a voter may believe that her vote "counts" more in a close election than in a less competitive race. Voter turnout also runs high in competitive elections because the parties and other campaign organizations work harder to get out the vote when they think they have a chance at winning but know that victory is not guaranteed.

Competitive races also draw ratcheted-up media attention. A tightly competitive local mayoral race might get greater than usual regional news attention, and a close race for the White House brings nearly nonstop media reports and candidate advertisements. The barrage of media coverage increases public awareness and may also boost voter efficacy by conveying the message that every vote counts.

The impact of this fierce party competitiveness was clearly evident in the 2004 presidential voting, when more than 120 million Americans cast their ballots. In absolute numbers, this is the largest number of voters of any race in history, although the **turnout rate,** the proportion of eligible voters who actually voted, was only 59 percent. The 2004 turnout rate was less than the 60.2 percent level seen in the 1992 election between George H. W. Bush and Bill Clinton, which was also extremely competitive. But in the 2004 election, voter turnout rose significantly in the sixteen key battleground states where both parties believed they had a chance of winning: Arizona, Colorado, Florida, Iowa, Maine, Michigan, Minnesota, Missouri, Nevada, New Hampshire, New Mexico, Ohio, Oregon, Pennsylvania, West Virginia, and Wisconsin. In those states, the turnout rate was 65.3 percent, more than 6 percent higher than the national rate, highlighting the powerful role of party competitiveness in attracting voter interest and increasing turnout.[29]

How Voters Decide

When deciding for whom they will vote, some voters evaluate candidates on the basis of their positions on issues and then cast their ballots for those who best represent their views. Called **prospective voting,** this method of candidate evaluation focuses on what the candidates will do in the future. A more common form of candidate

Concept Summary

FACTORS INFLUENCING WHETHER AN INDIVIDUAL VOTES

Education

— As education increases, so too does the likelihood of voting.

— There is a measurable difference in likelihood of voting between those who have only attended college and those who have graduated.

Age

— Young adults are much less likely to vote than middle-aged and older adults.

Race

— Voter participation among African Americans nearly equals that of whites.

— Voting participation among Hispanic and Asian Americans lags behind that of whites and African Americans.

Income

— Income is one of the best predictors of whether an American will vote.

— As income increases, so too does the likelihood of voting.

Party Competitiveness

— In elections in which either party has a viable chance of winning, voter turnout typically is high.

— In competitive elections, voter efficacy is also high.

evaluation is **retrospective voting,** in which a voter evaluates an incumbent candidate on the basis of whether the incumbent's past decisions and actions are satisfactory to the voter.[30] If they are satisfactory, the voter will likely support the incumbent. If not, the voter will be disposed to support the incumbent's opponent. The prevalence of an incumbency advantage in election outcomes indicates that many voters have a favorable view of the decisions and actions of incumbent candidates for most offices.[31]

retrospective voting
a method of evaluating candidates in which voters evaluate incumbent candidates and decide whether to support them based on their past performance

The most important factor that plays into how a voter decides on a candidate and perceives specific candidates, however, is the voter's party identification. Other influential determinants include those specific to a given election, such as candidates' attributes and the impact of the candidates' campaigns.

Major Factors in Voter Decision Making

The strongest bearing on voter preference is party identification, with about half of all voters basing their candidate choice on which party they identify with. Table 9.3 shows that in the 2008 presidential election, party identification was a potent influence on how voters decided among candidates. As shown in the table, among voters who identified themselves as either Democrats or Republicans, loyalty to their party's candidate was high, with 90 percent of both Democrats and Republicans voting for their party's nominee for president. President Obama's victory came in part because of his support among the nation's independent or unaffiliated voters—those who do not identify themselves as either Democrats or Republicans.

TABLE 9.3	Party Loyalty in the 2008 Presidential Election		
		Voting for McCain (%)	Voting for Obama (%)
	Democrats	10	90
	Independents	45	51
	Republicans	90	9

Often a significant determinant in why people vote the way they do, policy priorities are to a certain extent aligned with party identification (or, even more generally, with ideology), because the political parties usually embrace differing viewpoints on issues. National issues that top the list of concerns among voters have remained consistent over many years and include several domestic policy matters, such as the health of the economy, education, crime, health care, and Social Security. Since the terrorist attacks of 2001, homeland security and issues related to terrorism and then the wars in Iraq and Afghanistan have also ranked high in the list of issue concerns on which voters base their vote choices.

But how do voters decide which party and which candidate to support at the polls, based on the issues? First and foremost, an issue must be **salient** to voters—that is, it must resonate with them and reflect something that they care deeply about, an issue they are willing to base their vote on.[32] The ability of voters to cast an issue-based vote increases when candidates differ in their positions on an issue.

salient
having resonance, in relation to a voting issue, reflecting intense interest

Incumbency, the situation of already holding an office or official position, as we've seen, is also a key factor influencing how people vote. Because an incumbent is a "known commodity" with demonstrated experience to serve in office, voters are much more likely to vote for incumbents than for their challengers. Thus, for most offices, incumbents are much more likely to be reelected than their challengers are to be elected. Indeed, in congressional elections, generally more than 90 percent of incumbent U.S. senators and 95 percent of incumbent members of the House of Representatives win reelection. But incumbency is also an influence in presidential elections, gubernatorial and state legislative elections, and probably even your local city council elections. Incumbents have notable advantages over challengers, namely, greater name recognition, a track record that voters can evaluate, and access to campaign contributions that help get their message out.

incumbency
the situation of already holding the office that is up for reelection

Campaign Influences on Voter Choice

As we have seen, parties and candidates conduct campaigns to influence voters' choices at the polls. Campaigns today vary a great deal in how they are waged. Whereas a candidate for a small town's board of selectmen might knock on the door of every voter in the community, a U.S. Senate or gubernatorial candidate might spend most of his or her time raising money to pay for expensive television and radio advertisements. Generally, the lower the level of office, the greater the likelihood that the candidate will rely on grassroots activism.

> "Going negative" is a common feature of many modern campaigns. In 2008, as the competition for the Democratic nomination wore on, the campaigns of both Senator Hillary Clinton and Senator Barack Obama became increasingly negative. A widely publicized Clinton ad questioned Senator Obama's foreign policy experience, asking voters to consider who they wanted to answer a 3:00 a.m. phone call at the White House, while their children sleep soundly in their beds.

Trends in modern campaigns, including a far deeper reliance on paid professional staffers and the prevalence of the media as a tool for communicating with voters, are catapulting the costs of campaigns sky-high. Voter choices are also affected by increasingly negative campaigns, one outcome of the modern political campaigns' reliance on paid professionals. Outside consultants typically have far fewer qualms about "going negative" than do activists in the all-community volunteer-run campaigns that were more typical of earlier times.

Consultants use negative campaign tactics for a simple reason: research shows that the approach sways voter opinion.[33] Although the candidates themselves often prefer to accentuate a positive message that highlights their background, experience, and qualifications, paid campaign consultants generally do not hesitate to sling the mud. Once a candidate establishes name recognition and credibility with voters, many consultants believe highlighting the opponent's negative qualities and actions is an effective campaign strategy.

But the impact of negative campaigning is not limited merely to swaying voters from one candidate to another. Research by political scientists shows that negative campaigning can suppress voter turnout in several ways. For example, Shanto Iyengar and Jennifer A. McGrady note that negative advertising may suppress voter turnout among the attacked candidate's supporters.[34] Other political scientists' research shows that negative campaigning undermines the democratic process by decreasing civic engagement among all voters. According to these findings, the electorate becomes disenchanted with the candidates (about whom voters get a barrage of negative information), with the campaigns (because campaigns serve as the primary messengers for delivering negative information about opponents), or with the entire electoral process that facilitates this negativity. Some voters view negative campaigning as being completely at odds with their idealized conception of the democratic process, and this may discourage them from voting.

Why Some People Do Not Vote

Negative campaigning is one reason why some people do not vote, but political scientists have proposed several others. Lack of civic engagement on the part of voters underlies many of these ideas. Other reasons have to do with the nature of campaigns and the structure of elections.

Lack of Efficacy

Some voters do not vote because they do not participate in civic affairs, either locally or at the national level. Many of these nonvoters lack efficacy.[35] They do not believe that the government listens to people like themselves nor that their vote actually matters in determining the outcome of elections and the business of government.[36]

Scholars have determined that individuals who lack efficacy exist across the social and economic spectrums but that poorer people are more likely than better-off individuals to feel that the government does not listen to people like them. Yet although it is a common notion that people are alienated from politics or think that the government does not listen to their concerns, a recent study estimated that only about 9 percent of the U.S. population feels this way.[37] This same survey indicated that people lacking efficacy—a group that the study called the "disaffecteds"—typically had a low level of educational attainment and were less likely to follow current events than more engaged citizens.

Voter Fatigue and Negative Campaigns

Another explanation for why some Americans do not vote stems from the nature of political campaigns. In the United States, campaigns tend to be long-drawn-out affairs. For example, presidential campaigns typically last for more than a year, with some candidates positioning themselves three or four years in advance of an election. Contrast this with many parliamentary systems, including Germany's, in which an election must be held within sixty days of the dissolution of parliament because of a "no confidence" vote of the chancellor (similar to a prime minister). Some scholars say that the lengthiness of the campaigns leads to **voter fatigue,** the condition in which voters simply grow tired of all candidates by the time Election Day arrives, and may thus be less likely to vote.

American journalist and humorist Franklin Adams commented that "elections are won by men and women chiefly because most people vote against somebody rather than for somebody." The prevalence of negative campaigning compounds the impact of voter fatigue. Even the most enthusiastic supporters of a candidate may feel their advocacy withering under the unceasing mudslinging that occurs in many high-level campaigns. And so while evidence shows that negative advertising is effective in swaying voters' opinions, sometimes it also succeeds in suppressing voter turnout by making voters less enthusiastic about voting.

voter fatigue
the condition in which voters grow tired of all candidates by the time Election Day arrives, and may thus be less likely to vote

The Structure of Elections

Political scientists also cite the structure of U.S. elections as a reason why more Americans do not vote. For years voting rights activists claimed that the registration requirements in many states were too complicated and discouraged people from voting by making it too difficult to register. In 1993, Congress sought to remedy this situation by passing the National Voter Registration Act, frequently called the "Motor Voter" Act, which allows eligible people to register to vote when they apply for a driver's license or enroll in a public assistance program or when they submit the necessary information by mail. Although there was enormous anticipation that the motor voter law would significantly boost voter registration and turnout, in fact its impact has been negligible.

Critics of the structure of elections also point to their frequency. In the United States, the number of elections varies from municipality to municipality, and local government charters may call for more than four elections for municipal offices alone. Although most federal offices require only two elections (a primary and a general), these elections are not always held in conjunction with state, county, and municipal elections.

The timing of elections also affects voter participation. Most general elections are held on a weekday—the first Tuesday after the first Monday in November. Moreover, although states decide when to hold primary elections, state legislative elections, and municipal and school board elections, these elections, too, typically occur on a weekday. Critics say that holding elections on weekends or over a two-day period instead, or establishing a national voting holiday, would increase voter turnout by ensuring that voters had ample opportunity to cast their ballots (see "Global Comparisons").

The Rational Abstention Thesis

A final explanation as to why some people do not vote is that they make a conscious choice that not voting is a rational, logical action. Called the **rational abstention thesis,** this theory states that some individuals decide that the "costs" of voting—in terms of the time, energy, and inconvenience required to register to vote, to become informed about candidates and elections, and actually to vote—are not worth the effort when compared to the expected "benefits," or what the voters could derive from voting.

In light of these cumulative "costs," it is perhaps surprising that so many people choose to vote.[38] One explanation for why they do is that most voters report that they derive psychological rewards from exercising this citizen's right—feelings of being civically engaged, satisfied, and patriotic. But when the costs associated with voting increase too much, turnout drops; more people choose not to vote when voting becomes too inconvenient. This

rational abstention thesis
a theory that some individuals decide the costs of voting are not worth the effort when compared to the benefits

GLOBAL COMPARISONS

ELECTIONS IN INDIA

While we may think that conducting elections in the United States is a large undertaking, holding elections in India is even more challenging. India is the largest democracy in the world and the second most populous country after China. Thus, the efforts associated with organizing the general election process are enormous.

The Indian Election Commission, an independent committee that is insulated from executive interference, has authority for running elections. The commission's job is to ensure free and fair elections. Since the beginning of India's democracy in 1947, free and fair elections have taken place at regular intervals, as the Indian constitution requires.

Indian elections today constitute the largest elections in human history. Eight hundred thousand polling stations span the country in widely varying climatic and geographic zones, giving accessibility to the vote to more than 668 million people. With such a large electorate, polling for the national elections extends to at least three days.

The entire election process takes five to eight weeks for the national election to the Lok Sabha (the House of the People), the lower house of India's Parliament, and four to six weeks for the state legislative assemblies. Elections begin with the announcement of the election schedule, usually at a press conference a few weeks before the formal election process begins, and with notifications calling upon the electorate to elect members of the House. Once the notifications are made, candidates can file their nominations. Candidates then get two weeks to campaign before the voting begins.

After the minimum three days set aside for voting, a later date is set for counting the votes, and the election commission compiles a complete list of the House members elected.

For more information on India's Parliament, visit the Parliament of India's Web site: http://rajyasabha.nic.in/. For more information on elections in India, visit www.indian-elections.com/.

Should the United States adopt a general election process like India's?

---

drop-off occurs, for example, when municipalities shorten voting hours and during inclement weather.

The Impact of Nonvoting

From a civic engagement perspective, nonvoting is both a symptom and a result of a lack of civic involvement on the part of individuals.[39] Your roommate might not vote because she is not civically engaged—because she feels that she has little to contribute and that the government does not listen to "people like her" anyway. But by not voting, she perpetuates this lack of efficacy by remaining outside the process rather than staking a claim to what is rightfully hers: the idea that every individual has the right to a voice in the composition and priorities of the government. Only by becoming civically engaged—learning about the candidates, discussing issues, and voting—can she break the cycle of inefficacy. Voting will make her pay more attention to campaigns, candidates, and issues.

Beyond the effects of nonvoting on individuals, low voter turnout affects the polity. When relatively few people vote in a given election, the outcome is likely to represent the will of only that subset of the electorate who voted. This impact is important: consider that polls indicate that the outcomes of the 2000 and 2004 presidential elections would have been different if voter turnout had been higher. In each of these elections, the Democratic nominee (Al Gore and John Kerry, respectively) was the favored candidate among several groups whose turnout falls below average, including voters under age 24, African American voters, and voters with lower incomes. The process becomes cyclical: these nonvoters who disagree with the outcome conclude that the government does not represent them, feel less efficacious, and are less inclined to vote in the future.

Moreover, some scholars assert that democracies with low voter turnout are more likely to generate threats to their own well-being.[40] In democracies with low turnout, these scholars say, charismatic, popular political figures may rise to power and become authoritarian leaders. Corruption, too, can be a problem in low-turnout democracies where government officials might feel relatively unconcerned about the disapproval of disgruntled constituents.

Other researchers, however, contend that nonvoting is not a big problem, especially in cases where large numbers in the electorate are relatively uninformed about candidates and issues.[41] A number of scholars in this camp argue that participation by the uninformed is undesirable, as it may lead to drastic changes in government. Opponents of this view counter that because of political parties' role in selecting candidates, the menu for voter choice is actually quite limited in most elections. Those who argue that nonvoting does not matter also ignore the fact that voting tends to produce more engaged citizens who, because they vote, feel a duty to be informed and involved.

Other scholars who claim that low voter turnout is not a problem argue that low voting rates are simply a function of people's satisfaction with the status quo: their nonvoting simply means that they do not seek change in government. This argument, however, does not explain why lower turnout is most likely to occur in populations that are least likely to be satisfied with their situation. For example, people with lower incomes are much less likely to vote than those with higher incomes. Whatever the reason—a lack of efficacy as argued by some, satisfaction as argued by others—nonvoters' best chances of having their views reflected in the policy process is to articulate them through voting.

CONCLUSION   *CONTINUING THE CONVERSATION*

The nature of political campaigns in the United States has continuously evolved, but the changes in recent decades have been especially dramatic. An era in which political parties and grassroots activism dominated campaigns has given way to the present-day realities where money, media, and mavens of strategy are key forces in shaping campaigns, which have grown increasingly candidate-centered. Prominently driving the changes are the simultaneous *decrease* in political party clout and *increase* in the need for money—money to pay for the small army of professional staffers that run the campaigns; and money to cover the expensive media buys that candidates, especially those running for national and state office, heavily depend on for communicating with the electorate.

Technology offers the potential to bring the politics of electoral campaigns back to the grassroots—now perhaps more appropriately called the netroots. Although campaigns' use of technology certainly is not free, digital communication is cost-effective and rapid. Campaigns' and candidates' option of communicating with voters through mediums such as social-networking sites, YouTube, e-mail, and instant messaging presents an exciting alternative to high-priced "campaigning-as-usual."

Through the new mediums of communication, there is great potential, too, for the inclusion of a variety of new voices in the political campaigning process. Groups that want to influence campaigns and voters have at their disposal a vast arsenal of new technology that makes such influence possible.

Summary

1. Civic Engagement and Political Participation
Active political engagement benefits both the individual and the polity. When it comes to elections, campaigns, and voting, the opportunities for civic engagement are numerous. Although some civic activities, such as working full-time on a campaign, might represent enormous commitments, others, including casting a ballot and engaging in political discourse, are less time-consuming and are manageable for even the busiest people.

2. Elections in the United States
U.S. elections include the primary election, in which a party's nominee to run in the general election is selected; the general election, in which the winning candidate attains the office being sought; and special-purpose elections such as the initiative, referendum, and recall, which are citizen-sponsored efforts to have a greater say in the political process.

3. The Act of Voting
Although all of the states rely on the Australian (secret) ballot, the types of ballots used in states vary significantly. The type of ballot can have an impact on election outcomes, as in the 2000 presidential election.

4. Running for Office: The Choice to Run
Most offices have formal eligibility requirements, but there are also more subjective requirements by which voters view candidates as qualified to hold a given office. Often these characteristics have to do with occupation, education, and experience.

5. The Nature of Political Campaigns Today
Today's political campaigns hire a wide variety of professionals who perform the tasks that were once accomplished by volunteer staffs. Office seekers' increasing reliance on electronic media, in particular television, has drastically changed both the ways in which campaigns are conducted and the costs of those campaigns. The widespread use of the Internet, too, continues to alter the nature of campaigns.

6. Regulating Campaign Contributions
Government efforts over the years to regulate campaign contributions have led to laws with numerous loopholes. The latest attempt to curtail the influence of money on politics is the Bipartisan Campaign Finance Reform Act of 2002.

7. Presidential Campaigns
Presidential campaigns are of increasing duration. They begin with the primary process, continue through the national party conventions, proceed to the general election campaign and voting, and end with the Electoral College vote.

8. Who Votes? Factors in Voter Participation
Influences on voter participation include education, age, race, income, and party competitiveness.

9. How Voters Decide
Party identification, policy priorities, incumbency, and campaigns are factors influencing how voters decide for whom to vote.

10. Why Some People Do Not Vote
The many reasons why people don't vote include a lack of efficacy, the impact of voter fatigue and negative campaigns, the structure of elections, and the rational abstention thesis. Whatever the reason, nonvoting has a harmful impact on individuals and the government.

Key Terms

For Review

1. What are some opportunities for civic engagement related to elections, campaigns, and voting?

2. What are the different kinds of elections in the United States? What is the difference between a primary election and a general election?

3. What is the difference between formal and informal eligibility requirements for political office?

4. Why is regulating campaign finance so difficult? Explain the various efforts to limit the impact of money on campaigns.

5. What factors influence whether a person will vote or not?

6. What factors influence how or for whom an individual will vote?

7. What is the rational abstention thesis? Is it rational? What factors might not be calculated into the costs and benefits of voting?

For Critical Thinking and Discussion

1. Why do formal and informal eligibility requirements for office differ? What are the informal eligibility requirements to run for the state legislature where you live? What are the requirements for the city or town council in your hometown or the community where your school is located? How do these differences reflect the nature of the constituency for the office being sought?

2. How has the increasing cost of political campaigns changed the nature of American politics? Why have costs escalated?

3. What has been the impact of the increasing negativity in American political campaigns?

4. Using the text discussion of factors influencing whether a person votes, assess a classmate's likelihood of voting based solely on those factors. Then ask the person if he or she votes. Was your assessment accurate?

5. In your view, what is the impact of nonvoting?

PRACTICE QUIZ

MULTIPLE CHOICE: Choose the lettered item that answers the question correctly.

1. A secret ballot prepared by the government, distributed to all eligible voters, and, when balloting is completed, counted by government officials in a nonpartisan fashion is called
   a. a British ballot.
   b. a Greek democratic ballot.
   c. an Australian ballot.
   d. a Nebraska ballot.

2. A type of primary that allows voters to vote only in the primary of the party in which they are registered, is called
   a. a caucus.   **c.** an open primary.
   b. a blanket primary. **d.** a closed primary.

3. The phenomenon by which candidates running for a lower-level office such as city council benefit in an election from the popularity of a top-of-ticket nominee is called
   a. the petticoat effect.
   b. the bustle effect.
   c. the trickle down theory.
   d. the coattail effect.

4. GOTV is
   a. get out the vote.
   b. governors on television.
   c. government of the vice president.
   d. grabbing on to volunteers.

5. A special election in which the computerized voter machine simulates the elimination of last place voter-getters to eventually decide a winner is called
   a. an instant recall.
   b. an instant runoff.
   c. an open primary.
   d. a voter initiative.

6. The proportion of eligible voters who actually voted is called
   a. the eligibility factor.
   b. voter turnout.
   c. voter sampling.
   d. the voting projection.

7. A campaign professional who works with the candidate in identifying likely contributors to the campaign and arranging events and meetings with donors is called
   a. a media consultant.
   b. a fund-raising consultant.
   c. a campaign manager.
   d. a pollster.

8. Tasks that involve direct contact with voters or potential voters are called
   a. negative campaigning.
   b. media outreach.
   c. constituent services.
   d. grassroots organizing.

9. An election that determines which candidates win the offices being sought is called
   a. a caucus.   **c.** a closed primary.
   b. an open primary.   **d.** a general election.

10. A method of candidate evaluation in which a voter evaluates an incumbent candidate and decides whether to support the incumbent or his or her opponent based on the incumbent's past performance is called
    a. retrospective voting.   **c.** reactionary voting.
    b. prospective voting.   **d.** negative voting.

FILL IN THE BLANKS.

11. The social networks and reciprocal relationships present in society are called _____ .

12. A _____ is a meeting of party leaders held to select delegates to the national convention.

13. The situation of already holding the office that one is seeking is called _____ .

14. The idea that some individuals decide that the costs of voting are not worth the effort when compared to the benefits is called _____ .

15. An issue that resonates with voters is said to be _____ .

Answers: 1. c; 2. d; 3. d; 4. a; 5. b; 6. b; 7. b; 8. d; 9. d; 10. a; 11. social capital; 12. caucus; 13. incumbency; 14. rational abstention thesis; 15. salient.

Internet Resources

American Democracy Now Web site

www.mhhe.com/harrison1e Consult the book's Web site for study guides, interactive activities, simulations, and current hotlinks for additional information on voting, campaigns, and elections in the United States.

The Living Room Candidate

www.livingroomcandidate.org This site, maintained by the Museum of the Moving Image, provides videos of television commercials run by presidential campaigns from 1956 to 2008.

Project Vote Smart

www.vote-smart.org This nonpartisan Web site provides independent, factual information on election procedures in each state.

Rock the Vote

www.rockthevote.org This nonprofit, nonpartisan organization encourages political participation by young people and provides resources on policies of interest, as well as voting information.

Vote, Run, Lead

www.voterunlead.org This is the Web site for an organization that encourages the civic engagement of young women as voters, activists, and candidates for political office.

Recommended Readings

Abramson, Paul R., John H. Aldrich, and David W. Rohde. *Change and Continuity in the 2004 and 2006 Elections.* Washington, DC: CQ Press, 2007. The latest in this series of election analyses examines how the tactics employed in the 2006 midterm elections could shape the 2008 races.

Bimber, Bruce, and Richard Davis. *Campaigning Online: The Internet in U.S. Elections.* New York: Oxford University Press, 2003. Describes how voters and political campaigns are increasingly relying on the Internet as a communication, fund-raising, and organizing tool.

Burns, Nancy, Kay Lehman Schlozman, and Sidney Verba. *The Private Roots of Public Action: Gender Equality, and Public Action.* Cambridge, MA: Harvard University Press, 2003. Explores the differences in political participation between men and women.

Faucheux, Ron. *Campaigns and Elections: Winning Elections.* New York: M. Evans and Company, 2003. A collection of the "best of the best" articles from *Campaigns and Elections* magazine; a practical guide to conducting campaigns.

Herrnson, Paul S., Richard G. Niemi, Michael J. Hanmer, Benjamin B. Bederson, and Frederick C. Conrad. *Voting Technology: The Not-So-Simple Act of Casting a Ballot.* Washington, DC: Brookings Institution Press, 2008. Explains the intricacies of voting technology, including the electoral implications of how votes are cast.

Jacobson, Gary C. *The Politics of Congressional Elections.* New York: Longman, 2008. A classic work explaining the process of congressional elections and demonstrating how electoral politics reflects and shapes other basic components of American democracy.

Leighley, Jan. *Strength in Numbers: The Political Mobilization of Racial and Ethnic Minorities.* Princeton, NJ: Princeton University Press, 2001. Examines the factors that influence political participation by African Americans and Hispanic Americans.

Maisel, L. Sandy. *The Parties Respond: Changes in American Parties and Campaigns,* 4th ed. Westview Press, 2002. Explains how political parties have changed their functions in response to the changing nature of American campaigns.

Patterson, Thomas E. *The Vanishing Voter.* New York: Knopf, 2002. An analysis of the decline in voter turnout, with recommendations for reversing the trend.

Wattenberg, Martin P. *Is Voting for Young People?* New York: Longman, 2007. Explains why young people have not voted historically and analyzes the importance of voter participation from the viewpoint of young Americans.

Zukin, Cliff, Scott Keeter, Molly Andolina, Krista Jenkins, and Michael X. Delli Carpini. *A New Engagement? Political Participation, Civic Life, and the Changing American Citizen.* New York: Oxford University Press, 2006. Describes the changing ways in which Americans are participating in the political life of their country and communities.

Movies of Interest

Bulworth (1999)

Warren Beatty stars in this offbeat skewering of the impact of money on political campaigns in the United States.

The Candidate (1972)

A character played by Robert Redford is convinced to run for the Senate on the premise that, with no chance at success, he can say whatever he wants. But success changes the candidate, so that his values shift as the prospect of winning becomes apparent.

National Journal

Looking Back: A 'Maverick' Nominee, but Still the Same GOP

John McCain achieved something that no GOP White House hopeful had been able to do in more than half a century—capture the party's nomination without carrying the party's base.

And that's true regardless of whether its "base" is defined as self-identified conservatives or as self-identified Republicans.

Three states were critical to McCain's success—New Hampshire, South Carolina and Florida. McCain won the Republican primaries in all three but, according to the exit polls, he did so without winning a majority or even a plurality of self-identified conservatives. What's more, McCain didn't attract a majority or even a plurality of the self-identified Republicans in any of those three contests.

In Florida, the senator from Arizona and former Massachusetts Gov. Mitt Romney each won 33 percent of the voters in the GOP primary who called themselves Republican. (Even though the primary was open only to registered Republicans, 17 percent of those surveyed said they usually think of themselves as something else, such as independents.) In New Hampshire and South Carolina, McCain's victories came from getting the support of solid pluralities of the independents and self-described moderates who voted in the GOP contest. In Florida, which gave him decisive momentum heading into the bonanza of primaries and caucuses on Super Tuesday, McCain won largely because of independents, moderates, and Latinos.

In the 13 states that held GOP caucuses—where appealing to grassroots conservatives and party regulars is critical to success—McCain came in first only in Hawaii and Washington, yet went on to clinch the GOP nomination.

"It wasn't the normal way to do it, but he did it," says former Republican National Committee Chairman Frank Fahrenkopf.

Most leading Republicans doubt that fundamental change is afoot. Yet, almost universally, they fervently hope that McCain can fundamentally change the way their party is perceived by an electorate that now gives the incumbent Republican president, George W. Bush, abysmal job-approval ratings.

And that's far from the only paradox about McCain's nomination. Many Republicans admit they don't particularly care for McCain or his maverick tendencies, but they readily acknowledge that he had a better chance of holding the presidency for their party than any other 2008 contender they could have nominated.

During the primary season, McCain tried to appeal to the base of a party that, if anything, has grown more conservative because it has bled moderates in recent years. On immigration, tax cuts, and offshore drilling, he shifted his stands to the right. But in doing so, he blurred the very thing that gives him his best chance of winning the independents who this year hold the keys to the White House—his maverick image. So, arguably, McCain has changed more than the party he now heads.

There's not much sense among Republicans that their party's base is shifting beneath them. "I think we are still the conservative political party. And McCain has adapted more to that fact than the party has moved toward some of McCain's more moderate tendencies," said Dick Wadhams, chairman of the Colorado Republican Party.

Conservative Gary Bauer said, "I don't think he's redefining the party ideologically, but I do think because of his persona he is bringing people into the Republican Party that may not have embraced conservative ideas if somebody else was selling them."

Other Republicans note that despite McCain's unconventional path to the nomination, the party base remains much what it has been since Ronald Reagan recast it on his way to winning the presidency in 1980—a coalition of defense and national security hawks, low-tax advocates, and Christian conservatives. "I don't see that any of these groups have dropped out of the party. Hence I don't see the party as having 'moved' anywhere," said California Republican Party Chairman Ron Nehring.

Some Republicans talk of the McCain nomination as though the candidate and his party serendipitously stumbled into something mutually beneficial.

As late as February 7, two days after the Super Tuesday contests gave McCain a huge delegate lead, some conservatives were still plotting to stop him. David Keene, chairman of the American Conservative Union, pulled together some 50 top conservatives during the Conservative Political Action Conference in Washington, in hopes of uniting them behind Romney. But it was too late. Shortly before Keene's group was scheduled to meet, Romney addressed CPAC and shocked the crowd by withdrawing. "It ended up being a goodbye meeting," one attendee recalls.

Not long after Romney spoke, McCain addressed the conservative gathering. Plenty of boos punctuated the applause.

Regardless of whether they supported McCain earlier this year, many Republicans now think that his nomination has thrown them something of a life preserver, given that the public is so hostile to the GOP brand these days. "As much as I liked some of the other candidates, they were in the traditional Republican mold and would probably not be faring as well right now against [Democratic presidential nominee Barack] Obama in this difficult national political environment," Wadhams said. "McCain has the ability to win this election on the strength of his appeal to independent voters, and can help our party across the board. In many ways, I think we lucked out with McCain winning our nomination."

Even though McCain catapulted his way to the top of his party on his strength among moderate Republicans and independents, the GOP remains firmly rooted in conservatism. One yardstick for measuring conservatives' clout within the party is the composition of the 168-member RNC, which consists of a party chair and a national committeeman and national committeewoman from each state, the District of Columbia, Puerto Rico, and four U.S. territories. Each person was elected by the party leadership or party convention in his or her locale.

"If you look at the RNC elections for national committee folks nationwide, most would argue the party is moving to the right," said Michigan Republican Party Chairman Saul Anuzis, who attributes McCain's triumph to the split among conservatives. Anuzis estimates that one-quarter of the RNC's members are new this year. "The ones that I know have all been elected as more conservative than the people they replaced," he said. Indeed, plenty of evidence backs him up.

Earlier this year, the Kansas Republican State Committee ousted two-term RNC member Alicia Salisbury and replaced her with Helen Van Etten, the president of the Kansas Republican Assembly, an anti-tax, anti-abortion group that described itself as "the Republican wing of the Republican Party" when moderates controlled the state GOP.

But perhaps nowhere was the conservative bloodletting more pronounced than in Iowa, where conservative Mike Huckabee made his dramatic breakout when he won the GOP presidential caucuses on the strength of his support from the born-again and evangelical Christians who swamped the party's precinct meetings. Those conservative Christians also elected delegates to county GOP conventions and then to the July state convention, where they bowled over two pillars of the party establishment, Steve Roberts and state Rep. Sandy Greiner, in elections to the RNC.

A former state party chairman and 20-year RNC member, Roberts was tossed out

Republicans talk of the McCain nomination as though the candidate and his party serendipitously stumbled into something mutually beneficial.

in favor of Steve Scheffler, president of the Iowa Christian Alliance. Roberts, a foe of abortion rights, came under fire for not being more vocal in condemning the Polk County judge who ruled last year that the state's ban on same-sex marriage is unconstitutional. The judge stayed his own decision within 24 hours, but his ruling set off a firestorm among Iowa conservatives.

Roberts' fate is indicative of how the battle for control of the party between hard-right conservatives and somewhat more moderate Republicans is unfolding. "In Iowa, we're in the middle of a real fork in a road, and maybe nationally," Roberts said.

Greiner, an eight-term member of the Iowa House who was endorsed for the RNC post by every one of her state House GOP colleagues, was defeated by Kim Lehman, the president of the Iowa Right to Life Committee. And Greiner is hardly known as a moderate. She was an early Reagan supporter, and in 2008 she served as a state co-chair for the presidential effort of former Sen. Fred Thompson of Tennessee.

"She's as conservative as they come," said retiring state Rep. Carmine Boal. "I've watched the woman vote for 16 years; it's ridiculous."

In Greiner's defeat, Boal sees a troubling aspect of how some conservative Christians and their allies conduct their politics—that is, without regard to whether they alienate many Republicans who agree with them on a host of issues, including social ones. "As far as the future of the party, do we take a sharp right [turn], and that's all we're going to have?" Boal wonders.

For the moment, Boal, like many other conservative Republicans, is prepared to embrace McCain as the GOP nominee, but only out of what she sees as necessity. "As much as I don't like it, in many ways he is the best candidate for us—not in the long term, but he's the best one right now," said Boal, acknowledging that the political environment is anti-Republican these days.

"McCain's got enough of the conservative viewpoints to bring along people, but yet enough of the renegade or independent streak to bring along independents and country-club Republicans," Boal said. "We'd love to have a Reagan Republican. But, at this time, he is the best we can do."

It's hard to predict what direction McCain will go next. "If he becomes the president because he's a safe pair of hands, then there's no new era and you're just reshuffling the deck a little bit," said University of Wisconsin political scientist Byron Shafer, an expert on party coalitions and the presidential nominating process. "Celebrity commercials—they're not a new direction; they don't involve anything that you will do if you win."

If McCain isn't elected, recriminations would likely divide the party: Conservatives would assert that the party should have nominated a true believer, while centrists would argue McCain should have made a sharper break with Bush and the party status quo.

That such a confrontation didn't happen during the nominating contest this year but could happen in a McCain presidency is deeply ironic. Still, maybe it shouldn't be surprising, given that John McCain has never been the first choice of most of his party.

THEN: John McCain was one of few presidential hopefuls to have won their party's nomination without winning their party's base supporters.

NOW: The Republican party grapples with what the McCain nomination signals for the future of the party.

NEXT: Will the GOP base change as a result of John McCain's campaign?
Will Christian conservatives continue to replace moderate Republicans in RNC positions?
How should political parties balance their imperatives to energize their base voters and draw in independents?

The Media

THEN

The relationship between the media and consumers was one-way.

NOW

Technology has created a two-way relationship between the media and consumers, involving the exchange of a seemingly limitless amount of information.

NEXT

Will the abundance and reach of the media overload people with information?

Will people select media sources that serve only to confirm their views?

Will the ever-increasing speed and volume of information affect its quality?

Bringing the Story of the Iraq War Home

As the war in Iraq continues, many people have lost sight of the stories of the soldiers on the ground in Mosul and Baghdad and Fallujah. It is the job of ABC News senior national security correspondent Martha Raddatz to keep the troops' experiences alive for American television viewers who have grown increasingly war weary. Prominent in this viewing audience, and always eager for information on the well-being of the troops, are the loved ones of those who serve. | In her coverage of the war, Raddatz understands that although the larger policy picture is important, the lives of the servicemen and servicewomen on the ground—their struggles, fears, and successes—matter deeply to the

> Martha Raddatz, then senior national security correspondent for ABC News, in Mosul, Iraq, last year.

American public's perceptions of the war and of the soldiers themselves. In her book *The Long Road Home: A Story of War and Family*, Raddatz tells the story of the battle of Sadr City, the first place where U.S. troops experienced insurgent violence, culminating in one of the bloodiest battles of that conflict. Her book tells of the terrible dilemma faced by soldiers who came under fire from insurgents and civilians using children as human shields. | Raddatz knows that covering the story from the ground means putting herself in harm's way. (Two of Raddatz's colleagues were seriously injured when the truck they were riding in hit an improvised explosive device, or IED.) "We have more than 135,000 U.S. troops in Iraq right now," she has explained. "It is so important for me to go over there and cover what they do, and you cannot do that from the Pentagon. I feel very strongly that you have to go over there."* | Advances in technology have meant that Raddatz and war correspondents like her can do their jobs with more immediacy and greater impact than the reporters who covered past wars. Using satellite and digital technology, Raddatz's reports from the front have been broadcast live, in real time. Videophones and related technology have allowed Raddatz and her fellow correspondents to travel into danger zones far less visibly than could reporters carrying traditional film cameras and sound equipment. | The war zone reporting of Raddatz and correspondents like her has made a valuable contribution to the larger American conversation about the war. The personal, "from the front" perspective of these journalists provides a powerful alternative to the sameness and anonymity that often characterize war coverage: "Three American soldiers died today in fighting in Iraq...." Raddatz understands the far-reaching implications of this war, but she also understands the smaller implications. Her daughter Greta Bradlee quotes an e-mail she received from her mother in 2005: "When we walked onto the plane, we saw in the middle four flag-draped coffins, stacked side by side. On the way home on Easter Sunday. The passengers were seated on the sides of them. Our luggage was next to the coffins. The retired general I was with walked back and touched the flags. I cannot describe how emotional it was to see those coffins so close to you ... not knowing who they were, but knowing how they probably died." | Raddatz's informed reporting—and that of the army of other journalists risking their lives to ensure that we the American public grasp and engage with the issues concerning the Iraq War—reflects the many important functions of the media. The mass media provide us with information about politics and our government. They help us to interpret events and developments that are significant for ourselves and our society. The information they disseminate is crucial to our ability to have meaningful conversations about our shared civic life and the policies that affect us.

*www.berkeley.edu/news/media/releases/2006/02/06_bradlee/shtml

If you are like most Americans

—and indeed like multitudes of people across the globe—the media are a fixture in your daily life. You may wake up to a radio show each morning or read a newspaper over breakfast or while commuting on a bus or train. You may watch televised news stories on the Iraq War as reported by Martha Raddatz and other journalists in the evening. You may receive real-time news updates on your cell phone, Internet news sites, and Weblogs or tune in to the twenty-four-hour news channels available virtually everywhere. There is no escaping that as a citizen of the twenty-first century, you are bathed in a sea of news and information. Some of what the media offer you is meant to entertain, some is meant to inform, but increasingly the lines between the two have blurred.

No one can dispute that the sheer amount of information and entertainment available courtesy of the media has increased immeasurably over the past few decades. Within a generation, the modern media have transformed American life. Where once people had to seek out news and information, today they are inundated with it, and they must develop the skill to filter the good from the bad.

Although this abundance of information at times may rise to the level of a blitz, information is empowering. It serves as the basis on which people shape well-founded opinions. These opinions are the building blocks for meaningful civic engagement and political participation. In this chapter's "American Democracy Now" vignette and in the discussion that follows, we see how the media continuously shape the ways we receive information and the ways we exercise the rights and privileges of our American democracy.

This chapter focuses on the contemporary U.S. media's role as both an information source and a conduit through which individuals convey information and opinions to others, and it explores the growing, shifting influence of the media on politics and civic life over time.

FIRST, we consider *the political functions of the media.*

SECOND, we explore *the press and politics,* taking *a historical view.*

THIRD, we focus on the origins and formats of the first of the electronic media with a look at *the radio and television revolutions.*

FOURTH, we examine the diverse and growing uses of the Internet as *the media revolution continues.*

FIFTH, we weigh *how the media influence government policy.*

SIXTH, we ponder charges that the U.S. media are *biased media.* Do most people believe that the media are too liberal or too conservative? Are they right?

FINALLY, we consider the government's *regulation of the media* and examine how the media's rapidly continuing transformation impacts government's ability to regulate new formats of communicating.

The Political Functions of the Media

In the United States today, the media in all their forms—including print, television, radio, and the Internet—fulfill several key functions. Much of what the media do revolves around entertaining us, whether that means watching *CSI* or reading the Sunday funnies. But the media perform important political functions as well and are a vital element of our democracy. Specifically, the media perform the following functions:

- provide political information;
- help us to interpret events and policies and are influential in setting the national policy agenda;
- provide a forum for political conversations;
- socialize children to the political culture.

Providing Information

One long-standing function of the mass media is to serve up a steady diet of news and information to readers, viewers, and listeners. Indeed, the media, particularly the electronic media, are the primary source of information for most individuals. Coverage includes everything from weather watches, to sports scores, to the latest legislative developments on Capitol Hill, to serious analysis of top domestic policy issues and international problems. From this steady diet arises the problem of information overload—the constant availability of news information to the point of excess, which may cause media consumers to ignore, dismiss, or fail to see the significance of particular events. Media critics fault the television networks in particular for injecting entertainment into news shows. They dub this combination

infotainment
news shows that combine entertainment and news, a hybrid of the words *information* and *entertainment*

sound bites
short audio or video clips taken from a larger speech

soft news
events or topics that are not serious or broadly important

infotainment (a hybrid of the words *information* and *entertainment*). More recent is the trend of uniting comedy with political content, as in Jon Stewart's *The Daily Show* and Stephen Colbert's *The Colbert Report,* both of which interpret news events with a comedic slant.

SOUND BITES AND SOFT NEWS   Journalists blame the public for a lack of interest in real issues and an addiction to negative news and **sound bites**—short audio or video clips taken from a larger speech. In turn, reporters must please the public in order to maintain ratings. Media representatives argue that today's media consumers prefer infotainment to a probing discussion of the issues. Those who are interested can find in-depth, balanced information online if they know where to look but are often hard pressed to locate it in the average newspaper or commercial radio or television broadcast.

Why do some news organizations dedicate so much coverage to events or topics that are not serious or broadly important—in other words, to **soft news**? Some scholars point to the profit-seeking motivations of media moguls. Indeed, it is no secret that most media outlets are in a race to increase their profits, and their typical strategy is to attract higher numbers of consumers. So television networks and cable television stations strive to boost their viewers; newspapers and magazines, their subscribers; radio stations, their listeners; and Internet sites, the number of hits they receive—often by disseminating material molded to mass tastes.

THE PROFIT MOTIVE   Media consumers generally do not directly create media profit. Instead, rising use by consumers means that media channels can charge advertisers more because their ads are reaching more people. Only public television and public radio (which are nonprofit institutions that depend on private and government grants and donations from viewers and listeners), as well as satellite radio providers such as Sirius and XM (which do not accept advertising but charge listeners subscription fees), do not rely on advertising dollars.

What influence does profit seeking have on the quality of political reporting and people's attitudes about government? Some analysts, including James Hamilton, say that profit seeking creates a kind of media bias.[1] They point out that media outlets may avoid political controversy in an effort not to offend their audiences. Other scholars, among them Matthew Robert Kerbel, argue that the media's emphasis on negativity—particularly the misdeeds and character flaws of government officials, which have a powerful attraction for the general public—contributes to the public's declining trust in governmental institutions.[2] Other commentators argue that the abundance of profit-making media outlets has negatively affected the quality and accuracy of the information they provide (see "Exploring the Sources"). For example, William V. Kennedy argues that reporters covering wars are often ill equipped to "ask the right questions," with the result that news consumers get misinformation about military actions and outcomes.[3]

Beyond the potent imprint of profit seeking on news content, scholars bemoan the influence of the sheer proliferation (and the expanded reach) of media sources in recent years. The exploding number of news sources, they say, has stifled the originality and quality of programming everywhere. In fact, evidence suggests that television networks get some of their major stories from newspapers as well as from the Internet. Newspaper reporters complain that network anchors "rip and read" stories for the nightly television news that have appeared in their newspapers that morning. Similarly, Internet bloggers charge that print journalists steal their blog scoops without crediting them.

Interpreting Matters of Public Interest and Setting the Public Agenda

As described in the opening "American Democracy Now" vignette, besides reporting information, the media help people to comprehend and interpret matters of public interest and to make informed decisions about public policies. Political scientists Shanto Iyengar asserts that the process of interpretation often begins with media **framing**—setting a context that helps consumers understand important events and matters of shared interest.

Political scientist Pippa Norris has analyzed the process of framing as it relates to gender. She asserts that gender has become a common frame through which journalists provide context for different kinds of political stories.[4] Norris explains that voters, candidates, public

framing
the process by which the media set a context that helps consumers understand important events and matters of shared interest

EXPLORING THE SOURCES

CONFIDENCE IN THE MEDIA

The Gallup Organization has asked the following question in surveys since 1972: "In general, how much trust and confidence do you have in the mass media—such as newspapers, T.V., and radio—when it comes to reporting the news fully, accurately, and fairly: a great deal, a fair amount, not very much, or none at all?"

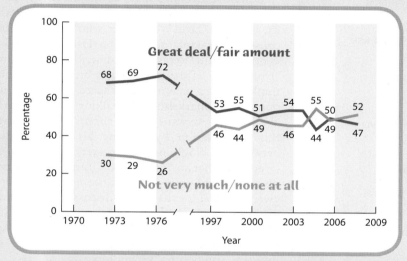

Source: The Gallup Poll, *Media Use and Evaluation*, www.galluppoll.com/poll/1663/Media-Use-Evaluation.aspx.

The line graph illustrates survey respondents' views on these questions, showing survey data at various times between May 1972 and September 2007. You can see that considerable changes have occurred in people's assessment of news organizations in this period.

---

opinion, and issues all may be viewed from a gender-based perspective. For example, in the 2008 presidential campaign, the media initially covered the race for the Democratic nomination by accentuating the gender of Senator Hillary Clinton (D-New York) and played up Clinton's potential to be the first woman president of the United States. Media reporting defined her opponent, Senator Barack Obama, as potentially the first African American president. Similarly, when Senator John McCain announced that Alaska governor Sarah Palin would be his running mate in the 2008 general election campaign, the media emphasized the gendered aspects of her nomination, particularly her role as a mother.

The media also help to shape the **public agenda**—public issues that most demand the attention of government officials. The media commonly influence the setting of the public agenda by **priming**—using their coverage to bring particular policies on issues to the public agenda.

public agenda
the public issues that most demand the attention of government officials

priming
bringing certain policies on issues to the public agenda through media coverage

Providing a Forum for Conversations About Politics

Throughout their existence, the media have provided an often lively forum for conversations about politics. The prominence of this role has reached new heights in the Internet era.

THE POLITICAL FUNCTIONS OF THE MEDIA

Providing Information

— The media, particularly the electronic media, are the primary source of information for most individuals.

— Because media corporations seek profits, media outlets often try to avoid political controversy so as not to offend their audiences.

Interpreting Matters of Public Interest and Setting the Public Agenda

— The media interpret matters of public interest and related policies—a process that involves framing the issues.

— The media help to shape the public agenda and use the tool of priming in this effort.

Providing a Forum for Conversations About Politics

— The Internet has facilitated two-way conversations between media and consumers.

Socializing Children to Political Culture

— The media socialize children to dominant cultural values.

— The media often reinforce democratic principles.

Historically, information flowed from the media—which through the years have included everything from the political broadsides and leaflets of colonial times to modern newspapers, radio news, and television programming—to the people. The people then formed opinions based on what they read, heard, and saw. This historical one-way tradition typically featured little give-and-take between media sources and their consumers. A notable exception has been the **letter to the editor,** in which a reader responds to a newspaper story, knowing that the letter might be published in that paper.

The advent of talk radio gave listeners one of their first regular opportunities to express their views publicly. Television took note, and call-in shows such as *Larry King Live* now are common fare on cable television stations.

But no other medium has expanded the ability of people to communicate their views to the degree that the Internet has. David Weinberger, who served as marketing consultant and Internet adviser to Democratic 2004 presidential hopeful Howard Dean, describes the phenomenon: "Don't think of the Internet as a broadcast medium . . . think of it as a conversational space. Conversation is the opposite of marketing. It's talking in our own voices about things we want to hear about."[5] Weblogs facilitate this conversation by inviting an ongoing dialogue between the blog hosts and posters. Discussion boards (even those that are "nonpolitical") are filled with political discussion and opinions. Chat rooms permit people of a given political persuasion to discuss and organize with like-minded thinkers. Social-networking sites such as MySpace, Facebook, BlackPlanet, MyBatanga, AsiaAve, and Faithbase allow individuals to share their stories, interests, and political viewpoints.

Socializing Children to Political Culture

The media also socialize new generations to the political culture. For young children, television remains the dominant medium for both entertainment and socialization. TV-viewing toddlers receive regular messages about important cultural values. Shows such as *Sesame Street* and *Barney* send powerful messages about the value of diversity in society. A song such as *Barney*'s "You Are Special" underscores the value of individualism in the culture. Young children's shows also subtly instruct watchers on the value of patriotism and of specific civic behaviors, such as voting.

letter to the editor
a letter in which a reader responds to a story in a newspaper, knowing that the letter might be published in that paper

> The media socialize individuals to key political values. On shows such as *American Idol,* principles of democracy prevail as viewers vote for their favorite contestant. What are some other popular television shows that reflect society's core political values?

TV programming for older children similarly takes on political issues. In *Arthur,* the main character comes face-to-face with censorship when adults in his town have the "Scare Your Pants Off" book series removed from the public library, thus providing a concise fifteen-minute lesson on civil liberties issues.

Even television and radio programs not specifically aimed at youth often reinforce democratic principles and practices. What is *American Idol* if not a televised election? And when the tribe speaks on *Survivor,* they do so through the process of voting. Talk radio and television call-in programs rest on the assumption that individuals' opinions

GLOBAL COMPARISONS

TALK RADIO, SAUDI STYLE—MUBASHER FM

When you think of Saudi Arabia, one thing that probably does not pop into your mind is talk radio. But every Monday night during prime-time hours, radio host Salama al-Zaid takes calls from about twenty listeners, most of whom are seeking help in dealing with the national bureaucracy or lodging complaints of corruption against government officials.

Saudi Arabia, bordered by the Persian Gulf on the east and the Red Sea on the west, is a kingdom ruled by King Abdullah and administered primarily through an enormous network of the royal family. The Muslim Shari'a is the basis of the nation's laws, although some secular laws have been enacted in recent years. Women do not have basic rights such as voting and driving. Although the country traditionally has enjoyed a high standard of living, poverty is a growing problem. Restrictions on the media abound, and criticism of the monarchy is especially frowned upon. It is in this environment that Zaid hosts his radio program. *Mubasher FM* ("Live FM" in Arabic) went on the air in 2006.

*Can the media genuinely open up closed societies?

Zaid claims that King Abdullah views Zaid's program as a useful tool in gauging public opinion. "The media has always been a red line in this country. But the king came and said this is the way to reach the people. And he sent a message to me: Keep going," explains Zaid, who fully supports the monarchy. Callers to the program get more than a sympathetic ear. Not only do government officials try to rectify problems aired on the program, but callers sometimes receive an audience with the king, who has issued decrees to address various issues broadcast on *Mubasher FM*.

Zaid is highly critical of corrupt officials, whom he has challenged to phone in and explain their behavior. Moreover, he is not afraid of speaking out on some of the most controversial issues in Saudi society, including those affecting the rights of women. During one program, he took Saudi schools and universities to task for failing to hire qualified women as teachers. Calling on the royal court to address this problem, he complained that "our daughters are being wronged by our universities and places of higher learning."

The optimistic Zaid believes that Saudis are advancing toward being a more open society. He takes heart that people are increasingly willing to come forward and complain about corruption of government officials and unacceptable problems such as the sexual harassment of women. That he must sift through thousands of calls each week indicates a willingness by individuals to voice their complaints without fear of reprisals, and Zaid characterizes that as progress.

> Radio Host Salama al-Zaid.

Source: Hassan M. Fattah, "Challenging Saudi Arabia's Powerful, One Caller at a Time," *New York Times*, May 5, 2007, p. A4.

---

matter and that they have the right to voice them (see "Global Comparisons"). These various kinds of programming may not directly spur a particular political behavior on the part of viewers. Nonetheless, television and other forms of media that we often think of as pure entertainment frequently reinforce and legitimize dominant American political values.

The Press and Politics: A Historical View

The sheer volume of information available today through the media makes the influence of the media in our times beyond dispute. Historically, too, the media have played an essential role in setting the political agenda and shaping public policy. The power of the media was evident, for example, as early as pre-Revolutionary times, such as when newspaper owners and readers rallied against the Stamp Act's (1765) imposition of taxes on newspapers and other kinds of legal documents. Newspaper publishers sympathetic to the colonists' cause of ejecting Great Britain from American shores used their "power of the pen" to arouse public opinion, and they strongly supported the patriot cause throughout the Revolution. Taking sides in an internal conflict was a new role for the press, one that would sow the seeds of future media influence on the country's domestic and foreign policy. The early history of media development also raised issues that continue to create conflict about the media's role in society.

The Early Role of the Press

Great leaders learned early how intimately their careers were linked to favorable press coverage and influence. From the 1790s to the 1830s, the press served primarily as a vehicle for the leaders of political parties, who expressed their opinions through newspapers known to reflect their particular viewpoints in reporting the news. Were these newspapers forerunners of today's liberal and conservative media outlets? Their circulation was small, but so was their audience; most people could not read and write and did not vote.

penny press
newspapers that sold for a penny in the 1830s

By the 1830s the environment had changed. For openers, the average American was now able to read. New technology made possible the **penny press**—newspapers that sold for a penny. Circulation increased, and the working class became interested in what the newspapers had to offer. Another reason newspapers reduced their price was the advent of advertising; newspaper owners figured out that if they sold advertising, they could increase both their profits and their papers' circulation. The 1830s was the first time advertising became part and parcel of the newspaper business, and although pressures from advertisers sometimes affected coverage and editorial opinion, few readers noticed this practice, and even fewer challenged it.

Over time the influence of advertising grew exponentially. Although today's major newspapers do not openly change their editorial opinions to please their advertisers, occasionally advertisers flex their muscles, as General Motors did when it withdrew its advertising from the *Los Angeles Times* after the newspaper recommended the firing of the company's CEO.[6]

> Yellow journalism can influence the national policy agenda. When the battleship *Maine* exploded in Havana harbor in February 1898, newspaper coverage significantly molded public opinion, and in turn Congress declared war on Spain. Can you think of examples of recent media coverage of events that have influenced public opinion

yellow journalism
irresponsible, sensationalist approach to news reporting, so named after the yellow ink used in the "Yellow Kid" cartoons in the *New York World*

Yellow Journalism and Muckraking

Throughout the last part of the nineteenth century, newspapers competed vigorously with each other for ever-greater shares of readership. Publishers found that stories about sex, gore, violence, and government corruption sold papers faster than reports about garbage collection and school budgets. Well-known publishers William Randolph Hearst and Joseph Pulitzer established their reputations and their fortunes at this time, Hearst with the *New York Journal American* and Pulitzer with the *New York World*. Along with Hearst and Pulitzer at the beginning of the twentieth century came the practice of yellow journalism, so named after the yellow ink used in the "Yellow Kid" cartoons in the *New York World*. The term **yellow journalism** has come to signify an irresponsible, sensationalist approach to news reporting and is used to this day to criticize certain elements of the press.

The most famous example of the impact of yellow journalism came with both Hearst's and Pulitzer's support of the United States' entry into the Spanish-American War (1898). This conflict is sometimes referred to as "the newspaper war" because of the major role of the press in President William McKinley's decision to invade Cuba and later the Philippines. Public sentiment in the United States, influenced by reports of Spanish cruelty toward the Cubans during and after the Cuban independence movement, strongly favored Cuba. Hearst and Pulitzer, followed by other newspapers across the country, fanned the flames of war with sensational and lurid anti-Spanish stories, dwelling on the brutality of the Spanish toward Cuban rebels. The precipitating event, the explosion of the U.S. battleship *Maine* in Havana harbor in February 1898, may or may not have been due to a Spanish torpedo according to recent evidence. But press reports, accompanied by the cry "Remember the *Maine*," galvanized the public and Congress. The president responded to the intensifying pressures, and Congress declared war on Spain in April. The press and the public had guided public policy.

Hard on the heels of the Spanish-American "newspaper war" came the era of **muckraking,** an about-face that placed journalists in the heroic role of exposing the dark underbelly of government and industry. The most famous of the muckrakers included Ida Tarbell, who exposed the oil industry in a series of articles running from 1902 to 1904 in *McClure's* magazine called "The History of the Standard Oil Company"; Lincoln Steffens, who published *The Shame of the Cities* in 1904; and Upton Sinclair, whose novel *The Jungle* (1906) revealed the horrors of the meat-processing industry, leading to passage of the Pure Food and Drug Act and later to the establishment of the Food and Drug Administration.[7]

muckraking
criticism and exposés of corruption in government and industry by journalists at the turn of the twentieth century

A Widening War for Readership

Yellow journalism died down after World War I, and newspapers entered a period that at least on the surface valued objectivity. Newspapers increasingly found themselves competing with the new media that were just coming into being: radio stations from 1920 to 1950; television from the 1940s to 1980; and from then on, the explosion of the **new media—** cable television, the Internet, blogs, and satellite technology.

This increased competition has had several impacts on the newspaper industry. First, newspaper readership has steadily declined, particularly the audience for local newspapers. For example, Figure 10.1 shows that between 1998 and 2006, the proportion of people who read a local newspaper every day or several times a week decreased from 68 percent to 57 percent. Figure 10.2 illustrates that although readership of national newspapers increased slightly after the terrorist strikes of September 11, 2001, since that time readership has ebbed to the same level as before the attacks. Partly as a result of a long-term decline in local newspaper readership, the number of daily newspapers has decreased dramatically, with many cities that used to support three or four "dailies" now typically have only one newspaper. Second, competition has resulted in consolidation of the newspaper industry so that today a single large parent company typically owns any local newspapers. For example, the Gannett Corporation, which publishes *USA Today,* also publishes numerous daily and weekly newspapers in towns throughout the country. Third, competition has forced nearly every newspaper to offer free online editions. Thus you can receive nearly any newspaper at no cost in your e-mail inbox each morning.

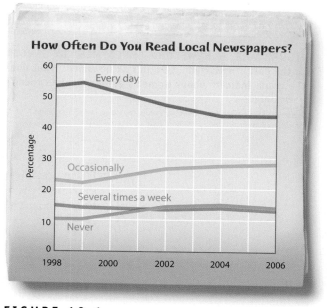

FIGURE 10.1

Declining Readership of Local Newspapers

Source: The Gallup Poll, *Media Use and Evaluation*, www.galluppoll.com/content/?ci=1663&pg=1,accessed May 3, 2007.

new media
cable television, the Internet, blogs, and satellite technology

FIGURE 10.2

Stagnant Readership of National Newspapers

Source: The Gallup Poll, *Media Use and Evaluation*, www.galluppoll.com/content/?ci=1663&pg=1,accessed May 3, 2007.

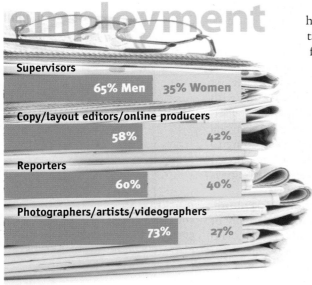

Supervisors
65% Men 35% Women

Copy/layout editors/online producers
58% 42%

Reporters
60% 40%

Photographers/artists/videographers
73% 27%

POLITICAL INQUIRY

FIGURE 10.3 ■ NEWSROOM EMPLOYMENT BY GENDER
In the past, "newsmen" were in fact news*men*. What does the graph indicate about women's employment in today's newsrooms?

Source: The American Society of Newspaper Editors, "Newsroom Employment Census," Table M, www.asne.org/index.cfm?id=5653, accessed June 19, 2007.

Beyond falling readership, the newspaper industry has changed as society has changed. Large cities are now likely to have smaller weekly publications targeted to specific demographic audiences—gays, women, African Americans, for example—and to publish foreign-language newspapers appealing to such diverse newcomers to the United States as Mexican, Brazilian, Vietnamese, Iranian, Nigerian, and Russian immigrants.

As the industry has changed, so, too, has the human face of the newsrooms. Figure 10.3 shows that in 2007, more than one third of all newsroom supervisors were women, as were some two fifths of all layout and copy editors and reporters. These figures reflect the societal changes from the times in which "newsmen" were in fact news*men*. Among all positions measured in the annual newsroom census, women were least likely to hold jobs in the visual arts, such as photographer and artist.

Table 10.1 shows another measure of how modern newsrooms have changed along with American society. The table illustrates the proportion of minority journalists working at newspapers in eight different circulation categories. From Table 10.1 we can see that minority journalists are much more likely to be employed at larger-circulation newspapers, with minorities constituting one fifth of the journalists at papers having a circulation of 250,000 to 500,000 (see "On the Job"). That proportion is nearly identical at the largest-circulation newspapers and steadily tapers off among newspapers with circulation of less than 250,000.

The Media Go Electronic: The Radio and Television Revolutions

It is impossible to overemphasize the transformative impact of the early electronic media. From the time of the first U.S. radio broadcasts in the early 1920s, radio allowed listeners to hear news in real time. This immediacy marked a drastic change from the standard, delayed method of

TABLE 10.1

Minority Journalists as a Percentage of the Professional Workforce of Newspapers in Eight Circulation Categories

NEWSPAPER CIRCULATION	YEAR				
	1980	**1992**	**1997**	**2002**	**2007**
Over 500,000	7.2	15.6	17.3	18.5	19.3
250,001 to 500,000	6.4	13.3	16.2	18.8	20.9
100,001 to 250,000	6.3	10.4	13.1	14.5	17.0
50,001 to 100,000	5.6	9.3	11.3	10.5	12.0
25,001 to 50,000	4.2	5.7	7.1	7.9	8.7
10,001 to 25,000	3.1	5.7	7.0	7.1	7.8
5,001 to 10,000	2.4	4.5	5.1	4.8	5.4
5,000 and Under	2.8	5.4	4.6	4.8	5.6

Source: The American Society of Newspaper Editors, "Newsroom Employment Census," Table F, www.asne.org/index.cfm?id=5653, accessed June 19, 2007. Copyright © 2008 The American Society of Newspaper Editors.

DAVID CHEN, JOURNALIST

<u>Name:</u> David Chen

<u>Age:</u> 41

<u>Hometown:</u> Montclair, New Jersey

<u>College attended:</u> Yale (BA in History) and Columbia (Master's in International Affairs)

<u>Major:</u> History (at Yale) and Media and Communications and East Asian Studies (at Columbia)

<u>Job:</u> City Hall Bureau Chief, *New York Times*

<u>Typical salary range for jobs in journalism:</u>
$28,000–$70,000

<u>Day-to-day responsibilities:</u> I cover Mayor Michael R. Bloomberg's administration from inside City Hall's vaunted Room Nine, where reporters from all the major newspapers converge in one cramped room. I am the leader of a three-person team, and my responsibilities are similar, if a bit more demanding and intense, to what I did for my previous job, as the paper's New Jersey State House bureau chief in Trenton. In any given week we produce a mix of breaking news stories, features, and analysis pieces, in an effort to keep readers apprised of government and political news.

<u>How did you get your job?</u> I first contacted the *Times* at a journalism conference, where I distributed my clips and met a few editors. A few months later, the *Times* asked me to fly to New York for interviews with even more editors; I was offered a job on the spot.

<u>What do you like best about your job?</u> The ability to meet people from all different backgrounds. The opportunity to make a difference in public policy or in people's lives. The chance to learn something new every day. And the luxury of changing beats or assignments every few years.

<u>What is your least favorite aspect of your job?</u>
The long hours (with nights and weekends often routine). The logistics of getting to a place to report a story, then struggling with technical issues to file that story.

<u>What advice would you give to students who would like to do what you're doing?</u>
Read as many different things as you can—newspapers, books, magazines, even junk mail. Travel as widely as possible. Never assume that you know what the story is before you actually report a story. Strive for fairness, balance, and thoroughness in every story. Try not to get rattled by people who criticize your work. And never forget that the most important person in a story is not you, or your subject, but the reader, because you have to earn the reader's trust and respect, every day.

receiving news, which was by reading the morning and evening editions of newspapers, plus the occasional "extra edition" published when important breaking news warranted it. Radio also altered the relationship between politicians—particularly presidents—and their constituents, as it enabled listeners to hear the voices of their elected leaders. Television further revolutionized this relationship by making it possible for people to see their leaders (though initially only in black and white).

How Radio Has Opened Up Political Communication

Radio was the first electronic medium that brought people into direct contact with their leaders. Beginning in the 1920s, radios became a fixture in American living rooms, and families who could not afford a radio of their own would often spend evenings at the homes of friends or neighbors who could.

FDR'S FIRESIDE CHATS   Franklin D. Roosevelt was the first politician to realize the value of radio as a device for political communication—and to exploit that value. As governor of New York (1928–1932), Roosevelt faced a Republican state legislature hostile to many of his liberal social welfare programs. To overcome the opposition, Roosevelt used radio addresses

> President Franklin Roosevelt was recognized as a master political communicator. Roosevelt relied on a folksy, conversational tone and the medium of radio to bring his message to the people.

> Some seventy-five years later, another president, Barack Obama, is widely recognized as a skilled political speaker. Unlike FDR, however, Obama uses lofty rhetoric and new technologies to drive his message home. How does a politician's ability to communicate successfully with the people influence his or her governing?

fireside chats
President Franklin Roosevelt's radio addresses to the country

talk radio
a format featuring conversations and interviews about topics of interest, along with call-ins from listeners

fairness doctrine
requirement that stations provide equal time to all parties regarding important public issues and equal access to airtime to all candidates for public office

to appeal directly to his constituents, who would then lobby the legislators for his policies. Indeed, after some of Roosevelt's radio addresses, legislative offices were flooded with letters from constituents asking lawmakers to support a particular policy.

By the time Roosevelt became president in 1933, he had grasped the importance of radio as a tool for communicating directly with the people. FDR often began his radio addresses to the country—his **fireside chats**—with the greeting, "Good evening, friends," highlighting the personal relationship he wished to cultivate between himself and his listeners. (You can download many of Roosevelt's fireside chats in MP3 format from the Vincent Voice Library at Michigan State University.) Through the folksy fireside chats, Americans learned about presidential initiatives on the banking crisis, New Deal social welfare programs, the declaration of war on Japan after that nation's attack on Pearl Harbor, and the progress of U.S. forces during World War II. In all, Roosevelt had thirty fireside chats with Americans over his twelve years as president.

During the golden age of radio—the period from the early 1920s through the early 1960s—radio was the dominant form of electronic entertainment. Radio programming included a wide array of shows, from newscasts, to serial dramas, to comedies, to variety shows. Although political and news radio programming remained popular during the 1950s and 1960s, radio generally took a backseat to television during this era.

TALK RADIO: TALKING THE POLITICAL TALK   Radio began to emerge from the shadows of television in the 1970s and 1980s. These decades brought a renaissance of sorts for radio, as the medium saw tremendous growth in **talk radio**—a format featuring conversations and interviews about topics of interest, along with call-ins from listeners. As many AM station owners switched to an all-talk format in these years, music programming migrated to the FM band.

In 1987 the Federal Communications Commission (FCC) repealed the **fairness doctrine,** which had required stations to provide equal time to all sides regarding important public issues and equal access to airtime to all candidates for public office. Since the law's repeal, partisan radio programming has grown dramatically. Today, listeners tend to tune in to radio hosts who share—many say, reinforce—their opinions, and they interact with them through call-in opportunities. Talk radio features numerous well-known personalities, including Rush Limbaugh, Sean Hannity, Mark Levin, Laura Ingraham, and Bill O'Reilly, whose shows are also available via the Internet and through podcasts, thus potentially reaching a significantly expanded number of listeners.

Figure 10.4 shows the rise in listenership for talk radio programs since 1995. Daily listenership of such programs has nearly doubled, increasing from 11 percent in 1995 to 20 percent in 2006. The percentage of people who listen to talk radio several times a week has also nearly doubled in that time.

Talk radio was one of the first forums that allowed media consumers to "talk back" to the host. At its best, talk radio allows for a natural, real-time exchange of information between the host and the audience; at its worst, it has given rise to developments such as the so-called primal scream format, which we consider later in the chapter. Scholars widely agree that talk radio programs promote citizen engagement in the form of civic discourse. Recall from earlier chapters that civic discourse means the sharing of viewpoints and the articulation of personal positions on public issues (along with the information gathering and reflective thinking that must accompany this expression). This information sharing is fundamental to a civic society. That is, without informed and shared opinions, people cannot be responsible, politically engaged citizens.

The appeal of talk radio, particularly as broadcast via the Internet, mirrors the allure of Internet blogs. The messages of both mediums have become highly personal and emotional, targeted to a narrow segment of the public. Conservative radio commentators tend to draw an audience dominated by middle-aged conservative males, while the much smaller liberal market segment tends to draw the coveted younger audience.

Television and the Transformation of Campaigns and Elections

Although radio predates television, TV nonetheless has been the centerpiece of U.S. home entertainment for a long time. Television began to make a mark on the American scene in the 1940s, when small TV sets—their screens flecked with static snowflakes—hit the market. Today, the images we view are crystal clear, as high-definition big-screen TVs increasingly dominate households. Hundreds of channels compete for audience share, ending the previous dominance of the three major networks, ABC, NBC, and CBS.

With all the new competition, network television is rapidly losing viewers. Along with announcing in July 2004 that cable television enjoyed 52 percent of the prime-time TV-viewing audience, Nielsen Media Research, publisher of the famous Nielsen ratings for television shows, reported that network television had just 44 percent (with public television having a 4 percent market share). In addition, total viewership for the television networks had fallen by 41 percent between 1977 and 2003, from 51 million viewers to 30 million.

Figure 10.5 shows the continuation of these changes. Viewership of nightly network news broadcasts on ABC, CBS, and NBC plummeted between 1996 and 2006. In 1996, well over a majority of Americans watched a nighttime network news broadcast; by 2006, only 35 percent did, and the number who never watched grew to 19 percent. Compare these figures with the data for the networks' cable news counterparts, where daily viewership has increased by more than 10 percent. Among the other categories of TV news (morning shows such as *Good Morning America* and the *Today* show, public television news broadcasts, and local news shows), viewership has essentially stagnated.

> Although political talk radio programs have been around for decades, technologies such as the Internet and podcasts expand the reach of talk radio hosts such as conservative commentator Laura Ingraham to a significantly larger audience.

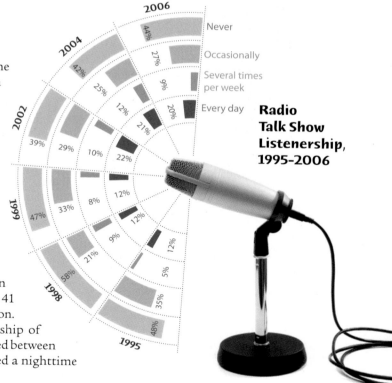

Radio Talk Show Listenership, 1995–2006

POLITICAL INQUIRY

FIGURE 10.4 ■ What has been the trend in talk radio listenership since 1995? What factors might explain this trend?

Source: The Gallup Poll, "Media Use and Evaluation," www.galluppoll.com/content/?ci=1663&pg=1, accessed May 3, 2007.

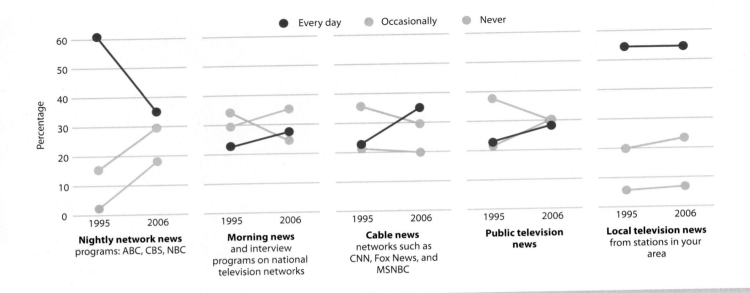

FIGURE 10.5

Where Do Americans Get Their News?

Source: The Gallup Poll, "Media Use and Evaluation," poll administered September 7–10, 2006, www.galluppoll.com/content/?ci=1663&pg=1, accessed June 21, 2007.

narrowcasting
the practice of aiming media content at specific segments of the public

media segmentation
the breaking down of the media according to the specific audiences they target

telegenic
the quality of looking good on TV

As cable news channels such as CNN and Fox News have increased their viewing audience, it is no wonder the word *broadcasting* has spawned the term **narrowcasting:** the practice of aiming political media content at specific segments of the public, divided according to political ideology, party affiliation, or economic interests. This winnowing of audiences has led to **media segmentation,** the breaking down of the media in general according to the specific audiences they target. Examples of segmented media include Black Entertainment Television (BET); the U.S.-based Spanish-language television network Telemundo; and the Lifestyle Network, which includes the Food Network and HGTV. Through media segmentation, advertisers can hone their advertising to the tastes of their targeted market.

Being **telegenic,** or looking good on TV, has become almost mandatory today for serious political candidates. It is unlikely that President William Howard Taft (1909–1913), who weighed over 300 pounds, would ever have been elected if he had been forced to appear on television. Nor would Abraham Lincoln, whose handlers would have marched him straight to a cosmetic surgeon to have the giant mole on his cheek removed. Richard Nixon might have won the presidency in 1960 had it not been for his nervous demeanor and the "five o'clock shadow" on his face that made him look sinister in the first-ever televised presidential candidate debates that year. His opponent, the handsome, relaxed, and articulate John F. Kennedy, won the visual debate hands down, even though in hindsight most analysts agree that Nixon "won" the debate on its verbal merits.

The Media Revolution Continues: The Internet

The modern media revolution continued with the birth of the Internet. As a medium of communication, a source of news and information, and a tool for political engagement and grassroots organizing, the Internet has had an incalculable—and a global—impact on the way people interact.

But access to the Internet is not equal, because affluent individuals are more likely than the less affluent to have computers and Internet connections. The term for this unequal access to computer technology is the **digital divide.** Sociologist Mark Wheeler has examined the digital divide, particularly when it comes to high-speed Internet connectivity. He has noted

digital divide
the inequality of access to computers and Internet connections

that income and wealth affect individuals' access to high-speed Internet service, even in the world's most affluent democracies.[8]

Yet even for those without computers of their own, the Internet has broadly transformed life in the United States. How the average U.S. citizen is educated, communicates, gets news, shops, receives information about politics, and participates in the political process all have changed because of the Internet. As political scientist Michael Cornfield noted, "I can't think of anything except kissing babies that you can't do online."[9] The influence of the Internet has been both positive and negative, and it continues to evolve.

The Internet and Civic Engagement

Over time, the Internet has transformed the media's function as a conveyor of information and a resource for civic engagement. Communications scholar Howard Rheingold argues that the digital media in particular serve as a key avenue by which young people can use their "public voice" to consume and share information.[10]

THE EVOLUTION OF THE INTERNET

In its early years, the Internet functioned in much the same way that traditional media formats such as newspapers and periodicals functioned: it provided a convenient but "one-way" means for people to get information at times determined by the publishers. As **bandwidth**—the amount of data that can travel through a network in a given time period—has increased, so, too, has the sophistication of Web content, as well as the venues and formats that serve as information sources. Today's news Web sites—including those of all the network and cable

How the Media Have Shaped Entertainment and the Information Highways

THEN (1960s)	NOW (2009)
Television programming matures and revolutionizes how the media entertain and provide information.	The Internet matures and revolutionizes how we are entertained and how we get information.
Television accentuates a new set of candidate qualities—including being telegenic—that had not mattered much in earlier political campaigns.	The Internet accentuates a new set of candidate qualities—including being tech savvy and Net organized—that were unheard of a generation ago.
Communication between the media and voters was one-way: people got information but could not "talk back."	Information flow is two-way, thanks to talk radio and the Internet—including blogs, YouTube, and social networking sites.

WHAT'S NEXT?

> What new media technologies will shape campaigns and political participation in the future?

> For individuals seeking information about policy issues and political campaigns, what might be the negative consequences of the abundance of information flowing through the electronic media?

> How will technology change political participation in the future?

news stations, plus sites maintained by Internet service providers such as AOL—give Internet users news stories when they want them instead of at predetermined times. Users can selectively search for specific information about public issues that matter to them, potentially building their knowledge base with a mouse click. Moreover, many contemporary news outlets, including magazines and radio programs, are now making available downloadable podcasts of content that users can view or listen to at their convenience. These podcasts are giving individuals even greater access to information, including reports on social issues, policy initiatives, and politics. Civic participation has been facilitated by the rise of these news Web sites and other sites, hosting blogs and forums that allow readers to engage in virtual civic discourse and even to form virtual communities.

bandwidth
the amount of data that can travel through a network in a given time period

THE INTERNET AS A SOURCE OF INFORMATION AND COMMUNITY

YouTube provides a compelling example of how the evolving Internet has worked to the benefit of civic engagement. This Web site, which debuted in February 2005 and is now owned by Google, allows individuals to post and watch original videos. The success of the YouTube experiment is inconceivable in the world of the dial-up Internet connection that was the norm

> Senator Hillary Clinton's off-key rendition of the national anthem, captured by an MSNBC news video crew, reached a worldwide audience via YouTube. The pervasiveness of video cameras and the technology of the Internet and YouTube mean that candidates and campaigns have little ability to manage campaign news.

vblog
a video Weblog

prosumers
individuals who simultaneously consume information and news and produce information in forms like videos, blogs, and Web sites

just a few years ago. YouTube's YouChoose '08 is an online network of YouTube members who upload political videos related to the 2008 presidential campaign so that others may view them. And so if you want to watch a political advertisement, see an interview with the French president or participate in Citizen Tube (YouTube's video Weblog, or **vblog**), today's technology makes it possible for you to do so in seconds. In 2007, YouTube partnered with CNN to host both Democratic and Republican presidential primary debates, promoting civic engagement by making it possible for Web site users not only to watch the debates but also to submit questions to the candidates. The interactivity embodied in viewing, commenting, posting, and vblogging has revolutionized civic discourse.

Today's Internet technology also facilitates the formation of virtual communities. These networks of interested participants, while different from their IRL (in real life) counterparts, share features with those real-world groups. Many blogs, for example, have community leaders, regular contributors, expert commentators, and participants with established roles. Blogs promote civic engagement by disseminating information, exposing readers to the viewpoints of others, providing a forum allowing bloggers to share their own views, serving as a venue for the formation of online communities that can foster feelings of efficacy among participants, and channeling activism, both virtual and real.* In short, the Internet has led to the phenomenon of the **prosumer**—the individual who simultaneously consumes information and news and produces information in forms such as videos, blogs, and Web sites.

The Internet as a Source of News

Internet users in the United States spend an average of three hours per day online, according to research conducted in 2005 by the Stanford Institute for the Quantitative Study of Society (SIQSS)—far more than they spend watching TV or reading newspapers.[11] Perhaps

---

* A note about content: The authors recognize the enormous variation in the quality of information available on the Internet in general and in blogs in particular. So when using the Internet as a source of information, a healthy dose of skepticism can be quite useful.

more important, the number of individuals using the Internet as a source of news continues to increase dramatically. Figure 10.6 shows that in the eleven-year span from 1995 to 2006, the proportion of Americans who get news from the Internet has grown exponentially. In fact, by 2006 a majority of Americans got news from the Internet at least sometimes, and over one fifth used the Internet as a news source daily. It is no wonder Nielsen TV ratings and newspaper subscriptions have declined.

The old adage that a "week is an eternity in politics" has become an understatement in the age of the Internet and the twenty-four-hour news cycle. Things happen in the click of a mouse button, and increasingly politicians are making snap statements in front of ever-present cell phone video cameras and regretting them later. Vermont governor Howard Dean, a candidate for the 2004 Democratic nomination for president, certainly regretted his wild scream to a crowd during a campaign stop, the video of which was later played and replayed on the Internet and on TV screens around the world.

Internet news sites could be doing some things better, though. For example, many news outlets present a news story as either an article or a video, but few major media outlets offer hotlinks to original source data that would aid interested site users in delving more deeply into the story. Instead of a synthesized news article on a Supreme Court decision, for instance, media outlets could provide links to the original opinions on the case as well as links to audio recordings of the arguments before the court, records of lower court decisions, and briefs filed with the court, supporting or opposing one side or the other, which are available elsewhere online *if* one is willing to search for them. Instead, most outlets offer only broad coverage with links to related stories—an approach that does not make it easy for an individual to research a matter of interest more deeply.

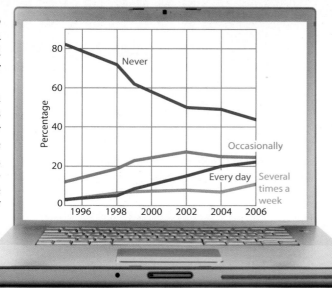

FIGURE 10.6

Increasing Percentages of Americans Get News from the Internet

Source: The Gallup Poll, "Media Use and Evaluation," poll administered September 7–10, 2006, www.galluppoll.com/content/?ci=1663&pg=1, accessed June 21, 2007.

The Internet's Influence on Political Participation and Campaigns

Even more than talk radio, the Internet has made politics participative. People can express their preferences online on issues from health reform to term limits, from income tax credits to repealing the inheritance tax. But besides acting as a gauge for public opinion, the Internet can also be a useful tool for citizens' political activism. The traditional media have not had nearly the impact on political participation that the Internet has had. For example, the left-of-center wing of the Democratic Party has not achieved the same media dominance in radio as the conservative wing of the Republican Party. One radio station targeting liberal listeners, Air America, was formed in 2004, but it has never succeeded in attracting a competitive share of the radio audience. What *has* worked in attracting the liberal wing of the youth vote are blogs and Web sites such as www.moveon.org.

USING THE INTERNET TO MOBILIZE VOTERS Jesse Ventura, a professional wrestler who served as the governor of Minnesota from 1999 to 2003, credits the Web for opening up the political process by enabling grassroots mobilization through **e-campaigning,** the practice of mobilizing voters using the Internet, which allowed an outsider like himself to be elected governor. Winning half of the under-thirty vote, Ventura conducted a campaign without any physical headquarters—at least at first. Armed with a large e-mail list, he enlisted pledges of support that short-circuited the traditional doorbell ringing and telephone calls that go with the territory when running for office. His tactics gave him the final surge of voters that he needed to win. Ventura's victory testifies to the power of the Internet as a political campaign tool.

The potential of the Internet as a force in political campaigns came into sharp focus again in 2004, when liberal Democratic governor Howard Dean of Vermont used the Web extensively for recruiting volunteers and raising money. Dean's efforts proved so successful that other candidates quickly followed his strategy. By the 2008 campaign, every major presidential

e-campaigning
the practice of mobilizing voters using the Internet

HOST A BLOG

FACT:

Blogs are today's tools for sharing information and opinions as well as for political organizing. No matter what your political persuasion, position, or passion, a personal blog will allow you to communicate your views with like-minded people (as well as with those who disagree with your perspectives).

Act!

The organizer of one blog called *Students for Barack Obama* saw it grow into a real-world political organization made up of over 60,000 members at eighty colleges and universities. It boasts a political action committee, a finance director, a field director, an Internet director, and a blog team director. Says twenty-one-year-old Bowdoin College organizer Meredith Segal, "Young people are on the Web. That's how we're organizing."*

You can start your own blog, either individually or with a group of friends. Focusing your blog on a specific theme or person—an ideology, an issue, a candidate, or a cause—will attract more hits and comments than will random observations or general information. You also can attract people to your blog through Web communities such as Facebook.com and MySpace.com.

Where to begin

Blogger—an automated Weblog publishing tool—allows you to create your own blog for free using a free Google account password. Go to www.blogger.com/start. Blogger comes complete with templates that allow you to structure your blog and generates traffic to it through the blogger.com Web site.

Not ready to start your own blog? Then visit one of these political blogs and express your ideas:

Daily Kos (www.dailykos.com): liberal
Instapundit (www.instapundit.com): conservative/libertarian

See you in the blogosphere!

*Jose Antonio Vargas, "Young Voters Find Voice on Facebook," *Washington Post*, February 17, 2007, A1.

candidate had a staff of Web site designers, Internet campaign managers, and blog managers. The Internet has even changed how candidacies are announced and presidential campaigns unfold. A campaign video of former senator John Edwards announcing his candidacy in New Orleans ran on YouTube, and both Senator Barack Obama and Senator Hillary Rodham Clinton announced their candidacies via their Web sites, followed by the posting of the corresponding videos on YouTube.

HOW THE INTERNET CAN AFFECT A POLITICAL CAMPAIGN The Internet has also changed the nature of political organizing. On the day that Senator Obama announced his bid for the presidency, Farouk Olu Aregbe, a student government adviser at the University of Missouri, logged on to www.facebook.com and announced the formation of a group called "One Million Strong for Barack." Within a month, Aregbe's Facebook group had over a quarter of a million members, and other Facebook users had formed more than 500 groups supporting the candidate (see "Doing Democracy").

But the rapid expansion of Internet technology has also made it more difficult for presidential campaigns (and administrations) to manage the news.[12] As a case in point, in January 2007, just after Senator Clinton launched her White House bid, a video appeared on YouTube featuring her singing an off-key rendition of the national anthem (the moment had been captured by an MSNBC news video crew). After the blog site *The Drudge Report* featured a link to the video, it logged nearly 800,000 hits. What was the campaign to do? Ignore the video? Apologize for the senator's inadequate singing voice? Promise that she would not sing publicly again? The campaign decided to ride it out and do nothing, and this strategy seemed to work, as the story and video soon fizzled. Wrote Patrick Healy of the *New York Times:* "The video clip may have been trivial, but the brief episode surrounding it illustrated how visual and audio technologies like video streaming have the potential to drive political news in unexpected directions, and how White House candidates are aggressively monitoring and trying to master them."[13]

Today's Blogosphere

Clearly, the widespread use of the Internet has also contributed to the spread of blogs. A new language has sprouted to incorporate this development, beginning with **blogosphere**—the community, or social network, of bloggers. The owner of the Dallas Mavericks basketball team, Mark Cuban, says that he runs his Internet blog as a means of correcting all the media accounts about him. As in every other corner of the Internet, there are no checks on what he posts: Cuban has called sports columnists "clueless," "morons," and purveyors of "slime reporting," yet he claims an audience of 300,000 readers.[14]

Estimates indicate that the number of blogs has doubled every five months since 2003 to a current level of over 20 million individual blogs.[15] As the number has multiplied, their variety and credibility have increased. Bloggers received press credentials at both the Democratic and the Republican conventions in 2008. Traditional television and print media outlets now host blogs as well.

The blog's rise as a tool of grassroots organizing has given birth to the term **netroots** to describe Net-centered political efforts on behalf of candidates and causes. A blog makes information available to large numbers of users immediately, spreading news and energizing supporters more rapidly than any other medium. It also differs from traditional media in one important way: bloggers make no attempt to be impartial. A blog is an opinion journal, offering a specific perspective and appealing to a specific segment of the public. In that respect, it cannot replace traditional journalism, especially because there is no check on whether the facts it presents are correct. But blogs continue to change the face of political campaigning and grassroots organization—for better and for worse.

Media Convergence

The concept of convergence has taken hold among media observers today. **Convergence** refers to the merging of various forms of media—newspapers, television stations, radio networks, and blogs—under one corporate roof with one set of business and editorial leaders. The emergence of Politico, a multimedia start-up that debuted in Washington, D.C., in January 2007, is an example of this concept come to life. What would have been regarded in the past as a violation of antitrust laws is now considered the wave of the future. Politico's mission is to report on the daily politics on Capitol Hill and in the White House. Politico is a publication of Capital News Corp., which is financed by Allbritton Communications, which used to own a now-defunct newspaper called the *Washington Star.*

The Negative Political Impact of the Internet

The explosion of the Internet in politics has also opened a Pandora's box of problems. One key problem is misinformation. Unlike newspapers, magazines, and television networks, where editors and fact-checkers are responsible for ensuring accuracy, the Internet is almost entirely unmonitored. In political campaigns, misinformation can be devastating.

Another problem is that the Internet has contributed to the decline in civility in political discourse. Some bloggers and anonymous messageboard posters seek to destroy their opponents' reputations. The nature of the Internet means that lies and slanderous accusations can often be leveled with no consequence to the poster. This problem occurs not just in national politics but in community politics as well.

The Internet also poses a host of unknown potentialities. What will be the crossover effects, for example, of such present-day crimes as identity theft and the stealing of social security numbers and state secrets, both of which have been "hacked into" via the Net? Consider the problems of a national election conducted through computer terminals. How

blogosphere
a community, or social network, of bloggers

netroots
the Internet-centered political efforts on behalf of candidates and causes

convergence
the merging of various forms of media, including newspapers, television stations, radio networks, and blogs, under one corporate roof and one set of business and editorial leaders

➤ In 2008, bloggers at the national party conventions were granted press credentials. Blogs spread news—though sometimes *inaccurate* news—and opinions very quickly. Their drawbacks aside, blogs have changed the landscape of political campaigning and grassroots organizing.

would a recount be managed? Would the outcome be fair? Would the losers view it as fair? Would the average citizen trust the results?

And although new communications tools allow politicians substantially to reduce the amount of legwork and "flesh pressing" required in a typical campaign, the absence of such glad-handing could also destroy the flavor of local politics. Politicians would no longer have to stand in front of supermarkets and kiss babies, but neither would the voters be able to get to know the candidates or to probe into their views on the issues.

The Internet and Free Speech

The rise of the Internet has been faster than society's ability to digest its impact and has overwhelmed our guarantees of free speech. In Europe, for example, hate speech on the Internet is forbidden and carefully regulated; in the United States it is not. As a result, a large number of hate sites register their domains in the United States, where they can operate freely and spew their venom throughout the world without fear of government interference. Americans and others often abuse this freedom—which, for example, allows groups to gather the names and addresses of physicians who perform abortions, post them on anti-abortion Web sites, and urge people to protest against these doctors.

> Media support for the war in Iraq ran high at the time of this May 1, 2003, speech aboard the aircraft carrier USS *Abraham Lincoln* off the California coast. In his remarks, President George W. Bush declared the end of major combat operations in Iraq.

The danger is that some of these activities might lead to acts of violence, including murder. In spring 2005, U.S. District Court judge Joan Humphrey Lefkow returned home from work to find the murdered bodies of her husband and mother in the basement of her home on Chicago's North Side. Their killer, an unemployed electrician, had found Judge Lefkow's name and address posted on several hate Web sites, where readers were encouraged to take justice into their own hands. The day after the murders, Bill White, editor of one of the hate sites, posted his approval: "Everyone associated with the Matt Hale trial [over which Judge Lefkow had presided] has deserved assassination for a long time. I don't feel bad that Judge Lefkow's family was murdered. . . . In fact . . . I laughed."[16]

The availability of cheap worldwide communications technology makes the Internet an ideal tool for terrorists and other haters who hide among the world's 533 million users, including about 133 million Americans. The murder of Judge Lefkow's husband and mother introduced a new dimension to the nation's debate over the limits of free speech. The Internet has allowed extremists to seize on new technologies to spread their messages far more effectively than the soapboxes of earlier days; it also enhances their ability to promote and recruit supporters to their causes.

The United States is wedded to the principle of freedom of speech, refusing to regulate the Internet or any other vehicle of free speech. Throughout the nation's history, speech of all kinds has been protected, with periodic exceptions for sedition in war as well as for child pornography in peacetime. Americans have great tolerance for language and believe that fringe groups can flourish freely in a democracy without risking tears in the fabric of society. But the world has changed since 9/11, and as the threat of terrorism grows, many citizens expect lawmakers to do whatever is necessary—including setting limits on free speech—to curb violence spawned by the prevalence of hate on the Internet.[17]

How the Media Influence Government Policy

There is no doubt that media reporting can have an effect on government policy making, as coverage of the wars in Afghanistan and Iraq shows. In the patriotic cultural climate following September 11, 2001, public confidence in the Bush White House's policy grew as favorable media reporting increased significantly. The media heavily covered the Bush administration's plan

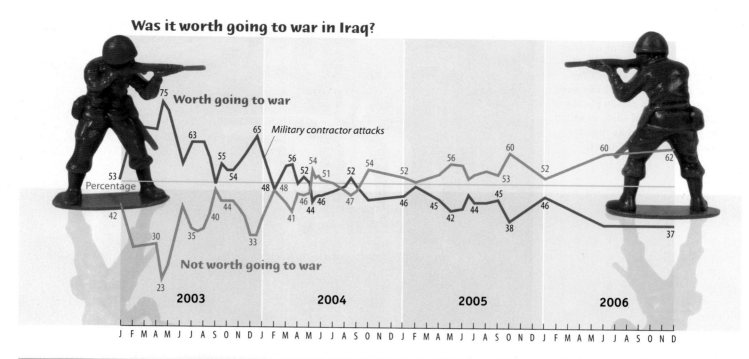

Was it worth going to war in Iraq?

Worth going to war

Military contractor attacks

75 63 55 65 56 54 51 52 54 52 56 60 52 60 62
53 54 48 48 52 46 47 46 46 45 44 45 53 46
Percentage
42 44
40 42 44 38 37
30 35 33 41
23

Not worth going to war

2003   2004   2005   2006

J F M A M J J A S O N D J F M A M J J A S O N D J F M A M J J A S O N D J F M A M J J A S O N D

POLITICAL INQUIRY

FIGURE 10.7 ▪ **What did Americans think in April 2003 about the worth of the United States' going to war with Iraq, according to Gallup polling? How did attitudes change by late 2006, according to updated polling? What main reasons do you think explain the shifts in popular opinion? Was media coverage a factor?**

Source: The Gallup Poll, "Gallup's Pulse of Democracy: Iraq," www.galluppoll.com/content/?ci=1663&pg=1, accessed June 27, 2007.

to invade Afghanistan, with its objective to overthrow the Islamic fundamentalist Taliban regime that was allowing the operation of al-Qaeda terrorist training there and to track down terrorist leader Osama bin Laden. There was also saturated media reporting on the intent to invade Iraq, as the Bush administration claimed that Iraqi president Saddam Hussein's regime was manufacturing weapons of mass destruction.

Initially, media and public support for Bush policy and the military invasions was strong. Figure 10.7 shows that in April 2003, 73 percent of Americans surveyed by the Gallup organization believed it was "worth going to war." On May 1, 2003, the media approvingly covered President Bush's triumphant announcement on the USS *Abraham Lincoln* that "major combat operations had ended," and Americans widely cheered. Clearly, media coverage had cultivated powerful public support for policy initiatives.

If positive media coverage of a policy can create favorable public opinion, can negative coverage create unfavorable opinion? For example, would the 73 percent of people who thought it was worth going to war in Iraq change their minds if media coverage turned negative, or would they hold fast to their views? Figure 10.7 shows the impact that negative media coverage can have on policy. Table 10.2, which tracks responses from 2003 to 2008 to the question of whether the Iraq War was a mistake, further illustrates this downturn in support. Clearly, as the war in Iraq has dragged on, public support has dwindled. Although support has sagged for numerous reasons, including the escalating body count, the war's protracted nature, and the failure to find the weapons of mass destruction that motivated the war, both the graph

TABLE 10.2

Was War in Iraq a Mistake?
In view of the developments since we first sent our troops to Iraq, do you think the United States made a mistake in sending troops to Iraq, or not?

	YES (%)	NO (%)
Sept, 2008	58	41
Apr, 2007	57	41
Apr, 2006	57	42
Apr, 2005	49	48
Apr, 2004	42	57
Mar, 2003	23	75

Source: The Gallup Poll, "Gallup's Pulse of Democracy: Iraq," www.galluppoll.com/content/?ci=1663&pg=1, accessed June 27, 2007.

> In this sobering photo, U.S. soldiers carry the coffin of a soldier killed in Afghanistan. Because of the emotional impact of such images, the Pentagon has banned news photographers from taking photos of flag-draped coffins of soldiers killed in Iraq or Afghanistan as they are returned to the United States.

and the table show that media coverage of one event sparked a significant decline in public support for the war. That event was the spring 2004 attacks on four U.S. military contractors who were killed, mutilated, and burned in Fallujah by a band of Iraqi insurgents.

Media coverage also influences policy making by prioritizing issues for both the public and the government—as does the *absence* of media coverage in some cases. For example, the families of some servicemen and servicewomen in Afghanistan have complained about the comparatively scarce coverage of military events there. They have worried that the lack of a spotlight would leave their loved ones without adequate supplies and equipment to complete their missions. Other families have decried the defense department's policy of banning "arrival ceremonies for, or media coverage of, deceased military personnel returning to or departing from Ramstein [Germany] airbase or Dover [Delaware] base, to include interim stops."[18] Some observers speculate that the dissemination of photos of such rites would have unleashed even stronger negative opinions of Bush military policy. To get around the restrictions, many newspapers, including the *New York Times,* the *Washington Post,* and *USA Today,* have run photo listings of Americans killed in Iraq and Afghanistan.

A Biased Media?

A recent joke about how the media will cover the end of the world stereotyped the nation's major newspapers while also emphasizing their importance in reporting world events. As the story goes, the *New York Times* headline would be: "World Ends; Third World Hit Worst." The *Washington Post*'s front page would blare: "World Ends; Unnamed Source Says White House Had Prior Knowledge." In *USA Today,* a newspaper with a huge national and international circulation, the story would be titled "We're Dead; State-by-State Analysis, page 4D; Sports, page 6C." And the *Wall Street Journal*? "World Ends; Stock Market Goes Down."

Media critics today are everywhere. All of them claim that both print and electronic media exhibit bias in their reporting, in their selection of what issues to cover, and in favoring one side of an issue (or one politician) over another. One of the most common complaints is that the media have an ideological bias.

THE QUESTION OF IDEOLOGICAL BIAS A long-standing complaint is that the media—particularly big-city newspapers—evidence a liberal bias. For example, former House majority leader Tom DeLay (R-Texas) protested the liberal leanings of two of the country's major newspapers, the *New York Times* and the *Washington Post*, for running stories about his ethics problems. Those media, he claimed, ignored the same practices when Democrats such as Nancy Pelosi (D-California), then House minority leader, engaged in them. The day after the *New York Times* published an article revealing that DeLay's congressional campaign had paid his wife and daughter more than $500,000 for their services, DeLay lashed out, stating that the article was "just another seedy attempt by the liberal media to embarrass me."

The notion that the media have a liberal bias is an often-heard criticism. In 1964, former president Dwight D. Eisenhower, in his address to the Republican National Convention, condemned a liberal media bias:

> My friends, we are Republicans. If there is any finer word in the field of partisan politics, I have not heard it. So let us particularly [scorn] the divisive efforts of those outside our family, including sensation-seeking columnists and commentators, who couldn't care less about the good of our party.[19]

Many conservatives point to studies indicating that a majority of newsroom reporters identify themselves as liberal or Democrat. Conservatives charge that the ideological bent of the journalists carries through to the topics covered and to the perspectives of the stories. But studies conducted by various political scientists, including C. Richard Hofstetter, Michael J. Robinson, and Margaret A. Sheehan, refute the idea that journalists' personal viewpoints tinge the content of the news in a liberal way.[20] Indeed, studies suggest that most news stories take the form of a debate, with the journalist presenting the various sides of an issue and leaving the conclusion to the reader's interpretation.

Changes in the nature of the mass media have led to increasingly vocal charges, especially by Democratic elected officials, that newer media outlets, particularly talk radio and the blogosphere, are dominated by conservatives. Among the most vocal critics of the alleged conservative media bias was former Democratic president Bill Clinton. Clinton blamed the media for his troubles over Whitewater—an investment scandal involving shady real estate dealings by Clinton and his wife, Hillary Rodham Clinton—and later for his woes over his affair with White House intern Monica Lewinsky. Hillary Clinton included the press in her ill-considered remarks about the existence of a "vast right-wing conspiracy" that sought to discredit her husband's presidency.

THE PUBLIC'S VIEW ON MEDIA BIAS What does the public think about partisan bias? Figure 10.8 shows that when asked the question "In general, do you think the news media are — ?" (the survey rotated the potential responses: "too liberal," "just about right," and "too conservative"), 45 percent responded that they thought the news media were too liberal. Thirty-five percent said they thought the media were "just about right" ideologically, while nearly 20 percent said they believed the news media were too conservative.

Thus more than half (65 percent) of those surveyed believed that the media are biased (either liberally or conservatively). Yet research by William P. Eveland Jr. and Dhavan V. Shah into people's perception of media bias concluded that it is often linked to whether people have conversations with others whose views differ from theirs. When they do not have such dialogues, they are more likely to believe that the media are biased against their view.[21]

THE ISSUE OF CORPORATE BIAS Most professional journalists hold journalistic objectivity to be important, and that principle well serves the interests of the large corporations that dominate the U.S. media industry today. Within the giant media conglomerates, motivated as they are by the drive for profits, there is strong disincentive for ideological bias on the part of their reporters. Newspapers and television stations rely on advertisers, and advertisers want not only to attract the largest number of readers or viewers but also to avoid offending the largest numbers. Thus, given the corporate nature of today's media, neutrality is generally a guiding principle.

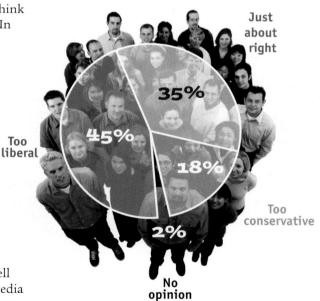

FIGURE 10.8

Public Opinion of Partisan Media Bias

Source: The Gallup Poll, "Media Use and Evaluation," poll administered September 7, 2006. www.gallup.com/content/?ci=1663&pg=1, accessed June 21, 2007.

Critics on the left, however, argue that these corporate structures create their own bias and that this bias has altered what is considered news and how that news is covered.[22] Corporate bias—and the desire to attract, keep, and please an audience—produces skewed programming. Will corporate conglomerates be willing to report on situations that may put themselves and their advertisers in a negative light? How does the drive for profits influence what is in the news? Are viewers being fed "news" that is not particularly newsworthy? There is no doubt that profits influence the media to cover the kinds of stories that viewers and readers want. In particular, violence dominates most local news programming, so much so that the principle of "if it bleeds, it leads" now extends into the first fifteen minutes of many local news broadcasts. Fires; political, sport, and sex scandals; and celebrity-heavy news are also powerful audience attractors.

"Why don't the media report good news?" is an oft-repeated question from those who feel scarred by bad publicity. Are the media biased in favor of the negative? If the sun comes up in the morning, is that news? In fact, although many individuals bemoan the emphasis on the negative, good news typically does not attract the audience that bad news does.

Regulation of the Media: Is It Necessary?

The framers of the Constitution had to be concerned only with print media when they guaranteed freedom of the press—one of the fundamental liberties they ensured in the Bill of Rights. As the media evolved beyond print into electronic formats, so, too, did thinking about the government's role in regulating the media, especially media outlets such as radio and television stations. But technology has outpaced the ability of the government to regulate certain forms of electronic media, including the Internet and satellite radio services such as Sirius and XM. Nonetheless, television and regular radio transmissions are still subject to government regulation.

Control of the Business Side of the Media

Through the independent regulatory agency known as the Federal Communications Commission (FCC), founded in 1934, the government regulates and controls the ownership of radio and television stations. Most of the FCC's rules have concerned ownership, such as the number of outlets a network may own.

> Should telecommunications giants such as Verizon and Comcast be allowed to use their market power to control information flowing over the Internet or to favor certain online clients?

In 1996, Congress passed the Telecommunications Act, which opened the communications markets to telephone companies. This sweeping law allowed competition in the communications industry. It presented new (often confusing) options for consumers, as individual companies began to offer a suite of services, from local and long-distance telephone service, to Internet access, to cable and satellite television.

With the combination of all of these services under single companies, large corporate conglomerates have increasingly gained control of the media. Firms such as Disney, Viacom, News Corporation, and Time Warner exert a powerful influence over what news the average American sees and reads on a given day. The advent of these media titans has given rise to concerns about whether this type of control will deter balanced reporting of the news and unbiased presentations of issues. In addition, public conversations about our democracy are probing into the question of whether the relative lack of competition (because there are so few competitors) means that a valuable check on what the media do and how they do it has been lost.

Congress is currently considering another question of control over the business of the media. The issue, a controversial one, centers on **Net neutrality**: the idea that Internet traffic—e-mail, Web sites, videos, and phone calls—should flow through the Internet pipeline without interference or discrimination by those who own or are running the pipeline (see "The Conversation of Democracy"). *Should* these broadband behemoths be able to use their market power to control information or to favor certain clients online? Critics charge that congressional passage of legislation supporting the service providers would destroy the neutrality and openness of the Internet. Tim Berners-Lee, the inventor of the World Wide Web, says, "The neutral communications medium is essential to our society. . . . It is the basis of democracy, by which a community should decide what to do."[23] Do you agree with Berners-Lee? In what ways would you say that neutral media are the basis of a democracy?

Control of Media Content

To avoid government regulation, the broadcasting industry has established its own code of conduct, although the National Association of Broadcasters' code remains purely voluntary. The Telecommunications Act of 1996, however, did provide for the inclusion of V-chip technology in television sets. The **V-chip,** an electronic chip installed in all TV units thirteen inches or larger in size and made for the U.S. market since January 1, 2000, lets parents block programming they consider unsuitable for children. A further provision of the act, aimed at limiting the transmission of pornographic materials on the Internet so that minors could not access them, was struck down by the courts as an unconstitutional limitation of freedom of speech. Consequently, the broadcast media, as well as Internet sites, have been free to provide whatever content they believe will draw an audience—often to the detriment of civil discourse.

The reflective, respectful citizen debate that once was the media norm is increasingly a thing of the past. It has largely given way to a **primal scream format** featuring the loud, angry argument and commentary that characterize television and radio talk shows today. In an effort to attract listeners and viewers, hosts often push the envelope on what is defined as acceptable speech. One case in point: In 2007, radio talk show host Don Imus incited public and media outrage by using racially insensitive language to describe the Rutgers University women's basketball team. CBS Radio subsequently sacked him. Several weeks later, shock jocks Opus and Anthony netted a thirty-day suspension from XM satellite radio when they and a guest described a fantasy of raping Secretary of State Condoleezza Rice, Queen Elizabeth II, and First Lady Laura Bush.

One problem with such aggressive programming by these radio and television talk shows is that they may turn

Net neutrality
the idea that Internet traffic—e-mail, Web site content, videos, and phone calls—should flow without interference or discrimination by those who own or run the Internet pipeline

V-chip
required by the Telecommunications Act of 1996, a computer chip in television sets that lets parents block programming they consider unsuitable for children

primal scream format
the loud, angry argument characteristic of many television and radio talk shows

> Talk radio hosts often push the envelope on what is defined as acceptable speech. When Don Imus used racially insensitive language to describe the Rutgers University women's basketball team in 2007, his words sparked public outrage. Imus's show was canceled after many sponsors pulled their advertisements. By the end of that year, Imus returned to the airwaves on ABC Radio.

SHOULD CONGRESS REGULATE THE INTERNET INFRASTRUCTURE?

The Issue: The technological revolution has brought ongoing, exponential growth in Internet traffic. As rising numbers of people turn to the Internet for more and more uses—from viewing videos online to sending pictures to Grandma, and from buying gifts and personal items to calling friends and relatives—the volume of information that the broadband infrastructure of the Internet must transmit is becoming overwhelming. The owners of that infrastructure—corporate giants such as AT&T, Verizon, and Comcast—seek legislation that would allow them to charge companies that produce high volumes of traffic. In effect this legislation would set up a two-tiered system of broadband access in which one tier is an "express lane" with tolls, and the other an older, slower lane with free access. One problem is that many of today's services require the faster access to make them effective.

Yes: Congress should regulate the Internet infrastructure. We need a two-tiered system of broadband access. The telecommunications titans in command of the Internet infrastructure argue that in order to keep up with the increasing demand for broadband space, they will have to expand and improve the system continually. Corporate advocates of a two-tiered system of broadband access are also interested in providing premium-quality broadband service to their own clientele. Thus, for example, Verizon wants to ensure that its Internet subscribers (rather than the subscribers of its competitors) have high-quality access to the broadband infrastructure technology that Verizon owns, so that its subscribers do not get caught in an Internet traffic jam.

No: "Fast lane" services are a bad idea, as they would hurt both businesses and consumers. In fact, a broad coalition of businesses and interest groups, including savetheinternet.org, oppose measures that would enable broadband providers to charge for their services. The opposing entities also include firms such as Microsoft, Google, eBay, and Yahoo and powerful citizen organizations such as the American Association of Retired People (AARP). Senator Ron Wyden (D-Oregon) has introduced legislation that would prevent broadband providers from creating for-fee "fast lane" services.

It is the very accessibility of the Internet that has fostered strong business growth. Start-ups such as YouTube and Vonage Internet phone service are examples of ventures that may not have been able to compete and survive in a tiered broadband system. A paying system could also prevent future Internet business development.

Other approaches: Without essential maintenance and expansion, the Internet infrastructure cannot keep up with soaring demand. In addition, the security of the system is crucial to continued business activity and corporate financial growth, as well as to national economic health. Broadband availability is a national security issue because if law enforcers, airports, hospitals, nuclear power plants, and first responders do not have adequate or immediate access to the information they need in order to perform their jobs, human lives are at risk. Because of these critical financial and security implications, a tax or user fee could be instituted that would pay for Internet infrastructure improvements.

What do you think?

① Do you believe that Congress should reject proposals to create a for-fee fast lane for Internet traffic? If so, why? Or do you think the marketplace should determine which services get faster access to broadband lines? If so, why would the latter be preferable?

② What impact would the creation of a two-tiered Internet structure have on Internet business development? On national security?

③ Should the federal government help to defray the costs of improvements to the Internet infrastructure? Why, or why not?

many listeners away from this type of programming in general. The leading television show of this type was CNN's *Crossfire*, in which the liberal Democrat and conservative Republican cohosts fired questions at the guest—a politician, an author, or an activist—who was often interrupted well before he or she could take a breath and offer an opinion or consider the next question. After many years on the air, *Crossfire* was scrapped by CNN, although many others remain in its wake to continue the noisy, uncivil pattern. On PBS's *The McLaughlin Group*, a panel of otherwise serious journalists responds to John McLaughlin, a former priest and Nixon administration official, who throws questions at them; they yell back at him and at each other, appearing not to notice that the level of dialogue continues to sink throughout the course of the show.

The lack of civility in discourse so characteristic of modern media also distorts elections, which the members of the press corps often cover as if they were reporting the Kentucky Derby, complete with winners, losers, and very large stakes. The erosion of dialogue and the devaluation of ideas feed into this process and turn policies that call for careful analysis into horse races, with everything scrutinized from the starting gate to the finish line.

CONCLUSION
CONTINUING THE CONVERSATION

The surge in the number and variety of media outlets—along with the changes in the nature of the media and in people's interactions with them—has affected politics and government in many ways. Once defined as a one-way relationship, the relationship between the media and consumers has evolved in unforeseen ways. Even the nature of the "old media" has changed, although many would ask whether the change has been for the better. On the one hand, narrowcasting and the resulting segmentation of media markets, a central feature of media growth, might raise the comfort level of many people, who no longer have to throw soft objects at their television sets in protest but can instead pick and choose what they watch. On the other hand, media segmentation also limits the exposure of many people to new ideas. Like gated communities, segmented media are also segregated media, detached environments that expose people only to viewpoints with which they agree, thus cordoning them off from society and from many of its problems. Segmented media also confuse genuine political participation with mere ranting. After all, sounding off on a radio talk show is much easier and more entertaining than attending a zoning board meeting to fight urban congestion or becoming civically engaged in other ways.

Technology has created a two-way relationship between the media and consumers, involving the exchange of seemingly limitless information in a vast conversation of democracy. The openness and easy accessibility of the new media have led to considerable criticism of them, but the good news is that almost all public—and to a lesser extent, private—institutions have become much more transparent in recent years. Supreme Court justice Louis Brandeis (1856–1941) once said that sunlight was the best disinfectant, that public scrutiny was the best step toward genuine reform. This two-way relationship has also meant that citizens are afforded greater opportunities to use their public voice to influence government and the policies it creates.

Can we predict the future of the media by examining the past and the present? Certainly we can foretell increasing transparency because of the pervasive nature of today's media and the steady trend in that direction, but we cannot predict the forms media will take. What we can guarantee is continued change in the forms and usage of media, and steadily increasing access to information. Will this expanding access overload people with information? It appears that many of us are developing new skills to cope with the abundance of information, much in the way that our grandparents may have developed the skill of skimming a newspaper, selecting only those stories that mattered to them. The question remains as to whether we will select only information that confirms what we already think. One trend is clear: the ever-increasing volume of information and the speed of its delivery will yield an abundance of both poor-quality and high-quality information.

The modern media have opened the door more widely to citizens' direct participation in the democratic process. In light of Americans' high levels of cynicism about their elected leaders, might this powerful new opportunity to be heard make our democracy more participatory than the Constitution's framers ever intended or imagined? Will the availability of the Internet as a forum for citizens and a tool for organizing lead to a meaningful expansion of participation in civic life and in the conversation of democracy? Will citizens use the new technology productively?

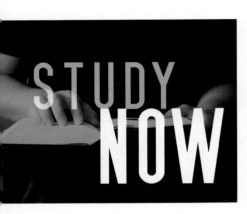

Summary

1. The Political Functions of the Media
The media perform several key political functions, including disseminating information, helping to interpret matters of public interest and to set the national policy agenda, providing a forum for political conversations, and socializing children to the political culture.

2. The Press and Politics: A Historical View
Since early in American history, the press has played a vital role in shaping the political context. As the format of the media has evolved over the centuries, so has media impact on politics and policy making.

3. The Media Go Electronic: The Radio and Television Revolutions
The advent of the electronic media marked a revolutionary change with respect to the impact of media on politics. Television has altered the nature of politics and campaigning, affecting everything from how campaigns for office are conducted to how candidates look and dress. Talk radio, too, has had a significant impact on politics and government by providing a forum for political discourse that is open to participation by virtually everyone.

4. The Media Revolution Continues: The Internet
The Internet has drastically altered the political landscape by making available, in a keystroke, an abundance of information and by serving as a powerful medium for the broad, rapid dissemination of information and opinion. The Internet has changed how political campaigns are conducted, including aspects such as fund-raising, voter mobilization, candidacy announcements, and campaign strategy.

5. How the Media Influence Government Policy
The media exert an impact on government policy making by creating popular support or disapproval for government policies and by covering some public issues but not others. Media coverage of the wars in Afghanistan and Iraq shows this influence and its effect on subsequent policy.

6. A Biased Media?
In considering the question of media bias, we must consider the issues both of content bias and ideological bias. A frequent complaint is that the media—particularly big-city newspapers—have a liberal bias. However, studies by various political scientists conclude that journalists' personal views do not color news content in a liberal way. This research stresses, rather, that most news stories take the form of a debate that presents the various sides of an issue and leaves the conclusion to the reader's interpretation.

7. Regulation of the Media: Is It Necessary?
The Federal Communications Commission is the government agency charged with regulating radio and TV stations and controlling their ownership. The Telecommunications Act of 1996 allowed competition in the communications industry and presented new options for consumers, as individual companies began to offer a suite of services. With the combination

of all of these services under single companies, large corporate conglomerates increasingly have gained control of the media. Thus, in an era of new media technologies, the FCC's job has become more complex.

For Review

1. What functions do the media perform? How have these functions changed over time?

2. Describe the evolution of the press in the United States. How do newspapers today differ from newspapers in earlier centuries?

3. What impact has television had on how people get information? On how political campaigns are waged?

4. How have changes in technology influenced political participation? In particular, what has been the impact of the Internet and blogs?

5. What public policy challenges have arisen with the advent of new technologies?

6. What has been the impact of the media on the political and policy-making processes?

7. What evidence is there to support claims of media bias? Is all bias ideological?

8. In what specific ways does the government regulate media? What aspects of the media and their coverage does the government not regulate?

For Critical Thinking and Discussion

1. Has the Internet changed how you personally participate in politics? Does virtual activism make real-world activism less likely or more likely? Explain.

2. What do you think are the *most important* functions the media perform? Why? Does the diversity of media outlets hinder the media's ability to serve some of their more traditional functions? Explain.

3. Compare and contrast the penny papers of the nineteenth century with today's blogs. What are the similarities and differences between the two? How will blogs evolve given the evolution of other media forms?

4. Discuss the dangers of the unchecked Internet in the political world. Can these dangers be combated? If so, how?

5. What difficulties are associated with government regulation of the media in an era of cable television, the Internet, and satellite radio?

MULTIPLE CHOICE: Choose the lettered item that answers the question correctly.

1. Merging various media forms (newspapers, television stations, radio networks, and blogs) under one roof is called
   a. networking.
   b. convergence.
   c. media relations.
   d. blogosphere.

2. Short audio or video clips taken from a larger speech are called
   a. e-campaigns.
   b. sound bites.
   c. infotainment.
   d. digital snippets.

3. Individuals who simultaneously consume information and news and produce information in forms like videos, blogs, and Web sites are called
   a. bloggers.
   b. net audience.
   c. Web makers.
   d. prosumers.

4. President Franklin Roosevelt's radio addresses to the country were called
   a. great communications.
   b. White House communiqués.
   c. roundtable conversations.
   d. fireside chats.

5. The idea that Internet traffic—e-mails, Web site content, videos, and phone calls—can be transmitted through the Internet pipeline without interference or discrimination by those who own or run the pipeline is called
   a. Net neutrality.
   b. Internet objectivity.
   c. the neutral frontier.
   d. absolute Web domain.

6. The practice of aiming media messages at specific segments of the public is called
   a. limited media.
   b. media messaging.
   c. narrowcasting.
   d. information limitation.

7. The requirement that stations provide equal time to all parties regarding important public issues and equal access to airtime to all candidates for public office is called
   a. Net neutrality.
   b. the limited media.
   c. the fairness doctrine.
   d. information objectivity.

8. The TV computer chip that allows parents to block programming they consider unsuitable for children is the
   a. PG-scope.
   b. PG14-html.
   c. V-chip.
   d. X-chip.

9. The practice of mobilizing voters using the Internet is called
   a. I-rallying.
   b. e-campaigning.
   c. netroots.
   d. Web mobilization.

10. Events or topics that are not serious or broadly important are called
   a. infotainment.
   b. soft news.
   c. media fluff.
   d. softnet.

FILL IN THE BLANKS.

11. Public issues that most demand the attention of government officials are called the _____.

12. A _____ is a video weblog.

13. The journalists who criticized and exposed corruption in government and industry at the turn of the twentieth century were called _____.

14. The requirement that stations provide equal time to all parties regarding important public issues and equal access to airtime for all candidates is called _____.

15. A person who looks good on TV is called _____.

Answers: 1. b, 2. b, 3. d, 4. d, 5. a, 6. c, 7. c, 8. c, 9. b, 10. b, 11. public agenda, 12. vblog, 13. muckrakers, 14. the fairness doctrine, 15. telegenic.

382 **CHAPTER 10** | The Media

RESOURCES FOR RESEARCH AND ACTION

Internet Resources

American Democracy Now Web site
www.mhhe.com/harrison1e Consult the book's Web site for study guides, interactive activities, simulations, and current hotlinks for additional information on the media and politics in the United States.

State of the Media
www.stateofthemedia.org Run by the Project for Excellence in Journalism, this site features an annual report on the media and tracks trends in media usage and confidence in the media.

The Pew Research Center for People and the Press
http://people-press.org This site provides independent research, surveys, data sets, and commentary on the media and issues of media interest.

Media Watch
www.mediawatch.com Visit this site to learn about the initiatives of an activist group that monitors media content and seeks to combat stereotypes and violence in the media.

Recommended Readings

Arnold, R. Douglas. *Congress, the Press, and Political Accountability.* Princeton, NJ: Princeton University Press, 2004. Analyzes how local newspapers cover members of Congress in their districts throughout a legislative session.

Bennett, W. Lance. *News: The Politics of Illusion.* 7th ed. New York: Longman, 2006. Offers a behind-the-scenes tour of the media in politics while grappling with the question, How well does the news, as the core of the national political information system, serve the needs of democracy?

Cavanaugh, John William. *Media Effects on Voters.* Lanham, MD: University Press of America, 1995. Explores how traditional and new media influence voting choices.

Cook, Timothy E. *Governing with the News: The News Media as a Political Institution.* Chicago: University of Chicago Press, 1998. Examines the media as the "fourth branch" of government, including how the media shape public policy and how policy makers respond to the media's agenda setting.

Crouse, Timothy. *The Boys on the Bus.* New York: Random House, 1973. A classic tale of the presidential campaign press corps.

Graber, Doris. *Media Power and Politics.* Washington, DC: CQ Press, 2006. Analyzes the influence of the media on opinions, elections, and policies, as well as efforts to shape the content and impact of media coverage.

Iyengar, Shanto, and Jennifer A. McGrady. *Media Politics: A Citizen's Guide.* New York: W.W. Norton, 2006. Surveys how politicians use the media to get elected, wield power in office, and achieve policy goals.

Jamieson, Kathleen Hall, and Paul Waldman. *The Press Effect: Politicians, Journalists, and the Stories That Shape the Political World.* Oxford: Oxford University Press, 2003. Demonstrates how the national press molds the news through its reporting, using the examples of the 2000 presidential election, the Supreme Court's decision on the Florida vote that year, and the press's response to national politics after 9/11.

Plissner, Martin. *The Control Room: How Television Calls the Shots in Presidential Elections.* New York: Free Press, 1999. Describes the effect of television news and advertising on presidential elections.

Movies of Interest

All the President's Men (1976)
Starring Dustin Hoffman and Robert Redford, this film, based on Bob Woodward and Carl Bernstein's best-selling book of the same title, tells the saga of the two *Washington Post* reporters' investigation of the Watergate scandal that rocked the Nixon White House.

Citizen Kane (1941)
This classic, directed by and starring Orson Welles, is Welles's fictionalized version of newspaper scion William Randolph Hearst, who purportedly attempted to halt release of the film.

Good Night and Good Luck (2005)
Directed by George Clooney, this film tells the story of famed CBS newsman Edward R. Murrow, who takes on Senator Joseph McCarthy and the House Un-American Activities Committee's communist witch hunt during the 1950s despite pressure from corporate sponsors and from McCarthy himself.

Live from Baghdad (2002)
This movie demonstrates the differences in tactics between twenty-four-hour news channels and network news shows, telling the story of CNN's coverage of the U.S. invasion of Iraq in 1990.

Network (1976)
Faye Dunaway, Peter Finch, William Holden, and Robert Duvall star in this classic satirizing the nature of newscasting in the 1970s.

Shattered Glass (2003)
Stephen Glass was a staff writer for the *New Republic* and was also freelancing for other prominent publications when it was discovered that he had fabricated stories. This film depicts his career and his downfall.

Veronica Guerin (2003)
Starring Cate Blanchett, this film is based on the true story of Veronica Guerin, a crime reporter for the *Dublin Sunday Independent,* who was murdered in 1996.

NEW MEDIA AS THE MESSAGE

During Super Bowl broadcasts just days before the Super Tuesday primaries, Barack Obama appeared in a 30-second campaign ad that was unremarkable in its presentation save for three words and a number that appeared midway through the footage of the candidate surrounded by excited crowds. As Obama's long arms reached out to grasp outstretched hands, viewers received an invitation: Text HOPE to 62262.

In an around-the-clock media environment fixated on all things political, Obama has experimented with new tools for communication in a media climate so diffuse that it's difficult for any candidate to shape a message let alone hold it for a few hours. He and his team have exploited the elite media's enthusiasms for the history-making features of his campaign, while also making adroit use of technology to push information to supporters using a network that some describe as "off-line."

The people who sent text messages to the campaign that Sunday were greeted with a request to provide some information about themselves: "Welcome to Obama mobile news and updates. Reply with your ZIP code to get local Obama info."

This 2008 twist on political message delivery seized the power of two communications technologies at once: the ability of television to engage a broad audience using emotion, music, and moving images; and the capacity of text messaging to establish social links that can help transform citizen engagement into political support, one person at a time.

Campaigns understand that the quirky electronic new-media platforms can easily spark coverage or help candidates play defense against rivals. Online news aggregators collect establishment reporting but are willing to be guided by what's popular. Many blogs mix opinion with reporting and analysis. And a handful of cliquish, minutia-obsessed political websites follow hour-by-hour developments in polling, horse race predic-

tions, and he-said/she-said sparring among rival candidates.

YouTube and the social-networking sites Facebook and MySpace did not exist as political forces four years ago, and it's anyone's guess how technology will have altered "news" dissemination and voter persuasion by 2012. It's not ridiculous to imagine computer-generated, three-dimensional hologram "candidates" conversing interactively with individual voters in their living rooms.

Obama's Internet savvy and willingness to spend millions of dollars to forge fast new electronic connections with supporters have helped his campaign to set online fundraising records, and enriched his voter-turnout organizations in key states.

Ari Fleischer, a spokesman for candidate George W. Bush during the 2000 election and later his White House press secretary, said that it's possible to get carried away in the midst of a tight, contested race. "The wonderful thing about all these changes is that you can communicate better and faster, but the enduring factor is that you have to have something to communicate," he cautioned. "You have to connect with the voters on something the voters care about. Substance and character come first, and speed comes second."

Dee Dee Myers, who writes a blog for Vanity Fair and appears as a Democratic political analyst on MSNBC, believes that Obama opponent Hillary Clinton's approach to campaign communications reflects what a twice-successful team was familiar with light-years ago. In the 1990s, the media mix was easier to peg; there was a defined news "cycle" during a 24-hour day; and it was possible to pinpoint the power hitters who controlled political information that influenced voter choices.

"A lot of people who are running Hillary Clinton's campaign came of age during Bill Clinton's campaign, so I think a lot of the approaches that they use, the way they see campaigns and the way they see the world,

were defined 16, 18, 20 years ago," Myers said. "The Obama campaign culture was created in 2007, not in 1992."

Obama has demonstrated his ease with traditional news outlets and electronic media, but he has also shown his willingness to use alternative outlets. For instance, he posted a written defense of his controversial pastor, the Rev. Jeremiah Wright, on The Huffington Post a political website, before responding to the establishment press. Appearing on the Huffington site showed deference to his younger constituents, who do everything on the Web.

The public's online reactions to the Wright videos were part of the blowback that convinced the Obama campaign that an important speech about race was necessary. And the candidate's March address in Philadelphia got heavy replay of its own on YouTube and was "rebroadcast" as text and video on the mainstream media—seemingly enough exposure to blunt the intense news-industry dissection of Wright's most objectionable video excerpts. After Obama's damage-control speech, public opinion polls indicated that he held his ground with voters, with 10 primary contests left on the calendar.

Obama's approach to media and message complements his personality, his "change" agenda, and his young, educated, and tech-savvy upper-income supporters. "Obama and Clinton have different audiences, and if Hillary Clinton were just as smart about using the new media, it wouldn't do her as much good," analyst Kathleen Hall Jamieson suggested, "because it's not her natural audience. It's not as if the new media alone is able to persuade an audience and bring them in."

If Internet prowess and the swooning of young people were what it took to get to the White House, former Vermont Gov. Howard Dean or Rep. Ron Paul of Texas would have done better against their opponents. Even wealthy Mitt Romney, who tapped a documentary filmmaker, Michael Kolowich, to create a "Mitt TV" video channel for his campaign, could not overcome GOP reservations that he was inauthentic and squishy on core conservative issues.

In a blog post titled "Ten Lessons From Mitt TV," written after the former Massachusetts governor withdrew from the race, Kolowich predicted, "What we're learning from the use of tactical Web video in the 2008 presidential campaign will inform and inspire marketing and communications well beyond politics in 2008." But how a campaign can win more votes with clever videos of a flawed candidate, he did not say.

New forms of information-sharing for election purposes via the Internet, talk radio, and entertainment TV go back at least to the early 1990s, a period when the networks' news programming had already shed millions of viewers and candidates were jostling to find alternatives. Bill Clinton famously appeared on MTV and on Arsenio Hall's late-night talk show, while President George H.W. Bush, seeking a second term, resisted such exposure, believing that it was unpresidential.

Sixteen years later, presidential contenders know they need websites to present themselves. Some have turned to the Internet first to announce their candidacies. And in 2008, no leading presidential candidate would dream of rejecting an opportunity to appear before today's voter-rich talk-show audiences.

The latest research by political scientists is inconclusive about whether candidates' use of new-media technologies and approaches can or will deliver new political outcomes. Did voters turn thumbs-down when some presidential candidates thought that it was silly to answer debate questions posed via citizen-created YouTube videos, one of which featured a talking snowman? Can candidates woo new voters with personalized e-mail? With e-mail carrying videos?

Anyone using the Internet can become a game-changer.

Will voters' opinions be shaped more by political attack ads on TV or passed around in cyberspace, or by the truth-squading of those same ads by media organizations?

"The big story of this campaign cycle is citizen-generated media," said Diana Owen, a Georgetown University political scientist. Citizen-generated media can be blogs, video, text, recordings, photos, research, pass-around issue papers, Facebook propaganda, text-messaging—virtually anything. Examples this year include the Yes We Can music video that was done for Obama but not by his campaign, and "Obama Girl," the cheeky, scantily clad young woman who appears on BarelyPolitical.com. Owen cautions, however, that these pass-around messages have not yet been transforming; mainly, they've been additives. "What does it take to move the agenda?" she asked. "At this stage, citizen-generated media still has to make it into the mainstream media."

If the diffusion of information and the individualization of political communication on the Internet enlarges participation in the political process, particularly among the 18-to-29-year-olds who year after year always seem to fall short of the turnout forecasts, that expansion could recast the types of candidates and public policies taking center stage.

Keep in mind that social networking on the Web is almost exclusively an interest of young people: 67 percent of those ages 18 to 29 have used the sites, and 27 percent said they used them to get campaign news, Pew has reported.

"This may be an audience in search of a candidacy," Jamieson said. A media era

of electronic politics and interactive communications could slice through the establishments of both parties. "It may wipe an entire generation out of politics," Jamieson suggested.

Some 42 percent of adults 29 and younger cite the Internet as a regular source of campaign news for the '08 race. For voters 50 and older, the Internet figure is just 15 percent but even that has doubled since 2004. The people in between also made a big leap in tapping political news on the Internet—up from 16 percent in 2004 to 26 percent now.

Because the coverage surrounding the 2008 race has been especially event-sensitive, anyone using the Internet can become a game-changer. "There's the potential for one blogger, one person with a video camera to have a huge impact," said Amy Mitchell, deputy director of the Project for Excellence in Journalism.

One final thought for 2009: How will the next president be tempted to take advantage of today's communications complexities? Will he use social-networking sites to gin up support for a bill in Congress? Will he stop begging reluctant TV networks to open their prime time to East Room speeches—and instead take every word to YouTube's POTUS channel? Obama pledged in January that if he's elected he will throw open the West Wing to C-SPAN to broadcast his negotiations with "all parties" to get health care legislation.

"We can easily put too much attention on the techniques of delivering a message, rather than focusing on the message itself," warned Martha Joynt Kumar, a Towson University scholar who writes extensively about White House communications. In politics, the new media may have become a message. But in governing, the message is still the message.

■ THEN: Presidential campaigns used television as the dominant medium to reach the people.

■ NOW: New media allow candidates to reach different constituencies in differing ways, but candidates and campaigns vary in their effectiveness in using these media.

■ NEXT: How do today's campaign tactics foreshadow new ways campaigns and government will adapt to the new media environment? What impact will citizen-generated media have on voter preferences and turnout in future elections? Will new technology benefit local and state campaigns in the same way it has benefited candidates running in national campaigns?

CHAPTER

11

Congress

THEN

The framers granted to Congress certain explicit powers, as well as key implied powers by which the national government strengthened and broadened its authority.

NOW

A much more demographically diverse Congress exercises wide powers, its decision making influenced by shifting constituencies in a fast-growing, fast-changing country.

NEXT

Will technology significantly affect the ability of "average" citizens to influence Congress?

Will the composition and policy making of Congress more broadly reflect the changing face of the United States?

What pressing new issues will Congress be forced to consider?

Fighting for Military Medical Care

Staff Sgt. John Daniel Shannon, 43, was a reconnaissance and land-navigation expert who led the 2nd Infantry Division's Ghost Recon Platoon. In November 2004, in Ramadi, Iraq, a round of fire from an insurgent's AK-47 blew away Shannon's left eye and part of his skull. The soldier suffered severe brain injuries. Following emergency treatment, Shannon was airlifted to the Walter Reed Army Medical Center in Washington, D.C., where he underwent surgery. | After having recovered from his operation, brain-injured and suffering from post-traumatic stress disorder, Shannon staggered around Reed's hospital grounds in search of his outpatient accommodations. So began a torturous two-year-long journey through a maze of military medical care. Shannon later described his initial ordeal before the House Oversight Committee:

> Upon my discharge, hospital staff gave me a photocopied map of the installation and told me to go to the Mologne House where I would live while in outpatient. I was extremely disoriented and wandered around while looking for someone to direct me to the Mologne House. Eventually, I found it. | I had been given a couple of weeks' appointments and some other paperwork upon leaving Ward 58, and I went to all of my appointments during that time. After these appointments, I sat in my room for another couple of weeks wondering when someone would contact me about my continuing medical care.*

As days turned into weeks of waiting, Shannon grew more and more exasperated. "I thought, 'Shouldn't they contact me? I didn't understand the paperwork.' I'd start calling phone numbers, asking if I had appointments," he explained to *Washington Post* reporters. "I finally ran across someone who said: 'I'm your case manager. Where have you been?' [I said] 'Well, I've been here! Jeez Louise, people, I'm your hospital patient!'"** | In February 2007, *Washington Post* reporters Dana Priest and Anne Hull wrote a series of investigative reports documenting the travails of returned veterans. Their coverage brought to light the bureaucratic nightmare of Sgt. Shannon and vets like him. It was a story of having to deal with military and veterans' health care databases that were not integrated with one another. It was a story of having to complete paperwork for a raft of different agencies—most soldiers are required to submit twenty-two different documents to different command posts in order to receive medical care, the *Post* reported. | The *Post* coverage attracted widespread interest not only from the general public but also from members of Congress. Committee hearings were scheduled for the purposes of getting to the bottom of the problems of returned veterans and creating guidelines for eliminating the bureaucratic snafus. Observed House Oversight chair Representative Bob Filner (D-California), "We have to have a different . . . level of oversight. And the resources that ought to be used for these returning young men and women are just not there. I mean, we spend for the war, but we don't spend for the warrior. We are spending a billion dollars every two-and-a-half days in the war in Iraq. But we have to fight for every disability dollar for some soldier who is mentally scarred. We are just not seeing [sufficient resources] with this administration or the Congress—treating these young men and women who come home is part of the cost of war. And we have got to have those resources. We're going to have tens of thousands coming back from Iraq and Afghanistan, hopefully soon, with physical maiming and mental scars. We have got to have the resources in place, and right now we do not."***

> Staff Sgt. John Daniel Shannon, testifying before the House Oversight Committee.

*Testimony of Staff Sgt. John Daniel Shannon before the Government Reform and Oversight Committee of the U.S. House of Representatives, March 5, 2007, http://oversight.house.gov/documents/20070305110147-84033.pdf.
**Dana Priest and Anne Hull, "Soldiers Face Neglect, Frustration at Army's Top Medical Facility," *Washington Post*, February 18, 2007, p. A01.
***"Congress Responds to Walter Reed Reports," PBS, *Online News Hour*, broadcast February 22, 2007, available at www.pbs.org/newshour/bb/military/jan-june07/walterreed_02-22.html.eq.

The "American Democracy Now"

vignette illuminates the initiative of two talented reporters, and of the brave veterans who came forward to be interviewed, in seeking to fix a veterans' health care system that was badly broken. As concerned citizens, the reporters and their sources hoped that the media coverage would help bring about desperately needed changes in veterans' medical care and significantly improve the quality of life for returning soldiers and Marines. But beyond the personal stories of heroic veterans and the documentation of a crippled military medical bureaucracy, the vignette also illustrates the nature of Congress, the legislative branch of the national government.

First and foremost, Congress is an institution shaped by the people elected to serve there, men and women acting as the trusted representatives of the constituents who voted them into office. Congress and the policies it sets are molded by the times; laws passed in one generation may seem antiquated to the next. And Congress and the policies it creates are influenced by a wide variety of other factors, including the legislative body's institutional history, the lawmaking process, and the internal and external actors—congressional leaders, political parties, interest groups, the president, staff members, ordinary citizens, and the media, who seek to influence congressional actions.

The Constitution's framers structured the government so that Congress—more so than the two other institutions of the federal government—would be responsive to the needs and will of the people. In representing their constituents, members of Congress provide an easily accessed point of contact for people to connect with their government and to have their voices heard.

Citizens today have countless opportunities to participate in shaping Congress's agenda and influencing how the members of Congress vote. Individuals and groups of constituents communicate by e-mail, the Internet, and telephone and meet face-to-face with members of Congress on issues that concern them. Constituents meet with congressional staff members for help in understanding how to deal with government bureaucracy. Through congressional campaigns and elections, citizens learn about issues of national importance and can participate in a variety of ways, such as volunteering in support of a candidate's run for office, contributing to the individual's campaign, becoming informed about the candidates and issues, and casting a ballot on Election Day.

Throughout this chapter, we view Congress through the lens of civic engagement, seeing that Congress—the people's branch of the federal government—while imperfect, is structured to empower citizens to play a role in determining public policy priorities. And ultimately it is the people, through their choices at the ballot box, who decide who the creators of those policies will be.

This chapter provides a foundation for your study of Congress.

FIRST, we examine *the origins of Congress.*

SECOND, we explore the process of *congressional elections.*

THIRD, we consider the *powers of Congress.*

FOURTH, we survey the *functions of Congress,* including representation, policy making, oversight, agenda setting and civic engagement, and management of societal conflict.

FIFTH, we take stock of the similarities and differences between the two chambers of the national legislature as we look at *the House and the Senate compared.*

SIXTH, we focus on how a bill becomes a law by examining *the legislative process.*

SEVENTH, we analyze how the *congressional leadership* affects the legislature's ability to perform its functions.

EIGHTH, we consider *decision making in Congress,* with a particular eye to *the legislative context.*

NINTH, we examine the similarities and differences between *the people and their elected representatives.*

The Origins of Congress

For the United States' founders, creating the national Congress was a crucially important task. Fearful of a powerful executive, but having endured the problems stemming from the weak national government under the Articles of Confederation, the framers of the Constitution believed that the legislature should be the key branch of the newly formed national

GLOBAL COMPARISONS

JAPAN'S NATIONAL DIET, 国会

✳Should the U.S. House of Representatives have the ultimate decision-making power in the event of policy disagreements, like the Japanese Shūgiin?

Much like the United States, Japan has a bicameral legislature. The Japanese call this body the *Kokkai,* or National Diet. Japan's post–World War II constitution created the current legislative structure, which eliminated the power held by the emperor in the previous constitution and granted the legislature the exclusive power to create laws. It also bestowed on the legislature the power to select the country's prime minister.

Japan's lower house, like that of the United States, is the House of Representatives (*Shūgiin*), which has 480 members. Of these members, 300 are elected in district elections, in which the candidate with the most votes wins the seat. The remaining 180 seats are elected in a proportional representation system, in which candidates in eleven separate blocs are elected in proportion to the percentage of the votes their party receives.

Japan's upper house, the House of Councilors (*Sangiin*), is the equivalent of the U.S. Senate. Of its 242 members, 146 are elected from districts through a single nontransferable vote system. This means that each voter (in Japan the voting age is 20) may cast a vote for only one candidate and that candidates cannot transfer extra votes to other members of their party, but the top several candidates with a plurality of votes win. The other 96 members of the Senate are elected in a proportional representation system, in which rank-ordered candidates are awarded seats based on the percentage of the vote their party receives in national balloting.

If the *Sangiin* and the *Shūgiin* disagree on policy matters such as the ratification of treaties, the national budget, and the designation of the prime minister, the Japanese Constitution grants the ultimate decision-making power to the House of Representatives, the *Shūgiin*. But outside those policy matters, the *Shūgiin* needs a two-thirds majority vote to override action taken by the House of Councilors, or *Sangiin*.

government. In their vision, the Congress would be the institution responsible for making laws that would create effective public policy. In structuring the Congress, the framers strove to create a legislative branch that was at once powerful enough to govern and to check the power of the president and yet not so powerful that the legislature itself would exercise tyrannical rule. (See "Global Comparisons" for an example of how a different constitution structured Japan's legislature.)

As they debated the shape of the Congress, the Constitution's framers had to balance the desires of representation of two opposing groups. The Constitution created a bicameral, or two-house, legislature in which one house, the House of Representatives, would be based on population, and the other chamber, the Senate, would be based on state representation.[1] The constitutionally specified duties of each house of Congress reflect the framers' views of the essential nature of the two chambers and the people who would serve in them.

The House of Representatives, with the smallest constituencies of any federal office (currently about 647,000 people reside in each congressional district), is the chamber closer to the people. As such, the framers intended the House to closely represent the people's views. The Constitution thus requires, for example, that all revenue bills (bills that would create taxes) must originate in the House of Representatives. In the framers' eyes, unwarranted taxation was an egregious offense. By placing the power to tax in the hands of the members of the House of Representatives—the officials who face more frequent federal elections—the framers sought to avoid the types of unpopular, unfair taxes that had sparked the American Revolution. A short electoral cycle, they reasoned, would allow disfavored politicians to be voted out of office. Like all other bills, revenue bills must be passed in identical form by both the House and the Senate to become law, but requiring revenue bills to originate in the House reflected a victory by the large states at the Constitutional Convention (smaller states wanted taxation power to reside with the Senate).

Although the framers viewed the House as the "people's chamber," they conceived the Senate to be a more elite, more deliberative institution, one not subject to the whims of mass politics like its lower-house counterpart. Today the Senate remains a more deliberative body than the House. This quality is made possible by the Senate's smaller size and the less frenetic electoral schedule of its members, who face elections less frequently than House representatives. In addition, because of the specific constitutional duties mandated to the upper house, particularly the requirement that treaties must be ratified in the Senate, many U.S. senators have specialized in U.S. foreign policy issues. (See "The House and the Senate Compared" later in this chapter for further discussion of House-Senate differences.)

The framers' vision was to structure the Congress to embody republican principles, ensuring that in its central policy-making responsibilities, the national legislature would be responsive to the needs and will of the people. Both historically and continuing in the present day, civically engaged citizens have exerted a strong influence on the outcome of the policy-making process. One important avenue by which individuals influence Congress and its acts is through congressional elections, a topic we now consider.

Congressional Elections

The timetable for congressional elections reflects the framers' views of the differing nature of the House of Representatives and the Senate. House members, as public servants in the legislative body that the framers conceived as closer to the people, are elected every two years, in even-numbered years (2008, 2010, and so on). But the framers also sought to check the power of the people, who they believed could be irrational and unruly, and so members of the Senate originally were chosen by state legislators. Ratification of the Seventeenth Amendment to the Constitution in 1913 shifted the election of senators to popular election within the states. Senators serve six-year terms, which are staggered so that one-third of the Senate is elected every two years. Thus in any given congressional election year, thirty-three or thirty-four members of the Senate are up for election. Usually, the two senators from a given state will not be elected in the same cycle, unless the death or resignation of a sitting senator requires a special election. As we saw in Chapter 2, the Constitution requires the number of seats in the House of Representatives awarded to each state be based on that state's population and that each state has two U.S. senators. On average, a successful campaign for a seat in the House of Representatives cost about $966,000 in 2006. This is a veritable bargain compared to the price tag for a successful bid for the U.S. Senate, which averaged about $7.8 million that year. Compare this to the annual salary of $165,200 that rank and file members of the House and Senate collect.

Incumbency

The status of already holding office—known as incumbency—strongly influences a candidate's ability to raise money and is probably the most important single factor in determining success in a congressional campaign. Indeed, in any

Favorability Ratings of Congress

How would you rate the overall performance of Congress today?

☐ Favorably

☐ Unfavorably

☐ Neither favorably nor unfavorably

Source: "Democratic Party's Favorables Rise, Congress Still Unpopular," http://people-press .org/reports/display.php3?ReportID=426.

>A testimony to the power of incumbency: Representative Charles Rangel (D-New York), who has served in Congress for nearly forty years, waves to the crowds as he rides along New York City's Fifth Avenue in the 2007 National Puerto Rican Day parade.

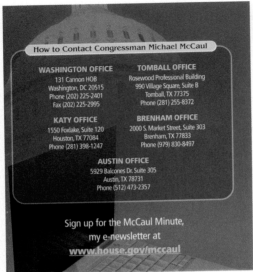

> A piece of franked mail from a congressional office. Note the signature of the sending member of Congress, which serves as a postage stamp.

reapportionment
reallocation of seats in the House of Representatives to each state based on changes in the state's population since the last census

redistricting
redrawing of congressional district boundaries within each state, based on the reapportionment from the census

gerrymandering
the drawing of legislative district boundaries to benefit an incumbent, a political party, or another group

majority-minority district
a legislative district composed of a majority of a given minority community—say, African Americans—the intent of which is to make it likely that a member of that minority will be elected to Congress

election year, about 95 percent of incumbent members of the House of Representatives running for reelection win, and about 88 percent of their Senate counterparts do. These outcomes may indicate what *individual* members of Congress are doing right: representing their own constituencies effectively, engaging with their constituents, and listening to and addressing their needs. But voters typically think about Congress in terms of *a whole*, rather than individuals, viewing it as a body that is overwhelmingly composed of "other people's" representatives, who do not reflect their views.[2] Thus the voting public frequently attacks Congress as a collective entity.

Why do incumbents so often win reelection? Several factors make it more likely that someone already in office will be returned to that office in a reelection bid:

- **Stronger name recognition.** Having run for election before and served in government, incumbents tend to be better known than challengers.
- **Easier access to media coverage.** Media outlets routinely publicize the activities of elected congressional officials, rationalizing that they are covering the institution of Congress rather than the individuals. Nonincumbent challengers face an uphill battle in trying to get coverage of their campaigns.
- **Franking.** The privilege of sending mail free of charge is known as *franking.* Federal law allows members of Congress free mailings to every household in their state or congressional district. These mailings make it easy for members of Congress to stay in touch with their constituencies throughout their tenure in office.
- **Campaign contributions.** Political action committees and individuals are interested in supporting candidates who will be in a position to help them once the election is over. Because donors are aware of the high reelection rates of incumbent candidates, incumbents garner an enormous proportion of contributions, sometimes as much as 80 percent in any given congressional election year.
- **Casework.** When an incumbent personally helps constituents solve problems with the federal bureaucracy, the resulting loyalty and good-word-of-mouth reputation helps to attract support for that candidate during a run for reelection.

Thus, incumbency is a powerful obstacle for outsiders who seek to unseat an elected member of Congress. Despite the incumbency advantage, in each congressional election, many individuals challenge incumbent members of Congress, often doing so knowing that the odds are stacked against them but believing in giving voters a ballot choice. Others run because they seek to bring attention to a particular issue or to shape the policy agenda—or sometimes because they simply underestimate the power of incumbency.

Reapportionment and Redistricting

Sometimes the advantages of incumbency can be diminished, as in election years after reapportionment and redistricting. **Reapportionment** is the reallocation of seats in the House of Representatives on the basis of changes in a state's population since the last census. Every ten years, in the year ending in zero (2000, 2010, and so on), the federal government counts the number of people in the country as a whole. If the census indicates that a state's population has changed significantly, that state may gain or lose seats in the House of Representatives. **Redistricting,** the redrawing of congressional district boundaries within a state, is based on the reapportionment from the census.

>The term *gerrymander* originated from this Gilbert Stuart cartoon of a Massachusetts electoral district. To Stuart, the district looked like a salamander. A friend christened it a "Gerry-mander," after Massachusetts governor Elbridge Gerry, a signer of the Declaration of Independence and the politician who approved redrawing district lines for political advantage.

What point does this famous historical cartoon of 1812, representing Massachusetts legislative districts, make about the nature of a gerrymander? What do people today mean when they talk about gerrymandering? What are your own views on the practice?

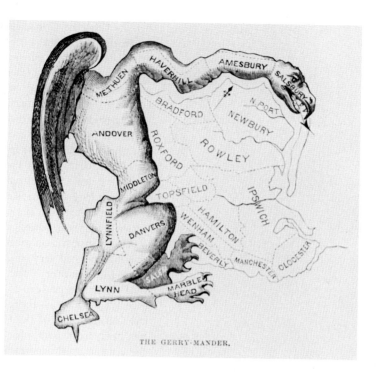

THE GERRY-MANDER.

Because the composition of a given congressional district can change as a result of reapportionment and redistricting, this process can mitigate the impact of incumbency. Frequently the greatest shifts in the composition of the House of Representatives occur in election years ending in 2 (2002, 2012, and so on), when the first elections take place that incorporate the changes from reapportionment and redistricting. As a result of reapportionment in 2002, for example, New York and Pennsylvania each lost two House seats. Five states in the Midwest lost one House seat each, while several states in the South and Southwest gained seats. When a state loses a seat, the result is that an incumbent member of Congress is likely to lose a seat. When a state gains a seat, a new member of Congress can be elected to the open seat.

In some states, the goal of congressional redistricting is to protect House incumbents. The redrawing of congressional boundaries for the purpose of political advantage is a form of **gerrymandering,** the practice of drawing legislative district boundaries to benefit an incumbent, a political party, or some other group. The term was coined in reference to Massachusetts governor Elbridge Gerry after a district shaped like a salamander was created to favor his party in 1811. The illustration shows the first gerrymander.

Most forms of gerrymandering are legal. The U.S. Supreme Court ruled in 1986 that a gerrymandering plan is unconstitutional only when it eliminates the minority party's influence statewide.[3] Because of the strict standards, only one partisan gerrymandering plan filed after the 1990 census was successfully challenged.

State legislatures have attempted to address the issue of racial imbalance in the House of Representatives by constructing a kind of gerrymander called a majority-minority district. A **majority-minority district** is composed of a majority of a given minority community—say, African Americans—and the creators' intent is to make it likely that a member of that minority will be elected to Congress. The Supreme Court has ruled that such racial gerrymandering is illegal unless the state legislature redrawing the district lines creates majority and minority districts at the expense of other redistricting concerns. Typically these concerns include preserving the geographic continuity of districts, keeping communities within one legislative district, and reelecting incumbents.

Powers of Congress

The primary source of congressional authority is the U.S. Constitution. As shown in Table 11.1, the Constitution enumerates to Congress a number of different powers. The nature of these responsibilities

TABLE 11.1

Enumerated Powers of the Congress

JUDICIAL POWERS
Establish the federal court system

Punish counterfeiters

Punish illegal acts on the high seas

ECONOMIC POWERS
Impose taxes

Establish import tariffs

Borrow money

Regulate interstate commerce

Coin and print money, determine the value of currency

NATIONAL SECURITY POWERS
Declare war

Raise and regulate national armed forces

Call up and regulate state national guard

Suppress insurrections

Repel invasions

REGULATORY POWERS
Establish standards of weights and measures

Regulate copyrights and patents

ADMINISTRATIVE POWERS
Establish procedures for naturalizing citizens

Establish post offices

Govern the District of Columbia

reveals that the Constitution is both very specific in describing congressional powers (as in punishing illegal acts on the high seas) and at the same time quite vague (as in its language establishing the federal court system). Many of the specific duties of Congress reflect Americans' bitter experience in the colonial era, in that the framers granted powers to Congress that they did not want to place in the hands of a strong executive. For example, the economic powers granted to Congress, including the ability to tax and spend, to establish tariffs, and to borrow money, all limit the power of the president.

Powers specifically granted to Congress still have a distinct impact on our everyday lives. For example, Congress regulates currency, establishes weights and measures, and administers post offices. As we have seen, the connection between Congress, particularly the House, and the people was crucial to the framers, and so the Constitution requires that all taxation and spending measures originate in the House because the framers believed this chamber would be nearest to the people—and that House members would therefore ensure that the people's will was done.

The Constitution moreover imbues the Congress with an additional source of power, one that has proved very important in the expansion of legislative authority over time. As discussed in Chapter 2, the necessary and proper—or elastic—clause states that the Congress shall have the power to "make all Laws which shall be necessary and proper for carrying into Execution the foregoing powers, and all other Powers vested by this Constitution in the Government of the United States, or in a Department or Officer thereof." This clause has been responsible for Congress's ability to legislate in many matters not described in the enumerated powers. Deciding whether oil companies should be allowed to drill for oil in the Arctic National Wildlife Refuge, determining the powers of law enforcement in investigating terrorism, and regulating stem cell research are all examples of powers not enumerated in the Constitution but that Congress exercises because of the broad scope of authority provided by the necessary and proper clause.

In addition to the Constitution, Congress derives power from Supreme Court decisions, the media, and the people. Supreme Court decisions often uphold the constitutionality of a law, in a sense verifying Congress's ability to create policy on a given subject. The media grant Congress power by providing members with a forum in which to communicate with constituents, sway public opinion, and create a favorable climate for the passage of legislation. The people are a key source of congressional power through civic participation in the electoral and legislative processes. Citizens communicate their views and priorities to their representatives, who then can claim public support in their endeavors to enact policy.

> The Constitution says nothing about the power of Congress to create policy concerning issues like stem cell research, but because of the Constitution's elastic clause, Congress has exerted broad authority over a wide range of policy issues.

Functions of Congress

The Constitution is far more explicit in defining the responsibilities of the national legislature than it is in describing the function of the other branches of the government.[4] In its shaping of congressional functions, the Constitution's concerns with limited government, checks and balances, the separation of powers, and the creation of a federal system are all readily apparent.

Representation Comes in Many Forms

In delineating the composition of the federal legislature and the procedures for electing its members, the Constitution shapes the congressional function of representation in several ways. Representation traditionally involves a House or Senate member's articulating and voting for the position that best represents the views of his or her constituents.[5] But sometimes a member of Congress may speak for other constituencies as well. For example, a feminist legislator might "represent" feminists nationwide,[6] just as a gay legislator might "represent" the collective interests of gays across the United States.

Often Congress's policy-making function is at odds with its representation function. A legislator may be pressured—by his or her political party or own conscience—to vote for a policy that clashes with constituents' interests or views. In representing constituents, legislators frequently follow one of two models of representative behavior.

MODELS OF REPRESENTATION According to the **trustee model** of representation, a member of the House or the Senate is articulating and voting for the position that best reflects constituents' views. This model was espoused by British political theorist Edmund Burke (1729–1797), who served in Parliament as a representative of Bristol, England. Explaining his conception of representation, Burke emphasized to his constituents, however, that a member of Parliament "is not a member of Bristol, he is a member of Parliament."[7] Burke accordingly argued that a member of Parliament should follow his conscience when making decisions in the legislature: "Your representative owes you, not his industry only, but his judgement [sic]; and he betrays, instead of serving you, if he sacrifices it to your opinion."[8] In this trustee view, a legislator may act in opposition to the clear wishes of his or her constituents, such as in cases where an action is "for their own good" or the good of society.

Such was the case in 1993 when Representative Marjorie Margolies-Mezvinsky, a freshman Democratic legislator from a predominantly Republican district in Pennsylvania, voted with her party for a series of tax hikes proposed by the Bill Clinton administration. Margolies-Mezvinsky, who had been elected on Clinton's coattails with a large number of other women legislators, recognized that the vote could damage her political career, as did Republicans in the House who waved white handkerchiefs and chanted, "Bye-bye, Margie, bye-bye!" during the House vote. Many constituents did in fact resent what they perceived as a rejection of their views on the tax proposals, which were unpopular in Margolies-Mezvinsky's district. When she sought reelection in 1994, she lost her House seat.

Another model of representation is the **instructed delegate model,** the idea that a legislator, as a representative of his or her constituents, should vote in keeping with the constituents' views, *even if those views contradict the legislator's personal views*. This model of representation conceives of legislators as the agents of their constituents. A legislator hewing to the instructed delegate model faces a dilemma when his or her constituency is evenly divided on an issue.

Given these two different models of representation, which one do legislators typically follow? Most analyses of representation indicate that legislators are likely to combine the approaches. Specifically, with regard to many important or high-profile issues, legislators act as instructed delegates, whereas for more mundane matters about which their constituents are less likely to be aware or to hold a strong position, they rely on the trustee model.

PORK BARREL AND EARMARKS Members of Congress also represent their constituencies through pork barrel politics. **Pork barrel** (also called simply *pork*) refers to legislators' appropriations of funds for special projects located within their congressional district. Because pork brings money and jobs to a particular district, reelection-seeking legislators work aggressively to earmark monies for their states or districts—to "bring home the bacon."[9] Members frequently use transportation bills as a means of creating pork barrel projects for their districts. One analysis estimates, for example, that every $1 billion spent on highway and mass transit projects creates about 47,500 jobs, and members of Congress are happy to take credit for the jobs and for highway and mass transit improvements when running for reelection.[10]

trustee model
a model of representation in which a member of the House or Senate should articulate and vote for the position that best represents the views of constituents

instructed delegate model
a model of representation in which legislators, as representatives of their constituents, should vote in keeping with the constituents' views, even if those views contradict the legislator's personal views

>Representative Marjorie Margolies-Mezvinsky (left, D-Pennsylvania), elected to the House of Representatives in 1992, lost her bid for reelection in 1994 because of the unpopularity of her votes for tax increases. Should Margolies-Mezvinsky have followed the instructed delegate model rather than the trustee model of representation?

pork barrel
legislators' appropriations of funds for special projects located within their congressional district

> The politics of pork: a representative from Alaska attempted to secure $223 million in funding to construct a bridge that would connect the remote Gravina Island (left) with the town of Ketchikan. Because of vocal public opposition, the earmarks were removed from the budget.

earmark
a designation within a spending bill that provides for a specific expenditure

casework
personal work by a member of Congress on behalf of a constituent or group of constituents, typically aimed at getting the government to do something the constituent wants done

ombudsperson
a role in which an elected or appointed leader acts as an advocate for citizens by listening to and investigating complaints against a government agency

Members of Congress also use **earmarks** as a means of representing constituent interests: a designation within a spending bill that provides for a specific expenditure. A striking example of both pork barrel politics and an earmark is the infamous Bridge to Nowhere in Ketchikan, Alaska, a city with 8,000 residents but a large tourist industry. City leaders want to make the land of nearby Gravina Island (currently accessible via a seven-minute ferry ride) available for development by constructing a huge bridge that would allow tourist-carrying cruise ships to pass under. Ketchikan officials had an ally in Representative Don Young (R-Alaska), chair of the House Committee on Transportation and Infrastructure, who earmarked $223 million as a federal contribution to the bridge in a federal highway and mass transit bill, the Transportation Equity Act. Steve Ellis, of the taxpayer watchdog group Taxpayers for Common Sense, called the project "an abomination."[11] A thunderous public uproar followed media coverage of the appropriation, and the earmark was removed from the budget. But Young succeeded in keeping the allocation, so the state of Alaska could still choose to spend the money on the bridge project. The issue became a lightning rod in the 2008 presidential race when critics alleged that as governor of Alaska, Republican vice presidential nominee Sarah Palin had supported the project before reversing her position.

CASEWORK   A special form of representation called **casework** refers to providing representation in the form of personal aid to a constituent or group of constituents, typically by getting the government to do something the constituent wants done (see "On the Job"). Members of Congress and their staffs commonly assist constituents in dealing with bureaucratic agencies. In doing so, they serve in the capacity of an **ombudsperson,** an elected or appointed representative who acts as a citizens' advocate by listening to their needs and investigating their complaints with respect to a particular government agency. For example, a member of Congress might intervene with the Immigration and Naturalization Service (INS) to request that a constituent's relative in a foreign country be granted a visa to travel to the United States.

According to political scientist Morris Fiorina, casework is a valuable tool for legislators. Fiorina points out that servicing constituents is relatively easy for members of Congress, because bureaucrats—who depend on Congress for their funding—typically respond quickly to the requests of legislators.[12] The loyalty derived from assisting constituents is one aspect of the incumbency advantage that makes incumbent members of Congress more likely to be elected than their challengers, who do not enjoy that source of constituent loyalty.

Casework benefits constituents when, for example, a member of Congress's staff works with a local branch of a Veterans' Administration clinic to secure services for a retired veteran, whose family members derive a sense of efficacy—a feeling that they can get things done and that the government works for people like them. They perceive that their individual member of Congress genuinely represents them and protects their interests, with the result that these constituents not only feel engaged but also are likely to advocate for their member's reelection bid.

But casework is not without its costs, as noted by Walter F. Mondale. Mondale, who served as a member of both the House and the Senate, as well as vice president of the United States, warns that casework can take a legislator's time away from his or her legislative responsibilities:

> Good constituent service is, of course, necessary—and honorable—work for any member of Congress and his [sic] staff. Citizens must have somewhere to turn for help when they become victims of government bureaucracy. But constituent service can also be a bottomless pit. The danger is that a member of Congress will end up as little more than an ombudsman between citizens and government agencies. As important as this work is, it takes precious time away from Congress' central responsibilities as both a deliberative and a law-making body.[13]

In describing the constituent service dilemma, Mondale raises questions worthy of citizens' reflection. For example: Is the national interest served when a congressional staff member has to track down your grandma's Social Security check? Does doing so result in a missed opportunity for government officials to create policy with broad, significant implications?

ON THE JOB

THOMAS LAMBERT, CONGRESSIONAL INTERN

Name: Thomas Lambert

Age: 21

Hometown: Fairfield, Connecticut

College: Pepperdine University, Malibu, California

Major: Political Science

Job title: Intern, Office of Congressman Christopher Shays (R-Connecticut), Washington, D.C.

Salary range for jobs like this: $0–$17,000

Day-to-day responsibilities: Each day I avail myself to members of the staff who need high-priority special projects completed in a timely fashion. These include deliveries to other offices, attendance at briefings on certain subjects that members of the staff cannot attend, and research on topics relevant to upcoming legislation. I also answer calls from constituents in our district, sort mail and faxes, give tours of the U.S. Capitol, and maintain parts of the congressman's Web site.

How did you get your job? Pepperdine has a strong Washington, D.C., internship program. I pursued this opportunity and, considering my major and my interests, applied to work for my local congressman, Republican representative Christopher Shays. After going through the application process, I was notified via e-mail that I had the internship. I have prior experience working on home-state campaigns for local politicians and for one semester interned in Hartford, Connecticut, at the state Capitol; so working in Washington was always the next logical step.

What do you like best about your job? The best part is knowing that the work I do in Washington is positively and directly affecting my neighbors and members of my community. Each day, I talk to constituents, and I know my job influences the workings of my hometown, county, and state. When I go home, reflect on my day, and know for a fact that what I and others in my office did improved my community, I feel a tremendous sense of fulfillment.

What is your least favorite aspect of your job? You have to have incredibly thick skin to work in a legislative office, especially as an intern who is on the front line of calls and visitors. While many are grateful for the work we do, it is not uncommon to get an irate constituent call with a rant about the congressman's position on an issue. The worst is when the rage is directed toward the intern, but I know it just comes with the territory.

What advice would you give to students who would like to do what you are doing? Go for it! Interning on Capitol Hill is a lot different from college, and the city demands much of its workers, but the experience adds a whole new dimension to one's education. There is nothing like living the real thing, and elements of my job add a component to my overall education I could never learn from just reading a textbook. I feel infinitely more prepared for the working world as a result of my internship.

And is the use of congressional staff members as ombudspeople a prudent application of taxpayers' money?

Policy Making: A Central Responsibility

Each year Congress passes laws determining everything from incentives for the creation of alternative energy sources, to what restrictions should govern gun purchases, to what law enforcers can do when they suspect someone of being a terrorist. The Constitution invests Congress with other policy-making powers as well, including the authority to tax and spend, to declare war, to establish courts, and to regulate the armed forces. This policy-making function is the central responsibility that the Congress carries out, and nearly all of its other functions are related to its policy-making role. Congressional policy-making power also extends to the operations and priorities of governmental departments and agencies. For example, Congress has directed the State Department to select a domestic secure production facility to create ePassports, next-generation passports with an embedded microchip.

Oversight: A Check on the Executive Branch

One of Congress's significant functions is described in this chapter's opening vignette, in which returning service members testified before the House Oversight Committee regarding their difficulties in securing quality health care. In creating a system of checks and balances in the Constitution, the framers established the key congressional function of oversight.[14] **Oversight** is the process by which Congress "checks" the executive branch to ensure that the laws Congress passes are being administered in keeping with legislators' intentions. Congressional oversight is a check on the executive branch because the federal bureaucracy that implements laws is part of the executive branch.

In carrying out their oversight function, members of Congress use a variety of tools, some of which are listed here:

oversight
the process by which the legislative branch "checks" the executive branch to ensure that the laws Congress has passed are being administered in keeping with legislators' intent

- congressional hearings, in which government officials, bureaucrats, and interest groups testify as to how a law or policy is being implemented and examine the impact of its implementation;
- confirmation hearings on presidential appointees to oversee executive departments or governmental agencies;
- investigations to determine whether a law or policy is being implemented the way Congress intended it to be, and inquiries into allegations of wrongdoing by government officials or bureaucrats;
- budgetary appropriations that determine the level of funding of an executive department or a government agency.

agenda setting
determination by Congress of which public issues the government should consider for legislation

These tools ensure that Congress has some say in how the executive branch administers the laws that Congress creates. Members of Congress increasingly have viewed their role of checking the executive branch as crucially important.

Agenda Setting and Civic Engagement

Congress engages continuously in **agenda setting**: determining which public policy issues the federal legislature should consider.[15] Indeed, political scientists such as Cox and McCubbins assert that agenda setting relieves the pressure parties face in getting their members to vote with the party.[16] At the beginning of a congressional term, House and Senate leaders announce their goals for the coming session. These goals reflect the issues and positions that predominated during the electoral campaign and that congressional leaders perceive to represent the people's priorities.

In setting the national agenda, Congress serves as a key agent in molding the scope of civic engagement and discourse, as people learn about, discuss, and form positions about issues. Frequently, agenda setting is itself influenced by public discourse, as when constituents complain to a member of Congress about a problem that needs to be solved or when an interest group contacts a legislator about a policy its membership would like to see implemented. When enough members (or one very influential member) of an interest group press for a particular action, legislators in Congress might introduce a bill concerning the issue or conduct a hearing to investigate it.

Concept Summary

FUNCTIONS OF CONGRESS

Representation

— In representing the needs and views of their constituents, members of Congress sometimes act as trustees, as instructed delegates, or as a combination of the two roles.

Policy Making

— Policy making is a key responsibility of Congress, and many of its other functions are related to its policy-making authority.

Oversight

— Through oversight, Congress "checks" the executive branch to ensure that laws are being administered in keeping with legislators' intentions.

Agenda Setting and Civic Engagement

— Congress continuously focuses on agenda setting— that is, determining which public policy issues the federal legislature should consider.

Managing Societal Conflict

— Through compromise, Congress mediates the conflict inherent in a society with diverse people.

There are many ways by which people can become educated about Congress in the course of its day-to-day business. At any given time, you can learn about the issues currently on the congressional agenda on C-SPAN, a twenty-four-hour cable news service that broadcasts congressional hearings and roll call votes. Through C-SPAN and other media coverage, you can hear about the issues that are being debated and various legislators' stands on them. Whenever a big issue has been on the agenda—such as committee hearings on the renewal of the USA PATRIOT Act, acceptable tactics for interrogating enemy detainees, the Senate Judiciary hearings on Supreme Court confirmations, and even President Clinton's impeachment hearings—Congress has asked questions, provided opinions, and conducted investigations that further the people's civic education.

Managing Societal Conflict

Congress also has a significant influence in managing the societal conflict inherent in a divided society such as the United States. Some citizens want policies benefiting rural areas, and others give higher priority to urban areas. Some want more money for programs for senior citizens; others seek funding for children's programs. With respect to abortion policy, some people are pro-life, and others are pro-choice. In addition, there are divisions related to social class, race, geography, gender, sexual orientation, religion, and so on. Congress manages these conflicts by representing a wide range of views and interests.

The House and the Senate Compared

Although the House of Representatives and the Senate share numerous functions, the two chambers of Congress differ in significant ways. As President Woodrow Wilson remarked, the "House and Senate are naturally unalike."[17] Constitutionally, the two houses are conceived as unique organizations, and the framers designated their duties to match the strengths and expertise of the people who would come to hold office in each chamber. Table 11.2 highlights these major differences. For example, the Constitution empowers the House of Representatives, as the legislative body closer to the people, with initiating any bills that result in taxes; whereas it empowers the Senate, as the more deliberative house, to give the president advice and consent on appointments and the ratification of treaties. The differences between the House and Senate are not limited merely to their functions, however. The electoral and legislative structures are also sources of differences between the two houses.

The 435 current members of the House of Representatives each represent a legislative district determined by the reapportionment and redistricting process that occurs every ten years, as we considered earlier in this chapter. In more populated areas, these congressional districts are often homogeneous, cohesive units in which a House member's constituency is likely to have fairly unified positions on many issues.[18] Senators, however, are elected by the population of an entire state, and although the political culture in some states is somewhat cohesive (for example, Massachusetts voters are more liberal on most issues than are Kansas voters), in many states there are notable differences in constituents' views, ideology, and policy priorities. For instance, senators Barbara Boxer and Dianne Feinstein both represent the entire state of California, and both are Democrats. Although California is generally viewed as a very liberal political culture, Boxer and Feinstein also must represent the interests of both liberal voters in the western coastal areas of the state and more conservative voters inland to the east. At times, moreover, the interests of a senator's

TABLE 11.2

Differences Between the House and the Senate

House	Senate
Larger (435 members)	Smaller (100 members)
Shorter electoral cycle (two-year term)	Longer electoral cycle (six-year term)
Narrow constituency (congressional districts)	Broad constituency (states)
Less prestigious	More prestigious
Originates all revenue bills	Ratifies treaties; confirms presidential nominees
Less reliant on staff	More reliant on staff
Power vested in leaders and committee chairs	Power more evenly distributed

> California senators must balance the views not only of surfers and Hollywood stars, but also of farmers and ranchers. They must take into account the concerns of liberal urban coastal dwellers along with the more conservative views of those who live in the state's heartland to the east, including the significant agricultural interests in those areas. Agribusiness interests and farmers often lobby for government support of irrigation programs, for example. Here, sprinklers irrigate a cotton field at pre-bloom stage.

bill
a proposed piece of legislation

hopper
a wooden box that sits on a desk at the front of the House of Representatives, into which House members place bills they want to introduce

joint referral
the practice, abolished in the 104th Congress, by which a bill could be referred to two different committees for consideration

lead committee
the primary committee considering a bill

seniority system
the system in which the member with the longest continuous tenure on a standing committee is given preference when the committee chooses its chair

constituents divide over a given issue: in California, for example, environmental activists and fishers have argued against programs that divert water from lakes and streams so that it can be used for irrigation on commercial farms, while affluent agribusinesses advocate water diversion. A U.S. senator must balance such conflicting positions when making policy decisions.

The differing length of representatives' and senators' terms of service affects how members of each chamber of Congress relate to their constituents. Given their short two-year terms, members of the House of Representatives naturally are reluctant to defy the will of the electorate on a given issue because of the likelihood that their opposition will be used against them during their reelection campaign. As the framers structured it, the House remains "the people's house," the chamber in which civically engaged individuals can effectively have their interests represented. And although U.S. senators naturally also want to please their constituents, they recognize that voting against their constituents' will on a particular issue might be less significant than such an action would be for a House member, especially if the issue arises early in their term and is not important enough for people to hold against them six years down the road.

The size of the chambers and length of terms also affect the relative prestige of each chamber. In general, the smaller Senate is considered more prestigious than the House of Representatives, although some individual House members may enjoy more prestige than some senators.

Although the House and Senate differ in their constitutionally determined duties, both must pass any piece of legislation before it can become law. But the way in which legislation is considered and voted upon differs in each house of Congress.

The larger size of the House of Representatives, with its 435 members, necessitates a more formal legislative structure in order to prevent unruliness. The House, for example, generally has more, and more formal, rules guiding debate than the Senate. Despite the differences between the two chambers, the legislative process is remarkably similar in both.

The Legislative Process

Article I, Section 1, of the Constitution states, "All Legislative Powers herein granted shall be vested in a Congress of the United States, which shall consist of a Senate and House of Representatives." A **bill** is a proposed piece of legislation. As shown in Figure 11.1, every bill must be approved by *both houses* (the House and the Senate) *in identical form*. In general, bills must pass through five steps in order to become law:

1. **Introduction.** A member of the House of Representatives or the Senate formally proposes the bill.

2. **Committee review.** Subgroups within the House and Senate, composed of legislators who have expertise in the bill's subject matter, review the bill.

3. **House and Senate approval.** If the bill makes it out of committee, a majority of members in the House and Senate must approve it.

4. **Conference Committee reconciliation.** The Conference Committee reconciles the bill when different versions have passed in the House and the Senate.

5. **Presidential approval.** If the president signs the bill, it becomes law. But even after this arduous process, a presidential veto can kill the bill.

Introducing a Bill

Bills are introduced differently in each chamber of Congress. In the House of Representatives, a member of a legislator's staff drafts the proposed legislation, and the House member puts the bill into the **hopper,** a wooden box that sits on a desk at the front of the House chamber. Upon introduction, a bill is referred to as "H.R.," meaning House of Representatives, followed by a number that indicates the order in which it was introduced in a given legislative session, for example, "H.R. 207."

In the Senate, the process is less formal. Here, senators can announce proposed legislation to colleagues in a speech on the Senate floor (see "Exploring the Sources"). Alternatively, a senator can submit a written draft of the proposed legislation to an official known as the Senate clerk, or sometimes a senator will propose legislation simply by offering it as an amendment to an already pending piece of legislation. Once a bill is introduced in the Senate, it is referred to as "S.," or "Senate," followed by its number reflecting the order in which it was introduced in a given legislative session—for example, "S. 711."

Before 1995, a bill introduced in the House of Representatives could be subject to **joint referral,** the practice of referring the bill simultaneously to two different House committees for consideration. But the 104th Congress abolished joint committee referrals. Today bills introduced in the House are referred to one committee, called the **lead committee.** Occasionally, when the substance of a bill warrants additional referrals to other committees that also have jurisdiction over the subject of the bill, the bill might be subsequently referred to a second committee.[19] In the Senate, bills typically are referred to only one committee.

The Bill in Committee

After introduction by a member of the House or Senate, a bill is read into the *Congressional Record,* a formal record of all actions taken by Congress. Because of the large number of bills introduced, both chambers rely on an extensive committee structure that facilitates the consideration of so high a volume of bills.[20] Most bills that are introduced "die" in committee. That is, a committee does not consider the bill (sometimes because the committee does not have the time in a legislative session to take up the measure) or declines to forward the bill to the full chamber.

Each congressional committee and subcommittee is composed of a majority of members of the majority party in that chamber. For example, if 218 or more members (a majority in the House) elected to the House of Representatives are Republicans, then every committee and subcommittee in the House has a majority of Republicans. The parties in each chamber decide members' committee and subcommittee assignments.

Though the selection of committee chairs varies between chambers and parties, committee chairs are often chosen using the **seniority system,** by which the member with the longest continuous tenure on a standing committee receives preference when the committee chooses its chair. The committee chairs run committee meetings and control the flow of work in each committee. Although the seniority system is an institution in Congress, it is an informal system, and seniority does not always determine who will be the committee chair.[21] Chairs are chosen by a secret ballot, and in recent years junior members sometimes have won out over senior committee members.

FIGURE 11.1 ◼ What do you notice about the initial stages of the legislative process whereby a bill becomes a law? How do the Senate and the House resolve differences in versions of a bill passed in each chamber? What outcomes are possible once a bill goes to the president for approval?

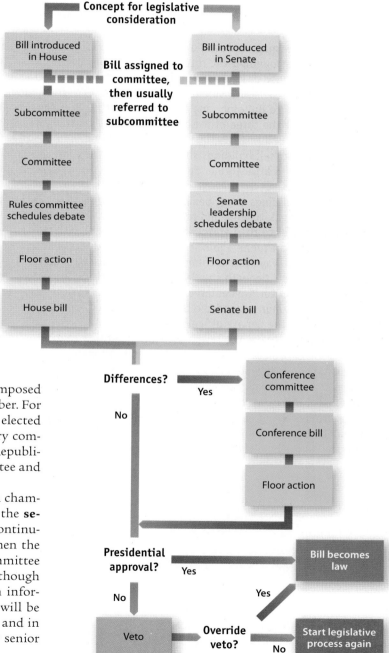

The Legislative Process

NAVIGATING CONGRESS

When we think of Congress, we typically picture the gleaming white dome of the Capitol building. This image is appropriate, because the Capitol Rotunda is a highly important place for members of Congress and the people whom they represent. The Capitol is home to the House and Senate chambers where issues are debated on the floor and where votes are cast.

As shown in the map, however, a large part of Congress's work takes place in the office buildings surrounding the rotunda that are considered part of "Capitol Hill." Members of the House of Representatives are typically assigned an office in one of three buildings on the south side of the Capitol Rotunda: the Cannon Office Building, the Longworth Office Building, and the Rayburn Office Building. Senators work out of an office in one of the three office buildings located on the north side of the rotunda: the Russell Office Building, the Dirksen Office Building, and the Hart Office Building. The Cannon and Russell buildings share essentially the same design. The House office buildings are named after former Speakers of the House of Representatives, while the Senate office buildings are named after prominent U.S. senators.

Many of the buildings boast beautiful architecture and amenities such as gymnasiums, post offices, kitchens, and recording studios. In the Rayburn Office Building, members can travel to the Capitol via a subway tunnel with two cars, and pedestrian tunnels join it to the Longworth Building. A double-track subway system connects Dirksen, Russell, and the Capitol, and tunnels beneath the Cannon and Russell buildings connect to the Capitol. Immediately east of the Capitol Rotunda is the Library of Congress, and the U.S. Supreme Court Building sits just south of the Senate office buildings.

Although office space and layout are not something that political scientists typically analyze, the proximity of members of Congress to their office neighbors, along with the common facilities they share, surely has an impact on the legislative process. In the Capitol Hill office buildings, just as in any other kind of office or group setting, senators and representatives of diverse backgrounds become familiar with colleagues whom they see regularly in the hallways, elevators, gyms, kitchens, and subway trains between buildings.

Evaluating the Evidence

1. Like a member of Congress, you also have a network of relationships based on your daily activities. What people do you see regularly because of your work or school schedule? What unlikely relationships have you formed because of your daily activities?

2. In what ways might the time spent in their Capitol Hill offices and common facilities breed familiarity among federal legislators? What different kinds and backgrounds of people might this daily contact bring together?

3. In what specific ways do you think legislators' interactions in their office buildings might affect their political decision making in the chambers of the House and the Senate?

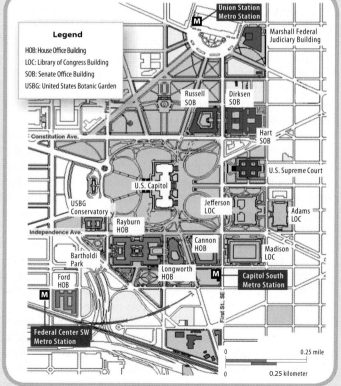

Source: www.aol.gov/cc/cc-map.cfm

Legend

HOB: House Office Building
LOC: Library of Congress Building
SOB: Senate Office Building
USBG: United States Botanic Garden

Standing committees are permanent committees with a defined legislative jurisdiction. The House has twenty-four standing committees, and the Senate has twenty. The House Committee on Homeland Security and the Senate Armed Services Committee are examples of standing committees.

Select committees are specially created to consider a specific policy issue or to address a particular concern. In 2005 the House formed a select committee, the Select Bipartisan Committee to Investigate the Preparation for and Response to Hurricane Katrina, which examined what went wrong in the preparations for and response to that killer storm. Other select committees have focused on such issues as homeland security and terrorism, aging, and transportation.

Joint committees are bicameral committees composed of members of both chambers of Congress. Sometimes these committees offer administrative or managerial guidance of various kinds. For example, one joint committee oversees the presidential inauguration, and another supervises the administration of the Library of Congress.

In addition to the congressional committees, the House has more than ninety subcommittees, and the Senate has sixty-eight. **Subcommittees** typically handle specific areas of the committees' jurisdiction. For example, the Committee on Homeland Security is a standing committee in the House. Within the committee, there are six subcommittees: the Subcommittee on the Prevention of Nuclear and Biological Attack; Subcommittee on Intelligence, Information Sharing, and Terrorism Risk Assessment; Subcommittee on Economic Security, Infrastructure Protection, and Cybersecurity; Subcommittee on Management, Integration, and Oversight; Subcommittee on Emergency Preparedness, Science, and Technology; and Subcommittee on Investigations. Each subcommittee handles bills relevant to its specified jurisdiction.

When a committee or subcommittee favors a measure, it usually takes four actions:

- **Agency review.** During **agency review,** the committee or subcommittee asks the executive agencies that would administer the law for written comments on the measure.
- **Hearings.** Next the committee or subcommittee holds **hearings** to gather information and views from experts, including interest groups, concerned citizens, and sometimes celebrity spokespersons.
- **Markup.** During **markup,** the committee "marks up" the bill with suggested language changes and amendments. The committee does not actually alter the bill; rather, members recommend changes to the full chamber. In a typical bill markup, the committee may eliminate a component of the proposal or amend the proposal in some way.
- **Report.** After agreeing to the wording of the bill, the committee issues a **report** to the full chamber, explaining the bill and its intent. The bill may then be considered by the full chamber.

In the House of Representatives, a special measure known as a **discharge petition** is used to extract a bill from a committee in order to have it considered by the entire House. A discharge petition requires the signature of a majority (218) of the members of the House.

Debate on the House and Senate Floor

Table 11.3 shows some key differences in the legislative process between the House and Senate. For example, if a House bill is "discharged," or makes it out of committee, it then goes to the **Rules Committee,** one of the most important committees in the House, which decides on the length of debate and the scope of amendments that will be allowed on a bill. The Rules Committee sets the structure for the debate that ensues in the full House. For important bills, the Rules Committee tends to set

standing committee
permanent committee in Congress, with a defined legislative jurisdiction

select committee
congressional committee created to consider specific policy issues or address a specific concern

joint committee
bicameral committee composed of members of both chambers of Congress

subcommittee
a subordinate committee in Congress that typically handles specific areas of a standing committee's jurisdiction

agency review
part of the committee or subcommittee process of considering a bill, wherein committee members ask executive agencies that would administer the law for written comments on the measure

hearings
sessions held by committees or subcommittees to gather information and views from experts

markup
the process by which members of legislative committees "mark up" a bill with suggested language for changes and amendments

report
a legislative committee's explanation to the full chamber of a bill and its intent

discharge petition
a special tactic used to extract a bill from a committee in order to have it considered by the entire House

Rules Committee
one of the most important committees in the House, which decides the length of debate and the scope of amendments that will be allowed on a bill

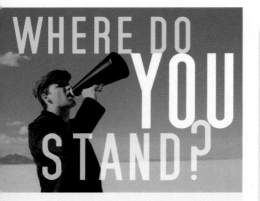
TABLE 11.3 Differences in the Legislative Process in the House and Senate

House	Senate
Bill introduced by member placing bill in hopper	Bill introduced by member
Relies on Rules Committee to schedule debate on House floor and to establish rules for amendments	Relies on unanimous consent agreements to determine rules for debate and amendments
Has a rule barring nongermane amendments	No rule banning nongermane amendments
Does not allow filibusters	Allows filibusters
Discharge petition can be used to extract a bill from a committee	No discharge petitions allowed

strict limits on the types of amendments that can be attached to a bill. In general, the Rules Committee also establishes limits to floor debate in the House.

The Senate does not have a committee to do the work of the Rules Committee, but the Senate's small size allows members to agree to the terms of debate through **unanimous consent** agreements. Unanimous consent must be just that: every senator needs to agree to the terms of debate (including time limits on debate), and if even one senator objects, unanimous consent does not take effect. Senators do not look favorably on objections to unanimous consent, and so such objections are rare. Objecting to unanimous consent agreements can potentially undermine a senator's ability to get legislation passed by provoking the ire of other senators.

If the Senate does not reach unanimous consent, the possibility of a **filibuster** arises—a procedural move that attempts to halt passage of the bill.[22] Sometimes the mere threat of a filibuster is enough to compel a bill's supporters to alter a bill's content. During a filibuster, a senator can speak for an unlimited time on the Senate floor. Filibustering senators do not need to restrict themselves to speaking only on the subject of the bill—they just need to keep talking. Some senators have read the Bible, cookbooks, and even the Nynex Yellow Pages into the *Congressional Record*. In the 1930s, Senator Huey P. Long (D-Louisiana) filibustered many bills, once speaking for fifteen hours to block one that he viewed as "helping the rich get richer and the poor get poorer." Long, viewed as a character by many of his Senate colleagues, was a favorite among visitors to the Senate galleries, where he would entertain onlookers with New Orleans recipes for "pot-likkers" and with his articulations of Shakespeare in a Louisiana drawl. Former Republican South Carolina senator Strom Thurmond holds the Senate record for the longest filibuster. In an attempt to block passage of the Civil Rights Act of 1957, Thurmond filibustered for twenty-four hours and eighteen minutes. A filibuster can end by a vote of **cloture,** in which a supermajority of sixty senators agrees to invoke cloture and end debate. Cloture is initiated if sixteen senators sign a cloture petition.

After a bill is debated by the full chamber, the members vote on it. Before a bill can become law, identical versions of the bill must pass in both the House and the Senate. If only one chamber passes a bill during a congressional term, the bill dies. If both the House and Senate pass bills on the same topic, but with differences between the bills, the bills are then sent to a **conference committee,** a bicameral, bipartisan committee composed of legislators whose job is to reconcile the two versions of the bill. Typically, the legislators appointed to the conference committee will be members of the standing committees that considered the bill in their chambers. After the committee develops a compromise version of the bill, the bill then goes back to both chambers for another vote. If the bill does not pass in both chambers during a congressional term, the bill is dead, although it can be reintroduced in the next session. If both chambers approve the bill, it then goes to the president for signature or veto.

unanimous consent
an agreement by every senator to the terms of debate on a given piece of legislation

filibuster
a procedural move by a member of the Senate to attempt to halt passage of or change a bill, during which the senator can speak for an unlimited time on the Senate floor

cloture
a procedural move in which a supermajority of sixty senators agrees to end a filibuster

conference committee
a bicameral, bipartisan committee composed of legislators whose job is to reconcile two versions of a bill

Presidential Action

When both the House and Senate manage to pass a bill in identical form, it proceeds to the president, who may take one of three actions. First, the president may sign it, in which case the bill becomes a law. Second, the president may choose to do nothing. If the president does nothing and Congress is in session, the bill becomes law after ten days without the president's signature. A president may take this route if he or she does not support the bill but knows that Congress would override a veto. If, however, the Congress has adjourned (that is, the bill was passed at the end of a legislative session), the president may exercise a pocket veto. A **pocket veto** occurs when Congress has adjourned and the president waits ten days without signing the bill; the president effectively "puts the bill in his pocket," and the bill dies. Finally, a president may exercise the executive power of a *vote:* rejecting the bill and returning it to Congress with a message explaining why the bill should not become law. Congress can vote to override the veto by a two-thirds vote in both houses, in which case the bill becomes law. But overriding a presidential veto is a difficult and rare achievement.

pocket veto
a special presidential veto of a bill passed at the conclusion of a legislative session, whereby the president waits ten days without signing the bill, and the bill dies

Congressional Leadership

The House and the Senate alike choose the majority and minority leaders for their adept negotiating skills, their finely honed ability to guide compromise, and their skills of persuasion. A majority leader nurtures compromise in the legislative process by knowing the members' positions on legislation well enough to recognize which issues are negotiable and which are deal-breakers; by engineering trade-offs between players; and by convincing committee chairs that a negotiated compromise is the best outcome they can expect.

In earlier eras, forceful leaders rose to the position of majority leader in both houses and strongly influenced congressional priorities and legislation.[23] But as political parties have come to play a less important role in the election of members of the House and Senate, allegiance to party leaders in these institutions has dwindled.[24] The era has long passed in which individuals could essentially control what Congress did through their assertive personalities.[25] Today's congressional power brokers face members whose loyalty to the party and the leadership is tempered by the need to please constituencies that themselves are less loyal to the parties than in bygone times.[26] Nonetheless, despite the evolution in the role of congressional leader, partisanship remains a strong aspect of congressional politics, particularly since 1994. Table 11.4 shows the leaders of the 110th Congress (2007–2009).

Leadership in the House of Representatives

Although Article I, Section 2, of the Constitution states, "The House of Representatives shall choose their Speaker and other Officers," and all members of the House vote for the Speaker, it is really the members of the majority party who select their **Speaker of the House.** Second in the line of presidential succession (after the vice president), the Speaker serves as the presiding officer and manager of the House. In this capacity, the Speaker chairs floor debates, makes majority party committee assignments, assigns members to the powerful Rules Committee, negotiates with members of the minority party and the White House, and guides legislation through the House.[27] But the Speaker is also the leader of his or her party in the House, and a key duty associated with this role is helping party members get reelected. Finally, the Speaker is himself or herself an elected member of the House.

TABLE 11.4

The Leaders of the 110th Congress (2007-2009)

HOUSE OF REPRESENTATIVES	
Speaker of the House	Nancy Pelosi (D-California)
House Majority Leader	Steny Hoyer (D-Maryland)
House Majority Whip	James E. Clyburn (D-South Carolina)
House Minority Leader	John Boehner (R-Ohio)
House Minority Whip	Roy Blunt (R-Missouri)
U.S. SENATE	
Senate Majority Leader	Harry Reid (D-Nevada)
Senate Majority Whip	Dick Durbin (D-Illinois)
Senate Minority Leader	Mitch McConnell (R-Kentucky)
Senate Minority Whip	Trent Lott (R-Mississippi)

Speaker of the House
the leader of the House of Representatives, chosen by the majority party

The House leadership—which, in addition to the Speaker, includes the majority leader, the minority leader, and the party whips—is chosen at the beginning of each session of Congress through a conference also known as a *caucus.* During a caucus, all of the members of the political party meet and elect their chamber leaders, approve committee assignments, and elect committee chairpersons. Party leaders also may call a party caucus during a legislative session to shore up support on an issue being voted upon or to formulate the party's position on an issue on the agenda.[28] One issue before Congress is the problem of controlling greenhouse gas emissions, which is considered in "The Conversation of Democracy."

In 1999, the then-majority Republican Party caucus elected Representative Dennis Hastert (R-Illinois) Speaker of the House. Hastert was little known on the national scene, particularly when compared with his predecessor, Newt Gingrich (R-Georgia), whose abrasive leadership style was often highlighted in the national media. But the mild-mannered Hastert's tenure as Speaker came to an abrupt end in 2006, when Republicans failed to win a majority in the House elections. With this turn of events, many commentators faulted Hastert for being weak and ineffectual. As the Democrats swept into office that year, they also made history, electing Representative Nancy Pelosi (D-California) the first woman to serve as Speaker. Pelosi is an unabashed liberal who railed against the Bush administration, particularly its policies in Iraq, during the 2006 congressional elections. But Pelosi recognized early that the Speaker's role is one of leading not just her own political party, but the entire House of Representatives, with its wide span of views and interests: "You have to govern from the center. We are in a completely different place now. We are setting our legislative agenda."[29]

During Pelosi's tenure in the House, she has earned a reputation for integrity and the ability to form a coalition within her party—nurturing the loyalty of junior members; unifying moderate, liberal, and conservative Democrats; building coalitions composed of representatives from different districts, generations, ethnicities, and sexes. These skills are essential attributes for the Speaker of the House.

The Speaker relies on the **House majority leader** to help develop and implement the majority party's legislative strategy, work with the minority party leadership, and encourage unity among majority party legislators. In this last task, the Speaker and the House majority leader are assisted by the **majority whip,** who acts as a go-between with the leadership and the party members in the House. The term *whip* comes from the English hunting term *whipper-in,* a hunter whose job is to keep the foxhounds in the pack and to prevent them from straying during a fox hunt. Similarly, the job of the party whip is to keep party members together, encouraging them to vote with the party on issues and preventing them from straying off into their own positions. The minority party in the House also elects leaders, the **House minority leader** and the **minority whip,** whose jobs mirror those of their majority party colleagues but without the power that comes from holding a majority in the House.

Leadership in the Senate

In the Senate, the vice president of the United States serves as the president of that body, according to the Constitution. But in actual practice, vice presidents preside over the Senate only rarely. Vice presidents, however, have one power in the Senate that, although rarely exercised, is enormously important. If a vote in the upper house of Congress is tied, the vice president breaks the tie. Such a situation occurred in 2005 when Vice President Dick Cheney cast the tie-breaking vote on a major budget bill that slashed federal spending by nearly $40 billion by allowing states to impose new fees on Medicaid recipients, cutting federal funds that enforce child-support regulations, and imposing new federal work requirements on state welfare recipients.

The majority party in the Senate elects a Senate leader called the **president pro tempore.** Meaning "president for the time," this position is often referred to as "president pro tem." The job of the president pro tem is to chair the Senate in the vice president's absence. Historically, this position has been honorary in nature, with the majority party senator who has the longest record of continu-

House majority leader
the leader of the majority party, who helps the Speaker develop and implement strategy and work with other members of the House of Representatives

majority whip
a go-between with the majority leadership and party members in the House of Representatives

House minority leader
the leader of the minority party, whose job mirrors that of the majority leader but without the power that comes from holding a majority in the House of Representatives

minority whip
go-between with the minority leadership, whose job mirrors that of the majority whip but without the power that comes from holding a majority in the House of Representatives

president pro tempore
(also called *president pro tem*) theoretically, the chair of the Senate in the vice president's absence; in reality, an honorary title, with the senator of the majority party having the longest record of continuous service being elected to the position

THE CONVERSATION OF DEMOCRACY

SHOULD CONGRESS LIMIT GREENHOUSE GAS EMISSIONS?

The Issue: One policy issue taken up in several recent sessions of Congress is emissions of carbon dioxide (CO_2), a "greenhouse gas" believed to contribute to global warming. These emissions, produced by public utilities, industries, and motor vehicles' burning of fossil fuels, have been an increasingly hot-button issue since the Democrats took control of Congress in 2006. After former vice president Al Gore won the Nobel Peace Prize for his contributions to raising public awareness about global climate change, many members of Congress felt pressure from their constituents to address the problem of carbon dioxide emissions. In this "Conversation of Democracy," we consider the question, should Congress limit greenhouse gas emissions?

Yes: The United States generates 22 percent of the world's CO_2 emissions, excluding gases that are the by-product of foreign countries' production of goods for U.S. consumption. Given this volume of consumption, Americans should take responsibility for protecting the global environment. Failure to curb greenhouse gas emissions will have terrible long-term consequences for the environmental and the economic health of not only the United States but also the wider world. Failure to reduce CO_2 emissions promotes global warming, resulting in the melting of the polar ice caps, higher tides throughout the world, and drastic changes in weather patterns and ecology, all of which can have a devastating impact on humans' as well as other species' ability to survive and thrive.

No: There is no need to create a massive regulatory structure to compel industry to reduce CO_2 emissions. Some political leaders maintain that carbon dioxide is not a pollutant and does not threaten public health. Furthermore, Senator James Inhofe (R-Oklahoma) has said that global warming is a hoax and has faulted environmental groups for duping the American public.* Forcing regulations on industry will significantly harm the U.S. economy. Regulating CO_2 emissions will drive up costs for gasoline, utilities, and various products we use every day.

Other approaches: Instead of mandating curbs directly, Congress could take a cue from states such as California and use the federal government's role as an energy customer to encourage companies to curb emissions and become more green. For example, it could require national parks or other federally owned properties to purchase electricity from sources that meet certain emissions standards. It should also further encourage the development of alternative, renewable sources of energy—such as wind, solar, and geothermal energy—by continuing to extend tax credits for these promising industries.

What do you think?

① Do you support legislation that would limit industrial output of carbon dioxide? Why or why not?

② What businesses and industries could be hurt by such legislation? Would you be willing to pay more at the pump to curb greenhouse emissions?

③ If limiting the production of greenhouse gases is crucial, what role should other countries play? What are some challenges of getting other countries to reduce their emissions of carbon dioxide?

*"Senate Rejects Global Warming Bill," www.cbsnews.com/stories/2003/10/30/politics/main580915.shtml.

---

ous Senate service being elected to the office. Despite the honorary nature of the position, the Senate's president pro tem is third in the line of presidential succession (following the vice president and the Speaker of the House). Robert Byrd (D-West Virginia), who has served in the Senate since 1959, is the current president pro tem.

The real power in the U.S. Senate is held and wielded by the **Senate majority leader,** whose job is to manage the legislative process so that favored bills are passed; to schedule debate on legislation in consultation with his or her counterpart in the minority party, the **Senate minority leader;** and to act as the spokesperson for the majority party in the Senate. The majority and the minority leaders both play crucial roles in ushering bills through the Senate, and the majority leader facilitates the numerous negotiations that arise when senators bargain over the content of a given piece of proposed legislation.[30]

Senate majority leader Harry Reid (D-Nevada) was elected after the Democrats won a majority of seats in the 2006 Senate elections. Reid is a soft-spoken politician who was

Senate majority leader
the most powerful position in the Senate; the majority leader manages the legislative process and schedules debate on legislation

Senate minority leader
the leader of the minority party in the Senate, who works with the majority leader in negotiating legislation

elected partly because of his talent at building consensus, a necessary skill given his desire to tackle some highly partisan and controversial issues when he assumed his leadership role, including ethics reform, funding for stem cell research, and an increase in the federal minimum wage.

Decision Making in Congress: The Legislative Context

When deciding whether to "tow the party line" on a legislative vote, members of Congress do not operate independently and in isolation. Throughout the legislative process, they face a variety of external pressures that influence their views. Some of these influences are subtle; others are more pronounced. Moreover, the impact of the influence varies according to the timing and type of legislation being considered. For example, political scientist Barry C. Burden has noted that the personal experiences of legislators sometimes have a bearing on their policy stances on issues.[31] Among the most important influences on members of Congress with respect to the legislative process are political parties, members' colleagues and staff, interest groups, the president, and of course their constituents—the people who elected them to serve as their representatives in our system of republican government.

Political Parties and Partisanship in Decision Making

Figure 11.2 shows the party breakdown in Congress since 1985. The data show that 1994 was a pivotal year, ending Democratic control in the House and Senate. For nearly all of the next twelve years, Republicans retained control over both the House and the Senate. (Republicans lost their narrow majority in the Senate in 2001 when one Republican senator switched parties, but they regained control in the 2002 elections.) But in 2006, the balance of power shifted back to the Democrats, who won majorities in both houses, squeaking out a majority in the Senate with a one-member lead. That year, Democratic candidates benefited from President George W. Bush's unpopularity and public weariness with the war in Iraq. As shown in Figure 11.3, in 2008 Democrats increased their majorities in both houses, benefitting from George W. Bush' unpopularity and—for some Democratic congressional candidates—from Barack Obama's coattails. While significantly increasing their numbers

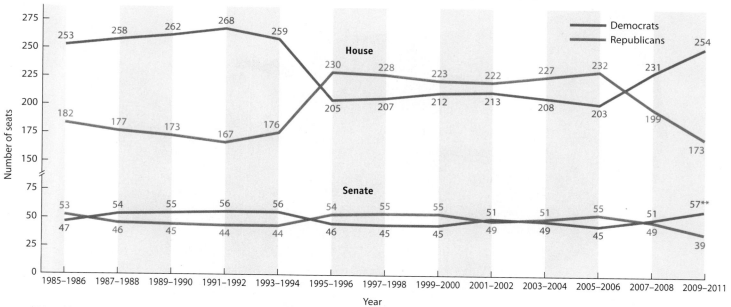

Party Breakdowns in the House and Senate, 1985–2011*

* At publication time, the outcome of four Senate and six House elections is yet to be decided.
** Two Independent members of the Senate typically vote Democratic.

FIGURE 11.2 ■ What trends does this table show with respect to party representation in the House of Representatives since 1985? What trends does it indicate for the Senate? Generally speaking, do the patterns for the House resemble those for the Senate?

in both houses, the Democrats fell short of the sixty members necessary for a filibuster-proof majority in the Senate.

The partisan breakdown of Congress is important because most major legislative votes cast are "party votes," meaning that most members of one political party vote one way, while most members of the other party vote the other way. In some cases, this divide is due to the differing ideologies the parties represent. In other instances, party voting is simply pure partisanship: Democrats vote against something because Republicans vote for it and vice versa.

Partisan voting increased after the Watergate scandal in the 1970s and rose again after the 1994 congressional elections, in which Republicans took control of Congress. Partisan voting tends to be particularly acrimonious immediately before congressional and presidential elections. It occurs more often when members are voting on domestic policy issues, such as environmental or economic regulatory policy and entitlement programs, that tend to crystallize ideological differences between the parties. But often partisan votes are politically motivated, plain and simple. One of the most partisan votes on record in Congress was the 1998 vote on whether President Bill Clinton should be impeached. In that vote, 98 percent of all members of Congress voted the party line—Republicans for impeachment, Democrats against.

Scholars believe that changes in how congressional district maps are drawn partly explains increased partisan voting in the House of Representatives. In earlier times, redistricting occurred through a simple redrawing of the lines of a congressional district to accommodate population changes. But today, with the widespread use of computer-driven mapmaking technology, congressional seats can be configured to ensure a "safe seat"—one in which the party identification of the majority of a district's voters makes it likely that a candidate from a given party will win election. Sometimes, for example, more than 60 percent of a district's population identifies with one political party. The advent of safe seats means that a House member generally can be partisan with immunity because his

Priorities for Congressional Legislators

What issue is of more concern to you today, and is one that the members of Congress urgently need to address—the economy or national security?

☐ The economy—issues such as jobs and economic growth

☐ National security—issues such as the Iraq war and the war on terror

☐ Other issues

Source: "Economy Tops National Security as New Voter Concern," www.rasmussenreports .com/public_content/politics/election_20082/ 2008_presidential_election/economy_tops _national_security_as_new_voter_concern.

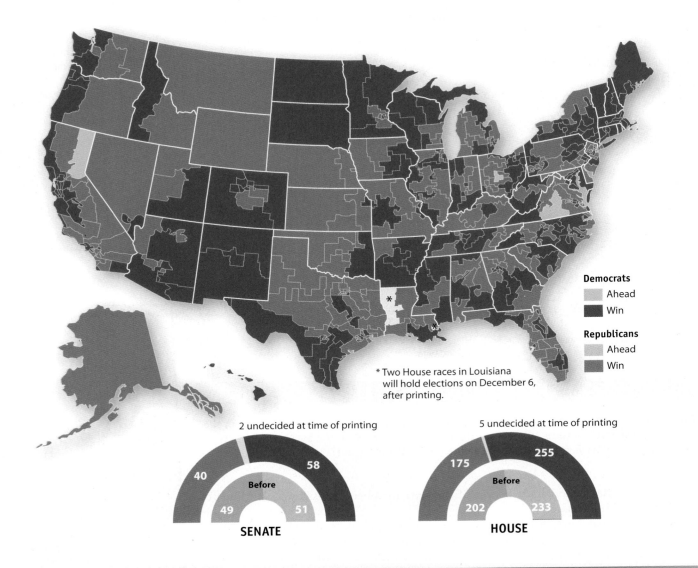

Democrats
Ahead
Win

Republicans
Ahead
Win

* Two House races in Louisiana will hold elections on December 6, after printing.

2 undecided at time of printing

SENATE

40
58
Before
49
51

5 undecided at time of printing

HOUSE

175
255
Before
202
233

POLITICAL INQUIRY

FIGURE 11.3 ■ PARTY REPRESENTATION IN THE HOUSE OF REPRESENTATIVES, 2008 How many seats in the House do the Republicans have as a result of the 2008 election? How many seats do the Democrats have? Which party has the majority? Given the party of the new president, how do you think the new House composition might affect lawmaking?

or her constituency so often agrees with the representative's partisan stance. In contrast, when congressional districts were more competitive, a House member typically would have to temper partisan impulses to placate the sizeable proportion of his or her constituency that identified with the opposing party. Today that is no longer the case, and it appears that Republicans in the House of Representatives have become more conservative and their Democratic counterparts have become increasingly liberal. Consequently, House members are less likely to compromise or to be moderate in their positions in negotiating issues with the opposition.

Many scholars assert that a similar bifurcation of political ideology has not occurred in the Senate. They claim that because state populations as a whole tend to be more ideologically diverse and less homogeneous than House districts, U.S. senators often must temper their views to reflect the wider range of their constituents' perspectives. Thus senators tend to be more willing to compromise and to take a more moderate stance in negotiating with the opposing party than their House counterparts. Nonetheless, on some issues, other scholars note that the Senate is increasingly dividing along strongly partisan lines.[32] In the 2006 Senate confirmation hearings for Supreme Court nominee Samuel Alito, Democrats opposed Alito's nomination, fearing that the conservative judge would provide the swing vote to overturn the landmark Supreme Court ruling *Roe v. Wade,* which legalized abortion in the United States. In the Senate's vote to confirm Alito, forty out of forty-four Democratic senators voted against Alito's confirmation, whereas all but one of the fifty-four Republicans (Rhode Island senator Lincoln Chafee) voted for Alito's confirmation.

Colleagues and Staff: Trading Votes and Information

Congressional colleagues provide cues for members of the House and Senate in their decision making over whether to vote for a pending piece of legislation. Members may seek the opinions of like-minded colleagues in determining how to vote on a proposed bill. In addition, legislators may consult with peers who are policy experts, such as Senator John Warner (R-Virginia), a recognized authority on military affairs.

Members of Congress also engage in **logrolling,** the practice of trading votes between members. Logrolling is a reciprocal tactic by which a member agrees to vote on one piece of legislation in exchange for a colleague's vote on another.

In addition, House and Senate members rely on their staffs to inform their decision making on legislation.[33] Staff members frequently have policy expertise that can guide a legislator's decision on an upcoming vote. They also figure in the legislative voting process by communicating with legislators about the desires of constituents and interest groups with respect to a pending piece of legislation.

Partisanship in Congress

THEN (1980s)	NOW (2009)
Congress is divided; Democrats control the House of Representatives, and Republicans control the Senate.	Democrats control both houses of Congress.
Although incumbents enjoy a considerable advantage, many congressional districts are a mix of constituents of both major parties.	Fewer congressional districts are competitive. Many districts are more homogeneous because district boundaries can be drawn with sophisticated computer programs.
Partisan voting is evident, but legislators are often forced to base their positions on constituent preferences in addition to their own party loyalty.	With the advent of less competitive districts, legislators are more partisan than their predecessors.

WHAT'S NEXT?

> Has the outcome of the 2008 elections increased or decreased party tensions, in your view? Why?

> In recent years, partisanship has increased when there has been a president of one party and a Congress of another. Does such a scenario exist today? What implications does that have for the future of partisanship in Congress for the next several years?

> Increases in technological sophistication could make redistricting an even more exact science. What impact would this have on partisanship in Congress?

Interest Groups: Influence Through Organization

In various ways, interest groups also influence congressional elections. They can affect electoral outcomes, for example, through an endorsement process by which a group notifies its members that it backs a certain candidate in the hope that members get on the bandwagon and express their support at the polls. In addition, through their political action committees, interest groups make financial contributions to congressional campaigns. And interest groups whose memberships are mobilized to support or oppose a candidate often provide grassroots activists to political campaigns.[34]

As we considered in Chapter 7, interest groups also shape the legislative process. They make their mark by influencing congressional campaigns, by providing information to members of Congress as they try to decide whether to vote for a particular piece of legislation, and by lobbying members of Congress to support or oppose legislation.[35]

logrolling
the practice in which members of Congress agree to vote for a bill in exchange for their colleague's vote on another bill

DOING DEMOCRACY

LOBBY CONGRESS FOR STUDENT AID

FACT:

The costs of U.S. higher education have shot up in recent years. Between 1986–1987 and 2004–2005, the average costs of tuition, fees, books, and room and board have nearly tripled at four-year colleges, increasing from just over $4,000 to just under $12,000, while costs at two-year colleges have doubled from an average of about $3,000 to over $6,000. Meanwhile, the average costs at private four-year schools have escalated from just over $10,000 in 1986–1987 to over $26,000 in 2004–2005.* State colleges and universities and community colleges are often hit the hardest; state budget shortfalls can mean lower budget appropriations for public institutions of higher learning. In Massachusetts, for example, tuition at public four-year colleges increased 24 percent between the 2001–2002 and 2002–2003 academic years.**

Do you feel the crunch? When you've completed your studies, will you be saddled with overwhelming debt?

Act!

At Columbia University Teachers College in New York City, student Nathan Walker (who has accumulated over $100,000 worth of student loan debt in order to pay for his education) went to Washington, D.C., and testified before a congressional committee to promote passage of the National Tuition Endowment Act. If enacted, this law could generate more than $30 billion in tuition relief for higher education over a ten-year period. Walker says that he learned in interviews with Department of Education (DOE) officials that the interest generated by student loans was given to other programs rather than used to subsidize DOE programs. The aim of the National Tuition Endowment Act is to direct all income generated from student financial aid into the tuition endowment program.

You can help to see that a bill like the National Tuition Endowment Act is passed by registering your opinion with your representatives in Congress and by mobilizing other students on your campus. E-mail campaigns to members of Congress are an easy way of communicating your views. You can also write an op-ed piece or a letter to the editor of your campus or community newspaper, invite a member of Congress to your campus to discuss the issue with students, or have your student government endorse the bill and then convey that support to your representatives in Congress.

Where to begin

- The National Tuition Endowment Act Web site (www .columbia.edu/cu/senate/committees/student_affairs/nte/) provides research on the bill and information on how to get started in working for its passage, including tools like a downloadable endorsement form.
- The Pell Institute for the Study of Opportunity in Higher Education (www.pellinstitute.org/default.htm) is a research center that provides policy analysis that can be used to persuade policy makers. Its goal is to improve educational opportunities for low-income, first-generation, and disabled college students in particular.
- The American Student Association of Community Colleges (www.asacc.org/) makes available a wealth of information geared to educational equity for the 12 million community college students across the United States. The organization also runs an annual National Student Advocacy Conference.

*U.S. Department of Education, National Center for Education Statistics, Digest of Education Statistics 2005.
**William Trombley, "The Rising Price of Higher Education," The National Center for Public Policy and Higher Education (Winter 2003), www.highereducation.org/reports/affordability _supplement/affordability_1.shtml.

The President's Effect on Decision Making

As we have seen, the president determines whether to sign or to veto legislation that reaches his desk. But often, before a bill reaches the signing stage, the president's position on it carries enough influence to sway members of Congress, particularly members of his political party, to vote for or against the proposed legislation.

The president can be a lightning rod with respect to some legislative matters. In 2006, President George W. Bush's support for proposed legislation awarding a contract to manage U.S. ports to Dubai (a nation on the Persian Gulf) generated enormous congressional opposition. The bill's opponents included not only Democrats but also some members of

Bush's own political party, who saw the bill as an opportunity to distance themselves from an unpopular president in a congressional election year.

Constituents: The Last Word

Of all the players with a voice in the legislative process, congressional constituents—the people whom the members of Congress represent—wield perhaps the strongest, if indirect, influence with respect to congressional decision making. Most members of Congress want to be reelected, and representing constituents' views (and being able to convince voters that their views are represented well) is a major avenue to reelection to Congress. Thus, constituents influence the legislative process by ensuring that their representatives in Congress work hard to represent their perspectives and policy interests, whether those concerns are over environmental pollution, crime, or (like Nathan Walker, the focus of "Doing Democracy") the soaring cost of higher education.

In fact, some research shows that the public's "potential preferences" can motivate legislators to espouse a policy position likely to be embraced by constituents.[36] But other research shows that most voters are not especially vigilant when it comes to monitoring their elected officials in Congress. In fact, only a very small percentage of voters, sometimes called the **attentive public,** pay careful attention to the public policies being debated by Congress and to the votes cast by their representatives and senators. But the fact that the attentive public is a relatively small minority does not mean that votes taken in Congress are insignificant as far as constituents' opinions go. Indeed, if a member of Congress should disregard constituents' views in voting on a major issue, it is quite likely that an opposing candidate or political party will bring this misstep to the public's attention during the individual's next congressional campaign.

The People and Their Elected Representatives

Although members of Congress may make it a priority to represent the viewpoints and interests of their constituents, demographically speaking, they do not represent the American public at large. As Table 11.5 shows, Congress, especially the Senate, is older, whiter, more educated, wealthier, and more likely to be male than the population as a whole. That said, Congress is not designed to be a perfect sampling of American demographics.[37] It is logical that the leaders of government would more closely resemble individuals who have achieved leadership positions in other realms, such as the corporate world and academia.

attentive public
the segment of voters who pay careful attention to political issues

TABLE 11.5

Demographic Characteristics of the 110th Congress Compared to the U.S. Population

	House (%)	Senate (%)	Population (%)
PARTY			
Democrat	53	49	33
Republican	47	49	29
Independent Unaffiliated	0	2	38
AVERAGE AGE	56 years	62 years	36 years
SEX			
Male	83	84	49
Female	17	16	51
RACE			
White	85	95	81
Black	9	1	13
Hispanic (any race)	5	3	14
Asian/Pacific Is.	1	1	3.5
Native American	.22	0	0.7
EDUCATION			
Bachelor's degree	91	98	27
Master's degree	28	19	7
Law degree	41	58	1
PhD	5	0	1
MD	3	4	2
RELIGION^			
Protestant	58	57	44
Roman Catholic	29	24	25
Jewish	6	11	1.5
Muslim	.22	0	0.5
Buddhist	0	0	0.5
WEALTH^*			
Net assets over $1 million (household)	16	33	7

* Excludes primary residence.
^ Data for 109th Congress.

Sources: Mildred L. Amer, *Membership in the 110th Congress: A Profile* (Washington, DC: Congressional Research Service); U.S. Census Bureau, *The Statistical Abstract of the United States, 2004–05* (Washington, DC: Author, 2004); The Pew Research Center for the People and the Press, "Democrats Gain Edge in Party Identification," July 26, 2004, http://peoplepress.org/commentary/display.php3?AnalysisID=95.

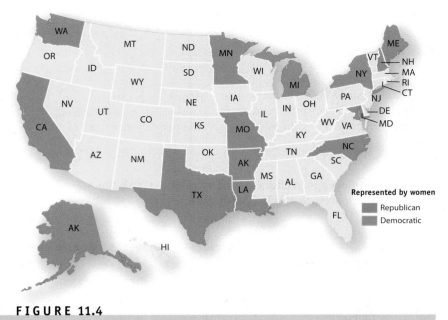

FIGURE 11.4

States Represented by Women in the U.S. Senate

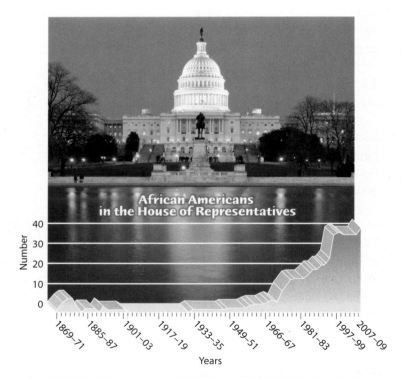

FIGURE 11.5 ■ What explains the rise in African American representation in the House from 1871 through 1887? Why did blacks' representation fall after 1877? What pattern do you see since the late 1960s, and what political and social changes explain it?

Yet importantly, Congress is more diverse today than at any other point in history. Figure 11.4 shows that women represent 14 states in the U.S. Senate (three states, California, Maine, and Washington have two women senators), but the proportion of women in Congress is not nearly equal to their proportion in the national population. In 2008, a record of at least 74 women (or 17 percent of the House) were elected to the House of Representatives. Despite this upward trend, the United States lags behind many industrialized democracies with respect to the proportion of women serving in the national legislature.

Similarly, African Americans have historically been underrepresented in Congress. To date, only five African Americans have served in the Senate, including two, Hiram Revels and Blanche Bruce, who served during the Reconstruction era that followed the Civil War. After Bruce left the Senate in 1881, no other African American would be elected to the Senate until 1967, when Senator Edward Brooke (R-Massachusetts) was elected for one term. More recently, Senator Carol Moseley Braun (D-Illinois) was elected in 1992 and served for one term, and Barack Obama was elected from the state of Illinois in 2004, but with his election to the presidency in 2008, no African Americans currently serve in the U.S. Senate.

Figure 11.5 traces the increasing success of African Americans in getting elected to the House of Representatives. The figure shows that as in the Senate, African Americans' initial service in the House came about in the Reconstruction period. But the successes of that era were short-lived, and the numbers of African Americans in Congress would not match those of the immediate post-Reconstruction period until after the civil rights movement of the 1960s. Today, as in the case of women, more African Americans serve in Congress than at any other point in U.S. history.

Latinos' success at winning election to Congress still drastically lags behind their proportion of the population, with Latinos constituting nearly 14 percent of the population but just 5 percent of the members of the House of Representatives and 3 percent of the Senate. But many states, including New Mexico, California, Texas, and Arizona, are seeing rising numbers of Latinos elected to state legislatures, providing a pool of candidates who could move on to run for Congress. As women, African Americans, and ethnic minorities take up an increasing proportion of the eligibility pool—the group of people deemed qualified for office—diversity in Congress is sure to grow.

Congress is an ever-evolving institution. The national legislature is shaped by the framers' vision that created it; by the groups and individuals that seek to, and do, influence it; and by the broader electorate who vote for the representatives who serve in it. The Constitution's framers ingeniously created a strong legislative system designed to dominate the national government. In doing so they simultaneously—and significantly—checked the power of the executive.

The framers ensured that the legislative branch of the federal government would be responsive to changing times. Today, Congress is more demographically diverse than ever before in history. It has also responded to modern challenges by exercising a wider scope of powers, concerned with issues that were unimaginable even two decades ago, let alone more than two centuries ago. Congressional decision making today is influenced by shifting constituencies in a country that is rapidly growing more diverse.

For groups and individuals alike, Congress stands as a crucial resource for civic engagement, political participation, and efficacy. The digital technologies of today and tomorrow will continuously provide citizens with powerful tools for communicating with congressional policy makers and influencing policy. With Congress well structured to respond to constituents' needs, ongoing technological advances and the spread of cheap technology to more and more citizens mean that members of Congress and their staffs should be increasingly accessible to the people. And representatives' district offices will continue to provide constituents another easily accessed channel through which to convey their needs and interests to their representatives—and through which their representatives, in turn, can monitor the opinions of their constituents so that they may better represent them.

Congress has proved itself to be a remarkably flexible institution, responding to changes in society, shifting constituencies, and increasingly diverse members, particularly in recent times. That Congress will become even more diverse is relatively assured.

Summary

1. The Origins of Congress

The Constitution's framers intended Congress to be the strongest and most important branch of the federal government, a body both representative and deliberative. They structured the national legislature in such a way as to ensure both a check on the power of the executive and a voice for the people. The Constitution provided a flexible framework for the evolution of Congress to meet changing times. That framework continues to this day to shape the structural and procedural differences between the House of Representatives and the Senate, including the two houses' respective sizes, rules, and processes.

2. Congressional Elections

One of the most important factors shaping congressional elections is incumbency, which confers numerous advantages to those already serving in elective office. Congressional elections are also shaped by the processes of reapportionment and redistricting, which occur every ten years.

3. Powers of Congress

The Constitution enumerates certain powers for Congress, including judicial, economic, national security, regulatory, and administrative powers. Other powers of the federal legislature have evolved through national legislators' interpretation of the Constitution's necessary and proper clause, which has been a mechanism for the expansion of congressional authority.

4. Functions of Congress

The primary functions of Congress are public policy making, popular representation, oversight of the executive branch to ensure the proper administration of laws, civic education, and management of societal conflict. In their representation function, members of Congress might follow the instructed delegate model or the trustee model of representation.

5. The House and the Senate Compared

Members of the House of Representatives and the Senate serve different constituencies for different terms of office. House members are elected for a two-year term from a congressional district, and senators serve for a six-year term and represent an entire state. With respect to the legislative structure and environment, the House, with its larger size (435 members today), is more formal, and the Senate (100 members) is less formal.

6. The Legislative Process

A bill, the precursor to a law, can be introduced by a member of the House or the Senate. Once proposed, the bill is then referred to a committee, where it is debated, reviewed, and amended. If it passes out of committee, it is debated by the full chamber; if it passes in both the House and Senate, the president may sign the bill, veto it, or take no action. By far, most bills introduced do not become law.

7. Congressional Leadership

House leadership consists of the Speaker of the House of Representatives and the House majority and minority leaders, plus the majority and minority whips. In practice the Senate majority leader wields the power in the upper chamber of the national legislature. Frequently, the skills demonstrated by various leaders in Congress are a reflection of the needs of their chambers—quiet fortitude in some circumstances, adept partisanship in others.

8. Decision Making in Congress: The Legislative Context

Political parties, congressional colleagues, interest groups, the president, and constituent viewpoints all play roles in influencing members of Congress. In recent years, partisanship has increased in Congress, making legislators' debates more rancorous and divisive.

9. The People and Their Elected Representatives

Although Congress is not demographically representative of the United States, it is more demographically diverse than the leadership structure of other institutions. Nonetheless, Congress is becoming increasingly diverse, with higher proportions of women, African Americans, and Latinos serving today than ever before.

Key Terms

agency review 403
agenda setting 398
attentive public 413
bill 400
casework 396
cloture 404
conference committee 404
discharge petition 403
earmark 396
filibuster 404
gerrymandering 392
hearings 403
hopper 400
House majority leader 406
House minority leader 406

instructed delegate model 395
joint committee 403
joint referral 400
lead committee 400
logrolling 411
majority whip 406
majority-minority district 392
markup 403
minority whip 406
ombudsperson 396
oversight 398
pocket veto 405
pork barrel 395
president pro tempore 406

reapportionment 392
redistricting 392
report 403
Rules Committee 403
select committee 403
Senate majority leader 407
Senate minority leader 407
seniority system 400
Speaker of the House 405
standing committee 403
subcommittee 403
trustee model 395
unanimous consent 404

For Review

1. Why was Congress created in the way it was?
2. What impact does incumbency have on congressional elections?
3. What is the difference between reapportionment and redistricting?
4. Historically, what has been the impact of the necessary and proper (elastic) clause?
5. What are the two types of congressional powers?
6. What impact do the constitutionally enumerated duties of the House and Senate have on the expertise of each chamber?
7. Outline the basic steps of the legislative process.
8. What factors influence the legislative process? How?
9. Why are so many bills introduced but so few passed?
10. How do the qualities of congressional leaders differ today from the ones needed in earlier eras?
11. Why has party-line voting increased in Congress in recent years?

For Critical Thinking and Discussion

1. If you were serving in Congress, would you tend to follow the instructed delegate model of representation or the trustee model? Why? What might be the likely outcome of your choice?
2. How does the legislative process differ in the House and Senate? In which chamber is the process more streamlined? More deliberative? Why?
3. What do you and the people you know think about the work and contributions of Congress? Would you give Congress high or low approval ratings as an institution, or something in between? Who is your own congressional representative, and what rating would you give her or him? Why?
4. Log on to the Library of Congress Web site (http://thomas.loc.gov/) and read about issues currently on the floor of the House of Representatives. Can you see the impact of any of the external influences mentioned in this chapter on the legislative process? Describe these influences and discuss how they are shaping the process.
5. Why do you think so few women and racial and ethnic minorities have been elected to Congress? Why is this situation changing? What do you imagine that Congress will look like, demographically speaking, in the year 2050?

MULTIPLE CHOICE: Choose the lettered item that answers the question correctly.

1. The drawing of legislative district boundaries to benefit an incumbent, a political party, or another group is called
   a. earmarking.
   b. gerrymandering.
   c. reapportioning.
   d. logrolling.

2. A legislative power held by the chief executive whereby the president can reject a piece of congressional legislation with reasons provided for his rejection is called
   a. a markup.
   b. a veto.
   c. a logroll.
   d. cloture.

3. The process by which the members of legislative committees edit a bill with suggested language for changes and amendments is called
   a. cloture.
   b. logrolling.
   c. markup.
   d. agency review.

4. When an elected or appointed leader acts as an advocate for citizens by listening to and investigating complaints against a government agency, that official is called
   a. an ombudsperson.
   b. a whip.
   c. an overseer.
   d. the president pro tempore.

5. A special tactic used to extract a bill from a committee in order to have it considered by the entire House is called
   a. a discharge petition.
   b. oversight.
   c. cloture.
   d. unanimous consent.

6. Personal work by a member of Congress on behalf of a constituent or group of constituents, typically aimed at getting the government to do something the constituent wants done, is called
   a. oversight.
   b. pork barrel politics.
   c. casework.
   d. logrolling.

7. The process of allocating seats in the House of Representatives to each state based upon changes in the state's population since the last census is called
   a. gerrymandering.
   b. redesigning.
   c. redistricting.
   d. reapportionment.

8. The model of representation in which a member of the House or the Senate should articulate and vote for the position that best represents the views of constituents is called the
   a. instructed delegate model.
   b. trustee model.
   c. expediency model.
   d. casework model.

9. A designation within a spending bill that provides for a specific expenditure is called
   a. an earmark.
   b. gerrymandering.
   c. reapportionment.
   d. logrolling.

10. The process by which the legislative branch "checks" the executive branch to ensure that the laws Congress has passed are being administered in keeping with congressional legislators' intent is called
   a. oversight.
   b. pork barrel politics.
   c. casework.
   d. logrolling.

FILL IN THE BLANKS.

11. The _____ theoretically is the chair of the Senate; in reality this title has been an honorary one, with the senator of the majority party having the longest record of continuous service in the Senate being elected to the position.

12. _____ is the determination by Congress of which public issues the government should consider for legislation.

13. The wooden box that sits on a desk at the front of the chamber of the House of Representatives, into which a House member places a bill he or she would like to introduce, is called the _____.

14. A congressional committee created to consider a specific policy issue or address a specific concern is called a _____.

15. The practice, abolished in the 104th Congress, by which a bill could be referred to two different committees for consideration was called _____.

Answers: 1. b; 2. b; 3. c; 4. a; 5. a; 6. c; 7. d; 8. a; 9. a; 10. a; 11. president pro tempore; 12. Agenda setting; 13. hopper; 14. select committee; 15. joint referral.

RESOURCES FOR RESEARCH AND ACTION

Internet Resources

American Democracy Now Web site
www.mhhe.com/harrison1e Consult the book's Web site for study guides, interactive activities, simulations, and current hotlinks to additional information on Congress.

Congressional Quarterly
www.cq.org *Congressional Quarterly (CQ)* is an important provider of news and analysis for Washington insiders, but its Web site is a subscriber site. Nonetheless, free trial subscriptions are available. Its job opportunities site, www.cq.com/corp/show.do?page=corp _hilljobs, is not password protected.

C-Span
www.c-span.org The cable television network C-Span provides a plethora of information on Congress, including Internet video, audio, and podcast programs of congressional hearings, committee meetings, C-Span video series, and a wide variety of public affairs information.

Library of Congress
http://thomas.loc.gov (note the absence of www) Thomas (named for Thomas Jefferson) is the Web site for the Library of Congress, the most important clearinghouse for information about Congress, legislation, hearings, votes, and other federal matters.

Roll Call
www.rollcall.com This Web site for *Roll Call,* the "newspaper of Capitol Hill since 1955," offers an insider's look at the world of Capitol Hill, including issue analysis, politics, and opinions.

U.S. Senate and U.S. House of Representatives
www.senate.gov and **www.house.gov** These Web sites for the Senate and House provide information about members of Congress, votes, pending legislation, committees, and session schedules, plus information about the Capitol building and information for visitors.

Recommended Readings

Ahuja, Sunil and Robert Dewhirst (eds.). *The Roads to Congress.* Belmont, CA: Wadsworth, 2006. A reader examining several key congressional races, including safe seats, open seats, and contested seats in the House and Senate.

Dodd, Lawrence C. and Bruce J. Oppenheimer. *Congress Reconsidered,* 8th ed. Washington, DC: CQ Press, 2004. The most recent edition of a classic series providing comprehensive coverage of the evolution of the American Congress.

Fenno, Richard F., Jr. *Home Style: House Members in Their Districts.* New York: Longman, 2002. Fenno traveled the United States observing members of Congress at home in their districts and explains how constituent interaction affects congressional decision making.

Hastert, Dennis. *Speaker: Lessons from Forty Years in Coaching and Politics.* Washington, DC: Regnery Books, 1993. A political memoir/how-to book that is part political autobiography of one of the nation's least-known high-ranking elected officials and part handbook for those interested in learning from his experiences.

Loomis, Burdett and Wendy J. Schiller. *The Contemporary Congress.* Belmont, CA: Wadsworth, 2005. A concise yet comprehensive analysis of Congress, particularly the legislative context that influences the legislative process.

Martin, Janet M. *Lessons from the Hill: The Legislative Journey of an Education Program.* New York: St. Martin's Press, 1994. A case study of one piece of legislation, in which the author illuminates the various influences on the legislative process.

O'Neill, Thomas P. *Man of the House: The Life and Political Memoirs of Speaker Tip O'Neill.* New York: Random House, 1987. The political memoir of a long-term Speaker of the House of Representatives, providing a fascinating glimpse into the "real world" of Capitol Hill politics from the 1960s through the 1980s.

Sulkin, Tracy. *Issue Politics in Congress.* New York: Cambridge University Press, 2005. An examination of the issue of representation through the rubric of issue politics—that is, why legislators adopt the issue stances they do.

Thomas, Sue. *How Women Legislate.* New York: Oxford University Press, 1994. Ground-breaking analysis of the differences and similarities between how men and women approach the task of legislating.

Movies of Interest

The Congress (1988)
This Ken Burns documentary provides a fine introduction to the U.S. Congress (both the institution and the Capitol building). Burns traces the history of the institution and the people who have served in it, including nineteenth-century statesmen Henry Clay and Daniel Webster and continuing to Congress's modern leaders.

The Ugly American (1963)
This drama stars Marlon Brando as Harrison Carter MacWhite, who, after surviving an acrimonious Senate confirmation hearing, becomes ambassador to a Southeast Asian nation on the brink of civil war.

Mr. Smith Goes to Washington (1939)
This classic Frank Capra movie features Jimmy Stewart as Jefferson Smith, who, after the death of a senator, is appointed to serve in the U.S. Senate despite his political naïveté. Stewart's depiction of a filibuster informs most Americans' perception of this political maneuver.

National Journal

A Rookie Congressmen: Savvy, Minus the Seniority

Freshman Rep. Peter Welch, D-Vt., knew immediately who was calling when he picked up the phone in his congressional office a few days before last year's August recess. "Pee-tah," bellowed Sen. Bernie Sanders, I-Vt., "I need your help."

Sanders was asking his successor in the House to perform a daunting task—and with less than 24 hours' notice. He wanted Welch to add to the House version of a sweeping energy bill a Sanders amendment that encouraged universities to support energy-efficiency projects. The Senate had approved the proposal—which was of great interest to environmentally friendly Vermont—but House committees had dropped it. To help Sanders, Welch would have to bump up against Energy and Commerce Committee Chairman John Dingell, D-Mich., the dean of the House who is not accustomed to taking suggestions from the Senate, let alone from a newcomer in his own chamber.

"I had to get Chairman Dingell to be agreeable." Welch recounted in a recent interview. "He agreed that I could call his committee staff, though they objected [to adding Sanders's amendment] because they wanted more leverage in the conference committee with the Senate." Ultimately, Welch used the parliamentary leverage of the Rules Committee, on which he sits, to get the provision inserted into the House-passed package, and it was part of the broader energy bill enacted in December. He explained that the feat was possible because "I had built some relationship at the Rules Committee with Mr. Dingell, who is a very gracious man."

At a time when many freshman House Democrats are worrying about a tough re-election campaign—or are still trying to find their way around the Capitol—Welch acts like a veteran. He has drawn on his background as a lawyer who served two lengthy stretches in the Vermont Senate, including eight years as president pro tem, to comfort-ably maneuver through Washington's legislative channels. He has already taken on substantial energy and environmental issues and procurement reforms that Speaker Nancy Pelosi, D-Calif., and committee chairmen have highlighted in their agenda.

"He's very smart, and he takes the initiative," Oversight and Government Reform Committee Chairman Henry Waxman, D-Calif., said of Welch. "He speaks with a great deal of authority. He has a very bright future."

A veteran House Democratic leadership aide added, "It's like [Welch] has been here for years. He is connected in every way. . . .

He's always looking for something to do. He knows that it will help him to be involved."

Involved indeed. When Democrats regained control of Congress, they decided that as an inducement to serve on the Rules Committee, they would permit its members to serve on another prominent House committee as well. Welch used the opportunity to join Waxman's Oversight panel, which has wide-ranging investigative authority. The two have worked together on numerous issues.

Welch's influence was apparent, when the House passed his bill to close a potential loophole on government contracts. He initiated the measure after learning that the Justice Department had published a proposed regulation in November that would have exempted overseas contracts from federal reporting requirements. Even though Bush administration officials later acknowledged and fixed what they described as an unin-tentional error, Welch said, "I don't totally trust the administration to get it right, and I'm skeptical of their explanation that this was, quote, a mistake."

Despite the administration's opposition, the House passed Welch's legislation by voice vote. Rep. Tom Davis, R-Va., the ranking member on the Oversight Committee, said he enjoyed working with Welch, and he praised the freshman's handling of the bill, including his willingness to accept some technical changes. "He is thoughtful, nice, and earnest," said a GOP aide who has watched Welch in action. "He clearly wants to learn and has respect for others' views."

At a time when many freshman House Democrats are worrying about a tough re-election campaign—or are still trying to find their way around the Capitol—Welch acts like a veteran.

Welch, who recalls with nostalgia the less partisan tone of the Vermont Senate, said, "My goal is to protect taxpayers. And I have more confidence that will happen when there is bipartisan agreement." Although he succeeded a socialist, Sanders, in the House, Welch takes a more pragmatic, middle-of-the-road approach. His score in National Journal's 2007 vote ratings made him the 77th-most-liberal House member, while Sanders was the fourth-most-liberal senator.

Top Democrats took notice of Welch soon after he arrived in Washington. Only a few weeks after he was sworn in, he announced that he had become the first House member to make his congressional office carbon-neutral. By providing financial support for renewable-energy projects in Vermont, he said, he was offsetting the greenhouse-gas emissions generated by his D.C. office.

After Welch discussed his actions with Pelosi aides and with Dan Beard, the House's chief administrative officer, Pelosi and other Democratic leaders announced a "greening the Capitol" initiative last June to make Congress carbon-neutral. "Peter Welch has been a leader on this issue," Pelosi said in unveiling the plan. "The House must lead by example, and Congressman Welch exemplifies this key model."

Welch has been out front on two other major energy and environmental policy initiatives. Working with co-sponsors from California, he took the lead in September in urging the Environmental Protection Agency to grant California a waiver for its stricter tailpipe-emissions standards. That issue has generated significant attention in Vermont and other states that have adopted the California standard; Vermont's attorney general spearheaded a lawsuit against EPA after Administrator Stephen Johnson rejected the application.

More recently, Welch has provided talking points to party leaders to support their call for the president to stop filling the Strategic Petroleum Reserve, because of soaring gasoline prices. With Democratic Caucus Chairman Rahm Emanuel, D-Ill., and Rep. Edward Markey, D-Mass., who chairs the Select Committee on Energy Independence and Global Warming, Welch filed a bill in February to suspend purchases for the reserve. "We should stop paying record prices to top off a reserve that is nearly full," Welch said at the time. "History shows that the result will be lower oil and gas prices."

In advocating his energy proposals, Welch has cited the onerous burden of high fuel prices on his home state and what he has called the "Enron loophole" that has allowed energy speculators to "rip off" his constituents who struggle to heat their homes each winter. "My work is all about Vermont," he said.

At the Rules Committee, Welch has managed 17 House rules, which govern floor deliberations on legislation by, for instance, setting the length of debate and the amendments allowed. The panel has long been viewed as a "leadership arm" where politically secure members perform vital housekeeping tasks on behalf of majority-party leaders. Given the leadership's increasingly centralized control, entrepreneurial panel members can be highly productive, as long as their efforts are politically attuned. As the leadership aide noted, the Rules Committee freshmen are "very valuable to the speaker."

While some might find it surprising that a freshman would exert influence at the committee, which was once the bastion of more-senior members, a notable generational shift has taken place on the panel. Rules Chairwoman Louise Slaughter, D-N.Y., is the only Democratic member who served there before the party lost its majority in 1994. Of the panel's eight other Democrats, four are freshmen, two joined the House after 2002, and the two others have served a bit more than a decade.

Republicans started the move toward putting junior lawmakers on Rules when they took control in 1995, although only one GOP member was then a freshman. Perhaps the GOP's most significant internal change at Rules came in 2005, when four veteran members departed to join Ways and Means, Energy and Commerce, and other more-influential House panels. Asked about the exodus from the supposedly prestigious panel, Rep. Deborah Pryce, R-Ohio, said at the time that sitting on the Rules Committee limits members because they "don't get involved as much in the substance" of legislation.

Some committee veterans have viewed these moves with dismay as a downgrading of the panel's influence. "The result is good for individual members, but it distracts from the prestige that the Rules Committee once had," said Don Wolfensberger, a former GOP chief of staff at Rules who is now director of the Congress Project at the Woodrow Wilson International Center for Scholars.

So far, the Rules Committee has clearly been "good" for Welch. But he is modest in refusing to discuss his prospects for advancing in the House. "This is a target-rich environment," he said. "I am philosophical. We work hard, and things will take care of themselves."

He reacted with mock horror to the suggestion that he might be in line to succeed either of his home-state senators, each of whom is several years older than he. "That gets me in trouble," Welch said. "I am very, very friendly with Patrick [Leahy] and Bernie. We have an excellent working relationship. . . . Patrick's seniority has been very helpful to me." In particular, Leahy, who chairs the Judiciary Committee, has told Welch that he enthusiastically supports his contractor-abuse measure and wants to secure Senate passage.

Although Welch noted, "I am old for a freshman," he said his age adds to his comfort level. "I am settled and I don't look at other rungs on the ladder." The death in 2004 of his wife, Joan Smith—who was a dean at the University of Vermont—after a long struggle with cancer "gave me perspective," he added. "She was from Chicago and she loved politics. She would love Congress." Welch appears to be drawing pleasure for the two of them.

THEN: Freshman members of Congress were appointed to positions on less prestigious committees.

NOW: Both parties are seeing the value of placing freshman representatives on more influential committees.

NEXT: Will the informal legislative system in which seniority rules and influence is traded back and forth remain an inevitable aspect of Congress?
Will future newcomers to congress experience similar difficulties in getting things done?
How will the ability to navigate the complicated hierarchy of the House of Representatives shape the congressional careers of those freshmen elected in the 2008 elections?

The
Presidency

THEN Presidential power grew over the centuries to "imperial" proportions and then ebbed in the late twentieth century in the wake of scandals.

NOW The imperial presidency has reemerged as a model for viewing presidents today.

NEXT Will future presidents continue down the path of an imperial presidency?

What checks will constrain future presidents' exercise of power?

How will the relationship between presidents and the people change in the future?

Deciding the 2008 Democratic Nominee: Students for Obama

In November 2007, it was apparent to political scientists and the public at large that Senator Hillary Clinton (D-New York) would be the Democratic nominee for president of the United States the following fall. But apparently somebody forgot to tell the college students. Starting in January and continuing through the spring of 2008, Senator Barack Obama (D-Illinois) started outpolling Clinton in primaries and caucuses. During the protracted contest for the nomination, Clinton was never able to best Obama in the delegate count. | What happened? The answer is that Senator Obama's message of change resonated strongly with young voters. Largely through the efforts of Students for Obama chapters, college students influenced the outcome of the Democratic primary in several states. College students' participation in the primaries broke records in many states, and estimates based on exit polls indicated that they were much more likely to participate in electoral activities than their peers who did not attend college. And while many college students turned out to support Republican candidates in that party's primary, John McCain served up the Republican nomination relatively early. But the historic participation of young voters in the primaries played an important role. Their increased political participation and their attraction to Obama were key factors in his securing the nomination. | According to the Students for Obama Web site:

> Senator Obama's candidacy for President has inspired millions of young Americans to believe in their power to make America great again. Students for Barack Obama, founded in the summer of 2006, began with a few students using Facebook to petition Senator Obama to run for President in 2008. The passion and dedication of thousands of students has transformed that movement into the official student organization of Obama for America—and one of the largest grassroots student organizations in history.*

College students from San Diego State University to Eastern Maine Community College and even some high school students joined forces to form over 600 chapters of Students for Obama. In Billings, Montana, thirty students met one Thursday in May to eat pizza—and to plan a winning strategy for getting out the vote in that state's primary, which included leafleting downtown Billings with flyers reminding people to vote early. Robb Friedlander, 18, from Overland Park, Kansas, was one of the cofounders of "Hofstra for Obama." Members of that group traveled to Philadelphia to get out the vote during the Pennsylvania primary and phone-banked for Obama during the Ohio and Texas primaries. Those same efforts would be replicated in the November election, and Obama's strong support among college-age voters, gauged at 66 percent, would be instrumental in helping him win the presidency. "He really does inspire college-age students to believe that we can change something," Friedlander noted.** As one University of Iowa student said when Senator Obama visited the campus, "This is our campaign!"***

> College students were among Senator Barack Obama's most ardent supporters and most important groups of volunteers.

* http://students.barackobama.com/page/content/sfbohome.
** www.cbsnews.com/stories/2008/05/14/politics/uwire/main4097674.shtml.
*** http://students.barackobama.com/page/content/sfbohome.

The opening vignette illustrates

one channel by which individuals and groups can influence the presidency. Each presidency is shaped not only by the person who holds the office but also by the support of constituencies within the public, the support of Congress for presidential policy priorities, and the societal context of the day. Each presidential term can be molded and manipulated in many ways, with the result that one president may appear strong, and the next, weak—or a president may be both effective and ineffectual during the course of just one term. In looking at the roles presidents play in conducting their office, as well as the sources of their power, we consider in this chapter why some presidents are more effective than others.

The presidency is constantly evolving. The institution of the presidency that George W. Bush has left behind is not the one that George Washington left behind. In the discussion that follows, we examine the development of the presidency in order to gain historical perspective on how the individuals who have served as president have changed the nature of the institution over time and what the impacts of those changes are for presidents today.

The institution of the presidency has changed in part because of the evolution of the public expectations of the institution that, for many Americans, embodies their government.[1] It is fitting therefore that this chapter often looks through the prism of civic engagement to probe into the complicated relationship between the people and the presidency. We consider that even within this most "imperial" of the American institutions of government, the people, like the Students for Obama described in the vignette, play a vital part in determining not only who serves as president but also how effective and successful the president is in exercising the executive power.[2]

Presidential Elections

The relationship between Americans and their president begins well before a president takes the oath of office. In presidential election years, nonstop campaigning provides ample opportunities for the public to learn about presidential candidates and their positions on issues. Campaigns also present many avenues for participation by the people—for example, by volunteering in or contributing to candidates' campaigns or even just by debating candidates' views around the water cooler. Although these opportunities for citizen engagement are especially abundant during a presidential election year, similar chances to get involved arise well before, because potential candidates typically position themselves years in advance of election day to secure their party's nomination and to win the general election.

As discussed in Chapter 8, the delegates to the national conventions are chosen by citizens in each state who vote in their party's primary election. After the nominees have been decided, typically by late August, they and their vice-presidential running mates begin their general election campaign. Usually the parties' choice of nominee is a foregone conclusion by the time of the convention. Eligible incumbent presidents (that is, those who have served only one term) are nearly always renominated, and the nominee of the opposing party is often determined by the primary results.

The votes tallied on Election Day determine which presidential candidate's slate of electors will cast their ballots, in accordance with state law. There are 538 electors in the Electoral College because the number of electors is based on the number of members of Congress—435 in the House of Representatives, 100 in the Senate—plus three electors who

SHOULD WE ABOLISH THE ELECTORAL COLLEGE?

The Issue: The 2000 presidential election saw a historically unlikely but obviously possible occurrence: the candidate with the most popular votes, Democrat Al Gore, lost the presidential election to his opponent, Republican George W. Bush. In every other election for federal office, the candidate with the most popular votes wins that seat. But instead of the direct election of the president, the Constitution requires that the president be elected by the Electoral College. Essentially, the winner is determined by the cumulative results of fifty-one separate elections, one conducted in each state plus the District of Columbia, with the number of electoral votes determined in proportion to the size of the state's congressional delegation.

Is the Electoral College system unfair? Should we abolish it?

Yes: The Electoral College is exclusive and undemocratic. The nature of the Electoral College system demands that candidates focus nearly exclusively on key swing states that will be pivotal to their election and on populous states that carry the most electoral votes. The system is undemocratic because of its reliance on plurality elections within the states. In a plurality, the candidate with the most votes wins, even if that candidate does not receive a majority of the votes. The ultimate victory in the 2000 presidential election by the candidate (George W. Bush) whom the most people did not prefer highlights the undemocratic nature of the Electoral College. The Electoral College should be abolished.

No: The constitutionally mandated Electoral College system provides a crucial check on what would otherwise be the unchecked will of the people. In structuring the Electoral College as they did, the Constitution's framers devised a way of representing the views of both the *people* who elect the electors and the *states* because of the state-based nature of the elections. Other checks on the will of the people include staggered senatorial elections (in which one-third of that body is elected every two years) and appointed Supreme Court justices, and these are evidence of the framers' view that the will of the people needed to be tempered. If the Electoral College were abolished, the most populous geographical regions would dominate in presidential elections. Urban areas would have tremendous clout in presidential elections, and less densely populated rural areas would be virtually ignored. The current structure strengthens the power of the states and in this way ensures that our federal system remains strong.

Other approaches: Because of the difficulty of abolishing the Electoral College, various schemes have been proposed that would make it almost impossible for the loser of the popular vote to win the presidency, including awarding a state's electoral votes proportionally instead of on a winner-take-all basis, dividing electoral votes by congressional district (currently done in Maine and Nebraska), and awarding extra electoral votes to the winner of the popular vote. Legislation recently passed in Maryland, Hawaii, Illinois, and New Jersey would commit those states' electors to vote for the winner of the popular vote if states representing a 270-vote majority in the Electoral College enact similar legislation.

What do you think?

① Do you think that the Electoral College should be abolished, should remain the same, or should be reformed? Why? If your answer is "should be reformed," what changes would you implement?

② If the Electoral College were abolished, what impact would the change likely have on voters in your home state? Does that scenario influence your view?

③ Americans revere the Constitution as a near-sacred document. Typically, citizens are reluctant to advocate amending the "supreme law of the land." Does reluctance to amend the handiwork of the Constitution's framers influence your view?

represent the people of the District of Columbia. A presidential candidate today needs a simple majority of votes (270) to win the presidency. On the Monday following the second Wednesday of December, the slate of electors chosen in each state meet in their respective state capitals and cast their electoral votes. The results are then announced in a joint session of Congress in early January. In most presidential elections, however, the winner is known on election night because analysts tabulate the outcome in each state and predict the electoral vote. The winner takes the oath of office as president in inaugural ceremonies on January 20.

Presidential Roles in the Domestic Sphere

A newly elected president quickly discovers that the presidential office requires the performance of a variety of functions each day. Many of these roles involve leadership in domestic policy issues,[3] whether it is George W. Bush's priority of reforming schools, Bill Clinton's desire to overhaul health care, or all presidents' need to keep the economy sound and growing strongly. As leaders in the domestic sphere, presidents must interact with Congress, manage the economy, and serve as the leader of their party.[4]

Chief Legislator

Although the separation of powers precludes the president from actually creating laws, presidents nonetheless have significant legislative power.[5] Presidents can influence Congress by lobbying its members to support or oppose pending legislation and by defining the congressional agenda in the annual presidential State of the Union message. Presidents also "legislate" when they submit the budget for the entire federal government to Congress annually, although Congress ultimately passes the spending plan.

Today one of the most important legislative tools at a president's disposal is the authority either to sign legislation into law or to veto it,[6] as described in Chapter 2. Although a veto allows the president to check the power of Congress, it also provides Congress with the opportunity to check presidential power by overriding the veto with a two-thirds majority vote.[7] In giving the president the right to veto laws, the Constitution essentially integrates the executive into the legislative process.[8]

As discussed in Chapter 11, there are several variations on the veto. During a regular legislative session, if the president does not sign or veto a bill within ten days after receiving it from Congress, the bill becomes law even without the president's consent. But if the president receives a congressional bill for his signature and Congress is scheduled to adjourn within ten days, the president can exercise a pocket veto by taking no action at all. Further, during the presidency of Bill Clinton, Congress statutorily equipped the president with a new kind of veto power: the **line-item veto** allowed the president to strike out specific line items on an appropriations bill while allowing the rest of the bill to become law. In 1997, however, the Supreme Court declared the line-item veto unconstitutional, asserting that it violated the separation of powers because the Constitution grants Congress the inherent power to tax and to spend.

Figure 12.1 shows that the use of the veto varies widely from president to president. Modern presidents are generally much more likely to veto legislation than their earlier counterparts were. A primary determinant of whether a president will regularly exercise veto power is whether the president's party has a majority in Congress.

An exception to this trend was the presidency of Franklin D. Roosevelt. As Figure 12.1 shows, during Roosevelt's twelve-year term in the White House, he issued 372 vetoes, or 12 percent of all presidential vetoes. Roosevelt chalked up this exceptional record despite having strong Democratic majorities in Congress throughout his tenure. But Roosevelt used the veto much differently than most presidents do. Because he was such a strong president, he exercised his veto power to prevent the passage of even small pieces of legislation with which he disagreed. Most presidents save the veto for important legislative matters, as they are unwilling to offend members of Congress over smaller laws that they do not favor.

President George W. Bush vetoed relatively few (nine) pieces of legislation during his two terms of office. His first veto came in 2006, when a congressionally passed measure that would have eased restrictions on federal funding for stem cell research reached Bush's desk. One explanation for Bush's scant use of vetoes is that while the Republicans controlled Congress, Bush did not need to veto legislation often because he effectively convinced Congress to act on his legislative priorities. Indeed, eight of President Bush's nine vetoes occurred after the Democrats took control of Congress in 2006.

But President Bush used a different tactic—the signing statement—to put his mark on the way policies were to be administered during his tenure of office. A presidential

line-item veto
power of the president to strike out specific line items on an appropriations bill while allowing the rest of the bill to become law; declared unconstitutional by the Supreme Court in 1997

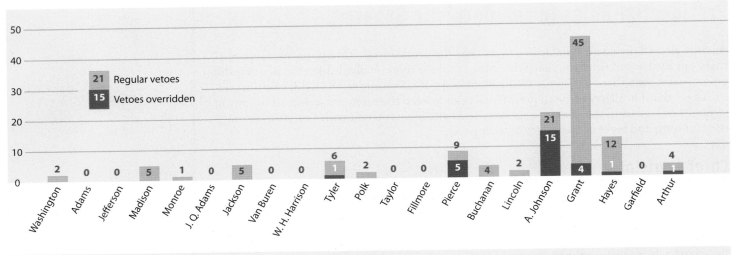

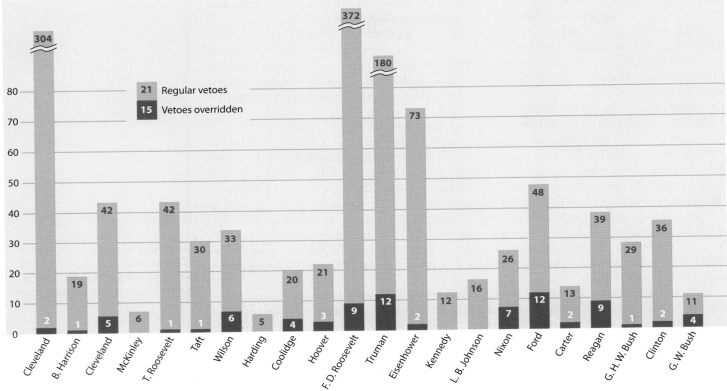

FIGURE 12.1 ■ **PRESIDENTIAL VETOES, 1789–2008** What does this table generally indicate about the use of the presidential veto over time? What trend is evident in presidents' use of the veto from the administration of Franklin Roosevelt to the present? Why do you think a president is more likely to veto legislation when one party controls Congress and the other controls the presidency?

signing statement
a written message that the president issues upon signing a bill into law

signing statement is a written message that the president issues upon signing a bill into law. A presidential signing statement may, for example, direct executive departments in how they should implement a law, taking into account constitutional or political considerations. Controversy arose over the perception that the president used the tool of the signing statement to modify the intent of the laws. Critics, including the American Bar Association, complained that by using signing statements, President Bush was asserting unconstitutional legislative authority, and some critics compared the presidential directives to invoking the line-item veto in some pieces of legislation.[9] In all, President Bush issued more than 750 signing statements during his two terms of office.

Chief Economist

Although the Constitution makes no mention of presidential responsibilities with respect to the economy, the president's submitting a budget to Congress reflects what has become another key presidential role: the manager of the economy. Of course, the president does not exert a great deal of control over the enormous national economy, but presidents have numerous tools at their disposal that powerfully influence the country's economic performance. For example, in 2008 when Wall Street reacted unfavorably to ongoing financial crises in the banking, mortgage, insurance, and financial services sector, the Bush administration was at the forefront in urging Congress to shore up the corporations with a bailout plan. In addition, by submitting a budget to Congress, presidents set the economic priorities of the legislative agenda. Presidents also help to establish the regulatory and economic environment in which businesses must operate, and in this way they can influence economic growth and employment levels.

Central in presidents' oversight of economic performance is the appointment of the Federal Reserve Board ("the Fed") and its chair, who play a crucial role in managing the economy. The position of Fed chair tends to be less partisan than many other appointments, and a given chair often serves under presidents of both political parties. In 2005, President Bush named Ben Bernanke as Fed chair, replacing Alan Greenspan, who had served for eighteen years under both Democrats and Republicans.

The appointment of a Fed chair has a lot to do with consumer confidence, as well as with support from economically influential individuals on Wall Street, including investment bankers, stockbrokers, and mortgage lenders. The fact that a Fed action (such as increasing the interest rate) can send the stock market plummeting sheds light on why presidential appointments to the Fed are watched so closely.

Party Leader

One of the most important domestic roles for the president is political: the function of party leader. As chief of one of the two main parties, the president is a symbolic leader for the party members and asserts influence in the party's operations by selecting the national party chair and serving as the party's premier fund-raiser. The presidential function of party leader has become even more significant in recent White House administrations, with presidents working ever more aggressively to promote

> One way presidents try to affect the nation's economy is through the appointment of the "Fed Chief," who oversees the board that plays a crucial role in managing the economy. Federal Reserve Chairman Ben Bernanke is frequently called upon to testify before Congress on the state of the economy and monetary policy, as he does here before the House Financial Services Committee in February 2008.

> In the president's role as party leader, former President George W. Bush (R) formally endorsed Republican presidential nominee John McCain in an attempt to shore up McCain's support within the Republican party base. But the unpopular president's support of McCain was viewed negatively by some general election voters, and McCain lost his bid for the presidency.

GLOBAL COMPARISONS

PARLIAMENTARY SYSTEMS

In the many nations of the world that have parliamentary systems, the country's chief executive—the *prime minister* or *premier*—is elected not by the people but by the members of the majority political party in the legislature. Parliamentary

When will the United States' electoral system produce a woman president?

systems distinguish between the head of government and the head of state. The *head of government* is the prime minister or premier, the individual who leads the government in its work. The *head of state* is frequently a constitutional monarch whose duties are primarily ceremonial and symbolic. In Great Britain, Prime Minister Gordon Brown is the head of government, and Queen Elizabeth II is the head of state.

When compared with a presidential system like that of the United States, parliamentary systems are viewed as being more responsive to the will of the people. Although the people do

not directly elect the prime minister, the desire of members of a parliament to serve the needs of their constituents ensures that the prime minister remains responsive as well.

Although the United States' presidential system has not yet produced a woman president, female members of many parliaments around the world have succeeded in getting elected to the chief executive post—prime minister. This is the case even in nations where the political culture places less emphasis on women's equality than Americans do. Women have served as prime minister in Sri Lanka, India, Israel, the Central African Republic, Great Britain, Portugal, Bolivia, Dominica, Norway, Yugoslavia, Netherlands Antilles, New Zealand, Bermuda, Guyana, Bangladesh, Haiti, Turkey, Rwanda, Canada, Burundi, France, Nicaragua, Lithuania, and Pakistan.

Parliamentary systems lack the separation of powers between the legislative and executive branches that characterizes presidential systems. In addition, parliamentary systems are seen as more unstable than presidential systems because the governments they form often depend on coalitions made up of members of two or more parties. When those parties disagree, the coalition sometimes disintegrates.

the reelection of candidates from their party by ensuring that enough money is available for their campaigns.

The president also acts as party head in the day-to-day operations of the executive branch, as many of the staff appointments to the White House Office, cabinet, subcabinet, ambassadorships, and judiciary typically come from party ranks. Finally, at the end of a president's term, he likely campaigns on behalf of his party's presidential nominee.

Presidential Roles in the Foreign Policy Sphere

Presidential responsibilities also extend to setting and executing foreign policy. The president's foreign policy powers are for the most part constitutionally derived.[10] Specifically, the Constitution gives the president the authority with which to carry out the roles of chief diplomat and commander in chief of the U.S. armed forces.

Chief Diplomat

Serving in the capacity of chief diplomat, the president (along with advisers) shapes and administers the nation's foreign policy. Supported by a wide array of foreign policy resources, including the State Department, the National Security Council, the Central Intelligence

Agency, and the various branches of the U.S. military, the president creates and administers foreign policy. In setting foreign policy, the president can act more unilaterally than with most domestic policies. Presidents are much less likely to be challenged in the foreign policy arena by members of Congress, who, in reflection of their constituents' main interests, tend to be primarily concerned with domestic policy issues.

As chief diplomat, the president, in conjunction with his or her staff, negotiates treaties and other international agreements with foreign nations and represents the United States at international summits. The president also has the authority to enter into an **executive agreement,** a kind of international agreement. Executive agreements are based on the constitutional authority vested in the president, and, unlike treaties, they may not be binding on future presidents nor do they require Senate approval.

The Constitution also empowers the president to appoint ambassadors to other nations. As high-ranking diplomats, ambassadors are the official representatives of the United States in their host nation. Ambassadors' duties vary widely, depending upon the locale of their appointment. Some ambassadors play an influential, highly visible role in carrying out U.S. foreign policy, but others remain in the background.

The president, acting in the role of chief diplomat, is the leader of the diplomatic corps. In the capacity of chief diplomat, the president also hosts state dinners at the White House and formally receives the ambassadors of other nations.

Commander in Chief

As commander in chief, the president is the supreme military commander of the U.S. Army, Navy, Air Force, Marines, and Coast Guard. Counseled by advisers, the president decides when to send troops into battle (although only Congress can formally declare war) and sets military strategy in times of both peace and war.[11]

In the George W. Bush administration, the president's role as commander in chief was an understandably important one. During Bush's first term, the nation's military actions in Afghanistan and Iraq came to define his presidency. By 2004, the president's role as commander in chief was viewed as a political asset. The *Washington Post* noted in the weeks preceding the 2004 presidential election that "administration officials disclosed plans . . . that show the many ways Bush will try to emphasize his role as commander in chief."[12] The administration's strategy included interrupting Bush's campaign-related travel so that the president could meet with then-interim president of Afghanistan, Hamid Karzai, at the United Nations and welcome Iraq's then-interim prime minister, Ayad Allawi, in the White House Rose Garden. These kinds of gestures aim to demonstrate that as commander in chief, the president commands the respect both of the U.S. military and of the foreign nations dependent upon U.S. military power.

> In the administration of George W. Bush, the president's role as commander in chief was particularly important. Here Bush and President Hamid Karzai of Afghanistan shake hands after dedicating the new U.S. Embassy building in Kabul, the Afghan capital.

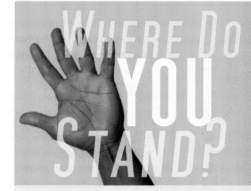

Meeting with the Enemy

Is it a good idea or a bad idea for a president to meet with leaders of foreign countries that are widely viewed to be enemies of the United States?

☐ Good idea

☐ Bad idea

Source: "Americans Favor President Meeting with U.S. Enemies," www.gallup.com/poll/107617/Americans-Favor-President-Meeting-US-Enemies.aspx.

Overlap in the Domestic and Foreign Policy Roles: Chief Executive and Chief of State

Some presidential functions overlap the domestic and foreign policy spheres. This spillover notably exists in the president's role as chief executive—in which the president, as head of the executive branch, appoints his advisers and staff—and the role of chief of state, the ceremonial function of the president.

Chief Executive

As the nation's leader in domestic and foreign policy initiatives, the president serves as chief executive. In this capacity, the president appoints the *secretaries* (top administrators) of the cabinet—the fifteen departments of the federal government—as well as the heads of other federal government agencies charged with developing and implementing the administration's policy. As chief executive, the president also appoints other staff members and numerous advisers, including staff in the Executive Office of the President. In the capacity of chief executive, the president determines how the bureaucracy will implement the laws Congress has passed and which policies—those concerning education, crime, social welfare, and so on—will be emphasized.[13]

Chief of State

The president's role as chief of state reflects the chief executive's embodiment of the values and ideals of the nation, both within the United States and abroad. The function of chief of state is similar to the ceremonial role played by the constitutional monarch in parliamentary systems such as Great Britain's. In the United States, the role of symbolic leader of the nation enhances the president's image and authority and promotes national unity. We may experience this sense that we are one indivisible nation, for example, when the president, as chief of state, makes a formal state visit to another nation, hosts Olympic medalists at the White House, and visits the sites of national tragedies such as Ground Zero after the terrorist attacks of September 11, 2001, and the devastated cities on Texas' Gulf coast after Hurricane Ike in September 2008.

The President and the Executive Branch

Because daily news reports so often showcase the president acting as head of state and chief diplomat, one of the president's primary responsibilities—administering the federal government—is easily overlooked. As chief

DOING DEMOCRACY

VOLUNTEER THROUGH THE USA FREEDOM CORPS

FACT:

Former President George W. Bush launched the USA Freedom Corps (USAFC) in the aftermath of the September 11, 2001, terrorist attacks on the United States. Seeking to build on the "countless acts of service, sacrifice, and generosity" following 9/11, the President announced the formation of the USAFC in his 2002 State of the Union Address, during which he called on Americans "to serve a cause greater than themselves."

Over 65 million Americans volunteer each year, and the USAFC acts as a clearinghouse of information for those who would like to volunteer to improve their communities. The USAFC provides information on full-time service programs such as AmeriCorps and the Peace Corps. It also publicizes a volunteer network that matches potential volunteers with organizations that need their help.

Act!

In October 2006 Tulane University student Austin Marks became the 500,000th person to receive the President's Volunteer Service Award. Marks is a USAFC volunteer who returned to his hometown of New Orleans to help the city rebuild after Hurricane Katrina.

You can volunteer at an organization that reflects your individual concerns, priorities, and the level of commitment you are willing to make, whether that commitment is a life-altering change such as joining a Peace Corps program teaching children on the other side of the globe or simply volunteering two hours a month at a local domestic violence shelter.

Where to begin

The USA Freedom Corps Web site (www.usafreedomcorps.gov/) features a key word search that enables you to identify volunteer opportunities according to your interests. Its geographic locator allows you to focus on volunteer opportunities in specific communities. The Web site also has other tools to help you become an active volunteer, including "Ten Tips for Volunteering Wisely" and an interactive record of service log.

---

executive, the president is constitutionally charged with ensuring that the "laws be faithfully executed." Today this responsibility means that the president oversees a bureaucracy of more than 4 million government employees, including the members of the military, while presiding over an astonishing $3 *trillion* annual federal budget. In addition, as we now consider, the president is the leader of the executive branch of government, which includes the vice president, the cabinet, the offices within the White House, and the entire federal bureaucracy.

The Vice President's Role

John Nance Garner, Franklin D. Roosevelt's vice president from 1933 to 1941, vulgarly commented that "the vice presidency isn't worth a pitcher of warm piss."[14] This insider's observation on the vice-presidential office matches the perceptions of many Americans fairly well. But although the media and the public tend to ignore the vice presidency and to marginalize the responsibilities of the second-in-command, vice presidents have an enormously important function. They are first in the line of succession to the presidency if the president should die or become incapacitated. Only eight presidents have died while in office, and although presidential succession may not be the foremost consideration in selecting a running mate for many presidential candidates, it can be an issue. Bill Clinton, in describing his selection of Tennessee senator Al Gore as his running mate, explained that his choice of Gore in part reflected Clinton's belief that Gore would make a good president "if something happened to me."[15]

> Presidential candidates often choose a running mate who complements their attributes. Vice President Joe Biden, who served thirty-six years in the U.S. Senate, brought experience to Democratic President Barack Obama's ticket in 2008.

balanced ticket

the selection of a running mate who brings diversity of ideology, geographic region, age, gender, race, or ethnicity to the slate

cabinet

the group of experts chosen by the president to serve as advisers on running the country

THE VICE PRESIDENT'S JOB   Many vice presidents serve a largely ceremonial function that revolves around activities such as attending state dinners, visiting foreign nations, and attending the funerals of foreign dignitaries. But vice presidents may have more substantive responsibilities, depending upon their skills and the needs of the administration. Sometimes, for example, a vice president acts as legislative liaison with Congress, particularly if the vice president has more experience in dealing with the legislative branch than the president. Such was the case with Al Gore, who had served eight years in the House of Representatives and eight years in the Senate, whereas the president under whom he served, Bill Clinton, lacked Washington experience. In other instances, vice presidents' policy expertise is a crucial resource for the administration. In the case of Vice President Dick Cheney, experience in foreign policy and national security determined the pivotal role he played in developing the foreign policy of George W. Bush's administration.

Although vice presidents are only "a heartbeat away" from the presidency, their own election to the presidency (should they decide to run) is not ensured when their term as second-in-command has ended. It is true that several vice presidents—among them, George H. W. Bush and Lyndon B. Johnson—have won election to the presidency in their own right; but many other former vice presidents have failed.[16] Notably, Al Gore, Walter Mondale, and Gerald Ford (the vice presidents of Bill Clinton, Jimmy Carter, and Richard Nixon, respectively) all went down to defeat at the polls in their bid for the White House.

CHOOSING A VICE PRESIDENT   In selecting a vice-presidential running mate, presidential candidates weigh several considerations. Would-be presidents strive for a **balanced ticket;** that is, to broaden their appeal to the electorate and increase their chances of getting elected, they select a running mate who brings diversity of ideology, geographic region, age, gender, race, or ethnicity to the slate. For example, Jimmy Carter, a southern governor, selected as his running mate Senator Walter Mondale of Minnesota, who enjoyed strong ties with organized labor and could draw northern and midwestern voters' support for the ticket. And Republican John McCain's selection of Alaska governor Sarah Palin in 2008 was viewed by many analysts as an effort to attract the votes of women and cultural conservatives.

Presidential candidates also may base their vice-presidential selection on their own shortcomings, whether in policy expertise or governing experience. For example, it is widely believed that President George W. Bush selected Dick Cheney as his running mate because of Cheney's foreign policy knowledge and experience—credentials that then-candidate Bush was lacking as governor of Texas. Similarly, in the 2008 presidential election, Democratic nominee Barack Obama's selection of U.S. Senator Joseph Biden (D-Delaware) was viewed by many media pundits as an attempt to silence critics who bemoaned his relative lack of experience.

The Cabinet

Since George Washington's presidency, every president has depended upon the advice of a **cabinet,** the group of experts chosen by the president to serve as advisers on running the country. These advisers serve as the heads of each of the executive departments. Figure 12.2 shows the fifteen departments of the cabinet. Each cabinet member except the head of the Department of Justice is called the *secretary* of that department. In the administration of George W. Bush, Condoleezza Rice was head of the Department of State, and thus her title was secretary of state. The head of the Department of Justice is called the attorney general.

Figure 12.2 shows cabinet departments and their respective Web sites. The newest department, the Department of Homeland Security, was created by President George W. Bush in 2002. This department is charged with increasing the nation's preparedness, particularly with respect to catastrophic events such as terrorist attacks and natural disasters. George Washington's cabinet consisted of the heads of only four departments—justice, state, treasury, and war (the latter is now called the Department of Defense). Subsequent presidents added other departments.

Department of Agriculture
www.usda.gov

Department of Commerce
www.commerce.gov

Department of Defense
www.defenselink.mil

Department of Education
www.ed.gov

Department of the Interior
www.doi.gov

Department of Justice
www.usdoj.gov

Department of Labor
www.dol.gov

Department of State
www.state.gov

Department of Energy
www.energy.gov

Department of Health
& Human Services
www.hhs.gov

Department of
Homeland Security
www.dhs.gov

Department of Housing
& Urban Development
www.hud.gov

Department of
Transportation
www.dot.gov

Department of
the Treasury
www.ustreas.gov

Department of
Veterans Affairs
www.va.gov

POLITICAL INQUIRY

FIGURE 12.2 ■ THE DEPARTMENTS OF THE PRESIDENT'S CABINET The presidential cabinet consists of the heads of the fifteen departments shown in the figure. Which department is concerned with finding alternatives to the use of fossil fuels? Which one addresses the problems of the dedicated service men and women who serve in Iraq and Afghanistan? Which department arose as a result of the 9/11 terrorist strikes?

Table 12.1

Women and Minorities Appointed to Presidential Cabinets

President	Number of Women Cabinet Members	Number of Minority* Cabinet Members	Tenure
G. W. Bush	7	10	2001–2009
Clinton	13	11	1993–2001
G. H. W. Bush	4	3	1989–1993
Reagan	4	2	1981–1989
Carter	4	1	1977–1981
Ford	1	1	1974–1977
Nixon	0	0	1969–1974
Johnson	0	1	1963–1969
Kennedy	0	0	1961–1963
Eisenhower	1	0	1953–1961
Truman	0	0	1945–1953
F. Roosevelt	1	0	1933–1945

*Includes African American, Latino/a, and Asian Americans.

Sources: Brigid C. Harrison, *Women in American Politics: An Introduction* (Belmont, CA: Wadsworth Publishing, 2003); the Center for the American Woman and Politics, *National Information Bank on Women in Public Office*, Eagleton Institute of Politics, Rutgers University; www.whitehouse.gov, and various presidential library Web sites.

Each president may also designate cabinet rank to other advisers whose agencies are not permanent cabinet departments. Typically, presidents have specified that their national security adviser, director of the Office of Management and Budget, and administrator of the Environmental Protection Agency be included in their administration's cabinet.

Today, presidents and the public scrutinize presidential cabinet appointments to determine whether, in the words of Bill Clinton, they "look like America." As the data in Table 12.1 confirm, this is a relatively new gauge, as only three women and two members of ethnic minority groups had served in presidential cabinets until the Carter administration. Increasingly, however, as the table shows, presidential cabinets have become more diverse, with significant strides made during the Clinton administration.[17] President Clinton became the first president to appoint a woman to any of the "big four" posts when he named Janet Reno attorney general and Madeleine Albright secretary of state. George W. Bush named Colin Powell the first black secretary of state, and when Powell resigned, Bush replaced him with Condoleezza Rice, an African American woman who had served previously as national security adviser.

The Executive Office of the President

Executive Office of the President (EOP)
offices, counsels, and boards that help the president to carry out the day-to-day responsibilities of the office

Whereas the cabinet usually functions as an advisory board for the president, the **Executive Office of the President (EOP)** typically is the launch pad for the implementation of policy. The offices, counsels, and boards that compose the EOP help the president to carry out the day-to-day responsibilities of the presidency and similarly assist the First Lady and the vice president in their official activities. The EOP also coordinates policies among different agencies and departments.

Among the EOP offices, several are particularly important, including the White House Office, the National Security Council, the Office of Management and Budget, and the Counsel of Economic Advisers. These offices are crucial not only because of the prominent issues with which they deal but also because of their strong role in developing and implementing policy in these issue areas.[18]

White House Office (WHO)
the office that develops policies and protects the president's legal and political interests

chief of staff
among the most important staff members of the WHO; serves as both an adviser to the president and manager of the WHO

THE WHITE HOUSE OFFICE Playing a pivotal role in most presidential administrations, the **White House Office (WHO)** staff members develop policies favored by the presidential administration and protect the president's legal and political interests. They research policy and keep the president informed about policy issues on the horizon. WHO staffers also regularly interact with members of Congress, their primary goal being to get presidential policy priorities enacted into law. They strive to ensure that these policies, once passed into law, are administered in keeping with the president's expectations.

Because of the enormous influence of staff members in the White House Office, presidents take pains to ensure their loyalty and trustworthiness. Among the top staff members of the White House Office is the **chief of staff,** who serves as both an adviser to the president and the manager of the WHO. Other staff members with clout include the **press secretary,** the president's spokesperson to the media, and the **White House counsel,** the president's lawyer. The president's secretary and appointments secretary are also influential WHO employees; they act as gatekeepers by controlling access to the president by other staffers and by members of Congress and the cabinet.

NATIONAL SECURITY COUNCIL The president consults members of the **National Security Council (NSC)** on domestic and foreign matters related to national security. Since its creation in 1947 during the Truman administration,[19] the NSC has advised presidents on key national security and foreign policy decisions and assisted in the implementation of these decisions by coordinating policy administration among different agencies. For example, once the president has decided on a specific policy, the NSC might coordinate its implementation among the Department of State, the Central Intelligence Agency, various branches of the military, and diplomatic officials.

The president officially chairs the National Security Council. Its other regular members include the vice president, secretary of defense, secretary of state, secretary of the treasury, and the assistant to the president for national security affairs, who is responsible for administering the day-to-day operations of the NSC and its staff. Other administration officials serve the NSC in advisory capacities or are invited to meetings when matters concerning their area of expertise are being decided.

OFFICE OF MANAGEMENT AND BUDGET Once part of the Department of the Treasury, the **Office of Management and Budget** (**OMB**—originally called the Bureau of the Budget) has been a separate office within the WHO since 1939. Its chief responsibility is to create the president's annual budget, which the president submits to Congress each January. The budget outlines all of the anticipated revenue that the government will receive in the next year, usually from taxes and fees paid by businesses and individuals. The budget also lists the anticipated expenditures for the coming year, detailing how much money the various departments and agencies in the federal government will have available to spend on salaries, administrative costs, and programs. The OMB is among the president's most important agencies for policy making and policy implementation.

The director of the Office of Management and Budget, a presidential appointee confirmed by the Senate, has a staff of about 600 career civil servants. In recent decades the OMB director has figured prominently in presidential administrations and typically has been designated a member of the cabinet. The director's job is complex. He or she interacts intensively with Congress, trying to ensure that the budget that passes resembles the president's proposed budget as closely as possible. The director also lobbies members of Congress with the goal of ensuring that the key provisions of the budget that are important to the president remain intact in the congressionally approved version.

Once Congress approves the budget, the director of the OMB turns attention to its implementation, as it is the job of the OMB staff to manage the budget's execution by federal departments and agencies—to ensure that monies are spent on their designated purposes and that fraud and financial abuse do not occur. This managerial responsibility of the Office of Management and Budget was the reasoning behind the change in the office's name (from the Bureau of the Budget) in 1970.

Presidential Succession

No examination of the executive branch would be complete without considering the question, What happens if the president dies? Presidential succession is determined by the Presidential Succession Law of 1947. But sometimes incapacitation other than death prevents presidents from fulfilling their duties. In such cases the Twenty-Fifth Amendment, ratified in 1967, determines the course of action.

press secretary
the president's spokesperson to the media

White House counsel
the president's lawyer

National Security Council (NSC)
consisting of top foreign policy advisers and relevant cabinet officials, this is an arm of the EOP that the president consults on matters of foreign policy and national security

Office of Management and Budget (OMB)
office that creates the president's annual budget

ON THE JOB

DIANA M. SMITH, WHITE HOUSE MEDIA AFFAIRS INTERN

Name: Diana M. Smith

Age: 21

Hometown: Fort Worth, Texas

College: Texas Christian University

Major: Political Science

Job title: White House Office of Media Affairs Intern (September–December 2005)

Salary range for jobs like this: No salary, but the learning experience can pay great dividends.

Day-to-day responsibilities: Most of my duties were confidential. Some of my work entailed secretarial duties like running errands, answering the phone, and clipping news articles pertaining to the president and hot topics the administration was concerned about. My confidential duties took up most of my time and generally involved working on projects for White House Office spokespeople and doing different kinds of research.

How did you get your job? I got the application, printed it out, and sent in the packet. It was that simple. I sent in the completed application in late spring and got a phone call in July. Applications are filtered and then sent to the various White House offices, which then select applicants they would like to interview. In late July, the White House Intern Coordinator called and offered me the position to start in September.

What do you like best about your job? The best part of the job was the events that I could attend. Someone might say, "The president is landing on the South Lawn in Marine One; do you want to go over and watch?" The White House Intern Office also hosts brown bag lunch events where speakers address just the interns. Also, it was just amazing to walk the halls and see people you read about in the paper; knowing something from the inside out lets you connect the dots and really use your knowledge.

What is your least favorite aspect of your job? It was so neat to be there, and you want to do something, but you still are only an intern, there for a short time. You know it is important to do your job—that it's not menial and that doing it helps others to use their time better. It is hard when you know how to do something but you cannot because that is not your job.

What advice would you give to students who would like to do what you're doing? Just apply. I thought that you had to know somebody, but even people who do know somebody had to go through the same process. I also would recommend that people use a D.C.-based internship service like the Washington Center. The biggest complaint that other interns had was problems with housing, but by using the Washington Center, I eliminated that problem because they provide everything. So just go after it. It was a neat opportunity, and for most people, it is not something they think they can do. Do not limit yourself with that excuse. Always go after what you want—if you can live with yourself knowing you tried instead of wondering "what if"? I was blessed to have had such a memorable opportunity.

When the President Dies in Office

When the president dies, the course of action is clear in most cases: the vice president assumes the presidency. Such was the situation when Harry Truman became president upon Franklin D. Roosevelt's death from natural causes in 1945 and when Lyndon Johnson was sworn in as president after the assassination of John F. Kennedy in 1963. Vice presidents sometimes fill the unexpired term of their president for reasons other than the president's death, as when Gerald Ford acceded to the presidency upon the resignation of Richard Nixon after the Watergate scandal.

The Presidential Succession Law of 1947 determines presidential succession if the vice president also dies or is unable to govern. Table 12.2 shows that after the vice president, the next in line for the presidency is the Speaker of the House of Representatives, then the president pro tem of the Senate, followed by a specified order of the members of the cabinet. Notice that as new cabinet departments have been established, their secretaries have been added to the bottom of the line of succession. As a precaution, at the State of the Union address each year, one cabinet member is chosen not to attend the president's speech before Congress but rather to stay behind at the White House. This measure ensures that if a catastrophe should occur in Congress during the address, someone in the line of succession will be able to assume the duties of the president.

When the President Cannot Serve: The Twenty-Fifth Amendment

What happens when a president is alive but unable to carry out the responsibilities of the office? Until the ratification of the Twenty-Fifth Amendment in 1967, the course of action was not clear. Such was the case in 1881, when an assassin shot President James Garfield, and Garfield lived two and a half months before succumbing to his injuries. In another such instance, President Woodrow Wilson was so ill during his last months in office that he was incapacitated. First Lady Edith Wilson assumed some of his responsibilities and decision making. Questions about presidential health also arose toward the end of Franklin D. Roosevelt's tenure; and during the Eisenhower administration, the president authorized Vice President Richard Nixon to determine whether Eisenhower was competent to govern after battling a series of illnesses. President Kennedy, who suffered from a host of physical ailments including severe, chronic back pain and Addison's disease, similarly empowered Vice President Lyndon Johnson: in an informal agreement, the men arranged that if Kennedy was physically unable to communicate with Johnson, Johnson was authorized to assume the presidency.

After Kennedy's assassination, the ratification of the Twenty-Fifth Amendment (1967) finally put codified procedures in place for dealing with an incapacitated president. According to the Twenty-Fifth Amendment, if a president believes he or she is unable to carry out the duties of the office, the president must notify Congress, and the vice president becomes the acting president until the president can resume authority. The amendment would apply in the case when a president is anesthetized for surgery, for example, or perhaps recuperating from a debilitating illness.

In other situations, a president might be incapable of carrying out the duties of office and incapable of notifying Congress. In such a case, the Twenty-Fifth Amendment requires that the vice president and a majority of the cabinet notify Congress, and the vice president becomes the acting president. If a question arises as to whether the president is fit to reassume the duties of office, a two-thirds vote of Congress is required for the acting president to remain.

> When a president dies in office, the line of presidential succession is clear. Crowds watched the funeral procession for President Franklin D. Roosevelt, who died in office in 1945 and was succeeded by his vice president, Harry S Truman (1945–1953).

TABLE 12.2

The Line of Presidential Succession

1. Vice president
2. Speaker of the House of Representatives
3. President pro tem of the Senate
4. Secretary of state
5. Secretary of the treasury
6. Secretary of defense
7. Attorney general
8. Secretary of the interior
9. Secretary of agriculture
10. Secretary of commerce
11. Secretary of labor
12. Secretary of health and human services
13. Secretary of housing and urban development
14. Secretary of transportation
15. Secretary of energy
16. Secretary of education
17. Secretary of veterans affairs
18. Secretary of homeland security

Sources of Presidential Power

The presidency that Barack Obama assumed on January 20, 2009, scarcely resembled the one executed by the first president, George Washington, in the 1790s. In the interim, the powers of the president have evolved, reflecting the expansion of the federal government since that time, changes in public attitudes about the proper role of government, and the personalities and will of those who have served as president.

In describing the powers that would guide presidents for centuries to come, the framers of the Constitution created a unique office. These visionary authors had lived through a repressive era in which an authoritarian monarch had exercised absolute power. They subsequently had witnessed the new American nation's struggles under the ineffectual Articles of Confederation, in which the federal government had too little power and the states too much. Thus, the framers sought to establish an office that would balance the exercise of authority with the preservation of the rights and will of the people.

Given their colonial experience, it was no surprise that the framers granted the presidents both *expressed powers* and *inherent powers* in the Constitution. Congress grants presidents additional powers, called *statutory powers,* through congressional action. We consider these various powers in this section.

Additional presidential powers have emerged over time. These newer authorities reflect both changes in the institution of the presidency and shifts in popular views on the appropriate role of government and the president. These powers include emergency powers granted in Supreme Court decisions and powers that, while not formalized, are given to presidents by the public through election mandates, presidential popularity, or unified public opinion on a particular issue or course of action.

The Constitution: Expressed Powers

expressed powers
presidential powers enumerated in the Constitution

The primary source of presidential power comes from the Constitution in the form of the **expressed powers,** which are those enumerated in the Constitution. These powers, found in Article II, Sections 2 and 3, list the following powers:

- serve as commander in chief of the armed forces
- appoint heads of the executive departments, ambassadors, Supreme Court justices, people to fill vacancies that occur during the recess of the Senate, and other positions
- pardon crimes, except in cases of impeachment
- enter into treaties, with two-thirds consent of the Senate
- give the State of the Union address to Congress
- convene the Congress
- receive ambassadors of other nations
- commission all officers of the United States

The expressed powers outlined in the Constitution provide a framework for presidential responsibilities and an outline of presidential power. They also shape how presidents themselves develop their authority.

The Constitution: Inherent Powers

take care clause
the constitutional basis for inherent powers, which states that the president "shall take Care that the Laws be faithfully executed"

inherent powers
presidential powers that are implied in the Constitution

One of the principal ways by which the Constitution provides for presidents themselves to assert additional powers, beyond those expressed in the Constitution, is the **take care clause,** which states that "the executive Power shall be vested in a President of the United States of America" and that "he shall take Care that the Laws be faithfully executed." On the basis of this clause, presidents throughout U.S. history have asserted various **inherent powers,** which are powers that are not expressly granted by the Constitution but are inferred.

President Thomas Jefferson exercised inherent powers in his far-reaching Louisiana Purchase in 1803. Jefferson authorized this $15 million purchase of 800,000 square miles of land, even though the Constitution did not authorize any such action on the part of a president. Interestingly, in the civic discourse over the Constitution, Jefferson, an Anti-Federalist, had argued for states' rights and against a strong central government and a powerful presidency. Jefferson had believed that the powers enumerated in the Constitution defined the powers of the government. But Jefferson thought that the purchase of the Louisiana Territory was of crucial strategic and economic importance. He believed that the deal was key to the United States' averting war with France and to securing the port of New Orleans, which was essential for the new American republic's fortunes in trade. Jefferson could not wait for a constitutional amendment to authorize the transaction, and so he forged ahead with the purchase. Congress and many Americans of the day agreed with his actions, and so there were no negative consequences to them.

More recently, in the 1930s, President Franklin D. Roosevelt drew on the inherent powers when he expanded the size of the federal government in order to administer his New Deal programs, designed to relieve the economic and human distress of the Great Depression. Beginning in 2002, President George W. Bush used the inherent powers when he suspended the civil liberties of foreign nationals being held in a military prison at the U.S. naval base at Guantánamo Bay, Cuba, as part of the administration's war on terror. The individuals at Guantánamo Bay have been detained indefinitely for questioning about their possible terrorist activities. These instances of presidents' exercise of inherent powers generated varying degrees of controversy among Americans of the times.

Statutory Powers

The Constitution's expressed and inherent powers provided a foundation for presidential power that has evolved over time. These powers have been supplemented by additional powers—**statutory powers**—explicitly granted to presidents by congressional action.

An example of such a grant of statutory powers is the 1996 Line Item Veto Act, discussed earlier, which gave the president the power to strike down specific line items on an appropriations bill while allowing the rest of the bill to become law. As noted, in 1997 the Supreme Court declared the line-item veto unconstitutional on the grounds that the congressional action violated the separation of powers.

statutory powers
powers explicitly granted to presidents by congressional action

Special Presidential Powers

Presidents also have special powers that have evolved from various sources, including the Constitution, Supreme Court decisions, and congressional statutes. These powers, which numerous presidents have exercised, have come to be regarded as accepted powers and privileges of the presidency. They include *executive orders, emergency powers,* and *executive privilege.*

EXECUTIVE ORDERS The president has the power to issue **executive orders** that have the force of law. Executive orders carry the same weight as congressional statutes and have been used in a variety of circumstances to guide the executive branch's administrative functions.[20] In general, executive orders:

executive order
power of the president to issue orders that carry the force of law

- direct the enforcement of congressional statutes or Supreme Court rulings;
- enforce specific provisions of the Constitution;
- guide the administration of treaties with foreign governments;
- create or change the regulatory guidelines or practices of an executive department or agency.

Executive orders can be an important strategic tool, as they convey the president's priorities to the bureaucracy that implements the laws. For example, in 1948 President Harry Truman signed Executive Order 9981, which states, "It is hereby declared to be the policy of the President that there shall be equality of treatment and opportunity for all persons in the armed services without regard to race, color, religion, or national origin."[21] This executive order effectively banned segregation in the U.S. military. Why would Truman issue an executive order instead of working for congressional passage of a statute that would desegregate the military? Many analysts think the reason is that Truman, who ardently believed that the military should be desegregated, not only doubted that Congress would pass such a measure but also faced pressure from early civil rights activists who had pledged an African American boycott of military service if the military was not desegregated. President George W. Bush drew criticism for his extensive use of executive orders, which served to create policy in various areas. For example, one Bush executive order froze the assets of any person who threatened the efforts at stabilization in Iraq; another created a uniform system for classifying national security information.[22]

Executive orders have very few limitations and stipulations. One limitation is that presidents cannot use them to create new taxes or appropriate funds, because the Constitution reserves these powers for Congress.

emergency powers
broad powers exercised by the president during times of national crisis

EMERGENCY POWERS   Broad powers that a president exercises during times of national crisis have been invoked by presidents since Abraham Lincoln's claim to **emergency powers** during the Civil War. Lincoln used emergency powers during the war to suspend the civil liberties of alleged agitators, to draft state militia units into national service, and to federalize the governance of southern states after the war.

In 1936, the U.S. Supreme Court acknowledged the existence of presidential emergency powers in *United States v. Curtiss-Wright Export Corp.*[23] In this case, the U.S. government charged the Curtiss-Wright Corporation with conspiring to sell fifteen machine guns to Bolivia, in violation of a joint resolution of Congress and a presidential proclamation. Without congressional approval, President Franklin D. Roosevelt had ordered an embargo on the machine gun shipment. The Court supported Roosevelt's order, ruling that the president's powers, particularly in foreign affairs, are not limited to those powers expressly stated in the Constitution. The justices also stated that the federal government is the primary actor in foreign affairs and that the president in particular has inherent powers related to his constitutional duties in foreign relations.

But presidents' use of emergency powers goes beyond taking action in foreign policy matters, as emergency powers sometimes come into play in domestic crises. In 2005, in the aftermath of Hurricane Katrina, President George W. Bush used his emergency powers to issue an executive order that temporarily repealed the work standards set by the Davis-Bacon Act of 1931. This act requires federal contractors on federally funded construction contracts to pay workers at least the prevailing wages in the area where the work is conducted. By repealing the Davis-Bacon Act, Bush temporarily eliminated those work standards for federally funded reconstruction projects in Alabama, Florida, Louisiana, and Mississippi, thus lowering the federal government's cost of hiring workers to clean up in the aftermath of the hurricane. In notifying Congress of his decision, Bush cited the "national emergency" the hurricane had created, permitting him to take this action.[24]

executive privilege
the right of the chief executive and members of the administration to withhold information from Congress or the courts, or the right to refuse to appear before legislative or judicial bodies

EXECUTIVE PRIVILEGE   Presidents also can exercise **executive privilege,** the authority of the president and other executive officials to refuse to disclose information concerning confidential conversations or national security to Congress or the courts. In invoking executive privilege, presidents draw on the idea that the Constitution's framework of separation of powers justifies the withholding of certain information from Congress or the judiciary,[25] a claim initially asserted when George Washington refused to grant Congress access to all documents pertaining to treaty negotiations. Typically presidents claim executive privilege so they can get advice from aides without fear that such conversations might be made public or scrutinized by members of Congress or the judiciary. Presidents also have invoked executive privilege when negotiating foreign policies with other heads of state, to shield these leaders from having sensitive negotiations examined by the other branches of the federal government.

On occasion, the judicial branch of the federal government has successfully challenged executive privilege. For example, when President Richard Nixon refused to turn over tapes of Oval Office conversations to a special prosecutor investigating the Watergate scandal in 1974, the Supreme Court intervened. In *United States v. Richard M. Nixon,* the Court asserted that while executive privilege does exist, it was not applicable regarding the tapes because President Nixon's claim of executive privilege concerning the tapes was too broad.[26] (See pp. 448–449 for more on Watergate.)

More recent cases in which a president has invoked executive privilege are notable. President Bill Clinton attempted to do so to prevent White House aides from testifying before special prosecutor Kenneth Starr during the Monica Lewinsky scandal. (Clinton was accused of having extramarital relations with Lewinsky, a White House intern.) Clinton's maneuver failed, and his aides were compelled to testify. In 2007, President George W. Bush asserted executive authority in a showdown with Congress over the politically motivated firing of nine U.S. attorneys. Bush invoked executive privilege to prevent White House Counsel Harriet Miers and presidential adviser Karl Rove from testifying before Congress. The congressional inquiry continued without Miers's and Rove's testimony, however, and eventually Attorney General Alberto Gonzales stepped down as a result of the scandal.

In general, the courts have allowed executive privilege in cases where a clear issue of separation of powers exists—as with respect to international negotiations and conversations regarding matters of policy or national security. The courts have tended to limit the use of executive privilege when presidents have exercised it in an effort to prevent the revelation of misdeeds by members of the executive branch.

The People as a Source of Presidential Power

One of the most important sources of presidential power today comes from the people. Although one president generally will have the same formal powers as the next, presidents' ability to wield their power, to control the political agenda, and to get things done typically is a function of political skill, charisma, and what political scientist Richard Neustadt has called "the power to persuade."[27]

The President and the Bully Pulpit

Modern presidents work to persuade the public on a virtually continuous basis. They know that if they win popular support for their views and political agenda, they will have an easier time getting their policy priorities through Congress. In their efforts to persuade the people, they exploit the power of their office, using the presidency as a forum from which to speak out on any matter—and to have their views listened to. This ready access to the public ear and broad power of the president to communicate led President Theodore Roosevelt to exclaim, "I have got such a bully pulpit!"[28]

In using their bully pulpit, presidents seek to communicate that their stances on important issues are the right choices and that their actions, particularly controversial decisions, should be supported. Presidents also strive to persuade the public that they are doing a good job on key policy fronts such as economic and foreign policy. Sometimes presidents seek to mobilize the public to take specific actions or to adopt certain beliefs. In the week after the September 11, 2001, terrorist attacks, for example, President George W. Bush urged Americans to return to work so that the economy would not suffer further damage, and encouraged them to resume other normal activities. By appealing to people's patriotism—and defining that patriotism as resuming normal activities—the president persuaded Americans to do what was best for the country. Months later, the president would again ask for the support of the American people, this time support for military action to disarm weapons of mass destruction in Iraq. He succeeded in convincing many Americans that military intervention was necessary, as public opinion initially supported the war in Iraq. But as time passed with no evidence of weapons of mass destruction and with more and more troops losing their lives, public support for the war and confidence in the president's leadership diminished.

The reason why presidents work so tirelessly to win public support for their agenda is that they understand that getting Congress to act on policy priorities, to approve budgets, and to pass favored legislation depends heavily on the perception that the public supports presidential initiatives. Indeed, political scientist Richard Neustadt argues that the modern institution of the presidency is weak and that presidents in fact must rely on public and congressional support in order to enact their agendas.[29] Getting Congress to do what the president wants is more difficult when a president faces a divided government, the situation in which the president belongs to one political party and Congress is controlled by a majority of members of the other party. For example, when the Republicans lost control of both the House and Senate in the 2006 congressional elections, President Bush's chances of enacting his legislative priorities, such as privatizing Social Security, decreased significantly because the new Democratic majorities in Congress did not share these priorities.

But beyond partisan differences, presidents' ability to get things done in Congress also is a function of their popularity with the people. A popular president can use that clout to persuade members of Congress that his positions are the right ones; an unpopular president will face greater obstacles to having his legislative agenda enacted.

The President and Public Approval

approval ratings

the percentage of survey respondents who say that they "approve" or "strongly approve" of the way the president is doing his job

The flow and ebb of presidential popularity during the administration of George W. Bush illustrates how essential the people's support is to the success of a chief executive's initiatives. After the September 11, 2001, terrorist attacks and President Bush's rapid and dignified response to them, Bush enjoyed record high approval ratings. **Approval ratings** are the percentage of survey respondents who say that they "approve" or "strongly approve" of the way the president is doing his job. Figure 12.3 shows that immediately after September 11, President Bush's approval ratings hovered in the high 80s, occasionally reaching 90 percent, meaning that 90 percent of those surveyed indicated that they approved of the way the president was handling his job. (In contrast, the average presidential approval rating since the Franklin D. Roosevelt administration was 56 percent.) During this time, Bush had enormous legislative successes. These included the passage of the USA PATRIOT Act of 2001, which gave law enforcement officers greater authority in handling suspected terrorist acts, and the congressional declaration of a "war on terror." When Bush's popularity subsequently waned because of the people's dissatisfaction with the rate of progress in the war in Iraq, the high number of casualties in the war, and continued weakness in the American economy, so too did support decrease for the continuation of the war, the president's economic policies, and a proposed extension of the USA PATRIOT Act.

Presidential Approval Ratings

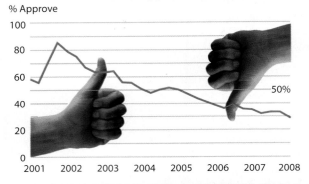

% Approve

FIGURE 12.3 ■ **What factors can influence presidential approval ratings? What explains the rise in President Bush's approval ratings toward the end of 2001? Why did his popularity and ratings fall steadily after that time?**

Source: The Gallup Poll, www.galluppoll.com/content/?ci=1663&pg=1.

In general, presidential approval ratings reveal that some presidents are simply more popular than others. For example, presidents Reagan and Clinton tended to enjoy high approval ratings, with President Clinton's second-term ratings running particularly high, especially in light of the Monica Lewinsky scandal and the subsequent impeachment proceedings against him. But presidential approval is also influenced by external events. In particular, all elected presidents tend to start out with a **honeymoon period,** a time early in a new president's administration characterized by optimistic approval by the public. And when the United States engages in a short-term military action or is the subject of an attack by terrorists, we see similar peaks of approval ratings, sometimes referred to as the **rally 'round the flag effect.** The state of the economy also affects approval ratings, as evidenced by the dwindling approval ratings of President George H. W. Bush near the end of his term in 1992–1993. During this period the economic policies of the 1980s were called into question as a recession set in, and Bush was forced to break his campaign promise of "read my lips; no new taxes," a shift that resulted in low approval ratings.

honeymoon period

a time early in a new president's administration characterized by optimistic approval by the public

rally 'round the flag effect

peaks in presidential approval ratings during short-term military action

A president rarely sustains high public approval continuously. Once achieved, however, high ratings help the chief executive to achieve his goals by demonstrating the people's support of the presidential agenda.[30]

The Media as a Tool of Presidential Influence

Modern presidents rely heavily on the mass media to convey their message to the people. The importance of the medium of television to presidents and would-be presidents was first realized in the televised presidential debates in 1960 between John F. Kennedy and Richard Nixon. After the debates, most of those who had listened to the two candidates on the radio judged Nixon to have won. But those who watched the contest of words on television came to a different conclusion (see "Exploring the Sources"). Years later, after having served as president, Nixon would comment on the influence of television in presidential campaigns, asserting that "in the television age, the key distinction is between the candidate who can speak poetry and the one who can only speak prose."[31]

Since the time of the Kennedy-Nixon debates, presidents' use of electronic media has increased significantly. Today's presidential candidates hire media consultants to assist them in preparing for televised debates. Teams of consultants create sophisticated media strategies that aim to integrate the presidential campaign's use of television, radio, and the Internet.

Once a president takes office, the expertise of the White House communications office kicks in to "spin" news in a favorable light for the administration. In particular, the White House communications director forges relationships with the most prominent media outlets by providing access, exclusive interviews, and scoops on breaking stories to reporters considered friendly to the administration.

Presidents use television to communicate directly with the American people. Important national speeches and the State of the Union address are televised, just as press conferences (usually) are. Interestingly, before the advent of television, presidential press conferences occurred more frequently than today, providing the best opportunity for the president to "talk to the people" and for reporters and their audiences to learn about presidential priorities.[32] On average, each president from Calvin Coolidge's administration starting in 1923 to the end of Harry Truman's in 1952 held at least one weekly press conference. During the Eisenhower administration, Eastman Kodak created high-speed film, an advance that permitted the filming of presidential press conferences without high-intensity lights. This invention proved a watershed with respect to the broadcasting of press conferences, as it prompted Eisenhower to establish the practice of monthly televised press conferences. John Kennedy further changed the nature of presidential press conferences by allowing television outlets to broadcast them live. Kennedy's ability to use press conferences and television to his advantage is legendary. Kennedy established the precedent of holding frequent televised press conferences, elevating them to a strategic weapon in the presidential arsenal for shaping public opinion.

Table 12.3 summarizes the number of presidential press conferences President Kennedy and his successors have held. Not surprisingly, the presidents who communicated best through the medium of television tended to hold more press conferences than others. For example,

> Modern presidents must rely heavily on the mass media to convey their message to the people, in ways their predecessors could not have imagined. Here, President Bill Clinton, who had a love/hate relationship with the press, talks with reporters during a photo op aboard Air Force One.

THE NIXON-KENNEDY DEBATES

This image shows Vice President Richard M. Nixon (right) shaking hands with Senator John F. Kennedy during their televised debate in 1960. The election was a close one, with Kennedy winning by only about 120,000 votes. Some analysts say that Kennedy's victory over Nixon in the televised debates was enough to cost Nixon the presidency that year, and they argue that the contrasting appearance and demeanor of the two candidates was a significant factor.

Evaluating the Evidence

① What physical characteristics of each man are apparent that may have helped or hurt his televised image?

② What other factors may have influenced the viewing audience? Do you think, for example, the men's clothing played a role? How about their ages? Anything else?

TABLE 12.3

Presidential Press Conferences

President	Months in Office	Number of Solo Press Conferences	Average Number of Solo Press Conferences per Month
Kennedy	34	65	1.91
Johnson	62	118	1.90
Nixon	66	39	.59
Ford	30	39	1.30
Carter	48	59	1.23
Reagan	96	46	.48
G. H. W. Bush	48	83	1.73
Clinton	96	62	.65
G. W. Bush	90	37	.41

Sources: Author's calculations based on data from www.whitehouse.gov and various news sources; Martha Joynt Kumar, "Presidential Press Conferences: The Importance and Evolution of an Enduring Forum," *Presidential Studies Quarterly* 35 (2005): 1.

compare the charismatic, persuasive John Kennedy or Lyndon Johnson with Richard Nixon, who was not telegenic and had an odd speaking voice. Yet sometimes the best communicators, including former actor Ronald Reagan—often called the Great Communicator—conducted few press conferences. Table 12.3 also shows that more recently, Bill Clinton held a below-average number of solo press conferences. Early in his tenure, George W. Bush was widely criticized for the rarity of his press conferences. In his first five years in office and after promising twice-monthly conferences, Bush held fewer solo press conferences than any other modern president. Later in his second term, Bush's number of solo press conferences increased to a nearly monthly rate, though the number tapered off toward the end of his term.

Although the nature of presidential press conferences and other media forums has evolved over time, the mass media have served as a key avenue by which modern presidents have communicated directly to the population at large. And because the nature of the president's relationship with his constituency is constantly evolving, so too is presidential power.

The Evolution of Presidential Power

Although the constitutional powers of the presidency have changed little over time, the power of the presidency has evolved a great deal.[33] In part, this development stems from some presidents' skillful use of powers not granted by the Constitution, such as the powers to persuade and to assert more authority. But the political environment within which presidents have governed has also contributed to the evolution of presidential power.[34]

The history of the early republic saw an incremental expansion of the power of the presidency, whereas the Great Depression of the 1930s and the election of Franklin D. Roosevelt in 1932 spawned an enormous growth of presidential authority.[35] As successor presidents inherited the large bureaucracy that Roosevelt built, presidential powers have further expanded—gradually creating what historian Arthur Schlesinger Jr. has called the "imperial presidency."

Early Presidents and the Scope of Presidential Power

Thomas Jefferson's election to the presidency in 1801 marks one of the earliest expansions of presidential power. Jefferson broadened the powers of the office despite his Anti-Federalist reluctance to delegate too much power to the national government. Jefferson increased presidential power in two significant ways. First, as we have seen, Jefferson established the principle of inherent powers of the presidency by undertaking the Louisiana Purchase. Second, Jefferson's tenure of office witnessed the first time that a president had to act as party leader. Jefferson had no choice but to assume this role: if he had not, he would not have been elected president given the dominance of the Federalist Party during this era (see Chapter 8).

Twenty-five years later, Andrew Jackson would also adopt the role of president-as-party-leader, but he would add a new twist. Jackson's emphasis on *populism,* a political philosophy that emphasizes the needs of the common person, spawned a new source of presidential power, as Jackson was the first president to derive real and significant power from the people. Whereas earlier politics had mostly emphasized the needs of the elite, Jackson's populism mobilized the masses of common people who traditionally had not been civically engaged. This populism augmented the power of the presidency by increasing the popularity of the president and investing him with power that came from the people's goodwill.

In the twentieth century, the nature and scope of presidential power changed as a consequence of the prevailing political environment. One of the most extraordinary shifts in the nature of the presidency occurred during Franklin D. Roosevelt's administration, which lasted from 1932 until his death in 1945. (Roosevelt was elected to an unprecedented four terms; the Twenty-Second Amendment to the Constitution, which allows only two elected presidential terms, was ratified six years after his death.)

Having come to power during the Great Depression, Roosevelt engineered a significant change in the function of the federal government. He called for a New Deal for the American people, a series of social welfare programs that would provide employment for many of the nation's unemployed workers. Roosevelt's New Deal was based on the ideas of economist John Maynard Keynes, who argued for temporary deficit spending by the government (that is, going into debt) to spur the economy during economic downturns.

Roosevelt's primary weapon in his New Deal arsenal was the **Works Progress Administration (WPA),** a federal government program that employed 8.5 million people at a cost of more than $11 million between 1935 and 1943. The idea was that government-funded employment would create economic growth in the private sector because those employed by the government would have the money to buy goods and services, thus creating spiraling demand. The rising demand for goods and services would mean that the private sector could then employ more people, and the cycle of recovery and growth would continue. For example, if during the 1930s, the government employed your great-grandfather to work on a road-building project in his town, he might have put his paycheck toward buying more bread and other baked goods than he previously could have afforded. If enough people in town could have similarly patronized the bakery, then the baker might have had to hire an assistant to keep up with demand, and consequently the

Works Progress Administration (WPA)
a New Deal program that would employ 8.5 million people at a cost of more than $11 million between 1935 and 1943

assistant would have had money to spend on, say, new shoes for his children. In this way the increased demand for products and services would continue, creating additional economic growth.

Roosevelt's New Deal was important to the presidency for two reasons. First, it dramatically changed people's views of the role of the federal government. People now tend to think of the federal government as the provider of a "safety net" that protects the most vulnerable citizens—a safeguard that did not exist before the New Deal, when those needing assistance had to rely on the help of family, friends, churches and private charities. Second, this popular perception and the programs that emerged—the Works Progress Administration, unemployment insurance, Social Security—meant that the federal government would have to grow larger in order to administer these programs. As a result, the president's role as chief executive would become much more important to modern presidents than it had been to those who served before Roosevelt.[36]

The Watershed 1970s: The *Pentagon Papers*, Watergate, and the "Imperial Presidency"

Americans' penchant for strong presidents modeled after Roosevelt diminished drastically in the 1970s. In 1971, an employee of the Department of Defense named Daniel Ellsberg leaked a classified, top-secret 7,000-page history of the nation's involvement in and thinking on Vietnam dating from the Truman administration in 1945 to the Nixon administration then installed in the White House. Called the *Pentagon Papers*, the work first appeared as a series of articles in the *New York Times*. When the Nixon administration in 1971 successfully petitioned the Department of Justice to prevent the publication of the remainder of the articles, the *Washington Post* assumed publication of them. When the Department of Justice sued the *Post*, the *Boston Globe* resumed their publication. Two weeks later, in an expedited appeals process, the U.S. Supreme Court ruled in *The New York Times Co. v. The United States* that the government "carries a heavy burden of showing justification for the imposition of such a restraint" and that the government had failed to meet that burden, thus allowing the continued publication of the papers.[37]

The *Pentagon Papers* tainted the public's view of the presidency. The published work revealed miscalculations by policy makers in presidential administrations from Truman's to Nixon's, as well as arrogance and deception on the part of policy makers, cabinet members, and presidents. Specifically, the *Pentagon Papers* revealed that the federal government had repeatedly lied about or misrepresented the fact of increasing U.S. military involvement in Southeast Asia. In particular, the analysis in the *Pentagon Papers* indicated not only that U.S. marines had conducted offensive military maneuvers well before the public was informed, but also that the U.S. military had engaged in other actions, including air strikes, over Laos and military raids throughout the North Vietnamese coastal regions. The Nixon administration's legal wrangling to prevent release of the *Pentagon Papers* cast a dark cloud over the public's perception of the presidency.

Cynicism about the presidency continued to grow in light of the **Watergate** scandal a year later. In 1972, men affiliated with President Nixon's reelection campaign broke into the headquarters of the Democratic National Committee (located in the Watergate Hotel in Washington, D.C.) to retrieve wiretaps that they had previously installed to monitor their opponents. *Washington Post* reporters Bob Woodward and Carl Bernstein, in a groundbreaking series of stories, traced the burglaries and the subsequent cover-up to high-level officials in the Nixon administration. This crime and the Nixon administration's attempts at cover-ups became known as the Watergate scandal. A Senate investigation revealed that President Nixon had secretly taped conversations in the Oval Office that would shed light on "what the president knew [about the break-in] and when he knew it."[38] Nixon claimed executive privilege and refused to turn the tapes over to a special prosecutor who had been appointed to investigate the scandal. When the U.S. Supreme Court ruled in *United States v. Richard Nixon* that Nixon must provide the tapes to the special prosecutor, one key tape was found to have a gap of almost twenty minutes where someone, reportedly his secretary, Rosemary Woods, had erased part of the recording.

> William Frazee, the chief of the presses for the *Washington Post*, makes the victory sign after learning of the Supreme Court's decision allowing newspapers to publish the *Pentagon Papers*. Applause broke out in the press room as the first print run began rolling.

Watergate
during the Nixon administration, a scandal involving burglaries and the subsequent cover-up by high-level administration officials

Meanwhile, all of the Watergate burglars had pleaded guilty and been sentenced, and only one refused to name the superiors who had orchestrated the break-in. But the testimony of burglar James W. McCord Jr. linked the crime to the Committee to Re-Elect the President (CREEP), Nixon's campaign organization, and to high-ranking Nixon White House officials. The disclosure prompted John Dean, Nixon's White House counsel, to remark, "We have a cancer within, close to the presidency, that is growing."[39] With indictments handed down for many of Nixon's top aides, and with a Senate investigation and a special prosecutor's investigation in progress, the House Judiciary Committee took up the matter of impeachment. The committee handed down three articles of impeachment against Nixon—one for obstruction of justice, a second for abuse of power, and a third for contempt of Congress. When a newly released tape documented that Nixon had planned to block the investigations by having the Federal Bureau of Investigation and the Central Intelligence Agency falsely claim that matters of national security were involved, the tape was referred to as a "smoking gun."[40] Nixon lost the support of his few loyalists in Congress and on August 8, 1974, announced that he would resign from office the following day.

From a historical perspective, Watergate might seem like a relatively insignificant event in the history of the American presidency. But the impact of the Watergate scandal on the presidency has been enormous. Watergate badly wounded the natural trust that many Americans held for their president and for their government. Combined with the unpopularity of the Vietnam War and the release of the *Pentagon Papers,* it created a deep cynicism that pervades many Americans' perception of their government even today—a pessimistic attitude that has passed from generation to generation.

Watergate also dramatically demonstrated how enormously the presidency had changed. Modern presidents had supplanted Congress as the center of federal power and in so doing had become too powerful. Historian Arthur Schlesinger Jr. and other presidential scholars have decried the problem of the growth of the executive branch and, in particular, the imperial "courts"—the rising number of Executive Office of the President staff members, many of whom are not subject to Senate confirmation and share a deep loyalty to the person who is president rather than to the institution of the presidency. In juxtaposition with an attitude like that expressed by Richard Nixon in his comment that "when the president does it, that means it is not illegal,"[41] the imperial presidency left much room for abuse.

The Post-Watergate Presidency

With the election of Jimmy Carter to the White House in 1976, many observers believed that the era of the imperial presidency had passed. Carter, the mild-mannered governor of Georgia and thus a Washington outsider, seemed to be the antidote the nation needed after the display of power-run-amok during Nixon's tenure. But given the significant challenges Carter faced during his term, many people believed that he did not exercise *enough* authority—that he acted weakly when faced with various crises.

Evolution of the Modern Presidency

THEN (1970s)	NOW (2000s)
The presidency has become an increasingly powerful institution, shaped by the predecessors of Richard Nixon, who assumes office in 1969.	Presidential power is bolstered as the tragedy of September 11 necessitates strong leadership.
The presidency supplants Congress as the epicenter of power in the federal government.	Presidential exercise of authority in the foreign policy realm serves to limit Congress's ability to rein in presidential power.
Backlash against abuses of executive power in the Nixon administration pave the way for the election of Jimmy Carter, a comparatively weak president.	Backlash against presidential policies leads to the election of Democratic Presdient Barack Obama, and Democrats increase their majorities in both houses of Congress.

WHAT'S NEXT?

> How do you anticipate that the election of 2008 will further shape the institution of the presidency?

> Will the new president continue on the path of the imperial presidency? Why or why not?

> What public policy issues will likely dominate in the months and years to come? How will these issues influence the ways presidential power is exercised?

Ronald Reagan's election in 1980 in some ways represented a return to a more powerful, "imperial" presidency. Reagan, a former actor, was Hollywood swagger personified, speaking tough talk that many Americans found appealing. His administration was not unlike an imperial court, featuring a group of advisers with deep loyalties to Reagan. But the era of unchecked presidential power was gone for good. Reagan and his successors, George H. W. Bush, Bill Clinton, and George W. Bush, attempted to set up administrations akin to imperial presidencies, each surrounding himself with a team of like-minded advisers and carving out strong policy agendas. But each also faced a much more aggressive media, dedicated to the kind of investigative reporting that had made Woodward and Bernstein famous.

It was an emboldened media, for example, that brought the Iran-contra scandal to light during the Reagan administration. This episode involved administration officials' sale of weapons to Iran and use of the proceeds to fund (illegally) the activities of anti-leftist "contra" rebels in Nicaragua. The media also relentlessly covered the Monica Lewinsky scandal during the Clinton administration, as well as the White House-CIA leak scandal during the George W. Bush administration. In the latter affair, Vice President Dick Cheney's chief of staff I. Lewis "Scooter" Libby leaked the identity of a CIA operative to a journalist as retaliation for an earlier incident involving the operative's husband. Libby was sentenced to thirty months in prison on charges of lying to investigators and obstruction of justice.

Each post-Watergate president has also faced a Congress that is often reluctant to follow his lead, as well as a frequently skeptical public that has come to believe that presidents might not always have citizens' best interests as their top goal. These factors all influence how the people evaluate the leadership of their president.

Impeachment: A Check on Abuses of Presidential Power

Although presidential powers are flexible and can be shaped by the individuals holding the office, these powers do not go unchecked. One crucial check on presidential power is **impeachment,** the power of the House of Representatives to formally accuse the president (and other high-ranking officials, including the vice president and federal judges) of crimes. The Constitution specifically refers to charges of "Treason, Bribery, or other high Crimes and Misdemeanors," an appropriately vague description of the potential offenses a president could commit. An impeachment can be thought of as an indictment: If a majority of the members of the House of Representatives vote to impeach the president, the charges against the president, called the **articles of impeachment,** are forwarded to the Senate. The Senate then tries the president and, in the event of conviction for the offenses, determines the penalty. In convicting a president, the Senate has the authority to punish the president by removing him from office.

Although the Senate can force a president to step down, it has never done so in practice, and only two presidents have been impeached by the House of Representatives. The first was Andrew Johnson, who succeeded Abraham Lincoln as president in 1865 upon the latter's assassination. When he assumed the presidency, Johnson faced not only a divided nation but also a government in turmoil. The eleven articles of impeachment against him had to do primarily with his removal of the secretary of war, Edwin Stanton, who was working with Johnson's congressional opponents to undermine Johnson's reconstruction policies in the South. The so-called Radical Republicans in the House believed that Johnson's policies were too moderate, and they sought to treat the Confederate states as conquered territories and to confiscate the land of slaveholders. These same House members wanted to protect their ally Stanton and prevent him from being removed from office. The Senate ultimately recognized the politically motivated nature of the articles of impeachment against Johnson and acquitted him on all counts.

impeachment
the power of the House of Representatives to formally accuse the president (and other high-ranking officials, including the vice president and federal judges) of crimes

articles of impeachment
charges against the president during an impeachment

> On the basis of an investigation by special prosecutor Kenneth Starr, the House impeached President Bill Clinton for committing perjury by lying to a grand jury about his relationship with White House intern Monica Lewinsky and for obstructing justice. The Senate voted to acquit Clinton on those perjury charges.

The most recent occurrence of the impeachment of a president was in 1998, when the House of Representatives approved two articles of impeachment against President Bill Clinton. On the basis of an investigation by a special prosecutor, the House impeached Clinton for lying to a grand jury about his relationship with White House intern Monica Lewinsky and for obstructing justice. The Senate acquitted Clinton on both counts.

During the Watergate scandal that rocked Richard Nixon's presidency, the House Judiciary Committee approved articles of impeachment against the president and sent them to the full House for a vote. Republican members of Congress convinced Nixon that the House would vote to impeach him and that the Senate would convict him and remove him from office. Faced with the inevitable, Nixon became the first president to resign from office before the House could vote to impeach him.

Evaluating Presidential Leadership

In 1998, while President Clinton was mired in impeachment hearings in Congress, his public approval ratings stood at 60 percent. Despite the Monica Lewinsky scandal and the risk that the president might be removed from office for lying about his relationship with the White House intern, a healthy majority of Americans separated Clinton's personal moral failings from his ability to govern successfully.

While a president is in office, people evaluate the president's performance on the basis of specific criteria. These include questions such as these: Does the president prioritize the same issues that I do? Is the president effectively managing the economy? Is the United States respected around the world? Is the president a strong leader, unafraid to exercise power? Does the president have a vision for the nation and for his administration? Is the president able to communicate that vision to the people? If presidents are successful in these areas, they tend to have generally high approval ratings. As we have seen, however, high approval ratings are difficult to sustain over the course of an administration.

In general, the average American's criteria for presidential greatness differ substantially from assessments by scholars of the presidency. The American public at large tends to emphasize recent presidents with strong communication skills, citing Ronald Reagan, John F. Kennedy, and Bill Clinton among the top four presidents in one survey (with Abraham Lincoln number three). Scholarly rankings tend to be more historically inclusive, with George Washington, Abraham Lincoln, Franklin D. Roosevelt, and Thomas Jefferson leading the list of the greatest presidents.

Women in the White House

Of the three branches of government, the executive branch has been the most challenging for women to gain entry into as formal participants. As we saw earlier in this chapter, no woman served as a cabinet member until the twentieth century, and to date, a woman has not been elected president. Yet cabinet positions are not the only place where women's influence in the executive branch has been felt. Historically, the women who have served as First Lady have influenced both presidents and policy.

Some recent First Ladies, among them Nancy Reagan and Hillary Clinton, have exercised undisguised public power. Upon President Obama's election, many Americans began to wonder whether First Lady Michelle Obama would take up the reigns as policy leader. And with women becoming an increasing proportion of the pool of candidates deemed eligible to be president, a woman's election to the presidency in the near future becomes nearly assured. Indeed, Senator John McCain's selection of Alaska Governor Sarah Palin was seen by many analysts as an acknowledgment of the importance of women voters and the inevitability of a woman president. As President Richard Nixon remarked, "Certainly in the next 50 years we shall see a woman president, perhaps sooner than you think. A woman can and should be able to do any political job that a man can do."[42]

WHERE DO YOU STAND?

The Greatest President

Whom do you regard as the greatest U.S. president overall?

Source: Table 3, www.harrisinteractive.com/harris_poll/index.asp?PID=869.

The First Lady

Much like the presidency itself, the office of the First Lady has been defined by the individuals who have occupied it. That women as different as Barbara Bush, the wife of President George H. W. Bush, and Hillary Clinton, the wife of President Bill Clinton, could consecutively and successfully serve as First Lady demonstrates the open-mindedness with which the American people view the role.

Although the role of First Lady has historically been ceremonial in nature, many modern First Ladies have used the position as a platform for favorite causes, policies, and views. President Ronald Reagan noted, "If the president has a bully pulpit, then the First Lady has a white glove pulpit . . . more refined, restricted, ceremonial, but it's a pulpit all the same."[43] Recent initiatives of the white glove pulpit include Laura Bush's advocacy of literacy and Nancy Reagan's anti-drug-abuse ("Just Say No") campaign.

Other First Ladies have used their proximity to the chief executive to influence policy concerns more broadly and more forcefully. Some have acted "behind the scenes," as was the case with Edith Wilson, the wife of Woodrow Wilson. Others have taken a more public role. Eleanor Roosevelt, the wife of Franklin D. Roosevelt, fought for many causes during her husband's administration, including human rights and civil rights for African Americans. Hillary Clinton transformed the office of First Lady by serving, at her husband's appointment, as the chair of a presidential task force on health care reform. Her role in the task force, and indeed throughout the Clinton administration, proved to be a lightning rod for critics who thought that a First Lady should not be so prominent. Laura Bush by contrast has been a more reserved and less public First Lady.

When a Woman Is Elected President

As First Lady, Barbara Bush speculated about the election of a woman president. She wryly commented, "Somewhere out in this audience may even be someone who will one day follow my footsteps, and preside over the White House as the president's spouse. I wish him well!"[44]

Over a period of time, pollsters have explored the possibility of whether Americans would vote for a qualified woman for president. Figure 12.4 shows that since 1937, when only 33 percent of Americans said they would cast their presidential ballot for a qualified woman, that figure has steadily risen. By 1999, the number rose to 92 percent of respondents who said they would vote for a female presidential candidate. Yet by 2005 that figured had declined to 89 percent. One explanation for this drop could be that Senator Hillary Clinton was frequently mentioned at the time of the poll as a likely 2008 presidential candidate and that respondents unwilling to support her candidacy responded that they were unwilling to vote for a woman for president.

Though Senator Clinton's bid for the White House was unsuccessful, inevitably, the United States will have to face the issue of the role of the First Gentleman. We can wonder about the dilemmas that might arise for the men who pioneer in this new role.

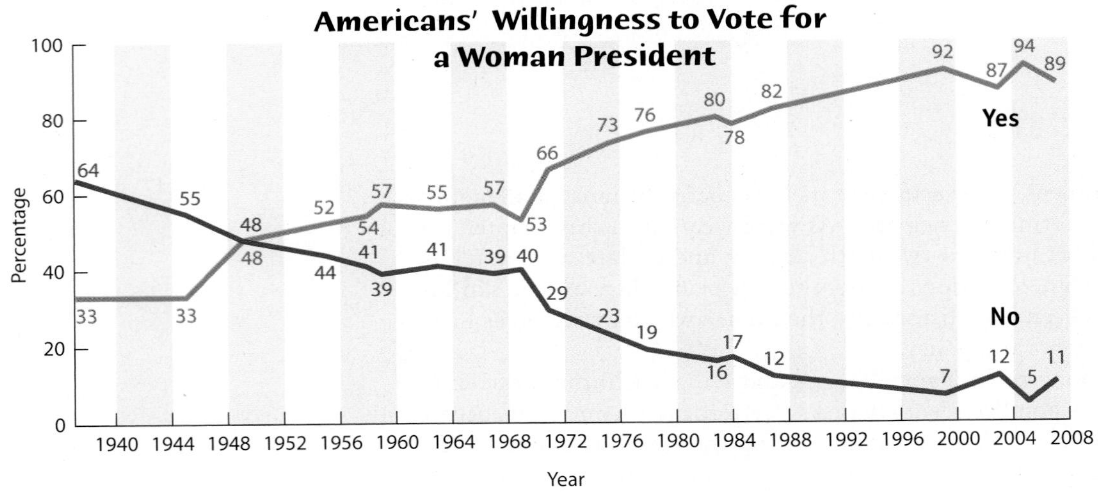

Americans' Willingness to Vote for a Woman President

POLITICAL INQUIRY

FIGURE 12.4 ■ What has been the trend since the late 1930s in the American electorate's willingness to vote for a woman president? What factors do you think explain this shift?

Source: The Gallup Poll, www.galluppoll.com/content/?ci=8611&pg=1 and www.gallup.com/poll/18937/, and www.gallup.com/poll/26875/Analysis=Impact=Personal=characteristics=Candidate=Support. aspx, accessed March 17, 2008.

Will the ceremonial functions of the first spouse remain the same? Will the First Gentleman choose the White House china; will he assist in the organization of state dinners and other social functions? Will he work in a private-sector job outside the White House? Will he have a voice in influencing administration policy?

We will learn the answers only when a married woman becomes president. In all likelihood, people's fascination with the role of First Gentleman will wane when the novelty of the office wears off. And similarly to the various interpretations of the role that First Ladies have created, it is likely that the role of First Gentleman will be flexible and adaptable, responding to the inclinations and the personalities of the men who occupy it, as well as to public preferences.

CONCLUSION *CONTINUING THE CONVERSATION*

The American presidency is a dynamic institution, one that is molded by the individuals who serve as president and by the American people—by their changing interests, viewpoints, struggles, and needs. The presidency has a symbiotic relationship with the larger culture in which it exists; it is at once shaped by, and shapes, the culture.

The executive branch of the federal government is also flexible, incorporating the needs of diverse constituencies and participants, particularly in recent times. The continued evolution of the presidency as a more diverse institution is relatively assured.

The presidency is a product of both the design of the framers and the desires of the citizenry. As the country's need for stronger presidents has increased, the resources and authorities of presidents have grown to accommodate new powers. But at what point does the presidency become, in the minds of Americans, *too* powerful?

Since the activist administration of Franklin D. Roosevelt, the characterization of the presidency as an "imperial" institution has dogged numerous presidents, most recently former president George W. Bush. For many Americans, their vote in the 2008 presidential election was a reflection of their views on the Bush administration and its legacy. Looking ahead, how will the citizens of the future view the scope of presidential power? The answer will depend in large part on the people themselves, particularly those who vote. It will depend on whom citizens elect to the highest office in the land; on how the people's opinions shape (or, in some cases, fail to shape) presidential actions; and on how the people's relationship with their presidents develops. For although the Constitution created a system in which presidential powers can institutionally be checked, the framers did not foresee the most significant checks on modern presidents: the will of the people and a ruthlessly investigatory media, both of which ensure that presidential power is not unrestrained.[45]

Summary

1. Presidential Elections

Campaigns are the primary mechanism by which candidates for the presidency outline their priorities and their positions on issues. It is during campaigns that the people's relationship with the president is initially forged. Campaigns are key avenues by which individuals can become involved in the electoral process, such as through participating in nominating conventions, voting on Election Day, and voicing their opinions about the formal selection of the president through the Electoral College system.

2. Presidential Roles in the Domestic Sphere

As chief legislator, the president helps to define Congress's agenda through the annual State of the Union address and influences congressional legislation, particularly concerning the federal budget. Presidents also "legislate" when they veto legislation. As chief economist, the president uses a variety of tools, including the federal budget and the appointment of the chair of the Federal Reserve, to shape economic policy. As party leader, the president acts as the chief of his own party and helps party members get elected to federal, state, and local offices.

3. Presidential Roles in the Foreign Policy Sphere

As chief diplomat, the president and his administration shape the foreign policy of the United States. As commander in chief, the president is the leader of all branches of the armed forces.

4. Overlap in the President's Domestic and Foreign Policy Roles

The president's roles of chief executive and chief of state encompass both domestic and foreign policy spheres. The responsibility as chief executive includes the job of chief administrator of the entire executive branch of government, including the cabinet departments. As chief of state, the president is the ceremonial head of state, a function that is carried out by a separate officeholder in many other nations.

5. The President and the Executive Branch

Leading the executive branch of the federal government is among the president's top responsibilities. Key executive branch offices are the vice president, the cabinet, and the Executive Office of the President (EOP). The EOP includes the White House Office, the Office of Management and Budget, the National Security Council, and the Council of Economic Advisers. Each office assists the president in devising and implementing policy.

6. Presidential Succession

If a president dies in office, he or she is succeeded by the vice president, the Speaker of the House, the president pro tem of the Senate, and then by a specified order of cabinet officials, according to the Presidential Succession Act of 1947. When a president becomes incapacitated in office, the Twenty-Fifth Amendment to the Constitution prescribes the course of action.

7. Sources of Presidential Power

Article II, Sections 2 and 3, of the U.S. Constitution enumerate the expressed powers of the president. Inherent powers emanate from the "take care" clause of the Constitution and have been asserted by presidents as constitutionally implied. Statutory powers include powers that the Congress grants presidents, and special presidential powers include emergency powers, executive privilege, and the power to issue executive orders.

8. The People as a Source of Presidential Power

Because the people are a major source of presidential power, presidents continuously seek to nurture and secure public support. To this end, presidents exploit their easy access to the "bully pulpit" and the media. High public approval ratings can serve as an important source of presidential power and are of particular help in getting popular presidential proposals enacted by Congress.

9. The Evolution of Presidential Power

The presidential powers of George Washington contrast strikingly with the powers of contemporary presidents. Presidential power first expanded during the administration of Thomas Jefferson, and this authority continued to grow through Andrew Jackson's tenure of office. Franklin D. Roosevelt's administration witnessed the greatest expansion in executive power to date, to the point that modern presidencies have been characterized as "imperial presidencies." The notion of the imperial presidency was significantly damaged by the Watergate scandal in 1973. Since then, presidents have fought hard to secure the public trust while often facing a media skeptical of their integrity and motivations.

10. Evaluating Presidential Leadership

Significant differences separate scholarly assessments of specific presidents from the views of the general population. In general, nonacademics tend to name modern presidents who have been effective communicators as among the greatest presidents, whereas scholars cite a number of earlier presidents as most effective.

11. Women in the White House

Traditionally, the most prominent role for women in the White House has been that of First Lady. Some First Ladies, among them Eleanor Roosevelt and Hillary Clinton, have been much more powerful and visible public figures than others. As the pool of potential female presidential candidates increases, there is a growing likelihood that a woman will be elected president.

For Review

1. Explain the process of presidential elections. What role do states play in the electoral procedures?
2. List the various roles of the president, and provide an example of each.
3. What are the sources of presidential power?
4. How has presidential power evolved over time?
5. Explain the organization and functions of the Executive Office of the President.
6. What is the trend with regard to Americans' willingness to vote for a qualified woman for president?

For Critical Thinking and Discussion

1. What is your opinion about the presidential election process? Would you favor a constitutional amendment eliminating the Electoral College in favor of a popularly elected president? Why or why not?
2. What do you think are the most important roles for presidents today? Why do these roles matter more than others?
3. Who do you think has been the greatest president in U.S. history? What characteristics do you admire about the president you choose?
4. What factors affect how frequently presidents veto legislation? Does vetoing legislation signify presidential strength or weakness? Explain.
5. What impact did Watergate have on people's perception of the presidency and of government? Have there been lasting effects from this scandal? Explain.
6. Would the people you know be willing to vote for a woman for president? Which demographic groups do you think would be more willing? Why? Which would be less willing, in your opinion—and why?

MULTIPLE CHOICE: Choose the lettered item that answers the question correctly.

1. The power of the House of Representatives to formally accuse the president (and other high-ranking officials, including the vice president and federal judges) of crimes is called
   a. oversight.
   b. impeachment.
   c. divided government.
   d. judicial review.

2. The presidential powers enumerated in the Constitution are the
   a. expressed powers.
   b. inherent powers.
   c. executive powers.
   d. emergency powers.

3. The right of the chief executive and members of the administration to withhold information from Congress or the courts, or the right to refuse to appear before legislative or judicial bodies, is called
   a. emergency power.
   b. executive privilege.
   c. expressed power.
   d. an executive order.

4. A key White House Office (WHO) staff member who serves as both adviser to the president and the manager of the WHO is the
   a. vice president.
   b. White House counsel.
   c. chief of staff.
   d. National Security Adviser.

5. An agreement between the United States and another nation that is in effect during the administration of the president who negotiates the agreement and may not be binding on future presidents is called
   a. a treaty.
   b. a negotiated standard.
   c. a presidential pact.
   d. an executive agreement.

6. A written message that the president issues upon signing a bill into law is
   a. an executive order.
   b. a signing statement.
   c. a veto message.
   d. an executive agreement.

7. It is harder for presidents to achieve their legislative agendas when they belong to one political party and Congress is controlled by a majority of members of the other party. This situation is called
   a. divided government.
   b. bipartisanship.
   c. bicameralism.
   d. bifurcated institutionalism.

8. The name for a presidentially issued rule or regulation that has the force of law is an
   a. emergency order.
   b. executive privilege.
   c. expressed order.
   d. executive order.

9. Presidential powers that are implied in the Constitution are called
   a. expressed powers.
   b. inherent powers.
   c. executive powers.
   d. emergency powers.

10. A peak in presidential approval ratings during a short-term military action reflects
    a. for God and country effect.
    b. homeland security effect.
    c. pledge of patriotism effect.
    d. rally 'round the flag effect.

FILL IN THE BLANKS.

11. _____ is the arm of the EOP that enables presidents to consider matters of foreign policy and national security with their top national security advisers and relevant cabinet officials.

12. _____ was a scandal involving burglaries and the subsequent cover-up by high-level administration officials during the Nixon administration.

13. The group of experts that counsels the president on running the country is called the _____.

14. The office that creates the president's annual budget is the _____.

15. When the president seeks to prevent a piece of legislation from becoming law by taking no action if the legislation is submitted for his signature within ten days of the end of a legislative session, this tactic is called a _____.

Answers: 1. b; 2. a; 3. b; 4. c; 5. d; 6. b; 7. a; 8. d; 9. b; 10. d; 11. The National Security Council; 12. The Watergate scandal; 13. cabinet; 14. Office of Management and Budget; 15. pocket veto.

RESOURCES FOR RESEARCH AND ACTION

Internet Resources

American Democracy Now **Web site**

www.mhhe.com/harrison1e   Consult the book's Web site for study guides, interactive activities, simulations, and current hot-links for additional information on the American presidency.

270 to Win

www.270towin.com   This interactive Web site demonstrates how the Electoral College outcome is determined; users can experiment with altering the results of elections. It also contains past voting information for all states.

Center for the Study of the Presidency

www.thepresidency.org   This research center analyzes presidential leadership and offers seminars and symposia for presidential research-ers, including the Center Fellows program for undergraduate students.

Presidential Libraries

You can find the Web sites of the libraries of recent presidents, which typically include a wealth of information about individual presiden-cies and archival resources:

William J. Clinton Presidential Library: www.clintonlibrary.gov/

George (H. W.) Bush Presidential Library: bushlibrary.tamu.edu/

Ronald Reagan Presidential Library: www.reagan.utexas.edu/

Jimmy Carter Library and Museum: www.jimmycarterlibrary.org/

Gerald R. Ford Presidential Library: www.fordlibrarymuseum.gov/

Richard Nixon Presidential Library: www.nixonfoundation.org/

Lyndon Baines Johnson Presidential Library: www.lbjlib.utexas.edu/

John F. Kennedy Presidential Library: www.jfklibrary.org/

The White House

www.whitehouse.gov   You can visit the White House Web site for information about current issues and news, the text of presidential speeches, links to cabinet departments, the EOP, and information about the First Lady and the vice president.

Recommended Readings

Barber, James D. *The Presidential Character: Predicting Performance in the White House.* Englewood Cliffs, NJ: Prentice-Hall, 1985. Focuses on the psychology of presidents and the character traits that influence their ability to succeed in office.

Borrelli, MaryAnne. *The President's Cabinet: Gender, Power, and Repre-sentation.* Boulder, CO: Lynne Rienner, 2002. Analysis of the evolu-tion of presidential cabinets in terms of gender representation.

Ehrenhalt, Alan. *The United States of Ambition: Politicians, Power and the Pursuit of Office.* New York: Times Books, 1991. Interesting account of the importance of personal drive and ambition in catapulting would-be presidents to the White House.

Halberstam, David. *The Best and the Brightest.* Fawcett Books, 1993. Riveting analysis of how the Kennedy and Johnson administrations entrenched the United States in the war in Vietnam.

Hughes, Karen. *Ten Minutes from Normal.* New York: Viking, 2004. Unique insider's view of the George W. Bush White House and of the author's struggles to balance work, family, and church obligations.

Neustadt, Richard E. *Presidential Power and the Modern President.* New York: The Free Press, 1990. Update of the author's classic 1960 vol-umes, explaining the evolution of power in the modern presidency and probing, in particular, presidents' ability to persuade.

Schlesinger, Arthur M., Jr. *The Imperial Presidency.* Boston: Houghton Mifflin, 1973. Classic volume describing how the presidency has become a rarely checked, "imperial" institution.

Suskind, Ronald. *The Price of Loyalty: George W. Bush, the White House, and the Education of Paul O'Neill.* New York: Simon & Schuster, 2004. Criti-cal account of decision making in the George W. Bush White House.

Woodward, Bob, and Carl Bernstein. *All the President's Men,* 2nd ed. New York: Simon & Schuster, 1994. Classic work that launched investigative journalism, particularly concerning the presidency, in which the authors describe their investigation of the Watergate scandal that led to President Richard Nixon's resignation.

Movies of Interest

Recount (2008)

This movie chronicles the 2000 presidential election, focusing on the controversy surrounding ballot counting in Florida that cul-minated in the U.S. Supreme Court case *Bush v. Gore.*

Air Force One (1997)

In this suspense thriller, the president of the United States, played by Harrison Ford, is forced to do battle with terrorist hijackers aboard Air Force One.

The American President (1995)

Rob Reiner directed this comedic drama about an unmarried male president (portrayed by Michael Douglas) and a lobbyist (Annette Bening), who fall in love.

All the President's Men (1976)

In this 1976 film adaptation of the book by the same name, Robert Redford and Dustin Hoffman star as *Washington Post* reporters Bob Woodward and Carl Bernstein (respectively), who uncover the details of the Watergate scandal that led to President Nixon's resignation.

In addition, there are numerous biographical movies of American presidents, including many that air on the A&E network's *Biography* series. You can find these programs at www.biography.com.

National Journal

BUSH'S LEGACY

Worst. President. Ever." That succinct judgment, received not long ago via e-mail from a political scientist, sums up a good deal of what conventional wisdom has to say about President Bush. In an unscientific online poll of 109 historians, more than 60 percent rated Bush's presidency as the worst in U.S. history. In his 2007 book, Second Chance: Three Presidents and the Crisis of American Superpower, former National Security Adviser Zbigniew Brzezinski titles his chapter on Bush "Catastrophic Leadership." "A calamity," Brzezinski wrote. "A historical failure."

One hypothesis is at odds with the prevailing wisdom that **Bush, whatever you think of him,** has been a president of major consequence.

And he was referring to just the Iraq war. The litany of disasters and failures commonly attributed to Bush has grown familiar enough to summarize in checklist format: WMD; Guantanamo; Abu Ghraib; waterboarding; wiretapping; habeas corpus; "Osama bin Forgotten"; anti-Americanism; deficits; spending; Katrina; Rumsfeld; Cheney; Gonzales; Libby. In this view, George W. Bush is at least as destructive as was Richard Nixon, a president whose mistakes and malfeasances took decades to undo.

Though a smaller band, Bush's defenders parry that he will look to history more like Harry Truman, a president whose achievements took decades to appreciate. In this view, Bush will be remembered as the president who laid the strategic groundwork for an extended struggle against Islamist terrorism; who made democratization the cen-

terpiece of foreign policy; who transformed the federal-state relationship in education; who showed that a candidate can touch the "third rail" of Social Security and still get elected (twice).

Notice what those two views assume in common: Bush has been a game-changing president. For better or worse, he has succeeded in his ambition of being a transformative figure rather than one who plays "small ball," in Bush's own disdainful phrase. Hasn't he?

Perhaps not. Bush may go down in history as a transitional and comparatively minor figure. His presidency, though politically traumatic, may leave only a modest policy footprint. In that sense—though by no means substantively or stylistically—Bush's historical profile may resemble Jimmy Carter's more than Truman's or Nixon's.

Odd as it may sound today, this president entered office as a proponent of bipartisanship. Bush brought off a bipartisan education reform, and after the September 11 terrorist attacks, he did what even his critics agreed was a masterful job of rallying the country. His public approval rose to a dizzying 90 percent.

The fruits of this early period of two-party government were considerable: a new campaign finance law, the USA PATRIOT Act's revisions to domestic-security law, the Sarbanes-Oxley corporate accountability law, the creation of the Homeland Security Department, and more. "Seventeen major legislative acts were passed in the first two years of the Bush presidency—the second-highest among first-term presidents in the post-World War II period," writes Charles O. Jones, a presidential historian.

But 2002 also marked the Bush administration's transition to a more rigidly partisan governing style. That January, Karl Rove, Bush's top political adviser, signaled that Republicans would "make the president's handling of the war on terrorism the centerpiece of their strategy to win back the Senate," as The Washington Post reported. This

represented a distinct change in tone: "Until now," The Post noted, "Bush has stressed that the fight against terrorism is a bipartisan and unifying issue for the country."

That year's midterm election, which gave Republicans control of the Senate and consolidated their margin in the House, vindicated their strategy but also trapped the party within it.

In firm control of both branches, Bush and congressional Republicans embarked on an experiment in one-party government. What followed was a period of substantive excess and stylistic harshness that came to define Bush's presidency in the public's mind, obliterating memories of the "compassionate conservative."

Profligate spending and a major Medicare expansion disgusted conservatives. Efforts to reform Social Security and immigration policy collapsed embarrassingly; Bush's sluggish response to Hurricane Katrina cratered Americans' faith in his competence. Abroad, Abu Ghraib, Guantanamo, waterboarding, and extrajudicial detentions called the country's basic decency into question.

By 2006, the president's approval rating was in the 30 percent range and falling. The Democrats swept control of Congress in November. If Bush's presidency had ended in January 2007, his reputation as our era's Nixon might have been assured.

But Bush has used his last two years as, in effect, a third term, behaving as if he were his own successor.

"There was unquestionably a sharp change in their approach to the world and in their policies," says Kenneth Pollack, a senior fellow at the Brookings Institution. Frequently cited examples include the Iraq surge, patient but rigid dealings with Iran, a relaunch of Israeli-Palestinian peace talks, a denuclearization deal with North Korea, and a promise to halve greenhouse-gas emissions by 2050.

What changed? "I think we learned a bit," Stephen Hadley, Bush's national security adviser, told reporters in June.

But ever protective of Bush's trademark steadfastness, the White House takes issue with any talk of U-turns. "I think there's actually remarkable continuity," says Tony Fratto, the deputy press secretary. He asserts that reality has caught up with the administration rather than the other way around.

Whatever the explanation, Bush hands the next president a healing rather than a broken Iraq, diplomatic processes rather than deadlocks in the Middle East and the Korean Peninsula, and a position on global warming that is widely viewed as moving the United States past obstructionism.

"I think what you see here is a guy who has learned to be as effective as possible in reduced circumstances," says political scientist Steven Schier. Paradoxically, this chief executive who prided himself on assertive, even aggressive, leadership proved to be a weak strong president but a surprisingly strong weak one.

The harder question is where Bush will leave matters after eight years, not after just the past two. One hypothesis is at odds with the prevailing wisdom that Bush, whatever you think of him, has been a president of major consequence. Consider, again, the five problems mentioned earlier. The situation in Iraq in January 2001 was unstable and dangerous but not critical, and the same is true today. With regards to Iran, the Israeli-Palestinian conflict, North Korea, and global warming, the country is in roughly the same place it was when Bill Clinton left office.

Two other areas, the war on terrorism and fiscal policy, deserve a closer look.

September 11, 2001, it is often said, "changed everything." It certainly changed Americans' attitudes, convincing the public that Al Qaeda and its affiliates are a threat rather than a nuisance, and that the United States must apply military as well as civilian tools to confront terrorism. September 11 thereby triggered a cascade of policy changes, ranging from the PATRIOT Act to the Iraq war.

The threat was pre-existing, however, as Bush's supporters tirelessly repeat (adding that the Clinton administration failed to deal with it). The question is whether Bush, like Truman, has set up a lasting strategic and institutional architecture for managing the conflict. "If we wait for threats to fully materialize, we will have waited too long," Bush said in June 2002. That statement, the core of the Bush Doctrine, is hardly controversial today.

Similarly, the Detainee Treatment Act, the Military Commissions Act, the PATRIOT Act, and the new Foreign Intelligence Surveillance Act have put in place mechanisms that subsequent presidents may revise but will not repudiate.

Bush's critics, meanwhile, argue that he trashed the country's finances. He cut taxes steeply, waged an expensive war without paying for it, engineered a costly expansion of Medicare (also without paying for it), and untethered federal spending, thus turning healthy surpluses into chronic deficits—all while failing to come to grips with an imminent crisis in entitlement programs.

"We're in much worse fiscal shape today than we were in 2001," says David Walker, who until recently headed the Government Accountability Office and is now president of the Peter G. Peterson Foundation.

As for Bush's tax cuts, viewed in historical perspective they were a blip, not a turning point. Overall, taxes went down early in this decade but then bobbed back up again, though not all the way.

Bush failed to deal with the long-term entitlement problem. He left the ledger in worse shape than he found it, and his botched effort to reform Social Security may have made entitlement reform more difficult politically. "I think we've lost a tremendous opportunity during the Bush period and, really, over the last part of the Clinton period," says Stuart Butler, an analyst at the Heritage Foundation.

Still, as Butler's comment implies, Bush's failure in this regard is not unique. His predecessors ducked the entitlement problem and his would-be successors are all but promising to do the same. Bush's fiscal failing, in short, arguably lies not in being exceptional but in being all too ordinary.

Indeed, what is most striking about the Bush presidency is not the new problems it has created (though Iraq may yet change that verdict) or the old problems it has solved (though Iraq may yet change that verdict, too). What is striking, rather, is that Bush will pass on to his successor all the major problems and preoccupations he inherited: Iraq, Iran, Israel and the Palestinians, North Korea, global warming, Islamist terrorism, nuclear proliferation, health care, entitlement costs, immigration. What is remarkable, in other words, is not how much Bush has done to reshape the agenda but how little.

Reagan removed inflation from the agenda; he and George H.W. Bush (still sadly underrated) removed the Cold War; Clinton removed welfare and the deficit. Bush, as of now, ends up more or less where he started—not exactly, of course (he resurrected the deficit, for example), but about as close as history's turbulence allows. The biggest surprise of the Bush presidency is its late-breaking bid to join the middling ranks of administrations that are judged not by their triumph or tragedy but by their opportunity cost: What might a greater or lesser president have done with Bush's eight years?

In his recent book The Bush Tragedy, Jacob Weisberg mentions the he was "originally going to call this book The Bush Detour, thinking of the Bush presidency simply as lost time for the country." His original title may have been closer to the mark. If so, history's ironic judgment on this singularly ambitious president will be that his legacy was small ball, after all.

THEN: Judging the legacy of a president is measured by both its short- and long-term impact.

NOW: George W. Bush leaves the White House with record low approval ratings.

NEXT: Will the eight years of the Bush administration be viewed as a transformative presidency? What will be the future policy implications of Bush's legacy of one-party government? How will the Bush legacy shape the Obama presidency?

The
Bureaucracy

THEN

The federal bureaucracy under President George Washington had three departments and two offices serving a national population of 4 million.

NOW

Almost 3 million civilian federal bureaucrats—plus 35 to 40 million state, local, private for-profit, and non-profit bureaucrats—serve a national population of over 300 million.

NEXT

Will the volume of public service outsourced to private for-profit contractors continue to soar?

Will contracting-out boost the efficiency and effectiveness of public service delivery and save taxpayer dollars over time—or not?

Will the bureaucracy remain a target of criticism from citizens, candidates, and elected officials?

Protecting Taxpayer Dollars for Four Decades

In 1965, the U.S. Air Force hired A. Ernest Fitzgerald as a civilian cost analyst and management systems deputy. Three years later, Fitzgerald was defying his Air Force superiors by testifying before Congress about cost overruns, technical difficulties, and the concealment of these problems by government contractor Lockheed. As a public servant, he felt obligated to blow the whistle on the waste of taxpayer money he was witnessing firsthand. At the root of the problems were mismanagement and corruption on the part of both the government and government contractors. As a result of Fitzgerald's testimony, the Air Force decreased its order for C-5A jet transports from 115 to 81—yet the cost of the 81 transports was still $1 billion more than the initially contracted cost for 115 transports. Fitzgerald's testimony cost him dearly: his superiors stripped him of his duties, denied him his promised civil service job protections, and, at the urging of President Richard Nixon, fired him. I Fitzgerald subsequently sued the national government to regain his position. Four years later, his legal battle (at a cost close to $1 million) ended when a federal judge ruled that the Air Force had to give him back his job. Once reinstated, Fitzgerald continued to find and report fraud and corruption in the government's relations with contractors. Fitzgerald's concern for taxpayers again made headlines in 1988 when he shared his knowledge of government mismanagement with the nonprofit government watchdog group the Project for Military Procurement (the Project). The Project released Fitzgerald's mismanagement revelations to the media, which informed citizens about the government's purchase of coffee pots costing $7,622 and hammers with a price tag of $200. The media also reported the government's purchases of wildly overpriced spare parts that it did not need and other spare parts that did not work.* I Whistle-blowers such as A. Ernest Fitzgerald risk their careers for the public good. Their revelations of unethical behavior and the waste of taxpayer dollars have given rise to a skeptical public that grows ever less trusting of government officials and ever more demanding of government transparency—the disclosure of information about budgets and practices, in the interest of accountability and openness. In response to the ballooning public mistrust sparked by Fitzgerald's 1968 testimony, elected officials passed laws, collectively known as sunshine laws, promoting openness in government and greater accountability to citizens. One such law, the Whistle-blower Protection Act, aims to protect government employees who come forward to report government mismanagement and corruption. The importance of these laws became glaringly apparent after the terrorist attacks of September 11, 2001, as a new wave of whistle-blowing exposed serious flaws in U.S. defenses. The revelations spawned calls to strengthen whistle-blower protections. I Upon Fitzgerald's retirement from public service in February 2006, acting Department of Defense inspector general Thomas Gimble honored his career of waging war on wastefulness and fraud in government. Gimble characterized Fitzgerald's successful fight to regain his job as "a landmark moment in the effort to protect the rights of whistleblowers" who assist Congress in holding the bureaucracy accountable when they "identify potential deficiencies in [government] programs and operations, or potential misconduct by federal employees and contractors."**

The C-5 jet transport, about which public servant—and whistle-blower—A. Ernest Fitzgerald testified in 1968.

* A. Ernest Fitzgerald, *The Pentagonists: An Insider's View of Waste, Mismanagement and Fraud in Defense Spending* (Boston: Houghton Mifflin, 1989).
** www.dodig.mil/IGInformation/archives/Ernie FitzgeraldRetirement022806.htm.

In the year of his retirement,

A. Ernest Fitzgerald was one of almost 3 million national civilian bureaucrats providing public services. Public servants conduct vital and varied work for citizens. Air traffic controllers ensure safety in the skies and on the runways. Meat inspectors keep diseased meat from the dinner table. Meteorologists watch for developing tornadoes and hurricanes so that they can warn people in time to evacuate. More visible are the mail carriers who deliver our mail. Beyond the legions of federal public servants, almost 20 million state and local bureaucrats assist in implementing national public policies. In addition, through grants and contracts with the national government, millions of employees in private for-profit businesses and in nonprofit organizations help to do the work of government. President George W. Bush (2001–2009) estimated the cost of providing national public services in his proposed 2009 budget to be about $3.1 trillion.[1] This staggering sum amounts to $7.3 billion per day and $5.07 million per minute.

Americans expect the millions of government and nongovernment employees to provide public services and benefits efficiently and effectively. In our democracy, citizens also expect accountability. They want assurance that their tax dollars are spent properly and in furtherance of the public good. But such accountability is hindered by the complexities of public service delivery. Moreover, assessing performance is difficult when the services bureaucrats provide include ensuring justice and domestic tranquility, defending the nation, and promoting the general welfare.

In this chapter we focus on civilian *bureaucrats*, the public servants who put public policies into action, and on *bureaucracies*, the government organizations in which they work. We also look at how citizens help to improve government performance and ensure bureaucratic accountability.

FIRST, we discuss who and what constitute *bureaucrats and bureaucracy.*

SECOND, we focus on *federal bureaucrats* by examining three categories of such public servants: political appointees, civil servants, and members of the senior executive service.

THIRD, we consider that through grants and contracts, various nonfederal bureaucrats—*state, local, and shadow bureaucrats*—also administer national public policies.

FOURTH, we survey the historical growth in size, cost, and complexity of national public service delivery by reviewing the *evolution and organization of the federal bureaucracy.*

FIFTH, we investigate the multiple ways in which bureaucrats influence the development, approval, implementation, and evaluation of public service through a review of *federal bureaucrats' roles in public policy.*

SIXTH, we look into the multiple mechanisms outside and inside government to foster *federal bureaucratic accountability.*

SEVENTH, we explore the perennial question, *can bureaucratic performance be improved?*

Bureaucrats and Bureaucracy

Most people think of government agencies when they hear the word *bureaucracy,* and they think of government employees when they hear the word *bureaucrat*—and their thoughts are often negative. They typically focus on a large government organization with inefficient, dehumanizing procedures that require tedious paperwork. They visualize long lines at the Department of Motor Vehicles as lazy and uncaring workers (who they believe cannot be fired) slowly process mounds of forms.

Taxpayers are not the only people who think and speak negatively of the bureaucracy. Even our presidents—who rely on bureaucrats and bureaucracies to implement their policy promises—historically have not hesitated to criticize bureaucrats. In describing his initiative to improve the performance of the national bureaucracy, President Bill Clinton (1993–2001) stressed that his goal was "to make the entire federal government both less expensive and more efficient, and to change the culture of our national bureaucracy away from complacency and entitlement toward initiative and empowerment."[2]

Are the negative images and the criticisms of bureaucrats and bureaucracies fair? Before we can answer, we must understand who the bureaucrats are, what they are hired to do, and how they are expected to accomplish their work.

Who Are the Bureaucrats?

Who was the last government employee with whom you had a face-to-face interaction? Who was the last government worker to make a decision that directly affected you? Chances are it was not an elected official such as the president or a member of the Senate. It was probably not an appointed federal judge. Rather, the government employees that you (and the people around you) interact with and are affected by on a daily basis are those individuals who

bureaucrats
people employed in a government executive branch unit to implement public policy; public administrators; public servants

are hired into executive branch agencies to implement public policy—that is, **bureaucrats.** Bureaucrats include government employees such as the administrator who reviews college students' Pell Grant applications, the Food and Drug Administration (FDA) inspector who monitors food and drug quality, and the Equal Employment Opportunity Commission (EEOC) lawyer who argues that an employer allowed sexual harassment of its workers. Bureaucrats provide the public services that elected officials authorize, and in doing so they make decisions that affect people daily.

Because of perpetual criticism of bureaucracies and bureaucrats on the part of elected officials and ordinary citizens, individuals working in the national bureaucracy do not take being called a bureaucrat as a compliment. Bureaucrats prefer the term *public servant,* because that phrase captures how they see themselves and their essential job goal.[3] Even as people love to bash bureaucrats, data from the International Social Survey Programme (ISSP) indicate that 63.9 percent of U.S. respondents agreed that "public service" in the United States is "somewhat committed" to serving the people, and another 11.6 percent agreed that public service is "very committed" to serving the people.[4] See "Global Comparisons" for a cross-national look at citizens' perceptions of the public service commitment of the bureaucracy in their country.

Charles Goodsell, a respected scholar of public administration and public policy, notes that studies show government employees to be very hard workers who are motivated by the recognition of the importance of public service. This public service motivation is distinct from the motivation of private-sector employees, for whom salary levels and shorter work hours provide key incentives.[5] Compared to private-sector employees, public servants have higher levels of formal education, must comply with more stringent codes of behavior, and express a greater concern for serving the public.[6] In addition, government bureaucrats tend to report somewhat higher levels of job satisfaction than do their private-sector counterparts.[7]

Very few children say that they want to be a bureaucrat. Yet millions do aspire to careers as public servants, including teachers, police officers, lawyers, and health care professionals. National, state, and local governments hire professionals such as these to implement public policy—to do the business of government. Chances are, whatever your major in college, you can get a job as a public servant. Almost 23 million national, state, and local bureaucrats, engaged in every job and career imaginable, implement national public policy.

Joining the millions of government bureaucrats are the so-called **shadow bureaucrats**—employees on the payroll of private for-profit businesses and private nonprofit organizations with government contracts. Through a process of **contracting-out** (also called *outsourcing* or *privatizing*), the government signs work contracts with these organizations to assist in the implementation of national policy. In other words, shadow bureaucrats do the work of government, but they do not receive a government paycheck.

In summary, today, a mix of national, state, and local bureaucrats, as well as shadow bureaucrats, deliver national public services. In addition to having in common the delivery of public services, public and shadow bureaucrats also share a similar work environment. That is, they work in bureaucratic organizations.

shadow bureaucrats
people hired and paid by private for-profit and nonprofit organizations that implement public policy through a government contract

contracting-out
also called *outsourcing* or *privatizing;* a process by which the government contracts with a private for-profit or nonprofit organization to provide public services or resources needed by the government

Bureaucracy: An Organizational Structure

Max Weber (1864–1920), the "father of sociology," coined the word *bureaucracy* to describe large organizations, such as government, with the following features: a division of labor, specialization of job tasks, hiring systems based on worker competency, hierarchy with a vertical chain of command, and standard operating procedures. Weber argued that these features enhance the performance and accountability of large organizations. In our discussion, **bureaucracy** is any organization with a hierarchical structure, although most commonly used to designate a government agency or the collection of all national executive branch organizations.

Organizations with these bureaucratic features are not unique to government. For example, colleges and universities are also bureaucratic organizations. They have a division of

bureaucracy
any organization with a hierarchical structure, although most commonly used to designate a government agency or the collection of all national executive branch organizations

GLOBAL COMPARISONS

PUBLIC SERVICE COMMITMENT TO SERVING THE PEOPLE

Criticism of bureaucrats in the private and public sectors is widespread. Yet research by political scientists David J. Houston and Lauren K. Harding reveals that the majority of citizens in European countries, Canada, and the United States think that the public service in their own country is at least somewhat committed to, if not very committed to, serving the people.*

COUNTRY	PERCENTAGE OF CITIZENS WHO THINK THE PUBLIC SERVICE IN THEIR COUNTRY IS SOMEWHAT OR VERY COMMITTED TO SERVING THE PEOPLE
Austria	80.3%
Ireland	77.1%
United States	**75.4%**
Switzerland	71.8%
Canada	69.9%
Great Britain	68.9%
Norway	67.9%
Belgium	66.5%
Germany-West	63.9%
Denmark	60.3%
Germany-East	59.5%
Netherlands	56.7%
France	56.1%
Finland	55.6%
Sweden	55.0%
Spain	50.3%
Portugal	39.3%

The research results reveal certain patterns. In most countries—the United States being an exception—there is a significant positive correlation between a person's being employed as a public servant himself or herself and thinking that public service is committed to serving the public. In addition, younger and older citizens are generally more likely than middle-aged citizens to perceive that their national bureaucracies have a distinct public service motivation. But most important to thinking that one's national bureaucracy is committed to public service is a person's overall attitudes about government. Individuals who believe that politicians are self-interested, that their government does not care what they think, and that they themselves have no say in what their government does are significantly less inclined to say that their national bureaucracies have a public service motivation. In contrast, citizens with a relatively greater sense of political efficacy report higher trust in public service, as measured by their belief that the bureaucracy is committed to public service. Moreover, those who think that democracy is working well in their nation are more likely to report that their public servants are committed to serving the public.

So, although bureaucrat-bashing is common, research indicates that at least in the majority of European nations, Canada, and the United States, the majority of people believe that public servants have a public service motivation—in other words, that bureaucrats are committed to serving the public.

* David J. Houston and Lauren K. Harding, "Trust in the Public Service: A Cross-National Examination," presented at the 66th Annual National Conference of the Midwest Political Science Association, Chicago, April 3–6, 2008, p. 24.

---

labor with specialization of tasks (consider the various academic departments, each specializing in a different discipline). They hire employees (such as professors, computer technicians, and student affairs staff) with the knowledge, skills, and abilities essential to doing their jobs well. Colleges and universities also have a hierarchy with a chain of command (faculty members report to chairpersons, who report to a dean, who reports to the vice president for academic affairs, who reports to the president, who makes final decisions). University employees implement standardized procedures to register students for classes, determine financial aid eligibility, and punish violations of the conduct code.

So, although most people think of government when they hear the word *bureaucracy,* a bureaucracy is *any* organization with Weber's bureaucratic structure. Yet in this chapter, as is appropriate to our study of American government, we focus on the departments and agencies that compose the national government bureaucracy. And even though most people think of government employees when they hear the term *bureaucrat,* nongovernment employees, as we have seen, may also be paid with taxpayer money to serve the public, and so it is appropriate that we consider them, too.

Federal Bureaucrats

Political scientists distinguish among national bureaucrats according to several factors, including the process by which they are hired, the procedures by which they can be fired, and the grounds for which they can be fired. On the basis of these factors, we can differentiate among three categories of national civilian bureaucrats: political appointees, civil servants, and senior executive service employees.

Political Appointees

In 1863, President Abraham Lincoln, suffering from smallpox, told his secretary to "send all the office seekers in here. I finally have something I can give to them all." Indeed, before the creation of the civil service system in 1883, presidents had the authority to hire bureaucrats, selecting whomever they wanted and establishing whatever qualifications they desired, in a noncompetitive hiring system known as *patronage*. Under the patronage system, hordes of men seeking government jobs presented themselves to the president after each election.

Government has come a long way since 1863. Today federal agencies hire the majority of bureaucrats based on **merit**—a system of hiring and promotion based on an individual's competence—rather than patronage. Out of the 2.7 million bureaucrats in the national government today, only about 7,000 political appointees are hired through patronage.[8]

After the election of a new president, Congress publishes the **plum book,** which lists the top jobs in the bureaucracy to which the president will appoint people through the patronage system. As we've seen, there is no standard process for assessing the knowledge, skills, and abilities needed for appointive positions, nor is there open competition for these patronage jobs. Further, because citizens expect presidents to be responsive and accountable to them, and presidents rely on their political appointees to support their efforts to meet these expectations, presidents tend to appoint people who support their policy preferences to these top positions.

Patronage positions come with a downside for the appointees: no job security. The president not only hires but can also fire political appointees at his pleasure. More common than firing is the resignation or retirement of appointees who no longer enjoy presidential approval.

Civil Servants

During the first century of U.S. history, all national bureaucrats got their jobs through patronage. Then in 1883, mobilized by the assassination of President James Garfield (whose brief administration lasted from March to September 1881) by an unsuccessful seeker of a patronage position, Congress and President Chester Arthur (1881–1885) approved the Pendleton Civil Service Act. This law introduced a merit-based civil service system to the national government. The hiring principles of the **merit-based civil service** system are open competition, competence, and political neutrality. **Civil servants** are bureaucrats hired through the merit-based personnel system. The 1978 Civil Service Reform Act reinforced these merit principles and legislated the right to unionize for many federal civil servants.

OPEN COMPETITION AND COMPETENCE Today merit-based civil service jobs, which compose at least 85 percent of the national bureaucracy, are open and accessible to all who wish to compete for a position. (See "Doing Democracy" on page 469 to learn more about becoming a public servant.) The competition requires that candidates prove their competence to do the job (their merit). Jobs covered by the merit-based civil service system are analyzed and ranked on the basis of the knowledge, skills, and abilities needed to do the job competently. A job's rank determines its salary. The pay scales offer equal pay for jobs

---

merit
a system of hiring and promotion based on an individual's competence

plum book
a publication that lists the top jobs in the bureaucracy to which the president will appoint people via the patronage system

> Secretary of State Condoleezza Rice is sworn into office by Associate Supreme Court Justice Ruth Bader Ginsburg on January 28, 2005. Secretary Rice was only the second woman, and the first African American woman, to serve as secretary of state. Justice Ginsburg was only the second woman ever appointed to the U.S. Supreme Court.

merit-based civil service
a personnel system in which bureaucrats are hired on the basis of the principles of competence, equal opportunity (open competition), and political neutrality; once hired, these civil servants have job protection

civil servants
bureaucrats hired through a merit-based personnel system who have job protection

of equal worth, as determined by the job analysis. (See Table 13.1 for the pay scales and education requirements for white-collar government jobs for which education alone can be qualifying.) Today the national civil service comprises more than 900 occupational titles.

Several national laws have helped to make today's civil servants, as a group, look more like the U.S. population at large than they did in the past. Title VII of the 1964 Civil Rights Act, as amended, prohibits employers, including the government, from making personnel decisions based on factors irrelevant to job competence, such as sex, race, color, ethnicity, age, and disabilities, that can be reasonably accommodated. The merit principles of the 1978 Civil Service Reform Act (CSRA) reiterate this prohibition against discrimination in personnel practices. The bans against discrimination in Title VII and the CSRA do not apply to the positions of elected officials or political appointees.

Title VI of the 1964 Civil Rights Act prohibits discrimination based on race, color, religion, and ethnicity in educational opportunities offered by institutions receiving federal funding. Title IX, which was added to the act in 1972, extended this prohibition to sex-based discrimination. Enforcement of these laws has increased the diversity of people who are able to gain the education and experience needed to do government jobs competently. The interaction of Titles VI, VII, and IX has fostered greater *descriptive representation* among civil servants than among any other category of government worker. This means that the people serving resemble the larger population whom they serve in terms of demographic characteristics such as race, age, ethnicity, sex, religion, and economic status. "Exploring the Sources" on page 470 considers the influence these laws have had on the national civil service.

POLITICAL INQUIRY

>This engraving depicts President James Garfield's assassination. Shot in July 1881, Garfield died two and a half months later of a fatal heart attack brought on by his doctors' attempts to find the assassin's bullet in his body.

Who assassinated President Garfield? What was the killer's motivation? How did the tragedy change the process of choosing civil servants?

Education Requirements and Salary Ranges for White-Collar Federal Civil Service Positions (2008)

Level	Salary Range	Qualifying Education
GS-1	$17,046–21,324	No high school diploma required
GS-2	$19,165–24,115	High school graduation or equivalent
GS-3	$20,911–27,184	One academic year above high school
GS-4	$23,475–30,522	Two academic years above high school, or associate's degree
GS-5	$26,264–34,139	Four academic years above high school leading to a bachelor's degree, or a bachelor's degree
GS-7	$32,534–42,290	Bachelor's degree with superior academic achievement or one academic year of graduate education or law school
GS-9	$39,795–51,738	Master's (or equivalent graduate degree) or two academic years of progressively higher level graduate education
GS-11	$48,148–62,593	PhD or equivalent degree or three academic years of progressively higher level graduate education
GS-12	$57,709–75,025	Completion of all requirements for a doctoral or equivalent degree (for research positions only)

TABLE 13.1

Source: www.govcentral.com/benefits.

The Federal Civilian Nonpostal Bureaucracy

THEN (1789)	NOW (2008)*
Public servants got jobs through a patronage system.	Civil servants get jobs through a merit-based system or by contract (the latter in the case of nonprofit and private for-profit employees).
Public servants were all white males.	The civil service workforce is 17.2% black, 7.4% Hispanic, 5.0% Asian, and 2.1% Native American, and 56% of civil servants are male.
Public service jobs were strictly clerical.	Civil service jobs are 34.5% administrative, 24.0% professional, 30.2% technical and clerical, and 11.0% blue collar.
Public servants worked exclusively in New York City.	About 15% of civil servants work in the Washington, D.C.–Maryland–Virginia–West Virginia metropolitan area; 82% work elsewhere in the United States; and about 3% work outside the country.

WHAT'S NEXT?

> Will the number of shadow bureaucrats continue to rise? Why or why not?

> Will the percentage of federal employees working outside the United States continue to grow as a result of globalization?

> How will minimum job qualifications for public service change with continuing technological advances and globalization?

* www.opm.gov/feddata/html/prof0906.asp.

POLITICAL NEUTRALITY Merit-based civil servants cannot be fired merely because someone with different political beliefs is elected or appointed to supervise them. They can be fired due to poor quality of work (misfeasance), or nonperformance of their work (nonfeasance), or for violating the rules or regulations that guide their work (malfeasance). The system thus gives civil servants job protection and does not require them (unlike political appointees) to adhere to the president's policy preferences. Hence the civil service system supports political neutrality to ensure efficient and effective public service delivery.

In 1939 Congress approved the Hatch Act, limiting civil servants' rights to engage in political activity. The rationale behind this law's passage was that if civil servants stayed out of politics, they would be less inclined to allow party loyalty to influence their job performance. Over time, however, civil servants have contested the constitutionality of the legal limits on their political engagement. As a result, the Hatch Act has been modified in the last few decades to loosen the restrictions on civil servants' political activities. This easing of limits on political engagement has allowed civil servants to exercise their First Amendment rights of expression, including political expression more freely and fully.

CIVIL SERVICE REFORM ACT (1978)

"There is widespread criticism of federal government performance. The public suspects that there are too many government workers, that they are underworked, overpaid, and insulated from the consequences of incompetence."[9] With these words, President Jimmy Carter (1977–1981) announced proposed civil service reforms in 1978. The resulting Civil Service Reform Act of 1978 (CSRA) reaffirmed and expanded the merit principles established by the Pendleton Act and reorganized the management of the national civil service. Carter's reforms also eliminated the Civil Service Commission (CSC), the central personnel office created by the Pendleton Act.

Three new independent administrative agencies—the Office of Personnel Management (OPM), the Merit System Protection Board (MSPB), and the Federal Labor Relations Authority (FLRA)—replaced the old Civil Service Commission. Today the OPM is the central personnel office, responsible for developing and implementing merit-based civil service personnel policies and procedures. The MSPB ensures proper implementation of the merit system. The CSRA also legislated for the collective bargaining rights (unionization rights) of national civil servants and created the FLRA to monitor the relations between unionized bureaucrats and the federal government.

UNIONIZED CIVIL SERVANTS Three out of every five U.S. federal civil servants belong to labor unions.[10] The American Federation of Government Employees (AFGE) is the largest such union, representing 600,000 national bureaucrats. The level of union membership varies dramatically from agency to agency. Whereas about 90 percent of U.S. Postal Ser-

DOING DEMOCRACY

BECOME A PUBLIC SERVANT

FACT:

Like the U.S. population as a whole, the bureaucracy is "graying" as the average age of civil servants is increasing. Close to 40 percent of the bureaucratic workforce is now eligible for retirement.* This development means growth in job opportunities, especially for college graduates.

The national government actively recruits interns and employees via the Internet. Recruitment programs target college students, minority citizens, and persons with disabilities in efforts to diversify the federal workforce. For Sonia Paola Ayerdi, a first-generation Latina with a disability, an internship with the National Resources Conservation Service turned into a full-time job through SCEP (Student Career Experience Program).**

Act!

With Internet access, you can research and apply for federal internship openings (as Sonia Ayerdi did) and employment opportunities. You can also complete online interest questionnaires to determine which national government positions suit you best. National Web sites even offer assistance with developing résumés. You can post your résumé online with the government for agency recruiters to view. After you identify the opportunities you are interested in (and qualify for), follow the application instructions that accompany the announcements.

Where to begin

- The Office of Personnel Management (OPM) serves as a one-stop official job site of the national government. Here you can find job announcements, assistance with developing a résumé, and answers to frequently asked questions regarding government employment: **www.usajobs.opm.gov/.**
- The Office of Personnel Management's Web site includes the "Career Interest Questionnaire and Interest Guide," which helps respondents determine which jobs best fit their knowledge, skills, abilities, and interests, **www.usajobs.opm .gov/careers/index.asp?ic=1.**
- The OPM has a site that provides information on educational opportunities in the federal government, including apprenticeships, fellowships, and internships, **www.studentjobs .gov/e-scholar.asp.**

* www.opm.gov/feddata/html/prof0906.asp.
** Personal interview.

---

vice employees are union members (not AFGE members but members of one of several unions for postal employees), the level of union membership among bureaucrats in the State Department is close to zero. Part of the explanation for the range of unionization levels across national agencies is the percentage of each agency's workers that is composed of blue-collar workers. In general, blue-collar workers are likelier to be union members than are white-collar workers.

Unionized civil servants have leverage to negotiate certain conditions of work. For example, they may bargain for improved training opportunities and enhanced due process protections in disciplinary matters. National civil service employee unions cannot negotiate salaries or work hours, however. And unlike private-sector unions, national civil servant unions do not have the legal right to strike. The prohibition of strikes by national civil servants is typically justified by the

> Members of the American Federation of Government Employees (AFGE), the largest federal employee union, rally outside the U.S. Army Tank Automotive Command in May 2003 to oppose President Bush's attempts to remove collective bargaining and other union protections from 800,000 civilian workers in the name of national security. The president succeeded in restricting collective bargaining rights and civil service protections for civil servants employed by the Department of Homeland Security.

EQUAL EDUCATIONAL AND EMPLOYMENT OPPORTUNITY AND STRATIFIED OCCUPATIONAL SEGREGATION

Laws prohibit race-based and sex-based discrimination in educational and employment opportunities. In addition, affirmative action requires most governments (as employers) and private businesses with government contracts to adopt and implement personnel plans detailing how they will actively recruit qualified women and minorities for open positions.

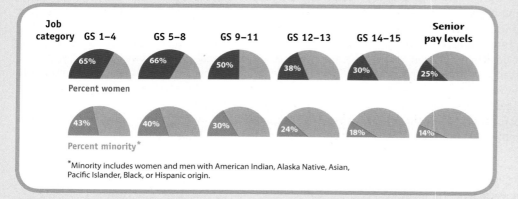

Job category: GS 1–4 (Percent women 65%, Percent minority* 43%), GS 5–8 (66%, 40%), GS 9–11 (50%, 30%), GS 12–13 (38%, 24%), GS 14–15 (30%, 18%), Senior pay levels (25%, 14%)

*Minority includes women and men with American Indian, Alaska Native, Asian, Pacific Islander, Black, or Hispanic origin.

COLLEGE DEGREES CONFERRED BY SEX AND RACE/ETHNICITY			
DEMOGRAPHIC	BACHELOR'S	MASTER'S	DOCTOR'S*
Men	42.5%	41.2%	52.9%
Women	57.5%	58.2%	47.1%
White	70.0%	60.3%	56.2%
Black	8.7%	7.8%	5.1%
Hispanic	6.3%	4.4%	3.2%
Asian/Pacific Islander	6.2%	4.8%	4.9%
Native American	0.7%	0.5%	0.4%

* Doctor's degrees are the highest degree a student can earn for graduate study and include EdD, JD, PhD.
Source: U.S. Department of Education, National Center for Education Statistics, http://nces.ed.gov/fastfacts/display.asp?id=72.

Evaluating the Evidence

① Review the accompanying chart and table. Do equal educational and equal employment laws work? Explain.

② Are there additional data you would want to review before answering question 1? If so, what kind of information would this supplementary data provide? Why?

③ Sex-based and race-based occupational segregation occurs when women and minority men dominate low-paying, low-status jobs and white men dominate high-paying, high-status jobs. Based on the data presented here, does occupational segregation exist in the national civil service? Explain.

---

senior executive service (SES)
a unique personnel system for top managerial, supervisory, and policy positions offering less job security but higher pay than the merit-based civil service system

fact that these workers provide essential services that are vital to public safety. A strike by these workers would therefore threaten public safety and health.

THE SENIOR EXECUTIVE SERVICE One additional CSRA-mandated change to the national bureaucracy was the creation of a new category of civil servant, the **senior executive service (SES)** bureaucrat. SES positions are hybrids of political appointee and civil service positions. The SES includes most of the top managerial, supervisory, and policy positions that are not patronage positions.

At least 90 percent of SES bureaucrats are career civil servants (hired through an open competition based on competence) who have given up some job security for positions with higher pay. These employees can be moved from job to job and from agency to agency (less job security), but they are immune from firing except for proven misfeasance, nonfeasance, or malfeasance. The remaining SES bureaucrats are typically hired from outside the merit-based civil service system. Appointed with approval of the OPM and the White House Office of Presidential Personnel, these SES noncareer bureaucrats do not face open competition and do not have the job protection of merit-based civil servants.[11]

Supplementing the work of national political appointees, civil servants, and SES bureaucrats are armies of state, local, and shadow bureaucrats. The volume of national public policy executed by these non-national bureaucrats has been increasing dramatically since the 1960s due to devolution and a rise in contracting-out.

State, Local, and Shadow Bureaucrats

Today, the overwhelming majority of the almost 20 million state and local bureaucrats, and possibly as many as 15 million shadow bureaucrats, provide various national public services. Through devolution and contracting-out, the national government relies on these non-national bureaucrats to serve the people's daily needs. National bureaucrats monitor these state, local, and shadow bureaucrats' compliance with the rules and regulations that come with devolution and outsourcing.

As you may recall from Chapter 3, devolution is the federal government's shifting of greater responsibility for financing and administering public policies to state and local governments, putting the implementation of national policy in the hands of state and local bureaucrats. Mandates in federal laws require state and local governments to implement national policies. In cases where national law preempts (takes precedence over) state and local law, state and local bureaucrats have to implement federal policy instead of state or local programs. Preemption is common, for example, in the area of environmental protection, where state and local officials must ensure private- and public-sector compliance with federal air, water, and landfill standards.

As we've seen, the national government also contracts with shadow bureaucracies—private for-profit and nonprofit organizations—to provide vital services as well as to produce certain resources needed to serve the public. Outsourcing, for example, includes the federal government's contracting-out with Lockheed Martin and Boeing for the production of defense resources such as helmets, fighter planes, and laser-guided missiles. Traditionally, too, the government undertakes large capital projects such as the construction of roads and government buildings through contracts with private businesses. Further, the federal government outsources medical as well as social research to cure disease and address the ills of society. And through government contracts, the Red Cross has dispensed disaster relief for decades.

The national government expects that contracting-out will reduce the expense of government by eliminating the overhead costs (including employee benefits and basic operating costs) of producing public goods and services. Outsourcing also provides a means by which the government can hire experts and specialists when they are needed and keep them off the payroll at other times. The government can eliminate these contracted personnel and their costs more easily than it can fire civil servants, who have job protection. The expectation is that the private- and nonprofit-sector employees and organizations will be more efficient and effective than government bureaucracies.

Some government contracts and grants-in-aid flow to faith-based organizations (FBOs). This development has sparked concerns about the preservation of the constitutionally mandated separation of church and government (see "The Conversation of Democracy").

Even with the increased use of state, local, and shadow bureaucrats, the national bureaucracy itself is neither small nor streamlined. It is composed of thousands of bodies with a variety of names and organizational structures. The national bureaucracy, an evolving organism, continues to grow in complexity even as it privatizes and devolves more of its work.

SHOULD FAITH-BASED ORGANIZATIONS RECEIVE PUBLIC FUNDING TO DELIVER SOCIAL SERVICES?

The Issue: In 2006, $2.2 billion of federal grants-in-aid went to 3,000 nonprofit faith-based organizations (FBOs) to provide social services.* For example, the Young Men's Christian Association (YMCA) and the Salvation Army both received taxpayer money to provide services ranging from housing, to counseling, to after-school programs. The First Amendment of the Constitution, however, establishes religious freedom, and the courts have interpreted this civil liberty as requiring the separation of religious organizations and government. But since the advent of a provision called Charitable Choice, part of the Welfare Reform Act of 1996, state and local governments have been encouraged to use national grants to contract with faith-based organizations to provide social welfare services. Beginning in 2001, President George W. Bush issued several executive orders giving federal government assistance to faith-based organizations interested in applying for national grants to dispense social services. Should faith-based organizations be receiving public funds?

Yes: Faith-based hospitals, nursing homes, and children's institutions, as well as the YMCA and the Salvation Army, have received government funds for decades. These FBOs provide vital services to those in need and in some cases do a superior job at distributing these services. People in need of assistance for housing, food, and clothing—and individuals seeking treatment for an addiction—feel more comfortable turning to a familiar local religious organization than to a complex government bureaucracy. In addition, because volunteers compose a large percentage of the FBO labor force, providing social services through FBOs is cheaper than paying government workers. Moreover, FBOs can provide social services and resources in a nonreligious way.

No: First, it is unconstitutional for the government to support a religion. Providing funding to any FBO flagrantly does exactly this. Further, we cannot ensure that the FBO employee who has a strong faith will not include religious education or preaching in delivering services. Nor can we prevent such an individual from using a religious test to determine whom he or she will serve. Government bureaucrats who monitor the grant rules will have difficulty ensuring that public money is not supporting religious activities. We should eliminate the problem by not funding FBOs.

Other approaches: President George W. Bush's executive orders eliminated the requirements that FBOs keep separate accounts for the public funds they receive. Such separate accounts ensured that FBOs did not spend public funds on religious activities. Even though they no longer need to maintain separate accounts, FBOs are still restricted from spending public funds on religious activities. But how can we know whether FBOs are abiding by the restriction on spending public dollars on religious programs? If the mandate for separate accounts is put back in place, we can hold FBOs accountable for spending public money only on nonreligious endeavors. Therefore, if the government reverts to requiring separate accounts, providing public funds to FBOs is OK.

What do you think?

① Reflecting back on the discussion in Chapter 4 of the First Amendment's religious freedom guarantee, do you think the public funding of social services delivered by faith-based organizations violates the Constitution? Explain.

② Just as opponents of public funding of FBOs claim that FBO employees may push their religious beliefs on clients or use a religious test to deny services to some clients, do you think that some government employees may also behave this way? How might the government prevent such behavior among its bureaucrats as well as publicly funded FBO employees?

* www.whitehouse.gov/government/fbci/fs_strength-nonprofit.html.

The Evolution and Organization of the Federal Bureaucracy

Four million people resided in the United States in 1789, the year George Washington was sworn in as the first president. Most of them lived off the land and were self-sufficient; they expected few services from the national government. The federal bureaucracy consisted of the Department of War, Department of Foreign Affairs, Treasury Department, Attorney General's Office, and Postal Services Office. These three departments and two offices handled the core functions demanded of the national government at that time: respectively, providing defense; managing foreign affairs; collecting revenues and paying bills; resolving lawsuits and legal questions; and delivering mail. Initially, other than for military personnel, the work of public servants was mostly clerical in nature.

Today, as the U.S. population tops 300 million, more than 2,000 executive branch units, employing 4 million bureaucrats (2.7 million civilian bureaucrats and about 1.3 million military personnel), implement volumes of national policies. The number of bureaucrats is equal to the nation's population in 1789. Figure 13.1, the organizational chart of the federal government, provides a window on the breadth of the federal bureaucracy today. Figures 13.2 and 13.3 show the growth in size and cost of the national bureaucracy since the 1960s.

Political scientists distinguish among five categories of executive branch organizations based on their structure and the type of work they perform: (1) departments, (2) independent administrative agencies, (3) independent regulatory commissions, (4) government corporations, and (5) agencies in the Executive Office of the President.

FIGURE 13.1

U.S. Government Organizational Chart

U.S. Government Manual (Washington, DC: U.S. Government Printing Office, 2007), p. 21.

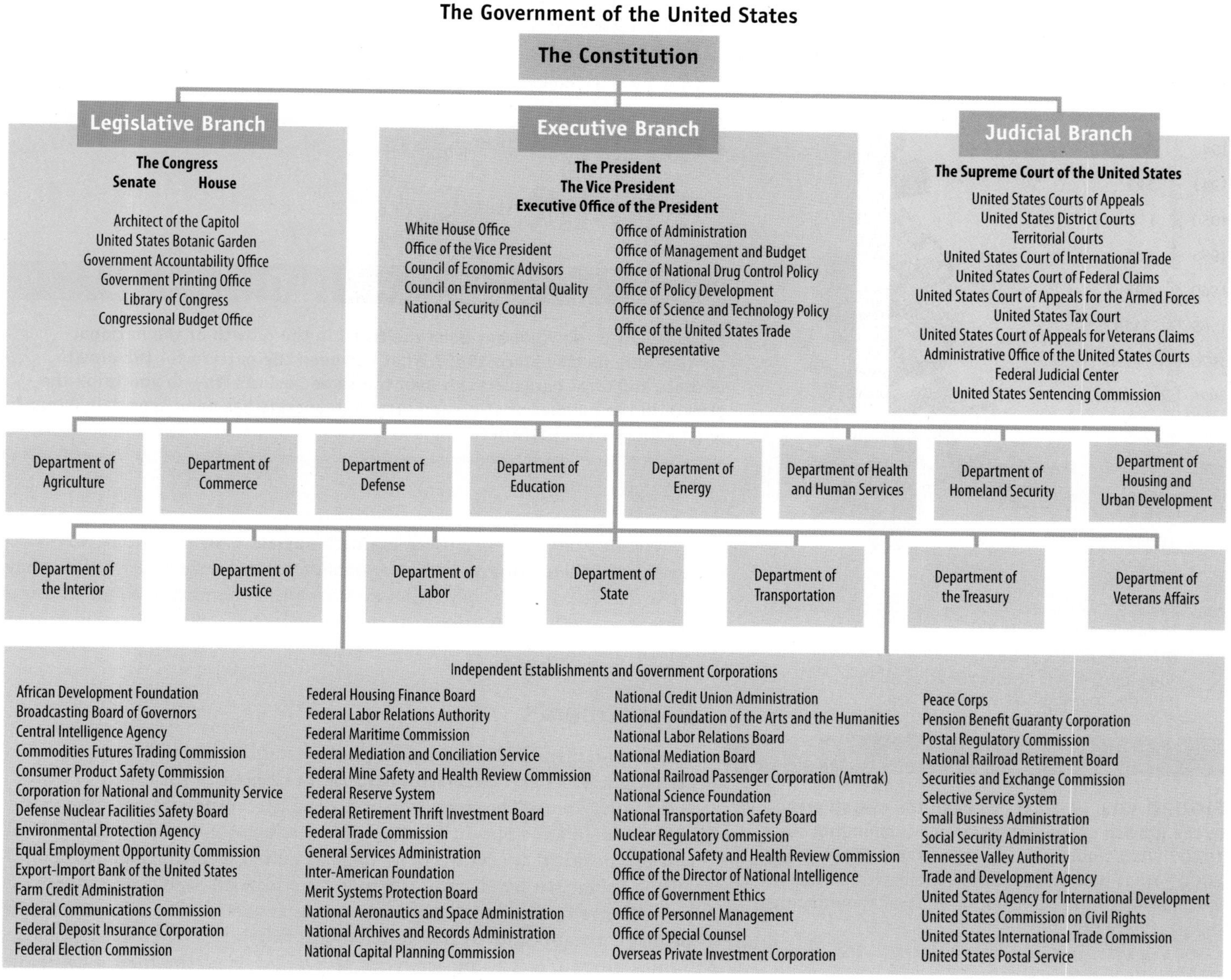

The Government of the United States

The Constitution

Legislative Branch

The Congress
Senate   House

Architect of the Capitol
United States Botanic Garden
Government Accountability Office
Government Printing Office
Library of Congress
Congressional Budget Office

Executive Branch

The President
The Vice President
Executive Office of the President

White House Office
Office of the Vice President
Council of Economic Advisors
Council on Environmental Quality
National Security Council

Office of Administration
Office of Management and Budget
Office of National Drug Control Policy
Office of Policy Development
Office of Science and Technology Policy
Office of the United States Trade Representative

Judicial Branch

The Supreme Court of the United States

United States Courts of Appeals
United States District Courts
Territorial Courts
United States Court of International Trade
United States Court of Federal Claims
United States Court of Appeals for the Armed Forces
United States Tax Court
United States Court of Appeals for Veterans Claims
Administrative Office of the United States Courts
Federal Judicial Center
United States Sentencing Commission

Department of Agriculture
Department of Commerce
Department of Defense
Department of Education
Department of Energy
Department of Health and Human Services
Department of Homeland Security
Department of Housing and Urban Development

Department of the Interior
Department of Justice
Department of Labor
Department of State
Department of Transportation
Department of the Treasury
Department of Veterans Affairs

Independent Establishments and Government Corporations

African Development Foundation
Broadcasting Board of Governors
Central Intelligence Agency
Commodities Futures Trading Commission
Consumer Product Safety Commission
Corporation for National and Community Service
Defense Nuclear Facilities Safety Board
Environmental Protection Agency
Equal Employment Opportunity Commission
Export-Import Bank of the United States
Farm Credit Administration
Federal Communications Commission
Federal Deposit Insurance Corporation
Federal Election Commission

Federal Housing Finance Board
Federal Labor Relations Authority
Federal Maritime Commission
Federal Mediation and Conciliation Service
Federal Mine Safety and Health Review Commission
Federal Reserve System
Federal Retirement Thrift Investment Board
Federal Trade Commission
General Services Administration
Inter-American Foundation
Merit Systems Protection Board
National Aeronautics and Space Administration
National Archives and Records Administration
National Capital Planning Commission

National Credit Union Administration
National Foundation of the Arts and the Humanities
National Labor Relations Board
National Mediation Board
National Railroad Passenger Corporation (Amtrak)
National Science Foundation
National Transportation Safety Board
Nuclear Regulatory Commission
Occupational Safety and Health Review Commission
Office of the Director of National Intelligence
Office of Government Ethics
Office of Personnel Management
Office of Special Counsel
Overseas Private Investment Corporation

Peace Corps
Pension Benefit Guaranty Corporation
Postal Regulatory Commission
National Railroad Retirement Board
Securities and Exchange Commission
Selective Service System
Small Business Administration
Social Security Administration
Tennessee Valley Authority
Trade and Development Agency
United States Agency for International Development
United States Commission on Civil Rights
United States International Trade Commission
United States Postal Service

Growth in National Civilian Bureaucrats and State and Local Bureaucrats

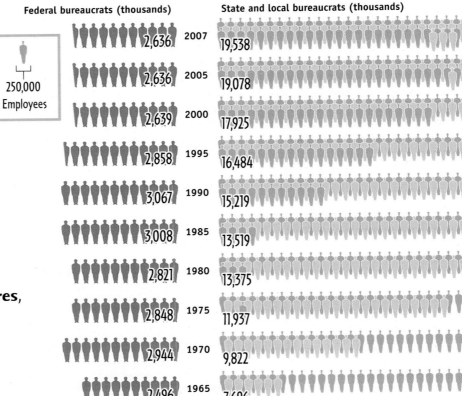

Federal bureaucrats (thousands)		State and local bureaucrats (thousands)
2,636	2007	19,538
2,636	2005	19,078
2,639	2000	17,925
2,858	1995	16,484
3,067	1990	15,219
3,008	1985	13,519
2,821	1980	13,375
2,848	1975	11,937
2,944	1970	9,822
2,496	1965	7,696

250,000 Employees

POLITICAL INQUIRY

FIGURE 13.2 ■ What has been the trend in the growth of the national civilian bureaucracy since 1965? What has been the pattern for the growth of state and local bureaucracies over the same period? Why do you think the growth in the number of state and local bureaucrats has been especially steep? What explains the pattern?

Source: Table 17.5 in *Fiscal Year 2009 Historical Tables,* www.whitehouse.gov/omb/budget/fy2009/pdf/hist.pdf.

Growth in Federal Expenditures, 1940–2009

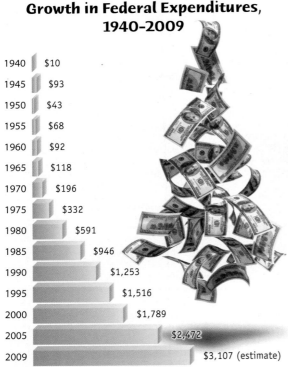

Year	Budget (billions)
1940	$10
1945	$93
1950	$43
1955	$68
1960	$92
1965	$118
1970	$196
1975	$332
1980	$591
1985	$946
1990	$1,253
1995	$1,516
2000	$1,789
2005	$2,472
2009	$3,107 (estimate)

Budget in billions of current dollars (rounded to nearest billion)

POLITICAL INQUIRY

FIGURE 13.3 ■ What has been the overall trend in the growth of federal government spending since 1940? What would you say about the pattern since 2000? What political factors—domestic and international—explain the trend in federal spending over the past decade?

Source: Table 3.1 in *Historical Tables Fiscal Year 2009*, www.whitehouse.gov/omb/budget/fy2009/pdf/hist.pdf.

Within each category there is much variation in size, structure, and function. When Congress and the president authorize a new policy, they must decide whether they will assign its implementation to an existing agency or create a new agency. If they choose the latter option, they must determine which type of agency to create.

Departments

The Department of Homeland Security, established in 2002, is the newest of fifteen federal **departments,** each responsible for one broadly defined policy area. The president holds the fifteen departments accountable through the appointment of a head official. *Secretary* is the title of this top political appointee in all departments except the Department of Justice, where the head is the attorney general. Although the Senate must confirm them, these top appointees serve at the president's pleasure. In addition to appointing the department secretaries, the president also names bureaucrats to positions in several levels of the hierarchy below the secretaries. These political appointees have titles such as *deputy secretary, assistant deputy secretary, agency director,* and *deputy director.* Table 13.2 lists the fifteen departments and gives the number of employees and budget outlay for each in 2007.

Independent Administrative Agencies

Whereas each executive branch department has authority for a broadly defined policy area, a host of **independent administrative agencies** are each responsible for a more narrowly defined function of the national government. Congress and the president create these agencies to fulfill one of several purposes. Some of them, such as the Smithsonian Institution, were established to handle new governmental functions that did not easily fall within the purview of existing departments. Other independent administrative agencies support the work of existing departments and agencies, including recruiting and training employees

department
one of fifteen executive branch units responsible for a broadly defined policy area and whose top administrator (secretary) is appointed by the president, is confirmed by the Senate, and serves at the discretion of the president

independent administrative agency
an executive branch unit created by Congress and the president that is responsible for a narrowly defined function and whose governing board is intended to be protected from partisan politics

TABLE 13.2

Evolution of Federal Government Departments

Department and Year Created	Civilian Employees (September 2007)	Budget Outlay in Billions of Dollars (2007)
State, 1789	35,105	$13.8
Treasury, 1789	103,596	$490.6
Interior, 1849	71,657	$10.5
Justice, 1870 (attorney general's office 1789; department status 1870)	107,292	$23.4
Agriculture, 1889	103,293	$84.4
Commerce, 1913 (separated from Department of Commerce and Labor, which had been created in 1903)	40,920	$6.5
Labor, 1913 (separated from Department of Commerce and Labor, which had been created in 1903)	12,328	$47.5
Defense, 1947 (previously, Department of War, created 1789; Army Department and Navy Department, created 1798)	673,319	$529.9
Housing and Urban Development, 1965	9,665	$45.6
Transportation, 1966	54,221	$61.7
Energy, 1977	14,754	$20.1
Health and Human Services, 1979 (created from Department of Health, Education and Welfare, established in 1953)	62,502	$672.0
Education, 1979 (created from Department of Health, Education and Welfare, established in 1953)	4,201	$66.4
Veterans Affairs, 1988	254,183	$72.8
Homeland Security, 2003	159,447	$39.2

Sources: Civil employee statistics from U.S. Office of Personnel Management (www.opm.gov/feddata/html/2007/september/table14.asp); budget information from *Historical Tables: Budget of U.S. Government FY 2009* (http://whitehouse.gov/omb/budget/fy2009/pdf/hist.pdf).

Homeland Security

Do you think the United States is safer with the creation of the Department of Homeland Security?

☐ Yes, we're safer

☐ No, we're not safer

☐ Made no difference

Source: "Homeland Security: Do Americans Feel Safer?" www.gallup.com/poll/7321/Homeland-Security-Americans-Feel-Safer.aspx.

independent regulatory commission

an executive branch unit responsible for developing standards of behavior within specific industries and businesses, monitoring compliance with these standards, and imposing sanctions on violators

economic regulation

government constraints on business practices to ensure competition in the marketplace and a healthy economy

government corporation

an executive branch unit that sells a service and is expected to be financially self-sufficient

(Office of Personnel Management) and managing government properties and records (General Services Administration). Still others, such as the National Science Foundation and the National Aeronautics and Space Administration, focus on research and preservation of national resources.

Congresses and presidents create independent administrative agencies when they want to protect the agencies' decision making or functions from partisan politics. Thus the structure of these agencies differs from the organization of the federal departments. A director, nominated by the president and usually needing Senate confirmation, heads each agency's board. The board is composed of members affiliated with both political parties, who are appointed by the president for a fixed term of a specified number of years. The expectation is that this structure will limit the president's influence over the independent agency, because it relieves the director of the need to be loyal to the president's preferences to keep the job. Hence these agencies are supposed to be "independent" of partisan politics. Yet ultimately such agencies still need to earn the support of those who authorize the spending of money and who have the authority to restructure the agency or its mission—Congress and the president.

Independent Regulatory Commissions

Over time, Congress and presidents have recognized the need for expertise in regulating the country's diverse economic activities and their impact on the overall economy, workers, consumers, and the environment. Acknowledging their own lack of such expertise, they have created numerous **independent regulatory commissions,** bureaucracies with the authority to develop standards of behavior for specific industries and businesses, to monitor compliance with these standards, and to impose sanctions on those it finds guilty of violating the standards.

Initially such government regulation centered on **economic regulation**—matters such as setting the prices of goods and services and ensuring competition in the marketplace. The first independent regulatory commission, the Interstate Commerce Commission (ICC, 1887), was set up to oversee the prices and services of the railroad industry. Beginning in the 1960s, Congress turned more in the direction of *social regulation,* establishing regulatory commissions that focused on how business practices affected the environment, and the health and safety of consumers and workers. For example, legislation created the Environmental Protection Agency (EPA) in 1970 and the Consumer Product Safety Commission (CPSC) in 1972.

Independent regulatory agencies are under the direction of bipartisan boards whose members do not need to be loyal to the president's preferences. Typically the president nominates and the Senate confirms an odd number of board members. Board members serve staggered fixed terms. This structure allows the agency to make decisions based on the expertise of its board members, not on the preferences of the president or Congress. Still, the agencies need both presidential and congressional support to survive.

Government Corporations

Like private businesses, **government corporations** sell a service or product; but unlike private businesses, they are government owned. Congress and the president create government corporations when they believe it is in the public interest for the national government to engage in a commercial activity, such as selling stamps to pay for the cost of delivering mail. (In fact, the best-known U.S. government corporation is the United States Postal Service.) Unlike the other categories of bureaucracies, government corporations are expected to make enough money to cover their costs.

A bipartisan board typically directs each government corporation. The president appoints the board members to serve for staggered fixed terms. Typically, the Senate is not required to confirm the board members. Like regulatory commissions and administrative agencies, government corporations are structured to be independent.

Executive Office of the President

By 1939, the national bureaucracy for which the president serves as chief executive officer had grown tremendously in size and diversity of structure and functions. Acknowledging that the president needed help to manage this constellation of departments, independent administrative agencies, independent regulatory commissions, and government corporations, President Franklin Roosevelt (1933–1945) and the Congress created the Executive Office of the President (EOP).

The EOP is composed of dozens of offices and councils that assist the president in managing the complex and sprawling executive branch of the bureaucracy. The EOP has evolved into the locomotive of the national government—the engine driving the development and implementation of presidential policies and programs. The president appoints the top-level bureaucrats in EOP agencies, and the majority of these appointments are not subject to Senate confirmation. The president has the authority to fire these appointees at his pleasure. Therefore the EOP serves the president; it is in fact the presidential bureaucracy. (See Chapter 12 for a detailed discussion of the EOP.)

Hybrids

Although political scientists commonly talk about five categories of bureaucracies, not all bureaucracies fit neatly into a given category. In addition to the five categories of bureaucracy we have considered, the executive branch also features hybrid agencies that have characteristics of more than one category. The Food and Drug Administration (FDA) is one such hybrid. The FDA regulates the food and pharmaceutical industries to ensure the safety of food and drugs on the market and hence is a regulatory agency. Yet it is not an independent regulatory commission, because it is housed within the Department of Health and Human Services.

In this section we took stock of the executive branch organizations in which national bureaucrats implement policy. We next consider the nature of the essential roles bureaucrats play in all stages of public policy.

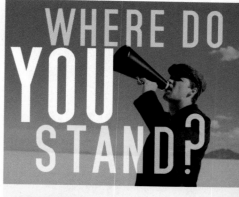

Federal Bureaucrats' Roles in Public Policy

Although the primary work of bureaucrats is implementation—putting public policy into action—bureaucrats play an active, vital role in all six stages of the public policy cycle. These stages are (1) agenda setting, (2) policy formulation, (3) policy approval, (4) resource allocation, (5) policy implementation, and (6) policy evaluation.

According to the **politics-administration dichotomy,** there is a clear line between *politics* (the formulation and approval of public policy, and the allocation of resources to put the policy into effect) and the *administration* of public policy (the real-world implementation of the policy). The dichotomy says that elected officials (whom citizens hold accountable through the ballot box) have authority for politics and that competent bureaucrats (hired through merit-based civil service) have authority for policy administration. Theoretically, this arrangement fosters not only responsive government but also efficient and effective public services.

The politics-administration dichotomy may sound good, but the reality of public policy processes does not allow for such a clean separation between those who "do politics" and those who administer policy. Although bureaucrats are hired to implement policy made by elected officials, elected officials tap the expertise of bureaucrats throughout the other five

politics-administration dichotomy
the concept that elected government officials, who are accountable to the voters, create and approve public policy, and then competent, politically neutral bureaucrats implement the public policy

stages of the policy process, allowing bureaucrats to influence and even make policies themselves, as we now shall see.

Agenda Setting

In the first stage of the public policy cycle, elected officials place issues on their agendas to discuss, if not to address by formulating a *policy*—a plan of government action to deal with a particular public concern. Citizens, interest groups, political parties, state and local elected officials, and bureaucrats from all levels of government, as well as shadow bureaucrats, all lobby to get their concerns on the agendas of national elected officials. Although many of the individuals and groups lobbying elected officials may have similar concerns, they typically do not agree on how the government should address these matters of common interest.

Bureaucrats play an instrumental role in setting the policy agenda. Because their focus is to implement public policy at the grassroots level, bureaucrats have a clear view of the societal problems that citizens are looking for the government to address and strong views on how best to address these problems. Political scientists use the term *iron triangle* to describe long-term collaborative efforts among bureaucrats in a government agency, the members of an interest group, and the members of a legislative committee to get their mutual concerns on the agenda and then to formulate the policies they deem necessary to address these concerns. *Issue networks,* which are temporary collaborations among bureaucrats, elected officials, and the members of several interest groups, also engage in lobbying to set the agenda, as well as to influence policy formulation. Bureaucrats, who want to get their concerns and proposed programs on the agenda, may work to create issue networks as well as iron triangles. For more about iron triangles and issue networks, see Chapter 7.

> Bureaucrats lobby government on behalf of the citizens they serve as well as on their own behalf. Members of the American Postal Workers Union, supported by other union members, protested Bush Administration plans in 2003 to privatize parts of the U.S. Postal Service, which would have meant a loss of jobs for postal workers.

Policy Formulation

The second stage of the policy process, policy formulation, involves defining a problem that has made it to the agenda and setting a plan of action (a policy) to address the problem. (Note, however, that not all concerns that reach an elected official's agenda—or even the agendas of numerous elected officials—go farther in the policy process.) Although anyone can formulate a public policy, only elected officials can officially introduce policy proposals into the lawmaking process. Thus individuals and groups outside government, as well as bureaucrats, must identify members of Congress to introduce policy proposals for legislative action. The president can also make policy by issuing an executive order, an authority that lies outside the legislative process (see Chapter 12).

Because bureaucrats often have specialized knowledge of societal problems, elected officials rely on bureaucrats when formulating policies. House and Senate committees frequently call on bureaucrats to review and comment on bills that, if approved, they will implement and to testify in the hearings in which congressional members investigate and study problems. Thus bureaucrats regularly take part in policy formulation, whether at their own impetus or at the request of elected officials.

In recognition of bureaucrats' expertise, Congress often includes vague or ambiguous language in bills and relies on bureaucrats to fill in the program details after a bill is passed, during the policy implementation stage. Vague legislative language may also reflect the congressional sponsors' need to win majority votes in both the House and the Senate and to secure presidential approval of the policy. Fuzzy language means that if the bill becomes law, bureaucrats will need to discern what the policy is directing them to do before they can implement it.

Policy Approval

When Congress and the president vote to approve or reject the formulated policy, which is in the form of a proposed piece of legislation—a bill—they have reached the third stage, policy approval. Bills detailing the government's plan to address a problem are called authorization bills; when Congress and the president, or Congress alone over a president's veto, approves such bills, the laws thus created authorize government action. **Authorization laws** not only provide the plan of action to address a given societal concern but also identify the executive branch unit that will put the plan into effect. The law may authorize an existing executive unit to carry out the policy, or it may establish a new unit to do the job. Presidential executive orders, another form of public policy, direct bureaucrats in how to implement policy. Yet bureaucracies cannot implement a public policy until they have legal authority to spend money.

authorization law
a law that provides the plan of action to address a given societal concern and identifies the executive branch unit that will put the plan into effect.

Resource Allocation

In the next phase of the policy process, resource allocation, Congress and the president specify how much money each bureaucracy will be authorized to spend during the budget year. Through the budget process (see Chapter 15), Congress and the president formulate appropriation bills, which are plans for the distribution of government revenue to government entities, including bureaucracies, legislative bodies, and judicial bodies. Approved appropriation bills—**appropriation laws**—give bureaucracies the legal authority to spend money.

Bureaucrats play three key roles in the budget process. First, at the request of the president, bureaucrats develop an annual budget request for their agencies. Second, before Congress approves the appropriation bills that distribute government revenues to the agencies, it calls upon bureaucrats to justify their budget requests. In turn, bureaucrats lobby members of Congress to allocate to their agencies the funds they requested. With limited money available, bureaucracies typically do not receive all the funding they request. Therefore, bureaucracies compete with one another for their piece of the limited budget pie. Once Congress and the president approve the appropriation bills, bureaucrats take on their third role in the budget process; they spend money to put the public policy into action.

appropriation law
a law that gives bureaucracies and other government entities the legal authority to spend money.

Policy Implementation

Bureaucrats are at the center of the second-to-last stage of the policy cycle, policy implementation. In this phase, bureaucrats must first interpret the law and then carry it out. Congress and the president delegate to bureaucrats the authority to determine the best way to implement the policy; this authority is called **administrative discretion.** Applying administrative discretion, bureaucrats make the day-to-day decisions related to executing policy programs and enforcing the necessary rules and standards. Elected officials risk the loss of control over the content of public policy when they delegate administrative discretion to bureaucrats. However, they have numerous tools to limit this risk, which we discuss later in this chapter's section on federal bureaucratic accountability.

Elected officials and ordinary citizens alike expect that bureaucrats will exercise administrative discretion. When pulled over by a police officer for speeding, for example, you hope the officer will use administrative discretion in your favor by giving you a warning instead of a ticket. In addition to being a break for you, a warning takes less time to issue than a ticket and thus puts the police officer back in action sooner. This outcome may better serve the public.

Bureaucrats, specifically those in independent agencies, use administrative discretion to establish programs, rules, regulations, and standards necessary for the effective and efficient implementation of policy. **Administrative law** is the name given to agencies' rule making and resolution of conflicts regarding their rules.

administrative discretion
the authority delegated to bureaucrats to use their expertise and judgment when determining how to implement public policy

administrative law
the name given to agencies' rule making and resolution of conflicts regarding their rules

administrative rule making
the process by which an independent commission or agency fills in the details of a vague law by formulating, proposing, and approving rules, regulations, and standards that will be enforced to implement the policy

administrative adjudication
the process by which agencies resolve disputes over the implementation of their administrative rules

The process by which bureaucrats translate vague law into concrete plans of action is a quasi-legislative ("as-if legislative") process. It is "quasi-legislative" because bureaucrats in the executive branch, not legislators, make policy as they fill in the details needed to implement legislation. **Administrative rule making** is the name of this process by which upper-level bureaucrats use their administrative discretion and their expertise in the policy area to create rules, regulations, and standards that the bureaucracy will then enforce. For example, recognizing its lack of expertise in the specifics of how to prevent air and water pollution, Congress delegated to the Environmental Protection Agency (EPA) the authority to establish policy. The EPA sets specific pollution emissions standards in order to implement the Clean Water and Clean Air acts. Although Congress does not approve these EPA administrative standards, importantly, the standards have the force of law.

Agencies involved in administrative rule making also have a quasi-judicial ("as-if judicial") role. Through **administrative adjudication**, they determine when their rules are violated, and they impose penalties on the violators. Citizens who disagree with an agency's application of its administrative rules or those whom an agency finds guilty of violating its rules may challenge the agency's decisions through a lawsuit. Indeed, several states successfully sued the EPA in 2007 for its failure to set carbon dioxide emissions standards and hence its inadequate implementation of the Clean Air Act. Claiming that "the EPA's failure to act in the face of [the Supreme Court's 2007 ruling and] these incontestable dangers is a shameful dereliction of duty," Massachusetts attorney general Martha Coakley, along with the attorneys general of seventeen other states, as well as two cities and eleven environmental interest groups, sued the EPA in April 2008.[12]

CITIZENS' ROLE IN IMPLEMENTING EFFECTIVE POLICY Bureaucrats' ability to provide public services efficiently and effectively depends on many factors that are out of their control. First, the effectiveness of a public policy rests on the soundness of the theory behind the policy. This means that those who formulated the policy had to understand the cause(s) of the problem addressed by the policy and know how to respond to the cause(s). In the case of crime, for example, policy makers need to know what causes crime and how public servants can eliminate the cause in order to solve the crime problem (if it can be solved at all).

Second, policy makers must be willing and able to provide the money needed to hire the appropriate number of qualified public servants and to purchase the technology and equipment required. For example, Congress must fund the Food and Drug Administration at the appropriate level so that it has enough inspectors and investigators to enforce the regulations it approves to implement food and drug safety legislation. Government money comes from taxpayers. Although taxpayers expect the government to serve them and to resolve societal problems, their willingness to pay taxes is limited. Therefore, the government does not always have all the money needed for hiring and for the procurement of essential resources. A lack of resources will limit the effectiveness of public policy.

But even if the government knows how to solve a given problem and has all the necessary resources, it will fail without the participation and compliance of the people it serves. The effectiveness of public policies depends on people's knowledge of and compliance with the law. It depends on their applying for the government programs for which they qualify and their conformity to the directions and prescriptions of bureaucrats.

A medical analogy illustrates the factors that are essential to a successful policy outcome: a doctor's effectiveness depends on the soundness of the science behind the medicine or treatment prescribed, the patient's ability to pay for the treatment, and the patient's willingness to follow the prescribed treatment. Similarly, bureaucrats' effectiveness rests on the soundness of the theory behind the policy or program, the availability of the financial resources to pay for its full implementation, and the compliance of the people targeted by the program.

NEIGHBORHOOD CRIME WATCH

We immediately report all SUSPICIOUS PERSONS and activities to our Police Dept.

Bureaucrats' effectiveness and hence, government's success, thus depends on many factors, and surely a crucial one is citizens' active involvement in implementing policy by knowing and complying with policy programs. People benefit when bureaucrats implement public policies, and bureaucrats benefit when people are aware of and comply with public policies. This symbiotic relationship is essential to the success of public service.

Policy Evaluation

The last stage of the policy process is policy evaluation—the assessment of the intended and unintended effects of policy implementation. People do not assess government success by the number of laws passed or by the promises made in the language of the laws. Rather, the effectiveness and efficiency of public service delivery are what matter to the public. The implementation of policy by bureaucrats is thus the key to citizens' satisfaction with government—and the key to government success.

Since the 1970s, U.S. taxpayers have called for increased transparency in government, including evaluations of public policy implementation to determine how effectively government is using their tax dollars. The corruption of the administration of President Richard Nixon—which featured Nixon's misuse of the Internal Revenue Service to collect information on opponents, as well as the infamous White House cover-up of the break-in at the Democratic Party headquarters in the Watergate Building—partially explains the call for greater transparency in government. A. Ernest Fitzgerald's revelations of mismanagement and corruption also fueled citizen outcries for increased transparency and evaluations. So did the publication in 1973 of political scientists Jeffrey L. Pressman and Aaron B. Wildavsky's study of a federally funded economic development program.[13] Their landmark research concluded that it is "amazing that federal programs work at all" given the hurdles that policy implementers encounter.

As a result, policy evaluation has become a larger component of the workload of legislators and bureaucrats in recent decades than it ever was before. Because elected officials and citizens want proof of the efficiency and effectiveness of implemented policies, agencies must document what they do and its impact. Because citizens do not elect bureaucrats, they do not have the opportunity to fire civil servants whose performance is unsatisfactory. Therefore, citizens defer the responsibility for bureaucratic accountability to members of Congress, the president, and the judges who preside over the courts because these elected and appointed government officials have legal means to monitor bureaucrats' work and to hold them accountable.

Federal Bureaucratic Accountability

When it comes to public service, everyone is watching. The courts, through the mechanism of lawsuits, review the actions of the executive and legislative branches to ensure that they are constitutional and legal. Congress and the president, as the creators and funders of bureaucracies, can threaten to revamp or eliminate any bureaucracy, or to decrease its funding, if its performance falls short of expectations. Congress and the president not only structure bureaucracies to foster efficient, effective, and accountable public service but also pass laws to increase self-policing by bureaucrats.

People outside government, including many ordinary citizens, also keep a close eye on bureaucracies. To make it easier for government outsiders to hold bureaucracies accountable, President George W. Bush strongly supported the use of the Internet to extend the clout of **sunshine laws**—legislation ensuring the public's "right to know" about government business and government decision making. But these laws are effective only if citizens know about and take advantage of them.

Accountability to the People

American government today offers a variety of tools and resources to ensure that bureaucracies serve the people efficiently, effectively, and legally. National sunshine laws mandate transparency and openness in government and provide an opportunity for citizens to give input before government agencies make policy decisions. Interest groups and the media also use sunshine laws to watch government officials and bureaucracies.

SUNSHINE LAWS One of the first national sunshine laws for the enhancement of bureaucratic accountability to the people was the Administrative Procedure Act (APA) of 1946. The APA responded to citizens' and interest groups' concerns about the fast growth in the number of agencies involved in administrative rule making and about the lack of transparency and accountability of the bureaucratic rule makers. The APA, which applies to all federal agencies except those specifically excluded by legislation, standardized rule-making procedures and requires bureaucracies to publicize their proposed rules in the *Federal Register,* a daily national government publication. They also must publish an invitation for people to offer comments on the agency's proposals.

Once the agency collects and reviews the people's comments, it must publish its approved rules in the *Federal Register.* To facilitate this open process, the national government Web site www.regulations.gov posts proposed administrative rules and accepts electronically submitted comments on the rules. In this way people can have a voice in administrative rule making. Such citizen input is essential to democracy, because bureaucrats propose and approve more administrative rules each year than the pieces of legislation proposed and approved by Congress and the president.

The Freedom of Information Act (FOIA) is a 1966 amendment to the APA. The FOIA requires national agencies to give citizens access to government documents upon request and at a reasonable cost. Since 9/11, however, the national government has denied an increasing percentage of such requests in the name of national security. President George W. Bush, through executive order, expanded the types of information that the government can label as "classified," meaning that nongovernment officials are denied access to it. Christopher Oakley Hofius (see "On the Job") notes the importance of balancing government transparency with national security.

The decreased access to government documents has heightened tensions between people advocating government confidentiality on the one hand, and individuals cherishing democratic openness and those dedicated to holding the national bureaucracy accountable on the other hand. The American Society of Newspaper Editors is so concerned about the diminished access that it established Sunshine Week (first held March 13–20, 2005) to educate citizens about their right to know and to request information about what the bureaucracy is doing.

Another law that aims to make the federal bureaucracy open and responsive to the people is the Government in the Sunshine Act of 1976. This act of Congress requires all multiheaded national agencies, except those in the Executive Office of the President (EOP), to conduct open, public meetings where citizens can testify and present their concerns about these agencies' actions (past, current, and potential) and the procedures by which they make decisions.

National agencies are now also using the Internet to make government more transparent. In September 2000, the General Services Administration office of the national government launched FirstGov at www.firstgov.gov. This site provides government information

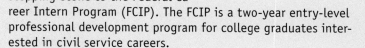

ON THE JOB

CHRISTOPHER OAKLEY HOFIUS, PROGRAM ANALYST

Name: Christopher Oakley Hofius

Age: 23

Hometown: Born in Guatemala City, Guatemala; longtime resident of Fullerton, California.

College: California State University, Fullerton

Majors: International Business (Spanish concentration) and Latin American Studies (BA)

Job title: Program Analyst, Information Security Oversight Office (ISOO), a component of the National Archives and Records Administration

Salary range for jobs like this: $48,000–$108,000

Day-to-day responsibilities: I support the general implementation and oversight of the information security policies and practices of federal executive branch agencies. More specifically, I assist in conducting on-site inspections, evaluations, and analyses of the security classification programs of federal agencies that create or handle classified information. I also assist in preparing inspection and evaluation reports. And with other analysts, I conduct periodic briefings concerning the government's security classification program. Classification decisions can affect current government operations, the well-being of citizens, and the writing of our nation's history.

How did you get your job? I first worked for ISOO as a summer intern in the Hispanic Association of Colleges and Universities' (HACU) National Internship Program. That experience was a stepping-stone to the Federal Career Intern Program (FCIP). The FCIP is a two-year entry-level professional development program for college graduates interested in civil service careers.

What do you like best about your job? I love working with high-level public policy, especially policy that determines the balance between government transparency and the protection of information that's sensitive to national security.

What advice would you give to students who would like to do what you are doing? Pay attention daily to the actions of the federal government if you are interested in a career in information security and national security. Keeping up-to-date with the rapidly evolving world of security requires discipline and constant reading of journals and periodicals. Motivated and skilled college students interested in serving their country should take advantage of government agency internship opportunities.

and services at your fingertips by offering a comprehensive Internet search of government, with both English-language and Spanish-language Web portals. The site assists visitors in identifying and contacting elected officials and provides easy access to data collected by governments, to laws and regulations, and to government forms. FirstGov even has links to national government employment opportunities and information on applying for jobs. The expectation is that e-government will streamline communications between the people and government so that government can be more responsive and efficient. Taxpayer dollars pay for these e-government sites. In other words, you are paying for them, so take advantage of them!

WATCHDOG GROUPS   Private organizations that monitor and evaluate the activities of bureaucrats have certainly taken advantage of sunshine laws and e-government. For example, in 2007, Congress passed legislation to establish an independent, bipartisan commission to investigate U.S. wartime contracting in Iraq and Afghanistan. Senator Claire

McCaskill (D-Missouri), the bill's cosponsor, praised "POGO's [the Project on Government Oversight] work in supporting these provisions, along with the support of other watchdog groups including Taxpayers for Common Sense, the Government Accountability Project, OMBWatch, Common Cause, U.S. PIRG and Iraq and Afghanistan Veterans of America."[14] In addition to taking advantage of their right to government documents under the FOIA, watchdog groups are also likelier than is the average citizen to use government Web sites such as www.regulations.gov to track bureaucratic rule-making activities.

In a democracy, bureaucrats, like elected officials, operate in a fishbowl. Working face to face, or computer screen to computer screen, with the people whom they serve, they are in full view of anyone interested in monitoring them. Sunshine laws provide citizens with the means to find out what is going on in the bureaucracy. When citizens or watchdog groups identify a problem with bureaucratic operations, they frequently turn to the media to bring public attention to the issue, as the media are always ready to report on bureaucratic inefficiency and impropriety. A more expensive option for citizen and interest group action against bureaucratic waste and misconduct is the filing of a lawsuit.

Accountability to the Courts

As bureaucratic agencies implement policy, they must comply with constitutional guarantees of due process and equal protection of laws. A citizen believing that bureaucrats have violated these rights can challenge bureaucratic actions through the agency's quasi-judicial processes, discussed earlier. If the citizen is not satisfied with the result of this quasi-judicial recourse, he or she can sue the agency through the courts.

Through the litigation process, the U.S. judicial system seeks to ensure that administrative agencies conduct their quasi-legislative and quasi-judicial functions in compliance with the constitutional guarantees of due process (in the Fifth and Fourteenth amendments) as well as the Administrative Procedure Act of 1946. In 2006, for example, federal district judge Richard Leon ruled that the Federal Emergency Management Agency (FEMA) procedures and notices to Hurricane Katrina victims were so difficult to understand that evacuees were deprived of due process because they were unable to determine what the process was. According to the lawyer for ACORN, a housing advocacy group that brought the lawsuit, as many as 11,000 families may have been wrongfully denied long-term housing assistance by the lack of due process in FEMA procedures.[15]

> Individual citizens and interest groups frequently pressure the government to investigate scandals and disasters in order to find out what went wrong and what the government can do to prevent future misbehavior and disasters. Sally Regenhard, founder of the Skyscraper Safety Campaign, participates in a vigil in front of the White House urging the formation of an independent commission to investigate the terrorist attacks of September 11, 2001. Ms. Regenhard's son, a probationary New York City firefighter, perished in the World Trade Center collapse.

Accountability to Congress

Bureaucrats must always keep in mind the preferences and agenda of Congress if they want to survive, for Congress approves the legislation that creates, regulates, and funds bureaucracies. The Senate has an additional mechanism for promoting bureaucratic accountability, in that more than one-quarter of the president's appointees are subject to Senate confirmation. The confirmation process for top bureaucrats gives senators a degree of influence over the leadership and direction of executive departments and agencies.

Another lever by which Congress encourages bureaucratic accountability is the monitoring of bureaucracies' policy implementation, a form of legislative oversight. When the media, citizens, or interest groups bring concerns about a bureaucracy's policy implementation to the attention of legislators, Congress might launch an investigation. If, consequently, Congress and the president are dissatisfied with that bureaucracy's performance or behavior, they can cut its budget, modify its legal authority, or even eliminate the agency.

In most cases, oversight does not occur unless citizens, interest groups, and the media push for congressional action, as occurred in the aftermath of 9/11 when public pressure forced Congress to create the 9/11 Commission to investigate the terrorist attacks on the World Trade Center in New York City. An evaluation of bureaucratic performance can also be required in the authorization legislation by a **sunset clause,** which forces the expiration of the program or policy after a specified number of years unless Congress reauthorizes it through new legislation.

sunset clause
a clause in legislation that sets an expiration date for the authorized program/policy unless Congress re-authorizes it

Accountability to the President

The president also has several tools for holding bureaucracies accountable. Like Congress, the president can use the authorization and appropriation processes to ensure accountability. In addition, because most top political appointees serve at the president's pleasure, they are responsive to the president's policy preferences—and in this way they and their agencies are accountable to the president.

Today the Office of Management and Budget, an EOP agency, is the key lever in the president's efforts to hold the bureaucracy accountable. The OMB evaluates bureaucratic performance for the president. Based on OMB performance assessments, the president proposes budget increases or decreases, agency growth or elimination, or even a reorganization of the executive branch in which agencies are consolidated. President George W. Bush reported in his 2007 budget message that his President's Management Agenda (PMA) initiative, an OMB-implemented strategy to evaluate and improve the management and performance of the national government, had identified 141 programs that "should be terminated or significantly reduced in size" because they were "not getting results and not fulfilling essential priorities."[16]

In addition to overseeing performance evaluations of bureaucratic agencies, the OMB spearheads the development of the president's budget, controls the implementation of appropriation laws, and regulates administrative rule making. Through its Office of Information and Regulatory Affairs (OIRA), the OMB ensures that regulations created by executive branch agencies are not "unnecessarily costly"[17] and support the president's policy preferences.

Presidents can also ensure bureaucrats' accountability by exercising their authority to reorganize agencies and to modify executive branch procedures. During his first term of office, President Bill Clinton assigned to Vice President Al Gore the task of "reinventing" the national government. Gore responded with his plan for a National Performance Review (NPR). Implementing Gore's NPR recommendations, Clinton cut the federal workforce by more than 370,000 positions and eliminated unnecessary paperwork and regulations (red tape), simplifying many rules by which bureaucrats functioned.[18]

Internal Accountability

The president, Congress, the courts, and ordinary citizens have multiple means by which to hold bureaucrats accountable. But bureaucrats, who themselves are taxpayers, also worry about inefficiency and waste in public service, as A. Ernest Fitzgerald's story highlights. Legislated codes of behavior and whistle-blower protections help to foster accountability from within bureaucracies.

CODES OF BEHAVIOR AND THE ETHICS IN GOVERNMENT ACT To ensure the best public service, bureaucracies have codes of behavior. These codes specify guidelines for ethical, efficient, and effective behavior on the part of bureaucrats. Each government agency has its own such code. In addition, in 1992, the Office of Government Ethics published a comprehensive set of ethical standards for national bureaucrats. Moreover, many of the professions in which bureaucrats are members (lawyers, doctors, nurses, accountants, engineers, and so on) also have established codes of behavior. Importantly, however, codes of behavior are just guidelines. They do not stipulate what a bureaucrat should do in a given situation. Thus bureaucrats must use discretion when applying such codes to their daily work of providing public service.

The Ethics in Government Act of 1978 established the United States Office of Government Ethics (OGE), which is charged with preventing conflicts of interest by bureaucrats (political appointees, SES bureaucrats, and civil servants). A **conflict of interest** arises when a public servant is in a position to make a decision or take an action from which he or she can personally benefit. In such a situation, the public servant's private interest is in conflict with his or her responsibility to serve the public interest. A key to the prevention of conflicts of interest is the requirement that top government officials must disclose their finances.

WHISTLE-BLOWER PROTECTIONS AND INSPECTORS GENERAL
Whistle-blower laws offer an additional means of internal accountability in the national bureaucracy. The 1978 Civil Service Reform Act provided some protections to civil servant **whistle-blowers**—employees who disclose government misconduct, waste, mismanagement, abuse of authority, or a threat to public health or safety. The CSRA established the Office of Special Counsel to protect whistle-blowers' job security. Then in 1986, thanks to the lobbying efforts of many groups, including the Project on Government Oversight, Congress approved the False Claims Act. This law allows for a monetary reward for government whistle-blowers who expose fraud that harms the U.S. government. The reward is contingent upon the government's litigation of the alleged perpetrators and receipt of monetary compensation. In addition, the Sarbanes-Oxley Act of 2002 established whistle-blower protections for employees at publicly traded private companies who report threats to public safety or health or the mismanagement of government-contracted work.

In another attempt to improve internal accountability, Congress approved the Inspector General Act in 1978. This law aims to ensure the integrity of public service by creating government watchdogs, called **inspectors general,** appointed by the president and embedded in government agencies to monitor policy implementation and investigate alleged misconduct. The law requires the appointment of the inspectors general without regard to their

conflict of interest
in the case of public servants, the situation when they can personally benefit from a decision they make or an action they take in the process of doing their jobs

whistle-blower
a civil servant who discloses mismanagement, fraud, waste, corruption, and/or threats to public health and safety to the government

inspectors general
political appointees who work within a government agency to insure the integrity of public service by investigating allegations of misconduct by bureaucrats

> The underground tunnel of Boston's Central Artery/Tunnel Project, better known as the Big Dig, opened in 2003. In July 2006, four concrete slabs, each weighing at least three tons, fell from the tunnel's ceiling, crushing a woman to death. The ceiling collapse—the latest in a long series of problems with the private contractors that have included cost overruns, construction defects and delays, fraud, and the use of substandard concrete—sparked investigations by the state police, the Federal Highway Administration, the Massachusetts attorney general, and the U.S. attorney general.

political affiliation and strictly on the basis of their abilities in accounting, auditing, or investigation. "We're supposed to check our politics at the door and call things as we see them. If we uncover things that reflect badly on the government, we're legally and morally obliged to report it. We're obliged to do that for the good of the country." So explained Clark Ervin, who held the position of inspector general at the State and Homeland Security departments.[19]

In summary, whistle-blower protection laws and inspectors general enhance the ability of the bureaucrats themselves to police the agencies in which they work, and sunshine laws give government outsiders various instruments for monitoring the bureaucracy. But many citizens and government officials believe that more needs to be done to improve bureaucrats' record of performance.

Can Bureaucratic Performance Be Improved?

In the United States, bureaucrats perform every job imaginable. They generally do their job so well that we rarely think about how their work positively affects us around the clock. We and our elected officials are nevertheless trigger-quick to bash the bureaucracy at the slightest hint of inefficiency. Similarly, the media seize upon any opportunity to report on problems with bureaucrats and bureaucracies. Our public discourse infrequently covers bureaucrats' *good* performance. When was the last time you heard a news report or were a party to a friendly conversation that praised a public servant?

Yet the U.S. Postal Service delivers hundreds of millions of pieces of mail six days a week, and rarely is a letter or package lost. Thousands of planes safely take off from and land at U.S. airports every hour, guided by federal bureaucrats in the person of air traffic controllers. Millions of senior citizens receive a monthly Social Security check on time every month. Even more people travel the interstate highway systems without incident each day.

Public administration and policy scholar Charles Goodsell has found that two-thirds to three-fourths of Americans report their encounters with government bureaucrats and bureaucracy as "satisfactory."[20] However, research consistently shows that some national agencies perform better than do others.

The Best-Performing Bureaucracies

Political scientists William T. Gormley and Steven Balla reviewed national performance data and summarized the characteristics of national agencies that perform well.[21] They found that numerous factors correlate with better-performing bureaucracies—factors that individual bureaucrats have little control over. They include legislative language that clearly states the goal of the legislation and provides high levels of administrative discretion, allowing bureaucrats to determine the best way to achieve the goal. Better-performing bureaucracies tend to be those with easily measured goals, especially goals that include providing resources to citizens (such as Social Security checks) as opposed to taking resources (tax collection). Another factor correlated with good performance is high levels of support from elected officials, the media, and diverse groups of citizens for the legislated goal and the implementing agency. High levels of support typically result in an agency receiving ample resources. Effective leaders who develop and maintain high levels of support from government officials and interested parties outside of government are also important to well-performing bureaucracies.

After Hurricane Katrina, many ordinary citizens and government officials blamed President Bush's top FEMA appointee, director Michael Brown, for FEMA's poor response to the hurricane's victims. The media as well as members of Congress focused their attention on the background of Brown and other FEMA appointees, noting their lack of relevant job experience. (In truth, earlier cuts in FEMA funding and the denial of requests for funds to improve New Orleans' levees also negatively affected public service delivery in this case.) Brown quickly resigned amid the political firestorm. Clearly, bureaucratic leadership and

Government Efficiency

Would you agree or disagree that when programs are run by the federal government, they tend to be wasteful and inefficient?

☐ Agree

☐ Disagree

Source: "Trends in Political Values and Core Attitudes: 1987–2007," http://people-press.org/reports/pdf/312.pdf.

sufficiency of resources, both of which are controlled by the president and Congress, are key factors in bureaucratic success.

Does Contracting-Out Improve Performance?

In addition to analyzing citizen satisfaction with public bureaucracies, Charles Goodsell has also analyzed the body of research that assesses the efficiency of public policy implementation by government bureaucrats compared to the efficiency of private organizations. He has found that "the assumption that business always does better than government is not upheld."[22] In fact, Goodsell reports that "despite antigovernment rhetoric to the contrary, the federal government achieves essentially the same degree of satisfaction for its services as corporate America does for its products."[23] Nevertheless, many commentators and elected officials argue that private businesses are more efficient than are governments and therefore that more public service should be outsourced to private businesses.

Contracting-out to private businesses certainly decreases the number of bureaucrats on the national payroll. But does outsourcing foster more efficient and effective public service? Does it save taxpayer dollars? The evidence strongly suggests otherwise.

> Federal Emergency Management Agency (FEMA) chief Michael Brown briefs President George W. Bush at a U.S. Coast Guard Base in Mobile, Alabama, before they tour the devastation left by Hurricane Katrina. Brown resigned as head of FEMA following the political and media firestorm over the poor federal response to the Hurricane Katrina disaster.

As the experience of A. Ernest Fitzgerald (see "American Democracy Now") highlights, outsourcing government work can lead to waste, fraud, overpricing, and corruption. In its evaluation of contract waste and fraud in Hurricane Katrina relief, the House of Representatives Government Reform Committee reported that "the main problems were no-bid contracts, layers of subcontracting that inflated costs, and a lack of oversight on the completion of work."[24] What causes these inefficiencies?

First, for-profit organizations must make a profit to survive. As contract law experts note, for many private government contractors, overestimating the costs of the work and then reaping illegally high profits are a common reality. Second, holding bureaucrats accountable for their performance is not easy in general, and determining whom to hold accountable for delays, cost overruns, and quality issues is complicated when policy implementation occurs through the shadow bureaucracy.[25] Unlike government bodies, private businesses can legally function behind closed doors—unless and until concerned citizens, watchdog groups, the media, and government officials force the doors open through congressional investigations or lawsuits.

Citizens' Role in Bureaucratic Performance

Citizens turn to the government to provide services and solve problems. As we have discussed, the government's success in serving the people well depends on many factors. Ultimately, even if all other factors correlated with a well performing bureaucracy are in place, the bureaucracy will fail without the participation and compliance of the people it serves. The effectiveness of public policies depends on people's knowledge of and compliance with the law. It depends on their applying for the government programs for which they qualify and their conformity to the rules, regulations, standards, and directions of bureaucrats. This symbiotic relationship is essential to the success of government.

In 1789, the federal bureaucracy was small in size and limited in scope. Bureaucrats hired through the patronage system staffed its three departments and two offices, and their work was primarily clerical. They collected revenues, paid bills, resolved lawsuits, supported diplomatic affairs, and provided for the country's defense.

Today, a sprawling, complex network of federal, state, local, and shadow bureaucrats distributes a huge number and diversity of public services that would have been unthinkable to the nation's early generations. A small percentage of today's public service jobs are clerical, with the majority of government work, including the work done by shadow bureaucrats, requiring high levels of education, specialization, and professional training. Hiring based on merit, not patronage; the devolution of service to state and local bureaucrats; and outsourcing to shadow bureaucrats are now the norm in the federal bureaucracy.

Indeed, over time, the federal government has relied more and more on state, local, and shadow bureaucrats to provide public services. The hope and expectation have been that the work of the shadow bureaucrats would be more efficient and effective than that provided by federal bureaucrats. But whistle-blowers as well as scholars have regularly challenged the idea that the shadow bureaucracy does a superior job of delivering vital services. Criticism of the federal bureaucracy and bureaucrats has been a constant chorus. Fraud, waste, secrecy, and overpriced contract work are common complaints. Yet most citizens report satisfactory interactions with government bureaucrats and sufficient public services.

Some intriguing questions about the federal bureaucracy arise for citizens and office-holders alike. Will the bureaucracy's growing reliance on e-government, which makes its operations more transparent and provides citizens with easier access to public servants and services, satisfy some of its critics? Or will the replacement of face-to-face interactions with screen-to-screen contacts decrease citizen satisfaction? Will continuing reports of fraud, waste, and mismanagement by private contractors force the government to reconsider outsourcing public services—and perhaps prompt the public to better appreciate, and even to praise, the work of federal bureaucrats?

Summary

1. Bureaucrats and Bureaucracy

Traditionally, bureaucrats are defined as employees in the executive branch of government who are hired to deliver public services. Today, however, many private-sector employees—the so-called shadow bureaucrats—also implement public policy. Although most people think of government agencies when they hear the word *bureaucracy,* a bureaucracy is any large, hierarchical organization featuring a division of labor, specialization of tasks, standard operating procedures, and a chain of command.

2. Federal Bureaucrats

The national government hires almost 3 million civilians into the executive branch to administer public policies. The president appoints a small percentage of these bureaucrats. The government hires the overwhelming majority of national bureaucrats on the basis of merit, using a hiring process that includes open competition and equal opportunity. As a result,

the national bureaucracy features a more diverse representation of the people than do the elective institutions of the federal government.

3. State, Local, and Shadow Bureaucrats
The overall number of national bureaucrats has been stable over the past few decades. However, the number of state, local, and shadow bureaucrats has grown significantly due to the proliferation of grants-in-aid and the practice of contracting-out more and more public service.

4. The Evolution and Organization of the Federal Bureaucracy
The federal bureaucracy has grown tremendously in size, scope, and complexity since 1789. Political scientists typically put government agencies in one of five categories—departments, independent administrative agencies, independent regulatory commissions, government corporations, and Executive Office of the President agencies. But this categorization oversimplifies the diversity of structure, size, and function of the thousands of national bureaucracies.

5. Federal Bureaucrats' Roles in Public Policy
Federal bureaucrats do much more than implement policy. Bureaucrats lobby elected officials in all stages of the policy cycle to get their concerns, and the concerns of the citizens who are their clients, addressed. Elected officials frequently defer to the expertise of bureaucrats when it comes to determining the detailed programs, rules, and standards that are needed to serve the people. Citizen satisfaction with government is deeply dependent on the efficient and effective work of bureaucrats.

6. Federal Bureaucratic Accountability
Elected officials delegate administrative discretion to bureaucrats. Interested parties inside and outside government closely scrutinize bureaucrats' use of this discretion. Taxpayers, clients, the media, and interest groups, as well as the president, Congress, and the courts, hold bureaucrats accountable. In addition to sunshine laws and ethics codes, the structure of national bureaucracies lends itself to accountability.

7. Can Bureaucratic Performance Be Improved?
All those who scrutinize bureaucracies are quick to find fault and slow to offer praise. Certainly not every agency is evaluated as performing well, but for the most part, citizens report that their interactions with government bureaucrats are at least satisfactory.

Key Terms

administrative adjudication 480

administrative discretion 479

administrative law 479

administrative rule making 480

appropriation law 479

authorization law 479

bureaucracy 464

bureaucrats 464

civil servants 466

conflict of interest 486

contracting-out (privatizing, outsourcing) 464

department 475

economic regulation 476

government corporation 476

independent administrative agency 475

independent regulatory commission 476

inspectors general 486

merit 466

merit-based civil service 466

plum book 466

politics-administration dichotomy 477

senior executive service (SES) 470

shadow bureaucrats 464

sunset clause 485

sunshine laws 482

whistle-blower 486

For Review

1. List and describe the structural characteristics of bureaucratic organizations.

2. Compare and contrast the following categories of bureaucrats: political appointees, civil servants, senior executive service bureaucrats, and shadow bureaucrats.

3. What accounts for the fact that the national budget and the scope of its responsibilities have continued to grow in recent decades, yet the number of its civilian employees has remained stable?

4. Differentiate the five categories of national bureaucracies by discussing differences in their structures and the type of services they provide.

5. Describe the role that bureaucrats play at each stage of the policy process.

6. Distinguish between internal and external means of bureaucratic accountability and give some examples of each.

7. According to Gormley and Balla, what are three or four characteristics of bureaucracies that perform well?

For Critical Thinking and Discussion

1. Do citizens expect too much from government and hence from bureaucrats and bureaucracies? Explain your answer.

2. Does the profit motive of private businesses threaten the efficient use of taxpayer money when public services are contracted-out? Why or why not?

3. Identify at least one public service that you believe the national government should not contract-out to private-sector organizations, and defend your choice(s).

4. How often do you interact with national bureaucrats? What about state bureaucrats? Local bureaucrats? Give some recent examples of each interacting. Can you identify some shadow bureaucrats that have provided you with public services?

5. Compose a list of public services provided to you since you woke up this morning. Which of these services do people generally take for granted?

MULTIPLE CHOICE: Choose the lettered item that answers the question correctly.

1. Who hires and signs the paychecks for shadow bureaucrats?
   a. federal government
   b. state governments
   c. local governments
   d. private and nonprofit employers

2. The youngest department in the nation bureaucracy is the department of
   a. energy.
   b. homeland security.
   c. state.
   d. veterans affairs.

3. The demographics of what category of federal employee is most comparable to those of the population as a whole?
   a. elected officials
   b. civil servants
   c. political appointees
   d. senior executive service employees

4. The legislation that created the merit-based civil service system was the
   a. Civil Rights Act (1964).
   b. Civil Service Reform Act (1978).
   c. Pendleton Act (1883).
   d. Title IX (1972).

5. The independent administrative agency that is the central personnel office for the federal bureaucracy today is the
   a. EOP.   c. MSPB.
   b. FLRA.   d. OPM.

6. In what category of federal bureaucracies are secretaries the top appointed officials?
   a. department
   b. independent administrative agency
   c. independent regulatory commission
   d. government corporation

7. Bureaucracies in which category are expected to make enough money to cover their costs?
   a. department
   b. independent administrative agency
   c. independent regulatory commission
   d. government corporation

8. Bureaucrats make policy, using the administrative discretion that Congress delegates to them, at the stage of the policy process that is called
   a. policy formulation.
   b. policy approval.
   c. policy implementation.
   d. policy evaluation.

9. All of the following are merit principles except
   a. competence.
   b. open competition.
   c. political neutrality.
   d. Senate confirmation.

10. For what role is A. Ernest Fitzgerald famous?
    a. assassinating President Garfield
    b. the first commissioner of the Civil Service Commission
    c. inspector general
    d. whistle-blower

FILL IN THE BLANKS.

11. A _____ is an organization with the following characteristics: a division of labor; workers hired based on competence to do a specialized task; standard operating procedures; and a vertical chain of command.

12. The hiring system initially used by the federal government, which allowed the president to hire anyone he wanted based on whatever qualifications he decided on, is the _____ system.

13. Do most federal bureaucrats work in Washington, D.C., or outside of Washington, D.C.?

14. The idea that elected officials make policy and bureaucrats hired based on their merit neutrally implement that policy is known as the _____.

15. Laws that force the government to be transparent by holding open meetings and providing citizens with requested information at a reasonable cost are collectively known as _____.

Answers: 1. d; 2. b; 3. b; 4. c; 5. d; 6. a; 7. d; 8. c; 9. d; 10. d; 11. bureaucracy; 12. patronage; 13. outside; 14. politics-administration dichotomy; 15. sunshine laws.

RESOURCES FOR RESEARCH AND ACTION

Internet Resources

American Democracy Now Web site
www.mhhe.com/harrison1e   Consult the book's Web site for study guides, interactive activities, simulations, and current hotlinks for additional information on bureaucracy in government.

Office of Management and Budget
www.whitehouse.gov.omb   This Web site provides access to the current and previous federal budget documents and historical budget tables.

Regulations.gov
www.regulations.gov   You can review proposed and approved rules, regulations, and standards of federal executive agencies and submit your comments about them.

U.S. Government Printing Office
www.gpoaccess.gov/gmanual/browse   This Web site allows you to view the most current U.S. Government Manual as well as several older editions of the manual.

USA.gov
www.firstgov.gov   Use this site as a one-stop portal to national, state, and local government officials, agencies, and documents.

Recommended Readings

Devine, Tom. *Courage Without Martyrdom: A Survival Guide for Whistleblowers.* Washington, DC: Project on Government Oversight and the Government Accountability Project, 1989. Presents details of eight survival strategies to guide bureaucrats and shadow bureaucrats contemplating blowing the whistle on fraud, corruption, and mismanagement. (Now available in PDF format at www.whistleblower.org/template/page.cfm?page_id=43.)

Fitzgerald, A. Ernest. *The Pentagonists: An Insider's View of Waste, Mismanagement, and Fraud in Defense Spending.* Boston: Houghton Mifflin, 1989. Fitzgerald's own story of blowing the whistle on waste, fraud, and mismanagement in the military's procurement system from the late 1960s through the 1980s.

Goodsell, Charles T. *The Case for Bureaucracy: A Public Administration Polemic,* 4th ed. Washington, DC: CQ Press, 2004. A review of the common myths and criticisms of bureaucracy, with evidence to show that they are indeed unsupported.

Gormley, William T., Jr. and Steven J. Balla. *Bureaucracy and Democracy: Accountability and Performance.* Washington, DC: CQ Press, 2004. Uses case studies and examples to illustrate what the national bureaucracy does and why it is important, and draws on social science theories to describe how bureaucracy works and the complex and conflicting demands put on it.

Kettl, Donald F. *System Under Stress: Homeland Security and American Politics.* Washington, DC: CQ Press, 2004. Analysis of the environmental factors that led to the creation of the newest cabinet-level department, the Department of Homeland Security, with an examination of the intergovernmental nature of the endeavor to protect homeland security.

Stillman, Richard. *The American Bureaucracy: The Core of Modern Government.* Chicago: Nelson-Hall Publishers, 1996. A comprehensive introductory textbook in public administration, with excellent description and analysis of bureaucracies (national, state, and local) in the United States.

Wilson, James Q. 1989. *Bureaucracy: What Government Agencies Do and Why They Do It.* New York: Basic Books, 1989. A classic treatise on what government agencies do and why they function as they do, with analysis on how they might become more responsible and efficient.

Movies of Interest

Pentagon Papers (2003)
In this made-for-TV movie, a Department of Defense bureaucrat, Daniel Ellsberg, has access to classified documents that he decides should be brought to the public's attention. The documents detail the secret history of U.S. involvement in Vietnam, which includes bureaucrats misinforming decision makers and the public. Ellsberg risks his career and his freedom to try to get the truth to the public. Based on a true story.

Mississippi Burning (1989)
Two committed FBI agents, with very different personal styles, investigate the disappearance of three civil rights workers during the 1960s. Based on a true story.

Serpico (1973)
The story of a New York City police officer who is living his dream of being a cop. His dream job turns life threatening when he blows the whistle on corruption in the police force, the existence of which shows that not all of Serpico's coworkers are as committed to public service as he is. Based on a true story.

BIRTH OF A NUMBER

On March 11, the Centers for Disease Control and Prevention announced that one in four teenage girls has a sexually transmitted disease.

This eye-opening statistic landed like a dead rat on the doorsteps of America's 37 million households and 30 million teenagers. The *New York Times,* among other papers, put the news on the front page. CBS news anchor Katie Couric told her viewers that "at least one in four teenage girls in America has a sexually transmitted disease," and she ended by saying, "I know what I'll be talking about at the dinner table tonight."

The one-in-four number "really caught every parent in America's attention," said Cecile Richards, the president of the Planned Parenthood Federation of America, because it is so simple and "so stunning." Richards said that her 17-year-old daughter read it "and personalized it, and said, 'There are some girls I know who have an STI'"—shorthand for sexually transmitted infection. "It really brought it home."

Rival Washington advocates pounced on the CDC's startling statistic. One faction, led by Planned Parenthood and other groups that get federal grants, said the number shows that the Bush administration's abstinence-promotion programs don't work and that funding should be transferred to sex-education and condom-distribution programs. The rival faction, led by social conservatives, said that the one-in-four number demonstrates the failure of condoms and sex-education classes.

An April 23 hearing of the House Oversight and Government Reform Committee showcased this dispute. Chairman Henry Waxman opened the hearing by declaring: "A few weeks ago, the CDC released data showing that one in four teenage girls in the U.S. has a sexually transmitted infection. . . . We will hear today from multiple experts that after more than a decade of huge government spending, the weight of the evidence doesn't demonstrate abstinence-only programs to be effective."

But how useful or valid is that one-in-four number? Are 25 percent of America's teenage girls really in imminent danger from HIV/AIDS, gonorrhea, and the human papillomavirus (HPV) that leads to cervical cancer?

A close examination of the CDC's star statistic reveals several serious shortcomings that undermine its validity, as well as its usefulness to parents, legislators, health officials, and advocacy groups on the left and the right.

Some of **the CDC's statements fall neatly in line** with liberal stances on sex policy.

For instance, Couric's and Waxman's shorthand summaries were misleading. The CDC's study referred to "infections," but most biological infections never turn into diseases; the body suppresses them before symptoms appear. Most news accounts, including the first line of an Associated Press story that ran in many newspapers, likewise referred to "diseases" rather than infections. The CDC did little to correct this inflated interpretation.

Other problems were numerous. For instance, the infections referred to in the study are not the ones that leap to people's minds when they worry about sexually transmitted diseases. The data excluded the two most-feared diseases, HIV/AIDS and syphilis. The most common infection was from HPV, which can have serious consequences but in the vast majority of cases disappears on its own.

The focus on "teenagers," moreover, covers a broad age range, from those who are 14 (only 13 percent of whom have had sexual intercourse, according to other studies) to women of 18 and 19 (70 percent of whom have had sex before their 19th birthday). CDC officials declined to describe to *National Journal* the infection rates in each of the two-year age groupings, even though they have the data.

Perhaps most critical, the CDC's March 11 news conference, and the materials distributed there, failed to put the numbers into historical context. Other CDC research shows that infection rates for most serious sexual diseases, including syphilis, gonorrhea, and chancroid, are sharply below 1990 levels—syphilis reached a historic low in 2000. The CDC's tests showed that none of the 18- and 19-year-old women in the study were infected with HIV or syphilis, but officials did not mention this success in the press release. Teenagers' exposure to STDs has also dropped because their sexual activity declined from 1998 to 2002.

CDC officials say they acted appropriately when they prepared and released the one-in-four number. "The last thing we want is for people to believe that 25 percent of girls have something that will bring them serious harm," John Douglas, director of the CDC's STD prevention division, told the *Chicago Tribune* in April. Asked about the substitution of "disease" for "infection," CDC officials replied in an e-mailed statement: "We use STD because it is more widely understood than STI among both health professionals and the lay public."

CDC Director Julie Gerberding declined to be interviewed for this article. In a statement to *National Journal,* she said, "As the nation's health protection agency . . . we pride ourselves in following three core values—accountability, respect, and integrity. In all my years as director, I have never been pressured or asked to make any decisions which were not based on the sound scientific research that the world expects from CDC."

Officials at the CDC's Division of STD Prevention at the National Center for HIV/AIDS, Viral Hepatitis, STD, and TB Prevention arrived at the one-in-four number in 2007. Officials already knew the approximate STI rates among teenagers, but they sought to reframe the existing data on young women. Douglas told *NJ,* "They're the cutting edge of prevention."

To get the new number, CDC researcher Sara Forhan turned to a database—the CDC's National Health and Nutrition Examination Survey—that goes back to the 1960s. The CDC's Center for Health Statistics, which collects information on the health and nutritional status of Americans, sends a mobile laboratory to 15 counties every year to survey and give laboratory tests to approximately 5,000 randomly selected volunteers. Since the 1960s, officials have used the NHANES database to expose problems caused by iron deficiency, cholesterol, lead, and many other hazards. Its data served as the basis for children's growth charts, for guidelines to reduce exposure to lead, and for awareness of obesity as a public health hazard.

Forhan examined the 2003–04 database for the age groups covering 14 to 19. She found good records on 615 women, of whom 18.3 percent had HPV, 3.9 percent carried chlamydia, 2.5 percent had trichomoniasis, and 1.9 percent had HSV-2 (herpes simplex virus). The four mini-surveys were combined, and CDC officials determined that 25.7 percent of the 615 women had one or more of the four diseases, according to a CDC briefing chart.

CDC officials, including Douglas, announced the number in Chicago at the CDC's biannual National STD Prevention Conference, which is attended by many experts, state officials, and reporters. The subsequent media reports and editorials generally echoed the recommendations of CDC officials, and their advocacy allies, for greater government-funded testing and intervention.

The one-in-four figure immediately became fodder in the ongoing debate over whether the government should support comprehensive sex education or fund advocacy for sexual abstinence until marriage.

Sex-education advocates were first out of the gate, announcing even before the press conference (in time for initial news reports) that funding should be transferred from "failed" abstinence-only programs to education that includes lessons on the use of contraceptives.

Proponents for abstinence and marriage programs countered that the CDC's number demonstrates just the opposite. "The half [of the adolescents] that weren't having sex did not have STIs," said the Family Research Council's Gaul. The CDC's one-in-four number "represents a failure of contraceptive-based education," Rep. Mark Souder, R-Ind., said at the Waxman hearing. The statistic "verifies that what we've been saying is true—the only safe sex is inside marriage." Souder announced that he's campaigning for a health warning on condom packages, akin to the warning on cigarette packs.

Boonstra, a comprehensive-education advocate at Guttmacher, responds that abstinence-until-marriage programs nearly always fail because, surveys show, 95 percent of people have sex before marriage.

Under the Bush administration, the federal government has spent about $180 million a year on classroom programs that promote abstinence until marriage (and don't train in condom use) to more than 2 million youths. The federal government also gives at least $300 million to federal agencies and states to fund comprehensive sex education, STI testing, and condom distribution. In the fiscal year ending June 2007, Planned Parenthood and its state affiliates received $337 million in government money, and the group's activities included spending $48 million on sexuality education programs, according to its annual report.

CDC officials try to stay clear of politics, Douglas said. They present scientific conclusions, he said, and "let the chips fall where they may politically." Yet some of the CDC's

statements fall neatly in line with liberal stances on sex policy.

The March 11 study was, moreover, closely associated with the CDC's funding aspirations. On the day it was released, CDC officials used the study to tout their sexually transmitted disease programs. "Continued commitment to STD prevention is essential," Kevin Fenton, the director of the CDC's STD division and Douglas's boss, said at the beginning of the press conference. "CDC estimates that approximately 19 million new [sexually transmitted] infections occur every year in the United States, [and] our task is to maximize the use of these new tools—from vaccines to innovative STD screening and treatment."

Because of the study, "we got some really good press, and we've been able to get the [budget] discussion on the table," said Don Clark, the executive director of the National Coalition of STD Directors, which is pushing to increase the STD budget. The CDC's STD programs have been reduced since 2003, and they're now stuck at about $150 million, he said. Last year, the agency asked for $267 million a year.

Overall, the CDC's primary budget—excluding vaccine programs—has been cut 15 percent since 2005, says Karl Moeller, the executive director of the Campaign for Public Health, an industry-funded coalition formed in 2004 to boost the CDC's core budget from $6.3 billion in 2005 to $15 billion by 2012.

The CDC is a science agency, yet it is expected to advocate for policies that aid public health, said Jeffrey Koplan, the CDC's director from 1998 to 2002. Science demonstrates that seat belts and air bags reduce automobile deaths, so "it would be irresponsible for public health leaders not to advocate for them," said Koplan, who is now the executive director of Emory University's Global Health Institute. "Large parts of public health are political."

■**THEN:** Federal agencies have been expected to act with non-partisan, non-political intentions.

■**NOW:** Political and budgetary interests may appear to color the neutral actions of federal agencies.

■**NEXT:** Should we be troubled by the political implications of the statistics released by federal agencies?

Will we conclude from the CDC's statistic that abstinence-only or safe-sex programs are more effective in fighting the spread of sexually transmitted diseases?

Will sunshine laws prove useful in clarifying statistics used by politicians as well as expert bureaucrats in policy debates?

The Judiciary

A common-law tradition imported from England dominated in the U.S. legal system.

Through code law and further interpretation of common law, the courts respond to unprecedented developments, from a torrent of technology to a continuing terrorist threat.

Will new laws successfully address the complexities of issues like technological advance and the terrorist menace?

Will shifting Supreme Court ideology influence government actions in response to the ever-present threat of terrorism?

Will courts with specific policy expertise supplant legislatures' policy making in areas such as technology?

Shaping the Judicial Context: Howard University Students

On a chilly morning in December 2006, the U.S. Supreme Court began considering two cases, *Community Schools v. Seattle School District No. 1* and *Meredith v. Jefferson Board of Education*. Both cases centered on the legality of a school district's decision—in an effort to foster classroom diversity—to admit a student to a high school on the basis of that student's race. Outside the Court chambers, hundreds of students, many from the historically black college Howard University, demonstrated. ▮ Delegations of other students—from Harvard University, the University of California at Berkeley, the University of Louisville, Fayetteville State University, Lincoln University, Morehouse College, and Spelman College—joined their Howard counterparts. Lincoln University students wore T-shirts with the image of the late Supreme Court justice and Lincoln alumnus Thurgood Marshall, the first African American appointed to the Court. Marshall had argued the groundbreaking 1954 *Brown v. Board of Education* case that resulted in the desegregation of U.S. schools. ▮ In considering the case, the Supreme Court weighed the following separate questions:*

> ▶ **Howard University students demonstrate outside the U.S. Supreme Court.**

1. Do previous judicial decisions concerning the use of racial criteria in *higher education* admissions apply to public *high school* students?
2. Is racial diversity a compelling public interest that justifies the use of race in selecting students for admission to public high schools?
3. The Constitution's equal protection clause guarantees all citizens equal protection under the law. Does a school district that normally permits a student to attend the high school of the student's choice violate the Constitution by denying the student admission to the chosen school because of his or her race, in an effort to achieve a desired racial balance?**

The student demonstrators favored retaining the racial criteria, under the assumption that the use of such criteria, on the whole, would benefit minority students. But when the Court issued its opinion, the justices disagreed. They ruled that previous decisions concerning affirmative action in higher education programs did not dictate the ruling regarding high schools because the programs varied so greatly. The Court also ruled that racial diversity as defined by the school board in these cases did not constitute a compelling interest, and that using such criteria did violate the Fourteenth Amendment's equal protection clause. ▮ Were the efforts of the student demonstrators worthless? Should they simply have stayed in bed? Certainly not. Indeed, one of the most important checks on the judiciary—which is the least democratic (and the only nonelected) branch of government—is the power of the people to make their views heard. Like the student protesters, people sometimes express their opinions about legal questions through demonstrations. At other times, they give expression to their views by bringing cases before the courts. And sometimes they even make themselves heard by violating the law—by not complying with legal decisions. ▮ Howard professor Gregory Carr acknowledged that while the Court might rule against the protesters, the act of demonstrating itself was important: "Somebody in this crowd will be sitting on one of those seats one day, even if we cannot see the change today," Carr said, pointing to the Supreme Court building behind him. "And [he or she will] make sure that this building represents the justice that this building is supposed to represent."***

* www.law.cornell.edu/supct/cert/05-908.html.

** The Oyez Project, *Parents Involved in Community Schools v. Seattle School District No. 1*, 551 U.S. ___ (2007), www.oyez.org/cases/2000-2009/2006/2006_05_908/.

*** http://media.www.thehilltoponline.com/media/storage/paper590/news/2006/12/05/Campus/Howard.Students.Lead.Protest.At.Supreme.Court-2522799.shtml?norewrite200612152160&sourcedomain=www.thehilltoponline.com.

We think of the courts primarily

as places where citizens turn when they have a dispute that they need to resolve. We venture into a courtroom when we encounter some difficult legal issue with either the government or a private individual or group. The resolution of disputes is indeed the primary function of the courts in the United States. But courts and judges are concerned with other, more significant and far-reaching endeavors. In this chapter, we consider how the judiciary, consisting of the federal and state court systems, provides one of the most important defenses that citizens have against abuses of power by the executive and legislative branches. The judiciary's role as protector of civil liberties and civil rights does not escape the recognition of the American people: courts typically receive higher approval ratings than the other institutions of government.[1]

In *Federalist* No. 78, Alexander Hamilton explains that the Constitution intentionally structures the judiciary to be the weakest branch of government. But the judiciary has evolved significantly, to the point that it shares an equal role with the other two branches. Today the courts play a central role in ensuring that power remains in balance among the three branches of government on the federal level, as well as between the federal government and the states.

Judges have powers that go well beyond the immediate case they are considering. This authority allows them to make law for future generations. In fact, on both the national and state level, lawmaking is a shared enterprise among the three branches—legislative, executive, and judicial. Although the Constitution created a government characterized by a separation of powers, lawmaking is far less compartmentalized.[2] It is simplistic to think that legislatures make law, executives enforce it, and courts interpret it; rather, lawmaking is a part of what all three branches are empowered to do.

The Origins of the U.S. Judiciary

The foundations of the U.S. **judiciary**—the branch of government comprising the state and federal courts and the judges who preside over them—reach back to American colonial history and the early years of the republic that took shape after the colonies broke with England. The U.S. Constitution created the framework for the judiciary. The structure and authority of the federal judiciary have evolved further, and continuously, through compromises forged over the last 200-plus years.

The Constitution and the Judiciary Act of 1789: Establishing the Supreme Court and the Federal District Courts

During the debates over the ratification of the Constitution, the Anti-Federalists and Federalists had sparred over what the powers of the national judiciary should be. The Anti-Federalists had warned that a too powerful national judiciary would erode states' rights. For their part, the Federalists had contended that a strong national court would be necessary to moderate conflicts between the states. Ultimately, the Constitution named the **U.S. Supreme Court** as the high court of the land, but the framers intentionally did not make the Court's powers specific. Only by saying little about the specific powers of the Supreme Court were they able to reach agreement on the judiciary.

One of the most important of the framers' compromises was to establish only one court, the Supreme Court, and to empower Congress to create all lower courts. Congress accordingly set up these inferior courts in the earliest days of its first session, when it passed the

In this chapter, we survey the foundations, structure, and workings of the contemporary U.S. judiciary. We examine how the courts are responding to the ongoing, and sometimes unprecedented, changes occurring in contemporary society. We conclude by looking at how individuals, as well as the other branches of the government and the courts themselves, check judicial power.

FIRST, we examine *the origins of the U.S. judiciary.*

SECOND, we consider *the basis of U.S. law,* including common law and code law.

THIRD, we focus on the *sources of U.S. law,* including constitutions, statutes, judicial decisions, executive orders, and administrative law.

FOURTH, we examine the structure of *the federal court system.*

FIFTH, we look at the criteria used in *selecting judges for the federal bench.*

SIXTH, we survey *the U.S. Supreme Court today,* including its jurisdiction and the procedures by which the Court chooses, considers, and decides a case.

SEVENTH, we examine *judges as policy makers.*

EIGHTH, we probe the various *checks on U.S. courts.* These checks come from the executive and legislative branches of the government, police and other law enforcement agents, interest groups, the courts themselves, and the ordinary citizens who most directly experience the impact of a court decision.

judiciary
the branch of government comprising the state and federal courts and the judges who preside over them

U.S. Supreme Court
high court with a limited original jurisdiction whose decisions may not be appealed; it serves as the court of last resort in the U.S. judiciary

Judiciary Act of 1789, creating the federal district courts.[3] The federal district courts' geographic jurisdictions matched state boundaries, with at least one federal court in every state. Congress intended that these courts would have strong ties to the states in which they were located and expected that in many cases federal judges would apply state, not federal, law. These federal district courts drew strength from their ties to the states, but the federal judiciary was quite weak, with little authority.

Marbury v. Madison and the Principle of Judicial Review

Shortly after his election in 1800, President Thomas Jefferson barred the Supreme Court from meeting in the 1801–1802 term. Jefferson was concerned about the out-of-power Federalists' potential use of the federal judiciary to maintain control in the national government. Jefferson was perhaps right to worry, because in the following term, in the landmark case *Marbury v. Madison* (1803), the Federalist-led Supreme Court grasped for itself the power of judicial review.[4] As we saw in Chapter 2, judicial review is the Court's authority to review and to strike down laws passed by the other branches of the national government.

In the *Marbury* case, the Court argued something that it had never argued before: that it had the power not only to review acts of Congress and the president but also to decide whether these laws were consistent with the Constitution, and to strike down those laws that conflicted with constitutional principles. Legal scholar Joel B. Grossman observes that in *Marbury*, "[John] Marshall made it abundantly clear that the meaning of the Constitution was rarely self-contained and obvious and that those who interpreted it—a role he staked out for the federal courts but one that did not reach its full flowering until the mid-twentieth century—made a difference."[5] Judicial review is the most significant power the Supreme Court exercises. Over time, the Court has extended this power to apply not only to acts of Congress and the chief executive but also to laws passed by state legislatures and executives, as well as to state court rulings.[6]

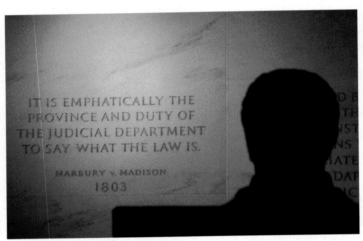

> Prominent on the façade of the U.S. Supreme Court building, this quotation from the landmark decision in the case of *Marbury v. Madison* demonstrates the importance of John Marshall's tenure as chief justice and Marshall's role in shaping the judiciary.

The Judiciary Act of 1891: Expanding the Federal Courts

circuit courts
also known as *courts of appeals*; the middle level in the federal court structure, the courts of appeals

circuit riding
the practice of traveling around the circuits by early Supreme Court justices and district court judges to hear appeals cases

courts of appeals
intermediate appellate courts in the federal system that review previous decisions made by courts in the federal or state judicial system

The middle level in the federal court structure, the courts of appeals, also known as **circuit courts** of appeals, were created some 100 years after the *Marbury* decision, through the Judiciary Act of 1891. This law sought to relieve the heavy caseload that the U.S. Supreme Court faced after Congress had gradually expanded the jurisdiction of the federal courts to include criminal cases during the nineteenth century.

Until the advent of separate circuit courts of appeals, federal district court judges and even Supreme Court justices had needed to ride by horseback around the circuits to hear intermediate-level appeals cases. They sometimes traveled thousands of miles in a year in the practice, which became known as **circuit riding.** Over time, they began to bitterly bemoan the hardships they faced in servicing the geographically expanding country and the increasing case docket. But it took a long time for the states and their representatives in Congress to become convinced of the necessity of **courts of appeals**—courts that review previous decisions made by courts in the federal or state judicial system. These courts were charged exclusively with reviewing the application of law in previous court decisions rather than reviewing evidence or facts of the cases.

The Judiciary Act of 1891 divided the courts of appeals into nine geographic units, with each unit number corresponding to a circuit. The assumption in carving out these units was that each state should be grouped with states likely to have similar political cultures. Today, there are twelve courts of appeals covering designated regions, and the thirteenth hears specific kinds of cases, among them cases involving international trade, governmental contracts, and patents. By creating these separate courts of appeals, Congress significantly reduced the Supreme Court's workload: in 1890, 623 cases were filed with the Court, but just two years later, after passage of the Judiciary Act, that number fell by more than half, to 275. The act also eliminated the requirement of circuit riding, thus easing the burden on Supreme Court justices. Significantly, in using statutes rooted in the common-law tradition, the Congress itself was creating a relatively new form of law: code law.

The Basis of U.S. Law

U.S. law combines two different kinds of law: *common law,* which is made principally by judges reaching decisions in cases, and *code law,* enacted primarily by legislators (and often referred to as *statutory law*) and by chief executives.[7] Although the U.S. legal system has roots in a common-law system, most legal disputes today center on disagreements involving the interpretation of code law. In contrast, most other countries use *either* code law *or* common law—sometimes in combination with other kinds of law such as customary rules or religious law (see "Global Comparisons").

The Language of U.S. Law

Understanding the language of the U.S. legal system is tricky. What do all the names mean in these cases? Who is opposing whom? What determines where a case is being heard? What is meant by that commonly heard word *litigation*? Let's begin with the last question. **Litigation** refers to the process by which cases are brought and decided in the American legal system. Every court case has a title, and the title is the shorthand way of naming the main parties in a case. For example, in 2000 the U.S. Supreme Court decided the case *Bush v. Gore.* In this case George W. Bush (the first name in the case) is the **plaintiff,** that is, the person or organization bringing the case. Al Gore (the second name) is the **defendant,** the individual who is defending himself or herself against the plaintiff's accusation.

In the U.S. judicial system, there are two main types of cases. The first category, **civil law cases,** involve a conflict between private individuals in which the plaintiff alleges that some action or inaction by the defendant has caused harm to him or her. The second type, **criminal law cases,** are brought by the government or a prosecutor against a defendant, alleging that he or she has engaged in conduct resulting in injury to another person and that this injury is so significant, it harms not only the individual but also the larger society.

Because criminal cases are concerned with the breach of an obligation owed by the individual to the larger society, criminal cases always involve either a state government or the national government (though sometimes civil cases can involve a government entity). For example, when the baseball legend and home run–record breaker Barry Bonds was indicted for allegedly having lied to federal authorities investigating the sale of steroids, the criminal case was filed as *The United States of America v. Barry Lamar Bonds.* In contrast, civil cases typically pit individual against individual, as in *Kevin Federline v. Britney Spears,* a lawsuit involving the custody of the celebrities' two sons. Civil cases typically center on the breach of some obligation owed by one individual to another. The most common civil cases are concerned with the family, a contractual matter, or a negligent injury to a person or property (known as a **tort**).

The names in the case title may also reveal the stage of litigation. At the trial stage, the case names a plaintiff and a defendant. Subsequent changes in the order of names suggest that a case has moved to the appeals stage. To clarify: When one party believes that the trial court judge has misapplied or misinterpreted the law, that party has a right to appeal this decision to an appellate court. In the filing of this appeal, the names of the parties change. The party bringing the appeal becomes the **petitioner** (also called *appellant*) and is the first party named in a case name. The person arguing against the appeal becomes the **respondent** (also called *appellee*) and is the second name in the case title. For example, in 2005, when AT&T sued Microsoft in a patent dispute, the case was *AT&T Corp. v. Microsoft* and was heard in the U.S. District Court for the Southern District of New York. Microsoft later

litigation
the process by which cases are brought and decided in the American legal system

plaintiff
the party bringing the case to court

defendant
a person defending himself or herself against a plaintiff's accusation

civil law case
a conflict between private individuals in which the plaintiff alleges that some action or inaction by the defendant has resulted in harm to him or her

criminal law case
a case brought by the government or a prosecutor against a defendant, alleging that he or she has engaged in conduct resulting in injury to another person, and that this injury is so significant, it harms not only the individual but also the larger society

tort
a wrongful act involving a personal injury or harm to one's property or reputation

petitioner
also called *appellant;* the party seeking to have a lower court's decision reviewed by an appellate court

respondent
also called *appellee;* the party opposing the hearing of a case by an appellate court

GLOBAL COMPARISONS

LEGAL SYSTEMS AROUND THE WORLD

An examination of legal systems around the world reveals that different societies incorporate key beliefs, ideologies, and religious ideals in their legal structures and that they do so in a variety of ways. For example, China's legal system, founded on code law, embodies a cultural heritage and a socialist legal tradition that emphasize economic equality and the government's control and management of resources. The scope of Chinese law—the realms of life that the laws can regulate—is broad and reflects the importance of society over the individual. For instance, the Chinese government regulates how many children a couple can have, in order to ensure adequate resources—food, clothing, education—to support the country's massive population. The Chinese state mandates that most couples in urban areas have only one child, although those who produce a first-born daughter may sometimes have a second child (in the hope that it will be a son); in many rural areas, farming couples may have two children. These laws reflect the socialist influence on the legal system, with its wide scope of authority to regulate what most Americans would consider strictly private matters. The legal system also reveals aspects of the Chinese cultural heritage, such as the state's emphasis on the value of male offspring, who have a filial obligation to provide for their parents in old age.

*Will increasing global connections weaken traditional cultural foundations of law, such as tribal and religious law?

In contrast, many countries in Africa mix various tribal customs with code law. Sometimes these traditions complement one another, but at other times they conflict. Take Kenya, for example, home to the Luo tribal tradition of wife inheritance, in which a member of a dead man's family, typically a brother or an uncle, "inherits" the widow. This practice, which is legal in Kenya, conflicts with laws passed by the Kenyan legislature that allow a widow to inherit her husband's property. (Wife inheritance was traditionally a means by which a husband's family could keep all of his assets.)*

In many Islamic countries, such as Saudi Arabia, code law and the Islamic legal tradition coexist. In a Saudi Arabian case

> Laws in many African countries mix tribal customs such as wife inheritance with code law, often to the detriment of women's rights.

in 2007, for example, the law's dual basis called for the trial of men who were alleged to have raped a woman, but also dictated a lashing for the woman because she had violated Islamic law by being alone with a male who was not a family member.

When scholars talk about different systems of law, they mean not only the form that the law takes (that is, code law versus common law) but also the underlying principles and goals upon which the legal system is based. So for countries blending code law and the Islamic legal tradition, *religious law* (Shari'a) informs much of the civil and criminal code. In other societies, *custom* strongly influences the law and helps to fill in gaps in code law. In countries with a socialist legal tradition, law functions to advance the *economic system* and to offer *defense against external threats;* the protection of individual rights, the hallmark of many other code law countries, is far less important.

Do some research into the laws that are in place in China, Kenya, or Saudi Arabia to see how traditions, religion, and ideology influence the legal structure. The Global Legal Information Network (GLIN) is a database of the laws, regulations, and judicial decisions of other countries (www.glin.gov/search .action). GLIN allows you to search these laws thematically. The Library of Congress also hosts a Web site that indexes the laws of all countries at www.loc.gov/law/guide/nations.html. For example, you can investigate the legal system of Kenya at the Library of Congress's Kenya Law section (www.loc.gov/law/guide/kenya.html). Or look at some of the laws adopted in China to get a glimpse of how the Chinese socialist ideology influences the creation of law (www.loc.gov/law/guide/china.html).

* www.plusnews.org/Report.aspx?ReportId=72821.

appealed the decision to the U.S. Court of Appeals for the Federal Circuit and finally to the U.S. Supreme Court. In 2007, the Supreme Court heard *Microsoft* (appellant) *v. AT&T* (appellee), as Microsoft was appealing the district court's decision in favor of AT&T, which the appeals court had affirmed (the Supreme Court ruled in favor of Microsoft).

Common Law

Law created by courts through the cases they decide is called **common law,** and it binds all courts considering similar cases in the future. To understand how common law functions in the American legal system, consider the 2005 case of Terri Schiavo, the woman at the center of a very controversial debate about an individual's right to die. When Schiavo became ill and collapsed in 1990, her brain lost oxygen and she lapsed into what doctors call a persistent vegetative state, or PVS. A person in a PVS can breathe on his or her own but has very limited brain activity and requires artificial food and hydration. Terri remained in this terrible state for years. Then in 1998, Terri's husband, Michael Schiavo, asked a Florida state court to issue an order that would allow the discontinuance of artificial food and hydration. When the state court issued the order, Terri's family filed a motion to block the removal of the feeding tube. Over the next seven years, the disputing parties battled out the case of Terri Schiavo in the state and federal courts. The courts had to determine whether Terri would have wanted to terminate life support. This determination must have been difficult for the judges, who had to puzzle out Terri's intent by listening to her loved ones' testimony on Terri's comments, before her accident, about how she would have wanted to live if she were ever in such a state.

Competent individuals have a right to discontinue food and hydration without government interference. The Supreme Court recognized this right in the case *Cruzan v. Missouri Department of Health* (1990). The *Cruzan* case concerned Nancy Cruzan, who also was in a persistent vegetative state and for whom the family sought to discontinue food and hydration. The state of Missouri had intervened, arguing that the family had not provided sufficient evidence that Ms. Cruzan would have wanted this termination. Ultimately, however, the family prevailed.

The *Cruzan* case is important because it created new law. The Supreme Court's decision in this case established that the Constitution's due process clause, which states, "No state shall make or enforce any law which shall abridge the privileges or immunities of citizens of the United States; nor shall any state deprive any person of life, liberty, or property, without due process of law," protected the right to discontinue food and hydration. This right was assumed in the *Schiavo* case. The courts were not trying to puzzle out whether Terri Schiavo had the right to discontinue food and hydration, as *Cruzan* had already established this right. Instead, the judicial deliberations focused solely on whether this was a choice that Terri herself would have made if she had been competent.[8] The law that established the right to discontinue food and hydration is now part of U.S. common law.

HISTORICAL BASIS OF COMMON LAW   England began using the common law as a means of unifying the country after the Norman invasion of 1066. In the 1100s, local courts began to write down this national, or "common," law to make it easy to use. Nobles soon realized that the law might be applied to limiting the power of the king and could protect the nobles against unfair and arbitrary actions by the monarchy. Most significant in the creation of common law was the Magna Carta ("Great Charter") of 1215, the first document to list the rights and protections granted to individuals in England. The Magna Carta is one of the core documents in the evolution of constitutional law.

In the common-law system, the jury provides a key check on the powers of the government. The English colonists of North America and later the framers of the Constitution embraced the right to a jury trial. This right rests on the belief that a jury of one's peers is best able to place itself in the shoes of the accused and to make a determination about whether a wrong has been committed. Serving on a jury, like voting in an election or volunteering for an interest group, is an important form of citizen engagement.

THE PRINCIPLE OF *STARE DECISIS*   In the evolution of the American judicial system, the colonists relied on the principle of *stare decisis,* a Latin phrase that means "let the

common law

law made by judges who decide cases and articulate legal principles in their opinions; based on the British system

stare decisis
from the Latin "let the decision stand," the principle that binds judges to rely upon the holdings of past judges in deciding cases

precedent
legal authority established by earlier cases

code law
laws created by legislators to regulate the behavior of individuals and organizations

decision stand." ***Stare decisis*** means that in deciding cases, judges must abide by the legal **precedent,** that is, the legal authority that earlier cases established, even in the instance of laws handed down hundreds of years before and in a society that was far different. The principle of *stare decisis* ensures that common law is not very quick to change. *Stare decisis* also ensures a consistency of legal expectations for individuals and the legal community. Common law was the predominant form of law in the United States in the nineteenth century.

Code Law

By the early twentieth century, rapid changes in society and the economy demanded much faster responses in the law than what common law could provide. Legislators in Congress and the states responded to these changes by creating laws to regulate the behavior of individuals and organizations and to deal with a vast array of new issues. The kind of law they developed is known as **code law.**

A similar, continuously changing social environment prevails today. Because of the steady flow of change and the fast pace of contemporary life, particularly due to nonstop technological advances, the prior body of law has become inadequate to deal with unprecedented developments in commerce, communication, and even crime. In creating code law responsive to these new realities, legislators have had to become more knowledgeable and specialized about the topics of the laws they write. They have had to rely heavily on experts—police attempting to enforce laws; business and industry leaders; other specialists—to help shape how laws are written.

Code law functions very differently from common law. When legislatures or executives make law, they can move quickly in response to some pressing crisis or problem. They can decide to change course and even take a totally unprecedented approach to a situation. Consider how quickly Congress and President George W. Bush acted in response to the terrorist strikes on the United States on September 11, 2001. Within one month of the attacks, Congress had passed the first USA PATRIOT Act, which significantly broadened the investigative and prosecutory powers of federal and state law enforcement officials. Within six months, President Bush had proposed a new federal agency, the Office of Homeland Security; called for the radical restructuring of federal administrative agencies; and issued an executive order establishing the use of military tribunals in cases involving enemy noncombatants. The swift and dramatic response of governmental agencies in the wake of 9/11 exemplifies how the government can use code law proactively to deal with a situation as it unfolds.

Sources of U.S. Law

We have seen that code law and common law coexist in the United States and that judges, legislators, and presidents all contribute to lawmaking. What's more, these officials often cooperate in the lawmaking enterprise, interacting to clarify ambiguous provisions in the code law or to apply the common law to more specific situations. These lawmakers collectively create law that is distinct, but they do so in different ways, as we consider in this discussion.

In this section we examine the five different sources of laws in the United States:

- the U.S. and state constitutions
- statutes
- judicial decisions
- executive orders
- administrative and regulatory law

These sources differ not only in terms of who makes the law, but also in their place in the hierarchy of the U.S. legal system. Moreover, lawmakers create law not only at the national level but in all fifty state governments as well.

The Federal and State Constitutions

Atop the hierarchy of the sources of U.S. law are constitutions—the U.S. Constitution and the constitutions of the fifty states. Constitutions are the highest form of law, taking precedence over all other laws, and they are the primary organizational blueprint for the federal and state governments. Constitutions delineate the powers of the government and the limitations on those powers. They also establish the structure and function of each of the branches—executive, legislative, and judicial—and define the relationship between the federal and state governments and between the government and the individual.

The body of law that comes out of the courts in cases involving constitutional interpretation is known as **constitutional law.** In cases concerning a provision of the federal Constitution, the high court is the U.S. Supreme Court, and its decisions bind all Americans, including Congress and the president.

If the president or the members of Congress do not like the outcome of a particular case, they may test the Supreme Court's ruling by passing a law challenging the decision. (In the instance of state high court cases, a governor or the state legislature can take a similar action.) Legislatures and executives also may try to circumvent a Court decision by changing the law through a constitutional amendment. For example, since 1963, some members of Congress have sought to blunt the impact of a series of Supreme Court decisions establishing that prayer in public schools violates the Constitution's separation of church and state. These legislators have introduced into the House and Senate various constitutional amendments that would allow vocal prayer or mandate a "moment of silence" in public schools. None of these proposed amendments has garnered the two-thirds supermajority vote in Congress necessary to move the amendment to the next stage in the ratification process. Yet some representatives in Congress continue to seek to negate the Court's decision by amending the Constitution.

constitutional law
the body of law that comes out of the courts in cases involving the interpretation of the Constitution

Statutes

Laws written by legislatures are called **statutes.** Statutory lawmaking is the hallmark of any code law system. In such a system, legislative law reflects the core principles of the government system. For example, the **U.S. Code** is a compilation of all the laws ever passed by the U.S. Congress, and it reflects this body's priorities and concerns. The U.S. Code has fifty sections spanning a range of issues including agriculture, bankruptcy, highways, the postal service, and war and defense.

statute
a law enacted by Congress or state legislatures to deal with particular issues or problems, sometimes more detailed and comprehensive than the common law

U.S. Code
a compilation of all the laws passed by the U.S. Congress

Judicial Decisions

When a judge or a panel of judges decide a case, they sometimes write an opinion that justifies their decision and explains how they have applied principles of *stare decisis*. These judicial opinions then become part of the common law.

Under what circumstances do judges write an opinion? To answer that question, we must consider the resources for appealing cases on the federal and state levels. The federal court system comprises two levels of appeals, or appellate, court: the circuit courts of appeals, previously described, and the U.S. Supreme Court, which has the final say in cases. The state systems generally feature two appeals levels, and the final appellate court is the court of last resort, performing much the same function as the U.S. Supreme Court.[9] Judges serving in *courts of last resort*—that is, the U.S. Supreme Court and the state high courts—almost always write opinions in cases, and these opinions have the force of law. The Supreme Court's decisions govern all similar cases heard in all the federal courts and become the law of the land; a state high court's decisions become law in that state.

Executive Orders

Article II, Section 1, of the U.S. Constitution states that "the executive power shall be vested in [the] president of the United States." This power has been interpreted to allow the president to issue orders that create and guide the bureaucracy in implementing policy.

Because executive orders have the force and effect of law, they represent a crucial tool in the president's lawmaking tool box. Historically, presidents have sometimes used executive orders to create policy that may not have garnered sufficient legislative support. For example, Chapter 12 describes President Harry Truman's use of executive orders to desegregate the military in 1948.

A president or governor can enact an executive order without input from the other branches of government, though executive orders are subject to judicial review and depend on Congress for funding. As described in Chapter 12, President Bush used executive orders extensively to address a wide range of issues. These included prohibiting new investment in Burma to punish that nation's repressive regime and improving the coordination and effectiveness of bureaucracies administering youth programs in the United States.[10]

Administrative Law

In addition to the executive order, presidents and governors have another source of lawmaking power: they head a vast bureaucracy of agencies that have their own lawmaking authority. As we saw in Chapter 13, bureaucrats get their power directly from the Congress or the state legislatures. By delegating significant power to bureaucratic administrators with expertise in specific policy areas, Congress and the state legislatures help to ensure the effective implementation of the laws they pass.

Why, specifically, must legislators delegate such power? The reason is that lawmakers typically write vague or ambiguous bills. They do so to increase the chances that representatives and senators with differing ideologies will find a given bill acceptable for passage into law. But the result of vague or ambiguous wording might be that the law, once passed, is difficult to implement. Thus legislators must turn to bureaucrats with expertise and specialized knowledge to help them to administer the law.

This delegation of authority gives administrators substantial power. It allows them to act as quasi- ("as if") legislators in creating administrative rules, implementing them, and interpreting those rules as well. Administrative rule-making fleshes out the broad principles in the statutory law, much of which is interpreted by the federal courts.

The Federal Court System

Article III of the Constitution created only one court—the Supreme Court—and left it to Congress to create any additional federal courts that the country might need. As we saw earlier in this chapter, Congress responded with a series of laws that created inferior (or lower) courts in the form of federal district courts and federal appellate courts (or courts of appeals).

In addition to these constitutionally and legislatively created courts, each state has its own independent state court system structured by state constitutions. Because the U.S. judicial system has both federal and state courts,

Concept Summary

SOURCES OF LAW IN THE UNITED STATES

Federal and State Constitutions

— Constitutions are the highest form of law.

— They outline the structure of the federal and state governments.

— They delineate the powers of the government and the limitations on those powers.

Statutes

— Statutes are laws created through the legislative process.

— Statutes create the code law system.

— They reflect the core principles of the government system.

Judicial Decisions

— Judicial decisions are based on the principle of *stare decisis*.

— They include an opinion that justifies a judge's decision.

— Judicial opinions then become part of the common law.

Executive Orders

— The authority to issue an executive order is the law-making power held by presidents and governors.

— The U.S. and state constitutions grant this power.

Administrative Law

— Administrative law centers on rule-making authority that legislators grant to bureaucrats.

— Administrative law allows bureaucrats to act as quasi-legislators in creating, implementing, and interpreting administrative rules.

it is said to be a **dual court system.** Figure 14.1 shows that nearly every case, whether tried in a federal or state court, originates in a **trial court**—the court in which a case is first heard and which determines the facts of a case.[11]

Jurisdiction of Federal Courts

The ability of a court to hear a case depends on whether that court has **jurisdiction**—the authority of a court to hear and decide a case. Federal jurisdiction is strictly defined by Article III, Section 2, of the Constitution. In this passage, federal courts are empowered to hear only cases involving a federal question or a diversity of citizenship. A **federal question** is a question of law based on interpretation of the U.S. Constitution, federal laws, or treaties. **Diversity of citizenship** means that the parties in the case are individuals from different states or that the case involves a U.S. citizen and a foreign government. It may also mean that the suit centers on the complaint of one or more states against another state or states.

When a court has **original jurisdiction** over a case, that court is the first court to hear the case—no other court has yet considered the legal issues in this case. In instances of original jurisdiction, the court must decide what happened in the case and must apply the existing law to resolve the dispute. In contrast, **appellate jurisdiction** empowers a court to review the decision of the court that has already heard a case. Usually, the appellate court is called upon to decide not what happened but rather whether the first court correctly applied or interpreted the law.

In the federal courts, the federal district courts have original jurisdiction in most cases. The U.S. courts of appeals handle first-level appeals of decisions made in those federal district courts. Most cases that reach the Supreme Court come to it under its appellate jurisdiction.

The Structure of the Federal Courts

The U.S. court system is a dual system in two ways. First, as noted above, parallel federal and state court systems operate largely independently of each other and make law in specific areas. Second, each of these systems has both trial courts and appellate courts. In the brief discussions that follow, we consider the different kinds of courts in the federal system.

FEDERAL DISTRICT COURTS The federal judiciary is structured hierarchically, similar to a pyramid. There are ninety-four federal district courts at the bottom of this pyramid. These are the trial courts in this system, and they do much of the work of the federal judiciary. The function of trial courts is straightforward: judges or juries decide what happened in a case and then apply the law. For example, in a terrorism case, the judge or the jury assesses whether the defendant is guilty of committing acts of terror as defined by federal law. If the defendant is found guilty, the court then looks to the law to impose a penalty. Federal district courts operate throughout the United States; every state must have at least one.

U.S. COURTS OF APPEALS At the middle level of the federal judicial pyramid are thirteen courts of appeals. As Figure 14.2 shows, twelve of these courts cover specific regions (circuits) plus the Federal Circuit located in the District of Columbia. The thirteenth court

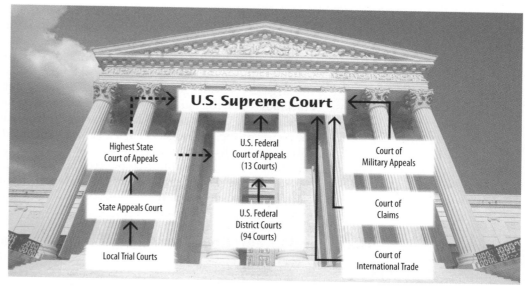

FIGURE 14.1

The U.S. Court System

dual court system
a two-part judicial system such as that of the United States, which has both federal and state courts

trial court
the court in which a case is first heard and which determines the facts of a case

jurisdiction
The power of a court to hear a case and to resolve it, given to a court by either a constitution or a statute

federal question
A question of law based on interpretation of the U.S. Constitution, federal laws, or treaties

diversity of citizenship
The circumstance in which the parties in a legal case are from different states or the case involves a U.S. citizen and a foreign government

original jurisdiction
the power of a court to hear a case first, before other courts have decided it

appellate jurisdiction
the authority of a court to review the decision reached by another court in a case

of appeals covers specific kinds of cases, involving such matters as international trade, government contracts, and patents. Congress has authorized 179 judgeships for these courts of appeals, though typically there are vacancies.

The size of each circuit varies depending on the size of the court's constituency and its caseload. Today, the smallest circuit is the First Circuit, which consists of six judgeships; the largest, the Ninth, has twenty-eight.[12] Each circuit court of appeals is supervised by a chief judge. The chief judge is the individual on the bench who has the most seniority but is under age 65. The judges who hear a case typically include a three-judge panel made up of the courts of appeals judges. They are sometimes joined by visiting judges (usually from the corresponding federal district of the court of appeals) and retired judges. In deciding cases, the judges read briefs submitted by lawyers, which argue their clients' case, and then hear oral arguments. During this process, no new facts are admitted into evidence; instead, the court of appeals focuses on questions of procedure or the application of law that occurred in a decision of the lower court.

The Federal Circuit Courts of Appeals

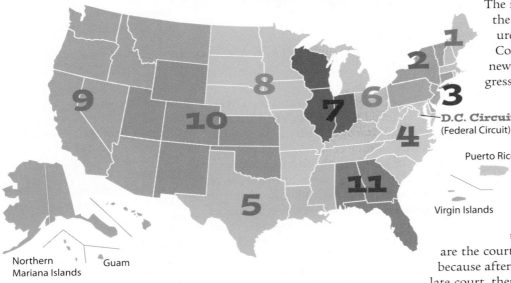

POLITICAL INQUIRY

FIGURE 14.2 ■ **How many U.S. circuit courts of appeals are there today? What are the circuits (regions) they cover, and what determines the size of each circuit? What kinds of cases does an additional, special court of appeals (not shown in the map) cover?**

The Judiciary Act of 1891 carved out only nine geographic units for the courts of appeals. The increased number of circuit courts to the thirteen of the present day (see Figure 14.2) through a process by which Congress split up existing circuits. Each new division has typically reflected Congress's desire to keep together states with similar legal and political cultures.

Courts of appeals have no original jurisdiction—that is, these courts do not decide the facts of a case. Rather, as appellate courts, they review the legal procedures of a preceding case and decide whether the law was applied appropriately given the facts already admitted into evidence. Courts of appeals are the courts of last resort for most federal cases because after a case has been decided by the appellate court, there is no automatic right to an appeal. Although some cases may be appealed to the U.S. Supreme Court, the Court ultimately chooses to hear only a small fraction of these.

SPECIAL COURTS In addition to the federal district courts and the courts of appeals, Congress, acting under Article I of the Constitution, created several specialized courts. These include the Court of International Trade, the U.S. Court of Military Appeals, the U.S. Tax Court, and the U.S. Court of Veterans' Appeals.

Recent media coverage has highlighted the activities of another kind of specialized court, the Foreign Intelligence Surveillance Act (FISA) court. It was established by Congress in a 1978 act that spells out the procedures for the collection of human and electronic intelligence.[13] During the George W. Bush administration, FISA courts were charged with determining whether an individual could be subject to warrantless surveillance of his or her communications (see Chapter 4).

FISA courts are evidence of a notable trend in how the judicial branch is coping with the growing complexity of the types of cases that come before the courts. This trend involves increasing specialization, both by law, as in the creation of special courts such as FISA courts, and by practice, as when judges develop an "informal" expertise in a policy area—say, DNA testing or software patent law. Legal scholar Lawrence Baum assesses this trend as an effort by the courts to gain and apply the kind of expertise characteristic of the administrative agencies of the government:

> Whether judicial specialization is established by law or develops in practice, it reflects an effort to gain the perceived strengths of administrative agencies while retaining the form and name of the courts. The efficiency and expertise that are ascribed to specialization can help courts keep up with their caseloads and perhaps improve the quality of decision-making.[14]

Although this specialization may occur in both state and federal courts, it is not possible for the highest court in the land, the U.S. Supreme Court, to limit its expertise.

THE U.S. SUPREME COURT WITHIN THE FEDERAL SYSTEM At the top of the federal judicial pyramid sits the U.S. Supreme Court. Although this court has a very limited original jurisdiction (which we examine later in this chapter), it hears appeals from both the federal and the state courts when cases decided there concern a federal constitutional question or when federal law is involved.

Nine judges, called **justices,** sit on the Supreme Court. One of these justices has been specially selected by the president to serve as the **chief justice,** the judge who provides both organizational and intellectual leadership on the Court. The chief justice has the same voting power as the other justices, called the associate justices. But he or she has an important, distinctive role in the decision-making process. When the chief justice agrees with the majority, he or she chooses whether to write the majority opinion or assign it to another justice. The current chief justice is John Roberts, whom President George W. Bush appointed in 2005.

Changing Caseloads: Fraud on the Internet

	THEN (2001)*	NOW (2007)**
Number of complaints processed by the federal government's Internet Fraud Complaint Center and referred to law enforcement agencies	33,940	90,008
Cumulative losses by victims of cybercrimes whose cases were processed by the federal government's Internet Fraud Complaint Center	$17.8 million	$239.1 million
Top three reported offenses	Internet auction fraud (63%)	Internet auction fraud (36%)
	General merchandise sales (11%)	Nondelivery of purchased goods (25%)
	Nigerian money offers (9%)	Confidence fraud (7%)

WHAT'S NEXT?

> Have you been, or do you know anyone who has been, a victim of Internet fraud?

> Will cyberfraud continue to grow, in keeping with the present trend? What will be the impact of any growth on the court system?

> What new forms might Internet crime take in the future?

* www.ic3.gov/media/annualreport/2001_IFCCReport.pdf.
** www.ic3.gov/media/annualreport/2007-IC3Report.pdf.

Selecting Judges for the Federal Bench

On July 19, 2005, President George W. Bush announced his nomination for the seat that had been occupied by Supreme Court Justice Sandra Day O'Connor, who retired at the end of the Court's 2004–2005 term. The president and many others had long anticipated a retirement on the Court, where no vacancies had opened up for more than a decade. Bush named circuit court of appeals judge John Roberts to fill the vacancy created by O'Connor's retirement. Then, shortly after the Roberts nomination, Chief Justice William Rehnquist died. Suddenly, Bush had to look for a successor to Rehnquist, who had served on the Court since 1972. The president decided to elevate Roberts's nomination to that of chief justice, and the Senate overwhelmingly confirmed him with a vote of 78–22.

justice
any of the nine judges who sit on the Supreme Court

chief justice
the leading justice on the Supreme Court, who provides both organizational and intellectual leadership

> Former Supreme Court Justice Sandra Day O'Connor was the first woman appointed to the high court. Chief Justice John Roberts was nominated to replace her upon her retirement, but then President George W. Bush appointed Roberts as chief justice upon the death of William Rehnquist. Roberts and O'Connor both attended Rehnquist's funeral in 2005.

senatorial courtesy

A custom that allows senators from the president's political party to veto the president's choice of federal district court judge in the senator's state

Once federal court judges are confirmed by the Senate, they serve for life, as long as they do not commit any impeachable offenses. This lifetime tenure is controversial (see "The Conversation of Democracy"). Chief Justice Roberts, who was appointed at the age of 50—and, assuming good health, who likely will serve on the Court for more than thirty years—will probably be the longest-lasting legacy of the Bush administration.

The Senate's Role in Appointment and Confirmation

The president and the Senate share power in the selection of federal court judges and Supreme Court justices. In this way, the nomination and confirmation process serves as a check on the respective powers of the presidency and the Senate.

In the case of the federal district court judges, a custom known as **senatorial courtesy** gives senators—though only those who are of the same political party as the president—a powerful voice in choosing the district court judges who will serve in their state. Under this tradition, a senator from the same political party as the president can veto the president's choice of a federal district court judge in the senator's state.

Because circuit courts of appeals judges and Supreme Court justices serve more than one state, the individual senators from any one state play a far less powerful role in the appointment of these judges than they do in the selection of district court judges. Rather, in the selection procedure for circuit court judges and U.S. Supreme Court justices, the Senate Judiciary Committee, composed of eighteen senators, takes the lead. Committee members are charged with gathering information about each nominee and providing it to the full Senate. The Senate Judiciary Committee also typically votes on the nominee, and the full Senate uses this vote to signal whether the nominee is acceptable. Sometimes the judiciary committee does not make a recommendation about a candidate, as when members split their vote 7–7 on the nomination of Clarence Thomas to be a U.S. Supreme Court justice in 1991.

Judicial Competence

Just as political service is a key to becoming a successful federal district court nominee, so competence is of central concern for nominees to the circuit courts of appeals and the Supreme Court. Appeals court judges and Supreme Court justices first and foremost must be qualified, and some nominees in recent decades have been rejected because of senatorial doubts about their qualifications. The Senate rejected two nominees of President Richard Nixon because of such concerns. And when President George W. Bush nominated his White House counsel Harriet Miers as an associate Supreme Court justice in 2005, he was forced to withdraw his nomination because of concerns about Miers's lack of qualifications. These objections strongly indicated that Miers would face a steep uphill climb in achieving Senate confirmation. (Some in the media argued, however, that the questions about Miers's competence were in part a political smoke screen—a ploy by certain conservative Republican senators who would be voting on her nomination to reject the Republican nominee because her ideological outlook may not have been conservative enough for them.[15])

Ideology and Selection to the Bench

Once the Senate establishes the competence of a circuit court or Supreme Court candidate, attention shifts to the nominee's ideology—his or her worldview. Mindful that federal judges typically serve far beyond their own tenure, presidents often regard these nominations as

SHOULD THERE BE A CONSTITUTIONAL AMENDMENT MANDATING A RETIREMENT AGE FOR SUPREME COURT JUSTICES?

The Issue: Some states require top judges to retire at age 70 or 75, but a Supreme Court justice has a lifetime tenure. Thus a Supreme Court justice can potentially serve well beyond the age at which most people retire from their professional lives. In 2006, Justice Sandra Day O'Connor stepped down from the Court at age 76. But O'Connor was an exception. For example, Oliver Wendell Holmes Jr. retired at age 90. At 88, John Paul Stevens continues to sit on the Court. Chief Justice William Rehnquist presided until his death at age 80 in 2005. Such precedents—given the cognitive and physical problems generally associated with old age—have given rise to questions about the wisdom of allowing justices to serve on the Supreme Court for life. Some Americans believe that the country needs a constitutional amendment to mandate a specific retirement age for the justices. Others outright disagree, although some of these naysayers propose alternative means of ensuring judicial competence.

Should there be a constitutional amendment mandating a retirement age for Supreme Court justices? Here is what the various camps have to say.

Yes: The country needs a constitutional amendment that modifies the framers' specification of a life term for Supreme Court justices. Relevant is the work of legal scholar David J. Garrow. His research on Supreme Court justices' "mental decrepitude" has emphasized that many former Supreme Court justices themselves, including Earl Warren and Potter Stewart, did not oppose a constitutional amendment limiting tenure to age 75—*if* such an age limit were imposed on members of Congress and the president as well. Moreover, in *Gregory v. Ashcroft* (1991), which addressed the constitutionality of a mandatory retirement age of 70 for state court judges, Justice Sandra Day O'Connor opined that a mandatory retirement age of 70 could be in the public interest.*

No: A constitutional amendment requiring a mandatory retirement age for Supreme Court justices constitutes age discrimination. Such an amendment violates the framers' intentions, as the Constitution explicitly states that justices may serve for life. Through such an amendment, the United States would lose the expertise, wisdom, and perspective of older jurists. Thus the Constitution should not be amended to set a specific age for retirement from the Court.

Other approaches: A constitutional amendment that would apply across the board to all Supreme Court justices, regardless of their health status, denies citizens the invaluable experience of some older justices whose health may not be in decline.

Society can address the challenge of ensuring competence on the Court by other means. For example, the ever-watchful media could publicize the behaviors of justices whose health seems to be impeding their ability to perform their duties. In addition, or alternatively, Congress could aggressively monitor the mental and physical health of Supreme Court justices by requiring the justices to provide health information to a special congressional monitoring committee.

What do you think?

① Do the potential advantages of preventing an elderly, mentally diminished Supreme Court justice from serving outweigh the benefits (wisdom, experience, and so on) that might come from the continued service of this jurist or other aging justices? Explain.

② Should the country pass a constitutional amendment setting a mandatory retirement age for Supreme Court justices? Why or why not?

③ What alternative solutions beyond those proposed in the "Conversation" might address the problem of ensuring competence on the Court?

* *Gregory v. Ashcroft*, 501 U.S. 452 (1991).

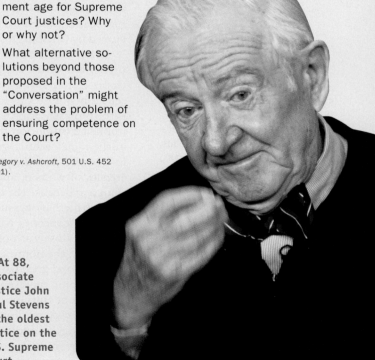

> At 88, Associate Justice John Paul Stevens is the oldest justice on the U.S. Supreme Court.

Diversity on the Supreme Court

Do you think the president should consider gender and racial diversity when naming a potential Supreme Court judge to the bench?

☐ Should consider

☐ Should not consider

Source: Newsweek Poll/Princeton Survey Research Associates International, www.pollingreport.com/court2.htm.

symbolic representation
the attempt to ensure that the Supreme Court includes representatives of major demographic groups, such as women, African Americans, Jews, and Catholics

a way of cementing their own legacies. They give the nod to judges, and more significantly, to Supreme Court justices, with whom they are ideologically compatible. When George W. Bush nominated John Roberts, he chose an individual who shared the president's own policy views, particularly with regard to issues such as abortion, church and state relations, and criminal due process protections.

A Supreme Court justice's (and a circuit court judge's) ideology can shift over time, however. President Richard Nixon selected Justice Harry Blackmun to serve on the Supreme Court because of Blackmun's conservative record in deciding cases involving civil rights and civil liberties. But Blackmun, who authored the Court's opinion in *Roe v. Wade*—the decision guaranteeing a woman's right to abortion—and who was a vocal critic of capital punishment once seated on the Court, was a serious disappointment to Nixon. Still, in most instances, a justice's worldview remains fairly constant. Justices' ideologies are reinforced by the presence of stable ideological blocs on the Supreme Court, which may bolster long-held beliefs and discourage the rethinking of issues from a completely new perspective. This reality underscores why the nomination and confirmation process is so important: the president and the Senate are banking on their assumption that the nominee's demonstrated ideology or perspective will color how he or she sees issues and cases that come before the Court in the future.[16]

Representation of Demographic Groups

When President George H. W. Bush nominated Clarence Thomas, an African American, to the Supreme Court, the justice whom Thomas would be replacing was the retiring jurist Thurgood Marshall, the first African American judge appointed to the Court (by President Lyndon Johnson, in 1967).[17] As noted at the beginning of the chapter, Marshall had argued the groundbreaking case *Brown v. Board of Education* (1954), which desegregated U.S. schools. Even though the federal courts effectively underrepresent the population at large, because judges are overwhelmingly male, white, Protestant, and upper middle class, the current Supreme Court has a relatively diverse composition. In recent decades, an informal demographic composition of the Court has evolved with an African American seat (currently occupied by Associate Justice Clarence Thomas), a Jewish seat (both Associate Justices Stephen Breyer and Ruth Bader Ginsburg are Jewish), a Roman Catholic seat (now actually several such seats, with Chief Justice John Roberts and Associate Justices Anthony Kennedy, Antonin Scalia, Clarence Thomas, and Samuel Alito all being Catholic), and a woman's seat (occupied by Ginsburg).

Given that Latinos are the fastest-growing ethnic group in the U.S. population, there is pressure to create a Latino seat on the Court as well. The appointment of a Latino Supreme Court justice is thus likely in the near future. The impulse to recognize specific seats that reflect major groups in the population serves the goal of **symbolic representation,** which is the representation on the Court of the country's leading demographic groups. There is an implicit assumption that a justice occupying one of these seats will best serve the concerns of the racial, ethnic, gender, or other group to which he or she belongs. That is, the Latino justice will take the perspective of Latinos, the female justice will consider the policy preferences of women, and so on. In fact, however, the representation may be more symbolic than real because the issues of importance to Latinos, women, or any other group are hardly monolithic. These issues are so multidimensional that no one person could speak for all the members' concerns. Nevertheless, many public figures and citizens say that the Court should mirror as closely as possible the main contours of the national demographic profile.

Clearly, the nomination and confirmation of federal judges does not take place in a vacuum. Beyond presidents' and senators' concerns about judicial qualifications, ideology, and demographic representation, these players are acutely aware of what their constituencies will think of any nominee and of what might happen at the confirmation hearings. For this reason they continuously gauge public opinion throughout the nomination and confirmation process. In addition to being mindful of the voters, the president and the senators calculate how interest groups, particularly those that helped to put them in office, will view the nominee. In nominating John Roberts, George W. Bush sought to ensure that his nominee would be acceptable to one of his core constituencies, conservative voters.

Interest groups often have a significant voice in the confirmation hearings. Some groups almost always participate in the hearings, among them the American Bar Association, labor and civil rights organizations, law enforcement groups, and business interests. These groups do not hesitate to let the members of the Senate Judiciary Committee know clearly whether they support or oppose a given candidate.

The U.S. Supreme Court Today

The decisions of the U.S. Supreme Court's nine justices are binding on all other courts in the country, and no other court may overturn them. Decision making on the Court is a multistep process that provides many opportunities for conflict and compromise. As a **collegial court,** which means it is made up of a panel of justices, Supreme Court justices must work closely together as they navigate the process. The need for compromise on the Court is especially intense because of the sheer number of cases it hears and the fact that its decisions are final.

collegial court
a court made up of a group of judges who must evaluate a case together and decide on the outcome; significant compromise and negotiation take place as members try to build a majority coalition

The Supreme Court's Jurisdiction

In the vast majority of cases, the Supreme Court is reviewing a decision made by a lower court rather than exercising original jurisdiction. The framers limited the Supreme Court's original jurisdiction to only those cases that concern ambassadors, public ministers, and consuls, and those involving two or more states. But over time, Congress, in cooperation with the Court, has decided that the Court should retain original jurisdiction only in cases involving suits between two or more states.

>The current U.S. Supreme Court. Front from left are Associate Justices Anthony Kennedy and John Paul Stevens, Chief Justice John Roberts, and Associate Justices Antonin Scalia and David Souter. Top from left are Associate Justices Stephen Breyer, Clarence Thomas, Ruth Bader Ginsburg, and Samuel Alito.

Choosing Cases for Review

Approximately 7,000 petitions are filed with the Court each year, each asking for the review of a case already decided. Each case is one that a party or parties are appealing from some other court because one or both sides dispute the decision in the case. Ultimately, the justices write decisions in only 80 to 90 cases, however. How do they decide which cases to hear? Like the other stages of the decision-making process, "deciding to decide," as Supreme Court scholar H. W. Perry puts it, is a joint activity.[18]

The decision to place a case on the Supreme Court's agenda is a collaborative one. Important in this process is the role of Supreme Court clerks. These young lawyers, who are recommended for the positions by certain "feeder professors" at selective law schools, are charged with drafting a **pool memo,** a description of the facts of the case, the pertinent legal arguments, and a recommendation as to whether the case should be taken.

The chief justice distributes a list of selected cases, the **discuss list,** to the other justices before a regularly scheduled conference. A chief justice's decision as to whether to include a given case on the discuss list is primarily based on review of the Supreme Court clerks' pool memos. On Fridays throughout the Court's term, which lasts from October to June, the justices meet in conference to discuss the cases on the list.[19] At this point, they vote on whether to issue a writ of *certiorari*—a Latin term roughly translated as "a request to make certain"—for specific cases. The **writ of *certiorari*** is a higher court's order to a lower court to make available the records of a past case so that the higher court can determine whether mistakes were made during the lower court trial that would justify a review of the case.[20] The writ of *certiorari* falls within the Court's discretionary jurisdiction, meaning that the Court can choose whether to hear such cases (unlike those cases that have a mandatory appeal to the U.S. Supreme Court).

The justices determine whether they will consider a case according to a practice known as the **Rule of Four,** under which the justices will hear a case if four or more of nine justices decide they want to hear it. They do not need to give reasons for wanting or not wanting to hear a case—they simply must vote. The vast majority of the cases the Court hears reach the justices through a writ of *certiorari*, reflecting its role as primarily an appellate court.

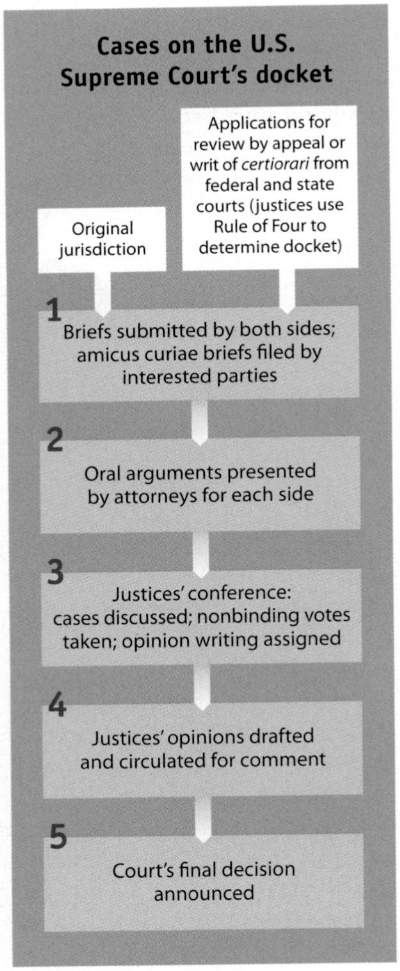

On the Docket: Considering the Case

When a case makes its way onto the Court docket, the parties in the litigation shift into high gear (see Figure 14.3). The petitioner (the party that sought the Court's review in the first place) usually has forty-five days to file a written **brief**—a document detailing the legal argument for the desired outcome—with the Court. After the filing of this brief, the opposing party, the respondent, has thirty days to file its own brief with the Court.

Today, *amicus curiae* briefs are a common part of Supreme Court litigation. Filed within a specified time period by a person or group that is not party to the lawsuit, an ***amicus curiae* brief,** or **"friend of the court" brief,** is a document that aims to influence the Court's decision. Some cases trigger the filing of many *amicus* briefs; the largest number of such briefs (ninety) ever filed in a Supreme Court case came in two cases involving affirmative action at the University of Michigan.[21]

pool memo
description written by Court clerks of the facts of a case filed with the Court, the pertinent legal arguments, and a recommendation as to whether the case should be taken

discuss list
compiled by the chief justice, the list of cases on review that he thinks may be appropriate for the Court to hear

writ of *certiorari*
latin for "a request to make certain"; this is an order to a lower court to produce a certified record of a case so that the appellate court can determine whether any errors occurred during trial that warrant review of the case

Rule of Four
practice by which the Supreme Court justices determine if they will hear a case if four or more justices want to hear it

brief
a document detailing the legal argument for the desired outcome in a court case

***amicus curiae* brief ("friend of the court" brief)**
document submitted by parties interested in a certain case or issue in an attempt to provide the Court with information that may be used to decide the case

Cases on the U.S. Supreme Court's docket

Original jurisdiction

Applications for review by appeal or writ of *certiorari* from federal and state courts (justices use Rule of Four to determine docket)

1 Briefs submitted by both sides; amicus curiae briefs filed by interested parties

2 Oral arguments presented by attorneys for each side

3 Justices' conference: cases discussed; nonbinding votes taken; opinion writing assigned

4 Justices' opinions drafted and circulated for comment

5 Court's final decision announced

FIGURE 14.3

Decision Making on the Supreme Court

DOING DEMOCRACY

FILE AN AMICUS CURIAE *BRIEF TO BRING ABOUT A POLICY CHANGE*

FACT:

You have probably heard some version of the cliché that Americans are "sue happy"—likely to file a lawsuit for even the most trivial inconvenience. Although Americans are more litigious than most other nationalities, the reality is that the U.S. legal system offers a bona fide method by which individuals can take steps to change policies they disagree with. It was citizens' lawsuits that ended school segregation, supported the freedom of the press, and clarified the nation's laws on many issues of high social importance, such as abortion, affirmative action, and the death penalty.

Act!

Kenyon College senior Matthew Segal understands that in making a decision in a case, judges consider its impact broadly because they recognize that the decision has policy consequences beyond the interests of plaintiffs and defendants. One way in which judges come to understand the larger influence of their decisions is by reading *amicus curiae* briefs, filed as testimony assessing the impact of a court ruling on various individuals or groups. Segal is the founder of the Student Association for Voter Empowerment, one of several youth organizations that recently filed an *amicus* brief with the U.S. Supreme Court. These briefs argued that an Indiana law requiring voter identification at the polls will place an unfair burden on young people, especially college students who move frequently.* In arguing cases with broad implications, some legal organizations seek out individuals, communities, and organizations (such as Segal's student association) that will be affected by pending litigation. In this way, legal professionals inform the courts about the potential effects of judicial rulings.

Where to begin

If you would like to investigate taking part in the filing of an *amicus* brief in regard to a court case of interest to you, start with these resources:

- **www.mountainstateslegal.org/index.cfm** The Mountain States Legal Foundation is a conservative organization interested in litigation involving access to federal land, environmental laws, limited and ethical government, private property issues, constitutional liberties, and freedom of enterprise.

- **www.aclu.org/scotus/index.html** The American Civil Liberties Union is a liberal organization that litigates and lobbies on a wide variety of civil liberties issues. Its "Action Center" link provides opportunities to engage with policy makers on a variety of legal issues.

* Ben Adler, "Young Activists Mobilize Against ID Law," The Politico, January 21, 2008.

Amicus curiae briefs seek to provide information that jurists need to resolve cases and can be very influential. In the University of Michigan cases, a wide variety of interested parties, ranging from the MTV network to the Law School Admissions Council, filed briefs describing their views on how racial equality has been and can be achieved in various settings. Judges often use the information or the legal arguments contained in *amicus curiae* briefs to decide cases.[22] The use of these briefs democratizes the judicial system by opening it up to lobbying that is similar to lobbying in the other branches of government. And the participation of interest groups and other organized interests in the judicial decision-making process provides an avenue for citizen engagement and civic discourse[23] (see "Doing Democracy"). But the playing field for these groups is not level: like lobbyists in the other branches of government, some groups are more influential than others. Elite interest groups, benefiting from members' influence and richer resources, are likelier to have their views heard in a court case than groups with less privileged members.[24]

In docketing a case, the clerk of the court selects a date for **oral arguments**—attorneys' formal spoken arguments that lay out why the Court should rule in their client's favor. Heard in the Supreme Court's public gallery, oral arguments give the justices the opportunity to ask the parties and their lawyers specific questions about the arguments in their briefs. In typical cases, each side's lawyers have thirty minutes to make a statement to the Court and to

oral arguments
the stage when appeals court judges or Supreme Court justices meet with the petitioner and the respondent to ask questions about the legal interpretations or information contained in their briefs

answer the justices' questions. Although the public gallery is very grand, and the mood is often somber and formal, the justices can sometimes be less than polite toward each other and the lawyers during the oral arguments. The justices frequently interrupt the attorneys during their opening statements and responses to questions and sometimes seem to ignore the lawyers entirely, instead talking with each other. This discourse takes place entirely within public view, and transcripts (and sometimes even tapes) are readily available to the public.

Meeting in Conference: The Deliberative Stage

After the justices have listened to the oral arguments in the case, they meet in conference to deliberate. At this point, each justice will signal his or her likely vote on the case and discuss the legal issues in play. We have few clues as to how the justices interact in conference, as these proceedings are entirely closed to the public. The late chief justice William Rehnquist once described conferences in which the most junior associate justice was seated closest to the door and was charged with answering any knocks on the door that might come about during deliberation.[25] But other than the anecdotal descriptions we have from justices, once a case enters this phase, it is in a kind of black box. We can only guess about how the justices deliberate and make their decisions, because there is no public record of these proceedings.

We do know that the justices must work together at the deliberation stage if they hope to reach a decision that a majority of them will sign. Because cases are decided by majority rule, there is a strong incentive to cooperate. The chief justice plays a vital role in this process. After the likely votes of the other justices are tallied in the conference, the chief justice decides whether he is with the majority. If he is, he chooses whether he wants to write the majority opinion. If he declines, he can assign the task to one of the other justices in the likely majority. If the chief justice is not with the majority, the senior member of this majority decides whether to write the opinion or assign the opinion to another justice. By the time the justices have finished with the conference, they will have already read the briefs in the case, heard the oral arguments, and listened to each other's views. In assigning the majority opinion, the senior member is effectively giving a stamp of approval to the view of the case that either he or she or some other member of the Court has articulated.

The assignment of the opinion is a crucial stage. The justice who writes the opinion must consider the position of the other justices, especially those who are likely to vote with him or her in the majority. No justice who is assigned with writing the majority opinion can afford to ignore the policy views of the other justices. At the opinion-writing stage, the justices must cooperate and try to hammer out a decision that at least five of them will agree to. Their discussion about the case often centers on the legal arguments that the parties have advanced or on the underlying factual issues.

Deciding How to Vote: Voting Blocs on the Court

How does each justice decide how to vote in a particular case? Frequently the justices vote in blocs—those with similar views tend to vote together, especially in similar cases. By the late 1990s and early 2000s, Supreme Court watchers could predict with a great deal of certainty how specific justices would line up to vote in cases involving abortion restrictions, for example.

These voting blocs work as a kind of shorthand for the justices, who often look to other, like-minded justices to decide how they should vote in certain cases.[26] In cases involving broad areas of the law, such as civil rights and civil liberties, and in cases concerned with the separation of powers, the justices are remarkably predictable[27] (see "Exploring the Sources"). Their decision making follows patterns, with many justices voting together term after term. For example, in case after case brought before the Rehnquist Court (from 1986 to 2005, when William Rehnquist was chief justice), four of the nine justices lined up on each side and Justice Sandra Day O'Connor was the swing vote whose decision determined the outcome in these closely divided cases.[28]

In terms of political stance, we tend to talk about the justices as either conservative or liberal, with conservative justices tending to favor the state and state interests in cases involving civil liberties or civil rights, and liberal justices tending to favor the individual in

THE IDEOLOGICAL BALANCE ON THE SUPREME COURT

> In this cartoon by David Horsey, Justice Anthony Kennedy acts as the fulcrum between the four liberal-leaning justices, Ruth Bader Ginsburg, David Souter, John Paul Stevens, and Stephen Breyer *(right)*, and the four conservative-leaning justices, Clarence Thomas, Antonin Scalia, Samuel Alito, and Chief Justice John Roberts *(left)*.

David Horsey, July 4, 2007. Copyright © Seattle Post-Intelligencer. Used with permission.

Evaluating the Evidence

1 What does Kennedy's posture indicate about the cartoonist's views of the ideological balance of the court?

2 Kennedy is not the chief justice of the Supreme Court, yet his "position" matters. Explain. In light of the composition of the current Supreme Court, does the "swing vote" matter?

3 Given the outcome of the 2008 presidential election, how is the ideology of the Supreme Court likely to tilt in the next few years if the president has the opportunity to fill vacancies on the Supreme Court?

these cases. The justices are arrayed in groups on a kind of spectrum, and Justice O'Connor occupied the central position for many years. Because the Court was so closely divided, she exercised significant power in the decision-making process.

Writing the Opinion

At the opinion-writing stage, give-and-take comes into play among the justices, especially if the case is particularly close so that the justice writing the majority opinion must lock in all the available votes. This is an important consideration because at this point the justices are still free to change their minds about how they will vote or whose opinion they will join.[29] Although there are no records of the justices' deliberations, it is likely that the first draft of most majority opinions is modified to reflect the desires of at least some of the justices who agree to sign it.

There are significant incentives for the author of the draft opinion to take into account the perspectives not only of the justices who agree with his or her conclusions, but also of

concurring opinion

judicial opinion agreeing with how the majority decides the case but disagreeing with at least some of the legal interpretations or conclusions reached by the majority

dissenting opinion

judicial opinion disagreeing both with the majority's disposition of a case and with their legal interpretations and conclusions

those who disagree. The reason is that the majority draft may not be the only draft circulating among the justices. When the justices disagree about a decision, it is likely that other drafts also circulate. Some of these drafts may become concurring opinions; others may become dissenting opinions. **Concurring opinions** agree with how the majority opinion decides the case but disagree with at least some of the legal arguments or conclusions reached in this majority opinion. **Dissenting opinions** not only disagree with these arguments and conclusions but also reject the underlying decision in the case.[30]

As drafts of the majority, concurring, and dissenting opinions circulate, the justices continue to gauge the level of support for each. It does not appear to be unusual for majority opinions to become concurring opinions and vice versa. Again, the ability of the justices to persuade their colleagues on the Court is the primary indicator of which opinion will prevail as the majority decision.

After the opinions are written and signed off on, the Court announces the decision by publishing it. On rare occasions, the justices read their majority opinions, and sometimes their concurring and dissenting opinions, from the bench.

The Supreme Court Today: The Roberts Court

Although it is still early in the tenure of Chief Justice John Roberts, we can make some observations about his leadership and ideology on the basis of decisions to date by the Roberts Court. Many legal scholars say the Roberts Court, particularly in the absence of the moderate O'Connor and with the addition of the conservative Alito, is tilting more conservatively than the Rehnquist Court in which Justice Sandra Day O'Connor played the pivotal balancing role.[31] Figure 14.4 shows the shifts in public opinion that have accompanied these changes in the composition of the court. Today about one-third of Americans view the Supreme Court as "too conservative," and the percentage of people who say that the Court's ideology is "about right" dropped from nearly 50 percent in 2000 to about 42 percent in 2007.[32]

The "American Democracy Now" vignette on p. 498 illustrates one such case that is evidence of this increasingly conservative tilt—the ruling in which the Roberts Court made significant changes to high school affirmative

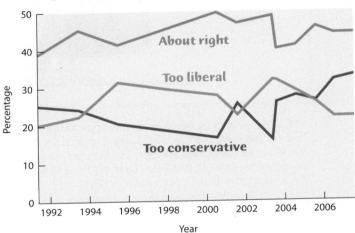

FIGURE 14.4

Citizens' Views on Supreme Court Ideology

Source: Gallup News Service, October 2, 2007.

action programs. This decision illuminates a distinct trend of the Court today: the justices' willingness to limit the exercise of authority by the states and the other branches of government. In another example, the Roberts Court weakened a key provision of a landmark campaign finance law, the Bipartisan Campaign Finance Reform Act of 2002, by loosening restrictions on campaign television ads. The Court's recent conservatism is also evident in a case in which the justices upheld a federal ban on partial birth abortion, a procedure in which labor is induced and suction is used to remove a fetus.[33]

Figure 14.5 shows the ideological distribution of the Supreme Court today and highlights its slight tilt toward the conservative side, with Justices Clarence Thomas, Antonin Scalia, Samuel Alito, and Chief Justice Roberts reflecting a conservative viewpoint and Justices John Paul Stevens, David Souter, and Ruth Bader Ginsburg taking a more liberal stance on many issues. In the center is Justice Anthony Kennedy, a moderate conservative, and Justice Stephen Breyer, a moderate liberal.

The Politics of the Court

Do you think the current Supreme Court is too liberal, just right, or too conservative?

☐ Too liberal

☐ Just right

☐ Too conservative

Source: "1/3 of Americans Say U.S. Supreme Court Too Conservative," www.gallup.com/poll/28861/OneThird-Americans-Say-US-Supreme-Court-Too-Conservative.aspx.

Judges as Policy Makers

Courts make law—common law—by deciding cases and establishing legal principles that bind future litigants and judges. The lawmaking function of courts ensures that judges have a powerful role as public policy makers.[34] This is particularly true of judges who serve in appellate courts such as the state supreme courts, the federal circuit courts of appeals, and the U.S. Supreme Court.

Because of their policy-making role, judges participate in a larger political discourse that goes far beyond the concerns of individual litigants. As we consider in this section, judges are not free to act completely independently of the other branches of the government, but they *are* able to weigh in on some of the country's most important issues. Supreme Court Justice Antonin Scalia has colorfully described the crucial role that judges play in using the law to create policy. As Scalia sees it, the ideal judge is "one who has the intelligence to discern the best rule of law for the case at hand and then the skill to perform the broken-field running through earlier cases that leaves him free to impose that rule: distinguishing one prior case on the left, straight-arming another on the right, high-stepping away from another precedent about to tackle him from the rear, until (bravo!) he reaches the goal—good law."[35] Most recently, the courts have been called upon to resolve issues related to the war on terror, the death penalty, the powers of the chief executive, freedom of speech, abortion, euthanasia, and affirmative action.

What does it mean to be a policy maker? Recall from Chapter 13 that policy makers are individuals who have authority to influence, or to determine, solutions—public policies—that address the issues and problems a society faces. After choosing a policy, the policy maker must stand ready to adapt it to changed situations or new challenges.

FIGURE 14.5 ■ **THE IDEOLOGICAL DISTRIBUTION OF THE SUPREME COURT TODAY**
In what direction does today's Supreme Court tilt with respect to ideology? How could that slant change? Given the current presidential administration, what is the likelihood that it will?

Stevens Souter Ginsburg Breyer Kennedy Roberts Alito Scalia Thomas

judicial activism
an approach to judicial decision making whereby judges apply their authority to bring about specific social goals

Activism Versus Restraint

When considering the courts' role as policy makers, legal analysts often categorize judges and justices as exercising either judicial activism or judicial restraint. **Judicial activism** refers to the courts' practice of applying their authority to bring about particular social goals. It reflects the notion that the role of the courts is to check the power of the federal and state executive and legislative branches when those governmental entities exceed their authority.

During the Warren Court (the tenure of Chief Justice Earl Warren, from 1953 to 1969), the Supreme Court took an activist stance, most notably in rejecting the constitutionality of racial segregation. By barring southern states from segregation in a variety of contexts—including schools and other public facilities—the activist Warren Court powerfully bolstered the efforts of civil rights activists. The activism of the Warren Court was also instrumental in shaping the modern rights of the accused. During Warren's tenure, the Supreme Court established *Miranda* rights for individuals accused of a crime[36] and mandated that states provide counsel to such defendants when they cannot afford an attorney.[37] The Warren Court's

>The activist Warren Court rejected the constitutionality of racial segregation, including in schools. Here students integrating Little Rock (Arkansas) Central High are escorted to an Army station wagon waiting to drive them home after school in 1957.

judicial restraint
an approach to judicial decision making whereby judges defer to the democratically elected legislative and executive branches of government

activism also shaped modern definitions of the privacy rights of individuals,[38] which would later form the framework for the Court's thinking about abortion rights (see Chapter 4 for further discussion of these cases). Supported by presidents who enforced its rulings, the Warren Court took on a leadership role in changing the nature of U.S. society.

Some judges reject the idea that the courts' role is to actively check legislative and executive authority. Noting that officials in those branches are elected to carry out the people's will, these judges observe **judicial restraint**—the limiting of their own power as judges. Practitioners of judicial restraint believe that the judiciary, as the least democratic branch of government, should not check the power of the democratically elected executive and legislative branches unless their actions clearly violate the Constitution.[39]

By tradition, judicial activism and judicial restraint are linked, respectively, with the liberal and conservative ideologies. That neat categorization, however, breaks down when one tries to apply it to recent courts. The Rehnquist Court (1986–2005) was both conservative and activist.[40] That Court chose to hear a case, *Planned Parenthood of Southeastern Pennsylvania v. Casey* (1992), that checked the authority of the state of Pennsylvania to implement a state law that limits access to abortion. In its decision, the Court laid the framework for the tightening of abortion laws in many states by clarifying what measure the states could take in restricting abortions.

Competing Legal Interpretations

When judges and lawyers consider a case, the common-law tradition—specifically, the principle of *stare decisis*—means that they must consider past cases with similar facts and legal questions. They must be guided by how courts in these cases have interpreted the underlying legal issues. As we have seen, the legal principles that come out of these cases constitute case law.

But even though *stare decisis* binds jurists and attorneys to prior case law, this does not mean that judges, in ruling on new cases, simply apply previous decisions to new circumstances. Rather, in interpreting the legal precedent, they typically choose among several cases related to the legal issues at stake, and their choice often determines the outcome of the present case. For this reason, law school students become skilled at identifying the line of cases that might help them to succeed in making a particular argument. They must assume, however, that the lawyer on the other side of the courtroom will also select cases that best support that attorney's chances for success.

Checks on the Courts

The U.S. judiciary is a powerful institution. It operates as the equal of the legislative and executive branches of government yet is insulated from the influence of these other institutions. An impartial, independent judiciary is a key cog in the wheel of the U.S. system, with its separation of powers and checks and balances. The power of the federal judiciary extends to individual judgeships, too, because once appointed to the federal bench, judges cannot be removed except for impeachable offenses. They are not responsible to any electorate, ideally having only the law and their conscience to guide their decision making.

Despite the authority and power of the courts, judges and justices face checks and constraints that limit how they decide cases, make law, and act as policy makers. Among the most important checks on the judiciary's power are the other branches of government. But the law enforcement community, lawyers, interest groups, and individual citizens also check the courts and constrain their activism, as we next consider.

The Inner Ring: Legislatures and Chief Executives

Formidable checks on the judiciary come from what some analysts call the *inner ring*—the other core institutions of the government, namely, the legislative and executive branches. Article II of the Constitution explicitly gives the legislative and executive branches crucial checks on the structure of the courts. It grants Congress the power to create all federal courts other than the Supreme Court and gives both the president and the federal legislature important powers in determining who sits on all federal courts. Indeed, the procedures for choosing the judges who will serve on the federal bench afford both of these branches significant control over the judiciary. Executives check the judiciary through their appointment authority, and the legislature does so through the confirmation process.

Beyond giving the president a check on the judiciary by specifying the executive's power to appoint judges, the Constitution also empowers the chief executive to grant pardons to individuals for violations of the law. A further check on judges results from the courts' reliance on the executive branch for the enforcement of their decisions. Specifically, if presidents fail to direct the bureaucracy to carry out judicial decisions, those decisions carry little weight. Frequently, it is executive implementation that gives teeth to the judiciary's decisions.

The Constitution also creates a legislative check on the judiciary given because the framers established only the Supreme Court and left it up to Congress to create the lower federal courts. In addition, Article I allows Congress to control the Supreme Court's appellate docket and even to remove whole categories of cases from the Court's consideration. Congress also can control the number of judges or justices who serve on the federal judiciary and can increase this number to get a majority of judges or justices to choose a preferred policy outcome. The two houses of Congress moreover have a central role in deciding whether to impeach federal judges. The House issues the articles of impeachment, and the Senate conducts the impeachment trial. Finally, Congress initiates the process of constitutional amendment. In fact, in several cases Congress has embarked on such amendment procedures in direct response to a Court decision with which members of Congress or their constituencies have disagreed. For example, the Twenty-Sixth Amendment, which standardized the voting age to 18 years of age, came about after the Supreme Court ruled that states could set their own age limits for state elections.[41]

Additional constitutional checks also limit the power of the judges. So although the courts can check the lawmaking power of the legislative and executive branches by exercising judicial review (which, to recap, is the courts' power to decide whether the laws passed by the other branches are constitutional), the legislature and the executive can check the courts' power of judicial review through the creation of new laws. For example, Title VII of the 1964 Civil Rights Act bars sex discrimination in employment. In decisions reached in 1974 and 1976, the Supreme Court interpreted this prohibition narrowly, concluding that Congress did not mean to bar discrimination on the basis of pregnancy when it passed Title VII. Many legislators were angered by these decisions. Consequently, in 1976, Congress passed the Pregnancy Discrimination Act, which amended Title VII to state explicitly that sex discrimination encompassed pregnancy discrimination. The Court could do nothing to respond to this new law because Congress used the law specifically to clarify the Civil Rights Act. Only if the new act had been in conflict with the Constitution could the Court have taken action.

> Congress and the president can check the courts' power of judicial review by enacting new laws. In 1976, Congress passed the Pregnancy Discrimination Act, which amended Title VII of the 1964 Civil Rights Act to state explicitly that sex discrimination encompassed pregnancy discrimination, after the Supreme Court had narrowly interpreted Title VII's bans on sex discrimination.

The Gatekeepers: Participants in the Judicial Process

Participants in the judicial process—especially law enforcement officers and interest groups concerned with issues of law—also provide checks on how judges and justices decide cases, make law, and act as policy makers.

LAW ENFORCERS' CHECKS ON THE JUDICIARY One way in which law enforcement officials check the judiciary is through the exercise of *discretion*. Every day, police officers face situations in which they must decide whether to investigate wrongdoing and whether to arrest suspects engaged in illegal acts. The use of discretion by the police and others who are in the front line of law enforcement means these citizens are effectively deciding how and whether to enforce the laws made by courts, legislatures, and chief executives.

ON THE JOB

LESLY M. MENDOZA, EXECUTIVE ASSISTANT, LEGAL SERVICES

Name: Lesly M. Mendoza

Age: 27

Hometown: Los Angeles

College: University of Southern California, Los Angeles

Major: Psychology; minor in Business and Children & Families in Urban America (BA)

Job title: Executive Assistant, Bet Tzedek Legal Services

Average salary for jobs like this: $48,000

Day-to-day responsibilities: My day-to-day responsibilities are broken up into three categories. First, I support the Development Department, which includes managing the donor database, sending acknowledgement letters, and assisting in the preparation of special annual events. Second, I assist the firm's president by setting up meetings and fielding the calls of distressed and potential clients. Third, I help with general administrative tasks, which includes working directly with Bet Tzedek's Board of Directors. Bet Tzedek is a nonprofit law firm that helps thousands of Angelenos gain new access to employment, housing, and healthcare; promotes empowerment for the physically and developmentally disabled; and provides advocacy for communities victimized by discrimination and civil rights abuses.

How did you get your job? While completing my undergraduate degree, I decided to pursue a career in the field of law. I began Web searching for a position at a law firm, preferably a nonprofit. Bet Tzedek offered me hands-on experience and access to public interest attorneys, so I accepted a job there.

What do you like best about your job? The highlight is my opportunity to translate for the attorneys at Bet Tzedek. I am extremely interested in public interest and social justice. By being able to translate English to Spanish—using my native language as a link between the attorneys and indigent clients—I am helping bring justice to these people's lives. Although I am not a lawyer and thus cannot offer legal advice, I do have the opportunity to speak with distraught clients. Most of these calls end with the clients' heightened sense of optimism from having someone help them or refer them to another agency. To know that I can make a difference in someone's life, even indirectly, makes my job a service to the community.

What is your least favorite aspect of your job? I sometimes come in direct contact with clients who are irritated or under duress. Lacking the tools to help them 100 percent of the time can give me a sense of failed responsibility. Another less-appealing aspect of my job is the "office congestion" I face in juggling special events, completing general tasks, and replying to numerous e-mails all at once. The job can become hectic, making for very long hours.

What advice would you give to students who would like to do what you are doing? Students interested in law school should first dedicate time to early LSAT preparation courses along with gaining personal experience. With so many applicants, your GPA and LSAT score and work experience are critical. If you are considering law as a career, a position at a law firm can test your interest in the field. So I encourage students to apply to a law firm—or, alternatively, to a government agency focused on social justice. There, like at Bet Tzedek, you may be able to assist attorneys with their jobs, and you will hear about current cases and learn more about what various lawyers do for the general public. Working at Bet Tzedek provided me direct contact with interested and encouraging staff who offered valuable advice and support in my journey to law school.

For many years, local law enforcement agents closed their eyes to spousal abuse, for example. If they investigated domestic violence, they often treated the perpetrator much more leniently than they would have if the person had not been married to the victim. This decision to be less aggressive in enforcing the law against assault and battery in such cases made some sense, because police knew that entering a home where spousal abuse was occurring was dangerous and that the victim would be unlikely to cooperate in prosecuting his or her attacker. Police often acted on their own, disregarding what the lawmaking institutions, including the courts, required them to do. Only when victims or their families successfully sued police departments for their failure to act did agencies throughout the country begin to treat spousal abuse cases more seriously.

INTEREST GROUPS' CHECKS ON THE JUDICIARY   Legal scholar Andrew Jay Koshner argues that interest groups have transformed how the judiciary operates.[42] Often, lawyers and law firms assist interest groups in bringing their concerns to the judiciary (see "On the Job"). For example, when lawyers for the National Association for the Advancement of Colored People (NAACP) hit a roadblock in their attempts to persuade state legislatures to eliminate segregation in public schools, they pressed civil rights advocacy groups to go to court. The result was the landmark Supreme Court ruling in *Brown v. Board of Education* (1954), which established that segregation in public schools violated the equal protection guarantees in the Fourteenth Amendment.[43]

Experienced and trusted interest groups also constrain the courts by providing them with essential information. Courts need such information, especially in highly complex or technical cases involving issues far outside judges' expertise. Depending on what information and arguments they provide, these groups can constrain the courts' options in a case. When a court decides, for example, to rely on information detailed in the brief of the American College of Obstetrics and Gynecology, a mainstream physicians' group, and virtually to ignore information provided by the pro-life group Physicians for Life, the court is legitimizing one group over the other and giving special access to the preferred group. This favored group's lawyers can provide information that helps them to advance their legal argument and that, in so doing, can limit the court's options and effectively constrain the judges in their decision making.

Intra-Court Constraints

Confirmed judges and justices also face powerful internal constraints on their judicial actions. For lower-court judges, the higher courts, or those courts' decisions in previous cases, impose limitations. Federal district court and appeals court judges, for example, do not diverge far from Supreme Court precedent because if they did so, they would risk having their decisions overturned.

Even the Supreme Court faces substantial constraints, some of which arise from dynamics inside the Court itself. The relationships and interactions among the justices seem to place serious restrictions on their decisions. We have seen, for example, that compromise and negotiation are a central part of the Court's decision making, particularly at the opinion-writing stage. Justices who can persuade others to sign their opinions exercise significant power. This power takes a different form than it does in the other branches. Whereas in the executive and legislative branches the players exercise the power of the purse and engage in overt forms of vote trading, in the judiciary this power is based on legal reasoning and persuasion.

The Outer Ring: The Users

In addition to these various other influences on the courts, an "outer ring" of *users*—the people whom a law directly affects—can considerably constrain the actions of judges. In the many cases where these users are the general public, the courts must consider how this public will receive their decisions and interpretations.

Indeed, public opinion seems to have a distinct impact on what the courts do, especially appellate courts such as the U.S. Supreme Court. The Court rarely issues a decision that is completely out of step with the thinking of the majority of the population. This trend is confirmed by the comparatively high levels of approval of the Court among Americans, illustrated in Figure 14.6. In fact, most cases seem to follow public opinion.

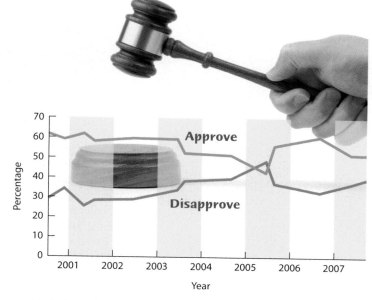

FIGURE 14.6

The Supreme Court's high approval ratings mirror the fact that it rarely breaks with public opinion in its decisions.

Source: Gallup News Service, October 2, 2007.

When the Court does break with public opinion, as it has in prohibiting prayer in the public schools, it opens itself up to harsh criticism by the president, Congress, interest groups, and the general public.

But sometimes in the case of a landmark decision that is out of touch with public sentiment, the Court's ruling and people's opinions align over time. This shift can occur either because later courts adjust the original, controversial decision or, less commonly, because the Supreme Court's decision changes public opinion. One example of the interplay between public opinion and judicial decisions can be seen in Court rulings concerning the death penalty. In the case of *Furman v. Georgia* (1972), the Supreme Court prohibited capital punishment as it was practiced at the time, finding that it violated the Eighth Amendment prohibition against cruel and unusual punishment. The *Furman* decision evoked a public outcry that led many state legislatures to modify their laws governing capital punishment. In 1976 the Court upheld this new generation of laws in *Gregg v. Georgia,* and public opinion has continued to be central to how the Court handles cases involving capital punishment. In the many cases brought to trial since *Gregg,* the justices have used the public opinion polls to justify the Court's decision to uphold capital punishment in general but to bar states from imposing it on juveniles and people with mental retardation.

>In the many capital punishment cases decided since *Gregg v. Georgia* (1976), the justices have upheld capital punishment in general but have barred states from imposing it on juveniles and people with mental retardation, using public opinion polls to justify their rulings. The lethal injection death chamber in the prison in Huntsville, Texas, shown here, is one of the most active in the nation.

Users can also constrain the courts by threatening to ignore their rulings. When members of the public disagree with judicial decisions, or with any law for that matter, they can engage in civil disobedience. In acts of civil disobedience, individuals or groups flout the law to make a larger point about its underlying unfairness. Keep in mind that the courts have little ability to enforce their decisions, and if people refuse to recognize those decisions and the other branches of the government fail to enforce them, the courts risk losing their authority and power. Fear of losing authority may partly explain why judicial decisions rarely fall out of step with the larger public stance on an issue. Like the inner ring and the gatekeepers, the outer ring imposes significant constraints on courts and probably limits how judges handle cases and interpret laws. These constraints may not be written into the U.S. Constitution as the checks are, but they are nonetheless very powerful and probably have a significant impact on how judges decide cases.

CONCLUSION *CONTINUING THE CONVERSATION*

The American judiciary—"the model for securing the rule of law," in the words of Chief Justice John Roberts—has evolved powerfully over the past two-plus centuries to accommodate a broad spectrum of societal changes in a continuously growing country. Rooted in a common-law tradition and framed by the Constitution, the judiciary in its early form strongly reflected its English heritage, with its emphasis on law made by judges.

The judiciary has proved remarkably responsive to the sweeping societal changes that have occurred since those early beginnings. Specifically, the judicial branch has expanded to reflect both the rising population and citizens' increased use of courts to settle disputed matters. At the same time, the body of law that the courts interpret and apply has developed well beyond its common-law origins into a system based heavily on more explicit code law.

In the coming years, the judicial system will face questions that are likely to grow in number and complexity. Future courts will be challenged to interpret new laws addressing a host of thorny issues, including many currently unresolved dimensions of technology and terrorism. For example, how can the courts effectively apply laws—dealing with everything from child pornography to hate speech—given the anonymity and global reach of the Internet? How will the courts balance issues of privacy with the urgent need to provide common security? Furthermore, *entirely new* problems, arising from forces in play today and to come in the future, will require the wisdom of the best and brightest judges. Deciding cases centered on these currently unknown issues also will vitally involve the input of experts and well-informed citizens. These issues may include, for example, new legal questions emerging as a result of the tide of new immigrants, related demographic shifts, and the country's mounting energy problems.

We can anticipate how the judicial branch will meet these and other new demands by examining the strategies the courts have brought to bear in the past. We can see that the judiciary has responded to societal changes in incremental ways, through both revisions in code law and increased judicial specialization. Today, special FISA courts are determining whether the domestic wiretapping of personal communications is warranted. Perhaps it will come to pass that activist courts with expertise in the technology of terrorism will play a more central role in policy making. A key question is, will the incremental change in judicial specialization that has thus far characterized the courts be sufficient in a world that is rushing forward at so high a rate of speed? And another important question is, how will shifting Supreme Court ideology figure into the mix?

Despite the uncertainties, the courts will remain a bastion in defense of individual liberties and rights. And public opinion of the judiciary will likely continue to run high, particularly when this institution is compared with the other branches of the government.

Summary

1. The Origins of the U.S. Judiciary

The Constitution and the Judiciary Act of 1789 created a weak judiciary. The Constitution specified only the Supreme Court and left it to Congress to establish lower courts. In the landmark case *Marbury v. Madison* (1803), the Court asserted the principle of judicial review, which empowered the courts to check the democratically elected branches of government. The Judiciary Act of 1891 expanded the federal court system by creating federal appellate courts.

2. The Basis of U.S. Law

The American legal system has its basis in both common law and code law. Common law is created when judges reach decisions and write opinions in cases. Code law is made by the legislative and executive branches when they pass statutes or create regulations. There are advantages and disadvantages to both common law and code law. Common law has the advantage of stability over time, but it is also slow to change when social, political, or economic conditions shift. Code law has the advantage of being quickly amendable to meet the needs of a rapidly changing society, but the resulting instability can undercut well-established principles.

3. Sources of U.S. Law

There are five sources of law in the American system: the federal and state constitutions, statutes, judicial decisions, executive orders, and administrative law. Constitutions take precedence over all other laws, in that when a conflict arises between a constitutional provision and some other law, the constitutional provision prevails and the other law is struck down. Both the federal government and the fifty state governments all take part in the lawmaking enterprise. There are also fifty-one legal systems in operation: the federal court system and the systems in place in the fifty states.

4. The Federal Court System

Some of the framers pressed strongly for a powerful national court system, and others argued that the state courts should be most prominent. The federal court system is a product of compromise and cooperation among the two factions. The Constitution expressly established the Supreme Court alone, and Congress created the appeals and district courts in a series of laws, beginning in 1789. The Supreme Court has almost total control over the cases it will hear, and compromise and negotiation mark deliberations among the justices. This Court is the United States' highest court, and its decisions are binding on both the lower federal courts and all the state courts.

5. Selecting Judges for the Federal Bench

Federal judges and justices are nominated by the president and confirmed by the Senate. In evaluating nominees, senators examine the nominee's competence and ideology and consider how the nominee's demographic characteristics might represent the population at large.

6. The U.S. Supreme Court Today

Although the Supreme Court has limited original jurisdiction, it is the highest court in the land. The justices choose to hear only a fraction of cases that come before them. The cases they select tend to have broad repercussions in their application. To date, the current Supreme Court, headed by Chief Justice John Roberts, has been conservative in its ideology and activist in its willingness to check the states and other branches of government.

7. Judges as Policy Makers

Judges are influential actors in the policy-making enterprise. They choose among several policy options in deciding cases. Although U.S. legal culture encourages the view that there is only one way that a case can be decided, the reality is that judges often draw from multiple legal interpretations in deciding cases and weigh these options in determining which best promotes the goal or social good that they think should receive priority.

8. Checks on the Courts

Powerful constraints limit what judges and justices in the U.S. legal system may do. The influences that can constrain policy making come from both outside and inside the judiciary. Outside influences include an inner ring consisting of legislatures and executives, a ring of gatekeepers comprising law enforcers and interest groups, and an outer ring of users, the people whom the laws directly affect. Within the judicial system, on the Supreme Court itself, legal precedent and the need to build coalitions restrict the justices' actions. Even in light of these various constraints, however, U.S. courts and judges play a crucial role in lawmaking and policy making.

Key Terms

amicus curiae brief ("friend of the court" brief) 514
appellate jurisdiction 507
brief 514
chief justice 509
circuit courts 500
circuit riding 500
civil law case 501
code law 504
collegial court 513
common law 503
concurring opinion 518
constitutional law 505
courts of appeals 500
criminal law case 501

defendant 501
discuss list 514
dissenting opinion 518
diversity of citizenship 507
dual court system 507
federal question 507
judicial activism 519
judicial restraint 519
judiciary 499
jurisdiction 507
justice 509
litigation 501
oral arguments 515
original jurisdiction 507
petitioner 501

plaintiff 501
pool memo 514
precedent 504
respondent 501
Rule of Four 514
senatorial courtesy 510
stare decisis 504
statute 505
symbolic representation 512
tort 501
trial court 507
U.S. Code 505
U.S. Supreme Court 499
writ of *certiorari* 514

For Review

1. What is the basis of the American legal system? Why is it unusual for a nation-state to blend the two traditions that are the core of this system? What are the advantages and disadvantages of these two traditions?

2. What are the five sources of law in the U.S. legal system? What is the relationship among these five sources?

3. What is the structure of the federal court system? Why do we say that conflict and compromise characterize this system? Does this system have more or less power than the state court system? Explain.

4. How are federal judges chosen? Who tends to be chosen? How does the selection process differ for federal district court judges, circuit court judges, and Supreme Court justices? In what ways do conflict and compromise characterize the selection process for all of these judges?

5. Outline the stages by which the Supreme Court decides cases. Why do we say that negotiation and compromise are a part of every one of these stages?

6. In what ways do federal judges participate in civic discourse as policy makers? Outline the ways in which this participation is either checked by the Constitution or constrained by internal and external actors.

For Critical Thinking and Discussion

1. How did the American legal system come to be a blend of the common law and code law traditions? Which tradition better suits today's political, social, and economic realities? Why?

2. What is your view on the shared lawmaking by the three branches of American government? Are you satisfied that this shared system benefits the country? Can you think of some negatives to the U.S. system?

3. The Supreme Court has the power of judicial review, that is, the power to strike down federal and state laws that it views as in conflict with the U.S. Constitution. Can you think of any reasons why it would not be a good thing to allow the Court to overturn laws passed by the democratically elected branches?

4. When a president nominates a prospective federal judge, a number of factors are at play, and the nominee's qualifications are only one of these. What are these other factors? Should they be in play? Why or why not? In what ways do these factors reinforce or undermine democratic principles?

5. Which do you think impose greater limitations on policy making by federal courts: constitutional checks or intra-court and external constraints? Why?

MULTIPLE CHOICE: Choose the lettered item that answers the question correctly.

1. *Marbury v. Madison*
   a. created the U.S. Supreme Court.
   b. established the separate but equal doctrine.
   c. established the principle of judicial review.
   d. created the U.S. courts of appeals.

2. Courts that review previous decisions made by courts in the federal or state judicial system are called
   a. petit courts.
   b. federal district courts.
   c. review courts.
   d. courts of appeals.

3. The process by which cases are brought and decided in the American legal system is called
   a. tort.
   b. litigation.
   c. civil action.
   d. riding circuit.

4. *Stare decisis* means
   a. "seize the day."
   b. "buyer beware."
   c. "let the decision stand."
   d. "bring the body."

5. The compilation of all the laws passed by the U.S. Congress is called
   a. tort law.
   b. the U.S. Code.
   c. majority opinions.
   d. the Public Record.

6. Code law is also known as
   a. statutory law.
   b. appellate law.
   c. regulatory law.
   d. *stare decisis*.

7. The authority of a court to hear and decide a case is called
   a. standing.
   b. diversity of citizenship.
   c. jurisdiction.
   d. judicial right of review.

8. _____ gives senators—though only those who are of the same political party as the president—a powerful voice in choosing the district court judges who will serve in their state.
   a. Judicial review
   b. Senatorial courtesy
   c. Tort reform
   d. Diversity of citizenship

9. A question of law based on interpretation of the U.S. Constitution, federal laws, or treaties is called
   a. U.S. Code.
   b. a federal question.
   c. criminal law.
   d. civil law.

10. The notion that the role of the courts is to check the power of the federal and state executive and legislative branches when those governmental entities exceed their authority is called
    a. judicial dynamism.
    b. judicial activism.
    c. judicial restraint.
    d. writ of *certiorari*.

FILL IN THE BLANKS.

11. The practice whereby Supreme Court justices and district court judges would travel throughout the country to hear appeals cases was called _____.

12. The list compiled by the chief justice of the Supreme Court of those cases on review that he thinks may be appropriate for the Court to hear is called the _____.

13. The attempt to ensure that the Court is representative of major demographic groups such as women, African Americans, Jews, and Catholics is known as _____.

14. According to the _____, the Court will agree to hear a case that comes to it under its discretionary jurisdiction if four or more justices vote to hear it.

15. _____, a Latin term meaning "a request to make certain," refers to an order to a lower court to produce a certified record of a case so that the appellate court can determine whether any errors occurred during trial that warrant review of the case.

RESOURCES FOR RESEARCH AND ACTION

Internet Resources

American Democracy Now Web site
www.mhhe.com/harrison1e   Consult the book's Web site for study guides, interactive activities, simulations, and current hotlinks for additional information on the U.S. judiciary.

FindLaw
www.findlaw.com   This Web site provides a wealth of information about lawmaking in the federal and state judiciaries, as well as ongoing cases in the news. It allows users easy access to federal and state code law, case law, and regulatory law. It also helps pre-law and law students stay connected to helpful information about legal education and practice.

Oyez
www.oyez.org/oyez/frontpage   This interactive Web site allows you to access recordings of the oral arguments in a select group of cases. You can also visit the site to take a virtual tour of the Supreme Court building and to learn interesting trivia about the Court, including a list of the most active lawyers before the Court.

Legal Information Institute (LII)
http://straylight.law.cornell.edu   This is a valuable resource for doing research not only on the U.S. Supreme Court but also on the other courts in the federal and state judiciaries. The site provides an excellent catalog of statutory, regulatory, and administrative laws, as well as executive orders. It also allows you to search for all sources of law in a particular area of the law, including not only federal and state court decisions but laws coming out of the other branches as well.

U.S. Supreme Court
www.supremecourtus.gov   The official Web site of the U.S. Supreme Court is an excellent resource for doing research on the Court. You can access the briefs and oral argument transcripts for cases currently before the Court, as well as cases recently decided. The site also allows easy access to nearly all cases that the Court has decided, including historical decisions.

Recommended Readings

McGuire, Kevin T. *Understanding the Supreme Court: Cases and Controversies.* New York: McGraw-Hill, 2002. A book that uses real cases to examine the selection of justices, the Supreme Court's decision-making procedures, the influence of interest groups, and the impact of Court rulings.

O'Brien, David M., ed. *Judges on Judging: Views from the Bench.* Chatham, NJ: Chatham House, 1997. An exploration by judges and justices of judicial review, decision making, constitutional interpretation, and the role of courts in the American system.

Samuels, Suzanne U. *Law, Politics and Society: An Introduction to American Law.* Boston: Houghton Mifflin, 2006. A comprehensive survey of the foundations of the American legal system, lawmaking by institutions and groups, and law and public policy.

Tarr, G. Alan. *Judicial Process and Judicial Policymaking.* Belmont, CA: Thomson/Wadsworth, 2006. A broad outline of the institutions and main actors in the U.S. judicial system, explaining both judicial decision making and policy making.

van Geel, T. R. *Understanding Supreme Court Opinions.* New York: Pearson/Longman, 2005. An introduction to Supreme Court opinions and to the justices' use of different schools of legal argument and interpretation in these opinions.

Movies of Interest

A Comedy of Power (2006)
In this French film (with English subtitles), a judge finds that a case involving corporate corruption extends to high-level government officials. Based on a true story, it depicts the real-life danger that judges sometimes face.

The Runaway Jury (2003) and *12 Angry Men* (1957)
These films provide critical examinations of the role of the jury in the American judicial system, with both ultimately skeptical in their assessment of juries.

Monster's Ball (2001)
Probing the issues of capital punishment and racism in a personal way, this film explores the relationships among a white executioner, his African American prisoner, and their families.

A Civil Action (1998)
Based on a real-life story, this engrossing film takes the viewer through the pitfalls of civil litigation in a series of cases involving the pollution of a Massachusetts town's water supply by several corporations and businesses.

Gideon's Trumpet (1980)
This classic film starring Henry Fonda traces the true story of Clarence Gideon's fight to have a counsel appointed to his case at the expense of the state. *Gideon v. Wainwright* was the 1963 Supreme Court's decision that extended state-appointed attorneys to all criminal defendants.

National Journal

BRAINS IN THE DOCK

The MacArthur Foundation will spend at least $10 million over the next several years to infuse the legal system with high-tech research from brain scientists.

MacArthur's Law and Neuroscience Project, advocates say, will provide scientific, legal, and philosophical advice to judges now facing a wave of courtroom claims that are based on early, and often shaky, research into the workings of the human brain. Lawyers and academic advocates are citing brain research to validate witness statements, strengthen claims for injury and clemency, break contracts, bolster an Illinois curb on the sale of violent video games, and even shift the goal of sentencing away from retribution toward crime prevention.

The project began last October following a proposal from Stanford University neuroscientist Robert Sapolsky, said Jonathan Fanton, president of the John D. and Catherine T. MacArthur Foundation in Chicago, which annually gives more than $260 million to mostly liberal causes and is best known for its "genius grants" to individuals. The foundation had been looking for novel projects to fund, Fanton told National Journal, and Sapolsky's proposal held out the promise of fundamentally changing criminal law and the justice system.

Critics contend that the project may prove counterproductive. If people believe that behavior and beliefs are controlled by brain physiology and chemistry rather than by the traditional notions of mind, soul, and character, that could boost the view that people can't control their decisions and desires, said Yuval Levin. He is a fellow at the Ethics and Public Policy Center, a think tank dedicated to promoting traditional ethics in policy debates, and until last year served as a White House domestic policy adviser. "If you believe you can't control your behavior, you don't work at controlling your behavior," he said. That belief, he said, could increase crime and prompt judges to regard

some citizens as patients best treated by long-term confinement; it could even lead to more death-penalty sentences for people who have what are considered irredeemably damaged brains.

For decades, scientists have tried to peer inside the living brain. In recent years, they have developed technology that can detect the movement of oxygen-rich blood and track which parts of the brain are most active when a person is making a particular decision or reacting to a threat. Manufacturers and advocates of the technology are using these early results to sell lie-detection services, persuade juries, and sway politicians, even though the reliability and relevance of the devices are unproven.

The technology is most frequently used to show apparent damage to, or incomplete development of, a person's brain. Attorneys are employing these high-tech images of brain problems, whether caused by genes, wounds, age, or early-childhood deprivation, to argue that their clients were not fully responsible for their actions and thus deserve clemency. Some attorneys have contended that the criminal justice system should treat teenage defendants leniently because the brain's amygdala—which reacts strongly to perceived threats—is active in teenagers, but the frontal cortex—which is thought to restrain aggression—does not fully develop until ages 18 to 21.

These arguments fit uneasily with traditional standards of responsibility, which assume that young people gradually learn from their parents, community, and culture how to govern their behavior, and that when they are no longer children, they should be liable for their actions.

Yet the new views have won some arguments. Congress supplemented funding for early-childhood programs in the 1990s after hearing from Vice President Gore and others that brain scans show that the first few years of a child's life deeply shape later edu-

cational achievement. Similarly, in 2005, the Supreme Court cited the new science in its 5-4 decision in Roper v. Simmons, which ruled that executing those convicted of committing murder before their 18th birthday is unconstitutional. During the oral argument, the justices focused 16 of their 20 questions to the condemned man's attorney on scientific evidence concerning juvenile development. MacArthur can claim some credit for the Roper decision, Fanton said, because the foundation helped to focus attention on the limited competence of juveniles.

The honorary chairwoman of the MacArthur project is Sandra Day O'Connor, a former Supreme Court justice who disagreed with the Roper decision. The six-year effort will include seminars for students, lawyers, judges, and politicians, and will also draft guideline for judges, Fanton said. "It is important to get the best neuroscience connected to the law," he said, "so this is properly used and not misused."

Eventually, the project will likely bring in politicians, said neuroscientist Michael Gazzaniga, director of the Sage Center for the Study of Mind at the University of California (Santa Barbara) and a co-director of the project. The 50 or so scientists, lawyers, judges, and academics working on the effort were chosen for the variety of their perspectives. The project has no agenda whatsoever, said Stephen Morse, a law professor at the University of Pennsylvania and a co-director of the project's panel on addiction and antisocial behavior.

So far, the new science is being cited in a tiny fraction of legal proceedings, mostly death-penalty cases and civil lawsuits, said Hank Greely, a Stanford law professor who is involved in the MacArthur project. But over the next 10 or 20 years, the use of the technology will broaden, he said. Brain-scanning equipment might be used to detect the early signs of Alzheimer's disease, Greely said, and the resulting information could impact the health insurance industry, spur states to cancel older peoples' driver's licenses, and guide investment by the nursing home industry. "The legal implications of this will be much broader than the courtroom," he said.

One likely early use for the technology in the legal system, according to Greely, could be to tailor treatments for drug-addicted criminals or to measure pain in people claiming injury or disability. Some evidence indicates that today's technology can detect brain patterns consistent with pain, and could help judges and juries to identify the "nontrivial chunk of those people [who] are exaggerating or flat-out lying," he said. Lawyers could someday also employ the technology in civil disputes to argue that their clients were unable to understand a complex contract or were not competent to sign a will.

Attorneys are already citing the technology in seeking to protect convicted defendants from execution. "Retribution is not proportional if the law's most severe penalty is imposed on one whose culpability or blameworthiness is diminished, to a substantial degree, by reason of youth and immaturity," the Supreme Court said in the Roper decision, which included four citations to a journal article about juveniles' developmental immaturity that was written by a MacArthur-funded psychologist.

The new science is also shaping cultural attitudes toward personal responsibility, Gazzaniga said. "Neuroscience is oozing into the public consciousness," especially through the universities, he said. The result, he argues, is that increasing numbers of people believe that free will is an illusion of brain mechanics, and that people can't be blamed for doing what their brain determined that

Increasing numbers of people believe that free will is an illusion of brain mechanics, and that people can't be blamed for doing what their brain determined that they would do.

they would do. "That idea is around in every college bull session and every defense attorney's 'Can we try that out?' " he said.

Some experts in the MacArthur project—including Sapolsky, who serves on the governing board—hold that view, according to Gazzaniga. Greely says, "A lot of philosophers and neuroscientists say this will be revolutionary." He added, "I'm skeptical because I don't think the neuroscientists have convinced us there is no free will."

"Everyone agrees that we should be locking up people that are dangerous to other people," said one of the determinists on the project, Joshua Greene, an assistant professor of psychology at Harvard University. If the technological advances persuade citizens and judges to embrace a new view of the brain, he said, they will be more likely to forgo their desire for retribution—inflicted in the form of long sentences in harsh prisons—and accept shorter sentences similar to those imposed in Europe.

The materialistic argument may lead to different results if it gains ground, said O. Carter Snead, an associate law professor

at the University of Notre Dame. Judges and citizens could discard traditional notions of mercy, in his view, and support severe penalties for murderers who can't show that their brain is damaged, as well as for criminals whose damaged brains make them more likely to commit crimes if they are released from prison.

Anthony Daniels, a former psychiatrist in British prisons, warned against any claim that people are wholly controlled by the biological workings of their brain. "If you take it seriously, it has the most illiberal consequences possible, at least as long as there is no cure [because each brain-damaged prisoner] needs to be locked up forever since he cannot control himself," said Daniels, who has cited his prison experiences in books and articles under the pen name Theodore Dalrymple.

Morse responds that the deterministic view of the brain can be made compatible with traditional notions of responsibility. This view holds that even if brains are soulless machines, people can still distinguish between right and wrong, and what is legal and illegal. Science needn't change the legal system, he argues. Plenty of room remains for advocates to persuade the public to accept or reject the contention that society could discard its claim to retribution for crimes, he said. "It's up for grabs."

And even if science eventually proves the determinists correct, the people and the politicians have the right and ability to reject scientists' prescriptions, Greely said. "My doctor, every time I see him, tells me to lose weight, but I'd rather have the cheeseburger than the apple."

■ **THEN:** Judges and juries worked with common standards for evidence, proof, and responsibility.

■ **NOW:** Judges and juries must preside over trials that present complex, scientific evidence and arguments beyond the scope of a common expertise.

■ **NEXT:** Will brain science change the definition of culpability for defendants?
Will neuroscience affect our understanding of cruel and unusual punishment?
Will science, not commonly held values, settle the question of free will in the courtroom?

Economic Policy

THEN

The federal government played a limited role in the economy, and there was consensus about the need for a balanced federal budget.

NOW

The federal government makes policy to achieve national economic health, and borrowing to balance the federal budget is the norm.

NEXT

Will continuing globalization impede the government's ability to maintain a healthy national economy?

Can the United States retain its dominance in the world economy?

Will your generation and future generations achieve the American dream?

3719

Helping Children Throughout the World

Iqbal Masih had a dream. His dream was for all children to be free from forced labor and able to get an education. His dream grew out of his own life experiences. Unable to repay a loan, Iqbal's father sold him to a carpet factory when he was 4 years old. From age 4 to age 10, Iqbal worked twelve hours a day, chained to a carpet-weaving loom. If he did not work fast enough, he was beaten. After escaping from his bondage, this tiny Pakistani boy—his development stunted and his body bent over due to years of immobility in front of his loom—captured world attention as an international activist against child labor. In 1994, at the age of 12, Iqbal traveled from his home in Pakistan to Boston, Massachusetts, to receive the Reebok Human Rights Youth in Action Award. I While in Massachusetts, he visited with students at Broad Meadows Middle School. Iqbal shared his dream with the students and asked for their help in educating people about forced child labor and in trying to stop people from buying rugs imported from countries that allowed this practice. Seventh graders Amanda Loos and Amy Papile organized their classmates in response to Iqbal's request, educating policy makers, friends, and their community about forced child labor. When Iqbal returned to Pakistan he had with him 670 letters addressed to Pakistani Prime Minister Benazir Bhutto that raised concerns about child labor, which Amanda, Amy, and their classmates had collected.* I Two years after his escape from forced labor and his activism began, and just a few months after his visit to Broad Meadows, Iqbal was shot to death while riding his bike. Shocked, then angry and determined to keep Iqbal's dream alive, the students decided to build a school in Pakistan. To raise money for the school, Amanda wrote a letter that told Iqbal's story, and she and her classmates e-mailed it to all the junior high schools they knew, asking that each class contribute $12 to "A School for Iqbal." Amanda explains the $12 request by stating, "He was 12 when he came, he was 12 when he won the Reebok human rights award, and he was 12 when he passed away."* I Amanda's class raised $150,000, and in 1997, a five-room school for Iqbal, which also functions as a community center, was opened in Kasur, Pakistan. In addition, the class established a program that loans Pakistani mothers money to buy back their children from forced labor.** Students at Broad Meadows Middle School continue to work toward making Iqbal's dream a reality. Since 1995, students have engaged in petition drives to change policies; interviewed store managers about child labor; testified before congressional panels; represented the United States in the Global March Against Child Labor; given keynote addresses at international conferences; and lobbied for the successful ratification of the 1999 International Labour Convention No. 182, which outlaws the worst forms of child labor. I Current Broad Meadows students, Broad Meadows graduates including Amanda, and students throughout the world are actively engaged in a network of children and young people—a global youth movement—that is working to end the causes of child labor. Amanda says, "Once you meet kids who've been through [what Iqbal went through], you can't just talk about it. You have to go out and do something."***

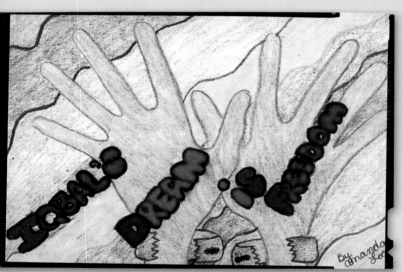

> Broad Meadows student Amanda Loos drew this poster in honor of Iqbal Masih and his dream of ending the horrors of child labor.

* "The New Design Interview," *New Designs for Youth Development Magazine* 14, no. 3, Fall 1998, www.mirrorimage.com/iqbal/media/newdesign/ndesign2.html.

** Arana Rubin and Courtney Rubin, "Girl Power: You're Never Too Young to Change the World," *Marie Claire*, September 2000, www.mirrorimage.com/iqbal/media/marieclaire/mcpage2.html.

*** Ron Adams, Personal Communications, July 29 and 30, 2008.

Why are 158 million children work-

ing in economic activities that keep them from attending school and, in many cases, threaten their health and development? The answer is that, in the competition to make profits, some firms hire children who are cheaper to pay, easier to control, and less likely to strike than are adult workers. Moreover, in today's global economy, where according to the World Bank 2.7 million people live in poverty and 1.1 million live in extreme poverty,[1] parents may be compelled to send their children to work for pay, no matter how low the wage, as they try to meet their families' most basic needs.

But isn't such child labor illegal? The overwhelming majority of nations do prohibit labor by children under age 15. In the United States, for example, state governments have been limiting children's work since Massachusetts enacted the first child labor law in 1836. The federal government began regulating child labor in 1938. Yet in many other nations where the economy is far less prosperous than that of the United States, the paid labor of all family members, including children, may be required for the family to sustain itself, and governments may believe that weak enforcement of child labor laws is best for the economic prosperity of the nation and its people.

All governments have an *economic policy,* a body of diverse policies geared toward promoting national economic health. Today, the U.S. national government enacts a variety of laws that seek to ensure economic prosperity. These include tax laws, laws that regulate economic activity in the domestic and international marketplaces, laws that protect the health and safety of workers, and spending policies that encourage job creation. In addition, the United States, like other nations, has policies that affect the amount of money in circulation and hence consumer prices.

Economic Health and the American Dream

The American national government seeks a healthy economy so that it can raise the revenue it needs to serve the people in compliance with the mission laid out in the Preamble to the Constitution: to establish justice, ensure domestic tranquility, provide for the common defense, promote the general welfare, and secure the blessings of liberty. On a more personal level, many U.S. citizens desire a healthy economy so that they can achieve the **American dream**—a financially secure, happy, and healthy life, with upward social mobility, attained through an individual's hard work and persistence.

Despite its name, the American dream's promise is not limited to Americans: people around the globe widely aspire to these same ideals. Hundreds of thousands of foreigners immigrate to the United States each year—most legally, some illegally—in search of the American dream. The decade of the 1990s saw the highest levels of immigration in U.S. history, with approximately 9.8 million immigrants gaining permanent legal status and an estimated 4.9 million immigrants entering and remaining in the United States without authorization.[2] The primary cause of immigration is the same as the cause of child labor: poverty. Foreign peoples come to the United States to get jobs that will provide more for them and their families than the jobs that their home country can provide. U.S. immigration policy (see Chapter 16) accommodates immigration on a limited basis, imposing an annual cap on the number of immigrants allowed legal entrance and giving preference to immigrants with family members living permanently in the United States, as well as those with high-level job skills needed in select segments of the economy.

American dream
the belief that in the United States hard work and persistence will reap a financially secure, happy and healthy life, with upward social mobility

The desire for enough money to buy not only what we require to meet our basic needs (food, shelter, and clothing), but also what many people would consider luxuries, seems natural to most Americans. In developed countries such as the United States, "luxuries" typically include owning a home instead of renting, owning a car or two, dining at a nice restaurant now and then, taking vacations, and sending children to good schools. The American dream includes sustaining this middle-class lifestyle through retirement and expecting our children's lives to be even better than our own.

Clearly, it takes money to live the American dream. For some, being born into a wealthy family or just dumb luck (winning the lottery!) may provide the means to live the American dream. For most individuals, however, the ability to earn enough money to attain the American dream is the product of several factors, including their education level, work ethic, and the availability of well-paying jobs.

Why are you attending college? Are you taking classes to develop your intellectual capacities? To better understand yourself and the world around you? To get a better-paying job so you can live the American dream? If you read your college's mission statement, you will find that your institution hopes to facilitate all of these accomplishments. Probably the easiest accomplishment to measure is gaining a well-paying job, and personal income is a logical measure of a well-paying job. Table 15.1 shows that personal income is positively correlated with educational attainment; generally, the more education you acquire, the higher your personal income will be. In addition, Table 15.1 shows that race and sex—two factors that you cannot control—are also correlated with personal income. So earning a college degree is the best step you can take in your quest to live the American dream. However, for women and nonwhite men, the income benefits of a college education are muted.

Although you may be able to increase your level of education, and you have some control over your work ethic, the availability of well-paying jobs commensurate with your level of education is not within your control. The health of the national economy determines the availability of jobs and their compensation (pay and benefits). So, although achieving the American dream depends on individual attributes and opportunities to develop those attributes, the health of the national economy also plays a major role.

A healthy national economy—with low unemployment, stable prices, and high productivity—supports a nation's ability to raise sufficient revenue to serve its people. The better the economy's performance, the greater the **tax base:** the overall wealth (income and assets, such as property) of citizens and corporations that governments tax in order to raise revenue.

TABLE 15.1

Education, Race, Sex, and Mean Personal Income

	High School	Associate's Degree	Bachelor's Degree	Master's Degree	Doctoral Degree
All groups	$ 27,915	$ 35,958	$ 51,206	$ 62,514	$ 88,471
Female	$ 21,659	$ 29,537	$ 38,447	$ 48,205	$ 73,516
Male	$ 33,266	$ 43,462	$ 63,084	$ 76,896	$ 95,894
Black	$ 23,777	$ 31,415	$ 42,968	$ 57,449	$ 81,457
Female	$ 19,623	$ 27,054	$ 41,066	$ 49,344	$ *
Male	$ 28,102	$ 38,234	$ 45,635	$ 69,557	$ *
Hispanic	$ 23,472	$ 31,032	$ 43,676	$ 56,486	$ *
Female	$ 18,967	$ 26,535	$ 37,550	$ 48,433	$ *
Male	$ 26,652	$ 35,896	$ 49,298	$ 63,026	$ *
White	$ 28,708	$ 36,881	$ 52,259	$ 62,981	$ 89,640
Female	$ 22,028	$ 30,099	$ 37,739	$ 48,388	$ 70,536
Male	$ 34,224	$ 44,557	$ 65,264	$ 77,845	$ 99,015

* Too few earning PhDs to meet statistical standards for reliability.

Source: U.S. Census Bureau, *Statistical Abstract of the United States: 2006*, 125th ed. (Washington, DC: 2005), Table 217.

tax base
the overall wealth (income and assets of citizens and corporations) that the government can tax in order to raise revenue

economy
the system of transactions by which goods and services are distributed in the marketplace

The Nature of the American Economy

In the United States and other countries, national government policies influence the **economy,** the system of transactions by which goods and services are produced, distributed, and consumed. Economic policies are those aimed at creating and/or maintaining a healthy economy. Economists view a healthy economy as one in which unemployment is low, the price of consumer goods is relatively stable, and the productivity of individual workers, and of the economy as a whole, is increasing.

Although labeled as a capitalist economy, the U.S. economy is not an example of pure capitalism. In a **pure capitalist economy,** private individuals and companies own the modes of producing goods and services, and the government does *not* enact laws aimed at influencing the marketplace transactions that distribute these goods and services. In other words, a pure capitalist economy has a government-free marketplace. Although private ownership of the modes of production dominates the U.S. marketplace, it is not a government-free marketplace. National government policies in some cases encourage, and in other cases mandate, certain business practices that the government deems essential to sustain a healthy economy, as well as a clean environment and a safe and productive citizenry. Because of the many national policies enacted to influence the economy, the U.S. economy is an example of a **regulated capitalist economy (mixed economy),** not a pure capitalist economy.

People around the world want their governments to engage in actions that ensure a healthy economy. Yet the actions a government takes to ensure a healthy economy depend on the economic theories its lawmakers follow. In the United States, Democrats and Republicans traditionally disagree on economic policies, each justifying their policy preferences with different economic theories. Next, we survey several economic theories that have influenced U.S. national economic policy in various historical periods.

pure capitalist economy
private individuals and companies own the modes of producing goods and services, and the government does not enact laws aimed at influencing the marketplace transactions that distribute these goods and services

regulated capitalist economy (mixed economy)
an economy in which the government enacts policies to influence the health of the economy

Economic Theories That Inform Economic Policy

Debates about the proper role for the national government in the economy have been ongoing since the birth of the American republic. The initial consensus was that the national government should follow a *laissez-faire* economic policy, playing a very limited role in the economy. But as the national economy evolved and experienced ups and downs, citizens and corporations sought greater government involvement in the economy, and economists developed new theories about the proper role for governments in creating and maintaining a healthy economy: Keynesian economics, supply-side economics, and monetarism.

Laissez-Faire Economics: An Unrealized Policy

Until the late 1800s, a majority of the American people believed that the national government should take a relatively **laissez-faire,** or "hands-off," stance with regard to the marketplace. That is, they thought that the government should neither encourage nor discourage (through its laws) business practices that affected economic health. In his *Wealth of Nations* (1776), economist Adam Smith described the principles underlying the theory of laissez-faire. Smith's classical capitalist argument emphasized that the most effective means of supporting a strong and stable economy in the long term is to allow unregulated competition in the marketplace. According to Smith, people's pursuit of their self-interest in an unregulated marketplace would yield a healthy economy. While supporting a hands-off approach in general, the national government became involved in economic activity not long after the Constitution went into effect in 1789.

Alexander Hamilton, who would become the country's first secretary of the treasury, argued in *The Federalist* No. 11 that regulation of commerce by the national government may "oblige foreign countries to bid against each other, for the privileges of our markets" leading to prosperity of the United States. In addition, Hamilton argued in *The Federalist* No. 12 that import taxes, which traders and businesses would pass on to the consumer, could both raise revenue and influence consumer behavior. In 1789, Congress approved and President George Washington (1789–1797) signed the first import tariff.

As a manufacturing economy replaced the farming-dominated economy during the nineteenth century, the general laissez-faire stance of the national government disappeared. Technological advances fueled industrialization and the movement of workers from farms to manufacturing jobs in the cities. As immigrants flocked to the United States in search

laissez-faire
hands-off stance of a government in regard to the marketplace

of the American dream, the supply of cheap labor ballooned. Giant corporations formed, and individuals with money to invest accumulated great wealth. Monopolies and trusts also developed, limiting competition in a variety of industries. **Income inequality,** the gap in the proportion of national income held by the few at the top of the income ladder compared to the many on the lower rungs, grew. At the same time, the quality of life for the majority of working-class citizens deteriorated as additional family members, including children, needed to work to pay for life's basic necessities. As fewer and fewer people achieved the American dream, even with all family members working, many Americans began to look to the federal government for solutions.

In the late nineteenth century, the federal government began to respond to workers' demands for better wages and working conditions and to business owners' calls for uniform (national) rules and regulations for business practices to replace the existing hodgepodge of state-imposed regulations. Moreover, by the early twentieth century, the national government took steps to protect public health by passing laws regulating the processing of foods and drugs, and the cleanliness and safety of manufacturing plants. Though not directed at the health of the economy, such regulations increased the costs of doing business, hence affecting the economy. In addition to regulating working conditions, the national government began to use the tool of immigration policy to bolster the national economy and the wages of American-born workers. For example, the Chinese Exclusion Act of 1882 disallowed immigrants from China, who were willing to work to build the railroads for lower wages than American-born workers. The contemporary public debate about the impact of immigrants on the U.S. economy—in terms of wages, working conditions, and the cost of health, education, and welfare policies—is discussed in Chapter 16.

Clearly, the national government never fully implemented laissez-faire. Moreover, as the national economy grew with industrialization, Americans accepted and even called for a mixed economy featuring regulated capitalism. Today, consensus continues on the need for some level of government involvement in the marketplace in order to ensure a healthy and sustainable economy, environment, and standard of living. But debate continues as well over how much government involvement is appropriate and what specific policies the government should enact.

income inequality
the gap in the proportion of national income held by the richest compared to that held by the poorest

> At the turn of the twentieth century, child labor was common because laws did not prohibit it and many families needed their children's income to help pay for life's necessities. Here a young boy works in a glass factory in 1910.

Keynesian Economics

Before the Great Depression of the 1930s, government officials and economists believed that a **balanced budget,** a budget in which the government's expenditures (costs of doing business) are equal to or less than its revenues (money raised), was important for a healthy economy. Yet officials and economists recognized that during wartime the government might need to engage in **deficit spending,** spending more than is raised through taxes, to pay for the military effort.

During the Great Depression, unemployment rates soared to 25 percent. That changed when President Franklin D. Roosevelt (1933–1945) and Congress supported deficit spending to address this severe economic depression that engulfed the nation. The Roosevelt administration implemented numerous economic regulations and a number of innovative work and public assistance programs. These policies drove up government spending at a time of shrinking government revenues. A key objective of the government's increased spending was to trigger economic growth by lowering unemployment rates, thereby increasing demand for goods (because more employed people means more people with money to spend), thus boosting the national economy. Deficit spending, Roosevelt said, would provide the solution to the American people's economic woes.

balanced budget
a budget in which the government's expenditures are equal to or less than its revenues

deficit spending
government expenditures costing more than is raised in taxes, leading to borrowing and debt

The new economic theory of John Maynard Keynes supported Roosevelt's unprecedented peacetime deficit spending. **Keynesian economics** recommends that during a **recession**—an economic downturn during which unemployment is high and the production of goods and services is low—the national government should increase its spending (to create jobs) and decrease taxes (so that people have more money to spend) to stimulate the economy. Based on this theory, during a **depression,** which is a long-term and severe recession, deficit spending is justified. During times of rapid economic growth—an **economic boom,** which is the opposite of a recession/depression—Keynesian theory recommends cutting government spending and possibly increasing taxes. In the long term, deficit spending during recessions and collecting a surplus when the economy is booming should lead to a balanced budget. Hence, Keynesian economic theory advocates using **fiscal policy,** the combination of tax policy and spending policy, to ensure a healthy economy.

Roosevelt's use of fiscal policy to reinvigorate the national economy was followed by passage of the landmark Full Employment Act in 1946, which established the national government's responsibility for ensuring the low unemployment rate characteristic of a healthy economy. Keynesian economics has informed the economic policies of Democratic and Republican administrations since Roosevelt's administration, but it did not provide a clear direction for economic policy during the economic downturn beginning in the late 1970s. Labeled **stagflation,** the economy during the late 1970s and most of the 1980s experienced the high unemployment of a recession and large increases in the prices of consumer goods (high inflation) typical of an economic boom. Republican President Ronald Reagan (1981–1989) implemented a different economic theory in his efforts to deal with stagflation.

Supply-Side Economics

President Reagan introduced the nation to a competing economic theory, **supply-side economics,** which advocates tax cuts and a decrease in government regulation to stimulate the economy in times of recession. Supply-siders argue that the government collects so much money in income taxes from workers that they are discouraged from working more than they absolutely need to (as any extra effort will just mean they pay more in taxes). In addition, high taxes drain the economy because they diminish people's ability to save and corporations' ability to invest to increase productivity. Therefore, the theory goes, if the government cuts taxes, workers will be more productive and people will have more money to save and invest, thus stimulating economic growth. Supply-siders also argue that because government regulation increases the cost of producing goods,

Keynesian economics
theory that recommends that during a recession the national government should increase its spending and decrease taxes, and during a boom, it should cut spending and increase taxes

recession
an economic downturn during which unemployment is high and the production of goods and services is low

depression
a long-term and severe recession

economic boom
rapid economic growth

fiscal policy
government spending and taxing and their effect on the economy

stagflation
an economic condition in which the high unemployment of a recession occurs along with large increases in prices of consumer goods (high inflation) typical of an economic boom

supply-side economics
theory that advocates cutting taxes and deregulating business to stimulate the economy

>During his campaign in 1988, presidential candidate George H. W. Bush told voters to "Read my lips. No new taxes." As president, Bush broke this promise in an attempt to address the growing national debt. At the 2000 Democratic National Convention, a democratic supporter reminds delegates of Bush's broken promise.

deregulation—reducing or eliminating restrictions on business—will contribute to increased production at the same cost, thus increasing the supply of goods.

Republican President George H. W. Bush (1989–1993) initially continued the supply-side economic policies of Reagan, but before the end of his presidency, Bush broke his promise not to raise taxes in an attempt to begin to address the growing **national debt**—the total amount of money owed to others due to borrowing. In addition to increasing taxes, he signed into law new regulations. Democratic President Bill Clinton (1993–2001) battled a Republican-dominated Congress for most of his presidency. Clinton's proposed spending increases were muted by Congress, and Congress pushed for tax cuts. As a result of these policies and economic growth, by the end of the 1990s, the national government was no longer engaging in deficit spending.

President George W. Bush (2001–2009), working with a Republican-dominated Congress for most of his presidency, pursued supply-side economics by cutting taxes and deregulating. During his first term in office, Bush succeeded in winning tax cuts for corporations, the wealthiest Americans, and the lowest-earning Americans. One result of these tax changes was that taxpayers who made more than $1 million in 2004 saw their tax bill fall by an average of $123,592.[3]

Monetarism

Economist Milton Friedman, a onetime supporter of Keynesian economics, is today best known for yet another economic theory, **monetarism,** which advocates that the government's proper role in promoting a healthy economy is the regulation of the money supply to ensure that the rate of inflation remains low. **Inflation** refers to a rising price level for consumer goods, which decreases the purchasing power of money. The Bureau of Labor Statistics provides an inflation calculator (www.bls/gov) that allows you to determine what yesterday's dollar is worth today due to inflation. For example, according to the calculator, $1.60 in 2007 bought what $1.00 in 1990 could buy.

Monetarists believe that *too much* money in circulation leads to a high inflation rate, which slows economic growth as people spend less because of higher prices. In addition, as the rate of inflation increases, investors begin to worry about the health of the economy, and investments may decline as a result, ultimately limiting economic growth. On the flip side, the monetarists say, *too little* money in circulation means there is not enough for new investments and that consequently new jobs are not created; this situation, too, retards economic growth. Today, monetarists target an inflation rate of 1–3 percent

Concept Summary

ECONOMIC THEORIES

— **Laissez-faire economics** proposes that the government should neither encourage nor discourage (through its laws) business practices; the government should have a hands-off stance with regard to the marketplace.

— **Keynesian economics** advocates the use of fiscal policy (taxing and spending policies) to create and maintain a healthy economy. According to Keynesian economics, during a recession the government should increase its spending and decrease taxes; during an economic boom the government should decrease spending and increase taxes.

— **Supply-side economics** calls for the government to cut taxes and deregulate to stimulate economic growth.

— **Monetarism** relies on the government's ability to influence the amount of money in circulation to maintain price stability and a healthy economy.

per year to ensure an adequate money supply for a healthy economy. They believe that the national government must use its monetary policy to maintain this level of inflation.

Should One Economic Theory Predominate?

Although economists, government officials, and citizens broadly agree that the government should act to ensure a healthy economy, there is perpetual debate over how involved the government should be in the economy and what specific policy actions it should take. Where people stand in this debate depends on which economic theory they advocate. Each theory supports the use of different government policies to promote a healthy economy. Before we discuss these various policies that theoretically promote economic health, we consider how governments measure economic health. Once we know what a healthy economy looks like, we can then consider the effects that various policies have on the health of the economy.

Measuring Economic Health

Economists and government officials describe a healthy economy as one that has the following characteristics: expanding gross domestic product (GDP); increasing level of worker productivity; low unemployment rate; low inflation rate.

These traditional measures of economic health together provide a useful snapshot of how the national economy is doing. Other measures of economic health focus on the general well-being of the people by accounting for factors such as rates of poverty and literacy and the financial situation of households. These less traditional measures include the United Nations Human Development Index, real median household income, income inequality, and the poverty rate.

Traditional Measures of Economic Health

Most economists assume that growth in the gross domestic product translates into a prosperous nation with improving living standards—hence, progress toward living the American dream. **Gross domestic product (GDP)** is the total market value of all goods and services produced by labor within a country's borders. Another assumption made by most economists is that high productivity, or output per worker, also fosters improved living standards. Rising GDP and productivity are signs of an expanding economy, which means the production of more goods and services—and thus the availability of more goods and services for consumers.

Economists also expect a healthy economy to correlate with a low level of inflation. When inflation rises, consumers' purchasing power falls and they cannot buy as much this year with the same amount of money they spent last year. The government agency known as the Bureau of Labor Statistics publishes the **consumer price index (CPI),** which measures the average change in prices over time of a "market basket" of goods and services, including food, clothing, shelter, fuel, transportation costs, and selected medical costs. The CPI is the most commonly used measure of inflation's impact on people. According to economists, when the economy is healthy, the inflation rate (measured by the change in CPI) ranges between 1 and 3 percent.

A low unemployment rate, 5 percent or less, is also characteristic of a healthy economy, according to economists. When more people are working, the financial situation of families overall should improve. In addition, in a growing economy with falling unemployment, government revenues should increase (as there is more corporate and personal income to tax), and government spending for social welfare programs should decrease (as fewer people should need public assistance). These trends create a healthier financial situation for government.

In sum, a high or rising GDP, high or increasing rate of productivity, low inflation rate, and low unemployment rate suggest a healthy national economy. Yet as the U.S. Department of Commerce's Bureau of Economic Analysis points out, "While the GDP is used as

deregulation
reduction or elimination of regulatory restrictions on firms and industries

national debt
the total amount of money the national government owes to its creditors

monetarism
theory that says the government's proper economic role is to control the rate of inflation by controlling the amount of money in circulation

inflation
the decreased value of money as evidenced by increased prices

gross domestic product (GDP)
the total value of all goods and services produced by labor within a country's borders

consumer price index (CPI)
the most common measure of inflation, it gauges the average change in prices over time of a "market basket" of goods and services including food, clothing, shelter, fuels, transportation costs, and selected medical costs

GLOBAL COMPARISONS

NATIONAL ECONOMIES AND HUMAN DEVELOPMENT

In recognition of global integration, and in an effort to make the world more secure, representatives from the world's governments met at the United Nations in New York City at the beginning of the new millennium to discuss common concerns. The participating governments signed the Millennium Declaration, pledging to eradicate "the abject and dehumanizing conditions of extreme poverty" by 2015. The agreement signaled a new global partnership working toward creating a world order that is more secure and just, due to improvements in human development.

Will a growing proportion of the world's population enjoy the benefits of the global economy?

In its 2007 annual report, the United Nations Development Programme (UNDP) noted that the average worldwide per capita (per person) income is growing and significant improvement has occurred in well-being measures, which include the Human Development Index (HDI).* The UN had created the HDI out of the recognition that a nation's gross national product, the most commonly used measure of economic health, does not indicate much about the quality of life for a nation's people. The HDI aims to fill this gap by measuring how well a country's economy is providing for three basic dimensions of human development. The first dimension is a long and healthy life, as measured by life expectancy at birth. The second is knowledge, as measured by adult literacy rates and enrollment in primary, secondary, and tertiary schools. The third dimension is a decent standard of living, which is measured by GDP per capita.

The closer to 1 a country's HDI score is, the better the aggregate living standard in the country. The accompanying table provides information on the top five and bottom five nations,

TOP FIVE NATIONS:	2006 HDI	BOTTOM FIVE NATIONS:	2006 HDI
1. Norway	0.963	174. Chad	.341
2. Iceland	0.956	175. Mali	.333
3. Australia	0.955	176. Burkina Faso	.317
4. Luxembourg	0.949	177. Sierra Leone	.298
5. Canada	0.949	178. Niger	.281

based on their HDI scores in 2006.** (The United States ranks tenth, with a rating of 0.944.) Note that the HDI, like GDP, is an average, *summary* indicator. That is, it indicates what is happening to the hypothetical average person in a country, not the average poor or average rich person.

At the same time that broad measures of well-being are improving globally, however, income inequality is growing around the globe. Today, 2 percent of the world's adult population owns more than 50 percent of the world's wealth.* The UNDP's 2007 annual report highlights the fact that globally, women are worse off than are men. "Women are consistently paid less than men, have a weaker political voice, often have access to fewer educational opportunities, and generally benefit least from the use of natural resources. [Moreover], 60 percent of the one billion poorest people are women."***

The UNDP and other United Nations agencies work to bring together governments, international organizations, profit-making corporations, and nonprofit civic groups to collaborate in eradicating these inequalities. The goal is to ensure that a growing proportion of the world's population enjoys the benefits of the global economy.

* United Nations Development Programme, *Making Globalization Work for All: United Nations Development Programme Annual Report 2007*, www.undp.org/publications/annualreport2007/IAR07-ENG.pdf.
** www.nationmaster.com/graph/eco_hum_dev_ind-economy-human-development-index.
*** *Making Globalization Work for All*, p. 4.

Human Development Index (HDI)
UN-created measure to determine how well a country's economy is providing for a long and healthy life, educational opportunities, and a decent standard of living

an indicator of economic progress, it is not a measure of well-being."[4] Therefore we need to review other measures that attempt to assess the well-being of the people.

Other Measures of Economic Health

The United Nations (UN) created the **Human Development Index (HDI)** to measure the standard of living of the people of various nations. As discussed in the "Global Comparisons" box, the HDI assesses three dimensions of human development that people in prosperous nations should be able to enjoy: a long and healthy life, educational opportunities, and a decent standard of daily living. These measures of economic health shed light on the ability of people to earn enough to *enjoy a decent quality of life.* Thus they are probing into something quite different from the traditional measures of national economic health that we have just discussed.

With an HDI score of .944 (1.0 is the highest score possible) based on data for 2006, the United States ranked tenth out of 178 nations. How do we know what this rank means to American households and their ability to live the American dream? Additional measures—looking at household income, income inequality, and the level of poverty within the population—can help us answer this question.

Real median household income is an important measure of the financial well-being of American households. **Real income** is income adjusted for inflation so that it can be compared across years. **Household income** is the total pretax earnings of all residents over the age of 15 living in a home. **Median household income** is the income level in the middle of all household incomes; 50 percent of the households have incomes less than the median and 50 percent have incomes greater than the median. An increase in real median household income should characterize a healthy, expanding economy if we assume that increases in workers' productivity will translate into increases in workers' incomes.

To determine whether people at all income levels are benefiting from a healthy economy, the government calculates changes in the percentage of the total national income possessed by households in five income groups. Specifically, the government divides U.S. households into five *quintiles,* each composed of 20 percent of the households in the nation, based on total household income. The bottom group (bottom quintile) is composed of the 20 percent of households with the lowest incomes, and the top quintile comprises the 20 percent of households with the highest incomes. The government then determines the percentage of the total national income possessed by each quintile. Changes in the percentage of the total income held by each quintile over time indicate whether income inequality is growing or shrinking. The ideal is to see a shrinking of income inequality as the national economy expands.

The ideal healthy economy would also ensure that all workers earn enough to stay out of **poverty**—the condition of lacking sufficient income to purchase the necessities for an adequate living standard. The **poverty rate** is the percentage of the population with income below the nationally designated poverty level. The U.S. Census Bureau calculates the poverty rate by using its **poverty thresholds**—an annually updated set of income measures (adjusted for family size) that define who is living in poverty. According to the poverty thresholds for 2006, a family of four, with two children under the age of 18 years, earning less than $20,444 was living in poverty. A family of the same size and makeup earning $20,445 was not living in poverty.

So we have seen that not only traditional economic measures such as GDP, productivity, inflation, and employment serve as indicators of national economic health, but also other measures shed light on the quality of life of people in the United States. With this context in mind, we next explore the way the national government uses fiscal policy to promote a healthy national economy that provides benefits to individuals and households.

real income
earned income adjusted for inflation

household income
total pretax earnings of all residents over the age of 15 living in a home

median household income
the middle of all household incomes—50 percent of households have incomes less than the median and 50 percent have incomes greater than the median

poverty
the condition of lacking sufficient income to purchase the necessities for an adequate living standard

poverty rate
proportion of the population living below the poverty line as established by the national government

poverty thresholds
an annually updated set of income measures (adjusted for family size) that defines who is living in poverty

Fiscal Policy and Its Impact on the Health of the Economy

As noted earlier, fiscal policy comprises spending policy and tax policy. The national government, through its budget process, annually approves a twelve-month plan for raising and spending revenue. The twelve months in which the fiscal policy plan is implemented is a **fiscal year (FY),** running from October 1 through September 30 of the following calendar year. A government's fiscal year is named for the calendar year in which it ends. FY 2009 began on October 1, 2008, and ends on September 30, 2009.

National government expenditures accounted for 19 percent of the GDP of the United States in 2007—unquestionably, a substantial percentage of national economic output. While

fiscal year (FY)
the twelve months in which the government implements its annual budget, which for the national government begins on October 1 and ends on September 30 of the following year

government spending certainly can create jobs, its primary goal is to provide the services necessary to fulfill the Constitution's mission. The other side of the coin, tax policy, raises revenue needed by the national government to serve the people. While the main goal of tax policy is to collect revenue, taxation also decreases the amount of money taxpayers have to spend in the marketplace and corporations have to invest. Hence, taxation may reduce consumer demand for goods and services, with possible effects on the unemployment rate as well as company profits. It may also impact investment in economic growth. Thus tax policy, like spending policy, powerfully affects the economy.

To understand fiscal policy, we look next at the sources of the funds the federal government uses to run the nation, as well as the spending decisions that Congress and the president must make.

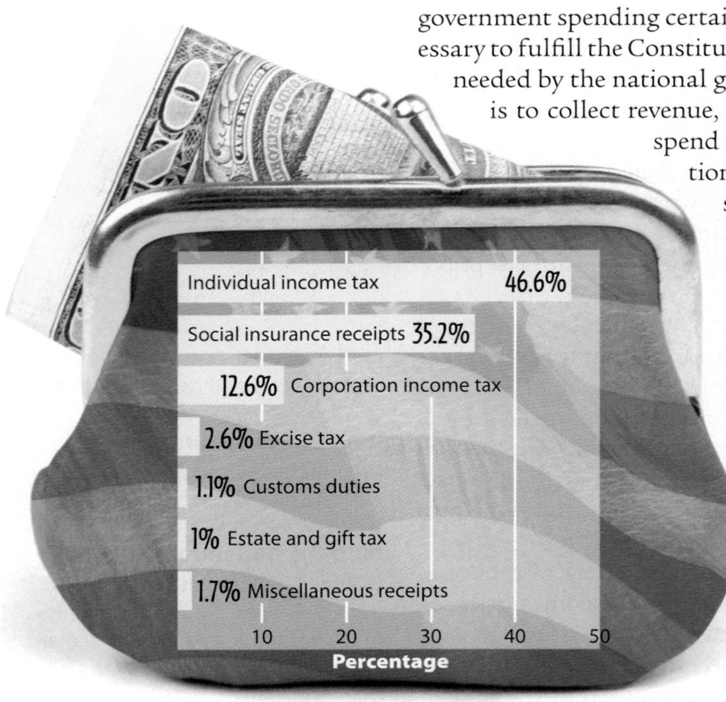

Tax Policy

The Constitution delegates the power of the purse to Congress. By the authority of the Constitution, Congress formulates and approves *tax laws* to raise money along with *appropriation laws*—legislation that authorizes the spending of government money for a fiscal year. The Constitution specifies that the House must introduce revenue-raising bills before the Senate can consider them. The House Ways and Means Committee and the Senate Finance Committee are the congressional standing committees from which tax bills emerge.

The Sixteenth Amendment (1913) authorized the use of a national income tax. Before this amendment, the national government relied on other taxes, with import taxes being the primary single revenue source. Figure 15.1 presents the tax mix proposed in the FY 2009 budget. Today, the national tax on individual income is the largest revenue source for the national government. The federal individual income tax is imposed on each individual's *earned income* (salaries and wages) and *unearned income* (profits made from investments).

Individual income tax 46.6%

Social insurance receipts 35.2%

12.6% Corporation income tax

2.6% Excise tax

1.1% Customs duties

1% Estate and gift tax

1.7% Miscellaneous receipts

10   20   30   40   50
Percentage

FY 2009 Executive Budget

POLITICAL INQUIRY

FIGURE 15.1 ■ What is the government's top source of revenue in the FY 2009 executive budget? Do you project that the revenue from this source will remain high in future budgets? Why or why not? What are the other two main sources that provide national revenue?

progressive tax
a tax that takes a larger percentage of the income of wealthier taxpayers and a smaller percentage of the income of lower-income taxpayers

proportional tax (flat tax)
a tax that takes the same percentage of each taxpayer's income

regressive tax
a tax that takes a greater percentage of the income of lower-income earners than of higher-income earners

tax expenditures
also called *tax breaks* or loopholes; government financial supports that allow individuals and corporations to pay reduced taxes, to encourage behaviors that foster the public good

The second-largest revenue category, social insurance, includes taxes collected for Social Security, Medicare, and unemployment compensation. Because employers deduct from workers' paychecks the amount they owe for social insurance taxes, these taxes are referred to as *payroll taxes*. The federal government's third-largest revenue source is corporate income taxes. The national government also collects *excise taxes,* which are taxes levied against a specific item such as gasoline or liquor, *estate and gift taxes,* and *customs duties* (import taxes).

Taxes levied by the federal government do not affect the income of all taxpayers in the same way. The national income tax is a **progressive tax** because it takes a larger percentage of the income of wealthier taxpayers and a smaller percentage of the income of less-well-off taxpayers. Most taxpayers view a progressive tax, theoretically based on a person's ability to pay, as fair and equitable. Some people believe that a **proportional tax (flat tax),** which takes the same percentage of each taxpayer's income, is fairer than a progressive tax. A flat tax of 10 percent would equal $3,500 for a person earning $35,000 and $13,500 for a person earning $135,000. Although these two taxpayers pay a different amount of money in taxes, the *proportion* of their income collected is the same—hence the name proportional tax. The third impact a tax can have is regressive. A **regressive tax** takes a greater percentage of the income of lower-income earners than of higher-income earners. States' sales taxes are the prime example of a regressive tax.

Another reason why taxes affect various taxpayers differently is the government's practice of granting **tax expenditures** (better known as *tax breaks* or *tax loopholes*). These are government financial supports to individuals and corporations to encourage behaviors that ostensibly enhance the public good. Tax breaks and loopholes allow these taxpayers to pay lower taxes on their income than they would otherwise pay. For example, to encourage home ownership, the government gives tax breaks to individuals paying interest on a home mortgage. One reason the federal government wants to promote homeownership is that the demand for new home construction often leads to job creation. Because of the government's interest in maintaining a low unemployment rate, it also offers tax breaks to businesses for job creation and worker retraining.

State and local governments, as well as nonprofit organizations that provide a public service, pay no federal taxes. Thus we say that they are exempt from federal taxes. Included in this group of tax exempt organizations are the overwhelming majority of colleges and universities, which are public or nonprofit institutions. They are tax exempt because they provide the public good of higher education without making a profit; they must invest any surplus money back into the institution. Given the soaring costs of college, Senator Charles Grassley (R-Iowa) and Senator Max Baucus (D-Montana) have raised questions about the legitimacy of tax exemption for some schools.

Tax expenditures and tax cuts would not be such a big concern if the government raised enough money to balance its budget. Unfortunately, deficit spending is the norm for the national government. How is the government spending all this money?

Spending Policy

Federal government spending decisions significantly affect both the national economy and the ability of individuals to achieve their American dream. Although setting the budget is an annual process, with Congress and the president approving a spending plan one fiscal year at a time, not all national government spending is approved on an annual basis.

Mandatory spending pays for government programs, such as Social Security, that were created and authorized by legislation that also obligates the government to spend the money necessary to meet that program's commitments for as long as the program exists. For a mandatory spending program, the **budget authority**—the authority provided by law for agencies to obligate government spending—is established at the birth of the program and does not need to be reestablished each fiscal year; this is open-ended budget authority. Interest payments on the national debt are also included in the category of mandatory spending; the government is legally obligated to pay back the money it borrows. Mandatory spending is *uncontrollable spending,* which means that current law requires the government to spend money to meet these obligations no matter what the cost. As Figure 15.2 shows, the majority of the national budget pays for uncontrollable, mandatory spending.

Today, the number of retirees is increasing rapidly because of the aging baby boomer generation (individuals born between 1946 and 1964), and the costs of medical care are skyrocketing. Thus national mandatory expenditures grow ever larger for Social Security and Medicare and Medicaid (health insurance for the elderly and low-income individuals, respectively,

Tax Brackets for Those Filing as Single Taxpayers*

THEN (2001)	NOW (2008)
15% for taxable income $0–27,050	10% for taxable income $0–8,025
27.5% for taxable income $27,050–65,550	15% for taxable income $8,025–32,550
30.5% for taxable income $65,550–136,750	25% for taxable income $32,550–78,850
35.5% for taxable income $136,750–297,350	28% for taxable income $78,850–164,550
39.1% for taxable income $297,350 and above	33% for taxable income $164,550–357,700
	35% for taxable income $357,700 and above

WHAT'S NEXT?

> Will calls for a more simplified tax structure result in legislation that replaces the six progressive tax brackets with a flat tax? Explain.

> Will the calls for a fairer tax structure encourage Congress to approve additional tax brackets? Why or why not?

> Will the growing national debt force an increase in the tax rates? Justify your answer.

*www.moneychimp.com/features/tax_brackets.htm.

mandatory spending
payment for debt and government programs for which the legislation that created the program also obligate the government to spend the money necessary to meet the program's commitments as long as the program is in existence

budget authority
authority provided by law for agencies to obligate government spending

Discretionary
nonsecurity
spending
17.3%

Discretionary
security spending
21.7%

Mandatory spending
61%

Social security
20.9%

Medicare
13.3%

Interest
8.4%

Other
18.4%

FIGURE 15.2

Federal Expenditures by Budget Categories: FY 2009 Executive Budget

Source: The Budget for FY 2009, Historical Tables, Tables 3.1 and 8.3, www.whitehouse.gov/omb/budget/fy2009/pdf.hist.pdf.

discretionary spending

payment on programs for which Congress and the president must approve budget authority each year in appropriation legislation

which are discussed in Chapter 16). As the mandatory spending slice of the budget pie has grown, citizens, Congress, and the president are deliberating, debating, and making hard choices about which policies deserve a shrinking percentage of the national budget.

Programs without open-ended budget authority in their authorizing legislation have their budget authority approved on an annual basis. Programs granted budget authority year by year in the annual budget process are **discretionary spending** programs with *controllable* spending. Each year, Congress and the president deliberate over how much budget authority to provide to these programs. Typically, Democrats and Republicans differ on their spending priorities, and when the percentage of the budget over which Congress has control (discretionary spending) shrinks, the partisan battles over spending become ever more intense. Although the number of programs covered by discretionary spending far exceeds the number of mandatory spending programs, a smaller percentage of the budget is spent on these programs.

The national government divides discretionary spending programs into two major categories: security spending and nonsecurity spending. As Figure 15.2 indicates, security spending is a bigger piece of the budget pie than is nonsecurity spending. Security spending includes expenditures for the Department of Defense—including military personnel, operations, maintenance, and procurement—for Homeland Security, and for international affairs. (Excluded in the FY 2009 budget proposal were funds for the global war on terror, which were added to the spending plan later as supplemental expenditures.) Nonsecurity spending covers an array of activities and programs, including: the administration of justice, agriculture, education, energy, health, housing, income security for the poor and disabled, transportation, and veterans' benefits and services.

In the annual budget process, Congress and the president do not make annual decisions about most of the money spent by the national government because the majority of expenditures are mandatory. Other than interest payments on the debt, mandatory spending could be controlled by Congress and the president by rewriting the legislation that established these open-ended budget obligations. As recent attempts to rewrite the legislation that created the Social Security retirement program have shown, however, many mandatory programs are politically difficult to change. This is partly because elected officials fear the impact such changes would have on their reelection prospects, and partly because of partisanship. Not only do Democrats and Republicans disagree on the proper reforms, neither party can agree among themselves on specific reforms. Hence, mandatory spending continues to grow as a percentage of the federal budget.

Creating Fiscal Policy Through the National Budget Process

The federal government creates its programs through authorization legislation that specifies the program's goals and establishes whether its budget authority is obligated for the life of the program (mandatory spending) or must be set annually (discretionary spending). In an annual appropriation process, Congress and the president establish yearly funding for discretionary spending programs and possibly change tax policy to increase revenue raised—to pay the bills—or to cut taxes in an effort to stimulate the economy. This process begins in the executive branch.

THE PRESIDENT'S EXECUTIVE BUDGET   The budget process officially starts about a year and a half before the beginning of the fiscal year for which budget authority will be obligated. For example, work on the budget for FY 2009 began during the spring of 2007. The process begins when the Office of Management and Budget (OMB) sends the president's budget priorities (policy and financing preferences) to the executive branch agencies. Executive branch agencies use the president's guidelines to formulate their funding requests. Typically, these requests are incremental changes (small increases) to their current fiscal year's budget authority.

The budget requests work their way back up the executive branch hierarchy to the OMB. The OMB reviews the budget requests, conducts hearings in which the agencies justify their requests, and analyzes the requests in light of economic forecasts. The OMB then submits its budget recommendations to the president, who works with the OMB to create a proposed fiscal plan for the entire national government for the upcoming fiscal year. The OMB drafts a budget document and a budget message, collectively labeled the **executive budget,** which explains the president's fiscal plan. The president is required by law to submit the executive budget to Congress by the first Monday in February, eight months before the fiscal year begins.

CONGRESSIONAL ACTION   Once Congress receives the president's executive budget, the Congressional Budget Office (CBO), the legislative branch's counterpart to the OMB, swings into action. The CBO analyzes the executive budget in light of economic forecasts and predicted government revenues. The House Budget Committee and the Senate Budget Committee use the CBO's analysis, along with reports from other congressional committees, to develop the **concurrent budget resolution,** which establishes a binding expenditure ceiling (the maximum amount that can be spent) and a binding revenue floor (the minimum amount that must be raised) as well as proposed expenditure levels for major policy categories. The House and the Senate must both agree to the concurrent budget resolution. This agreement is to occur by April 15, less than six months before the fiscal year begins.

After approval of the concurrent budget resolution, the House and the Senate Appropriations Committees each draft appropriation bills to provide budget authority for discretionary programs. In order to comply with the concurrent budget resolution, Congress may also need to revise the legislation that authorized selected government programs. For example, the House and Senate may have to agree to change the open-ended budget authority in existing legislation in order to comply with the expenditure ceiling in the concurrent budget resolution. Or they may have to agree to changes in tax legislation to meet the revenue floor specified in the concurrent resolution. **Budget reconciliation** is the annual process of rewriting authorization legislation to comply with the concurrent budget resolution. The deadline for completion of the reconciliation process is June 15, less than four months before the fiscal year begins.

Congress has until the end of June to approve the twelve appropriation bills that fund the national government for the upcoming fiscal year. This timetable leaves two months for the president to approve the bills so that by October 1 the national government can begin the new fiscal year with budget authority for discretionary spending programs. If Congress and the president fail to approve one or more of the appropriation bills by October 1, Congress must approve a **continuing resolution** to authorize agencies not covered by approved appropriation laws to continue to spend money within their previous budget year's levels.

The nature of the annual budget process is such that, at any given time, some government body in the executive or legislative branch is preparing a future budget, even as the executive branch is implementing the current budget. At the same time, the Government Accountability Office (GAO) is evaluating the implementation of the previous fiscal year's

> Photographers point their cameras at a stack of copies of President George W. Bush's FY 2009 budget in February 2008. Bush's executive budget for FY 2009 included a record-high spending plan of $3.1 trillion and a projected $408 billion deficit.

executive budget
the budget document and budget message that explains the president's fiscal plan

concurrent budget resolution
document approved by the House and Senate at the beginning of their budget process that establishes a binding expenditure ceiling and a binding revenue floor as well as proposed expenditure levels for major policies

budget reconciliation
the annual process of rewriting authorization legislation to comply with the expenditure ceiling and revenue floor of the concurrent budget resolution for the upcoming fiscal year

continuing resolution
an agreement of the House and Senate that authorizes agencies not covered by approved appropriation laws to continue to spend money within their previous budget year's levels

budget. Thus, budgeting is a perpetual government activity, one that takes up a great deal of national officials' time.

Deficit Spending, Debt, and Economic Health

Most Americans highly value the ideal of a balanced budget, in which, as we have seen, the government spends no more than the revenues that it raises. Although the nation had a **budget surplus** (money left over when all expenses are paid) for several years at the end of the 1990s, **budget deficits** (more money spent than collected through revenues) recurred as the first decade of the twenty-first century unfolded. Indeed, deficit spending has become the norm, not the exception (see Figures 15.3 and 15.4). What impact does fiscal policy dominated by deficit spending have on the nation's economic health?

A government that engages in deficit spending borrows money and hence goes into debt. Even as politicians, some economists, and many concerned citizens call for a balanced budget—with some people even proposing a constitutional amendment mandating this objective—deficit spending continues, and so the national debt grows. The long-term impact of debt is the legal obligation to pay back not only the money initially borrowed (the *principal*) but also *interest*. The additional amount of money in interest, typically equal to a percentage of the amount initially borrowed, means the borrower ultimately pays back more than the amount borrowed. In the case of government borrowing, future generations must pay back the

budget surplus
money left over after all expenses are paid

budget deficit
more money spent than collected through revenues

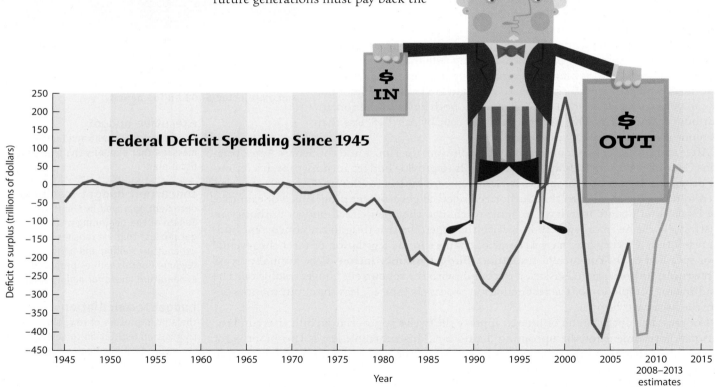

POLITICAL INQUIRY

FIGURE 15.3 ■ What do we mean by a budget deficit and a budget surplus? What trend in deficit spending does the graph indicate? In what recent years has there been a surplus rather than a deficit? What government expenditures do you think explain the rise in deficit spending since 2002?

debt of their parents and grandparents. Today, to pay off the national debt, each citizen would have to chip in about $32,000.[5]

Public debate is ongoing about the economic impact of long-term deficit spending and the colossal national debt, which hovers near $10 trillion. This gigantic sum is almost three times the amount of money the national government spends in one year. Some economists argue that the more money the national government borrows, the less money businesses can borrow in order to invest and expand the economy. In addition, many citizens grow increasingly concerned that today's deficit spending will burden future generations with the bill for current policies. Complicating the picture, as the debt incurred from decades of deficit spending accumulates, the debt payment is becoming a larger proportion of the annual federal budget, increasing the percentage of the budget that pays for mandatory spending.

In order for the government to stop its deficit spending and ultimately reduce its debt, it must increase taxes, cut expenditures, or both. Elected officials do not like to reduce spending, however, because budget cuts often mean that some of their constituents will lose a service or their jobs. In turn, the marketplace suffers because unemployed workers cannot afford to purchase as much as employed workers—and citizens who have been affected by unemployment may express their grievances on election day. Nor do federal fiscal decision makers like to raise taxes, because higher taxes mean that some citizens must give even more of their income to the government and thus have less to spend, invest, or save. Both the health of the economy and officeholders' reelection bids are likely to suffer.

As difficult as these budget decisions are for the elected officials—the president and Congress—they are further influenced by monetary policy making. It is *appointed* officials who have the decision-making power in this realm.

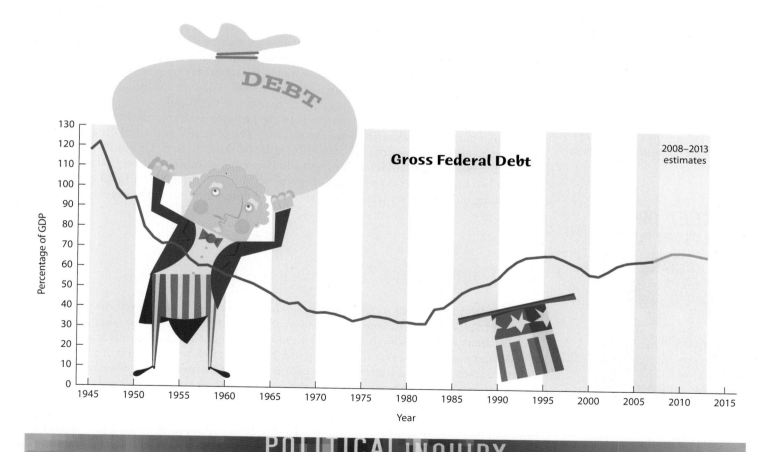

POLITICAL INQUIRY

FIGURE 15.4 ■ **What is the federal debt? What trend does the graph show with respect to the federal debt since the late 1980s?**

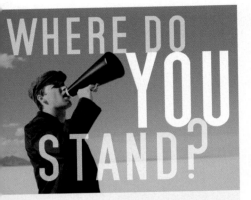

Monetary Policy and the Federal Reserve System

The federal government seeks to influence the value of money by controlling its availability. When more money is in circulation, it is lower in value. The rate of inflation indicates changes in the value of money. When prices are increasing, and consequently consumers need to spend more money to keep buying the same goods and services, inflation is at work. As prices go up, especially on necessities, many people have a tougher time maintaining their quality of life. The costs of running a business also increase with inflation. As a result of increased costs and decreased sales (because fewer people can maintain their level of spending), businesses may choose to lay off workers. Because of these potential problems, the national government tries to control the rate of inflation by gearing its monetary policy to maintain a healthy economy with low unemployment and low rates of inflation. Indeed, controlling inflation is the top priority of the Federal Reserve System, according to its current and past governors.[6]

The Federal Reserve System ("the Fed"), created in 1913, is responsible for setting U.S. **monetary policy**—the body of government policies aimed at maintaining price stability. The Federal Reserve System is composed of a Board of Governors (whose members the president nominates and the Senate must confirm), an Open Market Committee, 12 Federal Reserve Banks (and 25 branch banks), and about 3,000 member banks (all national government–chartered commercial banks and certain state government–chartered financial institutions). The "On the Job" features a Federal Reserve Bank of New York employee.

The Fed has three means by which it influences the supply of money. It can raise or lower the *reserve requirement*—the amount of money that financial institutions must keep out of circulation. In times of high inflation, the Fed may raise the reserve requirement to decrease the amount of money available through credit, hence decreasing the money supply. The Fed can also raise or lower the *discount rate*—the interest charged to financial institutions that borrow money from the Federal Reserve bank—and thereby make it more or less costly to borrow money. The Fed action that most influences the money supply, however, is its decision to buy or sell U.S. Treasury bonds, which are certificates indicating that the holder loaned the government money by purchasing the bond. The Fed sells bonds when it wants to decrease the money supply and buys bonds to increase the supply.

Beyond its authority to set monetary policy, the Fed also exerts regulatory authority over its member banks and other financial institutions. The objective of the Fed's regulatory authority is to create and maintain confidence in the banking system. This authority reaches back to the Fed's origins; indeed, Congress and President Woodrow Wilson (1913–1921) created the Fed during a period when the economy was unstable and the national government was moving away from its laissez-faire stance and embarking on a new course: economic regulation.

Regulatory Policy to Prevent Market Failure

As stated by Adam Smith in 1776, in theory, the competition that characterizes a free, unregulated market serves the public good by producing the range of high-quality and affordable products and services that citizens need or demand. Free-market advocates assume that competition provides for the public good. Yet at times, the competition of a free, unregulated market may fail a nation and its people. **Market failure** occurs when marketplace competition harms consumers, workers, the environment, or the economy as a whole.

Indeed, competition among private entities, each trying to make a profit, may threaten public safety and health. Consider, for example, the unsafe products, including dangerous food and drugs, that may be manufactured and sold to make a profit. Think about production and manufacturing processes that may pollute the air, water, and land, creating conditions that are injurious to public health. Competition may also lead firms to cut salaries and benefits to ensure their profits, or their very survival. Such cuts decrease workers' ability to earn wages and benefits that keep them in the middle class, or even out of poverty. Un-

Your Standard of Living Today

Is your personal standard of living better or worse today than it was five years ago, or is it about the same?

☐ Better
☐ Worse
☐ The same
☐ No opinion

Source: "Four in 10 Americans See Their Standard of Living Declining," www.gallup.com/poll/107749/Four-Americans-See-Their-Standard-Living-Declining.aspx.

monetary policy
the body of government policies, controlled by the Federal Reserve System, aimed at influencing the supply of money in the marketplace to maintain price stability

market failure
a condition in which competition for profits in the marketplace causes harm to society, such as environmental degradation, unsafe working conditions, and low pay

ON THE JOB

DAVID KADEN, FEDERAL RESERVE BANK EMPLOYEE

Name: David Kaden

Age: 22

Hometown: New York City

College: Harvard University, Cambridge, Massachusetts

Major: Social Studies (BA)

Job title: Assistant Chief of Staff, Federal Reserve Bank of New York

Salary for jobs like this: $40,000

Day-to-day responsibilities: In general, my assignment is to provide policy and administrative support to the chief of staff, deputy chief of staff, first vice president, and president of the Federal Reserve Bank of New York. My responsibilities include monitoring policies in development, helping to draft internal and external documents, and making recommendations about policy and management issues.

How did you get your job? I wrote my senior thesis on the politics of international financial crises. In the course of my research, I interviewed a number of current and former Federal Reserve officials. Toward the end of my senior year, I approached the New York Fed about a potential opportunity.

After several conversations and a couple of interviews, they offered me a position.

What do you like best about your job? The pace and variety of the issues I work on and the opportunity to help extraordinarily talented people analyze and execute complex decisions make my job interesting and provide a terrific education.

What is your least favorite aspect of your job? Not all of my assignments are equally engaging. Maintaining a consistent level of intensity and quality of effort is sometimes challenging.

What advice would you give to students who would like to do what you are doing? Develop a strong interest and thorough understanding of the economics and politics that undergird the U.S. economy and the global financial architecture. The more you know about the Federal Reserve, macroeconomic policy issues, financial markets and institutions, and the global economy, the better off you will be.

---

safe and unhealthful working conditions may be another "cost" that workers "pay" so that firms can hold down or reduce production expenses. Moreover, if marketplace competition leads to the elimination of all competitors, a monopoly develops, leaving consumers with goods that are overpriced and possibly of poor quality.

In the U.S. economy today, the government regulates marketplace practices to protect the public from market failure. This regulation occurs in two broad categories: business regulation and social regulation. **Business regulation** includes government policies that aim to preserve competition in the marketplace. **Social regulation** refers to government policies directed at protecting workers, consumers, and the environment from the harm caused by marketplace competition. In Chapter 13, we surveyed the administrative rule-making process by which executive branch agencies establish business and social regulations. In this discussion, we trace the evolution of these two types of regulatory policy.

Business Regulation

The federal government created the first agency for the purpose of regulating business, the Interstate Commerce Commission (ICC), in 1887. The ICC initially regulated the prices of and services provided by the railroad industry to protect the livelihood of farmers who

business regulation
government rules, regulations, and standards directed at protecting competition in the marketplace

social regulation
government rules and regulations aimed at protecting workers, consumers, and the environment from market failure

> The bankruptcy of Enron, an American energy company, in 2001, caused thousands of employees to lose their jobs, thousand of investors to lose their life savings, and the Security and Exchange Commission (SEC) to tighten its rules and regulations for stock transactions.

relied on the nation's rail lines to transport their goods to distant markets. Next, in 1914, the federal government established regulations to prevent large corporations from engaging in business practices that harmed marketplace competition and established the Federal Trade Commission (FTC) to oversee these regulations.[7]

In 1934, during the Great Depression, the government created the Securities and Exchange Commission (SEC) to regulate and make transparent the nation's stock markets and financial markets. Decades later, in 2002, the SEC reformed its rules and regulations to close loopholes in the regulation of stock transactions. These loopholes had been brought to light by the collapse of Enron, a giant U.S. energy corporation based in Houston. Enron disintegrated following the discovery of systematic internal accounting fraud, causing thousands of its employees to lose their jobs and (along with thousands of investors) their life savings. Because it took a toll on investor confidence generally, Enron's fall posed a threat to investments in the larger economy, and so the federal government toughened its regulation of financial markets.

Another regulation of the Depression era, the National Labor Relations Act of 1935 (commonly known as the Wagner Act), authorized the national government to regulate interactions between management and labor unions. For almost one hundred years before the law's passage, American workers had protested dangerous working conditions and wages so low that often entire families—including children as young as 5 years old—had to work seven days a week in order to earn enough to pay for basic needs. The Wagner Act empowered union members by creating the right of workers to unionize and elect representatives to bargain collectively with management for improved wages and working conditions. Moreover, the Wagner Act outlawed certain management practices that Congress considered unfair to labor—and hence a potential threat to the economy. Then in 1947, Congress overrode President Harry Truman's (1945–1953) veto and passed the Labor-Management Relations Act (Taft-Hartley Act), which identified and outlawed labor practices Congress deemed unfair and restricted the right to unionize to nonsupervisory employees only.

Thus within fifty years of the creation of the first regulatory agency, the ICC, the national government had put in place a full range of business regulations. From regulating prices and standards in industries, to criminalizing business practices that impinge on marketplace competition, to making stock transactions transparent, to regulating labor-management relations—today the government regulates the marketplace in a wide variety of ways in the interest of creating and maintaining a healthy economy.

Social Regulation

The national government also uses social regulatory policy—which aims to protect the public's health and safety—to safeguard workers, consumers, and the environment from the potential harm created by the competitive quest for profits in the marketplace. Like business regulation, social regulation has an economic impact because it increases the costs of doing business.

EARLY SOCIAL REGULATION   Scholars see precedents for social regulation in two 1906 laws that protected *public* health—the Pure Food and Drug Act and the Meat Inspection Act. Upton Sinclair's descriptions of the dangerous and unsanitary conditions in the Chicago meatpacking industry in his novel *The Jungle* motivated President Theodore Roosevelt (1901–1909) to sign these two laws. The Pure Food and Drug Act created the Food and Drug Administration (FDA) and charged it with testing all foods and drugs produced for human consumption. It also requires individuals to present prescriptions from licensed physicians in order to purchase certain drugs and mandates the use of warning labels on habit-forming drugs. The Meat Inspection Act requires government inspection of animals that are slaughtered and processed for human consumption and establishes standards of cleanliness for slaughterhouses and meat processing plants.

The federal government first addressed working conditions that jeopardized *workers'* health when it enacted the Fair Labor Standards Act (FLSA) in 1938. The FLSA established standards for a legal workweek, overtime pay for those working more than the standard workweek, minimum wages, record keeping of workers' hours, and limits on child labor. President Franklin D. Roosevelt characterized the law as the "most far-reaching, far-sighted program to the benefit of workers ever adopted."[8]

CONSUMER AND ENVIRONMENTAL PROTECTION

Whereas the national government's early social regulation in the 1930s principally aimed to address inequities and dangers in the workplace, in the 1960s the government focused anew on growing concerns about product quality and safety. In his 1965 book *Unsafe at Any Speed,* attorney and consumer advocate Ralph Nader warned that "a great problem of contemporary life is how to control the power of economic interests which ignore the harmful effects of their applied science and technology."[9] Although Nader's book targeted the unsafe cars rolling off the assembly lines of the U.S. auto industry, his warning was equally relevant to the countless American industries that were discharging chemicals and toxins into the environment. Nader's book ignited a consumer safety movement, and a related environmental movement was born with the first Earth Day in 1970.

Lobbying by concerned citizens and interest groups led to passage of the Environmental Protection Act of 1970 and the Consumer Product Safety Act (CPSA) of 1973. These far-reaching federal laws aimed to regulate business practices that threatened consumers' health and safety as well as the environment. The federal Consumer Product Safety Commission (CPSC), created through the CPSA, is charged by law with protecting the public from unreasonable risk of injury associated with more than 15,000 consumer products, including toys, products for children, products for inside and outside the home, and products made for sports and recreation. The CPSA can recall such products if it deems them unsafe, just as the FDA can recall food and prescription medicines it judges to be unsafe. The CPSC and the FDA post recall information on their Web sites (www.cpsc.gov/; www.fda.gov/opacom/Enforce.html).

> Ralph Nader, an attorney, lecturer, author, and political activist, speaks at the Kennedy School of Government at Harvard University during his fifth presidential election campaign in 2008. Nader's five decades of political activism have centered on concerns for consumer rights, government accountability, participatory democracy, environmental protection, and the economic and humanitarian effects of globalization.

THE COSTS OF REGULATION   National social regulation has unquestionably lowered the risk of harm to citizens and the environment caused by marketplace competition. But the burden of government regulations has driven up the cost of doing business, and in the end, consumers pay for this cost. In many industries, this increased cost poses greater problems for smaller firms than for larger ones. The higher costs caused by regulation may also put U.S. industries and firms at a competitive disadvantage in the global marketplace because many other countries do not impose regulations. Therefore, the production costs of firms in other countries are often lower than those in the United States.

The lack of regulations imposed by governments in other nations is a growing concern in the United States. The FDA and the CPSC are recalling numerous products manufactured in foreign countries, and even some products manufactured in the United States that use ingredients or components from foreign sources. Because of these concerns, trade policy and the interdependence of the global economy are prominent contemporary issues.

Trade Policy in the Global Economy

The next time you are shopping, try to purchase only American-made products. Is it possible? Stores in the United States offer products that are domestic (that is, American-made) as well as imported (made overseas by American or foreign companies). Moreover, many American-made products have imported components and ingredients. For example, U.S. International Trade Commission data show that ingredients for food products are imported from more than 100 countries.[10] Today, marketplaces in every country offer products grown and produced in countries from throughout the world. Hence national economies are integrated and interdependent—holistically forming the **global economy.**

To navigate in this global economy, each nation has its own **trade policy**—a collection of tax laws and regulations that support the country's international commerce. In addition, international organizations whose mission is to establish trade rules for all nations to follow have created a global trade policy. The goal of trade policy, like the other economic policies we have discussed, is ostensibly to promote prosperous economies.

Trade Policy: Protectionist or Free Trade?

A government's trade policy takes one of two basic forms: free trade or protectionism. **Protectionist trade policy** aims at protecting domestic producers and businesses from foreign competition through tariffs and nontariff trade barriers. A **tariff** is a special tax on imported goods. **Nontariff trade barriers** include government social and business regulations as well as government **subsidies**—tax breaks or another kind of financial support that encourages business expansion or decreases the cost of doing business so that businesses can be more competitive. Proponents of national government subsidies to U.S. farmers argue that to decrease these subsidies would place the farmers at a competitive disadvantage because European farmers receive even larger subsidies from their governments. Regulations include restrictions such as quotas on the number of imports allowed into the country and bans on the sale of imports that the government deems unsafe. For example, in 2007 the national government blocked imports of wheat gluten from a company in China after the FDA recalled a brand of pet food manufactured in Canada that contained this wheat gluten. The pet food caused cats and dogs throughout the United States to become ill and even to die.

From the 1790s until the 1930s, protectionism was the aim of U.S. trade policy. As the first secretary of the treasury, Alexander Hamilton argued successfully that taxes on imported goods could be set high enough to protect American-made products in the domestic marketplace. In 1930, even as the American economy was failing, Congress hiked tariffs 20 percent—so high that it set off an international tariff war. This tariff hike fueled the Great Depression, whose economic toll was global in scope.

After World War II, the United States and its international partners gradually shifted toward a **free trade policy,** which aims at lowering or eliminating tariffs and nontariff barriers to trade. Free trade policies decrease the costs of bringing products to markets throughout the world and, in this way, open markets to a greater diversity of products and brisker competition. When other nations eliminate tariffs, American companies can participate in the global marketplace at a lower cost. These opportunities encourage an increase in the supply of U.S. goods and thus lead to an expansion of the U.S. economy. By the same token, when the United States eliminates its tariffs, more foreign products make their way into the American marketplace, increasing the diversity of consumer goods and producer competition and decreasing consumer prices in the United States.

International Trade Agreements

In 1947, the United States and twenty-three other nations signed the General Agreement on Tariffs and Trade (GATT). This multilateral agreement on guidelines for conducting international trade had three basic objectives. One,

global economy
the worldwide economy created by the integration and interdependence of national economies

trade policy
a collection of tax laws and regulations that supports the country's international commerce

protectionist trade policy
establishment of trade barriers to protect domestic goods from foreign competition

tariff
a special tax on imported goods

nontariff trade barrier
business and social regulations as well as subsidies aimed at creating a competitive advantage in trade

subsidy
a tax break or another kind of financial support that encourages business expansion or decreases the cost of doing business so that businesses can be more competitive

free trade policy
elimination of tariffs and nontariff trade barriers so that international trade is expanded

the signatory countries would not discriminate against each other in trade matters. Two, the signatory countries would work toward eliminating all tariff and regulatory barriers to trade among their countries. Three, the signatory countries would consult and negotiate with each other to resolve any trade conflicts or damages caused by trading activities of another signatory country. Through multilateral negotiations, the GATT established the guidelines for international trade and resolved trade disputes from 1947 to 1995.

Then in 1995, the World Trade Organization (WTO) came into being. The WTO continues the GATT's advocacy of free trade and punishment of protectionism. Specifically, the WTO monitors adherence to international trade rules and resolves charges of rule violations raised by its member countries, of which there are over 130. The WTO Ministerial Conference meets every two years to discuss and deliberate on international trade rules. The meetings have become magnets for massive and sometimes violent demonstrations by protesters from around the world who believe that free trade is harming the environment, impeding human development in developing countries, and hurting the poor in all countries. Opponents of free trade argue that the deregulation of nontrade barriers has exacerbated deplorable working conditions, child labor problems, and poverty (see "The Conversation of Democracy").

In the 1990s, bipartisan support for free trade in the U.S. Congress produced regional trade agreements such as the North American Free Trade Agreement (NAFTA), which the United States, Canada, and Mexico signed in 1993. NAFTA eliminated barriers to trade and financial investments across the economies of the three nations. Yet by the beginning of the twenty-first century, congressional legislators' concerns about possible damage to living standards and the health of the global environment, which many argue are caused by free trade, were growing, as was the nation's **trade deficit.**

Throughout President George W. Bush's administration, congressional Democrats, led by Representatives Charles Rangel (New York) and Sandra Levin (Michigan), fought for worker and environmental protections in trade agreements. Rangel and Levin called for protection of basic worker rights such as those advocated by the International Labor Organization. Among these rights are bans on forced labor and child labor, prohibitions against discrimination in personnel decisions and policies, and safeguards for workers' rights to organize and to bargain collectively with employers—all forms of social regulation.[11] Americans across the country are also fighting for workers rights (see "Doing Democracy").

The debate over free trade versus protectionism goes on worldwide. Groups concerned about human development, especially in developing countries, worry that free trade agreements ignore the economic status of small family farmers, craftspeople whose goods are sold in local markets, and poor people in general. Americans wonder what free trade means for their prospects of living the American dream.

Foreign Trade

Do you view foreign trade as a positive opportunity for U.S. businesses or as a threat to the U.S. economy?

☐ Positive opportunity

☐ Threat to economy

Source: "More Americans See Threat, Not Opportunity, in Foreign Trade," www.gallup.com/poll/17605/More-Americans-See-Threat-Opportunity-Foreign-Trade.aspx.

trade deficit
a negative balance of trade in which imports exceed exports

The Global Economy, the U.S. Economy, and the American Dream Today

Owning a home, providing your children with good educational opportunities so they can advance in life, and saving for retirement—these are main ingredients of the American dream. Today, Americans tell pollsters that they are living better than their parents did. At the same time, Americans tell pollsters that today's children will *not* be able to live better than *their* parents did.[12] Indeed, *New York Times* columnist Bob Herbert summarizes several recent studies of the millennial generation (those born between 1980 and 2000) by stating that it "is in danger of being left out of the American dream—the first American generation to do less well economically than their parents."[13]

In contrast, Kishore Mahbubani, the dean of Singapore's Lee Kuan Yew School of Public Policy, reports that the American mantra of each generation living better than their parents is alive among Asian young people who are convinced that "they will do much better than their parents."[14] The economic situation of the U.S. millennial generation as well as that of its Asian counterpart may be explained by the fact that "the global economy has been growing at more than twice the pace of the United States economy," with Asian countries leading the way.[15]

IS FREE TRADE MERELY A RACE TO THE BOTTOM?

The Issue: Since World War II, world powers—including governments such as the United States and influential nongovernmental organizations (NGOs) such as the World Bank and the International Monetary Fund—have worked to expand international trade. Although the founders of this globalization movement, among them economist John Maynard Keynes, envisioned a "race to the top" with respect to living standards, today a global debate rages on the pros and cons of free trade. Supporters of free trade argue that it is the path out of poverty. Opponents insist that free trade has set off a brutal "race to the bottom" because of market failures.

Yes: Free trade sets off a race to the bottom. Big companies set up shop in foreign countries to hike up their profits, not to improve people's standards of living. Free trade encourages today's corporations to move their jobs to other countries where business and social regulation is weak or nonexistent. Consequently, the workers in producer nations lose jobs to lower-paid foreign workers toiling in deplorable conditions. Foreign plants, with weak or nonexistent environmental regulations to follow, are also creating major environmental hazards that spill across national borders. So, while the profits of multinational corporations are increasing due to free trade, the standard of living of the majority of people around the globe is stagnating at best. Like the United States at the dawn of the twentieth century, countries that are rapidly changing from an agrarian to an industrialized economy experience a race to the bottom in terms of wages, working conditions, and living standards.

No: Free trade spreads wealth. Free trade opens new markets for products from all countries. New markets increase demand for products, hence creating jobs in the producing countries. This job creation sparks a transition from an agrarian-based economy to an industrialized economy with improved living standards. Free trade also allows multinational companies to establish plants in foreign countries, bringing with them better salaries and working conditions as well as democratic values. As consumers enjoy a greater variety of products at lower costs, the standard of living improves, especially for lower-income households. History shows that in the long term this type of economic transition—economic development—improves the quality of life for workers as every-one benefits financially. As a nation's population becomes wealthier, it is in a better position financially to focus on environmental protection. Hence, free trade is good for the people and the environment.

Other approaches: Creative capitalism can ameliorate a race to the bottom. Civic-minded corporations practicing what Bill Gates, the recently retired head of Microsoft, calls "creative capitalism" use the power of the marketplace to help the world's poor.* Under creative capitalism, governments, businesses, and nonprofit organizations work together to ensure that current global economic forces benefit profit-making corporations while also addressing societal problems. For example, the (RED) Campaign is a coordinated effort in which corporations have pledged a percentage of their profits from select products to purchase medications needed to fight AIDS in Africa. The (RED) Manifesto states that "(RED) is not a charity. It is simply a business model."** In 2007, (RED) generated $50 million for the Global Fund to Fight AIDS, Tuberculosis, and Malaria.* Creative capitalism does not tinker with free trade, but it does encourage corporations to develop a social consciousness for which consumers reward them. The profits of free trade benefit the poor as well as the corporations.

What do you think?

① Are U.S. companies that create jobs in foreign countries interested in improving those countries' working conditions and pay and in protecting the environment? Explain.

② Do the greater diversity and availability of cheaper imported goods as a result of free trade improve or worsen the living standards of the world's peoples, in your opinion? Defend your position.

③ In the long term, what effect will a global laissez-faire policy have on the quality of life of the world's population as a whole?

④ How can the benefits of global economic development decrease income inequality?

* http://go.philly.com/gatestalk.
** www.joinred.com/manifesto.

DOING DEMOCRACY

LOBBY YOUR UNIVERSITY TO SUPPORT FAIR TRADE

FACT:

American workers, consumers, human rights groups, and students across the country are flexing their civic engagement muscle in campaigns advocating guarantees of worker rights. In 1998, pressure from such activists forced the Federation Internationale de Football Association (FIFA), the group that oversees the World Cup, to adopt a code stating that it would not use soccer balls made with child labor. In addition, various nonprofit organizations have secured certification of certain imported goods, such as coffee and tea, as "fair trade" products, which means that their producers must comply with basic workers' rights standards, including living wages and bans on child labor. And U.S. college students on over 200 campuses have joined United Students Against Sweatshops (USAS) to fight for improved working conditions and guaranteed workers' rights.

Act!

On April 10, 2007, University of Southern California students joined the growing ranks of college students fighting for fair trade. Thirteen students staged a sit-in at the USC president's office, emphatically continuing an eight-year student call for USC to affiliate with the Worker Rights Consortium (WRC), an independent group that monitors working conditions in foreign factories that produce university-themed apparel. The students also demanded that USC adopt the Designated Supplies Program (DSP), which ensures that university apparel is produced in factories where workers have the right to unionize and earn a living wage. The students' sit-in ended when the threat arose that they would be suspended immediately if they did not leave the office. Senior philosophy major Ana Valderrama explained, "We were prepared for arrest, but not suspension." Another student protester, junior international relations major Meher Talib, commented with frustration, "I'm upset that we didn't win the campaign. But that doesn't mean the campaign is over."*

Where to begin

If you are interested in learning more about fair trade and/or lobbying your university to affiliate with WRC and to adopt the DSP, numerous resources are available:

- **http://studentsagainstsweatshops.org**—The Web site for United Students Against Sweatshops (USAS) provides information on work conditions overseas as well as details on how to develop a chapter of USAS on your campus.

- **http://uscwatch.org**—This Web site traces the activities of USCWatch, a student group working to ensure that USC acts with the highest ethical principles in its local community and around the world.

- **www.freethechildren.com/youthzone/media/SevenSteps .pdf**—On this Web site, Free the Children provides a step-by-step guide to social involvement, from researching an issue you are passionate about through developing the agenda for, and running, a meeting of peers, to creating a blueprint for social action.

* Angie Green, *Los Angeles Times*, April 11, 2007, file://C:/DOCUME~1/jean/LOCALS~1/ Temp/XZR&%)AM.htm.

Between 2000 and 2007, according to traditional measures of economic health, the U.S. economy was expanding; however, it was the weakest economic expansion since World War II.[16] The GDP and productivity rose an average of 2.8 percent over this period. In addition, corporate profits as a share of the economy stood at record heights.[17] In this same time interval, the percentage of the population employed declined by 1.5 percent, and the unemployment rate fluctuated from a low of 4.0 percent in 2000 to a high of 6.0 percent in 2003. In early 2008, the unemployment rate was 4.9 percent.[18] As for the inflation rate, it was 3.38 percent in 2000, dropped to a low of 1.59 percent in 2002, and rose to 4.3 percent between January 2007 and January 2008.[19] Overall, economists and politicians typically interpret these levels as signs of a healthy economy.

During the same period, the real median household income in American households decreased. In 2007, hourly and weekly wages fell, after adjusting for inflation, by about 1 percent.[20] In addition to the decline in income, the poverty rate crept up from 11.3 percent in 2000 to 12.3 percent in 2006.[21] Moreover, income inequality grew. According to the U.S. Census Bureau, by 2007 the bottom quintile possessed just 3.4 percent of the total national

EXPLORING THE SOURCES

RACE, ETHNICITY, AND THE AMERICAN DREAM

In his November 26, 2007, opinion piece, Paul Krugman, an economist and noted columnist, commenting on a recent Gallup Poll reported that "Americans' economic pessimism reaches record highs . . . [and] the real explanation for the public's pessimism is that whatever good economic news there is hasn't translated into gains for most working Americans. One way to drive this point home is to compare the situation for workers today with that in the late 1990s, when the country's optimism was almost as remarkable as its pessimism today. . . . [In the 1990s, Americans] felt they were sharing in the country's prosperity."* Were all Americans able to share in the prosperity of the 1990s? Consider the data presented in the graphs below.

Evaluating the Evidence

① Considering the data presented in the graphs here, as well as in Table 15.1, how did race and ethnicity influence a person's share of the prosperity of the 1990s? Explain.

② The importance of earning a college degree to achieving the American dream is a reality. In the prosperous 1990s, did race and ethnicity influence a person's ability to pay for college? Explain.

③ What can data for different demographic groups, such as the data presented here, reveal that data for all Americans as one group cannot reveal? Explain.

④ What questions about the U.S. economy and the ability to achieve the American dream in the "prosperous" 1990s come to mind when you review the data in these graphs and tables?

PERCENTAGE OF PERSONS BELOW POVERTY 1990–2000 BY RACE/ETHNICITY

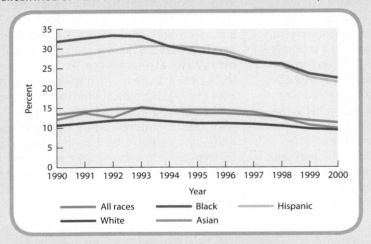

MEDIAN HOUSEHOLD INCOME IN CONSTANT (2004) DOLLARS BY RACE/ETHNICITY

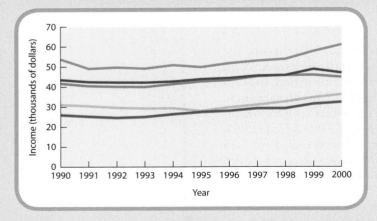

AVERAGE COST OF COLLEGE TUITION, ROOM, AND BOARD 1990–2000

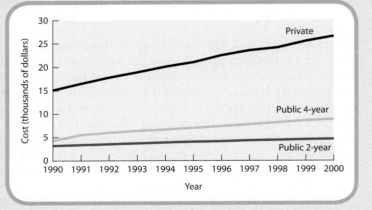

* Paul Krugman, "Winter of Our Discontent," *New York Times*, November 26, 2007.

Sources: www.census.gov/compendia/statab/tables07s0692.xls; www.census.gov/compendia/statab/tables07s0672.xls; www.census.gov/compendia/statab/tables07s0282.xls.

income, while the top quintile held 50.5 percent, which is the largest share of the national income held by the top quintile since 1967.[22] These data indicate that 20 percent of the population held more than 50 percent of the national income. See "Exploring the Sources" for a consideration of the situation in the 1990s.

On the basis of these statistics, so far in the twenty-first century, the prosperous U.S. economy has benefited corporations and people at the top of the income scale more than anyone else. Alan Greenspan, the renowned economist who chaired the Federal Reserve from 1987 to 2005, testified to Congress's Joint Economic Committee in 2005 about this paradox of a growing economy that disproportionately benefits those at the top: "This is not the type of thing which a democratic society—a capitalist democratic society—can really accept without addressing." He went so far as to suggest that this income gap seriously threatens the stability of the U.S. economy.[23]

Indeed, by February 2008, some in the media were forecasting stagflation as consumer prices increased, with energy prices climbing and food prices following suit, at the same time that economic growth (as measured by change in the GDP) was stagnating.[24] Senator Christopher Dodd (D-Connecticut), chairman of the Senate Banking Committee, stated, "The current economic situation is more than merely a 'slowdown' or a 'downturn.' It is a crisis of confidence among consumers and investors."[25] President Bush and Congress attempted to use fiscal policy to address this economic situation. In February 2008, they approved tax rebates totaling $168 billion and tax cuts for select businesses. Between September 2007 and March 2008, the Fed cut interest rates six times in efforts to stimulate economic growth. But the interest rate cuts were beginning to create fears of growing inflation during this period of economic slowdown, hence the stagflation forecast.

Economists and politicians blamed the economic stress on several factors, including years of risky housing loans and investments that by the summer of 2007 resulted in a jump in loan defaults and bankruptcies, followed by losses and failures in the financial investment industry. Senator Dodd's acknowledged "crisis of confidence among consumers and investors" sparked a call in spring 2008 for the Fed to increase its regulation of the banking and financial investment industries. By late September 2008 the federal government had pledged $300 billion to bring back to financial health two top mortgage companies (Freddie Mac and Fannie Mae) and American International Group (AIG), a top international insurance and financial services organization. The Bush administration then proposed an additional $700 billion bailout for Wall Street.

In a prime-time address on September 24, 2008, President Bush told the nation that "our entire economy is in danger" and warned that Congress must act quickly on his $700 billion bailout plan to prevent a "long and painful recession." Reflecting taxpayers' fears and disgust over the excesses of high-paid financial industry executives, Congressional Democrats and Republicans worked with the Bush administration to modify its bailout plan. The modifications called for greater oversight and accountability of government officials overseeing the bailout as well as accountability for those believed responsible for the financial crisis. In addition, Congress wrote taxpayer protections into the plan. Moreover, calls for new regulations for the banking and financial investment industries grew louder as the ability to achieve the American dream diminished.

The prizes of the American dream—a home of one's own, a college education for your children, and a comfortable retirement—are the prizes of middle-class America. Today, many labor experts consider $20 per hour (or an annual income of $41,600) to be the minimum income needed by a family of four to achieve this dream.[26] Unfortunately, fewer workers are able to find work that pays enough for them to afford the American dream. Even a growing percentage of college graduates are finding themselves in jobs for which they are overqualified and for which the pay is less than $20 per hour. Frank Levy, a labor economist at

The United States' #1 Economic Problem Today

In your opinion, what is the United States' most serious economic problem today?

☐ Prices of gas and oil
☐ Cost of housing/mortgages
☐ Unemployment/jobs
☐ Personal finances
☐ Government spending on the war and defense
☐ Other

Source: "Americans' Views of the Economy and the State of the Country," www.cbsnews.com/htdocs/pdf/Mar08c-economy.pdf.

Massachusetts Institute of Technology, notes that in today's economy, people worry first about having a job; then they worry about the rate of pay and the fact that they are not keeping up with the cost of living.[27] What accounts for the shrinking of the middle class?

In the global economy, U.S. workers must compete for jobs with workers in other nations where the cost of doing business is lower because of factors such as less government regulation and higher levels of government subsidies to businesses. In the United States, unionized workers compete with lower-paid nonunionized workers. Many U.S. workers (unionized and not) have begun to give back benefits and have agreed to salary cuts in order to keep their jobs. In addition, some unionized manufacturing plants have closed, with the jobs moving to nonunionized plants. At the same time, many companies are earning record-breaking profits, and their chief executive officers are collecting record-setting salaries and bonuses.

Since World War II, the United States has experienced ten periods of economic expansion,[28] which typically meant that a greater percentage of the population could afford the American dream. The economic expansion of 2001–2007 has been the weakest. For a growing number of citizens, the American dream is one of the casualties of this weak expansion.

CONCLUSION
CONTINUING THE CONVERSATION

On January 2, 2008, White House counsel Ed Gillespie told reporters that "we cannot take economic growth for granted" and that the Bush administration would therefore do "what we think is appropriate to continue to foster economic growth."[29] From President George Washington's administration to the current regime, the national government's involvement (some would say interference) in the domestic economy has dramatically evolved. The variety, complexity, and volume of economic policies have grown strikingly since 1789, when Washington took office. But as the federal government's role in the economy has expanded, its ability to balance the national budget has diminished. Today, the federal government's debt stands at the staggering sum of more than $8 trillion.

The president and Congress use fiscal policy, trade policy, and regulatory policy to achieve a prosperous economy, safe working conditions and consumer products, a healthy environment, and access to the American dream. The Fed aims to maintain price stability and high rates of employment through its control of monetary policy. Enacting the right mix of fiscal, trade, regulatory, and monetary policy to ensure a healthy and sustainable economy, environment, and standard of living is not easy, however, and the federal government does not always meet its economic targets. As current costs of housing, fuel, food, education, and other necessities rise to new heights, Americans are no longer confident that their children will live a better life than they. The American dream remains a dream, not a reality, for a growing proportion of the U.S. population.

Adding to the complexity of achieving and maintaining a prosperous U.S. economy is the interdependence of today's global economy. The economic activities of other countries, as well as political conflicts across the globe, affect the U.S. economy more acutely and rapidly then ever before. Conflicts in oil-producing countries drive up the price of oil, and the increased cost leads in turn to higher-priced U.S. consumer goods. The lack of regulation in many countries that produce goods for the U.S. market, as well as the ever-rising number of foreign-produced components used in U.S.-made goods, threatens the quality and safety of consumer products. Moreover, as foreign companies that manufacture products more cheaply compete with U.S.-made products, the number of well-paying manufacturing jobs in the United States is declining.

Since World War II, the United States has been the dominant economic force in the world. But the 2008 World Economic Forum—an annual meeting of thousands of corporate chief executive officers, government officials, and intellectuals—brought sobering conclusions. The consensus was that the United States has fallen from its pedestal as the world's economic leader,[30] the victim of its colossal national debt, deep reliance on imported oil, and a crisis in confidence among its own citizens about the state of the economy.

The new president, Congress, and the American people face a tangle of economic problems. Will we draw on our manifold strengths as a people and a nation to solve them successfully?

Summary

1. Economic Health and the American Dream
Though work ethic and education level influence personal income, a healthy national economy is essential to the ability of people to live a financially secure, happy, and healthy life—to realize the American dream. The health of the economy influences the availability of jobs with adequate levels of compensation (salaries and benefits).

2. The Nature of the American Economy
The national government's economic policy is aimed at establishing and maintaining a healthy economy so that it can raise the money necessary to fulfill its mission of serving the people. Because the government implements many policies that encourage, and sometimes mandate, certain business practices in the interest of creating and maintaining a healthy economy, the United States has what is known as a regulated capitalist economy.

3. Economic Theories That Inform Economic Policy
The national government's efforts to achieve and maintain a healthy economy have expanded as lawmakers have supported a variety of economic theories, among them Keynesian economics, supply-side economics, and monetarism. The specific policies implemented by the government depend on the particular economic theories government officials embrace. In recent decades Democrats and Republicans have followed different economic theories, with the result that taxing, spending, and regulatory policies have frequently shifted.

4. Measuring Economic Health
Traditional measures of economic health include worker productivity, GDP, rate of inflation, and rate of unemployment. Other measures include real median household income, income inequality, rate of poverty, and the Human Development Index. Together, they can be used to assess how well a prosperous national economy translates into the ability of people to live the American dream. Unfortunately, many times this diversity of measures yields conflicting assessments of economic health: the nation's economy may be growing at the same time that the financial status of households is stagnating or even declining.

5. Fiscal Policy and Its Impact on the Health of the Economy
Taxing and spending decisions by the president and Congress influence how much money consumers have to spend, save, and invest; how much profit firms make and how much they have to invest in expanding business; and how much the government has to spend in order to serve the people. Deficit spending is a persistent reality of U.S. fiscal policy, creating economic problems in the long term.

6. Monetary Policy and the Federal Reserve System
The Fed, directed by a group of appointed officials, works to keep inflation and unemployment low by regulating the amount of money in circulation in the economy. Aimed at creating and maintaining price stability, monetary policy is a component of U.S. economic policy.

7. Regulatory Policy to Prevent Market Failure
By the late 1800s the laissez-faire ideal concerning government regulation of marketplace competition and business practices was clearly not the reality. Today, business regulation (to ensure competition) and social regulation (to protect workers, consumers, and the

environment) are pervasive components of the U.S. economy, despite ongoing calls by business, some economists, and politicians (more apt to be Republicans than Democrats) to deregulate.

8. Trade Policy in the Global Economy

Protectionist trade policy dominated the United States until after World War II. Then free trade policy became the goal of international agreements and U.S. trade policy. Today, debate continues over the domestic and global effects (positive and negative) of free trade policy in the global economy.

9. The Global Economy, the U.S. Economy, and the American Dream Today

Although the United States economy looks healthy at the beginning of the twenty-first century, as indicated by traditional economic measures, for many individuals and households it is not translating into achievement of the American dream. Moreover, the United States' ability to maintain its leading role in the global economy is being questioned by politicians, corporate leaders, and intellectuals around the world.

Key Terms

American dream 535
balanced budget 538
budget authority 545
budget deficit 548
budget reconciliation 547
budget surplus 548
business regulation 551
concurrent budget resolution 547
consumer price index (CPI) 541
continuing resolution 547
deficit spending 538
depression 539
deregulation 541
discretionary spending 546
economic boom 539
economy 536
executive budget 547
fiscal policy 539
fiscal year (FY) 543

free trade policy 554
global economy 554
gross domestic product (GDP) 541
household income 543
Human Development Index (HDI) 542
income inequality 538
inflation 541
Keynesian economics 539
laissez-faire 537
mandatory spending 545
market failure 550
median household income 543
monetarism 541
monetary policy 550
national debt 541
nontariff trade barrier 544
poverty 543
poverty rate 543
poverty thresholds 543

progressive tax 544
proportional tax (flat tax) 544
protectionist trade policy 554
pure capitalist economy 537
real income 543
recession 539
regressive tax 544
regulated capitalist economy (mixed economy) 537
social regulation 551
stagflation 539
subsidy 554
supply-side economics 539
tariff 554
tax base 536
tax expenditures 544
trade deficit 555
trade policy 554

For Review

1. What is the American dream? Describe one impact each of the following national policies can have on the American dream: tax policy, spending policy, business regulation, social regulation, monetary policy, trade policy, immigration policy.
2. What distinguishes a pure capitalist economy from a regulated capitalist economy?
3. Differentiate among Keynesian economics, supply-side economics, and monetarism.
4. Explain at least six measures of economic health.
5. What is fiscal policy and who makes it?
6. What is monetary policy and who makes it?
7. Distinguish between business regulation and social regulation. Indicate how each type of regulation affects the economy.
8. Differentiate between the goals as well as the techniques of free trade policy and protectionist trade policy.
9. What is the health of the U.S. economy as well as the American dream at the beginning of the twenty-first century?

For Critical Thinking and Discussion

1. If you were president of the United States and wanted to balance the annual budget, what programs' cost cuts do you think you could get American taxpayers to support? What tax increases or new taxes do you think you could get American taxpayers to support? Explain your choices.
2. Consider your family's financial situation. What economic policy would you propose the national government implement to improve your family's financial situation? Explain.
3. Which type of tax do you think is the most fair, progressive, proportional, or regressive? Explain your choice.
4. If the national government deregulates with regard to environmental protection, product safety, and/or working conditions, would there be negative consequences? Give some examples, or explain why there would not be any.
5. Some politicians have suggested that a flat income tax of about 17 percent could raise about the same amount of revenue for the national government as the current progressive income tax and should replace it. Politically speaking, who would support such a proposal, and who would oppose it?

MULTIPLE CHOICE: Choose the lettered item that answers the question correctly.

1. The economic theory that advocates the use of fiscal policy to create and maintain a healthy economy is called
   a. Keynesian economics.
   b. laissez-faire economics.
   c. monetarism.
   d. supply-side economics.

2. Which of the following is *not* included in the mandatory spending category of the national government?
   a. debt payments
   b. education
   c. Medicare
   d. Social Security

3. The officials that approve fiscal policy are
   a. Congress (on its own).
   b. Congress and the president.
   c. Congress, the president, and the Fed.
   d. the Fed (on its own).

4. The officials that approve monetary policy are
   a. Congress (on its own).
   b. Congress and the president.
   c. Congress, the president, and the Fed.
   d. the Fed (on its own).

5. The policy that decreases the costs of bringing products to markets throughout the world by lowering or eliminating tariffs and deregulating is called
   a. free trade policy.
   b. monetary policy.
   c. protectionist trade policy.
   d. regulatory policy.

6. The policy in which the national government engages in order to protect consumers, workers, and the environment from the harm of marketplace competition (market failure) is called
   a. business regulation.
   b. deregulation.
   c. protectionist trade policy.
   d. social regulation.

7. Based on its impact on taxpayers' income, what type of tax is the state sales tax?

a. flat
b. progressive
c. proportional
d. regressive

8. The largest revenue source for the national government is
   a. corporate income taxes.
   b. import taxes.
   c. individual income taxes.
   d. social insurance taxes.

9. During what president's administrations did the national government first adopt Keynesian economic principles to create and maintain a healthy national economy?
   a. George Washington
   b. Franklin Delano Roosevelt
   c. Ronald Reagan
   d. George W. Bush

10. During what president's administrations did the national government attempt to address stagflation using the principles of supply-side economics?
    a. George Washington
    b. Franklin Delano Roosevelt
    c. Ronald Reagan
    d. George W. Bush

FILL IN THE BLANKS.

11. When it spends more money than it collects in taxes, the government is engaging in _____.

12. _____ refers to the rising prices of consumer goods, which means the value of the dollar has decreased.

13. The date on which the national 2009 fiscal year (FY 2009) began is _____.

14. The _____ is a nongovernmental organization that advocates for free trade policy, monitors adherence to international trade rules, and resolves charges of trade rule violation raised by its member countries.

15. The collection of national tax policies and spending policies is referred to as _____ policy.

Answers: 1. a; 2. b; 3. b; 4. d; 5. a; 6. d; 7. d; 8. c; 9. b; 10. c; 11. deficit spending; 12. Inflation; 13. October 1, 2008; 14. World Trade Organization (WTO); 15. fiscal.

RESOURCES FOR RESEARCH AND ACTION

Internet Resources

American Democracy Now Web site
www.mhhe.com/harrison1e   Consult the book's Web site for study guides, interactive activities, simulations, and current hotlinks for additional information on economic policy in the United States.

American Enterprise Institute (AEI)
www.aei.org   The AEI sponsors research on government policy and economic policy and advocates limited government involvement in the marketplace.

American Institute for Economic Research
www.aier.org   This nonprofit research and educational organization provides studies and information on economic and financial issues.

Broad Meadow Middle School Students' Web Sites
www.mirrorimage.com/iqbal/index.html (*The Kids' Campaign: A School for Iqbal*) and **www.odwusa.org** (*Operation: Day's Work-USA*)   Web sites maintained by the student activists at Broad Meadow Middle School to raise awareness about child labor and funds to promote education.

Bureau of Economic Analysis (BEA)
www.bea.doc.gov   The BEA, an agency in the Department of Commerce, produces and disseminates data on regional, national, and international economies.

Economic Policy Institute
http://epinet.org   This nonprofit organization aims to broaden public debate on strategies to achieve a prosperous and fair economy.

Office of Management and Budget (OMB)
www.whitehouse.gov/omb   The OMB's site has links to the most recent executive budget and historical budget documents.

Tax Foundation
www.taxfoundation.org   The Tax Foundation conducts policy research that monitors fiscal issues at the federal, state, and local levels. It collects and analyzes data related to taxes and tax burdens on U.S. citizens and corporations.

U.S. Census Bureau
www.census.gov   The Census Bureau, a bureau in the Department of Commerce, collects and disseminates data about the people and economy of the nation.

Recommended Readings

Birnbaum, Jeffrey, and Alan Murray. *Showdown at Gucci Gulch: Lawmakers, Lobbyists and the Unlikely Triumph of Tax Reform.* New York: Random House, 1987. An easy-to-read and insightful study of the tax reforms of 1982, painting a richly detailed picture of the personalities, debates, lobbying, and gimmicks that gave taxpayers a less complicated and fairer tax policy, with fewer loopholes for corporations and the affluent.

Derber, Charles. *People Before Profit.* New York: Picador, 2003. A disturbing analysis of globalization to date with a blueprint for a new form of globalization that will lead to a more stable and just global community.

Lieberman, Carl. *Making Economic Policy.* Englewood Cliffs, NJ: Prentice Hall, 1991. A concise yet comprehensive overview of economic policies, including spending policy, tax policy, monetary policy, economic regulation, and economic subsidies.

Schick, Allen. *The Federal Budget.* Washington, DC: Brookings Institute, 2000. A comprehensive, in-depth consideration of the national budget process.

Tolchin, Susan J., and Martin Tolchin. *Dismantling America: The Rush to Deregulate.* New York: Houghton Mifflin, 1983. The premier assessment of deregulation in the American economy during the 1970s and early 1980s.

Woodward, Bob. *Maestro: Greenspan's Fed and the American Boom.* New York: Simon & Schuster, 2000. A probing look into how the Fed operated under the leadership of Alan Greenspan from 1987 to 2000. The effect of the evolving global economy on the economic health of the United States is an intriguing part of Woodward's account.

Movies of Interest

Cinderella Man (2005)
Based on the life of prizefighter Jim Braddock, this film movingly depicts the common person's struggle to survive the Great Depression and the hopes and inspiration that one person's rise from the bottom can evoke in the population at large.

Enron: The Smartest Guys in the Room (2005)
Based on the best-selling book of the same title, this documentary spotlights the human drama of Enron's fall—the biggest corporate scandal in American history—including the company's collapse, the elimination of thousands of jobs, and the loss of $60 billion in market value and $2 billion in pension plans.

Commanding Heights: The Battle for the World Economy (2002)
This documentary exploration of the political side of today's global economy looks at the people, ideas, and events that fostered the liberalization of trade policies around the globe.

Bread and Roses (2000)
Two Mexican sisters, one a recent illegal immigrant, strive to unionize the janitorial workers that clean downtown Los Angeles office buildings. This human drama explores the dynamics of unionizing efforts: managerial intimidation, workers' efforts to build public support, and individuals' struggles as they try to determine what course of action is best for their career or family in the short term.

BUBBLE WATCH

National Journal

As Congress looks for culprits in the collapse of the subprime mortgage market, some lawmakers have fingered the man who has been portrayed as an economic genius and the leading architect of American prosperity for the past 15 years: former Federal Reserve Board Chairman Alan Greenspan.

In March, Senate Banking Committee Chairman Christopher Dodd, D-Conn., criticized a 2004 speech in which Greenspan urged lenders to help more consumers become homeowners by coming up with alternatives to traditional fixed-rate mortgages. The Fed "seemed to encourage the development and use of adjustable-rate mortgages that today are defaulting and going into foreclosure at record rates," Dodd said.

That is just the latest entry in a growing rap sheet that critics are compiling to document the Federal Reserve's role in what looks to be the second major asset bubble in a decade. The first was a boom in high-tech and Internet-based stock prices during the late 1990s, which ended with the NASDAQ Composite Index losing 78 percent of its value between March 2000 and October 2002.

Although there's no hard-and-fast definition of an asset bubble, the term typically describes a rapid run-up in prices that is driven more by buyers' expectations that prices will keep rising than by any conventional measure of underlying value.

The Fed, some experts say, ignores bubbles when they're inflating and then overreacts when they burst, lowering interest rates to cushion the effects on the broader economy. Easy credit may indeed ease a fall, but it also can set the stage for another spike in asset prices.

The Federal Reserve risks becoming "something of a serial bubble creator," says economist Nouriel Roubini, part of a mounting chorus of economists begging to differ with Greenspan and his successor as Fed chairman, Ben Bernanke, in their view that central banks should consider only growth and inflation when setting interest rates.

In recent decades, the Federal Reserve's Open Market Committee has ignored major increases in asset prices (for financial instruments such as stocks, or real property such as houses) unless they spark inflation or an ensuing bust seems likely to drag down the rest of the economy.

The debate began as a somewhat academic affair in 1999, when Bernanke, then an economist at Princeton University, wrote a paper with fellow economist Mark Gertler that laid out the arguments against modifying Fed policy to try to lessen bubbles. At the time, some critics, including some members of the Federal Reserve Board, had been suggesting that the Fed should raise rates to dampen the Internet stock frenzy.

By the time Bernanke took his views public in a speech to business economists shortly after joining the Fed's Board of Governors in 2002, the matter was no longer academic: The price of tech stocks had already tumbled, the economy had gone into recession, and the shock of 9/11 had put the board on a course that would drop interest rates to a minuscule 1 percent.

The Fed cannot identify a bubble with certainty early enough to make a difference, Bernanke argued in 2002. Even if it could, raising interest rates to tamp down demand for an asset would be dangerous—a small rate increase would have no effect, and a large hike could jeopardize the economy. "In short, we cannot practice 'safe popping,' at least not with the blunt tool of monetary policy," Bernanke said.

Instead, he argued, the Fed would do better to use some of its more pointed tools, including its rule-making and supervisory oversight of some financial institutions, to prevent bubbles from forming in the first place.

Bernanke contended that a reinterpretation of the events leading to the Great Depression bolstered his case: Rather than the stock market crash causing the Depression, several scholars have concluded recently that the drop in stock prices was merely a response to a slowing economy—which was

caused by the Fed's decision in 1928 to raise interest rates to slow a giddy rise in the financial markets. Instead of repeating such missteps, Bernanke said, the Federal Reserve should stand ready to counter any damage that falling asset prices wreak on the broader economy. That is, in fact, the approach the Fed took in 2001.

By 2002, however, the academic debate was gathering steam. Nearly half a dozen economists weighed in with papers challenging Bernanke's arguments on theoretical grounds, and Bernanke occasionally fired back. The challengers argued that the Fed, even if it wasn't sure a bubble was forming, could produce a better outcome by factoring asset prices into its policy equation than by ignoring them.

Those who want the Federal Reserve to be more bubble-conscious aren't looking for radical changes. "No one is in favor of aggressively using monetary policy to prick bubbles," Roubini said. Some observers just want the Fed to take "a more nuanced view." Roubini and others agree that the Fed should start by using some of the more refined tools in its workshop: the power of the podium— since lenders and financial markets closely follow the Fed's pronouncements—and the power to curb credit, whether by limiting investors' ability to buy securities on margin, or by scrutinizing the lending standards of the mortgage lenders it oversees.

The Fed has failed to use either of these tools, the challengers say. Despite Greenspan's famous remark in 1996 about the "irrational exuberance" of the stock markets, many observers viewed him as a cheerleader for the idea of a "New Economy" that encouraged the mania for high-tech and Internet-based corporate stocks.

During the run-up in housing prices, Greenspan was likewise blithe—referring to some "froth" in the housing market only shortly before his retirement in early 2006. "He should have put the facts out, and said that these sorts of prices were not likely to be sustainable, and that people should realize that they are taking a big risk," said Dean Baker, co-director of the Center for Economic and Policy Research. The markets, and homebuyers, would have given such cautions "lots of respect," Baker said.

The Fed likewise never used its power to restrain margin investing in the late 1990s, critics say, or to scrutinize mortgage-lending standards or the newfangled mortgage products being offered to higher-risk borrowers. "This was more than a failure of monetary policy; it was also failure of appropriate supervision," Roubini said. The regulators "were asleep at the wheel; they did nothing."

Many analysts note that the housing market is different than the stock market in key respects. For one, it is really made up of many different housing markets, which vary greatly by region. Moreover, houses are not merely an asset; they provide shelter for their owners. Faced with declining prices, would-be sellers will often choose to retain their homes—which protects against a downward price spiral.

In a 2005 study, researchers at the Federal Deposit Insurance Corp. noted that "the lion's share of home price booms have not ended in busts historically," but rather in price stagnation. The report noted, however, that "there are reasons to think that history might be an imperfect guide to the present situation" because changes in financial products, including subprime mortgages, are pushing these markets into "uncharted territory."

Even steeply falling housing prices might not chasten supporters of the Bernanke-Greenspan hands-off view. The key, for this camp, is whether a large price decline leads to broader economic woes, as people begin to feel poorer and cut back on spending.

"If you look back to the first bubble, to me what ratifies mopping up was how little damage the evaporation of $8 trillion did to the economy," says Princeton economist and

The Federal Reserve **risks becoming something of a** serial bubble creator.

former Fed board member Alan Blinder, referring to the loss of on-paper value of stocks from the dot-com bubble. A recession followed, he said, but it was extremely short-lived. "I call it a recessionette."

"If we look back and see the same reaction" to decline in house prices, Blinder says, he would consider that as "pretty much clinching the argument" for the current Fed policy of ignoring asset price run-ups. Although some asset-holders get hurt when bubbles pop, he acknowledges, "it may well be a requirement of exuberant capitalism—which is the kind we want—that it goes overboard now and then."

Although Bernanke has said that the Federal Reserve would pay attention to the impact of a housing boom on overall inflation, former New York Federal Reserve economist Stephen Cecchetti says that quirks in the way the government measures housing costs may have led the Fed to misread the economic cues both during the current boom and as prices decline. Government statisticians use "a fiction that homeowners rent from themselves, and treat renters and homeowners the same way," he says. Because rents tend to rise more slowly than home prices during a housing boom, the Consumer Price Index understates actual housing costs. With housing costs making up nearly 24 percent of the CPI, this measure thus understates inflation during a housing boom. And once home prices cool and rents rise, the CPI looks artificially high.

The lag could lead the Fed to keep rates unnecessarily low during a housing boom, thereby fueling the boom. During a housing

bust, the Fed might keep interest rates high to fight phantom inflation, thereby exacerbating problems in the housing market.

Even if housing prices merely stagnate for 10 years, the costs for individuals could be severe, according to Baker. Baby Boomers who counted on rising home prices to finance their retirement could find themselves in straitened circumstances, he argues. That, in turn, could lead to lower consumer spending and a slower-growing economy—albeit too far down the road to be blamed on Greenspan and Bernanke.

As yet, the Federal Reserve Board hasn't officially embraced a change of heart on the wisdom of more-aggressive bubble management.

But Greenspan, now on the speaking circuit as a civilian, has darkened his views of the seriousness of a potential housing bust. "If prices go down from here, I think we're going to have problems that could spill over to other areas," he told the Futures Industry Association in mid-March. He has also suggested that a recession is possible later this year. But he blames subprime lenders rather than easy credit for the decline in prices.

Bernanke, whose job precludes much public doomsaying, has waved off Greenspan's suggestions of an impending recession and remained fairly quiet about the housing market. At a mid-March hearing of Congress's Joint Economic Committee, he said that slower economic growth reflected a "correction" in the housing sector. He blamed poor lending practices for the turmoil in the subprime market and said that the problems in the housing arena seemed unlikely to spread to the broader economy. The Fed was continuing to monitor the situation closely, he said.

If a bursting housing bubble does drag the economy down, will the Federal Reserve lower rates aggressively, potentially feeding yet another asset bubble? Bernanke hasn't had to face that question—yet.

■ **THEN:** The Federal Reserve, under Greenspan, considered only growth and inflation when setting interest rates.

■ **NOW:** The growth-only policy may be leading to volatile bubbles in the economy that burst, causing greater harm than good.

■ **NEXT:** Will the Fed increase its regulation of the mortgage lending and financial investment industries?

What actions should the government take to prevent the current recession from turning into a depression?

Should the Fed take an active hand in controlling bubbles or let the market work itself out?

CHAPTER

16

Domestic Policy

THEN

In the 1930s, radical new federal government policies created a safety net by which economically distressed citizens could provide for their basic needs.

NOW

The federal government faces a host of domestic policy issues, from the high cost of maintaining the safety net to environmental degradation, scarce energy supplies, homeland security threats, and soaring immigration.

NEXT

Will Social Security survive—and fund the retirement checks of *your* generation?

Will global warming and worldwide environmental degradation force U.S. policy makers to sign on to international treaties?

Will demographic change owing to high immigration today bring new issues to tomorrow's policy agenda?

Taking Their Health into Their Own Hands: The Story of Love Canal

It was December 19, 2007, almost thirty years after she had learned that her children's school was sitting next to a toxic waste site, and Lois Gibbs was pleased. The occasion for her satisfaction was the signing by President George W. Bush of legislation calling for the Environmental Protection Agency (EPA) to develop the nation's first guidelines to ensure that schools are not built on or near toxic waste sites. Gibbs hopes that the national guidelines (with which compliance is voluntary) will encourage the forty-five states without laws preventing the building of schools on toxic sites to pass such state legislation.* Yet for this to happen, Gibbs knows that the Center for Health, Environment & Justice (CHEJ), the nonprofit group she founded in 1981 and still directs, must continue the work she started in 1978. I In April 1978, the *Niagara Gazette* ran a series of alarming articles exposing health problems in the Love Canal neighborhood of Niagara Falls, New York.** For then–27-year-old housewife Lois Gibbs, the articles revealed the probable cause of the various illnesses her two young children were suffering: 20,000 tons of toxic waste buried near her home and the school that her 5-year-old son attended. Hooker Electrochemical Company had *legally* dumped the waste in the partially dug Love Canal between 1942 and 1947. I Jolted by the reports, Gibbs sprang into action. Gibbs went door-to-door, talking with her neighbors to see whether they had experienced any unusual illnesses. She learned of abnormally high incidences of birth defects, miscarriages, cancers, and other health problems in the neighborhood. When the government failed to respond to the residents' escalating fears and urgent requests for assistance with medical problems and relocation, a frustrated Gibbs organized and led a collective grassroots effort to bring relief to the beleaguered Love Canal families. I Gibbs and her neighbors banded together in the Love Canal Homeowners Association (LCHA). The LCHA fought, and ultimately won, a three-year battle with the city, county, state, and national governments to relocate 833 Love Canal families. I The zealous activism of Gibbs and the LCHA made national headlines and forced Americans to recognize the link between toxic wastes and health problems. An important outcome was the national government's creation in 1980 of the landmark Superfund program to clean up toxic waste sites throughout the country. For Gibbs personally, the Love Canal crisis inspired and empowered her to found the Center for Health, Environment & Justice. CHEJ's mission is to "level the playing field so that people can have a say in the environmental policies and decisions that affect their health and well-being."** I In 2002, CHEJ created the National Model School Siting Policy guidelines. By 2005, five states responded to the CHEJ model by approving state school siting laws. Because the 2007 national law calls for guidelines, not mandated regulations, the remaining forty-five states have the discretion to establish (or not to establish) school siting laws. Gibbs continues to press her case, arguing that "locating a school near a toxic waste site is utterly inexcusable. Exposing children to known, harmful chemicals is not something that should ever happen in America."*

>A father and his children sit in front of a boarded-up house in Love Canal in Niagara Falls, New York, after hearing news that the development will close down because of toxic waste contamination.

* www.chej.org/documents/energy_bill_school_sitings_final.pdf.
** For a timeline and description of the crisis at Love Canal, go to www.chej.org. Additional information can be found at www.epa.gov/history/topics/lovecanal/.

According to the Declaration of

Independence and the U.S. Constitution, American government must ensure a just and safe society in which citizens can live their lives freely, in pursuit of their happiness. Essential to the achievement of these goals are the preservation and protection of the natural environment so that future generations can enjoy a quality of life comparable to today's. And implicit in these founding documents is that government policy makers must recognize the long-term impact of their policies, as well as their lack of policies, on citizens, their communities, and the nation at large.

In the Love Canal case, the *absence* of a viable public policy to deal with the disposal of chemicals had a harmful long-term impact on natural resources and human health. Once forced by the activism of Lois Gibbs and her neighbors to do so, the state and national governments worked together to address the toxic waste problems in Love Canal—and in the wider nation.

In our federal system, when citizens bring societal problems to the attention of government officials, the ensuing legislative and public debates typically revolve around several key questions. First, government officials must decide whether the problem is one that government should address. If the answer to this fundamental question is yes, then additional questions follow. What level of government has legal authority to address the problem? What level of government has the financial resources? What is the most cost-effective means to deal with the problem? Beyond the expected positive effects of a policy's implementation, what unexpected costs and negative consequences might occur?

Citizen Engagement and Domestic Policy

The Constitution established a government that is by and for the people. Previous chapters have explored the many ways that individuals and groups engage with government officials and political processes in order to influence what government does and does not do. Yet a widespread national affliction is *NIMBY,* or "not-in-my-backyard" syndrome. People with NIMBY syndrome decline to participate in politics until a government action or inaction threatens them directly. As we saw in the story of Lois Gibbs and her neighbors, when citizens experience a negative effect in their own backyard, they get involved. Lobbying government officials is a common first step in citizen engagement, and it may be as basic as making a phone call, sending an e-mail, or writing a letter. In the case of the Love Canal Homeowners Association and the CHEJ, lobbying eventually meant mobilizing large groups for activism. Citizens may also use lawsuits to press government officials to focus on issues of concern and to address them through policy making.

Complicating the work of U.S. policy makers, the diversity of citizens' needs and expectations for government action means that almost every call for government action sparks a call for either a different action or no action. The plurality of citizens' needs, individuals' constantly changing priorities, and their range of political ideologies make for an ongoing public conversation and legislative debate over which policies warrant government spending and who will pay the taxes to cover the bills. Democrats and Republicans frequently disagree on these matters. Democrats typically are liberal in inclination and tend to support **safety nets**—programs ensuring that every citizen's basic physiological needs (food, water, shelter, health care, and a clean environment) are met. Republicans more commonly have a conservative ideology and focus more on public safety and national security issues. Ultimately, elected officials—whose career goal, after all, is to get reelected—find it much easier

In this chapter, we survey national domestic policies that are most directly related to the basic needs of a sustainable, safe country where citizens can live healthy lives in pursuit of their happiness.

FIRST, we review the role of *citizen engagement* in establishing *domestic policy.*

SECOND, we consider the *tools of domestic policy,* the array of public programs by which the government provides for citizens' basic needs.

THIRD, we look at *environmental policy,* the government's efforts to preserve the environment, conserve scarce resources, and control pollution.

FOURTH, we examine *energy policy,* specifically looking at the problems of rising energy consumption and Americans' reliance on nonrenewable fossil fuels.

FIFTH, we consider *income security programs*—in particular, safety-net policies for citizens in financial need.

SIXTH, we probe *health care policy,* where soaring costs are prompting ongoing research and experimentation with new models.

SEVENTH, we explore the nation's new, centralized focus on *homeland security*—its origins, objectives, and intergovernmental basis.

EIGHTH, we examine legislators' efforts at reforming *immigration policy* to address citizens' concerns over the masses of unauthorized immigrants streaming into the country.

safety net
a collection of public policies ensuring that the basic physiological needs of citizens are met

to add new policies and programs, and consequently to drive up government expenses, than to eliminate programs or to decrease program costs.

As we have seen in preceding chapters, the government makes policy in several ways. For one, Congress and the president set policy by approving *authorization bills,* which establish a policy and identify who will implement it, and *appropriation bills,* which authorize the spending of national revenue. Federal, state, local, and shadow bureaucrats also make policy, through both the administrative rule-making process and their daily use of administrative discretion. In addition, the presidential power of the executive order amounts to making policy, as it gives the president the authority to tell bureaucrats how to carry out a national policy. Finally, the federal judiciary, through the various cases that come before the courts, has policy-making power by virtue of its authority to declare unconstitutional the laws made by the legislative and executive branches of national, state, and local government (the authority of judicial review). The courts also resolve conflicts over the meaning and proper implementation of laws. In summary, each of the three branches of the national government has policy-making authority that it uses to fulfill the government's constitutionally established mission to serve present and future generations.

Since 1788 (when the states ratified the U.S. Constitution), the national government's scope of responsibility for addressing domestic matters has gradually expanded as citizens and groups have lobbied to press for their interests. Federal authority now covers a diverse collection of public policies. Today's national budget lists seventeen superfunctions of the federal government (see Table 16.1).[1] The numbers in the table show that the majority of federal government functions and most government spending are directed at *domestic* policy

TABLE 16.1

National Budget Superfunctions and Expenditures: Total Proposed National Budget Authority, 2009—$3,107,355 million ($3.1 trillion)

Defense and Foreign Policy ($713,111 million; 22.9% of budget outlays)*	National defense ($675,084 million; 21.7%)
	International affairs ($38,027 million; 1.2%)
Domestic Policy ($2,214,943 million; 71.3%)	General science, space, and technology ($29,170 million; 0.9%)
	Energy ($3,104 million; 0.1%)
	Natural resources and environment ($35,546 million; 1.1%)
	Agriculture ($19,070 million; 0.6%)
	Commerce and housing credit ($4,182 million; 0.1%)
	Transportation ($83,901 million; 2.7%)
	Community and regional development ($23,345 million; 0.9%)
	Education, training, employment, and social services ($88,313 million; 2.8%)
	Health ($299,393 million; 9.6%)
	Medicare ($413,324 million; 13.3%)
	Income security ($401,711 million; 12.9%)
	Social Security ($649,332 million; 20.9%)
	Veterans benefits and services ($91,875 million; 3.0%)
	Administration of justice ($51,143 million; 1.7%)
	General government ($21,534 million; 0.7%)
Net Interest	($243,947 million; 7.9%)

* Numbers in parentheses represent (1) total outlay for each function and (2) percentage of total budget outlay, rounded to the nearest tenth of a percent.

Source: Budget of the United States Fiscal Year 2009, Historical Tables, Table 3.2, www.whitehouse.gov/omb/budget/fy2009/pdf/hist.pdf.

matters: 71.3 percent for domestic policies and 22.9 percent for foreign and defense policies. The remaining percentage pays the interest on the national debt incurred by past borrowing to cover deficit spending.

Because it would be impossible for us to examine every domestic policy program, we limit our focus in this chapter to a subset of national homeland policies. Specifically, we concentrate on policies that address the most basic of human needs and are essential to sustaining life, liberty, and opportunities to pursue happiness: environmental, energy, income security, health care, and homeland security policies. We also look at the controversial policy area of immigration, defined by some as a national security concern, by others as an economic issue, and by still others as a humanitarian cause reflecting the United States' roots and highest ideals.

Tools of Domestic Policy

The national government attempts to address citizens' problems and to provide benefits and services to the people by using various policy tools. Domestic policy tools include laws and regulations, direct provision of public goods, cash transfer payments, loans, loan guarantees, insurance, and contracting-out the provision of public goods to nongovernmental entities.

Laws and Regulations

At the federal, state, and local levels alike, government strives to accomplish its policy goals by creating laws with which individuals and organizations must comply. These include environmental laws, national narcotics laws, and laws addressing work standards and conditions. Many laws assign administrative agencies the authority to establish the specific rules, regulations, and standards that are essential to effective implementation of the laws.

The overwhelming majority of people and organizations comply with most laws and regulations. But because some individuals and organizations fail to do so, the government must monitor compliance. For example, the government hires inspectors to monitor adherence to rules that limit industrial plants' emissions of pollutants, and hires police officers to monitor compliance with laws that prohibit narcotic drug use. The government counts on citizens, interest groups, and the media to assist in overseeing compliance—and in reporting violators. Environmental interest groups such as Lois Gibbs's CHEJ provide grassroots citizens' organizations with information on how to identify possible violations of environmental laws—and hence how to monitor the pollution in their communities.

>National, state, and local governments hire public servants to monitor compliance with their laws and regulations. It is common for public servants from two or more levels of government, such as federal Drug Enforcement Administration (DEA) agents and state police officers, to work together in intergovernmental efforts to serve the public efficiently and effectively, as they do here in helping to transfer a Colombian drug lord to U.S. custody (several agents' faces are obscured for their safety).

Direct Provision of Public Goods

In addition to creating rules of behavior through law and regulations, governments provide services and benefits. Using the policy tool of **direct provision,** governments hire public servants—bureaucrats who receive a government paycheck—to dispense the service. For example, veterans hospitals hire doctors, nurses, and physical therapists to administer health care to veterans; the U.S. Postal Service hires mail carriers, postal clerks, and postal processing machine operators to deliver billions of pieces of mail each week. To provide for the country's common defense, the national government employs millions of military personnel. The workers hired by the national government to provide these services directly are on the payroll of the national government.

direct provision
the policy tool whereby the government that creates a policy hires public servants to provide the service

cash transfer
the direct provision of cash (in forms) including checks, debit cards, and tax breaks) to eligible individuals or to providers of goods or services to eligible individuals

in-kind assistance
a benefit program in which the recipient shops for a service provider who will accept payment from the government for the service or item purchased

noncontributory program
a benefit provided to a targeted population, paid for by a proportion of the money collected from all taxpayers

contributory program (social insurance program)
a benefit provided only to those who paid the specific tax created to fund the benefit

entitlement program
a government benefit guaranteed to all who meet the eligibility requirements

direct subsidy
a cash transfer from general revenues to particular persons or private companies engaged in activities that the national government believes support the public good

Cash Transfers

Another instrument of government policy is the **cash transfer**—the direct provision of cash (in various forms) to eligible individuals or to the providers of goods or services to eligible individuals. **In-kind assistance** is a form of a cash transfer in which the government provides cash to those who provide goods or services to eligible individuals. Approximately 60 percent of the money spent by the national government goes toward cash transfers to citizens. Today, the majority of U.S. citizens receive cash payments of some kind from the federal government at some time during their lives.

Examples of cash transfers include unemployment and Social Security checks, Pell grants to college students, grants-in-aid to state and local governments (see Chapter 3), and tax breaks and subsidies to individuals and corporations (see Chapter 15). Medicaid, the government program that provides health care for the poor, is an example of an in-kind assistance, cash transfer program. The Medicaid recipient receives medical care at no cost or at a reduced cost because the government pays health care providers for their services.

>The federal government assists college students through cash transfers such as Pell grants, student loans, and loan guarantees. College financial aid offices play a role in administering these grant and loan programs.

The main cash-transfer programs are of two kinds, depending upon their sources of revenue. For **noncontributory programs,** the general revenues collected by the government pay for the program. This means that a proportion of the money collected from all taxpayers funds the cash transfer. Temporary Assistance to Needy Families, the income security program for families with children who have no or very low income, is an example of a noncontributory cash-transfer program. In contrast, **contributory programs,** or **social insurance programs,** are funded by revenue collected specifically for these programs, and they benefit only those who have paid into the programs. Social insurance programs are **entitlement programs,** meaning the government guarantees the program's benefits to all who meet the eligibility criteria. Thus, workers who pay the payroll tax for Social Security will receive Social Security checks when they retire.

With a **direct subsidy,** another type of cash transfer, the government provides financial support to specific persons or organizations that engage in activities that the government believes benefit the public good. Individual farmers and agricultural corporations, for example, receive money from the government to grow specified crops or to limit how much they grow. College students receiving Pell grants, which do not need to be paid back, are also recipients of direct subsidies funded through the federal government's general revenue.

Loans, Loan Guarantees, and Insurance

In addition to using tax breaks and grants to encourage behaviors that accomplish its goals, the national government lends money to individuals and organizations, and it guarantees loans made by private organizations. Some examples are government loan programs

NONCONTRIBUTORY AND CONTRIBUTORY CASH TRANSFER PROGRAMS

— **Noncontributory cash transfer programs:** The general revenues collected from all citizens pay for these programs. The beneficiaries of these programs are individuals who meet the eligibility requirements, whether they paid taxes or not. Noncontributory cash transfer programs may be entitlement programs.

— **Contributory cash transfer programs (social insurance programs):** Designated tax contributions pay for these programs. The beneficiaries of these programs are the individuals who contribute to them. Social insurance programs are entitlement programs.

to assist individuals in purchasing homes, reflecting the widespread belief that home-ownership promotes the general welfare and domestic tranquility, and Perkins loans, which pay some of the college expenses of students from very low income families. In addition, the government guarantees banks that it will repay the loans they provide to college students if the students cannot repay the loans themselves; these guaranteed loans are called Stafford loans. If the government did not guarantee them, do you think that banks, which are profit-making organizations, would loan thousands of dollars to unem-ployed young people to pay for college costs? Probably not!

The national government is also in the insurance business. The Federal Deposit Insurance Corporation (FDIC) is one example of a national insurance program. The FDIC insures bank deposits of up to $100,000 in member banks. Through the tool of FDIC insurance, the government seeks to encourage people to save money not only for their own well-being but also for the good of the national economy.

> Depositors, fearful that the money they had deposited had been lost, besieged banks such as this one in Passaic, New Jersey, after Wall Street crashed and the Great Depression began in 1929. To protect depositors' money, in 1933 the federal government created the Federal Deposit Insurance Corporation (FDIC), which insures bank deposits. Depositors who besieged the failed IndyMac banks in the summer of 2008 found that the FDIC had insured their deposits for up to $100,000 and their individual retirement accounts for up to $250,000.

Contracting-Out

The government also contracts with private and nonprofit organizations to produce essential resources or to deliver services historically provided by the government. One example of contracting-out, or outsourcing (see Chapter 13), is its contracts with corporations such as Lockheed Martin and Boeing to build the planes and missiles it needs to defend the country.

By means of contracting-out and the other various tools we have surveyed, the government delivers goods and services to its citizens now and in the future. In the rest of this chapter, we examine how government uses these tools to implement overall policy in several domestic policy areas, including the environment, health care, and homeland security.

Environmental Policy

At the most basic level, providing for the general welfare means ensuring that people have the basic necessities for sustaining life. These needs include clean and drinkable water, breathable air, and unpolluted land on which to grow food safe for consumption. No one argues against a clean environment. Yet there is no consensus on how to achieve and maintain one. In addition, appeals for environmental protection often conflict with demands for ample supplies of energy and for economic development. For example, the extraction of coal and oil from the earth, as well as the development of nuclear energy, poses immediate as well as long-term threats to the environment. Government officials must balance the need to protect the water, air, and land with the need to ensure an ample supply of energy and economic development. For policy makers, this is a complex balancing act.

Environmental protection includes conserving natural resources and limiting the pollution emitted into the air and water and onto the land. By the late 1960s and 1970s,

>In 1936, floating oil and debris ignited, causing the first Cuyahoga River fire in Cleveland, Ohio. The most serious Cuyahoga River fire, pictured here, occurred in 1952. The river caught fire several more times before the 1969 fire that finally helped inspire the national government to place water pollution on its policy agenda.

several environmental crises had brought the harm humans had caused to the natural environment, plants, animals, and people into stark view.

Environmental Degradation

Since the 1940s, farmers have used chemicals to destroy insects, weeds, fungi, and other living organisms that harm their crops. The threats such pesticides pose to air, water, and land became the focus of public concern and political debate after the publication of Rachel Carson's eye-opening best seller *Silent Spring* in 1962. Carson's book documented how pesticides were contaminating the environment and getting into human food. The use of chemicals, she warned, threatened the existence not only of birds—whose extinction would mean a silent spring—but of humankind itself. Although the chemical industry tried to discredit Carson's findings, President John F. Kennedy (1961–1963) established a special panel to investigate them, and the panel found support for Carson's concerns.

Then, in 1969, these growing apprehensions became a spectacular reality when the heavily polluted Cuyahoga River in northeastern Ohio caught fire (again!). Around the same time, arsenic was found in the Kansas River, and millions of fish went belly-up in major waterways such as Lake Superior, killed by the chemicals and untreated waste emitted by industrial plants and local sewage systems. In response, state and local governments banned fishing in many waterways, including Lake Erie, due to their excessive pollution.

The mounting environmental crises (including the Love Canal incident examined in the "American Democracy Now" vignette) and additional governmental studies brought amplified calls to action from both citizens' groups and elected officials during the 1960s and 1970s. U.S. Senator Gaylord Nelson (D-Wisconsin) responded by founding Earth Day. He later recollected that "all across the country, evidence of environmental degradation was appearing. . . . The people were concerned, but the politicians were not. . . . Suddenly, the idea occurred to me—why not organize a huge grassroots protest over what was happening to our environment?"[2]

Nelson's vision of a day of educational rallies in Washington, D.C., became a reality on April 22, 1970, when more than 200,000 people gathered on the National Mall. Millions more congregated across the country to draw attention to environmental concerns. Earth Day 1970 was so successful at bringing attention to the environmental cause that many consider it the beginning of the environmental movement. Celebrated every year with rallies and teach-ins involving millions of people worldwide, Earth Day keeps concerns about environmental degradation on the public policy agenda.

Environmental Protection

A cascade of groundbreaking national legislation followed the first Earth Day. The Environmental Protection Act of 1970 established the Environmental Protection Agency (EPA) to oversee the implementation of laws protecting the quality of air, water, and land. The Environmental Protection Act mandates that all construction projects receiving federal funding must begin with an environmental impact study analyzing the project's effects on the environment and on endangered species. The act also has a sunshine component requiring the government to invite citizens' comments on proposed projects. Under these provisions of the law, environmental interest groups frequently bring lawsuits challenging the quality and accuracy of environmental impact studies and developers' lack of compliance with the sunshine provisions. Developers and parties probing into new energy sources view such lawsuits as a waste of time and money. But in fact, this litigation, combined with the broader work of various environmental groups, has become a driving force in environmental protection today.

CLEAN AIR The landmark Clean Air Act of 1970 delegates authority to the EPA to set air quality standards while giving state governments enforcement responsibility. Today, states in turn typically delegate some of their enforcement responsibilities to local governments. If states and their local governments do not enforce compliance with the national standards, the EPA can take over.

To bolster compliance with the Clean Air Act, the law gives citizens the right to sue those who are violating the standards. Citizens also have the right to sue the EPA if it does not enforce the Clean Air Act. Citizens and environmental interest groups have availed themselves of their right to sue, pushing the government and industries to comply with the law. For example, in 2007, Massachusetts and eleven other states, three cities, and several environmental groups successfully challenged the EPA and President George W. Bush's interpretation of the law, when the U.S. Supreme Court determined that carbon dioxide is a pollutant that the EPA has the authority to regulate.[3]

CLEAN WATER The Clean Water Act is actually the 1972 Federal Water Pollution Control Act as amended over the years. This law, which has the goal of making waterways clean enough to swim in and to eat fish from, authorizes the EPA to set water quality standards and to require permits for anyone discharging contaminants into any waterway. However, the direct discharge of pollutants into waterways is not the only source of water pollution. Runoff from farms, which carries animal waste and pesticides into waterways, contributes heavily to the problem. The Department of Agriculture joins forces with the EPA to prevent this indirect source of pollution.

Under the Clean Water Act, state and local governments must monitor water quality, issue permits to those discharging waste into waterways, and enforce the national standards. If states and localities fail to carry out these mandated responsibilities, the EPA can step in and do the job. The law also provides for federal loans to local governments, funneled through state governments, for building wastewater treatment plants.

The Safe Drinking Water Act of 1974 authorizes the EPA to establish purity standards for drinking water. Because states or localities typically operate water systems, this act effectively requires the EPA to regulate state and local governments. The act provides for national grants to state and local governments for research and for improving their water systems.

Water problems extend far beyond U.S. borders. For insight into international efforts to address water issues, see "Global Comparisons."

CLEAN LAND The United States produces more solid waste—from household garbage to toxic by-products of manufacturing such as the chemicals buried at Love Canal—per person than any other country. If not properly disposed of or treated, all waste has the potential to harm the environment, as well as plants, animals, and people.

Some toxic by-products, such as the radioactive nuclear wastes produced in manufacturing nuclear weapons and generating nuclear power, cannot be treated or disposed of, but they dissipate over time—from 100 years for low-level radioactive waste to hundreds of thousands of years for high-level radioactive waste. In 2004, a federal appeals court ruled that the developers of the nuclear repository being built at Yucca Mountain, Nevada, to store nuclear waste for the long term had to ensure it would function successfully for hundreds of thousands of years.[4]

Citizens with resources, including money and the time to organize or to join an existing organization, are able to fight the location of such undesirable land uses in their communities. Other citizens, much like the residents of Love Canal, find out about the toxic waste deposits in their neighborhoods only after a crisis occurs. Lower-income communities are more likely than more affluent cities and towns to bear the burden of housing waste storage facilities. **Environmental racism** is the term used to describe the higher incidence of environmental threats and subsequent health problems in lower-income communities, which frequently are also communities dominated by people of color.[5]

The Resource Conservation and Recovery Act of 1976, administered by the EPA, regulates the disposal of solid and hazardous wastes and encourages recycling. Although this act authorized the cleanup of toxic waste sites, and the government identified thousands of such sites in the 1970s, no national funding was made available for the cleanup. Then in 1980, as Congress was debating how to prevent crises such as Love Canal, an abandoned

environmental racism
the term for the higher incidence of environmental threats and subsequent health problems in lower-income communities, which frequently are also communities dominated by people of color

YOUTH ACTIVISTS TAKE ON THE WORLD WATER CRISIS

In Nepal, civic-minded 13-year-old Suresh Baral organized a school club that, with UNICEF funding, established a micro-finance program to help villagers install toilets.

Dolly Akhter, a similarly civically engaged 15-year-old living in a slum in Khaka, Bangladesh, established a hygiene group whose efforts resulted in the installation of new latrines in the local school. Once the latrines were in place, many of the teenage girls who had stopped coming to school due to the lack of privacy for hygiene, returned to school. For several of these teenagers, returning to school meant they did not have to marry this early in their lives.

* Can we cut the proportion of the world's population without safe drinking water in half by 2015?

Fifteen-year-old Mekhriniso Saidiso, a resident of Chapaev, Tajikistan, leads a student group that monitors the safe handling of drinking water in her community and school. She notes that this student group has provided girls in her community with their first opportunity to exercise leadership skills.

Smitha Ramakrishna returned to her Arizona home from a trip to India wondering how she could help the impoverished, water-deprived Indian children whom she had seen. Her solution was to organize the group Arizona Water Activists Karing for the Environment (AWAKE). AWAKE-sponsored walkathons raised money to purchase reverse-osmosis treatment systems to provide safe drinking water to thousands of children living in slums in India.

These are just a few examples of what young activists around the world are doing to address the spreading water crisis—an emergency that most people in developed nations are unaware of as they take for granted their access to toilets and drinkable water. But more than one out of six people in the world lack access to drinkable water. More than one in three people worldwide do not have access to toilets or latrines. As a result, water-related diseases cause more than 3 million global deaths a year, most of them children under 5 years of age. Moreover, women and children in the poorest countries and regions of the world frequently must walk long distances, up to four miles a day, to obtain safe water and carry it back to their homes. Currently, the water crisis is limited to certain countries and regions. Yet with the world's population poised to grow by at least 40 percent over the next fifty years, and with increased economic development and urbanization, the demand for drinkable water and clean water for agriculture has the potential to develop into a worldwide crisis.

At the 2nd Children's World Water Forum, held in conjunction with the 4th World Water Forum in Mexico City in 2006, 107 young activists from twenty-nine countries met to share their stories of children's efforts to address their communities' water problems. They drafted a document calling on all adult decision makers to "involve children in local actions to overcome the critical global challenge facing our water and sanitation environment . . . to fulfill the human right to sustainable, safe drinking water supplies and basic sanitation."*

The United Nations' Millennium Development Goals are eight objectives that almost 200 UN member nations around the world have agreed to achieve by 2015. The goals include the target of cutting in half the proportion of people in the world without safe drinking water by 2015. With the efforts of governments, nongovernmental organizations, and young activists, UNICEF—an organization dedicated to the protection, survival, and development of children and mothers—predicts that this target will be met.

> More than one out of six people in the world lack drinkable water, and so they drink water from polluted wells or wells infested with parasites, such as this one in the Ivory Coast. The lack of safe drinking water results in more than 3 million global deaths each year caused by water-related diseases.

* www.unicef.org/voy/explore/wes/explore_2711.html.

Sources: www.worldwatercouncil.org; Elisabeth Malkin, "At World Forum, Support Erodes for Private Management of Water," *New York Times*, March 20, 2006: A-11; www.unicef.org/voy/explore/wes/explore_2706.html.

DOING DEMOCRACY

TURN YOUR CAMPUS GREEN

FACT:

Environmental studies programs and "green" initiatives are popping up on college campuses all over the country. Harvard University replaced old toilet handles with new handles that help to conserve water. St. Mary's College of Maryland distributed refurbished bicycles across its campus to encourage students to ride bikes to class instead of cars. At the University of Arizona, undergraduate Emilie Brill-Duisburg won an award from the Association for the Advancement of Sustainability in Higher Education (AASHE) for her involvement in creating a course on rainwater harvesting. Colleges and universities, from Columbia University in New York to Lane Community College in Oregon, are hiring environmental experts to coordinate campus environmental projects.* Moreover, students at a growing number of colleges are lobbying for "green fees," which are increases in student fees to support environmentally sustainable projects.** In addition, by June 2007, 280 college presidents had signed the American College and University Presidents Climate Commitment, which commits them to reduce gas emissions that contribute to pollution and global warming.***

Act!

Do you know what your school is doing to address environmental challenges? One way to find out is to do an audit of its green initiatives. Start by looking around your campus for recycling bins and in your college's catalog for academic courses and programs in environmental studies. These may be the most visible signs of your college's environmental concern, but they may also be just the tip of the iceberg. Would you know a toilet that conserves water from one that does not? Is your campus using power from renewable sources such as wind and the sun? How would you know? Whom should you ask?

Where to begin

- Using your institution's Web site and search tool, you should be able to identify committees, task forces, and student organizations committed to environmental issues. There may even be a list of green initiatives.

- To read about how one undergraduate student, Aaron Allen, successfully lobbied for Tulane University to hire an environmental coordinator, go to **www2.tulane.edu/ EditorialNewsDetails.cfm?EditorialID=24.**
- To find out more about the Association for the Advancement of Sustainability in Higher Education, a membership-based association of colleges and universities working to promote sustainability in all its forms ("human and ecological health, social justice, secure livelihoods, and a better world for all generations"), visit **www.aashe.org/about/about.php.**

* "At Colleges, the Environment Is Hot," *Inside Higher Ed.,* October 24, 2006, www .insidehighered.com/news/2006/10/24/environment.
** "Cents and Sustainability," *Inside Higher Ed.,* May 18, 2007, www.insidehighered.com/ news/2007/05/18/fees.
*** "Presidents and Their Green Pledge," *Inside Higher Ed.,* June 13, 2007, www .insidehighered.com/layout/set/print/news/2007/06/13/climate.

---

site for the storage, treatment, and disposal of hazardous waste in Elizabeth, New Jersey, exploded.[6] Shortly thereafter, Congress approved the Comprehensive Environmental Response, Compensation and Liability Act of 1980 (known as the Superfund law) to pay for cleanup of the nation's most toxic waste dumps.

Because U.S. air quality and water quality have improved tremendously since the 1970s, many citizens and government officials have shifted their attention to other societal concerns. At the same time, U.S. industries have become more resistant to legislative proposals to stiffen environmental standards and are increasingly challenging the implementation of environmental laws. In addition, a growing private property rights movement is challenging restrictions on land use that have been put in place in the name of environmental protection. On the other hand, environmental protection is a hot topic on college campuses, for students, administrators, faculty, and presidents (see "Doing Democracy").

Although no one is arguing against a clean environment, tensions persist between the need for environmental protection and other policy areas. The increasing demand for cheap energy is one such area.

Energy Policy

Energy creation—the production of electricity and heat, as well as fuels to power automobiles, trucks, planes, trains, and other transport vehicles—is essential to the prosperity of the U.S. economy and to the American way of life. The United States uses more energy than any other country in the world, and its demand for energy continues to rise. What underlies this increasing demand? Industrial and commercial expansion, the construction of larger houses, and soaring computer use all have contributed to the ballooning demand for electricity. Robust sales of trucks for personal use, as well as of gas-guzzling sport utility vehicles (SUVs), have driven up consumers' demand for gasoline. The ever-rising energy demands of the U.S. economy and the lifestyle of U.S. residents are problematic for several reasons, as we shall see.

Energy and Global Warming

greenhouse effect
the heating of the earth's atmosphere as a result of humans' burning of fossil fuels and the resultant buildup of carbon dioxide and other gases

global warming
rising temperature of the earth as a result of pollution that traps solar heat, keeping the air warmer than it would otherwise be

The majority of energy consumed in the United States (about 85 percent) is produced by burning fossil fuels—oil, coal, and natural gas. Burning fossil fuels produces air pollution. The pollution produced by U.S. reliance on fossil fuels is not just a national problem; it is a global problem. Mounting evidence indicates that pollution from burning fossil fuels has increased temperatures worldwide creating a **greenhouse effect**—so-called because in a greenhouse, the walls and roof trap solar heat, keeping the temperature inside warmer than it is outside. **Global warming,** the gradual average increase in the earth's temperature, is the result of pollution that traps solar heat in the earth's atmosphere.

International fears about the potential harm of global warming led to a treaty called the Kyoto Protocol of 1997. Countries that ratify the Kyoto Protocol agree to work toward eliminating the greenhouse effect by reducing their emissions of carbon dioxide and other gases believed to cause it. Although 163 countries have ratified the treaty, the United States has not. Despite Vice President Al Gore's (1993–2001) role in negotiating the treaty, the U.S. Senate failed to ratify it. Subsequently, President George W. Bush challenged concerns about global warming and argued that the Kyoto Protocol threatened U.S. economic prosperity while not obligating other major polluting countries, such as China, to reduce their emissions of carbon dioxide and five other greenhouse gases.

Even though the federal government has opted not to ratify the Kyoto Protocol, many state and local governments are collectively working to meet its provisions, with the goal of showing the national government the benefits of abiding by it. Currently, nine northeastern states (Maine, Massachusetts, New Hampshire, Vermont, Rhode Island, Connecticut, New York, New Jersey, and Delaware) have agreed to the Regional Greenhouse Gas Initiative (RGGI). The RGGI commits these states to capping emissions from power plants. In 2005, seven of these states announced their agreement to go even further and reduce carbon dioxide emissions from power plants. Mayors in almost 200 cities have responded positively to the call of Seattle mayor Greg Nickels to meet the Kyoto Protocol's goal of reducing greenhouse gas emissions to 7 percent less than 1990 levels by 2012.[7]

> The daily struggle to breathe in densely polluted parts of China, including Beijing, threatened the health and participation of athletes from around the world in the 2008 Summer Olympics. Beginning several weeks before the Olympics started, the Chinese government limited the number of cars on the road in Beijing—cars with even-numbered license plates could drive one day and those with odd-numbered plates the next—and shut down manufacturing plants in areas near the Olympic venues in an effort to decrease air pollution during the games.

The environmental threats and damage created by energy production, accidents during transport (such as oil spills), and energy consumption are evident worldwide. International, national, state, and local policies are focusing on limiting these threats. An additional energy concern for the United States is the reliance on nonrenewable energy sources, as we next consider.

National Energy Policy

Until the 1950s, the United States produced almost all the oil it consumed.[8] Today it imports almost half the oil it uses (see Figure 16.1). Moreover, about 38 percent of all energy consumed in the United States comes from burning oil, meaning that about 19 percent of U.S. energy comes from imported oil. This heavy reliance on foreign oil concerns citizens and the government because of the volatile political environments in some oil-producing countries in the Middle East and South America and because of conflicts between U.S. policies and the policies of some of these countries.

THE OPEC EMBARGO AND CARTER'S RESPONSE In 1973, for example, the Arab members of the Organization of Petroleum Exporting Countries (OPEC) implemented an embargo on oil supplies. This embargo was a reaction to U.S. support of Israel

Top Suppliers of U.S. Crude Oil Imports, 2006

49.8%

Non-OPEC

United Kingdom 47
Colombia 52
Other non-OPEC nations 329
Angola 187
Mexico 575
Canada 651

50.2%

OPEC

Other OPEC nations 32
Ecuador 99
Kuwait 65
Algeria 130
Iraq 202
Nigeria 381
Venezuela 416
Saudi Arabia 519

Imports to U.S. in millions of barrels

POLITICAL INQUIRY

FIGURE 16.1 ■ What percentage of U.S. crude oil comes, respectively, from OPEC and non-OPEC countries? Which OPEC country is the top source of this oil? What stands out about the OPEC countries that are shown, in terms of their location in the world? Which non-OPEC country provides the most crude oil to the United States?

in that nation's Yom Kippur War of 1973 against Egypt and Syria over disputed lands. Outraged by what they saw as U.S. interference, OPEC member nations refused to sell oil to the United States and western European nations that supported Israel in the war. This five-month oil embargo, followed by OPEC production limits that kept oil prices high, and produced hours-long waits in gas station lines, forced the United States to set national energy policies.

In 1975 the national government established the Strategic Petroleum Reserve, a growing supply of crude oil stored away in case of a future energy emergency or an interruption in the U.S. supply of imported oil. That same year Congress also set fuel-efficiency standards for passenger cars and light trucks, the Corporate Average Fuel Economy (CAFÉ) standards. In 2007, more than thirty-five years after establishing CAFÉ, Congress significantly increased the fuel efficiency standards for the first time. Automobile producers must meet the new 35-miles-per-gallon standard, up from 25 miles per gallon, by the year 2020.[9]

In 1976 the federal government established the Department of Energy to develop and oversee a comprehensive national energy plan. In 1977, President Jimmy Carter (1977–1981) declared an "energy crisis" and announced policies stressing energy conservation through measures such as the regulation of temperature settings in public buildings and tax incentives to insulate homes. In addition, government regulation of oil and natural gas prices was curtailed during Carter's presidency.[10] Although the government had historically regulated the prices of these energy resources, the expectation was that if prices rose on the basis of supply and demand, people would conserve. Carter's energy policies also included increased financial support for research and development of alternative energy sources such as solar, wind, geothermal (produced by the earth's internal heat), and renewable biomass (fuels created from plant life, such as corn and switchgrass).

With deregulation, oil prices jumped by 1980 to more than ten times their 1972 level. But by 1986, oil prices began to fall. With lower prices through the 1990s came reduced federal government support for research and development of alternative energy sources. The public, too, lost interest in energy conservation, and the demand for energy grew, as did the production of gas-guzzling automobiles.

AN ENERGY POLICY FOCUSED ON FOSSIL FUELS   In 2001, Secretary of Energy Spencer Abraham sounded an alarm: "America faces a major energy-supply crisis over the next two decades. The failure to meet this challenge will threaten our nation's economic prosperity, compromise our national security, and literally alter the way we live our lives."[11] In response, President George W. Bush appointed Vice President Dick Cheney—a former oil company executive—to preside over a task force charged with formulating a new national energy policy. The result was an energy policy emphasizing the increased production of fossil fuels. This policy was in stark contrast to the conservation approach developed in the 1970s. Moreover, Bush's 2002 budget drastically cut funding for conservation initiatives and for research on alternative, renewable energy sources.

By the winter of 2005, government officials and citizens were increasingly concerned over the price and availability of oil. Hurricane Katrina had taken a toll on domestic oil production. The Iraq War and tensions with Iran jeopardized the stability of imports from the Middle East. President Hugo Chavez of Venezuela, the number 3 U.S. oil supplier, was also threatening to limit the availability of his country's oil.

FUTURE DIRECTIONS   In response, President Bush emphasized in his 2006 State of the Union address how essential affordable energy is to the United States' success in the world economy. He stressed that Americans' "addiction" to oil must be reduced. Bush called for a 22 percent increase in funding for research in alternative renewable energy sources such as solar and wind, as well as in nuclear energy, and recommended increased use of coal. The president also called for expanded research in alternative means to power automobiles, including electricity, hydrogen, and ethanol (produced from corn, wood chips, and switchgrass). Yet by the summer of 2008, oil and gasoline prices were hitting historic heights, as were food prices in response to increasing transportation costs. The public conversation focused more and more on conserving energy, drilling for oil in national preserves in Alaska, and discontinuing deposits into the Strategic Petroleum Reserve for a limited time so that U.S. consumers could use the fuel.

Today, limited supplies and high costs of traditional energy sources, along with the environmental impact of the continuing use of fossil fuels, threaten the quality of life of Americans and people around the globe. Americans are looking to national and state government for public policy solutions to these energy-related and environmental concerns. In a similar way, during the 1930s, Americans had turned to the national government to address the economic downturn that was impeding millions of Americans' ability to enjoy a decent quality of life, as we next consider.

Income Security Programs

Before the Great Depression of the 1930s, Americans who could not provide for their basic needs relied on relief from family, friends, charities, and, in some cases, local or state government. During the Depression, however, the excessively weak economy left one-quarter of the U.S. labor force unemployed. Families lost jobs, savings, and homes. Charities were overwhelmed. State and local governments lacked the resources to assist the millions of people without incomes. Citizens, as well as state and local governments, looked to the federal government for assistance.

Within his first one hundred days in office, President Franklin D. Roosevelt (1933–1945) proposed a sequence of revolutionary bills to stimulate and regulate the depressed economy and to provide income to the needy. His administration's radical proposals placed the national government at the center of issues it had historically left to local and state governments. These and the subsequent New Deal policies approved in Roosevelt's first few years in office created jobs, established a government-regulated economy (see Chapter 15), and provided income security for retired citizens and a safety net for people in financial need. Many of the New Deal programs are still in place today, though in modified form.

Noncontributory safety-net programs, which are funded through general tax revenues, engender a good deal of debate. Conservatives typically oppose these programs on the grounds that hard work, not government handouts, should be the source of the income individuals need to sustain themselves. Liberals are more inclined to support noncontributory safety-net programs. They make the case that marketplace failures, not individual characteristics, prevent many people from earning enough income to sustain themselves. Although you would be hard pressed to find someone who argues against contributory safety-net programs (also called *social insurance programs*), there is an ongoing conversation of democracy over the best means of funding such programs and the proper level of benefits. The largest contributory income security program, in terms of cost and people served, is the Old-Age and Survivors component of Social Security.

Social Security

The Social Security Act of 1935, a centerpiece of the New Deal, established a range of landmark income security programs. To this day, these programs provide financial assistance to the elderly, disabled, dependent, and unemployed.

OLD-AGE AND SURVIVORS INSURANCE The Social Security Act established the Old-Age and Survivors Insurance (OASI) Program, which initially provided income to individuals or families when a worker covered by the program retired. This contributory cash transfer program is the traditional retirement insurance component of Social Security; most people are aware of it and anticipate benefiting from it in retirement. OASI is a social insurance entitlement program, funded by contributions that employees as well as employers make. Each year the federal government establishes the amount of earnings subject to the Social Security tax, which is called the *covered income*. Employees and employers each pay 6.2 percent (for a total of 12.4 percent) of the employee's covered income for Social Security. In 2008, income up to $102,000 was subject to the tax.

A formula that accounts for how much individuals paid into Social Security over their years of employment determines the amount of each beneficiary's monthly Social Security

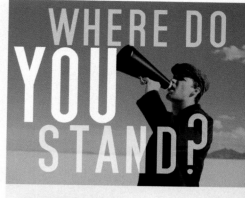

WHERE DO YOU STAND?

To Drill, or Not to Drill?

To reduce the price of gasoline, should the U.S. government allow drilling in coastal areas and wilderness preserves that are currently closed to development?

☐ Yes

☐ No

☐ No opinion

Source: "Majority of Americans Support Drilling in Off-Limits Areas," www.gallup.com/poll/108121/Majority-Americans-Support-Drilling-OffLimits-Areas.aspx.

> In January 1940, Ida Mae Fuller, a retired law clerk from Vermont, became the first person to receive a monthly Social Security retirement check. On October 5, 2007, Kathleen Casey-Kirschling, a retired teacher from New Jersey, used the Internet to file for Social Security. She will be the first baby boomer to receive a monthly retirement check.

indexed benefit
a government benefit with an automatic cost of living increase based on the rate of inflation

check. The more money invested, the greater the check. Because OASI is an **indexed benefit,** the government makes regularly scheduled, automatic cost of living adjustments (COLAs), increasing the benefit based on the rate of inflation. The 1937 Federal Insurance Contribution Act (FICA) established the pay-as-you-go funding mechanism for OASI. Through FICA contributions, current workers and employers deposit money in the Social Security Trust Fund, and the government uses the money contributed today to pay today's beneficiaries. The money left over after today's payments are made is invested so that the trust fund will grow; income from investments will be combined with future FICA revenues to pay for future Social Security checks.

The first person to receive a Social Security check—the momentous date was January 31, 1940—was Ida Mae Fuller. Ms. Fuller paid a total of $22 into the Social Security insurance program from 1937, when the FICA tax was first collected, to her retirement in 1940. Her first check was for $22.54. Over the next thirty-five years, she collected a total of $22,000, or 1,000 times what she paid into the system.[12] Because Social Security is an entitlement, and because the government cannot predict how long a Social Security recipient will live—and therefore how many checks the recipient will receive during his or her lifetime—the government cannot control or predict the annual cost of Social Security.

Most people (like Ms. Fuller) collect more from Social Security than they pay into the fund, and the number of retirees is growing. On October 15, 2007, Kathleen Casey-Kirschling became the first of the baby boomer generation (persons born between 1946 and 1964) to file for Social Security retirement benefits. With the increasing number of retirees and with those retirees living longer lives, the pay-as-you-go system will eventually reach the point of not covering the full costs of OASI. The surplus money in the Social Security Trust Fund is already shrinking. This situation generates intense public debate over what the national government should do to ensure that Social Security funds are available for workers who are currently contributing to the program (see "The Conversation of Democracy").

AMENDMENTS TO THE SOCIAL SECURITY ACT Congress amended the Social Security Act in 1939 to provide benefits to the dependents and surviving spouse of a deceased worker. In 1956 the act was further amended to assist workers who, due to physical or mental disabilities, had to stop working after age 50 but before the OASI-designated retirement age. The new benefit program thus created, called Social Security Disability

SHOULD THE SOCIAL SECURITY SYSTEM BE PRIVATIZED?

The Issue: Swift and steep population growth (especially due to the post–World War II baby boom) and steadily increasing life expectancy have created an untenable situation for the Social Security pay-as-you-go funding system. Instead of 16 workers paying for every retiree receiving Old-Age and Survivors Insurance benefits from the Social Security program, as in Franklin D. Roosevelt's day, today 3.3 workers pay for every retiree's benefits. The Congressional Budget Office, the Social Security Trustees, and many economists forecast that OASI, as presently structured, is not sustainable. Yet these forecasters disagree on the exact year when OASI will begin to pay out more than it brings in through its payroll tax, eventually depleting the accumulated surplus.

The federal government must formulate a policy now to save OASI. The proposed reform that has received the most attention is *privatization*—allowing workers to invest their Social Security taxes (or some part thereof) in private, individual accounts, and in this way to gain a measure of control over their retirement nest egg. How should government fix Social Security? Is privatization the answer?

Yes: Privatizing OASI will allow workers to invest some of their payroll tax money in stocks and bonds. Today's rate of return on Social Security is from 1 percent to 1.5 percent. The forecasted return on long-term investments in bonds is 3 percent to 3.5 percent, and in stocks it is 7 percent to 7.5 percent. According to these forecasts, with private accounts, workers who can afford to invest in stocks and bonds will accumulate more retirement savings in the long term than Social Security can provide. Privatization will especially benefit low-wage workers, who are less likely to have employer-provided pension plans and who typically cannot afford to invest in stocks and bonds and so must rely solely on OASI for their retirement income. In addition, the U.S. economy will benefit from privatization because retirees will have more money to spend—unless the predicted returns on private investments do not come to pass!

No: About one-third of householders entering retirement today rely solely on OASI for their retirement income. For these recipients, a long-term economic downturn could erode their private investments, with an outcome akin to another Great Depression. Privatization is not an option for these retirees. Instead, legislators should sustain OASI by amending the law to decrease the benefits for the two-thirds of recipients who do not rely solely on OASI in retirement. Recipients get back all the money they paid into OASI within their first three to four years of retirement. Legislators should change the formula so that after recipients recoup their OASI investment, only those who genuinely need the money will continue to receive a Social Security check.

Other approaches: Cutting benefits for those who do not depend on Social Security for survival increases the complexity of administering the program because with the inevitable ups and downs of the economy, retirees may need to move on and off Social Security. Therefore, to sustain Social Security, the federal government could increase the Social Security payroll tax rate to bring in more money. This policy, however, would harm low-wage workers far more than higher-wage workers.

Another option is to increase the covered income that is taxed for OASI; perhaps the OASI tax should be levied on all earned income. Still another approach is to change the flat Social Security tax rate (6.2 percent on all covered income) to a progressive tax rate—that is, one that levies a greater tax on individuals who earn income above a specified level. With this solution, higher-wage earners bear more of the burden, with little threat to their ability to afford their basic necessities.

What do you think?

① Which of the above approaches to reform do you think is best for workers? Why?

② How would you balance the interests of low-wage workers, who are more likely to depend on Social Security in retirement, against those of higher-income workers?

③ Should Social Security be a *means-tested benefit*—that is, a benefit based on financial need? Why or why not?

④ Is there a particular Social Security reform, or combination of reforms, that you believe the majority of U.S. citizens would support? Explain.

Adriel Bettelheim, "Social Security," in *Issues in Social Policy* (Washington, DC: CQ Press, 2000), 79–96.

Insurance (SSDI), provides income to those covered by the Social Security program and to their families if they meet the guidelines for disability. Similarly to OASI, SSDI is a contributory (social insurance) program.

In 1972, Congress again amended the Social Security Act by establishing the Supplemental Security Income (SSI) program, a noncontributory program. Recipients of SSI include low-income elderly people whose Social Security benefits are so low they cannot provide for themselves, individuals with disabilities, and blind people. Unlike other Social Security programs, SSI is a **means-tested benefit,** meaning that the eligibility criteria to receive the benefit include a government-specified income level, which is very low.

The Social Security Act of 1935 created other income security programs, including unemployment compensation and Aid to Dependent Children. Three years after passage of the Social Security Act, the Roosevelt administration also enacted a minimum wage, and several decades later, in 1975, Congress established an additional income security program known as the Earned Income Tax Credit. We now turn to these other income security programs.

Unemployment Compensation

Together, employees, employers, the federal government, and state governments fund the unemployment compensation program created by the Social Security Act of 1935. Through this program, employees who lose their jobs through no fault of their own can collect unemployment compensation for up to twenty-six weeks. An employee fired for cause (not doing the job, doing it poorly, or violating work rules or the law) cannot receive unemployment compensation.

Unemployment benefits differ by state. Each state government administers the program for its own citizens and determines how much an unemployed worker is eligible to collect. However, in all states, the amount of a person's unemployment benefit is based on a formula that takes into account the salary earned in the previous job. During economic recessions, the national government has sometimes extended the twenty-six-week benefit period if the unemployment rate remains high for a long time.

Minimum Wage

In addition to guaranteeing some income for workers who lose their jobs through no fault of their own, Congress in 1938 enacted the Fair Labor Standards Act, which established a minimum wage. The aim was to guarantee most employed workers a **living wage**—a wage high enough to keep them out of poverty. The federal government has amended this law several times to expand minimum wage coverage to additional job categories, yet there are still various exceptions to it. Workers not guaranteed the federal minimum wage include full-time students, youths under 20 years of age for the first ninety days of their employment, workers who earn tips, commissioned sales employees, farm laborers, and seasonal and recreational workers. (Why do you think these workers are excluded from the minimum wage?) For workers guaranteed the minimum wage, employers must pay overtime (equal to one and a half times an employee's regular hourly rate) for all hours over 40 worked during a workweek.

In 1938, the government set the federal minimum wage at twenty-five cents per hour. Unlike the Social Security retirement program, OASI, the minimum wage benefit is not indexed to other economic factors and so does not automatically receive a COLA to keep up with inflation. Congress and the president must approve new legislation if the minimum wage is to increase. (Why do you think OASI is indexed to receive automatic COLAs and the minimum wage is not?)

Proposals to raise the minimum wage are always controversial, as revealed by the intense debate that preceded legislation in May 2007 that increased the national minimum wage from $5.15 (the wage set in 1997) to $7.25 per hour. Senate Democrats, led by Senator Edward Kennedy (D-Massachusetts), included the provision for the minimum wage hike in a bill to continue funding for the Iraq War. In this way, they won needed votes from those who did not support the wage increase but did support the war funding. Speaker of the

House Nancy Pelosi (D-California) said of the increase, "We are raising wages for the hardest-working Americans."[13]

State and local governments can establish a minimum wage higher than the federal minimum for covered workers, and they can extend a minimum wage to workers not covered by the federal minimum wage. In 2007, more than half the states had minimum wages higher than the national $5.15 an hour.[14] But even in instances of these more generous benefits, the harsh reality is that many minimum wage workers, as well as many people earning several dollars over the national minimum wage—whom we collectively call the working poor—are still living in poverty. Hence, today's minimum wage is not a living wage. To reduce the financial hardship of minimum and low-wage workers, the national government established the Earned Income Tax Credit program.

Earned Income Tax Credit

In addition to providing cash transfers and regulating wages, the government supports income security through programs offering tax breaks. One of these is the Earned Income Tax Credit (EITC) program, established in 1975.

Citizens with low to moderate earned income from employment or from self-employment who file an income tax return are eligible for EITC benefits. Working parents are eligible for larger tax credits than are workers without children. The amount of the tax credit decreases (eventually reaching zero) as earned income increases. For example, in 2007, a parent with two children who earned $15,000 received an EITC of $4,716, and a parent with two children who earned $38,000 received no EITC.[15]

According to the Center on Budget and Policy Priorities, a research organization concerned with the status of poor people, the national EITC keeps more than 4 million people, the majority of whom are children, out of poverty each year and is the "nation's most effective antipoverty program for working families."[16] Yet the antipoverty program with which many Americans are most familiar began in 1935 as Aid to Dependent Children.

Temporary Assistance to Needy Families

The Social Security Act established Aid to Dependent Children (ADC), which evolved into Aid to Families with Dependent Children (AFDC) and was then replaced by Temporary Assistance to Needy Families (TANF). Initially supporting stay-at-home single widows with children, the ADC program evolved into TANF, with its emphasis on assisting needy female-headed households, as well as two-parent families. The focus moreover has changed from one of encouraging women to stay home with their children to one of requiring recipients to work (those in single- and dual-parent households) and requiring fathers (particularly those not living with their children) to take on greater financial responsibilities for their children.

Federal grants and state funds paid for the ADC and AFDC noncontributory cash transfer, entitlement programs, and a formula in the national law determined what percentage of each state's annual program cost the federal government would cover. The federal law also gave each state discretion to determine the level of benefits as well as the eligibility criteria for program recipients in that state. (See "Exploring the Sources" for data on the level of state benefits.) However, as mandated by federal law, eligibility criteria for AFDC in every state included the presence of children under the age of 18 and a means test indicating no or very low family income.

Due to the rise in the number of female-headed households with children living in poverty during the 1950s and 1960s—a development referred to as the **feminization of poverty**—the number of AFDC recipients increased during those decades. So did the controversy over AFDC. Although the overwhelming majority of AFDC beneficiaries were children, myths about a poor work ethic and irresponsible sexual practices on the part of their typically single mothers fueled many calls for reform.

Grassroots welfare rights organizations sprang up to fight for greater assistance in meeting the basic needs of poor families. One such group was Aid to Needy Children–Mothers

feminization of poverty
the phenomenon of increasing numbers of unmarried, divorced, and separated women with children living in poverty

EXPLORING THE SOURCES

DO TANF MONTHLY BENEFITS KEEP FAMILIES OUT OF POVERTY?

Each state establishes the TANF benefit levels for its recipients. The map indicates the 2003 TANF per-month benefit levels in each state for a family of three (one adult and two children) with no income. Is there any state whose benefit level you think provides a family of three with an adequate living standard?

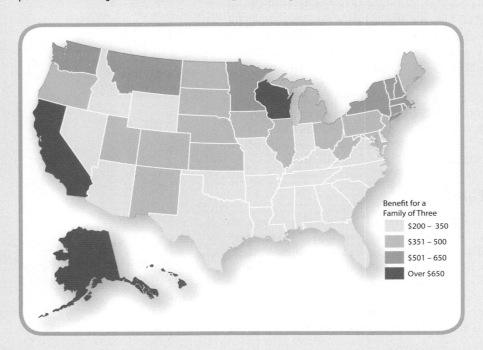

Benefit for a Family of Three

$200 – 350
$351 – 500
$501 – 650
Over $650

Evaluating the Evidence

① On the basis of the information in the map, determine the annual income provided to a family of three in your home state; in the state with the highest benefit; and in the state with the lowest benefit. How does your home state's benefit compare to the highest and lowest state benefits?

② Compare the annual incomes you identified in item 1 with the data supplied in Table 16.2 to determine whether the family of three in these three states would be defined as living in poverty according to the Department of Health and Human Services (HHS) poverty guidelines. Report your findings.

③ Do a second comparison to see whether the families in these states would be eligible for programs available to families based on 185 percent of the income in the HHS poverty guidelines, found in Table 16.2. Report your findings.

Anonymous, established in 1963 by AFDC recipient Johnnie Tillmon of the Watts section of Los Angeles. Tillmon and her organization pushed for government programs that would promote AFDC mothers' self-sufficiency by providing adequate income, job training, and child care that would allow them to transition off welfare. They also pressed for a minimum wage that was a living wage.

With passage of the Family Support Act (FSA) of 1988, the federal government implemented Tillmon's ideas for cultivating self-sufficiency in AFDC recipients. The FSA drove up the expense of the aid programs substantially, at least in the short term. Providing job training, child care, and health benefits to help people get off welfare costs more than issuing them a monthly income security check. In the long-term, the FSA was expected to decrease in costs as welfare recipients became self-sufficient workers. The short-term cost spike, however, led to calls for further welfare reform. In response, the federal government offered states waivers from some of the AFDC grant conditions to encourage experimentation with new forms of income security for low-income families with children.

On the national level, in 1996, President Bill Clinton (1993–2001) signed the Personal Responsibility and Work Opportunity Reconciliation Act (PRWORA), which radically changed both the nature and the provision of income security for low-income families with children. PRWORA replaced the AFDC entitlement program and several other grant assistance programs for low-income families with one grant, Temporary Assistance to Needy Families (TANF). Unlike AFDC, TANF is not an entitlement program.

Although PRWORA gives state governments a great deal of flexibility in determining TANF eligibility, benefits, and programs, it comes with several very specific regulations. For example, a family can receive benefits only for two consecutive years and a lifetime maximum of five years. Moreover, program beneficiaries must work or be enrolled in an educational or a training program that prepares them for work. In addition, female TANF recipients must identify their children's fathers so that these men can be required to provide financial support for their children. Ultimately, the success of this radical approach to welfare reform depends on the availability of jobs that pay well and offer benefits; hence its success depends on the overall health of the U.S. economy.

Government Definitions of Poverty

Despite the various income security programs we have considered, tens of millions of Americans, including millions who work full-time, live in *poverty*—the condition of lacking sufficient income to purchase the necessities for an adequate living standard. Millions of others are one problem away from poverty, meaning that a health emergency, significant car repair, family relations issue, or job layoff could land them in poverty. The government defines poverty using two measures: *poverty thresholds* and *poverty guidelines.*

POVERTY THRESHOLDS: COUNTING THE POPULATION LIVING IN POVERTY
Since the 1960s, the U.S. Census Bureau has used the gauge of *poverty thresholds*—an annually updated set of income measures (adjusted for family size) that define who is living in poverty (see Chapter 15). The government uses these thresholds to collect data on how many families and individuals are living in poverty.

According to the Census Bureau, in 2006, 36.5 million individuals (12.3 percent of the U.S. population) were living in poverty.[17] Just under 13 million children below the age of 18 years (17.4 percent) were in poverty, and almost 3.5 million people over the age of 65 (9.4 percent) were as well. The poverty rate among blacks was 24.3 percent; Hispanics, 20.6 percent; Asians, 10.3 percent; and non-Hispanic whites, 8.2 percent.

Government agencies that offer additional safety-net programs beyond the ones we have considered so far do not use the Census Bureau's poverty thresholds to determine eligibility. Instead, many use the Department of Health and Human Services' (HHS) **poverty guidelines,** a version of the poverty thresholds simplified for administrative use. Table 16.2 presents the HHS Poverty Guidelines for 2006.

Most (in-kind assistance) safety-net programs allow families with incomes of a certain percentage above the HHS poverty guidelines (say, 185 percent) to receive benefits. Administrators recognize that families with even those income levels experience difficulties in meeting their basic needs. Programs that use the HHS poverty guidelines as the basis for determining eligibility include the Food Stamp Program and the National School Lunch Program. These programs target the problem of **food insecurity,** the situation in which people have limited or uncertain ability to obtain, in socially acceptable ways, enough nutritious food to sustain a healthy and active life.

poverty guidelines
a simplified version of the Census Bureau's poverty thresholds developed each year by the Department of Health and Human Services; used to set financial eligibility criteria for benefits

food insecurity
situation in which people have limited or uncertain ability to obtain, in socially acceptable ways, enough nutritious food to live a healthy and active life

TABLE 16.2

Poverty Guidelines, 2006 ($ per year)

Persons in Family or Household	Forty-Eight Contiguous States and Washington D.C.	Alaska	Hawaii
1	9,800	12,250	11,270
2	13,200	16,500	15,180
3	16,600	20,750	19,090
4	20,000	25,000	23,000
5	23,400	29,250	26,910
6	26,800	33,500	30,820
7	30,200	37,750	34,730
8	33,600	42,000	38,640
For each additional person add	3,400	4,250	3,910

Source: *Federal Register*, vol. 71, no. 15 (January 24, 2006): 3848–3849.

ON THE JOB

CHRISTINA COREA, ASSISTANT, DEPARTMENT OF HOMELESS SERVICES

Name: Christina Corea

College: Boston College

Major: International Studies/Political Science (BA)

Job title: Assistant to the Deputy Commissioner for Policy & Planning, New York City Urban Fellows Program, Department of Homeless Services

Salary for jobs like this: $25,000

Day-to-day responsibilities: I assisted the deputy commissioner and her staff to reshape NYC's rental assistance program for homeless and formerly homeless clients; instituted a tracking process for Section 8 application referrals to the NYC Housing Authority; and did volunteer recruitment, data analysis, and report writing for the commissioner and her staff.

How did you get your job? I wanted to apply to law school right after undergraduate study but realized that many law schools like to see work experience and that I could probably do better on my LSATs if I took some time to study for them after college. I thought the best way to pursue a "gap year" was to apply for jobs that were part of a national fellowship program. During my senior year of college, I applied for the NYC Urban Fellows program, the Emerson Congressional Hunger Fellows Program, the Coro Fellows program, and Teach for America. The NYC Urban Fellows program had an extensive application process and then multiple rounds of interviews.

What did you like best about your job? I was placed in a learning community with twenty-four other recent college graduates. Though we did not directly work together, we were able to discuss different policy initiatives and support one another when the work was difficult.

What was your least favorite aspect of the job? Because I was weak in quantitative skills after college, I had a difficult time adjusting to the policy unit's work during the beginning of my fellowship. Though I struggled with these skills, in the end I was happy to have built a new skill set that I hope to refine in graduate school.

What advice would you give to students who would like to do what you did? I advocate that everyone seriously consider taking at least one year off after undergraduate study to explore personal interests and really consider the next step. Also, there is no better way to get a sense of different public service atmospheres than to intern while in college or during summer breaks. Definitely seek out alumni at your college who have positions that you would like to emulate or learn more about, and ask them for informational interviews. Last, be sure to keep in touch with all of the interesting people you meet in your internships, in on-campus activities, and on your informational interviews.

---

housing insecurity
situation in which people have limited or uncertain ability to obtain, in socially acceptable ways, affordable, safe, and decent-quality permanent housing

Housing insecurity—the condition in which people have limited or uncertain ability to obtain, in socially acceptable ways, housing that is affordable, safe, of decent quality, and permanent—is another problem for a growing proportion of the U.S. population. According to the Joint Center for Housing Studies at Harvard University, "The nation's housing challenges are escalating. Affordability is worsening, inadequate conditions persist, and crowding is more common."[18] The National Coalition for the Homeless estimates that more than 3 million people (1 percent of the entire U.S. population) experience homelessness in a given year.[19] About 40 percent of the homeless are children under the age of 18. Forty-nine percent are African American (compared to 11 percent of the general population). Twenty-three percent are veterans (compared to 13 percent of the general population).

Today the overwhelming majority of federal revenue spent on housing assistance is in the form of tax breaks to homeowners, developers, and property owners who rent to low-income householders. But the programs that are most in the public eye are means-tested public housing and housing voucher (Section 8 rent subsidy) programs for which low-income households can apply. According to the Department of Housing and Urban Development (HUD), the availability of these forms of housing assistance is very limited, not close to meeting the demand.[20] Read "On the Job" for an insider's view of the efforts of the Department of Homeless Services of New York City to address unmet housing needs.

Health Care Policy

Lack of health insurance is an additional problem for low-income households. Further, it is a growing challenge for middle-income households because the number of employers providing medical insurance for their employees (at no cost or a shared cost) has decreased in recent years as the cost of medical care has skyrocketed.

According to the U.S. Census Bureau, in 2006, 47 million people in the United States (15.8 percent) were without health insurance.[21] Among these uninsured, 8.7 million (11.7 percent) were under 18 years of age. Approximately 70 percent of those with insurance had private insurance plans, and the rest had government-provided plans, including Medicaid and Medicare. These two programs were established in 1965 as part of President Lyndon Johnson's (1963–1969) "Great Society" plan, which included government programs to address the effects of poverty during a time of national economic prosperity. Medicare and Medicaid are part of today's safety net.

Medicaid

Title XIX, added to the Social Security Act in 1965, created Medicaid—a joint federal-state entitlement program providing health care to people meeting the means test. Because the national legislation delegates substantial discretion to state governments regarding eligibility and benefits, there are really fifty different Medicaid programs.

In this cash transfer program, state governments pay health care providers, and then the national government reimburses the states for a percentage of these bills. The national government's share of each state's cost is based on a formula that takes into account the state's wealth. The national government pays as little as 50 percent of the Medicaid bill in the fourteen wealthiest states and as much as 77 percent in the poorest state, Mississippi.[22]

Medicaid beneficiaries fit in one of three broad categories: (1) low-income pregnant women, infants, and children up to age 6 in families with income less than 133 percent of the poverty guideline, and children up to 18 in families with income less than 100 percent of the poverty guideline; (2) low-income disabled citizens receiving SSI; and (3) low-income elderly people requiring nursing home or long-term care services or requiring assistance in meeting health care costs not covered by Medicare (a program of health insurance for the elderly; see below). States have the discretion to provide Medicaid to some additional groups, as defined by the national government. Although AFDC recipients were automatically eligible for Medicaid, today's TANF recipients are not.

The soaring cost of health care has drawn much attention to the Medicaid program. In the 1980s and 1990s, when the cost of Medicaid grew at an average annual rate of 20 percent, Congress tried to cut back its Medicaid costs by clarifying the health care fees for which the national government would reimburse state governments. At the same time, the rise in the percentage of *children* without health insurance generated bipartisan congressional support for the State Children's Health Insurance Program (SCHIP). Established in 1997, SCHIP covers medical costs for low-income uninsured children under the age of 19 who are not eligible for Medicaid. In this joint federal-state cash transfer program, eligibility is based on a family income that is generally less than 200 percent of the HHS poverty guideline. States participating in SCHIP can expand their current Medicaid program to cover these children,

or they can create a new program that provides the standard coverage mandated by the national government.

Although the majority of persons benefiting from Medicaid are women and children, the bulk of Medicaid spending covers the health care costs of the elderly. The largest percentage of Medicaid spending pays for nursing home and long-term care services, which Medicare does not cover.

Medicare

In 1965, President Lyndon Johnson signed legislation enacting Medicare, a program that provides health insurance to persons over age 65 and those under 65 who have been receiving SSDI for at least two years. Today, Medicare has four components.

Part A, Medicare's Hospital Insurance Program, is a social insurance program funded by a 1.45 percent tax paid by employees and employers that helps to pay for hospital stays. (This tax and the Social Security tax make up the "FICA" deduction from your paychecks.) All who pay into Medicare are eligible for Part A benefits when they reach the age of 65.

> California governor Arnold Schwarzenegger and Bill Novelli, CEO of the Association for the Advancement of Retired Persons (AARP), hold a town hall meeting with AARP members to discuss health care reform, including the governor's plan for universal health coverage in California.

Also eligible for Part A are persons under age 65 who have been receiving SSDI for at least two years.

All persons eligible for Part A and any persons over age 65, even if they are not eligible for Part A, can opt into *Part B,* Medicare's Supplemental Medical Insurance. Part B covers a percentage of physician costs and other outpatient health care expenses, such as laboratory fees and ambulance services.

In 1997, Congress established a third Medicare component, *Part C,* Medicare + Choice. This component allows Medicare beneficiaries to choose private health plans that provide them with the same coverage found in Medicare Parts A and B.

Under pressure from the American Association of Retired Persons (AARP) and other senior citizen interest groups, Congress proposed and President George W. Bush signed the Medicare Prescription Drug, Improvement, and Modernization Act in 2003. This act established Medicare *Part D,* the core of which is a prescription drug plan that took effect in 2006. A complicated program, Part D requires Medicare beneficiaries to choose a prescription drug plan provided by a private insurer if they do not already have prescription coverage through another health plan.

The Future of Health Care

In sum, the federal government, working hand-in-hand with state and local governments, helps to provide health insurance to millions of Americans who cannot afford it. Taxpayers generally accept the notion of government-funded health care for the elderly, persons with disabilities, and infants and children in poverty. Controversy continuously brews, however, over the question of who, if anyone, should guarantee health insurance coverage for *all* working Americans. Business interests lobby against legislation that mandates employer-provided health insurance, even if employees share the cost. At the same time, Massachusetts, California, and other states are experimenting with state laws that mandate health care coverage funded by innovative employer-employee-government programs. In 2007, California governor Arnold Schwarzenegger introduced his plan for universal health coverage in his state by asserting that "everyone in California must have health insurance."[23]

Homeland Security

The government's responsibility does not stop with ensuring basic necessities such as a clean environment, affordable energy, a secure income, sufficient food, shelter, and health care. Federal, state, and local governments also cooperate to prevent threats to personal safety, home, and health. Such threats may come from natural disasters such as hurricanes and earthquakes or from human-made calamities such as terrorist attacks.

The Importance of Intergovernmental Coordination

President George W. Bush and Congress established the Department of Homeland Security in 2002 in response to the September 11, 2001, terrorist attacks. The department's mission is to improve the coordination of efforts to prevent and respond to disasters, both human-made and natural, within U.S. borders. Homeland security is a central theme in contemporary U.S. domestic policy and an ever-present concern in Americans' daily lives.

Homeland security can succeed only as an intergovernmental effort. The prevention of attacks relies on intelligence collected by local and state law enforcement as well as federal agencies such as the Central Intelligence Agency (CIA), the National Security Agency (NSA), and the Federal Bureau of Investigation (FBI). Typically, the first responders to attacks and natural disasters are police officers, firefighters, emergency medical technicians, and other public servants hired by local governments. Federal and state agencies, when necessary, support first responders. The Department of Homeland Security agencies that back up first responders can include the Federal Emergency Management Agency (FEMA), the Office of Domestic Preparedness, and the National Biological Warfare Defense Analysis Center.

Three Dilemmas for Policy Makers

Three significant dilemmas present themselves in homeland security policy deliberations. The first deals with the question of how much intrusion into citizens' lives, in the name of prevention, is acceptable. The second dilemma is over the appropriate level and distribution of national grants-in-aid to state and local governments for improved communication systems and response capabilities. In 2005, controversy over grant distribution spurred the Department of Homeland Security to change its grant formula. Resulting cuts to New York City's homeland security funding led New York City mayor Michael Bloomberg and New York senators Hillary Clinton and Charles Schumer to protest the reduced funding. In light of the homeland security department's claim that the city had no national icons or monuments that were at risk, government officials and city residents bombarded homeland security secretary Michael Chertoff with postcards showing revered New York City landmarks such as the Statue of Liberty and the Empire State Building.

A third dilemma has to do with the intergovernmental aspect of homeland security. The issue is, how much discretion should devolve to state and local governments with the federal grants-in-aid? Although this is a common concern with respect to intergovernmental efforts for any policy area, the stakes can be very high and the finger-pointing and blaming can be especially vigorous when homeland disasters arise.

Katrina: A Test Case for National Preparedness

Hurricane Katrina and its aftermath in September 2005 presented the first real test of the response capacity of the Department of Homeland Security. The department failed the test according to citizens living in the states damaged by the hurricane, along with local and state government officials, the media, and Bush administration investigators. According to the Bush administration's *Fact Sheet: The Federal Response to Hurricane Katrina: Lessons Learned,* the hurricane and subsequent flooding of New Orleans "exposed significant flaws in our national preparedness for catastrophic events and our capacity to respond

Education as the Path to Solving Domestic Problems

	1985–1986 (%)	2005–2006 (%)
Percentage of persons 25 years and over with a bachelor's degree or higher*	19.4	28.0
Percentage of bachelor's degrees by field**		
Humanities	13.5	17.7
Social and behavioral sciences	13.6	16.8
Natural sciences	7.7	7.0
Computer sciences & engineering	14.1	8.7
Education	8.8	7.2
Business	24.0	21.4
Other	18.3	21.1

WHAT'S NEXT?

> Should the government enact laws facilitating more students' study of the "natural sciences" (which include biological and biomedical sciences, mathematics and statistics, and physical sciences and science technologies) as one approach to solving the nation's environmental and energy problems? How might doing so help the country to solve these domestic problems?

> What effect do you think the decrease in the percentage of students earning bachelor's degrees in computer sciences and engineering will have on the United States' homeland security?

* *Digest of Education Statistics 2007*, National Center for Education Statistics, Table 8, http://nces.ed.gov/programs/digest/d07/tables/dt07_008.asp.
** *Digest of Education Statistics 2007*, National Center for Education Statistics, Table 264, http://nces.ed.gov/programs/digest/d07/tables/dt07_264.asp.

to them."[24] The report highlights the crucial need for the integration of homeland security plans across national, state, and local government, as well as across organizations in the private and nonprofit sector.

Clearly, intergovernmental efforts are essential to a secure home, health, and opportunities to pursue happiness within the borders of the United States—the mission of domestic policy. The efforts of individual citizens are also vital.

Another facet of the Department of Homeland Security's work is the implementation of immigration policy and border security. Continuing concerns about potential acts of terrorism on U.S. soil, as well as debates over the economic effects of the increasing number of immigrants coming to the United States, have placed immigration policy reform high on the national agenda.

Immigration Policy

The majority of immigrants to the United States are young people seeking two goals: reunification with family members residing here and work that will provide a better quality of life than they are able to achieve in their home countries. U.S. immigration policy, the collection of laws that specify which people the government will authorize to immigrate to the United States, allows approximately one million immigrants, in four categories, to immigrate legally each year. Figure 16.2 shows that these legal immigrants come from around the globe. In addition to the legal newcomers, about 500,000 unauthorized immigrants come into the United States annually. After 9/11, citizens and their elected representatives, concerned about the impact of both authorized and unauthorized immigrants, began to analyze immigration policy anew. Debate on immigration policy reform has been ongoing ever since.

Authorized and Unauthorized Immigration

Federal immigration policy determines who may immigrate to the United States as permanent residents and as temporary visitors (such as tourists, students, and guest workers). Since the Immigration and Nationality Act of 1965, the largest category of immigrants authorized to come to the United States permanently are those seeking to reunify with family members who are either U.S. citizens or authorized permanent residents. The second-largest category comprises individuals welcomed for their employment skills; this group includes highly skilled professionals and wealthy entrepreneurs expected to invest in job creation. Persons to whom the United States offers humanitarian protection from perse-

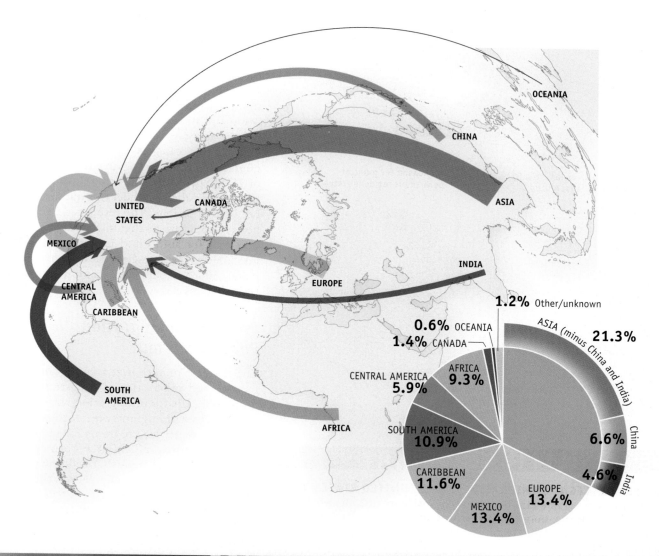

FIGURE 16.2 ■ GLOBAL SCOPE OF U.S. IMMIGRATION What world region is the source of most U.S. immigrants today? With respect to the Americas, what country or larger geographical unit is the source of most immigrants to the United States?

cution (or likely persecution) because of race, religion, nationality, membership in a particular social group, or political views compose the third-largest category of authorized immigrants. The smallest category of permanent authorized immigrants gain entry through the country-quota system, which allows up to 25,000 people per country per year (selected by lottery) to enter the United States legally.[25] Figure 16.3 presents the breakdown of authorized and unauthorized immigrants for 2006.

Who is *not* eligible for permanent authorized immigration to the United States? In addition to foreigners who do not fall within one of the categories described above, foreign nationals perceived to be anarchists or political extremists have been excluded since 1901, when a Polish anarchist assassinated President William McKinley (1897–1901). More recently, in 2002, the USA PATRIOT Act established new criteria for denying entry to the United States. Today, the national government can deny authorized immigration to foreigners who are perceived as a security or terrorist threat, have a criminal history, have previously been removed from the United States, or present a health risk.[26]

Why do half a million immigrants enter the United States without authorization each year? The answer to this question has several dimensions. One major dimension has to do

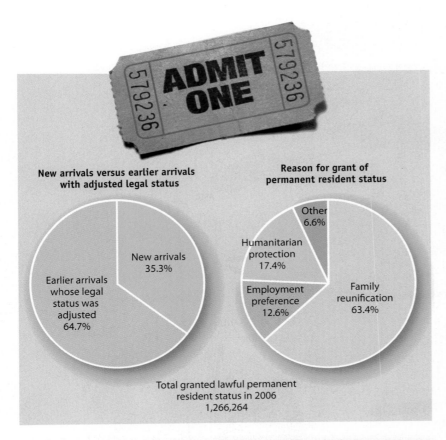

New arrivals versus earlier arrivals with adjusted legal status

- New arrivals 35.3%
- Earlier arrivals whose legal status was adjusted 64.7%

Reason for grant of permanent resident status

- Other 6.6%
- Humanitarian protection 17.4%
- Employment preference 12.6%
- Family reunification 63.4%

Total granted lawful permanent resident status in 2006
1,266,264

POLITICAL INQUIRY

FIGURE 16.3 ■ LEGAL IMMIGRATION TO THE UNITED STATES For immigrants who were granted lawful permanent residence in 2006, what percentages, respectively, were (1) new arrivals and (2) earlier arrivals whose legal status was adjusted? What factor accounted for the most grants of permanent status?

with economic opportunities—the lure of jobs that are better than those available in the home country. Yet unless an individual fits into one of the four categories for authorized immigration, he or she has no basis on which to apply for permanent, legal entry into the United States. Another reason for the large volume of unauthorized immigration is that individuals applying for immigration under the family reunification category or through their country's quota system come up against the annual U.S. quota of 25,000 per country. There is a wide gap between the number allowed under this quota and the number of applications. The result is a backlog of millions of applications that may mean up to a twenty-year wait for authorized immigration.[27] These are just some of the obstacles that explain why approximately 500,000 unauthorized immigrants enter the United States each year.

Proposed Immigration Policy Reforms

The flood of unauthorized immigrants creates financial and other stresses and strains that have prompted calls for immigration reform. Although unauthorized immigrants are not eligible for safety-net benefits such as programs for income security and food security, all children born on U.S. soil—even those born to unauthorized immigrants—are citizens and hence are eligible for these benefits. Moreover, the government guarantees a public education to all children, citizens and unauthorized immigrants alike. State and local governments cover approximately 92 percent of the cost of public education, and the national government funds the remaining 8 percent. And with respect to legal rights, the Fourteenth Amendment to the Constitution guarantees all people, not just citizens, due process before the government can infringe on their life, liberty, or pursuit of happiness, as well as equal protection of the law. Typically, the costs of these constitutional guarantees fall to state and local governments. Most unauthorized immigrants *do* pay taxes and so are contributing to government revenues collected to pay these bills. Yet their tax contributions do not cover these costs, just as the taxes collected from low-income citizens and authorized immigrants do not cover the costs of their safety-net benefits.

Given the financial burden of supporting the 10 million unauthorized immigrants residing in the United States in 2005, and in light of concerns about the ease with which terrorists (posing as well-intended immigrants) might gain entry into the country, Congress and President Bush worked intensively to reform immigration policy. Nonetheless, in May 2007, the reform bill that Senator Edward Kennedy described as the "best possible chance we will have in years to secure our borders and bring millions of people out of the shadows and into the sunshine" failed to win congressional approval.[28]

Although the various reforms proposed by the House, the Senate, and President Bush between 2005 and 2007 differed in detail, they had several common elements. One point of common ground was the proposal to secure the U.S.-Mexico border by building hundreds of miles of reinforced fence along it and hiring thousands of additional border patrol agents.

The most controversial component of the proposed reforms, put forth by the Senate in 2007, was a process by which the millions of unauthorized immigrants living in the United States could become authorized permanent residents and eventually apply for citizenship. Many Americans complained bitterly that the process would be unfair to the millions of foreign nationals who have been waiting out the application and authorization process so that they can legally enter the country. Others argued that unauthorized immigrants are inherently criminals and thus should not gain the benefit of legal permanent residence. On the other side of the debate were the countless employers who rely on the labor of immigrant workers (authorized and unauthorized), as well as some economists who stress the importance of immigrant labor to the continued prosperity of the U.S. economy. Others supporting the pathway to authorized permanent residency remind opponents of the essential role of immigration in the development of the United States—which is truly a "nation of nations"—since its founding.

> Members of the U.S. Army install part of the fence along the border near Puerto Palomas, Mexico. The federal government is building a 745-mile fence along the U.S.-Mexico border to reduce the flow of illegal migrants into the United States.

CONCLUSION   *CONTINUING THE CONVERSATION*

Before the Great Depression of the 1930s, the national government's domestic policy commitment was limited. State and local governments played the dominant role in addressing the day-to-day needs of the people. The Depression's nationwide scope and the inability of state and local governments to respond effectively to citizens' financial crises forced the national government to develop radical policies to achieve income security.

Today, the objectives of U.S. domestic policy are twofold: (1) maintenance of a safety net that assists citizens in meeting their basic needs and (2) the protection of Americans' lives, homes, and natural environment from perils—human-made and natural. The challenges of achieving these vital objectives are great. The increasing costs of safety-net programs and health care have prompted questions about the sustainability of these programs. Policy makers not only in the United States but throughout the world have environmental degradation on their agendas. Revising (some would say reestablishing) a national energy policy as well as reforming immigration policy are frequent topics in public and legislative conversations. In addition, gaps in homeland security are a persistent concern.

As the U.S. population grows and diversifies over the twenty-first century and beyond, what problems, both known and not yet anticipated, will citizens press the federal government to address? Will Congress and the president agree on a program for Social Security reform? Will the American government join with the governments of other nations to target global warming? Will Americans change their way of life in order to conserve energy and preserve and protect the environment? Will revolutionary new domestic policies be the solution, as they were in addressing the country's ordeal during the Great Depression?

Summary

1. Citizen Engagement and Domestic Policy

U.S. domestic policy addresses internal problems that threaten the people's well-being, domestic tranquility, civil liberties, and a decent standard of living. The exponential growth in the number and range of domestic policies since the Constitution's ratification in 1788 is the product of the responses of elected representatives to citizens' and interest groups' lobbying efforts as well as national crises.

2. Tools of Domestic Policy

The national government accomplishes its domestic goals through a variety of policy tools, including laws, regulations, direct provision of public goods, cash transfers, loans, loan guarantees, insurance plans, and contracting-out.

3. Environmental Policy

Since the 1970s, the federal government has assumed the primary role in formulating environmental policy. Through its regulatory policy, supplemented with grants-in-aid and loans, the national government has devolved the implementation of environmental protection to state and local governments. The tensions between the competing goals of environmental protection, economic development, and ensuring an ample supply of affordable energy are ongoing.

4. Energy Policy

Economic development and the high standard of living that is the American way have driven up energy demand. Given U.S. reliance on imported oil, much of it from politically unstable foreign nations, the internal situation of other countries strongly affects U.S. energy supplies and hence prices. Most U.S. energy is produced by the burning of nonrenewable fossil fuels, which harms the natural environment. This damage has led to an energy policy that includes funding for research and the development of alternative, renewable energy sources for the long term and conservation efforts for the short term.

5. Income Security Programs

The idea that the government should provide a safety net for citizens in financial need took shape through key components of President Franklin D. Roosevelt's New Deal. The government expanded this safety net with President Lyndon Johnson's Great Society programs. The national government meets its responsibility to provide a safety net through income security, food security, and housing security policies.

6. Health Care Policy

Health care costs are rising steadily for all. Even with the protections of Medicare and Medicaid, and even with the recent expansion of these programs, millions of people, including many employed adults, do not have health insurance. Given the steeply rising national and state expenditures for health care, and the large percentage of citizens lacking health insurance, research into and experimentation with new health care policies is ongoing.

7. Homeland Security

The Department of Homeland Security's mission is to prevent terrorist attacks and to respond to domestic disasters (human-made and natural). To accomplish this mission, the national government uses the policy tools of direct provision and grants-in-aid, working in collaboration with state and local governments.

8. Immigration Policy

Approximately 1.5 million authorized and unauthorized immigrants come to the United States each year seeking family reunification, asylum from persecution, and a better quality of life. Concerns over taxpayer costs to provide for immigrants and over the ease with which terrorists might gain entrance into the United States have sparked new efforts for immigration policy reforms.

Key Terms

For Review

1. Explain the NIMBY syndrome using the Love Canal case as an example.

2. Describe four or five of the domestic policy tools used by the federal government.

3. Discuss how the federal policy tools used for environmental protection make intergovernmental relations a key component of environmental policy.

4. Explain how concerns about environmental protection, as well as the political situation in oil-producing countries, influence national energy policy.

5. Use the following terms to distinguish between OASI and TANF: contributory program, noncontributory program, means-tested program, and entitlement program.

6. Which Americans are least likely to have health insurance? Why?

7. What is the mission of the Department of Homeland Security?

8. For what reasons do hundreds of thousands of foreigners come to the United States as unauthorized immigrants each year?

For Critical Thinking and Discussion

1. Many critics of current environmental policy argue that government regulation of pollution amounts to ineffective policy. Some claim that using cash transfer tools, including tax expenditures, grants, and direct subsidies, would be more effective. Explain how the government could use at least one of the cash transfer tools to protect the environment.

2. Which cash transfer programs (including tax expenditures) will the majority of Americans benefit from at some point in their lives? Explain.

3. Explain how at least two of the programs discussed in this chapter are important to a sustainable community.

4. What might explain why Social Security and Medicare are entitlements but TANF is not an entitlement? Keep in mind the nature of the programs (contributory or noncontributory) and the populations each program targets.

5. Frequently, a crisis or disaster is the catalyst for revolutionary, new public policies. Discuss one or two crises or disasters that have occurred in your lifetime and that led to major changes in public policy.

MULTIPLE CHOICE: Choose the lettered item that answers the question correctly.

1. The largest national cash transfer program is
   a. Food Stamps.
   b. Social Security.
   c. Temporary Assistance to Needy Families (TANF).
   d. unemployment compensation.

2. The largest component (in terms of cost and number of people served) of Social Security is
   a. COLA.
   b. OASI.
   c. SSDI.
   d. SSI.

3. Pell grants and financial support to farmers for growing or limiting the growth of crops are two examples of the policy tool of
   a. contributory cash transfer.
   b. direct subsidy.
   c. insurance.
   d. loan guarantee.

4. All of the following safety-net programs were created during President Franklin D. Roosevelt's administrations *except*
   a. Medicaid.
   b. the minimum wage.
   c. Social Security's Old-Age and Survivors Insurance.
   d. unemployment compensation.

5. The environmental movement began in the
   a. 1890s.
   b. 1930s.
   c. 1970s.
   d. 1990s.

6. The official who participated in writing the Kyoto Protocol (which the United States has not signed) is
   a. President Bill Clinton.
   b. President George W. Bush.
   c. Vice President Al Gore.
   d. Vice President Dick Cheney.

7. The disaster that prompted the national government to establish the Department of Homeland Security is
   a. the Great Depression.
   b. Hurricane Katrina.
   c. Love Canal.
   d. the terrorist attacks on 9/11.

8. The largest category of immigrants to the United States consists of
   a. authorized immigrants seeking family reunification.
   b. authorized immigrants with professional skills and/or wealth.
   c. authorized immigrants seeking humanitarian protection from persecution.
   d. unauthorized immigrants.

9. The entitlement retirement income program created in 1935 is
   a. EITC.
   b. OASI.
   c. SSDI.
   d. TANF.

10. The income security program that is subject to a regular COLA is
    a. minimum wage.
    b. OASI.
    c. TANF.
    d. unemployment compensation.

FILL IN THE BLANKS.

11. _____ is the national program that provides health insurance to the elderly.

12. _____ is the national program that provides health insurance to low-income citizens.

13. A (An) _____ program guarantees a benefit to all who meet the program's eligibility criteria, regardless of the total cost to the government.

14. An indexed benefit is one that automatically increases to keep up with inflation. The increase is a COLA, which stands for _____.

15. A (An) _____ benefit has a government-specified income level (typically based on the poverty guidelines) as one of its eligibility criteria.

Answers: 1. b; 2. b; 3. b; 4. a; 5. c; 6. c; 7. d; 8. a; 9. b; 10. b; 11. Medicare; 12. Medicaid; 13. entitlement; 14. cost of living adjustment; 15. means-tested.

RESOURCES FOR RESEARCH AND ACTION

Internet Resources

American Democracy Now Web Site
www.mhhe.com/harrison1e   Consult the book's Web site for study guides, interactive activities, simulations, and current hotlinks for additional information on domestic policy in the United States.

Catalog of Federal Domestic Assistance
http://12.46.245.173/cfda/cfda.html   This online version of the catalog provides easy access to information on all federal programs available to state, local, and territorial governments; individuals; and nonprofit and for-profit organizations.

Center for Budget and Policy Priorities
www.cbpp.org   The center focuses on the impact of public policies on low-income households. On the Web site, you will find links to numerous reports elaborating on the effects of public policies on such households.

Center for Health, Environment, and Justice
www.chej.org   This site, formerly the Citizens Clearinghouse for Hazardous Waste, was established by Lois Gibbs. This organization assists grassroots groups with organizing.

Environmental Protection Agency
www.epa.gov/history/topics   This section of the EPA's Web site provides historical overviews of toxic waste sites that the government has worked to clean up.

U.S. Census Bureau
www.census.gov/statab   This link on the Census Bureau's Web site contains the *Statistical Abstract,* an annually published volume with summary statistics illuminating the social, political, and economic status of the United States.

USA Government Information
www.usa.gov   This easy-to-use first stop for government information offers links to government agencies and their programs.

Recommended Readings

Carson, Rachel. *Silent Spring.* New York: Houghton Mifflin, 1990. Thorough and alarming description of how the pesticide DDT harmed the food chain, caused cancer and genetic damage, and threatened the world as we know it.

Ehrenreich, Barbara. *Nickel and Dimed: On (Not) Getting By in America.* New York: Henry Holt, 2001. Documentation of the author's experiences when she joined the millions of Americans working full-time, year-round, for wages higher than the minimum wage ($6 to $7 per hour) in jobs with no benefits.

Gore, Al. *Earth in the Balance: Ecology and the Human Spirit.* Boston: Houghton Mifflin, 1992. Comprehensive assessment of the major post–Cold War threat to the United States and the world: planetary destruction due to overpopulation, deforestation, soil erosion, air pollution, and water pollution. Written before his more popularly known *An Inconvenient Truth,* Gore recommends far-reaching and specific governmental and corporate actions.

Kettl, Donald. *System Under Stress: Homeland Security and American Politics,* 2nd ed. Washington, D.C.: CQ Press, 2007. Comprehensive presentation of the massive bureaucratic reorganization that created the Department of Homeland Security. The effectiveness of this reorganization is assessed in light of the disastrous governmental response to Hurricane Katrina.

Peters, B. Guy. *American Public Policy: Promise and Performance.* Washington, D.C.: CQ Press, 2004. A readable account of the policy-making process, with chapters on specific policy areas: economy, taxes, health care, income maintenance, education, energy, environmental protection, defense, law enforcement, and social regulation.

Movies of Interest

An Inconvenient Truth (2006)
A rallying cry for citizens and government to address the problem of global warming, this documentary presents the science of global warming as it follows Al Gore's environmental advocacy from his college years to today.

United 93 (2006)
An account of the fate of United Flight 93—the fourth plane hijacked on September 11, 2001—this fact-based film documents the plight of the passengers (who had become aware of the other hijackings) and their struggle to prevent another catastrophe. It also reveals the national government's lack of preparedness for the emergency.

A Civil Action (1998)
This movie highlights the enormous expense (financial and emotional) of proving in a court of law that a large corporation's chemical waste pollution caused the leukemia that killed children from eight families.

The China Syndrome (1979)
Released thirteen days before the nation's first nuclear accident at Three Mile Island in Pennsylvania, this film describes a meltdown at a nuclear power plant, a reporter's efforts to tell the public of the company's purposeful violation of safety standards, and the company's attempts to silence the reporter.

The Grapes of Wrath (1940)
The winner of two Academy Awards, this movie, set during the Great Depression, tells the story of the Joad family (and their acquaintances) as they struggle to meet their basic needs, first in the Oklahoma Dust Bowl and later in California.

Global Warming: From Lukewarm to Hot

Reps. Rick Boucher, D-Va., and Edward Markey, D-Mass., are two key players in the global-warming debate who have significantly different policy views, political styles, and legislative roles. But they've voiced surprising agreement that major action on the issue is increasingly likely this year, despite the conventional wisdom about holding off until a new president is in the White House.

"I think this is achievable" in 2008, said the low-profile Boucher, a moderate subcommittee chairman who emphasizes the need for bipartisan, industry-supported global-warming legislation. "Some Democrats would rather wait until 2009. Among the key reasons to act now are that we can have a U.S. position sooner in international negotiations. And industry is waiting for the rules before they make financial investment. The sooner we do that, the sooner we have a green industry to export to the rest of the world."

Markey, an often-fervent liberal whom Speaker Nancy Pelosi, D-Calif., tapped to promote wide-ranging legislation to address climate change, echoed the case for immediacy. "It's preferable to give everything that you can when you have the opportunity," he said. "The issue is too urgent to treat as an item on the political agenda."

Markey even suggested that President Bush could become part of an international breakthrough on global warming, akin to the bold strides on nuclear weapons reduction that President Reagan discussed with Soviet President Mikhail Gorbachev in 1986. Although those talks foundered, the summit was eventually seen as helping pave the way for a major arms treaty the following year. "The experts were dumbfounded when the Berlin Wall came down two years later," Markey said.

Most environmental groups contend that global-warming legislation is needed now because scientific research has shown that the problem has become more urgent. And political momentum has mounted considerably as the public has become more acutely aware of the threat, they argue. "There is no time for delay," Fred Krupp, the president of Environmental Defense, told a Senate hearing in November.

Still, the odds that Bush and the Democratic-controlled Congress will agree on a plan to reduce greenhouse gases seem at least as long as when Reagan and Gorbachev were trying to thaw the Cold War. The global-warming debate is highly complex, and the solutions would impose major costs on the public and on businesses. Plus, expectations are low for Congress getting much of anything.

The House has barely begun its legislative work on climate change, although the Senate is further along, after the Environment and Public Works Committee in December approved a comprehensive, bipartisan bill. Sponsored by Sens. Joe Lieberman, ID-Conn., and John Warner, R-Va., the legislation would cap greenhouse-gas emissions, provide emission allowances to polluters, and set up government auctions for a small portion of the allowances.

Proponents of the Lieberman-Warner bill face widespread skepticism that they can garner the 60 votes needed on the Senate floor to overcome hard-line foes. Although some prominent Republicans—including Sen. John McCain of Arizona and California Gov. Arnold Schwarzenegger—support global-warming legislation, many others in their party are dubious. A House GOP leadership aide dismissed the Senate measure as "focusing more on message than on substance," and added, "Republicans can show that Democrats are hitting consumers in the pocketbook without tangible benefit."

Barack Obama has endorsed similarly sweeping reductions in greenhouse gases. "I don't believe that climate change is just an issue that's convenient to bring up during a campaign," Obama said in an Iowa speech. "I believe it's one of the greatest moral challenges of our generation."

Some Republicans, though, contend that Democrats are poised to force what could become a fruitless debate merely to score political points. Legislative deadlock on global warming—either at the hands of filibustering Senate Republicans or a veto-wielding Bush—could provide fodder for Democrats' campaign attacks. But Pelosi's chief of staff, John Lawrence, brushed aside such talk of disingenuousness.

"We will try our best to send a bill to the president," Lawrence said in an interview. "We want a bill, not an issue."

Those who advocate action this year point to the bipartisan success on energy legislation—including the first statutory increase in automobile fuel-efficiency standards since 1975—that Bush signed into law on December 19.

Just a year ago, the prospects for that measure were bleak. Its backers didn't achieve all of their initial goals, but the effort showed Democratic leaders' deep commitment to reducing the nation's oil consumption and confronting global warming.

Pelosi, in particular, has been actively involved in making the environmental challenge what she calls her "flagship issue." At a pre-holiday roundtable discussion in her office, she reminded reporters, "Many people said to me" that the energy bill could not be done, and she described the result as "a Christmas present to the American people."

It showed that "change is possible," she asserted, while conceding that the next steps on climate change will be complicated.

Pelosi has not set a timetable for global-warming action this year. Key lawmakers are aware of "the imperative of getting it done," Lawrence said, and added that the speaker will likely discuss details with members soon after the House returns to work on January 15.

Pelosi could once again find herself at odds with the venerable House Energy and Commerce Committee Chairman John Dingell, D-Mich., a longtime auto-industry champion whom she successfully steered toward supporting the tougher fuel-efficiency standards last year. He emphasized the challenges facing the global-warming legislation in a year-end conference call with reporters.

"Working with the administration has been very difficult for me," Dingell said. "I truthfully and honestly don't know" about the chances for a bill. He also contended that the enactment of last year's energy legislation makes it unlikely that Congress can impose additional demands on his home state's auto manufacturers. "We have now squeezed the auto industry just about as hard as I think we can," he said. "We're going to try to see to it that everybody makes their proper contribution."

Dingell seemed more upbeat about the legislative prospects on global warming. "The chances of moving the bill are good," he said. "The country wants it. The legislation is needed. Members are supportive." Dingell acknowledged that the issues will be tough to address and that "a high level of bipartisanship" will be required.

Scientific experts generally agree that U.S. greenhouse-gas emissions should be reduced by 60 to 80 percent from current levels by 2050. The Senate committee's highly prescriptive global-warming bill would achieve a roughly 70 percent goal for U.S. emissions. In the most broadly co-sponsored House legislation on the issue—whose chief sponsor is Rep. Henry Waxman, D-Calif.—the explicit goal is an 80 percent cut, although the measure largely delegates to the Environmental Protection Agency the steps to achieve that objective. According to Markey, the energy bill signed by Bush will achieve about 25 percent of the required reduction in emissions by 2030.

The debate over the 2007 energy bill offers insight into the potential stumbling blocks

The global-warming debate is highly complex, and **the solutions would impose major costs** on the public and on businesses.

that lie ahead on global-warming legislation. The Senate, heeding objections from Southern-based utility companies, rejected a House-passed plan to require utilities to produce a larger share of electric power from renewable sources. Markey contended that removing that provision significantly lowered the potential to cut greenhouse gases. He vowed that the issue will come up again this year, "forcing the Senate to be accountable."

One of the leading foes of the renewable-fuels requirements for utilities was Boucher, who led the opposition to the House's 220–190 passage of that amendment during the August debate. "Wind and solar energy are less available in the South," said Boucher, who represents a rural western Virginia district where coal is king. "The proposal would require more taxes for our ratepayers and would not be a fair cost to impose." He noted that only 53 senators were willing to support the House-passed provision, seven votes short of what is needed to break a filibuster.

Boucher has focused on technologies to make coal cleaner and reduce pollution, and Pelosi and others have encouraged some of his proposals. He describes the looming climate-change measure as "the most complex legislation in the nation's history," in both substance and politics. He is seeking a consensus-driven approach and has conducted

extensive discussions with lawmakers and private-sector leaders. "I have spoken with everyone in the White House at every level of responsibility," Boucher added, but he would not disclose whether he had spoken with Bush.

Waxman, the No. 2 Democrat on Energy and Commerce who worked closely with Dingell in crafting the landmark 1990 Clean Air Act, is among those whom Boucher describes as an "essential" player on global warming. The two have had two lengthy meetings in Waxman's office on the prospective legislation. "I anticipate his support," Boucher said. "He and I have always had a very cordial relationship."

Waxman has a decidedly more liberal viewpoint in the global-warming debate, though he says he respects Boucher's work. "I have a very high regard for him," Waxman said in an interview. "He wants to develop a consensus proposal, though his goals are not as ambitious as mine. . . . My sense is that the American public is ready for strong legislation."

Waxman's history of contentious dealings with the Bush administration—including on energy issues—makes him somewhat more skeptical of chances for securing an agreement this year. "My view is that if we can get a strong bill, we should go for it," he said. He speculated, however, that some industry groups might prefer to resolve the issue with Bush in office this year, rather than face what likely would be more-rigorous demands from a Democratic president.

Should Congress actually get global-warming legislation near the finish line this fall, Boucher suggested that final action might require a lame-duck session after the election. If he and other proponents succeed in this campaign year, that would be an extraordinary result.

■ **THEN:** The impact of greenhouse-gas emissions on the climate was disputed.

■ **NOW:** Scientific experts generally agree that U.S. greenhouse-gas emissions should be reduced by 60 to 80 percent from current levels by 2050.

■ **NEXT:** Will a new generation of voters force Congress to pass comprehensive global-warming legislation?
Should government compensate industries for complying with new global-warming regulations?
Will President Obama become part of an international breakthrough on global warming?

Foreign
Policy and
National
Security

THEN

The emergence of the United States as a superpower and the Cold War dominated U.S. foreign policy in the aftermath of World War II.

NOW

The war on terror defines U.S. foreign and national security policy.

What long-term repercussions will the wars in Iraq and Afghanistan and ongoing tensions with Iran and North Korea have on the future of U.S. foreign policy and the United States' role as world leader?

How will the continuing threat of terrorism against the United States influence foreign and national security policy in the future?

Will U.S. foreign policy in the coming years increasingly reflect a clash of civilizations between Western democracies and fundamentalist Islamic states?

NEXT

Carrying Out Foreign Policy:
Chief Warrant Officer 4 (Ret) John Wimberg

In early 2004, John Wimberg was living a life not uncommon for a 43-year-old guy in suburban New Jersey. He enjoyed his job as a helicopter pilot at the New Jersey State Forest Fire Service. He spent weekends boating with his two daughters, Katie and Kirsten, and his wife, Linda. I In his younger days, Wimberg had served in the U.S. Navy. When his active duty ended, he joined the Army National Guard. In spring 2004, rumors began circulating that Wimberg's B Co. 150th Aviation Regiment would be called into active duty. In April, his unit was activated to the Army base at Fort Dix, New Jersey—and in November, Wimberg left McGuire Air Force base for Iraq. I Wimberg led the detachment that flew one of the Army's two-star generals around the war zone. "As the senior pilot, it was my job to review the flight plan and make sure we kept him in a safe area. . . . When we came under fire upon landing, I felt that the plans had gotten out. Once, the general had just gotten out of the helicopter and a mortar round exploded. We got out of there quickly."* Occasionally, Wimberg and his colleagues would fly "hero flights," the designation given to transporting the bodies of soldiers killed in action to Balad Air Base in Iraq. I Ask Wimberg what he missed while serving in Iraq, and he will tell you that he "missed a whole year of my kids' life. I missed Katie's eighth grade graduation. I missed Christmas morning. I missed everything that happened to them that year." Such sacrifice is common fare for the women and men of the United States armed forces. I Indeed, today, just as during the two World Wars and the wars in Korea and Vietnam, some of our friends and neighbors, and perhaps even we ourselves, may be directly and deeply involved in carrying out the military operations that are a component of foreign policy. Today people such as John Wimberg are not uncommon heroes in towns throughout the United States, as about 500,000 men and 165,000 women have served in Iraq and Afghanistan and have returned home. And more than 4,200 have not.**

> Chief Warrant Officer John Wimberg's life was changed when his unit was sent to Iraq in 2004.

* Telephone interview with John Wimberg, January 14, 2008.
** www.projects.washingtonpost.com/fallen/.

The conventional view is that

foreign policy is all about wizened old statesmen negotiating treaties and about sophisticated ambassadors clinking wine glasses at chic cocktail parties. It is true that top government officials in Washington, D.C., formulate foreign policy—the politics and programs by which the United States conducts its relations with other countries and furthers American interests around the globe. But the broader, everyday reality of U.S. foreign policy is that individual American citizens play an important part in shaping and implementing the programs decided upon by foreign policy makers. Citizens play their part by staying informed about policy makers' decisions on war, peace, trade issues, and policies that ensure national security in the post-9/11 world, and expressing their personal views to their representatives in government and through the ballot box. Or they play a more direct part by carrying out an aspect of the country's foreign policy, as John Wimberg did through his military service as a helicopter pilot in Iraq.

Of all the country's policy arenas, the foreign policy arena is the most volatile. During the past sixty years, the goals of U.S. foreign policy have shifted significantly, ranging from preventing the spread of communism in the post–World War II era, to redefining the national foreign policy agenda as the world's only superpower in the 1990s, to responding to the terrorist attacks on U.S. soil of September 11, 2001. As the objectives and worldviews of policy makers have changed in concert with unprecedented world developments, so too have their priorities and the instruments available to them in implementing U.S. foreign policy.

The Tools of U.S. Foreign Policy

Government officials use a variety of instruments to shape foreign policy. Among these are diplomacy, trade and economic policies, and military options.

Diplomacy

Covering a gamut of situations, diplomacy is often foreign policy makers' tool of choice. **Diplomacy** can be generally defined as the conduct of international relations, particularly involving the negotiation of treaties and other agreements between nations. It can include an occurrence as mundane as the communication between two embassies when a citizen of one country commits a crime in another. Or it can involve an event as significant as a major summit attended by world leaders. When diplomacy works, we typically do not hear about it.

Among the central figures in the diplomatic dance are **foreign service officers,** the diplomatic and consular staff at American embassies abroad. Foreign service officers, who are employees of the Department of State, conduct formal communications among nations. They are frequently responsible for negotiating many different types of international agreements, including economic and trade policies.

Trade and Economic Policies

U.S. foreign policy makers rely on trade policies, economic aid (foreign aid), and economic penalties to compel foreign governments to conform to the United States' will. Consider the example of most favored nation status. In international trade, conferring **normal trade relations (NTR) status** means that a country grants to a particular trading partner the same, least restrictive trade conditions (that is, the lowest tariff rates) that the country offers to its other favored trading partners—its "most favored nations." U.S. foreign policy

This chapter provides a framework for your study of foreign policy and national security in this textbook.

FIRST, we examine *the tools of U.S. foreign policy.*

SECOND, we analyze the question of *who decides: the creators and shapers of foreign policy.*

THIRD, we look at *U.S. foreign policy in historical context,* tracing its development from the ratification of the Constitution until World War II.

FOURTH, we analyze *the postwar era* and the status of *the United States as superpower.*

FIFTH, as it has become clear that Cold War policies are no longer relevant, we consider *U.S. foreign policy after 9/11.*

SIXTH, we take a look at *future challenges in American foreign policy.*

diplomacy
the conduct of international relations, particularly involving the negotiation of treaties and other agreements between nations

foreign service officers
the diplomatic and consular staff at U.S. embassies abroad

normal trade relations (NTR) status
the international trade principle holding that the least restrictive trade conditions (best tariff rates) offered to any one national trading partner will be offered to every other nation in a trading network (also known as *most favored nations*)

makers can bestow most favored nation status on a country to influence it to enact policies the United States prefers. Conversely, they can withhold this status to punish a nation that does not institute policies supportive of the United States' goals. For example, the United States withheld most favored nation status from Vietnam for many years, in an attempt to get the Vietnamese to account for American prisoners of war and soldiers missing in action in the Vietnam War.

Governments also use trade agreements as a tool of foreign policy. Among the most important of these agreements in the United States is the North American Free Trade Agreement (NAFTA), whose members include the United States, Mexico, and Canada. NAFTA eliminated barriers to trade and financial investments across the economies of the three nations (see Chapter 15 for further discussion).

Beyond trade policy, American diplomats frequently use economic enticements in the form of foreign aid to pressure other countries into enacting and enforcing policies that the United States supports. After the terrorist attacks of 9/11, for example, the George W. Bush administration sought the cooperation of the Pakistani government in Operation Enduring Freedom, the U.S. military offensive in neighboring Afghanistan. The United States sought to overthrow the Islamic fundamentalist Taliban regime, which had harbored and provided training grounds for terrorists, and to capture 9/11 mastermind Osama bin Laden, who was believed to be hiding in Afghanistan. Before the 9/11 terrorist strikes on domestic U.S. targets, Pakistan had received comparatively little aid from the United States. In fact, the United States had imposed sanctions on Pakistan because of its pursuit of nuclear weapons, its history of domestic coups, and its track record of defaulting on international loans. But after 9/11 and because of Pakistan's proximity to Afghanistan (they share a 1,500-mile-long border), Pakistan became a focal point of the U.S. war on terror. In order to encourage (and finance) the country's cooperation, the Bush administration waived the sanctions on Pakistan.[1] Moreover, whereas Pakistan had received only about $3.4 million in aid from the United States in the year before the terrorist attacks, in 2002 the country was the beneficiary of over $1 billion in U.S. aid. Although aid levels tapered off to between $400 million and $600 million annually between 2003 and 2007, the Bush administration requested $785 million for Pakistan in 2008.[2] The aid proved effective in paving the way for warmer Pakistani-U.S. relations: the United States regularly used Pakistani air bases to launch attacks into Afghanistan, and it continues to rely on Pakistani intelligence for information about terror network activity.

American foreign policy officials also use economic strategies to punish countries whose policies or behavior the U.S. government disapproves of. In May 2007, the United States imposed **sanctions**—penalties that halt economic exchanges (and that may include boycotts, trade embargos, the suspension of financial flow from investments, and the cessation of cultural exchanges) on Iran. The George W. Bush administration and Congress objected to a laundry list of Iran's activities, including the pursuit of nuclear weapons, financial and intellectual support of terrorist organizations, the country's opposition to the Mideast peace process, and its role in destabilizing both Iraq and Lebanon.[3] However, as Senator Christopher Dodd (D-Connecticut), chair of the Banking, Housing, and Urban Affairs Committee, has noted, "Economic sanctions are a critical element of U.S. policy toward Iran. But sanctions alone are not sufficient. They must be used as effective leverage, undertaken as part of a coherent, coordinated, comprehensive diplomatic and political strategy which firmly seeks to deter Iran's nuclear ambitions and other actions which pose a threat to regional stability."[4]

Almost a century ago, President Woodrow Wilson made this observation:

> A nation that is boycotted is a nation that is in sight of surrender. Apply this economic, peaceful, silent, deadly remedy and there will be no need for force. It does not cost a life outside the nation boycotted, but it brings a pressure upon the nation which, in my judgment, no modern nation could resist.[5]

sanctions
penalties that halt economic relations

But others argue that sanctions actually may worsen conditions, particularly for the poorest people in a sanctioned nation.[6] And given the high levels of **globalism,** or interconnectedness, among the world's countries today, a nation on which boycotts or sanctions are imposed often has recourse—sometimes in the form of aid from allies—to withstand the pressure of the economic penalty. Thus, as Senator Dodd observed, sanctions are frequently only a part of a wider diplomatic and political strategy.

The Military Option

Since September 11, 2001, the United States has been involved in a multifront war that prominently features military actions in Iraq and Afghanistan. The September 11 terrorist strikes and subsequent U.S. government actions demonstrate how the creators of foreign policy use the military option as an instrument of foreign policy. Hungry for an enemy after the deadly attacks on American soil, the United States targeted Afghanistan's Taliban regime. The Taliban had supported and harbored members of **al-Qaeda,** the radical international Islamic fundamentalist terror organization that took credit for the 9/11 bloodshed. Foreign intelligence had pointed to Osama bin Laden, a Saudi millionaire living in Afghanistan, as the engineer of the attacks. U.S. military action in Afghanistan continues today.

But the bases of world terrorist activity today transcend national borders. The nineteen 9/11 terrorists themselves were not citizen-soldiers of any one country but rather nationals from Saudi Arabia, the United Arab Emirates, Egypt, and Lebanon. They had trained in various nations, including Afghanistan, and had been supported by citizens of still other countries. Thus no single, clear nation-state was the enemy. Without a concrete enemy (over which a victory could be defined and declared), the Bush administration requested, and Congress passed, a formal declaration of a "war on terror."

Then–Secretary of State Colin Powell subsequently made a case to the United Nations and to the American people alleging that U.S. intelligence indicated that the Saddam Hussein regime in Iraq was harboring **weapons of mass destruction (WMDs)**—nuclear, chemical, and biological weapons.[7] In response to what at the time appeared to be a credible threat, on March 18, 2003, American troops invaded Iraq. The military strike toppled the Hussein regime, which the United States had supported for years through foreign aid.[8] Following the invasion, weapons inspectors conducted a thorough search of suspected weapons sites, but no WMDs were ever found, leaving many critics of the Bush administration to question the administration's motives and to ask whether the intelligence community had been pressured by administration officials to find intelligence rationalizing the war in Iraq.[9] Nonetheless, the military effort continues today.

When they use the military as an instrument of foreign policy, policy makers send a strong signal. When military conflict occurs on a grand scale—for the United States, that would include today's wars in the Mideast, as well as the Gulf War (1990-1991), the Vietnam War (1965-1975), the Korean War (1950-1953), and the two World Wars (1914-1918 and 1939-1945), the goal often is **regime change,** the replacement of a country's government with another government by facilitating the deposing of its leader or leading political party. That is, rather than attempting to change another nation's policies, the wars are fought to end the reign of the enemy nations' leaders. On the other hand, most military action by the United States in the past century has occurred on a smaller scale, as policy makers have sought to change

globalism
the interconnectedness between nations in contemporary times

al-Qaeda
a radical international Islamic fundamentalist terror organization

weapons of mass destruction (WMDs)
nuclear, chemical, and biological weapons

regime change
the replacement of a country's government with another government by facilitating the deposing of its leader or leading political party

TOOLS OF FOREIGN POLICY

Diplomacy

— Tool used to conduct international relations, particularly involving the negotiation of treaties and other agreements between nations

— The foreign policy makers' tool of choice

Trade and Economic Policies

— Trade policy, including granting most favored nation status to another country, to give it trade advantages

— Economic aid (foreign aid), involving financial incentives intended to compel foreign governments to conform to the United States' will

— Economic penalties, including sanctions or other forms of punishment against nations that have taken actions to which the United States objects

The Military Option

— The use of military force, often in a multifront war

— Tool used to send a strong signal to other nations

— Tool whose nature has changed drastically since 9/11 because of the advent of an enemy without national borders

Concept Summary

the policy in another country or perhaps to protect U.S. interests or allies. For example, in 1999 during the Clinton administration, the United States took military action in Kosovo in the former Yugoslavia to halt ethnic cleansing in that region. Other military actions—in Somalia (1992–1994), Bosnia (beginning in 1993), and Panama (1989)—have also been on a limited scale with specific and smaller goals than those of the major conflicts.

Who Decides? The Creators and Shapers of Foreign Policy

In the United States, the executive and legislative branches are the primary foreign policy makers, with the president and the executive branch playing the dominant role. That said, a wide variety of interests—from the media, to interest groups, to other nations, and even private individuals—provide the context of the foreign policy process and contribute to shaping the policy outcomes of that process.

The President and the Executive Branch

The president of the United States is the foremost foreign policy actor in the world. This vast power partially derives from the constitutionally prescribed duties of the president, particularly the role of commander in chief of the U.S. armed forces. But presidents' foreign policy powers also have roots in the way the institution of the presidency has evolved and continues to evolve. Other government institutions, especially the U.S. Congress, have some ability to rein in the foreign policy authority of the president. But presidential resources such as cabinet departments and the national intelligence community, as well as the executive prestige that supplements presidents' legal and administrative powers, mean that U.S. presidents in the twenty-first century are the central figures in the foreign policy arena.

THE DEPARTMENTS OF STATE AND DEFENSE   In the executive branch, the departments of State and Defense take the lead in advising the president about foreign and military policy issues. Specifically, the Department of State, headed by the secretary of state, has more than 30,000 employees located both within the United States and abroad. (State Department employees work at more than 300 U.S. consular offices around the world.) These staff members are organized according to topical specialty (trade policy, environmental policy, and so on) and geographic area specialty (the Middle East or Southeast Asia, for example). Political appointees hold many of the top ambassadorial posts. These ambassadors and the career members of the foreign service who staff each **country desk**—the official operation of the U.S. government in each country with diplomatic ties to the United States—help to shape and administer U.S. foreign policy in that country.

country desk
the official operation of the U.S. government in each country that has diplomatic ties to the United States

The Department of Defense, often referred to as the Pentagon for its five-sided headquarters, is headed by the secretary of defense. The modern Department of Defense traces its history to the end of World War II, although it is the successor of the Department of War established at the nation's founding. The Defense Department is the cabinet department that oversees all branches of the U.S. military. Thus, although the Army, Navy, Marines, Air Force, and Coast Guard operate independently, administratively they are part of the Department of Defense. The commanding officers of each branch of the military, plus a chairperson and vice chairperson, make up the Joint Chiefs of Staff, important military advisers to the president. Increasingly both the State and Defense departments rely on private contractors to perform some functions typically associated with these respective departments, particularly overseas.

THE NATIONAL SECURITY COUNCIL AND THE INTELLIGENCE COMMUNITY
As discussed in Chapter 12, the National Security Council, consisting of the vice president, the secretary of state, the secretary of the treasury, the secretary of defense, and the national security adviser, advises and assists the president on national security and foreign policy.

Through the input of the National Security Council, the president's administration considers the country's top security matters. The NSC also coordinates foreign policy approaches among the various government agencies that will implement them. A recent addition to the foreign policy apparatus, the national security adviser has traditionally competed with the secretary of state for influence over foreign policy—and for influence over the president as well. The tension between the two advisers also stems from the differing approaches each agency takes in shaping foreign policy. Frequently the State Department has a long-term view of world affairs and advocates for foreign policies in keeping with long-term goals. In contrast, the National Security Council focuses more on short-term crises and objectives. These competing viewpoints have at times sparked media wars between the leaders of these foreign policy bureaucracies. Perhaps none of these battles was more contentious than the one between President Jimmy Carter's (1977–1981) secretary of state Cyrus Vance and Zbigniew Brzezinski, his national security adviser. Brzezinski publicly attacked Vance because he disagreed with Vance's push for increased diplomacy with the Soviet Union, advocating instead a tougher, more hawkish strategy.

A key resource in presidential foreign policy making is the intelligence community. Chief among the agencies in this community is the Central Intelligence Agency (CIA). This independent agency of the federal government is responsible for collecting, analyzing, evaluating, and disseminating foreign intelligence to the president and senior national policy makers. The CIA's roots are the World War II–era Office of Special Services. Like the NSC, the modern CIA was created by the National Security Act of 1947 at the dawn of the Cold War to monitor the actions of the expansionist Soviet Union. Since that time, the CIA has expanded its mission, using agents to penetrate the governments of foreign countries, influence their politics, and foment insurrections when the president has deemed such tactics necessary to promote American interests.

The clandestine nature of the CIA's activities prompted some members of Congress to raise questions about the agency's operations abroad. In 1975, the Select Committee to Study Governmental Operations with Respect to Intelligence—called the Church Committee after its chair, Senator Frank Church (D-Idaho)—began investigations into whether the CIA and the FBI had engaged in illegal activities while gathering intelligence. These probes led to a series of reforms aimed at increasing Congress's oversight of the CIA's activities.

> Two members of former President George W. Bush's National Security Council, Bush's secretaries of Defense, Robert M. Gates (far left), and State, Condoleezza Rice (second from left), along with Bush's Chairman of the Joint Chiefs of Staff General Peter Pace (third from left), Commander of Multinational Forces-Iraq General David Petreaus (fifth from left), and other military officers depart Al Asad Air Base after advising President Bush during a 2007 meeting with members of the Iraqi government.

Primary among the reforms was creation of the Senate Select Committee on Intelligence. Today this committee and the House Intelligence Committee are the congressional watchdogs that oversee intelligence operations. Then, in the mid-1990s, following the collapse of communism, members of Congress again challenged the CIA's mission and operations. These critics complained that the agency was behind the times in remaining focused on an enemy that no longer existed. Evidence that operatives working for foreign governments had infiltrated the CIA led to even louder congressional demands for reform of the agency's operations.

These calls for reform gained strength in the aftermath of the 9/11 attacks. Congress, the media, and the independent 9/11 Commission pointed fingers at both the domestic intelligence service—the Federal Bureau of Investigation (FBI)—and the Central Intelligence Agency for failing to anticipate and to avert the terrorist strikes. Both agencies came under heavy scrutiny by Congress for lapses in intelligence and apprehension. Because the CIA and the FBI had been seriously understaffed in Arabic translators, neither agency had had the means to interpret intercepted messages that might have enabled them to prevent the tragedy.

In the agency's own investigation, the CIA inspector general also cited the CIA's failures to share intelligence with other governmental agencies and to view counterterrorism operations strategically.[10] A particular shortcoming identified by the inspector general was the agency's failure to develop its human intelligence (human spying networks) as fully as its electronic intelligence-gathering capabilities. And according to the 9/11 Commission, which in 2004 issued a report detailing the agency's failures, the CIA was also responsible for providing the information that Iraq possessed weapons of mass destruction.[11] The CIA director at the time, George Tenet, called it a "slam-dunk" case, which led President Bush to decide to invade that country and depose its president, Saddam Hussein, in March 2003. Later investigations determined, however, that no weapons of mass destruction existed and that the CIA had relied too heavily on information from Iraqi exiles eager to rid their country of Hussein. Some commentators even maintain that CIA analysts were under White House pressure to report that Iraq was developing weapons of mass destruction. But this allegation has never been proved.

Spurred by the 9/11 Commission's findings, in 2005 President Bush announced the appointment of a national intelligence czar, called the **director of national intelligence (DNI).** This individual is responsible for coordinating and overseeing all the intelligence agencies within the executive branch.

But even since the appointment of the first DNI, other controversial policies used by the CIA have come under fire. Specifically, the CIA used **extraordinary rendition,** apprehending an individual believed to be a terrorist and transferring the person to another nation. Using this practice, the CIA transported alleged terrorists to countries where interrogation methods include methods of torture forbidden in the United States. At a press conference on March 16, 2005, President Bush was asked about U.S. involvement in "rendition," particularly the practice of taking suspects to countries where, according to the State Department, police routinely torture people held in custody. In "the post-9/11 world," President Bush responded, "the United States must make sure to protect our people and our friends from attack. That was the charge we have been given. And one way to do so is to arrest people and send them back to their country of origin with the promise that they won't be tortured. That's the promise we receive. This country does not believe in torture. We believe in protecting ourselves"[12] (see "The Conversation of Democracy").

director of national intelligence (DNI)
the person responsible for coordinating and overseeing all the intelligence agencies within the executive branch

extraordinary rendition
apprehending an individual believed to be a terrorist and transferring the person to another nation

Congress

Along with the president, Congress also enjoys significant constitutional authority in foreign policy making. The constitutional provisions that outline congressional authority with respect to foreign relations include, prominently, Congress's power to declare war. In modern times, however, presidential administrations have circumvented this congressional power by using U.S. troops without a formal congressional declaration of war. Such was the case in the Vietnam War, for example.

DO THE GENEVA CONVENTIONS APPLY WHEN TERRORISTS HAVE SO DRASTICALLY ALTERED THE RULES OF WAR?

The Issue: The Geneva Conventions are a set of four treaties signed in Geneva, Switzerland, in 1949, in the aftermath of World War II. The conventions established standards for the protection of humanitarian concerns under international law. They apply to injured or ill members of the armed forces, prisoners of war, and civilians. Article 13 of the Third Geneva Convention, which specifically guides the treatment of prisoners of war, states that "prisoners of war must at all times be humanely treated. Any unlawful act or omission by the Detaining Power causing death or seriously endangering the health of a prisoner of war in its custody is prohibited, and will be regarded as a serious breach of the present Convention. In particular, no prisoner of war may be subjected to physical mutilation or to medical or scientific experiments of any kind which are not justified by the medical, dental or hospital treatment of the prisoner concerned and carried out in his interest. Likewise, prisoners of war must at all times be protected, particularly against acts of violence or intimidation and against insults and public curiosity. Measures of reprisal against prisoners of war are prohibited."*

Beginning in 2002, U.S. military authorities at the United States' Guantánamo Bay Naval Base in Cuba have detained about 775 "enemy combatants" whom the Bush administration accused of being terrorist operatives or of having information about terrorist operations. Captured primarily in Afghanistan, these individuals were transported to Guantánamo for questioning. Although authorities have released nearly two-thirds of the prisoners, over 270 remain. As designated enemy combatants, the prisoners have not enjoyed the legal rights granted to individuals charged with a crime in the United States. In effect, the Bush administration claimed that detainees at Guantánamo do not have the legal rights that those charged with a crime in the United States typically enjoy— no right to a lawyer, a trial, or *habeas corpus* (which, as you may recall, is a petition that allows a prisoner to go to a court where a judge will determine whether he or she is being held illegally).

Yes: The Geneva Conventions clearly apply in this situation. As many human rights organizations, including Amnesty International, argue, the detention of prisoners at Guantánamo amounts to a violation of the Geneva Conventions. Specifically, as these critics cite, there have been emphatic allegations of torture by individuals who have been released. Furthermore, the indefinite nature of the detentions—combined with the captors' acknowledged practices of sleep deprivation and constant light exposure, plus the disrespect of the Muslim religion on the part of some—constitutes the abuse of their human rights in violation of the Geneva Conventions. The moral high ground usually occupied by the United States is at stake, and if the United States does not accord these prisoners' rights consistent with the Geneva Convention, our own soldiers will be at risk of having their rights denied when they are captured by enemy forces.

No: The Geneva Conventions do not apply when the rules of engagement of war have changed so drastically. The Bush administration convincingly argued that the Geneva Conventions apply only to "prisoners of war" (POWs) and not to "unlawful combatants." Because the nature of the war on terror and of the tactics used by terrorists is in stark contrast to accepted international conventions of war, the treatment of combatants in that war should also vary. Donald Rumsfeld, the secretary of defense during President Bush's first term, frequently expressed in public his disdain for the Geneva Conventions. The Supreme Court has thus far agreed with the Bush administration's assessment that holding enemy combatants is legal.**

Other approaches: The Geneva Conventions do not apply to detainees at Guantánamo because they are not conventional enemy combatants, but the detainees should be afforded their human rights. In times like these, when international terrorist organizations do not follow centuries-old rules of engagement in warfare, the United States cannot follow antiquated rules and expect to keep its citizens safe. Therefore, detention can prevent further terrorist attacks if potential terrorists are prevented from carrying them out. Nevertheless, the detainees are entitled to humane treatment and to a hearing before an impartial judge to determine if they are truly a threat.

What do you think?

① Are the prisoners held at Guantánamo different from the prisoners of war held in other wars? If so, how?

② Are the Geneva Conventions, drafted soon after the conclusion of World War II, still applicable in the post-9/11 world, in which terrorism is such an urgent problem in international affairs?

* You can read the rules and explore other topics at this International Committee of the Red Cross site: www.icrc.org/ihl.nsf/7c4d08d9b287a42141256739003e636b/ 6fef854a3517b75ac125641e004a9e68.
** *Hamdi v. Rumsfeld*, 542 U.S. 507 (2004).

War Powers Act

law that limits presidential use of military forces to sixty days, with an automatic extension of thirty additional days if the president requests such an extension

In response to this presidential tactic, Congress in 1973 passed the **War Powers Act.** This law limits presidential use of military forces to sixty days, with an automatic extension of thirty additional days if the president requests such an extension. But the nature of modern warfare has quickly made the War Powers Act less effective than in the days of traditional warfare, as most modern warfare (the Iraq War being an exception) is measured in weeks rather than months. Thus it has been possible for modern presidents to wage full-scale wars without congressional involvement. Because of this reality, some critics have argued that designating war powers to the president is a cowardly decision. Representative Ron Paul (R-Texas), a conservative Republican presidential candidate in 2008, observed that "Congress would rather give up its most important authorized power to the President and the [United Nations] than risk losing an election if the war goes badly."[13] Other critics contend that the war powers law itself violates the constitutional provision for the separation of powers by mitigating both the president's power as commander in chief and Congress's authority to declare war.

But Congress's ability to shape foreign policy does not rest merely with its authority to declare war. Congressional powers with respect to foreign relations also include the authority of the U.S. Senate to ratify treaties, as well as to confirm presidential appointees to ambassadorial posts and to cabinet positions (including those of the secretaries of defense and state). Furthermore, one of Congress's greatest powers is its national legislature's control of the purse strings. This control means that although the president can order troops into action, the members of Congress must authorize spending for such an operation. This tension between Congress and the president is plainly evident in the numerous congressional votes to allocate funds for the war in Iraq, particularly after the Democratic Party won control of Congress in the midterm elections of 2006. Although the Democrats in Congress would have preferred not to allocate as much money to the war effort, their hands were tied because they did not want to relinquish their obligations to the troops already deployed in Iraq, nor did they want to alienate constituents in the military or defense communities who were benefiting from the increased expenditures.

The Military-Industrial Complex

In his farewell address, President Dwight D. Eisenhower (1953–1961), Supreme Allied Commander of Europe during World War II, warned the nation of the influence of the burgeoning military-industrial complex. Eisenhower stressed that the American people and their representatives in government must "guard against the acquisition of unwarranted influence" and noted that "only an alert and knowledgeable citizenry can compel the proper meshing of the industrial and military machinery of defense with our peaceful methods and goals so that security and liberty may prosper together."[14]

Eisenhower was describing the mutually advantageous—and potentially corrupting—collusion among the U.S. armed forces, the defense industry, and Congress. These three entities have the potential to develop "unwarranted influence" over foreign policy in general and defense spending in particular, for several reasons. First, the goals of the military and the goals of the defense industry often intersect. Consider for example the military's need to supply soldiers with the appropriate equipment to fight wars. Both the military complex and the defense industry benefit from doing so: the military wants to protect its troops and help ensure their success on the battleground, and the defense industry seeks to sell such goods to the military—and reap a healthy profit.

A second reason why the military-industrial complex has the potential to be so highly influential is the close personal and professional relationships that flourish between the individuals in the military and their counterparts in the defense industry. These relationships are similar to the associations that develop in the case of iron triangles (see Chapter 13). Indeed, many retired military personnel often put their military expertise to work in "retirement jobs" with defense contractors or as congressional lobbyists.

For many congressional districts throughout the United States, spending by the federal government for military bases, personnel, and defense contracts represents an important

> Governments attempt to shape public opinion, especially in wartime. During World War II, posters urged Americans to buy war bonds, but during the Vietnam War, journalists—especially television reporters—allowed Americans to see a harsher image of war. In an indelible 1972 image of that war, 9-year-old Kim Phuc, who had stripped off her burning clothes, flees an aerial napalm attack. Kim Phuc is now a Canadian citizen, and her spoken essay, "The Long Road to Forgiveness," was broadcast on National Public Radio in 2008.

infusion of money into the local economy. When this economic influence is combined with the clout members of the military, veterans, their interest groups, and their families can wield, we can see why many members of Congress support the military-industrial complex.

The Media

Because of the pervasiveness and reach of the media, foreign policy decisions provide prime fodder for news reporting. But the media go well beyond monitoring and reporting on foreign policy; they also frequently play a role in shaping the country's foreign policy and in influencing the conduct of that policy.

Since the beginning of the twentieth century, the U.S. government has used the news media in an organized way to promote its foreign policy priorities. During World War I, newspapers ran ads calling on Americans to take all kinds of actions to help the war effort, from cleaning their plates and planting "victory gardens" (to conserve food supplies for soldiers) to buying war bonds to help finance the war. By World War II, filmmakers spurred Americans to action, from enlisting in the armed services to conserving food fats and saving scrap metal for the war effort. In these various wartime initiatives, the media worked hand in hand with the government and took a generally highly patriotic and supportive stance. By the era of the Vietnam War, however, journalists, particularly television reporters stationed among U.S. troops in the faraway Asian country, painted a grimmer, more realistic canvas, focusing on the ravages of war that most Americans had never before seen.

As for the news media's influence over the conduct and substance of foreign policy, it can take a variety of forms including the following:

- *Agenda setting and public awareness.* By focusing public attention on policy makers in a certain area of the world or on a particular aspect of foreign policy, the media have an impact on setting the policy agenda. During the current conflict in Iraq, for

> The media play an important role in keeping tabs on those who carry out foreign policy on the ground. In April 2004, the news magazine program *60 Minutes II* broadcast an investigation of prisoner abuses at the Abu Ghraib prison in Baghdad, Iraq. Among the images shown was this one from late 2003 showing Pfc. Lynndie England holding a leash attached to an Iraqi detainee. England and several other soldiers serving at the prison were convicted by the Army courts-martial. England served 521 days for inflicting sexual, physical, and psychological abuse on Iraqi prisoners of war. Though the soldiers claimed they were instructed by superiors to engage in the abuse, no commanding officers were convicted.

example, the news media highlight the war's casualties on a daily basis. Newspapers report the names and sometimes print the photographs of soldiers killed in action; TV news specials scroll the names and hometowns of fallen U.S. troops and civilians. This coverage reminds policy makers and the American public alike about the human costs of war and can have an effect on subsequent policy-making decisions.

■ *Investigations.* The media play a powerful role in determining that U.S. foreign policy is being implemented in a way that the policy makers intended. The news media also help to ensure that the men and women who carry out foreign policy "in the trenches" of real life cease to commit or rectify any abuses they may be committing. Consider the media coverage surrounding U.S. soldiers' scandalous abuse of enemy prisoners at the Abu Ghraib prison in Iraq. Graphic photos published in print and online of American soldiers tormenting naked captives reached readers all over the world. These photos heightened public awareness of the culture that appeared to be prevalent at the prison and led to the court-martial of twelve soldiers.

Public Opinion

Some observers would point to the U.S. public's widespread opposition to the war in Iraq—and to the war's continuation despite that opposition—as evidence of what little impact public opinion has on foreign policy. But public opinion, particularly negative opinion with respect to military conflicts such as the Vietnam War and the current war in Iraq, does have the effect of constraining the actions of foreign policy makers. In particular, public support of foreign policy is valuable if that policy requires a substantial commitment of resources—say, troops or large sums of government aid—as in the beginning of the war in Iraq. But because of eroding public support for the war, the notion of a timeline for the withdrawal of troops is part of the national policy agenda. And with shrinking public support for the war came loud and escalating criticism of the Bush administration's Iraq policies, which forced the administration to change its course (creating the environment in which President Bush ordered additional troops to Iraq as part of a military surge designed to create more security there).

Hot-button foreign policy issues such as the abuse of prisoners and the fighting of costly wars generate high levels of media coverage. The public might voice strong opinions on these issues in the wake of the saturated media reporting. Yet when it comes to foreign policy matters, public opinion is rarely the strong force that it can be in setting the domestic policy agenda. In general, people tend to be less concerned, less informed, and less interested in foreign policy matters than in domestic issues. Thus, the public at large is likely to accept the views and actions of the individuals who make their country's foreign policy.

Public opinion plays a comparatively small role in shaping foreign policy for a variety of reasons. First, foreign policy is made incrementally, over years and decades, and keeping up with international developments in different parts of the world is not something that many individuals or even news organizations do. Often, international issues must reach crisis proportions before media coverage becomes significant and exerts an impact on public opinion.

Many Americans also feel less connected to foreign policy decisions than they do to domestic policy issues. Individuals may feel empathetic toward Chinese citizens who endure human rights violations at the hands of their government or might express sympathy to-

ward North Korean famine victims. Yet their compassion only goes so far because those incidents have less bearing on their own lives than, say, whether their mortgage payments will increase because of Federal Reserve policy or whether more student loans will be available to pay their tuition. Despite the disconnect between most people's everyday lives and pressing issues in foreign policy, individuals nonetheless can and do influence foreign policy decisions, as we now consider.

Private Citizens

Individuals can have an influential voice in foreign policy decision making. As we saw earlier in this chapter, the U.S. government can compel behavior by other nations by bestowing or withholding most favored nation status. Similarly, in their daily household decisions, private citizens can use the power of the purse to influence foreign policy, by rewarding and punishing other countries through their consumption choices.

THE POWER OF THE PURSE   Many consumers who seek to improve the lives of African people living with AIDS are purchasing Product (RED) items, for which corporations contribute a portion of their profits to buy antiviral drugs. The Product (RED) Manifesto boldly articulates the power that individuals possess: "As first world consumers, we have tremendous power. What we collectively choose to buy or not buy, can change the course of life and history on this planet."[15] By purchasing Product (RED) shirts, shoes, iPods, phones, and other merchandise, consumers raised over $57 million by 2008 to purchase urgently needed AIDS drugs.

Alternatively, consider how the recent scares over the presence of lead in some Chinese-manufactured toys have led many individual consumers to boycott the purchase of toys made in China, resulting in plummeting sales and falling prices for the imports. As a result, Congress has considered a measure that would not only strengthen the regulations guiding the importation of toys by requiring companies to test and certify that these products are safe before selling them to American consumers, but also grant the Consumer Product Safety Commission greater enforcement authority.

MICRO-LENDING   It is also through the efforts and contributions of private citizens that private nonprofits and nongovernmental organizations change conditions in foreign nations, and those changed international conditions can have an impact on foreign policy. Consider, for example, the practice of **micro-lending,** or loaning poor entrepreneurs small amounts of money that enable them to buy what they need to create a business. In Cape Coast, Ghana, Millicent Eshun is a 53-year-old mother of four who, using capital raised through micro-lending, has been able to rent a storefront and is now selling groceries. Contributors on Kivo.org, a micro-lending Web site, have donated $875 so she can increase her inventory. Eshun is part of a group in her town whose members have agreed to guarantee each group member's loan. How does micro-lending affect foreign policy? Since the end of World War II when U.S. foreign policy included aid to help Western European nations rebuild, the philosophy of micro-lending has informed the policy behind foreign aid. And when micro-lending succeeds, it changes the international environment in which nations create policy.

micro-lending
loaning poor entrepreneurs small amounts of money that enable them to buy what they need to create a business

INDIVIDUALS AS ADVOCATES   Individuals can have a more public impact on the foreign policy process as well. Consider the various educational exchange programs that arrange for students from one country to visit another. In effect, such visitors act as **public diplomats**—individuals who promote their country's interests by shaping the host country's perception of their homeland, not only through educational but also through business or entertainment initiatives that advance mutual understanding.

A world conflict can become an influence in American foreign policy, too, when individuals take personal causes that are related to their ethnic origins to the White House and Congress. The influence of domestic interests on foreign policy, called **intermestics,** plays a distinct part in foreign policy making.

public diplomat
an individual outside government who promotes his or her country's interests and thus helps to shape international perceptions of that nation

intermestics
the influence of domestic interests on foreign policy

> Individuals can have an impact on the foreign policy process. Here, Music Director Lorin Maazel conducts the New York Philharmonic Orchestra near a North Korean flag during a rehearsal at the East Pyongyang Grand Theater in Pyongyang, North Korea, in 2008. The Philharmonic was the first major American cultural group to visit North Korea and the largest delegation from the United States ever to visit this isolated nation.

isolationism
a foreign policy characterized by a nation's unwillingness to participate in international affairs

interventionism
a foreign policy characterized by a nation's willingness to participate and intervene in international situations, including another country's affairs

Among the most powerful examples of intermestics is the importance of large numbers of Cuban immigrants in Florida, many of them refugees or descendants of refugees from the regime of Fidel Castro. This influential group has swayed U.S. policy toward the imposition of an embargo against the Castro government since 1962, as well as encouraged tightened travel and currency restrictions between the United States and Cuba. And the considerable political clout wielded by individuals in the Irish-American community in the United States spurred the Clinton administration to assist in the Northern Ireland Peace Process, which brought the easing of decades-long tensions and violence in that region.

U.S. Foreign Policy in Historical Context: Isolationism and Intervention

As those who make and shape U.S. foreign policy continue to confront the challenges of a new century, they can look back on two broad historical traditions with respect to American foreign relations: isolationism and intervention. Historically, an initial policy of **isolationism,** a foreign policy characterized by a country's unwillingness to participate in international affairs, gave way to **interventionism,** the willingness of a country to take part and intervene in international situations, including another country's affairs.

The Constitutional Framework and Early Foreign Policy Making

In drafting the Constitution, the founders sought to remove the United States from international affairs. They reasoned that it was best for the new American republic to stay out of the deadly wars that had plagued Europe for centuries and because of which many Americans had left their native lands. Because of this isolationist outlook, the founders structured the Constitution so that responsibility for conducting foreign affairs rests exclusively with the national government rather than with the states.

THE CONSTITUTION AND FOREIGN POLICY POWERS The Constitution provides for shared responsibility for foreign policy making in the national government between the executive and legislative branches. The Constitution grants the president very specific powers. These include powers related to the role of commander in chief, to making treaties, and to appointing and receiving ambassadors. In comparison, Congress's powers in foreign policy making are broader. Moreover, the Constitution structures executive and legislative powers as complementary. Note that the Constitution provides for checks and balances: although the president is commander in chief, Congress declares war and raises and supports an army and navy. Political scientist Roger Davidson has termed the give-and-take between presidential and congressional power "an invitation to struggle," reflecting the founders' attempt to ensure that neither entity dominates the process.[16]

EARLY ISOLATIONISM In keeping with the founders' emphasis on isolationism, President George Washington's Farewell Address in 1796 warned the young government against involving the United States in entangling alliances. Washington feared that membership in such international associations would draw a war-weary people and a war-weakened nation into further conflicts. He refused to accept the advice of either his secretary of state, Thomas Jefferson, who favored an alliance with France, or his treasury secretary, Alexander Hamilton, who wanted stronger ties to Great Britain. As a general who knew firsthand

about the ravages of war and who also was the first American leader to connect foreign and defense policy, Washington set the tone for the United States' role in the world for the next 200 years.

FOREIGN TRADE AND THE EROSION OF U.S. ISOLATIONISM During Washington's tenure as president and in successive administrations, the United States' primary activity in the international arena was trade. Rich in natural resources and blessed with an industrious labor force, the United States sought to increase its wealth by selling raw materials and supplies to all sides in the Napoleonic wars (1792–1815), the latest in the never-ending series of European conflicts. The French empire took exception to the United States' provision of supplies to its enemies, and when France captured ships that it alleged were bound for enemy ports, the United States was forced into an undeclared naval war with France in the 1790s.

Neutral international trade was a difficult feat to accomplish in the American republic's early years. American ships had to cross sea lanes where neutrality was not the governing principle; instead, pirates, warring nations, and the allies of warring nations controlled the seas, and nationality counted for little. When pirates off the Barbary Coast of Africa seized ships and their crews, which they held for ransom, the United States fought the Barbary Wars (1801–1805 and 1815) against the North African Barbary states (what are now Morocco, Algeria, Tunisia, and Libya).

> *Burning of the Frigate Philadelphia in the Harbor of Tripoli, February 16, 1804,* a painting by Edward Moran (1829–1901), shows the USS *Philadelphia* aflame in Tripoli Harbor during the Barbary Wars.

Throughout the early part of the nineteenth century, the seas proved a difficult place for American sailors. During that time, the British Navy began the practice of **impressment,** or forcing merchant sailors off U.S. ships—in effect, kidnapping them—on the spurious grounds that American sailors were "deserters" from the British Navy. In protest of this policy, Congress passed the Embargo Act of 1807, which forced U.S. ships to obtain approval from the American government before departing for foreign ports. But the British continued impressments, and the Embargo Act seriously curtailed the amount of U.S. goods being exported. Overall, the Embargo Act harmed the U.S. economy, as the decline in trade spurred more economic woes.

impressment
the forcible removal of merchant sailors from U.S. ships on the spurious grounds that the sailors were deserters from the British Navy

The tensions between the United States and Great Britain escalated as the practice of impressment continued. When the United States sought to increase its territory northward into Canada (then still part of the British Empire), the United States and Great Britain fought the War of 1812 over the United States' desire to annex portions of Canada and to put a halt to the practice of impressments. The war was relatively short-lived, ending with the signing of the Treaty of Ghent in 1814, when the British decided that their military resources could be better used against France in the Napoleonic wars.

Hegemony and National Expansion: From the Monroe Doctrine to the Roosevelt Corollary

After the conclusion of the War of 1812 in 1814 and of the Napoleonic wars in 1815, peace settled over the United States and Europe. Still, some American politicians feared that European nations—especially France, Spain, and Russia—would attempt to assert or reassert their influence in the Western Hemisphere. Thus, the view arose in American foreign policymaking circles that the United States should establish hegemony over its own hemisphere. In 1823 President James Monroe declared that "the American continents by the free and

Monroe Doctrine
President James Monroe's 1823 declaration that the Americas should not be considered subjects for future colonization by any European power

manifest destiny
the idea that it was the United States' destiny to spread throughout the North American continent; used to rationalize the expansion of U.S. territory

Roosevelt Corollary
the idea, advanced by President Theodore Roosevelt, that the United States had the right to act as an "international police power" in the Western Hemisphere in order to ensure stability in the region

balance of power system
a system of international alliances that, in theory, would balance the power of one group of nations against the power of another group and thus discourage war

independent condition which they have assumed and maintain, are henceforth not to be considered as subjects for future colonization by any European power." Known as the **Monroe Doctrine,** this declaration sounded more like bravado than policy, because the United States was still too weak militarily to chase a European power away from South America, Central America, or the Caribbean. But the United States' interest in preventing the colonization of the Americas was consistent with the interest of the British, who did not want to see European rivals dominating in the Americas. Thus Monroe's doctrine had the backing of the still-formidable British fleet.

With the Americas out of play, European countries were expanding their colonial empires in Africa and the Middle East during the first half of the nineteenth century. Meanwhile, the United States also extended its territories westward and solidified its borders. Supporters of the theory of **manifest destiny**—the idea that it was the United States' destiny to expand throughout the North American continent—used this concept to rationalize the spread of U.S. territory. As the philosophy of manifest destiny took hold on the popular imagination, the United States expanded west to the Pacific Ocean, as well as south and southwest.

During this era, too, the United States became increasingly active in profitable international trade, particularly with China and Japan. To facilitate this Pacific trade—which was a primary goal of American policy makers—the United States acquired the islands of Hawaii, Wake, and Midway and part of Samoa in the 1890s. In 1898, on the pretext of ending Spanish abuses in Cuba and instigated by a jingoistic (extremely nationalistic and aggressive) President William McKinley and press, the United States decided to fight Spain, which by then was the weakest of the colonial powers. The United States won the Spanish-American War handily, and the victory increased the country's international prestige.

Theodore Roosevelt, who later became president, achieved enormous national popularity during the Spanish-American War for his leadership of the Rough Riders, a cavalry regiment. Their charge up San Juan Hill in Cuba in 1898 was the war's bloodiest and most famous battle. As spoils, the United States obtained the Philippines, Guam, Puerto Rico, and—temporarily—Cuba from Spain. Roosevelt supported the United States' entry into the war and later, as president (1901–1909), added his own famous dictum to the Monroe Doctrine: the **Roosevelt Corollary.** He announced that to ensure stability in the region, the United States had the right to act as an "international police power" and intervene in Latin America—and indeed, the entire Western Hemisphere—if the situation in any country warranted the intervention of a "civilized society."

After Roosevelt became president, the United States intervened in Panama, where U.S.-backed revolutionaries there won independence from Colombia in 1903. The United States then immediately began construction on the Panama Canal in 1904. The canal improved the flow of trade by reducing the length of time ships took to travel between the Atlantic and Pacific oceans. It also accomplished one of Roosevelt's more cherished dreams: to show off U.S. naval power. At one point, Roosevelt decided to send the navy around the world strictly for public relations reasons, as a "show of force." Congress protested the cost of this endeavor, however. In order to outsmart Congress, Roosevelt, who had enough funds in the treasury for half the trip, sent the troops as far as Tokyo Bay. To "bring the boys home," Congress had to ante up the rest of the money.

World War I and the End of U.S. Isolationism

Encouraged by its successful efforts at colonization and strong enough by this time to ignore George Washington's admonition about avoiding foreign entanglements, the nation became embroiled in two major European wars in the twentieth century: World War I and World War II. The United States' isolation from the world ended with these two wars, even though strong isolationist forces in Congress and the White House continued to play a role during the first half of the twentieth century.

World War I came about primarily because of the balance of power system that dominated the world's foreign policy decisions from the end of the Napoleonic wars in 1815 until the conclusion of World War I in 1918. The **balance of power system** was a system of international alliances that, in theory, would balance the power of one group of nations against

the power of another group and thus discourage war. For nearly a century, this attempt to bring order to international relations worked, and Europe enjoyed a long period of peace. But a flaw of the balance of power system was that a relatively small skirmish could escalate into a major international incident because of agreements for **collective defense**—the idea that allied nations agree to defend each other in the face of invasion—that were inherent in the system. Such was the case in 1914 in Sarajevo when a young Bosnian Serb student assassinated Archduke Ferdinand, heir to the Austro-Hungarian throne. The assassin was a member of a group seeking Bosnia's independence from the Austro-Hungarian empire. The empire demanded that Serbia respond to the assassination, and when it determined that Serbia had not so responded, it declared war. Austria-Hungary's declaration of war led to a sweeping domino effect that had the European continent in full-scale war within weeks of that initial declaration because of those alliances and collective defense obligations between nations.

The United States entered World War I in

> The Panama Canal improved the flow of international trade by reducing the length of time ships took to travel between the Atlantic and Pacific oceans. This is an aerial view of the Gatun Locks.

1917, three years after the conflict began and largely at the behest of Britain. U.S. participation led President Woodrow Wilson to formulate the first conceptual framework for world governance that had ever been articulated. The most effective way to maintain peace, Wilson believed, was through **collective security**—the idea that peace could be achieved if nations agreed to collectively oppose any nation that attacked another country. By using this approach, nations at peace could prevent war by working together to restrain the lawlessness inherent in more unstable parts of the world.

Internationalism and the League of Nations

In negotiating the end of World War I at the Paris Peace Conference, Wilson sought to organize a **League of Nations,** a representative body that would ensure the collective security of nations. Wilson was successful in convincing representatives at the Paris meetings of the need for such an organization. But he was less successful in convincing Congress of the merits of the League of Nations. In 1918 the Republican-controlled Senate—Wilson was a Democrat—refused to ratify the Treaty of Versailles, which included among the terms for ending World War I the formation of the League of Nations. Without the United States, the League died a natural death before being replaced near the end of World War II by the United Nations.

In the dawning days of World War I, the United States was still heeding George Washington's call to avoid entangling alliances. At the war's conclusion, isolationism remained a key tenet of U.S. foreign policy. In the years immediately following the war, trade reasserted itself as the key component of U.S. foreign policy. The industrial revolution was in full swing, and the United States depended upon the import of raw materials and the export of manufactured goods to grease the wheels of its prosperous economy in the 1920s. During this time, however, Europe was healing from the ravages of World War I, and growth in its manufacturing sector meant serious competition for American industry.

The U.S. economy suffered another blow in 1929 when the stock market crashed, marking the beginning of the Great Depression. To protect American industry from international competition, in 1930 Congress passed the Smoot-Hawley Tariff, which imposed a significant tax on imported goods. Confronted with this measure, other nations responded

collective defense
the concept that allied nations agree to defend one another in the face of an invasion

collective security
the idea that peace could be achieved if nations agreed to collectively oppose any nation that attacked another country

League of Nations
a representative body founded in the aftermath of World War I to establish the collective security of nations

in kind, placing tariffs on American goods imported into their countries. The result? International trade dropped dramatically, and the economies of various nations, burdened by lower demand for the goods they produced, faltered. Industrialists, as well as citizens who saw the economic impact of an isolated United States, began to question the isolationism that had characterized U.S. foreign policy to date—from the era of Washington to the era of Smoot-Hawley.

World War II: U.S. Foreign Policy at a Crossroads

World War I was supposed to be the "war to end all wars." In hindsight, however, many observers believed that the victors only sowed the seeds of World War II (1939-1945). By impoverishing the defeated Germany through the imposition of huge reparations (compensation paid by a defeated nation to the victors for war damages) and the loss of 13 percent of its territory, the Treaty of Versailles (1919) created the environment that gave Adolf Hitler, the fascist leader of Germany, the opportunity to succeed politically. With his aggressive foreign policy, Hitler aimed to expand the German homeland at the expense of non-Germanic populations.

Influenced by a strong isolationist group in Congress, the United States waited until two years after the official start of the war in 1939 to declare war. Following a deadly Japanese attack on the U.S. naval base at Pearl Harbor, Hawaii, in December 1941, the United States declared war first on Japan and then on the other Axis powers (Germany and Italy) after those countries declared war on the United States. Following years of fighting on multiple fronts, in August 1945 the United States dropped two atomic bombs on the Japanese cities of Hiroshima and Nagasaki. These devastating attacks ended the war.

The question remains whether the United States would have joined the efforts of the Allies (the United States, England, France, China, and the Soviet Union) sooner had policy makers known about the **Holocaust**—the murder by Hitler and his subordinates of six million Jews, along with political dissidents, Catholics, homosexuals, the disabled, and gypsies. Newspapers did not report the genocide until 1943, well after the war was under way. The experience of fighting World War II and dealing with its aftermath forced U.S. policy makers to reassess the country's role in the world, as well as the policies that governed its entire approach to foreign affairs.

Holocaust
the genocide perpetrated by Adolf Hitler and the Nazis against six million Jews, along with political dissidents, Catholics, homosexuals, the disabled, and gypsies

The Postwar Era: The United States as Superpower

The post–World War II era saw the emergence of two of the Allied victors, the United States and the Soviet Union, as **superpowers**—leader nations with dominating influence in international affairs. The United States' role as superpower in a new international system, and the relationship between these superpowers, would shape America's foreign policy for the remainder of the twentieth century. Increasingly important in this new era was the role that **multilateral** (many-sided, or supported by numerous nations) organizations and agreements would play.

superpowers
leader nations with dominating influence in international affairs

multilateral
many-sided; having the support of numerous nations

International Agreements and Organizations

In the aftermath of World War II, the United States was intent on avoiding the mistakes of the Treaty of Versailles, which many policy makers felt had led directly to the conditions that produced the war. They proceeded to address these mistakes one by one, often forming international organizations equipped to respond to the public policy challenges confronting the postwar world.

A key component of the postwar recovery effort was the **Marshall Plan.** Named for Secretary of State George Marshall, the program provided the funds necessary for Western European countries—even the United States' enemies from World War II—to rebuild. War-ravaged nations, including defeated (West) Germany, soon became economic powerhouses, thanks to initial help from the Marshall Plan. Ironically, by forcing the Germans to

Marshall Plan
the U.S. government program that provided funds necessary for Western European countries to rebuild after World War II

demilitarize as a condition of their surrender, the Allies freed Germany from spending large amounts of its own tax money on defense, thus enabling the German people to devote more of their resources to economic development. Other countries impoverished by war also benefited from the Marshall Plan (see Figure 17.1), creating new markets for U.S. products. Eastern European nations, now securely under Soviet influence, were prevented from participating. Because of the plan's success in Western Europe, the United States recognized that economic development and peace were intertwined, that economic stability was critical if future wars were to be prevented, and that an international approach was preferable to isolationism in foreign policy.

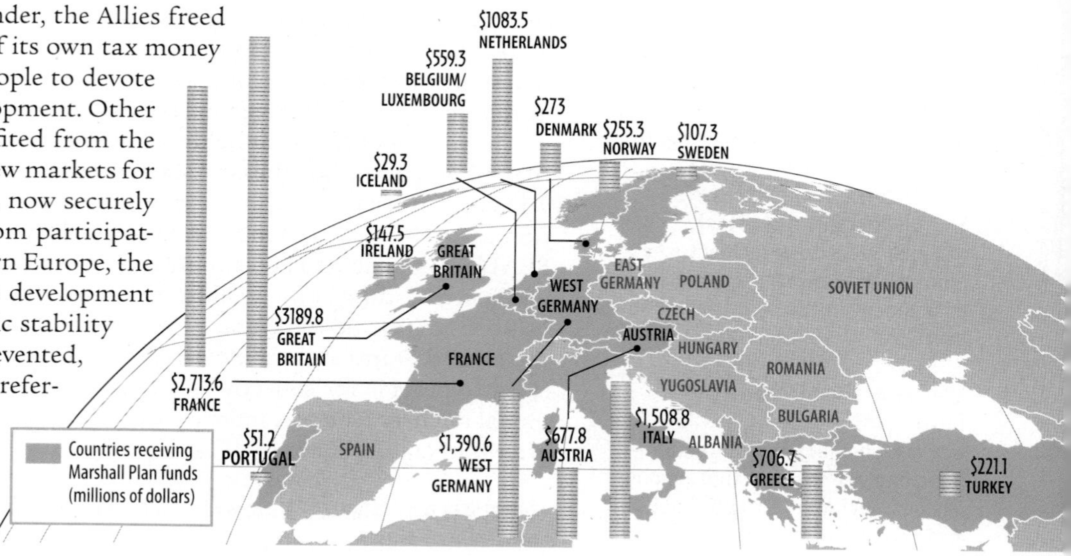

THE UNITED NATIONS   The Allied victors of World War II recognized the need for a structure to ensure collective security. In that spirit, U.S. officials organized a meeting in San Francisco in 1945 with fifty U.S. allies, all of whom agreed to create the **United Nations (UN).** Participants hoped that this international body, through collective security, would develop the capacity to prevent future wars. The charter of the United Nations created these components:

FIGURE 17.1

Recipients of Marshall Plan Aid, 1948–1951

Source: www.cnn.com/SPECIALS/cold.war/episodes/03/maps/.

- A Security Council with eleven members, five of which—including the United States, the Soviet Union (now Russia), China, Great Britain, and France—are permanent members with the power to veto any action taken by the council. Today the Security Council consists of fifteen members, with the permanent members and their veto power remaining unchanged.
- A General Assembly consisting of all the member nations, each with a single vote (in 1945, there were 51 member nations; today there are 192).
- A Secretariat headed by a secretary-general with a staff at UN headquarters in New York. The secretary-general in 2008 is Ban Ki-moon of South Korea.
- Several specialized organizations to handle specific public policy challenges, including the Economic and Social Council, the Trusteeship Council, and the International Court at The Hague.

The United Nations' mission includes the promotion of economic and social development. Since its founding it has added peacekeeping to its functions and has had some limited success in this endeavor in areas of the former Yugoslavia, the Middle East, and Africa. But in the immediate post–World War II era, the ability of the United Nations in general, and of the Security Council in particular, to provide for collective security was seriously undermined by the presence of the Soviet Union on the Security Council. Because the Soviet Union was a permanent member with veto power, any attempt by the Security Council to thwart Soviet aggression was blocked by the Soviets' veto.

NATO   It did not take long for the United States and the Western democracies to be disappointed by the inability of the United Nations to provide for collective security. The UN's failure to halt the militaristic expansion of the Soviet sphere of influence particularly troubled them. Their frustrations led the United States and its Western allies to attempt to bring order to international relations through the creation of regional security alliances. **Regional security alliances** typically involve a superpower and nations that are ideologically similar in a particular area of the world.

The first regional security alliance was the **North Atlantic Treaty Organization (NATO).** Established in 1949, NATO created a structure for regional security for its fifteen member nations through a declaration that "an armed attack against one or more NATO nations . . .

United Nations (UN)
established in 1945, an international body whose founders hoped would develop the capacity to prevent future wars by achieving collective security and peace

regional security alliance
an alliance typically between a superpower and nations that are ideologically similar in a particular region

North Atlantic Treaty Organization (NATO)
an international mutual defense alliance formed in 1949 that created a structure for regional security for its fifteen member nations

Warsaw Pact

regional security structure formed in 1955 by the Soviet Union and its seven satellite states in Eastern Europe in response to the creation of NATO

Southeast Asia Treaty Organization (SEATO)

regional security agreement whose goal was to prevent communist encroachment in the countries of Southeast Asia

International Monetary Fund (IMF)

institution charged with regulating monetary relationships among nations, including establishment of exchange rates for major world currencies; established in 1944 by the Bretton Woods Agreement

World Bank

international financial institution created by the Bretton Woods Agreement of 1944 and charged with lending money to nations in need

World Trade Organization (WTO)

organization created in 1995 to negotiate, implement, and enforce international trade agreements

shall be considered an attack against them all."[17] Through the formation of NATO, the United States made a specific commitment to defend Western Europe in the event of a Soviet attack. In response to the creation of NATO, the Soviet Union and its seven satellite states in Eastern Europe formed a similar regional security alliance, the **Warsaw Pact,** in 1955.

The success of NATO at holding Soviet expansion into Western Europe at bay motivated the creation of the **Southeast Asia Treaty Organization (SEATO),** whose goal was to prevent communist encroachment in Southeast Asia. SEATO was a decidedly weaker organization than NATO; decisions had to be reached unanimously and rarely were. For example, SEATO was unable to agree to intervene in Cambodia, Laos, or Vietnam because member nations, including France, Pakistan, and the Philippines, objected to intervention.

Both NATO and the Warsaw Pact reflected the tensions and rivalry that existed between the United States and the Soviet Union. They also reflected the failure of the United Nations to provide for collective security, that is, the security of *all* nations. Instead, the regional security alliances more closely resembled the balance of power alliances established after the Napoleonic wars.

INTERNATIONAL FINANCIAL ORGANIZATIONS In addition to establishing the United Nations and NATO for the purposes of conflict management and security, the United States recognized the need to relinquish a great deal of its own economic power in exchange for the economic stability that would come from international financial institutions. Doing so would benefit the global economy in general but also the U.S. economy in particular.

To this end, in 1944, an international agreement made in Bretton Woods, New Hampshire—the Bretton Woods Agreement—established the International Monetary Fund. The delegates to the meeting charged the **International Monetary Fund (IMF)** with regulating the monetary relationship among nations, including the establishment of exchange rates for major currencies around the world. To the present day, IMF member states provide the resources the IMF needs to operate through a formula by which nations pay amounts roughly proportional to the size of their economies. Based on these IMF contribution quotas, nations are then allocated votes proportional to their contributions. Thus the IMF perpetuates the dominance of the high-contributing economic powerhouses. Today the United States has nearly 20 percent of the IMF votes. The Bretton Woods agreement also established the institution that would become the **World Bank,** which initially focused on lend-

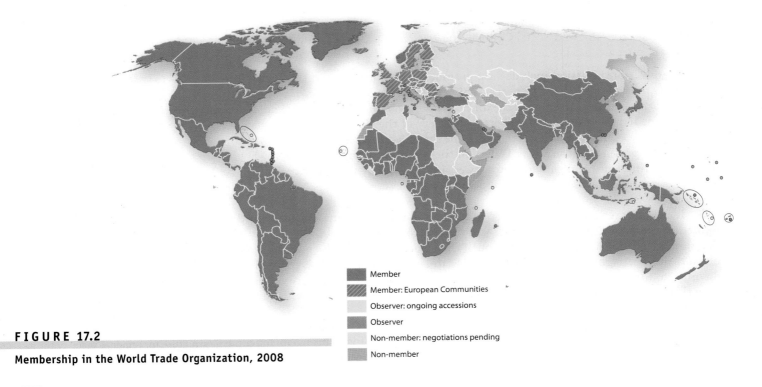

FIGURE 17.2

Membership in the World Trade Organization, 2008

Member

Member: European Communities

Observer: ongoing accessions

Observer

Non-member: negotiations pending

Non-member

POLITICAL INQUIRY

ing money to countries devastated in World War II. Today the World Bank lends money to developing nations in order to help them become self-sufficient.

Still reeling from the effects of high tariffs on international trade during the Depression, the United States also encouraged an international agreement that would heal the economies of nations by lowering tariffs and promoting international trade. In 1948, twenty-three nations signed the General Agreement on Tariffs and Trade (GATT). The GATT is based on the most favored nation principle.

In 1995, the **World Trade Organization (WTO)** replaced the GATT. Whereas the GATT was a series of agreements among nations, the WTO is an actual organization that negotiates, implements, and enforces international trade agreements. Today the WTO consists of 151 member nations (see Figure 17.2). Although it has a one-nation, one-vote policy, this policy is moot because the largest economies have the greatest say. The organization's goal—to remove all types of trade barriers, including obstacles to investment—is more ambitious than that of the GATT.

The Cold War: Superpowers in Collision

During World War II, the United States, Great Britain, and the Soviet Union were allies against the Nazis. But events at the wartime Yalta Conference in 1945—the second of three wartime conferences among British, U.S., and Soviet leaders—sowed the seeds of what would become known as the Cold War. The **Cold War** refers to the political, ideological, and military conflict that lasted from 1945 until 1990 between communist nations, led by the Soviet Union, and Western democracies, led by the United States. Each leader came to the Yalta Conference with an agenda. The United States' Franklin Roosevelt needed Soviet help in battling Japan in the naval wars of the Pacific. England's Winston Churchill sought democratic elections in Eastern Europe. And Soviet Premier Joseph Stalin wanted Eastern Europe as a Soviet sphere of influence, arguing that the Soviet Union's national security depended on its hegemony in the region.

At the conference, Stalin agreed to allow free elections in the region, but he later broke that promise. In response, former British prime minister Churchill warned Americans in a 1946 speech that the Soviets were dividing Europe with an "Iron Curtain." Churchill's characterization was accurate, because Stalin's brutal dictatorship, combined with the force of

Lead or Follow?

Do you think the United States should be a leader among the most powerful countries in the world, or should it stay out of international affairs?

☐ Be a leader

☐ Stay out

Source: "America's Place in the World," http://people-press.org/reports/display .php3?ReportID=263.

Cold War
the political, ideological, and military conflict that lasted from 1945 until 1990 between communist nations led by the Soviet Union and Western democracies led by the United States

the Soviet Red Army, would install a communist government in every Eastern European nation. When Stalin also refused to cooperate in the planned cooperative allied occupation of Germany, the result was the division of Germany into separate zones, one administered by the Soviet Union and the other three by the United States, Great Britain, and France. In 1948, when the Soviets backed communist guerillas who were attempting to take over Greece and Turkey, U.S. president Harry Truman (1945–1953) committed the United States to "support free people who are resisting attempted subjugation by armed minorities or by outside pressures."[18] This policy—the United States' foreign policy commitment to assist efforts to resist communism—was called the **Truman Doctrine.**

U.S. Efforts to Contain Communism: Korea, Cuba, and Vietnam

The Truman Doctrine reflected the ideas of George F. Kennan, the State Department's Soviet expert at the time. Specifically, Kennan advocated the principle of **containment,** the policy of preventing the spread of communism, mainly by providing military and economic aid as well as political advice to beleaguered countries that were vulnerable to communist takeover. Kennan argued, "It is clear that the main element of any United States policy toward the Soviet Union must be that of a long-term vigilant containment of Russian expansive tendencies."[19] The idea of containment would spur the United States to fight in two protracted wars, the Korean War and the Vietnam War, in order to contain communism.

THE KOREAN WAR, 1950–1953 The first military effort the United States engaged in to check the spread of communism occurred in 1950. In June of that year, North Korea, with the backing of Stalin and the Soviet Union, invaded South Korea in an attempt to reunify the Korean peninsula under communism. During that summer, the United States sent in forces as part of a United Nations force to help the South Koreans repel the attack. The defensive strategy quickly succeeded, but by October the United States changed military strategy. Instead of merely containing the spread of communism, the United States sought to reunify North and South Korea—and, in doing so, to depose the communists from North Korea. But as U.S. and South Korean forces edged north, they also came closer and closer to the North Korea–China border.

That October, China, wary of a potential invasion, came to the aid of fellow communists in North Korea. The two countries' combined forces repelled the United Nations forces back to the 38th parallel, the original border between North and South Korea. Over the next two years, U.S. forces (as part of the UN contingent), North and South Koreans, and Chinese soldiers would continue to do battle, with very little territory changing hands. When an armistice was reached in July 1953, the border established was the 38th parallel—exactly what it had been before the war—although a demilitarized zone (DMZ) was created. Today U.S. and South Korean troops still patrol one side of the DMZ, while North Korean troops patrol the other.

The Korean War marked an escalation and expansion of the Cold War. Not only was the war the first occasion in which the two superpowers clashed militarily, but it also brought the Cold War outside the boundaries of Europe. Significantly, the outbreak of the Korean War also gave rise to the concept of **limited war**—a combatant country's self-imposed limitation on the tactics and strategy it uses, particularly its avoidance of the deployment of nuclear weapons. The idea of limited war would set the stage for subsequent conflicts.

THE CUBAN MISSILE CRISIS, 1962 Another element of U.S. foreign policy during the Cold War involved the practice of brinkmanship, a phrase coined by John Foster Dulles, the secretary of state under President Dwight D. Eisenhower (1953–1961). In essence, **brinkmanship** meant fooling the enemy by going to the edge (the brink), even if the party using the brinkmanship strategy had no intention of following through to its logical conclusion.

The Cuban Missile Crisis in October 1962 turned out to be a perfect example of brinkmanship, even though that was not the intention of President John F. Kennedy (1961–1963). Reacting to Soviet premier Nikita Khrushchev's decision to put ballistic missiles in Cuba, Kennedy imposed a naval blockade around that island nation and warned the Soviet Union

---

Truman Doctrine
articulated by President Harry Truman, a foreign policy commitment by the United States to assist countries' efforts to resist communism in the Cold War era

containment
Cold War–era policy of preventing the spread of communism, mainly by providing military and economic aid as well as political advice to countries vulnerable to a communist takeover

limited war
a combatant country's self-imposed limitation on the tactics and strategy it uses, particularly its avoidance of the use of nuclear weapons

brinkmanship
Cold War–era practice of fooling the enemy by going to the edge (the brink), even if the party using the strategy had no intention of following through

to withdraw its missiles, or else—never specifying what he meant by "or else." Although this confrontation seemed like brinkmanship, it was no bluff; rather, it was an act of bravado that could easily have led to nuclear war. Luckily for the United States and the rest of the world, the Soviets backed down, withdrew their missiles, and entered a period of improved relations with the United States.[20]

THE VIETNAM CONFLICT, 1965–1975   The United States' involvement in the war in Vietnam was motivated in large part by policy makers' acceptance of the **domino theory,** the principle that if one nation fell to communism, other nations in its geographic vicinity would also succumb. As described by President Dwight Eisenhower, "You have broader considerations that might follow what you would call the 'falling domino' principle. You have a row of dominoes set up, you knock over the first one, and what will happen to the last one is the certainty that it will go over very quickly. So you could have a beginning of a disintegration that would have the most profound influences."[21]

domino theory
the principle that if one nation fell to communism, other nations in its geographic vicinity would also succumb

And so the United States again sought to contain the spread of communism in Southeast Asia. Although Vietnam was not of particular strategic importance to the United States, it represented the second "domino" in the faraway region. U.S. involvement in Vietnam started in the late 1950s, and by 1963, the United States became enmeshed in an all-out ground, naval, and air war there. The United States supported the South Vietnamese against the North Vietnamese in the decade-long civil war that would take the lives of almost 60,000 U.S. soldiers (see "Doing Democracy") and at least 3 million Vietnamese soldiers and civilians. On April 29, 1975, when the South Vietnamese capital, Saigon, fell to the North Vietnamese Vietcong forces, the event marked the first military failure by the United States in its efforts to contain communism.

> A widow is comforted as she watches a stoneworker carve the name of her husband on the Vietnam Veterans Memorial in Washington, D.C., in 2005. Names appear on the wall according to the date the service member was killed in action.

Détente: A Thaw in the Cold War Chill

Richard M. Nixon (1969–1974) was elected to the presidency in 1968, largely on his promise to conclude the war in Vietnam. Although several years would pass before the war ended, Nixon's approach to the top foreign policy issues of the day marked a departure from that of his predecessors. Specifically, the **Nixon Doctrine** emphasized the responsibility of U.S. allies to provide for their own national defense and security and sought to improve relations with the two communist world powers, the Soviet Union and China. As early as 1970 his administration sought **détente,** or the easing of tensions between the United States and its communist rivals. In keeping with this idea, the Nixon administration normalized diplomatic relations with China and began a series of nuclear arms control talks that would occur throughout the 1970s. Critics of the Nixon Doctrine argued that President Nixon's approach to foreign policy was accommodationist—that it sought the easy solution and ignored the moral and philosophical implications of improving relations between the Western democracies and their communist rivals.

Part of the motivation for détente was the recognition that any escalation of tensions between the superpowers would increase the probability of nuclear war. Since the early 1960s, the United States and the Soviet Union had engaged in a nuclear arms race in which each country attempted to surpass the other's nuclear capability. According to the doctrine of

Nixon Doctrine
policy emphasizing the responsibility of U.S. allies to provide for their own national defense and security, aimed at improving relations with the communist nations, including the Soviet Union and China

détente
easing of tensions between the United States and its communist rivals

DOING DEMOCRACY

LISTEN TO, RECORD, AND ARCHIVE A VETERAN'S STORY

FACT:

If you read the obituaries in your local newspaper, you may be aware of a stark reality: the generation of veterans who served in World War II—the men and women whom former NBC television news anchor Tom Brokaw termed "the greatest generation"—is slowly passing away into history. With their demise is the potential that the often remarkable personal stories of their World War II experiences will be lost for posterity. Scholars will long note what President Franklin Roosevelt said when Japan bombed Pearl Harbor and what Prime Minister Winston Churchill said at Yalta. But the full story of American foreign policy should also take into account the selfless contributions of the men and women who served their country in World War II, as well as in Korea, Vietnam, the Gulf War, and the UN peacekeeping missions in Eastern Europe. That story also would have to document the courage and patriotism of those serving in Afghanistan and Iraq today.

Act!

You can help preserve these vital histories by interviewing a veteran of any war, recording his or her story, and archiving it with the Library of Congress's Veterans History Project. Although a few veterans prefer not to relive their wartime experiences, many others, particularly older veterans, relish the opportunity to share their stories and the life lessons they learned while serving in wartime. Asking specific questions will prompt more detailed responses than general questions about their experiences. You might try, "What was your job during the war?" "When and where were you deployed?" "What did you miss the most?" What were your greatest hardships?"

Where to begin

- The Web site of the Library of Congress's Veterans History Project, **www.loc.gov/vets/kit.html,** provides simple guidance on how to get started in participating in this ongoing project and includes registration forms. It explains what kinds of media formats are accepted, how to conduct the interview, and how to submit the materials for archiving.
- To identify a subject for your interview, start with your own family, friends, and neighbors. Ask your grandparents, aunts, and uncles, perhaps even your parents, about their service in the military.
- If no one you know has served in the nation's armed forces, contact a veterans' organization (such as the Veterans of Foreign Wars, or VFW, post) in your town. You can find your local VFW post by entering your zip code at **http://emem .vfw.org/findpost.aspx.**

---

mutual assured destruction (MAD)
the doctrine that if one nation attacked another with nuclear weapons, the other would be capable of retaliating and would retaliate with such force as to assure mutual annihilation

deterrence
the idea that nations would be less likely to engage in nuclear war if adversaries each had first-strike capability

strategic arms limitation talks (SALT talks)
discussions between the United States and the Soviet Union in the 1970s that focused on cooling down the nuclear arms race between the two superpowers

mutual assured destruction (MAD), if one nation attacked another with nuclear weapons, the other would be capable of retaliating, and *would* retaliate, with such force as to assure mutual annihilation. The advent of intercontinental ballistic missiles (ICBMs) meant that both the United States and the Soviet Union were capable of sending nuclear warheads through space to targets in their rivals' homelands. The goal of the arms race (which would continue through the 1980s) was first-strike capability, meaning that each nation sought the ability to use nuclear weapons against another nation and eliminate the possibility of that nation's retaliating in a second-strike attack.

Many foreign policy makers in both the United States and the Soviet Union believed in the power of **deterrence,** the idea that nations would be less likely to engage in nuclear war if the adversaries each had first-strike capability. But Nixon and his primary foreign policy adviser, Henry Kissinger (who served first as Nixon's national security adviser and then as his secretary of state), sought negotiations with the Soviets that would dampen the arms race.

SALT I AND SALT II In 1972, the United States and the Soviet Union concluded two and a half years of **strategic arms limitation talks (SALT talks)** that focused on cooling the superheated nuclear arms race between the two superpowers. The resulting treaty,

SALT I, limited the two countries' antiballistic missiles (ABMs) and froze the number of offensive missiles that each nation could have at the number they already possessed, plus the number they had under construction.

The SALT II strategic arms limitation talks, begun during the Nixon administration and continuing through the Jimmy Carter presidency (1977–1981), resulted in the signing of the SALT II treaty in 1979. The **SALT II** treaty set an overall limit on all strategic nuclear launchers, including ICBMs, submarine-launched ballistic missiles (SLBMs), and cruise missiles. SALT II also limited the number of missiles that could carry multiple independently targeted reentry vehicles (MIRVs) with nuclear warheads, and limited each nation to the development of only one new type of ICBM.

Later in 1979, however, the Soviet Union invaded Afghanistan, sparking a new round of U.S-Soviet tensions. In response, President Jimmy Carter withdrew the SALT II treaty from consideration for ratification by the Senate. Nevertheless, Carter announced (as did his successor, Ronald Reagan) that the United States would abide by all of the terms of SALT II as long as the Soviet Union complied as well. During his one term in office, Carter also sought to engage the world in a campaign for human rights, while at the same time attempting to convert the vast U.S. military apparatus to peacetime functions—a policy known as **defense conversion.**

The Reagan Years and Soviet Collapse

Ronald Reagan's presidency (1981–1989) marked a pivotal time in U.S.-Soviet relations. On the one hand, the Reagan administration pushed for a *reduction* in missiles and nuclear warheads, not merely a limitation on increases. Because of this new direction, Reagan named these arms reduction talks the **strategic arms reduction talks (START talks).** Despite this overture, the Reagan administration was passionate in the pursuit of a ballistic missile defense system, called the **strategic defense initiative (SDI, or "Star Wars").** In protest of the development of this system, the Soviet Union walked out of the START meeting in 1983. The two superpowers would return to the table in 1985, after Reagan won reelection with a resounding victory.

In 1987, the United States and the Soviet Union signed the Intermediate-Range Nuclear Forces Treaty (INF), the first agreement that resulted in the destruction of nuclear weapons. It eliminated an entire class of weapons—those with an intermediate range of between 300 and 3,800 miles. A pathbreaking treaty, the INF shaped future arms control talks. It provided for reductions in the number of nuclear weapons, established the principle of equality because both nations ended up with the same number of weapons (in this case, zero), and, through the establishment of on-site inspections, provided a means of verifying compliance.

In retrospect, many analysts credit the Soviet Union's eventual collapse to President Reagan. During his tenure, Reagan ratcheted up the rhetoric with his many speeches referring to the Soviet Union as "the Evil Empire." Under his administration the U.S. defense budget also doubled, with much of the expenditure going toward the SDI. The Soviets reacted with fear and a surge in spending. These developments all came at a time when the Soviet Union was dealing with dissatisfied nationalities within its borders, as the fifteen republics that eventually would break away pressed for secession. The last straw, however, was the country's troubled economy, because in order to compete with the United States, the Soviet Union had increased its military budget to the point where its economy collapsed—and with it, the government.

Post-Soviet Times: The United States as Solo Superpower in an Era of Wars

The START talks, which had resumed in 1985, resulted in a long-awaited agreement that reduced the number of long-range strategic nuclear weapons to 3,000 for each side. In 1991, the agreement was signed by U.S. president George H. W. Bush and Soviet president Mikhail Gorbachev, whose tenure had ushered in the ideas of *glasnost* (openness) and *perestroika* (economic

SALT I
treaty signed in 1972 by the United States and the Soviet Union limiting the two countries' antiballistic missiles and freezing the number of offensive missiles that each nation could have at the number they already possessed, plus the number they had under construction

SALT II
treaty signed in 1979 by the United States and the Soviet Union that set an overall limit on strategic nuclear launchers, limited the number of missiles that could carry multiple independently targeted reentry vehicles (MIRVs) with nuclear warheads, and limited each nation to the development of only one new type of intercontinental ballistic missile (ICBM)

defense conversion
President Jimmy Carter's attempt to convert the nation's vast military apparatus to peacetime functions

strategic arms reduction talks (START talks)
talks between the United States and the Soviet Union in which reductions in missiles and nuclear warheads, not merely a limitation on increases, were negotiated

strategic defense initiative (SDI, or "Star Wars")
a ballistic missile defense system advocated by President Ronald Reagan

Defining U.S. Foreign Policy

THEN (1984)	NOW (2009)
The Cold War is the defining feature of U.S. foreign policy.	The war on terror is the defining feature of U.S. foreign policy.
The United States and the Soviet Union compete as the two world superpowers.	The United States is the world's only superpower.
The arms race results in unprecedented military spending.	A multifront war and national security needs result in unprecedented military and national defense spending.

WHAT'S NEXT?

> What new realities will shape U.S. foreign and national defense policy?

> Will the United States continue as the world's only superpower? How will a superpower be defined in the future? Will the term refer to military or economic might or a combination of these (and/or other) factors?

> What impact will continued spending have on the U.S. and global economy?

restructuring) in the Soviet Union. That same year, after an attempted coup failed, the Soviet Union ended and Russia had its first democratically elected president, Boris Yeltsin.

Upon Yeltsin's election, in another series of talks called START II, Yeltsin agreed to even deeper cuts in nuclear weapons. Importantly, he also assented to the eventual elimination of all land-based missiles with multiple warheads (MIRVs). The START II agreement of 1992 between the superpowers was fully implemented in 2003 and significantly decreased the likelihood of a massive nuclear attack.

The 1990s proved to be a novel time in U.S. foreign relations. For the first time in over half a century, the United States was without an enemy, and it found itself the world's lone superpower. The tumult following the collapse of communism ushered in an era of wars—many of them fueled by long-standing ethnic rivalries or disputes—and the creation of new borders and new nations. By the start of the new century, fourteen wars were going on around the globe. Some, like the decades-long conflict in Northern Ireland, now seem to be resolved. Others seemed intractable, like the conflict in the Middle East over the Palestinian question. Still others, like the tribal wars in Africa, were all too often manipulated by foreign interests and by corrupt indigenous leaders who were reluctant to give up their power. And other events—such as fighting that erupted between UN and U.S. forces against Somali militia fighters loyal to warlord Mohamed Farrah Aidid in 1993; the 1998 attacks on U.S. embassies in Nairobi, Kenya, and Dar es Salaam, Tanzania; and the 2000 suicide bombing of the U.S. Navy guided missile destroyer USS *Cole* in the port of Aden, Yemen—were harbingers of clashes to come. It was as if a giant hand had lifted a rock at the end of the Cold War, freeing long-submerged problems to crawl out again and presenting new challenges for U.S. foreign policy makers as the United States assumed its role as the world's leader.

U.S. Foreign Policy After 9/11

American foreign policy makers' challenges in the 1990s pale in comparison to those they have faced since the terrorist attacks of September 11, 2001. The incidents on that day have profoundly defined and determined recent American foreign policy.

One prism for viewing the 9/11 attacks is that posited by political scientist Samuel P. Huntington. He asserts that "the clash of civilizations will be the battle lines of the future."[22] Huntington's **clash of civilizations** thesis asserts that bitter cultural conflict will continue and escalate between modern Western democracies and fundamentalist Islamic states. Huntington, whose thesis remains controversial, argues that the ideological divisions that characterized the twentieth century—the clash between communism and democratic capitalism, for example—will be replaced by an older source of conflict: cultural and religious identity. Huntington initially posited his ideas in 1993, and his theories seemed particularly relevant during the 1990s when ethnic and religious warfare broke out in Bosnia and in

clash of civilizations thesis
Samuel Huntington's idea that bitter cultural conflict will continue and escalate between modern Western democracies and fundamentalist Islamic states

parts of Africa. Since 9/11, Huntington's neoconservative theory appears to have significantly shaped the foreign policy of the George W. Bush administration.

Huntington's clash of civilizations thesis provides one explanation of *why* contemporary U.S. foreign policy has focused on the areas that it has. President George W. Bush himself articulated his views on the *how* of that policy's implementation. According to the **Bush Doctrine,** unilateral action (action by the United States alone) directly targeted at enemies is both justifiable and feasible. The Bush Doctrine also asserted that the United States should use its role as the world's only remaining superpower to spread democracy and to create conditions of security that will benefit itself and its allies.

Bush Doctrine
the argument, articulated by President George W. Bush, that unilateral action directly targeted at an enemy is both justifiable and feasible

War in Afghanistan

The United States' first response to the 9/11 attacks was based on the connection of Osama bin Laden and the al-Qaeda terror network to the masterminding and execution of those attacks. For several years before 9/11, the fundamentalist Taliban regime in Afghanistan had allowed al-Qaeda training camps to operate in that country. In retaliation for the 9/11 strikes, in late 2001 the United States, a coalition of allies, and anti-Taliban rebels from within Afghanistan attacked the training camps and the Taliban government itself. Within weeks the Taliban government fell. By toppling the Taliban as the leaders of Afghanistan, the United States fulfilled the policy goal of regime change.

The multilateral forces worked to create first an interim government in Afghanistan and then, in 2004, a democratically elected government. Nonetheless, U.S. forces and those of its allies must still deal with continued attacks from Taliban forces, and Osama bin Laden, believed to have escaped to the mountains of neighboring Pakistan, remains at large. Although the U.S. invasion of Afghanistan occurred largely in response to the Taliban's support of al-Qaeda, the invasion also demonstrated the potential consequences for nations that support terrorism against the United States.

> One impact of the war in Afghanistan in 2001 has been increased educational opportunities for women. Here Afghan girls listen to their teacher during language class in an open-air classroom after space ran out in their school. Shortages of supplies and overcrowded classrooms are commonplace as the nation's girls, who had been prohibited from attending school under the Taliban regime, now may receive an education, though they are often still at great risk.

War in Iraq

After the Taliban's fall, President Bush set his sights on changing another regime: that of Iraq's Saddam Hussein. During the presidency of Bush's father, George H. W. Bush (1989–1993), the United States had gone to war with Iraq when that country invaded Kuwait, an ally of the United States. During the younger Bush's 2003 State of the Union address, the president claimed that Iraq possessed weapons of mass destruction (WMDs) and said that the Iraqis were attempting to purchase the components of nuclear weapons. In the ensuing weeks, the Bush administration made a case for going to war with Hussein's regime to both the UN Security Council and the American people. In doing so, Bush introduced the concept of **preventive war,** the strategy of waging war on countries regarded as threatening to the United States in order to avoid future conflicts.

The concept of preventive war represents a shift in policy from responding to attacks to anticipating attacks. The idea of preventive war is in part an outgrowth of the drastically altered nature of warfare. The biological, chemical, and nuclear weapons of today can cross borders with far deadlier efficiency than troops, ships, or aircraft. In addition,

preventive war
the strategy of waging war on countries regarded as threatening in order to avoid future conflicts

WHERE DO YOU STAND?

The Future of Iraq

Do you think Iraq will eventually be better off or worse off than before the U.S. invasion?

☐ Better off
☐ Worse off

Source: "Gallup's Pulse of Democracy: The War in Iraq," www.gallup.com/poll/1633/Iraq.aspx.

U.S. enemies no longer declare themselves as openly as they did before. The national defense policy makers who advocate preventive war thus argue that the only way to defend the country against these various new threats is to invade *before* the fact, in hopes of deterring another attack.

EARLY SUCCESS, FOLLOWED BY STALEMATE The invasion of Iraq in March 2003 was initially successful in toppling Saddam Hussein's regime. Despite insurgency violence that has prevented peace from taking root, elections were finally held in 2004 and 2005, and power officially passed to an elected government. In the face of continued violence, the Bush administration enacted a military surge policy, resulting in the addition of more than 20,000 troops in Baghdad and Al Anbar province. While not ending the conflict, the surge strategy has been credited with quelling much of the insurgent violence in these areas.

The United States launched its invasion of Iraq without the support of two of its major allies, France and Germany. Indeed, the "coalition of the willing" turned out to be a group of small nations, some of which have already withdrawn their troops, while the commitment of others was minimal. Some countries, for example, gave their verbal support to the war but sent few troops. Great Britain alone was firmly committed to the U.S. initiative in Iraq, despite the unpopularity of the war among the British people, according to polls.

International support for the U.S. military action in Iraq, which was never very high, plummeted in light of evidence that U.S. soldiers had abused prisoners at the Abu Ghraib prison, discussed earlier in this chapter. Ironically, the United States, which had initially launched the campaign against human rights abuses, now found itself under attack from many parts of the world for not abiding by its own rules.

PROBLEMS WITH NATION BUILDING As the war in Iraq stretched on for more than half a decade, support for the Bush administration policy dwindled. What many Americans thought would be a quick and incisive victory turned into a protracted and deadly war, costing more than 4,200 U.S. soldiers their lives (as of October 2008), nearly 4,000 of whom were killed after President Bush declared "mission accomplished" in May 2003.

Nation building in Iraq proved troublesome—far more so than the rebuilding of Japan after World War II, for example. There, U.S. general Douglas MacArthur undertook the task of reconstructing the nation and creating a system of democratic self-governance. It took four years, but when MacArthur left for duty in Korea, Japan was as close to democracy as any Far Eastern country. Japan's feudal aristocracy was abolished, the country had a new constitution that empowered the legislature to make laws, civil liberties and collective bargaining were guaranteed, the legal equality of the sexes was established, and citizens had been given the right of *habeas corpus*. MacArthur also suspended banks that had financed the war, destroyed (at least temporarily) the giant monopolies, and refused to allow "war profiteers" to invade Japan at the expense of local businesses.

Fifty years later, as the United States sought to rebuild Iraq's war-torn infrastructure and feed its people after toppling Hussein's regime, a powerful insurgency thwarted American efforts. Unlike MacArthur, the U.S. military had allowed widespread looting in the early days of the occupation, including the looting of munitions warehouses. These munitions later helped to arm the insurgents. Also unlike MacArthur, who had some familiarity with Japanese culture, few commanders knew either the Arabic language or Iraqi culture and rituals. Even fewer knew how to stem the war profiteering of the multinational corporations that had also "invaded" the country.

Iran and North Korea

In the twilight days of the Bush administration, the president continued to use antagonistic rhetoric toward two other nations that appeared to be on his list for regime change: Iran and North Korea (see "Global Comparisons"). In his 2002 State of the Union speech, Bush had referred to Iraq, Iran, and North Korea as players in an "axis of evil," regimes that sponsored terrorism and were seeking weapons of mass destruction. Bush's characterization is in keeping with (or has shaped) the American public's perception of these nations (see "Exploring the Sources").

GLOBAL COMPARISONS

THE UNITED STATES AND IRAN—A COMPLEX HISTORY

We can trace today's tense and complex relations between the United States and Iran back to 1951. That year, the democratically elected prime minister of Iran, Mohammed Mossadegh, nationalized the country's oil reserves, meaning that the government took over ownership of reserves that had been held by private corporations. Mossadegh's bold stroke set off a furious reaction by then–British prime minister Winston Churchill. Churchill and President Dwight Eisenhower, who was concerned about the increasing Soviet influence in Iran, agreed to enlist the Central Intelligence Agency in orchestrating a coup to depose Mossadegh in 1953.* The coup attempt eventually succeeded, and Mohammad Reza Pahlavi, Iran's monarch (Shah), installed as prime minister Fazlollah Zahedi, the choice of Great Britain and the United States.

Are Western democracies and fundamentalist Islamic states such as Iran destined to clash?

With continued British and U.S. support, the Shah modernized Iran's infrastructure. His autocratic rule, however, opened him to criticism by Ayatollah Ruhollah Khomeini, an influential Islamic Iranian cleric. Khomeini was exiled from the country but remained a vocal critic of both the Shah and the United States, which he characterized as "the Great Satan."

In early 1978, individuals from a broad coalition of Iranians— including students, Marxists, and pro-democracy activists—took to the streets protesting the Shah's oppressive government and calling for Khomeini's return. The demonstrations evolved into what became known as the Iranian revolution and forced the Shah to flee Iran in January 1979. When a victorious Khomeini returned to Iran shortly after, many Iranians embraced the stern cleric. And although various groups had sought to depose the Shah, the Iranian people at large soon voted to make Iran an Islamic republic with Khomeini as its leader.

During the Iranian uprisings in 1979, students had seized control of the U.S. embassy in Tehran and taken its personnel as hostages. The students claimed that the diplomats were CIA agents plotting a coup against the Khomeini government, as indeed had occurred in 1953. During this time tensions between the United States and Iran were sky-high, and fifty-two Americans were held hostage for 444 days. Khomeini supported the students' actions. Part of the American response was to freeze more than $12 billion in Iranian assets in the United States. Although the United States later returned a sizeable portion of these as-

sets, other parts remain frozen as the United States awaits the resolution of property disputes that arose out of the revolution. To the present day, this issue is a point of sharp contention between the two countries.

Closely monitoring the bitter relations between the United States and its allies and Iran, Saddam Hussein, the president of neighboring Iraq, decided to exploit the ill will that Westerners felt for the Khomeini regime and the chaos that had accompanied the Iranian revolution. Hussein's Iraqi army invaded Iran in 1980, setting off the Iran-Iraq War. The United States backed Iraq in this six-year war, in which Hussein used chemical weapons against Iranian soldiers and civilians.

Over the next fifteen years, relations between the United States and Iran remained contentious. The United States denounced Iran's support of terrorist organizations and its pursuit of nuclear weapons. In 1995, the Clinton administration imposed economic sanctions on Iran. These sanctions were expanded with the passage of the Iran-Libya Sanctions Act of 1996, which penalized foreign corporations that invested in Iran's energy industry. This measure was a severe blow to the Iranian economy. In 1997, reformist Mohammad Khatami was elected president of Iran with a platform of strengthening democracy in Iran. Khatami made overtures to the United States, and for several years, the icy American-Iranian relations seemed to be thawing. When the terrorist attacks of September 11 occurred, young Iranians took to the streets in spontaneous demonstrations of support for the U.S. victims of the attacks.

That the good will had dissolved, however, was apparent when George W. Bush characterized Iran as part of an "axis of evil" in his 2002 State of the Union speech. Relations chilled primarily because of Iran's pursuit of nuclear weapons. Since that time the harsh rhetoric has continued between the United States and Iran.

> Iranian women light candles in Mother Square in Tehran on September 18, 2001, in memory of victims of the September 11th terrorist attacks on the United States.

* www.nytimes.com/library/world/mideast/041600iran-cia-index.html.

EXPLORING THE SOURCES

U.S. PUBLIC OPINION OF VARIOUS COUNTRIES

This figure provides a visual interpretation of data collected from Americans by the Gallup polling organization in February 2007 in response to the question "Is your overall opinion of [the country whose name appears on the left] very favorable, mostly favorable, mostly unfavorable, or very unfavorable?"

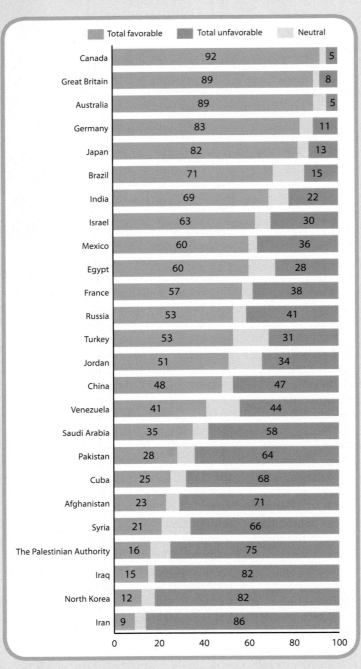

Legend:
- Total favorable
- Total unfavorable
- Neutral

Country	Total favorable	Total unfavorable
Canada	92	5
Great Britain	89	8
Australia	89	5
Germany	83	11
Japan	82	13
Brazil	71	15
India	69	22
Israel	63	30
Mexico	60	36
Egypt	60	28
France	57	38
Russia	53	41
Turkey	53	31
Jordan	51	34
China	48	47
Venezuela	41	44
Saudi Arabia	35	58
Pakistan	28	64
Cuba	25	68
Afghanistan	23	71
Syria	21	66
The Palestinian Authority	16	75
Iraq	15	82
North Korea	12	82
Iran	9	86

Source: http://brain.gallup.com/content/default.aspx?ci=1624.

Evaluating the Evidence

① In analyzing these data, what can you say about the United States' historic relationship with some of these countries and about the role that relationship might play in people's favorability ratings today?

② Is there evidence from these data that Cold War–era anticommunist sentiment among Americans still has a bearing on people's perceptions? Explain.

③ Do the data suggest that there is, in the phrasing of Samuel Huntington, a "clash of civilizations"? Is there evidence to dispute this suggestion? Explain.

Future Challenges in American Foreign Policy

The volatility and complexity of events in the global arena show no sign of abating. In the foreseeable future and beyond, U.S. foreign policy makers will undoubtedly continue to face a number of pressing issues. Certainly among the most urgent of these problems is the ongoing, acute threat of further terrorism directed at domestic and foreign targets. Issues such as the environment, human rights, and technology promise to remain a fixture on the U.S. foreign policy agenda in the years to come.

The Ongoing Threat of Terrorism

As the terrorist attacks of 9/11 tragically demonstrated, foreign affairs can be unpredictable. There are nonetheless some clear challenges that U.S. foreign policy makers are certain to confront in the years to come. First among these is the continued threat of terrorism. As a tactic, terrorism has proven enormously effective in accomplishing the goals of the attackers. Specifically, terrorism breeds terror—it has disrupted economies, created instability, and acted as a polarizing force.

The advent of chemical and biological weapons also promises to be a tough challenge for U.S. and other foreign policy makers. The potential, enormous damage of these weapons of mass destruction cannot be underestimated. Consider but one example: the death of five people and the panic that ensued after traces of the anthrax virus were found in letters mailed in the United States in the autumn of 2001.

Not all challenges to come are new ones, however. The continued proliferation of nuclear weapons presents a serious problem to foreign policy makers throughout the world (see "On the Job"). Figure 17.3 shows that eight nations have a declared nuclear weapons capability, including India and Pakistan; that another, Israel, has the undeclared potential; and that yet another, Iran, is seeking such potential. The fact that dangerous WMDs are in such wide distribution increases the likelihood of their use—either accidentally or intentionally.

POLITICAL INQUIRY

FIGURE 17.3 ■ THE NUCLEAR CLUB What, if anything, do most or all of the countries that gave up or ended their nuclear programs have in common, either among themselves or with the countries that have nuclear capability? What do most or all of the countries that have nuclear capability—either declared or undeclared—have in common? What conclusions can you draw about these commonalities?

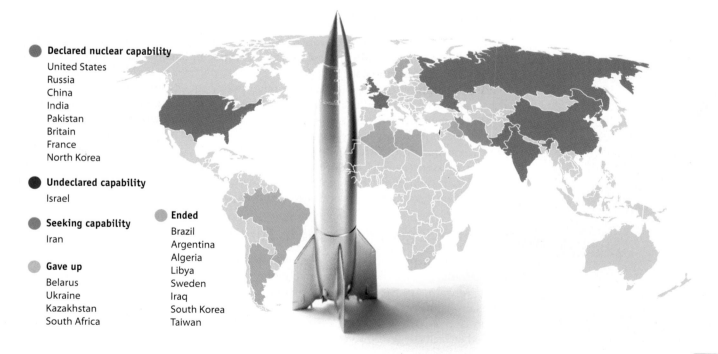

Declared nuclear capability
United States
Russia
China
India
Pakistan
Britain
France
North Korea

Undeclared capability
Israel

Seeking capability
Iran

Gave up
Belarus
Ukraine
Kazakhstan
South Africa

Ended
Brazil
Argentina
Algeria
Libya
Sweden
Iraq
South Korea
Taiwan

ALEX BOLLFRASS, PEACE FELLOW

<u>Name:</u> Alex Bollfrass

<u>Age:</u> 23

<u>Hometown:</u> Santa Barbara, California

<u>College:</u> University of California, Berkeley

<u>Major:</u> Political Science (BA)

<u>Job title:</u> Herbert Scoville Jr. Peace Fellow at the Arms Control Association

<u>Salary range for jobs like this:</u> $20,000–$25,000

<u>Day-to-day responsibilities:</u> About half my time is spent reporting and writing for our magazine *Arms Control Today*, mostly about the Middle East and chemical weapons. The rest of the time I write background memos about current issues and analyze the effects of new congressional legislation.

<u>How did you get your job?</u> The summer before my senior year of college, I interned at the Center for Nonproliferation Studies and discovered my interest in the nuclear security field. I stayed in touch with the people I worked for, who told me about various job opportunities, including the Scoville Fellowship. I applied and was flown to D.C. for an interview.

<u>What do you like best about your job?</u> Almost every minute of my time is spent working on something interesting. I am learning how our government makes laws and decisions and occasionally get to influence that process in a small way.

<u>What is your least favorite aspect of your job?</u> I work long hours for little pay.

<u>What advice would you give to students who would like to do what you are doing?</u> Look for people who are doing what you want to be doing in five or ten years. Send them an e-mail or call them to ask how they got there. Don't be shy—most people love talking about their work and will be happy to give you specific, useful advice. And, especially in the policy world, it is much easier to break into the field if you know someone.

Environmental Issues

In 2007, former vice president Al Gore won the Nobel Peace Prize for his work in raising public awareness of the critically important issue of rapid global climate change. This problem and other environmental concerns that by their very nature are worldwide challenges promise to remain on the United States' foreign policy agenda deep into the future. Specifically, the failure of the United States to ratify the Kyoto Protocol—an international agreement whose objective is to reduce global warming by lowering the amount of greenhouse gas emissions—makes it likely that the warming of Planet Earth will be a continuing and increasingly urgent focus of U.S. foreign policy makers. Other environmental concerns that are sure to have a secure place in foreign policy makers' agendas for the future include the massive world consumption of fossil fuels, the deterioration of the oceans, worldwide deforestation, and ongoing air and water contamination.

Technology's Potential in Foreign Affairs

Although there are many uncertainties about what's next in the foreign policy arena, one certainty is that the impact of technology—as a tool in foreign policy and in citizens' efforts to influence the policies and institutions of government—will continue to increase. For example, in recent years a number of countries have thrown off the shackles of one-person or one-party rule due to the revolution in communications technology, which has enabled citizens to see how governments in other countries work. Finding Western democracy preferable to their own form of government, in 2004 48 million voters in the Ukraine overturned dubious election results and ousted the first victor, Prime Minister Viktor Yanukovych, installing in his stead another Viktor: Viktor Yushenko. The electronic media broadcast the "orange revolution" in the Ukraine—so called for the orange flags and orange garments of the protesters—for viewers around the world to see. The increasing inability of countries, including China and North Korea, to limit access to technology and information from around the world will prove empowering to people everywhere.

CONCLUSION CONTINUING THE CONVERSATION

In retrospect, the development of the United States' foreign policy over time seems to have followed a natural progression as the nation itself grew and changed. The nation's initial isolationism, spawned by a healthy suspicion of foreign powers and their motives, gave way to international relations in the limited sphere of trade. Then, in both World War I and World War II, the importance of global alliances in helping to shape U.S. foreign policy became evident. With the end of World War II, the United States emerged as a superpower whose foreign policy came to be defined largely by its relations with its chief rival in the global arena, the Soviet Union. After the collapse of the Soviet empire in the 1990s, the foreign policy arena was murky, and evidence of how U.S. and world policy makers searched for a new prism through which to view the nations of the world.

On September 11, 2001, U.S. foreign policy instantly acquired a new focus. Their morning hardly going according to their daily planners, a shaken president and his aides scrambled to respond appropriately to the unforeseen and unprecedented terrorist attacks on U.S. soil. They asked the same question that the millions of Americans who watched the unbelievable events unfold on television asked: Why? Ultimately the administration's responses to the terrorist strikes showed that significant cultural and political differences separate the United States and the other Western democracies on the one hand, and fundamentalist non-Western states that harbor terrorists on the other hand. The attacks crystallized perceptions both among U.S. policy makers and in the general public that no longer could the terrorist states be viewed simply as potential threats or as insignificant to the United States' interests.

The outcome and repercussions of the U.S. responses to the attacks will undoubtedly be felt in the United States, in Iraq, and throughout the world for years to come. Will the U.S. military actions in Iraq succeed in creating the first Arab democracy in the Middle East, or will the chances of that fledgling democracy crumble to dust at the hands of extremists or clashing Islamic sects? Will postwar U.S. initiatives to help the Iraqis rebuild their shattered nation bring the same kind of successes that the Marshall Plan brought to post–World War II Europe? How will continuing tensions between the United States and nations such as Iran and North Korea affect the United States' status as world leader? Will the court of world public opinion support U.S. foreign policy regarding those two nations?

The threat of further terrorist attacks on America is the strongest evidence that the United States is engaged in a clash of civilizations. If that is the case, how will that clash play out? Given the distinctive nature of those who practice terrorism—their lack of geographic boundaries and their refusal to abide by the conventional rules of war—such a conflict surely would differ starkly from the last major clash of ideologies, the Cold War.

Finally, in view of the unique qualities of terrorism, it is difficult to anticipate how the continued threat of terrorist acts will shape U.S. foreign policy. The randomness of terrorism confounds policy makers and other experts and prevents them from making accurate predictions and determining adequate modes of defense. Nonetheless, given the high stakes of another potential attack, the threat of terrorism—and the imperative to prevent it—clearly will remain a defining characteristic of U.S. foreign policy in the decades to come.

STUDY NOW

Summary

1. The Tools of U.S. Foreign Policy
The government officials who formulate U.S. foreign policy rely on diplomacy, by which nations conduct political negotiations with one another and settle disagreements. They also rely on economic policy to cajole other nations into enacting policies that the United States supports, and on military force, if needed, to force other countries to align with U.S. interests.

2. Who Decides? The Creators and Shapers of Foreign Policy
Because the Constitution grants important foreign policy making powers to the president, the President along with the executive branch is the primary foreign policy maker in the United States. Congress also plays an important role in creating foreign policy, particularly through its decision making with respect to declaring war and appropriating funds. Interest groups, the media, and private individuals also influence the foreign policy process.

3. U.S. Foreign Policy in Historical Context: Isolationism and Intervention
The conduct of foreign policy was at first influenced by a suspicion of foreign affairs. As the U.S. economy developed, statesmen and business interests primarily concentrated on maximizing profits through international trade. In the twentieth century, the balance of power system drew the United States into global conflict in World War I. Although the United States retreated into an isolationist position during the Great Depression, an alliance with the British and Japan's attack on the U.S. naval base at Pearl Harbor, Hawaii, precipitated U.S. entry into World War II.

4. The Postwar Era: The United States as Superpower
After the Second World War, the United States and the Soviet Union emerged as competing superpowers locked in a Cold War of clashing ideologies. This rivalry defined U.S. foreign policy for half a century. During this period, international organizations charged with ensuring security and facilitating economic relations among nations were established. During the Cold War, the United States also attempted to curb the spread of communism on the Korean peninsula, in Cuba, and in Vietnam. President Richard Nixon initiated a period of détente; President Ronald Reagan outspent the Soviets and forced the collapse of the Soviet economy. The end of communism in the Soviet Union and Eastern Europe meant drastic changes in the context of international relations.

5. U.S. Foreign Policy After 9/11
With the terrorist attacks of September 11, 2001, a new era in U.S. foreign policy commenced, seeming to reflect acceptance of the theory that a clash of civilizations—warfare over cultural and religious differences—was inevitable. In espousing the tenets of the Bush Doctrine, administration officials promoted the strategy of preventive war. After 9/11, foreign policy officials also pursued a program of regime change in both Afghanistan and Iraq, while also setting their sights on the regimes in Iran and North Korea.

6. Future Challenges in American Foreign Policy
Among the greatest challenges for the United States in the foreign policy arena are the continued threat of terrorism and the accumulation of nuclear, chemical, and biological weapons. The highly interdependent global economy will also serve as a focal point in the future as will environmental challenges and the impact of technology.

Key Terms

Key Terms

For Review

1. What are the primary tools that policy makers use in the foreign policy process?

2. Why is the president the primary foreign policy maker in the United States? What tools do presidents have to assist them in creating foreign policy? Who are the other actors in foreign policy decision making?

3. How did the United States evolve from a nation that emphasized isolationism in its early years to internationalism in the post–World War II era? What factors spurred this transformation?

4. How did the Cold War between the United States and the Soviet Union affect U.S. foreign policy? How did it influence relations between the United States and other nations?

5. September 11, 2001, led to a significant shift in how the United States viewed itself and the world. What theories best explain how the United States now sees itself in the post-9/11 global context?

6. What specific, major challenges will U.S. foreign policy makers face in the years to come?

For Critical Thinking and Discussion

1. How have the 9/11 terrorist attacks changed the structure of the foreign policy-making apparatus in the executive branch?

2. How did World War II change the way the United States was perceived by other nations around the world? How did the war alter U.S. policy makers' perceptions of what the international order should look like?

3. In retrospect, was the theory of containment an accurate description of how the United States should have attempted to stem the tide of communism during the Cold War? Why or why not?

4. Does Samuel Huntington's clash of civilizations theory accurately reflect the current state of world affairs? Explain. What present-day realities are in keeping with Huntington's theory? What other realities defy it?

5. What additional challenges, beyond those we examined in the text, are likely to face the makers of U.S. foreign policy in the next decade (2010–2020)?

MULTIPLE CHOICE: Choose the lettered item that answers the question correctly.

1. The strategy of creating a system of international alliances that would equalize the power of one group of nations with the power of another group, and thus discourage war, is called
   a. containment.
   c. balance of power.
   b. détente.
   d. multilateralism.

2. _____ argues that unilateral action directly targeted at an enemy is both justifiable and feasible.
   a. The Bush Doctrine
   b. The clash of civilizations theory
   c. Containment theory
   d. The Roosevelt Corollary

3. The political, ideological, and military conflict that lasted from 1945 until 1990 between communist nations led by the Soviet Union and Western democracies led by the United States is called
   a. *glasnost*.
   c. World War I.
   b. the Cold War.
   d. World War II.

4. The idea that if one nation fell to communism, other nations in that geographic vicinity would also succumb is called
   a. risk theory.
   c. domino theory.
   b. monopoly theory.
   d. checkers theory.

5. The United States' foreign policy commitment to assisting efforts to resist communism was called
   a. the Monroe Doctrine.
   b. the Truman Doctrine.
   c. the Nixon Doctrine.
   d. the Bush Doctrine.

6. The idea that it was the United States' destiny to expand throughout the North American continent is called
   a. the Monroe Doctrine.
   b. the Roosevelt Corollary.
   c. manifest destiny.
   d. containment.

7. The ballistic missile defense system advocated by President Ronald Reagan was known as
   a. SALT.
   c. GATT.
   b. START.
   d. Star Wars.

8. The institution established in 1949 to create a structure for regional security for its fifteen member nations through a declaration of mutual defense is
   a. the World Bank.
   b. NATO.
   c. the United Nations.
   d. the World Trade Organization.

9. The institution, created by the Bretton Woods Agreement, that lends money to nations in need is
   a. the World Bank.
   b. NATO.
   c. the United Nations.
   d. the World Trade Organization.

10. The first agreements between the United States and the Soviet Union that focused on limiting the nuclear arms race between the two superpowers were called
    a. the Warsaw Pact.
    c. START.
    b. SALT.
    d. GATT.

FILL IN THE BLANKS.

11. The strategy of proactively waging war on a threatening country in order to avoid future conflicts is called _____.

12. The idea that peace could be achieved if nations agreed to collectively oppose any nation that attacked another country is called _____.

13. _____ are alliances such as NATO and the Warsaw Pact, and these alliances typically are made between a superpower and nations that are ideologically similar in a particular region of the world.

14. The easing of tensions between the United States and its communist rivals was _____.

15. The replacement of a country's government with another by facilitating the removal of its leader or leading political party is called _____.

Answers: 1. c; 2. a; 3. b; 4. c; 5. b; 6. c; 7. d; 8. b; 9. a; 10. b; 11. preventive war; 12. collective security; 13. Regional security alliances; 14. détente; 15. regime change

RESOURCES FOR RESEARCH AND ACTION

Internet Resources

American Democracy Now Web site
www.mhhe.com/harrison1e   Consult the book's Web site for study guides, interactive activities, simulations, and current hotlinks for additional information on American foreign policy.

Central Intelligence Agency
https://www.cia.gov   This is the official Web site of the CIA. Its *World Factbook,* available online at this site, is an excellent resource for research on various nations. The site also hosts news and information, history, and career opportunities.

Cold War
www.coldwar.org   This interactive Web site allows you to revisit the Cold War in a virtual museum. You can view relics of the Cold War, learn about the culture of the time, and play spy games.

North Atlantic Treaty Organization
www.nato.int   This site hosts an informative eLibrary as well as an impressive multimedia collection of documentation about NATO-related events and history.

State Department and Defense Department
www.state.gov and **www.defenselink.mil**   These government sites offer a plethora of information from these two cabinet departments. Included are news and information, policy statements, career opportunities, virtual tours, and reports.

World Bank
www.worldbank.org   This site explains the World Bank's policy priorities and offers data, research reports, and a wide variety of related international news.

Recommended Readings

Allison, Graham. *Nuclear Terrorism: The Ultimate Preventable Catastrophe.* New York: Times Books, 2004, and *The Essence of Decision: Explaining the Cuban Missile Crisis,* Boston: Little Brown, 1971. This key scholar of U.S. foreign policymaking uses the Cuban Missile Crisis as a model to explain foreign policymaking. In his more recent work, he analyzes the foreign policy dilemma of nuclear terrorism.

Cameron, Fraser. *U.S. Foreign Policy after the Cold War.* New York: Routledge, 2002. This introduction to U.S. foreign policy looks at some aspects of U.S. foreign policy from the perspective of their domestic origins. Critical of the United States' unilateralism, Cameron also details relations between the United States and the European Union.

Cohen, Warren I. *The Cambridge History of American Foreign Relations: Vol. 4, America in the Age of Soviet Power, 1945–1991.* New York: Cambridge University Press, 1993. Written from a post-Cold War perspective, this book explains the major foreign policy events since World War II, including Soviet-American tensions, the Korean and Vietnam wars; détente and U.S.-Soviet relations in the 1980s.

Jervis, Robert. *American Foreign Policy in a New Era.* New York: Routledge, 2005. A noted foreign policy scholar explains the issues and influences on American foreign policy in today's international cricumstances.

Keohane, Robert. *Neo-Realism and Its Critics,* New York: Columbia University Press, 1986. This classic work explains neorealism, a theory that emphasizes the power of state actors in international affairs.

Movies of Interest

The Good Shepherd (2006)
Directed by Robert De Niro and starring Matt Damon, Alec Baldwin, and Angelina Jolie, this film traces the creation of the CIA and its evolution through the Cold War.

The Killing Fields (1984)
Based on a true story, this film tells the story of an American journalist and his Cambodian guide during the vicious genocide by Cambodia's Khmer Rouge regime during the Vietnam War.

Breaker Morant (1980)
Based on a true story, this courtroom drama tells the story of three Australian soldiers who are court-martialed for shooting prisoners during the Boer War in South Africa (1899–1902).

Dr. Strangelove or: How I Learned to Stop Worrying and Love the Bomb (1964)
This Stanley Kubrick film probes the dangers of the Cold War when an insane army general tries to start a nuclear war over the objections of political leaders and other generals.

The Mouse That Roared (1959)
This Peter Sellers comedy takes a satirical look at how the United States used foreign aid to ensure the support of allies. It features a fictional impoverished European nation that invades the United States with the goal of losing so that it can receive foreign aid.

National Journal

ENEMY OF MY ENEMY

On paper, the Mujahedeen-e Khalq sounds like the sort of group the United States government might like to cultivate: well-organized Iranian exiles concentrated in Europe and Iraq who share Washington's antipathy to the theocracy in Iran. The group—whose name translates as "warriors for the people of Iran"—has its own "parliament in exile," the National Council of Resistance of Iran, and says it supports a secular government, democracy, human rights, and women's rights in Iran.

In practice, however, the Iranian group has some major shortcomings in the ally department. For the past decade, the State Department has listed the MEK as a "foreign terrorist organization," and more recently has argued that the group displays "cult-like characteristics."

The MEK has been waging a spirited campaign to persuade the U.S. to drop the terrorist designation—which would require either the secretary of State's say-so or an act of Congress.

Although the group can't make its own case directly, in the past several years two prominent former U.S. government officials have been publicly touting the MEK's virtues and arguing that the United States should remove it from the terrorist list.

At the moment, the more high-profile and influential of these advocates is former House Majority Leader Dick Armey, R-Texas, a senior policy adviser at the global law and lobbying firm DLA Piper. Last year, Armey wrote two op-eds for Washington newspapers urging the State Department to drop the MEK's terrorist designation.

"Never has the old adage 'The enemy of my enemy is my friend' been more true than in the case of the MEK," he wrote in The Hill in July. And in The Washington Times in December, Armey wrote, "With a stroke of the pen, the secretary of State could, and should, remove the Mujahedeen-e-Khalq and the National Council of Resistance of Iran from the list of foreign terrorist organizations."

Another public advocate for the MEK is Raymond Tanter, who was a senior staff member at the National Security Council in the Reagan administration and is now an adjunct professor at Georgetown University. In 2005, Tanter co-founded the nonprofit Iran Policy Committee, which lists as directors or advisers a half-dozen former executive branch, military, and intelligence officials and describes its mission as promoting a "central role for the Iranian opposition" in bringing about "democratic change" in Iran. The committee's publications, conferences, and congressional briefings routinely urge the U.S. to take the MEK off its terrorist list, as well as to meet with and fund the group.

The MEK began as an anti-shah leftist group in the 1960s. It got on the wrong side of the United States when members assassinated several of the shah's American advisers in the 1970s. In the three decades since Iran became an Islamic regime, the State Department says, the MEK has waged violent attacks inside that country, and it maintains the "capacity and will to commit terrorist acts in Europe, the Middle East, the United States, Canada, and beyond."

A charismatic husband-and-wife team leads the group: Massoud Rajavi, whose whereabouts are unknown, is the military leader, and Maryam Rajavi heads the political wing from France. The MEK's size is also unknown, but the Council on Foreign Relations estimates that it could have as many as 10,000 members worldwide.

In 2005, Human Rights Watch issued a report detailing complaints from a dozen former MEK members that they suffered physical and psychological abuse while they were in the group. The State Department says that members undergo indoctrination and weekly "ideological cleansings," are separated from their young children, and must vow "eternal divorce"—that is, to remain unmarried or to divorce their spouse.

The U.S. invasion of Iraq in 2003 took a toll on the MEK, which had set up operations there after being driven out of Iran and, later, France in the 1980s. Because Saddam Hussein had been providing the bulk of its military and financial support, the State Department says, the MEK subsequently began to use "front organizations" to solicit contributions from expatriate Iranian communities.

The U.S. military disarmed the group's foot soldiers in Iraq and now holds some 3,500 of them as "protected persons" under the Geneva Conventions at an encampment there. "We are not embracing them, we just don't know how to [disperse] them" without putting their lives in danger, says Brookings Institution senior fellow Peter Rodman, who was an assistant Defense secretary through 2006.

MEK supporters argue that the group has renounced violence, poses no terrorist threat, and, in fact, presents a viable alternative to the theocracy in Tehran. The terrorist designation, they say, was a futile Washington sop to appease that regime. "The U.S. government at any moment can make that decision, and decide [that the designation] is unwarranted," says Alireza Jafarzadeh, the former representative in Washington for the NCRI, and now a self-described consultant and a commentator on Fox News. Jafarzadeh blames "politics" for Washington's failure to act and says that the MEK spends about 80 percent of its resources "to counter the consequences of the designation."

MEK supporters argue that the group provided vital intelligence about Iran's covert nuclear program in 2002, as well as about Iranian-sponsored attacks on U.S. soldiers in Iraq.

Although more than 220 members of Congress signed a letter in 1998 protesting the group's terrorist designation, the MEK's several legal challenges to the designation have failed, and legislative efforts to remove it have gone nowhere.

Despite the Bush administration's tough line on the Tehran regime, the MEK's political fortunes in the U.S. have declined in recent years. The NCRI was once allowed to maintain an office, hire lobbyists, hold press conferences, and generally operate openly in the United States. But in late 2003, the administration got tough and the Justice Department shut down the office. The group still has some congressional supporters.

Armey's history as an outspoken advocate for the MEK is murky. DLA Piper has received $860,000 in fees over the past four and a half years from Saeid Ghaemi, whom the firm identifies as an "Iranian-American businessman who works closely with the Iranian-American community in the U.S. to promote human rights and democracy in Iran." Public records identify Saeid Ghaemi as a used-car dealer in the Denver area, but an Internet search turned up no information about his political work with the Iranian-American community. When National Journal reached him by phone to ask about his hiring of Armey and DLA Piper, Ghaemi said he was busy and would return the call. He failed to return that or subsequent calls.

Last year, Armey and the other lobbyists also worked on Ghaemi's behalf for a House measure urging the secretary of State to designate the Quds Force of Iran's Islamic Revolutionary Guards Corps as a foreign terrorist organization. Shortly after a broader measure targeting Iran and the Quds Force overwhelmingly passed the House last fall, Secretary of State Condoleezza Rice designated the force a terrorist group.

DLA Piper also lobbied in the Senate for the Iran Human Rights Act of 2007 that would, among other things, expand U.S. support for Iranian opposition groups to include those outside Iran, and would establish a State Department envoy to reach out to such groups.

Tanter, like some other MEK defenders, says he supports the group because it is the only opposition organization that really worries the mullahs in Tehran. "I did an analysis of all the opposition groups and found that the [Islamic Iranian] regime paid attention to [the MEK] 350 percent more than all the others. I am not here to lobby on behalf of groups on the foreign terrorist organization list. I am an American trying to

MEK supporters argue that the group has renounced violence, poses no terrorist threat, and, in fact, presents a viable alternative to the theocracy in Tehran. The terrorist designation, they say, was a futile Washington sop to appease that regime.

preserve American national security abroad and save lives."

Tanter's tax-exempt Iran Policy Committee has raised a substantial amount of money in a short period of time. The law prohibits anyone in the United States or subject to its laws from providing "material support or resources" to a designated foreign terrorist organization. But these financial sanctions don't prohibit "U.S. citizens from expressing their views on economic sanctions matters—and that includes the designation of the MEK—to Congress or the Executive Branch" according to the Treasury Department, whose Office of Foreign Assets Control oversees the sanctions. Bill Livingstone, who worked with his brother Neil on the 2006 report, said that the authors made sure the report did not violate Treasury's rules.

"The First Amendment protects Dick Armey to make his opinions known, and protects the Iran Policy Committee's educational mission to find options to reinforce our diplomacy" toward Iran, Tanter said. He has hired an attorney who specializes in the arcane Treasury rules and contends that his group tries "to vet our money to make sure we're not getting any" from prohibited groups. Tanter also points out that several of his group's advisers and directors are retired military and intelligence officers with security clearances that they would do nothing to jeopardize.

The effect of Armey's and Tanter's efforts is unclear. So far, the MEK's efforts to shed its terrorist designation have met with far more success in Europe than here. The group has won court decisions mandating that the European Union unfreeze the group's assets and that Great Britain remove it from that country's list of terrorist groups. The British government says it intends to appeal.

Although the State Department is required to review its designation of the MEK later this year, the group's supporters fear that the decision will reflect a political climate that has become less sympathetic to their cause. Administration hard-liners, who have lost ground to pragmatists, have been further undercut by the recent National Intelligence Estimate stating that Iran stopped its nuclear weapons program in 2003—a conclusion that the MEK disputes. "This so-called hard-line [Bush] administration is more interested in striking a grand bargain with Iran than the E.U. is," Tanter said. He and other MEK boosters also contend that if relations with Tehran worsen, the MEK's prospects could revive.

The neoconservative community, where the MEK has found support in the past, has become sharply divided, with critics becoming as vocal as supporters in conservative publications. "I don't think any administration is going to want to include them," said Rodman, who describes himself as a hard-line opponent of the Tehran regime. "Everyone has rejected [the MEK]. They're not the kind of people we want to work with."

■ **THEN:** Since World War II, the United States has allied itself with the enemy of its enemies in order to defeat their common adversary.

■ **NOW:** The formation of unpredictable and uncontrollable terrorist organizations has led the United States to exercise more caution when allying itself with the enemy of an enemy.

■ **NEXT:** Will the Obama administration lift MEK's "foreign terrorist organization" designation?
Will the strategy of relying on groups opposed to regimes that the United States opposes continue as a useful foreign policy model?
What role will American citizens have in determining whether the United States supports militant opposition groups like MEK?

State and Local Government

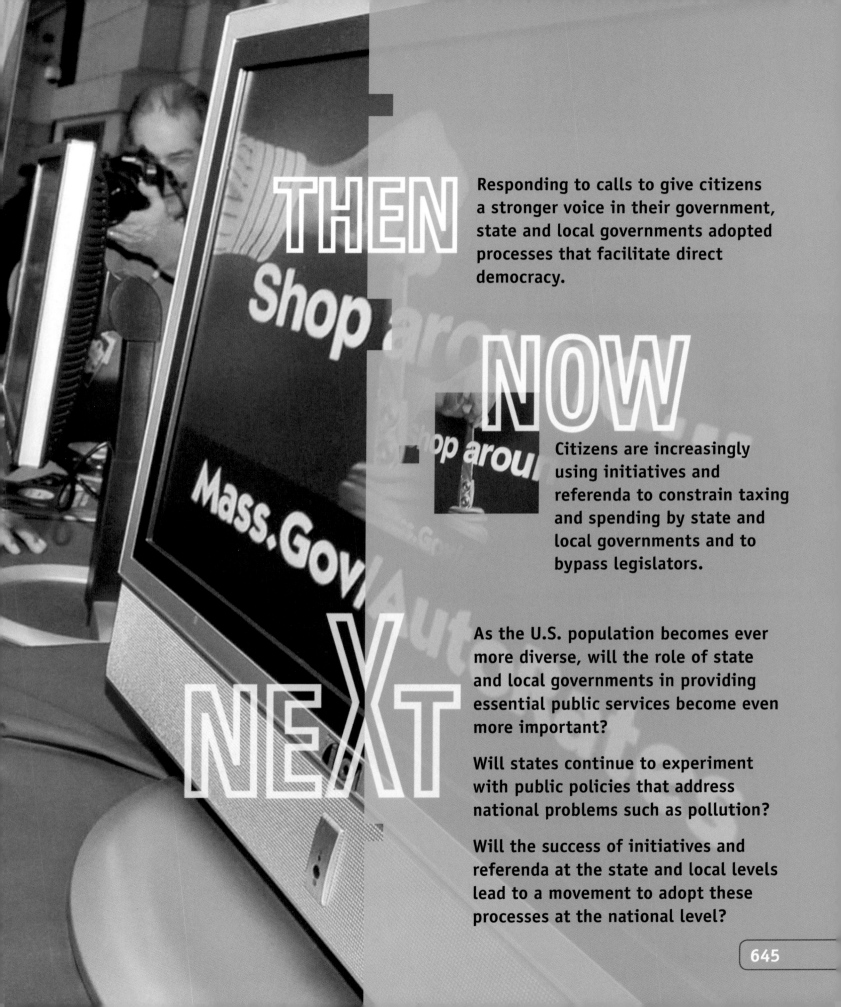

THEN

Responding to calls to give citizens a stronger voice in their government, state and local governments adopted processes that facilitate direct democracy.

NOW

Citizens are increasingly using initiatives and referenda to constrain taxing and spending by state and local governments and to bypass legislators.

NEXT

As the U.S. population becomes ever more diverse, will the role of state and local governments in providing essential public services become even more important?

Will states continue to experiment with public policies that address national problems such as pollution?

Will the success of initiatives and referenda at the state and local levels lead to a movement to adopt these processes at the national level?

Fighting for College Affordability: A Student-Led Ballot Initiative

I'm worried that I'm going to be spending the rest of my life repaying [college] loans," laments Juan Vazquez, a cultural-studies major at the University of California, San Diego (UCSD).* "The higher the fees, the more students have to work and the less [time] they spend on their studies. It shouldn't be this hard to get an education," argues Erin Keim, anthropology major at California State University, Long Beach.** Utsav Gupta, a bioengineering, biotechnology major at UCSD, claims, "When you raise tuition you're really affecting socioeconomic diversity at our campuses.* Vazquez, Keim, and Gupta are just three of the thousands of students who worked to get California's College Affordability Act of 2008 enacted. I Frustrated by failed attempts to get the California state legislature to enact a law freezing tuition, California students, their families, and others concerned about college affordability turned to the ballot initiative process. This process allows citizens to bypass the legislature by drafting a law and having it placed on the Election Day ballot for voters to approve or reject. Tuition Relief Now, a student-led ballot initiative project, drafted the College Affordability Act in 2007. To place the act on the November 2008 ballot, its supporters had to collect the signatures of 434,000 registered California voters to meet the legal requirement of 5 percent of the number of ballots cast in the last California gubernatorial election. I As established by California law, from the day in December 2007 that it introduced the College Affordability Act to the state government, Tuition Relief Now had 150 days to collect the required signatures. The campaign differed from most recent California ballot initiatives in several ways. First, it was student led and staffed by volunteers. Tuition Relief Now did not pay people to collect signatures, which is the norm for California ballot initiatives today. Tuition Relief Now also relied on Internet technology to recruit volunteers to circulate, and registered voters to sign, their petitions. As its Web site claims, "We know something most political consultants don't . . . how to reach every one of our friends using new technology. We're one of the first ballot initiative campaigns to blaze the trail."*** I As the petition deadline approached, California Assembly member Joe Coto introduced a proposal in the legislature, also called the College Affordability Act, that was identical to the ballot initiative. Chris Vaeth, campaign director for Tuition Relief Now, responded to Coto's proposal by saying, "We welcome passage of the College Affordability Act through the legislature or on the ballot, or in any way that enacts the first long-term tuition policy in decades."** I In June 2008, Vaeth reported, "Unfortunately we didn't gather enough signatures in time—but we were in the hundreds of thousands, something we're proud of for an all-volunteer effort. Our student/parent volunteer base is ready to re-file for 2010."**** In the meantime, Tuition Relief Now organizers are encouraging students and their families to write letters and e-mails to, or meet face-to-face with, their legislators to request they vote for the College Affordability Act.

> A student volunteer for Tuition Relief Now collects signatures on a petition to place the College Affordability Act on California's 2008 ballot.

* Tanya Sierra, "Students Try to Get Fee Freeze on Ballot," *San Diego Union-Tribune,* February 10, 2008.
** Serafina Costanza, "Coalition Takes It to the Capitol to Fight Tuition Increases," www.daily49er.com/home/index.cfm?event+displayArticlePrinterFriendly&uStory_id=51fef386-41cb-4a72-998d-b9c6cc0146df.
*** www.tuitionreliefnow.org/campaign/how_different/.
**** Personal communication, June 16, 2008.

Although U.S. citizens cannot

vote on proposed *national* laws, all state governments provide for some form of direct democracy that allows citizens to approve or reject *state* propositions formulated by government officials (such as proposed laws and constitutional amendments). Moreover, California and twenty other states allow citizens to place citizen-formulated propositions directly on the Election Day ballot for voters to approve or reject. In most states, too, citizens can use mechanisms of direct democracy to address issues in local government.

Therefore, the place where you reside in the United States—the state and locality—affects your options with respect to how you can take action for or against an issue that concerns you. Where you live also determines which state and local governments are obligated to serve you, and to which governments you have obligations such as the responsibilities to pay taxes and to serve on jury duty. Chapter 3 described the evolution of the U.S. federal system into today's complex arrangement of intergovernmental relations among the more than 89,000 distinct yet interdependent governments in the United States. This chapter focuses on the diversity of people, environments, resources, and cultures across the fifty states of the United States and the impact of this diversity on the functions and structures of state and local governments.

State and local governments influence our daily lives in myriad ways as they create and implement a dizzying array of policies. Thus an understanding of state and local government is an essential foundation for a well-developed sense of political efficacy—the belief that you can influence politics—and for political participation that brings results. Indeed, when people engage with government, they typically do so by way of their state and local governments.

Direct Democracy: Letting the People Decide

In the United States, governments at the national, state, and local levels are all representative democracies in which citizens elect officials to create and approve public policies for them. To verify that representative democracy functions properly, governments have enacted sunshine laws that open their processes to public view and participation. For example, national, state, and local governments all have **open meeting laws** requiring legislative bodies, as well as executive agencies, to conduct their policy-making meetings in public. Open meeting laws typically require advance public notice of the meetings of policy-making bodies in a general circulation newspaper.

Many state and local governments couple representative democracy with **direct democracy**—a system of procedures that allow citizens to vote directly to approve or reject proposed public policies or to force an elected official from office before the completion of his or her term. This chapter's "American Democracy Now" vignette describes how California students exercised their right to direct democracy. (In contrast to states and localities, the U.S. national government does not provide for direct democracy.)

Although many local governments have provided for direct democracy since their creation, South Dakota in 1898 became the first state to adopt direct democracy. Subsequently, between 1898 and 1918, twenty-four states adopted some form of direct democracy as a result of the Progressive movement, a mass movement that called for changes in state and local government processes to expand citizens' ability to have a voice in policy making and to hold their elected officials accountable. Progressives argued that these reforms would force government at all levels to be more responsive to the people and less

This chapter surveys the institutions and policies of state and local governments. We also look at the roles of state government in national politics.

FIRST, we examine citizen engagement in state and local government by way of the exercise of *direct democracy* at the state and local levels.

SECOND, we review the constitutional documents of state and local government, specifically the common principles and constructs of *state constitutions and local charters.*

THIRD, we consider the *diversity in political cultures, people, environments, and resources* that affect the processes and policy making of state and local governments.

FOURTH, we focus on *state and local government budgets* to understand what goods and services they provide to citizens and how they pay for them.

FIFTH, we look at the *responsibilities of state and local governments in national politics:* both the formal and informal responsibilities that have developed over the years.

SIXTH, we focus on the *institutions of state government,* examining the commonalities and differences from state to state and contrasting state and federal institutions.

SEVENTH, we survey *local governments* and differentiate among general-purpose and single-purpose local governments.

open meeting laws
laws requiring legislative bodies and executive agencies of government to conduct policy-making meetings in public

> Attendance at open meetings swells when officials are debating or voting on a controversial policy. Citizens who believe the policy will affect them negatively are much more apt to attend than citizens who support the policy or who do not fear a negative impact.

direct democracy

a system of government that allows citizens to vote directly to approve or reject proposed public policies or to force an elected official from office before the completion of his or her term

ballot measure

any proposed policy that, as the result of an initiative or a referendum, wins a place on the ballot for voters to approve or reject

legislative referendum

a ballot measure whereby voters approve or reject a law or amendment proposed by state officials

popular referendum

a measure that allows citizens, by collecting signatures in a petition drive, to put before voters specific legislation that the legislature has previously approved

beholden to well-funded special interest groups. The benefit, the Progressives said, would be a more democratic government. President Theodore Roosevelt (1901–1909) argued that direct democracy should be used to "correct [representative government] whenever it becomes misrepresentative."[1]

Referenda and Initiatives

Direct democracy takes various forms. Whatever the form, the final stage involves citizens' voting on a **ballot measure**—a proposed piece of legislation, a constitutional amendment, or some other policy proposal placed on the Election Day ballot for voters to approve or reject. The various forms of direct democracy differ in who formulates the proposed law and what process is required for getting it on the ballot.

The *referendum* is a ballot measure that gives citizens veto power by allowing them to vote to approve or reject legislation or a constitutional amendment that the state legislature has proposed. All fifty states allow for a **legislative referendum,** a ballot measure whereby voters approve or reject a law or an amendment *proposed* by state officials. States use the legislative referendum (among other procedures), for example, to amend their constitutions. In this process, proposed amendments to a state constitution must appear on the ballot for citizens to approve or reject (in all states except Delaware, where legislators, not citizens, approve constitutional amendments). Twenty-four states also use the **popular referendum,** a measure that allows citizens, by collecting signatures in a petition drive, to put before voters specific legislation that the legislature has *previously approved.* In effect, the popular referendum allows voters to repeal laws that their legislators already have passed.

The *initiative* is a ballot measure, formulated by an individual or a group such as Tuition Relief Now, that allows citizens themselves to propose legislation or state constitutional amendments through petitions signed by a specified number of registered voters. By using the tool of the initiative, citizens in twenty-one states and in almost 60 percent of U.S. cities can write legislative bills and force their state or local governments to place the bills on the ballot for citizens to approve or reject on Election Day. Twenty-four states allow their citizens to use the initiative process to place proposed state constitutional amendments on the ballot. Through the initiative procedure, citizens can bypass their elected officials to create and approve laws. Figure 18.1 identifies the states that have initiative and/or referendum processes.

Referenda and initiatives are a large (and growing) factor in state policy making, and citizens use them even more frequently in local policy making. State ballots featured about 500 initiatives in the eighty years between 1900 and 1980, or an average of about six per year; but between 1980 and 2003—a span of only twenty-three years—more than 1,400 initiatives appeared on state ballots, or an average of about sixty per year.[2] The success of California's Proposition 13 (1978) ignited this tremendous, continuing growth in ballot measures. The People's Initiative to Limit Property Taxation (Proposition 13) amended California's constitution. It set a cap on local property tax increases and required a supermajority vote of state legislators to approve increases in tax rates, thus making it more difficult for lawmakers to raise revenues.

In November 2008, there were 59 initiatives and 85 referenda on state ballots, with Colorado having the most ballot measures (14).[3] Some key issues that citizens in multiple states placed on the general election ballot included expanding legal gambling, limiting abortion, natural resource conservation, labor and employment rights, energy research and conservation, fighting crime, environmental protection, banning same-sex marriage, extension of voting rights, and taxation.

Clearly, citizens are increasingly using initiatives and referenda as means to participate personally and to influence public policy making. Some scholars attribute the rising use of direct democracy to citizens' growing frustration with government and to their willingness to take policy matters into their own hands. Others note that an "initiative industry" has arisen, featuring professionals whom citizens and interest groups can hire to collect signatures and coordinate media campaigns in support of or opposition to initiatives. Although they come with a high price tag, such professionals make it easier for citizens to initiate ballot measures and may even encourage them to attempt to influence their state and local governments by exercising their right to direct democracy.[4]

The increased use of direct democracy is not limited to the United States. European nations also have direct democracy provisions in their laws. However, the procedures typically used in Europe differ from those used by state and local governments in the United States (see "Global Comparisons").

Proponents of direct democracy applaud the growing use of these various means of increasing government responsiveness. They say that the availability of these tools fosters citizen engagement in policy making and that this trend is good for democratic government. Election Day ballot measures stimulate public conversations on public issues and mobilize voters, as indicated by higher voter turnout rates. Opponents of direct democracy note that citizens' drives to get signatures on petitions, as well as the campaigns to persuade voters to approve or reject ballot measures, are very costly, making it a tool for well-funded, well-organized special interests and wealthy individuals to influence government. Moreover, opponents argue that on Election Day voters cannot discern from the brief statement they read on the ballot the intricacies of proposed policies, and therefore they cannot cast an educated vote. The job of elected officials is to understand complex policy issues and to make the best decisions for their constituents. If voters do not like the decisions of their

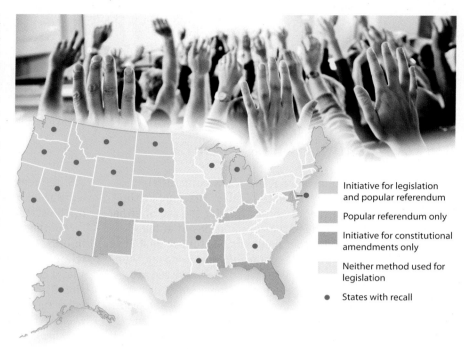

Initiative for legislation and popular referendum

Popular referendum only

Initiative for constitutional amendments only

Neither method used for legislation

● States with recall

FIGURE 18.1 ■ STATES WITH INITIATIVE, REFERENDUM, AND RECALL PROCESSES In what part(s) of the country do states tend to allow their citizens the most options for participating in the political process by affecting legislation or amending their state constitutions? Where do citizens have the least ability to do so? How might the history of these areas of the country have influenced these policies?

Note: All states except Delaware have referenda on state constitutional amendments.

GLOBAL COMPARISONS

DIRECT DEMOCRACY IN EUROPE

Direct democracy in European nations looks quite different from direct democracy in the United States. First, unlike the U.S. Constitution, which does not provide for the use of either an initiative or a referendum, the constitutions of at least thirty European countries contain provisions for national direct democracy. (Some European countries, among them Switzerland, have had national direct democracy since the early 1800s.) Moreover, in the United States, state and local governments have exercised various forms of direct democracy since before ratification of the U.S. Constitution, whereas in Europe, direct democracy is relatively new among local governments. Beyond the differences as to which levels of government use direct democracy, the direct democracy processes that local governments in Europe use contrast notably with those used by state and local governments in the United States.

* What issue will be the next common concern addressed by local referenda in Europe and in state and local ballot measures in the United States?

In European nations, a common component of direct democracy at the local level is the requirement that local governing councils must approve any ballot measure—whether it is initiated by citizens or formulated by a legislature—before the measure can appear on the ballot. There is no citizen initiative in European nations comparable to the U.S. initiative, which allows American citizens to bypass the local or state legislature by collecting the legally required number of signatures on a petition to place a proposal on the ballot. Direct democracy in Europe more closely resembles the U.S. referendum process, in which voters approve or reject legislation or a constitutional amendment proposed or passed by the state or local legislature.

Another difference between direct democracy in Europe and in U.S. state and local governments is a European requirement related to voter turnout. Specifically, European nations require that a certain percentage of registered voters turn out on Election Day in order for a referendum vote to be binding. If the voter turnout threshold is not met, the vote does not count. Even if the majority of voters approve the proposal, it will not become law. In most European countries, the voter turnout required is at least 50 percent of registered voters. There is no such turnout requirement for referendum or initiative votes in the United States, where once a measure makes it to the ballot, the vote will be valid.

One final difference between the referendum as it is applied in Europe and the United States relates to which policy matters can be placed on the ballot for citizens to approve or reject. In Europe, citizens cannot use direct democracy measures to propose changes in the local government's policies on taxation and borrowing money (through the selling of government bonds). In contrast, a review of referenda and initiatives in the United States in the last four decades indicates that tax issues and bond issues are very common ballot measures. In fact, it was Proposition 13—a 1978 tax initiative in California proposing a limit on increases in local property taxes—that sparked the explosion in ballot measures in the United States.

In recent years, environmental protection and conservation have become issues of common concern in U.S. state and local government ballot measures (initiatives and referenda) and local referenda in European countries. Citizens and interest groups on both continents are using direct democracy to encourage environmental protection and sustainability.

Source: Michael Smith, "Is Direct Democracy Good for the Environment? A Re-examination of the Link from the Perspective of Central and Eastern Europe," presented at the When Voters Make Laws: How Direct Democracy Is Reshaping American Cities Symposium at the University of Southern California, April 7, 2007.

elected officials, they can turn them out of office by not reelecting them and, in some states, by recalling them.

Recall of Elected Officials

Another instrument of direct democracy in the United States is *recall*—a procedure allowing citizens to remove an elected official from office before the end of the individual's term. The recall is unique to about one-third of the states and 60 percent of cities; Figure 18.1 indicates which states have recall. Recall requires a legally specified number of signatures on a petition to force a vote. The number of signatures required is typically a percentage of the number of registered voters who participated in the last election for that office; 25 percent is the most common requirement.[5]

States vary as to how they handle the recall procedure and how they replace a recalled official. For example, in Wisconsin when citizens vote to recall an elected official, the state holds a subsequent primary election for the position and, later, a general election. In contrast, in California, on the same day that citizens cast their ballot in the recall election, they also vote to elect an official to replace the incumbent if the majority of voters approve the recall.

In 2003, more than 1.5 million Californians (well over the state-required minimum of 12 percent of the 2002 turnout, which required 900,000 signatures) signed a recall petition.[6] The recall petition charged Governor Gray Davis with "gross mismanagement of California finances by overspending taxpayers' money, threatening public safety by cutting funds to local governments, failing to account for the exorbitant cost of energy, and failing in general to deal with the state's major problems until they get to crisis stage."[7] On the same day that California voters approved Davis's recall, they selected former actor Arnold Schwarzenegger of *Terminator* fame from a field of 135 candidates to replace Davis.[8]

Between 1996 and 2001, 10 percent of U.S. cities had recall elections for either mayors or city council members. At the local level, recall measures are successful about one-third of the time. In comparison, at the state level, there have been fewer than two dozen recall elections of governors or legislators over the past one hundred years. The 2003 recall of Governor Davis was the first gubernatorial recall since North Dakota Governor Lynn J. Frazier was recalled in 1921, and only the second recall of a governor in U.S. history.[9]

Whereas the Constitution of the United States does not recognize or provide for direct democracy, state constitutions do allow for political decision making by the people on the state and local levels. A review of state constitutions and local charters highlights additional differences between national, state, and local operations.

Trust in State Government

How much trust do you have in the ability of your state government to address the problems and concerns of your state?

☐ A great deal
☐ A fair amount
☐ Very little

Source: "Issues Facing State, Local Governments Affect Public Trust," www.gallup.com/poll/9487/Issues-Facing-State-Local-Governments-Affect-Public-Trust.aspx.

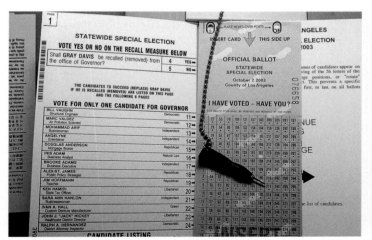

> The ballot for the 2003 special recall election of California Governor Gray Davis listed 135 candidates competing to replace Davis. To bolster their voter recognition, 5 of the 135 candidates, including the sitting lieutenant governor, Cruz Bustamante (first on the left) and syndicated columnist Arianna Huffington (second on the left), participated in a televised debate two months before the election.

State Constitutions and Local Charters

As we have seen, the U.S. Constitution gives legal authority to the national government for both the enumerated and the implied powers and distributes the reserved powers to the states. Each state's constitution, and the state laws written in compliance with it, defines that state's legal authority. This legal basis includes the state's authority to create local governments, which the U.S. Constitution does not mention at all. In this section, we first look at the basic components of state constitutions and their differences with respect to the U.S. Constitution. We then examine local **charters**—the constitutional documents approved by state governments to establish local governments.

charter
the constitution of a local government

The Elements of State Constitutions

Similarly to the U.S. Constitution, state constitutions include

- an enumeration of fundamental rights (bill of rights);
- a division of powers among three branches of government;
- an impeachment process;
- a constitutional amendment process.

Unlike the U.S. Constitution, the majority of state constitutions also contain

- allowances for direct democracy;
- provisions for the creation of local governments;
- provisions for public education;
- a balanced budget requirement;
- guidelines for conducting elections.

State constitutions typically offer greater fundamental rights than the U.S. Constitution guarantees. For example, although the U.S. Constitution does not prohibit discrimination in housing based on sexual orientation, the state constitutions of Connecticut, Hawaii, Maryland, Massachusetts, Minnesota, New Hampshire, New Jersey, New York, Rhode Island, Vermont, and Wisconsin do. Additional rights guaranteed by state governments do not violate the U.S. Constitution, which is the supreme law of the land, according to the principle of new judicial federalism (discussed in Chapter 3).

State constitutions are generally longer than the U.S. Constitution. The reason is that the U.S. Constitution presents only broad foundational principles and procedures, whereas the state constitutions spell out fundamental rights as well as details of policy matters—the latter, for example, in sections on educational policy and business regulation. In addition, state constitutions discuss local governments, which the U.S. Constitution does not mention at all.

Local Charters: How Much Local Discretion?

When a state government establishes a local government, the state government specifies the local government's structures, institutions, and responsibilities in a constitutional document called a charter. Traditionally, state governments wrote and approved local government charters that specified not only the structures but also the functions of local government. Under a court ruling that came to be known as **Dillon's rule,** articulated by Judge John Forrest Dillon in 1872, local governments are creatures of the state that created them, and as such,

Concept Summary

TWO FORMS OF ESTABLISHING LOCAL CHARTERS

— **Dillon's rule** limits the nature and extent of local government powers to those that the state-written and state-approved local government charter expressly enumerates as well as those necessarily implied by the expressed powers. In practice, Dillon's rule ensures that local governments have very little to no discretion over defining their powers and responsibilities.

— **Home rule** is a new relationship that has recently been created between states and the local governments they establish. Under home rule, states grant to citizens the opportunity to write, adopt, and amend local government charters, and in so doing, the state provides its citizens with some discretion in defining the nature and extent of the powers and structures of their local government.

they have only the powers expressly mentioned in their state-written and approved charters and those necessarily implied by the formally expressed powers.

In recent decades, however, most states have allowed for **home rule** by giving their citizens the opportunity to write, adopt, and amend local government charters at the city and county levels. A citizens' commission typically drafts these so-called **home rule charters,** which voters then accept or reject. These charters typically give the local government greater discretion in its activities than do state-developed charters. In comparison with local governments based on Dillon's rule, localities with home rule have discretion to determine the extent of their powers and responsibilities, as long as they comply with limits imposed by their state and by the U.S. Constitution.

Today, fifty state governments, each with its own constitution, and tens of thousands of local governments serve the diverse expectations and day-to-day needs of more than 300 million Americans.

Diversity in Political Cultures, People, Environments, and Resources

The national government is responsible for defense, foreign relations, interstate and foreign commerce, and promoting the general welfare—matters that affect the nation as a whole. By comparison, states and their local governments bear responsibility for the distinct day-to-day needs and demands of the people who live within their jurisdictions. Since the late 1970s, the federal government has relinquished much of its involvement in domestic issues, leaving state and local governments to step into the gap. The breadth of state and local policies, along with the size of their budgets and bureaucracies, is evidence of their increasingly central role in the lives of Americans.

The particular needs and demands each state and local government must address are the product of many factors, including residents' demographics (characteristics such as age, ethnicity, religion, income level, and educational attainment), the local environment, and resources. A state's resources (natural and financial resources alike), as well as its political culture, influence its capacity and willingness to meet the needs and demands of the people dwelling within its borders. The great diversity in people, environments, resources, and political cultures both within and across states affects the structures and public policies of state and local governments.

Political Culture and Its Effect on Governing

The dominant shared views among the people of a community concerning what the appropriate purposes and roles of government are, as well as who should participate in government, make up the *political culture*. Political scientist Joel Lieske has drawn on the work of Daniel Elazar, who distinguished among three types of political culture to explain state and regional differences in "political processes, institutional structures, political behavior, and policies and programs of state and local government."[10] The three political cultures Elazar identified are traditionalistic, individualistic, and moralistic.[11]

In a **traditionalistic political culture,** government's primary purpose is to preserve the status quo—to keep things as they currently are. Further, the expectation is that the participants in government should come from among society's elite, not from the population at large. States where a traditionalistic political culture dominates tend to have relatively lower voter turnout and lower levels of mass participation than other states. These states are also less likely to have provisions for direct democracy.

In an **individualistic political culture,** citizens view politics as a means by which an individual can improve his or her economic and social status. Those who participate in politics do so for their own benefit. In areas where an individualistic political culture dominates, the primary purpose of government depends on the goals of those who get involved,

Dillon's rule
the ruling articulated by Judge John Forrest Dillon in 1872 that local governments are creatures of the state that created them, and they have only the powers expressly mentioned in the charters written and approved by the state and those necessarily implied by the formally expressed powers

home rule
the opportunity provided by state government for citizens to write, adopt, and amend local government charters at the city and county levels

home rule charter
local government constitution written and approved by citizens following state-mandated procedures that include a referendum

traditionalistic political culture
the view that the purpose of government is to maintain the status quo and that participants in government should come from society's elite

individualistic political culture
the view that the decision to take part in government is an individual choice, and those who choose to participate determine the purpose of government and personally benefit from their participation

moralistic political culture
the view that the purpose of government is to serve the public good, including providing for those who are disadvantaged, and that all citizens should participate in government

so it is difficult to identify a pattern of government expenditures. These states also tend not to allow for direct democracy.

Concern for the collective good of society is the impetus for government action according to the **moralistic political culture.** In states dominated by this political culture, people feel an obligation to participate in government and to ensure that government is serving those who cannot provide for themselves. Mass political participation is common in such states, as are the processes of direct democracy. Voter turnout tends to be higher in states with a moralistic political culture than in those with traditionalistic or individualistic cultures.

Lieske extended Elazar's study of political culture to local governments. He identified ten subcultures that help to explain differences in political behaviors, policy preferences, and political institutions created by local governments. Lieske argued that the following socializing agents influence the political culture of a community of people: racial and ethnic kinship ties, value systems, and lifestyles.[12] In addition to these socializing agents, the local economy, distribution of income, life cycle, and environmental constraints, which include natural resources and climate, influence political culture.[13]

Because a community's political culture influences its governing processes, its people's political behavior and preferences, and ultimately public policy decisions, a diverse population and environmental factors yield a variety of public policies across states as well as within them.

People: Dealing with Demographics

Demographic differences from state to state and from locality to locality place varying demands on state and local governments. In Mississippi, 20 percent of the population live in poverty; in New Hampshire, about 6 percent do.[14] The greater the percentage of a state's population living below the poverty line, the greater the demand on state and local government budgets for safety-net provisions such as school lunch programs and subsidized housing. Similarly, the larger the proportion of children living in a state, the higher the demand for public elementary and secondary education. And the greater the proportion of a state's population that is elderly, the more extensive the need for Medicaid (the joint federal-state health insurance program for low-income citizens, which covers nursing home costs).

Another demographic difference that affects governmental expenditures can be seen in California, where about 40 percent of the residents speak a language other than English at home. This places demands on state and local governments to provide English as a Second Language (ESL) programs in public schools.[15] Because of this intrastate diversity, some school districts in California must cope with as many as forty different primary languages, while others need to handle two or three primary languages. Moreover, California residents need multilingual police officers, hospital workers, social workers, and emergency medical workers. West Virginia, where only about 3 percent of the residents speak a language other than English at home, does not have the same need for multilingual public servants and services.[16]

>Some states and localities are affected more than others by the growing number of people for whom English is not their first language. To provide services effectively to people who are not fluent in English, many state and local governments, as well as nonprofit organizations, must increasingly use the services of translators. In this health care clinic, a translator stands by during a well-baby exam of a Vietnamese child.

Environment and Resources: Variations in Needs and Tax Capacity

Climate significantly influences the demands citizens place on state and local governments and the services governments must provide for their citizens. States vulnerable to blizzards, tornadoes, and hurricanes all face unique demands, whether these be plowing and salting roadways in a snowstorm or alerting residents to a fierce approaching windstorm. State and local governments can address these localized problems more efficiently than the national government, but when climatic emergencies spread across state borders, the national government may need to step in.

Similarly, a region's natural resources affect public policies, the types of jobs available in the economy, and a government's ability to raise revenue (tax capacity). Oil is a natural resource that positively affects the economies of Texas and Alaska by creating jobs. Because the government can tax those who extract oil from the land, oil reserves also influence the tax policies in these states. A tax on the extraction of any natural resource, from fish in streams, to lumber in forests, to oil in the land, is a *severance tax*. Texas and Alaska raise so much revenue from their oil severance taxes that they are among the seven states that do not need to impose an individual income tax on their citizens in order to balance their budgets.

Many other examples illustrate the influence of climate and natural resources on a state's political and economic profile. The climate and natural resources of Hawaii have made tourism a vital industry there. The midwestern Plains states (Ohio, Indiana, Illinois, Michigan, Minnesota, and Wisconsin) are called America's breadbasket owing to the agricultural enterprise and related industries (such as food processing) that dominate the economies of those states. Compared with other states, Indiana has the greatest percentage of its labor force employed in manufacturing. The state policies needed to regulate and support each type of economic activity vary considerably, depending on whether farming, tourism, or manufacturing is the dominant industry.

Climate, natural resources, and the demographic profile of residents also affect a jurisdiction's tax base—its wealth, in the form of personal income, property, and other assets, that the government can tax. The financial resources of a government are a product of the tax base. Given the diversity of people, climate, and natural resources, as well as the diversity of political cultures that influences decisions about taxing and spending, it is not surprising that some states and localities have more money to spend than others do, which means that taxes and public services differ from state to state.

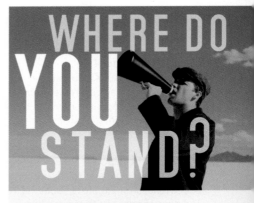

Oil and the Alaskan Wilderness

Would you support or oppose opening parts of the Alaska wilderness to explore for new sources of oil?

☐ Support

☐ Oppose

Source: FOX News/Opinion Dynamics Poll, www.pollingreport.com/energy2.htm.

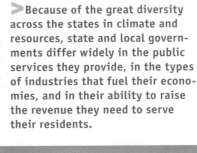

> Because of the great diversity across the states in climate and resources, state and local governments differ widely in the public services they provide, in the types of industries that fuel their economies, and in their ability to raise the revenue they need to serve their residents.

State and Local Government Budgets

operating budget
A budget that accounts for all the costs of day-to-day government operations and covers such items as salaries and benefits, utilities, office supplies, and rent

capital budget
A budget that accounts for the costs and revenues for expensive building and purchasing projects from which citizens will benefit for many years and for which governments can borrow money

essential services
Public services provided by state and local governments on a daily basis to prevent chaos and hazardous conditions in society

A government's budget is its central policy document. It reveals how the government is spending its financial resources and where it is getting the money to pay the bills. The constitutions of forty-nine states require state legislators to achieve a balanced budget. How do they approach this challenge? On what do state and local governments spend their money? From where do they get the revenue to balance their budgets?

Balanced Budgets

For forty-nine states and their local governments, the balanced budget requirement means that they must balance their **operating budgets,** which include all the costs of day-to-day government operations. That is, the government must raise enough money during the budget year, without borrowing, to pay for these expenses. In the case of governments, typical examples of operating budget expenditures include salaries and benefits, utility bills, office supplies, and rent. For a college student, food, entertainment, rent, car insurance, and gasoline are examples of operating expenditures.

Although state and local governments cannot borrow money to pay for their day-to-day operations, they can borrow money (go into debt) for *capital projects.* These include expensive building and purchasing projects from which citizens will benefit for many years. Because a state or local government typically cannot raise enough money through its taxes, user fees, and grants-in-aid in one year both to balance its operating budget and to build new highways, or to purchase new computer systems, states' laws allow them to borrow money to pay for these expensive projects. Such capital project expenditures and revenues are included in the **capital budget,** to which the annual balanced budget mandate does not apply. By comparison, the capital budget items of a college student include a car and college tuition.

State and Local Expenditures on Day-to-Day Domestic Matters

On what goods and services do state and local governments spend their money? Figure 18.2 shows the total expenditures of state and local governments in selected policy areas. This figure illustrates the diversity of services provided by state and local governments, most of them related to daily domestic matters, for these are the matters reserved to the states (and the local governments they create) by the Tenth Amendment of the U.S. Constitution.

State and local governments spend most of their money paying the salaries and benefits of their employees. The fifty state governments employ about 4 million people, and the 89,000-plus local governments employ more than 12 million.[17] These millions of state and local employees serve in just about every occupation imaginable, but many of them are involved in providing **essential services,** the everyday work required to prevent chaos and hazardous conditions in society. As long as they receive these services, citizens seldom think about them; but if they experience an interruption in even one essential service, they become alarmed, outraged, or seriously endangered or inconvenienced. Essential service providers include elementary and secondary schoolteachers, police officers, firefighters, sanitation workers, medical care personnel,

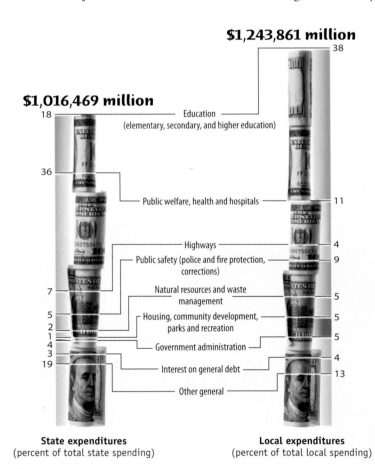

State expenditures
(percent of total state spending)

Local expenditures
(percent of total local spending)

FIGURE 18.2

Expenditures of State and Local Governments

Source: Calculated from U.S. Census Bureau, *Statistical Abstract of the United States: 2008,* *No. 422* (Washington DC: U.S. Government Printing Office, 2008).

and road and bridge maintenance crews. Let's take a close-up look at just a few of the essential services state and local workers provide: public education, public health, and public safety.

PUBLIC EDUCATION   State constitutions guarantee equal and effective education, and states typically create school districts (a type of local government) to provide elementary and secondary education. All states have a compulsory education law, which means that children must go to school until they achieve the age or grade level specified by their state government. The overwhelming majority of U.S. children attend public schools, with only about 10 percent in private schools and about 2 percent home schooled.[18] In view of the fact that almost 17 percent of the U.S. population is enrolled in public elementary and secondary schools at any given time, it is no wonder that the majority of local government employees are dedicated to providing elementary and secondary education.[19]

According to the National Center for Public Policy and Higher Education, in 2006, state and county governments provided higher education in 1,520 public colleges and universities, educating 78 percent of enrolled undergraduates.[20] The majority of these institutions (944) were two-year colleges. California had the highest number of public colleges and universities, with 110 two-year institutions and 34 four-year institutions. Rhode Island had the fewest, with 2 four-year public institutions and 1 two-year public institution.

In a comparison of policy costs, on average, educational policy makes up the largest proportion of state and local budgets. States vary widely, though, with respect to both the amount of money and the proportion of their budgets that they spend on public education. In the 2005–2006 school year, New Jersey spent the most—$13,781 per elementary and secondary school pupil. In that same year, Utah spent the least—$5,347 per pupil. Per-pupil state support of higher education in 2006 ranged from a high of $9,733 in Hawaii to a low of $2,361 in Colorado.[21]

Since the 1970s, lawsuits challenging state elementary and secondary school financing systems have become common. State courts have ruled intrastate inequities in spending between school districts to be in violation of state constitutions. More recently, state courts are determining whether states are providing an adequate education to all children. While courts focus on the results, states may need to increase their funding in order to provide the resources needed to offer an adequate educational experience.[22] "The Conversation of Democracy" explores the ongoing debate on the financing America's public schools.

PUBLIC HEALTH AND SAFETY   Another major responsibility of state and local governments is to ensure public health and safety, which involves a broad range of state and local government activity. Medicaid, for example, competes with education as the most expensive item in state budgets. Although rising Medicaid costs are ballooning state expenditures for public health, fewer state employees provide health services than education services.

Other public health- and safety-related protections funded at the state and local levels include the provision of safe drinking water and the proper disposal of garbage and sewage to prevent disease. State and local governments also establish building codes to ensure the safe construction of homes and other structures. They pass codes related to the use of smoke detectors, handrails on staircases, functioning fire escapes in high-rise buildings, and sanitary conditions in restaurants. They regulate personal behavior by means of criminal laws, speed limits, legal drinking ages, and laws specifying the blood alcohol content that defines "driving under the influence." State laws requiring the immunization of children before they are allowed attend school also promote public health and safety.

>State and local governments are responsible for essential services, including elementary and secondary education and the protection of public health and safety. One means of ensuring public safety is the regulation of individual behavior, such as the enforcement of state laws that prohibit driving under the influence of alcohol.

SHOULD STATE GOVERNMENTS BE RESPONSIBLE FOR FULLY FUNDING AN ADEQUATE PUBLIC ELEMENTARY AND SECONDARY EDUCATION FOR ALL CHILDREN?

The Issue: Children need a solid education in order to become financially self-sufficient adults who can contribute to society. The nation needs educated citizens to compete in the global economy. Historically, states delegated the responsibility for providing and funding elementary and secondary education to school districts or counties. Since the landmark Supreme Court decision in *Brown v. Board of Education of Topeka, Kansas* (1954; 1955), state governments have increased their involvement in education policy making and funding. Today, on average, approximately 48 percent of funding for schools comes from state, 43 percent from local, and 9 percent from national sources.* Many citizens are concerned about the range of spending per pupil across the states and even within each state. Nationwide, per-pupil expenditures range from $1,500 to $15,000.** This range suggests that not all children have access to a high-quality education. Therefore, parents, citizens, and some state courts have argued in favor of having state government be responsible for funding public education at the primary and secondary levels.

Yes: School districts where property values are low (poorer districts) do not collect the same amount of tax revenue as school districts where property values are high (richer districts), even if the tax rate in a poorer district is higher than the rate in a richer district. Therefore, relying on the property tax collected by school districts to fund a large proportion of public education leads to inequities in school funding. These funding inequities create unequal educational opportunities within a state and perpetuate class differences. This is a constitutional issue because each state constitution guarantees to all children in the state what numerous courts have described as an "adequate" education. Therefore, it is the responsibility of state governments, not local or national, to fully fund an adequate education for all children. Moreover, state governments have a greater capacity to raise revenue than do local governments.

No: Guaranteeing equal access to an adequate education does not mean that the state has to pay the full cost. State governments create local governments and delegate to them revenue-raising authority so that they can assist the state in serving the people. Therefore, the state government should first determine the cost of providing an adequate education and then grant money to school districts based on a formula that considers each district's property values and their tax rates—giving more money to poorer districts—to guarantee that all districts can meet the cost of an adequate education. Those districts that want to spend more than the state-determined "cost of providing an adequate education," and can raise more money through property taxes or some other means, will be allowed to do so. This method of sharing funds, based on a district's ability to pay, ensures that all children receive an adequate education and retains for the local governments policy-making leverage because they are contributing funding. If the state fully pays, the state will want to control policy.

Other approaches: The national government also has a responsibility to ensure that all children receive at least an adequate education. The national economy as well as the position of the United States among the world's leaders depend on it. In addition, the U.S. Constitution delegates to the national government the right to collect taxes to provide for the general welfare of the United States. Isn't the adequate education of all children vital to the general welfare? The national government has an even greater capacity to raise revenue than the states do. Because the national government has enacted laws requiring equal educational opportunities for all children, it should help to pay for that education.

What do you think?

① Typically, the government that funds the policy makes the policy. Which government do you think should make education policy, the national government, the state government, or the local school district? Explain your choice.

② What factors do you think a government would need to consider when calculating the cost of an "adequate" education? Would the cost be the same for every child? Would the cost be the same in every region of a state or the nation?

③ Should communities with more resources (richer communities) be able to spend more on public education, or should some of their resources be redistributed to poorer communities? Justify your answer.

* Kendra A. Hovey and Harold A. Hovey, *CQ's State Fact Finder 2007* (Washington, DC: CQ Press, 2007), p. 220.
** "Financing America's Public Schools," www.nga.org/cda/files/PUBLICSCHOOLS.pdf.

Since the terrorist attacks of 9/11, public safety—often now referred to as homeland security—has warranted increased attention from the national government. This attention has meant both new national policies and additional federal grant moneys for state and local governments, which employ first responders. The Department of Homeland Security, established in 2003, relies on the work of state and local police, firefighters, and emergency medical technicians to ensure domestic safety and security.

State Government Revenues

How do state and local governments raise the money needed to balance their operating budgets? Figure 18.3 shows the sources of state and local government revenues.

Other than grants-in-aid from the federal government, the largest revenue source for state governments (as a group) is the sales tax, although not all states impose a sales tax. Among the forty-five states that do collect a sales tax, the tax most commonly falls on purchases of goods, not on the costs of hiring someone—such as a lawyer, an accountant, or a hairdresser—to provide a service. Yet the states that tax purchased goods do not all tax the same goods or use the same tax rate. Take groceries, for example. Mississippi has a 7 percent sales tax on all groceries purchased. Virginia's sales tax on groceries is only 2.5 percent. Pennsylvania does not collect a sales tax on unprepared food purchased, but it does impose a 6 percent sales tax on ready-to-eat store- and restaurant-prepared foods.

Today debate is ongoing over the collection of sales taxes on Internet and online purchases. According to federal law, states can require only companies that have a physical presence in the state to collect sales taxes. So, if the vendor from which you make an Internet purchase is located in another state, your state government cannot force the vendor to collect a sales tax on the purchase. (Did you know that you, the purchaser, are legally obligated to pay this uncollected sales tax when you file your state taxes?) As the volume of Internet purchases continues to increase, and as citizens buy relatively fewer goods in local stores, many states are losing urgently needed sales tax revenue—and thus are vigorously lobbying for changes in the federal law. Another debate related to the sales tax is focusing on college textbooks. In this case, it is college students who are pressing for change (see "Doing Democracy").

State governments also raise money through excise taxes. These taxes on the purchase of gasoline, tobacco, alcohol, and other items aim not only to raise revenue, but also to reduce consumption of these products. In addition, state governments typically tax inheritances, large monetary gifts, and, as noted, the extraction of natural resources (severance taxes). Moreover, all but seven states—Alaska, Florida, Nevada, South Dakota, Texas, Washington, and Wyoming—collect personal income taxes.[23] How much money a state can raise through its mix of taxes (excluding the severance tax) is dependent on the income of its residents.

Beyond the variety of taxes they impose, states also raise revenue by charging fees for some of the services they provide, such as higher education (through tuition at state colleges and universities), hospital care, and solid waste removal and management. Some states, such as Pennsylvania and New Hampshire, even make money on the sale of liquor because they own the liquor stores in the state.

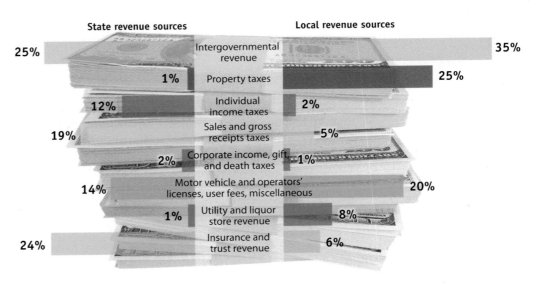

State revenue sources		Local revenue sources
25%	Intergovernmental revenue	35%
1%	Property taxes	25%
12%	Individual income taxes	2%
19%	Sales and gross receipts taxes	5%
2%	Corporate income, gift, and death taxes	1%
14%	Motor vehicle and operators' licenses, user fees, miscellaneous	20%
1%	Utility and liquor store revenue	8%
24%	Insurance and trust revenue	6%

FIGURE 18.3

State and Local Revenue Sources

Source: U.S. Census Bureau, *Statistical Abstract of the United States: 2008* (Washington, DC: U.S. Government Printing Office, 2007), Table 421.

DOING DEMOCRACY

LOBBY YOUR STATE LEGISLATORS FOR TAX-FREE TEXTBOOKS

FACT:

States vary as to whether they collect a sales tax on college textbooks. In addition to the five states that have no sales tax, eighteen states do not levy a sales tax on textbook purchases. Nine other states are considering dropping their sales tax on textbooks.* College students across Texas have been doing all they can to get the Texas state legislature either to drop the sales tax on textbooks entirely or to establish tax-free book-buying periods at the beginning of each college semester.

Act!

In November 2006, student government members from colleges throughout Texas convened in the state capital at Austin for the Texas Student Leaders Legislative Congress. The mobilized mass of students put the fight for tax-free textbooks at the top of their action agenda. On the designated "lobby day," student representatives met face-to-face with the legislators who represented the district where their college is located. Students unable to participate in lobby day were encouraged to lobby their legislators by sending postcards calling for tax-free textbooks. University of Texas students handed out packages of Ramen noodles—a widely consumed college survival food—outside the bookstore, along with informational sheets explaining that college students would save about $300 on average over the course of four years if they did not pay a sales tax on textbooks. The money saved would buy some 3,000 packages of Ramen noodles! Students at the University of Nebraska at Lincoln also staged a Ramen protest, building a mountain of noodles to draw attention to the high cost of textbooks. Texas Tech student body president Mark Laymon stressed that "this is one of the most important things you can

learn in college. Advocacy, how to get things done, how to organize people around issues, how to go about changing things in the political process. . . . This will really make a difference in students' lives."*

Where to begin

- Attend a student government meeting and request an opportunity to speak. Raise the issue of concern to you—whether it is tax-free college textbooks or something else—and encourage your student leaders to mobilize students to lobby legislators or to engage in public informational demonstrations such as the Ramen noodle mountain.
- **www.firstgov.gov**   You can link to your state government's Web site through this national government site. On your state's site you will find a tool that identifies state legislators based on addresses. Type in your school's address to find out which state legislator represents the district in which your school is located. Then start lobbying!

*Jon Schroeder, "Textbook Bills Gain Support Across Texas," *The Baylor Lariat*, March 1, 2007, www.baylor.edu/lariat/news.php?action=story&story=44369.

Local Government Revenues

How do local governments raise funds? A major revenue source for local governments is grants from their state government. The primary source of local government tax revenue, however, is the property tax. The property tax is imposed on the value of property a person owns (typically land and buildings, although some states also place a property tax on the value of household furnishings, clothing, and jewelry).

Unfortunately for local governments, the property tax is the most criticized tax, for several reasons. First, unlike the income tax, which (as a percentage of income) people view as based on their ability to pay, the property tax depends on the value of a person's property, which may not correlate with income and hence with that person's ability to pay. For people on a fixed income (such as Social Security), increases in property taxes mean they must pay a larger proportion of their income to hold on to their home. Further, unlike sales and income taxes, property taxes go up almost annually.

Owing to inflation, the operating costs of local governments rise every year. This increase occurs even when they are providing the same services as in the preceding year. Thus they need to raise more money each year if they are to balance their budgets. The way local governments collect more money is by increasing the property tax rate. Increases in the property tax rate take place through an annual vote (either by local government officials or by citizens in a referendum). Upon approval of the new tax rate, citizens receive a bill for their full property tax obligation and then write a check to pay the bill. This process makes the property tax a more "visible" burden to taxpayers than the sales tax, which people typically pay without much thought and do not track on an annual basis. It is also more visible than the income tax, which the government automatically deducts from individuals' paychecks, frequently without their close monitoring.

Recognizing that property taxes alone sometimes do not cover localities' full financial needs, state governments are increasingly allowing local governments to collect revenues through additional channels. Some state governments have given selected local governments the authority to collect sales taxes, and at least thirteen states allow some local governments to collect income taxes. The majority of states have authorized their local governments to collect fees for goods and services such as motor licenses, sewerage service, and utilities.

State and local governments differ with respect to the value of their available taxable resources, as well as in their decisions about which resources to tax, and at what rate. Because the governments of the fifty states and of the tens of thousands of U.S. localities have unequal financial capacities to provide for their citizens, they sometimes compete with each other for resources. For example, state and local governments vie with one another to attract new companies because the arrival of new firms means job creation, which expands the tax base. Newly created jobs mean more people working and thus more revenue raised through income taxes—and perhaps also through sales taxes because employed people usually have more money to spend than unemployed people do. To bring in new companies, state and local governments may provide tax breaks for businesses, or they may spend money on schools, parks, and improved public safety to enhance the quality of life in their communities. State and local governments also compete for national grant money that they can put toward balancing their budgets.

The Federal Government as a Fiscal Equalizer

The federal government offers state and local governments grants-in-aid to implement national policy preferences. It also provides grants to balance the interstate (among states) and intrastate (within a state) differences in financial capacity to meet the needs of the population at large. Through grant programs, which typically distribute more money to states and localities with the greatest mismatch between their resources and their citizens' needs, the federal government acts as a fiscal equalizer. Through its grants, the national government tries to ensure that all states can adequately serve their citizens.

For example, the national government distributes Medicaid grants to the states on the basis of a formula that ensures the greatest assistance goes to states with the lowest per capita income. Accordingly, in 2008, the federal budget covered 76 percent of Mississippi's Medicaid cost, based on data indicating that Mississippi had the lowest per capita income and the largest percentage of people in poverty among all the states. This was the highest national cost sharing for Medicaid among all the states. Twelve states received the lowest national cost sharing—50 percent—for Medicaid: California, Colorado, Connecticut, Delaware, Illinois, Maryland, Massachusetts, Minnesota, New Hampshire, New Jersey, New York, and Virginia.[24] Table 18.1 presents data on the amount of federal grant spending in ten states (the top and bottom five) for each dollar the state's citizens paid in federal taxes.

Recent decades have seen a decrease in federal assistance to state and local governments as the national government cuts back on its direct involvement in many domestic issues. State and local governments have had to increase their domestic policy efforts, forcing increases in their

TABLE 18.1

Federal Grant Spending per Dollar Paid by the State's Citizens in Federal Taxes, FY 2004

TOP FIVE: STATES RECEIVING THE MOST FEDERAL GRANT DOLLARS PER $1 OF FEDERAL TAXES PAID BY ITS CITIZENS

New Mexico	$2.00
Alaska	$1.87
West Virginia	$1.83
Mississippi	$1.77
North Dakota	$1.73

BOTTOM FIVE: STATES RECEIVING THE FEWEST FEDERAL GRANT DOLLARS PER $1 OF FEDERAL TAXES PAID BY ITS CITIZENS

Nevada	$0.73
Minnesota	$0.69
New Hampshire	$0.67
Connecticut	$0.66
New Jersey	$0.55

Source: Kendra A. Hovey and Harold A. Hovey, *CQ's State Fact Finder 2007* (Washington, DC: CQ Press, 2007), p. 139.

overall budgets and the size of their bureaucracies. In addition to increasing their role in domestic policy, states have obligations related to national politics that they share with their local governments.

Responsibilities of State and Local Governments in National Politics

The U.S. Constitution describes certain state obligations to the national government, and hence these are formal responsibilities. Other state responsibilities to the federal government have developed informally over time. In this section we explore the main formal and informal responsibilities of state and local governments to the national government.

States in National Politics: Formal Roles

The U.S. Constitution established state government authority in several areas of national import (all of which have been discussed in previous chapters):

- conducting national elections;
- determining the process by which electors for the Electoral College are selected;
- redrawing House districts (redistricting) after congressional reapportionment;
- ratifying amendments to the U.S. Constitution.

These are the formal roles of state governments in national politics. Today, most states delegate to local governments the responsibility of conducting elections, including those for national offices. In many states, there are ongoing efforts to reform the process of choosing electors for the Electoral College and redistricting. Both reform efforts are very controversial.

States in National Politics: Informal Functions

In addition to these constitutionally based roles for state governments, the states, by tradition, perform various informal functions in national politics and government. Two such functions are serving as a training ground for federal government officials and acting as a laboratory for innovative and experimental public policies.

TRAINING GROUNDS FOR NATIONAL OFFICE   Since 1921, the overwhelming majority of members of Congress have had prior local or state government experience, or both. In 2004, 61 percent of the candidates for the House of Representatives and 26 percent of Senate candidates were current or former state legislators. In 2005, 54 percent of the 435 House members had previously served as state legislators.[25] Presidents also develop experience serving in state government.

Political scientists have identified three common pathways to the presidency over the course of U.S. history: the Senate, the vice presidency, and a governorship. Four of the last five presidents—Jimmy Carter, Ronald Reagan, Bill Clinton, and George W. Bush—used their position as governor as a steppingstone to the White House. President Reagan said that being governor "was the best training school for" the presidency.[26] Reagan's vice president, George H. W. Bush, successfully ran for the presidency in 1988, but prior to his success, no sitting vice president had been elected to the presidency since Martin Van Buren in 1836. Yet Americans widely view their vice president as in training for the presidency because the second-in-command is only "a heartbeat away" from the office. Since 1960, forty-four senators have run for the presidency, and only two have won. Therefore, for the last four decades, governorships have served as the primary training ground for presidents.

Although career politicians typically advance from local to state to national positions, sometimes the movement occurs in the other direction—from national to state office. In 2008, ten sitting governors had previous experience serving in Congress.[27] That national officials are running for governor suggests a growing prestige for the gubernatorial office.

LABORATORIES FOR NEW PUBLIC POLICIES   State and local governments are worth watching if you are looking for new and innovative public policies. States and localities develop creative policies to deal with domestic matters that are reserved to them by the Constitution, as well as to carry out the authority for policy making that the national government devolves to them through mandates and grants (as discussed in Chapter 3). State and local governments also set policies for domestic problems they believe the national government is not addressing appropriately. In particular, state governments are leading the way with innovative programs for environmental protection and health care.

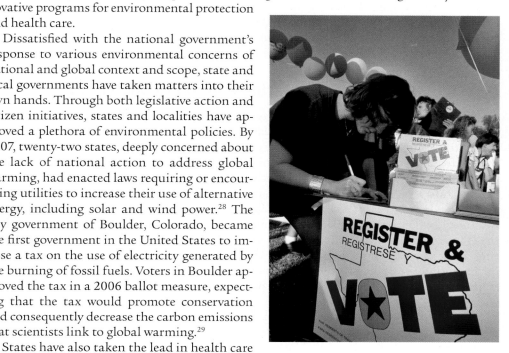

Dissatisfied with the national government's response to various environmental concerns of national and global context and scope, state and local governments have taken matters into their own hands. Through both legislative action and citizen initiatives, states and localities have approved a plethora of environmental policies. By 2007, twenty-two states, deeply concerned about the lack of national action to address global warming, had enacted laws requiring or encouraging utilities to increase their use of alternative energy, including solar and wind power.[28] The city government of Boulder, Colorado, became the first government in the United States to impose a tax on the use of electricity generated by the burning of fossil fuels. Voters in Boulder approved the tax in a 2006 ballot measure, expecting that the tax would promote conservation and consequently decrease the carbon emissions that scientists link to global warming.[29]

> Although the Constitution guarantees the right to vote to citizens 18 years old and older, each state government establishes the voter registration requirements for its citizens. These state-specific requirements typically include a residency requirement (for example, a person must live in the state for at least thirty days before registering to vote) and the need to register a specified number of days before the election (typically thirty days). A registered voter who moves must re-register in order to vote.

States have also taken the lead in health care policy making, stepping in when the national government has failed to deliver. While serving as First Lady (1993–2001), Hillary Rodham Clinton had worked diligently, but unsuccessfully, for a national universal health care plan. The plan was to institute publicly funded, national medical services that would cover most or all of the health care expenses of citizens who do not have their own, private health insurance. Subsequently, in 2006, Massachusetts became the second state, after Vermont, to pass legislation aimed at providing health care to all state residents. Minnesota, Maryland, and California are currently drafting their own universal health care plans.[30] In addition, with support from federal Medicaid funding, state governments across the country have experimented with programs that provide health insurance specifically to children.

States monitor each other's experiments closely. When policy makers in a given state see an innovative program working effectively, they often adopt it, making the necessary adjustments to meet the distinct needs of their own citizens. In turn, the national government sometimes adopts successful state programs, as in 1996 when Congress passed the Personal Responsibility and Work Opportunity Reconciliation Act, a national welfare reform bill that combined components of several experimental state welfare programs.

In summary, as the national government has placed ever-greater demands on state and local governments without always providing sufficient funding to address crucial policy issues, the states have become more creative in devising appropriate public policy solutions. States are also addressing problems when concerned citizens are not satisfied with the remedies provided—or not provided—by the national government. Finally, when an innovative policy works in one state, other states, and even the national government, are often inclined to adopt it.

Having surveyed the constitutional basis of state and local governments, as well as their responsibilities to their citizens and the nation, we now examine the structures and institutions by which state and local governments exercise their authority. Because no two states and no two local governments are identical, we will focus on the most common structures and institutions.

Institutions of State Government

The state constitutions in effect at the time of the ratification of the Articles of Confederation (1781) and the U.S. Constitution (1789) had all established three branches of government with a system of checks and balances. This state government structure became the model for the national government created by the U.S. Constitution. Although the constitutions of all the states have been amended numerous times over the centuries, and many have been totally replaced several times, the basic structures of state governments have not changed. Each state government's structure is unique, but the legislative, executive, and judicial institutions of all the states share several common characteristics that we now consider.

Legislative Branch: Formulating and Approving Policy

The basic functions of state legislatures resemble those of their federal counterpart, Congress. The primary functions of state legislatures are policy formulation and policy approval. In addition, state legislatures monitor the executive branch's implementation of policy. Further, individual state legislators, like members of Congress, assist their constituents in solving problems they may be experiencing with the various levels of government.

The state legislature, typically called the General Assembly, is bicameral (two chambered) in all states except Nebraska, which has a unicameral (single chamber) legislature. A state with a bicameral legislature commonly calls the chamber that has more members the House, and the smaller chamber the Senate. Nebraskans call their unicameral legislature the Senate. The number of legislators in each state legislature varies widely. The figure in "Exploring the Sources" presents the number of legislators per million people, for each state. As you can see from the graphic, the number of state legislators does not correlate with the state population.

State senators usually serve a four-year term of office; state representatives, a two-year term. Fifteen states have set term limits for legislators—incumbents can run for reelection for the same position only a set number of times. Not surprisingly, citizens (not state legislators) took the lead in establishing most of these term limits, using the state's initiative processes.

There is generally more diversity of gender, ethnicity, and race among state legislators than among national legislators. In 2007, for example, 23.5 percent of the total number of state legislators (7,382) were women (1,733 legislators). In Vermont, 37.8 percent of the legislators were women, but in South Carolina, only 8.8 percent of the lawmakers were women.[31] The predominance of a moralistic political culture (see page 654) appears to correlate with higher proportions of women elected to state legislatures, as does the presence in the population of relatively high numbers of educated, professional women—women who are more likely to have a sense of political efficacy and are more willing and able to run for office.

The racial and ethnic diversity within a state's population generally correlates with the diverse composition of its state legislature.[32] In 2007, about 8 percent of all state legislators were African American.[33] Mississippi, Alabama, and Georgia had the highest proportion of African Americans in their state legislatures: 24 percent. These states are first, third, and sixth (respectively), when states are ranked based on the proportion of African Americans in their population.[34] Nine states—Hawaii, Idaho, Maine, Montana, North Dakota, South Dakota, Utah, West Virginia, and Wyoming—had no African American legislators. All of these states, except West Virginia, are in the bottom ten states when ranked by the proportion of African Americans in their population.[35] As for Latino state lawmakers, in 2007 New Mexico's legislature had the largest representation, with 39 percent in the legislature.[36] New Mexico is also the state with the largest proportion of Latino residents.[37] Fourteen states had no Latino legislators. Overall, 3 percent of state legislators were Latino.[38]

Unlike members of the U.S. House and Senate, the overwhelming majority of state legislators (85 percent) serve on a part-time basis. Most state legislatures convene annually from January to May or June. Seven state legislatures convene only every other year.

Regardless of the variations from state to state with respect to the number of legislators, their terms of office, their demographic characteristics, and whether the job is full- or part-

EXPLORING THE SOURCES

HOW REPRESENTATIVE IS EACH STATE'S LEGISLATURE?

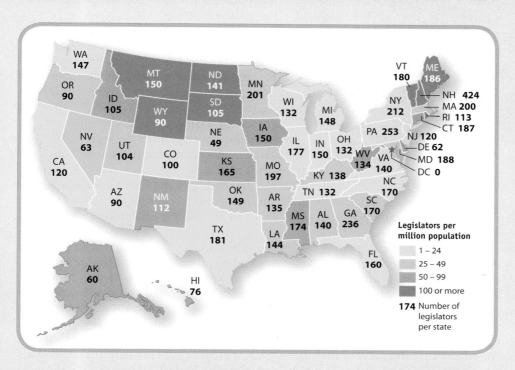

WA 147
OR 90
MT 150
ND 141
MN 201
VT 180
ME 186
ID 105
WY 90
SD 105
WI 132
MI 148
NY 212
NH 424
MA 200
RI 113
CT 187
NV 63
UT 104
NE 49
IA 150
PA 253
NJ 120
DE 62
CA 120
CO 100
KS 165
MO 197
IL 177
IN 150
OH 132
WV 134
VA 140
MD 188
DC 0
AZ 90
NM 112
OK 149
AR 135
KY 138
TN 132
NC 170
SC 170
TX 181
LA 144
MS 174
AL 140
GA 236
FL 160
AK 60
HI 76

Legislators per million population

- 1 – 24
- 25 – 49
- 50 – 99
- 100 or more

174 Number of legislators per state

As the map shows, the state's population does not determine the number of state legislators. In the case of New Hampshire residents, 324 legislators represent every 1 million people. For Californians, only 3 legislators represent every 1 million people.

Evaluating the Evidence

① After you examine the map, review Figure 18.1. Assuming that you are interested in having your voice heard by your elected officials, which state would you rather live in? Why?

② Considering all the figures in this chapter, discuss the geographic pattern of states that provide greater levels of democracy—as in government by and for the people.

③ On the basis of the figures in this chapter, which states would you characterize as having a moralistic political culture? Explain.

---

time, all state legislatures have the same primary function: to formulate public policy. Further, they all share with their state's governors the authority to approve public policy as part of the system of checks and balances that accommodates the separation of basic governing functions. Approved state policy is put into action by employees of the executive branch.

Executive Branch: Putting Policy into Action

The executive branch of state government implements public policy. Approximately 4 million people work in the executive branches of the fifty state governments. In addition to those who directly implement policy, states have numerous appointed and elected executive branch officials who assist in formulating policy and supervising its implementation.

Unlike citizens voting in the national presidential election, who elect individuals to only two executive branch positions (the presidency and the vice presidency), citizens in almost all states have the opportunity to elect people to *several* of the state executive branch positions. **Plural executive system** refers to a government structure in which citizens elect

plural executive system
A state and local government structure in which the citizens elect more than two people to top positions in the executive branch of government

FIGURE 18.4

Total Number of Statewide Elected Officials for Each State

Source: State totals from Kendra A. Hovey and Harold A. Hovey, *CQ's State Fact Finder 2007* (Washington, DC: CQ Press, 2007), p. 113.

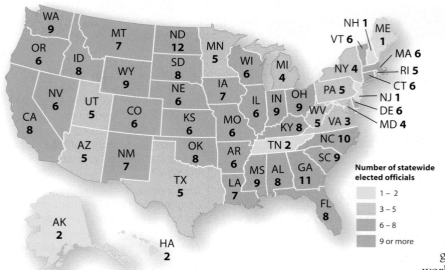

more than two officials to the executive branch (Figure 18.4). While the average number of statewide elected executive officials is seven, North Dakota elects the most (11). Each statewide elected executive branch official oversees a specific policy or functional area of state government, with the governor bearing responsibility for the remaining areas. The more elected statewide executive officials, the more people with whom the governor must share authority—and hence the weaker the governor.

GOVERNOR   The best-known elected official in state government is the governor. (Can you name your governor? What about your state legislators?) For one thing, unlike the majority of state legislators, the governor is a full-time official. Moreover, the governor gets more media coverage than do legislators. Thus citizens can more easily learn about and track the governor's positions and actions than they can the work of their elected state legislators. Once the majority of legislators approve a bill, the governor can sign it into law or reject it with a veto. The governor's one vote—to approve or to reject a bill—draws more media attention than does the vote of any individual legislator.

Just as the president launches the budget process by presenting Congress with a proposed budget, the majority of governors begin the state budget procedure by drafting an executive budget they put before the state legislature. Compared to Congress, state legislatures typically have more limits on their authority to modify the executive budget. On the basis of the modified executive budget, the legislature writes specific appropriation bills that provide for the spending of money by state departments and agencies. Most governors can use a line-item veto, the authority to eliminate one or more funding lines in appropriation bills while approving the remainder of the bill, on these appropriation bills. The line-item veto is a tool that governors can and do wield to balance the state budget.

Once a bill becomes law, the governor must ensure its efficient, effective, and legal implementation. To this end, governors have the authority to appoint numerous people to top positions in the executive branch. In addition, governors can reorganize the departments and agencies in the executive branch to improve their efficiency and performance in implementing the law. Governors can also mandate specific activities and procedures on the part of executive branch bureaucrats by issuing executive orders.

In another responsibility of gubernatorial office, the governor serves as commander in chief of the state's National Guard. In this capacity, the governor can call on the National Guard to respond to state emergencies and crises, including natural disasters (for example, floods, blizzards, landslides, and hurricanes), civil unrest (such as riots), and terrorist attacks (such as those on 9/11).

While the nation elected its first minority male president in 2008, and has never elected a woman to serve as president, a diversity of gender, race, and ethnicity is evident among the nation's governors. In 2008, eight of the fifty governors were women, and four were minority men (two African Americans, one Asian American, and one Latino).[39] Due to the plural executive structure of state government, there are many more opportunities for citizens to get elected to executive positions on the state than on the national level.

OTHER STATEWIDE ELECTED EXECUTIVES   States vary with respect to both how many elected executive branch officials they have and what positions these officials hold. All but eight states elect lieutenant governors, who typically have three constitutionally defined responsibilities, including being a heartbeat away from the governorship.

The lieutenant governor is in line to succeed the governor if the latter is unable to complete the term of office. States without the lieutenant governor position designate some other elected official to succeed a governor who cannot complete his or her term. Lieutenant governors also typically act as the president of their states' senates, presiding over Senate meetings and casting tie-breaking votes.

More than forty states have plural executive systems, which typically include the state attorney general, secretary of state, treasurer, and auditor. What are the responsibilities of these officials? The attorney general is the chief law enforcement officer in the state and represents the state in lawsuits. The secretary of state is the official record keeper. In addition to maintaining the legislative records, administrative rules, executive orders, and constitutional changes, the secretary of state keeps records of information relevant to elections, such as campaign finance reports, petitions by candidates to get on the Election Day ballot, and lists of registered voters. The state treasurer pays the state's bills, and the auditor reviews state spending to ensure that it is legal, efficient, and effective.

> On March 17, 2008, New York Lieutenant Governor David Paterson was sworn in as governor, replacing Eliot Spitzer after Spitzer resigned. Paterson, who is legally blind, became the first African American governor of New York. Governor Paterson stands beside New York City Mayor Michael Bloomberg, between the U.S. flag and the New York State flag.

The statewide executive officials elected by citizens do not serve under the governor. Elected independently of the governor, they may even be members of a political party other than the governor's party. Because they serve for fixed terms (usually four years) and must satisfy the voters, not the governor, if they are to win reelection, these officials need not be loyal to the governor's priorities. The majority of state executives elected statewide, including governors, have term limits—usually a limit of two consecutive terms.

Judicial Branch: Resolving Questions of Law

In addition to electing state legislators and (on average) seven state executive branch officials, citizens in most states also elect judges to serve in the state court system. Each of the fifty states has its own court system that is independent of the national judicial system. State judges must uphold their state's constitution and the U.S. Constitution. Lawsuits that involve state and local laws are resolved in state courts. If such cases also involve questions of federal law or the U.S. Constitution, they may move into the federal court system.

State courts hear thousands more criminal and civil cases than do the national courts. In the process of resolving these cases, state judges may have to interpret the meaning of laws and previous court decisions. State judges also have the authority of judicial review; that is, they can declare acts of the state and local legislative and executive officials to be unconstitutional.

STRUCTURE OF STATE COURT SYSTEMS   Although the primary responsibilities of the courts across the fifty states are the same, judicial structures and procedures differ from state to state. Here, we look briefly at certain commonalities in judicial organization and process.

Like the national government's court system, all state courts have either original jurisdiction or appellate jurisdiction. *Trial courts* have *original* jurisdiction: they are responsible for determining whether the accused person is guilty or not guilty based on the evidence presented in court. All states have two levels of trial courts. The lower-level trial courts hear

	Jurisdiction	Type	Judges
Court of last resort	Appellate	Bench only	Panel, most commonly elected
Intermediate appeals court	Mandatory appellate	Bench only	Panel, most commonly merit selection process
Major trial courts	Original and *de novo* from minor trial courts*	Jury or bench	One judge, most commonly elected
Minor trial courts	Original	Bench	Judge, most commonly elected

* Note: *De novo* because no written transcript is kept of the proceedings in minor trial courts; when there is an appeal there must be a new trial, and this is conducted in the major trial court.

POLITICAL INQUIRY

FIGURE 18.5 ■ STRUCTURE OF STATE COURT SYSTEMS Why are most judges in state courts elected, particularly at lower levels? How qualified are voters to select judges? What are the advantages and disadvantages of each type of selection?

nonpartisan election
an election in which candidates are not nominated by political parties and the ballot does not include party affiliations

partisan election
an election in which candidates are nominated by political parties and the ballot lists each candidate's political party affiliation

merit selection process
a process for selecting judges in which a nonpartisan committee nominates candidates, the governor or legislature appoints judges from among these candidates to a short term of service, and then the appointed judges face a retention election at the end of the short term

retention election
a noncompetitive election in which an incumbent judge's name is on the ballot and voters decide whether the judge should be retained

less serious cases than do the upper-level trial courts. In contrast to trial courts, *appellate courts* have *appellate* jurisdiction: they review the legality and fairness of trial and lower appellate court procedures and decisions in the cases brought to them through an appeal. Thus appellate courts do not determine guilt. Rather, they ensure due process through their review of judges' decisions made in lower courts—decisions on issues such as what evidence lawyers can submit for jurors to consider and what questions lawyers can ask of witnesses. The appellate judges review trial transcripts and lawyers' arguments to determine whether the judges made the correct decisions. The majority of states have two levels of appellate courts: the intermediate-level court and the court of last resort. Figure 18.5 summarizes the structure and selection process for the state court systems.

Judges decide what laws mean and ensure due process. How are judges selected to ensure that they have the proper qualifications for this essential role in our democracy?

JUDGES Whereas the president appoints and the Senate confirms national judges, the states use a variety of methods to select their judges. Some states use one selection process for trial judges and a different procedure for appellate judges. State judges may be (1) elected, (2) appointed, or (3) chosen through a process that combines an initial appointment with a subsequent retention election. Each state's law specifies the judicial selection procedure(s) the state will follow, which are the subject of frequent civic conversation and debate.

In states that grant judgeships through an electoral process, voters typically select judges through a nonpartisan election, a type of election not used at the national level of government. In a **nonpartisan election,** the candidates are not selected by a political party, and party affiliations do not appear on the ballot. In contrast, in a **partisan election,** political parties select candidates, and the ballot lists each candidate's party affiliation. State governments adopted nonpartisan judicial elections during the Progressive Era of the late 1800s and early 1900s—the same era when state governments were adopting direct democracy. Progressive reformers maintained that nonpartisan elections would encourage voters to pay greater attention to the candidates' qualifications than to their party affiliations and limit the influence of party organizations on both election outcomes and public policy.

Debates over appointing versus electing judges, and over partisan versus nonpartisan judicial elections, have led more and more states to adopt a **merit selection process,** which combines an initial appointment with a subsequent election. Proponents of this selection method believe that it combines the best of the electoral and appointive processes. Although merit selection procedures vary from state to state, they have some common elements. The process usually begins with the governor appointing citizens to a nonpartisan nominating committee. The nominating committee sends a list of qualified judicial candidates to the governor, who then appoints judges from the list of nominees. After a one- or two-year term, the appointed judge stands for a noncompetitive **retention election,** in which the judge runs unopposed and voters vote "yes" to keep the judge on the bench or "no" to remove the judge. Typically, a vote to retain the judge means a second term of eight or ten years. At the end of the term, the judge must again go through a retention election to remain on the bench.

The question of which government each judge actually works for can be a source of confusion for citizens. Even though voters elect trial judges to hear cases that arise in one city, borough, township, or county, the state government typically funds all of the trial courts, as well as the appellate courts, in the state. Hence individuals who appear to be city or county judges are in fact judges working in the state court system at large. Local governments do not have a separate judicial branch. Some local governments do not even have distinct legislative and executive branches. Instead, one governmental body (a council, a commission, a board, or an authority) has authority for both the legislative and executive functions, as we next consider.

Local Governments

Scholars categorize local governments as either *general-purpose* or *single-purpose* governments on the basis of the variety of services they dispense. Most citizens live within the borders of at least two general-purpose local governments (such as a county and a municipal government) and at least one single-purpose local government (typically a school district). In this section we differentiate among these general-purpose and single-purpose governments.

General-Purpose Local Governments

As the term suggests, **general-purpose government** provides numerous and varied services, in multiple policy areas, to the people living within its borders. The fifty states have 39,044 such governments, yet not all states have all varieties of general-purpose governments.[40] Municipal, township, and county governments are three forms of general-purpose governments.

Municipal governments are self-governing political jurisdictions created by states to provide goods and services to a densely populated area within the state. Municipal governments include city, borough, and town governments. These governments provide day-to-day services and benefits to citizens. **Townships,** which also deliver day-to-day services, are units of government that serve people living outside municipalities, in rural areas where the population is more dispersed than in areas served by municipal governments.

Day-to-day services provided by municipal and township governments include public safety, zoning regulations for land use, road maintenance, parks and recreation, and libraries. The larger the population of a municipality or township, the more numerous and diverse the services its government provides. Very large cities may have their own mass transportation systems, colleges, hospitals, and jails. Townships and smaller municipalities typically do not provide such services. Instead, county governments may provide these services in the less densely populated areas in which townships and smaller municipalities are located.

Most states initially created **county governments** to assist with the implementation of state policy in geographic subdivisions of the state. Although historically county governments were not self-governing and did not make many of their own public policies, the picture is changing. Today's county governments are taking on increased responsibilities and engaging in more policy making than in years past. County governments provide a growing list of services and benefits, including law enforcement, corrections, highway maintenance, property assessment, tax collection, the recording of legal documents (from voter registration to land transactions), higher education, nursing home care, parks and recreation, and land use planning. Because a single county typically contains numerous municipalities and townships, the services rendered by each of these general-purpose local governments somewhat depend on the services that are delivered by geographically overlapping governments.

There are three basic structures of general-purpose governments. These forms are differentiated by the way the executive and legislative functions are distributed among elected and appointed government officials.

In the **commission** form, which is more common in county and township governments than in other general-purpose governments, voters elect a body of officials who collectively hold the legislative and executive reins of the government. In this form of general-purpose government, there is no independently elected chief executive, and so the commission oversees day-to-day government affairs.

general-purpose government
a government providing services in numerous and diverse policy and functional areas to the residents living within its borders

municipal government
self-governing general-purpose government—including city, borough, and town governments—created by states to provide goods and services within a densely populated area

township
a unit of government that serves people living outside municipalities, in rural areas where the population is more dispersed than in areas served by municipal governments

county government
a general-purpose local government created by states to assist them in implementing policy in geographic subdivisions of the state

commission
a form of local government that is more common in county and township governments than in other general-purpose governments and for which voters elect a body of officials who collectively hold legislative and executive powers

ON THE JOB

JUSTIN TAYLOR, MAYOR

Name: Justin M. Taylor

Age: 30

Hometown: Carbondale, Pennsylvania

Colleges: Luzerne County Community College, University of Scranton

Majors: Fire Protection (AAS), Criminal Justice, Public Administration and Public Affairs (BA)

Job title: Mayor and city administrator (manager) of Carbondale, Pennsylvania

Salary range for jobs like this: $60,000–$80,000

Day-to-day responsibilities: As mayor, I'm responsible for executing, administering, and enforcing all city legislation; preparing and overseeing all fiscal operations; conducting research to improve city government; and developing procedures that promote efficiency in government. More specifically, I spend most of my days meeting with citizens, businesses, and other government officials and working on economic development projects and incentive legislation and programs.

How did you get your job? I won election to the position of mayor, which was a part-time office at the time. A referendum process gave me the position of city administrator as well, a full-time office for which I was qualified.

What do you like best about your job? Working with a great staff that understands that good, progressive government needs to run like a business and not a bureaucracy. I also like making real progress transforming one of Pennsylvania's greatest small communities.

What is your least favorite aspect of your job? Governing a small city that has limited resources. So many things need to be fixed or addressed, and the city has not reinvested in itself in about forty years. Knowing that we can't please everyone, I still wish we could take care of every problem that exists, because the vast majority of the problems are valid.

What advice would you give to students who would like to do what you are doing? I would say . . . get involved in your community—at a very early age! The more you know, and the more people you meet, the easier time you'll have getting into politics. Also, get educated—not just at college but locally. Understanding the history of certain issues and relating to what the people actually want will give you sound footing to start a life in public service.

---

council-mayor (council-executive)
a form of general-purpose local government comprising (1) a legislative body elected by voters and (2) an independently elected chief executive

strong mayor
an elected municipal government executive who holds the powers traditionally delegated to elected chief executives (veto power, power to formulate the budget, and power to appoint many executive branch officials)

weak mayor
an elected municipal government executive who holds few, if any, of the powers traditionally delegated to elected chief executives

The **council-mayor** form of municipal government is comparable to the **council-executive** form of county government, with both composed of a legislative body, elected by voters, and an independently elected chief executive. Within the council-mayor form of government, political scientists differentiate strong mayors from weak mayors. **Strong mayors** have the traditional powers delegated to elected chief executives (veto power, power to formulate the budget, and power to appoint many executive branch officials). **Weak mayors** have fewer, if any, powers traditionally delegated to elected chief executives.

The **council-manager** (also called **commission-administrator**) form of government, found in many counties and the majority of cities, features an elected body with legislative and executive powers; this council, or commission, hires a professional manager/administrator to oversee the government's daily operations. The appointed manager has no authority to vote on policy but does advise the elected council members on policy matters.

Of course, there are hybrids of these three basic forms of general-purpose government. One such hybrid exists in Carbondale, Pennsylvania, where the part-time, weak mayor successfully campaigned for a referendum in which the voters agreed to delegate to him the full-time position of city administrator (see "On the Job").

As national and state governments have devolved more responsibilities to general-purpose local governments, and as citizens' demands for services have mounted, general-purpose governments have sought to lighten their workload and decrease their spending. One approach they have used is to establish collaborative working relationships with one or more other local governments in their region. One type of collaborative relationship is a **Council of Governments (COG),** which is a regional agency composed of representatives from several local governments that are sharing resources to address one or more mutual problems. Another type of collaboration is the consolidation of services. In this case, two or more local governments provide services to their communities through one unit, such as a joint police department. In some cases, two local governments have also been consolidated into one. However, voters in most states must approve the consolidation of existing local governments through a referendum, and in the majority of cases, voters do not approve such consolidations because they do not want to lose the local government they know. Voters also fear consolidation will mean poorer quality services.[41]

In contrast to these collaborative approaches to lightening their burden, general-purpose governments (individually or collectively) can create a new government and delegate to it one specific responsibility, such as fire protection or the management of the sewer system. The newly created local government, with one specific responsibility—known as a single-purpose government—is an independently functioning entity.

Growth in Local Governments by Type

	1967*	1987*	2007**
National	1	1	1
State	50	50	50
County	3,049	3,042	3,033
Municipal, town, and townships	35,153	35,891	36,011
School districts	21,782	14,721	13,051
Single-purpose	21,264	29,532	37,381
Total	81,299	83,237	89,527

WHAT'S NEXT?

> Will the conditions that encourage general-purpose governments to create new single-purpose governments change any time in the near future?

> If the number of single-purpose governments continues to grow, what might cause citizens to become more aware of them and to pay more attention to them?

> Will cost concerns encourage citizens to support the consolidation of more local government services, and even consolidation of local governments?

* U.S. Census Bureau, *Statistical Abstract of the United States, 2006,* 125th ed. (Washington, DC: U.S. Government Printing Office, 2005), Table 415.
** U.S. Census Bureau, *2007 Census of Governments,* "Local Government and Public School Systems by Type and State," www.census.gov/govs/cog/GovOrgTab03ss.html.

Single-Purpose Local Governments

Tens of thousands of general-purpose local governments exist, but there are even more single-purpose governments, and the number keeps growing. A **single-purpose government** provides one service or function to the people living within its borders. The most visible of these governments are school districts. Political scientists usually discuss school districts separately from other single-purpose governments because there are so many of them and because state, not local, governments created them. The number of school districts varies tremendously from state to state; Texas has 1,089, and Virginia has only one. In addition to the 13,051 school district governments in the United States, there are 37,381 other single-purpose governments.[42]

Single-purpose governments typically have a structure comparable to the commission form of general-purpose government and fall into two types: districts and authorities. The most common distinction between a district and an authority is that a district can impose and collect taxes to pay for its services, but an authority cannot do so. Instead, the authority must raise money by selling or renting its services or resources. For example, a water authority sells water, a sewer authority charges for the use of sewers, and a parking authority charges for its parking spaces. In addition, because authorities do not have to deal with

council-manager (commission-administrator)
a form of general-purpose local government found in many counties and the majority of cities; it is composed of an elected body with legislative and executive powers whose members hire a professional manager to oversee the government's day-to-day operations

Council of Governments (COG)
a regional agency composed of representatives from several local governments who share resources to address one or more mutual problems

single-purpose government
a government providing services in one policy or functional area to residents living within its borders

the same personnel and financial constraints that general-purpose governments must confront, they have more flexibility in their operations.

Most people are aware of the general-purpose local governments under which they live. Few, however, know much about the single-purpose governments in their community, other than the school district. Moreover, because the NIMBY (not-in-my-backyard) syndrome is alive and well, people rarely take advantage of the open meetings conducted by government—national, state, general-purpose local government, or single-purpose local government—until or unless an action (or a proposed action) of government negatively affects them. Yet democratic governments rest on the principle that government is *by* and *for* the people. For many citizens, the *by* dimension creates an obligation to participate at least reactively, if not proactively. State and local governments provide countless, rich opportunities for citizen participation.

CONCLUSION   *CONTINUING THE CONVERSATION*

State governments were governing before the Articles of Confederation were ratified in 1781. The Tenth Amendment to the U.S. Constitution (1791) affirmed that state governments retained all the powers and responsibilities they had under the Articles that had not been delegated to the federal government through the Constitution. Therefore, state governments, and the local governments they create, have historically been the front-line providers of essential and daily domestic public services.

At the turn of the twentieth century, state and local governments began to adopt direct democracy processes (initiative, referendum, and recall) to enhance as well as check the outcomes of representative democracy—specifically, policy making by elected officials. Since California's Proposition 13 (1978), citizens increasingly are using direct democracy processes. In recent decades, state and local governments have experimented with more and more innovative policies to address nationwide problems. If a policy is successful, other local and state governments, as well as the national government, will often adopt it. Today, state and local governments are central to the American way of life. They are the focal points for much political conversation, policy innovation, and citizen attention and participation.

A more diverse population will necessarily require more from state and local governments, which will need to adapt essential and daily domestic public services to meet the needs of their specific populations. Can they continue to provide the quality and quantity of services citizens expect at a time when federal financial support is decreasing and ballot measures are calling for limits on taxing and spending? Will states continue to experiment with public policies that address nationwide problems, or will questions that have recently been raised about the constitutionality of state immigration and environmental policies allow the federal government to clamp down on state innovation? Will the successes of initiatives and referenda at state and local levels, coupled with recent economic downturns and discontent with national spending on the war on terrorism, encourage a conversation about adopting direct democracy processes at the national government level? How might the Internet foster such a conversation? Does the Internet remove some of the barriers to direct democracy at the national level?

Summary

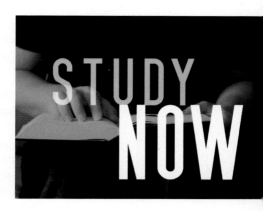

1. Direct Democracy: Letting the People Decide

State and local governments give U.S. citizens opportunities for direct democracy that are not available in the national government. All states provide for some form of referendum, and about 40 percent of the states also provide for citizen initiatives. In addition, about one-third of the states allow citizens to recall elected state officials with whom they are dissatisfied.

2. State Constitutions and Local Charters

Each state has its own constitution, which authorizes state legislators to create local governments through the process of approving local government charters. According to Dillon's rule, the responsibilities of local governments are limited to only those specified in their charters. In recent decades, state governments have expanded their use of home rule charters, approved by local voters, that provide local governments with greater discretion.

3. Diversity in Political Cultures, People, Environment, and Resources

The great diversity in the fifty states affects the demands placed on state and local governments. It also influences the political processes and the policy choices of these governments, as well as their financial capacity. The more than 89,000 state and local governments operating in the United States can better address this diversity than could one national government.

4. State and Local Government Budgets

Although the U.S. Constitution does not require the national government to balance its budget, state constitutions do mandate balanced state and local operating budgets. The ability of state and local governments to provide the day-to-day services for which they are responsible, many of which are essential to public safety and health, depends on their tax base. Because some states and localities have smaller tax bases than do others, the federal government takes on the role of fiscal equalizer to support those with weaker financial capacities.

5. Responsibilities of State and Local Governments in National Politics

The Constitution delegates to state governments a role in national elections, in the redistricting of national House districts, and in the ratification of amendments to the U.S. Constitution. In addition, state and local governments provide future national officials with government experience, and they test innovative public policies that, if successful, other state and local governments and even the federal government might adopt.

6. Institutions of State Government

Although the institutions of the fifty states share certain commonalities, such as a system that balances power among three branches of government, each state government is unique. In addition, state governments differ from the national government in that most states have a plural executive system and most elect rather than appoint state judges.

7. Local Governments

One useful way to differentiate among local governments in the United States is to categorize them as either general-purpose or single-purpose governments. General-purpose governments, which include cities, counties, boroughs, and townships, dispense a variety of services to their citizens. Single-purpose governments, such as school districts that provide elementary and secondary education, deliver one specific service to their citizens.

For Review

1. How does direct democracy differ from representative democracy?

2. Differentiate between Dillon's rule and home rule.

3. Explain how diversity in political culture, people, and resources puts different demands on state and local governments and hence leads to different policies.

4. What essential services do state and local governments provide?

5. Describe two informal functions of the states in national politics.

6. Identify some differences between the three branches of national government and the three branches of state governments.

7. Differentiate between general-purpose governments and single-purpose governments, and give examples of each.

For Critical Thinking and Discussion

1. Which of the many governments that you have interacted with has had the biggest impact on your life to date? What government will have the greatest impact on you after you graduate from college? In your retirement years?

2. Think about the distinctions the text makes among traditionalistic, individualistic, and moralistic political cultures. What would you say is the dominant political culture on your college campus? What is it in your home community? Do you think it would be possible to change these political cultures? Explain.

3. What would be the impact on state and local governments, as well as citizens, if the national government stopped acting as a fiscal equalizer?

4. Given the growth of the international direct democracy movement, do you think Congress would approve, and the states would ratify, an amendment to the U.S. Constitution that authorizes the use of direct democracy (initiative, referendum, and recall) at the national level of government? Explain why or why not.

5. Because the U.S. Constitution establishes minimums in terms of civil rights, states can establish additional rights, such as a voting age lower than 18. Some have called for states to lower the voting age to 16 years old for school board elections. Present an argument in support of this proposal. Present an argument against this proposal.

6. Given the fiscal stress that all governments (national, state, and local) are experiencing, note one national, one state, and one local public service that you are willing to have eliminated? Discuss the negative impacts of your proposed cuts.

7. Voter participation in state and local elections is lower than in national elections. What do you think explains this phenomenon? Discuss one proposal for local government action that you think might increase voter participation in local elections.

MULTIPLE CHOICE: Choose the lettered item that answers the question correctly.

1. All of the following are direct democracy processes except
   a. electing government officials.
   b. initiative.
   c. recall.
   d. referendum.

2. The direct democracy process that includes *citizens* drafting public policy, which is then placed on the Election Day ballot, is called
   a. initiative.
   b. legislative referendum.
   c. popular referendum.
   d. recall.

3. Higher levels of voter turnout occur in states dominated by a(n)
   a. individualistic political culture.
   b. moralistic political culture.
   c. traditionalistic political culture.
   d. libertarian political culture

4. A state's capital budget can include the costs for all of the following items except
   a. bridge and highway construction.
   b. computer systems purchases.
   c. state office buildings construction.
   d. salaries and benefits.

5. The primary source of tax revenue for state governments is
   a. excise taxes.
   b. personal income taxes.
   c. property taxes.
   d. sales taxes.

6. The primary source of tax revenue for local governments is
   a. excise taxes.
   b. personal income taxes.
   c. property taxes.
   d. sales taxes.

7. On average, citizens elect people to the greatest number of positions in
   a. the national executive branch.
   b. the national legislative branch.
   c. the state executive branch.
   d. the state legislative branch.

8. All of the following are examples of general-purpose local governments except
   a. boroughs.
   b. cities.
   c. counties.
   d. school districts.

9. The fastest growing category of government is
   a. municipal government.
   b. single-purpose government.
   c. state government.
   d. township.

10. Three branches of government are clearly identifiable in
    a. national, state, and local governments.
    b. national and state governments.
    c. state and local governments.
    d. only the national government.

FILL IN THE BLANKS.

11. The California tax-reform ballot measure known as _____ is credited with sparking an increase in citizen use of ballot measures that began in the 1980s and continues today.

12. In forty-nine states the _____ budget, which covers the costs of day-to-day government functions, must be balanced.

13. The everyday public services provided by state and local governments that are required to prevent chaos and hazardous conditions are collectively labeled _____ services.

14. The overwhelming majority of states have a _____ system that allows voters to elect, on average, seven state executive officials.

15. In a _____ election, candidates are not selected by political parties and the Election Day ballot does not list the candidates' party affiliations.

Answers: 1. a; 2. a; 3. b; 4. d; 5. d; 6. c; 7. c; 8. d; 9. b; 10. b; 11. Proposition 13; 12. operating; 13. essential; 14. plural executive; 15. nonpartisan.

RESOURCES FOR RESEARCH AND ACTION

Internet Resources

American Democracy Now Web site
www.mhhe.com/harrison1e   Consult the book's Web site for study guides, interactive activities, simulations, and current hot-links for additional information on state and local government.

Census Bureau's Quick Facts
http://quickfacts.census.gov   This site is your one stop for state-by-state statistics.

Council of State Governments
www.csg.org   A resource for state governments, this site offers training for state leaders and information on the best innovative approaches to the problems confronting states. This Web site also offers current news regarding government in all fifty states.

The Initiative and Referendum Institute
www.iandrinstitute.org   Located at the University of Southern California, this site offers up-to-date information on initiatives and referenda in the states as well as in various foreign nations. The site also provides information on the history and status of initiative and referendum mechanisms in all fifty states.

The National Council of State Legislators
www.ncsl.org   This site is a resource for state governments and individuals interested in improving state government operations and understanding state issues, as well as issues of federalism and intergovernmental relations.

The National Governors Association
www.nga.org   This site is a source of information on governors, collaborative lobbying efforts of governors, and the impact of national laws on state governments.

Stateline: Where state policy and politics news clicks
www.stateline.org   A public service funded by the Pew Charitable Trusts, Stateline reports on state-by-state politics and policy news. It publishes its reports every weekday except holidays.

Recommended Readings

Beyle, Thad L. *State and Local Government: 2007–2008.* Washington, DC: CQ Press, 2007. The most recent edition of an annually updated collection of news articles on the problems and concerns that state and local governments are confronting. Each section begins with an analysis of the most important issues relevant to that section's topic. Topics include politics, media, state institutions, and local governments.

Elazar, Daniel J. *American Federalism: A View from the States,* 2nd ed. New York: Harper & Row, 1972. The seminal work on the political cultures of states.

Hovey, Kendra A., and Harold A. Hovey. *CQ's State Fact Finder 2007.* Washington, DC: CQ Press, 2007. Sourcebook for information on all fifty states and the District of Columbia. Covers taxes, government employment, the impact of the national government's role as fiscal equalizer, and finances.

Kaufmann, Bruno, and M. Dane Waters. *Direct Democracy in Europe.* Durham, NC: Carolina Academic Press, 2004. A comprehensive guide to Europeans' more than 200 years of experience with the initiative and referendum processes.

Maddex, Robert L. *State Constitutions of the United States,* 2nd ed. Washington, DC: CQ Press, 2006. A comprehensive overview of the constitutions of all fifty states, U.S. territories, and Washington, D.C. Covers constitutional history, fundamental rights, branches of government, amendment procedures, special provisions such as direct democracy, and trends in constitutional reforms.

Van Horn, Carl. *The State of the States,* 3rd ed. Washington, DC: CQ Press, 1996. A collection of readings that provide a solid overview of the important issues confronting state governments and the behavior of state governmental institutions in the 1980s and early 1990s.

Movies of Interest

The Town That Was (2007)
This film tells the story of the battle in the 1980s between the people of Centralia, Pennsylvania, and the state government over the state's decision to raze the town and relocate its 1,600 citizens. State officials argued that these drastic measures would cost less than the estimated half-billion dollars needed to extinguish the coal mine fire burning below the town since 1962. The film centers on John Lokitis, the youngest of the eleven remaining Centralia residents.

All the King's Men (2006)
Based on a novel by Robert Penn Warren, this film follows the career of Willie Stark, a southern politician running for governor, who woos the citizens of Louisiana with promises of policies to support the lower economic classes. The novel loosely re-creates aspects of the life of Louisiana governor Huey Long.

Kingfish: A Story of Huey P. Long (1995)
This made-for-TV movie portrays the life and career of controversial Louisiana governor Huey Long. Was Long a hero working for the low-income and poorly educated citizens of Louisiana or a corrupt and dangerous politician whose radical policies led to his assassination in 1935?

Jaws (1975)
This popular super-thriller traces the battle between the new, yet experienced, police chief and the mayor over how to handle the crisis posed by a great white shark feasting in the waters off their small island resort town as the Fourth of July approaches. The chief, hired to protect the town's people and tourists, wants to close the beach. The mayor puts tourism and the needed revenue it will bring to the town above the people's safety.

National Journal

GENEROUS TO A FAULT

It's not that Vallejo doesn't need tough, experienced cops and seasoned firefighters. It's just that the midsize California city can't afford the jaw-dropping salaries it has been lavishing on them: Vallejo is broke.

Even within the pricey San Francisco Bay region, the city's generous payments to public safety workers stand apart: $306,000 a year in pay and benefits for a police captain (six times what the average schoolteacher in Vallejo earns); $171,000 for the average firefighter. Vallejo's city manager earns nearly $317,000, more than Vice President Cheney.

"All of our salaries are too high," says Mayor Osby Davis, a real estate and probate lawyer, whose part-time city job pays just $10,000 a year. The cure, he hopes, is to declare bankruptcy.

After nearly two years of contract talks and months of difficult debate, the mayor and council decided last month that it's worth the stigma of being the largest city in California history to seek bankruptcy protection if that gets Vallejo out from under its crushing financial commitments.

and greater demand for city services during hard times. But Vallejo's situation might turn out to be worse than most.

Bankruptcy lawyers are divided over whether Vallejo will become a trendsetter, especially during a rocky economic period. "It's anyone's guess," says Vallejo's bankruptcy adviser, Marc Levinson. "Whether other cities may be in such extremus, we don't know. The economy is what the economy is. Vallejo is not unique; it's just the first."

All California cities are in a special bind: They can't just jack up property taxes because their income isn't covering their bills. Proposition 13, which California voters passed in 1978, caps the taxes on residential property at 1 percent of the assessed value. And "assessed value" can rise only 2 percent a year until the property is sold.

"Proposition 13 is the third rail of politics in California," says Chris Hoene, director of policy and research for the National League of Cities. "You just don't touch it."

Hammered by the housing downturn, especially in the state's southern reaches,

nual survey of municipalities that it will release in July. "I don't think city finances are in the tank yet," Hoene said. "I don't know whether we'll see a round of bankruptcies in this case," he added, "but the circumstances will be similar around the country in terms of the revenue shortfalls that a lot of cities will be dealing with in the next few years."

Taking the temperature of city budgets can begin with a sweeping scan of state coffers. The Rockefeller Institute reports that nine states' tax revenues have plummeted compared with revenues for the first quarter of 2007. The states in trouble are Arizona, Florida, Georgia, Montana, North Carolina, Oklahoma, Rhode Island, South Carolina, and Utah.

Looking ahead to fiscal 2009, the Center on Budget and Policy Priorities examined projected shortfalls between what states need to maintain current services and the money they'll have on hand, plus the projected revenues they could tap. The center's analysts concluded that more than half the states will have to retrench to stay in the black.

"The problem started out with sales tax revenues being hit hard," said CBPP analyst Elizabeth McNichol. "People were not buying houses and not buying new materials for those houses, not consuming." Because the economy kept slowing and more people lost jobs, a more complete picture of the impact on states will emerge when the income-tax collection data from April are dissected. Many economists are anticipating dour news.

The responsibility for new schools, hospitals, and many social services rests largely with the states and cities, whose traditional sources of revenue are real estate and general sales taxes. In the last recession, Washington distributed more Medicaid money and other aid to the states to goose the economy and, as a result, helped localities avoid deeper cuts in health programs, McNichol added. That has not been the federal response this time, at least not yet.

The mayor and council decided last month that **it's worth the stigma of being the largest city in California history to seek bankruptcy protection** *if that gets Vallejo out from under its crushing financial commitments.*

Economists and budget-watchers who specialize in state and local governments say that although more than half the states are being squeezed, it's too early to know how much pain the economy's downturn will cause cities. Few are likely to escape unscathed, judging from the ominous mix of mounting costs for energy, food, and petroleum-based products (think asphalt); declining property-tax and sales tax revenues; rising pension and health care commitments to public workers;

California's state government is struggling to patch a $15 billion to $17 billion budget gap and is cutting programs in most areas, including education, welfare, and health care. Cities throughout the state are braced for the eventual effects.

Budget experts are waiting expectantly to get a better read on how cities are adjusting their balance sheets. The National League of Cities, for example, is gathering data about fiscal conditions as part of a large an-

Analysts believe that states will face added turmoil triggered by their long-range spending commitments for retiree health care and pensions—agreements reached in rosier times, when property values floated up like hot-air balloons. Cities are in the same situation.

Vallejo is not alone in its budget troubles. The National Conference of State Legislatures said that Georgia as a whole can weather the current downturn if it taps its reserve funds but that Atlanta might not be so fortunate. The city has flat or declining revenues and rising pension and health care costs that now swallow a quarter of its budget. For the fiscal year that begins on July 1, Atlanta officials anticipate a budget gap of about $140 million. Local news accounts describe the situation faced by Mayor Shirley Franklin as a "crisis."

Meanwhile, Alabama's Jefferson County informed banks late last winter that it would have trouble repaying debt for its sewer system and making payments on related interest-rate swaps. As credit markets faltered, Jefferson County was ensnared by financial products that became too rich for its dwindling budget.

In the Midwest, Detroit is in the fourth year of a structural deficit, now estimated at $58 million. "Detroit wasn't ever not struggling, but it's worse now," says Kim Rueben, an Urban Institute public finance economist.

On May 27, the Detroit City Council approved a $3 billion budget for fiscal 2009, opting to deficit-borrow its way out of the city's budget hole using $78 million in fiscal stabilization bonds to be sold late this year if officials fail to identify other revenue sources. The hope, however vague or overly optimistic, is that the revenue picture will somehow improve, justifying the decision to borrow rather than slash spending.

Cities with severe financial problems are nothing new, of course. More than 30 years ago, New York City memorably struggled with national economic stresses, dwindling revenue options, and urban upheaval. Local officials warned that with a $300 million shortfall and an inability to repay loans, the city risked insolvency and elimination of essential services if it did not get federal and state assistance. Bankruptcy was averted in 1975 with the grudging help of President Ford, the state Legislature, and other backers. But the city's obligations were spread out over years, and New York did not recover its preferred investment-grade ratings for two decades.

In 1991, Bridgeport, Conn., became the largest city ever to file for Chapter 9 bankruptcy protection. With 142,000 residents, Bridgeport faced a $12 million gap in a $304 million budget. The mayor and other city officials failed in their attempts to claw the $12 million out of the unions through contract concessions and saw bankruptcy protection as an alternative to what it anticipated would be an unwelcome state order to hike property taxes by as much as 18 percent. At the time, the city faced $220 million in general-obligation debt.

Although it never declared bankruptcy, San Diego weathered notorious budget problems. It went astray by repeatedly underfunding its pension obligations after being rocked by a recession in 1990 and losing much of its tax base when the defense industry shrank after the Persian Gulf War. With an approving wink from the unions, city officials survived the lean years by putting aside too little for future obligations, promising to add benefits to those contracts in the outyears. San Diego was like a condemned man who insists on tying his own noose.

By the summer of 2005, the city was in a crunch that residents could feel. Munici-

pal workers were laid off. Swimming pools closed. Libraries cut their hours. And San Diego abandoned hopes for new construction and basic maintenance. The municipal pension fund was in arrears by $1.7 billion. Mismanagement and misdeeds triggered federal investigations, litigation, and expensive settlements, all of it capped by a voter revolt, recounts journalist Roger Lowenstein.

Vallejo Mayor Davis believes that California cities are in for rougher times. "I think it's a matter of time before an awful lot of cities in this state consider this same thing, and it's because we all have the same sort of contracts," he says. The relevant unions are opposing bankruptcy, arguing that the city doesn't qualify and has other fiscal options.

Two fire stations had to be closed. Workers were laid off. Residents must leave messages with an automated emergency number when they call for help.

As far back as 1993, Vallejo's leaders realized that the costs of negotiated contracts were rising so sharply that they would outpace the city's revenues by 2010, the mayor added. A citizen's committee had studied the data and created a chart to illustrate precisely when the city would run out of money. Nothing happened. The general fund drained away, and Vallejo is now awash in $17 million of red ink, according to the city's filing with the court. By the time Davis became mayor in December, he says, the city was desperate for change: "Crisis is the time to re-evaluate."

A fresh start is what he hopes bankruptcy will give Vallejo. "Within five years, we'll see something totally different," he gushed, describing the city's ambition to build an orthopedic college, a cancer research center, and a convention center near the interstate.

"Come to Vallejo!" the mayor urged. "We're right by the water. We're in the middle of everything!"

■ **THEN:** Most local governments balanced their budgets and operated within their means despite economic difficulties.

■ **NOW:** Under the pressures of budget mismanagement and the economic downturn some cities are looking to escape their financial commitments.

■ **NEXT:** Will California repeal Proposition 13 or look for means other than raising property taxes to balance the budget?
Will bankruptcy offer an increasing number of cities an alternative means of resolving their financial obligations?
Will localities seek more help from the state or federal government to manage their finances in a tough economy?

THE DECLARATION OF INDEPENDENCE

In Congress, July 4, 1776

THE UNANIMOUS DECLARATION OF THE THIRTEEN UNITED STATES OF AMERICA

When in the Course of human Events, it becomes necessary for one People to dissolve the Political Bands which have connected them with another, and to assume, among the Powers of the Earth, the separate and equal Station to which the Laws of Nature and of Nature's God entitle them, a decent Respect to the Opinions of Mankind requires that they should declare the Causes which impel them to the Separation.

We hold these Truths to be self-evident, that all Men are created equal, that they are endowed, by their Creator, with certain unalienable Rights, that among these are Life, Liberty, and the Pursuit of Happiness.—That to secure these Rights, Governments are instituted among Men, deriving their just Powers from the Consent of the Governed, that whenever any Form of Government becomes destructive of these Ends, it is the Right of the People to alter or to abolish it, and to institute new Government, laying its Foundation on such Principles, and organizing its Powers in such Form, as to them shall seem most likely to effect their Safety and Happiness. Prudence, indeed, will dictate, that Governments long established, should not be changed for light and transient Causes; and accordingly all Experience hath shewn, that Mankind are more disposed to suffer, while Evils are sufferable, than to right themselves by abolishing the Forms to which they are accustomed. But when a long Train of Abuses and Usurpations, pursuing invariably the same Object, evinces a Design to reduce them under absolute Despotism, it is their Right, it is their Duty, to throw off such Government, and to provide new Guards for their future Security. Such has been the patient Sufferance of these Colonies; and such is now the Necessity which constrains them to alter their former Systems of Government. The History of the present King of Great-Britain is a History of repeated Injuries and Usurpations, all having in direct Object the Establishment of an absolute Tyranny over these States. To prove this, let Facts be submitted to a candid World.

He has refused his Assent to Laws, the most wholesome and necessary for the public Good.

He has forbidden his Governors to pass Laws of immediate and pressing Importance, unless suspended in their Operation till his Assent should be obtained; and when so suspended, he has utterly neglected to attend to them.

He has refused to pass other Laws for the Accommodation of large Districts of People, unless those People would relinquish the Right of Representation in the Legislature, a Right inestimable to them, and formidable to Tyranny only.

He has called together Legislative Bodies at Places unusual, uncomfortable, and distant from the Depository of their public Records, for the sole Purpose of fatiguing them into Compliance with his Measures.

He has dissolved Representative Houses repeatedly, for opposing with manly Firmness his Invasions on the Rights of the People.

He has refused for a long Time, after such Dissolutions, to cause others to be elected; whereby the Legislative Powers, incapable of Annihilation, have returned to the People at large for their exercise; the State remaining, in the mean Time, exposed to all the Dangers of Invasion from without, and Convulsions within.

He has endeavoured to prevent the Population of these States; for that Purpose obstructing the Laws for Naturalization of Foreigners; refusing to pass others to encourage their Migrations hither, and raising the Conditions of new Appropriations of Lands.

He has obstructed the Administration of Justice, by refusing his Assent to Laws for establishing Judiciary Powers.

He has made Judges dependent on his Will alone, for the Tenure of their Offices, and the Amount and Payment of their Salaries.

He has erected a Multitude of new Offices, and sent hither Swarms of Officers to harrass our People, and eat out their Substance.

He has kept among us, in Times of Peace, Standing Armies, without the Consent of our Legislatures.

He has affected to render the Military independent of and superior to the Civil Power.

He has combined with others to subject us to a Jurisdiction foreign to our Constitution, and unacknowledged by our Laws; giving his Assent to their Acts of pretended Legislation:

For quartering large Bodies of Armed Troops among us:

For protecting them, by a mock Trial, from Punishment for any Murders which they should commit on the Inhabitants of these States:

For cutting off our Trade with all Parts of the World:

For imposing Taxes on us without our Consent:

For depriving us, in many Cases, of the Benefits of Trial by Jury:

For transporting us beyond Seas to be tried for pretended Offences:

For abolishing the free System of English Laws in a neighbouring Province, establishing therein an arbitrary Government, and enlarging its Boundaries, so as to render it at once an Example and fit Instrument for introducing the same absolute Rule into these Colonies:

For taking away our Charters, abolishing our most valuable Laws, and altering fundamentally the Forms of our Governments:

For suspending our own Legislatures, and declaring themselves invested with Power to legislate for us in all Cases whatsoever.

He has abdicated Government here, by declaring us out of his Protection, and waging War against us.

He has plundered our Seas, ravaged our Coasts, burnt our Towns, and destroyed the Lives of our People.

He is, at this Time, transporting large Armies of foreign Mercenaries to complete the Works of Death, Desolation, and Tyranny, already begun with Circumstances of Cruelty and Perfidy, scarcely paralleled in the most barbarous Ages, and totally unworthy the Head of a civilized Nation.

He has constrained our fellow Citizens taken Captive on the high Seas to bear Arms against their Country, to become the Executioners of their Friends and Brethren, or to fall themselves by their Hands.

He has excited domestic Insurrections amongst us, and has endeavoured to bring on the Inhabitants of our Frontiers, the merciless Indian Savages, whose known Rule of Warfare, is an undistinguished Destruction, of all Ages, Sexes and Conditions.

In every Stage of these Oppressions we have Petitioned for Redress in the most humble Terms: Our repeated Petitions have been answered only by repeated Injury. A Prince, whose Character is thus marked by every Act which may define a Tyrant, is unfit to be the Ruler of a free People.

Nor have we been wanting in Attentions to our British Brethren. We have warned them, from Time to Time of Attempts by their Legislature to extend an unwarrantable Jurisdiction over us. We have reminded them of the Circumstances of our Emigration and Settlement here. We have appealed to their native Justice and Magnanimity, and we have conjured them by the Ties of our common Kindred to disavow these Usurpations, which would inevitably interrupt our Connections and Correspondence. They too have been deaf to the Voice of Justice and of Consanguinity. We must, therefore, acquiesce in the Necessity, which denounces our Separation, and hold them, as we hold the Rest of Mankind, Enemies in War, in Peace Friends.

We, therefore, the Representatives of the UNITED STATES OF AMERICA, in General Congress Assembled, appealing to the Supreme Judge of the World for the Rectitude of our Intentions, do, in the Name, and by Authority of the good People of these Colonies, solemnly Publish and Declare, That these United Colonies are, and of Right ought to be, Free and Independent States; that they are absolved from all Allegiance to the British Crown, and that all political Connection between them and the State of Great-Britain, is and ought to be totally dissolved; and that as Free and Independent States, they have full Power to levy War, conclude Peace, contract Alliances, establish Commerce, and to do all other Acts and Things which Independent States may of Right do. And for the Support of this Declaration, with a firm Reliance on the Protection of Divine Providence, we mutually pledge to each other our Lives, our Fortunes, and our sacred Honour.

John Hancock.

NEW-HAMPSHIRE
Josiah Bartlett
William Whipple
Matthew Thornton

MASSACHUSETTS BAY
Samuel Adams
John Adams
Robert Treat Paine
Elbridge Gerry

RHODE ISLAND
Stephen Hopkins
William Ellery

CONNECTICUT
Roger Sherman
Samuel Huntington
William Williams
Oliver Wolcott

NEW YORK
William Floyd
Philip Livingston
Francis Lewis
Lewis Morris

NEW JERSEY
Richard Stockton
John Witherspoon
Francis Hopkinson
John Hart
Abraham Clark

PENNSYLVANIA
Robert Morris
Benjamin Rush
Benjamin Franklin
John Morton
George Clymer
James Smith
George Taylor
James Wilson
George Ross

DELAWARE
Caesar Rodney
George Read
Thomas McKean

MARYLAND
Samuel Chase
William Paca
Thomas Stone
Charles Carroll

VIRGINIA
George Wythe
Richard Henry Lee
Thomas Jefferson
Benjamin Harrison
Thomas Nelson, Jr.
Francis Lightfoot Lee
Carter Braxton

NORTH CAROLINA
William Hooper
Joseph Hewes
John Penn

SOUTH CAROLINA
Edward Rutledge
Thomas Heyward, Jr.
Thomas Lynch, Jr.
Arthur Middleton

GEORGIA
Button Gwinnett
Lyman Hall
George Walton

November 22, 1787
JAMES MADISON

TO THE PEOPLE OF THE STATE OF NEW YORK:

Among the numerous advantages promised by a well constructed Union, none deserves to be more accurately developed than its tendency to break and control the violence of faction. The friend of popular governments never finds himself so much alarmed for their character and fate, as when he contemplates their propensity to this dangerous vice. He will not fail, therefore, to set a due value on any plan which, without violating the principles to which he is attached, provides a proper cure for it. The instability, injustice, and confusion introduced into the public councils, have, in truth, been the mortal diseases under which popular governments have everywhere perished; as they continue to be the favorite and fruitful topics from which the adversaries to liberty derive their most specious declamations. The valuable improvements made by the American constitutions on the popular models, both ancient and modern, cannot certainly be too much admired; but it would be an unwarrantable partiality, to contend that they have as effectually obviated the danger on this side, as was wished and expected. Complaints are everywhere heard from our most considerate and virtuous citizens, equally the friends of public and private faith, and of public and personal liberty, that our governments are too unstable, that the public good is disregarded in the conflicts of rival parties, and that measures are too often decided, not according to the rules of justice and the rights of the minor party, but by the superior force of an interested and overbearing majority. However anxiously we may wish that these complaints had no foundation, the evidence, of known facts will not permit us to deny that they are in some degree true. It will be found, indeed, on a candid review of our situation, that some of the distresses under which we labor have been erroneously charged on the operation of our governments; but it will be found, at the same time, that other causes will not alone account for many of our heaviest misfortunes; and, particularly, for that prevailing and increasing distrust of public engagements, and alarm for private rights, which are echoed from one end of the continent to the other. These must be chiefly, if not wholly, effects of the unsteadiness and injustice with which a factious spirit has tainted our public administrations.

By a faction, I understand a number of citizens, whether amounting to a majority or a minority of the whole, who are united and actuated by some common impulse of passion, or of interest, adversed to the rights of other citizens, or to the permanent and aggregate interests of the community.

There are two methods of curing the mischiefs of faction: the one, by removing its causes; the other, by controlling its effects.

There are again two methods of removing the causes of faction: the one, by destroying the liberty which is essential to its existence; the other, by giving to every citizen the same opinions, the same passions, and the same interests.

It could never be more truly said than of the first remedy, that it was worse than the disease. Liberty is to faction what air is to fire, an aliment without which it instantly expires. But it could not be less folly to abolish liberty, which is essential to political life, because it nourishes faction, than it would be to wish the annihilation of air, which is essential to animal life, because it imparts to fire its destructive agency.

The second expedient is as impracticable as the first would be unwise. As long as the reason of man continues fallible, and he is at liberty to exercise it, different opinions will be formed. As long as the connection subsists between his reason and his self-love, his opinions and his passions will have a reciprocal influence on each other; and the former will be objects to which the latter will attach themselves. The diversity in the faculties of men, from which the rights of property originate, is not less an insuperable obstacle to a uniformity of interests. The protection of these faculties is the first object of government. From the protection of different and unequal faculties of acquiring property, the possession of different degrees and kinds of property immediately results; and from the influence of these on the sentiments and views of the respective proprietors, ensues a division of the society into different interests and parties.

The latent causes of faction are thus sown in the nature of man; and we see them everywhere brought into different degrees of activity, according to the different circumstances of civil society. A zeal for different opinions concerning religion, concerning government, and many other points, as well of speculation as of practice; an attachment to different leaders ambitiously contending for pre-eminence and power; or to persons of other descriptions whose fortunes have been interesting to the human passions, have, in turn, divided mankind into parties, inflamed them with mutual animosity, and rendered them much more disposed to vex and oppress each other than to co-operate for their common good. So strong is this propensity of mankind to fall into mutual animosities, that where no substantial occasion presents itself, the most frivolous and fanciful distinctions have been sufficient to kindle their unfriendly passions and excite their most violent conflicts. But the most common and durable source of factions has been the various and unequal distribution of property. Those who hold and those who are without property have ever formed distinct interests in society. Those who are creditors, and those who are debtors, fall under a like discrimination. A landed interest, a manufacturing interest, a mercantile interest, a moneyed interest, with many lesser interests, grow up of necessity in civilized nations, and divide them into different classes, actuated by different sentiments and views. The regulation of these various and interfering interests forms the principal task of modern legislation, and involves the spirit of party and faction in the necessary and ordinary operations of the government.

No man is allowed to be a judge in his own cause, because his interest would certainly bias his judgment, and, not improbably, corrupt his integrity. With equal, nay with greater reason, a body of men are unfit to be both judges and parties at the same time; yet what are many of the most important acts of legislation, but so many judicial determinations, not indeed concerning the rights of single persons, but concerning the rights of large bodies of citizens? And what are the different classes of legislators but advocates and parties to the causes which they determine? Is a law proposed concerning private debts? It is a question to which the creditors are parties on one side and the debtors on the other. Justice ought to hold the balance between them. Yet the parties are, and must be, themselves the judges; and the most numerous party, or, in other words, the most powerful faction must be expected to prevail. Shall domestic manufactures be encouraged, and in what degree, by restrictions on foreign manufactures? are questions which would be differently decided by the landed and the manufacturing classes, and probably by neither with a sole regard to justice and the public good. The apportionment of taxes on the various descriptions of property is an act which seems to require the most exact impartiality; yet there is, perhaps, no legislative act in which greater opportunity and temptation are given to a predominant party to trample on the rules of justice. Every shilling with which they overburden the inferior number, is a shilling saved to their own pockets.

It is in vain to say that enlightened statesmen will be able to adjust these clashing interests, and render them all subservient to the public good. Enlightened statesmen will not always be at the helm. Nor, in many cases, can such an adjustment be made at all without taking into view indirect and remote considerations, which will rarely prevail over the immediate interest which one party may find in disregarding the rights of another or the good of the whole.

The inference to which we are brought is, that the *causes* of faction cannot be removed, and that relief is only to be sought in the means of controlling its *effects*.

If a faction consists of less than a majority, relief is supplied by the republican principle, which enables the majority to defeat its sinister views by regular vote. It may clog the administration, it may convulse the society; but it will be unable to execute and mask its violence under the forms of the Constitution. When a majority is included in a faction, the form of popular government, on the other hand, enables it to sacrifice to its ruling passion or interest both the public good and the rights of other citizens. To secure the public good and private rights against the danger of such a faction, and at the same time to preserve the spirit and the form of popular government, is then the great object to which our inquiries are directed. Let me add that it is the great desideratum by which this form of government can be rescued from the opprobrium under which it has so long labored, and be recommended to the esteem and adoption of mankind.

By what means is this object attainable? Evidently by one of two only. Either the existence of the same passion or interest in a major-

ity at the same time must be prevented, or the majority, having such coexistent passion or interest, must be rendered, by their number and local situation, unable to concert and carry into effect schemes of oppression. If the impulse and the opportunity be suffered to coincide, we well know that neither moral nor religious motives can be relied on as an adequate control. They are not found to be such on the injustice and violence of individuals, and lose their efficacy in proportion to the number combined together, that is, in proportion as their efficacy becomes needful.

From this view of the subject it may be concluded that a pure democracy, by which I mean a society consisting of a small number of citizens, who assemble and administer the government in person, can admit of no cure for the mischiefs of faction. A common passion or interest will, in almost every case, be felt by a majority of the whole; a communication and concert result from the form of government itself; and there is nothing to check the inducements to sacrifice the weaker party or an obnoxious individual. Hence it is that such democracies have ever been spectacles of turbulence and contention; have ever been found incompatible with personal security or the rights of property; and have in general been as short in their lives as they have been violent in their deaths. Theoretic politicians, who have patronized this species of government, have erroneously supposed that by reducing mankind to a perfect equality in their political rights, they would, at the same time, be perfectly equalized and assimilated in their possessions, their opinions, and their passions.

A republic, by which I mean a government in which the scheme of representation takes place, opens a different prospect, and promises the cure for which we are seeking. Let us examine the points in which it varies from pure democracy, and we shall comprehend both the nature of the cure and the efficacy which it must derive from the Union.

The two great points of difference between a democracy and a republic are: first, the delegation of the government, in the latter, to a small number of citizens elected by the rest; secondly, the greater number of citizens, and greater sphere of country, over which the latter may be extended.

The effect of the first difference is, on the one hand, to refine and enlarge the public views, by passing them through the medium of a chosen body of citizens, whose wisdom may best discern the true interest of their country, and whose patriotism and love of justice will be least likely to sacrifice it to temporary or partial considerations. Under such a regulation, it may well happen that the public voice, pronounced by the representatives of the people, will be more consonant to the public good than if pronounced by the people themselves, convened for the purpose. On the other hand, the effect may be inverted. Men of factious tempers, of local prejudices, or of sinister designs, may, by intrigue, by corruption, or by other means, first obtain the suffrages, and then betray the interests, of the people. The question resulting is, whether small or extensive republics are more favorable to the election of proper guardians of the public weal; and it is clearly decided in favor of the latter by two obvious considerations:

In the first place, it is to be remarked that, however small the republic may be, the representatives must be raised to a certain number, in order to guard against the cabals of a few; and that, however large it may be, they must be limited to a certain number, in order to guard against the confusion of a multitude. Hence, the number of representatives in the two cases not being in proportion to that of the two constituents, and being proportionally greater in the small republic, it follows that, if the proportion of fit characters be not less in the large than in the small republic, the former will present a greater option, and consequently a greater probability of a fit choice.

In the next place, as each representative will be chosen by a greater number of citizens in the large than in the small republic, it will be more difficult for unworthy candidates to practice with success the vicious arts by which elections are too often carried; and the suffrages of the people being more free, will be more likely to centre in men who possess the most attractive merit and the most diffusive and established characters.

It must be confessed that in this, as in most other cases, there is a mean, on both sides of which inconveniences will be found to lie. By enlarging too much the number of electors, you render the representatives too little acquainted with all their local circumstances and lesser interests; as by reducing it too much, you render him unduly attached to these, and too little fit to comprehend and pursue great and national objects. The federal Constitution forms a happy combination in this respect; the great and aggregate interests being referred to the national, the local and particular to the State legislatures.

The other point of difference is, the greater number of citizens and extent of territory which may be brought within the compass of republican than of democratic government; and it is this circumstance principally which renders factious combinations less to be dreaded in the former than in the latter. The smaller the society, the fewer probably will be the distinct parties and interests composing it; the fewer the distinct parties and interests, the more frequently will a majority be found of the same party; and the smaller the number of individuals composing a majority, and the smaller the compass within which they are placed, the more easily will they concert and execute their plans of oppression. Extend the sphere, and you take in a greater variety of parties and interests; you make it less probable that a majority of the whole will have a common motive to invade the rights of other citizens; or if such a common motive exists, it will be more difficult for all who feel it to discover their own strength, and to act in unison with each other. Besides other impediments, it may be remarked that, where there is a consciousness of unjust or dis-

honorable purposes, communication is always checked by distrust in proportion to the number whose concurrence is necessary.

Hence, it clearly appears, that the same advantage which a republic has over a democracy, in controlling the effects of faction, is enjoyed by a large over a small republic,—is enjoyed by the Union over the States composing it. Does the advantage consist in the substitution of representatives whose enlightened views and virtuous sentiments render them superior to local prejudices and schemes of injustice? It will not be denied that the representation of the Union will be most likely to possess these requisite endowments. Does it consist in the greater security afforded by a greater variety of parties, against the event of any one party being able to outnumber and oppress the rest? In an equal degree does the increased variety of parties comprised within the Union, increase this security? Does it, in fine, consist in the greater obstacles opposed to the concert and accomplishment of the secret wishes of an unjust and interested majority? Here, again, the extent of the Union gives it the most palpable advantage.

The influence of factious leaders may kindle a flame within their particular States, but will be unable to spread a general conflagration through the other States. A religious sect may degenerate into a political faction in a part of the Confederacy; but the variety of sects dispersed over the entire face of it must secure the national councils against any danger from that source. A rage for paper money, for an abolition of debts, for an equal division of property, or for any other improper or wicked project, will be less apt to pervade the whole body of the Union than a particular member of it; in the same proportion as such a malady is more likely to taint a particular county or district, than an entire State.

In the extent and proper structure of the Union, therefore, we behold a republican remedy for the diseases most incident to republican government. And according to the degree of pleasure and pride we feel in being republicans, ought to be our zeal in cherishing the spirit and supporting the character of Federalists.

Publius

THE FEDERALIST NO. 51

February 6, 1788

JAMES MADISON

TO THE PEOPLE OF THE STATE OF NEW YORK:

To what expedient, then, shall we finally resort, for maintaining in practice the necessary partition of power among the several departments, as laid down in the Constitution? The only answer that can be given is, that as all these exterior provisions are found to be inadequate, the defect must be supplied, by so contriving the interior structure of the government as that its several constituent parts may, by their mutual relations, be the means of keeping each other in their proper places. Without presuming to undertake a full development of this important idea, I will hazard a few general observations, which may perhaps place it in a clearer light, and enable us to form a more correct judgment of the principles and structure of the government planned by the convention.

In order to lay a due foundation for that separate and distinct exercise of the different powers of government, which to a certain extent is admitted on all hands to be essential to the preservation of liberty, it is evident that each department should have a will of its own; and consequently should be so constituted that the members of each should have as little agency as possible in the appointment of the members of the others. Were this principle rigorously adhered to, it would require that all the appointments for the supreme executive, legislative, and judiciary magistracies should be drawn from the same fountain of authority, the people, through channels having no communication whatever with one another. Perhaps such a plan of constructing the several departments would be less difficult in practice than it may in contemplation appear. Some difficulties, however, and some additional expense would attend the execution of it. Some deviations, therefore, from the principle must be admitted. In the constitution of the judiciary department in particular, it might be inexpedient to insist rigorously on the principle: first, because peculiar qualifications being essential in the members, the primary consideration ought to be to select that mode of choice which best secures these qualifications; secondly, because the permanent tenure by which the appointments are held in that department, must soon destroy all sense of dependence on the authority conferring them.

It is equally evident, that the members of each department should be as little dependent as possible on those of the others, for the emoluments annexed to their offices. Were the executive magistrate, or the judges, not independent of the legislature in this particular, their independence in every other would be merely nominal.

But the great security against a gradual concentration of the several powers in the same department, consists in giving to those who administer each department the necessary constitutional means and personal motives to resist encroachments of the others. The provision for defense must in this, as in all other cases, be made commensurate to the danger of attack. Ambition must be made to counteract ambition. The interest of the man must be connected with the constitutional rights of the place. It may be a reflection on human nature, that such devices should be necessary to control the abuses of government. But what is government itself, but the greatest of all reflections on human nature? If men were angels, no government would be necessary. If angels were to govern men, neither external nor internal controls on government would be necessary. In framing a government which is to be administered by men over men, the great difficulty lies in this: you must first enable the government to control the governed; and in the next place oblige it to control itself. A dependence on the people is, no doubt, the primary control on the government; but experience has taught mankind the necessity of auxiliary precautions.

This policy of supplying, by opposite and rival interests, the defect of better motives, might be traced through the whole system of human affairs, private as well as public. We see it particularly displayed in all the subordinate distributions of power, where the constant aim is to divide and arrange the several offices in such a manner as that each may be a check on the other—that the private interest of every individual may be a sentinel over the public rights. These inventions of prudence cannot be less requisite in the distribution of the supreme powers of the State.

But it is not possible to give to each department an equal power of self-defense. In republican government, the legislative authority necessarily predominates. The remedy for this inconveniency is to divide the legislature into different branches; and to render them, by different modes of election and different principles of action, as little connected with each other as the nature of their common functions and their common dependence on the society will admit. It may even be necessary to guard against dangerous encroachments by still further precautions. As the weight of the legislative authority requires that it should be thus divided, the weakness of the executive may require, on the other hand, that it should be fortified. An absolute negative on the legislature appears, at first view, to be the natural defense with which the executive magistrate should be armed. But perhaps it would be neither altogether safe nor alone sufficient. On ordinary occasions it might not be exerted with the requisite firmness, and on extraordinary occasions it might be perfidiously abused. May not this defect of an absolute negative be supplied by some qualified connection between this weaker department and the weaker branch of the stronger department, by which the latter may be led to support the constitutional rights of the former, without being too much detached from the rights of its own department?

If the principles on which these observations are founded be just, as I persuade myself they are, and they be applied as a criterion to the several State constitutions, and to the federal Constitution it will be found that if the latter does not perfectly correspond with them, the former are infinitely less able to bear such a test.

There are, moreover, two considerations particularly applicable to the federal system of America, which place that system in a very interesting point of view.

First. In a single republic, all the power surrendered by the people is submitted to the administration of a single government; and the usurpations are guarded against by a division of the government into distinct and separate departments. In the compound republic of America, the power surrendered by the people is first divided between two distinct governments, and then the portion allotted to each subdivided among distinct and separate departments. Hence a double security arises to the rights of the people. The different governments will control each other, at the same time that each will be controlled by itself.

Second. It is of great importance in a republic not only to guard the society against the oppression of its rulers, but to guard one part of the society against the injustice of the other part. Different interests necessarily exist in different classes of citizens. If a majority be united by a common interest, the rights of the minority will be insecure. There are but two methods of providing against this evil: the one by creating a will in the community independent of the majority—that is, of the society itself; the other, by comprehending in the society so many separate descriptions of citizens as will render an unjust combination of a majority of the whole very improbable, if not impracticable. The first method prevails in all governments possessing an hereditary or self-appointed authority. This, at best, is but a precarious security; because a power independent of the society may as well espouse the unjust views of the major, as the rightful interests of the minor party, and may possibly be turned against both parties. The second method will be exemplified in the federal republic of the United States. Whilst all authority in it will be derived from and dependent on the society, the society itself will be broken into so many parts, interests, and classes of citizens, that the rights of individuals, or of the minority, will be in little danger from interested combinations of the majority. In a free government the security for civil rights must be the same as that for religious rights. It consists in the one case in the multiplicity of interests, and in the other in the multiplicity of sects. The degree of security in both cases will depend on the number of interests and sects; and this may be presumed to depend on the extent of country and number of people comprehended under the same government. This view of the subject must particularly recommend a proper federal system to all the sincere and considerate friends of republican government, since it shows that in exact proportion as the territory of the Union may be formed into more circumscribed Confederacies, or States oppressive combinations of a majority will be facilitated: the best security, under the republican forms, for the rights of every class of citizens, will be diminished: and consequently the stability and independence of some member of the government, the only other security, must be proportionately increased. Justice is the end of government. It is the end of civil society. It ever has been and ever will be pursued until it be obtained, or until liberty be lost in the pursuit. In a society under the forms of which the stronger faction can readily unite and oppress the weaker, anarchy may as truly be said to reign as in a state of nature, where the weaker individual is not secured against the violence of the stronger; and as, in the latter state, even the stronger individuals are prompted, by the uncertainty of their condition, to submit to a government which may protect the weak as well as themselves; so, in the former state, will the more powerful factions or parties be gradually induced, by a like motive, to wish for a government which will protect all parties, the weaker as well as the more powerful. It can be little doubted that if the State of Rhode Island was separated from the Confederacy and left to itself, the insecurity of rights under the popular form of government within such narrow limits would be displayed by such reiterated oppressions of factious majorities that some power altogether independent of the people would soon be called for by the voice of the very factions whose misrule had proved the necessity of it. In the extended republic of the United States, and among the great variety of interests, parties, and sects which it embraces, a coalition of a majority of the whole society could seldom take place on any other principles than those of justice and the general good; whilst there being thus less danger to a minor from the will of a major party, there must be less pretext, also, to provide for the security of the former, by introducing into the government a will not dependent on the latter, or, in other words, a will independent of the society itself. It is no less certain than it is important, notwithstanding the contrary opinions which have been entertained, that the larger the society, provided it lie within a practical sphere, the more duly capable it will be of self-government. And happily for the *republican cause,* the practicable sphere may be carried to a very great extent, by a judicious modification and mixture of the *federal principle.*

Publius

Seneca Falls Conference, 1848

When, in the course of human events, it becomes necessary for one portion of the family of man to assume among the people of the earth a position different from that which they have hitherto occupied, but one to which the laws of nature and of nature's God entitle them, a decent respect to the opinions of mankind requires that they should declare the causes that impel them to such a course.

We hold these truths to be self-evident: that all men and women are created equal; that they are endowed by their Creator with certain inalienable rights; that among these are life, liberty, and the pursuit of happiness; that to secure these rights governments are instituted, deriving their just powers from the consent of the governed. Whenever any form of government becomes destructive of these ends, it is the right of those who suffer from it to refuse allegiance to it, and to insist upon the institution of a new government, laying its foundation on such principles, and organizing its powers in such form, as to them shall seem most likely to effect their safety and happiness. Prudence, indeed, will dictate that governments long established should not be changed for light and transient causes; and accordingly all experience hath shown that mankind are more disposed to suffer, while evils are sufferable, than to right themselves by abolishing the forms to which they are accustomed. But when a long train of abuses and usurpations, pursuing invariably the same object, evinces a design to reduce them under absolute despotism, it is their duty to throw off such government, and to provide new guards for their future security. Such has been the patient sufferance of the women under this government, and such is now the necessity which constrains them to demand the equal station to which they are entitled.

The history of mankind is a history of repeated injuries and usurpations on the part of man toward woman, having in direct object the establishment of an absolute tyranny over her. To prove this, let facts be submitted to a candid world.

He has never permitted her to exercise her inalienable right to the elective franchise.

He has compelled her to submit to laws, in the formation of which she had no voice.

He has withheld from her rights which are given to the most ignorant and degraded men—both natives and foreigners.

Having deprived her of this first right of a citizen, the elective franchise, thereby leaving her without representation in the halls of legislation, he has oppressed her on all sides.

He has made her, if married, in the eye of the law, civilly dead.

He has taken from her all right in property, even to the wages she earns.

He has made her, morally, an irresponsible being, as she can commit many crimes with impunity, provided they be done in the presence of her husband. In the covenant of marriage, she is compelled to promise obedience to her husband, he becoming, to all intents and purposes, her master—the law giving him power to deprive her of her liberty, and to administer chastisement.

He has so framed the laws of divorce, as to what shall be the proper causes, and in case of separation, to whom the guardianship of the children shall be given, as to be wholly regardless of the happiness of women—the law, in all cases, going upon a false supposition of the supremacy of man, and giving all power into his hands.

After depriving her of all rights as a married woman, if single, and the owner of property, he has taxed her to support a government which recognizes her only when her property can be made profitable to it.

He has monopolized nearly all the profitable employments, and from those she is permitted to follow, she receives but a scanty remuneration. He closes against her all the avenues to wealth and distinction which he considers most honorable to himself. As a teacher of theology, medicine, or law, she is not known.

He has denied her the facilities for obtaining a thorough education, all colleges being closed against her.

He allows her in church, as well as state, but a subordinate position, claiming apostolic authority for her exclusion from the ministry, and, with some exceptions, from any public participation in the affairs of the church.

He has created a false public sentiment by giving to the world a different code of morals for men and women, by which moral delinquencies which exclude women from society, are not only tolerated, but deemed of little account in man.

He has usurped the prerogative of Jehovah himself, claiming it as his right to assign for her a sphere of action, when that belongs to her conscience and to her God.

He has endeavored, in every way that he could, to destroy her confidence in her own powers, to lessen her self-respect, and to make her willing to lead a dependent and abject life.

Now, in view of this entire disfranchisement of one-half the people of this country, their social and religious degradation—in view of the unjust laws above mentioned, and because women do feel themselves aggrieved, oppressed, and fraudulently deprived of their most sacred rights, we insist that they have immediate admission to all the rights and privileges which belong to them as citizens of the United States.

In entering upon the great work before us, we anticipate no small amount of misconception, misrepresentation, and ridicule; but we shall use every instrumentality within our power to effect our object. We shall employ agents, circulate tracts, petition the State and national Legislatures, and endeavor to enlist the pulpit and the press in our behalf. We hope this Convention will be followed by a series of Conventions, embracing every part of the country.

Firmly relying upon the final triumph of the Right and the True, we do this day affix our signatures to this declaration.

Harriet Cady Eaton
Elizabeth M'Clintock
Mary M'Clintock
Margaret Pryor
Eunice Newton Foote
Margaret Schooley
Catherine F. Stebbins
Mary Ann Frink
Lydia Mount
Delia Matthews
Catharine C. Paine
Mary H. Hallowell
Sarah Hallowell
Catharine Shaw
Deborah Scott
Mary Gilbert
Sophrone Taylor
Cynthia Davis
Hannah Plant
Lucy Jones
Sarah Whitney
Elizabeth Conklin
Lucretia Coffin Mott
Mary Ann M'Clintock
Susan Quinn
Mary S. Mirror
Phebe King
Julia Ann Drake
Charlotte Woodard
Martha Underhill
Dorothy Matthews
Eunice Baker

Sarah R. Woods
Lydia Gild
Sarah Hoffman
Elizabeth Leslie
Martha Ridley
Rachel D. Bonnel
Betsey Tewksbury
Rhoda Palmer
Margaret Jenkins
Cynthia Fuller
Mary Martin
P. A. Culvert
Susan R. Doty
Rebecca Race
Martha Coffin Wright
Jane C. Hunt
Sarah A. Mosher
Mary E. Vail
Lucy Spaulding
Lavinia Latham
Sarah Smith
Eliza Martin
Maria E. Wilbur
Elizabeth D. Smith
Caroline Barker
Ann Porter
Experience Gibbs
Antoinette E. Segur
Hannah J. Latham
Sarah Sisson
Malvina Seymour
Phebe Mosher

Joel Bunker
Isaac Van Tassel
Thomas Dell
E. W. Capron
Stephen Shear
Henry Hatley
Amy Post
Frederick Douglass
Richard P. Hunt
Samuel D. Tillman
Justin Williams
Elisha Foote
Henry W. Seymour
David Salding
William G. Barker
Elias J. Doty
John Jones
William S. Dell
William Burroughs
Azaliah Schooley
Robert Smalldridge
Jacob Matthews
Charles L. Hoskins
Thomas M'Clintock
Saron Phillips
Jacob Chamberlain
Johnathan Metcalf
Nathan J. Milliken
S. E. Woodworth
Edward F. Underhill
George W. Pryor

GLOSSARY

A

absentee voting The casting of a ballot in advance by mail in situations where illness, travel, or other circumstances prevent voters from voting in their precinct.

administrative adjudication The process by which agencies resolve disputes over the implementation of their administrative rules.

administrative discretion The authority delegated to bureaucrats to use their expertise and judgment when determining how to implement public policy.

administrative law The name given to agencies' rulemaking and resolution of conflicts regarding their rules.

administrative rule making The process by which an independent commission or agency fills in the details of a vague law by formulating, proposing, and approving rules, regulations, and standards that will be enforced to implement the policy.

advice and consent The Senate's authority to approve or reject the president's top appointments.

affirmative action In the employment arena, intentional efforts to recruit, hire, train, and promote underutilized categories of workers (women and minority men); in higher education, intentional efforts to diversify the student body.

agency review Part of the committee or subcommittee process of considering a bill, wherein committee members ask executive agencies that would administer the law for written comments on the measure.

agenda setting The determination by Congress of which public issues the government should consider for legislation.

agents of socialization The individuals, organizations, and institutions that facilitate the acquisition of political views.

al-Qaeda A radical international Islamic fundamentalist terror organization.

American dream The belief that in the United States hard work and persistence will reap a financially secure, happy and healthy life, with upward social mobility.

amicus curiae **brief ("friend of the court" brief)** A document submitted by parties interested in a certain case or issue in an attempt to provide the Court with information that may be used to decide the case.

Anti-Federalists Individuals who opposed ratification of the Constitution because they were deeply suspicious of the powers it gave to the national government and of the impact these powers would have on states' authority and individual freedoms.

appellate jurisdiction The authority of a court to review the decision reached by another court in a case.

appropriation law A law that gives bureaucracies and other government entities the legal authority to spend money.

approval ratings The percentage of survey respondents who say that they "approve" or "strongly approve" of the way the president is doing his job.

articles of impeachment Charges against the president during an impeachment.

attentive public The segment of voters who pay careful attention to political issues.

Australian ballot A secret ballot prepared by the government, distributed to all eligible voters, and, when balloting is completed, counted by government officials in an unbiased fashion, without corruption or regard to individual preferences.

authoritarianism A system of government in which the government holds strong powers but is checked by some forces.

authorization law A law that provides the plan of action to address a given societal concern and identifies the executive branch unit that will put the plan into effect.

B

bad tendency test A standard established in the 1925 case *Gitlow v. New York*, whereby any speech that has the tendency to incite crime or disturb the public peace can be silenced.

balance of power system A system of international alliances that, in theory, would balance the power of one group of nations against the power of another group and thus discourage war.

balanced budget A budget in which the government's expenditures are equal to or less than its revenues.

balanced ticket The selection of a running mate who brings diversity of ideology, geographic region, age, gender, race, or ethnicity to the slate.

ballot measure Any proposed policy that, as the result of an initiative or a referendum, wins a place on the ballot for voters to approve or reject.

bandwidth The amount of data that can travel through a network in a given time period.

bicameral A legislative body composed of two chambers.

bill A proposed piece of legislation.

Bill of Rights The first ten amendments to the Constitution, which were ratified in 1791, constituting an enumeration of the individual liberties with which the government is forbidden to interfere.

Black Codes Laws passed immediately after the Civil War by the confederate states that limited the rights of "freemen" (former slaves).

blanket primary A type of primary that allows voters to vote in either party's primary, and voters can choose to vote in *both* parties' primaries for different offices.

block grant The intergovernmental transfer of money that has fewer conditions of aid than a categorical grant and is used for broadly defined policy areas; it is distributed based on complicated formulas.

blogosphere A community, or social network, of bloggers.

brief A document detailing the legal argument for the desired outcome in a court case.

brinkmanship The Cold War–era practice of fooling the enemy by going to the edge (the brink), even if the party using the brinkmanship strategy had no intention of following it through.

Brown v. Board of Education of Topeka This 1954 Supreme Court decision ruled that segregated schools violated the equal protection clause of the Fourteenth Amendment.

budget authority The authority provided by law for agencies to obligate government spending.

budget deficit More money spent than collected through revenues.

budget reconciliation The annual process of rewriting authorization legislation to comply with the expenditure ceiling and revenue floor of the concurrent budget resolution for the upcoming fiscal year.

budget surplus Money left over after all expenses are paid.

bureaucracy Any organization with a hierarchical structure, although most commonly used to designate a government agency or the collection of all national executive branch organizations.

bureaucrats People employed in a government executive branch unit to implement public policy; a public administrator; a public servant.

Bush Doctrine The argument, articulated by President George W. Bush, that unilateral action directly targeted at an enemy is both justifiable and feasible.

business regulation Government rules, regulations, and standards, directed at protecting competition in the marketplace.

C

cabinet The group of experts chosen by the president to serve as advisers on running the country.

campaign consultant A paid professional who specializes in the overall management of political campaigns or an aspect of campaigns.

campaign manager A professional whose duties comprise a variety of strategic and managerial tasks, from fund-raising to staffing a campaign.

campaign strategy The blueprint for the campaign, including a budget and fundraising plan, an advertising strategy, a staffing plan.

candidate committees Organizations that candidates form to support their individual election.

candidate-centered campaign A campaign in which the individual seeking election, rather than an entire party slate, is the focus.

capital budget A budget that accounts for the costs and revenues for expensive building and purchasing projects from which citizens will benefit for many years and for which governments can borrow money.

capitalism An economic system in which the means of producing wealth are privately owned and operated to produce profits.

casework Personal work by a member of Congress on behalf of a constituent or group of constituents, typically aimed at getting the government to do something the constituent wants done.

cash transfer The direct provision of cash (in forms including checks, debit cards, and tax breaks) to eligible individuals or to providers of goods or services to eligible individuals.

categorical formula grant The intergovernmental transfer of money for a specified program area for which the amount of money a government is eligible to receive is based on a legislated formula.

categorical project grant The intergovernmental transfer of money for a specified program area for which recipients compete by proposing specific projects they want to implement.

caucus A meeting of all members of the political party in one chamber in which they elect leaders, approve committee assignments, and elect committee chairpersons.

centralized federalism The relationship between the national and state governments whereby the national government imposes its policy preferences on state governments.

chad A ready-made perforation on a punch card ballot.

charter The constitution of a local government.

checks and balances The mechanisms by which each branch of government can monitor and limit the functions of the other branches.

chief justice The leading justice on the Supreme Court, who provides both organizational and intellectual leadership.

chief of staff Among the most important staff members of the White House Office (WHO); serves as both an adviser to the president and the manager of the WHO.

circuit courts Also known as *courts of appeals;* the middle level in the federal court structure.

circuit riding The practice of traveling around the circuits by early Supreme Court justices and district court judges to hear appeals cases.

citizens Those members of the polity who, through birth or naturalization, enjoy the rights, privileges, and responsibilities attached to membership in a given nation.

civic engagement Individual and collective actions designed to identify and address issues of public concern.

civil disobedience Active, but nonviolent, refusal to comply with laws or governmental policies that are morally objectionable.

civil law case A conflict between private individuals in which the plaintiff alleges that some action or inaction by the defendant has resulted in harm to him or her.

civil liberties Constitutionally established guarantees that protect citizens, opinions, and property against arbitrary government interference.

civil rights The rights and privileges guaranteed to all citizens under the equal protection and due process clauses of the Fifth and Fourteenth amendments; the idea that individuals are protected from discrimination based on characteristics such as race, national origin, religion, and sex.

civil servants Bureaucrats hired through a merit-based personnel system who have job protection.

clash of civilizations thesis Samuel Huntington's idea that bitter cultural conflict will continue and escalate between modern Western democracies and fundamentalist Islamic states.

clear and present danger test A standard established in the 1919 Supreme Court case *Schenck v. U.S.,* whereby the government may silence speech or expression when there is a clear and present danger that this speech will bring about some harm that the government has the power to prevent.

clear and probable danger test A standard established in the 1951 case *Dennis v. U.S.* whereby the government could suppress speech to avoid grave danger, even if the probability of the dangerous result was relatively remote; replaced by the imminent lawless action (incitement) test in 1969.

climate control The practice of using public outreach to build favorable public opinion of an organization.

closed primary A type of primary in which voting in a party's primary is limited to members of that party.

cloture A procedural move in which a supermajority of sixty senators agrees to end a filibuster.

coattail effect The phenomenon by which candidates running for a lower-level office such as city council benefit in an election from the popularity of a top-of-ticket nominee.

code law Laws created by legislators to regulate the behavior of individuals and organizations.

Cold War The political, ideological, and military conflict that lasted from 1945 until 1990 between communist nations led by the Soviet Union and Western democracies led by the United States.

collective defense The concept that allied nations agree to defend one another in the face of an invasion.

collective goods Outcomes shared by the general public; also called *public goods.*

collective security The idea that peace could be achieved if nations agreed to collectively oppose any nation that attacked another country.

collegial court A court made up of a group of judges who must evaluate a case together and decide on the outcome; significant compromise and negotiation take place as members try to build a majority coalition.

commercial speech Advertising statements that describe products.

commission A form of local government that is more common in county and township governments than in other general-purpose governments and for which voters elect a body of officials who collectively hold legislative and executive powers.

common law Law made by judges who decide cases and articulate legal principles in their opinions; based upon the British system.

concurrent budget resolution A document approved by the House and Senate at the beginning of their budget process that establishes binding expenditure ceilings and a binding revenue floor as well as proposed expenditure levels for major policies.

concurrent powers The basic governing functions of all sovereign governments; in the United States they are held by the national, state, and local governments and include the authority to tax, to make policy, to implement policy, and the power of eminent domain.

concurring opinion A judicial opinion agreeing with how the majority decides the case but disagreeing with at least some of the legal interpretations or conclusions reached by the majority.

confederal system A structure of government in which several independent sovereign governments agree to cooperate on specified governmental matters while retaining sovereignty over all other governmental matters within their jurisdictions.

confederation A national government composed of a league of independent states and in which the central government has less power than the member states.

conference committee A bicameral, bipartisan committee composed of legislators whose job is to reconcile two versions of a bill.

conflict of interest In the case of public servants, the situation when they can personally benefit from a decision they make or an action they take in the process of doing their jobs.

conflicted federalism The current status of national-state relations that has elements of dual and cooperative federalism, with an overall centralizing tendency at the same time that elements of policy are devolved.

Connecticut Compromise (Great Compromise) At the constitutional convention, the compromise between the Virginia Plan and the New Jersey Plan that created a bicameral legislature with one chamber's representation based on population and the other having two members for each state.

consent of the governed The idea that, in a democracy, the government's power derives from the consent of the people.

conservatism An ideology that emphasizes preserving tradition and relying on community and family as mechanisms of continuity in society.

constitution A document that describes three basic components of an organization: its mission, foundational structures, and essential processes.

constitutional law The body of law that comes out of the courts in cases involving the interpretation of the Constitution.

constitutionalism Government that is structured by law, and in which the power of government is limited.

consumer price index (CPI) The most common measure of inflation, it measures the average change in prices over time of a "market basket" of goods and services.

containment The Cold War–era policy of preventing the spread of communism, mainly by providing military and economic aid as well as political advice to countries vulnerable to a communist takeover.

continuing resolution An agreement of the House and Senate that authorizes agencies not covered by approved appropriation laws to continue to spend money within their previous budget year's levels.

contracting-out Also called *outsourcing* or *privatizing;* a process by which the government contracts with a private for-profit or nonprofit organization to provide public services or resources needed by the government.

contributory program (social insurance program) A benefit provided only to those who paid the specific tax created to fund the benefit.

convergence The merging of various forms of media, including newspapers, television stations, radio networks, and blogs, under one corporate roof and one set of business editorial leaders.

cooperative federalism The relationship between the national and state governments whereby the two levels of government work together to address domestic matters reserved to the states, driven by the policy priorities of the states.

Council of Governments (COG) A regional agency composed of representatives from several local governments who share resources to address one or more mutual problems.

council-manager (commission-administrator) A form of general-purpose local government found in many counties and the majority of cities; it is composed of an elected body with legislative and executive powers whose members hire a professional manager to oversee the government's day-to-day operations.

council-mayor (council-executive) A form of general-purpose local government comprising (1) a legislative body elected by voters and (2) an independently elected chief executive.

county government A general-purpose local government created by states to assist them in implementing policy in geographic subdivisions of the state.

country desk The official operation of the U.S. government in each country that has diplomatic ties to the United States.

courts of appeals The intermediate appellate courts in the federal system that review previous decisions made by courts in the federal or state judicial system.

creationism A theory of the creation of the earth and humankind that is based on a literal interpretation of the biblical story of Genesis.

criminal due process rights Safeguards for those accused of crime; these rights constrain government conduct in investigating crimes, trying cases, and punishing offenders.

criminal law case A case brought by the government or a prosecutor against a defendant, alleging that he or she has engaged in conduct resulting in injury to another person, and that this injury is so significant that it harms not only the individual but also the larger society.

cross pressuring The presence of two conditions or traits that pull a voter toward different political parties.

D

de facto segregation Segregation caused by the fact that people tend to live in neighborhoods with others of their own race, religion, or ethnic group.

de jure segregation Segregation mandated by law.

dealignment The situation in which fewer voters support the two major political parties, instead identifying themselves as independent, or splitting their ticket between candidates from more than one party

defendant A person who is defending himself or herself against a plaintiff's accusation.

defense conversion President Jimmy Carter's attempt to convert the nation's vast military apparatus to peacetime functions.

deficit spending Government expenditures costing more than is raised in taxes, leading to borrowing and debt.

democracy Government in which supreme power of governance lies in the hands of its citizens.

department One of fifteen executive branch units responsible for a broadly defined policy area and whose top administrator (secretary) is appointed by the president, is confirmed by the Senate, and serves at the discretion of the president.

depression A long-term and severe recession.

deregulation The reduction or elimination of regulatory restrictions on firms and industries.

détente The easing of tensions between the United States and its communist rivals.

deterrence The idea that nations would be less likely to engage in nuclear war if adversaries each had first-strike capability.

devolution The process whereby the national government returns policy responsibilities to state and/or local governments.

digital divide The inequality of access to computers and Internet connections.

Dillon's rule The ruling articulated by Judge John Forrest Dillon in 1872 that local governments are creatures of the state that created them, and they have only the powers expressly mentioned in the charters written and approved by the state and those necessarily implied by the formally expressed powers.

diplomacy The conduct of international relations, particularly involving the negotiation of treaties and other agreements between nations.

direct democracy A system of government that allows citizens to vote directly to approve or reject proposed public policies or to force an elected official from office before the completion of his or her term.

direct provision A policy tool whereby the government that creates a policy hires public servants to provide the service.

direct subsidy A cash transfer from general revenues to particular persons or private companies engaged in activities that the national government believes support the public good.

director of national intelligence (DNI) The person responsible for coordinating and overseeing all the intelligence agencies within the executive branch.

discharge petition A special tactic used to extract a bill from a committee in order to have it considered by the entire House.

discretionary spending Payment on programs for which Congress and the president must approve budget authority each year in appropriation legislation.

discuss list Compiled by the chief justice, the list of cases on review that he thinks may be appropriate for the Court to hear.

dissenting opinion A judicial opinion disagreeing both with the majority's disposition of a case and with their legal interpretations and conclusions.

diversity of citizenship The circumstance in which the parties in a legal case are from different states or the case involves a U.S. citizen and a foreign government.

divided government The situation that exists when Congress is controlled by one party and the presidency by the other.

divine right of kings The assertion that monarchies, as a manifestation of God's will, could rule absolutely without regard to the will or well-being of their subjects.

domino theory The principle that if one nation fell to communism, other nations in its geographic vicinity also would succumb.

double jeopardy To be tried again for the same crime that one has been cleared of in court; barred by the Fifth Amendment.

dual court system A two-part judicial system such as that of the United States, which has both federal and state courts.

dual federalism The relationship between the national and state governments, dominant between 1789 and 1932, whereby the two levels of government functioned independently of each other to address their distinct constitutional responsibilities.

dual sovereignty The existence of two governments, each with sovereignty over different matters at the same time; neither level is sovereign over the other.

due process The legal safeguards that prevent the government from arbitrarily depriving citizens of life, liberty, or property; guaranteed by the Fifth and Fourteenth amendments.

E

earmark A designation within a spending bill that provides for a specific expenditure.

e-campaigning The practice of mobilizing voters using the Internet.

economic boom Rapid economic growth.

economic incentives Motivation to join an interest group because the group works for policies that will provide members with material benefits.

economic regulation Government constraints on business practices aimed at ensuring competition in the marketplace and a healthy economy.

economy The system of transactions by which goods and services are distributed in the marketplace.

efficacy Citizens' belief that they have the ability to achieve something desirable and that the government listens to people like them.

electioneering Working to influence the election of candidates who support the organization's issues.

Electoral College A group of people elected by voters in each state to elect the president and the vice president.

elite theory A theory that holds that a group of wealthy, educated individuals wields most political power.

emergency powers Broad powers exercised by the president during times of national crisis.

eminent domain The authority of government to compel a property owner to sell private property to a government to further the public good.

entitlement program A government benefit guaranteed to all who meet the eligibility requirements.

enumerated powers The powers of the national government that are listed in the Constitution.

environmental racism The term for the higher incidence of environmental threats and subsequent health problems in lower-income communities, which frequently are also communities dominated by people of color.

equal protection clause The Fourteenth Amendment clause stating that no state shall "deny to any person within its jurisdiction the equal protection of the laws."

essential services Public services provided by state and local governments on a daily basis to prevent chaos and hazardous conditions in society.

establishment clause The First Amendment clause that bars the government from passing any law "respecting an establishment of religion"; often interpreted as a separation of church and state but increasingly questioned.

exclusionary rule The criminal procedural rule stating that evidence obtained illegally cannot be used in a trial.

executive agreement An international agreement between the United States and other nations, not subject to Senate approval and only in effect during the administration of the president who negotiates the agreement.

executive budget The budget document and budget message that explains the president's fiscal plan.

Executive Office of the President (EOP) The offices, counsels, and boards that help the president to carry out his day-to-day responsibilities.

executive order The power of the president to issue orders that carry the force of law.

executive privilege The right of the chief executive and members of the administration to withhold information from Congress or the courts, or the right to refuse to appear before legislative or judicial bodies.

exit polls Polls conducted at polling places on Election Day to determine the winner of an election before the polls close.

expressed powers Presidential powers enumerated in the Constitution.

extradition The return of a person accused of a crime to the state in which the crime was committed upon the request of that state's governor.

extraordinary rendition Apprehending an individual believed to be a terrorist and transferring the person to another nation.

F

fairness doctrine The requirement that stations provide equal time to all parties regarding important public issues and equal access to airtime to all candidates for public office.

federal question A question of law based on interpretation of the U.S. Constitution, federal laws, or treaties.

federal system A governmental structure with two levels of government and in which each level has sovereignty over different governmental functions and policy matters.

The Federalist Papers A series of essays, written by James Madison, Alexander Hamilton, and John Jay, that argued for the ratification of the Constitution.

Federalists Individuals who supported the new Constitution as presented by the Constitutional Convention in 1787.

feminization of poverty The phenomenon of increasing numbers of unmarried, divorced, and separated women with children living in poverty.

fighting words Speech that is likely to bring about public disorder or chaos; the Supreme Court has held that this speech may be banned in public places to ensure the preservation of public order.

filibuster A procedural move by a member of the Senate to attempt to halt passage of a bill, during which the senator can speak for an unlimited time on the Senate floor.

fireside chats President Franklin Roosevelt's radio addresses to the country.

fiscal policy Government spending and taxing and their effect on the economy.

fiscal year (FY) The twelve months during which the government implements its annual budget, beginning on October 1 and ending on September 30 of the following year.

527 A tax-exempt group that raises money for political activities, much like those allowed under the soft money loophole.

food insecurity The situation in which people have a limited or an uncertain ability to obtain, in socially acceptable ways, enough nutritious food to live a healthy and active life.

foreign service officers The diplomatic and consular staff at U.S. embassies abroad.

framing The process by which the media set a context that helps consumers understand important events and matters of shared interest.

free exercise clause The First Amendment clause prohibiting the government from enacting laws prohibiting an individual's practice of his or her religion; often in contention with the establishment clause.

free rider problem The phenomenon of someone deriving benefit from others' actions.

free trade policy The elimination of tariffs and nontariff trade barriers so that international trade is expanded.

freedom of assembly The right to form or join any type of organization, political party, or club without penalty.

full faith and credit clause The constitutional clause that requires states to comply with and uphold the public acts, records, and judicial decisions of other states.

fund-raising consultant A professional who works with candidates in identifying likely contributors to the campaign and arranging events and meetings with donors.

G

gender gap The measurable difference in the way women and men vote for candidates and in the way they view political issues.

general election An election that determines which candidates win the offices being sought.

general-purpose government A government providing services in numerous and diverse policy and functional areas to the residents living within its borders.

generational effect The impact of an important external event in shaping the views of a generation.

gerrymandering The drawing of legislative district boundaries to benefit an incumbent, a political party, or another group.

global economy The worldwide economy created by the integration and interdependence of national economies.

global warming The rising temperature of the earth as a result of pollution that traps solar heat, keeping the air warmer than it would otherwise be.

globalism The interconnectedness between nations in contemporary times.

GOTV Get out the vote.

government The institution that creates and implements policy and laws that guide the conduct of the nation and its citizens.

government corporation An executive branch unit that sells a service and is expected to be financially self-sufficient.

grandfather clause A clause exempting individuals from voting conditions such as poll taxes or literacy tests if they or their ancestor had voted before 1870, thus sparing most white voters in the South.

grant-in-aid (intergovernmental transfer) The transfer of money from one government to another government (or from a government to a nonprofit organization, for-profit organization, or individual) that does not need to be paid back.

grassroots organizing Tasks that involve direct contact with voters or potential voters.

Great Depression Between 1929 and 1939, a time of devastating economic collapse and personal misery for people around the world.

greenhouse effect The heating of the earth's atmosphere as a result of humans' burning of fossil fuels and the resultant buildup of carbon dioxide and other gases.

gross domestic product (GDP) The total value of all goods and services produced by labor and properties within a country's borders.

H

habeas corpus An ancient right that protects an individual in custody from being held without the right to be heard in a court of law.

hard money Regulated campaign contributions that can specifically advocate the election of a candidate.

hate crime A crime committed against a person, property, or society, where the offender is motivated, in part or in whole, by his or her bias against the victim because of the victim's race, religion, disability, sexual orientation, or ethnicity.

hearings Sessions held by committees or subcommittees to gather information and views from experts.

heightened scrutiny test (intermediate scrutiny test) The guidelines used most frequently by the courts to determine the legality of sex-based discrimination; on the basis of this test, sex-based discrimination is legal if the government can prove that it is substantially related to the achievement of an important public interest.

Holocaust The genocide perpetrated by Adolf Hitler and the Nazis of six million Jews, along with political dissidents, Catholics, homosexuals, and gypsies.

home rule The opportunity provided by state government for citizens to write, adopt, and amend local government charters at the city and county levels.

home rule charter A local government constitution written and approved by citizens following state-mandated procedures that include a referendum.

honeymoon period A time early in a new president's administration characterized by optimistic approval by the public.

hopper A wooden box that sits on a desk at the front of the House of Representatives, into which House members place bills they want to introduce.

horizontal federalism The state-to-state relationships created by the U.S. Constitution.

House majority leader The leader of the majority party, who helps the Speaker develop and implement strategy and work with other members of the House of Representatives.

House minority leader The leader of the minority party, whose job mirrors that of the majority leader but without the power that comes from holding a majority in the House of Representatives.

household income The total pretax earnings of all residents over the age of 15 living in a home.

housing insecurity The situation in which people have limited or uncertain ability to obtain, in socially acceptable ways, affordable, safe, and decent-quality permanent housing.

Human Development Index (HDI) A UN-created measure to determine how well a country's economy is providing for a long and healthy life, educational opportunity, and a decent standard of living.

I

imminent lawless action test (incitement test) A standard established in the 1969 *Brandenburg v. Ohio* case whereby speech is restricted only if it goes beyond mere advocacy, or words, to create a high likelihood of imminent disorder or lawlessness.

impeach Formally charging a government official with not fulfilling constitutional duties or with committing a high crime or misdemeanor.

impeachment The power of the House of Representatives to formally accuse the president (and other high-ranking officials, including the vice president and federal judges) of crimes.

implied powers The powers of the national government that are not enumerated in the Constitution but that Congress claims are necessary and proper for the national government to fulfill its enumerated powers in accordance with the necessary and proper clause of the Constitution.

impressment The forcible removal of merchant sailors from U.S. ships on the spurious grounds that the sailors were deserters from the British Navy.

income inequality The gap in the proportion of national income held by the richest compared to that held by the poorest.

incorporation The process by which the Bill of Rights protections were applied to state governments.

incumbency The situation of already holding the office that is up for reelection.

independent Often used as a synonym for unaffiliated voter.

independent administrative agency An executive branch unit created by Congress and the president that is responsible for a narrowly defined function and whose governing board is intended to be protected from partisan politics.

independent expenditures Outlays by PACs and others, typically for advertising for or against a candidate, but uncoordinated with a candidate's campaign.

independent regulatory commission An executive branch unit responsible for developing standards of behavior within specific industries and businesses, monitoring compliance with these standards, and imposing sanctions on violators.

indexed benefit A government benefit with an automatic cost of living increase based on the rate of inflation.

indirect democracy Sometimes called a *representative democracy,* a system in which citizens elect representatives who decide policies on behalf of their constituents.

individualistic political culture The view that the decision to take part in government is an individual choice and those who choose to participate determine the purpose of government and personally benefit from their participation.

inflation The decreased value of money as evidenced by increased prices.

information equilibrium The dissemination of information outside traditional channels of control.

infotainment News shows that combine entertainment and news, a hybrid of the words *information* and *entertainment.*

inherent characteristics Individual attributes such as race, national origin, religion, and sex.

inherent powers Presidential powers that are implied in the Constitution.

initiative A direct democracy process in which citizens draft a desired policy and get a state-specified number of signatures on a petition in support of the proposal so that it is placed on the ballot for voters to approve or reject.

in-kind assistance A benefit program in which the recipient shops for a service provider who will accept payment from the government for the service or item purchased.

inspectors general Political appointees who work within a government agency to ensure the integrity of public service by investigating allegations of misconduct by bureaucrats.

instant runoff election A special runoff election in which the computerized voting machine simulates the elimination of last-place voter-getters.

instructed delegate model A model of representation in which legislators, as representatives of their constituents, should vote in keeping with the constituents' views, even if those views contradict the legislator's personal views.

intelligent design The theory that the apparent design in the universe and in living things is the product of an intelligent cause rather than of an undirected process such as natural selection; its primary proponents believe that the designer is God and seek to redefine science to accept supernatural explanations.

interest groups Organizations that seek to achieve some of their goals by influencing government decision making.

intergovernmental lobbying Efforts by groups representing state and local governments to influence national domestic policy.

intergovernmental relations (IGR) The collaborative efforts of two or more levels of government working to serve the public.

intermestics The influence of domestic interests on foreign policy.

International Monetary Fund (IMF) The institution charged with regulating monetary relationships among nations, including establishment of exchange rates for major world currencies; established in 1944 by the Bretton Woods Agreement.

interstate compacts Agreements between states that Congress has the authority to review and reject.

interventionism A foreign policy characterized by a nation's willingness to participate and intervene in international situations, including another country's affairs.

iron triangle The interaction of mutual interests among members of Congress, executive agencies, and organized interests during policy making.

isolationism A foreign policy characterized by a nation's unwillingness to participate in international affairs.

issue network The web of connections among those concerned about a policy and those who create and administer the policy.

J

Jim Crow laws Laws requiring the strict separation of racial groups, with whites and "nonwhites" required to attend separate schools, work in different jobs, and use segregated public accommodations, such as transportation and restaurants.

joint committee A bicameral committee composed of members of both chambers of Congress.

joint referral The practice, abolished in the 104th Congress, by which a bill could be referred to two different committees for consideration.

judicial activism An approach to judicial decision making whereby judges apply their authority to bring about specific social goals.

judicial restraint An approach to judicial decision making whereby judges defer to the democratically elected legislative and executive branches of government.

judicial review Court authority to determine that an action taken by any government official or governing body violates the Constitution.

judiciary The branch of government comprising the state and federal courts and the judges who preside over them.

jurisdiction The power of a court to hear a case and to resolve it, given to a court by either a constitution or a statute.

justice Any of the nine judges who sit on the Supreme Court.

K

Keynesian economics The theory that recommends that during a recession the national government should increase its spending and decrease taxes, and during a boom, it should cut spending and increase taxes.

L

laissez-faire The hands-off stance of a government in regard to the marketplace.

lead committee The primary committee considering a bill.

League of Nations A representative body founded in the aftermath of World War I to establish the collective security of nations.

legislative referendum A ballot measure whereby voters approve or reject a law or amendment proposed by state officials.

legitimacy A quality conferred on government by citizens who believe that its exercise of power is right and proper.

***Lemon* test** A three-part test established by the Supreme Court in the 1971 case *Lemon v. Kurtzman* to determine whether government aid to parochial schools is constitutional; the test is also applied to other cases involving the establishment clause.

letter to the editor A letter in which a reader responds to a story in a newspaper, knowing that the letter might be published in that paper.

libel False written statements about others that harm their reputation.

liberalism An ideology that advocates change in the social, political, and economic realms to better protect the well-being of individuals and to produce equality within society.

libertarianism An ideology whose advocates believe that government should take a "hands off" approach in most matters.

liberty The most essential quality of American democracy; it is both the freedom from governmental interference in citizens' lives and the freedom to pursue happiness.

limited war A combatant country's self-imposed limitation on the tactics and strategy it uses, particularly its avoidance of the use of nuclear weapons.

line-item veto The power of the president to strike out specific line items on an appropriations bill while allowing the rest of the bill to become law; declared unconstitutional by the Supreme Court in 1997.

literacy test A test to determine eligibility to vote; designed so that few African Americans would pass.

litigation The process by which cases are brought and decided in the American legal system.

living wage A wage high enough to keep workers and their families out of poverty and to allow them to enjoy a basic living standard.

lobby To communicate directly with policy makers on an interest group's behalf.

logrolling The practice of members of Congress agreeing to vote for a bill in exchange for their colleague's vote on another bill.

loyal opposition A role that the party out of power plays, highlighting its objections to policies and priorities of the government in power.

M

majority rule The idea that in a democracy, only policies with 50 percent plus one vote are enacted, and only candidates that win 50 percent plus one vote are elected.

majority whip A go-between with the majority leadership and party members in the House of Representatives.

majority-minority district A legislative district composed of a majority of a given minority community—say, African Americans—the intent of which is to make it likely that a member of that minority will be elected to Congress.

mandates Clauses in legislation that direct state and local governments to comply with national legislation and national standards.

mandatory spending Payment for debt and government programs for which the legislation that creates the program also obligates the government to spend the money necessary to meet the program's commitments as long as the program is in existence.

manifest destiny The idea that it was the United States' destiny to spread throughout the North American continent; used to rationalize the expansion of U.S. territory.

Marbury v. Madison The 1803 Supreme Court case that established the power of judicial review, which allows the Court to strike down laws passed by the other branches that it views to be in conflict with the Constitution.

margin of error Also called *sampling error;* a statistical calculation of the difference in results between a poll of the sample and a poll of the entire population.

market failure A condition in which competition for profits in the marketplace causes harms to society, such as environmental degradation, unsafe working conditions, and low pay.

marketplace of ideas A concept at the core of the freedoms of expression and press, based on the belief that true and free political discourse depends upon a free and unrestrained discussion of ideas.

markup The process by which the members of legislative committees "mark up" a bill with suggested language for changes and amendments.

Marshall Plan The U.S. government program that provided funds necessary for Western European countries to rebuild after World War II.

McCullogh v. Maryland The 1819 case that established that the necessary and proper clause justifies broad understandings of enumerated powers.

means-tested benefit A benefit for which eligibility is based on having an income below a specified amount, typically based on a percentage of the poverty guideline.

media consultant A professional who brings the campaign message to voters by creating handouts and all forms of media ads.

media segmentation The breaking down of the media according to the specific audiences they target.

median household income The middle of all household incomes—50 percent of households have incomes less than the median and 50 percent have incomes greater than the median.

merit A system of hiring and promotion based on an individual's competence.

merit-based civil service A personnel system in which bureaucrats are hired on the basis of the principles of competence, equal opportunity (open competition), and political neutrality; once hired, these public servants have job protection.

merit selection process A process for selecting judges in which a nonpartisan committee nominates candidates, the governor or legislature appoints judges from among these candidates to a short term of service, and then the appointed judges face a retention election at the end of the short term.

micro-lending Loaning poor entrepreneurs small amounts of money that enable them to buy what they need to create a business.

minority whip The go-between with the minority leadership, whose job mirrors that of the majority whip but without the power that comes from holding a majority in the House of Representatives.

Miranda **rights** A criminal procedural rule, established in the 1966 case *Miranda v. Arizona,* requiring police to inform criminal suspects, on their arrest, of their legal rights, such as the right to remain silent and the right to counsel; these warnings must be read to suspects before interrogation.

monarchy A government in which a member of a royal family, usually a king or queen, has absolute authority over a territory and its government.

monetarism The theory that says the government's proper economic role is to control the rate of inflation by controlling the amount of money in circulation.

monetary policy The body of government policies, controlled by the Federal Reserve System, aimed at influencing the supply of money in the marketplace to maintain price stability.

Monroe Doctrine President James Monroe's 1823 declaration that the Americas should not be considered subjects for future colonization by any European power.

moralistic political culture The view that the purpose of government is to serve the public good, including providing for those who are disadvantaged, and that all citizens should participate in government.

muckraking Criticism and exposés of corruption in government and industry by journalists at the turn of the twentieth century.

multilateral Many-sided; having the support of numerous nations.

municipal government Self-governing general-purpose government—including city, borough, and town governments—created by states to provide goods and services within a densely populated area.

mutual assured destruction (MAD) The doctrine that if one nation attacked another with nuclear weapons, the other would be capable of retaliating and would retaliate with such force as to assure mutual annihilation.

N

narrowcasting The practice of aiming media content at specific segments of the public.

national debt The total amount of money the government owes to others due to borrowing.

National Security Council (NSC) Consisting of top foreign policy advisers and relevant cabinet officials, this is an arm of the Executive Office of the President that the president consults on matters of foreign policy and national security.

natural law The assertion that standards that govern human behavior are derived from the nature of humans themselves and can be universally applied.

natural rights (unalienable rights) The rights possessed by all humans as a gift from nature, or God, including the rights to life, liberty and the pursuit of happiness.

naturalization Becoming a citizen by means other than birth, as in the case of immigrants.

necessary and proper clause (elastic clause) A clause in Article I, section 8, of the Constitution that gives Congress the power to do whatever it deems necessary and constitutional to meet its enumerated obligations; the basis for the implied powers.

neoconservatism An ideology that advocates military over diplomatic solutions in foreign policy and is less concerned with restraining government activity in domestic politics than traditional conservatives.

Net neutrality The idea that Internet traffic—e-mail, Web site content, videos, and phone calls—should flow without interference or discrimination by those who own or run the Internet pipeline.

netroots The Internet-centered political efforts on behalf of candidates and causes.

New Deal Franklin Roosevelt's broad social welfare program in which the government would bear the responsibility of providing a "safety net" to protect the weakest members of society.

New Deal coalition The group composed of southern Democrats, northern city dwellers, immigrants, the poor, Catholics, labor union members, blue-collar workers, African Americans, and women that elected FDR to the presidency four times.

New Jersey Plan The proposal presented by states with smaller populations at the Constitutional Convention in response to James Madison's Virginia Plan.

new judicial federalism The practice whereby state judges base decisions regarding civil rights and liberties on their state's constitution, rather than the U.S. Constitution, when their state's constitution guarantees more than minimum rights.

new media Cable television, the Internet, blogs, and satellite technology.

Nixon Doctrine Policy emphasizing the responsibility of U.S. allies to provide for their own national defense and security, aimed at improving relations with the communist nations, including the Soviet Union and China.

noncontributory program A benefit provided to a targeted population, paid for by a proportion of the money collected from all taxpayers.

nonpartisan election An election in which the candidates are not nominated by political parties and the ballot does not include party affiliations.

nontariff trade barrier Business and social regulations as well as subsidies aimed at creating a competitive advantage in trade.

normal trade relations (NTR) status The international trade principle holding that the least restrictive trade conditions (best tariff rates) offered to any one national trading partner will be offered to every other nation in a trading network (also known as *most favored nations*).

North Atlantic Treaty Organization (NATO) An international mutual defense alliance formed in 1949 that created a structure for regional security for its fifteen member nations.

O

obscenity Indecent or offensive speech or expression.

Office of Management and Budget (OMB) The office that creates the president's annual budget.

office-block ballot A type of ballot that arranges all of the candidates for a particular office under the name of that office.

oligarchy A government in which an elite few hold power.

ombudsperson A role in which an elected or appointed leader acts as an advocate for citizens by listening to and investigating complaints against a government agency.

open meeting laws Laws requiring legislative bodies and executive agencies of government to conduct policy-making meetings in public.

open primary A type of primary in which both parties' ballots are available in the voting booth, and the voters simply select one on which to register their preferences.

operating budget A budget that accounts for all the costs of day-to-day government operations and covers such items as salaries and benefits, utilities, office supplies, and rent.

oral arguments The stage when appeals court judges or Supreme Court justices meet with the petitioner and the respondent to ask questions about the legal interpretations or information contained in their briefs.

ordinary scrutiny test The guidelines the courts used between 1873 and 1976 to determine the legality of sex-based discrimination; on the basis of this test, sex-based discrimination is legal if it is a reasonable means by which the government can achieve a legitimate public interest.

original jurisdiction The power of a court to hear a case first, before other courts have decided it.

outsourcing The situation in which the government signs contracts with private-sector employers to do work previously provided by government workers.

oversight The process by which the legislative branch "checks" the executive branch to ensure that the laws Congress has passed are being administered in keeping with legislators' intent.

P

partial preemption The authority of the national government to establish minimum regulatory standards that provide state and local governments the flexibility either to enforce the national standards or to establish their own more stringent standards, which they must enforce.

partisan election An election in which candidates are nominated by political parties and the ballot lists each candidate's political party affiliation.

party identifiers Individuals who identify themselves as a member of one party or the other.

party in government The partisan identifications of elected leaders in local, county, state, and federal government.

party in the electorate Individuals who identify with or tend to support a party.

party organization The formal party apparatus, including committees, party leaders, conventions, and workers.

party system The categorization of the number and competitiveness of political parties in a polity.

party-column ballot A ballot that organizes the candidates by political party.

patronage The system in which a party leader rewarded political supporters with jobs or government contracts in exchange for their support of the party.

penny press Newspapers that sold for a penny in the 1830s.

petitioner Also called *appellant;* the party seeking to have a lower court's decision reviewed by the Supreme Court under the Court's discretionary jurisdiction.

plaintiff The party bringing the case to court.

platform The formal statement of a party's principles and policy objectives.

Plessy v. Ferguson 1896 Supreme Court ruling creating the separate but equal doctrine.

plum book A publication that lists the top jobs in the bureaucracy to which the president will appoint people via the patronage system.

plural executive system A state and local government structure in which the citizens elect more than two people to top positions in the executive branch of government.

pluralist theory A theory that holds that policy making is a competition among diverse interest groups that ensure the representation of individual interests.

pocket veto A special presidential veto of a bill passed at the conclusion of a legislative session, whereby the president waits ten days without signing the bill, and the bill dies.

police powers The states' reserved powers to protect the health, safety, lives, and properties of residents in a state.

political action committee (PAC) A group that raises and spends money in order to influence the outcome of an election.

political culture The people's collective beliefs and attitudes about government and political processes.

political engagement Citizen actions that are intended to solve public problems through political means.

political ideology An integrated system of ideas or beliefs about political values in general and the role of government in particular.

political machines Big-city organizations that exerted control over many aspects of life and lavishly rewarded supporters.

political party An organization that recruits, nominates, and elects party members to office in order to control the government.

political socialization The process by which we develop our political values and opinions.

politics The process of deciding who gets benefits in society and who is excluded from benefiting.

politics-administration dichotomy The concept that elected government officials, who are accountable to the voters, create and approve public policy, and then competent, politically neutral bureaucrats implement the public policy.

poll tax A fee for voting; levied to prevent poor African Americans in the South from voting.

pool memo Description written by Court clerks of the facts of a case filed with the Court, the pertinent legal arguments, and a recommendation as to whether the case should be taken.

popular referendum A measure that allows citizens, by collecting signatures in a petition drive, to put before voters specific legislation that the legislature has previously approved.

popular sovereignty The theory that government is created by the people and depends on the people for the authority to rule.

population In a poll, the group of people whose opinions are of interest and/or about whom information is desired.

populism A philosophy supporting the rights and empowerment of the masses as opposed to elites.

pork barrel Legislators' appropriations of funds for special projects located within their congressional districts.

poverty The condition of lacking the income sufficient to purchase the necessities for an adequate living standard.

poverty guidelines A simplified version of the poverty thresholds developed each year by the Department of Health and Human Services; used to set financial eligibility criteria for benefits.

poverty rate The proportion of the population living below the poverty line as established by the national government.

poverty thresholds A set of income measures adjusted for family size that the Census Bureau establishes each year to define poverty for data collection purposes.

precedent Legal authority established by earlier cases.

preemption The constitutionally based principle that allows a national law to supersede state or local laws.

president pro tempore Also called *president pro tem;* theoretically, the chair of the Senate in the vice president's absence; in reality, an honorary title, with the senator of the majority party having the longest record of continuous service being elected to the position.

press secretary The president's spokesperson to the media.

preventive war The strategy of waging war on countries that are regarded as threatening in order to avoid future conflicts.

primal scream format Loud, angry argument characteristic of many television and radio talk shows.

primary election An election in which voters choose the party's candidates who will run in the later general election.

priming Bringing certain policies on issues to the public agenda through media coverage.

prior restraint A form of censorship by the government whereby it blocks the publication of news stories viewed as libelous or harmful.

privileges and immunities The Constitution's requirement that a state extend to other states' citizens the privileges and immunities it provides for its citizens.

progressive tax A tax that takes a larger percentage of the income of wealthier taxpayers and a smaller percentage of the income of lower-income taxpayers.

property Anything that can be owned.

proportional representation system An electoral structure in which political parties win the number of parliamentary seats equal to the percentage of the vote the party receives.

proportional (flat) tax A tax that takes the same percentage of each taxpayer's income.

proposition A proposed measure placed on the ballot in an initiative election.

prospective voting A method of evaluating candidates in which voters focus on candidates' positions on issues important to them and vote for the candidates who best represent their views.

prosumers Individuals who simultaneously consume information and news and produce information in forms like videos, blogs, and Web sites.

protectionist trade policy The establishment of trade barriers to protect domestic goods from foreign competition.

public agenda The public issues that most demand the attention of government officials.

public diplomat An individual outside government who promotes his or her country's interests and thus contributes to shaping international perceptions of the nation.

public goods Services governments provide that are available to everyone, like clean air, clean water, airport security, and highways.

public opinion The public's expressed views about an issue at a specific point in time.

public opinion poll A survey of a given population's opinion on an issue or a candidate at a particular point in time.

pure capitalist economy Private individuals and companies own the modes of producing goods and services, and the government does not enact laws aimed at influencing the marketplace transactions that distribute these goods and services.

purposive incentives Motivation to join an interest group based on the belief in the group's cause from an ideological or a moral standpoint.

push polls A special type of poll that both provides information to campaigns about candidate strengths and weaknesses and attempts to skew public opinion about a candidate.

Q

quota sample A method by which pollsters structure a sample so that it is representative of the characteristics of the target population.

R

rally 'round the flag effect The peaks in presidential approval ratings during short-term military action.

random sampling A scientific method of selection for a poll in which each member of the population has an equal chance at being included in the sample.

rational abstention thesis A theory that some individuals decide the costs of voting are not worth the effort when compared to the benefits.

rational choice theory The idea that from an economic perspective it is not rational for people to participate in collective action when they can secure the collective good without participating.

real income Earned income adjusted for inflation.

realignment A shift in party allegiances or electoral support.

reapportionment Reallocation of seats in the House of Representatives to each state based on changes in the state's population since the last census.

recall A direct democracy measure by which citizens can remove an elected official from office before the end of his or her term.

recession An economic downturn during which unemployment is high and the production of goods and services is low.

Reconstruction era The time after the Civil War between 1866 and 1877 when the institutions and infrastructure of the South were rebuilt.

redistricting The redrawing of congressional district boundaries within each state, based on the reapportionment from the census.

referendum A direct democracy measure that places public policy drafted by government officials on the ballot for voters to approve or reject.

regime change The replacement of a country's government with another government by facilitating the deposing of its leader or leading political party.

regional security alliance An alliance typically between a superpower and nations that are ideologically similar in a particular region.

regressive tax A tax that takes a greater percentage of the income of lower-income earners than of higher-income earners.

regulated capitalist economy (mixed economy) An economy in which the government enacts policies to influence the health of the economy.

regulatory law (administrative law) A law made by executive and regulatory agencies, often pursuant to a delegation of lawmaking power from Congress.

regulatory policies Policies that mandate individual and group (corporate) behaviors that foster the general welfare.

report A legislative committee's explanation to the full chamber of a bill and its intent.

reserved powers The matters referred to in the Tenth Amendment over which states retain sovereignty.

respondent Also called *appellee;* the party opposing the hearing of a case on the Supreme Court's discretionary docket.

responsible party model Political scientists' view that a function of a party is to offer a clear choice to voters by establishing priorities or policy stances different from those of rival parties.

retention election A noncompetitive election in which an incumbent judge's name is on the ballot and voters decide whether the judge should be retained.

retrospective voting A method of evaluating candidates in which voters evaluate incumbent candidates and decide whether to support them based on their past performance.

right to privacy The right of an individual to be left alone and to make decisions freely, without the interference of others.

Roosevelt Corollary The idea advanced by President Theodore Roosevelt, stating that the United States had the right to act as an "international police power" in the Western Hemisphere in order to ensure stability in the region.

Rule of Four The Supreme Court practice by which the Court will agree to hear a case that comes to it under its discretionary jurisdiction if four or more justices vote to hear it.

Rules Committee One of the most important committees in the House, which decides the length of debate and the scope of amendments that will be allowed on a bill.

run-off election A follow-up election that is held when no candidate receives the majority of votes cast in the original election.

S

safety net A collection of public policies ensuring that the basic physiological needs of citizens are met.

salient Having resonance, in relation to a voting issue, reflecting intense interest.

SALT I The treaty signed in 1972 by the United States and the Soviet Union limiting the two countries' antiballistic missiles and freezing the number of offensive missiles that each nation could have at the number they already possessed, plus the number they had under construction.

SALT II The treaty signed in 1979 by the United States and the Soviet Union that set an overall limit on strategic nuclear launchers, limited the number of missiles that could carry multiple independently targeted reentry vehicles (MIRVs) with nuclear warheads, and limited each nation to the development of only one new type of intercontinental ballistic missile (ICBM).

sampling error Also called *margin of error;* a statistical calculation of the difference in results between a poll of a randomly drawn sample and a poll of the entire population.

sanctions Penalties that halt economic relations.

select committee A congressional committee created to consider a specific policy issue or address a specific concern.

selective incorporation The process by which, over time, the Supreme Court applied those freedoms that served some fundamental principle of liberty or justice to the states, thus rejecting total incorporation.

Senate majority leader The most powerful position in the Senate; the majority leader manages the legislative process and schedules debate on legislation.

Senate minority leader The leader of the minority party in the Senate, who works with the majority leader in negotiating legislation.

senatorial courtesy A custom that allows senators from the president's political party to veto the president's choice of federal district court judge in the senator's state.

senior executive service (SES) A unique personnel system for top managerial, supervisory, and policy positions offering less job security but higher pay than the merit-based civil service system.

seniority system The system in which the member with the longest continuous tenure on a standing committee is given preference when the committee chooses its chair.

separate but equal doctrine Established by the Supreme Court in *Plessy v. Ferguson,* it said that separate but equal facilities for whites and nonwhites do not violate the Fourteenth Amendment's equal protection clause.

separation of powers The Constitution's delegation of authority for the primary governing functions among three branches of government so that no one group of government officials controls all the governing functions.

shadow bureaucrats People hired and paid by private for-profit and nonprofit organizations that implement public policy through a government contract.

signing statement A written message that the president issues upon signing a bill into law.

single-issue groups Groups that focus on one issue.

single-purpose government A government providing services in one policy or functional area to residents living within its borders.

slander False verbal statements about others that harm their reputation.

social capital The ways in which our lives are improved in many ways by social connections.

social contract An agreement between the people and their leaders in which the people agree to give up some liberties so that their other liberties are protected.

social contract theory The idea that individuals possess free will, and every individual is equally endowed with the God-given right of self-determination and the ability to consent to be governed.

social movement The organized action of a broad segment of society to demand and effect improvement in the treatment of a specific group.

social regulation The government rules and regulations aimed at protecting workers, consumers, and the environment from market failure.

socialism An ideology that advocates economic equality, theoretically achieved by having the government or workers own the means of production (businesses and industry).

soft money loophole The Supreme Court's interpretation of campaign finance law that enabled political parties to raise unlimited funds for party-building activities such as voter registration drives and get-out-the-vote (GOTV) efforts.

soft news Events or topics that are not serious or broadly important.

solidary incentives The motivation to join an interest group based on the companionship and the satisfaction derived from socializing with others that it offers.

sound bites Short audio or video clips taken from a larger speech.

Southeast Asia Treaty Organization (SEATO) A regional security agreement whose goal was to prevent communist encroachment in the countries of Southeast Asia.

sovereignty Having ultimate authority to govern, with no legal superior.

Speaker of the House The leader of the House of Representatives, chosen by the majority party.

spoils system The practice of rewarding political supporters with jobs.

stagflation An economic condition in which the high unemployment of a recession occurs along with large increases in prices of consumer goods (high inflation) typical of an economic boom.

standing committee A permanent committee in Congress, with a defined legislative jurisdiction.

standing to sue The ability to bring lawsuits in court.

stare decisis From the Latin "let the decision stand," the principle that binds judges to rely upon the holdings of past judges in deciding cases.

statute A law enacted by Congress and the state legislatures to deal with particular issues or problems, sometimes more detailed and comprehensive than the common law.

statutory powers Powers explicitly granted to presidents by congressional action.

steering The practice by which realtors steered African American families to certain neighborhoods and white families to others.

strategic arms limitation talks (SALT talks) Discussions between the United States and the Soviet Union in the 1970s that focused on cooling down the nuclear arms race between the two superpowers.

strategic arms reduction talks (START talks) Talks between the United States and the Soviet Union in which reductions in missiles and nuclear warheads, not merely a limitation on increases, were negotiated.

strategic defense initiative (SDI, or "Star Wars") A ballistic missile defense system advocated by President Ronald Reagan.

stratified sampling A process of random sampling in which the national population is divided into fourths and representative counties and metropolitan statistical areas are selected as representative of the national population.

straw poll A poll conducted in an unscientific manner, used to predict election outcomes.

strict scrutiny test Guidelines the courts use to determine the legality of all but sex-based discrimination; on the basis of this test, discrimination is legal if it is a necessary means by which the government can achieve a compelling public interest.

strong mayor An elected municipal government executive who holds the powers traditionally delegated to elected chief executives (veto power, power to formulate the budget, and power to appoint many executive branch officials).

subcommittee A subordinate committee in Congress that typically handles specific areas of a standing committee's jurisdiction.

subsidy A tax break or another kind of financial support that encourages business expansion or decreases the cost of doing business so that businesses can be more competitive.

sunset clause A clause in legislation that sets an expiration date for the authorized program/policy unless Congress reauthorizes it.

sunshine laws Legislation that opens up government functions and documents to the public.

Super Tuesday The Tuesday in early March on which the most primary elections are held, many of them in southern states; provided the basis for Super-Duper Tuesday in 2008.

superpowers Leader nations with dominating influence in international affairs.

supply-side economics The theory that advocates cutting taxes and deregulating business to stimulate the economy.

supremacy clause The paragraph in Article VI that makes the Constitution, and the treaties and laws created in compliance with it, the supreme law of the land.

supreme law of the land The U.S. Constitution's description of its own authority, meaning that all laws made by governments within the United States must be in compliance with the Constitution.

suspect classifications Distinctions based on race, religion, national origin, and sex, which are assumed to be illegitimate.

symbolic representation The attempt to ensure that the Supreme Court is representative of major demographic groups, such as women, African Americans, Jews, and Catholics.

symbolic speech Nonverbal "speech" in the form of an action such as picketing, flag burning, or wearing an armband to signify a protest.

T

take care clause The constitutional basis for inherent powers, which states that the president "shall take Care that the Laws be faithfully executed."

talk radio A format featuring conversations and interviews about topics of interest, along with call-ins from listeners.

tariff A special tax on imported goods.

tax base The overall *wealth* (income and assets of citizens and corporations) that the government can tax in order to raise revenue.

tax expenditures (Also, *tax breaks* or *loopholes*), government financial supports that allow individuals and corporations to pay reduced taxes, to encourage behaviors that foster the public good.

telegenic Looks good on TV.

third party A party organized in opposition or as an alternative to the existing parties in a two-party system.

Three-Fifths Compromise The negotiated agreement by the delegates to the Constitutional Convention to count each slave as three-fifths a free man for the purpose of representation and taxes.

ticket splitting The situation in which voters vote for candidates from more than one party.

time, place, and manner restrictions Regulations regarding when, where, or how expression may occur; must be content neutral.

tort A wrongful act involving a personal injury or harm to one's property or reputation.

total incorporation The theory that the Fourteenth Amendment's due process clause requires the states to uphold all freedoms in the Bill of Rights; rejected by the Supreme Court in favor of selective incorporation.

totalitarianism A system of government in which the government essentially controls every aspect of people's lives.

township A unit of government that serves people living outside municipalities, in rural areas where the population is more dispersed than in areas served by municipal governments.

tracking polls Polls that measure changes in public opinion over the course of days, weeks, or months by repeatedly asking respondents the same questions and measuring changes in their responses.

trade deficit Aa negative balance of trade in which imports exceed exports.

trade policy A collection of tax laws and regulations that supports the country's international commerce.

traditionalistic political culture The view that the purpose of government is to maintain the status quo and that participants in government should come from the society's elite.

trial court The court in which a case is first heard and which determines the facts of a case.

Truman Doctrine Articulated by President Harry Truman, a foreign policy commitment by the United States to assist countries' efforts to resist communism in the Cold War era.

trustee model A model of representation in which a member of the House or Senate should articulate and vote for the position that best represents the views of constituents.

turnout rate The proportion of eligible voters who actually voted.

U

umbrella organizations Interest groups that represent collective groups of industries or corporations.

unanimous consent An agreement by every senator to the terms of debate on a given piece of legislation.

unicameral A legislative body with a single chamber.

unilateralism One-sided action, usually in foreign policy.

unitary system A governmental structure in which one central government has sovereignty, although it may create regional governments to which it delegates responsibilities.

United Nations (UN) Established in 1945, an international body whose founders hoped would develop the capacity to prevent future wars by achieving collective security and peace.

U.S. Code A compilation of all the laws passed by the U.S. Congress.

U.S. Supreme Court High court with a limited original jurisdiction whose decisions may not be appealed; it serves as the court of last resort in the U.S. judiciary.

V

vblog A video Weblog.

V-chip Required by the Telecommunications Act of 1996, a computer chip in television sets that lets parents block programming they consider unsuitable for children.

veto An executive power held by the president, who can reject a bill and return it to Congress with reasons for the rejection.

Virginia Plan James Madison's proposal at the Constitutional Convention for a new governmental structure, which favored states with larger populations.

voter fatigue The condition in which voters grow tired of all candidates by the time Election Day arrives, and may thus be less likely to vote.

W

War Powers Act This law limits presidential use of military forces to sixty days, with an automatic extension of thirty additional days if the president requests such an extension.

Warsaw Pact A regional security structure formed in 1955 by the Soviet Union and its seven satellite states in Eastern Europe in response to the creation of the North Atlantic Treaty Organization (NATO).

Watergate During the Nixon administration, a scandal involving burglaries and the subsequent cover-up by high-level administration officials.

weak mayor An elected municipal government executive who holds few, if any, of the powers traditionally delegated to elected chief executives.

weapons of mass destruction (WMDs) Nuclear, chemical, and biological weapons.

whistleblower A civil servant who discloses mismanagement, fraud, waste, corruption, and/or threats to public health and safety to the government.

White House counsel The president's lawyer.

White House Office (WHO) The office that develops policies and protects the president's legal and political interests.

white primary A primary election in which a party's nominees for general election were chosen but in which only white people were allowed to vote.

winner-take-all An electoral system in which the candidate who receives the most votes wins that office, even if that total is not a majority.

Works Progress Administration (WPA) A New Deal program that would employ 8.5 million people at a cost of more than $11 million between 1935 and 1943.

World Bank The international financial institution created by the Bretton Woods Agreement of 1944 and charged with lending money to nations in need.

World Trade Organization (WTO) The organization created in 1995 to negotiate, implement, and enforce international trade agreements.

writ of *certiorari* Latin for "a request to make certain"; this is an order to a lower court to produce a certified record of a case so that the appellate court can determine whether any errors occurred during trial that warrant review of the case.

Y

yellow journalism An irresponsible, sensationalist approach to news reporting, so named after the yellow ink used in the "Yellow Kid" cartoons in the *New York World*.

REFERENCES

CHAPTER 1

1. Rogers Smith, *Civic Ideals: Conflicting Visions of Citizenship in U.S. History* (New Haven, CT: Yale University Press, 1997).
2. Robert A. Dahl, *Who Governs? Democracy and Power in an American City* (New Haven, CT: Yale University Press, 1961).
3. E. E. Schattschneider, *The Semi-Sovereign People* (New York: Holt, Rinehart, and Winston, 1960).
4. E. J. Dionne Jr., *Why Americans Hate Politics: The Death of the Democratic Process,* 2nd ed. (New York: Touchstone, 1992).
5. Gallup Poll, "Trust in Government," www.gallup.com/poll/5392/Trust-Government.aspx.
6. Institute of Politics at Harvard University, "Attitudes Towards Politics and Public Service: A National Survey of College Undergraduates," April 11–20, 2000, www.iop.harvard.edu/pdfs/survey/2000.pdf.
7. Ibid.
8. Ibid.
9. Ibid.
10. Barbara Roswell, "From Service-Learning to Service Politics: A Conversation with Rick Battistoni," http://reflectionsjournal.org/Articles/V3.N1.Battistoni.Rick.Roswell.Barbara.pdf.
11. www.18in08.com/about.
12. Though not active in the campaign, Citizen Change's mission was found at www.behaviordesign.com/work/case_studies/images/ctz/canned_site/about_citizen_change.html.
13. S. E. Finer, *The History of Government,* 3 vols. (London: Oxford University Press, 1997).
14. Martin A. Reddish, *The Constitution as Political Structure* (London: Oxford University Press, 1995).
15. Theodore Sky, *To Provide for the General Welfare: A History of the Federal Spending Power* (Newark, DE: University of Delaware Press, 2003).
16. David Epstein, *The Political Theory of the Federalist* (Chicago: University of Chicago Press, 1984).
17. Thomas Hobbes, *Leviathan* (1651; New York: Oxford University Press, 1996), chap. 14.
18. *New York Times,* "America Enduring," September 11, 2002, http://query.nytimes.com/gst/fullpage.html?res=9A00E0DE1431F932A2575AC0A9649C8B63&scp=1&sq=america+enduring&st=nyt.
19. Oscar Handlin and Mary Handlin, *The Dimensions of Liberty* (Cambridge, MA: Harvard University Press, 1961).
20. Richard Labunski, *James Madison and the Struggle for the Bill of Rights* (London: Oxford University Press, 2006).
21. Jack N. Rakove, *Original Meanings: Politics and Ideas in the Making of the Constitution* (New York: Knopf, 1996).
22. Ira Katznelson and Martin Shefter, eds., *Shaped by War and Trade: International Influences on American Political Development* (Princeton, NJ: Princeton University Press, 2002).
23. *Wing Hing v. City of Eureka* (Calif), 1886.
24. Clyde W. Barrow, *Critical Theories of the State: Marxist, Neo-Marxist, Post-Marxist* (Madison: University of Wisconsin Press, 1993).
25. Seymour Martin Lipset and Gary Marks, *It Didn't Happen Here: Why Socialism Failed in the United States* (New York: W. W. Norton, 2001).
26. Giovanni Sartori and Peter Mair, *Parties and Party Systems: A Framework for Analysis* (Oxford, England: European Consortium for Political Research.
27. Michael Delli Carpini, Director Pew Charitable Trusts, www.apa.org/ed/slce/civicengagement.html.

CHAPTER 2

1. Charles Hulse, "Filibuster Fight Nears Showdown," *New York Times,* May 8, 2005.
2. Quoted in Katherine Seelye, "Clinton Backer Points to Electoral College Votes as New Measure," *New York Times,* March 25, 2008.
3. www.u-s-history.com/pages/h1211.html.
4. www.yale.edu/lawweb/avalon/amerrev/parliament/stamp_act_1765.htm.
5. www.u-s-history.com/pages/h1221.html.
6. www.historyplace.com/unitedstates/revolution/rev-prel.htm.
7. J. Alan Rogers, "Colonial Opposition to the Quartering of Troops During the French and Indian War," *Military Affairs* (1970): 7.
8. www.manhattanrarebooks-history.com/declaratory_act.htm.
9. http://ahp.gatech.edu/townshend_act_1767.html.
10. Russell Bourne, *Cradle of Violence: How Boston's Waterfront Mobs Ignited the American Revolution* (Hoboken, NJ: Wiley, 2006).
11. www.u-s-history.com/pages/h675.html.
12. C. Brian Kelly, *Best Little Stories from the American Revolution* (Nashville, TN: Cumberland House, 1999).
13. www.bostonteapartyship.com/.
14. www.ushistory.org/declaration/related/intolerable.htm.
15. www.yale.edu/lawweb/avalon/resolves.htm.
16. For further discussion of the impact of *Common Sense* on colonial attitudes and beliefs, see Edmund S. Morgan, *The Birth of the Republic: 1763–89* (Chicago: University of Chicago Press, 1992), 71–76.
17. www.geocities.com/presfacts/8/lee.html.
18. Council of State Governments, *The Book of the States* (Lexington, KY: Author, 2004), 10–11.
19. www.fordham.edu/halsall/mod/iroquois.html.
20. Charles Beard, *An Economic Interpretation of the Constitution of the United States* (New York: Macmillan, 1913).
21. www.usconstitution.net/consttop_ccon.html.
22. www.africanaonline.com/slavery_timeline.htm.
23. Alexander Hamilton, "Federalist No. 9," *The Federalist Papers* (Cutchogue, NY: Buccaneer Books, 1992), 37.
24. James Madison, "Federalist No. 51," *The Federalist Papers* (Cutchogue, NY: Buccaneer Books, 1992), 261–65.
25. James Madison, "Federalist No. 10," *The Federalist Papers* (Cutchogue, NY: Buccaneer Books, 1992), 42–49.
26. Alexander Hamilton, "Federalist No. 84," *The Federalist Papers* (Cutchogue, NY: Buccaneer Books, 1992), 436–37.
27. Thomas Jefferson, Letter to James Madison on the Bill of Rights debate, March 15, 1789. Courtesy of Eigen's Political & Historical Quotations.
28. John P. Roche, "The Founding Fathers: A Reform Caucus in Action," *American Political Science Review,* LV (1961).
29. Alexander Hamilton, "Federalist No. 78," *The Federalist Papers* (Cutchogue, NY: Buccaneer Books, 1992), 395–96.
30. Courtesy of Eigen's Political and Historical Quotations, www.politicalquotes.org/Quotedisplay.aspx?DocID=22447.
31. Larry Sabato, *A More Perfect Constitution: 23 Proposals to Revitalize Our Constitution and Make America a Fairer Country* (New York: Walker Publishing, 2007).

32. *Plessy v. Ferguson,* 163 U.S. 537 (1896).

33. *Brown v. Board of Education,* 347 U.S. 483 (1954).

34. Linda Greenhouse, "For Justices Another Day on Detainees," *New York Times,* December 3, 2007.

35. *Boumediene v. Bush,* 533 U.S. ____ (2008).

36. Thomas Marshall, "Representing Public Opinion: American Courts and the Appeals Process," *Politics and Policy* 31, no. 4 (December 2003): 726–39.

CHAPTER 3

1. Kendra A. Hovey and Harold A. Hovey, *CQ's State Fact Finder: 2007* (Washington, DC: CQ Press, 2007), 220.

2. www.sss.gov.

3. *Marbury v. Madison,* 5 U.S. 137 (1803).

4. Joe R. Feagin and Clairece Booher Feagin, *Racial and Ethnic Relations,* 7th ed. (Upper Saddle River, NJ: Prentice Hall, 2003), p. 131.

5. Dennis L. Dresang and James J. Gosling, *Politics and Policy in American States and Communities,* 4th ed. (New York: Pearson Longman, 2004), 88.

6. *McCulloch v. Maryland,* 17 U.S. 316 (1819).

7. *Gibbons v. Ogden,* 22 U.S. 1 (1824).

8. *United States v. Lopez,* 514 U.S. 549 (1995).

9. www.oyez.org/cases/1990-1999/1994/1994_93_1260/.

10. *Helvering v. Davis,* 301 U.S. 619 (1937).

11. CNN, *CNN Reports: Katrina – State of Emergency* (Kansas City, KS: Andrews McMeel Publishing, 2005), 10.

12. Ibid., 11.

13. Ibid., 16.

14. Ibid., 176.

15. Ibid., 46.

16. *Pruneyard Shopping Center & Fred Sahadi v. Michael Robins et al.,* 447 U.S. 74, 100 S. Ct. 2035.

17. David B. Walker, *The Rebirth of Federalism,* 2nd ed. (New York: Chatham House, 2000).

18. *National League of Cities v. Usery,* 426 U.S. 833 (1976).

19. *Garcia v. San Antonio Transportation Authority,* 469 U.S. 528 (1985).

20. *United States v. Oakland Cannabis Buyers' Cooperative,* 532 U.S. 483 (2001).

21. www.drugpolicy.org/marijuana/medical/challenges/cases/conant/.

22. *Raich v. Gonzales,* 545 U.S. 1 (2005).

23. *Bush v. Gore,* 531 U.S. 98 (2000).

24. See for example David B. Walker, *The Rebirth of Federalism.*

25. *Massachusetts v. Mellon,* 262 U.S. 447 (1923).

26. *South Dakota v. Dole,* 483 U.S. 208 (1987).

27. U.S. Census Bureau, *Statistical Abstract of the United States 2006,* Table 421.

28. Jesse J. Holland, "Woman in Supreme Court Case Asks Congress to Step into Eminent Domain Case," Associated Press, September 20, 2005.

CHAPTER 4

1. Stephen L. Carter, *The Dissent of the Governed: Law, Religion, and Loyalty* (Cambridge, MA: Harvard University Press, 1998).

2. For an accessible and lively account of the central role of liberty in the American Revolution, see Thomas Fleming, *Liberty! The American Revolution* (New York: Viking, 1997).

3. For a history of civil liberties in wartime, see Geoffrey R. Stone, *Perilous Times: Free Speech in Wartime from the Sedition Act of 1798 to the War on Terrorism* (New York: W. W. Norton, 2004).

4. *Barron v. Baltimore,* 32 U.S. 243 (1833).

5. See *Hurtado v. California,* 110 U.S. 516 (1884) and *Turning v. New Jersey,* 211 U.S. 78 (1908) for a discussion of the standard the Court uses to determine whether a particular liberty should be incorporated into the Fourteenth Amendment.

6. *Gitlow v. New York,* 268 U.S. 652 (1925).

7. *Near v. Minnesota,* 283 U.S. 697 (1931).

8. *Palko v. Connecticut,* 302 U.S. 319 (1937).

9. Presidential Proclamation of September 24, 1862, by President Abraham Lincoln, suspending the writ of habeas corpus.

10. For two detailed accounts of the acts, see John C. Miller, *Crisis in Freedom: The Alien and Sedition Acts* (Boston: Little, Brown, 1951) and James Morton Smith, *Freedom's Fetters: The Alien and Sedition Laws and American Civil Liberties* (Ithaca, NY: Cornell University Press, 1956).

11. Ron Fournier, "Bush Orders Terrorist Trials by Military Tribunals," Associated Press, November 13, 2001. Executive order available at www.whitehouse.gov/news/releases/releases/2001/11/20011113-27.html.

12. *Schenck v. United States,* 249 U.S. 47 (1919).

13. *Gitlow v. New York.*

14. *Dennis v. U.S.,* 341 U.S. 494 (1951).

15. *Brandenburg v. Ohio,* 395 U.S. 444 (1969).

16. *U.S. v. O'Brien,* 391 U.S. 367.

17. *Tinker et al. v. Des Moines Independent Community School District et al.,* 393 U.S. 503 (1969).

18. For a discussion of *Tinker* and similar cases, see Jamin B. Baskin, *We the Students: Supreme Court Cases for and About Students* (Washington, DC: CQ Press, 2000).

19. *Texas v. Johnson,* 491 U.S. 397 (1989).

20. *U.S. v. Eichman,* 496 U.S. 310 (1990).

21. *Miller v. California,* 413 U.S. 15 (1973).

22. *Chaplinsky v. New Hampshire,* 315 U.S. 568 (1942).

23. *Reno v. ACLU,* 521 U.S. 844 (1997); *U.S. v. Playboy Entertainment Group,* 529 U.S. 803 (2000).

24. *Ashcroft v. Free Speech Coalition,* 535 U.S. 234 (2002).

25. James Risen and Eric Lightblau, "Bush Lets U.S. Spy on Callers Without Courts," *New York Times,* December 16, 2005.

26. *New York Times v. U.S.,* 403 U.S. 713 (1971).

27. www.gallup.com/poll/1690/Religion.aspx.

28. The phrase "wall of separation" first appeared in Thomas Jefferson's 1802 letter to the Danbury Baptist Association. This letter is available at the Library of Congress Web site: www.loc.gov/loc/lcib/9806/danpre.html.

29. For a discussion of the doctrine of accommodationism, see Kenneth D. Wald, *Religion and Politics in the United States,* 3rd ed. (Washington, DC: CQ Press, 1997). For a discussion of neutrality, see Robert Booth Fowler, Allen D. Hertzke, and Laura R. Olson, *Religion and Politics in America: Faith, Culture, & Strategic Choices,* 2nd ed. (Boulder, CO: Westview Press, 1999).

30. *Everson v. Board of Education,* 330 U.S. 1 (1947).

31. *Lemon v. Kurtzman,* 403 U.S. 602 (1971).

32. *Zelman v. Simmons-Harris,* 539 U.S. 639 (2002).

33. *Engel v. Vitale,* 370 U.S. 421 (1962).

34. See, for example, the U.S. District Court ruling in *Tammy Kitzmiller et al. v. Dover Area School District et al.,* 400 F. Supp. 2d 707 (M.D. Pa. 2005).

35. *Prince v. Massachusetts,* 321 U.S. 158 (1944).

36. *Employment Division, Department of Human Resources of the State of Oregon et al. v. Smith,* 494 U.S. 872 (1990).

37. *Griswold v. Connecticut,* 381 U.S. 479 (1965).

38. *Roberts v. U.S. Jaycees,* 468 U.S. 609 (1984).

39. *Roe v. Wade,* 410 U.S. 113 (1973).

40. *Planned Parenthood v. Casey,* 505 U.S. 833 (1992).

41. *Cruzan v. Director, Missouri Department of Health,* 497 U.S. 261 (1990).

42. Ibid.

43. *Bowers v. Hardwick,* 478 U.S. 186 (1986).

44. *Lawrence v. Texas,* 539 U.S. 558 (2003).

45. This is a point of agreement among the Court's opinion, the concurring opinion, and the dissenting opinion issued in *Lawrence v. Texas,* 539 U.S. 558 (2003).

46. *Weeks v. U.S.,* 232 U.S. 383 (1914).

47. *Mapp v. Ohio,* 367 U.S. 643 (1961).

48. See Chief Justice Warren E. Burger's dissent in *Coolidge v. New Hampshire,* 403 U.S. 443.

49. *Segura v. U.S.,* 468 U.S. 796 (1984).

50. *U.S. v. Leon,* 468 U.S. 897 (1984).

51. *California v. Greenwood,* 486 U.S. 35 (1988).

52. *Miranda v. Arizona,* 384 U.S. 436 (1966).

53. *Gideon v. Wainwright,* 312 U.S. 335 (1963).

54. *Furman v. Georgia,* 408 U.S. 238 (1972).

55. The de facto moratorium on the death penalty ended in 1976 in a series of cases starting with *Gregg v. Georgia,* 428 U.S. 153 (1976).

56. *Baze v. Rees,* 553 U.S. ____ (2008).

57. *Wilkerson v. Utah,* 99 U.S. 130 (1878).

58. For a strong argument against gun control, see John R. Lott Jr., *More Guns, Less Crime: Understanding Crime and Gun Control Laws* (Chicago: University of Chicago Press, 1998).

59. For a detailed look at different historical interpretations of the Second Amendment, see Carl T. Bogus, ed., *The Second Amendment in Law and History: Historians and Constitutional Scholars on the Right to Bear Arms* (New York: New Press, 2000).

60. For an articulation of this argument, see Carl T. Bogus, "What Does the Second Amendment Restrict? A Collective Rights

Analysis," *Constitutional Commentary* 18, no. 3 (Winter 2001): 485–516.

61. *District of Columbia v. Heller,* 554 U.S. (2008).

62. www.millionmommarch.org.

63. http://2asisters.org.

64. For a recent report, see ACLU, "History Repeated: The Dangers of Domestic Spying by Federal Law Enforcement," May 29, 2007, www.aclu.org/images/asset_upload_file893_29902.pdf.

65. ACLU, "No Real Threat: The Pentagon's Secret Database on Peaceful Protest," January 17, 2007, available at www.aclu.org/safefree/spyfiles/27988pub20070117.html.

66. Jo Mannies, "Ashcroft Defends Bush on Spying," St. Louis *Post-Dispatch,* February 10, 2008.

67. The full title of the law (H.R. 3162) is the Uniting and Strengthening America by Providing Appropriate Tools Required to Intercept and Obstruct Terrorism (USA PATRIOT) Act of 2001.

68. Protect America Act of 2007 (Pub.L. 110-55, S. 1927) signed into law by George W. Bush on August 5, 2007.

69. For an articulation of this argument, see Charles Krauthammer, "The Truth About Torture," *The Weekly Standard,* December 5, 2005.

70. For an articulation of this viewpoint, see Andrew Sullivan, "The Abolition of Torture," *New Republic,* December 19, 2005.

71. The full text of the Detainee Treatment Act of 2005 (H.R. 2863, Title X) is available at http://thomas.loc.gov/cgi-bin/query/R?r109:FLD001:S10909.

72. The full text of a statement delivered by Condoleezza Rice, the former U.S. secretary of state, at Andrews Air Force base in Maryland is available at www.timesonline.co.uk/tol/news/world/us_and_americas/article745995.ece.

73. European Parliament report, January 22, 2006, "Alleged Secret Detentions and Unlawful Inter-State Transfers Involving Council of Europe Member States."

74. David A. Harris, "'Flying While Arab,' Immigration Issues, and Lessons from the Racial Profiling Controversy," testimony before the U.S. Commission on Civil Rights (October 12, 2001).

75. OMB Watch, "Muslim Charities and the War on Terror: Top Ten Concerns and Status Update," revised March 2006, available at www.ombwatch.org//npadv/PDF/MuslimCharitiesTopTenUpdated.pdf.

CHAPTER 5

1. Rolan J. Pennock, "Rights, Natural Rights, and Human Rights—A General View," in *Human Rights,* eds. J. R. Pennock and J. W. Chapman (New York: New York University Press, 1981).

2. Raoul Berger, *Government by Judiciary: The Transformation of the Fourteenth Amendment* (Cambridge, MA: Harvard University Press, 1977).

3. Donald E. Lively, *The Constitution and Race* (New York: Praeger, 1992).

4. John Hope Franklin, *From Slavery to Freedom,* 7th ed. (New York: McGraw-Hill, 1994).

5. *Dred Scott v. Sandford,* 60 U.S. 393 (1857).

6. *Plessy v. Ferguson,* 163 U.S. 537 (1896).

7. August Meier, ed., *Black Protest Thought in the Twentieth Century* (Indianapolis, IN: Bobbs-Merrill, 1971).

8. George T. Blakey, *Hard Times and New Deal in Kentucky, 1929–1939* (Lexington: University of Kentucky Press, 1986).

9. Richard Kluger, *Simple Justice: The History of* Brown v. Board of Education *and Black America's Struggle for Equality* (New York: Knopf, 1976).

10. "Black/White & Brown: *Brown versus the Board of Education of Topeka,*" transcript of program produced by KTWU/Channel 11, Topeka, Kansas. Originally aired May 3, 2004. Transcript available online at http://brownvboard.org/video/blackwhitebrown/.

11. Ibid.

12. Raymond Wolters, *The Burden of Brown: Thirty Years of School Desegregation* (Knoxville: University of Tennessee Press, 1984).

13. Jo Ann Robinson, *The Montgomery Bus Boycott and the Women Who Started It* (Knoxville: University of Tennessee Press, 1987).

14. Taylor Branch, *Parting the Waters: America During the King Years, 1954–1963* (New York: Simon & Schuster, 1988).

15. *Browder v. Gale,* 142 F. Supp. 707 (1956).

16. Sudarshan Kapur, *Raising Up a Prophet: The African-American Encounter with Gandhi* (Boston: Beacon Press, 1992).

17. John Lewis, *Walking with the Wind: A Memoir of the Movement* (New York: Simon & Schuster, 1998).

18. David J. Garrow, *Protest at Selma: Martin Luther King, Jr., and the Voting Rights Act of 1965* (New Haven, CT: Yale University Press, 1978).

19. Taylor Branch, *Pillar of Fire: America in the King Years 1963–65* (New York: Simon & Schuster, 1998).

20. Stokely Carmichael, "What We Want," *New York Review of Books,* September 22, 1966: 5–7.

21. Stokely Carmichael and Mike Thelwell, "Toward Black Liberation," *Massachusetts Review* 7 (1966): 639–51.

22. Steven Lawson, *Black Ballots: Voting Rights in the South, 1944–1969* (New York: Columbia University Press, 1976).

23. www.census.gov/prod/2001pubs/statab/sec08.pdf.

24. *Bradwell v. Illinois,* 83 U.S. 130 (1873).

25. *Minor v. Happersett,* 88 U.S. 162 (1875).

26. www.now.org/history/purpos66.html.

27. *Reed v. Reed,* 404 U.S. 71 (1971).

28. *Craig v. Boren,* 429 U.S. 190 (1976).

29. *U.S. v. Virginia,* 518 U.S. 515 (1996).

30. Joe R. Feagin and Clairece Booher Feagin, *Racial and Ethnic Relations* (Upper Saddle River, NJ: Prentice Hall, 2003), 135.

31. Ibid., 149.

32. Ibid.

33. www.reuters.com/articlePrint?articleId=USN3061859320080131.

34. Roberto Suro, Richard Fry, and Jeffrey Passel, "Hispanics and the 2004 Election: Population, Electorate, and Voters" (Washington, DC: Pew Hispanic Center, 2005) p.4. http://pewhispanic.org/files/reports/48.pdf.

35. www.lulac.org/about/history.html.

36. Ibid.

37. *Mendez v. Westminister,* 64 F. Supp. 544 (1946).

38. Feagin and Feagin, *Racial and Ethnic Relations,* 218.

39. *Corpus Christi Independent School District v. Cisneros,* 404 U.S. 1211 (1971).

40. Texas State Historical Association, "The Handbook of Texas Online," www.tshaonline.org/handbook/online/articles/CC/jrc2.html.

41. U.S. Census Bureau, "Voting and Registration in the Election of November 2004," Table 8, www.census.gov/prod/2006pubs/p20-556.pdf.

42. Feagin and Feagin, *Racial and Ethnic Relations,* 278 and 310.

43. Ibid., 315.

44. *Sutton v. United Airlines,* 527 U.S. 471 (1999); *Murphy v. United Parcel Service, Inc.,* 527 U.S. 516 (1999).

45. *Bowers v. Hardwick,* 478 U.S. 186 (1986).

46. *Lawrence v. Texas,* 539 U.S. 558 (2003).

47. www.lambdalegal.org/our-work/publications/facts-backgrounds/recent-lgbt-advances.html.

48. *Romer v. Evans,* 517 U.S. 620 (1996).

49. *Regents of the University of California v. Bakke,* 438 U.S. 265 (1978).

50. Ward Connerly, "College Admissions, Let's Not Break the Law," 2007, www.acri.org/chairman.html.

51. www.acri.org/.

52. *Grutter v. Bollinger,* 539 U.S. 306 (2003).

53. *Parents Involved in Community Schools v. Seattle School District No. 1 et al.,* 551 U.S. _____ (2007) and *Meredith v. Jefferson County Board of Education,* 551 U.S. _____ (2007).

CHAPTER 6

1. Steven Pinker, *How the Mind Works* (W. W. Norton, 1997), viii.

2. Aaron Nelson, "Update: Kids Tell Adults to 'Go Vote,'" *The Brownsville Herald,* November 7, 2006.

3. V. O. Key Jr., *Public Opinion and American Democracy* (New York: Knopf, 1961), 8.

4. Mark Hugo Lopez, Peter Levine, Deborah Both, Abby Kiesa, Emily Kirby, and Karlo Marcelo, *The 2006 Civic and Political Health of the Nation: A Detailed Look at How Youth Participate in Politics and Communities* (College Park, MD: Circle: The Center for Information and Research on Civic Learning and Engagement, 2006), 4.

5. Ibid.

6. Sidney Verba, Kay Lehman Schlozman, and Henry E. Brady, *Voice and Equality: Civic*

Voluntarism in American Politics (Cambridge, MA: Harvard University Press, 1995), 439.

7. Frank Newport, "Clinton Has Edge Among Highly Religious White Democrats," The Gallup Organization, February 22, 2008, www.gallup.com/poll/104506/Clinton-Has-Edge-Among-Highly-Religious-White-Democrats.aspx.

8. Jeffrey M. Jones, "How Americans Voted," November 5, 2004, www.galluppoll.com/content/?ci=13957&pg=1.

9. Frank Newport and Joseph Carroll, "Religion Is Powerful Predictor of Vote in Midterm Elections," November 22, 2006, www.galluppoll.com/content/?ci=24319&pg=1.

10. David L. Leal, Matt A. Barreto, Jongho Lee, and Rodolfo O. de la Garza, "The Latino Vote in the 2004 Election," *PS: Political Science and Politics* (2005): 46.

11. Joseph Carroll, "Only 11% of Blacks Satisfied with State of the Nation Right Now," www.galluppoll.com/content/?ci=28039&pg=1.

12. Lopez et al., *The 2006 Civic and Political Health of the Nation,* 20–21.

13. Karlo Barrios Marcelo, Mark Hugo Lopez, and Emily Hoban Kirby, *Civic Engagement Among Young Men and Women* (College Park, MD: Circle: The Center for Information and Research on Civic Learning and Engagement, 2007), 12.

14. David W. Moore, "Death Penalty Gets Less Support from Britons, Canadians Than Americans," Gallup News Service, February 20, 2006.

15. Elizabeth Noelle-Neumann, *The Spiral of Silence: Public Opinion—Our Social Skin,* 2nd ed. (Chicago: University of Chicago Press, 1993).

16. Susan Herbst, *Numbered Voices: How Opinion Polling Has Shaped American Politics* (Chicago: University of Chicago Press, 1993).

17. Robert S. Erikson, Gerald C. Wright, and John P. McIver, *Statehouse Democracy: Public Opinion and Policy in the American States* (New York: Cambridge University Press, 1994).

18. Walter Lippmann, *Public Opinion* (1929; repr. London: Free Press, 1997), 114.

19. "George Gallup, 1901–1984: Founder, The Gallup Organization," http://gallup.com/content/?ci=21364.

20. Herbert Asher, *Polling and the Public: What Every Citizen Should Know* (Washington, DC: CQ Press, 2001).

21. Ibid., 2.

22. Joseph Carroll, "Many Americans Use Multiple Labels to Describe Their Ideology," December 6, 2006, www.gallup.com/poll/25771/Many-Americans-Use-Multiple-Labels-Describe-Their-Ideology.aspx.

23. Randolph Grossman and Douglas Weiland, "The Use of Telephone Directories as a Sample Frame: Patterns of Bias Revisited, *Journal of Advertising* 7 (1978): 31–36.

24. Stephen J. Blumberg and Julian V. Luke, "Coverage Bias in Traditional Telephone Surveys of Low-Income and Young Adults," *Public Opinion Quarterly* 71 (2007): 734–49.

25. Clyde Tucker, J. Michael Brick, and Brian Meekins, "Household Telephone Service and Usage Patterns in the United States in 2004: Implications for Telephone Samples," *Public Opinion Quarterly* 71 (2007): 3–22.

26. Blumberg and Luke, "Coverage Bias in Traditional Telephone Surveys of Low-Income and Young Adults," 734–49.

27. Ibid.

28. George Terhanian and John Bremer, "Confronting the Selection-Bias and Learning Effects Problems Associated with Internet Research," Harris Interactive white paper, August 16, 2000.

29. G. Terhanian, R. Smith, J. Bremer, and R. K. Thomas, "Exploiting Analytical Advances: Minimizing the Biases Associated with Internet-Based Surveys of Non-Random Samples," *ARF/ESOMAR: Worldwide Online Measurement* 248 (2001): 247–72.

30. Quoted by Robert Niles, "Margin of Error," www.robertniles.com/stats/margin.shtml.

31. Irving Crespi, *Pre-Election Polling: Sources of Accuracy & Error* (New York: Russell Sage Foundation, 1988).

32. Benjamin I. Page and Robert Y. Shapiro, *The Rational Public: Fifty Years of Trends in Americans' Policy Preferences* (Chicago: University of Chicago Press, 1992).

33. Frank Newport, *Polling Matters: Why Leaders Must Listen to the Wisdom of the People* (New York: Warner Books, 2004).

34. James A. Stimson, *Tides of Consent: How Public Opinion Shapes American Politics* (Cambridge: Cambridge University Press, 2004).

35. Frank Newport, "U.S. Satisfaction at 15%, Lowest Since 1992," April 14, 2008, www.gallup.com/poll/106498/US-Satisfaction-15-Lowest-Since-1992.aspx.

36. Frank Newport and Joseph Carroll, "Iraq Versus Vietnam: A Comparison of Public Opinion," August 24, 2005, www.galluppoll.com/content/default.aspx?ci=18097&pg=2.

37. Jeffrey M. Jones and Joseph Carroll, "National Satisfaction Level Dips to 25%, One of Lowest Since 1979," May 16, 2007, www.galluppoll.com/content/?ci=27601&pg=1.

38. George C. Edwards III, with Alec M. Gallup, *Presidential Approval: A Sourcebook* (Baltimore: The Johns Hopkins University Press, 1990).

39. David W. Moore, "Top Ten Gallup Presidential Approval Ratings," Gallup press release, September 24, 2001.

CHAPTER 7

1. Frank R. Baumgartner and Beth L. Leech, *Basic Interests: The Importance of Groups in Politics and in Political Science* (Princeton: Princeton University Press, 1998).

2. Peggy Daniels and Carol Schwartz, *Encyclopedia of Associations 1996* (Detroit, MI: Gale Research, 1995).

3. Alexis De Tocqueville, *Democracy in America: The Complete and Unabridged Volumes I and II* (1835–1840; New York: Bantam, 2000), 51.

4. Everett Carll Ladd, *The Ladd Report* (New York: Free Press, 1999).

5. Publius (James Madison), *Federalist #10,* 1787, www.ourdocuments.gov/doc.php?doc=10.

6. Robert D. Putnam, *Bowling Alone: The Collapse and Revival of American Community* (New York: Touchstone, 2000).

7. Claude S. Fischer, "Bowling Alone: What's the Score?" *Social Networks* 27 (May): 155–67.

8. Sylvia Hurtado and John H. Pryor, "The American Freshman: National Norms for Fall 2005," Cooperative Institutional Research Program (CIRP), Higher Education Research Institute (HERI) Graduate School of Education & Information Studies, University of California, Los Angeles, www.gseis.ucla.edu/heri/heri.html.

9. E. E. Schattschneider, *The Semi-Sovereign People* (New York: Holt Rinehart and Winston, 1960), 132.

10. Earl Latham, *The Group Basis of Politics* (Ithaca, NY: Cornell University Press, 1952).

11. David B. Truman, *The Governmental Process* (New York: Knopf, 1951).

12. Hugh Davis Graham, *The Civil Rights Era: Origins and Development of National Policy, 1960–1972* (London: Oxford University Press, 1990).

13. Sidney Verba, Kay Schlozman, and Nancy Burns, *The Private Roots of Public Action: Gender, Equality, and Political Participation* (Cambridge, MA: Harvard University Press, 2001).

14. Quoted in Mark P. Petracca, *The Politics of Interests* (Boulder, CO: Westview, 1992), 347.

15. Julie Greene, *Pure and Simple Politics: The American Federation of Labor and Political Activism, 1881–1917* (New York: Cambridge University Press, 1998).

16. Elizabeth Sanders, *Roots of Reform: Farmers, Workers, and the American State, 1877–1917* (Chicago: University of Chicago Press, 1998).

17. Sharon E. Jarvis, Lisa Montoya, and Emily Mulvoy, "The Civic Participation of Working Youth and College Students: Working Paper 36" (Austin, TX: The Annette Strauss Institute for Civic Participation, and CIRCLE, the Center for Information and Research on Civic Learning and Engagement, 2005).

18. James Q. Wilson, *Political Organizations* (New York: Basic Books, 1973).

19. Dennis Hastert, *Speaker: Lessons from Forty Years in Coaching and Politics* (Washington, DC: Regnery Publishing, 2004), 256.

20. Jeffrey Berry, *The Interest Group Society,* 3rd ed. (New York: Longman, 1997).

21. Martin J. Smith, *Pressures, Power and Policy: Policy Networks and State Autonomy in Britain and the United States* (Pittsburgh, PA: University of Pittsburgh, 1994).

22. Herbert Alexander, *Money in Politics* (Washington, DC: Public Affairs Press, 1972).

23. Frank Sorauf, *Money in American Elections* (New York: Little, Brown, 1988).

24. Frank Sorauf, *Inside Campaign Finance: Myths and Realities* (New Haven, CT: Yale University Press, 1992).

25. Gary C. Jacobson, *Money in Congressional Elections* (New Haven, CT: Yale University Press, 1980).

26. Allan J. Cigler and Burdett A. Loomis, *Interest Group Politics* (Washington, DC: CQ Press, 1991).

27. http://thomas.loc.gov/cgi-bin/bdquery/z?d110:h.r.02419.

28. Lucy G. Barber, *Marching on Washington: The Forging of an American Political Tradition* (Los Angeles: University of California Press, 2002).

29. www.cc.org/mission.cfm.

30. Material from example from Robert O'Harrow Jr. and Scott Higham, "Wife, Friend Tie Congressman to Consulting Firm," *Washington Post,* July 28, 2006, A1.

31. American Music Conference Newsletter, "Sesame Street's Elmo Visits Congress on Behalf of Music Education," www.amc-music.com/AMCNews/newsletterSp02/elmo_dc.html.

32. Louise Overacker, *Money in Elections* (New York: Macmillan, 1932), 378.

CHAPTER 8

1. E. E. Schattschneider, *Party Government* (New York: Farrar & Rinehart, 1942), 1.

2. L. Sandy Maisel and Kara Z. Buckley, *Parties and Elections in America,* 4th ed. (Lanham, MD: Rowman and Littlefield, 2004).

3. Jo Freeman, *A Room at a Time: How Women Entered Party Politics* (New York: Rowman & Littlefield, 2000).

4. Ibid.

5. Melanie Gustafson, Kristie Miller, and Elisabeth Israels Perry, *We Have Come to Stay: American Women and Political Parties, 1880–1960* (Albuquerque: University of New Mexico Press, 1999).

6. V. O. Key, *Politics, Parties, and Pressure Groups* (New York: Thomas Y. Crowell, 1964).

7. Seymour Martin Lipset and Stein Rokkan, *Party Systems and Voter Alignments* (New York: Free Press, 1967).

8. The Pew Research Center for the People and the Press, "Beyond Red vs. Blue: Republicans Divided About Role of Government—Democrats by Social and Personal Values" (Washington, DC: The Pew Research Center for the People and the Press, 2005).

9. Geoffrey Layman, *The Great Divide: Religious and Cultural Conflict in American Party Politics* (New York: Columbia University Press, 2002).

10. Walter Dean Burnham, *Critical Elections and the Mainsprings of American Politics* (New York: W. W. Norton, 1997).

11. John Aldrich, *Why Parties? The Origin and Transformation of Party Politics in America* (Chicago: University of Chicago Press, 1995).

12. *Buckley v. Valeo,* 424 U.S. 1 (1976).

13. Regina Dougherty, "Divided Government Defines the Era," in *America at the Polls: 1996,* eds. Regina Dougherty, Everett C. Ladd, David Wilber, and Lynn Zayachkiwsky (Storrs, CT: Roper Center for Public Opinion Research, 1997).

14. Richard Hofstadter, "A Constitution Against Parties: Madisonian Pluralism and the Anti-Party Tradition," *Government and Opposition* 4, no. 3 (1969), 345–66.

15. Jefferson and Washington quoted in Richard Hofstadter, *The Idea of a Party System: The Rise of Legitimate Opposition in the United States, 1780–1840* (Berkeley: University of California Press, 1969), 2, 123.

16. Hofstadter, *The Idea of a Party System.*

17. James L. Sundquist, *Dynamics of the Party System: Alignment and Realignment of Political Parties in the United States* (Washington, DC: Brookings, 1983).

18. Everett C. Ladd, *American Political Parties* (New York: W. W. Norton, 1970).

19. David R. Mayhew, *Electoral Realignments: A Critique of an American Genre* (New Haven, CT: Yale University Press, 2002).

20. William Nisbet Chambers, *Political Parties in a New Nation: The American Experience, 1776–1809* (New York: Oxford University Press, 1963).

21. Lance Banning, *The Jeffersonian Persuasion: Evolution of a Party Ideology* (Ithaca, NY: Cornell University Press, 1978).

22. Richard L. McCormick, *The Party Period and Public Policy: American Politics from the Age of Jackson to the Progressive Era* (New York: Oxford University Press, 1986).

23. Jules Witcover, *Party of the People: A History of the Democrats* (New York: Random House, 2003).

24. Lee Benson, *The Concept of Jacksonian Democracy* (Princeton, NJ: Princeton University Press, 1961).

25. Aileen Kraditor, *The Ideas of the Woman Suffrage Movement, 1890–1920* (New York: W. W. Norton, 1981).

26. Eric Foner, *Free Soil, Free Labor, Free Men: The Ideology of the Republican Party Before the Civil War* (New York: Oxford University Press, 1995).

27. William E. Gienapp, *The Origins of the Republican Party, 1852–1856* (New York: Oxford University Press, 1987).

28. Witcover, *Party of the People.*

29. McCormick, *The Party Period and Public Policy.*

30. Joel H. Silbey, *The Partisan Imperative: The Dynamics of American Politics Before the Civil War* (New York: Oxford University Press, 1985).

31. Lewis L. Gould, *Grand Old Party: A History of the Republicans* (New York: Random House, 2003).

32. Paul Kleppner, *The Third Electoral System, 1853–1892: Parties, Voters, and Political Cultures* (Chapel Hill: University of North Carolina Press, 1979).

33. Quoted in A. James Reichley, "Party Politics in a Federal Polity," in *Challenges to Party Government,* eds. John Kenneth White and Jerome M. Mileur (Carbondale: Southern Illinois University, 1992), 48.

34. Kristi Anderson, *After Suffrage* (Chicago: University of Chicago Press, 1996), 30.

35. John Petrocik, *Party Coalitions: Realignment and the Decline of the New Deal Party System* (Chicago: University of Chicago Press, 1981).

36. David G. Lawrence, *The Collapse of the Democratic Majority: Realignment, Dealignment, and Electoral Change from Franklin Roosevelt to Bill Clinton* (New York: Westview, 1997).

37. Thomas F. Schaller, *Whistling Past Dixie: How Democrats Can Win Without the South* (New York: Simon & Schuster, 2006).

38. Edward G. Carmines, John P. McIver, and James A. Stimson, "Unrealized Partisanship: A Theory of Dealignment," *Journal of Politics* 49 (1987): 376–400.

39. www.galluppoll.com/content/default.aspx?ci=24655&pg=2.

40. David Karol, Hans Noel, John Zaller, and Marty Cohen, "Polls or Pols? The Real Driving Force Behind Presidential Nominations," www.brookings.edu/articles/2003/summer_politics_cohen.aspx.

41. Arend Lijphardt, *Electoral Systems and Party Systems: A Study of Twenty-Seven Democracies, 1945–1990* (New York: Oxford University Press, 1994).

42. Lipset and Rokkan, *Party Systems and Voter Alignments.*

43. Maurice Duverger, *Political Parties* (New York: Wiley, 1951).

44. Gary Orren, "The Changing Styles of American Party Politics," in *The Future of American Political Parties: The Challenge of Governance,* ed. Joel L. Fleishman (Englewood Cliffs, NJ: Prentice Hall, 1982), 31.

45. This basis for this argument can be found in Larry J. Sabato and Bruce Larson, *The Party's Just Begun: Shaping Political Parties for America's Future,* 2nd ed. (New York: Longman, 2001).

46. Steven J. Rosenstone, Roy L. Behr, and Edward H. Lazarus, *Third Parties in America,* 2nd ed. (Princeton, NJ: Princeton University Press, 1996).

47. Stefan Halper and Jonathon Clarke, *America Alone: The Neo-Conservatives and the Global Order* (London: Cambridge University Press, 2004).

CHAPTER 9

1. V. O. Key, *The Responsible Electorate* (Cambridge, MA: Harvard University Press, 1966).

2. Samuel C. Patterson and Gregory A. Caldeira, "Getting Out the Vote: Participation in Gubernatorial Elections," *American Political Science Review* 77 (1983): 675–89.

3. Barbara Norrander, *Super Tuesday: Regional Politics and Presidential Primaries* (Lexington: University of Kentucky Press, 1992).

4. Thomas E. Cronin, *Direct Democracy: The Politics of Initiative, Referendum, and Recall* (Cambridge, MA: Harvard University Press, 1999).

16. Stephen Skowronek, *The Politics Presidents Make: Leadership from John Adams to George Bush* (Cambridge, MA: Belknap Press, 1997).

17. MaryAnne Borrelli, *The President's Cabinet: Gender, Power, and Representation* (Boulder, CO: Lynne Rienner, 2002).

18. Joel D. Aberbach and Mark A. Peterson, eds., *The Executive Branch* (New York: Oxford University Press, 2005).

19. William E. Leuchtenburg, *In the Shadow of FDR: From Harry Truman to Ronald Reagan* (Ithaca, NY: Cornell University Press, 1989).

20. Kenneth R. Mayer, *With the Stroke of a Pen: Executive Orders and Presidential Power* (Princeton, NJ: Princeton University Press, 2002).

21. www.trumanlibrary.org/9981.htm.

22. www.whitehouse.gov/news/releases/2007/07/20070717-3.html.

23. *U.S. v. Curtiss-Wright Export Corp.,* 229 U.S. 304 (1936).

24. Thomas B. Edsall, "Bush Suspends Pay Act in Areas Hit by Storm," *Washington Post,* September 9, 2005: D03.

25. Mark J. Rozell, *Executive Privilege: Presidential Power, Secrecy, and Accountability,* 2nd ed. rev. (Lawrence: University of Kansas Press, 2002).

26. *U.S. v. Richard M. Nixon,* 418 U.S. 683 (1974).

27. Richard Neustadt, *The Power to Persuade* (New York: Wiley, 1960).

28. *Outlook,* February 27, 1909.

29. Richard E. Neustadt, *Presidential Power and the Modern President* (New York: The Free Press, 1990).

30. George C. Edwards III with Alec M. Gallup, *Presidential Approval: A Sourcebook* [Eisenhower to Reagan] (Baltimore: Johns Hopkins University Press, 1990).

31. After 1984 presidential campaign between Ronald Reagan and Walter F. Mondale, *New York,* November 19, 1984.

32. Jeffrey K. Tulis, *The Rhetorical Presidency* (Princeton, NJ: Princeton University Press, 1988).

33. Harry A. Bailey Jr. and Jay M. Shafritz, *The American Presidency: Historical and Contemporary Perspectives* (Pacific Grove, CA: Brooks/Cole, 1988).

34. Marc Landy and Sidney M. Milkis, *Presidential Greatness* (Lawrence: University of Kansas Press, 2000).

35. Harold J. Laski, *The American Presidency* (New York: Harper & Row, 1940).

36. William M. Goldsmith, *The Growth of Presidential Power: A Documented History,* 3 vols. (New York: Chelsea House, 1974).

37. *New York Times Co. v. U.S.,* 403 U.S. 713 (1971).

38. Statement of Sen. Howard Baker (R-TN) during the Senate Committee investigation.

39. John Dean, the Nixon presidential transcripts, March 21, 1973.

40. http://nixon.archives.gov/find/tapes/excerpts/watergate.html.

41. David Frost, *I Gave Them a Sword* (New York: William Morrow, 1978).

42. http://blog.washingtonpost.com/the-trail/2007/08/29/a_party_in_disarray.html/.

43. Barbara Gamarekian, "Washington Talk: The Presidency; First Ladies Step Further Out of Shadows," *New York Times,* March 10, 1988: B5.

44. Barbara Bush, commencement address at Wellesley College, June 1, 1990.

45. Charles C. Thach Jr., *The Creation of the Presidency, 1775–1789: A Study in Constitutional History* (Baltimore: Johns Hopkins University Press, 1969).

CHAPTER 13

1. http://origin.www.gpoaccess.gov/usbudget/fy09/browse.html.

2. http://govinfo.library.unt.edu/npr/library/speeches/030393.html.

3. For a review of the literature on public service motivation, see David J. Houston, "'Walking the Walk' of Public Service Motivation: Public Employees and Charitable Gifts of Time, Blood, and Money," *Journal of Public Administration Research and Theory* 16, no. 1 (2005): 67–86.

4. David J. Houston and Lauren K. Harding, "Trust in the Public Service: A Cross-National Examination," presented at the 66th Annual National Conference of the Midwest Political Science Association, Chicago, April 3–6, 2008.

5. Charles T. Goodsell, *The Case for Bureaucracy: A Public Administration Polemic,* 4th ed. (Washington, DC: CQ Press, 2004): 104–106.

6. Norman J. Baldwin, "Public Versus Private Employees: Debunking Stereotypes," *Review of Public Personnel Administration* 12 (Winter 1991): 1–27.

7. Goodsell, *The Case for Bureaucracy,* 106.

8. www.gpoaccess.gov/plumbook/2004/index.html.

9. John T. Woolley and Gerhard Peters, "The American Presidency Project," www.presidency.ucsb.edu/ws/?pid=30436 (Santa Barbara: University of California, hosted, Gerhard Peters, database).

10. Robert B. Denhardt and Joseph W. Grubbs, *Public Administration: An Action Orientation* (Belmont, CA: Thomson Wadsworth, 2003), 231.

11. www.opm.gov/ses/features.asp.

12. www.msnbc.msn.com/id/23919234.

13. Jeffrey L. Pressman and Aaron Wildavsky, *Implementation: How Great Expectations in Washington Are Dashed in Oakland: Or, Why It's Amazing That Federal Programs Work at All* (Berkeley: University of California Press, 1973).

14. www.pogo.org/p/x/2007impact.html#contract.

15. Shaila Dewan, "FEMA Ordered to Restore Evacuees' Housing Aid," *New York Times,* November 30, 2006.

16. www.whitehouse.gov/omb/budget/fy2007/message.html.

17. William T. Gormley Jr. and Steven J. Balla, *Bureaucracy and Democracy: Accountability and Performance* (Washington DC: CQ Press, 2004), 67.

18. Albert Gore, "From Red Tape to Results: Creating a Government That Works Better and Costs Less," report of the National Performance Review (Washington, DC: U.S. Government Printing Office, 1993). Also at http://eric.ed.gov/ERICDocs/data/ericdocs2sql/content_storage_01/0000019b/80/14/0a/c1.pdf.

19. Matt Kelley, "Probes at NASA Plummet Under Its Current IG," *USA Today,* January 11, 2008.

20. Charles T. Goodsell, *The Case for Bureaucracy,* 139.

21. Gormley and Balla, *Bureaucracy and Democracy,* 164–78.

22. Goodsell, *The Case for Bureaucracy,* 54.

23. Ibid., 30.

24. www.house.gov/etheridge/Press-FEMAcontracts.htm.

25. Richard Stillman, *The American Bureaucracy: The Core of Modern Government* (Chicago: Nelson Hall Publishers, 1996), 308.

CHAPTER 14

1. "More Than Half of Americans Approve of the Job the Court Is Doing, Which Is Lower Than Approval Has Been at Some Recent Points but Still Much Higher Than Public Approval of President George W. Bush and Congress." Joseph Carroll, "1/3 of Americans Say U.S. Supreme Court Is 'Too Conservative,'" Gallup News Service, October 2, 2007.

2. Christopher N. May, *Constitutional Law—National Power and Federalism: Examples and Explanations* (New York: Aspen, 2004).

3. Morton J. Horowitz, *The Transformation of American Law, 1780–1860* (Cambridge, MA: Harvard University Press, 1977).

4. Charles D. Shipan, *Designing Judicial Review* (Ann Arbor: University of Michigan Press, 1997).

5. Joel B. Grossman, "Paths to the Bench: Selecting Supreme Court Justices in a 'Juristocratic' World," in *The Judicial Branch,* eds. Kermit L. Hall and Kevin T. McGuire (Oxford: Oxford University Press, 2005), 143.

6. Robert G. McCloskey, *The American Supreme Court,* 4th ed. (Chicago: University of Chicago Press, 2005).

7. Erwin Chemerinsky, *Constitutional Law: Principles and Policies* (New York: Aspen, 2006).

8. Robert A. Carp, Ronald Stidham, and Kenneth L. Manning, *Judicial Process in America* (Washington, DC: CQ Press, 2007).

9. Robert A. Carp and Ronald Stidham, *The Federal Courts,* 4th ed. (Washington, DC: CQ Press, 2001).

10. www.whitehouse.gov/news/releases/2008/05/20080517-2.html.

11. The exception is those cases whose original jurisdiction is the U.S. Supreme Court, which is not typically considered a trial court.